# THE WORKS OF THOMAS DICK, LL. D.

FOUR VOLUMES IN ONE.

VIZ.

AN ESSAY ON THE IMPROVEMENT OF SOCIETY
THE PHILOSOPHY OF A FUTURE STATE:
THE PHILOSOPHY OF RELIGION:
THE CHRISTIAN PHILOSOPHER:

OR,

THE CONNECTION OF SCIENCE AND PHILOSOPHY WITH RELIGION.

---

HARTFORD:
PUBLISHED BY A. C. GOODMAN & CO.
1850.

ON THE

# IMPROVEMENT OF SOCIETY

BY THE

# DIFFUSION OF KNOWLEDGE:

## AN ILLUSTRATION

OF THE

ADVANTAGES WHICH WOULD RESULT FROM A MORE GENERAL DISSEMINATION OF RATIONAL AND SCIENTIFIC INFORMATION AMONG ALL RANKS

ILLUSTRATED WITH ENGRAVINGS.

BY THOMAS DICK,

AUTHOR OF A VARIETY OF LITERARY AND SCIENTIFIC COMMUNICATIONS IN NICHOLSON'S PHILOSOPHICAL JOURNAL, THE ANNALS OF PHILOSOPHY, ETC. ETC.

"Knowledge is power." — *Lord Bacon.*

HARTFORD:
PUBLISHED BY A. C. GOODMAN & CO.

1850.

# PREFACE.

THE plan and outlines of the following work were sketched, and a considerable portion of it composed, about eighteen years ago. It was advertised, as preparing for the press, in 1823, when the author published the first edition of "The Christian Philosopher;" but various other engagements prevented its appearance at that period. The Introduction and the first two sections were published in a respectable quarterly journal in the year 1816; but they are now considerably modified and enlarged. This circumstance will account for the date of some of the illustrative facts to which reference is made in the first part of the volume, and in several portions of the Appendix.

Had the present work been published at any of the periods now referred to, the subject it discusses, and some of the illustrations, would have presented a more novel aspect than they can lay claim to at the present time, when the diffusion of knowledge has become an object of general attention. The author, however, is not aware that any work embracing so full an illustration of the same topics has yet made its appearance; and is, therefore, disposed to indulge the hope, that, in conjunction with the present movements of society, it may, in some degree, tend to stimulate those exertions which are now making for the melioration and mental improvement of mankind. Independently of the general bearing of the facts and illustrations on the several topics they are intended to elucidate, the author trusts that not a few fragments of useful knowledge will be found incorporated in the following pages, calculated to entertain and instruct the general reader.

In the numerous illustrations brought forward in this volume, it was found impossible altogether to avoid a recurrence to certain facts which the author had partially adverted to in some of his former publications, without interrupting the train of thought, and rendering his illustrations partial and incomplete. But, where the same facts are introduced, they are generally brought forward to elucidate a different topic. Any statements or descriptions of this kind, however, which may have the appearance of repetition, could all be comprised within the compass of three or four pages.

The general subject of the present work will be prosecuted in another volume, to be entitled "The Mental Illumination of Mankind, or an inquiry into the means by which a general diffusion of knowledge may be promoted." This work will embrace — along with a great variety of other topics — an examination of the present system of education, showing its futility and inefficiency, and illustrating the principles and details of an efficient intellectual syste[illegible]able of universal application; together with a variety of suggestions in [illegible] to the physical, moral, and intellectual improvement of society.

To his numerous correspondents who have been inquiring afte[illegible] work, "*The Scenery of the Heavens Displayed*, with the view of illustrating t[illegible]octrine of a *Plurality of Worlds*," which was announced at page 88 of the [illegible]ilosophy of a Future State," — the author begs respectfully to state, that, if [illegible]th permit, he intends to proceed, without delay, to the completion of that w[illegible]k, as soon as the volume announced above is ready for the press. It will form a volume of considerable size, and will be illustrated with a great number of engravings, many of which will be original.

*Broughty Ferry, near Dundee,*
*18th April,* 1833.

# CONTENTS.

## SECTION IV.

### ON THE PLEASURES CONNECTED WITH THE PURSUITS OF SCIENCE.



## SECTION V.

### ON THE PRACTICAL INFLUENCE OF SCIENTIFIC KNOWLEDGE, AND ITS TENDENCY TO PROMOTE THE COMFORTS OF GENERAL SOCIETY.

## SECTION VI.

### ON THE INFLUENCE OF KNOWLEDGE IN PROMOTING ENLARGED CONCEPTIONS OF THE CHARACTER AND PERFECTIONS OF THE DEITY.



## SECTION VII.

### ON THE BENEFICIAL EFFECTS OF KNOWLEDGE ON MORAL PRINCIPLE AND CONDUCT.



## SECTION VIII.

### ON THE UTILITY OF KNOWLEDGE IN RELATION TO A FUTURE WORLD.

## SECTION IX.

### ON THE UTILITY OF GENERAL KNOWLEDGE IN REFERENCE TO THE STUDY OF DIVINE REVELATION.



## SECTION X.

### MISCELLANEOUS ADVANTAGES OF KNOWLEDGE BRIEFLY STATED.



## SECTION XI.

### ON THE IMPORTANCE OF CONNECTING SCIENCE WITH RELIGION.

---

# APPENDIX.

ON THE

# GENERAL DIFFUSION OF KNOWLEDGE.

---

## INTRODUCTION.

When we take a restrospective view of the state of mankind during the ages that are past, it presents, on the whole, a melancholy scene of intellectual darkness. Although in every age men have possessed all the mental faculties they now or ever will enjoy, yet those noble powers seem either to have lain in a great measure dormant, or, when roused into action, to have been employed chiefly in malignant and destructive operations. Hence the events which the page of history records chiefly present to our view the most revolting scenes of war, rapine, and devastation, as if the earth had been created merely to serve as a theatre for mischief, and its inhabitants for the purpose of dealing destruction and misery to all around them. Such, however, are the natural consequences of the reign of *Ignorance* over the human mind. For the active powers of man necessarily follow the dictates of his understanding, and when the intellectual faculties are not directed to the pursuit and the contemplation of noble and benevolent objects, they will most frequently be employed in devising and executing schemes subversive of human happiness and improvement.

Amidst the darkness which, in ancient times, so long overspread the world, some rays of intellectual light appeared in Palestine, in Egypt, and in the Greek and Roman empires; but its influence on the nations around was extremely feeble, and, like a few tapers in a dark night, served little more than to render the surrounding darkness visible. The light of science which then shone was, however, doomed to be speedily extinguished. About the fifth century of the Christian era, numerous hordes of barbarians from the northern and the eastern parts of Europe, and the north-western parts of Asia, overran the western part of the Roman empire, at that time the principal seat of knowledge; and, in their progress, overturned and almost annihilated every monument of science and art which then existed. Wherever they marched, their route was marked with devastation and with blood. They made no distinction between what was sacred and what was profane—what was barbarous and what was refined. Amidst the din of war, the burning of cities, the desolation of provinces, the convulsion of nations, the ruin of empires, and the slaughter of millions, the voice of reason and of religion was scarcely heard; science was abandoned; useful knowledge was set at naught; every benevolent feeling and every moral principle was trampled under foot. The earth seemed little else than one great field of battle; and its inhabitants, instead of cultivating the peaceful arts and sciences, and walking hand in hand to a blessed immortality, assumed the character of demons, and gave vent to the most fiend-like and ferocious passions, till they appeared almost on the brink of total extermination.

For nearly the space of a thousand years posterior to that period, and prior to the Reformation, a long night of ignorance overspread the nations of Europe, and the adjacent regions of Asia, during which the progress of literature and science, of religion and morality, seems to have been almost at a stand; scarcely a vestige remaining of the efforts of the human mind, during all that period, worthy of the attention or the imitation of succeeding ages. The debasing superstitions of the Romish church, the hoarding of relics, the erection of monasteries and nunneries, the pilgrimages to the tombs of martyrs and other holy places, the mummeries which were introduced into the services of religion, the wild and romantic expeditions of crusaders, the tyranny and ambition of popes and princes, and the wars and insurrections to which they gave rise, usurped the place of every rational pursuit, and completely enslaved the minds of men. So great was the ignorance which then prevailed, that persons of the most distinguished rank could neither read nor write. Even many of the clergy did not understand the breviary, or book of common prayer, which they were daily accustomed to recite, and some of them could scarcely read it.* The records of past transactions were in a great measure lost, and legendary tales and fabulous histories, to celebrate exploits which were never performed, were substituted in place of the authenticated history of mankind. The learning which then prevailed, under the name of philosophy and of scholastic theology, consisted chiefly in vain disquisitions and reasonings about abstract truths, and incomprehensible mysteries, and in attempts to decide questions and points of theology, which lie beyond the reach of the human mind, and which its limited faculties are unable to resolve. Sophisms, falsehoods, and bold asseverations were held forth as demonstrations; a pompous display of *words* was substituted in the place of *things;* eloquence consisted in vague and futile declamations; and true philosophy was lost amidst the mazes of wild and extravagant theories and metaphysical subtleties. The sciences, such as they were, were all taught in the Latin tongue, and all books in relation to them were written in that language; the knowledge of them was therefore necessarily confined to the circle of the learned, and it would have been considered as a degradation of the subject, to have treated of it in any of the modern languages which then prevailed. The gates of the temple of knowledge were consequently shut against the great body of the people, and it was never once surmised that they had *any right* to explore its treasures. "During this period," says Dr. Robertson, "the human mind, neglected, uncultivated, and depressed, continued in the most profound ignorance. Europe, during four centuries, produced few authors who merit to be read, either on account of the elegance of their composition, or the justness and novelty of their sentiments. There are few inventions, useful or ornamental to society, of which that long period can boast." And, if those of the highest ranks, and in the most eminent stations in society, were so deficient in knowledge, the great mass of the people must have been sunk into a state of ignorance degrading to human nature.

About the time of the revival of letters, after the dark ages of monkish superstition and ignorance, the moral and intellectual state of the inhabitants of Europe began to experience a change auspicious of better times and of a more enlightened era. The diminution of the Papal power and influence, the spirit of civil and religious liberty which then burst forth, the erection of new seminaries of education, the discovery of the mariner's compass, the invention of the art of printing, the labours of Lord Bacon in pointing out the true method of philosophizing, and the subsequent discoveries of Galileo, Kepler, Boyle, and Newton, in the physical sciences,—gave a new and favourable impulse to the minds of men, and prepared the way for a more extensive communication of useful knowledge to persons of every rank. From this period knowledge began to be gradually diffused among most of the European nations; but its progress was slow, and its influence was chiefly confined to the higher circles of society, and to persons connected with the learned professions, till after the middle of the eighteenth century. About this time there began to issue from the press many popular works on Natural and Civil History, Geography, Astronomy, and Experimental Philosophy, divested of the pedantry of former times, and of the technicalities of science, which, along with periodical works that were then beginning to extend their influence, conveyed to the minds of the mechanic and the artizan various fragments of useful knowledge. It was not, however, till the era of the French Revolution, that the stream of knowledge began to flow with an accelerated progress, and to shed its influence more extensively on the middling and the lower orders of society. Though we cannot look back, without feelings of regret, and even of horror, at the revolting scenes of anarchy and bloodshed which accompanied that political convulsion, yet, amidst all its evils, it was productive of many important and beneficial results. It tended to undermine that system of superstition and tyranny by which most of the European nations had been so long enslaved; it roused millions, from among the mass of the people, to assert those rights and privileges, to which they are entitled as rational beings, and which had been withheld from them by the strong hand of power; it stimulated them to investigations into every department connected with the rights and the happiness of man, and it excited a spirit of inquiry into every subject of contemplation which can improve or adorn the human mind, which, we trust, will never be extinguished, till the light of useful knowledge shall extend its influence over all the inhabitants of the earth.

Striking, however, as the contrast is, between the state of knowledge in the present and in former ages, much still remains to be accomplished, till the great body of mankind be stimulated to the prosecution of intellectual acquirements. Though a considerable portion of rational information has of late years been dis

* As an evidence of the extreme ignorance of those times, it may be stated, that many charters granted by persons of the highest rank are preserved, from which it appears that they could not subscribe their name. It was usual for persons who could not write, to make *the sign of the cross*, in confirmation of a charter. Several of these remain, where kings and persons of great eminence affix *signum crucis manu propria pro ignoratione literarum*, "the sign of the cross made by our own hand, on account of our ignorance of letters." From this circumstance is derived the practice of making a × when signing a deed, in the case of those who cannot subscribe their names. See Robertson's Charles V. and Appendix, No. I.

seminated among a variety of individuals in different classes of society, yet, among the great majority of the population in every country, a degree of ignorance still prevails, degrading to the rank of intellectual natures. With respect to the great mass of the inhabitants of the world, it may still be said with propriety, that "darkness covers the earth, and gross darkness the people." The greater part of the continent of America, the extensive plains of Africa, the vast regions of Siberia, Tartary, Thibet, and the Turkish empire—the immense territories of New Holland, Sumatra, Borneo, and the Burman empire, the numerous islands which are scattered throughout the Indian and the Pacific oceans, with many other extensive regions inhabited by human beings—still lie within the confines of mental darkness. On the numerous tribes which people those immense regions of our globe, neither the light of science nor of revelation has yet shed its benign influence; and their minds, debased by superstition, idolatry, and every malignant passion, and enslaved by the cunning artifices of priests, and the tyranny of cruel despots, present a picture of human nature in its lowest stage of degradation. Even in Europe, where the light of science has chiefly shone, how narrow is the circle which has been enlightened by its beams! The lower orders of society on the continent, and even in Great Britain itself, notwithstanding the superior means of improvement they enjoy, are still miserably deficient in that degree of knowledge and information which every human being ought to possess; nor are there many even in the higher spheres of life who cultivate science for its own sake, who set a due value on intellectual acquisitions, or encourage the prosecution of rational inquiries.

There is, perhaps, no country in the world where the body of the people are better educated and more intelligent than in North Britain; yet we need not go far, either in the city or in the country, to be convinced, that the most absurd and superstitious notions, and the grossest ignorance respecting many important subjects intimately connected with human happiness. still prevail among the great majority of the population. Of two millions of inhabitants which constitute the population of the northern part of our island, there are not, perhaps, 20,000, or the hundredth part of the whole, whose knowledge extends to any subject of importance, beyond the range of their daily avocations. With respect to the remaining 1,800,000, it may perhaps be said with propriety, that of the figure and magnitude of the world they live in —of the seas and rivers, continents and islands, which diversify its surface, and of the various tribes of men and animals by which it is inhabited—of the nature and properties of the atmosphere which surrounds them—of the discoveries which have been made respecting light, heat, electricity, and magnetism—of the general laws which regulate the economy of nature—of the various combinations and effects of chymical and mechanical powers—of the motions and magnitudes of the planetary and the starry orbs —of the principles of legitimate reasoning—of just conceptions of the attributes and moral government of the Supreme Being—of the genuine principles of moral action—of many other subjects interesting to a rational and immortal being—they are almost as entirely ignorant as the wandering Tartar, or the untutored Indian.

Of eight hundred millions of human beings which people the globe we inhabit, there are not perhaps two millions whose minds are truly enlightened as they ought to be—who prosecute rational pursuits for their own sake, and from a pure love of science, independently of the knowledge requisite for their respective professions and employments. For we must exclude from the rank of rational inquirers after knowledge all those who have acquired a smattering of learning, with no other view than to gain a subsistence, or to appear fashionable and polite. And, if this rule be admitted, I am afraid that a goodly number even of lawyers, physicians, clergymen, teachers, nay, even some authors, and professors in universities and academies, would be struck off from the list of lovers of science and rational inquirers after truth. Admitting this statement, it will follow, that there is not one individual out of four hundred of the human race, that passes his life as a rational intelligent being, employing his faculties in those trains of thought and active exercises which are worthy of an intellectual nature! For, in so far as the attention of mankind is absorbed merely in making provision for animal subsistence, and in gratifying the sensual appetites of their nature, they can be considered as little superior in dignity to the lower orders of animated existence.

The late Frederick, king of Prussia, who was a correct observer of mankind, makes a still lower estimate of the actual intelligence of the human species. In a letter to D'Alembert, in 1770, he says, "Let us take any monarchy you please;—let us suppose that it contains ten millions of inhabitants; from these ten millions let us discount,—first the labourers, the manufacturers, the artizans, the soldiers, and there will remain about fifty thousand persons, men and women; from these let us discount twenty-five thousand for the female sex, the rest will compose the nobility and gentry, and the respectable citizens; of these, let us examine how many will be incapable of application, how many imbecile, how many pusillanimous, how many dissipated,—and from this calculation it will result, that out of what is called a civilized nation of nearly ten millions, you will hardly find a thousand well-informed persons, and even among them what inequality with regard to genius! If eight-tenths of the nation, toiling for their subsistence, never read—if another tenth are incapable of application, from frivolity, or dissipation, or imbecility,—it results, that the small share of good sense of which our species is capable, can only reside in a small fraction of a nation." Such was the estimate made by this philosophic monarch of the intelligence possessed by the nations of Europe, sixty years ago; and although society has considerably advanced in intellectual acquisitions since that period, the great body of the people, in every country, is still shrouded in the mists of folly and ignorance.

Such a picture of the intellectual state of mankind must, when seriously considered, excite a melancholy train of reflections in the breast both of the philanthropist and the man of science. That such a vast assemblage of beings, furnished with powers capable of investigating the laws of nature,—of determining the arrangement, the motions, and magnitudes of distant worlds,—of weighing the masses of the planets,—of penetrating into the distant regions of the universe,—of arresting the lightning in its course,—of exploring the pathless ocean, and the region of the clouds,—and of rendering the most stubborn elements of nature subservient to their designs: that beings, capable of forming a sublime intercourse with the Creator himself, and of endless progression in knowledge and felicity, should have their minds almost wholly absorbed in eating and drinking, in childish and cruel sports and diversions, and in butchering one another, seems, at first view, a tacit reflection on the wisdom of the Creator, in bestowing on our race such noble powers, and plainly indicates, that the current of human intellect has widely deviated from its pristine course, and that strong and reiterated efforts are now requisite to restore it to its original channel. Every lover of science and of mankind must, therefore, feel interested in endeavouring to remove those obstructions which have impeded the progress of useful knowledge, and to direct the intellectual energies of his fellow-men to the prosecution of objects worthy of the high station they hold in the scale of existence.

Were we to inquire into the external causes which have retarded the progress of the human mind, we should, doubtless, find them existing in the nature of those civil governments which have most generally prevailed in the world, and in several of the ecclesiastical establishments which have been incorporated with them. It has been a favourite maxim with all tyrants, that the people must be kept in ignorance; and hence we find, that in the empires of the East, which are all of a despotical nature, the people are debarred from the temple of science, and sunk into a state of the grossest ignorance and servility. Under such governments, the minds of men sink into apathy,—the sparks of genius are smothered,—the sciences are neglected,—ignorance is honoured,—and the man of discernment, who dares to vent his opinions, is proscribed as an enemy to the state. In the more enlightened governments on the continent of Europe, the same effects have followed, in proportion to the number of those tyrannical maxims and principles which enter into their constitution. Hence, we may frequently determine the degree of mental illumination which prevails among any people, from a consideration of the nature of the government under which they live. For the knowledge of a people is always in proportion to their liberty, and where the spirit of liberty is either crushed or shackled, the energies of the human mind will never be exerted with vigour, in the acquisition or the propagation of literature and science. Even in the mildest and most enlightened governments of modern Europe, the instruction of the general mass of society forms no prominent feature in their administration. Knowledge on general subjects is simply *permitted* to be disseminated among the people, its promoters are not sufficiently patronized and encouraged,—no funds are regularly appropriated for this purpose,—and its utility, in many instances, is even called in question. It is to be hoped, however, now that the din of war is in some measure hushed, that the attention of princes and their ministers will be more particularly directed to this important object: for it might easily be shown, were it necessary, that an enlightened population is the most solid basis of a good government, and the greatest security for its permanence,—that it will always form the strongest bulwark around every throne where the sceptre is swayed by wisdom and rectitude. That the establishment of the Popish religion in any state has a tendency to impede the progress of knowledge, it would be almost needless to illustrate. The mummeries which have been interwoven with its services, the grovelling and superstitious notions which it has engendered, the ignorance which prevails among the population of all those countries over which its influence extends, the alarms of its priestly abettors at the idea of free discussion, and of enlightening the minds of the people, the records of its Inquisitions, the history of the dark ages, when it prevailed in all its rigour, and the recent experience of our own times, show, that it is a system founded on the darkness and imbecility of the human intellect, and can flourish only where the spirit of liberty has fled, and where reason has lost its ascendency in the minds of men.*

* Let it be carefully remembered, that in these remarks it is merely the *system* of popery to which the author refers. He is aware that many indivi-

With regard to the internal causes of the ignorance which so generally prevails, they will be found in the general depravity of human nature; in the vicious propensities so prevalent among all ranks; in the indulgence of inordinate desires after riches and power; and in the general disposition of mankind to place their chief happiness in sensual gratifications,—evils which the spirit of Christianity only, in conjunction with every rational exertion, is calculated fully to eradicate. And therefore it is indispensable, that every attempt to diffuse intellectual light over the human race be accompanied with the most strenuous exertions to promote the *moral renovation* of mankind. For vice and ignorance, especially among the lower orders, generally go hand in hand; and experience demonstrates, that indulgence in evil passions, and in unhallowed gratifications, destroys the relish for mental enjoyments, and is one of the most powerful obstructions to the vigorous exercise of the intellectual powers.

That the general diffusion of knowledge among all ranks is an object much to be desired, will not, I presume, be called in question by any one who regards the intellectual powers of man as the noblest part of his nature,—and who considers, that on the rational exercise of these powers his true happiness depends. If ignorance be one of the chief causes which disturb the harmonious movements of the machine of society, by removing the cause we of course prevent the effects; and if knowledge be one of the mainsprings of virtuous conduct, the more it is diffused, the more extensively will be brought into action, on the stage of life, those virtues which it has a tendency to produce. A few Ferdinands and Wyndhams and Don Miguels may still remain, who regard the great mass of the people merely as subjects of legislation, or as the tools of tyranny and ambition, and that, therefore, they must be held in the chains of ignorance, lest they should aspire to the ranks of their superiors. But the general current of public opinion now runs counter to such illiberal and antiquated notions; and few persons of respectability, at least in this country, would hazard their reputation in defending a position so degrading and untenable. The more learning a people have, the more virtuous, powerful, and happy will they become; and to ignorance alone must the contrary effects be imputed. "There is but one case," says a French writer, "where ignorance can be desirable; and that is, when all is desperate in a state, and when, through the present evils, others still greater appear behind. Then stupidity is a blessing: knowledge and foresight are evils. It is then that, shutting our eyes against the light, we would hide from ourselves the calamities we cannot prevent." In every other case, knowledge must prove an inestimable blessing to men of every nation and of every rank.

That the period when a general diffusion of knowledge shall take place is hastening on, appears from the rapid progress which has been made in almost every department of science during the last half century; from the numerous publications on all subjects daily issuing from the press; from the rapid increase of theological, literary, and scientific journals, and the extensive patronage they enjoy from the numerous lectures on chymistry, astronomy, experimental philosophy, political economy, and general science, now delivered in the principal cities and towns of Europe; from the adoption of new and improved plans of public instruction, and the erection of new seminaries of education in almost every quarter of the civilized world; from the extensive circulation of books among all classes of the community; from the rapid formation of bible and missionary societies; from the increase of literary and philosophical associations; from the establishment of mechanics' institutions in our principal towns, and of libraries and reading societies in almost every village; from the eager desire now excited, even among the lower orders of society, of becoming acquainted with subjects hitherto known and cultivated only by persons of the learned professions; and, above all, from the spirit of civil and religious liberty now bursting forth, both in the eastern and the western hemispheres, notwithstanding the efforts of petty tyrants to arrest its progress. Amidst the convulsions which have lately shaken the surrounding nations, "many have run to and fro, and knowledge has been increased;" the sparks of liberty have been struck from the collision of hostile armies and opposing interests; and a spirit of inquiry has been excited among numerous tribes of mankind, which will doubtless lead to the most important results. These circumstances, notwithstanding some gloomy appearances in the political horizon, may be considered as so many preludes of a new and happier era about to dawn upon the world; when intellectual light shall be diffused among all ranks, and in every region of the globe; when Peace shall extend her empire over the world. when men of all nations, at present separated from each other by the effects of ignorance, and of political jealousies, shall be united by the bonds of love, of reason, and intelligence, and conduct themselves as rational and immortal beings.

In order that such a period may be gradually ushered in, it is essentially requisite that a com-

duals, distinguished for learning and piety, have been connected with the Romish church; and while he condemns the spirit and tendency of the peculiar dogmas and practices of that church, he deprecates every idea of persecution, and every attempt to deprive its members of those rights and privileges to which they are entitled as men and as citizens.

viction of the utility and importance of a general diffusion of knowledge be impressed upon the minds of the more intelligent and influential classes of society, and that every exertion and every appropriate mean should be used to accomplish this desirable object. In accordance with this idea, I shall endeavour, in the following work,

I. To illustrate the *advantages* which would flow from a general diffusion of useful knowledge among all ranks,—and shall afterwards follow out the investigation, by

II. An inquiry into the *means* requisite to be used in order to accomplish this important object.*

* As a particular illustration of the means by which a general diffusion of knowledge might be effected would render the present work too bulky,—this department of the subject will be prosecuted in a separate volume.

ON THE

# GENERAL DIFFUSION OF KNOWLEDGE.

---

## PART I.

### ON THE ADVANTAGES WHICH WOULD FLOW FROM A GENERAL DIFFUSION OF KNOWLEDGE.

THAT the intellectual faculties of man have never been thoroughly directed to the pursuit of objects worthy of the dignity of rational and immortal natures—and that the most pernicious effects have flowed from the perversion of their mental powers,—are truths which the history of past ages and our own experience too plainly demonstrate. That the state of general society would be greatly meliorated, were the mists of ignorance dispelled, and the current of human thought directed into a proper channel, might appear, were we to take an extensive survey of the evils which have been produced by ignorance, and its necessary concomitants,—and of the opposite effects which would flow from mental illumination, in relation to all those subjects connected with the improvement and the happiness of our species. Here, however, a field of vast extent opens to view, which would require several volumes fully to describe and illustrate: I shall, therefore, in the mean time, select, from the multitude of objects which crowd upon the view, only a few prominent particulars,—the elucidation of which shall occupy the following sections.

---

### SECTION I.

ON THE INFLUENCE WHICH A GENERAL DIFFUSION OF KNOWLEDGE WOULD HAVE IN DISSIPATING THOSE SUPERSTITIOUS NOTIONS AND VAIN FEARS WHICH HAVE SO LONG ENSLAVED THE MINDS OF MEN.

MY first proposition is, that the diffusion of knowledge would undermine the fabric of *superstition*, and remove those groundless fears to which superstitious notions give rise. Ignorance has not only debarred mankind from many exquisite and sublime enjoyments, but has created innumerable unfounded alarms, which greatly increase the sum of human misery. Man is naturally timid, terrified at those dangers whose consequences he cannot foresee, and at those uncommon appearances of nature whose causes he has never explored. Thus, he is led, in many instances, to regard with apprehension and dread those operations of nature which are the result of regular and invariable laws. Under the influence of such timid emotions, the phenomena of nature, both in the heavens and on the earth, have been arrayed with imaginary terrors. In the early ages of the world, a total eclipse of the sun or of the moon was regarded with the utmost consternation, as if some dismal catastrophe had been about to befall the universe. Believing that the moon in an eclipse was sickening or dying through the influence of enchanters, the trembling spectators had recourse to the ringing of bells, the sounding of trumpets, the beating of brazen vessels, and to loud and horrid exclamations, in order to break the enchantment, and to drown the muttering of witches, that the moon might not hear them. In allusion to this practice, Juvenal, when speaking of a loud scolding woman, says, that she was able to relieve the moon.

> "Forbear your drums and trumpets if you please,
> Her voice alone the labouring moon can ease."

Nor are such foolish opinions and customs yet banished from the world. They are said to be still prevalent in several Mahometan and Pagan countries.* Comets, too, with their blazing tails, were long regarded, and still are, by the vulgar, as harbingers of divine vengeance, presaging famines and inundations, or the downfall of princes and the destruction of empires.† The Auroræ Boreales, or northern lights, have been frequently gazed at with similar apprehensions, and whole provinces have been thrown into consternation by the fantastic coruscations of those lambent meteors. Some pretend to see, in these harmless lights, armies mixing in fierce encounter, and fields streaming with blood; others behold states overthrown, earthquakes, inundations, pestilences, and the most dreadful calamities. Because some one or other of these calamities formerly happened soon after the appearance of a comet, or the blaze of an aurora, therefore they are considered either as the causes or the prognostics of such events.

From the same source have arisen those foolish notions, so fatal to the peace of mankind, which have been engendered by *judicial astrology*. Under a belief that the characters and the fates of men are dependent on the various aspects of the stars and conjunctions of the planets. the most unfounded apprehensions, as well as the most delusive hopes, have been excited by the professors of this fallacious science. Such impositions on the credulity of mankind are founded on the grossest absurdity, and the most palpable ignorance of the nature of things; for since the aspects and conjunctions of the celestial bodies have, in every period of duration, been subject to invariable laws, they must be altogether inadequate to account for the diversified phenomena of the moral world, and for that infinite variety we observe in the dispositions and the destinies of men; and, indeed, the single consideration of the immense distances of the stars from our globe, is sufficient to convince any rational mind that their influence can have no effect on a region so remote from the spaces which they occupy. The planetary bodies, indeed, may, in certain cases, have some degree of *physical* influence on the earth, by virtue of their attractive power, but that influence can never affect the operation of moral causes, or the qualities of the mind. Even although it were admitted that the heavenly bodies have an influence over the destinies of the human race, yet we have no *data* whatever by which to ascertain the mode of its operation, or to determine the formula or rules by which calculations are to be made, in order to predict the fates of nations, or the individual temperaments and destinies of men; and consequently, the principles and rules on which astrologers proceed in constructing *horoscopes*, and calculating nativities, are nothing else than mere assumptions, and their pretensions nothing short of criminal impositions upon the credulity of mankind. With equally the same reason might we assert, that the earth, in different positions in its orbit, would have an influence in producing fools and maniacs in the planet Jupiter, or in exciting wars and insurrections among the inhabitants of Saturn, as to suppose, with Mr. Varley, the prince of modern astrologers, that "Saturn passing through the *ascendant*, causes dulness and melancholy for a few weeks," and that "Jupiter, in the third house, gives safe inland journeys and agreeable neighbours or kindred."

Notwithstanding the absurdity of the doctrines of astrology, this art has been practised in every period of time. Among the Romans, the people were so infatuated with it, that the astrologers, or, as they were then called, the *mathematicians*, maintained their ground in spite of all the edicts of the emperors to expel them from the capital; and after they were at length expelled by a formal decree of the senate, they found so much protection from the credulity of the people, that they still remained in Rome unmolested. Among the Chaldeans, the Assyrians, the Egyptians, the Greeks, and the Arabians, in ancient times, astrology was uniformly included in the list of the sciences, and used as one species of divination by which they attempted to pry into the secrets of futurity The Brahmins in India, at an early period, introduced this art into that country, and, by means of it, have rendered themselves the arbiters of good and evil hours, and of the fortunes of their fellow-men, and have thus raised themselves to great authority and influence among the illiterate multitude. They are consulted as oracles, and, like all other impostors, they have taken great care never to sell their answers without a handsome remuneration. In almost every country in the world this art is still practised, and only a short period has elapsed since the princes and legislators of *Europe* were directed in the most important concerns of the state by the predictions of astrologers. In the time of Queen Catharine de Medicis, astrology was so much in vogue, that nothing, however trifling, was to be done without consulting the stars. The astrologer Morin, in the seventeenth century, directed Cardinal Richelieu's motions in some of his journeys, and Louisa Maria de Gonzaga, queen of Poland, gave 2000 crowns to carry on an edition of his *Astrologia Gallica;* and in the reigns of Henry the Third and Henry the Fourth of France, the predictions of astrologers were the common theme of the court conversation. Even in the present day, and in the metropolis of the British empire, this fallacious art is practised, and its professors are resorted to for judicial information, not only by the vulgar, but even by many

* See Appendix, No. II. † Ibid.

in the higher spheres of life. The extensive annual sale of more than 240,000 copies of "Moore's Almanac," which abounds with such predictions, and of similar publications, is a striking proof of the belief which is still attached to the doctrines of astrology in our own age and country, and of the ignorance and credulity from which such a belief proceeds.* Parhelia, paraselenæ, shooting stars, fiery meteors, luminous arches, lunar rainbows, and other atmospherical phenomena, have likewise been considered by some as ominous of impending calamities.

Such are some of the objects in the *heavens*, which ignorance and superstition have arrayed with imaginary terrors.

On the *earth*, the objects which have given rise to groundless fears, are almost innumerable. The *ignes fatui*, those harmless meteors which hover above moist and fenny places in the night-time, and emit a glimmering light, have been regarded as malicious spirits, endeavouring to deceive the bewildered traveller, and lead him to destruction. The ticking noise of the little insect called the *death-watch*—a screech-owl screaming at the window—a raven croaking over a house—a dog howling in the night-time—a hare or a sow crossing the road—the meeting of a bitch with whelps, or a snake lying in the road—the falling of salt from a table—and even the curling of a fibre of tallow in a burning candle,† have been regarded with apprehensions of terror, as prognostics of impending disasters, or of approaching death.

In the Highlands of Scotland, the motions and appearances of the clouds were, not long ago, considered as ominous of disastrous events. On the evening before new-year's day, if a black cloud appeared in any part of the horizon, it was thought to prognosticate a plague, a famine, or the death of some great man in that part of the country over which it seemed to hang; and in order to ascertain the place threatened by the omen, the motions of the clouds were often watched through the whole night. In the same country, the inhabitants regard certain days as *unlucky*, or ominous of bad fortune. That day of the week on which the 3d of May falls, is deemed unlucky throughout the whole year. In the isle of Mull, ploughing, sowing, and reaping, are always begun on Tuesday, though the most favourable weather for these purposes be in this way frequently lost. In Morven, none will, upon any account, dig peat or turf for fuel on Friday. The age of the moon is also much attended to by the vulgar Highlanders; and an opinion prevails, that if a house take fire while the moon is in the decrease, the family will from that time decline in its circumstances, and sink into poverty.*

In England, it is reckoned a bad omen to break a looking-glass, as it is believed the party to whom it belongs will lose his best friend. In going a journey, if a sow cross the road, it is believed the party will meet either with a disappointment or a bodily accident before returning home. It is reckoned unlucky to see first one magpie, and then another; and to kill a magpie, it is believed, will certainly be punished with some terrible misfortune. If a person meet a funeral procession, it is considered necessary always to take off the hat, which keeps all the evil spirits that attend the body in good humour. If in eating, a person miss his mouth, and the victuals fall, it is reckoned very unlucky, and ominous of approaching sickness. It is also considered as unlucky to present a knife, scissors, razor, or any sharp cutting instrument, to one's mistress or friend, as they are apt to cut love and friendship; and to find a knife or razor, denotes ill luck or disappointment to the party.

Among the ancient nations, there was hardly any circumstance or occurrence, however trivial, from which they did not draw omens. This practice appears to have taken its rise in Egypt, the parent country of almost every superstition of paganism; but, from whatever source it may have derived its origin, it spread itself over the whole inhabited globe, even among the most civilized nations, and at this day it prevails more or less among the vulgar in every country. Even kings and emperors, sages and heroes, have been seized with alarm, at the most trivial circumstances, which they were taught to consider as ominous of bad fortune, or of impending danger. Suetonius says of Augustus, that he believed implicitly in certain omens; and that, *si mane sibi calceus perperam, ac sinister pro dextero induceretur, ut dirum*, "if his shoes were improperly put on in the morning, especially if the left shoe was put upon his right foot, he held it for a bad omen."

Thus it appears, that the luminaries of heaven, the clouds, and other meteors that float in the atmosphere, the actions of animals, the seasons of the year, the days of the week, the most trivial incidents in human life, and many other circumstances, have afforded matter of false alarm to mankind. But this is not all: Man, ever prone to disturb his own peace, notwithstanding the *real* evils he is doomed to suf-

* That the absurdities of astrology are still in vogue among a certain class, appears from the publication of such works as the following:—"A Treatise on Zodiacal Physiognomy, illustrated by engravings of heads and features, and accompanied by tables of the times of the rising of the twelve signs of the Zodiac, and containing also new *astrological* explanations of some remarkable portions of ancient mythological history. By John Varley. No. I., large 8vo., pp. 60, to be comprised in four parts. Longman and Co. 1828!" A specimen of some of the fooleries and absurdities gravely treated of by this sapient author, will be found in Nos. III. and IV. of the Appendix to this volume.

† Called in Scotland, the *dead speal*.

* Encyclopedia Britannica, Art. *Omen*.

-er, has been ingenious enough to form *imaginary* monsters which have no existence, either in heaven or on earth, nor the least foundation in the scenes of external nature. He has not only drawn false conclusions from the objects which have a real existence, to increase his fears; but has created, in his imagination, an *ideal world*, and peopled it with spectres, hobgoblins, fairies, satyrs, imps, wraiths, genii, brownies, witches, wizards, and other fantastical beings, to whose caprices he believes his happiness and misery are subjected. An old wrinkled hag is supposed to have the power of rendering miserable all around her, who are the objects of her hatred. In her privy chamber, it is believed, she can roast and torment the absent, and inflict incurable disorders both on man and beast;* she can transport herself through the air on a spit or a broomstick; or, when it serves her purpose, she can metamorphose herself into a cat or a hare; and, by shaking a bridle over a person asleep, can transform him into a horse; and, mounted on this new-created steed, can traverse the air on the wings of the wind, and visit distant countries in the course of a night. A certain being called a fairy, though supposed to be at least two or three feet high, is believed to have the faculty of contracting its body, so as to pass through the key-hole of a door; and though they are a distinct species of beings from man, they have a strong fancy for children; and hence, in the Highlands of Scotland, new-born infants are watched till the christening is over, lest they should be stolen or exchanged by those fantastic existences. The regions of the air have been peopled with apparitions and terrific phantoms of different kinds, which stalk abroad at the dead hour of night, to terrify the lonely traveller. In ruined castles and old houses, they are said to announce their appearance by a variety of loud and dreadful noises; sometimes rattling in the old hall like a coach and six, and rumbling up and down the staircase like the trundling of bowls or cannon-balls. Especially in lonely church-yards, in retired caverns, in deep forests and dells, horrid sounds are said to have been heard, and monstrous shapes to have appeared, by which whole villages have been thrown into consternation.†

Nor have such absurd notions been confined to the illiterate vulgar; men of considerable acquirements in literature, from ignorance of the laws of nature, have fallen into the same delusions. Formerly, a man who was endowed with considerable genius and knowledge, was reckoned a magician. Doctor Bartolo was seized by the Inquisition at Rome, in the sixteenth century, because he unexpectedly cured a nobleman of the gout; and the illustrious Friar Bacon, because he was better acquainted with experimental philosophy than most persons of the age in which he lived, was suspected, even by the learned ecclesiastics, of having dealings with the devil. Diseases were at those times imputed to *fascination*, and hundreds of poor wretches were dragged to the stake for being accessary to them. Mercatus, physician to Philip II. of Spain, relates, that he had seen a very beautiful woman break a steel mirror to pieces, and blast some trees, by a single glance of her eyes! Josephus relates, that he saw a certain Jew, named Eleazar, draw the devil out of an old woman's nostrils, by the application of Solomon's seal to her nose, in the presence of Vespasian. Dr. Mynsight is said to have cured several bewitched persons with a plaster of assafœtida. How the assafœtida was efficacious, was much disputed among the learned. Some thought the devil might consider such an application as an insult, and ran off in a passion; but others very sagely observed, that as devils were supposed to have eyes and ears, it was probable they might have *noses* too. James VI. who was famed for his polemics and theological acquirements, wrote a treatise in defence of witchcraft, and persecuted those who opposed

* The reader will find abundance of relations of this kind in "*Satan's invisible world discovered*," a book which was long read with avidity by the vulgar in this country, and which has frequently caused emotions of terror among youthful groups on winter evenings, while listening to its fearful relations, which could never be eradicated, and has rendered them *cowards* in the dark, during all the subsequent periods of their lives.

† That many of the superstitious opinions and practices above alluded to, still prevail even within the limits of the British empire, appears from the following extract from the "Monthly Magazine" for July 1813, p. 496.—"In Staffordshire, they burn a calf in a farm-house alive, to prevent the other calves from dying. In the same county, a woman having kept a toad in a pot in her garden, her husband killed it, and she reproached him for it, saying, she intended the next Sunday to have taken the sacrament, for the purpose of getting some of the bread to feed him with, and make him thereby a valuable familiar spirit to her. At Long Ashton, a young farmer has several times predicted his own end, from what he calls being *looked over*; and his mother and father informed a friend of mine, (says the relater) that they had sent to the White Witch Doctor, beyond Bridge Water, by the coachman, for a charm to cure him, (having paid handsomely for it;) but that he had now given him over, as her spells were more potent than his. If not dead, he is dying of mere fear, and all the parish of his class believe it. There is also, in that parish, an old man who sells gingerbread to the schools, who is always employed to cure the *red water* in cows, by means of charms and verses which he says to them. In the Marsh, we have water doctors, who get rich; at the mines, diviners with rods, who find ores and water; and at Weston-super-Mare, they see lights before funerals, and are agreed that the people in that parish always die by threes, *i. e.* three old, three young, three men, three women, &c. Such are a part only of the superstitions of the West in 1813!"

Every one who is much conversant with the lower ranks of society, will find, that such notions are still current and believed by a considerable portion of the population, which is the only apology that can be made for stating and counteracting such opinions.

his opinions on this subject. The pernicious effects in mines, occasioned by the explosion of hydrogen gas, were formerly imputed to the demons of the mine. Van Helmont, Bodinus, Strozza, and Luther, attributed thunder and meteors to the devil. Socrates believed he was guided by a demon. Dr. Cudworth, Glanvil, and others, wrote in defence of witchcraft and apparitions. But it would be endless to detail all the foolish opinions which have been imbibed and propagated even by men who pretended to genius and learning.

Besides the opinions to which I have now adverted, and which have a direct tendency to fill the mind with unnecessary apprehensions, there is also an immense variety of foolish and erroneous opinions which passed current for genuine truths among a great majority of mankind. That a man has one rib less than a woman,—that there is a certain Jew still alive, who has wandered through the world since the crucifixion of Christ,—that the coffin of Mahomet is suspended in the air between two loadstones,—that the city of Jerusalem is in the centre of the world,—that the tenth wave of the sea is greater and more dangerous than all the rest,—that all animals on the land have their corresponding kinds in the sea,—that there is a white powder which kills without giving a report,—that the blood of a goat will dissolve a diamond,—that all the stars derive their light from the sun,—that a candle made of human fat, when lighted, will prevent a person asleep from awaking, with many other similar unfounded positions,—are regarded as indisputable truths by thousands, whose adherence to tradition and authority, and whose indolence and credulity, prevent them from inquiring, with a manly independence, into the true state and nature of things.

Such are a few, and but a very few, of the superstitious notions and vain fears by which the great majority of the human race, in every age and country, has been enslaved. To have attempted a complete enumeration of such hallucinations of the human intellect, would have been vain, and could only have produced satiety and disgust. That such absurd notions should ever have prevailed, is a most grating and humiliating thought, when we consider the noble faculties with which man is endowed. That they still prevail, in a great measure, even in our own country, is a striking proof, that we are, as yet, but just emerging from the gloom of intellectual darkness. The prevalence of such opinions is to be regretted, not only on account of the groundless alarms they create, but chiefly on account of the false ideas they inspire with regard to the nature of the Supreme Ruler of the universe, and of his arrangements in the government of the world. While a man, whose mind is enlightened with true science, perceives throughout all nature the most striking evidences of benevolent design, and rejoices in the benignity of the Great Parent of the universe,—while he perceives nothing in the arrangements of the Creator, in any department of his works, which has a direct tendency to produce pain to any intelligent or sensitive existence,—the superstitious man, on the contrary, contemplates the sky, the air, the waters, and the earth, as filled with malicious beings, ever ready to haunt him with terror, or to plot his destruction. The one contemplates the Deity directing the movements of the material world, by fixed and invariable laws, which none but himself can counteract or suspend; the other views them as continually liable to be controlled by capricious and malignant beings, to gratify the most trivial and unworthy passions. How very different, of course, must be their conceptions and feelings respecting the attributes and government of the Supreme Being! While the one views Him as an infinitely wise and benevolent Father, whose paternal care and goodness inspire confidence and affection; the other must regard him, in a certain degree, as a capricious being, and offer up his adorations under the influence of fear.

Such notions have likewise an evident tendency to habituate the mind to false principles and processes of reasoning, which unfit it for forming legitimate conclusions in its researches after truth. They chain down the understanding, and sink it into the most abject and sordid state; and prevent it from rising to those noble and enlarged views which revelation and modern science exhibit, of the order, the extent, and the economy of the universe. It is lamentable to reflect, that so many thousands of beings endowed with the faculty of reason, who cannot by any means be persuaded of the motion of the earth, and the distances and magnitudes of the celestial bodies, should swallow, without the least hesitation, opinions ten thousand times more improbable; and find no difficulty in believing that an old woman can transform herself into a *hare*, and wing her way through the air on a broomstick.

But what is worst of all, *such notions almost invariably lead to the perpetration of deeds of cruelty and injustice.* Of the truth of this position, the history of almost every nation affords the most ample proof. Many of the barbarities committed in pagan countries, both in their religious worship and their civil polity, and most of the cruelties inflicted on the victims of the Romish inquisition, have flowed from this source.* Nor are the annals of our own coun-

* In the duchy of Lorraine, 900 females were delivered over to the flames, for being *witches*, by one inquisitor alone. Under this accusation, it is reckoned that upwards of *thirty thousand women* have perished by the hands of the Inquisition.—"*Inquisition Unmasked*," by Puigblanch.

try deficient in examples of this kind: The belief attached to the doctrine of witchcraft, led our ancestors, little more than a century ago, to condemn and to burn at the stake hundreds of unhappy women, accused of crimes of which they could not possibly have been guilty.* In New England, about the year 1692, a witchcraft phrensy rose to such excess as to produce commotions and calamities more dreadful than the scourge of war or the destroying pestilence. There lived in the town of *Salem*, in that country, two young women, who were subject to convulsions, accompanied with extraordinary symptoms. Their father, a minister of the church, supposing they were *bewitched*, cast his suspicions upon an Indian girl, who lived in the house, whom he compelled, by harsh treatment, to confess that she was a witch. Other women, on hearing this, immediately believed that the convulsions, which proceeded only from the nature of their sex, were owing to the same cause. Three citizens, casually named, were immediately thrown into prison, accused of witchcraft, hanged, and their bodies left exposed to wild beasts and birds of prey. A few days after, sixteen other persons, together with a counsellor, who, because he refused to plead against them, was supposed to share in their guilt, suffered in the same manner. From this instant, the imagination of the multitude was inflamed with these horrid and gloomy scenes. Children of ten years of age were put to death, young girls were stripped naked, and the marks of witchcraft searched for upon their bodies with the most indecent curiosity; and those spots of the scurvy which age impresses upon the bodies of old men, were taken for evident signs of infernal power. In default of these, torments were employed to extort confessions, dictated by the executioners themselves. For such fancied crimes, the offspring of superstition alone, they were imprisoned, tortured, murdered, and their bodies devoured by the beasts of prey. If the magistrates, tired out with executions, refused to punish, they were themselves accused of the crimes they tolerated; the very ministers of religion raised false witnesses against them, who made them forfeit with their lives the tardy remorse excited in them by humanity. Dreams, apparitions, terror, and consternation of every kind, increased these prodigies of folly and horror. The prisons were filled, the gibbets left standing, and all the citizens involved in gloomy apprehensions. So that superstitious notions, so far from being innocent and harmless speculations, lead to the most deplorable results, and therefore ought to be undermined and eradicated by every one who wishes to promote the happiness and the good order of general society.

Such, then, is the evil we find existing among mankind—false opinions, which produce vain fears, which debase the understanding, exhibit distorted views of the Deity, and lead to deeds of cruelty and injustice. Let us now consider the remedy to be applied for its removal.

I have all along taken it for granted, that ignorance of the laws and economy of nature is the great source of the absurd opinions to which I have adverted,—a position which, I presume, will not be called in question. For such opinions cannot be deduced from an attentive survey of the phenomena of nature, or from an induction of well-authenticated facts; and they are equally repugnant to the dictates of revelation. Nay, so far are they from having any foundation in nature or experience, that in proportion as we advance in our researches into Nature's economy and laws, in the same proportion we perceive their futility and absurdity. As in most other cases, so in this, a knowledge of the cause of the evil leads to the proper remedy. Let us take away the cause, and the effect of course will be removed. Let the exercise of the rational faculties be directed into a proper channel, and the mind furnished with a few fundamental and incontrovertible principles of reasoning—let the proper sources of information be laid open—let striking and interesting facts be presented to view, and a taste for rational investigation be encouraged and promoted—let habits of accurate observation be induced, and the mind directed to draw proper conclusions from the various objects which present themselves to view,—and then we may confidently expect, that superstitious opinions, with all their usual accompaniments, will gradually evanish, as the shades of night before the rising sun.

But here it may be inquired, *What kind of knowledge* is it that will produce this effect? It is not merely an acquaintance with a number of dead languages, with Roman and Grecian antiquities, with the subtleties of metaphysics, with pagan mythology, with politics or poetry: these, however important in other points of view, will not, in the present case, produce the desired effect; for we have already seen, that many who were conversant in such subjects were not proof against the admission of superstitious opinions. In order to produce the desired effect, the mind must be directed to the study of material nature, to contemplate the various appearances it presents, and to mark the uniform results of those invariable laws by which

* The Scots appear to have displayed a more than ordinary zeal against witches, and it is said that more deranged old women were condemned for this imaginary crime in Scotland, than in any other country. So late as 1722, a poor woman was burned for witchcraft, which was among the last executions in Scotland. A variety of curious particulars in relation to the trials of witches, may be seen in Pitcairn's "Criminal Trials, and other proceedings before the High Court of Justiciary in Scotland."—Part II. lately published. See also Appendix, No. V.

the universe is governed. In particular, the attention should be directed to those discoveries which have been made by philosophers in the different departments of nature and art, during the last two centuries. For this purpose, the study of natural history, as recording the various facts respecting the atmosphere, the waters, the earth, and animated beings, combined with the study of natural philosophy and astronomy, as explaining the causes of the phenomena of nature, will have a happy tendency to eradicate from the mind those false notions, and, at the same time, will present to view objects of delightful contemplation. Let a person be once thoroughly convinced that Nature is uniform in her operations, and governed by regular laws, impressed by an all-wise and benevolent Being, —he will soon be inspired with confidence, and will not easily be alarmed at any occasional phenomena which at first sight might appear as exceptions to the general rule.

For example,—let persons be taught that eclipses are occasioned merely by the shadow of one opaque body falling upon another—that they are the necessary result of the inclination of the moon's orbit to that of the earth—that the times when they take place depend on the new or full moon happening at or near the points of intersection—and that other planets which have moons, experience eclipses of a similar nature —that the *comets* are regular bodies belonging to our system, which finish their revolutions, and appear and disappear in stated periods of time—that the northern lights, though seldom seen in southern climes, are frequent in the regions of the North, and supply the inhabitants with light in the absence of the sun, and have probably a relation to the magnetic and electric fluids—that the *ignes fatui* are harmless lights, formed by the ignition of a certain species of gas produced in the soils above which they hover—that the notes of the death-watch, so far from being presages of death, are ascertained to be the notes of *love*, and presages of hymeneal intercourses among these little insects;* let rational information of this kind be imparted, and they will soon learn to contemplate nature with tranquillity and composure. Nay, a more beneficial effect than even this, will, at the same time, be produced. Those objects which they formerly beheld with alarm, will now be converted into sources of enjoyment, and be contemplated with emotions of delight.

"When from the dread immensity of space,
The rushing comet to the sun descends,
With awful train projected o'er the world;
——————— The enlighten'd few,
Whose god-like minds philosophy exalts,
The glorious stranger hail. They feel a joy
Divinely great; they in their powers exult;
They see the blazing wonder rise anew,
In seeming terror clad, but kindly bent
To work the will of all-sustaining Love."
*Thomson's Summer.*

Such are the sublime emotions with which a person enlightened with the beams of science contemplates the return of a comet, or any uncommon celestial appearance. He will wait the approach of such phenomena with pleasing expectation, in hopes of discovering more of the nature and destination of those distant orbs; and will be led to form more enlarged ideas of their omnipotent Creator.

Again, to remove the apprehensions which arise from the fear of invisible and incorporeal beings, let persons be instructed in the various optical illusions to which we are subject, arising from the intervention of fogs, and the indistinctness of vision in the night-time, which make us frequently mistake a bush that is near us for a large tree at a distance; and, under the influence of which illusions, a timid imagination will transform the indistinct image of a cow or a horse into a terrific phantom of a monstrous size. Let them also be taught, by a selection of well-authenticated facts, the powerful influence of the imagination in creating ideal forms, especially when under the dominion of fear—the effects produced by the workings of conscience, when harassed with guilt—by very lively dreams, by strong doses of opium, by drunkenness, hysteric passions, madness, and other disorders that affect the mind, and by the cunning artifices of impostors to promote some sinister or nefarious designs. Let them likewise be instructed in the nature of *spontaneous combustions and detonations*, occasioned by the accidental combustion and explosion of gases, which produce occasional noises and lights in church-yards and empty houses. Let the experiments of optics, and the striking phenomena produced by electricity, galvanism, magnetism, and the different gases, be exhibited to their view, together with details of the results which have been produced by various mechanical contrivances. In fine, let their attention be directed to the foolish, whimsical, and extravagant notions, attributed to apparitions, and to their inconsistency with the wise and benevolent arrangements of the Governor of the universe.*

That such instructions as those I have now hinted at would completely produce the intended effect, may be argued from this consideration, —*that they have uniformly produced this effect on every mind which has been thus enlightened.* Where is the man to be found, whose mind is enlightened in the doctrines and discoveries of

* This fact was particularly ascertained by Dr. Derham.—*Philosophical Transactions*, No. 291.

* See Appendix, No. VII. for an illustration of some of the causes which have concurred to propagate the belief of apparitions.

modern science, and who yet remains the slave of superstitious notions and vain fears? Of all the philosophers in Europe, is there one who is alarmed at an eclipse, at a comet, at an *ignis fatuus*, or the notes of a death-watch, or who postpones his experiments on account of what is called an unlucky day? Did we ever hear of a spectre appearing to such a person, dragging him from bed at the dead hour of midnight to wander through the forest trembling with fear? No: such beings appear only to the ignorant and illiterate; and we never heard of their appearing to any one who did not previously believe in their existence. But why should philosophers be freed from such terrific visions, if substantial knowledge had not the power of banishing them from the mind? Why should supernatural beings feel so shy in conversing with men of science? They would be the fittest persons to whom they might impart their secrets, and communicate information respecting the invisible world, but it never falls to their lot to be favoured with such visits. Therefore, it may be concluded, that the diffusion of useful knowledge would infallibly dissipate those groundless fears which have so long disturbed the happiness particularly of the lower orders of mankind.*

It forms no objection to what has been now stated, that the late Dr. Samuel Johnson believed in the existence of ghosts, and in the *second sight:* for, with all his vast acquirements in literature, he was ignorant of natural science, and even attempted to ridicule the study of natural philosophy and astronomy—the principal subjects which have the most powerful tendency to dissipate such notions,—as may be seen in No. 24 of his "Rambler;" where he endeavours to give force to his ridicule by exhibiting the oddities of an imaginary pretender to these sciences. He talks of men of science "lavishing their hours in calculating the weight of the terraqueous globe, or in adjusting systems of worlds beyond the reach of the telescope;" and adds, that "it was the greatest praise of Socrates, that he drew the wits of Greece from the *vain pursuit of natural philosophy* to moral inquiries, and turned their thoughts from stars and tides, and matter and motion, upon the various modes of virtue and relations of life." His opinions and conduct, therefore, can only be considered as an additional proof of the propriety of the sentiments above expressed.

Nor should it be considered as a thing impracticable to instruct the great body of mankind in the subjects to which I have alluded. Every man possessed of what is called common sense, is capable of acquiring all the information requisite for the purpose in view, even without infringing on the time allotted for his daily labours, provided his attention be once thoroughly directed to its acquisition, and proper means used to promote his instruction. It is not intended that all men should be made profound mathematicians and philosophers; nor is it necessary, in order to eradicate false opinions, and to enlarge and elevate the mind. A general view of useful knowledge is all that is necessary for the great mass of mankind; and would certainly be incomparably preferable to that gross ignorance, and those grovelling dispositions, which so generally prevail among the inferior ranks of society. And, to acquire such a degree of rational information, requires only that a taste for it, and an eager desire for acquiring it, be excited in the mind. If this were attained, I am bold to affirm, that the acquisition of such information may be made by any person who is capable of learning a common mechanical employment, and will cost him less trouble and expense than are requisite to a schoolboy for acquiring the elements of the Latin tongue.

To conclude this branch of the subject:—Since it appears that ignorance produces superstition, and superstitious notions engender vain fears and distorted views of the government of the Almighty,—since all fear is in itself painful, and, when it conduces not to safety, is painful without use,—every consideration and every scheme by which groundless terrors may be removed, and just conceptions of the moral attributes of the Deity promoted, must diminish the sum of human misery, and add something to human happiness. If therefore the acquisition of useful knowledge respecting the laws and the economy of the universe would produce this effect, the more extensively such information is propagated, the more happiness will be diffused among mankind.

## SECTION II.

### On the utility of knowledge in preventing diseases and fatal accidents.

It is a conclusion which has been deduced from long experience, "that mankind in their

* It would be unfair to infer from any expressions here used, that the author denies the possibility of supernatural visions and appearances. We are assured, from the records of Sacred History, that beings of an order superior to the human race, have "at sundry times, and in divers manners," made their appearance to men. But there is the most marked difference between vulgar apparitions, and the celestial messengers to which the records of Revelation refer. They appeared, not to old women and clowns, but to patriarchs, prophets, and apostles. They appeared, not to frighten the timid, and to create unnecessary alarm, but to declare "tidings of great joy." They appeared, not to reveal such paltry secrets as the place where a pot of gold or silver is concealed, or where a lost ring may be found, but to communicate intelligence worthy of God to reveal, and of the utmost importance for man to receive. In these, and many other respects, there is the most striking contrast between popular ghosts, and the supernatural communications and appearances recorded in Scripture.

opinions and conduct are apt to run from one extreme to another." We have already seen, that, in consequence of false conceptions of the Deity, and of his arrangements in the economy of nature, the minds of multitudes have been alarmed by the most unfounded apprehensions, and have been "in great fear where no fear was." On the other hand, from a similar cause, many have run heedlessly into danger and destruction, when a slight acquaintance with the powers of nature, and the laws of their operation, would have pointed out the road to safety. This leads me to the illustration of another advantage which would be derived from a general diffusion of knowledge,—namely,

*That it would tend to prevent many of those diseases and fatal accidents which flow from ignorance of the laws which govern the operations of nature.*

There are, indeed, several accidents to which mankind are exposed, which no human wisdom can foresee or prevent. Being furnished with faculties of a limited nature, and placed in the midst of a scene where so many powerful and complicated causes are in constant operation, we are sometimes exposed, all on a sudden, to the action of destructive causes, of which we were ignorant, or over which we have no control. Even although we could foresee a pestilence, a famine, an earthquake, an inundation, or the eruption of a volcano, we could not altogether prevent the calamities which generally flow from their destructive ravages. But, at the same time, it may be affirmed with truth, that a great proportion of the physical evils and accidents to which the human race is liable, are the effects of a culpable ignorance, and might be effectually prevented, were useful knowledge more extensively diffused. But it unfortunately happens, in almost every instance, that the persons who are exposed to the accidents to which I allude, are ignorant of the means requisite for averting the danger. To illustrate this point, I shall select a few examples, and shall intersperse a few hints and maxims for the consideration of those whom it may concern.

The first class of accidents to which I shall advert, comprises those which have happened *from ignorance of the nature and properties of the different gases*, and of the noxious effects which some of them produce on the functions of animal life.

We have frequently read in newspapers and magazines, and some of us have witnessed, such accidents as the following:—A man descends into a deep well, which had for some time been shut up. When he has gone down a considerable way he suddenly lets go his hold of the rope or ladder by which he descends, and drops to the bottom in a state of insensibility, devoid of utterance, and unable to point out the cause of his disaster. Another hastily follows him, to ascertain the cause, and to afford him assistance; but by the time he arrives at the same depth he shares the same fate. A third person, after some hesitation, descends with more cautious steps. But he soon begins to feel a certain degree of giddiness, and makes haste to ascend, or is drawn up by assistants. In the mean time, the unhappy persons at the bottom of the well are frequently left to remain so long in a state of suspended animation, that all means of restoration prove abortive; and the cause of the disaster remains a mystery, till some medical gentleman, or other person of intelligence, be made acquainted with the circumstances of the accident. Similar accidents, owing to the same cause, have happened to persons who have incautiously descended into brewers' vats, or who have entered precipitately into wine cellars and vaults, which had been long shut up from the external air, and where the process of fermentation was going on: They have been suddenly struck down, as by a flash of lightning; and, in some instances the vital spark has been completely extinguished. Many instances, too, could be produced, of workmen, who have incautiously laid themselves down to sleep in the neighbourhood of lime-kilns where they were employed, having, in a short time, slept the sleep of death. The burning of charcoal in close apartments has also proved fatal to many; more especially when they have retired to rest in such apartments, while the charcoal was burning, and before the rooms had received a thorough ventilation.

Numerous are the instances in which accidents have happened, in the circumstances now stated, and which are still frequently recurring; all which might have been prevented had the following facts been generally known and attended to:—That there exists a certain species of air, termed *fixed air*, or *carbonic acid gas*, which instantly extinguishes flame, and is destructive to animal life; that it is found in considerable quantities in places which have been shut up from the external atmosphere,—as in old wells, pits, caverns, and close vaults; that it is copiously produced during the fermentation of liquors in brewers' vats, where it hovers above the surface of the liquor; in cellars where wine and malt-liquors are kept; and by the burning of lime and charcoal; and, that being nearly twice as heavy as common air, it sinks to the bottom of the place where it is produced. The following plain hints are therefore all that is requisite to be attended to, in order to prevent the recurrence of such disasters. Previous to entering a well or pit which has been long secluded from the external air, let a lighted candle or taper be sent down; if it continues to burn at the bottom there is no danger, for air that will support flame, without an explosion, will also support animal life; but, should the taper be extinguished before it reaches the bottom, it would be attended with imminent danger to venture down till the foul air be expelled. The noxious air may be destroyed by throwing down a quantity of *quick lime*, and gradually sprinkling it with water; for as the lime slakes it will absorb the mephitic air, and a person may afterwards descend in safety. Where lime is not at hand, a bush, or such like bulky substance, may be let down and drawn up several times; or some buckets of water may be thrown into it, till the air be so purified, that a lighted taper will continue to burn at the bottom. These precautionary hints will apply to all the other cases referred to, where this species of gas may happen to exist. To which I may also add, as another hint, that in every situation where fixed air is supposed to exist, it is more dangerous to sit or to lie down, in such places, than to stand erect; for, as this gas is the heaviest of all the gases, it occupies the lowest place; and therefore, a person lying on the ground may be suffocated by it, while another standing at his side would feel no injury, his mouth being raised above the stratum of the noxious fluid.*—I shall only remark farther on this head, that several disorders have been contracted by persons sleeping under the branches of trees in the night-time, and in apartments where great quantities of fruit, or other vegetable matter, are kept,—from ignorance of the fact, that during the night, the leaves of trees, and all vegetable matter perspire a deleterious air, which, when it has accumulated to a certain degree, may induce a variety of serious complaints, and sometimes prove fatal.

*The disasters which have happened in coal mines, and other subterraneous apartments,* form another class of accidents, many of which have been the effects of ignorance. Of late years an immense number of men, boys, and horses, has been destroyed by the explosion of inflammable air in the coal mines in this country, particularly in the north of England, where the most affecting and tragical scenes have been presented to view. On the forenoon of Monday, 25th May, 1812, a dreadful accident took place at Felling, near Gateshead, in the mine belonging to C. T. Branding, Esq. When nearly the whole of the workmen were below,—the second set having gone down before the first had come up,—a double blast of hydrogen gas took place, and set the mine on fire, forcing up an immense volume of smoke, which darkened the air to a considerable distance, and scattered an immense quantity of small coal from the upcast shaft. In this calamity ninety-three men and boys perished. The mine was obliged to be closed up on the following Saturday, in order to extinguish the fire, which put an end to all hopes of saving any of the sufferers. On the 6th October, in the same year, and in the same county, (Durham,) a coal-pit, at Shiney Row, suddenly took fire, by explosion of the inflammable air; in consequence of which seven persons were severely scorched. And on the Saturday following, (October 10th,) the Harrington Mill pit, distant from the other about two or three hundred yards, also took fire; by which four men and nineteen boys were killed on the spot, and many people severely wounded and burned, and two boys were missing. This dreadful catastrophe was likewise occasioned by the explosion of fire-damp.† The above are only two or three examples of a variety of similar accidents which have happened, of late years, in the coal districts in the northern part of our island. That all such accidents could have been prevented by means of the knowledge we have hitherto acquired, would perhaps be too presumptuous to affirm; but that a great proportion of them were the effects of ignorance on the part of the miners, and might have been prevented by a general knowledge of the nature and causes of such explosions, and by taking proper precautionary measures, there is every reason to believe. That this is not a mere random assertion, will appear from the following extract from the Monthly Magazine for February 1814, p. 80:—"Mr. Bakewell, in his late lectures at Leeds, stated the following circumstance, which strongly evinces the benefits which arise from educating the working classes—that, in the coal districts of Northumberland and Durham, accidents are constantly taking place from explosions in the mines; so that not less than six hundred persons have been destroyed in the last two years. But, in one of the mines which was frequently subject to explosion, not an accident of any consequence had taken place for the last twelve years; the proprietors, besides other precautions, having for a considerable time past educated the children of the miners at their own expense, and *given them proper information respecting the nature of the danger to be avoided.*"‡

* The grotto del Cani, a small cavern in Italy, about four leagues from Naples, contains a stratum of carbonic acid gas. It has been a common practice to drive dogs into the cavern, where they suffer a temporary death, for the entertainment of strangers. But a man enters with perfect safety, and feels no particular inconvenience by *standing* in it, because his mouth is considerably above the surface of the stratum of deleterious air; but were he to lie down he would be instantly suffocated. The same precaution may also be useful in walking through certain caverns in our own country.

† See Monthly Magazine, vol. xxxiii. p. 580, and vol. xxxiv. p. 462.

‡ This section of the present work was written in 1816, and the facts referred to in it happened within three or four years of that date. Since that period Sir Humphrey Davy's ingenious contrivance, called the *safety lamp*, has been invented, by means of which, we have every reason to believe, many accidents in coal mines have been prevented, and many lives preserved from destruction. The peculiar property of this lamp is, that the miner may move about

Were the working miners carefully instructed in the nature and composition of the atmosphere, and its chymical properties, and particularly in the nature and composition of the different gases,—were such instructions illustrated by a judicious selection of chymical experiments, and were the proper practical hints and precautions deduced and clearly exhibited, there cannot be the least doubt that it would be attended with numerous beneficial results. When a person is ignorant of the noxious principles that may be secretly operating within the sphere of his labours, he will frequently rush heedlessly within the limits of danger; whereas, a man who is thoroughly acquainted with all the variety of causes which may possibly be in action around him, will proceed in every step with judgment and caution, and, where danger is apparent, will hasten his retreat to a place of safety.

*The injuries which are produced by the stroke of lightning form another class of accidents which are frequently owing to ignorance.* It is still to be regretted, that, notwithstanding the discoveries of modern philosophy, respecting the electric fluid and the laws of its operation, no *hunderguard* has yet been invented, which, in all situations, whether in the house, in the street, in the open field, in a carriage, or on horseback, shall serve as a complete protection from the ravages of lightning. Till some contrivance of this kind be effected, it is probable that the human race will still be occasionally subjected to accidents from electrical storms. Such accidents are more numerous and fatal, even in our temperate climate, than is generally imagined. From an induction of a variety of facts of this kind, as stated in the public papers and other periodical works, in the year 1811, the author ascertained that more than twenty persons were killed by lightning, or at the rate of a thousand persons every fifty years, during the summer months of that year, within the limits of our island; besides the violent shocks experienced by others, which did not immediately prove fatal, and the damage occasioned to

with it, and even work by its light in the midst of those explosive mixtures which have so often proved fatal when entered with a common lamp or a candle. It transmits its light, and is fed with air, through a cylinder of copper wire-gauze. The *apertures* in the gauze are about one-twentieth or one-twenty-fifth of an inch square, and the *thickness* of the wire from one-fortieth to one-sixtieth of an inch diameter. The parts of the lamp are:—1. The brass cistern which contains the oil. 2. The rim in which the wire-gauze cover is fixed, and which is fastened to the cistern by a moveable screw. 3. An aperture for supplying oil, fitted with a screw or cork, and a central aperture for the wick. 4. The wire-gauze cylinder, which consists of at least 625 apertures to the square inch. 5. The second top, three-fourths of an inch above the first, surmounted by a brass or copper plate, to which the ring of suspension is fixed. 6. Four or six thick vertical wires, joining the cistern below with the top plate, and serving as protecting pillars round the cage.

When the wire-gauze safety lamp is lighted and introduced into an atmosphere gradually mixed with fire-damp, the first effect of the fire-damp is to increase the length and size of the flame. When the inflammable gas forms one-twelfth of the volume of the air, the cylinder becomes filled with a feeble blue flame, but the flame of the wick appears burning brightly within the blue flame, and the light of the wick increases, till the fire-damp increases to one-fifth, when it is lost in the flame of the fire-damp, which fills the cylinder with a pretty strong light. As long as any *explosive* mixture of gas exists in contact with the lamp, so long will it give its light, and when it is extinguished, which happens when the foul air constitutes one-third of the volume of the atmosphere, the air is no longer proper for respiration, for though animal life will continue where flame is extinguished, yet it is always with suffering.

DAVY'S SAFETY LAMP.

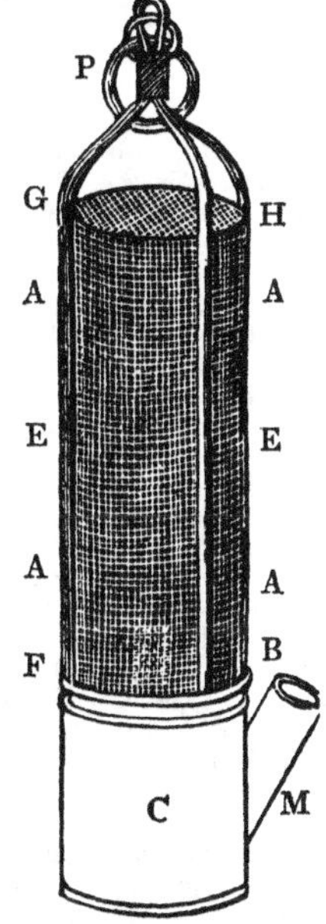


The following are the principal parts of the safety lamp:—F is the lamp throwing up a brilliant flame. C is the reservoir, supplied with oil by the tube M. E E is a frame of thick wire to protect the wire-gauze, A A A A, which has a double top G H. The frame has a ring P attached to it for the convenience of carrying it. The wire-gauze is well fastened to the rim B.

Notwithstanding the utility of this invention, such is the carelessness and apathy of the working miners, that they either neglect to use their safety lamps, or to attend to the means requisite to keep them in order,—which carelessness and apathy are the effects of that gross ignorance into which so many of them are sunk. Hence we find, that seldom a year passes in which we do not hear of destructive explosions happening in our coal mines, particularly in England.

sheep and cattle, and to public and private edifices; and it is worthy of notice, that most of the individuals who were killed by the lightning had either taken shelter under trees, or were in situations adjacent to bells or bell-wires. The experience of succeeding years proves that a similar number of disasters of this kind annually take place. It is, however, more than probable, that at least half the number of accidents arising from the same cause might have been averted, had the nature of lightning, and the laws which regulate its movements, been generally known. Seldom a year passes but we are informed by the public prints of some person or other having been killed by lightning, when taking shelter under a large tree,—of whole families have been struck down when crowding around a fire-place, during a thunder-storm,—of one person having been struck when standing beside a bell-wire, and another while standing under a bell connected with the wire, or under a lustre hanging from the ceiling.

There can be little doubt, that a considerable number of such accidents would have been prevented, had the following facts respecting the nature of lightning been extensively known:—That lightning is a fluid of the same nature, and is directed in its motions by the same laws which regulate the motions of the electric fluid in our common electrical machines;—that it is attracted and conducted by trees, water, moisture, flame, and all kinds of metallic substances;—that it is most disposed to strike high and pointed objects; and that, therefore, it must be dangerous to remain connected with or in the immediate neighbourhood of such objects when a thunder-cloud is passing near the earth.

Hence the following precautionary maxims have been deduced, by attending to which the personal accidents arising from thunder-storms might be in a great measure prevented. In the open air, during a storm, rivers, pools, and every mass of water, even the streamlets arising from a recent shower, should be avoided, because water being an excellent conductor, might determine the course of an electrical discharge towards a person in contact with it, or in its immediate neighbourhood. All high trees and similar elevated conductors should also be avoided, as they are in more danger of being struck than objects on the ground; and, therefore, a person in contact with them exposes himself to imminent danger, should the course of the lightning lie in that direction. But, to take our station at the distance of thirty or forty paces from such objects, or, at such a distance as may prevent us from being injured by the splinters of wood, should the tree be struck, is more secure than even in the midst of an open plain. Persons in a house not provided with thunder-rods, should avoid sitting near a chimney or fire-place, whether there be a fire in the grate or not. For when there is a fire in the grate, the fire contains the following conductors,—flame, smoke, rarefied air, and soot. Even when there is no fire, the soot with which the flue is lined is a conductor; and from the superior height of the chimney-shaft above every other part of the building, it is more liable than any other part of the house to be struck with lightning. In a house, too, gilt mirrors or picture-frames, lustres or burning candles, bell-wires, and all metallic substances, should be carefully avoided, as they afford so many points of attraction, which might determine the course of an electric discharge. The safest position is in the middle of the room, if not near a lustre, a bell, or any thing hanging from the ceiling; and if we place the chair on which we sit on a bed or mattress, almost every possible danger may be avoided.* Such are a few maxims easy to be recollected and put in practice, by attending to which, not a few accidents from electrical explosions might be averted.

In the next place, *various accidents have happened from ignorance of certain plain mechanical principles*. For example, serious accidents have sometimes occurred from the want of acquaintance with *the laws of motion*. Persons have heedlessly jumped out of moving vehicles, and got their legs and arms sprained or dislocated, and from one boat to another when both were in rapid motion, and run the risk of being either bruised, drenched, or drowned. But had the effects of *compound motion* been generally known and attended to, in all those cases where it occurs, it would have prevented many of those accidents which have happened from persons rashly jumping out of carriages when in rapid motion, or attempting to jump from the top of a moving cylinder, in which cases they are always precipitated with violence in a direction different from what they expected, from the obvious effects of a combination of forces. Boats and carriages have been sometimes overset by persons rising hastily when they were in danger of such accidents,—from ignorance of the principle, that the centre of gravity of the moving vehicle, by such a practice, is raised so as to endanger the line of direction being thrown beyond the base, when the vehicle must, of course, be overturned; whereas, had they clapped down to the bottom, they would have brought down the line of direction, and consequently the centre of gravity, farther within the base, so as to have prevented the accident and secured their safety.

* It has been generally thought that the cellar is the most secure situation during a thunder-storm, but this is true only in certain cases. When the lightning proceeds from the clouds, it is unquestionably the most secure position; but in the case of *a returning stroke*, or when the lightning proceeds from the earth, it is less secure than the higher parts of the building.

The reason of this will perhaps more plainly appear from the following explanations:—The *centre of gravity* is that point of a body about which all its parts are in *equilibrio*, or balance each other; and consequently, if this point be supported, the whole body will be at rest, and cannot fall. An imaginary line drawn from the centre of gravity of any body towards the centre of the earth is called *the line of direction*. Bodies stand with firmness upon their bases, when this line falls *within* the base; but if the line of direction falls *without* the base, the body will be overturned. Thus, the inclining body ABCD, whose centre of gravity is E, stands firmly on its base CDKF, because the line of direction EM falls within the base. But if a weight, as ABGH, be laid upon the top of the body, the centre of gravity of the whole body and weight together is raised up to I; and then as the line of direction ID falls without the base at D, the centre of gravity I is not supported, and the whole body and weight must tumble down together.

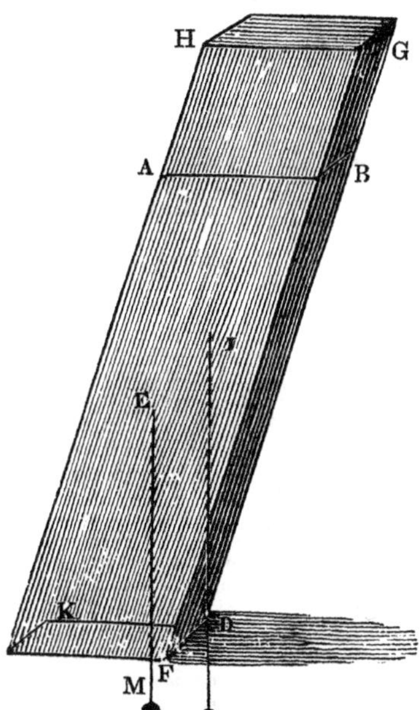


The tower of Pisa, in Italy, leans sixteen feet out of the perpendicular, so that strangers are afraid to pass under it; but as the plummet or line of direction falls *within its base or foundation*, it is in no danger of falling, if its materials keep together; and hence it has stood in this state for three hundred years. But were an additional erection, of any considerable elevation, to be placed upon its top, it would undoubtedly soon tumble into ruins.

To a somewhat similar cause, in combination with heedlessness and ignorance, may be ascribed many of those accidents which so frequently happen at spinning mills and other pieces of machinery, by which legs and arms are torn asunder, and the human frame sometimes mangled and destroyed.

Fatal accidents have likewise happened *from ignorance of the effects produced by the refraction of light*. It is a well-known optical fact, that when a ray of light passes from air into water, and is again refracted, the sine of the angle of incidence is in proportion to the sine of the angle of refraction as four to three. From this circumstance it happens, that pools and rivers appear shallower than they really are—their channels, when viewed from their brink, being apparently higher than their true position, in the proportion of three to four; so that a river eight feet deep will appear from its bank to be only six. This fact may be at any time perceived in a tub or pail full of water, where the bottom of the vessel will obviously appear to be raised a considerable space above its true position, and its apparent depth consequently diminished. In consequence of this optical illusion, which is not generally known, many a traveller as well as many a schoolboy has lost his life, by supposing the bottom of a clear river to be within his depth, as, when he stands on the bank, the bottom will appear one-fourth nearer the surface than it really is.

This will appear evident from the following illustrations:—If a ray of light AC passes obliquely from air into water, instead of continuing its course in the direct line CB, it takes the

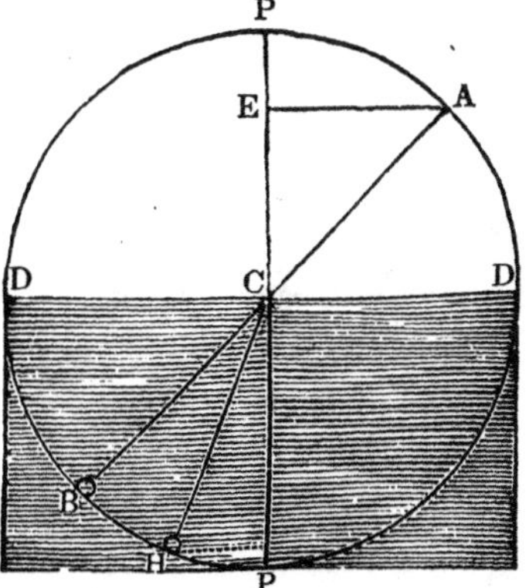


direction CH, and approaches the perpendicular PP, in such a manner, that the angle of refrac tion PCH is less than its angle of incidence ECA. AE is the *sine* of the angle of incidence, and HP the sine of the angle of refraction; and the proportion they bear to each other is as four to three. If a small body, therefore, were placed at H and viewed from the point A, it would appear as if it were raised to the point B, or one-fourth higher than it really is.

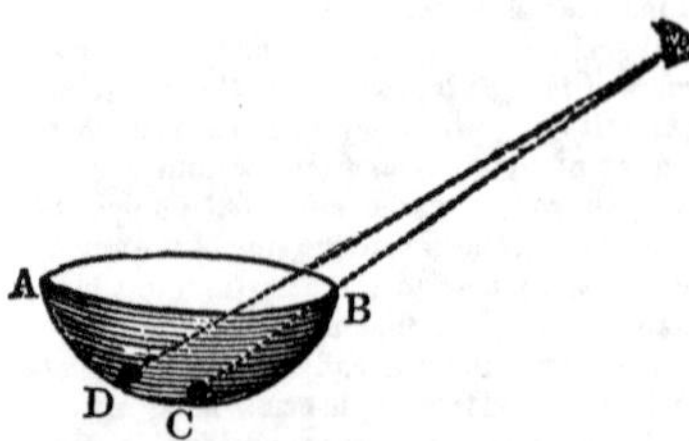


This may be farther illustrated by the following common experiment. Put a shilling into the bottom of an empty bason, at C, and walk backwards till it appear completely hid by the interception of the edge of the bason; then cause water to be poured into the bason, and the shilling will instantly appear as if placed at the point D; for, being now in a denser medium, it appears raised, or nearer to its surface. Before the water was poured in, the shilling could not be seen *where it was;* now it is seen *where it is not.* It is not the eye that has changed its place, but the ray of light has taken a new direction, in passing from the water to the eye, and strikes the eye as if it came from the piece of money. This experiment may be varied as follows:—Take an empty bason, and, along the diameter of its bottom, fix marks at a small distance from each other, then take it into a dark room, and let in a ray of light; and where this falls upon the floor, place the bason, so that its marked diameter may point towards the window, and so that the beam may fall on the mark most distant from the window. This done, fill the bason with water, and the beam which before fell upon the most distant mark, will now, by the refractive power of the water, be turned out of its straight course, and will fall two or three or more marks nearer the centre of the bason.

It is owing to the circumstance now stated, that an oar partly in and partly out of the water appears broken; that objects appear distorted when seen through a crooked pane of glass; that a fish in the water appears much nearer the surface than it actually is; and that a skilful marksman, in shooting at it, must aim considerably below the place which it seems to occupy. It is owing to the refractive power of the atmosphere, that the sun is seen before he rises above the horizon in the morning, and after he sinks beneath it in the evening; that we sometimes see the moon, on her rising, totally eclipsed, while the sun is still seen in the opposite part of the horizon; and that the stars and planets are never seen in the places where they really are, except when they are in the zenith, or point directly over our head.

Many affecting and fatal accidents have happened, and are frequently recurring, particularly to children, and females in the higher ranks of life, *from their clothes catching fire,* most of which might be prevented, were the two following simple facts universally known and practically applied, *that flame has a tendency to mount upwards;* and *that air is essentially requisite for supporting it.* When the clothes of females take fire, as the fire generally begins at the lower parts of their dress, so long as they continue in an upright posture the flames naturally ascend, and meeting with additional fuel as they rise, become more powerful in proportion; whereby the neck, the head, and other vital parts of the body are liable to be most injured; and, by running from one part of the room to another, or from one apartment to another, as is most frequently the case, the air, which is the fuel of fire, gains free access to every part of their apparel, and feeds the increasing flame. In such cases, the sufferer should instantly throw her clothes over her head, and roll or lie upon them, in order to prevent the ascent of the flames and the access of fresh air. When this cannot conveniently be effected, she may still avoid great agony, and save her life, by throwing herself at full length on the floor, and rolling herself thereon. Though this method may not, in every case, completely extinguish the flame, it will to a certainty retard its progress, and prevent fatal injury to the vital parts. When assistance is at hand, the by-standers should immediately wrap a carpet, a hearth-rug, a great coat, or a blanket, around the head and body of the sufferer, who should be laid in a recumbent position, which will prove a certain preventive from danger. During the year 1813, the author noted down more than ten instances, recorded in the public prints, of females who were burned to death by their clothes catching fire, all of which might have been prevented, had the simple expedients now stated been resorted to and promptly applied.

It may be remarked, in the next place, that *many of the diseases to which mankind are subject*—particularly fevers, small-pox, and other infectious disorders—might be prevented by the diffusion of knowledge in relation to their nature, their causes, and the means of prevention. It cannot have been overlooked, in the view of the intelligent observer, that fevers and other infectious disorders generally spread with the greatest facility and make the most dreadful havoc among the lower orders of society. This is owing, in part, to the dirty state in which their houses are kept, every part of which affords proper materials for the production and detention of pestilential effluvia, and their ignorance of the importance of pure atmospherical air to animal life, and the consequent necessity of daily ventilating their apartments. It is also owing in a great measure to the custom of persons crowding into the chambers of those who are labouring under such infectious diseases, and thereby not only increasing the strength of the infectious virus, but absorbing a portion of it in their own bodies, to spread its baleful influence in a wider circle. Such a conduct frequently proceeds from a want of conviction of the infectious nature of such disorders, and from ignorance of the rapid manner in which they are sometimes communicated from one to another, as well as from that obstinacy and from those inveterate prejudices which are always the accompaniments of ignorance. Though the *cow-pox* inoculation has been proved by experience to be an effectual preventive of that loathsome and often fatal disorder, the small-pox, yet numbers in the lower ranks of life cannot yet be persuaded to use this simple preventive, and will rather run the risk of experiencing all its disagreeable and dangerous effects both on their own persons and on those of their offspring. Their obstinate prejudices, in this and similar respects, are increased by their false views and reasonings respecting the doctrine of the divine decrees, and the providence of the Almighty. They imagine, that to induce one species of disease for the prevention of another is attempting to take the government of the world out of the hands of the Creator, and that no means of preventing disorders can be of any avail, if the Deity has otherwise decreed; not considering that the Almighty governs the world he has created by regular and invariable laws, and accomplishes his decrees through the intervention of those secondary causes, both natural and moral, which are continually operating in the physical and intellectual world. Were general knowledge more extensively diffused, and the minds of the multitude habituated to just principles and modes of reasoning, such fallacious views and opinions would be speedily dissipated, and consequently those physical evils and disorders which they produce would be in a great measure prevented.

Again, to ignorance we must likewise attribute, in a great measure, the *pernicious effects of contaminated air in dwelling-houses.* Pure air is essentially requisite to the health and vigour of the animal system as wholesome food and drink. When contaminated by stagnation, by breathing, by fires or candles, it operates as a slow poison, and gradually undermines the human constitution; yet nothing is less attended to in the economy of health by the great majority of mankind. Because air is an invisible substance, and makes little impression on the organs of sense, they seem to act as if it had no existence. Hence we find, that no attention is paid by the lower orders of society to the proper ventilation of their apartments. In some cases, the windows of their houses are so fixed in the walls as to be incapable of being opened; and in other cases, where the windows are moveable, they are seldom opened, except by accident, for weeks and months together; and were it not that a door and a chimney are to be found in every habitable apartment, the air would be rendered in many instances absolutely unfit for respiration. Crowds of tailors, weavers, shoemakers, and other mechanics, employed in sedentary occupations, are frequently pent up in close, and sometimes damp apartments, from morning till evening, without ever thinking of opening their windows for a single half hour for the admission of fresh air; and consequently, are continually breathing an atmosphere highly impregnated with the noxious gas emitted from the lungs, and the effluvia perspired from their bodies, which is most sensibly felt by its hot suffocating smell, when a person from the open air enters into such apartments. The sallow complexion of such persons plainly indicates the enervating effects produced by the air they breathe; and although its pernicious effects may not be sensibly felt, it gradually preys upon their constitutions, and often produces incurable asthmas, fevers, consumptions, and other dangerous disorders, which are frequently imputed to other causes. Nothing is more easy than to open the windows of an apartment, and other apertures that communicate with the external air, at meal hours, when the room is empty, in order to expel the contaminated air, and admit the pure vital fluid. No medicine or restorative is cheaper or of more importance to health and vigour than pure atmospherical air; yet, because it costs nothing, it is little regarded. Hints and admonitions in reference to this point are seldom attended to; for ignorance is always proud and obstinate, and the inconveniences supposed, in certain cases, to flow from the practice of ventilating particular apartments are seldom attempted to be remedied. It is, therefore, presumed, that were a knowledge of the nature of the atmosphere, of the ingredients that enter into its composition, of its indispensable necessity for the support and invigoration of animal life, of the circumstances by which it is deteriorated, and of the baleful effects which are produced by its contamination, more widely diffused, its use and importance would be more duly appreciated, and the disorders which flow from the circumstances now stated effectually prevented.*



* The following fact shows, in an impressive manner, the danger arising from the want of a free circulation and frequent change of air. "In the lying

Much benefit might also be prevented, were *a knowledge of the means of restoring suspended animation*, in cases of drowning, strangulation, &c., generally disseminated. As prompt measures in such cases are absolutely necessary, many fatal effects have happened from the delay occasioned by medical assistance having been at a distance; which might have been prevented, had the proper means of resuscitation been known and immediately resorted to by the persons present at such a juncture. Were the nature and importance of the function of *perspiration* generally known and attended to, it might likewise be the means of preventing those diseases and disasters which flow from making sudden transitions from heat to cold, which are the origin of many fatal disorders among the labouring classes. If a man is thoroughly convinced that more than the one-half of what he eats and drinks is thrown off by insensible perspiration, he will at once see the importance of avoiding every practice and every circumstance which has a tendency to obstruct the operations of this important function.

The last example I shall mention, though not of the least importance, is the fatal effects produced by ignorance of *the proper mode of treating children during the first stages of infancy*. It is a fact deduced from the annual registers of the dead, that one-half the number of children born, die under seven years of age. This extraordinary mortality is universally imputed, by medical writers, to wrong management during the first and second years of their infancy, and the practice of giving anodyne aromatic medicines. Instead of clothing infants in such a manner as to give free scope for the exercise of all the vital functions, as soon as they are ushered into the world, the midwives and officious matrons frequently vie with each other to improve upon nature, by attempting to model the head and to strengthen the limbs by the application of fillets, rollers, and swaddling-bands, of several yards in length; thus loading and binding them with clothes equal to their own weight, to the manifest injury of the motions of their bowels, lungs, limbs, and other animal functions. Instead of covering the head with a thin single cap, and keeping the extremities in a moderate degree of warmth, an opposite course is most frequently pursued, which is supposed to be one among the many existing causes of hydrocephalus or water in the brain. Instead of allowing the first milk that is secreted, which nature has endowed with a purgative quality, to stimulate the bowels, it is a common practice, immediately on the birth of a child, to administer a variety of purgative medicines in close succession, "as if," says a modern writer, "to prove that it has arrived in a world of physic and of evils." Instead of being exposed to the invigorating effects of pure air, and kept in a moderate degree of temperature, they are too frequently confined to a hot contaminated atmosphere, which relaxes their solids, impedes their respiration, and frequently induces fatal convulsions.* These are but a few examples out of many which could be produced of the improper treatment of children, from which multitudes of painful complaints and dangerous disorders derive their origin. It is therefore reasonable to believe, that were general information on such topics extensively disseminated, and a more rational mode of nurture during the first years of infancy adopted, not only fatal disorders, but many subsequent diseases in life, might either be wholly prevented, or at least greatly mitigated.

We have likewise reason to conclude, that a general dissemination of knowledge, by directing the mind to intellectual enjoyments, and lessening the desire for sensual pleasures, *would lead to habits of sobriety and temperance*. Intemperance has perhaps been productive of more diseases, misery, and fatal accidents, than all the other causes I have now specified. It has benumbed the intellectual faculties, debased the affections, perverted the moral powers, degraded man below the level of the brutes, and has carried along with it a train of evils destructive to the happiness of families, and to the harmony and order of social life. Wherever intemperance prevails, a barrier is interposed to every attempt for raising man from the state of moral and intellectual degradation into which he has sunk, and for irradiating his mind with substantial knowledge. But were the mind in early life imbued with a relish for knowledge and mental enjoyments, it would tend to withdraw it from those degrading associations and pursuits which lead to gluttony, debauchery, and drunkenness, and consequently prevent those diseases, accidents, and miseries, which invariably follow in their train. As the human mind is continually in quest of happiness of one description or another, so multitudes of the young and inexperienced have been led to devote themselves to the pursuit of sensual pleasures as their chief and ultimate object, because they have no conception of enjoyment from any

in hospital of Dublin, two thousand nine hundred and forty-four infants, out of seven thousand six hundred and fifty, died in the year 1782, within the first fortnight from their birth. They almost all expired in convulsions; many foamed at the mouth; their thumbs were drawn into the palms of their hands; their jaws were locked; their faces swelled; and they presented, in a greater or less degree, every appearance of suffocation. This last circumstance at last produced an inquiry whether the rooms were not too close and insufficiently ventilated. The apartments of the hospital were rendered more airy; and the consequence has been, that the proportion of deaths, according to the registers of succeeding years, is diminished from *three to one*."

* See the preceding note.

other quarter, and are altogether ignorant of the refined gratification which flows from intellectual pursuits. In the prosecution of knowledge, the rational faculties are brought into exercise, and sharpened and invigorated; and when reason begins to hold the ascendancy over the desires and affections, there is less danger to be apprehended that the mind will ever be completely subjected to the control of the sensitive appetites of our nature.

I might also have stated, that many physical evils might be prevented, were mankind at large acquainted with the characteristics of poisonous plants;—the means of detecting mineral poisons, and the mode of counteracting their effects;—the proper mode of extinguishing fires, and of effecting an escape, in cases of danger, from that element;—*the precautions requisite to be attended to in the management of steam-engines*,* &c. &c. But, as a minute acquaintance with some of these subjects supposes a greater degree of knowledge than could reasonably be expected in the general mass of society, I shall not further enlarge. The few examples I have selected will, it is presumed, be sufficient to prove and illustrate the position stated in the beginning of this section, "that knowledge would, in many cases, prevent dangers, diseases, and fatal accidents." If it be admitted, that several hundreds of persons are annually destroyed by noxious gases, by the explosions of fire-damp in coal-mines, by the stroke of lightning, by their clothes catching fire, and other accidents; and that several thousands are, during the same period, carried off by infectious diseases, and by those diseases which are the effects of contaminated air, and an improper mode of treatment during the first stages of infancy; and if a general diffusion of knowledge respecting the principles and facts adverted to above would have a tendency to prevent one-half the number of such physical evils as now happen, it will follow, that several hundreds, if not thousands, of useful lives might annually be preserved to the community, and a great proportion of human suffering prevented; and if so, the cause of humanity, as well as of science, is deeply interested in the general diffusion of useful knowledge among persons of every nation, and of every rank.

In the conclusion of this topic, it may be remarked, that the knowledge requisite for the purpose now specified is of easy acquisition. It requires no peculiar strength or superiority of genius, nor long and intricate trains of abstract reasoning; but is capable of being acquired by any person possessed of common sense, when his attention is once thoroughly directed to its acquisition. As the food of the body which is the most salutary and nourishing is the most easily procured, so that kind of knowledge which is the most beneficial to mankind at large, is in general the most easily acquired. Its acquisition would not in the least interfere with the performance of their regular avocations, as it could all be acquired at leisure hours. It would habituate them to rational reflections and trains of thought, and gradually unfold to their view new and interesting objects of contemplation. It would have a tendency to prevent them from spending their hours of leisure in folly or dissipation, and would form an agreeable relaxation from the severer duties of active life.

* See Appendix. No. VIII.

---

## SECTION III.

### On the Influence which a General Diffusion of Knowledge would have on the Progress of General Science.

We have already seen, that the diffusion of knowledge among the general mass of society would eradicate those false and superstitious opinions which have so long degraded the human intellect, would introduce just conceptions of the attributes of the Deity, and of his operations in the system of nature, and would avert, or at least greatly mitigate, many of those physical evils to which the human race has been subjected. Although these were the only advantages to be derived from the general dissemination of knowledge, they would be sufficient to warrant every exertion which the friends of science and of humanity can make to accomplish such an important object. But these are only a few of the many beneficial results which would, doubtless, flow from the progress of rational investigations and scientific pursuits. Knowledge, in its progress through the general mass of society, and among the various tribes of mankind, could not long remain confined within its present boundaries, but would, in all probability, enlarge its circumference nearly in proportion to the extent of its diffusion. The man of erudition and of science, who now exerts his influence and his talents to enlighten the minds of his fellow-men, would be laying a foundation for the expansion of his own intellectual views, and of those of his successors in the same pursuits, in future generations. As a small body of snow, by rolling, gradually accumulates to a large mass, so that portion of knowledge we already possess, in its progress through the various ranks of mankind, would have its volume increased, and its present boundaries extended, so that new scenes of intellectual vision and enjoyment would be continually opening to the view. In accordance with these views, I shall now proceed to illustrate the position,

That *a general diffusion of knowledge would tend to the rapid advancement of universal science.*

We are placed in the midst of a scene where a vast multiplicity of objects solicits our attention. Whether we look around on the surface of the earth, or penetrate into its bowels, or turn our eyes upwards to the surrounding atmosphere and the vault of heaven, we perceive an immense variety of beings, celestial and terrestrial, animated and inanimated, continually varying their aspects and positions, all differing from each other in certain points of view, yet connected together by various relations and resemblances.

*Science*, in the most general and extensive sense of the term, consists in a perception of the resemblances and differences, or the relations which these objects have to one another, and to us as rational beings. To ascertain the almost infinite number of relations which subsist among the immense variety of objects which compose the material and intellectual universe, requires an immense multitude of observations, comparisons, and deductions to be made by a vast number of observers placed in various circumstances and positions; or, in other words, *the discovery of an immense number of facts.* All science may therefore be considered as founded on *facts*; and perhaps there would be few exceptions to the truth of the position, were we to assert, that the most sublime truths and deductions, in every science, when stripped of all their adventitious circumstances, simplified, and expressed in the plainest and most perspicuous terms, may be reduced to so many facts. This position might be illustrated, were it necessary, by an induction of particulars from the various branches of mathematical and physical science. That "a whole is greater than any of its parts,"—that "the square described on the hypothenuse of a right-angled triangle is equal to the sum of the squares described on its remaining sides," are facts, the one deduced from observation or simple intuition, the other from a series of comparisons. That the sun is the centre, around which the planetary bodies revolve,—that a projectile describes a parabolic curve,—that the velocities of falling bodies are in proportion to the spaces run over,—that fluids press in all directions,—that the pressure of the atmosphere will support a column of water to the height of above thirty feet,—that the elastic spring of the air is equivalent to the force which compresses it,—that the angle of incidence of a ray of light is equal to the angle of reflection,—that the north pole of one magnet will attract the south pole of another,—that the air we breathe is a composition of oxygen and nitrogen; and a variety of similar truths,—are *facts*, deduced either from simple observation and experiment, or from a comparison of a series of phenomena and experiments with each other. Now, every comparison we make between two or more objects or ideas, is an act of the mind affirming a resemblance or a disgreement between the objects compared; which affirmation, if deduced from a clear view of the objects presented to the mind or senses, is the declaration of a fact.

If the above sentiments are just, it will follow, that every person possessed of an ordinary share of understanding, and whose organs of sensation are in a sound state, is capable of acquiring all the leading truths of the most useful sciences, since he enjoys the senses and faculties requisite for the observation of facts, and for comparing them with one another. And if such a person is capable of receiving into his mind truths already ascertained, he is also, for the same reason, qualified for discovering new truths or facts, provided he be placed in such circumstances as shall have a tendency to present the objects of his pursuit in the clearest point of view; that he have an opportunity of surveying them on all sides, and that his attention be firmly riveted on their several aspects and relations. That one man, therefore, excels another in these respects, is chiefly owing to his mind being more particularly directed to the contemplation of certain objects and relations, and his mental faculties concentrated upon them When a person, devoted to scientific investigation, discovers a new fact, it is not, in the majority of instances, because he possesses powers of intellect and organs of sensation superior to the ordinary endowments of humanity, but because he was placed in different circumstances, and had his attention directed to different objects, and was thus enabled to perceive relations and combinations which had been either unnoticed by others, or which were placed beyond the range of their observation. *Genius*, then, which is generally attributed to such characters, may be considered as consisting in a concentration of the rays of intellect upon any particular object, art, or science, arising from a lively taste we feel for that particular study. It may be compared to a *burning lens*, where the scattered rays of light are rendered powerful by being collected into a point.

In so far, then, as we are able to direct the faculties of the mind—however moderate a degree of vigour they may possess—to the fixed contemplation of scientific objects, in so far may we expect that new relations will be discovered, and new truths elicited. Sir Isaac Newton was one day asked, "How he had discovered the true system of the universe?" He replied, "By continually thinking upon it." He was frequently heard to declare, that "if he had done the world any service, it was due to nothing but *industry and patient thought*, that he kept the subject under consideration constantly before him, and waited till the first dawning opened gradually, by little and little, into a full and clear light." Had this illustrious philosopher been born of barbarous parents in the wilds of Africa,—had he been placed in circumstances widely different from those in which he actually existed, or had not his attention, by some casual occurrence, been directed to the grand object which he accomplished, in all probability, his mind would never have ranged through the celestial regions, nor have discovered the laws of the planetary motions.

Many important scientific facts require only a certain combination of circumstances to bring them to the view of any common observer. To discover the phases of the planet Venus, the satellites of Jupiter, and the elliptical figure of Saturn, after the telescope was invented, required no uncommon powers either of vision or of intellect in Galileo, who first brought these facts to view, however superior the faculties he actually possessed. It only required, that he had a previous knowledge of the existence of these planetary bodies, that his mind was interested in the extension of science, and that he foresaw a probability that new and interesting facts might be discovered by directing his new invented instrument to the starry regions. And when once he had descried from his observatory such new celestial wonders, every other person whose organs of vision were not impaired, with a similar tube, might discover the same objects. Yet, for want of the qualifications which Galileo possessed, the telescope might have long remained in the hands of thousands before such discoveries had been made; and it is a fact, that though the telescope was in use a considerable time before Galileo made his discoveries, no person had previously thought of directing it to the planets; at any rate, no discoveries had been made by it in the heavens.

The discovery of new truths in the sciences, therefore, is not, in most instances, to be ascribed to the exertions of extraordinary powers of intellect; but, in a great majority of cases, to the peculiar series of events that may occur in the case of certain individuals, to the various circumstances and situations in which they may be placed, to the different aspects in which certain objects may be presented to their view, and sometimes to certain casual hints or occurrences which directed their attention to particular objects. A spectacle-maker's boy, by an accidental experiment, led to the invention of the telescope; the remark of a fountain-player, who observed that water could rise only to thirty-two feet in the tubes of a forcing engine, led Galileo to calculate the gravity of the air. Newton's attention was first directed to a profound research into the laws of falling bodies, by the circumstance of an apple falling upon the head, as he was sitting under a tree in his garden, which led to the discovery of the grand principle which unites the great bodies of the universe. The well-known Mr. James Ferguson, author of several popular treatises on astronomy and mechanical philosophy, invented a system of mechanics, and ascertained the laws of the different mechanical powers, when only eight years of age, and before he knew that any treatise had ever been written on that subject. The accidental circumstance of seeing his father lift up the roof of his cottage, by means of a prop and lever, first directed his mind to these subjects, in which he afterwards made many useful improvements.

If, then, it be admitted, that an extraordinary degree of intellectual energy and acumen is not necessary, in every instance, for making useful discoveries,—that the concentration of the mental faculties on particular objects, and the various circumstances in which individuals may be placed, have led to the discovery of important facts,—it will follow, that the exertion of the ordinary powers of intellect possessed by the mass of society is sufficient for the purpose of prosecuting scientific discoveries, and that the more the number of scientific observers and experimenters is increased among the inferior ranks of society, the more extensively will interesting facts and analogies be ascertained, from which new and important principles of science may be deduced.

An ample field still remains for the exertion of all the energies of the human mind. The sciences are, as yet, far removed from perfection; some of them have but lately commenced their progress, and some of their elementary principles still require to be established by future observations. The objects of nature which science embraces are almost infinite; the existence of many of these objects has not yet been discovered, and much less their multiplied relations and combinations. The researches of ages are still requisite, in order thoroughly to explore the universe, and bring to view its hidden wonders. In order to bring to light, as speedily as possible, the undiscovered truths of science, we must endeavour to increase the number of those who shall devote themselves, either wholly or in part, to scientific investigation and research. And, were this object attained, in all probability, the number of useful truths and facts which would be discovered, would be nearly in proportion to the number of those whose attention is directed to such researches.

This might be illustrated from the history of the past progress of science. In those ages, when only a few solitary individuals, here and there, directed their attention to such pursuits, little or no progress was made in the various departments of human knowledge; nay, sometimes they appeared to have taken a retrograde course. During the dark ages, when the human mind, fettered by papal tyranny and superstition, and absorbed in sensual gratifications, seldom made excursions into the regions of science, no useful discoveries were brought to light,—science was not only at a stand, but the knowledge and improvements of preceding ages were even in danger of being entirely obliterated. But no sooner had the human intellect burst its fetters, and the number of rational investigators begun to increase,—no sooner had they formed themselves into regular associations for scientific purposes, than Science and Art were aroused from the slumber of ages, and began to move forward towards perfection with accelerated progress. This may easily be traced by those who have attended to the history of science during the last 160 years. About the commencement of this period, the Academy of Sciences at Paris, and the Royal Society of London, were established. These soon gave birth to similar societies in almost every country in Europe; and there can be no doubt, that the advanced state of knowledge in the present day is chiefly to be attributed to the investigations and discoveries made by the members of those associations, to their joint co-operation in the propagation of useful knowledge, and to the stimulus they afforded to intellectual pursuits.

Would we then accelerate the march of science far beyond the rate of its past and present progress,—would we wish to extend its range far beyond its present boundaries, nothing is so likely to effectuate this end, as an increase of the number of scientific experimenters and observers. Let a certain portion of rational information be imparted to the great mass of mankind,—let intellectual acquirements be exhibited to them as the noblest objects of pursuit, and let them be encouraged to form associations, for the purpose of mutual improvement and scientific research. By these means their attention would be directed to intellectual improvement, a taste would be excited for rational investigations, which would stimulate them to make farther progress; they would soon feel an interest in the objects of science; they would listen with pleasure to the accounts of discoveries which are gradually brought to light throughout the different regions of physical investigation; and would be stimulated, from a laudable ambition of distinguishing themselves as discoverers, as well as from an innate love to the pursuit of knowledge, to observe those facts, to make those researches, and to institute those experiments, that might have a tendency to enlarge the circle of human knowledge. Were the number of such persons increased but a thousand-fold, so that for every twenty scientific investigators now existing, twenty thousand were employed in surveying the various localities, aspects, and operations of nature, in the animal, vegetable, and mineral kingdoms, on the surface of the earth and the ocean, and in the celestial regions,—*hundreds* of new facts would, in all probability, be brought to light for *one* that is now discovered by the present contracted circle of scientific men; from which new and important conclusions in the arts and sciences might be deduced.

Nor let it be objected, that the great bulk of mankind, particularly the middling and the lower ranks of society, are incapable of making any important discoveries in science. If what we have already stated be correct, they are possessed of all the essential requisites, not only for acquiring the elementary principles of knowledge, but also for penetrating beyond the circle which marks the present boundaries of science. They are all organized in nearly the same manner, (a few insulated individuals only excepted,) and, consequently, have nearly an equal aptitude for the exercise of conception, judgment, and ratiocination. They have the same organs of sensation, and the same powers of intellect, as persons in the highest ranks of society. The grand scene of the universe is equally open to peasants and mechanics, as to princes and legislators; and they have the same opportunities of making observations on the phenomena of nature, and the processes of art,—nay, in many instances, their particular situations, and modes of life, afford them peculiar advantages in these respects, which are not enjoyed by persons of a superior rank. In short, they have the same innate curiosity and taste for relishing such investigations, provided the path of knowledge be smoothed before them, and their attention thoroughly directed to intellectual acquisitions.

Nor, again, should it be objected, that an attention to such objects, and an exquisite relish for mental enjoyments, would unfit them for the ordinary duties of active life. Every man, under a well-regulated government, enjoys a certain portion of leisure from the duties of his station, which, in too many instances, is wasted either in listless inaction, or in the pursuits of folly and dissipation. This leisure is all that is requisite for the purpose in view. It would only be requisite that, during its continuance, the train of their thoughts should be directed into a channel which would lead them to more pleasing associations, and more substantial pleasures, than the general current of human thought is calculated to produce. That those who are in the habit of exercising their faculties on rational subjects are thereby rendered more unfit for the common business of life, it would be absurd to suppose. He who habitually exercises his judgment on scientific objects, is gradually improving his mental powers, and must, from this very circumstance, be better qualified than others for exercising them in his particular trade or profession. For the habit of exerting the intellectual faculties in any one department, must necessarily fit them for vigorous exertion on any other object, whether mechanical, agricultural, social, or domestic, to which the attention may be directed. The evils which at present derange the harmony of society, so far from arising from a vigorous exertion of intellect, are to be ascribed, for the most part, to an opposite cause. The intellectual powers, in the case of the great bulk of mankind, lie in a great measure dormant, their energies are not sufficiently exerted in any department of active life; and when occasionally roused from their inactivity, they are too frequently exercised in the arts of deception, of mischief, and of human destruction. To direct the current of human thought, therefore, into a different channel, besides its influence on the progress of science, would be productive of many happy effects on the social and moral condition of mankind; and, as far as my experience goes, with a very few exceptions, I have found, that those who are addicted to rational pursuits are the most industrious and respectable members of civil and Christian society.

The above hints have been thrown out with the intention of showing, that, as all science is founded on facts, and as every person possessed of the common organization of human nature is capable of observing facts, and of comparing them with one another,—as the discovery of new truths is owing more to the concentration of the mental faculties on particular objects, and to several accidental circumstances, than to the exertion of extraordinary powers of intellect,—and as the sciences have generally improved in proportion to the *number* of those who have devoted themselves to their cultivation,—so there is every reason to conclude, that the diffusion of general knowledge and of scientific taste, and consequently, the increase of scientific observers, would ensure the rapid advancement of the different sciences, by an increase of the facts in relation to them which would thus be discovered.

I shall now endeavour to illustrate the positions stated above, by a few examples in relation to two or three of the physical sciences.

*Geology.*—This science is yet in its infancy; and some of its first principles require to be confirmed and illustrated by an induction of an immense number of facts of various descriptions. It is a branch of knowledge altogether founded upon facts palpable to the eye of every common observer. Its object is, to investigate the internal structure of the earth,—the arrangement of its component parts,—the changes which its materials have undergone since its original formation,—and the causes which have operated in the production of these changes. To determine such objects, it is requisite that an immense variety of observations be made on the form, position, and arrangement of mountains, —on the beds of rivers,—the interior of caverns,—the recesses of ravines,—the subterraneous apartments of mines,—the fissures and chasms which abound in Alpine districts,—and even on the bottom of the ocean, in so far as it can be explored; and that a multitude of facts be collected in relation to the materials and position, the elevation and inflexion, the fraction and dislocation of the earth's strata—calcareous petrifactions—metallic veins—decomposed rocks — mosses — rivers — lakes—sand-banks—sea-coasts—the products of volcanoes—the composition of stone, sand, and gravel—the organic remains of animal and vegetable matter,—in short, that the whole surface of the terraqueous globe, and its interior recesses, be contemplated in every variety of aspect presented to the view of man. The observations hitherto made in reference to such multifarious objects have been chiefly confined to a few regions of the earth, and the facts which have been ascertained with any degree of precision, have been collected, chiefly by a few individuals, within the last fifty or sixty years. From such partial and limited researches, general principles have been deduced, and theories of the earth have been framed, which could only be warranted by a thorough examination of every region of the globe. Hence one theory of the earth has successively supplanted another for more than a century past. The theories of Burnet, Whiston, Woodward, Buffon, and Whitehurst, have each had its day and its admirers, but all of them are now fast sinking into oblivion, and in the next age will be viewed only as so many philosophical rhapsodies, and ingenious fictions of the imagination, which have no solid foundation in the actual structure of the earth. Even the foundations of the Huttonian and Wernerian systems, which have chiefly occupied the attention of geologists during the last thirty years, are now beginning to be shaken, and new systems are constructing composed of the fragments of both. One principal reason of this diversity of opinion respecting the true theory of the earth, undoubtedly is, that all the facts in relation to the external and internal structure of our globe have never yet been thoroughly explored. Instead of retiring to the closet, and attempting to patch up a theory with scattered and disjointed fragments, our province, in the mean time, is, to stand in the attitude of surveyors and observers, to contemplate every aspect which terrestrial nature presents, to collect the minutest facts which relate to the object in view, and then leave to succeeding generations the task of constructing a theory from the materials we thus prepare.

Were we now to suppose, that, instead of one observer of geological facts that now exists, thousands were distributed throughout the different continents and islands, having their minds occasionally directed to such investigations; that the miners and labourers in coal-pits, iron-mines, and quarries, not only in Europe, but throughout Mexico and Peru, in the East and West Indies, in Canada, in New Holland, in Southern Africa, in the ranges of the Alps, the Andes, the Himalayas, and other quarters, observed with attention the various phenomena of nature subject to their inspection, with this object in view; that sailors, missionaries, and travellers of every description, contemplated the different aspects of nature in the regions through which they passed, and recorded the facts which came under their observation, for a similar purpose; and could we still farther suppose, that the great body of mankind in every clime might, at no distant period, have their minds directed to similar subjects, there cannot be the least doubt but an immense multitude of important facts would soon be accumulated, which would throw a striking light on the constitution of our planetary globe, and on the changes and revolutions through which it has passed, which would form a broad basis for the erection of a true theory of the earth, and tend either to establish or to overthrow the hypotheses which have hitherto been framed. Persons in the lower spheres of life have, in many cases, more frequent opportunities of ascertaining facts of the description to which I allude, than many others who are placed in an elevated rank. Colliers, quarriers, miners of every description, and the inhabitants of Alpine districts, are almost daily in contact with objects connected with geological research; and it is only requisite that their attention be directed to such inquiries—that the knowledge of a few elementary terms and principles be imparted to them—that they be directed to classify the facts which fall under their observation—and that a systematic list of queries, such as those published some years ago by the London "Geological Society," be put into their hands.*

*Natural History.*—It is evident that the extension and improvement of this department of knowledge depends almost entirely on observation. Although a considerable accession has of late years been made to our knowledge in this branch of study, yet much still remains to be accomplished before all the objects it embraces be thoroughly explored. Our acquaintance with the zoology, botany, and mineralogy of New Holland, Polynesia, Birmah, China, Tartary, Thibet, Africa, and America, is extremely limited; and even within the limits of Europe, numerous unexplored regions still lie open to the future researches of the natural historian. So numerous are the objects and investigations which natural history presents, that although its cultivators were increased ten thousand-fold, they would find sufficient employment in the prosecution of new discoveries for many centuries to come. Even those minute objects, in the animal and vegetable kingdoms, which lie beyond the natural sphere of human vision, and which the microscope alone can discover, would afford scope for the investigations of thousands of ingenious inquirers, during an indefinite series of ages. And it ought never to be forgotten, that every new object and process we are enabled to trace in this boundless field of observation, presents to us the Deity in a *new aspect*, and enables us to form more enlarged conceptions of that power and intelligence which produced the immense assemblage of beings with which we are surrounded.

Independently of the additions that might be made to our knowledge of animals, vegetables and minerals, there are several facts in natural history which might be more precisely ascertained and explained, were common labourers and others in the same rank of life inspired with the spirit of philosophical observation. For the illustration of this, I shall state only one particular circumstance. It is a fact, which, however inexplicable, must be admitted, that *toads* have been found alive in the heart of solid rocks, and in the trunks of trees, where they have been supposed to have existed for ages without any apparent access to nourishment or to air. Such facts are supported by so numerous and so respectable authorities, that it would be vain to call in question their reality; and they assume a more mysterious aspect, from the circumstance, that toads, when placed in the exhausted receiver of an air-pump, like all other animals, soon lose their existence. That the

* The queries to which I refer may be seen in the "Monthly Magazine" for June 1817, pp. 436—9. A few years ago, some interesting fossil remains, supposed to be the teeth and other bones of the extinct animal designated by the name of *Mammoth*, were almost entirely destroyed through the ignorance of some labourers in the parish of Horley, who happened to hit upon them when digging gravel. After cleaving them to pieces with their pick-axes, and finding it added nothing to their store of knowledge, "they threw away the fragments among the heaps of gravel, and the subject was consigned to oblivion; and it was only by accident that two entire teeth were found by a gentleman in the neighbourhood. The bones supposed to have been either destroyed or lost, are a very large bone, supposed to have been a thigh-bone; a huge blade-bone; and a tusk of ivory, perfect in its form, described as being about half a rod in length." Had these labourers been aware of the interesting nature of such fossils, they might have been all preserved entire; and this circumstance shows how important such occurrences, and the observations and researches of common labourers, might sometimes prove to the geologist and the general student of nature.

toad is not the only animal which has been found in similar instances, appears from a notice in the Monthly Magazine for April 1817, which states, that "a large lizard or serpent was found by some miners, imbedded in a stratum of mineral substance, and lived for some time after it was extricated." As the mineral substance in which this animal was found was at the bottom of a deep mine, and connected with the surrounding strata, we are almost under the necessity of concluding, that it must have existed in that state for many years. Now, it is proper to take into consideration, that such facts have been discovered, in the first instance, by labourers, quarriers, miners, and others engaged in laborious occupations, who, with the limited knowledge they presently possess, are unqualified for attending to all the circumstances which require to be noticed in conducting philosophical researches. Were persons of this description accustomed to examine every uncommon occurrence of this kind with a philosophic eye; were they, in such cases as those to which I have now referred, to examine, with accuracy, whether chinks or fissures, either horizontal or perpendicular, existed in the rocks, or were connected with the holes or vacuities of the old trees, where toads were found alive; and were every other circumstance, which a scientific investigator would take into account, accurately observed and recorded, such observations might ultimately lead to some rational explanations of such unaccountable facts. At any rate, as those who belong to that class of society to which I allude, have many opportunties of contemplating the various objects and operations of the material world, their accumulated observations, when scientifically directed, could not fail of enlarging our knowledge of facts in several departments of the history of nature.

*Meteorology.*—In this department of physical science, numerous facts still remain to be ascertained, before we can attempt to explain the causes of various interesting phenomena. We have hitherto been unable to collect with precision all the facts in relation to the diversified phenomena of the atmosphere, and are still at a loss to explain, on known principles, the causes which operate in producing many atmospherical appearances. We are still in a great measure ignorant of the *aurora borealis*, with respect to its nature and origin, its distance from the surface of the earth, what precise connexion it has with the magnetic and electric fluids, and why it has been frequently seen at some periods, and been invisible at others. We are in a similar state of ignorance in regard to *luminous and fiery meteors*,—as to their different species and varieties, the velocity and direction of their motions, their influence on other atmospherical phenomena, on vegetation, and on the weather, and the principles in nature which operate in their production. Although the general cause of *thunder-storms* is in some measure ascertained, yet we are ignorant of the causes of a variety of phenomena with which they are sometimes accompanied, and of some of the chymical agents by which they are produced. To determine the origin of *meteoric stones*, the particular regions in which they are produced, the causes of their extreme velocity, the oblique direction of their motion, and the agents which concur in their formation, has hitherto baffled the researches of the whole philosophical world. Even the nature of *the clouds*, their various modifications, their different electric states, the causes which combine to produce their precipitation into rain, the nature of evaporation, together with an immense number of facts requisite for laying the foundation of a correct theory of the weather, are still hid in obscurity.

It is obvious, that a thorough knowledge of atmospherical phenomena cannot be acquired, before we have ascertained not only the particular facts and appearances connected with the atmosphere, but all the preceding, concomitant, and consequent circumstances with which they are generally accompanied; and to determine such particulars requires an immense variety of observations, both by day and by night, through all the regions of the earth. Before such facts be more fully ascertained, our attempts to account for various atmospherical phenomena must prove unsatisfactory and abortive. Hence, the causes assigned by philosophers of the last century for the production of rain, hail, dew, fire-balls, and other meteors, are now considered nugatory and erroneous; and few will be bold enough to maintain that we have yet arrived at the knowledge of the true causes. If these sentiments be admitted, it will follow, that an increased number of observers of the scenery of the atmosphere, in different climates, with a scientific object in view, could not fail of increasing our knowledge both of the phenomena which take place in the regions of the atmosphere, and of the powers of nature which operate in their production

With respect to the *auroræ boreales*, some data might be ascertained for determining their height above the surface of the earth, which might lead to a discovery of their true cause, were a multitude of observers, in different places, at the same moment, to take the altitude and bearing of any particular coruscation, particularly of the modification of this phenomenon which assumes the form of a rainbow or luminous arch, which can instantly be done by noting the series of stars which appear about the middle or sides of the arc at any particular instant. By this means the parallactic angle might be found, and the distances of the places of observation, or their difference of latitude, if directly north and south of each other, would form base lines for determining the perpendicular elevation of the phenomenon. In reference to luminous meteors, as they are most frequently seen in the night-time, men of science and persons of elevated rank have seldom opportunities of observing their diversified phenomena, and the circumstances with which they are preceded and accompanied. But while persons of this class are reclining on beds of down, or regaling themselves at the festive board, hemmed in from the view of the surrounding sky by the walls and curtains of their splendid apartments, many in the lower walks of life are "keeping watch by night," or travelling from place to place, who have thus an opportunity of observing every variety of atmospherical phenomena; and it is not unlikely may have seen several species of luminous and fiery meteors unknown to the scientific world. Were persons of this description, particularly watchmen, soldiers, sailors, mail-coach guards, policemen, and such like, capable of observing such appearances with scientific interest and accuracy, and of recording their observations, various important additions might be made to the facts which compose the natural history of the atmosphere.

Similar additions might be made to our knowledge of thunder-storms, were their phenomena and concomitant circumstances accurately noted by a vast number of persons in different places. It might, for example, be determined, from a multitude of observations made with this special object in view,—at what distance from the earth a thunder-cloud may explode without danger?—in what circumstances, and at what elevation it generally attains its striking distance, and brings us within the range of its destructive influence?—what particular effects, hitherto unobserved, are produced by lightning on animal, vegetable, and mineral substances?—to what practical purposes its agency might be applied,—and how its destructive ravages might be averted or diminished? The same remarks will apply to the singular phenomenon of meteoric stones. These have seldom been observed at the instant of their descent by men addicted to philosophical research; but chiefly by peasants, labourers, and mechanics, who, at present, are generally unqualified for attending to every circumstance in the preceding and concomitant phenomena connected with their descent, with the discerning eye of a philosopher; and therefore, we may still be ignorant of certain important facts in the history of the fall of these bodies, which may long prevent us from forming any rational theory to explain their causes, or to determine the regions whence their origin is derived.

*Astronomy*.—My next illustration shall be taken from the science of astronomy. Though this is among the oldest of the sciences, and its general principles are established with greater precision than those of almost any other department of science, yet many *desiderata* requisite to its perfection, still remain to be ascertained. The late discovery of several new planets, both primary and secondary, leads us to conclude, that other globes of a similar nature, belonging to our system, may still lie hid in the distant spaces of the firmament. The spheroidal figure of some of the planets—their periods of rotation—the nature of the changes which appear to take place on their surfaces or in their atmospheres—the precise nature of the solar spots, the causes of their changes, and the influence which those changes produce on our earth or atmosphere—the parallax of the fixed stars—the rate of motion of the planetary system in absolute space—the gradual formation of nebulæ—the nature of variable stars—the number of comets, their periods, the nature of their tails and atmospheres, and their uses in the system of nature—with many other interesting particulars of a similar description, still remain to be ascertained. To determine such objects, requires a multiplicity of long-continued observations in every region of the heavens; and it must be evident, that the more we increase the number of astronomical observers, the greater chance we shall have of acquiring a more accurate and comprehensive knowledge of the bodies which roll in the distant regions of the universe, and of the relations they bear to one another, and to the whole system of nature.

This position might be illustrated by a few examples. The surface of Jupiter has been found to be diversified with a variety of spots and belts: the belts, which are considerably darker than the general surface of the planet, are observed to vary in their number, distance, and position. Sometimes only one or two, and sometimes seven or eight belts have been observed; sometimes they are quite distinct, and at other times they seem to run into each other; and, in some instances, the whole surface of this planet has appeared to be covered with small curved belts that were not continuous across his disk.

The following figures represent some of the diversified views which Jupiter sometimes exhibits.

Fig. 1, is copied from Dr. Long, and appears to be one of the views of this planet taken by the celebrated Cassini. It consists of about nine different belts. Fig. 2, is copied from Schroeter, and exhibits a view of Jupiter about the time of its occultation by the moon, on the 7th of April 1792. Fig. 3, is one of Sir W. Herschel's views of this planet, as it appeared on the 28th May 1780, when the whole disk of Jupiter appeared covered with small curved belts, or rather lines, that were not continuous across his disk. Fig. 4, contains a view which is nearly the appearance which Jupiter exhibits

at present, and which is not much different from his appearance for several years past. These appearances may be seen by a good achromatic telescope, magnifying from 80 to 150 times. These views demonstrate, that changes of considerable magnitude are occasionally taking place, either on the surface or in the atmosphere of this planet, which it would be of some importance to ascertain, in order to our acquiring a more intimate knowledge of the physical constitution of this globe. Now, were a number of observers, in different places, to mark these appearances, and to delineate the aspect of this planet during the space of two or three periodical revolutions,* marking the periods of the different changes, and noting at the same time the positions of his satellites—it might be ascertained, whether these changes are occasioned by tides, which are differently affected according to the position of his moons, or, by immense strata of clouds, or other changes that take place in his atmosphere, or by some great physical revolutions which are occasionally agitating the surface of this planet. The observers of such facts behooved to be numerous, in order that the deficiencies of one might be supplied by another, and the general conclusions deduced from a comparison of all the observations taken together; and it would be requisite, that the places of observation be in different countries, that the deficiency of observations in one place, occasioned by a cloudy atmosphere, might be compensated by those made in the serene sky of another. Such a series of observations, although they should not lead to satisfactory conclusions in relation to the particulars now stated, could scarcely fail of throwing some additional light on the nature and constitution of this planet.

With respect to the planet *Venus*, the author some time ago ascertained from observation,† that this planet may be distinctly seen in the day-time, at the time of its *superior* conjunction with the sun, when it presents to the earth a full enlightened hemisphere; provided its geocentric latitude, or distance from the sun's centre at the time be not less than 1° 43′. This is the only position (except at the time of a transit, which happens only once or twice in a

* The annual or periodical revolution of Jupiter is completed in about eleven years and ten months.

† See Nicholson's Phil. Journal, vol. xxxvi. for Oct. 1813.—Edin. Phil. Journal, No. v. for July 1820.—Monthly Mag. Feb. 1814, and August 1820, p. 63.—Scots Magazine for 1814, p. 84, &c.

hundred years) in which the polar and equatorial diameters of this planet can be measured, and their difference, if any, ascertained, so as to determine whether its figure, like that of the earth and several other planets, be *spheroidal*. But as this planet may not happen for a series of years to be in the precise position for such an observation, the attempt to determine the points now stated, even when the planet happens to be placed in the requisite circumstances, would, in all probability, fail, if a number of observers at the same time, in different places, were not engaged in the observation; on account of the uncertainty of enjoying a serene sky at one particular place, during the moments when the observation behooved to be made. Whereas, by a multitude of observations in different places, the object in view could not fail of being determined. The disputes respecting the period of rotation of this planet (whether it be 23 hours 20 minutes, or 24 days 8 hours) might also be settled, were a number of persons to observe its surface with equatorial telescopes in the day-time; particularly in those southern climes where the air is serene, and the sky exhibits a deep azure, where, in all probability, spots would be discovered, which could be traced in their motions for successive periods of twelve hours or more, which would determine to a certainty the point in question.

The following figure and explanation will perhaps tend to show the reason of the dispute which has arisen in reference to this point. Let A represent a spot on the surface of Venus.

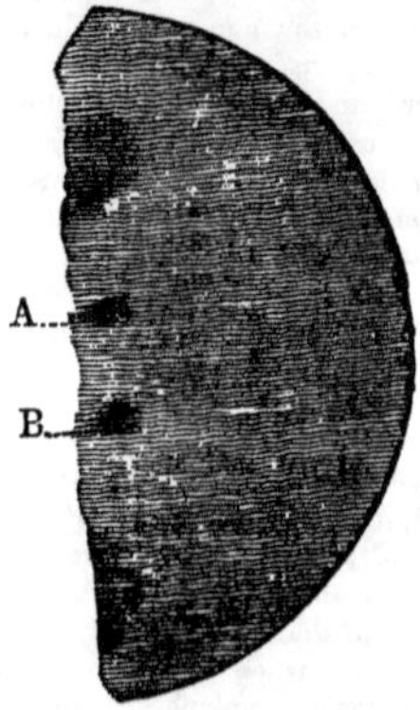


As this planet is seen, by the naked eye, only in the morning a little before sun-rise, or in the evening a short time after sun-set—the motion of the spot cannot be traced above an hour or two in succession; and, consequently, during that time, its progressive motion is almost imperceptible. Suppose the observation to have been made in the evening, after sun-set, the next observation cannot be made till about the same time, on the following evening, when it is found that the spot has moved from A to B. But it is still uncertain whether the spot has only moved from A to B, since the last observation, or has finished a complete revolution, and moved the distance A B as part of another revolution round the axis of the planet. This point can only be ascertained by tracing the motion of the spot without interruption for 10, 12, or 14 hours, when, if the rotation is performed in 23¼ hours, the motion of the spot could be traced without interruption across the whole disk of the planet. But such an observation could only be made in the day-time, in a serene sky, and by means of equatorial instruments, and by numbers of observers in different places, where the attention is directed to the same object. But the limits to which I am confined, in throwing out these cursory hints, prevent me from entering into minute details.

In regard to *comets*, it is scarcely necessary to remark, that were the number of those whose attention is directed to a survey of the heavens considerably increased, many of those eccentric bodies, which pass and repass within the orbits of the planets without being perceived, could not fail of being detected. Were multitudes of such persons engaged in exploring the celestial regions, on opposite sides of the globe, those comets which pass within the limits of our view, and which are above our horizon only in the day-time, and consequently invisible, would be detected, during the night, by our antipodes in the opposite regions of the globe. By this means the number of those bodies belonging to our system, the diversified phenomena they present, the form of their trajectories, the periods of their revolutions, the nature of their tails, and their ultimate destination, might be more accurately determined. With respect to the *fixed stars*, particularly those termed *variable stars*, the results of a multitude of observations made by different persons, might lead us to determine, whether those changes in brightness which they undergo, arise from the transits of large planets revolving around them, and thus furnish direct evidence of their being the centres of systems analogous to our own,—or whether they be occasioned by large spots which periodically interpose between our sight, and then disappear in the course of their rotation,—or whether the distance of such stars be changed by their revolving in a long narrow ellipse, whose transverse axis is situated nearly in our line of vision. In the several instances now stated, an immense variety of successive observations, by numerous observers at different stations, are requisite to accomplish the ends in view; but the limits of this section prevent me from entering into those details requisite for rendering the hints now suggested perspicuous to those who have not devoted their attention to this subject.

The *Moon* being the nearest celestial body to the earth, it might have been expected that the variety of scenery on her surface, and even some parts of her physical constitution, might have been ascertained and delineated. Yet all that has hitherto been discovered with certainty in relation to this body is, that her surface is strikingly diversified with mountains and valleys, with vast caverns or hollows surrounded with mountainous ridges, and with several elevated peaks, which rise, like a sugar loaf, from the middle of the plains. We have no accurate delineation of the lunar scenery, as exhibited in the various stages of the moon's increase and decrease, except those which have been published by Hevelius and Schroeter, which have never been translated into our language, and, consequently, are very little known. Most of our English books on astronomy contain nothing more than a paltry and inaccurate view of the *full moon*, which has been copied by one engraver from another, without any improvements, ever since the days of Ricciolus, and long before the telescope was brought to its present state of improvement. It is not from a telescopic view of the *full* moon that any specific deductions can be made respecting the appearance and arrangement of her diversified scenery; but from long-continued observations of her surface about the period of the quadratures, and at the times when she assumes a crescent or a gibbous phase; for it is only at such times that the shadows of her cavities and mountain-ridges can be distinctly perceived. As there is none of the celestial bodies whose constitution and scenery we have so excellent an opportunity of inspecting, had we a sufficient number of astronomical observers, furnished with good telescopes, the surface of this globe might be almost as accurately delineated as that of the earth, and the most prominent changes that take place on its surface plainly detected. In order to bring to light the minute parts of its scenery, it would only be requisite to distribute the entire surface of this luminary among a hundred or a thousand observers, allotting to each one or more spots as the particular object of his attention, with the understanding, that he is to inspect them with care through every variety of shade they may exhibit, and during the different stages of the moon's increase and decrease, and delineate the different aspects they may present. When we consider that, by means of a telescope which magnifies 200 times, an object on the moon that measures only 600 yards may be perceived as a visible point, and by one which magnifies 800 times, an object not larger than 150 yards in diameter may be distinguished—we can scarcely entertain a doubt, that a number of interesting discoveries might soon be made on the lunar surface, were such minute observations as those now suggested to be continued for a series of years, which might afford sensible and demonstrative evidence of the moon's being a habitable world. But before attention to such objects become general, and the number of astronomical observers be increased far beyond what it is at present, such discoveries can scarcely be expected.

I shall only remark farther on this head, that several discoveries have been made by accidentally directing a telescope to certain parts of the heavens. It is well known that Miss Herschell, while amusing herself in looking at the heavens through Sir William Herschell's telescope, discovered at different times a variety of comets, which might otherwise have passed unnoticed by the astronomical world; and several of the new planets which have been discovered within the last 50 or 60 years, were detected when the discoverers were employed making observations with a different object in view. The splendid comet which appeared in our hemisphere in 1811, was first discovered in this country by a *sawyer*,* who, with a reflecting telescope of his own construction, and from his *sawpit* as an observatory, descried that celestial visitant before it had been noticed by any other astronomer in North Britain. The author of this work detected this comet a day or two afterwards, before he had been informed of the discovery, while he was taking a random sweep over the northern region of the heavens. He had directed his telescope to a certain star in the neighbourhood of *Ursa Major*, and immediately afterwards, taking a general sweep upwards and downwards, and to the east and west, an uncommon object appeared in the field of view, which, after a little inspection, was perceived to be a comet, and he naturally concluded that he had made the first discovery, till the newspapers afterwards informed him that it had been detected a day or two before. It was while Sir W. Herschell was inspecting some small stars near the foot of *Castor*, with a different object in view, that he discovered the planet which bears his name, and which he at first took for a comet. It had been seen thirty years before, but for want of numerous observers to mark its motions, it had been marked in catalogues as a fixed star. It was while Mr. Harding of Lilienthal, near Bremen, was forming an atlas of the stars so far as the eighth magnitude, that, on the 1st September 1804, he discovered in the constellation Pisces the planet Juno, one of the four asteroids situated between the orbits of Mars and Jupiter.

If, therefore, instead of a few individuals occasionally engaged in surveying celestial phe-

* The name of this gentleman is Mr. Veitch, and I believe he resides in the neighbourhood of Kelso.

nomena, and chiefly confined to a small portion of Europe,—were thousands and ten thousands of telescopes daily directed to the sky from every region of the earth, and were distinct portions of the heavens allotted to distinct classes of observers, as the object of their more immediate research, every portion of that vast concave, with the numerous globes which roll within its wide circumference, as far as human vision assisted by art can penetrate, would ere long be thoroughly explored, and its hidden worlds disclosed to view. No comet could pass within the orbit of Jupiter without being detected,—the undiscovered planets belonging to our system, if any still remain, would be brought to view,—the periodical changes on the surfaces and in the atmospheres of the planets already discovered, with all their diversified phenomena, would be more accurately ascertained and delineated,—the path of the solar system in absolute space, the velocity of its motion, the distant centre about which it revolves, and the centre of gravity of the nebula to which it belongs, might be determined,—the changes and revolutions that are taking place among the fixed stars,—the undiscovered strata of *nebulæ*,—the old systems that are going into decay,—the new creations that may be emerging into existence, and many other sublime objects which at present lie concealed in the unexplored regions of space, might be brought within the range of human contemplation, and astronomy, the sublimest of all the sciences, approximate towards perfection.

For making the observations now supposed, a profound knowledge of the physical and mathematical principles of astronomy is not absolutely necessary. All the qualifications essentially requisite are,—a general knowledge of the elements of the science, of the celestial phenomena which have already been explored, and of the method of determining the right ascension and declination of any observed phenomenon,—qualifications, which every person of common understanding can easily acquire.

I might next have illustrated the general position laid down in the beginning of this section from the science of *chymistry*. This science, having for its object to ascertain the ingredients that enter into the composition of bodies, the nature of those ingredients, the manner in which they combine, and the properties resulting from their combination; or, in other words, an analytical examination of the material world, and the principles which concur to produce its diversified phenomena; it is apparent, at first view, that an immense number and variety of experiments are indispensably requisite for accomplishing such objects; and, consequently, that its progress towards perfection cannot be accelerated, unless multitudes of experimenters concur in observing the phenomena of nature, and the processes of the arts, in instituting analytical experiments, and in prosecuting every inquiry which has a tendency to promote its improvement. It is chiefly in consequence of the increased number of its cultivators that this science has risen to the distinguished rank it now holds among the useful departments of human knowledge, and that so many brilliant discoveries have rewarded the investigations of its votaries. Wrenched from the grasp of empirics and alchymists, and no longer confined to the paltry object of searching for the *philosopher's stone*, it extends its range over every object in the material world, and sheds its influence over all the other departments of physical science; and as its votaries increase in numbers and in perseverance, it will doubtless bring to light scenes and discoveries still more interesting and brilliant than those which have hitherto been disclosed. Illustrations of the same description might also have been taken from optics, electricity, magnetism, galvanism, pneumatics, and other departments of natural science; but having protracted this section to a disproportionate length, the instances already stated will, I presume, be sufficient to prove the truth of the position, "*that a general diffusion of knowledge would have a powerful influence on the progress of science.*"

From the few hints now given, and from many others that might have been suggested, had my limits permitted, it will appear, that much still remains to be accomplished till any science, even those which are farthest advanced, arrive at perfection. The reason is obvious; the scene of universal nature has never yet been thoroughly surveyed, and never will be, till the eyes and the intellects of millions be fixed in the contemplation of its multifarious and diversified objects and relations. Till the universe, in all its aspects, so far as it lies within the range of human inspection, be more particularly explored, clouds and darkness will continue to rest on many interesting departments of knowledge, and many of our most specious theories in the sciences must be considered as reposing on slender and unstable foundations. Prior to the introduction of the inductive method of philosophizing, men of science were extremely prone to the framing of hypotheses, before they had attentively surveyed and collected the requisite facts, and when only a few scattered fragments of nature were present to their view. Theory was reared upon theory, and system upon system; each of them obtained its admirers and its period of applause, but, in consequence of modern researches, they have now passed away like a dream or a vision of the night. The crystalline spheres with which Ptolemy had enclosed the heavens are now dashed to pieces; the vortices of Des Cartes have long since ceased their whirling; the terraqueous globe which Tycho had fixed in the centre of the universe is now set in rapid motion through the heavens, in company with the planetary orbs; and the abyss of water with which Burnet had filled the internal cavity of the earth is now converted into a mass denser than the solid rock. The *Terra Australis Incognito*, which served as a prop to certain theories, has completely evanished, and is now transformed into a dreary mass of water and ice. The subtile *ether*, which formerly accounted for so many phenomena, is now evaporated into electricity and heat. Whiston's idea of the cometary origin of our globe, and Buffon's fancy of the earth's being a splinter struck from the body of the sun, are fast sinking into oblivion; and such will be the fate of every theory, however specious, which is not founded on the broad basis of inductive evidence.

Even in the present day, there is still too great a propensity to generalize, without submitting to the trouble of observing phenomena, and noting their various modifications and attendant circumstances. The human mind is impatient, and attempts to reach the goal by the shortest and most rapid course, while observation and experiment are tedious and slow. Instead of surveying the material world with his own eyes, and investigating, by observation and experiment, its principles and laws, the man of genius frequently shuts himself up in his closet, and from a few scattered fragments of nature, constructs, in his imagination, a splendid theory, which makes a noise and a blaze for a little, like an unsubstantial meteor, and then evanishes into air. The system of nature, though directed in its general movements by a few simple laws, is too grand and extensive, and too complex in many of its parts, to be grasped by a few individuals, after a cursory survey; and, therefore, to attempt to comprehend its multifarious revolutions, phenomena and objects within the range of theories founded on a partial view of some of its detached parts, is not only an evidence of presumption and folly, but tends to damp our ardour in prosecuting the only sure path which leads to discovery, and to frustrate what appears to be one of the designs of the Creator, namely, *to grant to the intelligent inhabitants of our globe a gradual display of his stupendous plans in the universe as the reward of their incessant and unwearied contemplation of his wondrous works.*

Were the period arrived (and of its arrival I entertain no doubt, from the present movements of the human mind) when the majority of mankind shall devote a portion of their time and attention to the purposes of science, and to the contemplation of nature—then the different tastes of individuals, and the various situations in which they may be placed, would lead them to cultivate more particularly the science most congenial to their minds; and were distinct departments of the same science marked out for distinct classes of individuals, as the more immediate field of their investigation, on the principle of the division of labour, every leading principle and fact in relation to that science would soon be detected and illustrated in all its practical bearings. Even as matters presently stand, were the whole literary and scientific world to form itself into one great republic, and to allot the several branches of every department of knowledge to the different classes of such a community, according to their respective tastes and pursuits, as the object of their more particular attention, it might be followed by many interesting results, and important discoveries and improvements. But we live in too early a period in the history of science to expect a general interest to be taken in such objects; we are but just emerging from the gloom of ignorance and superstition; the great body of mankind still suffer their faculties to lie in a state of languor and inactivity, and those who are more vigorous and alert are too much engrossed in commercial speculations, in grasping at power and opulence, and in the indulgence of sensual gratifications, to think of attending to the interests of science and the progress of the human mind. Much, however, might be accomplished in this respect, with ease and pleasure, by various classes of society, and without interfering with their ordinary avocations, were their minds inclined and their attention directed to such pursuits. Sailors, in crossing the Atlantic, the Pacific, and the Indian oceans, have frequently excellent opportunities of observing the phenomena of the waters, the atmosphere, and the heavens, peculiar to the climates through which they pass; and were the facts presented to their view observed with care, classified, and recorded, they might, in many instances, contribute to the advancement of science. But thousands of such persons can sail twice "from Indus to the frozen pole, as ignorant as their *log*, and as stubborn as their compass," without importing one intellectual acquisition. The observations made during a single voyage across the Atlantic, by a single observer, M. Humboldt, on the aspect of the Antarctic region of the heavens—the peculiar azure of the African sky—the luminous meteors of the atmosphere—the tides, the currents, and the different colours of the ocean, and other phenomena which happened to present themselves to his view—are of more value to the scientific world than the observations of ten thousands of other beings who, for a series of years, have traversed the same regions. Yet these possessed, on an average, the same sentient organs, the same intellectual powers, though somewhat differently modified and directed, the same natural capacities for observation as this distinguished philosopher, which required only an impulse to be given in a certain direction, in order to accomplish the same ends. And was Humboldt more burdened and perplexed, or did he feel less comfortable and happy than his ignorant and grovelling associates in the ship that wafted them across the ocean? No. He felt emotions of delight and intellectual enjoyments to which they were utter strangers. While they were lolling on their hammocks, or loitering upon deck, viewing every object with a "brute unconscious gaze," and finding no enjoyment but in a glass of grog, —a train of interesting reflections, having a relation to the past, the present, and the future, passed through the mind of this philosopher. He felt those exquisite emotions which arise from perception of the beautiful and the sublime; he looked forward to the advancement of natural science as the result of his observations, and beheld a display of the wisdom and grandeur of the Almighty in the diversified scenes through which he passed. Such observations and mental employments as those to which I allude, so far from distracting the mind, and unfitting it for the performance of official duties, would tend to prevent that languor and *ennui* which result from mental inactivity, and would afford a source of intellectual enjoyment amidst the uniformity of scene, which is frequently presented in the midst of the ocean.

From the whole that has been now stated on this subject, it appears, that in order to make science advance with accelerated steps, and to multiply the sources of mental enjoyment, we have only to set the machinery of the human mind (at present in a quiescent state) in motion, and to direct its movements to those objects which are congenial to its native dignity and its high destination. The capacity of the bulk of mankind for learning mechanical employments, and for contriving and executing plans of human destruction, proves that they are competent to make all the researches requisite for the improvement of science. The same mental energies now exerted in mechanical labour and in the arts of mischief, if properly directed, and acting in unison, and accompanied with a spirit of perseverance, would accomplish many grand and beneficent effects, in relation both to the physical and moral world, and would amply compensate the occasional want of extraordinary degrees of mental vigour. Were only a hundred millions of eyes and of intellects, (or the tenth part of the population of our globe) occasionally fixed on all the diversified aspects, motions and relations of universal nature, it could not fail of being followed by the most noble and interesting results, not only in relation to science, but to social and moral order, and to the general melioration of mankind. Were this supposition realized, our travellers, merchants, and mariners, along with the produce of foreign lands, might regularly import, without the least injury to their commercial interests, interesting facts, both physical and moral, scientific observations, chymical experiments, and various other fragments of useful information for rearing the Temple of Science, and extending the boundaries of human knowledge.

---

## SECTION IV.

### ON THE PLEASURES AND ENJOYMENTS CONNECTED WITH THE PURSUITS OF SCIENCE.

MAN is a compound being; his nature consists of two essential parts, body and mind. Each of these parts of the human constitution has its peculiar uses, and is susceptible of peculiar gratifications. The body is furnished with external senses, which are both the sources of pleasure and the inlets of knowledge, and the Creator has furnished the universe with objects fitted for their exercise and gratification. While these pleasures are directed by the dictates of reason, and confined within the limits prescribed by the Divine law, they are so far from being unlawful, that in the enjoyment of them we fulfil one of the purposes for which our Creator brought us into existence. But the pursuit of sensitive pleasures is not the ultimate end of our being; we enjoy such gratifications in common with the inferior animals; and in so far as we rest in them as our chief good, we pour contempt on our intellectual nature, and degrade ourselves nearly to the level of the beasts that perish.

Man is endowed with intellectual powers, as well as with organs of sensation,—with faculties of a higher order, and which admit of more varied and sublime gratifications than those which the senses can produce. By these faculties we are chiefly distinguished from the lower orders of animated existence; in the proper exercise and direction of them, we experience the highest and most refined enjoyments of which our nature is susceptible, and are gradually prepared for the employments of that immortal existence to which we are destined. The corporeal senses were bestowed chiefly in subserviency to the powers of intellect, and to supply materials for thought and contemplation; and the pleasures peculiar to our intellectual nature, rise as high above mere sensitive enjoyments, as the rank of man stands in the scale of existence, above that of the fowls of the air, or the beasts of the forest. Such pleasures are pure and refined; they are congenial to the character of a rational being; they are more permanent than mere sensitive enjoyments; they can be enjoyed when worldly comforts are withdrawn, and when sensual gratifications can afford no delight; they afford solace in the hours of retirement from the bustle of business, and consolation amidst the calamities and afflictions to which humanity is exposed; and the more we acquire a relish for such pleasures, the better shall we be prepared for associating with intelligences of a higher order in the future world.

Before proceeding to the more particular illustration of this topic, let us consider the state and the enjoyments of the man whose mind is shrouded in ignorance. He grows up to manhood like a vegetable, or like one of the lower animals that are fed and nourished for the slaughter. He exerts his physical powers, because such exertion is necessary for his subsistence; were it otherwise, we should most frequently find him dozing over the fire, or basking in the sun, with a gaze as dull and stupid as his ox, regardless of every thing but the gratification of his appetites. He has perhaps been taught the art of reading, but has never applied it to the acquisition of knowledge. His views are chiefly confined to the objects immediately around him, and to the daily avocations in which he is employed. His knowledge of society is circumscribed within the limits of his parish, and his views of the world in which he dwells are confined within the range of the country in which he resides, or of the blue hills which skirt his horizon. Of the aspects of the globe in other countries—of the various tribes with which they are peopled—of the seas and rivers, continents and islands which diversify the landscape of the earth—of the numerous orders of animated beings which people the ocean, the atmosphere and the land,—of the revolutions of nations, and the events which have taken place in the history of the world, he has almost as little conception as the animals that range the forest, or bound through the lawns. In regard to the boundless regions that lie beyond him in the firmament, and the bodies that roll there in magnificent grandeur, he has the most confused and inaccurate ideas; and he seldom troubles himself with inquiries in relation to such subjects. Whether the stars be great or small, whether they be near us or at a distance, or whether they move or stand still, is to him a matter of trivial importance. If the sun give him light by day, and the moon by night, and the clouds distil their watery treasures upon his parched fields, he is contented, and leaves all such inquiries and investigations to those who have little else to engage their attention. He views the canopy of heaven as merely a ceiling to our earthly habitation, and the starry orbs as only so many luminous studs or tapers to diversify its aspect, and to afford a glimmering light to the benighted traveller. Of the discoveries which have been made in the physical sciences in ages past, of the wonders of creation which they have unfolded to view, of the instruments which have been invented for exploring the universe, and of the improvements which are now going forward in every department of science and art, and the prospects they are opening to our view, he is almost as entirely ignorant as if he had been fixed under the frozen pole, or chained to the surface of a distant planet. He considers learning as consisting chiefly in the knowledge of grammar, Greek and Latin; and philosophy and astronomy, as the arts of telling fortunes and predicting the state of the weather; and experimental chymistry, as allied to the arts of magic and necromancy. He has no idea of the manner in which the understanding may be enlightened and expanded, he has no relish for intellectual pursuits, and no conception of the pleasures they afford, and he sets no value on knowledge but in so far as it may tend to increase his riches and his sensual gratifications. He has no desire for making improvements in his trade or domestic arrangements, and gives no countenance to those useful inventions and public improvements which are devised by others. He sets himself against every innovation, whether religious, political, mechanical, or agricultural, and is determined to abide by the "good old customs" of his forefathers, however irrational and absurd. Were it dependent upon him, the moral world would stand still as the material world was supposed to do in former times; all useful inventions and improvements would cease, existing evils would never be remedied, ignorance and superstition would universally prevail, the human mind would be arrested in its progress to perfection, and man would never arrive at the true dignity of his intellectual nature.

It is evident that such an individual, (and the world contains thousands and millions of such characters) can never have his mind elevated to those sublime objects and contemplations which enrapture the man of science, nor feel those pure and exquisite pleasures which cultivated minds so frequently experience; nor can he form those lofty and expansive ideas of the Deity which the grandeur and magnificence of his works are calculated to inspire. He is left as a prey to all those foolish notions and vain alarms which are engendered by ignorance and superstition; and he swallows, without the least hesitation, all the absurdities and childish tales respecting witches, hobgoblins, spectres and apparitions, which have been handed down to him by his forefathers in former generations. And while he thus gorges his mind with fooleries and absurdities, he spurns at the discoveries of science as impositions on the credulity of mankind, and contrary to reason and common sense. That the sun is a million of times larger than the earth, that light flies from his body at the rate of two hundred thousand miles in a moment of time, and that the earth is whirling round its axis from day to day, with a velocity of a thousand miles every hour, are regarded by him as notions far more improbable and extravagant than the story of the "Wonderful Lamp," and all the other tales of the "Arabian Night's Entertainments." In his hours of leisure from his daily avocations, his thoughts either run wild among the most grovelling objects, or sink into sensuality or inanity, and solitude and retirement present no charms to his vacant mind. While human beings are thus immersed in ignorance, destitute of rational ideas, and of a solid substratum of thought, they can never experience those pleasures and enjoyments which flow from the exercise of the understanding, and which correspond to the dignity of a rational and immortal nature.

On the other hand, the man whose mind is irradiated with the light of substantial science, has views, and feelings, and exquisite enjoyments to which the former is an entire stranger. In consequence of the numerous and multifarious ideas he has acquired, he is introduced, as it were, into a new world, where he is entertained with scenes, objects, and movements, of which a mind enveloped in ignorance can form no conception. He can trace back the stream of time to its commencement; and, gliding along its downward course, can survey the most memorable events which have happened in every part of its progress from the primeval ages to the present day—the rise of empires, the fall of kings, the revolutions of nations, the battles of warriors, and the important events which have followed in their train—the progress of civilization, and of arts and sciences—the judgments which have been inflicted on wicked nations—the dawnings of Divine mercy towards our fallen race—the manifestation of the Son of God in our nature—the physical changes and revolutions which have taken place in the constitution of our globe—in short, the whole of the leading events in the chain of Divine dispensation from the beginning of the world to the period in which we live. With his mental eye he can survey the terraqueous globe in all its variety of aspects; contemplate the continents, islands and oceans which compose its exterior, the numerous rivers by which it is indented, the lofty ranges of mountains which diversify its surface, its winding caverns, its forests, lakes, sandy deserts, ice-islands, whirlpools, boiling springs, glaciers, sulphuric mountains, bituminous lakes, and the states and empires into which it is distributed, the tides and currents of the ocean, the ice-bergs of the polar regions, and the verdant scenes of the torrid zone. He can climb, in imagination, to the summit of the flaming volcano, listen to its subterraneous bellowings, behold its lava bursting from its mouth and rolling down its sides like a flaming river—descend into the subterranean grotto, survey, from the top of the Andes, the lightnings flashing and the thunders rolling far beneath him—stand on the brink of the dashing cataract and listen to its roarings—contemplate the ocean rearing its billows in a storm, and the hurricane and tornado tearing up forests by their roots, and tossing them about as stubble. Sitting at his fireside, during the blasts of winter, he can survey the numerous tribes of mankind scattered over the various climates of the earth, and entertain himself with views of their manners, customs, religion, laws, trade, manufactures, marriage ceremonies, civil and ecclesiastical governments, arts, sciences, cities, towns and villages, and the animals peculiar to every region. In his rural walks he can not only appreciate the beneficence of Nature and the beauties and harmonies of the vegetable kingdom, in their exterior aspect, but can also penetrate into the hidden processes which are going on in the roots, trunks and leaves of plants and flowers, and contemplate the numerous vessels through which the sap is flowing from their roots through the trunks and branches, the millions of pores through which their odoriferous effluvia exhale, their fine and delicate texture, their microscopical beauties, their orders, genera, and species, and their uses in the economy of nature.

With the help of his microscope, he can enter into a world unknown to the ignorant, and altogether invisible to the unassisted eye. In every plant and flower which adorns the field, in every leaf of the forest, in the seeds, prickles and down of all vegetables, he perceives beauties and harmonies, and exquisi e contrivances, of which, without this instrument, he could have formed no conception. In every scale of a haddock he perceives a beautiful piece of net-work, admirably contrived and arranged, and in the scale of a sole a still more diversified structure, which no art could imitate, terminated with pointed spikes, and formed with admirable regularity. Where nothing but a speck of *mouldiness* appears to the naked eye, he beholds *a forest of mushrooms* with long stalks, and with leaves and blossoms distinctly visible. In the eyes of a common fly, where others can see only two small protuberances, he perceives several thousands of beautiful transparent globes, exquisitely rounded and polished, placed with the utmost regularity in rows, crossing each other like a kind of lattice-work, and forming the most admirable piece of mechanism which the eye can contemplate. The small dust that covers the wings of moths and butterflies he perceives to consist of an infinite multitude of feathers of various forms, not much unlike the feathers of birds, and adorned with the most bright and vivid colours. In an animal so small that the naked eye can scarcely distinguish it as a visible point, he perceives a head, mouth, eyes, legs, joints, bristles, hair, and other animal parts and functions, as nicely formed and adjusted, and endowed with as much vivacity, agility and intelligence as the larger animals. In the tail of a small fish or the foot of a frog, he can perceive the variegated branchings of the veins and arteries, and the blood circulating through them with amazing velocity. In a drop of stagnant water he perceives thousands of living beings of various shapes and sizes, beautifully formed, and swimming with wanton vivacity like fishes in the midst of the ocean. In short, by this instrument he perceives that the whole earth is full of animation, and that there is not a single tree, plant or flower, and scarcely a drop of water that is not teeming with life and peopled with its peculiar inhabitants. He thus enters, as it were, into a new world, invisible to other eyes, where every object in the animal, vegetable and mineral kingdoms, presents a new and interesting aspect, and unfolds beauties, harmonies, contrasts and exquisite contrivances, altogether inconceivable by the ignorant and unreflecting mind.

In the invisible atmosphere which surrounds him, where other minds discern nothing but an immense blank, he beholds an assemblage of wonders, and a striking scene of Divine Wisdom and Omnipotence. He views this invisible agent not only as a *material* but as a *compound* substance—compounded of two opposite principles, the one the source of flame and animal life, and the other destructive to both, and producing by their different combinations, the most diversified and beneficent effects. He perceives the atmosphere, as the agent under the Almighty, which produces the germination and growth of plants, and all the beauties of the vegetable creation—which preserves water in a liquid state—supports fire and flame, and produces animal heat, which sustains the clouds, and gives buoyancy to the feathered tribes—which is the cause of winds—the vehicle of smells—the medium of sounds—the source of all the pleasures we derive from the harmonies of music—the cause of that universal light and splendour which is diffused around us, and of the advantages we derive from the morning and evening twilight. In short, he contemplates it as the prime mover in a variety of machines,—as impelling ships across the ocean, blowing our furnaces, grinding our corn, raising water from the deepest pits, extinguishing fires, setting power-looms in motion, propelling steam-boats along rivers and canals, raising balloons to the region of the clouds, and performing a thousand other beneficent agencies without which our globe would cease to be a habitable world. All which views and contemplations have an evident tendency to enlarge the capacity of the mind, to stimulate its faculties, and to produce rational enjoyment.

Again,—the man of knowledge, even when shrouded in darkness, and in solitude, where other minds could find no enjoyment, can entertain himself with the most sublime contemplations. He can trace the huge globe on which we stand flying through the depths of space, carrying along with it its vast population, at the rate of sixty thousand miles every hour, and, by the inclination of its axis, bringing about the alternate succession of summer and winter, spring and harvest. By the aid of his telescope he can transport himself towards the moon, and survey the circular plains, the deep caverns, the conical hills, the lofty peaks, the shadows of the hills and vales, and the rugged and romantic mountain scenery which diversify the surface of this orb of night. By the help of the same instrument, he can range through the planetary system, wing his way through the regions of space along with the swiftest orbs, and trace many of the physical aspects and revolutions which have a relation to distant worlds. He can transport himself to the planet Saturn, and behold a stupendous ring 600,000 miles in circumference, revolving in majestic grandeur every ten hours, around a globe nine hundred times larger than the earth, while seven moons larger than ours, along with an innumerable host of stars, display their radiance, to adorn the firmament of that magnificent world. He can wing his flight to the still more distant regions of the universe, leaving the sun and all his planets behind him, till they appear like a scarcely discernible speck in creation, and contemplate thousands and millions of stars and starry systems, beyond the range of the unassisted eye, and wander among suns and worlds dispersed throughout the boundless dimensions of space. He can fill up, in his imagination, those blanks which astronomy has never directly explored, and conceive thousands of systems and ten thousands of worlds, beyond all that is visible by the optic tube, stretching out to infinity on every hand,—new creations incessantly starting into existence—peopled with intelligences of various orders, and all under the superintendence and government of "the King Eternal, Immortal and Invisible," whose power is omnipotent, and the limits of his dominions past finding out.

It is evident that a mind capable of such excursions and contemplations as I have now supposed, must experience enjoyments infinitely superior to those of the individual whose soul is enveloped in intellectual darkness. If substantial happiness is chiefly seated in the mind, if it consists in the vigorous exercise of its faculties, if it depends on the multiplicity of objects which lie within the range of its contemplation, if it is augmented by the view of scenes of beauty and sublimity, and displays of infinite intelligence and power, if it is connected with tranquillity of mind, which generally accompanies intellectual pursuits, and with the subjugation of the pleasures of sense to the dictates of reason—the enlightened mind must enjoy gratifications as far superior to those of the ignorant, as man is superior, in station and capacity, to the worms of the dust.

In order to illustrate this topic a little farther, I shall select a few facts and deductions in relation to science which demonstrate the interesting nature and delightful tendency of scientific pursuits.

Every species of rational information has a tendency to produce pleasing emotions. There is a certain gratification in becoming acquainted with objects and operations of which we were formerly ignorant, and that, too, altogether independent of the practical tendency of such knowledge, of the advantages we may expect to reap from it, or the sensitive enjoyments with which it may be accompanied. A taste for knowledge, a capacity to acquire it, and a pleasure accompanying its acquisition, form a part of the constitution of every mind. The Creator has implanted in the human mind a principle of curiosity, and annexed a pleasure to its gratification, to excite us to investigations of the wonders of creation he has presented before us, to lead us to just conceptions of his infinite perfections, and of the relation in which we stand to him as the subjects of his government. We all know, with what a lively interest most persons peruse novels and romances, where hair-breadth escapes, mysterious incidents, and tales of wonder are depicted with all the force and beauty of language. But the scenes detailed in such writings produce only a momentary enjoyment. Being retraced as only the fictions of a lively imagination, they pass away like a dream or a vision of the night, leaving the understanding bewildered, and destitute of any solid improvement. In order to improve the intellectual faculties while we gratify the principle of curiosity, it is nly requisite, that we direct the attention to *facts* instead of fictions; and when the *real scenes* of the universe are presented in an interesting aspect, they are calculated to produce emotions of wonder and delight even superior to those excited by the most highly wrought tales of fiction and romance. The following facts and considerations will perhaps tend to corroborate this position.

In the first place, *the number of effects produced by a single principle in nature*, is calculated to excite emotions of admiration and delight. From the simple principle of *gravitation*, for instance, proceed all the beauties and sublimities which arise from the meandering rills, the majestic rivers, and the roaring cataracts—it causes the mountains to rest on a solid basis, and confines the ocean to its appointed channels—retains the inhabitants of the earth to its surface, and prevents them from flying off in wild confusion through the voids of space—it produces the descent of the rains and dews, and the alternate flux and reflux of the tides—regulates the various movements of all animals—forms mechanical powers—gives impulsion to numerous machines—rolls the moon round the earth, and prevents her from flying off to the distant regions of space—extends its influence from the moon to the earth, from the earth to the moon, and from the sun to the remotest planets, preserving surrounding worlds in their proper courses, and connecting the solar system with other worlds and systems in the remote spaces of the universe. When a stick of sealing wax is rubbed with a piece of flannel, it attracts feathers or small bits of paper; when a long tube of glass, or a cat's back is rubbed in the dark, they emit flashes of fire, accompanied with a snapping noise. Now is it not delightful to a rational mind to know, that the same principle which causes wax or amber to attract light substances, and glass tubes or cylinders to emit sparks of fire, produces the lightnings of heaven, and all the sublime phenomena which accompany a violent thunder-storm, and, in combination with other agents, produces also the fiery meteor which sweeps through the sky with its luminous train, and the beautiful coruscations of the aurora borealis? There are more than fifty thousand different species of plants in the vegetable kingdom, all differing from one another in their size, structure, flowers, leaves, fruits, mode of propagation, internal vessels, medicinal virtues, and the odours they exhale. Who would imagine that this immense assemblage of vegetable productions which adorns the surface of the earth in every clime, with such a diversity of forms, fruits and colours, are the result of the combination of four or five simple substances variously modified by the hand of the Creator? Yet it is an undoubted fact, ascertained from chymical analysis, that all vegetable substances, from the invisible mushroom which adheres to a spot of mouldiness, to the cedar of Lebanon and the Banian-tree, which would cover with its shade an army of ten thousand men,—are solely composed of the following natural principles,—Caloric, Light, Water, Air and Carbon.

Again, is it not wonderful, that the invisible atmosphere should compress our bodies every moment with a weight of more than thirty thousand pounds without our feeling it, and the whole earth with a weight of 12,043,468,800,000,000,000 of *pounds*, or five thousand billions of *tons*, that this pressure is essentially necessary to our existence, and that a small quantity of air within us, which would not weigh above a single ounce, by its strong elastic force, counteracts the effects of this tremendous pressure upon our bodies.

and prevents our being crushed to pieces—that the same cause prevents our habitations from falling upon us and crushing us to death, without which our glass windows would be shattered to atoms, and our most stately edifices tumbled into ruins!—that this atmosphere is at the same time performing an immense variety of operations in Nature and Art—insinuating itself into the pores and sap-vessels of plants and flowers—producing respiration in all living beings, and supporting all the processes of life and vegetation throughout the animal and vegetable creation—that its pressure produces the process of what is called *suction* and *cupping*—causes snails and periwinkles to adhere to the rocks on which they are found—gives effect to the adhesion of bodies by means of mortar and cements—raises water in our forcing-pumps and fire-engines—supports the quicksilver in our barometers—prevents the water of our seas and rivers from boiling and evaporating into steam—and promotes the action of our steam-engines while raising water from deep pits, and while propelling vessels along seas and rivers!

In the next place, science contributes to the gratification of the human mind *by enabling us to trace, in many objects and operations, surprising resemblances, where we should least of all have expected them.* Who could, at first sight, imagine, that the process of breathing is a species of combustion, or burning—that the diamond is nothing else than *carbon* in a crystallized state, and differs only in a very slight degree from a piece of charcoal—that water is a compound of two invisible airs or gases, and that one of these ingredients is the principle of flame!—that the air which produces suffocation and death in coal-mines and subterraneous grottos, is the same substance which gives briskness to ale, beer, and soda water, and the acid flavour to many mineral springs—that the air we breathe is composed of the same ingredients and nearly in the same proportions as nitric acid or aqua fortis, which can dissolve almost all the metals, and a single draught of which would instantly destroy the human frame—that the colour of *white* is a mixture or compound of all the other colours, *red*, *orange*, *yellow*, *green*, *blue*, *indigo*, and *violet*, and consequently, that the white light of the sun produces all that diversity of colouring which adorns the face of nature—that the same principle which causes our fires to burn, forms acids, produces the rust of metals, and promotes the growth of plants by night—that plants breathe and perspire as well as animals—that carbonic acid gas, or fixed air, is the product both of vegetation, of burning, of fermentation and of breathing—that it remains indestructible by age, and, in all its diversified combinations, still preserves its *identity*—that the air which burns in our street-lamps and illuminates our shops and manufactories, is the same which causes a balloon to rise above the clouds, and likewise extinguishes flame when it is immersed in a body of this gas—that the leaves of vegetables which rot upon the ground and appear to be lost for ever, are converted by the oxygen of the atmosphere into carbonic acid gas, and this *very same carbon* is, in process of time, absorbed by a new race of vegetables, which it clothes with a new foliage, and again renews the face of nature—and that the same principle which causes the sensation of *heat* is the cause of fluidity, expands bodies in every direction, enters into every operation in nature, flies from the sun at the rate of 195,000 miles in a second of time, and, by its powerful influence, prevents the whole matter of the universe from being converted into a solid mass!

What, then, can be more delightful, to a being furnished with such powers as man, than to trace the secret machinery by which the God of nature accomplishes his designs in the visible world, and displays his infinite power and intelligence—to enter into the hidden springs of Nature's operations, to follow her through all her winding recesses, and to perceive, from what simple principles and causes the most sublime and diversified phenomena are produced! It is with this view that the Almighty hath set before us his wondrous works, not to be overlooked, or beheld with a "brute unconscious gaze," but to be investigated, in order that they may be admired, and that in such investigations we may enjoy a sacred pleasure in contemplating the results of his Wisdom and Intelligence.

In the third place, science contributes to our enjoyment *by the grand and sublime objects she presents before us.* In consequence of the investigations which have been made to determine the distances and magnitudes of the heavenly bodies, objects of magnificence and grandeur are now presented to the view of the enlightened mind of which former ages could form no conception. These objects are magnificent in respect of *magnitude*, of *motion*, of *the vast spaces which intervene between them*, and of *the noble purposes for which they are destined.*

What a sublime idea, for example, is presented to the view by such an object as the planet *Jupiter*,—a globe fourteen hundred times larger than the world in which we dwell, and whose surface would contain a population a hundred times more numerous than all the inhabitants that have existed on our globe since the creation! And how is the sublimity of such an idea augmented when we consider, that this immense body is revolving round its axis at the rate of twenty-eight thousand miles in an hour, and is flying, at the same time, through the regions of space, twenty-nine thousand miles every hour, carrying along with it four moons, each of them larger than the earth, during its whole course round the centre of its motion! And if this planet, which appears only like a luminous *speck* on the nocturnal sky, presents such an august idea, when its magnitude and motions are investigated, what an astonishing idea is presented to the mind when it contemplates the size and splendour of the *sun*,—a body which would contain within its bowels nine hundred globes larger than Jupiter, and thirteen hundred thousand globes of the bulk of the earth,—which darts its rays, in a few moments, to the remotest bounds of the planetary system, producing light and colour, and life and vegetation throughout surrounding worlds! And how must our astonishment be still increased, when we consider the *number* of such globes which exist throughout the universe; that within the range of our telescopes more than eighty millions of globes, similar to the sun in size and in splendour, are arranged at immeasurable distances from each other, diffusing their radiance through the immensity of space, and enlivening surrounding worlds with their benign influence, besides the innumerable multitudes, which our reason tells us, must exist beyond all that is visible to the eyes of mortals!

But the *motions*, no less than the magnitudes of such bodies, present ideas of sublimity. That a globe* as large as the earth should fly through the celestial regions with a velocity of seventy-six thousand miles an hour,—that another globe† should move at the rate of one thousand seven hundred and fifty miles in a minute, and a hundred and five thousand miles an hour,—that even Saturn, with all his assemblage of rings and moons, should be carried along his course, with a velocity of twenty-two thousand miles an hour, —that some of the comets, when near the sun, should fly with the amazing velocity of eight hundred thousand miles an hour,—that, in all probability, the sun himself, with all his attending planets, besides their own proper motions, are carried around some distant centre at the rate of more than sixty thousand miles every hour; and that thousands and millions of systems are moving in the same rapid manner, are facts so astonishing, and so far exceeding every thing we behold around us on the surface of the earth, that the imagination is overpowered and confounded at the idea of the astonishing forces which are in operation throughout the universe, and of the power and energy by which they are produced; and every rational being feels a sublime pleasure in the contemplation of such objects which is altogether unknown to the ignorant mind.

The vast and *immeasurable spaces* which intervene between the great bodies of the universe likewise convey august and sublime conceptions. Between the earth and the sun there intervenes a space so vast, that a cannon ball, flying with the velocity of five hundred miles an hour, would not reach that luminary in twenty years; and a mail-coach, moving at its utmost speed, would not arrive at its surface in less than twelve hundred years; and, were it to proceed from the sun towards the planet Herschel, it would not arrive at that body after the lapse of *twenty-two thousand years*. And yet the sun, at that immense distance, exerts his attractive energy, retains that huge planet in its orbit, and dispenses light and colour, life and animation over every part of its surface. But all such spaces, vast as at first sight they appear, dwindle, as it were, into a span, when compared with those immeasurable spaces which are interposed between us and the regions of the stars. Between the earth and the nearest fixed star a space intervenes so vast and incomprehensible, that a ball flying with the velocity above mentioned, would not pass through it in four millions and five hundred thousand years; and as there are stars, visible through telescopes, at least a hundred times farther distant from our globe, it would require such a body four hundred millions of years, or a period 67,000 times greater than that which has elapsed since the Mosaic creation, before it could arrive at those distant regions of immensity.

The *grand and noble designs* for which the great bodies, to which I have adverted, are intended, suggest, likewise, a variety of interesting and sublime reflections. These designs undoubtedly are, to display the ineffable glories of the Eternal Mind,—to demonstrate the immensity, omnipotence and wisdom of Him who formed the universe,—and to serve as so many worlds for the residence of incalculable numbers of intelligent beings of every order. And, what an immense variety of interesting objects is presented to the mind when its views are directed to the numerous orders and gradations of intelligences that may people the universe,—the magnificent scenes that may be displayed in every world,—their moral economy, and the important transactions that may have taken place in their history under the arrangements of the Divine government!

Such are some of the scenes of grandeur which science unfolds to every enlightened mind. The contemplation of such objects has an evident tendency to enlarge the capacity of the soul,—to raise the affections above mean and grovelling pursuits, to give man a more impressive idea of the *dignity* of his rational and immortal nature, and of the attributes of that Almighty Being by whom he is upheld, and to make him *rejoice* in the possession of faculties capable of being exercised on scenes and objects so magnificent and sublime.

In the *fourth place*, science administers to our enjoyment by *the variety of novel and interesting objects it exhibits*. Almost every department of natural science presents to the untutored mind an assemblage of objects, new and strange, which

* The planet Venus † The planet Mercury

tend to rouse its faculties, and to excite to important inquiries and interesting reflections. The science of *mechanics* presents us with many curious combinations of mechanical powers, which, from the simplest principles, produce the most powerful and astonishing effects. "What can be more strange (says a profound and energetic writer*) than that an ounce weight should balance hundreds of pounds by the intervention of a few bars of thin iron?" And when we consider that all the mechanical powers may be reduced to the *lever*, the *wheel and axle*, the *pulley*, the *inclined plane*, the *wedge* and the *screw*, how astonishing are the forces exerted, and the effects produced, by their various combinations in wheel-carriages, mills, cranes, thrashing-machines, and pile-engines! *Hydrostatics* teaches us the wonderful fact, that a few pounds of water, without the aid of any machinery, will, by mere pressure, produce an almost irresistible force; or, in other words, that any quantity of fluid, however small, may be made to counterpoise any quantity, however large; and hence a very strong hogshead has been burst to pieces, and the water scattered about with incredible force, by means of water conveyed through a very small perpendicular tube of great length. On the same principle, and by the same means, the foundations of a large building might be shattered, and the whole structure overthrown. *Magnetism* discloses to us such singular facts as the following: —that a small piece of steel, when rubbed by the loadstone, and nicely poised, will place itself in a direction nearly north and south, so as to point nearly towards the poles of the world,—that the north and south poles of two loadstones will attract, and two north or two south poles repel each other; and that the power of a magnet will pass through a thick board, and turn round a compass-needle, with great velocity, though placed at a considerable distance.

The science of *optics* likewise disclose a variety of astonishing truths, and is no less replete with wonders. How wonderful the fact, that *light* proceeds from the sun, and other luminous bodies, with a velocity of 195,000 miles in a moment of time; that myriads of myriads of rays are flying off from visible objects towards every point of the compass, crossing each other in all directions, and yet accurately depicting the same images of external objects in thousands of eyes at the same moment,—that the thousands of millions of rays of light which proceed from any particular object must be compressed into a space not more than one-eighth of an inch in diameter, before they can enter the pupil of the eye, and produce vision,—that the images of all the objects which compose an extensive landscape are depicted on the bottom of the eye, in all their colours and relative proportions, within a space less than half an inch in diameter,—that the eye can perceive objects distinctly at the distance of six inches, and likewise at the distance of ten, fifty, or an hundred miles, serving the purpose both of a microscope and a telescope, and can be *instantaneously* adjusted to serve either as the one or as the other,—and that the variegated colouring which appears in the scenery of nature is not in the objects themselves, but in the light which falls upon them, without which all the scenes of creation would wear an uniform aspect, and one object would be undistinguishable from another!

The *instruments* which the science of optics has been the means of constructing, are also admirable in their effects and productive of rational entertainment. How wonderful, that, by means of an optic lens, an image is depicted in a dark chamber, on a white table, in which we may perceive the objects of an extensive landscape delineated in all their colours, motions and proportions, and so accurately represented, that we even distinguish the countenances of individuals at the distance of a mile,—that we can see objects distinctly when a thick board, or a piece of metal, is interposed between them and our eye,—that the images of objects can be made to hang in the air either upright or inverted, and that representations either of the living or of the dead can be made to start up instantly before the view of a spectator in a darkened room,—that, by admitting into a chamber a few rays of white light from the sun through a prism, all the colours of light may be seen beautifully painted on a piece of paper,—that a single object may be multiplied to an indefinite number, and that a few coloured bits of glass may be made by reflection to exhibit an infinite diversity of beautiful and variegated forms! How admirable the effects of the telescope, by which we may see objects as distinctly at the distance of two or three miles as if they were placed within a few yards of us, by which we can penetrate into the celestial regions, and behold the distant wonders of the planetary system, and the millions of stars dispersed through infinite space, as distinctly as if we were actually transported by a supernatural power several hundreds of millions of miles into the regions of the firmament! And how curious the circumstance, that we can, by this instrument, contemplate such objects in all directions and positions,—that we can view them either as *erect*, or as turned *upside down*,—that we can perceive the spires, houses and windows of a distant city when our backs are turned directly opposite to it, and our faces in a contrary direction—the rings of Saturn and the moons of Jupiter, when we are looking *downwards* with our backs turned to these objects,—that we can make an object on our right hand or our left, appear as if directly before us, and can cause a terrestrial landscape to appear above us, as if it were sus-

* Lord Brougham

pended in the sky.* By the help of the *microscope* we can exhibit to a number of spectators at the same moment, a small animal scarcely distinguishable by the naked eye, magnified to the size of ten or fifteen inches in length, and distinguish not only its limbs, joints, mouth and eyes, but even the motions of its bowels, and other internal movements; and in every department of nature can contemplate an assemblage of beauties, delicate contextures, and exquisite contrivances, which excite the highest admiration, and which would otherwise have appeared incredible and incomprehensible to the human mind.

The sciences of *electricity* and *galvanism* likewise display facts both curious and astonishing. How wonderful the operations of the electric fluid, which can suddenly contract the muscles of animals, and give a violent shock to a hundred or a thousand persons at the same moment—which moves with such amazing rapidity, that, in a few seconds of time, it might be made to fly to the remotest regions of the globe—which melts iron wire, sets fire to gunpowder and other inflammable substances, destroys the polarity of the magnetic needle, and promotes the vegetation of plants and the perspiration of animals—which can be drawn in vivid sparks from different parts of the human body, and made to descend from the clouds in streams of fire! And how powerful and astonishing the effects of the *galvanic* agency—which makes charcoal burn with a brilliant white flame, decomposes water into its elementary parts, and causes platina, the hardest and heaviest of the metals, to melt as readily as wax in the flame of a candle—which produces the most violent convulsions on the muscular system, causes a hare to move its feet, and a fowl to clap its wings, with force and energy, *after life is extinct*—throws the countenance, even of a dead man, into appalling grimaces and contortions, and excites the most rapid movements in his hands and limbs, to the horror and astonishment of all beholders!

The science of *chymistry*, throughout all its departments, is no less replete with wonders. How astonishing are many of the facts which it discloses, of which the following are merely specimens!—That all the productions of nature in

* This is effected by means of the "aerial reflecting telescope," lately invented by the author. The following is a general representation of this telescope in profile.

AB is a tube of mahogany about three inches long, which serves as a socket for holding the speculum; CD an arm attached to the tube, about the length of the focal distance of the mirror, consisting of two separate pieces C and D, the latter of which slides under the former, through the brass sockets EF. To the under part of the socket F is attached a brass nut with a female screw, in which the male screw *ab* acts by applying the hand to the nob *c*, which serves for adjusting the instrument to distinct vision. G is the brass tube which receives the eye-pieces. In looking through this telescope, the right eye is applied at the point H, the back is directly towards the object, and the observer's head is understood to be uncovered. When a diagonal eye-piece is applied, the object may be seen either to the right or to the left, or at right angles to its true position; or, it may be made to appear either upwards, as if hanging in the air, or downwards, as if below the surface of the earth. A particular description of this instrument may be seen in "The Edinburgh New Philosophical Journal" for July 1826, pp. 41—52, and in the "London Encyclopædia." Art. *Telescope.*

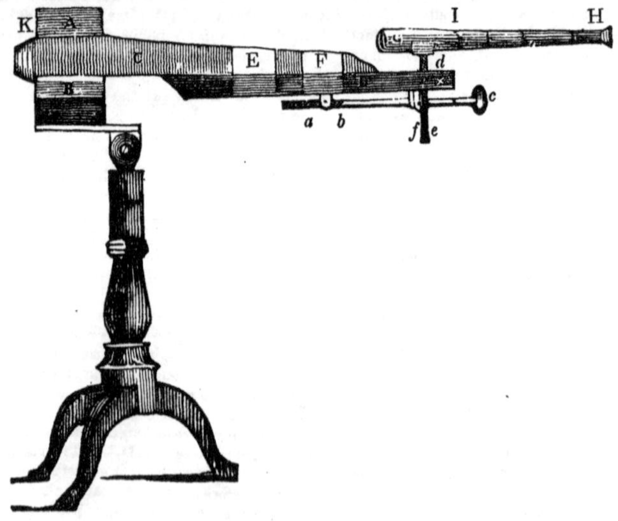

the animal and vegetable kingdoms, are composed of a very few simple substances, many of which are invisible gases—that water is chiefly composed of an *inflammable* principle—that the *acids*, such as aquafortis and oil of vitriol, are formed of different kinds of *air*—that an invisible fluid, one of the ingredients of the air we breathe, will cause a rod of iron to burn with brilliancy, and phosphorus to produce a splendour which dazzles the eyes of every beholder —that the *diamond*, notwithstanding its value and brilliancy, is composed of the same materials as *coal*—that oxymuriatic acid, or the bleaching gas, discharges all vegetable colours, and, in the course of a few minutes, will change a piece of printed calico into a pure *white;* and likewise burns all the metals, dissolves gold and platina, and suffocates all animals that breathe it, after one or two inspirations—that there are metals much lighter than water, which swim in that fluid and burn spontaneously with a bright red light, and when thrown into the mineral acids, inflame and burn on the surface, and in oxygen and oxymuriatic acid gas, produce a white flame, and throw out numerous bright sparks and scintillations,—that a certain kind of air, called the nitrous oxide, when inhaled into the lungs, produces an extraordinary elevation of the animal spirits, an irresistible propensity to laughter, a rapid flow of vivid ideas, and a thousand delightful emotions, without any subsequent feelings of debility or exhaustion—and, that it is not altogether improbable, according to the deductions of some modern chymists, that "*oxygen* and *hydrogen*, with the assistance of the *solar light*, are the only elementary substances employed in the constitution of the whole universe;" so that Nature, in all her operations, works the most infinitely diversified effects, by the slightest modifications in the means she employs.

Such are only a few *specimens* of the curious and interesting subjects which the physical sciences present to the reflecting mind. And is it conceivable that a rational being can make such objects as those I have now specified the subject of his frequent study and contemplation, and not feel pleasures and enjoyments far superior to those of the mass of mankind, who are either immersed in sensuality, or enveloped with the mists of ignorance? The man who has such subjects to study and investigate, and such objects to contemplate, can never be destitute of enjoyment. If happiness depends on the activity of the mind, and the range of objects presented before it, wherever he is placed,—whether at home or abroad, in the city or in the country, he can never be at a loss for means of mental gratification, and of increasing his stock of intellectual wealth. He needs not envy the rich and the noble, on account of the elegance of their mansions and the splendour of their equipage; for the magnificence and glories of the universe, and all the beauties of terrestrial nature lie before him, and are at all times ready to minister to his enjoyment. In investigating the admirable arrangements which appear in the economy of creation, in tracing throughout that economy the perfections of his Creator, and in looking forward to a nobler state of existence where his views of the divine empire shall be expanded, he can enjoy a satisfaction and delight which the wealth of this world cannot bestow, and which its frowns and calamities cannot destroy.

Besides the pleasures derived from a contemplation of the doctrines and the facts of science, —*there is a positive gratification in tracing the steps by which the discoveries of science have been made,—the reasonings and demonstrations by which its doctrines are supported, and the experiments by which they are proved and illustrated.* In this point of view, the study of several branches of mathematical science, however abstruse they may at first sight appear, will afford a high degree of gratification to the mind. When it is announced as a proposition in geometry, "that the square described on the hypothenuse, or longest side of a right angled triangle, is equal to the sum of the squares described on the other side,"*—it is pleasing to

* The following figure will convey an idea to the unlearned reader of the meaning of this proposition.

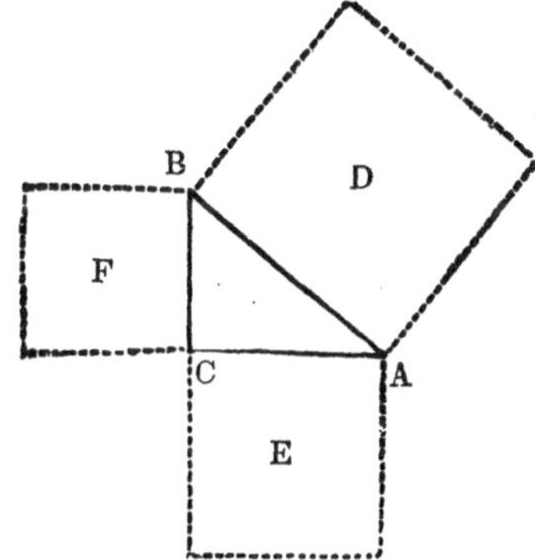


A B C is a right angled triangle, having the right angle at C, and A B is the hypothenuse, or longest side. By geometrical reasoning it can be demonstrated, that the square D, described on the longest side A B, is exactly equal to the sum of the squares E and F, described on the other two sides.—One of the uses of this proposition will appear from the following example. Suppose A C the height of a wall = 24 feet, B C the width of a trench = 18 feet; it is required to find the length of a ladder B A which will reach from the outside of the trench to the top of the wall. The square of 18 is 324; the square of 24 is 576, which added together make 900, equal to the square D; the square root of which is 30 = the length of the ladder. On this principle we can find

perceive, how every step of the demonstration proceeds with unerring certainty, and leads the mind to perceive the truth of the conclusion to which it leads, with as high a degree of demonstrative evidence as that 3 added to 6 make 9, or that 5 multiplied by 4 make 20. In like manner, when it is clearly demonstrated by mathematical reasoning, that "the three angles of every triangle, whatever be its size or the inclination of its sides, are exactly equal to two right angles, or 180 degrees," and that "the sides of a plane triangle are to one another as the sines of the angles opposite to them," the utility and importance of these truths may not at first view be appreciated, however convincing the evidence from which the conclusions are deduced. But when the student comes to know that on these demonstrated properties of a triangle depends the mode of measuring the height of mountains, and the breadth of rivers,—of determining the circumference of the earth, the distance of the sun and moon, the magnitudes of the planets, and the dimensions of the solar system,—it cannot but afford a positive gratification to perceive the important bearings of such truths, and that the astronomer, when he announces his sublime deductions respecting the sizes and distances of the heavenly bodies, does not rest on vague conceptions, but on observations conducted with the nicest accuracy, and on calculations founded on principles susceptible of the strictest demonstration.

"To follow a demonstration of a grand mathematical truth," says a powerful and enlightened writer,—"to perceive how clearly and how inevitably one step succeeds another, and how the whole steps lead to the conclusion,—to observe how certainly and unerringly the reasoning goes on from things perfectly self-evident, and by the smallest addition at each step, every one being as easily taken after the one before as the first step of all was, and yet the result being something, not only far from self-evident, but so general and strange, that you can hardly believe it to be true, and are only convinced of it by going over the whole reasoning,—this operation of the understanding, to those who so exercise themselves, always affords the highest delight."

It is likewise a source of enjoyment to contemplate the experiments by which the doctrines of science are supported, and the reasonings and deductions founded on experimental investigations. When a person is told that the atmosphere presses on every part of the surface of the earth with a force equal to two thousand one hundred and sixty pounds on every square foot, it must surely be gratifying to behold a column of water supported in a glass tube, open at the lower end,—and a square bottle connected with an air-pump, broken to pieces by the direct pressure of the atmosphere,—and from a comparison of the weight of mercury suspended in a tube with the diameter of its bore, to be able to calculate the atmospherical pressure on the body of a man, or even on the whole earth. When he is told that one ingredient of atmospheric air is the principle of flame, is it not curious and highly interesting to behold a piece of iron burning in this gas, throwing out brilliant sparks of white flame, and illuminating a large hall with a dazzling lustre?—and when he is informed that fixed air is the heaviest of the gases, and destructive to flame and animal life,—is it not gratifying to perceive this invisible fluid poured from one vessel to another, and when poured on the flame of a candle that it instantly extinguishes it? Many of the deductions of natural science are so wonderful, and so unlike every thing we should have previously conceived, that to the untutored mind they appear almost incredible, and little short of unfounded and extravagant assertions. When such a one is told that "any quantity of liquid, however small, will counterpoise any quantity, however great,"—that the rubbing of a glass cylinder against a cushion will produce the effect of setting fire to spirits of wine, or of bursting a bladder of air at the distance of a hundred feet from the machine—that the galvanic agency will produce a violent and uncommon effect upon the nervous and muscular system—and that in certain vegetable infusions, myriads of animals of various forms, may be seen a thousand times less than the smallest visible point—such assertions are apt to stagger his belief as improbable and extravagant. But when he actually sees in the first case, a large hogshead that would hold above a hundred gallons, filled with water, and a long tube whose bore is not half an inch in diameter, firmly inserted into its top, and a small quantity of water scarcely exceeding a quart, poured into the tube—and then beholds the top rapidly swelling, and in a few moments, the whole cask burst to pieces, and the water scattered in every direction,—or in the second case, when he sees alcohol suddenly taking fire, and a bladder filled with oxygen and hydrogen gas, exploding with a tremendous report, merely by the turning of the electrical machine at the other end of a long hall, and the interposition of a wire,—or, when in the third case, he sees a person drink a glass of porter which has a wire around it connected with a galvanic battery, and at a certain stage of the operation, receive a tremendous concussion, which makes him start and roar like a madman, or, in the last case, when he looks through a powerful microscope, and perceives hundreds of mites like so many young pigs, clambering among rocks of cheese, and thousands of fishes in a drop of water—such experimental illustrations of the truths of science, cannot fail to prove highly satisfactory, and to afford

the height of the mountains in the moon, when the length to their shadows is known.

no inconsiderable degree of entertainment and delight.

*The occasional performance of scientific experiments*, as opportunity offers, and *the construction of philosophical instruments*, may also be converted into a source of enjoyment. In the one case, the student of nature may derive gratification, in being the means of communicating entertainment and instruction to others; and in the other, he may whet his ingenuity, and increase his mental vigour, and be enabled, at a small expence, to gratify his curiosity in contemplating the various processes, and the beauties and sublimities of nature. Many of the instruments of science, when elegantly constructed, are beyond the reach of the general mass of mankind, on account of their expense; but a person of moderate reflection and ingenuity, during his leisure hours, can easily construct at an inconsiderable expense, many of the most useful instruments which illustrate the facts of science. For example, a powerful compound microscope, capable of enabling us to perceive the most interesting minute objects in the animal, vegetable, and mineral kingdoms, may be constructed at an expense of little more than a crown, provided the individual constructs the tubes and other apparatus of pasteboard, wood, or other cheap materials; and the occasional exercise of the mental powers in such devices, so far from being irksome or fatiguing, are generally accompanied with satisfaction and pleasure.

It is true, indeed, that the study of some of the subjects above mentioned, particularly the first principles of the mathematics, may, in the outset, be attended with some difficulties, and to some minds may wear a dry and uninteresting aspect. But as the mind proceeds onwards in its progress, and acquires clearer conceptions of what at first appeared difficult or obscure—every difficulty it is enabled to surmount gives a new relish to the subject of investigation, and additional vigour to the intellect, to enable it to vanquish the difficulties which still remain,—till at length it feels a pleasure and an interest in the pursuit, which no difficulties, nor even the lapse of time can ever effectually destroy. "Let any man," says Lord Brougham, "pass an evening in vacant idleness, or even in reading some silly tale, and compare the state of his mind when he goes to sleep or gets up next morning, with its state some other day when he has passed a few hours in going through the proofs, by facts and reasonings, of some of the great doctrines in Natural Science, learning truths wholly new to him, and satisfying himself by careful examination of the grounds on which known truths rest, so as to be not only acquainted with the doctrines themselves, but able to show why he believes them, and to prove before others that they are true;—he will find as great a difference as can exist in the same being,—the difference between looking back upon time unprofitably wasted, and time spent in self-improvement; he will feel himself in the one case listless and dissatisfied, in the other, comfortable and happy; in the one case, if he do not appear to himself humbled, at least he will not have earned any claim to his own respect; in the other case, he will enjoy a proud consciousness of having by his own exertions, become a wise, and therefore a more exalted creature."

The subjects to which I have now adverted, may be considered not merely in reference to the gratification they afford to the understanding, but likewise in reference to *the beneficial influence they would produce on the heart, and on social and domestic enjoyment.*

All the truths relative to the Creator's operations in the universe, when properly contemplated, are calculated to produce a powerful and interesting impression upon the affections. Is a person gratified at beholding *symmetry* and *beauty* as displayed in the works of art,—what a high degree of delightful emotion must be felt in surveying the beautiful arrangements of Infinite Wisdom, in the variety of forms, the nice proportions, the exquisite delicacy of texture, and the diversified hues which adorn the vegetable kingdom,—in the colours of the morning and evening clouds of a summer sky, the plumage of birds, the admirable workmanship on the bodies of insects, the fine polish of sea-shells, the variegated wavings and colouring of jaspers, topazes, and emeralds, and particularly in those specimens of divine mechanism in insects, plants, and flowers, which the unassisted eye cannot discern, and which the microscope alone can unfold to view! Has he a taste for the *sublime?* How nobly is he gratified by an enlightened view of the nocturnal heavens, where suns unnumbered shine, and mighty worlds run their solemn rounds! Such contemplations have a natural tendency, in combination with Christian principles and motives, to *raise the affections* to that Almighty Being who is the uncreated source of all that is sublime and beautiful in creation,—to enkindle the fire of *devotion*,—to excite *adoration* of his infinite excellences, and to produce *profound humility* in his presence. Such studies likewise tend to preserve the mind in calmness and *serenity* under the moral dispensations of Him whose wisdom is displayed in all his arrangements, and whose "tender mercies are over all his works,"—and to inspire it with *hope* and confidence in relation to the future scenes of eternity, from a consideration of his power, benevolence, and intelligence, as displayed throughout the universe, and of the inexhaustible sources of felicity he has it in his power to distribute among numerous orders of beings throughout an immortal existence. Contemplating the numerous displays of Divine munificence around us

—the diversified orders of delighted existence that people the air, the waters, and the earth, the nice adaptation of their organs and faculties to their different situations and modes of life, the ample provision made for their wants and enjoyments, and the boundless dimensions of the divine empire, where similar instances of beneficence are displayed—the heart is disposed to rest with confidence on Him who made it, convinced that his almighty power qualifies him to make us happy by a variety of means of which we have no adequate conception, and that his faithfulness and benevolence dispose him to withhold no real good "from them that walk uprightly."

Such studies would likewise tend to *heighten the delights of social enjoyment.* There is nothing more grating to the man of intelligence than the foolish and trifling conversation which prevails in the various intercourses of social life, even among the middling and the higher circles of society, and in convivial associations. The ribaldry and obscenity, the folly and nonsense, and the laughter of fools which too frequently distinguish such associations, are a disgrace to our civilized condition, and to our moral and intellectual nature. Without supposing that it will ever be expedient to lay aside cheerfulness and rational mirth, the lively smile, or even the loud laugh, it is surely conceivable, that a more rational and improving turn might be given to general conversation than what is frequently exemplified in our social intercourses. And what can we suppose better calculated to accomplish this end than the occasional introduction of topics connected with science and general knowledge, when all, or the greater part, are qualified so take a share in the general conversation? It would tend to stimulate the mental faculties, to suggest useful hints, to diffuse general information, to improve science and art, to excite the ignorant to increase in knowledge, to present interesting objects of contemplation, to enliven the spirits, and thus to afford a source of rational enjoyment. It would also have a tendency to prevent those shameful excesses, noisy tumults, and scenes of *intemperance* which so frequently terminate our festive entertainments. For want of qualifications for such conversation, cards, dice, childish questions and amusements, gossiping chit-chat, and tales of scandal are generally resorted to, in order to consume the hours allotted to social enjoyment. And how melancholy the reflection, that rational beings capable of investigating the laws and phenomena of the universe, and of prosecuting the most exalted range of thought, and who are destined to exist in other worlds, throughout an endless duration—should be impelled to resort to such degrading expedients, to wheel away the social hours!

*Domestic enjoyment might likewise be heightened and improved* by the studies to which we have adverted. For want of qualifications for rational conversation, a spirit of listlessness and indifference frequently insinuates itself into the intercourses of families, and between married individuals, which sometimes degenerates into fretfulness and impatience, and even into jars, contentions, and violent altercations; in which case there can never exist any high degree of affection or domestic enjoyment. It is surely not unreasonable to suppose, that were the minds of persons in the married state possessed of a certain portion of knowledge, and endowed with a relish for rational investigations—not only would such disagreeable effects be prevented, but a variety of positive enjoyments would be introduced. Substantial knowledge, which leads to the proper exercise of the mental powers, has a tendency to meliorate the temper, and to prevent those ebullitions of passion, which are the results of vulgarity and ignorance. By invigorating the mind, it prevents it from sinking into peevishness and inanity. It affords subjects for interesting conversation, and augments affection by the reciprocal interchanges of sentiment and feeling, and the mutual communication of instruction and entertainment. And in cases where malignant passions are ready to burst forth, rational arguments will have a more powerful influence in arresting their progress, in cultivated minds, than in those individuals in whose constitution animal feeling predominates, and reason has lost its ascendancy. As an enlightened mind is generally the seat of noble and liberal sentiments—in those cases where the parties belong to different religious sectaries, there is more probability of harmony and mutual forbearance being displayed, when persons take an enlarged view of the scenes of creation, and the revelations of the Creator, than can be expected in the case of those whose faculties are immersed in the mists of superstition and ignorance.

How delightful an enjoyment is it, after the bustle of business and the labours of the day are over,—when a married couple can sit down at each corner of the fire, and, with mutual relish and interest, read a volume of history or of popular philosophy, and talk of the moral government of God, the arrangements of his providence, and the wonders of the universe! Such interesting conversations and exercises beget a mutual esteem, enliven the affections, and produce a friendship lasting as our existence, and which no untoward incidents can ever effectually impair. A Christian pastor, in giving an account of the last illness of his beloved partner, in a late periodical work, when alluding to a book she had read along with him about two months before her decease, says, "I shall never forget the pleasure with which she studied the illustrations of the divine perfections in that interesting book. Rising from the contemplation of the variety, beauty, immensity, and order of the creation, she ex ulted in the assurance of having the Creator for her father, anticipated with great joy the vision of him in the next world, and calculated with unhesitating confidence on the sufficiency of his boundless nature to engage her most intense interest, and to render her unspeakably happy for ever." It is well known that the late lamented *Princess Charlotte*, and her consort Prince Leopold, lived together in the greatest harmony and affection; and from what her biographers have stated respecting her education and pursuits, it appears that the mutual friendship of these illustrious individuals was heightened and cemented by the rational conversation in which they indulged, and the elevated studies to which they were devoted. Her course of education embraced the English, classical, French, German, and Italian languages; arithmetic, geography, astronomy, the first six books of Euclid, algebra, mechanics, and the principles of optics and perspective, along with history, the policy of governments, and particularly the principles of the Christian religion. She was a skilful musician, had a fine perception of the picturesque in nature, and was fond of drawing. She took great pleasure in strolling on the beach, in marine excursions, in walking in the country, in rural scenery, in conversing freely with the rustic inhabitants, and in investigating every object that seemed worthy of her attention. She was an enthusiastic admirer of the grand and beautiful in nature, and the ocean was to her an object of peculiar interest. After her union with the prince, as their tastes were similar, they engaged in the same studies. Gardening, drawing, music, and rational conversation, diversified their leisure hours. They took great pleasure in the culture of flowers—in the classification of them —and in the formation, with scientific skill, of a *hortus siccus*. But the library, which was furnished with the best books in our language, was their favourite place of resort; and their chief daily pleasure, mutual instruction. They were seldom apart either in their occupations or in their amusements; nor were they separated in their religious duties. "They took sweet counsel together, and walked to the house of God in company;" and it is also stated, on good authority, that they had established the worship of God in their family, which was regularly attended by every branch of their household. No wonder, then, that they exhibited an auspicious and a delightful example of private and domestic virtue, of *conjugal attachment*, and of unobtrusive charity and benevolence. In the higher circles of society, as well as in the lower, it would be of immense importance to the interests of domestic happiness, that the taste of the Princess Charlotte was more closely imitated, and that the fashionable frivolity and dissipation which so generally prevail were exchanged for the pursuits of knowledge, and the delights of rational and improving conversation. Then those family feuds, contentions, and separations, and those prosecutions for matrimonial infidelity which are now so common, would be less frequently obtruded on public view, and examples of virtue, affection, and rational conduct, would be set before the subordinate ranks of the community, which might be attended with the most beneficial and permanent results, not only to the present, but to future generations.

In short, the possession of a large store of intellectual wealth would fortify the soul in the prospect of every evil to which humanity is subjected, and would afford consolation and solace when fortune is diminished, and the greater portion of external comforts is withdrawn. Under the frowns of adversity, those worldly losses and calamities which drive unthinking men to desperation and despair, would be borne with a becoming magnanimity; the mind having within itself the chief resources of its happiness, and becoming almost independent of the world around it. For to the individual whose happiness chiefly depends on intellectual pleasures, retirement from general society, and the bustle of the world, is often the state of his highest enjoyment.

Thus I have endeavoured briefly to illustrate the enjoyments which a general diffusion of knowledge would produce—from a consideration of the limited conceptions of the untutored mind contrasted with the ample and diversified range of view presented to the enlightened understanding—from the delightful tendency of scientific pursuits, in enabling us to trace, from a single principle, an immense variety of effects, and surprising and unexpected resemblances where we least expected to find them,—from the grand and sublime objects it presents before us—from the *variety* of novel and interesting scenes which the different departments of physical science unfold—from the exercise of tracing the steps by which scientific discoveries have been made—and from the influence of such studies on the affections and on social and domestic enjoyment.

For want of the knowledge to which I have alluded, it happens that few persons who have been engaged in commercial or agricultural pursuits feel much enjoyment, when, in the decline of life, they retire from the active labours in which they had been previously engaged. Retirement and respite from the cares of business afford them little gratification, and they feel a vacuity within which nothing around them or within the range of their conceptions can fill up. Being destitute of a taste for intellectual pursuits, and devoid of that *substratum* of thought which is the ground-work of mental activity and of rational contemplation, they enjoy nothing of that mental liberty and expansion of soul which the retreats of solitude afford to the contemplative mind; and, when not engaged in festive associations, are apt to sink into a species of listlessness and *ennui*. They stalk about from one place to another without any definite object in view—look at every thing around with a kind of unconscious gaze—are glad to indulge in trifling talk and gossip with every one they meet—and, feeling how little enjoyment they derive from their own reflections, not unfequently slide into habits of sensuality and intemperance.

From what we have stated on this topic, it evidently appears that the pursuits of science are fitted to yield a positive gratification to every rational mind. It presents to view, processes, combinations, metamorphoses, motions, and objects of various descriptions calculated to arrest the attention and to astonish the mind, far more than all the romances and tales of wonder that were ever invented by the human imagination. When the pleasures arising from such studies are rendered accessible to all, human happiness will be nearly on a level, and the different ranks of mankind will enjoy it nearly in an equal degree. As true enjoyment depends chiefly on the state of the mind, and the train of thought, that passes through it, it follows, that when a man prosecutes a rational train of thought, and finds a pleasure in the contemplation of intellectual objects, his happiness is less dependent on mere sensitive enjoyments, and a smaller portion of external comforts will be productive of enjoyment than in the case of those whose chief pleasure consists in sensual gratifications. When intellectual pursuits, therefore, shall occupy the chief attention of mankind, we may indulge the hope, that those restless and insatiable desires which avarice and ambition never cease to create, will seldom torment the soul, and that a noble generosity of mind in relation to riches will distinguish persons of every rank, and be the means of producing enjoyment wherever its influence extends.

---

## SECTION V.

### ON THE PRACTICAL INFLUENCE OF SCIENTIFIC KNOWLEDGE, AND ITS TENDENCY TO PROMOTE THE EXTERNAL COMFORTS OF GENERAL SOCIETY.

In the preceding section I have considered the beneficial tendency of knowledge and the pleasures it affords, chiefly in reference to the understanding and the affections. In the present section I shall consider it more particularly, in regard to its *practical effects* on the active employments and the external comforts of the middling and lower orders of the community.—Every art, being founded on scientific principles, and directed in its operations by the experimental deductions of philosophy, it follows, that a knowledge of the principles of science must be conducive to a *skilful* practice of the arts, and must have a tendency to direct the genius of the artist to carry them to their highest pitch of improvement. In illustrating this topic, I shall endeavour to show that an acquaintance with science would render mechanics, manufacturers, and labourers more expert and skilful in their different departments—would pave the way for future discoveries and improvements—and that the knowledge and spirit which produced such improvements would promote the external comforts of mankind.

I. A knowledge of the principles of science would render manufacturers, mechanics, and common labourers of all descriptions more skilful in their respective professions and employments.

In the arts of *dyeing* and *calico-printing*, every process is conducted on the principles of chymistry. Not a colour can be imparted but in consequence of the affinity which subsists between the cloth and the dye,—or the dye and the mordant employed as a bond of union between them; and the colours will be liable to vary, unless the artist take into account the changes which take place in them by the absorption of oxygen;—a knowledge of which and of the different degrees of oxidizement which the several dyes undergo, requires a considerable portion of chymical skill; and such knowledge is absolutely necessary to enable either the dyer or the calico printer to produce in all cases permanent colours of the shade he intends. To chymistry, too, they must be indebted for the knowledge they may acquire of the nature of the articles they use in their several processes—for the artificial production of their most valuable mordants—and for some of their most beautiful and brilliant colours. As an evidence of this, it is sufficient to state, that, to produce such colours as an olive ground and yellow figures, a scarlet pattern on a black ground, or a brown ground with orange figures, formerly required a period of many weeks; but by means of chymical preparations the whole of this work may now be done in a few days, and patterns more delicate than ever produced, with a degree of certainty of which former manufacturers could have no idea; and all this is effected by dyeing the cloth a self-colour in the first instance, and afterwards merely printing the pattern with a chymical preparation, which discharges a part of the original dye, and leaves a new colour in its stead.

The art of *bleaching* has likewise received so many important improvements from chymical science, that no one is now capable of conducting its processes to advantage who is ignorant of the scientific principles on which the present practice of that art is founded. Till about the close of the eighteenth century, the old *tedious* process of bleaching continued in practice. But, about that period the introduction of the *oxymuriatic acid*, combined with alkalis, lime and other ingredients, in bleaching cottons and linens, has given an entirely new turn to every part of the process, so that the process which formerly required several months for its completion can now be accomplished in a few days, and with a degree of perfection which could not previously be attained. Even in a few hours, that which formerly required nearly a whole summer, can now be effected, and that, too, merely by the action of an almost *invisible* fluid. As the whole process of bleaching, as now practised, consists almost entirely of chymical agents and operations, every person employed in this art, ought to possess a certain portion of chymical knowledge, otherwise many of its processes would run the risk of being deranged, and the texture of the materials undergoing the process of being either materially injured or completely destroyed.

The operation of *brewing* fermented liquors is likewise a chymical process. The student of chymistry will learn how the barley in the first instance is converted into a saccharine substance by malting; how the fermentative process converts the saccharine to a spirituous substance, and how the latter, by continuing the process, becomes changed into vinegar. He will also learn the means of promoting and encouraging this process, and how to retard and check it, when it is likely to be carried too far, so as to be sure of uniformly obtaining satisfactory results. In this and in every other process, it must therefore be of importance to acquire some knowledge of the principles of natural substances, and of the nature of those changes which take place in the materials on which we operate. In the *manufacture of soap*, it is reckoned by those intimately acquainted with the process, that many thousands per annum, now lost to the community, might be saved, were the trade carried on upon scientific principles. When a soap boiler is an accomplished chymist, he knows how to analyze barilla, kelp, potass, and other materials, so as to ascertain the proportion of alkali in each; and when these articles are at an exorbitant price, he will have recourse to various residuums, which he will decompose by chymical means, and use as substitutes. He will know how to oxydize the common oils and oil-dregs, so as to give them consistence, and render them good substitutes for tallow—and how to apportion his lime so as to make his alkali perfectly caustic, without using an unnecessary quantity of that article. The *manufacture of candles* might also derive advantage from chymical science. It is found that foreign tallows frequently contain a large portion of acid rendering them inferior to the English, which, by chymical means may be purified at a very small expense, and by the proper application of chymical agents, other brown tallows may be rendered beautifully white, and fit for the best purposes.*

The *tanning* of hides is now ascertained to consist in impregnating the animal matter with that peculiar principle taken from the vegetable kingdom, called *tan*, the effect of which is explained entirely on chymical principles. It is now known that many substances besides oak-bark, contains tan, and to chymistry we are indebted for the means of discovering with accuracy the quantity of tan which the several astringent vegetables contain. It is supposed not to be improbable, when the manufacturers shall have paid proper attention to chymical science, that the article in question may be prepared in chymical laboratories, so as entirely to supersede the use of oak bark, since the principle of tanning has already been formed *artificially* by a modern chymist.†—It is also well known, that to chymical research, the manufactures of *earthen-ware* and *porcelain* are indebted for the improved state in which they are now found. For, the successful management of all their branches, from the mixture of the materials which form the body of the ware, to the production of those brilliant colours with which such articles are adorned—is dependent on the principles of chymical science. The celebrated Wedgewood, to whom this branch of manufacture is so highly indebted, devoted his whole attention to the improvement of his art by the application of his chymical knowledge, of which few men possessed a larger share; and he has been heard to declare, "that nearly all the diversified colours applied to his pottery were produced only by the oxides of iron."

There are few persons to whom a knowledge of chymistry is of more importance than to the *Agriculturist.* It will teach him to analyse the soils on the different parts of his farm, and to subject to experiment the peat, the marle, the lime and other manures, in order to ascertain the advantages to be derived from them, and the propriety of applying them in particular instances. It will teach him when to use lime hot from the kiln, and when slacked, how to promote the putrefactive process in his composts, and at what period to check it, so as to prevent the fertilizing particles becoming unprolific and of little value. It will also teach him the difference in the properties of marle, lime, dung, mud, ashes, alkaline salt, soap-waste, sea-water and other manures, and, consequently, which to prefer in all varieties of soil. It is said that the celebrated Lavoisier

* For most of the above hints the author is indebted to Mr. Parkes.

† Segerin. See Nicolson's Phil. Journal, 4to vol. 1. p. 271.

cultivated 240 acres of land in La Vendee, on chymical principles, in order to set a good example to the farmers; and his mode of culture was attended with so much success, that he obtained a third more of crop than was procured by the usual method; and in nine years his annual produce was doubled.

I might also have illustrated the practical advantages of chymical science in relation to the *art of extracting metals from their ores*,—the conversion of iron into steel, and the metallic ore into malleable iron—the *manufacture of glass, alum, copperas, blue vitriol, soda, potash, Morocco-leather, paper, starch, varnish,* and *Prussian-blue*—the *refining of sugar, saltpetre, gold and silver*—the artificial *formation of ice*—the *method of preserving fish,* meat, and other articles of food, and various other processes connected with the practical departments of life, all of which are strictly chymical operations, and can be improved and brought to perfection chiefly by the knowledge and application of the doctrines and facts of chymical science.

With regard to the professions of the *physician, surgeon,* and *apothecary,* it is now universally admitted, that an extensive acquaintance with the principles and facts of chymistry is essentially requisite to the successful practice of these arts. The human body may be considered as a species of *laboratory,* in which the various processes of absorption, secretion, fermentation, composition and decomposition are incessantly going forward. Every article of food and drink we throw into the stomach, every portion of atmospheric air we receive into the lungs, every impression we derive from the surrounding elements, every motion of the heart and lungs, and every pulse that vibrates within us, may be considered as effecting a chymical change in the vital fluids, and in every part of the animal system; the nature of which it is of the utmost importance to the medical practitioner thoroughly to investigate and understand. For, how can he be supposed to be successful in his attempts to counteract the disorders to which the human frame is incident, and to produce a chymical effect on the constitution of his patient, if he is ignorant either of the processes which are going on in the system, of the chymical properties of the substances which he throws into it, or of the effects which they will certainly produce? If he is ignorant of the chymical affinities that subsist between the various articles of the Materia Medica, he may often administer preparations which are not only inefficacious, but even poisonous and destructive to his patient. When two chymical substances, each of which might be administered *separately* with safety, are combined, they sometimes produce a substance which is highly deleterious to the animal system. For example, although *mercury* and *oxygenized muriatic acid* have both been administered, and either of them may be taken separately without injury to the animal economy,—yet if a medical practitioner, ignorant of the chymical affinities of such substances, and of the quality of the compound, should give both of them in conjunction, the most dreadful consequences might ensue: since the product of this mixture, *oxygenized muriate of mercury,* is known to be a most corrosive poison; and there can be little doubt that hundreds of lives have been destroyed, by ignorant pretenders to medical science, in consequence of the injudicious administration of such deleterious preparations.

But chymistry is not the only science which is of utility in the arts which minister to the comfort and pecuniary interests of society. Geometry, trigonometry, conic sections, and other branches of mathematical knowledge; hydrostatics, hydraulics, mechanics, optics, botany, mineralogy and the other departments of the physical sciences, may be rendered of essential service to artisans and mechanics of various descriptions. All the sciences are, in some degree, connected, and reflect a mutual light upon one another; and consequently the man who has the most extensive acquaintance with science, is best qualified for carrying to perfection any one department of the useful arts.

*Practical Geometry* is highly useful to almost every mechanic and artisan, particularly to mill-wrights, bricklayers, carpenters and masons. It teaches them to form angles of any assigned number of degrees, to draw parallel and perpendicular lines, to proportion circumferences to diameters, to divide circular rims into any number of parts, to estimate the square or cubical contents of any piece of workmanship, and to calculate the price they ought to receive for any work they perform, according to its solid or superficial dimensions. In forming estimates of the expense of any proposed undertaking, the carpenter, bricklayer, and architect must find such knowledge essentially requisite, and even the common labourer who undertakes the formation of roads, the digging of pits, and the clearing away of rubbish, will find the principles of arithmetic and geometry of important service in estimating the rate at which he can perform such operations. The following geometrical theorems, besides many others, are capable of a variety of practical applications, in many departments of the arts. "If, from the two ends of any diameter of the circle, two lines be drawn to meet in any one point of the circle whatever, such lines are perpendicular to each other," or, in other words, they form a right angle at the point of contact.* Again, "The

* For example, if from the two ends of the diameter A and B, the lines A C, B C be drawn to the point C, these lines will be perpendicular to each other and consequently the angle at C will be a right an

areas of all circles are in exact proportion to the squares of their radii, or half diameters." If, for example, we draw a circle with a pair of compasses whose points are stretched 4 inches asunder, and another with an extent of 8 inches, the large circle is exactly *four times* the size or area of the small one. For the square of 4 is = 16, and the square of 8 is = 64, which is four times 16. And as the circumferences of the circles are in proportion to the radii, it will follow, that the length of a string which would go round the curve of the larger circle is exactly *double* the length of one which would go round the lesser. Mechanics, in recognising such theorems, will meet with many opportunities of reducing them to practice.—Again, there is a figure which Geometricians term a *parabola*, which is formed every time we pour water forcibly from the mouth of a tea-kettle, or throw a stone forward from the hand. One property of the parabola is, that if a spout of water be directed at half a perpendicular from the ground, or at an angle of elevation of 45 degrees, it will come to the ground at a greater distance than if any other direction had been given it, a slight allowance being made for the resistance of the air. Hence the man who guides the pipe of a fire-engine may be directed how to throw the water to the greatest distance, and he who aims at a mark, to give the projectile its proper direction.—To surveyors, navigators, land-measurers, gaugers and engineers a knowledge of the mathematical sciences is so indispensably requisite, that without it, such arts cannot be skilfully exercised.

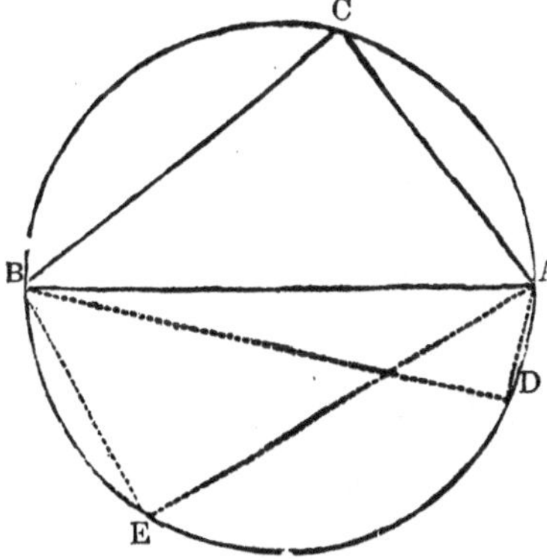


gle. In like manner the lines A D, and B D, A B and B E, will stand at right angles to each other; and the same will be the case to whatever point of the circle such lines are drawn. The practical application of this principle, in various operations, will, at once, be obvious to the intelligent mechanic, especially when he intends the two ends or sides of any piece of machinery to stand perpendicular to each other.

5

The *physical sciences* are also of the greatest utility in almost every department of art. To masons, architects, ship-builders, carpenters and every other class employed in combining materials, raising weights, quarrying stones, building piers and bridges, splitting rocks, or pumping water from the bowels of the earth,—a knowledge of the principles of *mechanics* and *dynamics* is of the first importance. By means of these sciences the nature of the lever and other mechanical powers may be learned, and their forces estimated—the force produced by any particular combination of these powers calculated—and the best mode of applying such forces to accomplish certain effects, ascertained. By a combination of the mechanical powers the smallest force may be multiplied to an almost indefinite extent, and with such assistance man has been enabled to rear works and to perform operations which excite astonishment, and which his own physical strength, assisted by all that the lower animals could furnish, would have been altogether inadequate to accomplish. An acquaintance with the experiments which have been made to determine *the strength of materials*, and the results which have been deduced from them, is of immense importance to every class of mechanics employed in engineering and architectural operations. From such experiments, (which have only been lately attended to on scientific principles) many useful deductions might be made respecting the best form of mortises, joints, beams, tenons, scarphs, &c.; the art of *mast making*, and the manner of disposing and combining the strength of different substances in naval architecture, and in the rearing of our buildings. For example,—from the experiments now alluded to it has been deduced, that the strength of any piece of material *depends chiefly on its depth*, or on that dimension which is in the direction of its strain. A bar of timber of one inch in breadth, and two inches in depth is *four times* as strong as a bar of only one inch deep; and it is *twice* as strong as a bar two inches broad and one deep, that is, a joint or lever is always strongest when laid on its edge. Hence it follows, that the strongest joist that can be cut out of a round tree is not the one which has the greatest quantity of timber in it, but such that the product of its breadth by the square of its depth shall be the greatest possible.—Again, from the same experiments it is found, that *a hollow tube is stronger than a solid rod containing the same quantity of matter*. This property of hollow tubes is also accompanied with greater stiffness; and the superiority in strength and stiffness is so much the greater as the surrounding shell is thinner in proportion to its diameter. Hence we find that the bones of men and other animals are formed hollow, which renders them incomparably stronger and stiffer, gives more room for the insertion of muscles, and makes them lighter and more agile, than if they were constructed of solid matter. In like manner the bones of birds, which are thinner than those of other animals, and the quills in their wings, acquire by their thinness the strength which is necessary, while they are so light as to give sufficient buoyancy to the animal in its flight through the aerial regions. Our engineers and carpenters have, of late, begun to imitate nature in this respect, and now make their axles and other parts of machinery hollow, which both saves a portion of materials and renders them stronger than if they were solid.*

The departments of *hydrostatics* and *hydraulics*, which treat of the pressure and motion of fluids, and the method of estimating their velocity and force, require to be thoroughly understood by all those who are employed in the construction of common and forcing-pumps, water-mills, fountains, fire-engines, hydrostatical presses, and in the formation of canals, wet-docks, and directing the course of rivers; otherwise they will constantly be liable to commit egregious blunders, and can never rise to eminence in their respective professions. Such principles as the following:—that fluids press equally in all directions,—that they press as much *upwards* as *downwards*,—that water, in several tubes that communicate with each other, will stand at the same height, in all of them, whether they be small or great, perpendicular or oblique,—that the pressure of fluids is directly as their *perpendicular height*, without any regard to their quantity,—and that the quantities of water discharged at the same time, by different apertures, under the same heigth of surface in the reservoir, are to each other nearly as the areas of their apertures,—will be found capable of extensive application to plumbers, engineers, pump-makers, and all who are employed in conducting water over hills or vallies, or in using it as a mechanical power, by a recognition of which they will be enabled to foresee, with certainty, the results to be expected from their plans and operations; for want of which knowledge many plausible schemes have been frustrated, and sums of money expended to no purpose.

The following figures and explanations will tend to illustrate some of the principles now stated:—1. Fluids press in proportion to their *perpendicular heights*, and the base of the vessel containing them, without regard to the quantity. Thus, if the vessel ABC, fig. 2, has its base BC equal to the base FG of the cylindrical vessel DEFG, fig. 1, but is much smaller at the top A than at the bottom, and of the same height; the pressure upon the bottom BC is *as great* as

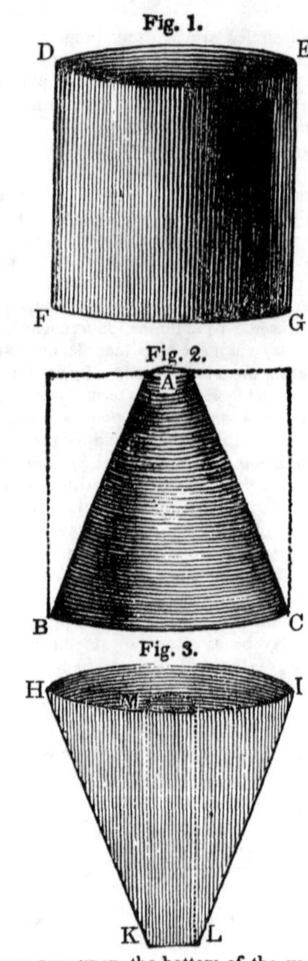


the pressure upon the bottom of the vessel DEFG, when they are filled with water, or any other liquid, notwithstanding that there will be a much greater quantity of water in the cylindrical than in the conical vessel; or, in other words, the bottom BC will sustain a pressure equal to what it would be if the vessel were as wide at the top as at the bottom. In like manner, the bottom of the vessel HIKL, fig. 3, sustains a pressure only equal to the column whose base is KL, and height KM, and not as the whole quantity of fluid contained in the vessel; all the rest of the fluid being supported by the sides. The demonstration of these positions would occupy too much room, and to many readers would appear too abstract and uninteresting; but they will be found satisfactorily demonstrated in most books which treat of the doctrines of hydrostatics.

2. The positions now stated form the founda-

* The mechanical reader who wishes particular information on this subject is referred to the article *Strength of materials* in *Ency. Brit.* 3d edit. which was written by the late Professor Robison.

tion of the hydrostatical paradox, namely, "that a quantity of fluid, however small, may be made to counterpoise a quantity, however great." Thus, if to a wide vessel AB, we attach a tube CD, communicating with the vessel, and pour

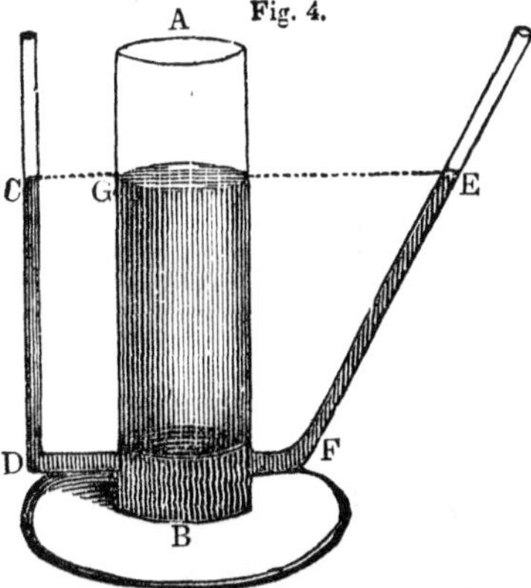

Fig. 4.

water into it, the water will run into the larger vessel AB, and will stand at the same height C and G in both. If we affix an inclined tube EF, likewise communicating with the large vessel, the water will also stand at E, at the same height as in the other two; the perpendicular altitude being the same in all the three tubes, however small the one may be in proportion to the other. This experiment clearly proves that the small column of water balances and supports the large column, which it could not do if the lateral pressures at bottom were not equal to each other. Whatever be the inclination of the tube EF, still the perpendicular altitude will be the same as that of the other tubes, although the column of water must be much longer than those in the upright tubes. Hence it is evident, that a small quantity of a fluid may, under certain circumstances, counterbalance any quantity of the same fluid. Hence also the truth of the principle in hydrostatics, that "*in tubes which have a communication, whether they be equal or unequal, short or oblique, the fluid always rises to the same height.*" From these facts it follows, that water cannot be conveyed by means of a pipe that is laid in a reservoir to any place that is higher than the reservoir.

These principles point out the mode of conveying water across valleys without those expensive aqueducts which were erected by the ancients for this purpose. A pipe, conforming to the shape of the valley, will answer every purpose of an aqueduct. Suppose the spring at A, fig. 5, and water is wanted on the other side of the valley to supply the house H, a pipe of lead or iron laid from the spring-head across the valley will convey the water up to the level of the spring-head; and if the house stand a little lower than the spring-head, a constant stream will pour into the cisterns and ponds where it is required, as if the house had stood on the other side of the valley; and, consequently, will save the expense of the arches BB, by which the ancient Romans conducted water from one hill to another. But, if the valley be very deep, the pipes must be made very strong near its bottom, otherwise they will be apt to burst; as the pressure of water increases in the rapid ratio of 1, 3, 5, 7, 9, &c. and is always in proportion to its perpendicular height.

Fig. 5.

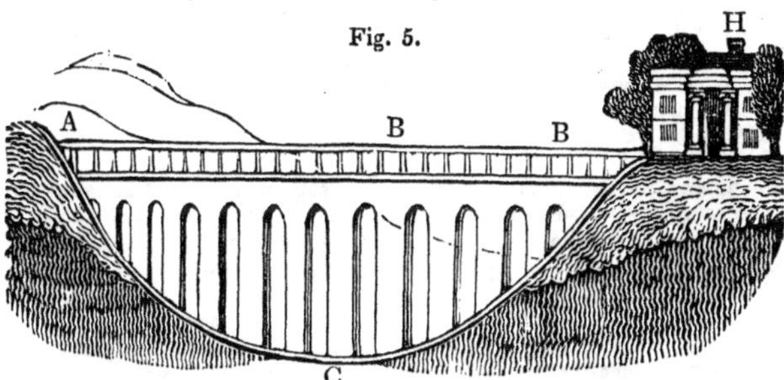


3. Fluids *press in all directions*, laterally and upwards, as well as downwards. That fluids press *laterally* may be seen by boring a hole in the side of a cask containing any liquid, when the liquid will run out in consequence of the lateral pressure. The *upward* pressure is not so obvious, but is clearly proved by the following experiment, with an instrument generally termed the hydrostatic bellows:—This machine consists of two thick oval boards, about 18 inches long and 16 inches broad, united to each other by leather, so as to open and shut like a pair of common bellows, but without valves. Into this instrument a pipe B, several feet high, is fixed at D. If we pour water into the pipe at its top C, it will run into the bellows and separate the boards a little. If we then lay three weights, each weighing 100 pounds, upon the upper

board, and pour more water into the pipe, it will run into the bellows, and raise up the board with all the weights upon it. And though the water in the tube should weigh in all only a quarter of a pound, yet the pressure of this small force upon the water below in the bellows shall support the weights, which are 300 pounds; nor will they have weight enough to make them descend, and conquer the weight of water, by forcing it out of the mouth of the pipe. The reason of this will appear from what has been already stated respecting the pressure of fluids of equal heights, without any regard to the quantities. For, if a hole be made in the upper board, and a tube be put into it, the water will rise in the tube to the same height that it does in the pipe; and it would rise as high (by supplying the pipe) in as many tubes as the board would contain holes. Hence, if a man stand upon the upper board, and blow into the bellows through the pipe, he will raise himself upward upon the board; and the smaller the bore of the pipe is, the easier will he be able to raise himself. And if he put his finger on the top of the pipe he may support himself as long as he pleases.

The uses to which this power may be applied are of great variety and extent; and the branches of art dependent upon it appear to be yet in their infancy. By the application of this power the late Mr. Bramah formed what is called the ***Hydrostatic Press***, by which a prodigious force is obtained, and by the help of which, hay, straw, wool, and other light substances, may be forced into a very small bulk, so as to be taken in large quantities on board a ship. With a machine, on this principle, of the size of a tea-pot, standing before him on a table, a man is enabled to cut through a thick bar of iron as easily as he could clip a piece of pasteboard with a pair of sheers. By this machine a pressure of 500 or 600 tons may be brought to bear upon any substances which it is wished to press, to tear up, to cut in pieces, or to pull asunder.

Upon the same principle, the tun or hogshead HI, fig. 7, when filled with water, may be burst, by pressing it with some pounds additional weight of the fluid through the small tube KL, which may be supposed to be from 25 to 30 feet in height. From what has been already stated, it necessarily follows, that the small quantity of water which the tube KL, contains, presses upon the bottom of the tun with as much force as if a column of water had been added as wide as the tun itself, and as long as the tube, which would evidently be an enormous weight.

A few years ago, a friend of mine, when in Ireland, performed this experiment to convince an English gentleman, who called in question the principle, and who laid a bet of fifty pounds that it would not succeed. A hogshead, above 3 feet high, and above 2 feet wide, was filled with water; a leaden tube, with a narrow bore, between 20 and 30 feet long, was firmly inserted into the top of the hogshead; a person, from the upper window of a house, poured in a decanter of water into the tube, and, before the decanter was quite emptied, the hogshead began to swell, and, in two or three seconds, burst into pieces, while the water was scattered about with immense force.

Hence, we may easily perceive what mischief may sometimes be done by a very small quantity of water, when it happens to act according to its perpendicular height. Suppose, that in any building, near the foundation, a small quantity of water, only of the extent of a square yard, has settled, and suppose it to have completely filled up the whole vacant space, if a tube of 20 feet long were thrust down into the water, and filled with water from above, a force of more than 5 tons would be applied to that part of the building, which would blow it up with the same force as gunpowder.* The same effect may sometimes be produced by rain falling into long narrow chinks, that may have inadvertently been left in building the walls of a house; which shows the importance of filling up every crevice and opening of a building, and rendering the walls as close and compact as possible. Hence, likewise, similar processes in nature, connected with pools of water in the bowels of the earth, may occasionally produce the most dreadful devastations. For, should it happen, that, in the interior of a mountain, two or three hundred feet below the surface, a pool of water thirty or forty square feet in extent, and only an inch or two in depth, was collected, and a small crevice or opening of half an inch in breadth were continued from the surface to the water in the pool; and were this crevice to be filled with rain or melted snow, the parts around the layer of water would sustain a pressure of more than *six hundred tons*, which might shake the mountain to its centre, and even rend it with the greatest violence. In this way, there is every reason to believe, partial earthquakes have been produced, and large fragments of mountains detached from their bases.

The principles now illustrated are capable of the most extensive application, particularly in all engineering and hydraulic operations. It is on the principle of the lateral and upward pressure of fluids that the water, elevated by the New River water-works, in the vicinity of London, after having descended from a bason in a vertical pipe, and then, after having flowed horizontally in a succession of pipes under the pavement, is raised up again through another pipe, as high as the fountain in the Temple Garden. It is upon the same principle that a vessel may be filled either at the mouth or at the bottom indifferently, provided that it is done through a pipe, the top of which is as high as the top of the vessel to be filled. Hence, likewise, it follows, that when piers, aqueducts, or other hydraulic works for the retention of water, are to be constructed, it becomes necessary to proportion their strength to the lateral pressure which they are likely to sustain, which becomes greater in proportion to the height of the water to be sustained. Walls, likewise, designed to support terraces, ought to be sufficiently strong to resist the lateral pressure of the earth and rubbish which they are to sustain, since this pressure will be greater as the particles of earth, of which the terraces are composed, are less bound together, and in proportion as the terraces are more elevated. The increase of pressure in proportion to the depth of any fluid likewise shows the necessity of forming the sides of pipes or masonry in which fluids are to be retained, *stronger towards the bottom*, where the pressure is greatest. If they are no thicker than what is sufficient for resisting the pressure near the top, they will soon give way by the superior pressure near the bottom; and if they are thick enough in every part to resist the great pressure below, they will be stronger than necessary in the parts above, and, consequently, a superfluous expense, that might have been saved, will be incurred in the additional materials and labour employed in their construction. The same principle is applicable to the construction of flood-gates, dams, and banks of every description, for resisting the force of water. When the strength and thickness requisite for resisting the pressure at the greatest depth is once ascertained, the walls or banks may be made to taper upwards, according to a certain ratio founded on the strength of the materials, and the gradual decrease of pressure from the bottom upwards; or, if one side be made perpendicular, the other may proceed in a slanting direction towards the top.

From the principles and experiments now stated, we may also learn the reason why the banks of ponds, rivers, and canals *blow up*, as it is termed. If water can insinuate itself under a bank or dam, even although the layer of water were no thicker than a half-crown piece, the pressure of the water in the canal or pond will force it up. In fig. 8, let A represent the section of a river or canal, and BB a drain running under one of its banks; it is evident, that, if the bank C is not heavier than the column of water BB, that part of the bank must inevitably give way. This effect may be prevented in artificial canals by making the sides very tight with clay heavily

* See fig. 8 p. 68.

rammed down, or by cutting a trench EF, about a foot and a-half wide, along the bank of the river or canal, and a little deeper than the bottom of the canal, which being filled up with earth or clay

Fig. 8.

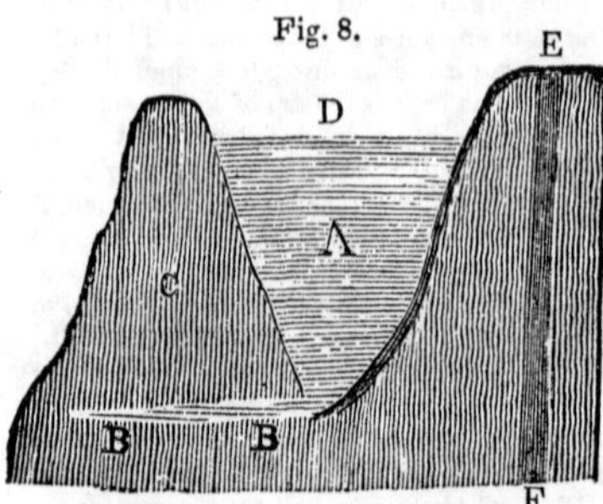


well moistened with water, forms, when dry, a kind of wall through which the water cannot penetrate. By inattention to such circumstances many disasters have happened, and much expense needlessly incurred; and, therefore, the scientific principles to which I have now adverted ought to be known, even by labourers of the lowest rank employed in operations carried on for the improvement of the country.

To the want of a recognition of these principles may be attributed the failure of the following scheme, and the disaster with which it was attended:—After the *diving-bell* was invented, it was considered desirable to devise some means of remaining for any length of time under water, and rising at pleasure without assistance. "Some years ago, an ingenious individual proposed a project, by which this end was to be accomplished. It consisted in sinking the hull of a ship made quite water-tight, with the decks and sides strongly supported by shores, and the only entry secured by a stout trap-door, in such a manner, that, by disengaging from within the weights employed to sink it, it might rise of itself to the surface. To render the trial more satisfactory and the result more striking, the projector himself made the first essay. It was agreed that he should sink in twenty fathoms water, and rise again without assistance at the expiration of 24 hours. Accordingly, making all secure, fastening down his trap-door, and provided with all necessaries, as well as with the means of making signals to indicate his situation, this unhappy victim of his own ingenuity entered, and was sunk. No signal was made, and the time appointed elapsed. An immense concourse of people had assembled to witness his rising, but in vain; for the vessel was never seen more. *The pressure of the water at so great a depth* had, no doubt, been completely under-estimated, and the sides of the vessel being at once crushed in, the unfortunate projector perished before he could even make the signal concerted to indicate his distress."*

Many other applications of the principles of hydrostatics might have been mentioned, but what has been now stated may serve to exemplify the practical utility of an acquaintance with such principles, not only to engineers and superintendants of public works, but to mechanics and artificers of every description.

The science of *Pneumatics*, which treats of the mechanical properties of the atmosphere, will likewise be found useful to mechanics and artists of various descriptions, to whom it is, in many cases, of importance to know something of the effects of the *resistance*, the *pressure*, and the *elasticity* of air. The construction of barometers, syphons, syringes, and air-pumps, depends upon the pressure of the atmosphere, and likewise water-pumps, fire-engines, and many other hydraulic machines; and, consequently, the constructors of such instruments and engines must frequently act at random, if they are unacquainted with the nature and properties of the atmosphere, and the agency it exerts in such mechanical contrivances.† Even the *carpenter* and the *mason* may be directed, in some of their operations, by an acquaintance with the doctrines of pneumatics. When two pieces of wood are to be glued together, they are first made as even and smooth as possible; the glue is then applied to one or both of the surfaces; they are then pressed together till the glue has become thoroughly dry. The use of the glue is to fill up every crevice in the pores of the wood, so as to prevent the admission of any portion of air between the pieces; and then the atmos-

* Herschel's "*Discourse on the Study of Nat. Philosophy.*"

† As an illustration of the importance of being acquainted with the atmospheric pressure, the following anecdote may be here inserted:—A respectable gentleman, of landed property, in one of the middle counties of Scotland, applied to a friend of mine, a Lecturer on Chymistry and Natural Philosophy, in order to obtain his advice respecting a pump-well which he had lately constructed at considerable expense. He told him, that, notwithstanding every exertion, he could not obtain a drop of water from the spout, although he was quite sure there was plenty of water in the well, and *although he had plastered it all around, and blocked up every crevice.* When my friend inspected the pump, he suspected that the upper part of the well was air-tight, and, consequently, that the atmospheric pressure could not act on the surface of the water in the well. He immediately ordered a hole to be bored adjacent to the pump, when the air rushed in with considerable force; and, on pumping, the water flowed copiously from the spout. The gentleman was both overjoyed and astonished; but it is somewhat astonishing, that neither he, nor his neighbours, nor any of the workmen who had been employed in its construction, should have been able to point out the cause of the defect; but, on the other hand, should have taken the *very opposite* means for remedying it, namely, by plastering up every crevice, so as to produce a kind of vacuum within the well. This and similar facts show how little progress scientific knowledge has yet made, even among the middle classes of the community

phere, with a force equal to 15 pounds on every square inch, presses the pieces firmly together. A knowledge of this principle will suggest the propriety of filling up every opening or crevice, and continuing the pressure for some time, as the air, wherever it gains admission, has a tendency, by its elastic force, to loosen every species of cement. The same principle might direct bricklayers and masons, in building either stone or brick-walls, in suggesting the propriety of filling up every crevice with the most tenacious cements, so as to prevent the access of the external air to the interior of the walls. For there can be no question that the firmness and stability of our houses and garden-walls depend, in part, upon the pressure of the atmosphere, after the interior crevices are thoroughly filled up. An extensive knowledge of this science would likewise direct them to the proper mode of constructing the flues of chimneys, so as to prevent that most disagreeable of all circumstances in dwelling houses, *smoky chimneys.* From ignorance of the effects of heat, of the experiments that have been made on rarefied air, and their relation to our common fires,—of the proper dimensions of funnels,—of the effects of winds and currents of air,—of the proper height and width of chimneys,—of the method of promoting a good draught, and making the air pass as near the fire as possible, and various other particulars requisite to be attended to in the construction of fire-places and their flues; many dwelling-houses have been bungled, and rendered almost uninhabitable. The workmen, in such operations, without any rational principle to guide them, carry up funnels in the easiest way they can, according to the practice of "use and wont," and leave the tenants or proprietors of the houses they erect to get rid of their smoke in the best way their fancy can contrive. Whereas, were chimneys and their flues constructed according to the principles of science, they might be rendered, almost with certainty, completely efficient for the purpose intended.

To all who are acquainted with the nature and properties of elastic fluids, it must be obvious, that the whole mystery of curing smoky chimneys consists in finding out and removing the accidental causes which prevent the heated smoke from being forced up the chimney by the pressure of the cool or heavier air of the room. These causes are various; but that which will be found most commonly to operate is, the bad construction of the chimney *in the neighbourhood of the fire-place.* "The great fault," says Count Rumford, "of all the open fire-places now in common use is, that they are much too large, or rather it is *the throat of the chimney*, or the lower part of its open canal, in the neighbourhood of the mantle, and immediately over the fire, which is too large." The following is a condensed view of some of the rules given on this subject, by this ingenious practical philosopher, and which are founded on the principles of science, and on numerous experiments:—1. The *throat* of the chimney should be perpendicularly over *the fire;* as the smoke and hot vapour which rise from a fire naturally tend *upwards.* By the *throat* of a chimney is meant the lower extremity of its canal, where it unites with the upper part of its open fire-place. 2. The nearer the throat of a chimney is to the fire the stronger will be its *draught*, and the less danger of its smoking; since smoke rises in consequence of its rarefaction by heat, and the heat is geater nearer the fire than at a greater distance from it. But the draught of a chimney may be too strong, so as to consume the fuel too rapidly; and, therefore, a due medium must be fixed upon, according to circumstances. 3. That *four inches* is the proper width to be given to the throat of a chimney, reckoning across from the top of the breast of the chimney, or the inside of the mantle to the back of the chimney, and even in large halls, where great fires are kept up, this width should never be increased beyond 4½ or 5 inches. 4. The width given to the back of the chimney should be about *one-third* of the width of the opening of the fire-place in front. In a room of a middling size, *thirteen inches* is a good size for the width of the back, and 3 times 13 or 39 inches for the width of the opening of the fire-place in front. 5. The angle made by the back of the fire-place and the sides of it, or covings, should be 135 degrees, which is the best position they can have for throwing heat into the room. 6. The back of the chimney should always be built *perfectly upright.* 7. Where the throat of the chimney has an end, that is to say, where it enters into the lower part of the open canal of the chimney, *there* the three walls which form the two covings and the back of the fire-place should *all end abruptly*, without any slope, which will render it more difficult for any wind from above to force its way through the narrow passage of the throat of the chimney. The back and covings should rise 5 or 6 inches higher than the breast of the chimney. 8. The current of air which, passing under the mantle, gets into the chimney, should be made *gradually to bend its course upwards*, by which means it will unite *quietly* with the ascending current of smoke. This is effected with the greatest ease and certainty, merely by *rounding off* the breast of the chimney, or back part of the mantle, instead of leaving it flat or full of holes and corners. Fig. 1 shows the section of a chimney on the common construction, in which *d e* is the throat. Fig. 2 shows a section of the same chimney altered and improved, in which *d i* is the reduced throat, four inches in the direction of *d i*, and thirteen inches in a line parallel to the mantle.

Fig. 1. Fig. 2.

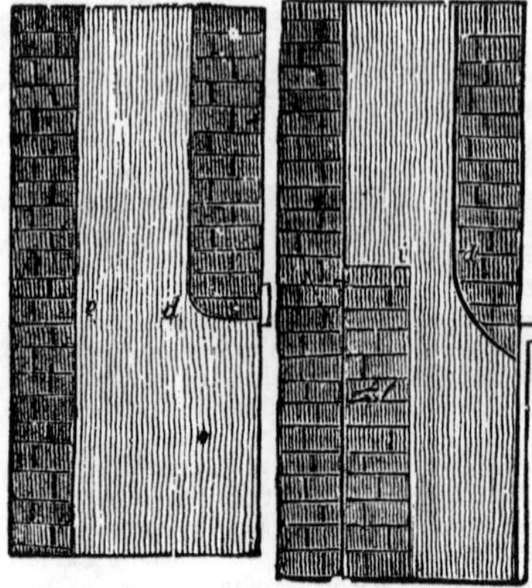

Masons, bricklayers and others, who are interested in this subject, would do well to procure and study Count Rumford's "Essay," which was originally sold for two shillings. His directions have seldom been accurately attended to in this country by those who have pretended to improve chimneys on the principles he has laid down, partly from carelessness, and partly from ignorance of the elements of science. When the grate is not set in its proper place, when its *sloping* iron back is retained,—when no pains have been taken to make its ends coincide with the covings of the fire-place,—when the mantle, instead of having its back rounded off, is a vertical plane of iron, cutting a column of smoke which rises beneath it; and, above all, when the throat of the chimney, instead of *four*, is made, as we often see, *fourteen* inches wide,—not one of the Count's directions has been attended to, and his principles have as little to do with the construction of such a chimney as with the building of the dykes of Holland, or the pyramids of Egypt.

A knowledge of the science of *Optics*, which explains the nature of vision, and the laws by which light is refracted and reflected, is essentially requisite to the makers of *telescopes*, *microscopes*, and all other dioptric and catoptric instruments, in order to carry them forward to their highest pitch of improvement. And yet how often do we find many of those employed in the construction and manufacture of such instruments glaringly deficient in the first principals of optical science? One maker imitates the instruments of another without discrimination, and while he sometimes imitates the excellencies, he as frequently copies the defects. Hence the glaring deficiencies in the construction of the eye-pieces of most of our pocket telescopes, and the narrow field of view by which they are distinguished, which a slight acquaintance with the properties of lenses would teach them to obviate. By a moderate acquaintance with the principles of this science, any ingenious mechanic might, at a small expense, be enabled to construct for himself many of those optical instruments by which the beauties of the animal and vegetable kingdoms, and the wonders of distant worlds have been explored.

Although, in the hands of mathematicians, the science of optics has assumed somewhat of a forbidding appearance to the untutored mind, by the apparently complex and intricate diagrams by which its doctrines have been illustrated, yet it requires only the knowledge of a few simple facts and principles to guide an intelligent mechanic in his experiments, and in the construction of its instruments. In order to the construction of a refracting telescope, it is only requisite to know, that the rays of light, passing through a convex-glass, paint an image of any object directly before it, at a certain point behind it, called its *focus;* and that this image may be viewed and magnified by another convex-glass, placed at a certain distance behind it. Thus, let CD, fig. 1, represent a convex-glass, whose focal distance CE is 12 inches; let AB represent a distant object directly opposite; the rays of light passing from this object, and crossing each other, will form an image of the object AB, at EF, in an *inverted* position. Let GH represent another convex-glass, whose focal distance is only one inch. If this glass is placed at one inch distant from the image EF, or 13

Fig. 1.

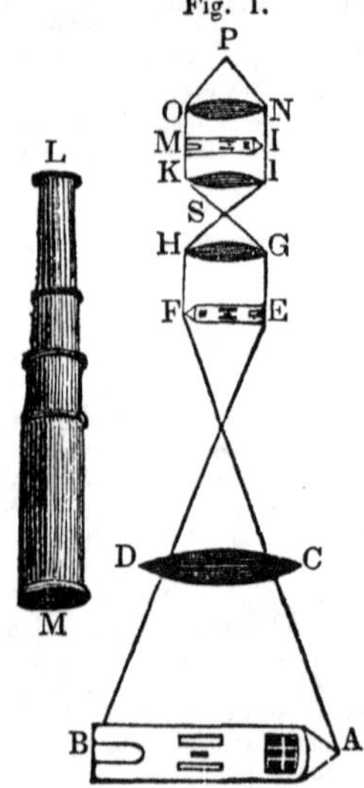

inches from the glass CD, and the eye applied at the point S, the object AB will be seen turned upside down, and magnified in the proportion of 1 to 12, or twelve times in length and breadth. This forms what is called an *Astronomical* telescope; but, as every thing seen through it appears inverted, it is not adapted for viewing terrestrial objects. In order to fit it for viewing land objects, two other eye-glasses, of the same focal distance, (namely, one inch,) are requisite; the second eye-glass IK is placed at 2 inches from GH, or double their focal distance, and the glass NO at the same distance from IK.* By this means a second image IM is formed in an *upright* position, which is viewed by the eye at P, through the glass NO, and the object appears magnified in the same proportion as before. The magnifying power of a telescope of this construction is found by dividing the focal distance of the object-glass by the focal distance of the eye-glass. Thus, if the object-glass be 36 inches in focal distance, and the eye-glass $1\frac{1}{2}$ inch, the magnifying power will be 24 times; if the focus of the eye-glass be 2 inches, the

Fig. 2.

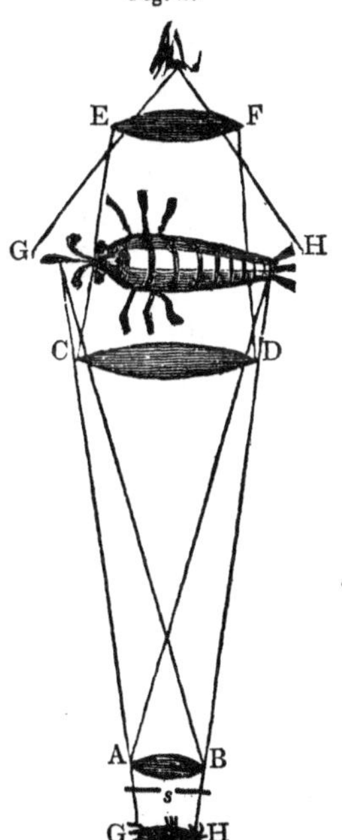


* This is not the best form of a terrestrial eye-piece; but it may serve for the purpose of illustration. The eye-piece now most generally used, consists of *four* lenses, combined on a different principle.

magnifying power will be 18 times, &c.—LM is the telescope fitted up for use.

A compound microscope might likewise be easily constructed by any ingenious artizan or mechanic, by attending to the following illustrations and directions. Fig. 2 represents the glasses of a compound microscope. AB is the glass next the object; CD is the amplifying glass for enlarging the field of view; EF is the glass next the eye. When a small object, as GH, is placed below the object-glass AB, at a little more than its focal distance from it, a magnified image of this object is formed by the glass AB at GH, which is magnified in proportion as the distance GG exceeds the distance of AG. This magnified image of the object is magnified a second time by the glass EF, to which the eye is applied at K. This instrument, when fitted up for use, is represented in fig. 3, where LM represents a box or pedestal on which it stands,

Fig. 3.

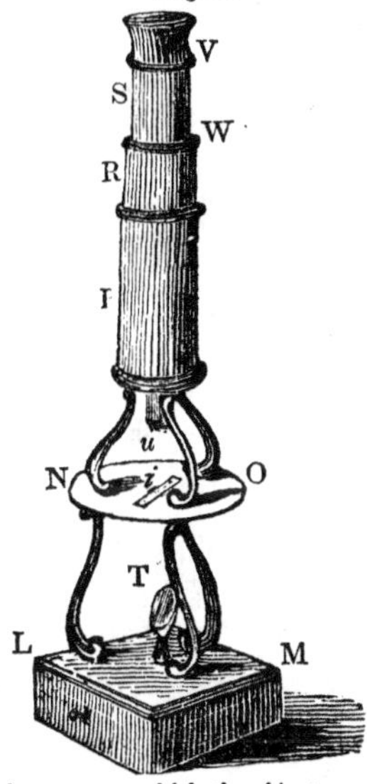


NO the stage on which the objects are placed, over the opening *i*, which is supported by 3 pillars fixed to the top of the box. P is a tube which is supported by 3 pillars fixed into the stage. Into this tube the tube R slides up and down for adjusting the focus. The small tube *u*, which carries the object-glass, is connected with the tube R, and slides up and down along with it. S is the tube which contains the two eye-glasses, and which may be made to slide up and down into the tube R, for increasing the magnifying power when occasion requires. T is a mirror, fixed on the pedestal, capable of moving up and down, and to the right or left, for throwing light upon the object placed over the hole *i*, which may be laid upon a slip of thin glass. The object-glass AB, fig. 2, is placed at *u*, fig. 3. The glass CD is placed opposite W, fig. 3, and the eye-glass EF opposite V.

Such are the essential parts of a compound microscope. Any common mechanic may construct one for himself by attending to the following directions: The object-glass AB, fig. 2, may be about ½, ¾, or 1 inch focal distance, and the aperture, or hole which lets in the light from the object, should not exceed 1-10th of an inch, otherwise it will cause a glare, which will produce an indistinct image of the object. The amplifying glass CD may be 2½ inches focal distance, and 1½ inch in diameter. This glass is not *essentially* necessary, but it serves to enlarge the field of view, and to render it more distinct near the border. The eye-glass EF should be about 1 inch focus, and about ¾ inch in diameter. With respect to the *distances* at which they should be placed from each other, the glass CD may be placed at about 5 or 6 inches from AB, and the glass EF about 2 inches, or 1⅞ inch from CD. The object-glass shoule be a *double* convex—the eye-glasses may be *plano-convex;* that is, plane on the one side and convex on the other, with the plane sides turned next the eye; but double convexes will do, if these cannot be procured. The tubes which contain the glasses may be made of pasteboard, and the stage, pillars, and box, of wood. The glasses may be procured for about 4 shillings; and if the individual fit them into the tubes, and perform all the other operations requisite, the expense of all the other materials will not exceed other four shillings. Suppose, now, that the object-glass AB is ½ inch focal distance, and the image GH is formed at the distance of 6 inches from it, this image will be larger than the object, nearly in the proportion of 6 to ½, or 12 times. Suppose the glass EF, considered in connexion with CD, to possess a magnifying power equal to 5 times, then the whole magnifying power will be $5 \times 12$, or 60 times. The object, therefore, will be magnified 60 times in length and in breadth, and, consequently, the surface will be magnified 3600 times, which is the square of 60. With such a microscope, the animalculæ in water, the circulation of the blood in frogs and fishes, the small feathers which compose the dust on butterflies' wings, and all the most interesting appearances of the minute parts of animals and vegetables, may be distinctly perceived.

Besides the discoveries in the heavens and in the minute parts of creation, to which the study of the science of optics has led,—its principles are capable of being directed to many important purposes in human life and society. By means of large burning mirrors and lenses the rays of the sun have been condensed, so as to increase their intensity more than seventeen thousand times, and to produce a heat more than four hundred times greater than that of our common fires, which would serve for the combustion and fusion of numerous substances, which are infusible in the greatest heat that can be produced in our common furnaces. The property of a convex lens, by which rays proceeding from its focus are refracted into parallel directions, has enabled us to throw, from light-houses, *a strong light* to great distances at sea. The large polyzonal, or *built up* lenses, contrived by Sir D. Brewster, which may be made of any magnitude, and the elegant lamp of Lieutenant Drummond,—the one producing the most intense light yet known, and the other conveying it undispersed to great distances,—promise to introduce improvements hitherto unthought of, and to diversify the nocturnal scenery both of sea and land. For, in the progress of extensive national improvements, they might be made subservient, in connexion with carburetted hydrogen gas, in enlivening and decorating the rural scene, in the absence of the sun, and in guiding the benighted traveller in all his journeyings. For, when we consider the improvements, in almost every department of the social state, which have been lately carried forward, it is surely not too much to expect, that, in the course of a century hence, our highways, villages, hamlets, and even some of our moors and mountains, shall be lighted up with gas lamps, connected with mirrors and lenses, analogous to those which illuminate our cities and towns, and which direct the mariner, when approaching our shores. The following figure shows the manner in which a large lens throws a light to great distances. Let AB, fig. 4, represent one of Sir D.

Fig. 4.

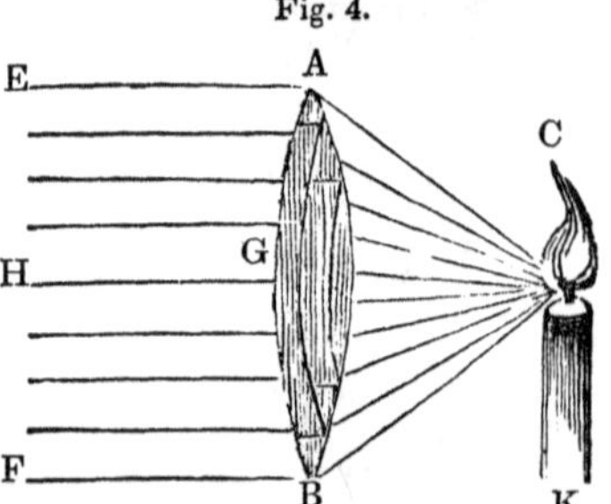


Brewster's polyzonal lenses, or any other large lens, and GK its focal distance; if a luminous body CK, as the flame of a lamp, be placed at the focal point K, the rays of light, diverging from CK, after passing through the lens AB, will proceed in a *parallel direction*, AE, GH, BF, and may illuminate objects at very considerable distances. AB, fig. 4, represents a section of the polyzonal lens built of ten different pieces. L, fig. 5 exhibits a *front* view of the

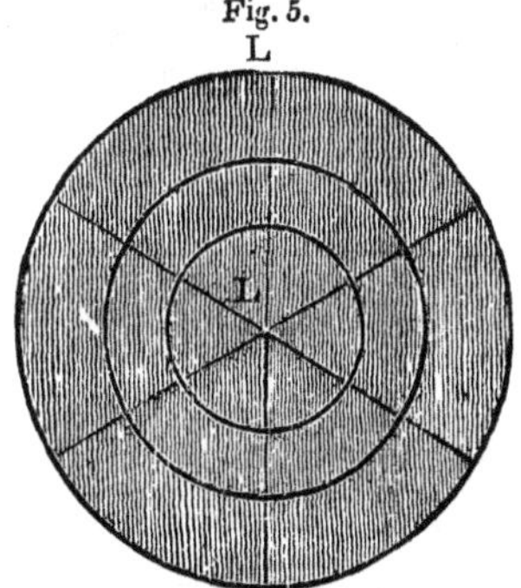


same lens. Could such lenses be constructed of the size of 6, 8, 10 or 12 feet diameter, they would produce a degree of heat from the solar rays far surpassing what has hitherto been effected, and be capable of throwing a brilliant light to immense distances.

Fig. 6, shows the manner in which a *concave mirror* TU reflects the light of a lamp VW, placed in its focus, to great distances. It is in this way that the light of the Bell Rock, and other light-houses, is reflected to more than thirty or forty miles distant.

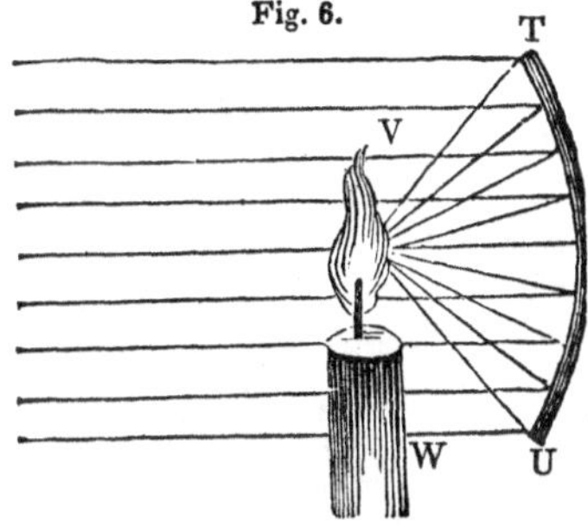


Even the sciences of *Electricity* and *Galvanism* might, in some instances, be rendered subservient to the operations of art. By means of the electrical fluid, models of corn-mills, water-pumps, and orreries, showing the diurnal motion of the earth, and the age and phases of the moon, have been set in motion; and there can be no question, that, in the hands of genius, it might be directed to accomplish much more important effects. Even the lightning of the clouds, which is only the electrical fluid acting on an ample scale, has been guided by the hand of art, to perform mechanical operations, by splitting large stones into shivers. This has been effected in the following manner. Suppose AB to represent a stone or portion of a rock, which is intended to be split into a number of pieces. Into the midst of this stone a long rod of iron, or conductor CD, is inserted, which terminates in a point. When a thunder-cloud, as EF, passes over the stone, within its striking

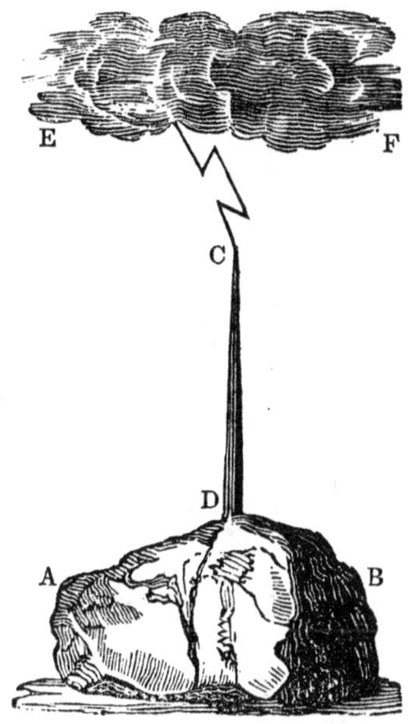


distance of the earth, the lightning from the cloud strikes the upper part of the pointed conductor, and is conducted downwards to the heart of the stone, which either rends it in different places, or splits it at once into a multitude of fragments. This experiment, which appears to have been first made in Prussia in 1811, was attended with complete success, during the first storm that passed over, after the bar of iron was inserted in the stone.

To braziers, tinsmiths, coppersmiths, and other workers in metals, a knowledge of *Galvanism* might suggest a variety of useful hints, especially where it is an object of importance to secure any piece of metallic workmanship from *rust*. It is found that when metals are pure and kept separate from each other, they remain for a long time untarnished; but when alloyed, or placed in contact with other metals, they soon undergo oxidation. Coins composed of one metal are found more durable than those composed of two; and the copper sheathing of ships which is fastened with iron nails soon undergoes corrosion. These effects are now explained on the principles of galvanism. When two metallic substances of different kinds are connected by moisture, they form what is called a *galvanic circle;* and, therefore, when one kind of metal is placed in contact with another, if either water or the moisture of the atmosphere adheres to them, a galvanic circle is formed, and oxidation is produced. On this ground the late Sir Humphrey Davy suggested the propriety of fastening the upper sheathing of ships with *copper* instead of *iron* nails. The same principle may be rendered of extensive application, and may afford many useful hints to every artizan employed in working and combining metals.

A knowledge of *magnetism* might also, in many cases, be directed to useful practical applications. This mysterious power, in connexion with its polarity, has already enabled the miner and surveyor to traverse the remotest corners of the largest mines, and to trace their way back in safety through all the windings of those subterraneous apartments, and has directed the navigator to steer his course with certainty, through the pathless ocean, to his "desired haven." Throughout all the regions of the globe the magnetic power extends its influence; and it is now found to have an intimate connexion with heat, electricity, and galvanism. Of late years, it has been ascertained that iron with its oxides and alloys are not the only substances susceptible of magnetic influence. The magnetism of *nickel*, though inferior to that of iron, is found to be considerable; and that of *cobalt* and *titanium* is quite perceptible. Nay, the recent discoveries of *Arago* have shown, "that there is no substance but which, under proper circumstances, is capable of exhibiting unequivocal signs of the magnetic virtue." In consequence of a recent discovery of *M. Oersted*, "we are now enabled to communicate, at and during pleasure, to a coiled wire, *of any metal indifferently*, all the properties of a magnet—its attraction, repulsion, and polarity, and *that* even in a more intense degree than was previously thought to be possible in the best natural magnets." This discovery tends to enlarge our views of the range of magnetic influence, and to lead us to the conclusion that its powers may hereafter be applied to purposes of which at present we can have no conception. Although the polarity of the magnet has been of incalculable service to mankind, particularly in promoting navigation and enlarging our knowledge of the globe, yet we have no reason to believe that this is the only practical purpose to which its powers may be applied, or the only reason why the Creator has so widely diffused its influence in the system of nature; since, in his diversified operations in the material world, he so frequently produces a variety of effects from one and the same cause. It remains with man to prosecute his observations still more extensively on this subject, and his industry will, doubtless, be rewarded with the discovery of new relations, laws, and combinations, which may be susceptible of the most important practical applications in the arts which minister to the comfort and convenience of mankind. Even in its present state, the attractive property of magnetism is capable of being applied as a *mechanical* power, in certain pieces of machinery, although its application in this way has never yet been attempted on an extensive scale.

The following fact shows how its attractive power has lately been applied to the prolongation of life, and the warding off of incurable disease, in the case of a useful class of our fellow men. "In needle manufactories the workmen are constantly exposed to excessively minute particles of steel which fly from the grindstones, and mix, though imperceptible to the eye, as the finest dust in the air, and are inhaled with their breath. The effect, though imperceptible, on a short exposure, yet being constantly repeated from day to day, produces a constitutional irritation, dependent on the tonic properties of the steel, which is sure to terminate in pulmonary consumption; insomuch, that persons employed in this kind of work used scarcely ever to attain the age of forty years. In vain was it attempted to purify the air, before its entry into the lungs, by gauzes or linen guards; the dust was too fine and penetrating to be obstructed by such coarse expedients, till some ingenious person bethought him of that wonderful power, which every child that searches for its mother's needle with a magnet, sees in exercise. Masks of magnetized steel wire are now constructed and adapted to the faces of the workmen. By these the air is not merely *strained* but *searched* in its passage through them, and each obnoxious atom arrested and removed."*

This interesting fact affords a striking proof of the useful purposes to which the powers and properties of natural substances may be applied, when the mind is directed to contemplate them in all their bearings, and to trace them to all their legitimate consequences. The attractive power of the magnet, considered not only in its relation to iron and steel, but to all other substances in which magnetical virtue is found in a greater or less degree to reside—might, therefore, in the hands of an ingenious mechanic, lead to many interesting experiments, which might pave the way for the most important practical results.

The facts connected with the science of *Geology* may likewise, in many instances, be directed to practical purposes. From the researches which, of late years, have been made in the interior of the earth, geologists are now pretty well

* Herschel's *Prelim. Dis. on Nat. Philos.*

acquainted with the position and alternation of its strata, and with the different fossils which may be expected to abound in any particular district. Although these researches were undertaken chiefly with a view to ascertain the changes which have happened in the structure of our globe, and to support certain theories of the earth—yet they may frequently be of use to landed proprietors, to engineers, and to speculators in *mining* operations, so as to direct them in their investigations, and prevent them from embarking in schemes that may ultimately blast their expectations, exhaust their resources, and lead to irretrievable ruin. The ruinous effects sometimes produced by ignorance of this subject are strikingly illustrated by the following fact:—

"It is not many years since an attempt was made to establish a colliery at Bexhill, in Sussex. The appearance of thin seams and sheets of fossil wood, and wood-coal, with some other indications similar to what occur in the neighbourhood of the great coal beds in the north of England, having led to the sinking of a shaft, and the erection of machinery, on a scale of vast extent,—not less than eight thousand pounds are said to have been laid out on this project, which, it is almost needless to add, proved completely abortive, as every geologist would have at once declared it must, the whole assemblage of geological facts being adverse to the existence of a regular coal bed *in* the Hastings' *sand;* while this on which Bexhill is situated, is separated from the *coal strata* by a series of interposed beds of such enormous thickness as to render all idea of penetrating *through* them absurd.—The history of mining speculations is full of similar cases, where a very moderate acquaintance with the *usual order of nature*, to say nothing of theoretical views, would have saved many a sanguine adventurer from utter ruin."*

The study of the various branches of *Natural History* might also be rendered productive of utility in different departments of the arts. It is quite evident that a scientific knowledge of *Botany* must be highly useful to gardeners and their labourers, and to all who take an interest in horticultural and rural operations. Not only a knowledge of the *classification* and arrangement of plants, but also of their physiological structure and functions, of their medicinal qualities, and of the chymical properties of soils and the different manures, will be found of considerable utility to such individuals.—*Zoology* and *Comparative Anatomy*, which describe the peculiar structure and habits of animals, both foreign and domestic, will convey various portions of interesting information to shepherds, cattle-dealers, and agriculturists of every description. An acquaintance with *Mineralogy*, which treats of the solid and inanimate materials of our globe,—the earthy, saline, inflammable, and metallic substances of which it is composed, must be interesting to lapidaries, jewellers, iron-founders, and all who are employed in working various metals. To know the nature of those substances on which they are operating, the materials with which they are united in their native ores, their combination with phosphorus, sulphur, and carbon, the changes produced upon them by oxygen and the different acids, their relations to heat, and the liquids with which they may come in contact, and the various compounds into which they may be formed, will have a direct tendency not only to increase their stock of general knowledge, but to render them more skilful and intelligent in their respective professions. *Meteorology*, which treats of the weather and the variable phenomena of the atmosphere, will, in many instances, be found a useful study to mariners, fishermen, travellers, and farmers, by which they may frequently be directed in their movements, and avoid many inconveniences and dangers. By carefully attending to the motions of the barometer and thermometer, and comparing them with the electrical state of the atmosphere, the direction of the winds, and the appearances of the clouds, the farmer may be warned of the continuance of rain or drought, and direct his operations accordingly, so as to protect his produce from danger.

There is no application of science to the arts of more importance, and more extensive in its effects, than that of the employment of *Steam* for driving all kinds of machinery, and for propelling vessels along rivers and across the ocean. "It has armed," says Mr. Jeffrey, "the feeble hand of man with a power to which no limits can be assigned—completed the dominion of mind over the most refractory qualities of matter, and laid a sure foundation for all those future miracles of mechanic power, which are to aid and reward the labours of after generations." The first person who appears to have entertained the idea of employing steam for propelling vessels, was Mr. J. Hulls, in the year 1736. But it was not till 1807, when Mr. Fulton launched, at New-York, the first steam-boat he had constructed, that navigation by steam was introduced to general practice, which may therefore be considered as the epoch of the invention. In a few years every river and bay in the United States became the scene of steam navigation. In 1822 there were more than 350 steam vessels connected with these States, some of them of eight and nine hundred tons burden, and by this time, doubtless, they are more than doubled. In 1819 an expedition left Pittsburg, descended the Ohio in steam-boats for 1100 miles, and then ascending the rapid Missouri, proceeded to the distance of no less than two thousand five hundred miles. They

* Herschel's *Discourse*, &c.

have now been introduced into every country in Europe. On the principal rivers and seas connected with the British Isles, and even in the Scottish lakes, these vessels are sweeping along in majestic pomp, against wind and tide, diversifying the scenery through which they pass, and transporting travellers and parties of pleasure to their destination, with a rapidity unexampled in former ages. On the Clyde alone more than fifty or sixty steam vessels are constantly plying. The scenery of the Rhine, the Rhone, the Elbe, the Seine, the Danube, the Wolga, the lakes of Constance and Geneva, and of many other rivers and inland seas, is now enlivened by these powerful machines, conveying goods and passengers in every direction. Even the Atlantic ocean, an extent of more than three thousand miles, has been traversed by a steam-boat in twenty days; and the period, we trust, is not far distant, when the Red Sea, the Persian Gulph, the Bay of Bengal, the Indian Ocean, the Mediterranean, the Euxine, the Gulph of Mexico, and even the wide Pacific, will be traversed by these rapid vehicles, conveying riches, liberty, religion and intelligence to the islands of the ocean, and forming a bond of union among all nations.

The admirable improvements in the construction of *steam carriages* which are now going forward, are no less worthy of attention. The rapid movements of these machines, which have been lately introduced on the Liverpool and Manchester railway, and the security and comfort with which they are attended, have excited the astonishment of every beholder. And no wonder,—since goods and passengers are now conveyed between these cities, with a velocity of nearly thirty miles an hour! so that it may be said, with the strictest propriety, that the steam engine is the most brilliant present ever made by philosophy to mankind.

The discovery of *carburetted hydrogen gas*, and its application to the purpose of illuminating our dwelling-houses, streets, and manufactories, may also be considered in reference to the arts. Every city, and every town of a moderate size, is now enlivened with the splendid brilliancy produced from this invisible substance ; pipes for its conveyance have been laid, of many hundred miles in extent, and diverging into numerous ramifications, and thousands of artists are employed in conducting its manufacture, and forming tubes and other devices for distributing it in all directions.

Now, since the inventions to which I am adverting are founded on chymical and mechanical principles, and on the discoveries of modern science, and since many thousands of mechanics are now employed in constructing the machinery connected with these inventions, and in conducting its operations both by sea and land, it is of the utmost importance, in order to their being fully qualified for their respective departments, that they understand the scientific principles which enter into the construction of such machines and engines, the peculiar uses of every part, the manner in which the chymical agents employed operate, and the effects which, in any given circumstance, they must necessarily produce. In particular, it is indispensably necessary, that *engine-men*, and others employed for directing these machines, when in operation, should be acquainted with every part of their structure, and the principles on which their movements depend; for the comfort and *safety* of the public are dependent on the caution and skill with which they are conducted. How could any man be qualified for such an office without some portion of scientific knowledge? and how could travellers in such vehicles consider their lives and property secure, if they were not guided by men of intelligence and prudence? To the want of such caution and skill are chiefly to be attributed most of the disasters and fatal accidents, connected with such operations, which have hitherto taken place.

Besides the agriculturists, manufacturers, mechanics, and artificers alluded to above, there are numerous other classes to which similar remarks will apply. In short, there is scarcely an individual, however obscure, in any department of society, but may derive practical benefit from an acquaintance with science. "The farm-servant or day labourer," says Lord Brougham, "whether in his master's employ, or tending the concerns of his own cottage, must derive great practical benefit,—must be both a better servant, and a more thrifty, and, therefore, comfortable cottager, for knowing something of the nature of soils and manures, which chymistry teaches, and something of the habits of animals, and the qualities and growth of plants, which he learns from natural history and chymistry together. In truth, though a man is neither a mechanic nor a peasant, but only one having a pot to boil, he is sure to learn from science lessons which will enable him to cook his morsel better, save his fuel, and both vary his dish and improve it. The art of good and cheap cookery is intimately connected with the principles of chymical philosophy, and has received much, and will yet receive more, improvement from their application."—Nay, even the *kitchen maid*, the laundry maid, and the mistress of every family, may derive many useful hints from the researches of science. The whole art of cookery is a chymical operation, and so are the arts of washing, dressing, bleaching, and dyeing. By a knowledge of the nature and properties of the acids and other chymical substances, they would learn how to eradicate stains of ink, grease, &c. from cotton, linen, woollen, and silks, in the safest and most effectual manner, and many other processes of great utility in domestic life. Even the art of kindling a fire, and of *stirring* it when kindled, depends on philosophical principles. For example, the stirring of a fire is of use, because it makes a hollow, where the air being rarefied by the adjacent heat, the surrounding air rushes into the partial vacuum, and imparting its oxygen, gives life to the fire and carries the flame along with it. On this principle the following rules are founded. 1. Never stir a fire when fresh coals are laid on, particularly when they are very small, because they immediately fall into the vacuum, and prevent the access of the oxygen of the atmosphere, which is the principle of combustion. 2. Always keep the bottom bar clear, because it is there chiefly that the air rushes in to nourish the fuel. 3. Never begin to stir at top, unless when the bottom is quite clear, and the top only wants breaking, otherwise the unkindled fuel may be pressed down in a body to the bottom, and the access of atmospheric air prevented.

Illustrations, of a similar kind, of the practical applications of science, might have been given to an almost indefinite extent; but the above specimens may suffice as corroborative of the general position—that scientific knowledge would render mechanics and manufacturers of all descriptions more skilful in the prosecution of their respective employments.

Some, however, may be disposed to insinuate, that it is quite enough for philosophers to ascertain principles, and to lay down rules founded upon them, for the direction of the mechanic or artizan;—or, that it is only requisite that the directors and superintendents of chymical processes and mechanical operations, should be acquainted with that portion of science which is necessary for their peculiar departments. But it is easy to perceive, that a mechanic who works merely by rules, without knowing the foundation or *reasons* of them, is only like a child who repeats his catechism by rote, without attaching a single idea to the words he utters, or like a horse driving a thrashing machine, without deviating from the narrow circle to which he is necessarily confined. When any accident occurs, when the circumstances of the case are somewhat changed, when the same principle on which he generally proceeds requires to be applied to a new object or mode of operation, he either blunders his work, or feels himself utterly at a loss how to proceed. The least deviation from his accustomed trammels puts him out, because he has no clear and comprehensive view of the principles on which his practice depends. Hence we uniformly find, that a man of scientific acquirements will easily comprehend the plan of any new machine or architectural operation, and be able to execute it, while he who works only by square and rule, will hesitate at every step, and perceive innumerable difficulties in his way. To confine artists to mere rules, without a knowledge of the principles on which they are founded, is to degrade their intellectual nature, to reduce them to something like mere machines, to render them less useful both to themselves and to their employers, and to prevent the improvement of the liberal and mechanical arts.

The following instance may be stated as a specimen of the advantages of chymical knowledge, and of the practical purposes to which it may be applied in different regions of the globe. A young Parisian, of the name of Léger went on a commercial adventure to Egypt in the year 1822; but during some of the convulsions of that unsettled country, he lost the little property with which he was intrusted, and was forced to make a precipitate retreat from Suez to Alexandria. He remained some time at Alexandria, destitute and almost hopeless. But the talent of observation, and the social habits characteristic of his countrymen, came to his aid; in a lucky moment he formed the resolution of retrieving his fortune by introducing the luxury of *ice* into the parched land of the Ptolemies. This common product of wintry regions is known to be as grateful to the languid natives of tropical climates as ardent spirits are to the benumbed inhabitants of the Polar circle. Having succeeded in effecting a return to his family, the enterprising Parisian was enabled by the friendly assistance of Gay Lussac and Thenard, to adopt the best means that chymistry could devise for the preservation of ice, both during the voyage, and after its arrival in a sultry latitude; and at length set out from Paris with his inventions, and arrived safely at Alexandria, in April 1823. The sovereign of Egypt, Mahommed Ali, was delighted at this novel addition to oriental luxuries; and, besides valuable presents, gave the inventor the exclusive right for five years of importing ice into his dominions. This privilege is estimated to be worth one million of francs, or nearly 50,000*l.* In ancient times the world was enlightened by the learning of Egypt; the greatest philosophers travelled thither, as to the fountain-head of science; but the land of Sesostres and Alexander has now become the prey of the ferocious Moslem; and whatever she enjoys of art, knowledge or civilization, she is compelled to receive from the once barbarous regions of the West.*

II. Scientific knowledge will not only render persons more skilful in their respective employments, but *will enable them to make improvements in the arts, and in the physical sciences with which they are connected.*

It has frequently been affirmed that many useful inventions have been owing to *chance*, and that persons ignorant of science have stumbled upon them without any previous investiga-

* Scots Mechan. Mag. 1825.

tion. It is not denied, that several inventions have originated in this way, but they are much fewer than is generally imagined; and, in almost every instance, where chance suggested the first hint of any invention, the future improvements were directed by the hand of genius and the aids of science. It is said, that the invention of the telescope was owing to a spectacle-maker's boy having accidentally taken up two convex glasses of different focal distances, and placed the one near his eye and the other at a considerable distance, when he perceived, on looking through them, the spire of a neighbouring church turned upside down, and much larger than its usual size. The father of the boy, amazed at this singular appearance, bethought himself of adjusting two glasses on a board, supporting them in two brass or wooden circles, which might be removed nearer to, or farther from each other at pleasure, as in the following figure, where A represents the object, B the lens next the object, *a* the inverted image

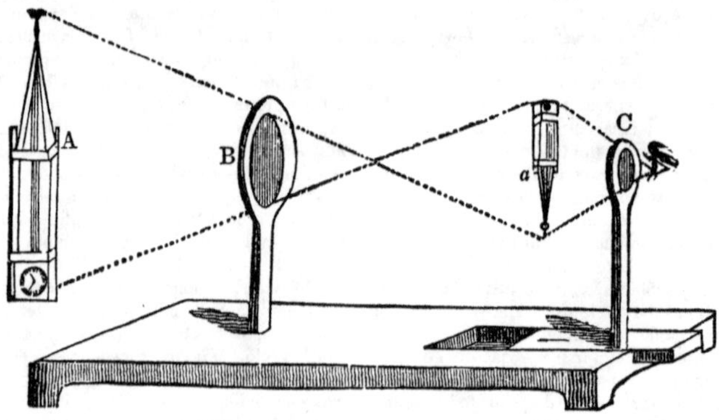


formed by it, C the glass next the eye, and D the sliding board on which it was fixed, for adjusting the focus. Such appears to have been the first rude construction of a telescope. But so long as the invention remained in this state, it was of little benefit to society. It was not before Galileo, a philosopher of Tuscany, heard of the circumstance, and entered into investigations on the refraction of light, and the properties of lenses, that this noble instrument was improved and directed to the heavens for the purpose of making astronomical discoveries; and all the subsequent improvements it has received, have been the result of reasonings, and experimental investigations, conducted by men of science. Sir Isaac Newton, *in consequence of his experiments and discoveries respecting light and colours*, detected the true cause of the imperfection of the common refracting telescope, and suggested the substitution of metalline specula instead of lenses, which led him to the invention of the *reflecting* telescope; and Mr. Dollond, *in consequence of his investigations and experiments respecting the different degrees of refraction and divergency of colour produced by different kinds of glass*, effected the greatest improvement that had ever been made on the *refracting* telescope, by producing an image free of the imperfections caused by the blending of the prismatic colours. And we have reason to believe, that the further improvement of this telescope will chiefly depend on ascertaining the true chymical composition of flint glass for achromatic purposes, and the proper mode of conducting its manufacture, which may lead to the construction of instruments of this kind, on a more extensive scale than has ever yet been attempted, and to discoveries in the celestial regions far beyond those which have hitherto been made. But such improvements can never be effected, unless by numerous experimental investigations, conducted by those whose minds are thoroughly imbued with the principles of chymical and optical science.*

One of the latest improvements on Achromatic object-glasses was made by a foreigner of the name of *Guinand*, who was originally a cabinet-maker. After acquiring a knowledge of the principles of optics, and of the mode of constructing telescopes, he applied himself particularly to ascertain the proper composition of *flint-glass* for achromatic purposes; and, after spending twenty or thirty years in making experiments—casting one pot of glass after another, and meeting with frequent disappointments,—he at length succeeded in obtaining glass for achromatic telescopes, of larger dimensions and of a quality superior to what could formerly be procured. Of this glass was formed the largest triple achromatic telescope ever constructed, which was lately erected in the observatory of the university at Dorpat, under the direction of M. Fraunhofer. This glass is perfectly free from veins, and has a greater dispersive power than any obtained before. The diameter of this object glass is almost ten inches, and its focal distance 15 feet. It has four eye-pieces, the lowest magnifying 175 times, and the highest 700 times. Mr. Tulley of Islington lately constructed, of similar materials,

With regard to the invention and improvement of the *steam-engine*—a story has been told "that an idle boy being employed to stop and open a valve, saw that he could save himself the trouble of attending and watching it, by fixing a plug upon a part of the machine which came to the place at the proper times, in consequence of the general movement." Whether or not this story has any foundation in truth—certain it is, that all the most useful improvements in this engine have been the result of the most elaborate researches and investigations of scientific truths. The first distinct notion of the structure and operation of this powerful machine appears to have been given by the Marquis of Worcester, in 1663, in his "Century of Inventions." Its subsequent improvements by Savary, Blackey, Newcomen, Beighton and Fitzgerald, were the results of physical knowledge, of mechanical skill, and of the most laborious investigations. Its latest and most important improvements by Mr. James Watt, were owing no less to the scientific knowledge which adorned his mind, than to his mechanical ingenuity. He was a man of a truly philosophical mind, eminently conversant in all branches of natural knowledge, and the pupil and intimate friend of Dr. Black, and had attended the lectures of that distinguished philosopher in the university of Glasgow. And he often acknowledged "that his first ideas on this subject were acquired by his attendance on Dr. Black's chymical lectures, and from the consideration of his theory of latent heat, and the expansibility of steam." We may therefore rest assured, that all the future improvements and new applications of this noble invention will be the result of physical and chymical knowledge combined with mechanical skill; and consequently, no artizan can ever expect to be instrumental in bringing the steam-engine to its highest pitch of improvement, and in directing its energies to all the purposes to which they may be applied, unless the pursuits of science occupy a considerable share of his attention.

The first hint of the *mariner's compass* is generally supposed to have been owing to chance. Some persons may have accidentally observed, that when a small loadstone is suspended in water on a piece of wood or cork, its ends pointed towards the south and north. Such experiments seem to have been applied at first for mere amusement, and to excite astonishment in the minds of the ignorant and illiterate. But it was not till some genius possessed of science and of reflecting powers seized the hint thus given, that it was applied to the important purpose of directing the mariner in his course through the pathless ocean. And to science we are indebted for the manner of determining the *declination* of the needle, in all parts of the world, by means of the azimuth compass, and thus rendering it an accurate guide to the navigator in every region through which he moves. The discovery of that peculiar principle termed *galvanism*, was partly owing to accident. Whilst Galvani, professor of anatomy at Bologna, was one day employed in dissecting a frog, in a room where some of his friends were amusing themselves with electrical experiments, one of them having happened to draw a spark from the conductor, at same time that the professor touched one of the nerves of the animal, its whole body was instantly shaken by a violent convulsion. Having afterwards suspended some frogs from the iron palisades which surrounded his garden, by means of metallic hooks fixed in the spines of their backs, he observed that their muscles contracted frequently and involuntarily, as if from a shock of electricity. Such facts, presented to the view of unscientific persons, might have produced nothing more than a gaze of wonder; perhaps supernatural powers might have been resorted to in order to account for the pheno-

manufactured by the same artist, a telescope whose object-glass is about seven inches diameter, and its focal length twelve feet, which is now in the possession of Dr. Pearson. The piece of flint-glass of which the concave lens was formed, cost Mr. Tulley about thirty guineas. Unfortunately for science, the ingenious artist (Guinand) is now dead, and it is uncertain whether he has left any particular details of his process behind him. The possibility, however, of procuring glass for the construction of very large achromatic telescopes is now put beyond a doubt.

The unscientific reader may acquire a *general* idea of an achromatic object-glass from the following figure,—where A D represents a double unequally convex lens of *crown glass*, C B a double concave of *flint glass*, and E F another convex lens of crown-glass. These are placed together in the manner represented in the figure, and form what is called

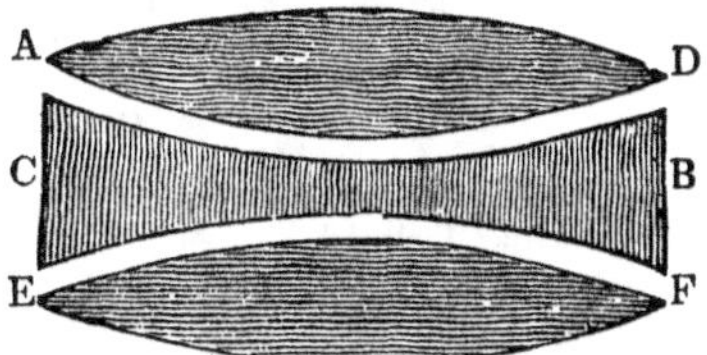


an achromatic object-glass, the term *achromatic* signifying *free of colour*. Sometimes only two lenses, a convex of crown, and a concave of flint-glass are combined for the same purpose. In the case of a single convex glass, the image formed is blended with the prismatic colours which come to foci at different distances from the lens, and consequently produce a comparatively indistinct image, which will not admit of a high magnifying power. But the achromatic lens, forming an image without colour, will bear a larger aperture, and a higher magnifying power, than a common refractor of the same length. So great is the difference—that an achromatic telescope of Dollond, only three feet ten inches in length, was found to equal, and even excel the famous aerial telescope of Huygens of 123 feet focal length, and the gentlemen present at the trial agreed that "the dwarf was fairly a match for the giant." The principal obstacle to their construction on a large scale, is, the difficulty of procuring large pieces of flint-glass free of veins, and of a proper dispersive quality.

mena, and in a short time they might have been forgotten as a vision of the night. But such scientific minds as those of Valli, Volta, Monro, Fowler, Davy, Humboldt and Wollaston, having seized upon these facts, having contemplated them in every point of view, and instituted experiments of every description in relation to them—most astonishing discoveries in science have been brought to light—the whole aspect of chymistry has been changed, and numerous improvements introduced into the practice of the useful arts. Alkalis have been decomposed, new metallic substances discovered, the cause of the *corrosion* of metals ascertained, and the means determined by which it may be effectually prevented.

It is a truth which the whole history of science fully corroborates, that very few important discoveries have been made by accident or by ignorant persons, whose minds were not directed to the particular object of research. On the other hand, we have every reason to believe, that there are many facts and circumstances which have passed under the inspection of untutored minds, which, had they come within the range of men of science, would have led to many useful inventions which are yet hid in the womb of futurity, and which will reward the industry of more enlightened generations. The inventions to which we have now adverted, and many others, where chance suggested the first rude hints, would, in all probability, have lain for ages in obscurity, without any real utility to mankind, had not the genius of science seized upon them, viewed them in all their bearings, and traced them to all their legitimate consequences and results. Had the telescope, the steam engine, and the mariner's compass, in their first embryo state, remained solely in the hands of ignorant empirics, they might have been reserved merely as play-things for the purpose of vulgar amusement, or exhibited by cunning impostors to aid their deceptions, or to produce a belief of their supernatural powers. But science snatched them from the hands of the ignorant and the designing, and having added the requisite improvements, bequeathed them to mankind as the means of future advancement in the paths of knowledge, and in the practice of the arts.

It may be laid down as a kind of axiom, to which few exceptions will occur, that great discoveries in science and improvements in art are never to be expected but as the result of knowledge combined with unwearied investigation. This axiom might be illustrated, were it necessary, from what we know of the past history of our most useful inventions. The celebrated M. Huygens, who first discovered the means of rendering clocks exact by applying the *pendulum*, and rendering all its vibrations equal by the cycloid—was one of the first mathematicians and astronomers of his age. He had long kept the object of his pursuit before his mind, he plied his mechanical ingenuity in adapting the machinery of a clock to the maintaining of the vibrations of a pendulum, and by his mathematical knowledge investigated the theory of its motion. By the aid of a new department of geometrical science, invented by himself, he showed how to make a pendulum swing in a cycloid, and that its vibrations in this curve are all performed in equal times, whatever be their extent. The ingenious Mr. Robert Hooke, who was the inventor of spring or pocket watches, and of several astronomical instruments for making observations both at sea and land—was eminently distinguished for his philosophical and mathematical acquirements. From his earliest years he discovered a genius for mechanics, and all his other knowledge was brought to bear upon his numerous inventions and contrivances.—Otto Guericke, who *invented* the *Air-pump*, was one of the first mathematicians of his time; and the Honourable Robert Boyle, who *improved* this valuable instrument, was one of the most illustrious philosophers of the age and country in which he lived.—Mr. Ferguson, the inventor of several orreries, the astronomiaal rotula, the eclipsarian, the mechanical paradox, and other astronomical machinery, had, from his earliest years, devoted the greatest part of his time to the study of mechanics, and the physical and mathematical sciences with which it is connected, as appears from the numerous popular works which he published on these subjects which are still in extensive circulation.—The late Mr. Arkwright, the inventor of the *spinning jennies*, devoted many years to the study of mechanics and to the improvement of his invention, till he was perfectly conversant in every thing that relates to the construction of machinery. This admirable invention, by which a pound of the finest cotton has been spun by machinery into a yarn extending more than 119 miles, was not the result of chance, but of the most unwearied study and attention in regard to every circumstance which had a bearing on the object of his pursuit: and as he had not originally received any thing like a *regular* scientific education, his acquirements were the result of his own application and industry.—"The new process of refining sugar, by which more money has been made in a shorter time, and with less risk and trouble, than was ever perhaps gained from an invention, was discovered by an accomplished chymist, E. Howard, brother of the Duke of Norfolk, and was the fruit of a long course of experiments, in the progress of which, known philosophical principles were constantly applied, and one or two new principles ascertained."

There are few inventions of modern times that have been more directly the result of philosophical knowledge and experiment, than the *safety-lamp*, invented by that accomplished chymist, the late Sir Humphrey Davy. He instituted a series of philosophical experiments, with the express purpose of constructing, if possible, a lamp by which the miner might walk through a body of fire-damp in his subterraneous apartments without danger of an explosion; and the success with which his investigations were attended, led to one of the most beautiful and useful inventions which distinguish the period in which we live.* Had this ingenious philosopher been ignorant of the nature and properties of carburretted hydrogen gas, of the composition of atmospheric air, of the nature of combustion, and of the general principles of chymical science, he could never have hit upon the construction of this admirable instrument, and the useful miner would still have been left to grapple with his invisible enemy (the fire-damp) without any means of escaping from its destructive agency.†

* See Appendix, No. IX.

† It is more than probable, that fatal accidents have occurred in coal mines where these lamps have been used, owing to the ignorance and inattention of some of those artists who have been employed in forming the *wire-gauze* with which they are surrounded. A friend of mine, who performed a great variety of experiments with this instrument, with every combination of explosive gas, informed me, that, with a lamp surrounded with wire-gauze, manufactured by an artist in a town in the north of England, and *who supplied it for the use of the miners*—an explosion uniformly took place when the instrument was placed in a body of inflammable gas. He suspected that the apertures in the wire-gauze were too large, and remonstrated with the artist on his want of accuracy; and it was not before he procured gauze with smaller apertures that his experiments succeeded; and they were attended with complete success in every future experiment, after the gauze was changed. So small was the difference in the contexture of the two pieces of the gauze, that, to a common eye, it was scarcely perceptible. It is found by experiment, that the apertures in the gauze should not exceed one twentieth of an inch square, and that wire from one fortieth to one sixtieth of an inch diameter, is the most convenient. Had the artist alluded to, known how to perform experiments with this instrument, and tried the effects of his gauze before he sold it for the purpose intended, such serious blunders would not have been committed. Who knows but the deficiency in the gauze alluded to might have been the cause of the destruction of several lives in the pits where it was used? for it is a certain fact that accidents from explosions are occasionally recurring, even in mines where these lamps are generally in use. Hence the necessity of chymical knowledge and attention to scientific accuracy in those who are the manufacturers of instruments of this description—on the accurate construction of which the lives and comforts of a useful body of the community may depend. I know not whether it be customary to put the safety-lamp into the hands of the miner, without first trying its efficiency for resisting the effects of explosive gases. If it is not, it is a most glaring and dangerous oversight; and there can be no question, that to the neglect of this precaution are to be attributed many of those explosions which have taken place in the mines where this lamp has been introduced. Besides, such neglects have a direct tendency to detract from the merits of this noble invention, to prevent its universal adoption, and to render uncertain its efficiency for warding off destructive explosions. But from the experiments alluded to above, which were performed with the greatest care, and with every possible combination of explosive gas, and frequently exhibited in private, and before large public audiences—the efficiency of this lamp for resisting the effects of fire-damp is put beyond the shadow of a doubt. It is known to be the practice of some miners, occasionally to screw off the top of their lamp, in order to enjoy the benefit of more light than what shines through the wire-gauze. Such a practice ought to be strictly prohibited, and the instrument, if possible, rendered incapable of being opened at top—a practice which may probably have been the occasion of several explosions. If the workmen in mines were carefully instructed in the general principles of chymistry, and particularly in the nature of combustion, explosions, and the qualities of the different gases, they would not dare to hazard such dangerous experiments.

We may farther remark, that the mechanic whose mind is enlightened with scientific knowledge, *has a much greater chance of being instrumental in improving the arts, than the mere chymist or philosopher*. While the mere philosopher is demonstrating principles and forming theories in his closet, and sometimes performing experiments, only on a *small* scale,—the workman, in certain manufactories, has a daily opportunity of contemplating chymical processes and mechanical operations on an *extensive* scale, and of perceiving numberless modifications and contrivances, which require to be attended to, of which the mere scientific speculator can form but a very faint and inadequate conception. Being familiar with the most minute details of every process and operation, he can perceive redundancies and defects imperceptible to other observers; and, if he has an accurate knowledge of the general principles on which his operations depend, he must be best qualified for suggesting and contriving the requisite improvements. As the mechanic is constantly handling the tools and materials with which new experiments and improvements may be made,—observing the effects of certain contrivances, and of deviations from established practice—and witnessing the chymical and mechanical actions of bodies on each other—he has more opportunities of observation in these respects, and, consequently, is more likely than any other class of society to strike out a new path which may lead to some useful invention in the arts, or discovery in the sciences.* But if his mind is not imbued with knowledge, he trudges on, like a mill-horse, in the same beaten track, and may overlook a thousand opportunities of performing experiments, and a thousand circumstances which might suggest new improvements.

In short, in so far as chance is concerned in new discoveries and improvements in the arts, the scientific mechanic has a hundred chances to one, compared with the ignorant artificer, that, in the course of his operations, he shall hit upon a new principle of improvement: his chances of such results are even superior to those of the most profound philosophers who never engage in

* See Appendix No. X

practical operations, as he is constantly in the way of perceiving what is useless, defective, or in any way amiss in the common methods of procedure. To use a common expression, "he is in the way of good luck, and if he possesses the requisite information, he can take the advantage of it when it comes to him." And should he be so fortunate as to hit on a new invention, he will probably enjoy not merely the honour which is attached to a new discovery, but also the pecuniary advantages which generally result from it.

We have, therefore, every reason to hope, that, were scientific knowledge universally diffused among the working classes, every department of the useful arts would proceed with a rapid progress to perfection, and new arts and inventions, hitherto unknown, be introduced on the theatre of the world, to increase the enjoyments of domestic society, and to embellish the face of nature. No possible limits can be assigned to the powers of genius, to the resources of science, to the improvement of machinery, to the aids to be derived from chymical researches, and to the skill and industry of mechanics and labourers when guided by the light which scientific discoveries have diffused around them. Almost every new discovery in nature lays the foundation of a new art; and since the recent discoveries of chymistry lead to the conviction, *that the properties and powers of material substances are only beginning to be discovered*—the resources of art must, in some measure, keep pace with our knowledge of the powers of nature. It is by seizing on these powers, and employing them in subserviency to his designs, that man has been enabled to perform operations which the whole united force of mere animal strength could never have accomplished. Steam, galvanism, the atmospheric pressure, oxygen, hydrogen, and other natural agents, formerly unnoticed or unknown, have been called into action by the genius of science; and, in the form of steam-boats and carriages, Voltaic batteries, gasometers and air-balloons, have generated forces, effected decompositions, diffused the most brilliant illuminations, and produced a celerity of motion both on sea and land which have astonished even the philosophical world, and which former generations would have been disposed to ascribe to the agencies of infernal demons. And who shall dare to set boundaries to the range of scientific discovery—or to say, that principles and powers of a still more wonderful and energetic nature, shall not be discovered in the system of nature, calculated to perform achievements still more striking and magnificent? Much has, of late years, been performed by the application and combination of chymical and mechanical powers, but much more, we may confidently expect, will be achieved in generations yet to come, when the physical universe shall be more extensively explored, and the gates of the temple of knowledge thrown open to all. Future Watts, Davys and Arkwrights will doubtless arise, with minds still more brilliantly illuminated with the lights of science, and the splendid inventions of the present age be far surpassed in the "future miracles of mechanic power," which will distinguish the ages which are yet to come. But, in order to this "wished for consummation," it is indispensably requisite that the mass of mankind be aroused from their slumbers, that knowledge be universally diffused, and that the light of science shed its influence on men of every nation, of every profession, and of every rank. And if, through apathy or avarice, or indulgence in sensual propensities, we refuse to lend our helping hand to this object, now that a spirit of inquiry has gone abroad in the world—society may yet relapse into the darkness which enveloped the human mind during the middle ages, and the noble inventions of the past and present age, like the stately monuments of Grecian and Roman art, be lost amidst the mists of ignorance, or blended with the ruins of empires.

III. The knowledge and mental activity connected with the improvement of the arts, *would promote the external comforts of mankind, particularly of the lower orders of society.*

Since the period when the arts began to be improved, and a spirit of inquiry after knowledge was excited among the middling and lower orders, many comforts and conveniencies have been introduced, and a new lustre appears on the face of general society. In many places the aspect of the country has been entirely changed; the low thatched cottage of the farmer has arisen into a stately mansion, the noisome dunghill which stood within two yards of his door, has been thrown into a spacious court at a distance from his dwelling, and his offices display a neatness and elegance which seem to vie with those of the proprietor of the soil. The gloomy parish church with its narrow aisle and tottering belfrey, has been transformed into a noble lightsome edifice, and adorned with a stately spire towering above all surrounding objects; and the village school, within whose narrow walls a hundred little urchins were crowded, like sheep in a fold, has now expanded into a spacious hall. Narrow dirty paths have been improved, roads formed on spacious plans, canals and railways constructed, streets enlarged, waste lands cultivated, marshes drained, and the interior of houses decorated and rendered more comfortable and commodious. In districts where nothing formerly appeared but a dreary waste, print-fields have been established, cotton mills, founderies, and other manufactories erected, villages reared, and the noise of machinery, the tolling of bells, the sound of hammers, the buzz of reels, and the hum of human voices and of ceaseless activity, now diversify the scene where nothing was formerly heard but the purling stream or the howlings of the tempest. In certain parts of the country where the passing of a chariot was a kind of phenomenon, mails and stage-coaches crowded with travellers of all descriptions, within and without, now follow each other in rapid succession, conveying their passengers with uninterrupted rapidity, and at one-half the expense formerly incurred. Even on the inland lake, where scarcely a small skiff was formerly seen, steam-vessels are now beheld sweeping along in majestic style, and landing fashionable parties, heroes, divines, and philosophers, to enliven the rural hamlet, the heath-clad mountain, and the romantic glen.

Much, however, is still wanting to complete the enjoyments of the lower ranks of society. In the *country*, many of them live in the most wretched hovels, open to the wind and rain, without a separate apartment to which an individual may retire for any mental exercise; in *towns*, a whole family is frequently crowded into a single apartment in a narrow lane, surrounded with filth and noxious exhalations, and where the light of day is scarcely visible. In such habitations, where the kitchen, parlour, and bed-closet are all comprised in one narrow apartment, it is next to impossible for a man to improve his mind by reading or reflection, amidst the gloom of twilight, the noise of children, and the preparation of victuals, even although he felt an ardent desire for intellectual enjoyment. Hence the temptation to which such persons are exposed to seek enjoyment in wandering through the streets, in frequenting the ale-house, or in lounging at the fire-side in mental inactivity. In order that the labourer may be stimulated to the cultivation of his mental powers, he must be furnished with those domestic conveniencies requisite for attaining this object. He must be paid such wages as will enable him to procure such conveniencies, and the means of instruction, otherwise it is next thing to an insult to exhort him to prosecute the path of science. *The long hours of labour, and the paltry remuneration which the labourer receives in many of our spinning-mills* and other manufactories, so long as such domestic *slavery* and avaricious practices continue, *form an insurmountable barrier to the general diffusion of knowledge.*

But were the minds of the lower orders imbued with a certain portion of useful science, and did they possess such a competency as every human being ought to enjoy, their knowledge would lead them to habits of *diligence* and *economy*. In most instances it will be found, that ignorance is the fruitful source of indolence, waste, and extravagance, and that abject poverty is the result of a want of discrimination and proper arrangement in the management of domestic affairs. Now, the habits of application which the acquisition of knowledge necessarily produces, would naturally be carried into the various departments of labour peculiar to their stations, and prevent that laziness and inattention which is too common among the working classes, and which not unfrequently lead to poverty and disgrace. Their knowledge of the nature of heat, combustion, atmospheric air, and combustible substances, would lead them to a proper economy in the use of fuel; and their acquaintance with the truths of chymistry, on which the art of a rational cookery is founded, would lead them to *an economical practice in the preparation of victuals*, and teach them to extract from every substance all its nutritious qualities, and to impart a proper relish to every dish they prepare; for want of which knowledge and attention, the natural substances intended for the sustenance of man will not go half their length in the hands of some as they do under the judicious management of others. Their knowledge of the structure and functions of the animal system, of the regimen which ought to be attended to in order to health and vigour, of the causes which produce obstructed perspiration, of the means by which pestilential effluvia and infectious diseases are propagated, and of the disasters to which the human frame is liable in certain situations, *would tend to prevent many of those diseases and fatal accidents* to which ignorance and inattention have exposed so many of our fellow-men. For want of attending to such precautions in these respects, as knowledge would have suggested, thousands of families have been plunged into wretchedness and ruin, which all their future exertions were inadequate to remove. As the son of Sirach has well observed, "Better is the poor being sound and strong in constitution, than a rich man that is afflicted in his body. Health and good estate of body are above all gold; there are no riches above a sound body, and no joy above the joy of the heart."

As slovenliness and filth are generally the characteristics of ignorance and vulgarity, so an attention to *cleanliness* is one of the distinguishing features of cultivated minds. Cleanliness is conducive to health and virtuous activity, but uncleanliness is prejudicial to both. Keeping the body clean is of great importance, since more than the one half of what we eat and drink is evacuated by perspiration, and if the skin is not kept clean the pores are stopped, and perspiration consequently prevented, to the great injury of health. It is highly necessary to the health and cheerfulness of children; for where it is neglected, they grow pale, meagre, and squalid, and subject to several loathsome and troublesome diseases. Washing the hands, face, mouth, and feet, and occasionally the whole body, conduces to health, strength, and ease, and tends to prevent colds, rheumatism, cramps, the palsy, the itch, the tooth-ache, and many other maladies. Attention to cleanliness of body would also lead to cleanliness in regard to clothes, victuals, apartments, beds and furniture. A knowledge of the nature of the mephitic gases, of the necessity of pure atmospheric air to health and vigour, and of the means by which infection is produced and communicated, would lead persons to see the propriety of frequently opening doors and windows to dissipate corrupted air, and to admit the refreshing breeze, of sweeping cobwebs from the corners and ceiling of the room, and of removing dust, straw, or filth of any kind which is offensive to the smell, and in which infection might be deposited. By such attention, fevers and other malignant disorders might be prevented, vigour, health, and serenity promoted, and the whole dwelling and its inmates present an air of cheerfulness and comfort, and become the seat of domestic felicity.

Again, scientific knowledge would display itself among the lower orders, in the tasteful *decorations of their houses and garden plots.* The study of botany and horticulture would teach them to select the most beautiful flowers, shrubs, and evergreens; to arrange their plots with neatness and taste, and to improve their kitchen-garden to the best advantage, so as to render it productive for the pleasure and sustenance of their families. A genius for mechanical operations which almost every person may acquire, would lead them to invent a variety of decorations, and to devise many contrivances for the purpose of conveniency, and for keeping every thing in its proper place and order—which never enter into the conceptions of rude and vulgar minds. Were such dispositions and mental activity generally prevalent, the circumstances which lead to poverty, *beggary*, and drunkenness, would be in a great measure removed, and *home* would always be resorted to as a place of comfort and enjoyment.

Again the study of science and art would incline the lower classes *to enter into the spirit of every new improvement, and to give their assistance in carrying it forward.* The want of taste and of mental activity, and the spirit of selfishness which at present prevails among the mass of mankind, prevent the accomplishment of a variety of schemes which might tend to promote the conveniences and comforts of general society. For example; many of our villages which might otherwise present the appearance of neatness and comfort, are almost impassable, especially in the winter season, and during rainy weather, on account of the badness of roads and the want of foot-paths. At almost every step you encounter a pool, a heap of rubbish, or a dunghill, and in many places feel as if you were walking in a quagmire. In some villages, otherwise well planned, the streets present a grotesque appearance of sandy hillocks and mounds, and pools of stagnant water scattered in every direction, with scarcely the vestige of a pathway to guide the steps of the passenger. In winter, the traveller, in passing along, is bespattered with mire and dirt, and in summer, he can only drag heavily on, while his feet at every step sink into soft and parched sand. Now, such is the apathy and indifference that prevail among many villagers as to improvement in these respects, that although the contribution of a single shilling or of half a day's labour might, in some instances, accomplish the requisite improvements, they will stand aloof from such operations with a sullen obstinacy, and even glory in being the means of preventing them. Nay, such is the selfishness of many individuals, that they will not remove nuisances even from the front of their own dwellings, because it might at the same time promote the convenience of the public at large. In large towns, likewise, many narrow lanes are rendered filthy, gloomy, and unwholesome by the avarice of landlords, and the obstinate and boorish manners of their tenants, and improvements prevented which would tend to the health and comfort of the inhabitants. But as knowledge tends to liberalise the mind, to subdue the principle of selfishness, and to produce a relish for cleanliness and comfort, when it is more generally diffused, we may expect that such improvements as those to which I allude will be carried forward with spirit and alacrity. There would not be the smallest difficulty in accomplishing every object of this kind, and every other improvement conducive to the pleasure and comfort of the social state, provided the majority of a community were cheerfully to come forward with their assistance and contributions, however small, and to act with concord and harmony. A whole community or nation acting in unison, and every one contributing according to his ability, would accomplish wonders in relation to the improvement of towns, villages, and hamlets, and of every thing that regards the comfort of civil and domestic society.

In short, were knowledge generally diffused, and art uniformly directed by the principles of science, new and interesting plans would be formed, new improvements set on foot, new comforts enjoyed, and a new lustre would appear on the face of nature, and on the state of general society. Numerous conveniencies, decorations, and useful establishments never yet attempted, would soon be realized. Houses on neat and commodious plans, in airy situations, and furnished with every requisite accommodation, would be reared for the use of the peasant and mechanic; schools on spacious plans for the promotion of useful knowledge would be erected in every village and hamlet, and in every quarter of a city where they were found expedient; asylums would be built for the reception of the friendless poor, whether young or old;

manufactories established for supplying employment to every class of labourers and artizans, and lecture-rooms prepared, furnished with requisite apparatus, to which they might resort for improvement in science. Roads would be cut in all convenient directions, diversified with rural decorations, hedge-rows, and shady bowers,—foot-paths, broad and smooth, would accompany them in all their windings, and gas-lamps, erected at every half-mile's distance, would variegate the rural scene and cheer the shades of night. Narrow lanes in cities would be either widened or their houses demolished; streets on broad and spacious plans would be built, the smoke of steam-engines consumed, nuisances removed, and cleanliness and comfort attended to in every arrangement. Cheerfulness and activity would everywhere prevail, and the idler, the vagrant, and the beggar would disappear from society. All these operations and improvements, and hundreds more, could easily be accomplished, were the minds of the great body of the community *thoroughly enlightened and moralized*, and every individual, whether rich or poor, who contributed to bring them into effect, would participate in the general enjoyment. And what an interesting picture would be presented to every benevolent mind, to behold the great body of mankind raised from a state of moral and physical degradation to the dignity of their rational natures, and to the enjoyment of the bounties of their Creator!—to behold the country diversified with the neat and cleanly dwellings of the industrious labourer,—the rural scene, during the day, adorned with seminaries, manufactories, asylums, stately edifices, gardens, fruitful fields and romantic bowers, and, during night, bespangled in all directions with variegated lamps, forming a counterpart, as it were, to the lights which adorn the canopy of heaven! Such are only a few specimens of the improvements which art, directed by science and morality, could easily accomplish.

---

## SECTION VI.

### ON THE INFLUENCE OF KNOWLEDGE IN PROMOTING ENLARGED CONCEPTIONS OF THE CHARACTER AND PERFECTIONS OF THE DEITY.

All the works of God speak of their Author, in silent but emphatic language, and declare the glory of his perfections to all the inhabitants of the earth. But, although " there is no speech nor language" where the voice of Deity is not heard, how gross are the conceptions generally entertained of the character of Him " in whom we live and move," and by whose superintending providence all events are directed! Among the greater number of pagan nations, the most absurd and grovelling notions are entertained respecting the Supreme Intelligence, and the nature of that worship which his perfections demand. They have formed the most foolish and degrading representations of this august Being, and have " changed the glory of the incorruptible God into an image made like to corruptible man, and to four-footed beasts and creeping things." Temples have been erected and filled with idols the most hideous and obscene; bulls and crocodiles, dogs and serpents, goats and lions have been exhibited to adumbrate the character of the Ruler of the universe. The most cruel and unhallowed rites have been performed to procure his favour, and human victims sacrificed to appease his indignation. All such grovelling conceptions and vile abominations have their origin in the darkness which overspreads the human understanding, and the depraved passions which ignorance has a tendency to produce. Even in those countries where Revelation sheds its influence, and the knowledge of the true God is promulgated, how mean and contracted are the conceptions which the great bulk of the population entertain of the attributes of that incomprehensible Being whose presence pervades the immensity of space, who " metes out the heavens with a span," and superintends the affairs of ten thousand worlds The views which many have acquired of the perfections of the Deity, do not rise much higher than those which we ought to entertain of the powers of an archangel, or of one of the seraphim; and some have been known, even in our own country, whose conceptions have been so abject and grovelling, as to represent to themselves " the King eternal, immortal, and invisible," under the idea of a " venerable old man." Even the more intelligent class of the community fall far short of the ideas they ought to form of the God of heaven, owing to the limited views they have been accustomed to take of the displays of his wisdom and benevolence, and the boundless range of his operations.

We can acquire a knowledge of the Deity only by the visible effects he has produced, or the *external manifestations* he has given of himself to his creatures; for the Divine Essence must remain for ever inscrutable to finite minds. These manifestations are made in the Revelations contained in the Bible, and in the scene of the material universe around us. The *moral* perfections of God, such as his justice, mercy, and faithfulness, are more particularly delineated in his word; for, of these the system of nature can afford us only some slight hints and obscure intimations. His natural attributes, such as his immensity, omnipotence, wisdom, and goodness, are chiefly displayed in the works of creation; and to this source of information the inspired writers uniformly direct our attention, in order that we may acquire the most ample and impressive views of the grandeur of the Divinity, and the magnificence of his operations. "Lift up your eyes on high and behold! who hath created these orbs? who bringeth forth their host by number? The everlasting God the Lord, by the greatness of his might, for that he is strong in power. He measureth the ocean in the hollow of his hand, he comprehends the dust of the earth in a measure, he weigheth the mountains in scales, and hath stretched out the heavens by his understanding. All nations before him are as the drop of a bucket, and are counted to him less than nothing, and vanity. Thine, O Lord, is the greatness, and the glory, and the majesty, for all that is in heaven and earth is thine." The pointed interrogatories proposed to Job,* and the numerous exhortations in reference to this subject, contained in the book of Psalms and other parts of Scripture, plainly evince, that the character of God is to be contemplated through the medium of his visible works. In order to acquire a just and comprehensive conception of the perfections of Deity, we must contemplate his character as displayed both in the system of Revelation and in the system of nature, otherwise we can acquire only a partial and distorted view of the attributes of Jehovah. The Scriptures alone, without the medium of his works, cannot convey to us the most sublime conceptions of the magnificence of his empire, and his eternal power and Godhead; and the works of nature, without the revelations of his word, leave us in profound darkness with regard to the most interesting parts of his character—the plan of his moral government, and the ultimate destination of man.

Would we, then, acquire the most sublime and comprehensive views of that invisible Being, who created the universe, and by whom all things are upheld, we must, in the first place, apply ourselves, with profound humility and reverence, to the study of the *Sacred oracles;* and, in the next place, direct our attention to the material works of God as *illustrative* of his Scriptural character, and of the declarations of his word. And, since the sacred writers direct our views to the operations of the Almighty in the visible universe, *in what manner* are we to contemplate these operations? Are we to view them in a careless, cursory manner, or with fixed attention? Are we to gaze on them with the vacant stare of a savage, or with the penetrating eye of a Christian philosopher? Are we to view them through the mists of ignorance and vulgar prejudice, or through the light which science has diffused over the wonders of creation? There can be no difficulty to any reflecting mind in determining which of these modes ought to be adopted. The Scriptures declare, that as "the works of Jehovah are *great,*" they must be "*sought out,*" or thoroughly investigated, "by all those who have pleasure therein;" and a threatening is denounced against every one who "disregards the works of the Lord," and "neglects to *consider* the operations of his hand."

Such declarations evidently imply, that we ought to make the visible works of God the subject of our serious study and investigation, and exercise the rational powers he has given us for this purpose; otherwise we cannot expect to derive from them a true and faithful exhibition of his character and purposes. For, as the character of God is impressed upon his works, that character cannot be distinctly traced unless those works be viewed in their *true light* and actual relations—not as they may appear to a rude and inattentive spectator, but as they are actually found to exist, when thoroughly examined by the light of science and of revelation. For example, a person unaccustomed to investigate the system of nature imagines that the earth is a *fixed* mass of land and water in the midst of creation, and one of the largest bodies in nature, and, consequently, that the sun, moon, and stars, and the whole material universe revolve around it every twenty-four hours. Such a conception of the material system might, indeed, convey to the mind an astonishing idea of the *power* of the Deity in causing such an immense number of orbs to revolve around our world with so prodigious a velocity as behoved to take place, were the earth in reality a quiescent body in the centre of the universe. But it would give us a most strange and distorted idea of his *intelligence.* While it tended to magnify his *omnipotence,* it would, in effect, deprive him of the attribute of *wisdom.* For, in the first place, such a conception would represent the Almighty as having devised a system of means altogether superfluous and preposterous, in order to accomplish the end intended; for it is the characteristic of wisdom to proportionate the means to the nature of the design which is to be accomplished. The design, in the case under consideration, is to produce the alternate succession of day and night. This can be effected by giving the earth itself a rotation round its axis, as is the case in other globes of much larger dimensions. But according to the conception to which we are now adverting, *the whole material creation* is considered as daily revolving around this comparatively little globe of earth, an idea altogether extravagant and absurd, and inconsistent with every notion we ought to entertain of infinite wisdom. In the next place, were the earth considered as at rest, the motions of the planets would present a series of looped curves without any marks of design, a scene of inextricable confusion, and the whole of the solar system would appear devoid of order and harmony, and, consequently,

* Job. ch. xxxviii. &c.

without the marks of wisdom and intelligence. So that when the arrangements of nature are contemplated through the mists of ignorance, they tend to obscure the glory of the Divinity, and to convey a *distorted* idea of his character. Whereas, when the system of the universe is contemplated in its true light, all appears arranged with the most admirable harmony, simplicity, and order, and every mean proportionate to the end it is intended to accomplish. Again, in so far as we consider the earth as the principal body, or among the largest bodies of the universe, in so far do we narrow our conceptions of the extent and magnificence of creation, and, consequently, limit our views of the plans and perfections of the Creator. For our conceptions of his attributes must, in some measure, correspond to the views we have acquired of the amplitude and grandeur of his empire.

Now, what is it that enables us to investigate the works of God, and to contemplate the system of nature *in its true light?* It is *Science* combined with observation and experiment. And what is science considered in a theological point of view? It is nothing else than a rational inquiry into the arrangements and operations of the Almighty, in order to trace the perfections therein displayed. And what are the truths which science has discovered? They may be regarded as so many rays of celestial light descending from the Great Source of Intelligence to illuminate the human mind in the knowledge of the divine character and government, and to stimulate it to still more vigorous exertions in similar investigations, just as the truths of revelation are so many emanations from the "Father of lights," to enlighten the darkness and to counteract the disorders of the *moral* world; and both these lights must be resorted to to direct our inquiries, if we wish to attain the clearest and most comprehensive views of the attributes of the Divine Mind. Revelation declares, in so many distinct propositions, the character of God, and the plans of his moral government. Science explains and illustrates many of those subjects to which revelation refers. It removes the veil from the works of the Creator; it dispels the mists which ignorance and superstition have thrown around them; it conducts us into the secret chambers of nature, and discloses to us many of those hidden springs which produce the diversified phenomena of the material world; it throws a light on those delicate and minute objects which lie concealed from the vulgar eye, and brings within the range of our contemplation the distant glories of the sky; it unveils the laws by which the Almighty directs the movements of his vast empire, and exhibits his operations in a thousand aspects of which the unenlightened mind can form no conception. If, then, science throws a light on the works and the ways of God, the acquisition of scientific knowledge, when properly directed, must have a tendency to direct our conceptions and to amplify our views of his adorable attributes, and of his providential arrangements.

Here it will naturally be inquired,—What are some of those views of the divine character which scientific investigation has a tendency to unfold? Our limits will not permit a full and explicit answer to this inquiry, the illustration of which would require a volume of no inconsiderable size, and therefore, we shall attempt nothing more than the statement of a few general hints.

1. The phenomena of the material world, as investigated by science, evince the *unity* of the Divine Being. There is such a *harmony* that prevails through the whole visible universe, as plainly shows it to be under the government of *one* Intelligence. Amidst the immense complication that surrounds us, we perceive *one set* of laws uniformly operating in accordance with which all things proceed in their regular courses. The same causes uniformly produce the same effects in every region of the world, and in every period of time. "Vegetables spring from the same seed, germinate by the same means, assume the same form, sustain the same qualities, exist through the same duration, and come to the same end." Animals, too, of the same species, are brought into existence in the same manner, exhibit the same life and vital functions, display the same active powers and instinct, and hasten to the same dissolution. Man has one origin, one general form, the same corporeal structure, the same vital functions, the same system of intellectual faculties, and comes to the same termination. All the elements around him, and every arrangement in this sublunary sphere, are made, in one regular manner, subservient to his sensitive enjoyment, and are evidently fitted, by one design, and directed by one agency, to promote his happiness. The connexion and harmony which subsist between the animal and vegetable kingdoms, plainly evince that *one* and the same Being is the former of both, and that in his contrivances with respect to the one, he had in view the necessities of the other. We know, that different sorts of plants, herbs, and flowers, are appointed for food to the several tribes of animals. That which is hurtful to one species is salutary to another. One creature climbs the highest rocks for herbs, another digs in the earth for roots, and we scarcely know a plant or leaf but what affords nourishment, and a place of nativity to some species or other of the insect tribes. This is the foundation of innumerable relations and connexions between these two departments of creation, which show the work to be *one*, and the result of the same *Power* and *Intelligence*. In like manner, day and night uniformly return with the utmost regularity, and by the operation of the same cause, and with the same regularity

and harmony the seasons revolve and appear in constant succession. The composition of the atmosphere is the same under every latitude, and light and heat are diffused by the same law in every region of the earth. One law causes a stone to fall to the ground, and by the operation of the same law, the moon is retained in her orbit around the earth, the planets directed in their revolutions round the sun, and the whole universe compacted into one harmonious system. In short, all the arrangements and operations of nature, so far as our knowledge extends, present to our view a single design, regularly executed by a single agency. The fair inference, therefore, is, that every part of the world in which we dwell, and every department of the solar system, are under the government of *one Intelligence*, which directs every movement throughout the universal system. And the more extensively our views of the universe are enlarged, the marks of unity in operation and design become more strikingly apparent. Now, if two or more intelligences had the government of the universe in their hands, and if they had equal power and contrary designs, their purposes would clash, and they could never become the parents of that harmony which we clearly perceive throughout the system of nature. Thus the operations of the visible world confirm and illustrate the declaration of the inspired oracles, that "*there is none other God but one.*"

2. A scientific investigation of the material world opens to us innumerable evidences of *Divine Wisdom.*

Wherever we turn our eyes in the visible world around us, and survey with attention the various processes of nature, we perceive at every step the most striking marks of intelligence and design. We perceive the wisdom of the great Author of nature, in the admirable constitution of the atmosphere, and the wonderful properties of the constituent principles of which it is composed,—in the motions of *light*, the inconceivable smallness of its particles, its adaptation to the eye, and the admirable manner in which vision is performed,—in the nature of *sound*, the laws by which it is propagated, and the various modifications of which it is susceptible,—in the process of *evaporation*, and the rains, dews, and fertility which are the results of this admirable part of the economy of nature,—in the utility of the mountains and valleys with which the earth is diversified, and the beautiful colouring which is spread over the face of nature,—in the morning and evening *twilight*, and the gradual approaches of light and darkness,—in the vast expanse of the *ocean* and its numerous productions,—in the grand, and picturesque, and beautiful landscapes with which our globe is adorned, —in the composition and specific gravity of *water*, and in the peculiar structure and density of the solid parts of the earth,—in the expansion of water in the act of freezing, and the nature and properties of heat and flame,—in the power of *steam*, the properties of the gases, the qualities of the magnet, and the agencies of the galvanic and electric fluids,—in the structure of *vegetables*, the adaptation of their seeds, roots, fibres, vessels, and leaves to the purpose of vegetative life,—the curious processes which are continually going on in their internal parts, their delicate contexture and diversified hues, and the important purposes they serve in the system of nature,—in the structure of the various *animated beings* which traverse the air, the waters, and the earth,—the provision made for the continuance of the species, their architective faculties, their wonderful instincts, and the *infinite diversity of organization* which appears among them, *suited to their various wants and modes of existence*,—in the admirable organization of the *human frame*, the numerous bones, muscles, ligaments, membranes, arteries, and veins which enter into its construction, the apt disposition of all its parts, the means contrived for the reception and distribution of nutriment, the effect which this nutriment produces in bringing the body to its full growth and expansion,—its self-restoring power when diseased or wounded, the provision made against evil accidents and inconveniences, the variety of muscular movements of which it is susceptible, the process of respiration, the circulation of the blood, the separation of the chyle, the exquisite structure of the different senses, and the nice adaptation of every organ and movement to the ends it was intended to subserve. The same wisdom is perceptible in the position which the sun holds in the solar system, in order to a due distribution of light and heat to surrounding worlds; in the distance at which the earth is placed from this luminary,—in the order and harmony of all the celestial motions, and in the wonderful and beautiful scenery, invisible to the unassisted eye, which the microscope displays, both in the animal and vegetable world. In short, there is not an object within us or around us, in the mountains or the plains, in the air, the ocean, or the sky,—among the animal or the vegetable tribes, when steadily contemplated in all its aspects and relations, but displays to the eye of reason and devotion the consummate intelligence and skill of its almighty Author, and calls upon every intelligent agent, in silent but emphatic language, to praise him "who made the earth, the sea, the fountains of water, and all that live in them, for whose pleasure they are and were created."

Let us just select one example out of the many thousands which might be brought forward on this subject. This example shall be taken from an *invisible* department of nature. In consequence of modern scientific discovery, it has been ascertained that the atmosphere, or the air we breathe, is compounded of two invisible substances, termed *oxygen* gas and *nitrogen* gas. Oxygen, as formerly stated, is the principle of vitality and combustion, nitrogen is destructive both to flame and animal life. Were we to breathe oxygen by itself, it would cause our blood to circulate with greater rapidity, but it would soon waste and destroy the human frame by the rapid accumulation of heat. Were the nitrogen to be extracted from the atmosphere, and the oxygen left to exert its native energies, it would melt the hardest substances and set the earth on flames. If the oxygen were extracted and the nitrogen only remained, every species of fire and flame would be extinguished, and all the tribes of animated nature instantly destroyed. The proportion of these two gases to each other is nearly as *one* to *four*. Were this proportion materially altered, a fluid might be produced which would cause a burning pain and instantaneous suffocation. The *specific gravity* of these two substances is nearly as 37 to 33, that is, the nitrogen is a small degree *lighter* than the oxygen. Were this proportion reversed, or, in other words, were the oxygen of the atmosphere a small degree lighter than the nitrogen, so that the nitrogen might become a little heavier than common air,—as this gas is thrown off continually by the breathing of men and other animals, it would perpetually occupy the lower regions of the atmosphere, and be productive of universal pestilence and death. Again, oxygen gas is separated from the nitrogen in the lungs; it is absorbed by the blood, and gives it its *red* colour, and is the source of animal heat throughout the whole system. It forms the basis of all the acids; it pervades the substance of the vegetable tribes, and enables them to perform their functions, and it forms a constituent part of the water which fills our rivers, seas, and oceans. And as the atmosphere is daily liable to be deprived of this fluid by combustion, respiration, and other processes, the leaves of trees and other vegetables give out a large portion of it during the day, which, uniting with the nitrogen gas thrown off by the breathing of animals, keeps up the equilibrium, and preserves the salubrity of the air in which we move and breathe.

These facts demonstrate the infinite knowledge and the consummate *wisdom* of the Contriver of the universe,—in the exquisitely nice adjustment of every minute circumstance, so as to preserve the balance of nature and secure the happiness of his sensitive and intelligent offspring. What an all-comprehensive intelligence does it indicate in the Divine Mind, to cause one single principle in different combinations to produce so immense a variety of important effects! What dreadful havoc would be produced throughout the whole of our sublunary system, if a substance like oxygen gas, which pervades every part of nature, *were not nicely balanced and proportioned.* All nature might soon be thrown into confusion, and all the tribes of the living world either be reduced to misery, or swept into the tomb. A material difference in the proportion of the two airs which compose the atmosphere, might be productive of the most dreadful and destructive effects. One of the most corrosive acids, *aquafortis*, is composed of 75 parts oxygen and 25 parts nitrogen. Were this the proportion of these fluids in the atmosphere, every breath we drew would produce the most excruciating pain, and, after two or three inspirations, the vital powers would be overcome, and life extinguished. Here then we perceive an *admirable adjustment of means to ends*, and an evidence of that comprehensive knowledge which penetrates into the energies of all substances, and foresees all the consequences which can follow from the principles and laws of nature, in every combination and in every mode of their operation. This is only one instance out of a thousand which the researches of science afford us of the admirable economy of the wisdom of God. From ignorance of such facts, the bulk of mankind are incapable of appreciating the blessings they enjoy, under the arrangements of infinite wisdom, and unqualified for rendering a grateful homage to Him "in whom they live and move, and have their being."

3. The contemplation of nature through the medium of science, affords innumerable displays of the *benevolence* of the Deity. Benevolence, or goodness, is that perfection of God which leads him, in all his arrangements, to communicate happiness to every order of his creatures. This attribute, though frequently overlooked is so extensively displayed throughout the scene of creation, that we feel at a loss to determine from what quarter we should select instances for its illustration. Wherever we find evidences of wisdom and design, we also find instances of benevolence; for all the admirable contrivances we perceive in the system of nature, have it as their ultimate end to convey pleasure, in one shape or another, to sensitive beings. If there are more than 240 bones in the human body variously articulated, and more than 440 muscles of different forms and contextures, such a structure is intended to produce a thousand modifications of motion in the several members of which it is composed, and to facilitate every operation we have occasion to perform. If the ear is formed with an external porch, a hammer, an anvil, a tympanum, a stirrup, and a labyrinth, this apparatus is intended to convey pleasure to the soul by communicating to it all the modifications of sound. If the *eye* is composed of three coats, some of them opaque and some transparent, with three humours of different forms and refractive powers, and a numerous assemblage of minute veins, arteries, *muscles*, nerves, glands, and lymphatics, it is in order that the images of

objects may be accurately depicted on the retina, that the ball of the eye may be easily turned in every direction, and that we may enjoy all the entertainments of vision.* If an atmosphere is thrown around the earth, it is for the purpose of attempering the rays of the sun, giving a lucid brightness to every part of the heavens, producing the morning and evening twilight, promoting evaporation and the respiration of animals, and causing the earth to bring forth abundance of food, by means of the rains and dews; all which effects produce happiness in a thousand different ways to every sentient being. If this atmosphere presses our bodies with a weight of thirty thousand pounds, it is in order to counterpoise the internal pressure of the circulating fluids, and to preserve the vessels and animal functions in due tone and vigour, without which pressure the elastic fluids in the finer vessels would inevitably burst them, and the spark of life be quickly extinguished. Thousands of examples of this description, illustrative of divine benevolence, might be selected from every part of the material system connected with our world, all of which would demonstrate that the communication of enjoyment is the great end of all the contrivances of infinite wisdom.

There is a striking display of benevolence *in the gratification afforded to our different senses.* As the eye is constructed of the most delicate substances, and is one of the most admirable pieces of mechanism connected with our frame, so the Creator has arranged the world in such a manner as to afford it the most varied and delightful gratification. By means of the solar light, which is exactly adapted to the structure of this organ, thousands of objects of diversified beauty and sublimity are presented to the view. It opens before us the mountains, the vales, the woods, the lawns, the brooks and rivers, the fertile plains and flowery fields, adorned with every hue,—the expanse of the ocean and the glories of the firmament. And as the eye would be dazzled, were a deep *red* colour or a brilliant *white* to be spread over the face of nature, the divine goodness has clothed the heavens with *blue* and the earth with *green*, the two colours which are the least fatiguing and the most pleasing to the organs of sight, and at the same time one of these colours is diversified by a thousand delicate shades which produce a delightful *variety* upon the landscape of the world. The ear is curiously constructed for the perception of sounds, which the atmosphere is fitted to convey; and what a variety of pleasing sensations are pro-

* As an evidence of the care of the Creator to promote our enjoyment, the following instance may be selected in regard to the *muscles* of the eye. Nothing can be more manifestly an evidence of contrivance

Fig. 1.

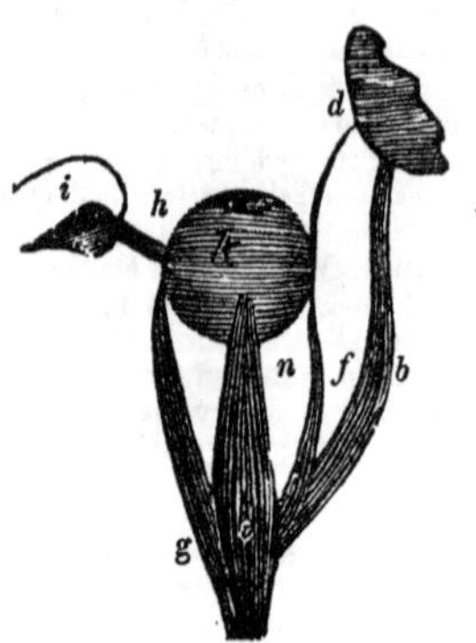


and design, and at the same time of benevolent intention, than these muscles, which are admirably adapted to move the ball of the eye in every direction, upwards, downwards, to the right hand, to the left, and in whatever direction we please, so as to preserve that parallelism of the eye which is necessary to distinct vision. In fig. 1. is exhibited the eyeball with its muscles; *a*, is the optic nerve; *b*, the *musculus trochlearis*, which turns the pupil downwards and outwards, and enables the ball of the eye to roll about at pleasure; *c*, is part of the *os frontis*, to which the trochlea or pulley is fixed, through which *d*, the tendon of the trochlearis, passes; *e*, is the *attolens oculi* for raising up the globe of the eye; *n*, the *depressor oculi*, for pulling the globe of the eye down; *f*. *adductor oculi*, for turning the eye towards the nose; *g*, *abductor oculi*, for moving the globe of the eye outwards, to the right or left; *h*, *obliquus inferior*, for drawing the globe of the eye forwards, inwards, and downwards; *i*, part of the

Fig. 2.

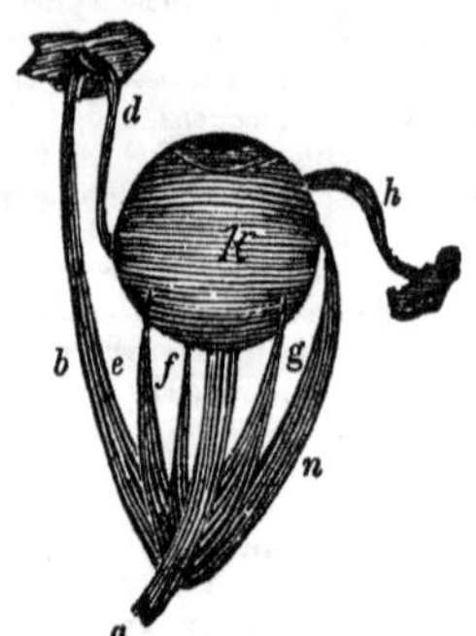


superior maxillary bone, to which it is fixed; *k*, the eyeball. Fig. 2. represents the same muscles in a different point of view, where the same letters refer to the same muscles.

All these opposite and antagonist muscles preserve a nice equilibrium, which is effected partly by their equality of strength, partly by their peculiar origin, and partly by the natural posture of the body and the eye, by which means the eye can be turned instantaneously towards any object, preserved in perfect steadiness, and prevented from rolling about in hideous contortions. This is only *one* out of a hundred instances in relation to the eye, in which the same benevolent design is displayed.

duced by the objects of external nature intended to affect this organ! The murmurings of the brooks, the whispers of the gentle breeze, the hum of bees, the chirping of birds, the lowing of the herds, the melody of the feathered songsters, the roarings of a stormy ocean, the dashings of a mighty cataract, and, above all, the numerous modulations of the human voice and the harmonies of music, produce a variety of delightful emotions which increase the sum of human enjoyment. To gratify the sense of *smelling*, the air is perfumed with a variety of delicious odours, exhaled from innumerable plants and flowers. To gratify the *feeling*, pleasing sensations of various descriptions are connected with almost every thing we have occasion to touch; and to gratify the sense of *taste*, the earth is covered with an admirable profusion of plants, herbs, roots, and delicious fruits of thousands of different qualities and flavours, calculated to convey an agreeable relish to the inhabitants of every clime. Now, it is easy to conceive, that these gratifications were not necessary to our *existence*. The purposes of vision, as a mere animal sensation for the use of self-preservation, might have been answered, although every trace of beauty and sublimity had been swept from the universe, and nothing but a vast assemblage of dismal and haggard objects had appeared on the face of nature. The purpose of hearing might have been effected although every sound had been grating and discordant, and the voice of melody for ever unknown. We might have had smell without fragrance or perfume; taste without variety of flavour; and feeling, not only without the least pleasing sensation, but accompanied with incessant pain. But, in this case, the system of nature would have afforded no direct proofs, as it now does, of divine benevolence.

*The remedies which the Deity has provided against the evils to which we are exposed*, are likewise a proof of his benevolence. Medicines are provided for the cure of the diseases to which we are liable; heat is furnished to deliver us from the effects of cold; rest from the fatigues of labour; sleep from the languors of watching; artificial light to preserve us from the gloom of absolute darkness, and shade from the injuries of scorching heat. Goodness is also displayed in the power of *self-restoration* which our bodies possess, in recovering us from sickness and disease, in healing wounds and bruises, and in recovering our decayed organs of sensation, without which power almost every human being would present a picture of deformity, and a body full of scars and putrefying sores. The pupil of the eye is so constructed, that it is capable of contracting and dilating by a sort of instinctive power. By this means the organ of vision defends itself from the blindness which might ensue from the admission of too great a quantity of light; while, on the other hand, its capacity of expansion, so as to take in a greater quantity of rays, prevents us from being in absolute darkness even in the deepest gloom, without which we could scarcely take a step with safety during a cloudy night. Again, in the construction of the human body, and of the various tribes of animated beings, however numerous and complicated their organs, there is no instance can be produced that any one muscle, nerve, joint, limb, or other part, is contrived *for the purpose of producing pain.* When pain is felt, it is uniformly owing to some derangement of the corporeal organs, but is never the necessary result of the original contrivance. On the other hand, every part of the construction of living beings, every organ and function, and every contrivance, however delicate and minute, in so far as its use is known, is found to contribute to the enjoyment of the individual to which it belongs, either by facilitating its movements, by enabling it to ward off dangers, or in some way or another to produce agreeable sensations.

In short, *the immense multitude of human beings which people the earth, and the ample provision which is made for their necessities*, furnish irresistible evidence of divine goodness. It has been ascertained, that more than sixty thousand species of animals inhabit the air, the earth, and the waters, besides many thousands which have not yet come within the observation of the naturalist. On the surface of the earth there is not a patch of ground or a portion of water, a single shrub, tree, or herb, and scarcely a single leaf in the forest, but what teems with animated beings. How many hundreds of millions have their dwellings in caves, in the clefts of rocks, in the bark of trees, in ditches, in marshes, in the forests, the mountains and the valleys! What innumerable shoals of fishes inhabit the ocean and sport in the seas and rivers! What millions on millions of birds and flying insects, in endless variety, wing their flight through the atmosphere above and around us! Were we to suppose that each species, at an average, contains four hundred millions of individuals, there would be 24,000,000,000,000, or 24 billions of living creatures belonging to all the known species which inhabit the different regions of the world, besides the multitudes of unknown species yet undiscovered,—which is *thirty thousand times* the number of all the human beings that people the globe.* Besides these, there

* As an instance of the *immense number* of animated beings, the following facts in relation to two species of birds may be stated. Captain Flinders, in his voyage to Australasia, saw a compact stream of stormy petrels, which was from 50 to 80 yards deep and 300 yards or more broad. This stream for a full hour and a half continued to pass without interruption with nearly the swiftness of the pigeon. Now, taking the column at 50 yards deep by 300 in breadth, and that it moved 30 miles an hour, and allowing nine cubic inches of space to each bird, the

are multitudes of animated beings which no man can number, invisible to the unassisted eye, and dispersed through every region of the earth, air, and seas. In a small stagnant pool which in summer appears covered with a green scum, there are more microscopic animalcules than would outnumber all the inhabitants of the earth. How immense then must be the collective number of these creatures throughout every region of the earth and atmosphere! It surpasses all our conceptions. Now, it is a fact that, from the elephant to the mite, from the whale to the oyster, and from the eagle to the gnat, or the microscopic animalcula, no animal can subsist without nourishment. Every species, too, requires a different kind of food. Some live on grass, some on shrubs, some on flowers, and some on trees. Some feed only on the roots of vegetables, some on the stalk, some on the leaves, some on the fruit, some on the seed, some on the whole plant; some prefer one species of grass, some another. Linnæus has remarked, that the cow eats 276 species of plants and rejects 218; the goat eats 449 and rejects 126; the sheep eats 387 and rejects 141; the horse eats 262 and rejects 212; and the hog, more nice in its taste than any of these, eats but 72 plants and rejects all the rest. Yet such is the unbounded munificence of the Creator, that all these countless myriads of sentient beings are amply provided for and nourished by his bounty! "The eyes of all these look unto Him, and he openeth his hand and satisfieth the desire of every living being." He has so arranged the world, that every place affords the proper food for all the living creatures with which it abounds. He has furnished them with every organ and apparatus of instruments for the gathering, preparing, and digesting of their food, and has endowed them with admirable sagacity in finding out and providing their nourishment, and in enabling them to distinguish between what is salutary and what is pernicious. In the exercise of these faculties, and in all their movements, they appear to experience a happiness suitable to their nature. The young of all animals in the exercise of their newly acquired faculties, the fishes sporting in the waters, the birds skimming beneath the sky and warbling in the thickets, the gamesome cattle browsing in the pastures, the wild deer bounding through the forests, the insects gliding through the air and along the ground, and even the earth-worms wriggling in the dust,—proclaim, by the vivacity of their movements and the various tones and gesticulations, that the exercise of their powers is connected with *enjoyment*. In this boundless scene of beneficence, we behold a striking illustration of the declarations of the inspired writers, that "the Lord is good to all,"—that "the earth is full of his riches," and that "his tender mercies are over all his works."

Such are a few evidences of the benevolence of the Deity as displayed in the arrangements of the material world. However plain and obvious they may appear to a reflecting mind, they are almost entirely overlooked by the bulk of mankind, owing to their ignorance of the facts of natural history and science, and the consequent inattention and apathy with which they are accustomed to view the objects of the visible creation. Hence they are incapacitated for appreciating the beneficent character of the Creator, and the riches of his munificence; and incapable of feeling those emotions of admiration and *gratitude* which an enlightened contemplation of the scene of nature is calculated to inspire.

4. An enlightened and comprehensive survey of the universe presents to us *a view of the vast multiplicity of conceptions and the infinitely diversified ideas which have been formed in the Divine Mind.*

As the conceptions existing in the mind of an artificer are known by the instruments he constructs, or the operations he performs, so the ideas which have existed from eternity in the

number would amount to 151 millions and a half. The migratory pigeon of the United States flies in still more amazing multitudes. Wilson, in his "American Ornithology," says, "Of one of these immense flocks, let us attempt to calculate the numbers, as seen in passing between Frankfort on the Kentucky and the Indian territory. If we suppose this column to have been one mile in breadth, and I believe it to have been much more, and that it moved four hours at the rate of one mile a minute, the time it continued in passing would make the whole length 240 miles. Again, supposing that each square yard of this moving body comprehended three pigeons, the square yards multiplied by 3 would give 2,230,272,000," that is, two thousand two hundred and thirty millions and two hundred and seventy-two thousand, nearly three times the number of all the human inhabitants of the globe, but which Mr. Wilson reckons to be far below the actual amount. Were we to estimate the number of animals by the scale here afforded, it would amount to several hundreds or thousands of times more than what I have stated in the text. For if a single flock of pigeons now alluded to in only one district of the earth, amounts to so prodigious a number, how many thousand times more must be the amount of the same species in all the regions of the globe! In the above calculations, it is taken for granted that pigeons fly at the rate of from 30 to 60 miles an hour, and it is found by actual experiment that this is the case. In 1830, 110 pigeons were brought from Brussels to London, and were let fly on the 19th July, at a quarter before nine A. M. One reached Antwerp, 186 miles distance, at 18 minutes past 2, or in 5 1-2 hours, being at the rate of 34 miles an hour. Five more reached the same place within eight minutes afterwards, and thirteen others in the course of eight hours after leaving London. Another went from London to Maestricht, 260 miles, in six hours and a quarter, being at the rate of nearly 42 miles an hour. The golden eagle sweeps through the atmosphere at the rate of 40 miles an hour, and it has been computed that the Swift flies, at an average, 500 miles a day, and yet finds time to feed, to clean itself, and to collect materials for its nest with apparent leisure. Such are the numbers of this species of animated beings, and such the powers of rapid motion which the Creator has conferred upon them, —powers which man, with all his intellectual faculties and inventions, has never yet been able to attain.

mind of the Creator are ascertained from the objects he has created, the events he has produced, and the operations he is incessantly conducting. The formation of a single object is an exhibition of the *idea* existing in the Creating Mind, of which it is a copy. The formation of a second or a third object exactly resembling the first, would barely exhibit the same ideas a second or a third time, without disclosing any thing *new* concerning the Creator; and, consequently, our conceptions of his intelligence would not be enlarged, even although thousands and millions of such objects were presented to our view,—just as a hundred clocks and watches, exactly of the same kind, constructed by the same artist, give us no higher idea of his *skill* and *ingenuity* than the construction of one. But, every *variety* in objects and arrangements exhibits a new discovery of the plans, contrivances and intelligence of the Creator.

Now, in the universe we find all things constructed and arranged on the plan of *boundless and universal variety*. In the animal kingdom there have been actually ascertained, as already noticed, about sixty thousand *different species* of living creatures. There are about 600 species of *mammalia*, or animals that suckle their young, most of which are quadrupeds—4000 species of *birds*, 3000 species of *fishes*, 700 species of *reptiles*, and 44,000 species of insects.* Besides these, there are about 3000 species of *shell-fish*, and perhaps not less than eighty or a hundred thousand species of animalcules invisible to the naked eye; and new species are daily discovering, in consequence of the zeal and industry of the lovers of natural history. As the system of animated nature has never yet been thoroughly explored, we might safely reckon the number of species of animals of all kinds, as amounting to at least *three hundred thousand*. We are next to consider, that the organical structure of each species consists of an immense multitude of parts, and that all the species are infinitely diversified—differing from each other in their forms, organs, members, faculties and motions.—They are of all shapes and sizes, from the microscopic animalculum, ten thousand times less than a mite, to the elephant and the whale.—They are different in respect of the construction of their sensitive organs. In regard to the *eye*, some have this organ placed in the front, so as to look directly forward, as in man; others have it so placed, as to take in nearly a whole hemisphere, as in birds, hares and conies; some have it fixed, and others, moveable; some have *two* globes or balls, as quadrupeds; some have *four*, as snails, which are fixed in their horns; some have *eight*, set like a locket of diamonds, as spiders; some have several *hundreds*, as flies and beetles, and others above *twenty thousand*, as the dragon-fly and several species of butterflies. In regard to the *ear*,—some have it large, erect and open, as in the hare, to hear the least approach of danger; in some it is covered to keep out noxious bodies; and, in others, as in the mole, it is lodged deep and backward in the head, and fenced and guarded from external injuries. With regard to their *clothing*,—some have their bodies covered with hair, as quadrupeds; some with feathers, as birds; some with scales, as fishes; some with shells, as the tortoise; some only with skin; some with stout and firm armour, as the rhinoceros; and others with prickles, as the hedgehog and porcupine—all nicely accommodated to the nature of the animal, and the element in which it lives. These coverings, too, are adorned with *diversified* beauties, as appears in the plumage of birds, the feathers of the peacock, the scales of the finny tribes, the hair of quadrupeds, and the variegated polish and colouring of the tropical shell-fish—beauties which, in point of symmetry, polish, texture, variety, and exquisite colouring, mock every attempt of human art to copy or to imitate.

In regard to *respiration*—some breathe through the mouth by means of lungs, as men and quadrupeds; some by means of gills, as fishes; and some by organs placed in other parts of their bodies, as insects. In regard to the *circulation of the blood*, some have but one ventricle in the heart, some two, and others three. In some animals, the heart throws its blood to the remotest parts of the system; in some it throws it only into the respiratory organs; in others, the blood from the respiratory organs is carried by the veins to another heart, and this second heart distributes the blood, by the channel of its arteries, to the several parts. In many insects, a number of hearts are placed at intervals on the circulating course, and each renews the impulse of the former, where the momentum of the blood fails. In regard to *the movements of their bodies*,—some are endowed with swift motions, and others with slow; some walk on two legs, as fowls; some on four, as dogs; some on eight, as caterpillars; some on a hundred, as scolopendræ or millepedes; some on fifteen hundred and twenty feet, as one species of sea-star; and some on two thousand feet, as a certain species of echinus.* Some glide along with a sinuous motion on scales, as snakes and serpents; some skim through the air, one species on two wings, another on four; and some convey themselves with speed and safety by the help of their webs, as spiders; while others glide with agility through the waters by means of their tails and fins.—But it would require volumes to enumerate and

* Specimens of all these species are to be seen in the magnificent collections in the Museum of Natural History at Paris.

* See Lyonet's notes to Lesser's *Insecto-Theology*, who also mentions that these *Echini* have 1300 horns, similar to those of snails, which they can put out and draw in at pleasure.

explain all the known varieties which distinguish the different species of animated beings. Besides the varieties of the species, there are not, perhaps, of all the hundreds of millions which compose any one species, two individuals precisely alike in every point of view in which they may be contemplated.

As an example of the numerous parts and functions which enter into the construction of an animal frame, it may be stated, that, in the human body there are 445 bones, each of them having *forty* distinct scopes or intentions; and 246 muscles, each having *ten* several intentions; so that the system of bones and muscles alone includes above 14,200 varieties, or different intentions and adaptations. But, besides the bones and muscles, there are hundreds of *tendons* and *ligaments* for the purpose of connecting them together; hundreds of *nerves* ramified over the whole body to convey sensation to all its parts; thousands of arteries to convey the blood to the remotest extremities, and thousands of *veins* to bring it back to the heart; thousands of *lacteal* and *lymphatic* vessels to absorb nutriment from the food; thousands of *glands* to secrete humours from the blood, and of *emunctories* to throw them off from the system—and, besides many other parts of this variegated system, and functions with which we are unacquainted, there are more than *sixteen hundred millions* of membranous cells or *vesicles* connected with the *lungs*, more than *two hundred thousand millions* of pores in the skin, through which the perspiration is incessantly flowing, and above a *thousand millions* of scales, which according to Leeuwenhoek, Baker, and others, compose the cuticle or outward covering of the body. We have also to take into the account, the compound organs of life, the numerous parts of which they consist, and the diversified functions they perform; such as the *brain*, with its infinite number of fibres and numerous functions; the *heart*, with its auricles and ventricles; the stomach, with its juices and muscular coats; the *liver*, with its lobes and glands; the *spleen*, with its infinity of cells and membranes; the *pancreas*, with its juice and numerous glands; the *kidneys*, with their fine capillary tubes; the *intestines*, with all their turnings and convolutions; the *organs of sense*, with their multifarious connexions; the mesentery, the gall-bladder, the ureters, the pylorus, the duodenum, the blood, the bile, the lymph, the saliva, the chyle, the hairs, the nails, and numerous other parts and substances, every one of which has diversified functions to perform. We have also to take into consideration *the number of ideas included* in the *arrangement and connexion* of all these parts, and in the manner in which they are *compacted* into one system of small dimensions, so as to afford free scope for all the intended functions. If, then, for the sake of a rude calculation, we were to suppose, in addition to the 14,200 adaptations stated above, that there are 10,000 veins great and small, 10,000 arteries, 10,000 nerves,* 1000 ligaments, 4000 lacteals and lymphatics, 100,000 glands, 1,600,000,000 vesicles in the lungs, 1,000,000,000 scales, and 200,000,000,000 of pores, the amount would be 202,600,149,200 different parts and adaptations in the human body; and if all the other species were supposed to be differently organised, and to consist of a similar number of parts, this number multiplied by 300,000, the supposed number of species—the product would amount to 60,780,044,760,000,000, or above sixty thousand billions,—the number of distinct ideas, conceptions or contrivances, in relation to the animal world—a number of which we can have no precise conception, and which, to limited minds like ours, seems to approximate to something like infinity; but it may tend to convey a rude idea of the endless multiplicity of conceptions which pervade the Eternal Mind.

That many other tribes of animated nature have an organization no less complicated and diversified than that of man, will appear from the following statements of M. Lyonet. This celebrated naturalist wrote a treatise on one single insect, the *cossus caterpillar*, which lives on the leaves of the willow,—in which he has shown, from the anatomy of that minute animal, that its structure is almost as complicated as that of the human body, and many of the parts which enter into its organization even more numerous. He has found it necessary to employ *twenty* figures to explain the organization of the *head*, which contain 228 different muscles. There are 1647 muscles in the body, and 2066 in the intestinal tube, making in all 3941 muscles; or nearly *nine* times the number of muscles in the human body. There are 94 principal *nerves* which divide into *innumerable ramifications*. There are two large tracheal arteries, one at the right, and the other at the left side of the insect, each of them communicating with the air by means of nine spiracula. Round each spiraculum the trachea pushes forth a great number of branches, which are again divided into smaller ones, and these further subdivided and spread through the whole body of the caterpillar; they are naturally of a silver colour, and make a beautiful appearance. The principal trachael vessels divide into 1326 different branches. All this complication of delicate machinery, with numerous other parts and organs, are compressed into a body only about two inches in length.

* The amazing extent of the ramification of the veins and nerves may be judged of from this circumstance, that neither the point of the smallest needle, nor the infinitely finer lance of a gnat can pierce any part without drawing blood, and causing an uneasy sensation, consequently without wounding, by so small a puncture, both a nerve and a vein: and therefore the number of these vessels here assumed may be considered as far below the truth.

Were we to direct our attention to the *vegetable* kingdom, we might contemplate a scene no less variegated and astonishing than what appears in the animal world. There have already been discovered more than *fifty-six thousand* species of plants, specimens of all which may be seen in the Museum of Natural History at Paris. But we cannot reckon the actual number of species in the earth and seas at less than *four or five hundred thousand*. They are of all sizes, from the invisible forests which are seen in a piece of mouldiness, by the help of the microscope, to the cocoas of Malabar fifty feet in circumference, and the banians, whose shoots cover a circumference of five acres of ground. Each of them is furnished with a complicated system of vessels for the circulation of its juices, the secretion of its odours, and other important functions somewhat analogous to those of animals. Almost every vegetable consists of a root, trunk, branches, leaves, skin, bark, pith, sap-vessels, or system of arteries and veins, glands for perspiration, flowers, petals, stamina, farina, seed-case, seed, fruit, and various other parts; and these are different in their construction and appearance in the different species. Some plants, as the oak, are distinguished for their strength and hardness; others, as the elm and fir, are tall and slender; some are tall, like the cedar of Lebanon, while others never attain to any considerable height; some have a rough and uneven bark, while others are smooth and fine, as the birch, the maple, and the poplar; some are so slight and delicate that the least wind may overturn them, while others can resist the violence of the northern blasts; some acquire their full growth in a few years, while others grow to a prodigious height and size, and stand unshaken amidst the lapse of centuries; some drop their leaves in autumn, and remain for months like blighted trunks, while others retain their verdure amidst the most furious blasts of winter; some have leaves scarcely an inch in length or breadth, while others, as the *tallipot* of Ceylon, have leaves so large that one of them, it is said, will shelter fifteen or twenty men from the rain.

The variety in the vegetable kingdom in respect of *flowers*, is apparent even to the least attentive observer. Every species is different from another in the form and hues which it exhibits. The carnation differs from the rose, the rose from the tulip, the tulip from the auricula, the auricula from the lily, the lily from the narcissus, and the ranunculus from the daisy. At the same time each ranunculus, daisy, rose or tulip, has its own particular character and beauty, something that is peculiar to itself, and in which it is distinguished from its fellows. In a bed of ranunculuses, or tulips, for example, we shall scarcely find two individuals that have precisely the same aspect, or present the same assemblage of colours. Some flowers are of a stately size, and seem to reign over their fellows in the same parterre, others are lowly or creep along the ground; some exhibit the most dazzling colours, others are simple and blush almost unseen; some perfume the air with exquisite odours, while others only please the sight with their beautiful tints. Not only the forms and colours of flowers but their *perfumes*, are different. The odour of southernwood differs from that of thyme, that of peppermint from balm, and that of the daisy from the rose, which indicates a variety in their internal structure, and in the juices that circulate within them. The *leaves* of all vegetables, like the skin of the human body, are diversified with a multitude of extremely fine vessels, and an astonishing number of *pores*. In a kind of box-tree called *Palma Cereres*, it has been observed that there are above *an hundred and seventy-two thousand* pores on one single side of the leaf. In short, the whole earth is covered with vegetable life in such profusion and variety as astonishes the contemplative mind. Not only the fertile plains, but the rugged mountains, the hardest stones, the most barren spots, and even the caverns of the ocean, are diversified with plants of various kinds; and, from the torrid to the frigid zone, every soil and every climate has plants and flowers peculiar to itself. To attempt to estimate their number and variety would be to attempt to dive into the depths of infinity. Yet, every diversity in the species, every variety in the form of the individuals, and even every difference in the shade and combination of colour in flowers of the same species, exhibits a distinct conception which must have existed in the Divine Mind before the vegetable kingdom was created.

Were we to take a survey of the *mineral* kingdom, we should also behold a striking exhibition of the "*manifold* wisdom of God." It is true, indeed, that we cannot penetrate into the interior recesses of the globe, so as to ascertain the substances which exist, and the processes which are going on near its central regions. But, within a few hundreds of fathoms of its surface, we find such an astonishing diversity of mineral substances as clearly shows, that its internal parts have been constructed on the same plan of *variety* as that of the animal and vegetable kingdoms. In the classes of *earthy*, *saline*, *inflammable*, and *metallic* fossils, under which mineralogists have arranged the substances of the mineral kingdom, are contained an immense number of genera and species. Under the *earthy* class of fossils are comprehended diamonds, chrysolites, menilites, garnets, zeolites, corundums, agates, jaspers, opals, pearl-stones, tripoli, clay slate, basalt, lava, chalk, limestone, ceylanite, strontian, barytes, celestine, and various other substances. The *saline* class comprehends such substances as the following, natron or natural soda, rock salt, nitre, alum, sal-ammoniac, Epmon salt, &c. The class of *inflammable* substances comprehends sulphur, carbon, bitumen, coal, amber, charcoal, naphtha, petroleum, asphalt, caoutchouc, mineral tar, &c. The *metallic* class comprehends platina, gold, silver, mercury, copper, iron, lead, tin, bismuth, zinc, antimony, cobalt, nickel, manganese, molybdenum, arsenic, scheele, menachanite, uran, silvan chromium, tungsten, uranium, titanium, tellurium, sodium, potassium, &c. All these mineral substances are distinguished by many varieties of species. There are *eight genera* of earthy fossils. One of these genera, the *flint*, contains 34 species, besides numerous varieties, such as chrysoberyls, topazes, agates, beryls, quartz, emery, diamond spar, &c. Another genus, the *clay*, contains 32 species, such as opal, pitch-stone, felspar, black chalk, mica, hornblende, &c. and another, the *calc*, contains 20 species, as limestone, chalk, slate, spar, fluor, marle, boracite, loam, &c. There are ten species of *silver*, five of *mercury*, seventeen of *copper*, fourteen of *iron*, ten of *lead*, six of antimony, three of bismuth, &c. All the bodies of the mineral kingdom differ from one another as to figure, transparency, hardness, lustre, ductility, texture, structure, feel, sound, smell, taste, gravity, and their magnetical and electrical properties; and they exhibit almost every variety of colour. Some of those substances are soft and pulverable, and serve as a bed for the nourishment of vegetables, as black earth, chalk, clay, and marl. Some are solid, as lead and iron; and some are fluid, as mercury, sodium, and potassium. Some are brittle, as antimony and bismuth, and some are malleable, as silver and tin. Some are subject to the attraction of the magnet, others are conductors of the electric fire; some are easily fusible by heat, others will resist the strongest heat of our common fires. Some are extremely ductile, as *platina*, the heaviest of the metals, which has been drawn into wires less than the two thousandth part of an inch in diameter,—and *gold*, the parts of which are are so fine and expansible, that an ounce of it is sufficient to gild a silver wire more than 1300 miles long.

In order to acquire the most impressive idea of the mineral kingdom, we must visit an extensive mineralogical museum, where the spectator will be astonished both at the beauty and the infinite diversity which the Creator has exhibited in this department of nature. Here it may be also noticed, that not only the external aspect of minerals, but also the *interior configuration* of many of them, displays innumerable beauties and varieties. A rough dark-looking pebble, which to an incurious eye appears only like a fragment of common rock, when cut asunder and polished, presents an assemblage of the finest veins and most brilliant colours. If we go into a lapidary's shop and take a leisurely survey of his jaspers, topazes, cornelians, agates, garnets, and other stones, we cannot fail to be struck with admiration, not only at the exquisite polish and the delicate wavings which their surfaces present, but at the variety of design and colouring exhibited even by individuals of the same species, the latent beauties and diversities of which require the assistance of a microscope to discern, and are beyond the efforts of the most exquisite pencil fully to imitate.

Not only in the objects which are visible to the unassisted eye, but also *in those which can only be perceived by the help of microscopes*, is the characteristic of *variety* to be seen. In the scales of fishes, for example, we perceive an infinite number of diversified specimens of the most curious workmanship. Some of these are of a longish form, some round, some triangular, some square; in short, of all imaginable variety of shapes. Some are armed with sharp prickles, as in the perch and sole; some have smooth edges, as in the tench and cod-fish; and even in the same fish there is a considerable variety; for the scales taken from the belly, the back, the sides, the head and other parts, are all different from each other. In the scale of a perch we perceive one piece of delicate mechanism, in the scale of a haddock another, and in the scale of a sole, beauties different from both. We find some of them ornamented with a prodigious number of concentric flutings, too near each other and too fine to be easily enumerated. These flutings are frequently traversed by others diverging from the centre of the scale, and proceeding from thence in a straight line to the circumference. On every fish there are many thousands of these variegated pieces of mechanism. The hairs on the bodies of all animals are found, by the microscope, to be composed of a number of *extremely minute tubes*, each of which has a round bulbous root, by which it imbibes its proper nourishment from the adjacent humours, and these are all different in different animals. Hairs taken from the head, the eye-brows, the nostrils, the beard, the hand, and other parts of the body, are unlike to each other, both in the construction of the roots and the hairs themselves, and appear as varied as plants of the same genus but of different species. The parts of which the *feathers* of birds are composed, afford a beautiful variety of the most exquisite workmanship. There is scarcely a feather but contains a million of distinct parts, every one of them regularly shaped. In a small fibre of a goose-quill, more than 1200 downy branches or small leaves have been counted on each side, and each appeared divided into 16 or 18 small joints. A small part of the feather of a peacock, one-thirtieth of an inch in length, appears no less beautiful than the whole feather does to the naked eye, exhibiting a multitude of bright shining parts, reflecting first one colour and then another in the most vivid manner. The *wings* of all kind of insects, too, present an infinite variety, no less captivating to the mind than pleasing to the eye. They appear strengthened and distended by the finest bones, and covered with the lightest membranes. Some of them are adorned with neat and beautiful feathers, and many of them provided with the finest articulations and foldings for the wings, when they are withdrawn and about to be folded up in their cases. The thin membranes of the wings appear beautifully divaricated with thousands of little points, like silver studs. The wings of some flies are *filmy*, as the dragon-fly; others have them stuck over with short *bristles*, as the flesh-fly; some have rows of feathers along their ridges, and borders round their edge, as in gnats; some have hairs and others have hooks placed with the greatest regularity and order. In the wings of moths and butterflies there are millions of small feathers of different shapes, diversified with the greatest variety of bright and vivid colours, each of them so small as to be altogether invisible to the naked eye.

The *leaves* of all plants and flowers when examined by the microscope, are found to be full of innumerable ramifications that convey the perspirable juices to the pores, and to consist of barenchymous and ligneous fibres, interwoven in a curious and admirable manner. The smallest leaf, even one which is little more than visible to the naked eye, is found to be thus divaricated, and the variegations are different in the leaves of different vegetables.—*A transverse section of a plant* not more than one-fourth of an inch in diameter, displays such beauties and varieties, through a powerful microscope, as cannot be conceived without ocular inspection. The number of pores, of all sizes, amounting to hundreds of thousands (which appear to be the vessels of the plant cut asunder,) the beautiful curves they assume, and the radial and circular configurations they present, are truly astonishing; and every distinct species of plants exhibits a different configuration. I have counted in a small section of a plant, of the size now stated, 5000 radial lines, each containing about 250 pores, great and small, which amount to *one million two hundred and fifty thousand* of these variegated apertures.—Even *the particles of sand* on the sea-shore, and on the banks of rivers, differ in the size, form, and colour of their grains; some being transparent, others opaque, some having rough and others smooth surfaces; some are spherical or oval, and some pyramidal, conical or prismatical. Mr. Hook, happening to view some grains of white sand through his microscope, hit upon one of the grains which was exactly shaped and wreathed like a shell, though it was no larger than the point of a pin. "It resembled the shell of a small water-snail, and had twelve wreathings, all growing proportionably one less than the other towards the middle or centre of the shell, where there was a very small round white spot." This gives us an idea of the existence of shell-fish which are invisible to the naked eye, and, consequently, smaller than a mite.

The variety of forms in which *animal life* appears, in those invisible departments of creation which the microscope has enabled us to explore, is truly wonderful and astonishing. Microscopic animals are so different from those of the larger kinds, that scarcely any analogy seems to exist between them; and one would be almost tempted to suppose that they lived in consequence of laws directly opposite to those which preserve man and the other larger animals in existence. When we endeavour to explore this region of animated nature, we feel as if we were entering on the confines of a new world, and surveying a new race of sentient existence. The number of these creatures exceeds all human calculation. Many hundreds of species, all differing in their forms, habits, and motions, have already been detected and described, but we have reason to believe, that by far the greater part is unexplored, and perhaps for ever hid from the view of man. They are of all shapes and forms: some of them appear like minute atoms, some like globes and spheroids, some like handbells, some like wheels turning on an axis, some like double-headed monsters, some like cylinders, some have a worm-like appearance, some have horns, some resemble eels, some are like long hairs, 150 times as long as they are broad, some like spires and cupolas, some like fishes, and some like animated vegetables. Some of them are almost visible to the naked eye, and some so small that the breadth of a human hair would cover fifty or a hundred of them, and others so minute, that millions of millions of them might be contained within the compass of a square inch. In every pond and ditch, and almost in every puddle, in the infusions of pepper, straw, grass, oats, hay and other vegetables, in paste and vinegar, and in the water found in oysters, on almost every plant and flower, and in the rivers, seas and oceans, these creatures are found in such numbers and variety as almost exceed our conception or belief. A class of these animals, called *Mudusæ*, has been found so numerous as to discolour the ocean itself. Captain Scoresby found the number in the olive-green sea to be immense. A cubic inch contains sixty-four, and consequently a cubic mile would contain 23,888,000,000,000,000; so that, if one person should count a million in seven days, it would have required that 80,000 persons should have started at the creation of the world to have completed the enumeration at the present time. Yet, all the minute animals to which we now allude are furnished with numerous organs of life as well as the larger kind, some of their internal movements are distinctly visible, their motions are evidently *voluntary*, and some of them appear to be possessed of a considerable degree of sagacity, and to be fond of each other's society.*

In short, it may be affirmed without the least hesitation, that the beauties and *varieties* which exist in those regions of creation which are invisible to the unassisted eye, are far more numerous than all that appears to a common observer in the visible economy of nature. How far this scene of creating Power and Intelligence may extend beyond the range of our microscopic instruments, it is impossible for mortals to determine; for the finer our glasses are, and the higher the magnifying powers we apply, the more numerous and varied are the objects which they exhibit to our view. And as the largest telescope is insufficient to convey our views to the boundaries of the great universe, so we may justly conclude, that the most powerful microscope that has been or ever will be constructed, will be altogether insufficient to guide our views to the utmost limits of the descending scale of creation. But what we already know of these unexplored and inexplorable regions, gives us an amazing conception of the intelligence and wisdom of the Creator, of the immensity of his nature, and of the infinity of ideas which, during every portion of past duration, must have been present before his All-Comprehensive Mind. What an immense space in the scale of animal life intervenes between an *animalcule* which appears only the size of a visible point, when magnified 500,000 times, and a *whale*, a hundred feet long and twenty broad! The proportion of bulk between the one of these beings and the other is nearly as 34,560,000,000,000,000,000 to 1. Yet all the intermediate space is filled up with animated beings of every form and order! A similar variety obtains in the vegetable kingdom. It has been calculated, that some plants which grow on *rose* leaves, and other shrubs, are so small that it would require more than a thousand of them to equal in bulk a single plant of *moss*; and if we compare a stem of moss, which is generally not above 1-60th of an inch, with some of the large trees in Guinea and Brazil of twenty feet diameter, we shall find the bulk of the one will exceed that of the other no less than 2,985,984,000,000 times, which multiplied by 1000 will produce 2,985,984,000,000,000, the number of times, which the large tree exceeds the rose-leaf plant. Yet this immense interval is filled up with plants and trees of every form and size! With good reason, then, may we adopt the language of the inspired writers,—"How *manifold* are thy works, O Lord! In wisdom hast thou made them all. O the depth of the riches both of the wisdom and the knowledge of God! Marvellous things doth He which we cannot comprehend."*

* The following extract from Mr. Baker's description of the *hair-like animalcule* will illustrate some of these positions. A small quantity of the matter containing these animalcules having been put into a jar of water, it so happened, that one part went down immediately to the bottom, while the other continued floating on the top. When things had remained for some time in this condition, each of these swarms of animalcules began to grow weary of its situation, and had a mind to change its quarters. Both armies, therefore, set out at the same time, the one proceeding upwards and the other downwards; so that after some time they met in the middle. A desire of knowing how they would behave on this occasion, engaged the observer to watch them carefully; and to his surprise, he saw the army that was marching upwards, open to the right and left, to make room for those that were descending. Thus, without confusion or intermixture, each held on its way; the army that was going up marching in two columns to the top, and the other proceeding in one column to the bottom, as if each had been under the direction of wise leaders.

* The figures of microscopical objects contained in the engravings Nos. I. and II., will convey a rude idea of some of the objects to which I have now alluded.

No. I. Fig. 1. represents the *scale* of a *sole-fish* as it appears through a good microscope. CDEF, represents that part of the scale which appears on the outside of the fish, and ABCD, the part which adheres to the skin, being furrowed, that it may hold the faster. It is terminated by pointed spikes, every alternate one being longer than the interjacent ones. Fig. 2, is the scale of a haddock, which appears divaricated like a piece of net-work. Fig. 3, represents a small portion or fibre of the *feather of a peacock*, only 1-30th of an inch in extent, as it appears in the microscope. The small fibres of these feathers appear, through this instrument, no less beautiful than the whole feather does to the naked eye. Each of the sprigs or hairs on each side of the fibre, as CD, DC, appears to consist of a multitude of bright shining parts which are a congeries of small plates, as *eee*, &c. The under sides of each of these plates are very dark and opaque, reflecting all the rays thrown upon them like the foil of a looking-glass; but their upper sides seem to consist of a multitude of exceedingly thin plated bodies, lying close together, which, by various positions of the light, reflect first one colour and then another, in a most vivid and surprising manner. Fig. 4, 5, 6, 7, represent some of the different kinds of feathers which constitute the dust which adheres to the wings of moths and butterflies, and which, in the microscope, appear tinged with a variety of colours. Each of these feathers is an object so small as to be scarcely perceptible to the naked eye.

*Explanation of the figures on No. II.*—Fig. 1. represents a *mite*, which has eight legs, with five or six joints in each, two feelers, a small head in proportion to its body, a sharp snout and mouth like that of a mole, and two little eyes. The body is of an oval form, with a number of hairs like bristles issuing from it, and the legs terminate in two hooked claws. Fig. 2. represents a microscopic animal which was found in an infusion of *anemony*. The surface of its back is covered with a fine mask in the form of a *human face*, it has three feet on each side, and a tail which comes out from under the mask. Fig. 3, is an animalcula found in the infusion of *old hay*. A, shows the head, with the mouth opened wide, and its lips furnished with numerous hairs; B, is its forked tail, D, its intestines, and C, its heart, which may be seen in regular motion. The circumference of the body appears indented like the teeth of a saw. Fig. 4, shows the *Wheel animal* or *Vorticella*. It is found in rain-water that has stood some days in leaden gutters, or in hollows of lead on the tops of houses. The most remarkable part of this animalcula is its *wheel work*, which consists of two semicircular instruments, round the edges of which many little fibrillæ move themselves very briskly sometimes with a kind of rotation, and sometimes

**Even** the *external aspect of nature*, as it appears to a superficial observer, presents a scene of *variety*. The ranges of mountains with summits of different heights and shapes, the hills and plains, the glens and dells, the waving curves which appear on the face of every landscape, the dark hues of the forests, the verdure of the fields, the towering cliffs, the rugged precipices, the rills, the rivers, the cataracts, the lakes and seas; the gulphs, the bays and peninsulas; the numerous islands of every form and size which diversify the surface of the ocean, and the thousands of shades of colouring which appear on every part of sublunary nature, present a scene of diversified beauty and sublimity to the eye of every beholder.—And if we lift our eyes to the regions of the firmament, we likewise behold a scene of sublimity and grandeur mingled with variety. The sun himself appears diversified with spots of various shapes and sizes, some a hundred, some a thousand, and some ten thousand miles in diameter—indicating operations and changes of amazing extent—and almost every new revolution on his axis presents us with new and varied clusters. Every planet in the solar system differs from another in its size, in its spheroidal shape, in its diurnal rotation, in the aspect of its surface, in the constitution of its atmosphere, in the number of moons with which it is surrounded, in the nature of its seasons, in its distance from the sun, in the eccentricity of its orbit, in the period of its annual revolution, and in the proportion it receives of light and heat. Every comet, too, differs from another in its form and magnitude, in the extent of its nucleus and tail, in the period of its revolution, in the swiftness of its motion, and in the figure of the curve it describes around the sun; and "one star differeth from another star in glory." But could we transport ourselves to the surfaces of these distant orbs, and survey every part of their constitution and arrangements, we should, doubtless, behold beauties and varieties of divine workmanship far more numerous, and surpassing every thing that appears in our sublunary system. We have every reason to believe, from the infinite nature of the Divinity, and from what we actually behold, that the mechanism and arrangements of every world in the universe are all different from each other; and we find that this is actually the case, in so far as our observations extend. The

in a trembling or vibratory manner. Sometimes the wheels seem to be entire circles, with teeth like those of the balance-wheel of a watch: but their figure varies according to the degree of their protrusion, and seems to depend upon the will of the animal itself; *a*, is the head and heels; *b*, is the *heart*, where its systole and diastole are plainly visible, and the alternate motions of contraction and dilatation are performed with great strength and vigour in about the same time as the pulsation of a man's artery. This animal assumes various shapes, one of which is represented at fig. 5, and becomes occasionally a case for all the other parts of the body.

Fig. 6, represents *an insect with net-like arms*. It is found in cascades where the water runs very swift. Its body appears curiously turned as on a lathe, and at the tail are three sharp spines, by which it raises itself and stands upright in the water; but the most curious apparatus is about its head, where it is furnished with two instruments, like fans or nets, which serve to provide its food. These it frequently spreads out and draws in again, and, when drawn up, they are folded together with the utmost nicety and exactness. When this creature does not employ its nets, it thrusts out a pair of sharp horns, and puts on a different appearance, as in fig. 7, where it is shown magnified about 400 times. Fig. 8, is the representation of an animalcula found in the infusion of *the bark of an oak*. Its body is composed of several ringlets, that enter one into another, as the animal contracts itself. At *a b*, are two lips furnished with moveable hairs; it pushes out of its mouth a *snout* composed of several pieces sheathed in each other, as at *e*. A kind of horn, *d*, is sometimes protruded from the breast, composed of furbelows, which slide into one another like the drawers of a pocket telescope. Fig. 9, is another animalcula, found in the same infusion, called a *tortoise*, with an umbilical tail. It stretches out and contracts itself very easily, sometimes assuming a round figure, which it retains only for a moment, then opens its mouth to a surprising width, forming nearly the circumference of a circle. Its motion is very surprising and singular. Fig. 10, is an animalcula, called *great mouth*, which is found in several infusions. Its mouth takes up half the length of its body; its inside is filled with darkish spots, and its hinder part terminated with a singular tail. Fig. 11, represents the *proteus*, so named on account of its assuming a great number of different shapes. Its most common shape bears a resemblance to that of a swan, and it swims to and fro with great vivacity. When it is alarmed, it suddenly draws in its long neck, transforming itself into the shape represented at *m*, and, at other times it puts forth a new head and neck with a kind of wheel machinery, as at *n*. Fig. 12, exhibits a species of animalcula shaped like bells with long tails, by which they fasten themselves to the roots of *duck weed*, in which they were found. They dwell in colonies, from ten to fifteen in number. Fig. 13, is the *globe animal*, which appears exactly globular, having no appearance of either head, tail or fins. It moves in all directions, forwards or backwards, up or down, either rolling over and over like a bowl, spinning horizontally like a top, or gliding along smoothly without turning itself at all. When it pleases, it can turn round, as it were upon an axis very nimbly without removing out of its place. It is transparent, except where the circular black spots are shown; it sometimes appears as if dotted with points, and beset with short moveable hairs or bristles, which are probably the instruments by which its motions are performed. Fig. 14, shows a species of animalculæ called *soles*, found in infusions of straw and the ears of wheat; *o*, is the mouth, which is sometimes extended to a great width, *p*, is the tail. Fig. 15, represents an anima. found in an infusion of citron flowers. Its head is very short, and adorned with two horns like those of a deer; its body appears to be covered with scales, and its tail long, and swift in motion. Fig. 16, represents the *eels* which are found in paste and stale vinegar. The most remarkable property of these animals is, that they are *viviparous*. If one of them is cut through near the middle, several oval bodies of different sizes issue forth, which are young *anguillæ*, each coiled up in its proper membrane. An hundred and upwards of the young ones have been seen to issue from the body of one single eel, which accounts for their prodigious increase.

It may not be improper to remark, that no engraving can give an adequate idea of the objects referred to above, and, therefore, whoever wishes to inspect nature in all her minute beauties and varieties, must have recourse to the microscope itself.

moon is the principal orb on whose surface particular observations can be made; and we find that its arrangements are materially different from those of the earth. It has no large rivers, seas, or oceans, nor clouds such as ours to diversify its atmosphere. It has mountains and plains, hills and vales, insulated rocks and caverns of every size and shape; but the form and arrangement of all these objects are altogether different from what obtains in our terrestrial sphere.—While, on our globe, the ranges of mountains run nearly in a line from east to west, or from north to south,—on the surface of the moon they are formed for the most part into *circular* ridges, enclosing, like ramparts, plains of all dimensions, from half a mile to forty miles in diameter. While on earth, the large plains are nearly level, and diversified merely with gentle wavings,—in the moon, there are hundreds of plains of various dimensions *sunk*, as it were, nearly two miles *below the general level of its surface*. On this orb we behold insulated mountains, more than two miles in elevation, standing alone, like monuments, in the midst of plains,—circular basins or caverns, both in the valleys, and on the summits and declivities of mountains, and these caverns, again, indented with smaller ones of a similar form, at the same time, there are plains far more level and extensive than on the earth. On the whole, the mountain-scenery on the lunar surface is far more diversified and magnificent than on our globe, and differs as much from terrestrial landscapes as the wastes and wilds of America from the cultivated plains of Europe. In short, while on the earth, the highest mountains are little more than four miles in height, on some of the planets mountains have been discovered, which astronomers have reckoned to be twenty-two miles in elevation.

If then, it is reasonable to believe, that all the worlds in the universe are different in their construction and arrangements, and peopled with beings of diversified ranks and orders—could we survey only a small portion of the universal system—what an amazing scene would it display of the conceptions of the Divine Mind and of "*the manifold wisdom of God!*" Such views, therefore, of the *variety of nature* are evidently calculated to expand our conceptions of the divine character, to excite us to admiration and reverence, to extend our views of the riches of divine beneficence, and to enlarge our hopes of the glories and felicities of that future 'inheritance which is incorruptible and which fadeth not away.'

5. The contemplation of nature, through the medium of science, is calculated to *expand our conceptions of the power of the Deity, and of the magnificence of his empire.* The power of God is manifested by its effects; and in proportion as our knowledge of these effects is enlarged, will our conceptions of this attribute of the Divinity be expanded. To *create* a single object implies an exertion of power which surpasses finite comprehension;—how much more the creation and arrangement of such a vast multiplicity of objects as those to which we have just now adverted! For, all that immense variety of beings which exists in the animal, vegetable, and mineral kingdoms, and in the invisible regions which the microscope has explored, evinces the omnipotence of the Deity, no less than his wisdom and intelligence. But the *magnitude*, as well as the number and variety of the objects of creation, displays the almighty power of the Creator. In this point of view, the discoveries of modern astronomy tend to aid our conceptions of the grandeur of this perfection, and to extend our views of the range of its operations far beyond what former ages could have imagined. When we take a leisurely survey of the globe on which we dwell, and consider the enormous masses of its continents and islands, the quantity of water in its seas and oceans, the lofty ranges of mountains which rise from its surface, the hundreds of majestic rivers which roll their waters into the ocean, the numerous orders of animated beings with which it is peopled, and the vast quantity of matter enclosed in its bowels from every part of its circumference to its centre, amounting to more than *two hundred and sixty thousand millions of cubical miles*—we cannot but be astonished at the greatness of that Being who first launched it into existence, who "measures its waters in the hollow of his hand, who weighs its mountains in scales, and its hills in a balance;" and who has supported it in its rapid movements, from age to age. But, how must our conceptions of divine power be enlarged when we consider, that this earth, which appears so great to the frail beings which inhabit it, is only like a small speck in creation, or like an atom in the immensity of space, when compared with the myriads of worlds of superior magnitude which exist within the boundaries of creation! When we direct our views to the planetary system, we behold three or four globes, which appear only like small studs on the vault of heaven, yet contain a quantity of matter more than two thousand four hundred times greater than that of the earth, besides more than twenty lesser globes, most of them larger than our world,* and several hundreds of *comets*, of various magnitudes, moving in every direction through the depths of space. The *Sun* is a body of such magnitude as overpowers our feeble conceptions, and fills us with astonishment. Within the wide circumference of this luminary more than a million of worlds as large as ours could be contained. His body fills a cubical space equal to 681,472,000,000,000,000 miles, and his surface more than 40,000,000,000, or forty thousand millions of square miles. At the

*The satellites of Jupiter, Saturn and Herschel are all reckoned to be larger than the Earth.

ate of sixty miles a-day, it would require more than a hundred millions of years to pass over every square mile on his surface. His attractive energy extends to several thousands of millions of miles from his surface, retaining in their orbits the most distant planets and comets, and dispensing light and heat, and fructifying influence to more than a hundred worlds.* What an astonishing idea, then, does it give us of the power of Omnipotence, when we consider, that the universe is replenished with *innumerable* globes of a similar size and splendour! For every star which the naked eye perceives twinkling on the vault of heaven, and those more distant orbs which the telescope brings to view throughout the depths of immensity, are, doubtless, *suns*, no less in magnitude than that which " enlightens our day," and surrounded by a retinue of revolving worlds. Some of them have been reckoned by astronomers to be even much larger than our sun. The star *Lyra*, for example, is supposed, by Sir W. Herschel, to be 33,275,000 miles in diameter, or thirty-eight times the diameter of the sun; and, if so, its cubical contents will be 36,842,932,671,875, 000,000,000 miles, that is, more than *fifty-four thousand times* larger than the sun. The *number* of such bodies exceeds all calculation. Sir W. Herschel perceived in that portion of the milky way which lies near the constellation *Orion*, no less than 50,000 stars large enough to be distinctly numbered, pass before his telescope in an hour's time; besides twice as many more which could be seen only now and then by faint glimpses. It has been reckoned that nearly a hundred millions of stars lie within the range of our telescopes. And, if we suppose as we justly may, that each of these suns has a hundred worlds connected with it, there will be found *ten thousand millions of worlds* in that portion of the universe which comes within the range of human observation, besides those which lie concealed from mortal eyes in the unexplored regions of space, which may as far exceed all that are visible, as the waters in the caverns of the ocean exceed in magnitude a single particle of vapour!

Of such numbers and magnitudes we can form no adequate conception. The mind is bewildered, confounded, and utterly overwhelmed when it attempts to grasp the magnitude of the universe, or to form an idea of the omnipotent energy which brought it into existence. The *amplitude of the scale* on which the systems of the universe are constructed tends likewise to elevate our conceptions of the grandeur of the Deity. Between every one of the planetary bodies there intervenes a space of many millions of miles in extent. Between the sun and the nearest star, there is an interval, extending in every direction, of more than twenty billions of miles; and, it is highly probable, that a similar space surrounds every other system. And, if we take into consideration the *immense forces* that are in operation throughout the universe—that one globe, a thousand times larger than the earth, is flying through the regions of immensity at the rate of thirty thousand miles an hour, another at the rate of seventy thousand, and another at a hundred thousand miles an hour, and that millions of mighty worlds are thus traversing the illimitable spaces of the firmament—can we refrain from exclaiming in the language of inspiration, " Great and marvellous are thy works, Lord God Almighty! Who can by searching find out God? Who can find out the Almighty to perfection? Who can utter the mighty operations of Jehovah? Who can show forth all his praise?"

Such a scene displays, beyond any other view we can take of creation, the *magnificence and extent of the divine empire*. Those countless worlds to which we have now adverted, are not to be considered as scenes of sterility and desolation, or as merely diffusing an useless splendour over the wilds of immensity, nor are they to be viewed as so many splendid toys to amuse a few astronomers in our diminutive world. Such an idea would be altogether inconsistent with every notion we ought to form of the wisdom and intelligence of the Deity, and with every arrangement we perceive in the scenes of nature immediately around us, where we behold every portion of matter teeming with inhabitants. These luminous and opaque globes dispersed throughout the regions of infinite space, must, therefore, be considered as the abodes of sensitive and intellectual existence, where intelligences of various ranks and orders contemplate the glory, and enjoy the bounty of their Creator. And what scenes of diversified grandeur must we suppose those innumerable worlds to display! What numerous orders and gradations of intellectual natures must the universe contain, since so much variety is displayed in every department of our sublunary system! What *boundless intelligence* is implied in the *superintendence* of such vast dominions! On such subjects the human mind can form no *definite* conceptions. The most vigorous imagination, in its loftiest flights, drops its wing and sinks into inanity before the splendours of the " King eternal, immortal, and invisible, who dwells in the light unapproachable," when it attempts to form a picture of the magnificence of the universe which he has created. But of this we are certain, that over all this boundless scene of creation, and over all the ranks of beings with which it is replenished, his moral government extends. Every motion of the material system, every movement among the rational

* The planetary system, including the *comets* contain more than a hundred bodies dependant on the sun.

and sentient beings it contains, and every thought and perception that passes through the minds of the unnumbered intelligences which people all worlds, are intimately known, and for ever present to his omniscient eye, and all directed to accomplish the designs of his universal providence and the eternal purposes of his will. "He hath prepared his *throne in the heavens*, his kingdom ruleth over all," and "he doth according to his will among the armies of heaven," as well as "among the inhabitants of the earth." "The host of heaven worshippeth him,—all his works, in all places of his dominions, praise him. His kingdom is an everlasting kingdom, and of his government there shall be no end." At the same moment he is displaying the glory of his power and intelligence to worlds far beyond the reach of mortal eyes,—presiding over the councils of nations on earth, and supporting the invisible animalcula in a drop of water. "In him" all beings, from the archangel to the worm, "live and move," and on him they depend for all that happiness they now possess, or ever will enjoy, while eternal ages are rolling on.

Such views of the omnipotence of the Deity and of the grandeur of his empire, are calculated not only to expand our conceptions of his attributes, but to enliven our hopes in relation to the enjoyments of the future world. For we behold a prospect boundless as immensity, in which the human soul may for ever expatiate, and contemplate new scenes of glory and felicity continually bursting on the view, "world without end."

Such are some of the views of the Deity which the works of nature, when contemplated through the medium of science, are calculated to unfold. They demonstrate the *unity* of God, his *wisdom* and intelligence,—his boundless *benevolence*,—the *vast multiplicity of ideas which have existed in his mind from eternity*,—his *almighty power*, and the *magnificence* of his empire. These views are in perfect unison with the declarations of the sacred oracles; they illustrate many of the sublime sentiments of the inspired writers; they throw a light on the moral government of God, and elevate our conceptions of the extent of his dominions; they afford a *sensible* representation of the infinity and immensity of the divine nature, in so far as finite minds are capable of contemplating such perfections; and, when considered in connexion with the scriptural character of Deity and the other truths of revelation, are calculated "to make the man of God perfect and thoroughly furnished unto every good work." As the works of God without the assistance of his word, are insufficient to give us a *complete* view of his character and the principles of his moral government, so the bare reading of the Scriptures is insufficient to convey to our minds those diversified and expansive conceptions of the Divinity to which we have adverted, unless we comply with the requisitions of the sacred writers, to "meditate on all his works, to *consider* the operations of his hands, to speak of the glory of his kingdom," and to talk of his "*power*," in order that we may be qualified "to make known to the sons of men his mighty operations, and the glorious majesty of his kingdom."

How very different, then, from the views now stated, must be the conceptions formed of the Divinity, by those whose range of thought is chiefly confined to the objects that lie within a few miles of their habitation, and how limited ideas must they entertain of divine perfection! For the view that any one entertains of the nature and attributes of God, must, in some degree, correspond to the knowledge he has acquired of the visible effects of his power, wisdom, and benevolence; since it is only by the sensible manifestations of Deity, either through the medium of nature or revelation, that we know any thing at all about his nature and perfections. And, therefore, if our views of the *manifestations* of the Divinity be limited and obscure, such will likewise be our views of the Divinity himself. It is owing to the want of attention to such considerations, that many worthy Christians are found to entertain very confused and distorted ideas of the character of the Deity, of the requisitions of his word, and of the arrangements of his universal providence. And is it not an object much to be desired, that the great body of mankind should be more fully enlightened in the knowledge of their Creator? The knowledge of God lies at the foundation of all religion, and of all our prospects in reference to the eternal world, and it must surely be a highly desirable attainment to acquire as glorious and expansive an idea of the object of our adoration, as the finite capacity of our intellects is capable of comprehending. Such views as we have now exhibited of the wisdom, power, and beneficence of the Deity, and of the magnificence and variety of his works, were they communicated to the generality of mankind and duly appreciated, would not only interest their affections and increase their intellectual enjoyment, but would enable them to understand the meaning and references of many sublime passages in the volume of inspiration which they are apt either to overlook or to misinterpret. Such views, likewise, would naturally inspire them with *reverence* and *adoration* of the Divine Majesty, with *gratitude* for his wise and benevolent arrangements,—with *complacency* in his administration as the moral Governor of the world,—with a firm *reliance on his providential care* for every thing requisite to their happiness, and with an earnest desire to yield a cordial *obedience* to his righteous laws. At the same time, they would be qualified to declare to others "the glorious honour of his

Majesty, to utter abundantly the memory of his great goodness, and to speak of all his wonderful works."

## SECTION VII.

### ON THE BENEFICIAL EFFECTS OF KNOWLEDGE ON MORAL PRINCIPLE AND CONDUCT.

Knowledge is valuable chiefly in proportion as it is practical and useful. It dispels the darkness which naturally broods over the human understanding, and dissipates a thousand superstitious notions and idle terrors by which it has been frequently held in cruel bondage. It invigorates and expands the intellectual faculties, and directs them to their proper objects. It elevates the mind in the scale of rational existence, by enlarging its views and refining its pleasures. It gratifies the desire of the soul for perpetual activity, and renders its activities subservient to the embellishment of life and the improvement of society. It unveils the beauties and sublimities of nature, with which the heavens and the earth are adorned, and sets before us the "Book of God," in which we may trace the lineaments of his character and the ways of his providence. It aggrandizes our ideas of the omnipotence of Deity, and unfolds to us the riches of his beneficence, and the depths of his wisdom and intelligence. And, in the exercise of our powers on such objects, we experience a thousand delightful emotions and enjoyments to which the unenlightened multitude are entire strangers. All such activities and enjoyments may be reckoned among the practical advantages of knowledge.

But there is no application of knowledge more interesting and important than its practical bearings on moral principle and action. If it were not calculated to produce a beneficial effect on the state of morals and the intercourses of general society, the utility of its general diffusion might, with some show of reason, be called in question. But, there cannot be the slightest, doubt, that an increase of knowledge would be productive of an increase of moral order, and an improvement in moral conduct. For truth, *in thought and sentiment*, leads to truth *in action*. The man who is in the habit of investigating truth, and who rejoices in it when ascertained, cannot be indifferent to its application to conduct. There must be truth in his actions; they must be the expression, the proof, and the effect of his sentiments and affections, in order that he may approve of them, and be satisfied that they are *virtuous*, or accordant with the relations which subsist among moral agents. There must likewise be a truth or harmony between his actions, so that none of them be incoherent with the rest. They must all be performed on the same principles, with the same designs, and by the same rule. To a man who perceives truth and loves it, every incongruity and every want of consistency between sentiment and action, produces a disagreeable and painful sensation; and, consequently, he who clearly perceives the rule of right, and acts in direct opposition to it, does violence to his nature, and must be subjected to feelings and remorses of conscience far more painful than those of the man whose mind is shrouded in ignorance. It is true, indeed, that proficiency in knowledge and in the practice of true morality, do not always proceed with equal pace. But, it is nevertheless true, that every action that is truly virtuous is founded on knowledge, and is the result of scrutiny and choice directed by truth; otherwise, what is termed virtue, would be only the effect of necessity, of constraint, or of mechanical habits. We need not, therefore, fear, that the dominion of virtue* will be contracted, or her influence diminished, by an enlargement of the kingdom of light and knowledge. They are inseparably connected, their empire is one and the same, and the *true* votaries of the one will also be the true votaries of the other. And, therefore, every one that sincerely loves mankind and desires their moral improvement, will diffuse light around him as extensively as he can, without the least fear of its ultimate consequences; since he knows for certain, that in all cases whatever, wisdom excels folly, and light is better than darkness. The following observations will perhaps tend more particularly to comfirm and elucidate these positions.

1. *Ignorance is one principal cause* of the want of virtue, and *of the immoralities which abound in the world.* Were we to take a survey of the moral state of the world, as delineated in the history of nations, or as depicted by modern voyagers and travellers, we should find abundant illustration of the truth of this remark. We should find, in almost every instance, that ignorance of the character of the true God, and false conceptions of the nature of the worship and service he requires, have led not only to the most obscene practices and immoral abominations, but to the perpetration of the most horrid cruelties. We have only to turn our eyes to Hindostan, to Tartary, Dahomy, Benin, Ashantee, and other petty states in Africa; to New Zealand, the Marquesas, the Sandwich islands, and to the Society isles in the Southern Pacific, prior to their late moral transformation, in order

* By *virtue*, in this place, and wherever the term occurs, I understand, conduct regulated by the law of God, including both the external action and the *principle* whence it flows; in other words, Christian morality, or that *holiness* which the Scriptures enjoin.

to be convinced of this melancholy truth. The destruction of new-born infants,—the burning of living women upon the dead bodies of their husbands,—the drowning of aged parents,—the offering of human victims in sacrifice,—the torturing to death of prisoners taken in battle,—the murder of infants and the obscene abominations of the societies of the *Arreoy* in *Otaheite* and other islands, and the dreadful effects of ambition, treachery, and revenge, which so frequently accompany such practices, are only a few specimens of the consequences of ignorance combined with human depravity. It is likewise to ignorance chiefly that the vices of the ancient pagan world are to be attributed. To this cause the apostle of the Gentiles ascribes the immoralities of the heathen nations. "The Gentiles," says Paul, "having the understanding darkened through the ignorance that is in them, have given themselves over unto lasciviousness, to work all manner of uncleanness with greediness."* And, in another part of his writings, he declares, "Because they did not like to retain God in their knowledge, they were given up to a reprobate mind," or a mind *void of judgment;* and the consequence was, "they were filled with all unrighteousness, fornication, wickedness, covetousness, maliciousness, envy, murder, deceit, and malignity;" they were "backbiters, haters of God, proud, boasters, inventors of evil things, disobedient to parents, without understanding, without natural affection, implacable, and unmerciful."† And, if we turn our eyes to the state of society around us, we shall find that the same cause has produced the same effects. Among what class do we find sobriety, temperance, rectitude of conduct, honesty, active beneficence, and abstinence from the grosser vices most frequently to prevail? Is it among ignorant and grovelling minds? Is it not among the wise and intelligent, those who have been properly instructed in their duty, and in the principles of moral action? And, who are those that are found most frequently engaged in fighting, brawling, and debauchery, in the commission of theft and other petty crimes, and in rioting in low houses of dissipation? Are they not, for the most part, the rude, the ignorant, and untutored,—those whose instruction has been neglected by their parents or guardians, or whose wayward tempers have led them to turn a deaf ear to the reproofs of wisdom? From all the investigations which of late have been made into the state of immorality and crime, it is found, that gross ignorance, and its necessary concomitant, grovelling affections, are the general characteristics of those who are engaged in criminal pursuits, and most deeply sunk in vicious indulgence. Now, if it be a fact that ignorance is one principal source of immorality and crime, it appears a natural and necessary inference, that the general diffusion of knowledge would tend to counteract its influence and operations. For when we remove the *cause* of any evil, we, of course, prevent the *effects;* and not only so, but at the same time bring into operation all those virtues which knowledge has a tendency to produce.

2. Knowledge is requisite for ascertaining the true principles of moral action, and the duties we ought to perform. Numerous are the treatises which have been written, and various the opinions which have been entertained, both in ancient and modern times, respecting the foundation of virtue and the rules of human conduct. And were we to investigate the different theories which have been formed on this subject, to weigh the arguments which have been brought forward in support of each hypothesis, and to balance the various conflicting opinions which different philosophers have maintained, a considerable portion of human life would be wasted before we arrived at any satisfactory conclusions. But if we take the system of revelation for our guide in the science of morals, we shall be enabled to arrive, by a short process, at the most important and satisfactory results. We shall find, that, after all the theories which have been proposed, and the systems which have been reared by ethical philosophers, the Supreme Lawgiver has comprised the essence of true morality under two commands, or fundamental principles, "Thou shalt love the Lord thy God with all thy heart," and "Thou shalt love thy neighbour as thyself." On these two commandments rests the whole duty of man.

Now, although the leading ideas contained in these commands are simple and obvious to every one who considers them attentively, yet it requires certain habits of reflection and a considerable portion of knowledge, to be enabled to trace these laws or principles to all their legitimate consequences, and to follow them in all their ramifications, and in their bearings on human conduct, and on the actions of all moral intelligences. For, it can easily be shown, that these laws are so comprehensive as to reach every possible moral action, to prevent every moral evil, and to secure the happiness of every moral agent,—that all the duties inculcated in the Bible, which we owe to God, to our fellow-creatures, and to ourselves, are comprehended in them, and are only so many ramifications of these general and fundamental principles,—that they are equally adapted to men on earth and to angels in heaven,—that their control extends to the inhabitants of all worlds,—that they form the basis of the order and happiness of the whole intelligent system—and that their authority and influence will extend not only through all the revolutions of time, but through all the ages of eternity. Here, then, we have a subject calcu-

* Ephes. iv. 18, 19. † Rom. i. 28. 3[illegible].

'ated to exercise the highest powers of intelligence, and the more we investigate it the more shall we admire the comprehensive nature of that "law which is exceeding broad," and the more shall we be disposed to comply with its divine requisitions. But unless we be, in some measure, acquainted with the first principles of moral action, and their numerous bearings upon life and conduct, we cannot expect to make rapid advances in the path of virtue, or to reach the sublimer heights of moral improvement.

3. Knowledge, combined with habits of thinking, would lead to inquiries into the *reasons* of those moral laws which the Creator has promulgated, and the *foundations* on which they rest. It is an opinion which very generally prevails, even among the more respectable portion of mankind, that the moral laws given forth to men are the *mere dictates of Sovereignty*, and depend solely on the *will* of the Deity, and, consequently, that they might be modified, or even entirely superseded, were it the pleasure of the Supreme Legislator to alter them or to suspend their authority. But this is a most absurd and dangerous position. It would take away from the *inherent excellence* of virtue, and would represent the Divine Being as acting on principles similar to those of an Eastern despot. If such a position were true, it would follow, that all the immoralities, cruelties, oppressions, wars, and butcheries that have taken place in the world, are equally excellent and amiable as truth, justice, virtue, and benevolence, and that the character of infernal fiends is just as lovely and praiseworthy as that of angels and archangels, *provided the Deity willed that such a change should take place.* Were such a change possible, it would not only overturn all the notions we are accustomed to entertain respecting the moral attributes of God, but might ultimately destroy our hopes of future enjoyment, and endanger the happiness of the whole moral universe. But, there is an inherent excellence in moral virtue, and the Deity has willed it to exist, because it is essential to the happiness and order of the intelligent system. It might be shown, that not only the two fundamental principles of religion and morality stated above, but all the moral precepts which flow from them, are founded on the nature of God, and on the relations which subsist among intelligent agents, and that, were they reversed, or their influence suspended, misery would reign uncontrolled through the universe, and in the course of ages the whole moral and intelligent system would be annihilated.*

Now, if men were accustomed to investigate the foundations of morality, and the reasons of those moral precepts which are laid before them as the rule of their conduct, they would perceive a most powerful motive to universal obedience. They would plainly see, that all the laws of God are calculated to secure the happiness of every moral agent who yields obedience to them,—that it is their *interest* to yield a voluntary submission to these laws,—and that *misery* both here and hereafter, is the certain and *necessary* consequence of their violation. It is a common feeling with a considerable portion of mankind, though seldom expressed in words, that the laws of heaven are too strict and unbending,—that they interfere with what they consider their pleasures and enjoyments, and that if one or more of them could be a little modified or relaxed, they would have no objections to attempt a compliance with the rest. But such feelings and sentiments are altogether preposterous and absurd. It would be inconsistent not only with the rectitude, but with the *benevolence* of the Deity, to set aside or to relax a single requisition of that law which is "*perfect*," and which, as it now stands, is calculated to promote the happiness of all worlds. Were he to do so, and to permit moral agents to act accordingly, it would be nothing less than to shut up the path to happiness, and to open the flood-gates of misery upon the intelligent universe. Hence we are told by Him who came to fulfil the law, that, sooner may "heaven and earth pass away," or the whole frame of nature be dissolved, than that "one jot or one tittle can pass from this law." For, as it is founded on the nature of God, and on the relations which subsist between Him and created beings, it must be absolutely perfect and of eternal obligation; and, consequently, nothing could be taken from it, without destroying its perfection, nor any thing added to it, without supposing that it was originally imperfect. Were the bulk of mankind, therefore, capable of entering into the spirit of such investigations, and qualified to perceive the true foundations of moral actions; were they, for example, clearly to perceive, that *truth* is the bond of society, and the foundation of all delightful intercourse among intelligent beings in every world, and that, were the law which enjoins it to be reversed, and rational creatures to act accordingly, all confidence would be completely destroyed,—the inhabitants of all worlds thrown into a state of universal anarchy, and creation transformed into a chaos,—such views and sentiments could not fail of producing a powerful and beneficial influence on the state of morals, and a profound reverence and respect for that law "which is holy, just, and good."

4. Knowledge, in combination with habits of reflection, *would lead to self-examination and self-inspection.* The indolent and untutored mind shuns all exertion of its intellectual faculties, and all serious reflection on what passes within it,

* For a full illustration of these positions, and a variety of topics connected with them, the author begs to refer his readers to a work which he lately published, entitled "*The Philosophy of Religion, or an Illustration of the Moral Laws of the Universe.*"

or has a relation to moral character and conduct. It is incapable of investigating its own powers, of determining the manner in which they should operate, or of ascertaining the secret springs of its actions. Yet, without a habit of reflection and self-examination, we cannot attain a knowledge of ourselves, and, without self-knowledge, we cannot apply aright our powers and capacities, correct our failings and defects, or advance to higher degrees of improvement in knowledge and virtue. In order to ascertain our state, our character, and our duty, such inquiries as the following must frequently and seriously be the subject of consideration. What rank do I hold in the scale of being, and what place do I occupy in the empire of God? Am I merely a sensitive creature, or am I also endowed with moral and intellectual powers? In what relations do I stand to my fellow-creatures, and what duties do I owe them? What is my ultimate destination? Is it merely to pass a few years in eating and drinking, in motion and rest, like the lower animals, or am I designed for another and a higher sphere of existence? In what relation do I stand to my Creator, and what homage, submission, and obedience ought I to yield to him? What are the talents and capacities with which I am endowed, and how shall I apply them to the purposes for which they were given me? What are the weaknesses and deficiencies to which I am subject, and how are they to be remedied? What are the vices and follies to which I am inclined, and by what means may they be counteracted? What are the temptations to which I am exposed, and how shall they be withstood? What are the secret springs of my actions, and by what laws and motives are they regulated? What are the tempers and dispositions which I most frequently indulge, and are they accordant with the rules of rectitude and virtue? What are the prejudices I am apt to entertain, and by what means may they be subdued? What are the affections and appetites in which I indulge, and are they regulated by the dictates of reason and the law of God? What are my great and governing views in life? Are they correspondent to the will of my Creator, and to the eternal destination that awaits me? Wherein do I place my highest happiness? In the pleasures of sense, or in the pleasures of intellect and religion,—in the creature or in the Creator? How have I hitherto employed my moral powers and capacities? How do I stand affected towards my brethren of mankind? Do I hate, or envy, or despise any of them? Do I grudge them prosperity, wish them evil, or purposely injure and affront them? Or do I love them as brethren of the same family, do them all the good in my power, acknowledge their excellencies, and rejoice in their happiness and prosperity?

Such inquiries and self-examinations, when seriously conducted, would necessarily lead to the most beneficial moral results. In leading us to a knowledge of our errors and defects, they would teach us the excellency of *humility*, the reasonableness of this virtue, and the foundation on which it rests, and of course, the folly of pride, and of all those haughty and supercilious tempers which are productive of so much mischief and unhappiness, both in the higher and the lower spheres of life. Pride is uniformly the offspring of self-ignorance. For, if a man will but turn his eyes within, and thoroughly scrutinize himself, so as to perceive his errors and follies, and the germs of vice which lodge in his heart, as well as the low rank he holds in the scale of creation, he would see enough to teach him humbleness of mind, and to render a proud disposition odious and detestable, and inconsistent with the relations in which he stands to his Creator, to his fellow-creatures, and to the universe at large. Such mental investigations would also lead to self-possession, under affronts and injuries, and amidst the hurry and disorder of the passions,—to charity, candour, meekness, and moderation, in regard to the sentiments and conduct of others, to the exercise of self-denial, to decorum and consistency of character, to a wise and steady conduct in life, and to an intelligent performance of the offices of piety and the duties of religion. But how can we ever expect that an ignorant uncultivated mind, unaccustomed to a regular train of rational thought, can enter, with spirit and intelligence, on the process of self-examination? It requires a certain portion, at least, of information, and a habit of reflection, before a man can be qualified to engage in such an exercise; and these qualifications can only be attained by the exercise which the mind receives in the acquisition of general knowledge.—If, then, it be admitted, that self-ignorance is the original spring of all the follies and incongruities we behold in the characters of men, and the cause of all that vanity, censoriousness, malignancy, and vice which abound in the world; and, if self-knowledge would tend to counteract such immoral dispositions, we must endeavour to communicate a certain portion of knowledge to mankind, to fit them for the exercise of self-examination and self-inspection, before we can expect that the moral world will be renovated, and "all iniquity, as ashamed, hide its head, and stop its mouth."

5. Knowledge, by expanding the mind, will enable it to take a clear and comprehensive view of the motives, bearings, tendencies, and consequences of moral actions. A man possessed of a truly enlightened mind, must have his moral sense, or conscience, much more sensible and tender, and more judiciously directed, than that of a person whose understanding is beclouded with ignorance. When he has to choose between good and evil, or between good and bet-

ter, or between any two actions he has to perform, he is enabled to bring before his mind many more arguments, and much higher and nobler arguments and motives, to determine the choice he ought to make. When he is about to perform any particular action, his mental eye is enabled to pierce into the remote consequences which may result from it. He can, in some measure, trace its bearings not only on his friends and neighbours, and the community to which he belongs, but also on surrounding nations, on the world at large, on future generations, and even on the scenes of a future eternity. For an action, whether good or bad, performed by an individual in a certain station in society, may have a powerful moral influence on tribes and nations far beyond the sphere in which it was performed, and on millions who may people the world in the future ages of time. We know that actions, both of a virtuous and vicious nature, performed several thousands of years ago, and in distant places of the world, have had an influence upon the men of the present generation, which will redound either to the honour or the disgrace of the actors, "in that day when God shall judge the world in righteousness, and reward every man according to his works." We also know, that there are certain actions which to some minds may appear either trivial or indifferent, and to other minds beneficial, which nevertheless involve a principle which, if traced to its remoter consequences, would lead to the destruction of the intelligent creation. Now, it is the man of knowledge and of moral perception alone, who can recognise such actions and principles, and trace them to all their natural and legitimate results. He alone can apply, with judgment and accuracy, the general laws of moral action to every particular circumstance, connect the present with the future, and clearly discern the mere semblance of truth and moral rectitude from the reality.

In short, the knowledge of divine revelation, and a serious study of its doctrines and precepts, must accompany every other species of information, if we wish to behold mankind reformed and moralized. It is in the sacred oracles alone, that the will of God, the natural character of man, the remedy of moral evil, the rules of moral conduct, and the means of moral improvement, are clearly and fully unfolded. And the man who either rejects the revelations of heaven, or refuses to study and investigate the truths and moral requisitions they contain, can never expect to rise to the sublime heights of virtue, and to the moral dignity of his nature. But, were the study of the scriptures uniformly conjoined with the study of every other branch of useful knowledge, we should, ere long, behold a wonderful transformation upon the face of the moral world. Pride, selfishness, malice, envy, ambition, and revenge, would gradually be undermined. The spirit of warfare and contention would be subdued; rioting, drunkenness, and debauchery, would be held in abhorrence by all ranks; kindness and affection would unite the whole brotherhood of mankind; peace, harmony, and subordination would be displayed in every department of social life; "our judges would be just, and our exactors righteous; wars would be turned into peace to the ends of the earth, and righteousness and praise spring forth before all the nations." Were moral principle thus diffused among the different classes of society, it could not fail of producing a beneficial influence on the progress of the arts and sciences, and on every thing that might tend to meliorate the condition of our fellow-creatures, and to promote the general improvement of mankind. For, in endeavouring to promote such objects, we meet with as great a difficulty in the *moral* as in the intellectual condition of mankind. The principles of *selfishness*, pride, ambition, and envy, and similar dispositions, create obstacles in the way of scientific and philanthropic improvements, tenfold greater than any which arise from pecuniary resources or physical impediments. But were such principles undermined, and a spirit of good-will and affection pervading the mass of society, the machinery of the moral world would move onward with smoothness and harmony; and mankind, acting in unison, and every one cheerfully contributing to the good of the whole, would accomplish objects, and beneficial transformations on the physical and moral condition of society, far superior to any thing that has hitherto been realized.

To what has been now stated, with regard to the influence of knowledge on moral conduct, it may, perhaps, be objected, that many instances occur of men of genius and learning indulging in dissolute and immoral habits, and that the higher classes of society, who have received a better education than the lower, are nearly as immoral in their conduct. In replying to such an objection, we have to consider, in the first place, *what is the nature of the education such persons have received.* Most of the higher classes have received a grammar-shcool education, and, perhaps, attended a few sessions at an academy or an university. There cannot, however, be reckoned above one in ten who pursues his studies with avidity, and enters into the spirit of the instructions communicated at such seminaries; as it is well known to every one acquainted with the general practice of such students in colleges and academies, that a goodly number of them spend their time as much in folly and dissipation, as in serious study. But, although they had acquired a competent acquaintance with the different branches to which their attention was directed, what is the amount of their acquisitions? A knowledge of the Greek and Latin Classics, and of pagan mythology, in the acquisition of which five years are generally spent at the grammar-school, and two at the university—and the elements of logic, ethics and mathematical philosophy. But such departments of knowledge, *in the way in which they have been generally taught*, have no necessary connexion with religion and moral conduct. On the contrary, by keeping the principles of Christianity carefully out of view, and even insinuating objections against them, some professors of these sciences have promoted the cause of infidelity, and consequently impeded the progress of genuine morality. What aid can be expected to morality from a mere grammar-school education, when the acquisition of words and phrases, and the absurd notions and impure practices connected with Roman and Grecian idolatry, form the prominent objects of attention; and when, as too frequently happens, no instructions in Christianity are communicated, and not even the forms of religion attended to in many of those seminaries? The mere acquisition of languages is not the acquisition of useful knowledge: they are, at best, but the *means* of knowledge; and although we would not discourage any one, who has it in his power, from prosecuting such studies, yet it is from other and more important branches of study that we expect assistance in the cause of moral improvement.

With regard to men of learning and genius, we have likewise to inquire into the nature and tendency of their literary pursuits, before we can ascertain that they are calculated to prevent the influence of immoral propensities and passions. Persons are designated men of learning, who have made proficiency in the knowledge of the Greek, Latin, French, German and other languages,—who are skilled in mythology, antiquities, criticism, and metaphysics, or who are profound students in geometry, algebra, fluxions, and other branches of the mathematics. But it is easy to perceive, that a man may be a profound linguist, grammarian, politician, or antiquarian, and yet not distinguished for virtuous conduct; for such departments of learning have no direct bearing upon moral principle or conduct. On the contrary, *when prosecuted exclusively, to the neglect of the more substantial parts of knowledge*, and *under the influence of certain opinions and prejudices*, they have a tendency to withdraw the attention from the great objects of religion, and consequently from the most powerful motives which excite to moral action.—We have likewise to inquire, whether such persons have made the Christian revelation one great object of their study and attention, and whether they are frequently employed in serious contemplations of the perfections of the Creator, as displayed in the economy of the universe. If such studies be altogether overlooked, we need not wonder that such characters should frequently slide into the paths of infidelity and dissipation; since they neglect an attention to those departments of knowledge which alone can guide them in the paths of rectitude. We may as soon expect to gather "grapes from thorns or figs from thistles," as to expect pure morality from those, however high they may stand in literary acquirements, who either neglect or oppose the great truths of religion.—We do not mean, however, to insinuate, that the subjects alluded to above are either trivial or unworthy of being prosecuted. On the contrary, we are fully persuaded, that there is not a subject which has ever come under human investigation, when prosecuted with proper views, and in connexion with other parts of knowledge, but may be rendered subservient, in some way or another, both to the intellectual and the moral improvement of man. But, when we speak of diffusing useful knowledge among the mass of mankind, we do not so much allude to the capacity of being able to translate from one language into another, of knowing the sentiments of the ancient Greeks and Romans, and the characters and squabbles of their gods and goddesses, or to the faculty of distinguishing ancient coins, fragments of vases, or pieces of armour—as to the facts of history, science, and revelation, particularly in their bearing upon the religious views and the moral conduct of mankind. And, if the attention of the great body of the people were directed to such subjects, from proper principles and motives, and were they exhibited to their view in a lucid and interesting manner, there cannot be the smallest doubt, that the interests of virtue and of pure and undefiled religion would be thereby promoted to an extent far beyond what has ever yet been realized.

---

## SECTION VIII.

### ON THE UTILITY OF KNOWLEDGE IN RELATION TO A FUTURE WORLD.

MAN is a being destined for eternity. The present world through which he is travelling is only a transitory scene, introductory to a future and an immortal existence. When his corporeal frame sinks into the grave, and is resolved into its primitive elements, the intellectual principle by which it was animated shall pass into another region, and be happy or miserable, according to the governing principles by which it was actuated in the present life. The world in which we now reside may be considered as the great nursery of our future and eternal existence, as a state of probation in which we are educating for an immortal life, and as preparatory to our entering on higher scenes of contemplation and enjoyment. In this point of view, it is of importance to consider that our present views and recollections will be carried along with us into that future world, that our virtues or vices will be as *immortal* as ourselves, and influence our *future* as well as our present happiness, and, consequently, that every study in which we engage, every disposition we now cultivate, and every action we perform, is to be regarded as pointing beyond the present to an unseen and eternal existence.

If, then, we admit that the present state is connected with the future, and that the hour of death is not the termination of our existence, it must be a matter of the utmost importance, that the mind of every candidate for immortality be tutored in those departments of knowledge which have a relation to the future world, and which will tend to qualify him for engaging in the employments, and for relishing the pleasures and enjoyments of that state. The following remarks are intended to illustrate this position.

We may remark, in the first place, in general, that *the knowledge acquired in the present state*, whatever be its nature, *will be carried along with us when we wing our flight to the eternal world.* In passing into that world we shall not lose any of the mental faculties we now possess, nor shall we lose our *identity*, or consciousness of being the same persons we now feel ourselves to be; otherwise, we behoved to be a different order of creatures, and consequently could not be the subjects either of reward or of punishment for any thing done in the present state. A destruction of our faculties, or a total change of them, or the loss of consciousness, would be equivalent to an annihilation of our existence. But, if we carry into the future state all our moral and intellectual powers, we must also, of necessity, carry along with them all the recollections of the present life, and all the knowledge, both physical and moral, which these faculties enabled us to acquire. We have an exemplification of this in the parable of our Saviour respecting the rich man and Lazarus, where Abraham is represented as addressing the former in these words; "Son, *remember*, that thou in thy lifetime receivedst thy good things, and likewise Lazarus evil things;" evidently implying, that the rich man retained the power of *memory*, that he possessed a consciousness that he was the same thinking being that existed in a former state, and that he had a perfect recollection of the conduct he pursued, and the scenes in which he was placed in this sublunary world. If, then, it be admitted, that we shall be, substantially, the same intellectual beings as at present, though placed in different circumstances, and that the ideas and moral principles we now acquire will pass along with us into futurity, and influence our conduct and happiness in that state,—it cannot be a matter of indifference whether the mind of an immortal being be left to grope amidst the mists of ignorance, and to sink into immorality, or be trained up in the knowledge of every thing that has a bearing on its eternal destination. On the contrary, nothing can be of higher value and importance to every human being, considered as immortal, than to be trained to habits of reasoning and reflection, and to acquire that knowledge of his Creator, of himself, of his duty, and of the relations in which he stands to this world and to the next, which will qualify him for the society in which he is hereafter to mingle, and the part he has to act in a higher scene of action and enjoyment. For, as gross ignorance is the source of immoral action, and as immoral principles and habits *unfit the soul* for the pleasures and employments of an immortal state, the man who is allowed to remain amidst the natural darkness of his understanding, can have little hope of happiness in the future world since he is destitute of those qualifications which are requisite in order to his relishing its enjoyments.

*Scientific knowledge*, as well as that which is commonly designated theological, *is to be considered as having a relation to the future world.* Science, as I have already had occasion to notice, is nothing else than an investigation of the divine perfections and operations as displayed in the economy of the universe; and we have every ground to conclude, both from reason and from revelation, that such investigations will be carried forward, on a more enlarged scale, in the future world, where the intellectual powers, freed from the obstructions which now impede their operation, will become more vigorous and expansive, and a more extensive scene of divine operation be presented to the view. There are certain *applications* of scientific principles, indeed, which may have a reference solely to the condition of society in the present life, such as, in the construction of cranes, diving-bells, speaking-trumpets, steam-carriages and fire-engines; but the general principles on which such machines are constructed, may be applicable to thousands of objects and operations in other worlds with which we are at present unacquainted. The views, however, which science has opened of the wisdom and benevolence of the Deity, of the multiplicity of ideas and conceptions which have existed in his infinite mind, of his almighty power, and of the boundless range of his operations—will not be lost when we enter into the eternal world. They will prepare the soul for higher scenes of contemplation, for acquiring more expansive views of divine perfection, and for taking more extensive and sublime excursions through the boundless empire of Omnipotence. The same may be affirmed of the principles of arithmetic, algebra, geometry, conic sections, and other departments of the mathematics, which contain truths that are eternal and unchangeable, and that are applicable in every mode of existence, and to the circumstances of all worlds. Such knowledge may form the ground work of all our future improvements in the world beyond the grave, and give to those who have acquired it, in conjunction with the cultivation of moral principle, a superiority over others in the employments and investigations peculiar to that higher sphere of existence; and, consequently, a more favourable and advantageous outset into the new and unknown regions of the invisible state. To suppose, that the leading principles of scientific knowledge are of utility only in the present world, is not only contrary to every enlightened idea we can form of the future state, either from reason or revelation, but would remove some of the strongest motives which should induce us to engage in the prosecution of useful knowledge. If science is to be considered as altogether confined in its views and effects, to the transitory scene of this mortal state, its attainment becomes a matter of comparatively trivial importance. To a man hastening to the verge of life, there could be no strong inducement to listen to its deductions or to engage in its pursuits. But, if the principles of science, when combined with the truths of revelation, extend to higher objects than the construction of machinery and the embellishment of human life,—if they point beyond the present to a future world, if they tend to expand our views of the attributes of the Divinity, and of the grandeur of his kingdom,—and if they prepare the mind for entering into more ample views and profound investigations of his plans and operations, in that state of immortality to which we are destined,—it must be a matter of importance to every human being, that his mind be imbued with such knowledge, as introductory to the employments of that eternal world which lies before him.—But, we may remark more particularly

In the second place, that *the acquisition of general knowledge, and habits of mental activity, would induce persons to serious inquiries into the evidences of a future state.* Although there are few persons, in a Christian country, who deny the existence of a future world, yet we have too much reason to believe, that the great majority of the population in every country are *not thoroughly convinced* of this important truth, and that they pass their lives just as if the present were the ultimate scene of their destination. Notwithstanding all the "church-going" which is so common among us, both among the higher and the lower classes, and the numerous sermons which are preached in relation to this subject, it does not appear, that the one-half of our population have any fixed and impressive belief of the reality of an eternal world. If it were otherwise, it would be more frequently manifested in their general temper, conversation and conduct. But we find the great mass of society as keenly engaged in the all-engrossing pursuit of wealth and honours, as if the enjoyments of this world were to last for ever. In general conversation in the social circle, the topic of a future world, and our relation to it, is studiously avoided. While a person may talk with the utmost ease about a projected voyage to America, the East Indies, or Van Diemen's Land, and the geographical peculiarities of these regions, and be listened to with pleasure—were he to talk, in certain respectable companies, of his departure to another world, and of the important realities to which he will be introduced in that state,—were he even to suggest a hint, that the scene of our eternal destination ought occasionally to form the subject of conversation,—either a sarcastic sneer or a solemn gloom would appear on every face, and he would be regarded as a wild enthusiast or a sanctimonious hypocrite. But why should men manifest such a degree of apathy in regard to this topic, and even an aversion to the very idea of it, if they live under solemn impressions of their connexion with an immortal existence? Every one who admits the idea of a future world, must also admit, that it is one of the most interesting and momentous subjects that can occupy his attention, and that it as far exceeds in importance the concerns of this life, as the ages of eternity exceed the fleeting periods of time. And, if so, why should we not appear as eager and interested in conversation on this subject, as we sometimes are in relation to a voyage to some distant land? Yet, among the majority of our fellow-men, there is scarcely any thing to which their attention is less directed, and the very idea of it is almost lost amidst the bustle of business, the acquisition of wealth, the dissipations of society, and the vain pageantry of fashionable life. Among many other causes of the indifference which prevails on this subject, *ignorance* and mental inactivity are none of the least. Immersed in sensual gratifications and pursuits, unacquainted with the pleasures of intellect, and unaccustomed to rational trains of reflection, multitudes pass through life without any serious consideration of the future scene of another world, resolved, at the hour of dissolution, to take their chance with the generations that have gone before them. But, were men once aroused to mental activity, and to the exercise of their reasoning powers on important objects, they would be qualified for investigating the evidences which demonstrate the immortality of man, which could not fail to impress their minds with a strong conviction of the dignity of their intellectual natures, and of their high destination. Those evidences are to be found in the Christian revelation which has "brought life and immortality to light," and thrown a radiance on the scenes beyond the grave. But, even independently of revelation, the evidences which prove the immortal destiny of man, from the light of nature, are so strong and powerful, that, when weighed with seriousness and impartiality, they must appear satisfactory to every candid and inquiring mind. When we consider *the universal belief* of the doctrine of man's immortality which has prevailed in all ages and nations—when we consider *the desire of future existence* implanted in the human breast—*the noble intellectual faculties* with which man is endowed, and the strong *desire of knowledge* which forms a part of his constitution—the *capacity of making perpetual progress* towards intellectual and moral perfection—*the unlimited range of view* which is opened to the human faculties throughout *the immensity of space and duration*—the *moral powers* of action with which man is endowed, and their capacity of perpetual expansion and activity—the apprehensions and *forebodings* of the mind, when under the influence of remorse—the *disordered state of the moral world* when contrasted with the systematic order of the material—the *unequal distribution of rewards and punishments* when viewed in connexion with the justice of God—the *absurdity* of admitting that *the thinking principle in men will ever be annihilated*—and the *blasphemous and absurd consequences* which would follow, if the idea of a future state of retribution were rejected; when we attend to these and similar considerations, we perceive an assemblage of arguments, which, when taken in combination with each other, carry irresistible evidence to the mind of every unbiassed inquirer, that man is destined to an immortal existence—an evidence amounting to a moral demonstration, and no less satisfactory than that on which we rest our belief of the existence of the Eternal Mind.* But the greater part of mankind, in their present untutored state, are incapable of entering into such inquiries and investigations. For want of moral and intellectual instruction, they may be said to "have eyes, but see not, ears, but hear not, neither do they understand," and hence, they pass through the scenes of mortality, almost unconscious of their relation to the eternal world, and altogether unprepared for its exercises and enjoyments.

In the next place, *the acquisition of knowledge, in connexion with the cultivation of moral principles and Christian affections, would tend to prepare the mind for the intercourse and employments of the future world.* From divine revelation, we are assured, that in the future state of happiness, the righteous shall not only join the company of "the spirits of just men made perfect," but shall also be admitted into "the general assembly of angels. With these pure and superior intelligences, and, doubtless too, with the inhabitants of other worlds, shall the redeemed inhabitants of our globe hold delightful intercourse, and join in their sublime conversation on the most exalted subjects. One of the employments in which they will be incessantly engaged, will be, to contemplate the divine works and administration, and to investigate the wonders of creating power, wisdom, and goodness, as displayed throughout the universe. For such are the representations given in scripture of the exercises of the heavenly world. Its inhabitants are represented as raising the following song of praise to their Creator, "Great and marvellous are thy works, Lord God Almighty! Just and true are thy ways, thou King of saints," which evidently implies, that both the wonders of his creation, and the plan of his moral government, are the subjects of their intense study and investigation. And, in another scene exhibited in the book of Revelation, they are represented in the sublime adorations they offer to "Him who liveth for ever and ever," as exclaiming, "Thou art worthy, O Lord, to receive glory, and honour, and power; for thou hast created all things, and for thy pleasure they are and were created," plainly indicating, that the scenes of the material universe, and the divine perfections as displayed in them, are the objects of their incessant contemplation.

Now, in order to our being prepared for such intercourses and employments, two grand qualifications are indispensably requisite. In the first place, the cultivation of moral principle and conduct, or in other words, the attainment of that *holiness* which the scriptures enjoin, "without which," we are assured, "no man can see the Lord," that is, can hold no delightful intercourse with him through the medium of his works and providential dispensations. Without this qualification, we are altogether unfit for being introduced into the assembly of angels and other pure intelligences, and for joining with them in their holy services and sublime adorations—as unfit as an ignorant Hotentot, a wild Bosheman, or the lowest dregs of society, would be to take a part in an assembly of learned divines, statesmen, or philosophers. In order to a delightful association with any rank of intelligences, there must exist a certain congeniality of disposition and sentiment, without which, an intimate intercourse would be productive of happiness to neither party. Persons of proud and revengeful dispositions, and addicted to vicious indulgence, could find no enjoyment in a society where all is humility and affection, harmony and love; nor could pure and holy beings delight in associating with them, without supposing the moral laws of the Creator, and the constitution of the intelligent universe entirely subverted. Such characters are as opposite to each other, as light and darkness; and, therefore, we may as soon expect to make the East and West points to meet together, or to stop the planets in their career, as to form a harmonious union be-

* For a full illustration of these and other evidences of a future state, along with various topics connected with this subject, the author respectfully refers his readers to a work which he lately published, entitled "*The Philosophy of a Future State.*"

tween the ignorant and vicious, and the enlightened and virtuous inhabitants of the celestial world. In the next place, a knowledge of the character of God, of his moral dispensations, and of his works of creation, must form a preparation for the exercises of the heavenly state; since these are some of the subjects which occupy the attention of "the innumerable company of angels and the spirits of just men made perfect." But how could we be supposed to engage in such studies, and to relish such employments, if we remain altogether unacquainted with them till our spirits take their flight from these tabernacles of clay? How could a man whose mind is continually grovelling among the meanest and the most trivial objects, whose soul never rises above the level of his daily labours, which necessity compels him to perform, whose highest gratification is to carouse with his fellows, to rattle a set of dice, or to shuffle a pack of cards, and who is incapable of prosecuting a train of rational thought—how could such a one be supposed qualified for entering, with intelligence and delight, into the sublime investigations, and the lofty contemplations which arrest the attention, and form the chief exercises "of the saints in light?" There is an utter incongruity in the idea, that a rude and ignorant mind could relish the enjoyments of the heavenly world, unless it be enlightened and transformed into the image of its Creator; and we have no warrant from revelation to conclude that such a transformation will be effected, after the spirit has taken its flight to the invisible state.

But it is easy to conceive what transporting pleasures will be felt by an enlightened and virtuous individual when he is ushered into a scene where his prospects will be enlarged, his faculties expanded, and the causes which now obstruct their energies for ever removed. He will feel himself in his native element, will resume his former investigations on a more enlarged scale, and with more vigour and activity, and enjoy the prospect of perpetually advancing from one degree of knowledge and felicity to another throughout an interminable succession of existence. Having studied the moral character of God as displayed in his word, and in the dispensations of his providence; having acquired, after all his researches, only a faint and imperfect glimpse of his moral attributes; having met with many difficulties and labyrinths in the movements of the divine government which he was altogether unable to unravel, which produced an ardent longing after a more enlarged sphere of vision—how gratifying to such a mind must it be, to contemplate the divine character in the fulness of its glory, to behold the apparent inconsistencies of the divine government reconciled, its intricate mazes unravelled, its wisdom and rectitude displayed, and the veil which concealed from mortals the reasons of its procedure for ever withdrawn! Having taken a cursory survey of the displays of divine wisdom and goodness, in the arrangement of our sublunary system, and in the construction of the animal and vegetable tribes with which it is furnished; having directed his views, by the light of science, to the celestial regions; having caught a glimpse of the astonishing operations of almighty power in the distant spaces of the firmament; having been overwhelmed with wonder and amazement at the extent and grandeur of the divine empire; having cast many a longing look towards distant worlds, mingled with many anxious inquiries into their nature and destination which he was unable to resolve, and having felt an ardent desire to learn the history of their population, and to behold the scene of the universe a little more unfolded—what transporting joys must be felt by such an individual, when he shall enter into a world where "he shall know even as also he is known;" where the veil which intercepted his view of the wonders of creating power shall be removed; where the cherubim and the seraphim, who have winged their flight through regions of immensity impassable by mortals, shall rehearse the history of other worlds; where the sphere of vision will be enlarged, the faculties invigorated, and the glories of divine goodness, wisdom and omnipotence displayed in all their effulgence! Having familiarized such objects to his mind, during this first stage of his existence, he will enter on the prosecution of new discoveries of divine perfection, with a renovated holy ardour, of which rude and grovelling minds are incapable, which will fill his soul with extatic rapture—even "with joy unspeakable and full of glory."

Let us suppose, for the sake of illustration, two individuals of opposite characters entering the future world at the same time—the one rude, ignorant, and vicious, and the other "renewed in the spirit of his mind," and enlightened with all the knowledge which science and revelation can furnish—it is evident, that, although they were both ushered into the same locality, their state and enjoyments would be altogether different. The one would sink, as it were, to his natural level, following the principles, propensities and passions which he previously indulged; and, although he were admitted into the society of pure and enlightened spirits, he would remain as a cheerless, insulated wretch, without intellectual activity, and destitute of enjoyment. Finding no pleasures suited to his benighted mind and his grovelling affections, he would be fain to flee to other regions and to more congenial associates, as the owl flies from the vocal grove and the society of the feathered choir, and prefers the shades of night to the beams of day. Like this gloomy bird, which delights in obscure retreats and rugged ruins, and has no relish for blooming gardens and flowery meads—the unenlightened and unsanctified soul would feel itself unhappy and *imprisoned*, as it were, even amidst triumphant spirits, and the splendours of immortal day. Whereas the other, having ardently longed for such a state, and having previously undergone the requisite preparation for its enjoyments, feels himself in a region suited to his taste, mingles with associates congenial to his disposition, engages in exercises to which he was formerly accustomed, and in which he delighted, beholds a prospect, boundless as the universe, rising before him, on which his faculties may be exercised with everlasting improvement and everlasting delight, and, consequently, experiences a "fulness of joy" which can never be interrupted, but will be always increasing "world without end."

Such are the views we must necessarily adopt respecting the state and enjoyments of these two characters in the life to come; and there is no resisting of the conclusion we have deduced respecting the ignorant and vicious individual, without supposing that something, equivalent to a miracle, will be performed in his behalf, immediately after his entrance into the invisible world, to fit him for the employments of a state of happiness. But, for such an opinion we have no evidence, either from scripture or from reason. It would be contrary to every thing we know of the moral government of God; it would strike at the foundation of all religion and morality; it would give encouragement to ignorance and vice; it would render nugatory all the efforts of a virtuous character to increase in knowledge and holiness during the present life, and it would give the ignorant and the licentious an equal reason for expecting eternal happiness in the world to come, as the most profound Christian philosophers, or the most enlightened and pious divines. Besides, we are assured by the "Faithful and True Witness," that, as in the future world, "he who is righteous shall remain righteous still," so "he who is unjust shall remain unjust still, and he who is filthy shall remain filthy still;" which expressions seem evidently to imply, that no more opportunities will be granted for reforming what had been amiss, and recovering the polluted and unrighteous soul to purity and rectitude. *

If, then, it appears, that we shall carry the knowledge and moral habits we acquire in this life along with us into the other world,—and if a certain portion of rational and religious information and moral principle is essentially requisite to prepare us for the employments and felicities of that state—by refusing to patronise every scheme by which a general diffusion of knowledge may be promoted, we not only allow our fellow-men to wander amidst the mists of superstition, and to run heedlessly into numerous dangers, both physical and moral, we not only deprive them of exquisite intellectual enjoyments, and prevent the improvement of the arts and sciences, but we deprive them, in a certain degree, of the chance of obtaining happiness in a state of immortality. For as ignorance is the parent of vice, and as vicious propensities and indulgences necessarily lead to misery, both here and hereafter, the man whose mind is left to grope amidst intellectual darkness, can enjoy no well-founded hope of felicity in the life to come, since he is unqualified for the associations, the contemplations, and the employments of that future existence. As in the material creation, light was the first substance created before the chaos was reduced to beauty and order, so, in the intellectual world, knowledge, or light in the understanding, is the first thing which restores the moral system to harmony and order. It is the commencement of every process that leads to improvement, comfort, and moral order in this life, and that prepares us for the enjoyments of the life to come. But ignorance is both the emblem and the prelude of "the blackness of darkness for ever." This is one of the most powerful considerations which should induce every philanthropist to exert every nerve, and to further every scheme which has for its object to diffuse liberty, knowledge and moral principle among all the inhabitants of the earth.

---

## SECTION IX.

### ON THE UTILITY OF GENERAL KNOWLEDGE IN RELATION TO THE STUDY OF DIVINE REVELATION.

Of all the departments of knowledge to which the human mind can be directed, there is none of greater importance than that which exhibits the real character and condition of man as a moral agent—his relation to the Deity—his eternal destiny—the way in which he may be delivered from the effects of moral evil—and the worship and service he owes to his Almighty Creator. On these and kindred topics, the

* Whatever opinion we may form as to the doctrine of *Universal Restoration*,—it will be admitted, even by the abettors of that doctrine, that an unholy and unenlightened soul is unfit for celestial happiness, *on its first entrance into the future world*, and thousands or millions of years, or a period equivalent to what is included in the phrase, "ages of ages," may elapse before it is fit for being restored to the dignity of its nature, and the joys of heaven. Even on this supposition, (although it were warranted by Scripture) the preparation of human beings in the present life for a state of future happiness, must be a matter of the highest importance, since it prevents the sufferings denoted by "devouring fire, weeping, wailing and gnashing of teeth," during the indefinite and long-continued period of "ages of ages."

Christian revelation affords the most clear and satisfactory information, and the details which it furnishes on these subjects are of the highest moment, and deeply interesting to every inhabitant of the globe. But ignorance, leagued with depravity and folly, has been the cause that the sacred oracles have so frequently been treated with indifference and contempt; and that those who have professed to recognise them as the intimations of the will of Deity have been prevented from studying them with intelligence, and contemplating the facts they exhibit in all their consequences and relations.

In order to a profitable study of the doctrines, facts and prophecies contained in the Bible, it is requisite, in the first place, that a deep and thorough conviction be produced in the mind, that they are indeed the revelations of heaven, addressed to man on earth to direct his views and conduct as an accountable agent, and a candidate for immortality. From ignorance of the *evidences* on which the truth of Christianity rests, multitudes of thoughtless mortals have been induced to reject its authority, and have glided down the stream of licentious pleasure, "sporting themselves with their own deceivings," till they landed in wretchedness and ruin. The religion of the Bible requires only to be examined with care, and studied with humility and reverence, in order to produce a full conviction of its celestial origin; and wherever such dispositions are brought into contact with a calm and intelligent investigation of the evidences of revelation, and of the facts and doctrines it discloses, the mind will not only discern its superiority to every other system of religion, but will perceive the beauty and excellence of its discoveries, and the absolute necessity of their being studied and promulgated in order to raise the human race from that degradation into which they have been so long immersed, and to promote the renovation of the moral world. And, those objections and difficulties which previously perplexed and harassed the inquirer will gradually evanish, as the mists of the morning before the orb of day.

The *evidences* of Christianity have been generally distributed into the *external* and the *internal.* The external may again be divided into *direct* or *collateral.* The *direct* evidences are such as arise from the nature, consistency, and probability of the facts; and from the simplicity, uniformity, competency and fidelity of the testimonies by which they are supported. The *collateral* evidences are those which arise from the concurrent testimonies of heathen writers, or others, which corroborate the history of Christianity and establish its leading facts. The *internal* evidences arise, either from the conformity of the announcements of revelation to the known character of God, from their aptitude to the frame and circumstances of man, or from those convictions impressed upon the mind by the agency of the Divine Spirit.

In regard to the *external* evidences, the following propositions can be supported both from the testimonies of profane writers, the Scriptures of the New Testament, and other ancient Christian writings; viz. 1, "That there is satisfactory evidence that many professing to be original witnesses of the Christian miracles, passed their lives in labours, dangers, and sufferings, voluntarily undergone in attestation of the accounts which they delivered, and solely in consequence of their belief of those accounts; and that they also submitted, from the same motives, to new rules of conduct." And, 2, "That there is *not* satisfactory evidence, that persons pretending to be original witnesses of any other miracles, have acted in the same manner, in attestation of the accounts which they delivered, and solely in consequence of their belief of the truth of these accounts." These propositions can be substantiated to the conviction of every serious and unbiassed inquirer; they form the basis of the external evidence of the Christian religion; and, when their truth is clearly discerned, the mind is irresistibly led to the conclusion, that the doctrines and facts promulgated by the first propagators of Christianity are true.

The following propositions can also be satisfactorily proved, viz. That the Jewish religion is of great antiquity, and that Moses was its founder—that the books of the Old Testament were extant long before the Christian era; a Greek translation of them having been laid up in the Alexandrian library in the days of Ptolemy Philadelphus—that these books are in the main genuine, and the histories they contain worthy of credit—that many material facts which are recorded in the Old Testament are also mentioned by very ancient heathen writers—that Christianity is not a modern religion, but was professed by great multitudes nearly 1800 years ago—that Jesus Christ, the founder of this religion, was crucified at Jerusalem during the reign of Tiberius Cæsar—that the first publishers of this religion wrote books containing an account of the life and doctrines of their master, several of which bore the names of those books which now make up the *New Testament*—that these books were frequently quoted and referred to by numerous writers from the days of the apostles to the fourth century and downwards—that they are genuine, or written by the authors whose names they bear—that the histories they contain are in the main agreeable to those facts which were asserted by the first preachers and received by the first converts to Christianity—that the facts, whether natural or supernatural, which they record, are transmitted to us with as great a degree of evidence (if not greater) as any historical fact recorded by historians of allowed character and reputation—and that these books were written under a superintendant inspiration. These and a variety of similar propositions intimately connected with them can be fully substantiated; and the necessary conclusion of the whole is, that Christianity is a revelation from God to man, and that its truths are to be believed, and its precepts practised by all to whom they are addressed.

*Miracles* form one part of the external evidence by which revealed religion is supported. If God, in compassion to our benighted and bewildered race, has thought fit to communicate a revelation of his will, there is no conceivable mode by which that revelation could be more powerfully attested, than by empowering the messengers whom he inspired to work miracles, as attestations of the truth of the doctrines they declared. Accordingly we find, that at the introduction both of the Jewish and the Christian dispensations, a series of uncontrolled miracles was exhibited to those to whom the messengers of revelation were sent, as evidences that they acted under the authority of the Creator of the universe. Under the administration of Moses, who founded the Jewish economy, the waters of Egypt were turned into blood, darkness covered all that country for three days, thunders and hail terrified its inhabitants and destroyed the fruits of their ground, and all their first-born were slain by a celestial messenger in one night—the Red Sea was parted asunder, the tribes of Israel passed in safety through its waves, while their enemies "sank as lead in the mighty waters;" water was brought from the flinty rock, manna from heaven was rained down to supply the wants of two millions of human beings in a barren wilderness; mount Sinai was made to tremble to its centre, and was surrounded with flames and smoke; Korah, Dathan, and Abiram, with all the thousands that joined their conspiracy, were by a miraculous earthquake swallowed up in a moment; Jordan was divided when its waters overflowed its banks, and at the sound of horns the strong walls of Jericho fell prostrate to the ground. When Jesus Christ introduced the gospel dispensation, he gave incontrovertible proofs of his divine mission, by curing diseases of every description merely by his word, causing the lame to walk, the deaf to hear, the dumb to speak, and the blind to see; raising the dead to life, stilling the tempestuous waves and the stormy wind; turning water into wine, feeding five thousand men in a wilderness on a few loaves and fishes; and, particularly, by his own resurrection from the dead, after he had been "crucified and slain." These, as well as the miracles wrought by Moses, were demonstrative evidences of the agency and interference of the Most High; they were completely beyond the power of mere human agency, and were altogether different from the tricks of jugglers and impostors. They were performed in the open face of day, in the presence of multitudes of persons of every description; they were level to the comprehension of every man whose faculties and senses were in a sound state; and the conclusion which every unbiassed mind behooved to draw from them, was, that "no man could do such miracles unless God was with him;" and, consequently, that the truths declared by those who were empowered to perform them, are the revelations of heaven; for it would be inconsistent with the nature of the Divine Being to suppose, that he would interpose his almighty power to control the laws of nature, for the purpose of giving his sanction to falsehood or imposture.

Of the reality of the miraculous events to which I have alluded, we have as high a degree of evidence as we have for the reality of any other fact recorded in the scriptures or in the history of the world. The single fact of *the resurrection of Christ*, a fact so important in the Christian system, and with which all its other facts and doctrines are essentially connected, rests upon a weight of evidence so great that the rejection of it would be almost equivalent to the adoption of universal scepticism. This fact does not rest upon the testimony of an unknown individual, or even of an unknown multitude, but on the twelve apostles who had been previously chosen for this purpose, who had accompanied their Master in all his journeys, who had been the witnesses of his miracles, sufferings, and crucifixion, and who affirmed, without the least hesitation, and in the face of every threatening and persecution, that they had seen him alive at different times, and held intimate converse with him after he had risen from the dead. It rests likewise on the testimony of the seventy disciples, and on that of the five hundred brethren who had seen the Lord after his resurrection. These persons had full opportunity of information as to the fact they asserted; they could not be deceived, for it was brought within the evidence of their senses. They *saw* the body of the Lord Jesus after he had been crucified and laid in the tomb—not with a passing glance, but at different times and in divers places; they had an opportunity of *handling* it to convince them it was no phantom; they *heard* him speak, and entered into intimate conversation with him on the subject of their future ministry. They saw him, not only separately, but together; not only by night, but by day, not at a distance, but immediately before them. And as they could not be deceived themselves, they could have no motive for deceiving others; for they were aware that, by so doing, they exposed themselves to scorn, persecution, sufferings, and death itself, without the most distant hope of recompense either in this world or in another. Their character and conduct were strictly watched and scrutinized. Their enemies had taken every precaution which human wisdom could devise, to prevent the dead body of their Master from being removed from the sepulchre, either by fraud or by violence, and to secure the public from being deluded by any attempt at imposture. And yet, only a few days after he was buried, and in the very place where he was crucified, his resurrection was publicly asserted and proclaimed; and no attempt was made on the part of the Jewish rulers to invalidate the testimony of the apostles, by producing the dead body of him whom they had crucified—on whose tomb they had set a seal and a guard of Roman soldiers. For it is evident, that if his body could have been found, they would have produced it as the shortest and most decisive confutation of the story of the resurrection. All these circumstances being considered, to suppose that the apostles either were deceived, or attempted to deceive the world, would be to admit a miracle as great as that of the resurrection itself. But if the fact of Christ's resurrection be admitted, the truth of the evangelical history and of the doctrines of Christianity follows as a necessary consequence.

*Prophecy* forms another branch of the external evidences of religion. As God alone can perceive with certainty the future actions of free agents, and the remote consequences of those laws of nature which he himself established—prophecy, when clearly fulfilled, affords the most convincing evidence of an intimate and supernatural communion between God and the person who uttered the prediction. It is evident, however, that prophecy was never intended as an evidence of an original revelation. From its very nature it is totally unfit for such a purpose, because it is impossible, without some extrinsic proof of its divine origin, to ascertain whether any prophecy be true or false, till the period arrive when it ought to be accomplished. But when it is fulfilled, it affords complete evidence, that he who uttered it spake by the spirit of God, and that the doctrines he taught were dictated by the same spirit, and, consequently, true. To us, therefore, who live in an age posterior to the fulfilment of many of the ancient prophecies, and while some of them are actually accomplishing, the fulfilment of these predictions forms a powerful and striking evidence of the divine authority of the writers both of the Old and the New Testament.

The first prophecy which was given forth in the garden of Eden, that "the seed of the woman should bruise the head of the serpent," and the predictions of the Jewish prophets respecting the appearance, the miracles, the sufferings, the death, resurrection, and subsequent glory of Messiah, and the opposition he was to endure from the people to whom he was sent, were literally accomplished, when Jesus Christ appeared in the world; and the narrations of the evangelists may be considered as a commentary upon these ancient prophecies. The deliverance of the Jews from the Babylonish captivity, and its accomplishment by Cyrus,—the conquest of Egypt by Nebuchadnezzar, foretold by Jeremiah,—the succession of the Assyrian, Persian, Grecian, and Roman monarchies,—the persecution of the Jews under Antiochus Epiphanes, and the erection of the papal kingdom foretold by Daniel,—and the destruction of Jerusalem and the dreadful miseries which should befall its inhabitants, foretold by Jesus Christ, have all received their accomplishment, according to the spirit and import of the original predictions, and this accomplishment is embodied in the history of nations.

But there are prophecies which were uttered several thousands of years ago, of the accomplishment of which we have *sensible evidence* at the present moment, if we look around us and consider the state of the nations and empires of the world. For example, it was prophesied respecting Ishmael, the son of Abraham, "that he should be a wild man; that his hand should be against every man, and every man's hand against him; that he should dwell in the presence of all his brethren; that he should be multiplied exceedingly, beget twelve princes, and become a great nation." This prediction has been literally accomplished in the *Arabs*, the undoubted descendants of Ishmael, who, for time immemorial, have been robbers by land and pirates by sea; and though their hands have been against every man, and every man's hand against them, they have always dwelt, and at this day, still dwell, in "the presence of their brethren," a free and independent people. The greatest conquerors in the world have attempted to subdue them, but their attempts uniformly failed of success. When they appeared on the brink of ruin, they were signally and providentially delivered. Alexander was preparing an expedition against them, when he was cut off in the flower of his age. Pompey was in the career of his conquest, when urgent affairs called him to another quarter. Gallius had penetrated far into their country, when a fatal disease destroyed great numbers of his men, and obliged him to return. Trajan besieged their capital city; but was defeated by thunder, and lightning, and whirlwinds. Severus besieged the same city twice, and was twice repelled from before it. Even the Turks have been unable to subdue the Arabs, or even to restrain their depredations; and they are obliged to pay them a sort of annual tribute for the safe passage of the pilgrims who go to Mecca to pay their devotions. The curse pronounced upon *Ham*; the father of Canaan, could also be shown to have been signally accomplished in the case of the Canaanites, and the Africans, their descendants, who have been literally "a servant of servants to their brethren." They were under the dominion, first of the Romans, then of the Saracens, and now of the Turks. And in what ignorance, barbarity, *slavery*, and misery do most of them remain? Many thousands of them are every year bought and sold, like beasts in the market, and conveyed from one quarter of the world to do the work of beasts in another. The present state of *Babylon* is also a striking accomplishment of the denunciations of ancient prophecy. When we consider the vast extent and magnificence of that ancient city, "the glory of kingdoms and the beauty of the Chaldee's excellency," we should have thought it almost *impossible* that it should have become "an utter desolation," that "the wild beasts should cry in its desolate houses, and dragons in its pleasant palaces," and that "it should never be inhabited nor dwelt in from generation to generation," as the prophet Isaiah had foretold, several hundreds of years prior to its destruction, and when it was flourishing in the height of its glory.* Yet we know for certain, that this once magnificent metropolis, whose hanging gardens were reckoned one of the seven wonders of the world, has become so complete a desolation, that the besom of destruction has left scarcely a single trace of its former grandeur; and it is a subject of dispute among travellers, whether the exact site on which it was built be yet ascertained.

In short, the present state of the Jews, compared with ancient predictions, is one of the most striking and convincing proofs of the literal fulfilment of the Old Testament prophecies. The following prediction respecting them was uttered more than 1700 years before the commencement of the Christian era: "The Lord shall scatter thee among all people from the one end of the earth even unto the other. And among those nations shalt thou find no ease, neither shall the sole of thy foot have rest, but the Lord shall give thee a trembling heart, and failing of eyes, and sorrow of mind."—"And thou shalt become an astonishment, a proverb, and a by-word among all the nations whither the Lord shall lead you."† The whole history of the Jewish nation since the destruction of Jerusalem, as well as the present state of that singular people, forms a striking commentary upon these ancient predictions, and shows, that they had been fully and literally accomplished. The Jews, it is well known, have been dispersed almost over the whole face of the globe for more than seventeen hundred years; they have been despised and hated by all nations; they have suffered the most cruel persecutions; "their life has hung in doubt before them, and they have feared day and night," both for their property and their lives; they have been sold in multitudes, like cattle in the market; they have been exposed on public theatres, to exhibit fights, or be devoured by wild beasts. So strong were popular prejudices and suspicions against them, that in the year 1348, on *suspicion* of their having poisoned the springs and wells, a million and a half of them were cruelly massacred. In 1492, 500,000 of them were driven out of Spain, and 150,000 from Portugal, and even at the present moment they are, in most places, subjected both to civil incapacities and unchristian severities. Yet, notwithstanding the hatred and contempt in which they are held, wherever they appear, they are most obstinately tenacious of the religion of their fathers, although their ancestors were so prone to apostatize from it; and although most of them seem to be utter strangers to piety, and pour contempt on the *moral* precepts of their own law, they are most obstinately attached to the *ceremonial* institutions of it, burdensome and inconvenient as they are. They have never been amalgamated with any of the nations among which they dwelt; they remain a distinct people, notwithstanding their numerous dispersions; their numbers are not diminished; and, were they collected into one body, they would form a nation as numerous and powerful as in the most flourishing periods of the Jewish commonwealth. The existence of the Jews in such circumstances, *as a distinct nation*, so contrary to the history of every other nation, and to the course of human affairs in similar cases, may justly be considered as *a standing miracle* for the truth of divine revelation. Such a scene in the conduct of the divine government, cannot be paralleled in the history of any other people on the face of the earth; and their being permitted so long to survive the dissolution of their own state, and to continue a distinct nation, is doubtless intended for the accomplishment of another important prediction, viz. that "they may return and seek the Lord their God, and David their king, and fear the Lord and his goodness in the latter days." In the present day, we perceive a tendency towards this wished-for consummation. Within these last thirty years, a greater number of Jews has been converted to the profession of the Christian faith than had happened for a thousand years before. And when they shall be collected from all the regions in which they are now scattered, and brought to the acknowledgment of Jesus Christ as the true Messiah, and to submission to his laws, and reinstated either in their own land or in some other portion of the globe, such an event will form a sensible demonstration of the divinity of our religion, level to the comprehension of all nations, and which all the sneers and sophisms of sceptics and infidels will never be able to withstand.

The *internal* evidences of Christianity are those which are deduced from the nature of the facts, doctrines and moral precepts which it reveals, and from the harmony and consistency of all its parts. The following is a brief summary

* Isaiah xiii. 19–22.
† Deut. ch. xxviii.

of the leading views which may be taken of this subject.

1. *The dignity and majesty of the style* in which many portions of the Scriptures are written, and *the sublimity of many of the ideas and sentiments* they contain, are strong presumptions of their divine original. This is strikingly exhibited in all those cases in which the perfections and operations of the Deity are brought into view, as in such passages as the following,—"He hangeth the earth upon nothing; he bindeth up the waters in his thick clouds; he hath compassed the waters with bounds, until the day and night come to an end; the pillars of heaven tremble and are astonished at his reproof. He divideth the sea by his great power; by his spirit he hath garnished the heavens. Lo, these are only parts of his ways, but how little a portion is heard of him, and the thunder of his power who can comprehend?"—"By the word of the Lord were the heavens made; he spake and it was done, he commanded and it stood fast." "Great is Jehovah and of great power, his greatness is unsearchable, his understanding is infinite; marvellous things doth he which we cannot comprehend." "The heaven, even the heaven of heavens cannot contain him; he hath prepared his throne in the heavens, and his kingdom ruleth over all. He doth according to his will in the army of heaven and among the inhabitants of the earth, and none can stay his hand, or say unto him, what dost thou?" "Who hath measured the ocean in the hollow of his hand, and meted out heaven with a span, and comprehended the dust of the earth in a measure, and weighed the mountains in scales and the hills in a balance. Who hath directed the spirit of the Lord, or being his counsellor hath taught him? Behold, the nations are as a drop of a bucket, and are counted as the small dust of the balance. Behold, he taketh up the isles as a very little thing. All nations before him are as nothing, and they are counted to him less than nothing and vanity." These, and many similar passages to be found in the sacred writings, far surpass, in dignity of language and sublimity of sentiment, every thing that is to be found in the writings of the most celebrated poets and philosophers of Greece and Rome. If we take the most animated poems of Homer, Virgil, or Horace, and read them in a prose translation, as we do the Scriptures, they appear flat and jejune, and their spirit is almost evaporated; and the words they put into the mouths of their deities, and the actions they ascribe to them, are frequently both ridiculous and absurd, calculated to excite hatred and contempt, instead of adoration and reverence. But the Scriptures preserve their sublimity and glory even in the most literal translation, and such a translation into any language is always found to be the best; and it has uniformly happened, that those who have presumed to heighten the expressions by a poetical translation or paraphrase, have failed in the attempt. It indicates an utter want of true taste in any man to despise or undervalue these writings. Were it not that the sacred penmen lay claim to the inspiration of the Almighty, and, consequently, set themselves in direct opposition to pride, lasciviousness, revenge, and every other unholy principle and passion, the bible, in point of the beauty and sublimity of its sentiments, and the *variety* of interesting information it conveys, would be prized more highly by every man of taste than all the other writings either of poets, philosophers or historians, which have descended to us from the remotest ages of antiquity.

2. The Christian religion *exhibits the most rational, sublime, and consistent views of the Divine Being.* It represents him as self-existent and independent, and as "the high and lofty One who inhabited eternity," before the universe was brought into existence, in whose sight "a thousand years are as one day, and one day as a thousand years." It represents him as filling the immensity of space with his presence, as having the most intimate knowledge of all creatures and events throughout the vast creation, as the Creator of heaven and earth, as possessed of uncontrollable power, infinite wisdom and intelligence, boundless benevolence and mercy, perfect rectitude and holiness, and inviolable faithfulness and truth. It represents his providential care as extending to all the creatures he has formed, and to all their movements, however numerous or minute; animating the vegetable and animal tribes, setting bounds to the raging billows, "thundering marvellously with his voice, sending lightnings with rain," having "his way in the whirlwind and the storm," making "the earth to quake at his presence," shining in the stars, glowing in the sun, and moving with his hands the mighty worlds which compose the universe. It represents him as governing the universe of minds which he has formed, as having the "hearts" and purposes "of all men in his hand," and as directing all the mysterious and wonderful powers of knowledge and moral action to fulfil his purposes throughout the whole extent of his immense and eternal empire. Such a being, when properly contemplated, is calculated to draw forth the love and adoration of all rational beings; and wherever Christianity has imparted a knowledge of these attributes of the divinity, idolatry and superstition, with all their absurdities, abominations, and horrid cruelties, have gradually disappeared.

3. Christianity has given us full assurance of *the immortality of man and of a future state of punishments and rewards.* Nothing can be of more importance to every human being than to be assured of his eternal destination. Without the discoveries of Christianity, we can attain to no absolute certainty on this momentous subject,

The greatest philosophers of the heathen world considered the arguments in favour of man's immortal destiny as amounting only to a certain degree of probability, and their minds were continually hanging in doubt and uncertainty, as to what might befall them at the hour of dissolution. The most powerful arguments in proof of a future retribution, are founded on the justice, the benevolence, and the wisdom of the Deity; but it is questionable whether we should ever have acquired clear conceptions of these attributes of the Divinity without the aid of the revelations of the Bible. On this most important point, however, Christianity dissipates every obscurity, dispels every doubt, and sets the doctrine of "life and immortality" beyond the grave, in the clearest light, not by metaphysical reasonings, unintelligible to the bulk of mankind, but by the positive declarations of him who hath "all power in heaven and on earth." It gives full assurance to all who devote themselves to the service of God, and conform to his will, that "when their earthly tabernacles are dissolved, they have a building of God, an house not made with hands, eternal in the heavens;" and that "the afflictions" to which they are now exposed "work out for them an eternal weight of glory." And, to console them in the prospect of dropping their bodies into the grave, they are assured, that the period is approaching, when their mortal frame "shall put on immortality," and when "all who are in their graves shall hear the voice of the Son of God, and shall come forth, they that have done good to the resurrection of life, and they that have done evil to the resurrection of condemnation."

4. Christianity clearly *points out the way by which pardon of sin may be obtained by the guilty.* Reason discovers that man is guilty, and at the same time perceives that a sinner deserves punishment. Hence, the remorse and the fears with which the consciences of sinners in every age have been tormented. "Wherewithal shall I come before the Lord? Shall I come with thousands of burnt offerings? Shall I offer my first-born for my transgressions, the fruit of my body for the sin of my soul?" are the anxious inquiries of every sinner who feels conscious that he has violated the laws of Heaven. Hence, the numerous modes by which Pagan nations have attempted to appease the wrath of their deities; hence, their sacrifices, their burnt-offerings, their bodily tortures, their human victims, and the rivers of blood which have flowed in their temples and upon their altars. But reason could never prove, that by any of these modes sin could be expiated, and the Deity rendered propitious. Christianity alone unfolds the plan of redemption, and the way by which guilty men may obtain forgiveness and acceptance in the sight of him whose laws they have violated. It declares, "that Christ Jesus died for our offences, and rose again for our justification;" that "God hath set him forth as a propitiation to declare his righteousness in the remission of sins," and that, having made so costly a sacrifice for the sins of the world, he will refuse nothing that can contribute to the present and everlasting happiness of the believer in Jesus. "He who spared not his own Son, but delivered him up for us all, how shall he not with him also freely give us all things?" Such declarations, when cordially received, are sufficient to allay all the fears of a guilty conscience, to inspire the soul with holy love and gratitude, and to produce "a peace of mind that passeth all understanding."

5. Christianity inculcates *the purest and most comprehensive system of morality.* Its moral requisitions are all comprehended under the two following rules or principles, "Thou shalt love the Lord thy God with all thy heart," and "thou shalt love thy neighbour as thyself," which diverge into numberless ramifications. It could easily be shown, that these principles are sufficient to form the basis of a moral code for the whole intelligent creation, that they are calculated to unite the creature to the Creator, and all rational beings with one another, wherever they may exist throughout the boundless empire of the Almighty; and that peace, order, and happiness would be the invariable and necessary results wherever their influence extended. If the love of God reigned supreme in every heart, there would be no superstition or idolatry in the universe, nor any of the crimes and abominations with which they have been accompanied in our world,—no blasphemy or profanation of the name of Jehovah,—no perjury, hypocrisy, arrogance, pride, ingratitude, nor murmurings under the allotments of Divine Providence. And, if every moral intelligence loved his fellow-creatures as himself, there would be no rivalships and antipathies between nations, and, consequently, no wars, devastation, nor carnage,—no tyranny, haughtiness, or oppression among the great, nor envy, discontent, or insubordination among the lower classes of society,—no systems of slavery, nor persecutions on account of religious opinions,—no murders, thefts, robberies, or assassinations,—no treacherous friendships, nor fraud and deceit in commercial transactions,—no implacable resentments among friends and relatives, and no ingratitude or disobedience among children or servants. On the other hand, meekness, long suffering, gentleness, humility, temperance, fidelity, brotherly kindness, and sacred joy, would pervade every heart, and transform our world from a scene of contention and misery to a moral paradise. The comprehensive nature of these laws or principles, and their tendency to produce universal order and happiness among all intelligences, form, therefore, a strong presumptive argument of their divine original.

There are certain Christian precepts, different from all that were ever taught by the sages of the Pagan world, and in direct opposition to their most favourite maxims, which might be shown to have the same beneficial tendency. For example, it is one of the precepts laid down by the Founder of our religion, "Resist not evil, but whosoever shall smite thee on the right cheek, turn to him the other also," &c.; and in accordance with this precept he propounds the following, "Love your enemies, do good to them that hate you, and pray for them who despitefully use you and persecute you." And he enforces it by one of the most sublime and beautiful motives, "That ye may be the children of your Father who is in heaven, for he maketh the sun to rise on the evil and on the good, and sendeth rain on the just and on the unjust." Now, these precepts of morality are not only original, and peculiar to the Christian system, but they are in direct opposition to all the virtues generally denominated *heroic*, and which are so much celebrated by the poets, philosophers, and historians of antiquity. While the annals of history proclaim, that the exercise of the heroic virtues (among which are classed implacability and revenge,) has banished peace from the world, and covered the earth with devastation and bloodshed, it could easily be shown, that, were the virtues inculcated by our Saviour universally practised, there would not be an enemy on the face of the globe, wars would cease to the ends of the earth, and the whole world would form one vast community of friends and brethren. Whereas, were the opposite dispositions *universal*, an uncontrolled by any counteracting principle, they would produce a scene of universal contention and misery throughout the moral universe.—Another disposition peculiar to the Christian system, and which is enforced throughout both the Old and the New Testament, is *humility*. So little was this disposition regarded by the ancient heathen world, that, in the classical languages of Greece and Rome, there is no word to denote the virtue of humility. It is a quality, however, which results so naturally out of the relation in which man stands to his Maker, and is so correspondent to the low rank which he holds in the scale of universal being, that the religion which so powerfully enjoins it may be said to have "a sign from heaven" that it proceeds from God. And, in his intercourses in society, a man will always find, that there is a far higher degree of quiet and satisfaction to be enjoyed, by humbling himself, than by endeavouring to humble others; for every arrogant and haughty spirit will uniformly smart under the feelings of wounded pride, and disappointed ambition.

The Christian virtues to which I have now adverted, ought not to be considered as the characteristics of a mean and unmanly spirit, or as contrary to the dignity and energy of the human character. The apostles and first Christians, who uniformly practised these virtues, were distinguished by undaunted fortitude and almost unparalleled intrepidity. They advocated their cause, before princes and rulers, with the utmost dignity and composure; they were ready to suffer the greatest persecutions, and even the most excruciating torments, rather than betray the sacred cause in which they had embarked; and one of them had the boldness, when brought before the Roman governor as a prisoner, to arraign the very vices for which he was notorious, and to make the profligate judge tremble in his presence.* So far from these virtues being mean or unmanly, they are the principal qualities that are justly entitled to the epithet *heroic;* for they are the most difficult to be acquired and sustained, as they run counter to the general current of human passion and feeling, and to all the corrupt propensities of the nature of man. A man may have sufficient heroism to bombard a town, or to conquer an army, and yet be altogether unable to regulate his temper, or subdue his boisterous passions. But, "he that is slow to anger, is better than the mighty, and he that ruleth his spirit than he that taketh a city." In the one case, we strive against the corrupt affections of our nature, in the other, (as in giving vent to implacability and revenge,) we give loose reins to our malignant passions. In the one case, we struggle against the stream, in order to obtain safety and repose; in the other, we allow ourselves to be hurried along with the current, regardless of the rocks against which we may be dashed, or the whirlpools in which we may be engulfed. In proportion, then, as the Christian virtues prevail in any community, will quarrels and contentions, and every thing destructive of human enjoyment, be effectually prevented, and happiness diffused among all ranks of society.

In short, Christianity, in its moral requisitions, enjoins every relative and reciprocal duty between parents and children, masters and servants, husbands and wives, governors and subjects, and, not only enforces the practice of justice and equity in all such relations, but inspires the most sublime and extensive charity,—a boundless and disinterested effusion of tenderness for the whole species, which feels for their distress, and operates for their relief and improvement. It prescribes no self-denial, except with regard to sinful lusts and depraved passions; no mortification, except of evil affections; it gives full scope to every feeling that contributes to the real enjoyment of life, while it guards, by the most awful sanctions, every duty the observance of which is necessary for our present and future happiness. It extends our views beyond the limits of the present state, and shows us, that the future happiness of man is connected with his present con-

* Acts xxiv. 25.

duct, and that every action of our lives should have a reference to that immortal existence to which we are destined. But it never insinuates, that earth and heaven are opposed to each other, as to their duties and enjoyments, or that we must be miserable here, in order to be happy hereafter. For while it prescribes rules which have for their ultimate object our happiness in a future world, the observance of these rules is calculated to secure our highest enjoyment even in the present life ; and every one who has devoted himself to the practice of genuine Christianity has uniformly found, that "godliness is profitable unto all things, having the promise both of the life that now is, and of that which is to come." On the characteristics of the moral code of Christianity, then, I should scarcely hesitate to rest almost the whole of the internal evidence of its divine original. For laws, which have a tendency to unite in a bond of affectionate union the whole intelligent creation,—which, if practised, would undermine every species of moral evil, and promote peace and happiness over all the earth, and which are equally calculated to produce true enjoyment in this world, and to prepare us for the higher felicities of the world to come,—must have had their origin in the mind of that Almighty Being whose omniscient eye perceives all the effects of every principle of action, and all the relations which subsist throughout the moral universe.

6. Christianity explains certain moral phenomena, which would otherwise have been inexplicable, and affords strong consolation under the evils of life. It throws a light on the origin of evil, and the disorders both of the physical and moral world, by informing us, that man has lost his original happiness and integrity, that the earth has been defiled by his sin and rebellion, and that it is no longer the beautiful and magnificent fabric which it appeared during the period of primeval innocence. On the same ground, it discovers the reason, why *death* has been permitted to enter our terrestrial system, and the cause of all those afflictions and calamities to which mankind are subjected. It presents before us principles, sufficient to explain most of the apparent irregularities and mysterious operations which appear in the moral government of the Almighty,—why storms and tempests, earthquakes and volcanoes are permitted to produce their ravages,—why the wicked so frequently enjoy prosperity, while the virtuous groan under the pressure of adversity,—why tyranny is established and vice enthroned, while virtue is despised, and love to truth and righteousness sometimes exposes its votary to intolerable calamities. All such occurrences, under the government of God, are accounted for on these general principles,—that they fulfil his counsel,—that they are subservient to the accomplishment of some higher designs of which we are partly ignorant, and that the justice and equity of his procedure will be fully displayed and vindicated in the future world, where "every man will be rewarded according to his works." And as Christianity explains the cause of the physical and moral evils which exist in our world, so it affords strong consolation to the minds of its votaries under the afflictions to which they are now exposed. For, what is death to that mind which considers immortality as the career of its existence? What are the frowns of fortune to him who claims an eternal world as his inheritance? What is the loss of friends to that heart which feels that it shall quickly rejoin them in a more intimate and permanent intercourse than any of which the present life is susceptible? What are the changes and revolutions of earthly things to a mind which uniformly anticipates a state of unchangeable felicity? As earth is but a point in the universe, and time but a moment in infinite duration, such are the hopes of the Christian in comparison of every sublunary misfortune.

7. Revelation communicates to us a knowledge of facts and doctrines which we could not otherwise have acquired. It informs, us that the Deity existed *alone* innumerable ages before Time began—that the material universe was brought into existence, at his command, and by the exertion of his Almighty power—and that the earth, *in its present form*, had no existence at a period seven thousand years beyond the present. It informs us of the manner in which this globe was first peopled, of the primeval state of its first inhabitants, of their fall from the state of innocence and purity in which they were at first created, of the increase of wickedness which followed the entrance of sin into the world, of the Deluge which swept away its inhabitants, and of which the most evident traces are still visible on the surface, and in the bowels of the earth,—and of the manner in which Noah and his family were preserved from this universal destruction, for the re-peopling of the world. It informs us of the time, manner and circumstances in which the various languages which now exist had their origin—a subject which completely puzzled all the ancient philosophers, which they could never explain, and on which no other history or tradition could throw the least degree of light. It unfolds to us views of the state of society in the ages that succeeded the deluge, of the countries into which mankind were dispersed, and of the empires wnich they founded. It records the history of Abraham, the legislation of Moses, the deliverance of the tribes of Israel from Egypt, their passage through the Red-sea, their journeyings through the deserts of Arabia, under the guidance of the pillar of cloud and of fire, and their conquest of the land of Canaan. It informs us of a succession of prophets that were raised up to announce the coming of Messiah, and to foretel the most

remarkable events that were to take place in the future ages of the world—of the appearance of Jesus Christ, of the promulgation of his gospel, and the miraculous effects with which it was accompanied. All which events, as explained and illustrated in the Sacred History, form one grand series of dispensations which is, in the highest degree, illustrative of the Power, Wisdom, Goodness and Rectitude of the Supreme Being,—and of which no other records can give us any certain information.

8. *The beneficial effects which Christianity has produced in the world* constitute a most powerful evidence of its divinity. One striking effect it has produced, is, the superior light it has thrown on the great objects of religion, and the knowledge it has communicated respecting its moral requisitions. Wherever it has been received, it has completely banished the absurd systems of polytheism and pagan idolatry, with all the cruel and obscene rites with which they were accompanied; and in their place, has substituted a system of doctrine and practice, not only pure and rational, but level to the comprehension of the lowest class of society. A mechanic or peasant, instructed in the leading principles of Revelation, now entertains more just and consistent notions of God, of his perfections, his laws, and the plan of his universal providence, than the most renowned philosophers of ancient times ever acquired. Christianity has produced an influence even on the progress of the arts and of rational science; for wherever it has been established, they have uniformly followed in its train; and the latest discoveries in philosophy, so far from being repugnant to its doctrines and facts, are in perfect consistency with all its revelations, and tend to illustrate many of its sublime annunciations. With regard to *practice*—it has introduced many virtues which were altogether unknown in the heathen world. Instead of sottish idolatry, lasciviousness, unnatural lusts, pride, ostentation, and ambition, it has introduced, among all who submit to its authority, rational piety, humility, moderation, self-denial, charity, meekness, patience under affronts and injuries, resignation to the will of God, brotherly kindness, and active beneficence. In the first ages of Christianity, such virtues were eminently conspicuous.—"See," said the heathen, "how these Christians love one another." Lactantius, one of the early Apologists, was able to say, in the face of his antagonists, "Give me a man who is wrathful, malicious, revengeful, and, with a few words of God, I will make him calm as a lamb; give me one that is a covetous, niggardly miser, and I will give you him again liberal, bountiful, and dealing out of his money by handfuls; give me one that is fearful of pain and death, and immediately he shall despise racks and crosses, and the most dreadful punishments you can invent."

Its influence on communities and nations is no less evident, in the changes it has introduced in the circumstances of domestic life, and the barbarous practices it has completely abolished. When it made its way through the Roman empire, it abolished the unnatural practice of polygamy and concubinage, reduced the number of divorces, and mitigated the rigour of servitude, which, among the Romans, was cruel and severe—masters being often so inhuman as to remove aged, sick or infirm slaves into an island in the Tiber, where they suffered them to perish without pity or assistance. Polished and polite, as the Romans have been generally considered, they indulged in the most barbarous entertainments. They delighted to behold men combating with wild beasts and with one another; and we are informed by respectable historians, that the fights of *gladiators* sometimes deprived Europe of twenty thousand lives in one month. Neither the humanity of Titus, nor the wisdom and virtue of Trajan, could abolish these barbarous spectacles, till the gentle and humane spirit of the gospel put a final period to such savage practices, and they can never again be resumed in any nation where its light is diffused, and its authority acknowledged. It humanized the barbarous hordes that overturned the Roman empire, and softened their ferocious tempers, as soon as they embraced its principles and yielded to its influence. It civilized, and raised from moral and intellectual degration, the wild Irish, and our forefathers the ancient Britons, who were classed among the rudest of barbarians till the time when they were converted to the religion of Jesus; so that the knowledge we now see diffused around us, the civilization to which we have advanced, the moral order which prevails, the beauties which adorn our cultivated fields, the comforts and decorations connected with our cities and towns, and the present improved state of the arts and sciences, may all be considered as so many of the beneficial effects which the Christian religion has produced among us.

In our own times, we have beheld effects no less powerful and astonishing, in the moral revolution which Christianity has lately produced in Tahiti, and the adjacent islands in the Southern ocean. In this instance, we behold a people who, a few years ago, were among the most degraded of the human race—who were under the influence of the most cruel superstitions and idolatries—who adored the most despicable idols—who sacrificed on their altars multitudes of human victims, and were plunged into all the vices and debaucheries, and vile abominations which can debase the character of man—we behold them now transformed into civilized and Christian societies—their minds enlightened in the knowledge of the true God, their tempers moulded into the spirit of the religion of Jesus,—their savage practices abolished,—industry, peace and moral order spreading their benign influence on all around, and multitudes rejoicing in the prospect of a blessed immortality. Where barrenness and desolation formerly prevailed, and where only a few savage huts appeared, open to the wind and rain, beautiful villages are now arising, furnished with all the comforts and accommodations of civilized life. Where pagan altars lately stood, and human victims were cruelly butchered, spacious temples are now erected for the worship of "the God and Father of our Lord Jesus Christ," and seminaries for the literary and religious instruction of the young. Where sanguinary battles were fought, amidst the furious yells of savage combatants, who cruelly massacred every prisoner of war—the voice of rejoicing and of thanksgiving is now heard ascending to Heaven from the peaceable "dwellings of the righteous,"—all which effects have been produced, within less than twenty years, by the powerful and benign agency of the Gospel of peace.*

Even *war* itself—the most disgraceful and diabolical practice in which mankind have indulged, and which will affix an eternal stigma on the human character—even war has assumed something of the spirit of mildness and humanity, compared with the savage ferocity with which it was conducted during the reign of heathenism. Prisoners are no longer massacred in cold blood; the conquered are spared, and their liberty frequently restored; and, were the principles of Christianity recognised, and universally acted upon by professing Christian nations, the spirit of warfare would soon be wholly exterminated, and Peace would extend its benign influence over all the kingdoms and families of the earth. The celebrated Montesquieu, in his "Spirit of Laws," has observed, "The mildness so frequently recommended in the gospel is incompatible with the despotic rage with which an arbitrary tyrant punishes his subjects and exercises himself in cruelty. It is the Christian religion which, in spite of the extent of empire and the influence of climate, has hindered despotism from being established in Ethiopia, and has carried into Africa the manners of Europe. The heir to the throne of Ethiopia enjoys a principality, and gives to other subjects an example of love and obedience. Not far from hence may be seen the Mahometan shutting up the children of the king of Senaar, at whose death the council sends to murder them in favour of the prince who ascends the throne."—"Let us set before our eyes, on the one hand, the continual massacres of the kings and generals of the Greeks and Romans, and on the other, the destruction of people and cities by the famous conquerors Timur Beg, and Jenghis Kan, who ravaged Asia, and we shall perceive, that we owe to Christianity in government a certain political law, and in war a certain law of nations, which allows to the conquered the great advantages of liberty, laws, wealth, and always religion, when the conqueror is not blind to his own interest."

But Christianity has not only abolished many barbarous practices, it has likewise given birth to numerous benevolent institutions and establishments altogether unknown in Pagan countries. Let us consider the numerous schools for the instruction of youth in useful knowledge and in the principles of religion, which are erected in all towns and villages in Christian countries, the numerous churches and chapels devoted to the worship of God, and to the instruction and comfort of individuals of every condition, age, and sex,—the colleges and caademies which have been founded for imparting knowledge in literature, and in arts and sciences,—the numerous philanthropic societies which have been formed for the relief of the aged, the infirm, and the destitute sick,—the education of the deaf and dumb,—the reformation of the criminal code,—the improvement of prison discipline,—the reformation of juvenile offenders,—the aiding of the friendless, the orphan, and the widow,—the literary and moral instruction of the children of the poor,—the relief of destitute imprisoned debtors,—the improvement of the domestic condition of the labouring classes,—the promotion of permanent and universal peace,—the diffusion of the knowledge of the Christian religion throughout every region of the globe, and for various other benevolent purposes, all calculated to alleviate the distresses of suffering humanity, to extend the blessings of knowledge, and to communicate enjoyment to all ranks of mankind; and we may challenge the enemies of our religion to point out similar institutions in any pagan country under heaven that has never felt the influence of Christianity. And if such beneficent effects are the native result of the benevolent and expansive spirit of Christianity, they form a strong presumptive evidence, independently of any other consideration, that it derived its origin from that Almighty Being who is good to all, and whose "tender mercies are over all his works."

In fine, Christianity is adapted to every country and every clime. Its doctrines and precepts are equally calculated to promote the happiness of princes and subjects, statesmen and philosophers, the high and the low, the rich and the poor. It is completely adapted to the nature and necessities of man; its rites are few and simple, and may be observed in every region of the globe. It forbids the use of nothing but what is injurious to health of body or peace of mind, and it has a tendency to promote a friendly and affectionate intercourse among men of a-

* For a particular account of this moral revolution which has recently taken place in the Society and other islands of the Pacific, the reader is referred to "Ellis' Polynesian Researches," 2 vols. 8vo.

nations. And, as it is calculated for being universally extended, so its prophets have foretold that its blessings shall ultimately be enjoyed by all nations. In the period in which we live, we behold such predictions more rapidly accomplishing than in former times, in consequence of the spirit of missionary enterprise which now pervades the religious world. And when it shall have extended a little farther in its progress, and shall have brought a few more kingdoms and islands under its authority, its beneficent effects will be more clearly discerned, and the evidences of its celestial origin will appear with a force and power which its most determined adversaries will not be able to gainsay or resist.

In proportion as the physical sciences advance, and the system of nature is explored, will the harmony between the operations of the Creator in the material world and the revelations of his word, become more strikingly apparent. Ever since philosophy began to throw aside its hypothetical assumptions and theoretical reasonings, and to investigate nature on the broad basis of *induction*, its discoveries have been found completely accordant with the Scriptures of truth, and illustrative of many of the sublime sentiments they contain. Geology, when in its infancy, was eagerly brought forward by a few sceptical and superficial minds, to subserve the cause of infidelity. A few pretended facts, of an insulated nature, were triumphantly exhibited, as insuperable objections to the truth of the Mosaic history and chronology. But later and more accurate researches have completely disproved the allegations of such sceptical philosophers, and were they now alive, they would feel ashamed of their ignorance, and of the fallacious statements by which they attempted to impose on the credulity of mankind. As geology advances in its investigations, along with its kindred sciences, the facts which it is daily disclosing appear more and more corroborative of the description given in the Bible of the original formation and arrangement of our globe, and of the universal deluge. And, therefore, we have every reason to conclude, that when science and art shall have arrived at a still higher point of perfection, and our terrestrial system shall have been more thoroughly explored throughout all its departments, arguments will be derived from philosophy itself in support of the divinity of our religion, which will carry irresistible conviction to every mind.

Such is a very brief summary of the internal evidences of the Christian religion. It is distinguished by the dignity and sublimity of the style and sentiments of the writings which contain its revelations,—it exhibits the most rational and consistent views of the attributes of the Divine Being,—it gives us full assurance of a future state of immortality,—it points out the way by which pardon of sin and deliverance from moral evil may be obtained,—it exhibits the purest and most comprehensive system of morality,—it explains certain moral phenomena which would otherwise have been inexplicable,—it affords strong consolation under the evils of life,—it communicates the knowledge of interesting facts and doctrines which can be found in no other record,—it has produced the most beneficial effects on the state of society wherever it has been received,—it is completely adapted to the necessities of man, and calculated for being universally extended over the world;—to which we might have added, that it is consistent in all its parts, when viewed through the medium of enlightened criticism, and harmonises with the principles of sound reason, and the dictates of an enlightened conscience. These are characteristics which will apply to no other system of religion that was ever proposed to the world; and if Christianity, accompanied with such evidences, is not divine in its original, we may boldly affirm that there is no other religion known among men that can lay claim to this high prerogative. But we do not think it possible that the mind of man can receive a more convincing demonstration of the truth of Christianity than is set before us in the authentic facts on which it rests, in its tendency to produce universal happiness, and in the intrinsic excellence for which it is distinguished. That man, therefore, by whatever appellation he may be distinguished, who sets himself in opposition to the spirit of this religion, and endeavours to counteract its progress, must be considered as not only destitute of true taste and of moral excellence, but as an enemy to the happiness of his species. If the religion of the Bible is discarded, we are left completely in the dark with regard to every thing that is most interesting to man as an intellectual being, and as a moral and accountable agent. We should, in this case, have the most imperfect conceptions of the attributes of Deity, and should know nothing of his designs in giving us existence, and placing us in this part of his empire,—we should remain in ignorance whether the world had a beginning or had existed from eternity, or whether we shall ever have an opportunity of beholding the grand system of the universe a little more unfolded,—we should be destitute of any fixed moral laws to direct us in our social transactions and intercourses,—we should be entirely ignorant of the principles and objects of the moral government of the Almighty,—we should be destitute of any consolation under the afflictions and calamities of life,—we should hang continually in doubt whether death is to put a final termination to our being, or convey us to another and an eternal state of existence; and, at length, we should be plunged into the gulf of universal scepticism, into which every rejecter of revelation ultimately sinks.

It may not be improper to remark, that the religion to whose characteristics I have now adverted, is not to be considered as precisely that form of Christianity which has been established in Italy, in Germany, in Russia, or in Britain; or as it is professed by Episcopalians, Presbyterians, Independents, or any other sectary; or as it is expounded in the catechisms, confessions, or systems of divinity, which have been published by the different denominations of the Christian world. In all these cases, its true glory has been obscured, its beauty defaced, and its purity contaminated, by passing through the atmosphere of human folly and corruption; and opinions and practices have been incorporated with its leading principles altogether repugnant to the liberal and expansive spirit for which it is distinguished. *It is to the Christianity of the Bible alone to which I refer.* It is there alone that it is to be seen in its native purity, simplicity, and glory; and he who neglects to study the Scriptures, unfettered by the trammels of human systems, will never be able fully to perceive or to appreciate the true excellence of that religion, which is "pure and peaceable, full of mercy and good fruits," and which breathes "good will towards men." For, in some of the forms which Christianity has assumed in certain countries, it has been so much blended with human inventions, as to be scarcely distinguishable from heathenism; and, consequently, in such cases, it has seldom been accompanied with those beneficial effects which it is calculated to produce. And, among almost all the sectaries in every country, either some of its distinguishing features have been overlooked, or its doctrines mixed up with metaphysical dogmas, or its practical bearings disregarded, or opinions respecting its forms and circumstantials set in competition with its fundamental truths and moral requisitions. "Nevertheless, the foundation of God standeth sure,"—and the Divine fabric of Christianity will remain unshaken and unimpaired, so long as the Scriptures are preserved uncontaminated and entire.

The evidences to which I have now adverted *are continually increasing* in their clearness and force. Time, which is gradually undermining the foundation of error, is enlarging the bulwarks of truth, and adding to their strength and stability. Opposition has tended only to clear away the rubbish which has been thrown around the Christian fabric, but is has shown its foundations to be firm and impregnable. The *historical* evidence has been gaining strength ever since the days of the apostles, and since the time when Herbert, Chubb, Tindal, Morgan, and other infidel writers attempted to undermine the cause of revealed religion. The defences which were published by Grotius, Stillingfleet, Butler, Leland, Watson, Paley, and others, have shown, that the more the arguments for Christianity have been opposed, sifted, and examined, the more irresistible have they appeared, and the more have they shone with increasing brightness; so that no infidel has ever attempted to meet them on fair grounds.—The evidence from *prophecy*, from its very nature, is continually progressive; and, in proportion as Scripture predictions are studied with judgment and intelligence, and compared with the history of past ages and the present state of the nations, will a new light be thrown on the prophetical writings, which will cause the evidence of their divinity to shine forth with a brighter, lustre, and enable every intelligent observer to read, in passing events and in the revolutions of empires, the faithfulness of the Almighty in accomplishing those declarations, which, "at sundry times and divers manners, he spake to the fathers by the prophets."—The *internal* evidence, which has been more overlooked than it ought to have been, is likewise increasing, and will continue to increase, in proportion as the Scriptures are perused with judgment and care, as nature is contemplated with humility and reverence, and as useful knowledge is diffused over the world. When the holy principles of our religion shall have acquired a greater influence over the tempers and conduct of its professors; when the deliberations of statesmen and the conduct of states and empires shall be directed by its maxims and laws; when Christianity shall be divested of the false drapery with which its pretended friends have attempted to adorn it, and freed from the corruptions which human folly has incorporated with its institutions; when all who recognise its leading doctrines, throwing aside party disputes and animosities, shall form themselves into one grand and harmonious association; when a few more portions of the heathen world shall have been brought into subjection to the Prince of Peace, and when the general happiness resulting from such events shall be felt and acknowledged—then, all who behold such blessed transformations will be enabled to read, in characters that cannot be mistaken, that the Creator of the universe is the original author of Christianity, and that the promotion of the best interests of mankind is the great end of all its revelations.

---

My intention in giving the preceding summary of the evidences of Christianity is, to show, that, without habits of rational thinking and a certain portion of general information, these evidences cannot be thoroughly investigated, nor their weight and importance duly appreciated. For, how can a mind unaccustomed to reading and reflection be supposed capable of entering into all the topics and considerations requisite to be attended to in such investigations,— of balancing arguments,—of comparing prophecies with their accomplishment in the history of nations,—of detecting sophisms, or of feeling the force of reasonings, however clear or powerful? It is destitute of those fundamental principles and general ideas on which all moral ratiocinations are grounded. On such a mind, the most weighty arguments and the most cogent reasonings make no sensible impression. It may be susceptible of being biassed against religion by the sneers and sarcasms of jovial companions, and the ridicule with which they may treat the truths of revelation, but it is unqualified either to rebut such impertinences, or to appreciate the excellencies of Christianity, the foundation on which it rests, and the benignant tendency of its doctrines and precepts. And if, in the present day, a man has no acquaintance with the grounds and reasons of revealed religion, and the evidences on which its truth and divinity rest, he will not only be indifferent to the observance of its precepts, and destitute of its supports and consolations, but will be constantly liable to be turned aside to the paths of folly and intemperance, and to become the prey of unthinking fools and scoffing infidels. Whereas, when a man can give a reason of the hope that is in him, his religion becomes a delightful and a rational service, and he is enabled to put to silence the scoffs and vain cavillings of foolish and unreasonable men.

Besides assisting us in investigating the evidences of religion—a certain portion of general information is highly useful, and even necessary *for enabling us to understand the Sacred writings.* It is true, indeed, that the leading doctrines of revelation, respecting the attributes of God, the mediation of Christ, the way in which salvation is to be obtained, the grand principles of moral action, and the duties connected with the several relations of life, are detailed with such plainness and perspicuity as to be level to the comprehension of every reflecting mind, however unskilled in literature or science. But there are certain portions of Revelation, necessary "to make the man of God perfect," the study of which requires the exertion of all our faculties, and the application of every branch of human knowledge we can possibly acquire. This arises from the very nature of the subjects treated of, and from the limited faculties of the human mind. To illustrate this idea is the object of the following remarks.

1. A considerable portion of Scripture is occupied with *prophetical declarations,*—in reference to events which have long since taken place, to those which are now happening, and to those which will hereafter happen in the future ages of the world. It contains a series of predictions which embrace the leading outlines of the history of the world, from its commencement to its final consummation. Now, in order to trace the accomplishment of these predictions, and to perceive clearly the events to which they refer, a minute acquaintance with *ancient and modern history* is indispensably requisite: for it is in history, either sacred or civil, that their accomplishment is recorded. And, could we, with one comprehensive glance, take a survey of all the leading events which the history of the world records, we should be enabled, when reading the prophetical writings, to perceive, at every step, the ideas and purposes of that All-Comprehensive Mind that "knoweth the end from the beginning," and his faithfulness in accomplishing the promises, and executing the threatenings of his word.—A knowledge of *Chronology* is also requisite, in order to ascertain the time in which predictions were uttered, and the periods to which they refer—and of *Ancient Geography,* to determine the localities of those tribes or nations to which the prophecies have a reference, and their relative positions with regard to each other.—In particular, it is necessary to be acquainted with the *Figurative style* in which prophecy is conveyed, in order to understand the writings of the ancient prophets. These writings, in common with those of most of the Eastern nations, are highly poetical, and abound in Allegories, Parables and Metaphors. The *Allegory* is that mode of speech in which the writer or speaker means to convey a different idea from what the words in their primary signification bear. Thus, "Break up your fallow-ground, and sow not among thorns,"* is to be understood, not of tillage, but of repentance; and these words, "Thy rowers have brought thee into great waters, the east wind hath broken thee in the midst of the seas,"† allude, not to the fate of a *ship,* but to the fate of a *city.*—Of all the figures used by the prophets, the most frequent is the *Metaphor,* by which words are transferred from their plain and primary, to their figurative and secondary meaning. One of the most copious sources of those metaphors to which the sacred writers resort, is *the scenery of Nature.* The Sun, Moon, and Stars, the highest and most splendid objects in the natural world, figuratively represent kings, queens, and princes or rulers, the highest in the political world, as in the following passages, "The moon shall be confounded, and the sun ashamed."‡ "I will cover the heavens, and make the stars thereof dark; I will cover the sun with a cloud, and the moon shall not give her light."§ *Light* and *darkness* are used figuratively for joy and sorrow, prosperity and adversity; as, "We wait for light, but behold obscurity, for brightness, but we walk in darkness;"‖—and likewise for knowledge and ignorance;—"The people that walked in darkness have seen a great light," &c. Immoderate rains, hail, floods, torrents, inundations, fire and storms, denote judgments and destruction; *Lebanon* remarkable for its height and its stately cedars, is used as an image of majesty and strength; Carmel, which abounded in vines and olives, as an image of fertility and beauty; and bullocks of Bashan, rams, lions,

* Jer. iv. 3. † Ezek. xxvii. 26. ‡ Isaiah xxiv 23. § Ezek. xxxii. 7. ‖ Isaiah lix. 9.

eagles, and sea-monsters, as images of cruel and oppressive conquerors and tyrants. Metaphors are likewise borrowed from history, from the scenery of the temple and its various utensils and services, and from the ordinary customs and occupations of life—the meaning and application of which require to be distinctly understood, in order to perceive the spirit and references of ancient prophecy. Those who would wish to study this subject with intelligence, would do well to consult the works of Lowth, Hurd, Sherlock, Kennicot, Newcome, and particularly "Newton's Dissertations on the Prophecies."

2. In studying the *historical parts of Scripture*—a knowledge of ancient history, and even of Pagan Mythology, tends, in many instances, to throw light on the narratives of the Sacred writers. We find, from heathen writers, who were strangers to the Jewish religion, that the most ancient tradition of all nations, respecting the early history of the world, is exactly agreeable to the relation of Moses, though expressed in a more abstruse, doubtful and imperfect manner. The description of the origin of the world, in the ancient Phenician history, translated by *Philo Biblius* from *Sanchoniathon's* collection, and transmitted to us by *Eusebius*, is materially the same, with that which is recorded in the Book of Genesis, when separated from the fabulous notions with which it is blended. The Egyptians, according to Laertius, acknowledged, "that originally the world was a confused chaos, from whence the four elements were separated, and living creatures made; and that the world had a beginning, and consequently would have an end." Hesiod, the most ancient writer whose works have reached us, says, that "all things had their origin from a rude chaos;" and Ovid, in the first book of his "Metamorphoses," tells us, "that before the seas, and the land, and the canopy of heaven existed, there was one appearance throughout the whole of nature, which they called *chaos*—a rude and indigested mass, in which earth and air, fire and water were indiscriminately mixed." In short, Thales, Anaxagoras, Aratus, Virgil and Homer, speak of the original of all things, comformable to the account given by Moses, though in a different phraseology; and we learn from Josephus, Philo, Tibullus, Clemens Alexandrinus, and Lucian, that the memory of the six days work was preserved, not only among the Greeks and Italians, by honouring the seventh day, but also among the Celtæ and Indians, who all measured their time by weeks.—Manetho, who wrote the history of the Egyptians, Berosus, who wrote the Chaldean history, Hierom, who wrote the history of Phenicia, and Hecatæus, Hillanicus and Ephorus, who wrote the history of Greece, all agree in asserting, "that those who descended from the first men, in the first ages of the world, lived many of them nearly a thousand years."—With regard to *the deluge*, we find most of the Greek and Roman writers, Ovid, Lucian, Berosus the Chaldean, Abydenus the Assyrian, and many others referring to that great event, and detailing the particular circumstances connected with it, in language nearly similar to that of the Sacred historian; such as, the preservation of Noah, the ark in which he was preserved, the mountain on which it rested, the dove and the raven which he is said to have sent out, and the wickedness of the Antediluvians, as the cause of that dismal catastrophe. We find, also, that the whole mythology of India is full of allusions to the general deluge, which appears to be the commencement of their present era; and that accounts of the same event are to be met with in China and Japan.*

An acquaintance with ancient history is necessary for enabling us to fill up the blanks left by the Sacred historians. From the time of Ezra and Nehemiah to the birth of Christ, there is an interval of about four hundred and fifty years, of the events which happened during which we have no account in any part of the inspired writings. A knowledge of the events which happened during this interval is necessary, in order to complete our views of the scheme of Divine Providence, and to unfold to us the series of God's dispensations in relation both to the Jews and the surrounding nations. During this period, too, many of the predictions of Daniel and the other prophets received their accomplishment,—particularly those which relate to the Medes and Persians, the Macedonian empire, the times of Alexander the Great, Ptolemy Philadelphus, Antiochus Epiphanes, Philip of Macedon, and the persecutions in the days of the Maccabees. In order, therefore, to obtain a clear and comprehensive view of the ways of Providence during this interval, such works as Shuckford's "Connexion of Sacred and Profane History," and Prideaux's "Connexions of the Old and New Testament," require to be studied with care, in many parts of which will be seen a running commentary on Daniel's vision of the "Ram and He-Goat," and of "the things noted in the Scripture of truth," which have a reference, among other things, to the kings of Persia, to Alexander and his successors, and the warlike expeditions in which they were engaged. For an elucidation of the general train of events from the Mosaic creation to the establishment of Christianity, "Stackhouse's History of the Bible," in six volumes 8vo, or in three volumes 4to, with the additional notes and dissertations of Bishop Gleig, will be found an invaluable treasure, and will amply repay the reader who gives it a diligent perusal.†

* See Maurice's "Indian Antiquities" and Bryant's System of Mythology."

† In Bishop Gleig's edition of Stackhouse's History, a long and useful dissertation, entitled, "An Appa-

3. A knowledge of the manners and customs, climate and seasons, arts and sciences of the Eastern nations, is essentially requisite, in many instances, in order to understand the allusions of the sacred writers, and the meaning of various portions of Scripture. For example, when an untutored reader peruses the account given in the Evangelists of the cure of the paralytic who was carried by four men on a bed, and who, finding it impossible to pass through the throng, ascended to the top of the house in which Jesus was, and let him down bed and all, "through the tiling," into the very room where he was sitting—he is apt to entertain a very confused and erroneous idea of the circumstances of the case, when his attention is directed solely to the mode of building in this country. But, when he is informed, that the houses in the country of Judea were low-built and flat-roofed, and surrounded with a parapet breast-high, that there was a ladder or pair of stairs which led to the top of the house from the outside, and a trap-door or hatchway in the middle of the roof—he will soon acquire a clear idea of the circumstances stated in this and other parts of the Evangelical history, and of the ease with which the paralytic man might be conveyed to the top of the building and let down through the roof. The same facts likewise illustrate the circumstance of Peter's going to the top of the house to pray, and the custom of making proclamations from the house-tops, to which there are several allusions in Scripture.—A knowledge of the weather and seasons of Judea, is frequently of use to illustrate the force of certain expressions of the sacred writers. It may seem to us nothing extraordinary that there should be "thunder and rain in harvest," or in the months of June and July, when Samuel said, "Is it not *wheat harvest* to day? I will call unto the Lord, and he shall send thunder and rain."* But Jerome, who lived in Judea many years, says, it never rained there at that season; so that the thunder and rain which happened at the intercession of Samuel were truly miraculous, and as such, "the people greatly feared the Lord and Samuel."—Again, in Luke xii. 55, it is said, "When ye see the south wind blow, ye say there will be heat, and it cometh to pass." In our climate, where the south wind seldom blows, this may not be always the case. But in Syria, Egypt, Judea and the adjacent countries, the effect here mentioned is striking and uniform. When the south wind begins to blow, the sky becomes dark and heavy, the air grev and thick, and the whole atmosphere assumes a most alarming aspect. The heat produced by these southern winds has been compared to that of a huge oven, at the moment of drawing out the bread, and to that of a flame blown upon the face of a person standing near the fire that excites it.

Thousands of illustrations of Sacred Scripture may be derived from such sources; and he who is unacquainted with them must remain a stranger to the beauties of the style of the inspired writers, and to the precise meaning of many portions both of the historical and the prophetical writings. The manners and customs of the Eastern nations have remained nearly the same for several thousand years; so that those which are found existing in the present day are exactly, or nearly the same, as those which prevailed in the times when the books of the Old and New Testaments were written. Modern oriental travellers, in their descriptions of the arts, sciences and manners of the East, have furnished us with a mass of invaluable materials for the elucidation of holy writ, and they have proved, in many cases, unintentionally, better commentators than the most profound critics and philologists. Many of their insulated remarks of this kind have lately been classified and arranged by various writers, particularly by Harmer, in his "Observations," Burder in his "Oriental Customs," Paxton in his "Illustrations," and Taylor, the late learned editor of the new editions of Calmet's Dictionary, in his *Fragmenta*, appended to that work, which contains an immense number of such observations, illustrated with a great variety of engravings.

4. An acquaintance with *Ancient Geography*, especially that part of it which relates to the Eastern countries, would enable a person to peruse many portions of Scripture with much greater interest and intelligence, than if he were altogether ignorant of this branch of knowledge. In the history of the Old Testament, and in the Prophetical writings, there are frequent references and allusions to Mesopotamia, Idumea, Egypt, Assyria, Chaldea, Arabia, Ethiopia, Lybia Parthia, Scythia, Persia, and other countries—to the cities of Jerusalem, Babylon, Nineveh, Damascus, Tadmor, Tyre, Sidon, &c.—to the great Sea, or the Mediterranean, the Dead Sea, the Sea of Tiberias, the Red Sea—the isles of Chittim, Cyprus, Crete, Melitâ—the rivers Jordan, Kishon, Jabbok, Euphrates, Hiddekel, Pison, Ulai, Abana, Pharpar, &c.—Now, a knowledge of the positions of such places with respect to the country of Judea, their relative situations with regard to each other, and of the outlines of their history, and of the warlike achievements and commerce of their inhabitants—is frequently necessary, in order to attain a clear and com

ratus to the History of the Bible," has been left out, without any reason being assigned for the omission. In other respects the original work appears to be complete. Bishop Gleig's improvements consist chiefly in bringing forward the discoveries of modern science for the purpose of elucidating certain Scriptural facts, and repelling the objections of infidels—and in various dissertations on some of the leading doctrines and historical facts of revelation, which form valuable additions to the original work of Stackhouse. See also *Horne's Introduction*, &c.

* Sam. xii. 17.

prehensive view of the passages in which there are allusions to such localities.—In reading the Evangelists, it is highly expedient to know, for example, the position of Samaria, Galilee, the lake of Gennesareth, and the river Jordan, with respect to that portion of the Holy Land, denominated Judea—the situations of Bethlehem, Nazareth, Jericho, Nain, Sychar, Bethsaida, Cana, Tyre and Sidon, with respect to Jerusalem, and their respective distances from that metroplis—and the characteristics of the inhabitants of these places; for, upon a knowledge of such circumstances, our perception of the beauty and appropriateness of our Saviour's discourses, and of the propriety of his actions, will, in a great measure, depend.—In reading the history of the journeyings of the Apostles, it is no less expedient that we have lying before us maps of Asia Minor, of Ancient Greece, of Palestine, of the Eastern parts of Africa, and of the islands of the Mediterranean, and that we have some accquaintance with the history and character of the tribes which inhabited these countries in the days of the Apostles. Without such knowledge and assistances, we must, in many instances, read their narratives without ideas—and shall be unable to appreciate their labours, the long journeys they undertook, the fatigues they endured, the dangers to which they were exposed by sea and land, and the allusions made to such circumstances in the Apostolic Epistles.*

5. An acquaintance with the facts of Natural History and Science, and with the general phenomena of Nature, would tend to throw a light on many passages of Scripture, and would enable persons to perceive a beauty and an emphasis in certain expressions, which they would otherwise be apt to overlook. For example, in the beginning of the hundred and thirty-fifth psalm, the servants of God are exhorted to "praise the name of Jehovah;" and in the sequel of the Psalm various *reasons* are assigned why we should engage in this exercise. One of these reasons is, that "*He causeth the vapours to ascend from the ends of the earth.*" Many persons who read or who may sing this portion of sacred poetry, would be apt to overlook the circumstance now stated as an argument of very inferior importance. But if we examine the subject attentively, we shall find, that this physical operation of the Almighty is not only very wonderful in its nature, but that upon it most of our comforts, and even our very existence, depend. *Evaporation* is a process by which water and other liquids are converted into vapour. The matter of *heat*, combining with water, renders it specifically *lighter*, by which means it rises and mixes with the atmosphere, where it remains either *invisible*, or assumes the appearance of clouds. In this state it occupies a space fourteen hundred times greater than in its ordinary liquid state, and consequently is much lighter than the atmospheric air into which it rises. It has been calculated, that, from an acre of ground, during twelve hours of a summer's day, more than 1600 gallons of water have been drawn up into the air in the form of vapour. From the whole surface of the ocean there arise, every twelve hours, no less than 30,320,500.000,000 or more than thirty millions of millions of cubic feet of water, which is more than sufficient to supply all the rivers that intersect the four quarters of the globe. This immense body of vapour is formed into clouds, which are carried by the winds over every part of the continents; and, by a process with which we are still unacquainted, is again condensed into rain, snow or dews, which water and fertilize the earth. Now, if this wonderful and extensive process of nature were to cease—we might wash our clothes, but centuries would not dry them, for it is evaporation alone that produces this effect—there would be no rains nor dews to fertilize our fields, and the consequence would be, the earth would be parched, and the vegetable productions which afford us subsistence would wither and decay,—the rivers would swell the ocean, and cause it to overflow a portion of the land, while, at the same time, their sources would soon be completely exhausted, and their channels dried up. In such a state of things, the whole system of terrestrial nature would be deranged, and man, and all the other tribes of animated nature—deprived of those comforts which are essential to their existence—would, in a short time, perish from the earth. So that it forms a powerful and impressive motive to excite us to praise the name of Jehovah, when we call to remembrance, that it is He "who causeth the vapours to ascend from the ends of the earth," and thus preserves the harmony of nature, and secures to all living creatures the blessings they now enjoy.

Again, we are informed by Solomon, (Eccles. i. 7.) that "all the rivers run into the sea; yet the sea is not full; *unto the place from whence the rivers come, thither they return again.*" It appears, at first sight, somewhat unaccountable, that the ocean has not long ere now overflown all its banks, when we consider that so many majestic streams are incessantly rolling into its abyss, carrying along with them into its caverns no less than thirteen thousand six hundred cubical miles of water every year. Solomon partly solves the difficulty, by informing us, that, "to the place whence the rivers come, thither they return again." But how do they return? Many expositors of Scripture attempt to explain this circumstance, by telling us that the waters of the ocean percolate through the earth, and in some

* The student of ancient geography will be assisted in his researches by a perusal of Wells' "Set of Maps of Ancient Geography," twenty-three in number—and Wells' "Sacred Geography," modernized by the Editor of Calmet's Dictionary, which is one of the most accurate and complete works of the kind

way or another, arrive near the tops of mountains, where springs generally abound. But such a supposition is not only highly improbable, when we consider the vast mass of earth and rocks, several hundreds of miles in thickness, through which the waters would have to percolate, but *directly contrary* to the known laws of nature; for *no fluid can rise in a tube above the level of its source*, which in this case it behoved to do. Modern experiments and discoveries, however, have satisfactorily accounted for this fact, on the principle of *evaporation*, to which I have just now adverted. From the surface of the ocean and of the rivers themselves, there is carried up into the atmosphere, in the form of vapour, nearly three times the quantity of water sufficient to replenish the sources of all the rivers in the world. The vapour thus raised is carried by the winds, in the form of clouds, over every region of the globe, and falls down in rains to carry on the various processes of nature. One part falls into the sea, another on the lowlands, and the remaining part is sufficient to replenish the sources of all the rivers. So that the assertion of Solomon is strictly and philosophically correct, that "to the place whence the rivers come, thither they return again." They first fall into the ocean; a portion of their waters is then raised by evaporation into the atmosphere; this portion of vapour, after traversing the regions of the air, falls down in rain, mists, and dews, and supplies the numerous springs "which run among the hills."

Such illustrations, which might be indefinitely extended, not only throw a light on the meaning of the sacred writers, but tend likewise to show the harmony that subsists between the discoveries of science and the truths of revelation. As the Author of Christianity and the Author of the system of nature is one and the same Being, there must exist a harmonious correspondence between *truth* in the one, and *fact* in the other; and the more they are studied with intelligence, and in connexion with each other, the more will their harmony be apparent.

It is a circumstance that has frequently forced itself upon my attention, that whatever scene of nature we contemplate, and however brilliant and unexpected the discoveries which modern science has brought to light,—however far they have carried our views into the wonders of the minute parts of creation, and into the immeasurable regions of space, where myriads of suns are lighted up,—and however much the mind may be lost in astonishment and wonder, at the magnificent scenes which they disclose,—we shall find sentiments and expressions in Scripture adequate to express every emotion of the soul when engaged in such contemplations.—Are we contemplating the expanse of the ocean, and the vast mass of waters which fill its mighty caverns? and do we wish to raise our thoughts in adoration of the power of that Almighty Being who formed it by his word? We are presented by the inspired penmen with expressions in which to vent our emotions. "He holds its waters in the hollow of his hand; he taketh up its isles as a very little thing." "He gathereth the waters of the sea together as a mass; he layeth up the depth as in storehouses." "He divideth the sea by his power; he hath compassed the waters with bounds, until the day and night come to an end." "Thou coveredst the earth with the deep as with a garment; the waters stood above the mountains:* At thy rebuke they fled; at the voice of thy thunder they hasted away. Thou hast set a boundary that they may not pass over, that they turn not again to cover the earth." "He hath placed the sand for the bounds of the sea, by a perpetual decree, that it cannot pass it; and though the waves thereof toss themselves, yet they cannot prevail; though they roar, yet can they not pass over it." He hath said to its rolling billows, "Hitherto shalt thou come, and no farther; and here shall thy proud waves be stayed."—Are we spectators of storms and tempests, especially in the terrific grandeur they display in southern climes? Our emotions will be expressed with the greatest emphasis in the language of inspiration, in which we are uniformly directed to view the agency of God in such phenomena. "Clouds and darkness are round about him: He hath his way in the whirlwind and the storm, and the clouds are the dust of his feet." "When he uttereth his voice, there is a sound of waters in the heavens; he causeth the vapours to ascend from the ends of the earth; he maketh lightnings with rain, and bringeth forth the winds out of his treasuries." "The God of glory thundereth; the voice of the Lord is full of majesty; the voice of the Lord divideth the flames of fire; yea, the Lord breaketh the cedars of Lebanon." "Who can stand before his indignation? The mountains quake before him, the hills melt, and rocks are shivered at his presence."

Again, when we contemplate the immense number and variety of animated beings which glide through the waters, move along the earth, and wing their flight through the air; together with the ample provision which is made for their accommodation and subsistence,—where can we find language more appropiate to express our feelings than in these words of the Psalmist? "How manifold are thy works, O Lord! In wisdom hast thou made them all; the earth is full of thy riches; so is the great and wide sea, wherein are things creeping innumerable, both small and great beasts. These all wait upon thee, that thou mayest give them their meat in due season. Thou givest them,—they gather; thou openest thine hand,—they are filled with good."—When we survey the structure of

* Referring to the deluge.

the human frame, and consider the vast number of bones, muscles, veins, arteries, lacteals, lymphatics, and other parts, all curiously combined, and calculated to facilitate every motion of our bodies, and to produce sensitive enjoyment,—along with the organs of sense, the process of respiration, and the circulation of the blood through the whole frame every four minutes,—can we refrain from adopting the expressive language of the Psalmist? "I will praise thee, for I am fearfully and wonderfully made! marvellous are thy works. My substance was not hid from thee when I was made in secret, and curiously wrought,"—or variegated like needle-work,—"in my mother's womb.* Thine eyes did see my substance when it was yet imperfect; and in thy book all my members were written, which in continuance were fashioned when as yet there was none of them. How precious are thy thoughts (or, thy wonderful contrivances) concerning me, O God! How great is the sum of them! If I should count them, they are more in number than the sand." To which may be added the words of Job, "Thine hands have made and fashioned me: thou hast clothed me with skin and flesh, and hast fenced me with bones and sinews; and thy visitation preserveth my spirit."—When we contemplate the minute wonders of creation, and are struck with astonishment at the inconceivable smallness of certain animated beings,—how can we more appropriately express our feelings than in the language of Scripture, "He is wonderful in counsel, and excellent in working; his wisdom is unsearchable, his understanding is infinite; marvellous things doth he which we cannot comprehend. There is none like unto thee, O Lord, neither are there any works like unto thy works. Thou art great, and dost wondrous things; thou art God alone."

When we contemplate the amazing structure of the heavens—the magnitude of the bodies which compose the planetary system, and the numerous orbs which adorn the nocturnal sky—when we penetrate with the telescope into the more distant regions of space, and behold ten thousand times ten thousand more of these bright luminaries rising to view from every region of the firmament—when we consider that each of these twinkling luminaries is a sun, equal or superior to our own in size and in splendour, and surrounded with a system of revolving worlds—when we reflect, that all this vast assemblage of suns and worlds, forms, in all probability, but a very small portion of Jehovah's empire, and when our minds are bewildered and astonished at the incomprehensible grandeur of the scene—where shall we find language to express our emotions more energetic and appropriate than in such passages as these? "Canst thou by searching find out God? Canst thou find out the Almighty to perfection? He is glorious in power, his understanding is infinite, his greatness is unsearchable. The heavens declare the glory of Jehovah, and the firmament showeth his handy-work. All nations before him are as nothing, and they are counted to him as less than nothing and vanity. He meteth out the heavens with a span, and comprehendeth the dust of the earth in a measure. Behold! the heaven and the heaven of heavens cannot contain him. By the word of the Lord were the heavens made, and all the host of them by the spirit of his mouth. He spake, and it was done; he commanded, and it stood fast. He doth great things past finding out, and wonders without number. Great and marvellous are thy works, Lord God Almighty! Touching the Almighty we cannot find him out; he is excellent in power, and his glory is above the earth and the heavens. Who can utter the mighty operations of Jehovah? Who can show forth all his praise?"

Are we led, from the discoveries of modern astronomy, to infer, that numerous worlds besides our own exist throughout the universe? This idea will be found embodied in numerous passages of Scripture, such as the following;—"Through faith we understand that *the worlds were framed* by the word of God." "In these last days he hath spoken to us by his Son, whom he hath appointed heir of all things, by whom also he made the worlds." "Thou hast made heaven, the heaven of heavens, *with all their host*, and thou preservest them all, and *the host of heaven worshippeth thee*." "He sitteth upon the circle of the earth, and the inhabitants thereof are as grasshoppers. All the inhabitants of the earth *are reputed as nothing in his sight*. The nations are as the drop of a bucket; and he doth according to his will *in the armies of heaven*,

* In our translation, the beauty and emphasis of this passage are partly lost. The expression, "curiously wrought," literally translated, signifies "flowered with a needle." The process of the formation of the human body in the womb is compared to that in a piece of delicate work wrought with a fine needle, or fashioned with peculiar art in the loom; which, with all its beautiful proportion of figure and variety of colouring, rises by degrees to perfection under the hand of the artist, from a rude mass of silk or other materials, and according to a pattern lying before him. In accordance with this idea, the Divine Being is here represented as working a shapeless mass, after a plan delineated in his book, into the most curious texture of muscles, bones, veins, ligaments, membranes, lymphatics, &c. most skilfully interwoven and connected with each other, till it becomes a structure with all the parts, lineaments, and functions of a man,—no one of which is to be seen at first, any more than the figures in a ball of silk, before it is fashioned with the needle. The wonders of this workmanship are farther enhanced from the consideration, that, while human artificers require the clearest light for accomplishing their work, the Divine Artist performs it "*in secret*," within the dark and narrow recess of the womb. The expression, "How precious are thy *thoughts to me*," should be rendered, "How precious are thy *contrivances respecting me*," namely, in reference to the exquisite structure and organalation of the corporeal frame, on which the Psalmist had fixed his meditations.

and among the inhabitants of the earth." "He hath prepared his *throne* in the heavens, and *his kingdom ruleth over all.*" "When I consider thy heavens—what is man, that thou art mindfull of him?" It would be easy to show, were it expedient in the present case, that all such expressions and representations, embody in them the idea of *a plurality of worlds*, without which they would appear either inexplicable, or as a species of bombast, unworthy of the character of inspired writers. So that, to whatever department of nature we direct our contemplations, we perceive its correspondence with the sentiments expressed in the sacred writings, and find in these writings the most sublime and appropriate language in which to express those emotions which the diversified scenes of the material world are calculated to inspire.

We may now ask, if such an assertion can be made, in truth, with regard to any other writings, ancient or modern, whose sentiments have not been derived from the sacred oracles? Can we find in the writings of all the poets, philosophers and orators of Greece and Rome, sentiments so dignified, appropriate and sublime, in relation to the objects to which we have alluded? Do not such writers frequently misrepresent and even caricature the system of nature? Are not their descriptions of the gods, and the actions they attribute to them, in many instances, mean, ridiculous, unworthy of the character of superior beings, and even in the highest degree immoral and profane? And, if we turn to the literature and the sacred books of the Chinese, the Persians, the Hindoos or the Japanese, shall we find any thing superior? And is not the circumstance to which we have adverted, a strong presumptive evidence that the Scriptures of the Old and New Testament were written under the inspiration of the Almighty; and consequently, that they are "profitable for doctrine, for reproof, and for instruction in righteousness, that the man of God may be made perfect, and thoroughly furnished unto all good works?"

Such is a brief view of some of the advantages which may be derived from history and general science in the study of the Scriptures. There is, indeed, scarcely a branch of useful knowledge, of whatever description, but may be rendered in some way or another, subservient to the elucidation of the sacred oracles, and in enabling us to take a wide and comprehensive view of the facts and doctrines they declare. Were the great body of mankind, therefore, instructed in general knowledge, and accustomed to rational investigations, they would be enabled to study the Scriptures with much greater interest and intelligence than they can now be supposed to do. They would perceive the beauty and sublimity of their language, the dignity and excellence of the sentiments they contain, the purity of their doctrines, and the beneficent tendency of their moral precepts; and, by familiarizing their minds with the numerous and multifarious facts they exhibit, and comparing them with the history of nations, and with passing events, they would gradually acquire an enlightened and comprehensive view of God's superintending providence. The study of the Scriptures, in their native simplicity, with the helps now alluded to, and without intermixture of the technical language of theologians, and of party opinions, would be of vast importance in religion. It would convince the unbiassed inquirer how little foundation there is in the Scriptures themselves, for many of those numerous disputes about metaphysical dogmas, which have rent the Christian world into a number of shreds and patches, and produced jealousy and animosity, where love and affection should have appeared predominant. He would soon be enabled to perceive, that the system of Revelation chiefly consists of a series of important *facts*, connected with the dispensations of God towards our race, and interwoven with a variety of practical and interesting truths; and that the grand design of the whole is to counteract the effects of moral evil, to display the true character of Deity, to promote love to God and man, to inculcate the practice of every heavenly virtue, and to form mankind into one harmonious and affectionate society. He would find none of the technical terms and phraseology which the schoolmen and others have introduced into their systems of theology; nor any of those anathemas, which one sectary has so frequently levelled at another, applied to any one, excepting to those "who love not our Lord Jesus in sincerity." He would naturally be led to the conclusion, that what is not clearly and explicitly stated in the Scriptures, or but obscurely hinted at, in reference to the external government of the church or any other subject, cannot be a matter of primary importance, and consequently, ought never to be the subject of virulent dispute, or the cause of dissension or separation among Christians—and that those things only are to be considered as the prominent and distinguishing truths of religion which are the most frequently reiterated, and expressed with such emphasis, and perspicuity, that "he who runs may read them."

Again, such an intelligent study of the Scriptures as would accompany the acquisition of general knowledge, would have a tendency to promote the union of the Christian church. Ignorance and distorted views of the truths of revelation are almost uniformly accompanied with illiberality and self-conceit; and where these prevail, silly prejudices are fostered, and party opinions tenaciously adhered to, and magnified into undue importance. But an enlightened mind,—the farther it advances in the path of knowledge and in the study of the Sacred Oracles, the more will it perceive the limited nature of its faculties, and the difficulty of deciding on certain mysterious doctrines; and consequently, the more will it be disposed to grant to every other mind a liberty of thought on subordinate religious subjects, and to make every allowance for those educational prejudices and other causes which have a tendency to warp the mind to certain favourite opinions. And, when such a disposition more generally prevails, and is accompanied with the exercise of Christian love and moderation--the spirit of party will be gradually undermined, and all who recognise the grand and essential features of genuine Christianity will unite in one lovely and harmonious society. But, so long as ignorance and habits of mental inactivity prevail among the great body of the population, such a happy consummation cannot be expected.*

In short, were the Sacred writings studied with reverence and attention, and those departments of knowledge to which I have alluded brought forward to assist in their investigation, Infidelity would soon feel ashamed of its ignorance and impertinence, and hide its head in retirement and obscurity. It is owing, in a great measure, to ignorance of the Scriptures, that so many avowed infidels are to be found in society. "They speak evil of the things which they know not;" "their mouth speaketh great swelling words" of vanity against truths which they never investigated, and which, of course, they do not understand. Even some of those who have attempted to *write* against revelation are not ashamed to avow, that they have never either read or studied the writings it contains. Paine, one of the most virulent adversaries of Christianity, had the effrontery to affirm, that, when he wrote the first part of his "Age of Reason," he was without a Bible. "Afterwards," he tells us, in schoolboy language, "I procured a *Bible* and a *Testament*." Who, but an arrant fool would have made such a declaration, and thus have proclaimed his own impertinence and folly? and who would have listened with patience to such an impudent avowal, had it been made in relation to any other subject? For, to attempt to answer a book which one had not read, is surely the height of presumption and impudence, and plainly indicates, that the mind was previously prejudiced against it, and determined to oppose its sentiments. Others have looked into the Bible, and skimmed over its contents, with the express purpose of finding faults and contradictions. Emerson the mathematician, having imbibed a disrelish for the Scriptures, endeavoured to satisfy his mind that they were not divine, by picking out a number of insulated passages, which he conceived to be contradictions, and set them, one opposite to another, in two separate columns, and then was bold enough to aver that he had proved the Bible to be an imposture. Is it any wonder that men who presume to act in this manner should never come to the knowledge of the truth? What book in the world would stand such an ordeal? There is no treatise on any subject whatever, which, if treated in this manner, might not be made to appear a mass of absurdities and contradictions. If the Bible is to be read at all, it must be perused both with reverence and with intelligence; and there is no one who enters on the study of it, in such a state of mind, but will soon perceive, that it contains "the witness in itself," that it is from God, and will feel, that it is "quick and powerful" in its appeals to the conscience, and a "searcher of the thoughts and intents of the heart." But he who reads it either with scorn, with negligence, or with prejudice, needs not wonder if he shall find himself only confirmed in his folly and unbelief. "For a scorner seeketh wisdom, and findeth it not; but knowledge is easy unto him that hath understanding.

I have dwelt, at considerable length, on the topic of Christianity, because it is a subject of peculiar interest and importance to every individual. If, in systems of education, and in the means by which mankind at large may be enlightened and improved, the knowledge of religion be overlooked, and its moral requisitions disregarded, more evil than good may be the result of the dissemination of general and scientific knowledge. We have a proof of this in the scenes of anarchy, licentiousness and horror which succeeded the first French revolution, when revealed religion was publicly discarded, and atheism, infidelity and fatalism, accompanied with legalized plundering, became "the order of the day." If knowledge is not consecrated to a moral purpose, and prosecuted with a reference to that immortal existence to which we are destined, the utility of its general diffusion might be justly called in question. But, when prosecuted in connexion with the important discoveries of revelation, it has a tendency to raise man to the highest dignity of which his nature is susceptible, and to prepare him for more exalted pursuits and enjoyments in the life to come.

---

## SECTION X.

### *Miscellaneous Advantages of Knowledge briefly stated.*

In this section, I shall briefly advert to several advantages which would flow from a general diffusion of knowledge, not directly included in those which have already been stated.

I. Minds tutored in knowledge and habits of reflection, *would be led to form just estimates of human character and enjoyment.*

The bulk of mankind are apt to form a false estimate of the characters of men, from consider

* For a more full illustration of this topic, see Section V.

ing only those adventitious circumstances in which they are placed, and those external trappings with which they are adorned. Wherever wealth and splendour, and high-sounding titles have taken up their residence, the multitude fall down and worship at their shrine. The natural and acquired endowments of the mind are seldom appreciated and respected, unless they are clothed with a dazzling exterior. A man of genius, of virtue and of piety, is not distinguished from the common herd of mankind, unless he can afford to live in an elegant mansion, to entertain convivial parties, and to mingle with the fashionable and polite. The poor and ignorant peasant looks up with a kind of veneration to my lord and my lady, as if they were a species of superior beings, though, perhaps, with the exception of a few trifling accomplishments, they are scarcely raised above the level of the vulgar whom they despise, in respect to intellectual attainments; and they are often far beneath them in those moral accomplishments which constitute the true glory of man,—being too frequently the slaves of many foolish caprices and unhallowed passions. To pay homage to mere titles, rank or riches, has a tendency to degrade the human mind, and has been the source of all that vassalage, slavery and despotism which have prevailed in the world. On the other hand, the man of rank and fashion looks down with a species of disdain, and considers as unworthy of his notice, the man of talent, or the rational inquirer after truth, if he is clad in a homely dress, and possessed of only a small share of wealth; because, forsooth, he is unqualified to accompany him to horse-races, assemblies, masquerades, and other fashionable entertainments. Many an individual of superlative worth and merit has been thus overlooked by his superiors in rank, and even by the great body of his fellow-men, and has passed through the world almost unnoticed and unknown, except by a few minds congenial to his own. For the beauties and excellencies of *mind* can only be perceived and appreciated by those whose mental faculties have been, in some degree, enlightened and improved, and who are qualified to estimate the value of a jewel, although its casket may be formed of coarse materials, and besmeared with sand and mud.

The multitude form no less erroneous estimates in regard to human happiness. Having felt little other misery than that which arises from poverty, want, or excessive labour, they are apt to imagine, that where riches abound, and the avenues to every sensitive enjoyment are free and unobstructed, there misery can scarcely gain admittance, and the greatest share of human happiness must be found; that where there is wealth there can be little sorrow, and that those who glide along in splendour and affluence can scarcely be acquainted with the cares and anxieties which press so heavily upon the rest of mankind. Hence the ruling passion, which distinguishes the majority of mankind, to aspire after elevated station and rank, and to accumulate riches, although it should be at the expense of trampling under foot every social duty, and every moral principle, and even at the risk of endangering life itself. Hence, the idle and the vicious are led to imagine, that if they can but lay hold of wealth, whether by fraud, by deceit, or by open violence, they will be able to administer nutriment to those desires which, when gratified, will complete their happiness.

It is evident, that nothing can be supposed more effectual for counteracting such fallacious tendencies of the human mind, than the cultivation of reason, the expanding of the intellectual faculties, and the habit of applying the principles of knowledge to the diversified phenomena of human character and conduct. The man whose mind is accustomed to investigation, and to take an extensive range through the regions of science, and who considers his mental powers as the chief characteristic by which he is distinguished in the scale of animal existence, will naturally be guided in his estimates of human character, by *moral* and *intellectual* considerations. His eye will easily penetrate through the thin veil of exterior and adventitious accompaniments, and appreciate what alone is worthy of regard in the characters of men, whether they be surrounded by wealth and splendour, or immersed in poverty or obscurity. And with respect to human happiness, a person of this description will easily enter into such a train of reasoning as the following, and feel its force:—That, in respect of wealth, what we cannot reach may very well be forborne; that the inequality of happiness on this account is, for the most part, much less than it seems; that the greatness which we admire at a distance, has much fewer advantages, and much less splendour, when we are suffered to approach it; that the happiness which we imagine to be found in high life, is much alloyed and diminished by a variety of foolish passions and domestic cares and anxieties, of which we are generally ignorant; and that the apparent infelicity of the lower stations in society is frequently moderated by various moral and domestic comforts, unknown to many of those who occupy the highest ranks of social life. There is a certain portion of external enjoyment without which no man can be happy; and there is a certain portion of wealth to procure this enjoyment which every rank of society ought to possess, and which even the lowest ranks would obtain, were the movements of the social machine properly conducted. But, to pursue riches, with all the violence of passion, as the chief end of our being, is not only degrading to our intellectual natures, and tends to block up the avenues to tranquil enjoyment, but is fraught with toil and anxiety and innumerable hazards. "Wealth," says a

Latin moral writer, "is nothing in itself; it is not useful but when it departs from us; its value is found only in that which it can purchase, which, if we suppose it put to its best use by those that possess it, seems not much to deserve the desire or envy of a wise man. It is certain, that with regard to corporeal enjoyment, money can neither open new avenues to pleasure, nor block up the passages of anguish. Disease and infirmity still continue to torture and enfeeble, perhaps exasperated by luxury, or promoted by softness. With respect to the mind, it has rarely been observed, that wealth contributes much to quicken the discernment, enlarge the capacity, or elevate the imagination; but may, by hiring flattery, or laying diligence asleep, confirm error and harden stupidity."

Such are some of the views and principles by which an enlightened mind will naturally estimate the characters and enjoyments of mankind. Were the great body of the population in every country qualified to enter into such reasonings, and to feel the force of such considerations, it could not fail of being accompanied with many beneficial effects. It would temper that foolish adulation which ignorance and imbecility so frequently offer at the shrine of wealth and splendour; and would undermine those envious and discontented dispositions with which the lower ranks are apt to view the riches and possessions of the great. As moral principles and conduct, associated with intelligence, are the only proper objects of respect in the human character, it would lead persons to form a judgment of the true dignity of man, not by the glitter of affluence, or the splendour of equipage, but by those moral and intellectual qualities and endowments, which, in every station, demands our regard, and which constitute the real glory of the human character. It would tend to counteract the principle of *Avarice*, which has produced so many miseries and mischiefs in society, and to promote that *Contentment* under the allotments of Divine Providence in which consists the chief part of the happiness of mankind. And while it would counteract the tendency to foolish and immoral pursuits, it would direct to those rational pursuits and enjoyments which are pure and permanent, and congenial to the high dignity and destination of man. In short, were the attention of the higher and influential classes turned away from hounding and horse-racing, masquerades, gambling, and such like frivolous amusements, and directed to the study of useful science, we might expect to behold them patronising philantrophic and scientific characters in their plans and investigations, and devoting a portion of their wealth to carry forward those improvements by which the comforts of mankind would be increased, and science and art carried nearer to perfection. The twentieth part of that wealth which is too frequently spent in fashionable follies, were it devoted to such purposes, would be of incalculable service to the interests both of humanity and of science.

II. The acquisition of general knowledge *would enable persons to profit by their attendance on public instructions.*

In the present day, lectures on popular philosophy, astronomy, chemistry, geology, and political economy are occasionally delivered in the principal cities and towns of Great Britain; but, out of a population of thirty or forty thousand, it frequently happens, that scarcely thirty or forty individuals can be collected to listen to instructions on such subjects. This, no doubt, is partly owing to the fee demanded for admission, which is sometimes beyond the reach of many intelligent persons in the lower walks of life. But it is chiefly owing to *the want of taste* for such branches of knowledge—to ignorance of the elements of general science—and to unacquaintance with the *terms* which require to be used in the explanation of such subjects, arising from the want of intellectual instruction in early life. Even of the few who generally attend such lectures, there is not perhaps the one half who can enter with intelligence into the train of reasoning and illustration brought forward by the lecturer, or feel much interest in the discussions, excepting when their eyes are dazzled with some flashy experiment. Hence it follows, that very little knowledge comparatively can be communicated in this way to the population at large, owing to the deficiency of previous instruction,—and that systems of intellectual education, more extensive and efficient than those which have hitherto been in operation, require to be adopted, before the great body of the people can be supposed to profit by attendance on courses of lectures on any department of knowledge.

The same remark will apply, with a few modifications, to the instructions, delivered by the teachers of religion. For want of a proper foundation being previously laid, in the exercise of the rational faculty, and the acquisition of general information, comparatively little advantage is derived from the sermons and expository lectures delivered by the ministers of the Gospel. Of a thousand individuals which may compose a worshipping assembly where religious instructions are imparted, there are seldom above two hnndred (and most frequently much fewer) that can give any intelligent account of the train of thought which has been pursued, or the topics which have been illustrated in the discourses to which they have professed to listen. This may be owing, in many instances, to the dry and abstract method by which certain preachers construct their discourses, and to the want of energy, and the dull and monotonous manner in which they are delivered. But, in the majority of instances, it is obviously owing to habits of *inattention* to subjects of an intellectual nature—to an incapacity for following a train of illustration or reasoning—and to the want of acquaintance with the meaning of many terms which theological instructors find it expedient to use in the construction of their discourses—and such deficiencies are to be ascribed to the mental faculties not having been exercised from infancy in the pursuit of knowledge and in rational investigations.

This deficiency of knowledge and intellectual culture seems to be virtually acknowledged by the ministers of religion; since, in their general discourses, they confine themselves, for the most part, to the elucidation of the *first principles* of religion. Instead of exhibiting a luminous and comprehensive view of the whole scenery of divine revelation, and illustrating its various parts from the history of nations, the system of nature, and the scenes of human life—they generally confine their discussions to a few topics connected with what are termed the fundamental doctrines of the Gospel. Instead of "going on to perfection," as the Apostle Paul exhorts, by tracing the elements of Christianity in all their bearings on moral conduct and Christian contemplation, and endeavouring to carry forward the mind to the most enlarged views of the perfections of God and the "glory of his kingdom"—they feel themselves under the necessity of recurring again and again to "the first principles of the doctrine of Christ"—feeding their hearers "with milk" instead of "strong meat." And the reason assigned for waiving the consideration of the more sublime topics of natural and revealed religion, and thus limiting the subject of their discussions, is that their hearers are unqualified to follow them in the arguments and illustrations which behoved to be brought forward on such subjects—that such an attempt would be like speaking to the winds or beating the air, and would infallibly mar their edification. If this reason be valid, (and that it is partly so there can be little doubt) it implies, that some glaring deficiency must exist in the mental culture of the great body of professing Christians, and that it ought to be remedied by every proper mean, in order that they may be qualified to advance in the knowledge of the attributes, the works, and the ways of God, and to "go on unto perfection."

It is foretold in the sacred oracles, that "men shall speak of the might of God's terrible acts," that "his saints shall speak of *the glory of his kingdom*, and talk of his *power*, to make known to the sons of men his mighty operations and the glorious majesty of his kingdom." This prediction has never yet been fulfilled in reference to the great body of the Christian church. For, where do we find one out of twenty among the hearers of the Gospel capable of rehearsing the "terrible acts" of God, either in his moral or his physical operations—of tracing the dispensations of his providence towards nations and communities, in a connected series, from the commencement of time, through the successive periods of history—and of comparing the desolations of cities and the ruin of empires with the declarations of ancient prophecy? Where do we find one out of a hundred capable of expatiating on the "power" of Jehovah, and on the most striking displays of this perfection which are exhibited throughout the vast creation? Or where shall we find those who are qualified to display the magnificence of that empire which is "established in the heavens," embracing within its boundaries thousands of suns and ten thousands of worlds—or "to speak," with intelligence, "of the glory of that kingdom which ruleth over all," and thus "to make known to others the mighty operations" carried on by Jehovah, "and the *glorious majesty* of his kingdom?" It is obvious that no such qualifications yet exist among the *majority* of members which compose the visible church. And yet the predictions to which we refer *must be realized*, at some period or another, in the history of the divine dispensations. And is it not desirable that they should, in some degree, be realized in our own times? And, if so, ought we not to exert all our influence and energies in endeavouring to accomplish so important and desirable an object? And, in what manner are our energies in this respect to be exerted, but in concerting and executing, without delay, plans for the universal *intellectual* instruction of mankind? For, without the communication of knowledge to a far greater extent, and much more diversified than what has even yet been considered necessary for ordinary Christians, we can never expect to behold in the visible church "saints" endowed with such sublime qualifications as those to which we have alluded, or the approach of that auspicious era when "all shall know the Lord," in the highest sense of the expression, "from the least even to the greatest."

To obtain a comprehensive, and as far as possible, a *complete* view of the system of revelation in all its parts and bearings, and to be enabled to comply with all its requirements, is both the duty and the interest of every man. But, in order to this attainment, there must be acquired a certain habit of thinking and of meditating. In vain does a person turn over whole volumes, and attempt to peruse catechisms, bodies of divinity, or even the Scriptures themselves,—he can never comprehend the dependencies, connexions and bearings of divine truth, and the facts they explain and illustrate, unless he acquire a habit of arranging ideas, of laying down principles, and deducing conclusions. But this habit cannot be acquired without a continued series of instructions, especially in the early part of life, accompanied with serious attention and profound application. For want of such pre-requisites the great body of Christians do not read half the benefit they otherwise might from the preaching of the Gospel; and "when for the time they ought to be teachers of others, they have still need that one teach them again, which be the first principles of the oracles of God." "Hence it is," says a celebrated preacher, "that the greatest part of our sermons produce so little fruit, because sermons are, at least they ought to be, connected discourses, in which the principle founds the consequence, and the consequence follows the principle: all which supposes in the hearers a habit of meditation and attention. For the same reason, we are apt to be offended when any body attempts to draw us out of the sphere of our prejudices, and are not only ignorant, but ignorant from gravity, and derive, I know not what glory from our own stupidity. Hence it is, that a preacher is seldom or never allowed to *soar* in his sermons, to rise into the contemplation of some lofty and rapturous objects, but must always descend to the *first principles* of religion, as if he preached for the first time, or as if his auditors for the first time heard. Hence our preachers seem to lead us into obscure paths, and to lose us in abstract speculations, when they treat of some of the attributes of God, such as his faithfulness, his love of order, his regard for his intelligent creatures. It is owing to this that we are, in some sense, well acquainted with some truths of religion, while we remain entirely ignorant of others. Hence also it is, that some doctrines which are true in themselves, demonstrated in our Scriptures, and essential to religion, become errors, yea sources of many errors in our mouths, because we consider them only in themselves, and not in connexion with other doctrines, or in the proper places to which they belong in the system of religion."

Were we then, without delay, to set on foot plans of universal instruction, on a rational principle—were the young generation to be universally trained up in rational exercises and habits of reflection, first at Infant Schools, and afterwards at seminaries of a higher order, conducted on the same intellectual principle, and this system of tuition continued to the age of manhood, we should, ere long, behold a wonderful change in the state of society, in the intelligence of the Christian people, and in the illustrations of religion which would be introduced into the pulpit. We should behold thousands of intelligent worshippers crowding our religious assemblies, with minds prepared for receiving instruction, and eagerly listening to arguments and illustrations in reference to the most sublime and important subjects. We should behold our preachers explaining the first principles of religion with such clearness and energy, that they should seldom need to recur to the subject, "soaring in their sermons," rising into "the contemplation of some lofty and rapturous objects"—displaying the majesty and supremacy of God in the operation of his moral government among the nations, descanting on his glorious attributes, exhibiting his wisdom in the arrangements of nature and the movements of his providence, illustrating his omnipotence and grandeur from the glories of the firmament, and the magnitude of the universe—directing their hearers to the contemplation of the works of his hand as illustrations of the declarations of his word—demonstrating the truth of revelation from its powerful and beneficient effects—enforcing the holy tempers and the duties which religion requires from every rational and scriptural motive—illustrating the effects of moral evil from the history of nations and the miseries in which it has involved individuals and societies—expatiating on schemes of philanthropy for the improvement of mankind, and the conversion of the heathen, and displaying the love and mercy of God towards our race, and the connexions and bearings of the work of redemption, in its relation to the angelic tribes and other beings, and in its glorious and happy consequences on unnumbered multitudes of mankind, throughout the ages of eternity. In such a state of Christian society we should have no dull monotonous preachers, skimming over the surface of an abstract subject, in a twenty minutes' sermon, and leaving their hearers as dull, and lifeless, and uninformed as they found them; but all our public services would be conducted with life, and energy, and pathos, and by men of sanctified dispositions and enlightened understandings, "not given to" idleness and "filthy lucre," but having their whole faculties absorbed in the study of the word, the ways, and the works of God. And, in order to expand the minds of the Christian people, and to prepare them for listening with intelligence to such instructions, we should have Courses of Lectures on Natural History, Philosophy, Astronomy, and General History, attended by *thousands* of anxious inquirers, instead of the *tens* which can now be induced to attend on such means of instruction. For knowledge, when it is clearly exhibited, and where a previous desire has been excited for its acquisition, is a source of enjoyment to the human mind in every stage of its progress, from the years of infancy to the latest period of mortal existence.

III. Such a diffusion of knowledge as that to which we have now adverted, *would introduce a spirit of tolerance and moderation, and prevent the recurrence of those persecutions for conscience' sake, which have so much disgraced the world.*

It is a striking and most melancholy fact in the history of man, that the most dreadful sufferings and tortures ever felt by human beings, have been inflicted on account of differences of opinion respecting the dogmas and the ceremonies of religion. Men have been suffered to remain villains, cheats and robbers, deceitful, profligate and profane, to invade the territories of their unoffending neighbours, to burn cities and towns, to lay waste provinces, and slaughter thousands of their fellow-creatures, and to pass with impunity; while, in numerous instances, the most pious, upright, and philanthropic characters have been hurried like criminals to stakes, gibbets, racks, and flames, merely for holding an opinion different from their superiors respecting a doctrine in religion, or the manner in which the Divine Being ought to be worshipped. In the early ages of Christianity, under the emperor Nero, the Christians were wrapped up in the skins of wild beasts, and some of them in this state worried and devoured by dogs; others were crucified, and others dressed in shirts made stiff with wax, fixed to axle trees, and set on fire, and consumed in the gardens at Rome. Such dreadful persecutions continued, under the heathen emperors, with a few intervals, to the time of Constantine, a period of more than two hundred and thirty years. It might not be so much to be wondered at that pagans should persecute the followers of Christ; but it was not long before pretended Christians began to persecute one another on account of certain shades of difference in their religious opinions. The persecutions to which the Waldenses and Albigenses were subjected by the Popish church, and strangling and burning of supposed heretics, and the tortures inflicted on those suspected of favouring the doctrines of Protestantism by the Spanish inquisition—a court whose history is written in flames, and in characters of blood,—exhibit a series of diabolical cruelties, the recital of which is enough to make "the ears of every one to tingle," and to make him feel as if he were degraded in belonging to a race of intelligences capable of perpetrating such dreadful enormities.

Even in the British isles such persecutions have raged, and such cruelties have been perpetrated, and that, too, in the name of the benevolent religion of Jesus Christ. In our times, the more appalling and horrific forms which persecution formerly assumed, have been set aside by the civil laws of the country, but *its spirit still remains*, and manifests itself in a variety of different shapes. What other name can be given to a power which prevents a numerous and respectable body of men from holding certain civil offices and emoluments, because they do not belong to an established church, and yet *compels* them to contribute to the maintenance of the ministers of that church, although they do not recognise them as their religious instructors? that denies to a dissenter, or his children, the privilege of being interred in what is called consecrated ground, and refuses to allow a bell to be tolled at their funerals?—that, in Scotland, prevents a person, however distinguished for moral qualifications and intellectual acquirements, from being eligible as teacher of a parochial school, if he is not connected with the established church? and in many other ways attempts to *degrade* thousands of individuals on account of their thinking and acting according to the dictates of their conscience? It is true, indeed, that fires, and racks, and tortures, and gibbets, and thumb-screws are no longer applied as punishments for differences of opinion in religion, for the strong hand of the civil law interposes to prevent them. But were no such power interposed, the principle which sanctions such deprivations as those now mentioned, if carried out to all its legitimate consequences, might soon lead to as dreadful persecutions as those which have already entailed idelible disgrace on the race of man.

Such a spirit of intolerance and persecution is directly opposed to every rational principle, to every generous and humane feeling, to every precept of Christianity, and to every disposition inculcated by the religion of Jesus. *It is the height of absurdity to enforce* belief in any doctrine or tenet, by the application of *physical power*, for it never can produce the intended effect; it may harden and render persons more obstinate in their opinions, but it can never convey conviction to the understanding. And if men had not acted like fools and idiots, as well as like demons, such a force, in such cases, would never have been applied. And, as such an attempt is *irrational*, so it is *criminal* in the highest degree, to aim at producing conviction by the application of flames, or by the point of the sword; being at direct variance both with the *precepts* and the *practice* of the Benevolent Founder of our holy religion.

We have, therefore, the strongest reason to conclude, that were the light of science and of Christianity universally diffused, the hydra of persecution would never dare, in any shape, to lift up its heads again in the world. As it was during the dark ages that it raged in its most horrific forms, so the light of intelligence would force it back to the infernal regions whence it arose, as the wild beasts of the forests betake themselves to their dens and thickets at the approach of the rising sun. Wherever reason holds its ascendancy in the mind, and the benevolence of Christianity is the great principle of human action, persecution will never be resorted to, either for extirpating error or enforcing belief in any opinions. An enlightened mind will at once perceive, that in punishing erroneous opinions by fines, imprisonment, racks, and flames, *there is no fitness* between the *punishment* and the supposed *crime*. The crime is a mental error, but penal laws have no internal operation on the mind, except to exasperate its feelings against the power that enforces them, and to confirm it more strongly in the opinions it has embraced. Errors of judgment, whether religious or political, can only be overturned by *arguments* and calm reasoning, and all the civil and ecclesiastical despots on earth, with all their edicts, and bulls, and tortures, will never be able to extirpate them in any other way. For the more that force is resorted to to compel belief in any system of opinions, the more will the mind revolt at such an attempt, and the more will it be convinced, that such a system is worthless and untenable, since it requires such irrational measures for its support. It can only tend to produce dissimulation, and to increase the number of hypocrites and deceivers. An enlightened mind will also perceive, that such conduct is no less *irreligious* than it is irrational; for, where persecution begins religion ends. Religion proclaims "peace on earth and good will to men;" all its doctrines, laws, and ordinances are intended to promote the happiness of mankind, both in "the life that now is and that which is to come." But actions which tend to *injure* men in their persons, liberty, or property, under the pretence of converting them from error, must be directly repugnant to the spirit of that religion which is "pure, and peaceable, gentle, and easy to be entreated," and to the character of that Benevolent Being whose "tender mercies are over all his works." If our religion *required* for its establishment in the world, the infliction of civil pains and penalties on those who oppose it, it would be unworthy of being supported by any rational being; and it is a sure evidence that it is not the genuine religion of the Bible, but error and human inventions, under the mask of Christianity, that are intended to be established, when such means are employed for its propagation and support. It requires very little reflection to perceive, that religion does not consist in mere opinions or ceremonial observances, but in the cultivation and excercise of those heavenly virtues and dispositions which tend to cement the family of mankind in brotherly affection, and to prepare them for the intercourses and employments of the celestial world; and if these are wanting or disregarded, religion becomes a mere inanity, and it is of little consequence what opinions men profess to entertain respecting it.

In short, in an enlightened state of society, men would be disposed to allow the utmost freedom of thought on every subject, not inconsistent with the good order of society, and would nevertheless hold the most friendly intercourse with each other. They would clearly discern, that the best way to reclaim the vicious, and to convert the erroneous, is, not to rail and to threaten, but to be affable and gentle, to bring forward cogent arguments, and "in meekness to instruct those who oppose themselves to the truth." They would see, that many of those opinions and dogmas, in regard to religion, which have created heart-burnings and dissensions, are comparatively of trivial importance,—that the doctrines in which all Christians agree are much more numerous, and of far greater importance, than those about which they differ,—that there are subjects on which the limited faculties of human beings are unable to form any clear or decisive opinions,—that the mind must form its opinions,—in accordance with the limited or the expansive range of its intellectual vision,—that where its mental view is narrow and confined, its conclusions must be somewhat different from those which are deduced by a mind qualified to take in a more extensive field of vision,—that the philosopher whose mind takes in at a grasp the general system of the world, and the diversified phenomena of the universe, must have ideas and modes of thinking materially different from those of the peasant, whose views are limited chiefly to the confines of his parish, and the objects immediately around him,—that there are are few men *wilfully* erroneous, and that ignorance and vice are the principal causes of false and untenable opinions,—that due allowance ought always to be made for educational biasses, local prejudices, social influence, and the range of thought to which individuals have been accustomed,—that the exercise of love towards God and man is of infinitely greater importance than mere coincidence in opinion, and that a complete unanimity of opinion on every subject is not to be expected in the present state, perhaps not even in the future world. Were such considerations taken into account, (and they would be all recognised in an enlightened state of society,) those contentions and animosities which now rankle in the Christian church, and separate the different sectaries, would be laid to rest, persecution in every shape would be held in universal abhorrence, and peace, moderation, and candour would distinguish the friends of religion and all classes of society.

IV.—A universal diffusion of knowledge would *vanquish the antipathies of nations*, and tend to produce *union and harmony among mankind.*

"God hath made of one blood all nations of men, for to dwell on all the face of the earth." But although they are all the offspring of one Almighty Being, and descended from one original human pair, they have hitherto lived, for the most part, in a state of strife and variance, of contention and warfare. The history of the world contains little else than details of the dissensions of nations, the feuds of chieftains, "the tumults of the people," the revolutions of empires, and the scenes of devastation and carnage which have followed in their train. If we go as far back in our researches as the earliest historical records can carry us, we shall find that wars have prevailed, almost without intermission, in every age, in every country, and among every tribe. No sooner has one series of battles terminated than preparations have been made for another; and, in such contests, magnificent cities have been tumbled into ruins, provinces desolated, kingdoms rent asunder, and thousands of thousands of human beings slaughtered with all the ferocity of infernal demons. It is not beyond the bounds of probability to suppose, that, in those scenes of warfare, the eighth part of the human race, in every age, has been destroyed, or, a number of mankind amounting to nearly *twenty thousand millions*, which is equal to twenty-five times the number of inhabitants presently existing in the world. And the leaders in such diabolical exploits, so far from repenting of their atrocities, have generally been disposed to glory in their crimes.

Hence the jealousies, the antipathies, and the hatred which have subsisted, and which still subsist, between neighbouring nations. The Turks hate the Greeks, and, as far as in their power, inflict upon them every species of cruelty and injustice. The Chinese hate the Europeans, cheat them if they can, and pride themselves in their fancied superiority over all other nations. The Moors of Africa hate the negroes, plunder their villages, and reduce them to slavery; the King of Dahomey wages almost continual war with the neighbouring tribes, and adorns the walls of his palace with the skulls of prisoners taken in battle. The Algerines and the emperors of Morocco live in a state of continual warfare with Christian nations, seize upon their ships, and reduce their crews to slavery. The *Monucaboes*, who inhabit the inland part of Malacca, live at variance with all around them, and never fail to set fire to the ripening grain in every field that is unprotected and uninclosed. The Arabians are set against every other nation, and roam through their deserts, attacking caravans and travellers of every description. The inhabitants of one part of New Zealand are almost in a continual state of enmity against those of another, and the natives of almost every island in the Indian and Pacific oceans, if not engaged in actual contests, are in a state of warlike attitude with regard to each other. Even nations advanced to high degrees of civilization, are found indulging the meanest and most unreasonable jealousies and antipathies in relation to one another. The French and the English, whom nature has separated only by a narrow channel of the sea, and who are distinguished above all other nations for their discoveries and improvements in the arts, have, for centuries, fostered a spirit of jealousy and rivalship which has produced political animosities, hatred, wars, and ruin to the financial and commercial interests of both nations. During the wars which succeeded the French revolution, this spirit of hatred and enmity rose to such a pitch, that a large portion of each nation would have, with pleasure, beheld the other hurled with fury into the infernal regions.*

Is there no prospect, then, that such antipathies shall ever be extirpated, and harmony restored to the distracted nations? Shall the earth be for ever swept with the besom of destruction? Shall war continue its ravages without intermission? Shall hatred still rankle among all nations, and Peace never wave its olive branch over the world? Are we to sit down in hopeless despair, that a union among the nations will ever be effected, because wars have continued since the beginning of the world? No,—we have no reason to despair of ultimate success, when the moral machinery, calculated to effectuate the object, shall be set in motion. As ignorance is the parent of vice, the nurse of pride, avarice, ambition, and other unhallowed passions, from which wars derive their origin, so, when the strongholds of ignorance shall be demolished, and the light of intelligence shall shed its influence over the world, and the opposite principles of humility, moderation, and benevolence shall pervade the minds of men, the foundations of the system of warfare will be shaken, and a basis laid for the establishment of universal peace. However long the ravages of war have desolated and convulsed the world, it is announced in the decree of heaven, that a period shall arrive "when *wars shall cease unto the ends of the earth.*" And the era when warriors "shall beat their swords into ploughshares and their spears into pruning hooks, and learn the art of war no more," is coeval with the period foretold in ancient prophecy, when "the knowledge of the Lord shall cover the earth, and when all shall know him from the least to the greatest."

Knowledge has a tendency to unite the hearts of all who are engaged in its pursuit; it forms a bond of union among its votaries more firm and permanent than that which unites princes and statesmen; especially if it is conjoined with Christian principles and virtuous dispositions. Congeniality of sentiments, and similarity of pursuits, gradually weaken the force of vulgar prejudices, and tend to demolish those barriers which the jealousies of nations have thrown around each other. True philosophers, whether English, Swedish, Russian, Swiss, German, or Italian, maintain an intimate and affectionate correspondence with each other on every subject of literature and science, notwithstanding the

* During the wars alluded to, a gentleman, (conversing with the author on the subject,) who was uttering the most virulent invectives against the French, concluded by saying, "After all I wish no great evil to the French, *I only wish they were all safely landed in heaven*," plainly intimating, that he considered them unworthy to live upon the earth, and that the sooner they were cut off from it and sent to the other world, so much the better, whether their fate should be to dwell in the shades of Tartarus or the abodes of Elysium.

antipathies of their respective nations. During the late long-continued and destructive warfare between the French and English, which was carried on with unprecedented hostility and rancour, the naturalists, mathematicians, astronomers, and chemists of the two countries, held the most friendly correspondence in relation to the subjects connected with their respective departments, in so far as the jealousies of their political rulers would permit. In the communication of the French and English philosophers respecting the progress of scientific discovery, we find few traces of nationality, and should scarcely be able to learn from such communications that their respective nations were engaged in warfare, unless when they lament the obstructions which interrupted their regular correspondence, and their injurious effects on the interests of science. It is a well known fact, that, during the late war, when political animosities ran so high, the National Institute of France announced prizes for the discussion of scientific questions, and invited the learned in other nations, not even excepting the English, to engage in the competition; and one of our countrymen, Sir Humphrey Davy, actually obtained one of the most valuable and distinguished of these honorary awards.

When knowledge is conjoined with a recognition of the Christian precept, "Thou shalt love thy neighbour as thyself," its possessor will easily be made to enter into such considerations as the following, and to feel their force:—That all men, to whatever nation or tribe they belong, are the children of one Almighty Parent, endowed with the same corporal organs, the same intellectual powers, and the same lineaments of the Divine image—that they are subject to the same animal and intellectual wants, exposed to the same accidents and calamities, and susceptible of the same pleasures and enjoyments—that they have the same capacities for attaining to higher degrees of knowledge and felicity, and enjoy the same hopes and prospects of a blessed immortality—that God distributes among them all, thousands of benefits, embellishing their habitations with the same rural beauties, causing the same sun to enlighten them, the same vital air to make their lungs play, and the same rains and dews to irrigate their ground, and ripen their fields to harvest—that they are all capable of performing noble achievements, heroic exploits, vast enterprises; of displaying illustrious virtues, and of making important discoveries and improvements—that they are all connected together by numerous ties and relations, preparing for each other the bounties of Nature and the productions of art, and conveying them by sea and land from one country to another; one nation furnishing tea, another sugar, another wine, another silk, another cotton, and another distributing its manufactures in both hemispheres of the globe—in short, that they are all under the moral government of the same Omnipotent Being, who "hath made of one blood all nations of men to dwell on the face of all the earth, who hath determined the boundaries of their habitations," who carries them yearly around the centre of light and heat, and who "gives them rain from heaven and fruitful seasons, filling their hearts with food and gladness." How various, then, the ties, how sacred and indissoluble the bonds, which should unite men of all nations! Every man, whether he be a Jew or a Greek, a Barbarian or a Scythian, a Turk or a Frenchman, a German or a Swede, a Hottentot or an Indian, an Englishman or a Chinese, is to be considered as our kinsman and our brother, and, as such, ought to be embraced with benevolence and affection. In whatever region of the globe he resides, whatever customs or manners he adopts, and to whatever religious system he adheres, he is a member of the same family to which we all belong. And shall we feel indifferent to our brethren, shall we indulge resentment and hostility towards them, because they are separated from us by a river, by a channel, by an arm of the sea, by a range of mountains, or by an arbitrary line drawn by the jealousy of despots, or because their government and policy are different from ours? Ought we not, on the contrary, to take a cordial interest in every thing that concerns them—to rejoice in their prosperity, to feel compassion on account of the ravages, desolation, and misery which error and folly, vice and tyranny may have produced among them; and to alleviate, to the utmost of our power, the misfortunes and oppressions under which they groan? Reason, as well as Christianity, spurns at that narrow-minded patriotism which confines its regards to a particular country, and would promote its interests by any means, although it should prove injurious to every other nation. Whatever tends to the general good of the whole human family, will ultimately be found conducive to the prosperity and happiness of every particular nation and tribe; while, on the other hand, a selfish and ungenerous conduct towards other communities, and an attempt to injure or degrade them, will seldom fail to deprive us of the benefits we wished to secure, and to expose us to the evils we intended to avert. Such appear in fact to be the principles of God's moral government among the nations, and such the sanctions by which the laws of natural justice are enforced.

Were such sentiments universally recognised and appreciated, the antipathies of nations would speedily be vanquished, and union and harmony prevail among all the kindreds of the earth. And what a multitude of advantages would ensue—what a variety of interesting scenes would be presented—what an immense number of delightful associations would be produced, were such a union effected among mankind! Were men over all the globe living in peace and harmony, every sea would be navigated, every region explored, its scenery described, its productions collected, its botanical peculiarities ascertained, and its geological structure investigated. The geography of the globe would be brought to perfection; its beauties, harmonies, and sublimities displayed, and the useful productions of every clime transported to every country, and cultivated in every land. Science would, of course, be improved, and its boundaries enlarged; new physical facts would be discovered for confirming and illustrating its principles, and a broad foundation laid for carrying it to perfection. While, at present, every traveller in quest of scientific knowledge in foreign lands, is limited in his excursions, and even exposed to imminent danger, by the rancour of savage tribes and the jealousy of despotic governments—in such a state of things, every facility would be given to his researches, and all the documents of history, and the treasures of nature and art, laid open to his inspection. He would be conducted, as a friend and brother, through every city and rural scene; the processes of arts and manufactures, the curiosities of nature, and the archives of literature and science, would be laid open to his view; and he would return to his native land loaded with whatever is curious and useful in nature and art, and enriched with new accessions to his treasures of knowledge. The knowledge and arts of one country would thus be quickly transported to another; agricultural, manufacturing and mechanical improvements would be gradually introduced into every region; barren wastes would be cultivated, forests cut down, marshes drained, cities founded, temples, schools and academies erected, modes of rapid communication between distant countries established, mutual interchanges of affection promoted, and "the once barren deserts made to rejoice and blossom as the rose."

We should then behold the inhabitants of distant countries arriving on our shores—not with tomahawks, clubs, spears, muskets, and other hostile weapons, but with the symbols of peace and the productions of their respective climes. We should behold the Malayans, the Chinese, the Cambodians, the Burmese, the Persians and the Japanese, unfurling their banners on our coasts and rivers, unloading their cargoes of tea, coffee, silks, nankeens, embroideries, carpets, pearls, diamonds, and gold and silver ornaments and utensils—traversing our streets and squares in the costume of their respective countries, gazing at our shops and edifices, wondering at our manners and customs, mingling in our assemblies, holding intercourse with our artists and philosophers, attending our scientific lectures and experiments, acquiring a knowledge of our arts and sciences, and returning to their native climes to report to their countrymen the information they had received, and to introduce among them our discoveries and improvements. "We should behold the tawny Indians of Southern Asia forcing their way up its mighty rivers in their leathern canoes, to the extremities of the north, and displaying on the frozen shores of the icy sea, the riches of the Ganges; the Laplander covered with warm fur arriving in southern markets, in his sledge drawn by rein-deer, and exposing for sale the sable skins and furs of Siberia; and the copper-coloured American Indian traversing the Antilles, and conveying from isle to isle his gold and emeralds." We should occasionally behold numerous caravans of Arabians, mounted on their dromedaries and camels, and tribes of Tartars, Bedouins, and Moors visiting the civilized countries of Europe, laden with the rarities and riches of their respective countries, admiring the splendour of our cities and public edifices, learning our arts and manufactures, acquiring a knowledge of our literature and sciences, purchasing our commodities, procuring specimens of our philosophical instruments, steam-engines, and mechanical powers—inviting agriculturists, artists, mechanics, teachers, ministers of religion, mathematicians and philosophers, to settle among them, for the purpose of improving their system of husbandry, rearing cities, towns and villages, disseminating useful knowledge, and introducing the arts and enjoyments of civilized society—at the same time inviting them to contract marriages with their sisters and daughters, and thus, by new alliances, *to reunite the branches of the human family*, which, though descended from one common parent, have been so long disunited,—and which disunion, national prejudices and antipathies, as well as climate and complexion, have tended to perpetuate. And, while we were thus instrumental in imparting knowledge and improvements to other nations, we ourselves should reap innumerable advantages. Our travellers and navigators, into whatever regions they might wish to penetrate, would feel secure from every hostile attack, and would recognise in every one they met a friend and a brother, ready to relieve their necessities, to contribute to their comfort, and to direct them in their mercantile arrangements and scientific researches. Our merchants and manufacturers would find numerous emporiums for their goods, and new openings for commercial enterprise, and would import from other countries new conveniences and comforts for the use of their countrymen at home.

From such friendly intercourses we should learn, more particularly than we have yet done, the *history* of other nations, and the peculiar circumstances in which they have existed, particularly of those tribes which have been considered as moving beyond the range of civilized society. All that we at present know of the history of many foreign nations, consists of a few insulated sketches and anecdotes, picked up at random by travellers who passed only a few days or weeks in the countries they describe, who were beheld with suspicion, and were imperfectly acquainted with the languages of the inhabitants. But, from a familiar and confidential intercourse, we should become acquainted with the whole series of their history, so far as it is known, which might not only be curious and interesting in itself, but might throw a light on the records of other nations, on the facts of sacred history, and on the general history of the world. We might thus know something of the circumstances which attended the early *dispersion* of mankind,—the motives which determined each tribe to choose its separate habitation in an unknown region, and which induced them to cross unknown arms of the sea, to traverse mountains which presented no path, and rivers which had not yet received a name, and whose commencement and termination were alike unknown. The information which distant tribes refuse us, when we approach them like warlike adventurers or ambitious merchants, would be freely communicated, when we mingled with them as friends and benefactors, and especially, after we had been instrumental in meliorating their physical and moral condition, and in communicating to them our improvements.

And, in the name of all that is sacred and benevolent, what should hinder such harmonious and affectionate intercourses between nations from being universally realized? Are we not all brethren of one family? Have we not all one Father? Has not one God created us? Does not the same planet support us, and the same atmosphere surround us? Does not the same sun cheer and enlighten us? Have we not the same physical organization, the same mental powers, and the same immortal destination? And is it not the interest of every individual of the human family that such a friendly intercourse should be established? Are there any *insuperable* obstructions, any *impassable* barriers, any *natural impossibilities*, that prevent such a union among the nations? No,—knowledge, combined with moral principle and true religion, if universally diffused, would speedily effectuate this wonderful transformation. Enlighten the understandings, direct the moral powers of man, extend the knowledge of Christianity through the world, and a broad foundation will be laid for universal improvement, and *universal friendship* among all nations.

But, in order that we may be instrumental in preparing the way for so desirable an event, our conduct towards other nations, and particularly towards uncivilized tribes, must be very different from what it has generally been in the ages that are past. We must become, not the plunderers and destroyers, but the instructors and the benefactors of mankind. Instead of sending forth the artillery of war, for the subjugation of distant nations, we must uniformly display the banner of love and the branch of Peace; instead of despatching crowds of needy adventurers, fired with the cursed love of gold, to plunder and to kill, like the Spaniards in their conquest of Mexico and Peru, —we must send forth armies of enlightened benefactors, to traverse the benighted nations, to carry the knowledge of divine truth within the region of Pagan darkness, to impart to them the blessings of instruction, and the comforts and conveniences of civilized life. Instead of landing on their shores swords and spears and musketry, —ploughshares, pruning hooks, and every other agricultural implement, must be plentifully supplied to all the inhabitants. Instead of carrying into slavery their children and relatives, and imbittering their lives with cruel treatment, like the Spaniards and the Portuguese, in reference to the African negroes, we must, proclaim "liberty to the captives, and the opening of the prison-doors to them that are bound." In short, our conduct must be almost diametrically opposite to that which political intriguers have generally pursued towards other states, if we would promote union among the nations. Our selfishness must be changed into beneficence, our pride into humility, our avarice into generosity, and our malignity into kindness and benevolence. Kindness and benevolent attentions will sometimes subdue even the most ferocious animals, and will seldom fail to soften the breast of the most savage people, and to win their affections. There is scarcely an individual within the range of the human species, or even within the range of animated nature, but is susceptible of the impressions of love; and if such principles and affections were to direct the future intercourses of nations, we might expect, ere long, to behold the commencement of that happy era, when "the wilderness and solitary place shall be glad, when nation shall no longer lift up sword against nation, when righteousness and praise shall spring forth before all the nations, and when there shall be nothing to hurt or destroy" among all the families of the earth.

V.—A general diffusion of knowledge would be one general mean of promoting ***union in the Christian Church.***

It is a lamentable fact, that throughout the whole world, there is no system of religion, the votaries of which are subdivided into so many sectaries as those who profess an adherence to the Christian faith. Within the limits of Great Britain, there are perhaps not much fewer than a hundred different denominations of Christians belonging to the Protestant church. We have Calvinists, Arminians, Baxterians, Antinomians, Arians and Unitarians, Episcopalians, Presbyterians, Methodists, Baptists, and Independents,—Seceders, Brownists, Sandemanians, Quakers, Moravians, Swedenborgians, Millenarians, Sabbatarians, Universalists, Sublapsarians, Supralapsarians, Dunkers, Kilhamites,

Shakers, &c. Of some of these there are several subdivisions. Thus, there are three or four denominations of Seceders, four or five of Baptists, three or four of Methodists, and two or three of Glassites or Sandemanians. Most of these denominations recognise the leading truths of divine revelation,—the natural and moral attributes of the Deity,—the fall of man, —the necessity of a Saviour,—the incarnation of Christ,—the indispensable duty of faith in him for the remission of sins,—the necessity of regeneration, and of holiness in principle and practice,—the obligation of the moral law,—the doctrine of a resurrection from the dead, and of a future state of rewards and punishments,—in short, every thing by which Christianity is distinguished from Mahomedanism, Pagan idolatary, and all the other systems of religion that prevail in the world. Yet, while agreeing in the leading doctrines of the Christian faith, they continue in a state of separation from each other, as if they had no common bond of union, and, as rival sects, are too frequently in a state of alienation, and even of open hostility. The points in which they differ are frequently so minute as to be incapable of being accurately defined, or rendered palpable to an impartial inquirer. Where the difference is most apparent, it consists chiefly in a diversity of opinion respecting such questions as the following:—Whether the election of man to eternal life be absolute or conditional,—whether Christ died for the sins of the whole world, or only for a limited number,—whether there be a gradation or an equality among the ministers of the Christian church,—whether every particular society of Christians has power to regulate its own affairs, or ought to be in subjection to higher courts of judicature,—whether the ordinance of the Lord's Supper should be received in the posture of sitting or of kneeling,—whether Baptism should be administered to infants or adults, or be performed by dipping or sprinkling, &c. Such are some of the points of dispute, which have torn the Christian church into a number of shreds, and produced among the different sectaries jealousies, recriminations and contentions. When we consider the number and the importance of the leading facts and doctrines in which they all agree, it appears somewhat strange and even absurd, that they should stand aloof from each other, and even assume a hostile attitude, on account of such comparatively trivial differences of opinion, especially when they all profess to be promoting the same grand object, travelling to the same heavenly country, and expect, ere long, to sit down in harmony in the mansions above. The grand principles of human action, which it is the chief object of Revelation to establish, and the precepts of morality which ought to govern the affections and conduct of every Christian, are recognised by all; and why then should they separate from each other, and remain at variance on account of matters of "doubtful disputation?"

The *evils* which flow from such a divided state of Christian society, are numerous and much to be deplored. A sectarian spirit has burst asunder the bonds of Christian love, and prevented that harmonious and affectionate intercourse among Christians which is one of the chief enjoyments of social religion. It has infused jealousies, fanned the flame of animosity and discord, set friends, brethren and families at variance, and shattered even civil communities into factions and parties. It has kindled contentions and heart-burnings, produced envyings, animosites, and hatred of brethren, burst asunder the strongest ties of natural affection, and has led professed Christians to violate the plainest dictates of humanity and of natural justice. It has excited a feverish zeal for the peculiarities of a sectary, while the distinguishing features of Christianity have either been overlooked or trampled under foot. It has wasted money unnecessarily in erecting separate places of worship, which might have been devoted to the promotion of the interests of our common Christianity. It has even corrupted our very *prayers*, infused into them human passions, and a spirit of party, and confined them to the narrow limits of our own sectary, as if the Omnipotent, whom we profess to adore, were biassed by the same prejudices as ourselves, and dispensed his favours according to our contracted views. Could we fly with the swiftness of an angelic messenger through the various assemblies convened on the Christian Sabbath, while they are offering up their prayers to heaven, what a repulsive and discordant scene would present itself, when we beheld the leaders of certain sectaries confining their petitions to their own votaries, imploring a *special* blessing upon themselves, as if they were the chief favourites of heaven, lamenting the errors of others, throwing out inuendos against rival sectaries, taking credit to themselves as the chief depositories of gospel truth, and thanking God for their superior attainments in Christian perfection! How unlike the noble, benevolent and expansive spirit which Christianity inculcates!—Nay, the intolerance which the divisions of the Christian church have engendered, has established Inquisitions for the purpose of torturing and burning supposed heretics,—has banished, imprisoned, plundered, hanged and committed to the flames, thousands and ten thousands, on account of their religious *opinions*; and many eminent characters, illustrious for piety and virtue, have fallen victims to such unchristian barbarities.

In particular, the divisions and contentions of Christians have been one of the chief causes of *the progress of infidelity*. The truth and excellence of our religion can only be exhibited to the world by its effects. And when, instead of love, union and harmony among its professors, we behold bitter envyings, schisms, contentions and animosities, there appears nothing to allure vicious and unthinking minds to examine its evidences, and to give it an impartial hearing. "First agree among yourselves," infidels reply, "and then we will consider the truth and importance of your opinions." Such a mode of reasoning and conduct is indeed both absurd and unfair, when the genuine doctrines and requisitions of Christianity are clearly stated in its original records, and which they ought to examine for themselves; but it is a circumstance much to be deplored, that Christians, by their sectarian animosities, should throw a stumbling-block in the way of rational investigation into the truths and foundations of religion, and cause thousands to stumble and fall to their destruction. But, what is perhaps worst of all, it has greatly retarded, and still retards, the universal propagation of Christianity through the world. Something has indeed been effected, of late years, by various sections of the Christian church, in the different Missionary enterprises which they have conducted, in their separate capacities; but it is not too much to affirm, that, had they acted in combination and in harmony, in the missionary cause, ten times more good would have been effected than has ever yet been accomplished. Besides, in our present mode of propagating the Gospel among the heathen, we are to a certain extent, sowing the seeds of those unhappy dissensions which have so long prevailed among ourselves. And, therefore, till the different religious denominations, in this and other Christian lands, be brought into a more general and harmonious union, we cannot expect to behold a rapid and extensive propagation of primitive Christianity throughout the Pagan world.

Such are some of the evils which a sectarian spirit has produced in the Christian Church. It is almost needless to say, that they do not originate in the genius of the Gospel, which is directly opposed to such a spirit, but in the corruption of human nature, and the perversion of true religion. They have their rise in *ignorance*,—in ignorance both of the revelations of the Bible, considered as one whole, and of those truths of history, philosophy, and general science, which have a tendency to liberalize and to enlarge the capacity of the human mind. This ignorance naturally leads to *self-conceit*, and an obstinate attachment to preconceived opinions and party prejudices, to attaching an undue importance to certain subordinate and favourite opinions, and overlooking the grand essentials of the Christian scheme; and thus prevents the mind from expanding its views, and taking a luminous and comprehensive ssuvey of the general bearings and distinguishing features of the religion of the Bible. And, if such numerous and serious evils have followed from the divisions of Christians, it becomes an important inquiry, whether they have ever been productive of advantages sufficient to counterbalance such pernicious effects. Is an obscure question, in relation to church-government, to be set in competition with Christian union? Is a metaphysical opinion about the sovereignty of God, and his councils during eternity past, to be obstinately maintained, although the strongest bonds of Christian love should thereby be burst asunder? Is the rigid adherence to an opinion respecting dipping or sprinkling in baptism, or the maintenance of a dogma in reference to the extent of Christ's redemption, under pretence of bearing a testimony in behalf of Divine truth, to be considered as sufficient to counterbalance the numerous evils which have flowed from a sectarian spirit? Can we suppose, that He whose law is *love*, who hath commanded us to "keep the unity of the Spirit in the bond of peace," and who hath declared, again and again, in the most explicit terms, "By this shall all men know that ye are my disciples, if ye love one another;" are we to suppose, that *He* will consider the maintenance of such opinions, under such pretences, as a warrant for the infringement of the law of charity, or the breach of Christian union, or that he sets a higher value on intellectual subtleties and speculative opinions, than on the practical requisitions of his word, and the manifestations of Christian temper and conduct? To answer these questions in the affirmative, would be little short of offering an insult to the King of Zion. Whatever is not so clearly revealed in Scripture, that every rational and serious inquirer does not plainly perceive it to be truth or duty, can scarcely be supposed to be of such importance, as to warrant the breach of the unity of the church. For the inspired writers, who wêre the vehicles of a revelation from heaven, can never be supposed to have used vague or ambiguous language in explaining and enforcing matters of the first importance.

If we consider the temper and conduct of many of those who are sticklers upon phrases, and zealous about matters of mere form, we shall be convinced how few beneficial practical effects are the result of a narrow sectarian spirit. While they appear fired with a holy zeal lest the purity of divine ordinances should be tainted by unwashen hands, you will sometimes find them immersed in the grossest sensualities and immoralities of conduct. While they are severe sticklers for what they conceive to be the primitive form and order of a Christian church, you will not unfrequently find *disorder* reigning in their families, the instruction of their children and servants neglected, and a sour and boisterous spirit manifested in all their intercourses with their domestics. Yea, you will find, in numerous instances, that they scruple not to practise *frauds* in the course of their business, and that you can have less dependance on their promises than on those of the men of the world, who make no pretences to religion. As an excellent writer has well observed. "An ardent temperament converts the enthusiast into a zealot, who, while he is laborious in winning proselytes, discharges common duties very remissly, and is found to be a more punctilious observer of his creed than of his word. Or, if his imagination is fertile, he becomes a visionary, who lives on better terms with angels and with seraphs, than with his children, servants, and neighbours; or, he is one who, while he reverences the 'thrones, dominions, and powers' of the invisible world, vents his spleen in railing on all 'dignities and powers on earth.'"*

What are the *remedies* then, which may be applied for healing the unhappy divisions which have arisen in the Christian church? It is evident, in the first place, that we must discard the greater part of those human systems of divinity, and those polemical writings and controversies, which have fanned the flame of animosity, and which have so frequently been substituted in the room of the oracles of God. We must revert to the Scriptures as the sole standard of every religious opinion, and fix our attention chiefly on those matters of paramount importance which are obvious to every attentive reader, and which enter into the essence of the Christian system. For, to maintain, that the Scriptures are not sufficiently clear and explicit in regard to every thing that has a bearing on the present comfort and the everlasting happiness of mankind, is nothing short of a libel on the character of the sacred writers, and an indignity offered to Him by whose Spirit they were inspired. We must also endeavour to discard the "vain janglings," the sophistical reasonings, and the metaphysical refinements of the schools, and the technical terms of polemical theology, such as *trinity*, *ypostatical union*, *sacraments*, &c. and, in our discussions, especially on mysterious or doubtful subjects, adhere as nearly as possible to the language of the inspired writers. In particular, more attention ought to be paid to the manifestation of *Christian love*, and the *practice* of religion, than to a mere coincidence of view with regard to certain theological dogmas. For it is easy to conceive, that a man may be animated by holy principles and dispositions, although he may have an obscure conception, or may even entertain an erroneous opinion, of some of the doctrines of religion; and we know by experience, that men may contend zealously for what are considered orthodox doctrines, and yet be destitute of the spirit of religion, and trample on its most important practical requirements. And, were the *spirit* of our holy religion thoroughly to pervade the different sections of the church —were Christian *affection* more generally manifested among all who bear the Christian name, and the practical injunctions of Christianity uniformly exemplified in their conduct, we should soon behold a general coincidence of opinion on every thing that can be deemed important in religion, and a mutual candour and forbearance, in regard to all subordinate opinions, that do not enter into the essence of religion, and which ought to be left to the private judgment of every inquirer.

But I entertain little hope that such measures will be adopted, and an object so desirable accomplished, while so much ignorance still pervades the minds of the majority of Christians, and while the range of their intellectual views is so much contracted. It is only when the effects of a general diffusion of knowledge shall be more extensively felt, that a more general and cordial union of the Christian world is to be expected. Light in the understanding is the source of all reformations, the detector of all evils and abuses, the corrector of all errors and misconceptions, and the stimulus to every improvement. It dispels the mists which prevented our distinct vision of the objects of our contemplation, discovers the stumbling-blocks over which we had fallen, points out the devious ways into which we had wandered, and presents before us every object in its just magnitude and proportions. The knowledge to which I allude consists, in the first place, in a clear and comprehensive view of the whole system of divine revelation, in all its connexions and bearings,—and, in the next place, in an acquaintance with all those historical, geographical, and scientific facts which have a tendency to expand the capacity of the mind, and to enlarge our conceptions of the attributes of God, and of the ways of his providence. Wherever the mind is thoroughly enlightened in the knowledge of such subjects, the tendency to bigotry and sectarianism will quickly be destroyed, and the partition walls which now separate the different sections of the church will gradually be undermined and crumble into dust. This might be illustrated from the very nature of the thing. A man whose mind is shrouded in comparative ignorance, is like a person who lands on an unknown country in the dusk of the evening, and forms his opinion of its scenery and inhabitants from the obscure and limited view he is obliged to take of them, during the course of a few hours,—while he whose mind is enlightened in every department of human and divine knowledge, is like one who has taken a minute and comprehensive survey of the same country, traversed its length and breadth, mingled with every class of its inhabitants, visited its cities, towns, and villages, and studied its arts and sciences, its laws, customs, and antiquities. The one can form but a very imperfect and inaccurate conception of the country he has visited, and could convey only a similar conception to others,—the other has acquired a correct idea of

* Natural Hist. of Enthusiasm, p. 14.

the scene he has surveyed, and can form an accurate judgment of the nature, the tendency, and bearings of the laws, institutions, and political economy which have been the subject of his investigations. So that the accounts given by these two visiters, of the same country, behoved to be materially different. The sectarian bigot is one who has taken a partial and limited view of one or two departments of the field of revelation, who fixes his attention on a few of its minute objects, and who overlooks the sublimity and the grand bearings of its more magnificent scenery. The man of knowledge explores it throughout its length and breadth, fixes his eye upon its distinguishing features, and brings all the information he has acquired from other quarters, to assist his conceptions of the nature, the bearings, and relations of the multifarious objects presented to his view. The luminous views he has taken of the leading objects and design of revelation, and the expansive conceptions he has acquired of the perfections of Him by whom it was imparted,—will never suffer him to believe, that it is agreeable to the will of God that a Christian society should be rent asunder in the spirit of animosity, because one party maintains, for example, that *dipping* is the true mode of performing baptism, and the other, that it should be administered by *sprinkling*, while they both recognise it as a divine ordinance, and symbolical of spiritual blessings,—or that such conduct can have a tendency to promote the glory of God, and the best interests of men. He can never believe that that incomprehensible Being who inhabiteth eternity, who superintends the affairs of ten thousand worlds, and who hath exhibited in his word the way to eternal life in the clearest light—should attach so great a degree of importance to such questions, that either the one party or the other should be considered as exclusive supporters of divine truth, while they infringe the law of Christian love, and forbear "to keep the unity of the spirit in the bond of peace." For, in reference to the example now stated, a few drops of water are equally a *symbol* or *emblem* as the mass of liquid in a mighty river;—and to consider the Almighty as beholding with approbation such speculations, and their consequent effects, would be little short of affixing a libel on his moral character. The man of knowledge is disposed to view in the same light, almost all the minute questions and circumstantial opinions, which have been the cause of separating the church of Christ into its numerous compartments.

If we attend to facts, we shall find, that, in ninety-nine cases out of a hundred, the man who is a violent party-partisan, is one whose ideas run in one narrow track, and who has taken a very limited and partial survey of the great objects of religion. He is generally unacquainted with the range of history, the facts of science, the philosophy of nature, and the physical and moral state of distant nations. His mind never ranges over the globe, nor contemplates the remote wonders of the Creator's empire. His reading is chiefly confined to the volumes and pamphlets published by the partisans of his own sect; he can run over the scriptures and arguments which support his opinions, like a racer in his course, but, if you break in upon his train of thought, and require him to prove his positions, as he goes along, he is at a stand, and knows not how to proceed. While he magnifies, with a microscopic eye, the importance of his own peculiar views, he almost overlooks the grand and distinguishing truths of the Bible, in which all true Christians are agreed. On the other hand, there is scarcely one instance out of a hundred, of men whose minds are thoroughly imbued with the truths of science and revelation, being the violent abettors of sectarian opinions, or indulging in party animosities; for, knowledge and liberality of sentiments almost uniformly go hand in hand. While we ought to recognise and appreciate every portion of divine truth, in so far as we perceive its evidence,—it is, nevertheless, the dictate of an enlightened understanding, that *those truths which are of the first importance, demand our first and chief attention.* Every controversy, agitated among Christians on subjects of inferior importance, has a direct tendency to withdraw the attention from the great objects which distinguish the revelations of the Bible; and there cannot be a more absurd or fatal delusion, than to acquire correct notions on matters comparatively unimportant, while we throw into the shade, or but faintly apprehend, those truths which are essential to religion, and of everlasting moment. Every enlightened Christian perceives the truth and importance of this position; and were it to be universally acted upon, sectarian divisions and contentions would soon cease to exist; for they have almost uniformly taken place in consequence of attaching too great a degree of importance to matters of inferior moment.

Were the minds of the members of the Christian church, therefore, thoroughly enlightened, and imbued with the moral principles of the religion of Jesus, we should soon behold, among all denominations, a tendency to union, on the broad basis of recognising the grand essential truths of Christianity, which formed the principal subjects of discussion in the sermons of our Saviour and his apostles—and a spirit of forbearance manifested in regard to all opinions on matters of inferior importance. Were this period arrived—and, from the signs of our times, its approach cannot be very distant—it would be attended with a train of the most glorious and auspicious effects. A merging of party differences, and a consequent union of enlightened Christians, would dissipate that spirit of trifling in religion by which so much time has been absorbed in discussing sectarian opinions, to the neglect of the great objects of the Christian faith; for when trivial controversies are quashed, the time and attention they absorbed would be devoted to more sublime and important investigations. It would have a powerful influence on the propagation of Christianity throughout the heathen world; for the whole Christian world would then become one grand Missionary Society, whose operations would be conducted with more efficiency and skill, whose funds would be much more ample, and whose Missionaries would be better educated than they now are—and those sectarian differences of opinion, which now produce so many unhappy dissensions, for ever prevented from disturbing the harmony of converts in distant lands. It would cherish the principle of Christian love, detach it from every unholy jealousy, and render it more ardent and expansive in its philanthropic operations. It would produce a powerful and beneficial influence upon the men of the world, and even upon infidels themselves; it would snatch from them one of their most powerful arguments against the religion of the Bible, and would allure them to the investigation of its evidences, by the exhibition it gave of its harmonious and happy effects. It would have an influence on the minds of the Roman Catholics, in leading them to an unbiassed inquiry into the grounds on which the Protestant church is established. At present, when called upon to examine the doctrines of Protestantism, they retort upon us—"You are divided into a hundred different sectaries, and are at variance among yourselves; show us which of these sects is in possession of the truth, and we will then examine your pretensions, and perhaps come over to your standard." It would have an influence on the Jewish people, in removing their prejudices against the religion of Jesus of Nazareth, especially, were it followed, as it likely would be, with a repeal of all those statutes which have imposed upon them disabilities, deprived them of the rights of citizenship, and subjected them to unchristian severities. In short—in connexion with the general manifestation of Christian principle—it would produce a benign influence on surrounding nations, and on the world at large. For a body of Christians, in such a country as ours, formed into one grand association, and acting in harmony, must exert a powerful influence on the councils of the nation; and our political intercourses with other states, being conducted on the basis of Christian principles and laws, would invite their attention to a religion productive of so much harmony and so many beneficial effects. Peace and unity in the church would have a tendency to promote peace and friendship among nations; the cause of universal education would be promoted, without those obstructions which now arise from sectarian prejudices; and a general diffusion of useful knowledge would soon be effected throughout every quarter of the civilized world, till the knowledge of Jehovah should cover the earth as the waters cover the channels of the seas.

The disunion of the Christian church is not to be perpetual. We are certain, that a period is hastening on, when its divisions shall be healed, when its boundaries shall be enlarged, and when "*the name of Jehovah shall be one throughout all the earth.*" At some period or other, therefore, in the lapse of time, a movement towards such a union must commence. It cannot take place before the attention of the religious world is directed to this object. And why should not such a movement commence at the present moment? Why should we lose another year, or even another month, before we attempt to concert measures, in order to bring about a consummation so devoutly to be wished? The present eventful period is peculiarly auspicious for this purpose; when the foundations of tyranny, injustice, and error are beginning to be shaken; when knowledge is making progress among every order of society; when reforms in the state, and in every subordinate department of the community, are loudly demanded by persons of every character and of every rank; when the evils attached to our ecclesiastical institutions are publicly denounced; when the scriptures are translating into the languages of every tribe; and when missionary enterprises are carrying forward in every quarter of the habitable globe. To attempt a union of all true Christians, at the present crisis, would, therefore, be nothing more than falling in with the spirit of the age, and acting in harmony with those multifarious movements, which are destined to be the means of enlightening and renovating the human race; and at no period since the Reformation could such an attempt have been made with more sanguine expectations, and greater prospects of success. All eyes are now turned towards some eventful and auspicious era, when the light of science shall shine refulgent, when abuses shall be corrected, evils remedied, society meliorated, and its various ranks brought into more harmonious association. And shall Christians alone remain shut up in their little homesteads, apart from each other, stickling about phrases, and contending about forms, without ever coming forth to salute each other in the spirit of union, and to give an impulse to the moral machinery that is hastening forward the world's improvement and regeneration? Such a surmise cannot be indulged: it would be a libel on the Christian world, and a reproach on the religion of which they profess themselves the votaries. I trust there are thousands in every department of the church, who are ardently longing to break down the walls of partition, which separate them from their brethren, and anxiously waiting for an opportunity of expressing their sentiments, and of giving the right hand of fellowship "to all who love our Lord Jesus in sincerity."

In any attempts that may be made to promote this great object, *mutual concessions behoved to be made by all parties.* One general principle, that requires to be recognised, is this:—*that every opinion and practice be set aside, which is acknowledged on all hands to have no direct foundation in scripture*, but is a mere human fabrication, introduced by accident or whim; such as, the observance of fast and preparation days previous to the participation of the Lord's Supper, kneeling in the act of partaking of that ordinance, repeating the Athanasian Creed in the regular services of the church, &c. &c. It is a striking and remarkable fact, that the chief points about which Christians are divided, are points on which the volume of inspiration is silent, and which the presumption and perversity of men have attached to the Christian system, and interwoven with the truths and ordinances of religion; and, therefore, were the line of distinction clearly drawn between mere human opinions and ceremonials, and the positive dictates of revelation, and the one separated from the other, the way would be prepared for a more intimate and harmonious union in the church of Christ. As a preparative measure to such a union, a friendly intercourse between the different sectaries* should be solicited and cherished. Enlightened ministers of different denominations should occasionally exchange pulpits, and officiate for each other in the public exercises of divine worship. This would tend to show to the world, and to each other, that there is no unholy jealousy or hostile animosity subsisting between them, which their present conduct and attitude too frequently indicate. It would also be productive of many conveniences, in the case of a minister being indisposed, or absent from home, as his place could frequently be supplied, without the least expense or inconvenience, by his brethren of other denominations. It would likewise show to the mass of professing Christians, that the doctrines promulgated, and the duties enforced, by ministers of different denominations, are substantially the same. What a disgrace to the Christian name, that such a friendly intercourse has never yet been established; or, when it occasionally happens, that it should be considered as an extraordinary and unlooked-for phenomenon! What a strange and unexpected report must be received by Christian converts in heathen lands, when they are told, that Christian ministers in this country, who were instrumental in sending missionaries to communicate to them the knowledge of salvation, are actuated by so much jealousy, and stand so much aloof from each other, that even at the very time they are planning missionary enterprises, they will refuse their pulpits to each other, for the purpose of addressing their fellow-men on subjects connected with their everlasting interests, and refrain from joining in unison in the ordinances of religion, although many of them expect, ere long, to join in harmony in the services of the sanctuary above! It is to be hoped, that such a disgrace to the Christian cause will soon be wiped away, and its inconsistency clearly perceived by all who are intelligent and "right-hearted men."

* By *sectaries*, in this place, and elsewhere, I understand, not only the different denominations of *Dissenters*, but the Church of England, the Church of Scotland, and all other national churches, which are all so many sectaries, or different compartments of the universal Christian church.

Such a friendly intercourse and correspondence as now suggested, would be far more efficient in preparing the way for a cordial union of Christians, than the deliberations and discussions of a thousand doctors of divinity, delegated to meet in councils to settle the points in dispute between the different sectaries. This object, I presume, will never be accomplished by theological controversy, or by any attempt to convince the respective parties of the futility or erroneousness of their peculiar opinions; but, on the ground of their being brought nearer to each other, and more firmly united in the mutual exercise of the Christian virtues, and in the bonds of Christian affection. And, when such a harmonious intercourse shall be fully effected, it will form a more glorious and auspicious era in the history of the Christian church, than has ever occurred since the "good tidings of great joy" were proclaimed in the plains of Bethlehem, or since the day of Pentecost, when "the whole multitude of them that believed were of one heart, and of one soul, and had all things common."*

---

## SECTION XI.

### *On the importance of connecting Science with Religion.*

In several of the preceding sections, I have exhibited sketches of the outlines of some of the branches of science, and of the objects towards which its investigations are directed. I have all along taken it for granted, that such knowledge and investigations ought to be combined with just views of religion, and an attention to its practical acquirements, and have occasionally interspersed some remarks on this topic. But as the subject is of peculiar importance, it may not be inexpedient to devote a section to its more particular elucidation.

Of late years, knowledge has increased, among the middle and lower ranks of society, with greater rapidity than in any preceding age, and Mechanics' Institutions, and other associations, have been formed, to give an impulse to the re-

* See *Appendix*, Note XI.

newed vigour of the human mind, and to gratify the desires which are now excited for intellectual pleasures and acquirements. Reason is arousing from the slumber of ages, and appears determined to make aggressions on the world of science, and to employ its faculties on every object which comes within the range of human investigation. The labourer, the mechanic and artisan,—no longer confined to trudge in the same beaten track in their respective professions, and to the limited range of thought which distinguished their predecessors in former generations—aspire after a knowledge of the principles on which their respective arts are founded, and an acquaintance with those scientific subjects, which were formerly confined to the cloisters of colleges and the higher orders of society. Lectures have been delivered in most of our towns and even villages, on the practice of the arts and the principles of the physical sciences, which have extended their intellectual views, and given them a higher idea of the nobleness and sublimity of the mental faculties with which they are endowed. This excitement to rational inquiry has partly arisen from the spirit of the age, and the political movements which have distinguished our times; but it has also been produced by the exertions of men of erudition, in concerting plans for the diffusion of knowledge, in giving a popular form to works of science, and divesting it of that air of mystery which it formerly assumed. And, should such excitement be properly directed, it cannot fail to raise the lower ranks of the community from intellectual degradation, and to prevent them from indulging in intemperance, and other sensual vices, which have so long debased our rational nature. At no former period has the spirit of science been so fully awakened, and so generally disseminated. On every side the boundaries of knowledge have been extended, the system of nature explored, the labours of philosophy withdrawn from hypothetical speculations to the investigation of facts, and the liberal and mechanical arts carried to a pitch of perfection, hitherto unattained.

But, amidst all the intellectual movements around us, it is matter of deep regret, that the knowledge of true religion, and the practice of its moral precepts, have not kept pace with the improvements and the diffusion of science. Not a few of those who have lately entered on the prosecution of scientific pursuits,—because their ideas have not been expanded a little beyond the limited range of thought to which they were formerly confined—seem now to regard revealed religion as little else than a vulgar superstition, or, at most, as a matter of inferior moment. Because their forefathers thought that the earth was the largest body in nature, and placed in a quiescent state in the centre of the universe, and that the stars were merely brilliant spangles fixed in the concave of the sky, to diversify the firmament—which notions are now proved to be erroneous—therefore they are apt to surmise, that the religion they professed rested on no better a foundation. Because their notions of that religion were blended with erroneous opinions and foolish superstitions, they would be disposed to throw aside the whole, as unworthy of the attention of men of enlightened understandings, whose minds have been emancipated from the shackles of vulgar prejudice and priestly domination. Such irreligious propensities have their origin, for the most part, in a principle of *vanity* and *self-conceit*, in that spirit of *pride* congenial to human nature, which leads the person in whom it predominates to vaunt himself on his superiority to vulgar opinions and fears—and, in the want of discriminating between what is of essential importance in religion, and the false and distorted notions which have been incorporated with it by the ignorance and perversity of men.

This tendency to irreligion has likewise been promoted by the modes in which scientific knowledge has been generally communicated. In the greater part of the best elementary treatises on science, there seldom occurs any distinct reference to the perfections and the agency of that Omnipotent Being, under whose superintendence all the processes of nature are conducted. Instead of directing the young and untutored mind to rise "from nature up to nature's God"—it is considered by many, as *unphilosophical*, when explaining natural phenomena, to advert to any but proximate causes, which reason or the senses can ascertain; and thus a veil is attempted to be drawn between the Deity and his visible operations, so as to conceal the agency of Him whose laws heaven and earth obey. In the academical prelections on physical science, in most of our colleges and universities, there appears a studied anxiety to avoid every reflection that wears the semblance of religion. From the first announcement of the properties of matter and the laws of motion, through all their combinations in the system of nature, and their applications to dynamics, hydrostatics, pneumatics, optics, electricity, and magnetism, the attention of the student is kept constantly fixed on secondary causes and physical laws, as if the universe were a self-existent and independent piece of mechanism; and it is seldom that the least reference is made to that Almighty Being who brought it into existence, and whose laws and operations are the subject of investigation. It is almost needless to add, that the harmony which subsists between the works of God, and the revelations of his word—the mutual light which they reflect upon each other—the views which they open of the plan of the Divine government,—and the moral effects which the contemplation of nature ought to produce upon the heart—are never, so far as we have learned, introduced, in such seminaries, as subjects which demand particular attention. Thus the Deity is carefully kept out of view, and banished, as it were, from his own creation; and the susceptible mind of the youthful student prevented from feeling those impressions of awe and reverence, of love and gratitude, which the study of the material world, when properly conducted, is calculated to produce.

The same principles and defects are perceptible in the instructions communicated in most of the *Mechanics' Institutions*, which have been lately formed for the improvement of the middle and lower classes of society. It has been publicly announced, in the speeches of gentlemen of science and erudition, who, with a laudable zeal, took a part in the organization of these institutions,—and the announcement has been re-echoed in every similar association, and transcribed into every literary journal,—that, "*Henceforward the discussions of science are to be completely separated from religion.*" I do not mean to accuse the highly respectable characters alluded to, as being hostile either to natural or revealed religion, from the circumstance of their having made this announcement; as I presume they only intended by it to get rid of those sectarian disputes about unimportant points in theology, which have so long disturbed the peace of the church and of the world. But, when I consider the use that will be made of it by certain characters and societies, and the bearing it may have on the mode of communicating scientific knowledge, I am constrained to pronounce the declaration as no less *unphilosophical*, than it is impious and immoral in its general tendency. It is *unphilosophical*; for science, when properly considered in relation to its higher and ultimate objects, is nothing else than an investigation of the power, wisdom, benevolence, and superintending providence of the Almighty, as displayed in the structure and movements of the universe,—of the relation in which we stand to this Great Being,—and of the duties which we owe him. To overlook such objects, is evidently contrary to the plainest dictates of reason and philosophy. Is it possible that an intelligent mind can contemplate the admirable and astonishing displays of divine perfection and munificence, throughout every part of creation, and not be excited to the exercise of love, and gratitude, and reverential adoration? Such feelings and emotions lie at the foundation of all true religion,—and the man who can walk through the magnificent scene of the universe, without feeling the least emotion of reverence and adoration, or of gratitude for the wise and benevolent arrangements of nature, may be pronounced unworthy of enjoying the beneficence of his Creator. It was doubtless for this end, among others, that the Almighty opened to our view such a magnificent spectacle as the universe displays, and bestowed upon us faculties capable of investigating its structure,—that we might acquire, from the contemplation of it, enlarged conceptions of the attributes of his nature, and the arrangements of his providence, and be excited to "give unto nim the glory due to his name." And, if we derive such impressions from our investigations of the material system, shall it be considered as inconsistent with the spirit of true philosophy, to endeavour to communicate the same impressions to the minds of those whom we are appointed to instruct? There can be little doubt, that the practice of setting aside all references to the character and perfections of the Deity, in physical discussions, has tended to foster a spirit of irreligion in youthful minds, and to accelerate their progress towards the gulf of infidelity and scepticism.

Again, philosophy, as well as religion, requires that the phenomena of nature be traced up to their *first cause*. There are no causes cognizable by the senses, which will account for the origin of the universe, and the multifarious phenomena it exhibits; and therefore we must ascend in our investigations to the existence of an invisible and eternal Cause, altogether impalpable to the organs of sense, in order to account for the existence and movements of the material world. To attempt to account for the harmony and order, and the nice adaptations which appear throughout creation, merely from the physical properties of matter, and the laws of motion, is to act on the principles of atheism; and is clearly repugnant to every dictate of reason, which declares, that to every effect we must assign an adequate cause. And, if in our physical investigations, we are *necessarily* led to the admission of a self-existent and eternal Being, the original source of life and motion, it must be deeply interesting to every one of us to acquire as much information as possible respecting his perfections, and the character of his moral government. From Him we derived our existence,—on Him we depend every moment "for life, and breath, and all things." Our happiness or misery is in his hands, and our eternal destiny, whether connected with annihilation or with a state of conscious existence, must be the result of his sovereign and eternal arrangements. Our comfort in the present life, and our hopes and prospects in relation to futurity, are therefore essentially connected with the conceptions we form of the attributes of Him who made and who governs the universe; and, consequently, that philosophy which either overlooks or discards such views and considerations, is unworthy of the name,—is inconsistent with the plainest deductions of reason, and, wherever it is promulgated, must prove inimical to the best interests of mankind. To regard science merely in its applications to the arts of life, and to overlook its deductions in reference to the Supreme Disposer of events, is *preposterous* and absurd, and unworthy of the character of the man who assumes to himself the name of a philosopher; for, in doing so, he violates the rules which guide him in all his other researches, and acts inconsistently with the maxim, that the most interesting and important objects demand our first and chief attention.

But the evil to which I have now adverted, is not the only one of which we have reason to complain. While the deductions of natural religion are but slightly adverted to in physical discussions, and in many instances altogether overlooked,—*the truths of Christianity are virtually set aside*; and it seems to be considered by some as inconsistent with the dignity of science, to make the slightest reference to the declarations of the sacred oracles. In many of our grammar schools, academies, and colleges, where the foolish and immoral rites of pagan mythology are often detailed, no instructions are imparted, to counteract the baneful influence which heathen maxims and idolatry may produce on the youthful mind. The superior excellence of the Christian religion, and the tendency of its principles and precepts to produce happiness, both here and hereafter, are seldom exhibited; and in too many instances the recognition of a Supreme Being, and of our continual dependance upon him, and the duty of imploring his direction and assistance, are set aside, as inconsistent with the spirit of the age, and with the mode of conducting a fashionable education. The superintendents of mechanics' institutions, following the prevailing mode, have likewise agreed to banish from their institutions and discussions, all references to religion, and to the peculiarities of the Christian system.

Now, we maintain, that Christianity in every point of view in which its revelations may be considered, is *a subject of paramount importance.* It is every thing, or it is nothing. It must reign supreme over every human pursuit, over every department of science, over every passion and affection, or be discarded altogether, as to its authority over man. It will admit of no compromises; for the authority with which it professes to be invested, is nothing less than the will of the Eternal, whose sovereign injunctions the inhabitants of earth and the hosts of heaven are bound to obey. If its claims to a divine origin can be disproved, then it may be set aside as unworthy of our regard, and ranked along with the other religions which have prevailed in the world. But, *if it is admitted to be a revelation from the Creator of the universe to man on earth*, its c aims are irresistible, it cannot be rejected with impunity, and its divine principles and maxims ought to be interwoven with all our pursuits and associations.

The importance of Christianity may be evinced by such considerations as the following:—It communicates to us the only certain information we possess of the character, attributes, and purposes of the Creator, to whose laws and moral government we are all amenable. It discloses to us our state and condition, as depraved creatures and violators of his righteous laws, and the doom which awaits the finally impenitent in the world to come. It informs us of the only method by which we may obtain forgiveness of sin, and complete deliverance from all the miseries and moral evils to which we are exposed. It inculcates those divine principles and moral precepts which are calculated to unite the whole human race in one harmonious and affectionate society, and to promote the happiness of every individual, both in "the life that now is, and in that which is to come." It presents before us sources of consolation, to cheer and support the mind, amidst the calamities and afflictions to which we are subjected in this mortal state. It unfolds to us, in part, the plan of God's moral government of the world, and the reasons of certain dispensations and moral phenomena, which would otherwise have remained inexplicable. In short, it proclaims the doctrine of a resurrection from the dead, and sets in the clearest light the certainty of a future state of punishments and rewards, subjects in which every individual of the human race is deeply interested—giving full assurance to all who comply with its requisitions, that when their corporeal frames are dissolved, they "shall have a building of God, an house not made with hands, eternal in the heavens," where they shall inherit "fulness of joy and pleasures for evermore."

These are only some of the important revelations which Christianity unfolds. And, if it be a truth which cannot be denied, that we are naturally ignorant of God, can we be happy without being acquainted with his moral attributes, purposes, and laws? If we be guilty and depraved —which the whole history of our race clearly demonstrates—can we feel true enjoyment, if our guilt is not cancelled, and our depravity not counteracted? Is it a matter of indifference, whether we acquire a knowledge of those moral principles, which will guide us in the path to wisdom and felicity, or be hurried along by heedless passions, in the devious ways of vice and folly? Is it of no importance, whether we obtain information respecting our eternal destiny, or remain in uncertainty whether death shall transport us to another world, or finally terminate our existence? Can any man, who calls himself a philosopher, maintain, with any show of reason, that it is *unphilosophical*, or contrary to the dictates of an enlightened understanding, that such subjects should form one great object of our attention—that they should be interwoven with all our studies and active employments—and that they should constitute the basis of all those instructions, which are intended for the melioration and improvement of mankind? To maintain such a position, would be to degrade philosophy in the eyes of every intelligent inquirer, and to render it unworthy of the patronage of every one who has a regard to the happiness of his species. That philosophy which truly deserves the name will at once admit, that concerns of the highest moment ought not to be set aside for matters of inferior consideration; but that every thing should be attended to in its proper order, and according to its relative importance. If such considerations have any weight, they prove, beyond dispute, that there is a glaring deficiency in our methods of education, where a foundation is not laid in the truths of Christianity, and where its authority is overlooked, and its claims disregarded.

Let us consider for a moment what would be the natural effects of *a complete separation* between science and religion—between the general diffusion of knowledge and the great objects of the Christian faith. Science might still continue to prosecute discoveries, to enlarge its boundaries, and to apply its principles to the cultivation of new arts, and to the improvement of those which have hitherto been practised. Its studies might give a certain degree of polish to the mind, might prevent certain characters from running the rounds of fashionable dissipation, and, in every gradation in society, might counteract, to a certain degree, the tendency to indulgence in those mean and ignoble vices to which the lower ranks in every age have been addicted. But, although the standard of morals would be somewhat raised, and the exterior of life polished and improved, the latent principles of moral evil might still remain rankling in the breast. Pride, ambition, avarice, and revenge, receiving no counteraction from religious principle, might be secretly harboured and nourished in the heart, and ready to burst forth, on every excitement, in all the diabolical energies in which they have so frequently appeared amidst the contests of communities and nations. The recognition of a Supreme intelligence, to whom we are accountable, would soon be considered as unnecessary in scientific investigations, and his natural perfections overlooked; and, consequently, all the delightful affections of love, gratitude, admiration, and reverence, which are inspired by the view of his moral attributes, and the transcendent excellence of his nature, would be undermined and annihilated. There would be no reliance on the superintending care of an unerring Providence, ordaining and directing every event to the most beneficial purposes, and no consolation derived, amidst the ills of life, from a view of the rectitude and benevolence of the Divine government. The present world would be considered as the only scene of action and enjoyment; the hope of immortality, which supports and gladdens the pious mind, would be exterminated, and every thing beyond the shadow of death involved in gloom and uncertainty. The only true principles of moral action, which revealed religion inculcates, being overlooked or discarded, every one would consider himself as at liberty to act according as his humour and passions might dictate; and, in such a case, a scene of selfishness, rapacity, and horror, would quickly ensue, which would sap the foundation of social order, and banish happiness from the abodes of men.

Such would be the necessary effects of a complete renunciation of revealed religion, and such a state of things our literary and scientific mode of education has a *natural tendency* to produce, *in so far as the truths of Christianity are set aside, or overlooked*, in our plans of instruction. Where should our youths receive impressions of the Deity, and of the truth of religion, unless in those seminaries where they are taught the elements of general knowledge? Shall they be left to infer, that religion is a matter of trivial importance, from the circumstance, that it is completely overlooked throughout the whole range of their instructions? It may be said, that they have opportunities of receiving Christian instruction elsewhere, particularly from the ministers of religion; but will their minds be better prepared for relishing such instructions, because the religion of the Bible has been carefully kept out of view in the other departments of tuition? Will they not rather come to such instructions, with their minds biassed against the truths of revelation; especially when we consider, that, in almost every instance, where religion is discarded in the process of secular instruction, Pagan maxims are introduced, and insinuations occasionally thrown out hostile to the interests of genuine Christianity? Notwithstanding all that I have stated in the preceding pages, respecting the beneficial effects of a universal diffusion of knowledge, I am fully persuaded, that, unless it be accompanied with a diffusion of the spirit of the Christian religion, and a corresponding practice, it will completely fail in promoting the best interests of mankind. If scriptural views of the character of the Deity—if the promotion of love to God and to man—if the cultivation of heavenly tempers and dispositions, and the practice of Christian morality, be entirely overlooked in seminaries devoted to the instruction of the great body of the community—such institutions, instead of being a blessing, would ultimately become *a curse* to the human species; and we should soon behold a vast assemblage of *intelligent demons*, furnished with powers and instruments of mischief superior to any that have hitherto been wielded, and which might, ere long, produce anarchy, injustice, and horror throughout every department of the moral world.

That these are not mere imaginary forebodings, might be illustrated from the scenes which were lately exhibited in a neighbouring nation. The first revolution in France in 1789, was a revolution not merely in politics and government, but in religion, in manners, in moral principle, and in the common feelings of human nature. The way for such a revolution was prepared by the writings of Voltaire, Mirabeau, Diderot, Helvetius, D'Alembert, Condorcet, Rousseau, and others of the same stamp—in which, along with some useful discussions on the subject of civil and religious liberty, they endeavoured to disseminate principles subversive both of natural and revealed religion. Revelation was not only impugned, but entirely set aside; the Deity was banished from the universe, and an imaginary phantom, under the name of the Goddess of Reason, substituted in his place. Every thing was reduced to a system of pure materialism; the celestial spark of intelligence within us was assimilated to a piece of rude matter, and the fair prospects of immortality, which Christianity presents, transformed into the gloom of an eternal night. Every previous standard of morals was discarded; every one was left to act as selfishness, avarice, and revenge might dictate; religion of every description fled from the torch of the prevailing philosophy; and, while "justice and morality" were proclaimed as "the order of the day," every moral principle, and every human feeling, were trampled under foot. It is stated, on good authority, that a little before the revolution, a numerous assembly of French *Literati*, being asked, in turn, at one of their meetings, by their president, "Whether there was any such thing as moral obligation," answered, in every instance, that *there was not*. Soon after that revolution, the great body of French infidels, who then ruled the nation, not only denied all the obligations which bind us to truth, justice, and kindness, but pitied and despised, as a contemptible wretch, the man who believed in their existence. Atheism was *publicly* preached, and its monstrous doctrines disseminated among the mass of the people, an occurrence altogether novel in the history of man. A professor was even named by Chaumette, to instruct the children of the state in the mysteries of Atheism. De la Metherie, the author of a Philosophical Journal, when discussing the doctrine of crystallization, made the wild and hideous assertion, "that the highest and most perfect form of crystallization *is that which is vulgarly called God*." In the National Convention, Gobet, archbishop of Paris, the rector Vangirard, and several other priests, abjured the Christian religion; and for this abjuration *they received applauses and the fraternal kiss*. A priest from Melun stated, that there is no true religion but that of nature, and that all the mummery with which they had hitherto been amused, is only old wives' fables; *and he was heard with loud applause*. The Convention decreed, that "all the churches and temples of religious worship, known to be in Paris, should be instantly shut up, and that every person requiring the opening of a church or temple should be put under arrest, as a suspected person, and an enemy to the state." The carved work of all religious belief and moral practice was boldly cut down by Carnot, Robespierre, and their atheistical associates, and the following inscription was ordered to be displayed in all the public burying-grounds—"*Death is only an eternal sleep*;" so that the dying need no longer be afraid to step out of existence. Nature was investigated, by these pretended philosophers, only with a view to darken the mind, to prevent mankind from considering any thing as real but what the hand could grasp or the corporeal eye perceive, and to subvert the established order of society.

The consequences of the operation of such principles were such as might have been expected. They are written in characters of blood, and in crimes almost unparalleled in the history of nations. A scene of inhumanity, cruelty, cold-blooded malignity, daring impiety, and insatiable rapacity, was presented to the world, which excited in the mind of every virtuous spectator amazement and horror. Savage atrocities were perpetrated which would have been shocking in the most barbarous and unenlightened age; and, perhaps, at no era has there been more wretchedness occasioned by licentious principles and moral degeneracy. The ties of friendship were cut asunder, the claims of consanguinity disregarded, and a cold-blooded selfishness pervaded the great mass of society. "The kingdom appeared to be changed into one great prison; the inhabitants converted into felons, and the common doom of man commuted for the violence of the sword, and the bayonet, and the stroke of the guillotine." Such was the rapidity with which the work of destruction was carried on, that, within the short space of ten years, not less than three millions of human beings (one half more than the whole population of Scotland) are supposed to have perished in that country alone, chiefly through the influence of immoral principles, and the seductions of a false philosophy. The following is a brief sketch of some of the scenes to which we allude, drawn by one who was an eye-witness of the whole, and an actor in several parts of that horrid drama. "There were," says this writer, "multiplied cases of suicide; prisons crowded with innocent persons; permanent guillotines; perjuries of all classes; parental authority set at nought; debauchery encouraged by an allowance to those called unmarried mothers; nearly six thousand divorces in the city of Paris within a little more than two years; in a word, whatever is most obscene in vice and most dreadful in ferocity."*

Notwithstanding the incessant shouts of "Liberty and Equality," and the boasted illuminations of philosophy, the most barbarous persecutions were carried on against those whose

* Gregoire.

religious opinions differed from the system adopted by the state. While infidelity was enthroned in power, it wielded the sword of vengeance with infernal ferocity against the priests of the Romish church, who were butchered wherever found—hunted as wild beasts—frequently roasted alive, or drowned in hundreds together, without either accusation or trial. At Nantz, no less than 360 priests were shot, and 460 drowned. In one night, 58 were shut up in a barge, and drowned in the Loire. Two hundred and ninety-two priests were massacred during the bloody scenes of the 10th August, and the 2d September, 1792; and 1135 were guillotined under the government of the National Convention, from the month of September 1792, till the end of 1795, besides vast numbers, hunted by the infidel republicans, like owls and partridges, who perished in different ways, throughout the provinces of France.

Such were some of the dismal effects which flowed from the attempt to banish religion from science, from government, and from the intercourses and employments of society. Were such principles universally to prevail, the world would soon become one vast theatre of mischief and of misery—an immense den of thieves and robbers—a sink of moral pollution—a scene of impiety, injustice, rapine, and devastation; a Golgotha, strewed with carcasses and "dead men's bones." All confidence and friendship between intelligent beings would be destroyed; the dearest and most venerable relations would be violated by incestuous pollutions; appetite would change every man into a swine, and passion into a tiger; jealousy, distrust, revenge, murder, war, and rapine would overspread the earth, and a picture of hell would be presented wherever the eye roamed over the haunts of men.

During the period when the atrocities to which we are adverting were perpetrating, the ruffians who bore rule in France were continually imputing to the illumination of philosophy, the ardour which animated them in the cause of liberty; and, it is a truth, that science was enlarging its boundaries even amidst the horrors with which it was surrounded. Chemistry was advancing in its rapid career of discovery, and the celebrated Lavoisier, one of its most successful cultivators, was interrupted in the midst of some interesting experiments, and dragged to the guillotine, where he suffered in company with 28 farmers-general, merely because he was rich. Physical astronomy, and the higher branches of the mathematics were advancing under the investigations of La Place; geodetical operations were carrying forward, on an extensive scale; and the physical sciences, in general, under the hands of numerous cultivators, were going on towards perfection. But, while this circumstance shows, that science may advance in the midst of irreligion—it proves, at the same time, that, *without being combined with religion*, it cannot, of itself, meliorate the morals of mankind, or counteract the licentiousness of society. Though it may be considered as a ray of celestial light proceeding from the original Source of intelligence, yet it will fail in producing its most beneficial effects, unless it be combined with "the light of the knowledge of the glory of God," as it shines in the word of Divine Revelation. Had such a connexion been formed between science and religion, certain it is, that the bonds which unite the social system would never have been burst asunder, nor the foundations of morality overturned by such a violent explosion as happened at the French revolution. And, although I am aware, that a variety of political causes combined to produce that great convulsion, and the effects which flowed from it, yet it cannot be denied, that the principles of atheism, and a false philosophy which had thrown off its allegiance to Christianity, were the *chief causes* which produced the licentiousness and impiety which characterized the rulers and citizens of France, under "the reign of terror."

It is therefore to be hoped, that those who now patronise the intellectual improvement of mankind, and who wish to promote the best interests of society, will take warning from the occurrences which so lately happened in the French nation, during the reign of infidel philosophy and impiety, and not suffer religion to be dissevered from those pursuits which should lead the mind to the contemplation of a Supreme Intelligence, and of the glories of an immortal existence. The moral Governor of the world has set before us the horrid scenes to which we have alluded, as a beacon to guard us from similar dangers, that society might not again be exposed to a ship vreck so dreadful and appalling. We have, surely, no reason to repeat the experiment, in order to ascertain the result. It is written in characters conspicuous to every eye, and legible even to the least attentive observer, and may serve as a warning both to the present age, and to every future generation. Its effects are felt even at the present moment, in the country where the experiment was tried, in the irreligion and profligacy which, in its populous cities, still abound, especially among the middle and higher ranks of society. Its effects are apparent even in our own country; for the sceptical principles and immoral maxims of the continental philosophy were imported into Britain, at an early period of the French Revolution, when the Bible was discarded by multitudes, as an antiquated imposture, and committed to the flames; and it is, doubtless, owing in part, to the influence of these principles, that, in organizing institutions for the diffusion of knowledge among the lower ranks, attempts have been made to separate science from its references to the Creator, and from all its connexions with revealed religion. It is, therefore, the duty of every man who loves his species, and who has a regard for the welfare and prosperity of his country, to use his influence in endeavouring to establish the literary and scientific instruction of the community on the broad basis of the doctrines of revelation, and of those moral laws which have been promulgated by the authority of the Governor of the universe, which are calculated to secure the moral order, and to promote the happiness of intelligent agents, throughout every province of the Divine empire.

"When we look at plans of education," (says an intelligent writer) "matured, or in progress, which are likely to concentrate the *national intellect*, and form the *national taste*, and engross the daily leisure of the peasant or artisan, on principles of virtual exclusion to every thing specifically Christian, when we see this grievous and deadly deficiency attaching to schemes of benevolence, which are otherwise pure and splendid, receiving the sanction of public recognition, countenanced or winked at by the mightiest of scholars, and most illustrious of statesmen, and thus put in condition for traversing the land, from the one end to the other, we do feel alarmed, in no ordinary degree, at the effects that are likely to follow it; and could we influence the consultations in which the whole originates, would entreat its projectors to pause and deliberate, lest they stir the elements of a latent impiety, instead of dispensing a national blessing. We dread not the light of science, nor any light of any kind which emanates from God to man. On the contrary, we hail it as a precious acquisition, provided it be mingled and seasoned with that which is revealed, as "the true light which lighteth every man that cometh into the world;" but, in a state of separation from this better light, and unattempered by its restoring influence, we are constrained to dread it, by all the concern we ever felt for the eternal well-being of our human kindred."*

To prevent any misconceptions that may arise respecting our views of the connexion of science and religion, it may be proper to remark, in the first place,—that we would consider it preposterous in the highest degree, to attempt the introduction of sectarian opinions in religion into the discussions connected with science and philosophy. It would be altogether irrelevant to the objects of scientific associations, to introduce the subjects of dispute between Calvinists and Arminians, Presbyterians, Episcopalians, and Independents; and we are of opinion, that the sooner such controversies are banished, even from *theology*, and from the Christian world at large, so much the better; for they have withdrawn the minds of thousands from the *essentials* to the mere *circumstantials* of religion; and, in too many instances, have exposed the Christian world to the sneers of infidels, and the scoffs of the profane.—Nor, in the next place, would we consider it as either judicious or expedient, to attempt to foist in even the essential doctrines of Christianity, on every occasion, when the subject of discussion did not *naturally* and *directly* lead to their introduction, or to some allusions to them. Such attempts generally frustrate the end intended, and are equally displeasing to the man of taste, and to the enlightened Christian.—What we understand by connecting science with religion, will appear in the following observations:—

I. As science has it for one of its highest objects to investigate the works of the Creator,—*an opportunity should be taken*, when imparting scientific instructions, *of adverting to the attributes of the Deity as displayed in his operations.* The character of the Divine Being, and the perfections he displays, are, in every point of view, the most interesting of all human investigations. The system of nature, in all its parts and processes, exhibits them to our view, and forces them, as it were, upon our attention, if we do not wilfully shut our eyes on the light which emanates from an invisible Divinity through his visible operations. The contemplation of this system, even in its most prominent and obvious appearances, has a natural tendency to inspire the most profound emotions of awe and reverence, of gratitude and admiration, at the astonishing displays it exhibits of Omnipotent energy, unsearchable wisdom, and boundless beneficence. Such studies, when properly directed, are calculated to make a powerful and interesting impression on the minds of the young; and it is doing them an incalculable injury, when their views are never elevated above proximate causes and physical laws, to the agency of Him who sits on the throne of the universe.—"If one train of thinking," says Paley, "be more desirable than another, it is that which regards the phenomena of nature, with a constant reference to a supreme intelligent Author. To have made this the ruling, the habitual sentiment of our minds, is to have laid the foundation of every thing which is religious. The world from henceforth becomes a temple, and life itself one continued act of adoration. The change is no less than this, that whereas formerly God was seldom in our thoughts, we can scarcely look upon any thing without perceiving its relation to him." And is such a train of thinking to be considered as unphilosophical? Is it not, on the contrary, the *perfection* of philosophy to ascend to a cause that will account for every phenomenon—to trace its incessant agency, and to acknowledge the perfections it displays? Bishop Watson has well observed, "We feel the interference of the Deity everywhere, but we cannot apprehend the *nature* of his agency anywhere. A blade of grass can-

* Rev. D. Young—Introductory Essay to Sir M. Hales' Contemplations.

not spring up, a drop of rain cannot fall, a ray of light cannot be emitted from the sun, nor a particle of salt be united, with a never-failing sympathy to its fellow, without him; every secondary cause we discover, is but a new proof of the necessity we are under of ultimately recurring to him, as the one primary cause of every thing."

Illustrations of the position for which we are now contending will be found in such works as the following :—Ray's "Wisdom of God in the Creation,"—Boyle's "Philosophical and Theological works,"—Derham's Astro and Physico-Theology,"*—Nieuwentyt's Religious Philosopher,"—Le Pluche's "Nature Displayed,"—Baxter's "Matho," or the principles of natural religion deduced from the phenomena of the material world,—Lesser's *Insecto-Theology*, or a demonstration of the Being and Attributes of God, from the structure and economy of insects, with notes by Lyonet,—Bonnet's "Contemplation of Nature,"—Euler's "Letters to a German Princess," *translated by Hunter*,—Pierre's "Studies of Nature,"—"Paley's Natural Theology,"—Adam's "Lectures on Natural Philosophy,"—Parkes' "Chemical Catechism," and several others. The chief object of *Ray* is to illustrate the wisdom of the Deity in the figure and construction of the earth, in the structure and symmetry of the human frame, and in the economy of the animal and vegetable tribes. The object of Derham, in his Astro-Theology, is to display the wisdom and omnipotence of Deity, as they appear in the structure, arrangement, and motions of the heavenly bodies; and his *Physico-Theology*, a work of much greater extent, demonstrates the being and attributes of God from the constitution of the earth and atmosphere,—the senses—the structure, motions, respiration, food, and habitations of animals—the body of man—the economy of insects, reptiles, and fishes, and the structure of vegetables. Though this excellent work is now considered as somewhat antiquated, yet we have no modern work that can fully supply its place. Paley's Natural Theology, however excellent in its kind, does not embrace the same extensive range of objects. *Nieuwentyt* enters into a minute anatomical investigation of the structure of the human body, which occupies the greater part of his first volume; and in the two remaining volumes, illustrates the Divine perfections from a survey of the atmosphere, meteors, water, earth, fire, birds, beasts, fishes, plants, the physical and chemical laws of nature, the inconceivable smallness of the particles of matter, and the structure of the starry heavens. The voluminous work of *Le Pluche* comprehends interesting descriptions of quadrupeds, birds, fishes, insects, plants, flowers, gardens, olive-yards, cornfields, woods, pasture-grounds, rivers, mountains, seas, fossils, minerals, the atmosphere, light, colours, vision, the heavenly bodies, globes, telescopes, microscopes, the history of navigation, systematic physics, &c.—interspersed with a variety of beautiful reflections on the Wisdom and Beneficence of the Deity in the arrangements of nature. *Euler's* Letters comprehend popular descriptions of the most interesting subjects connected with natural philosophy and ethics, interspersed with moral reflections, and frequent references to the truths of revelation. *Condorcet*, in his French translation of this work, carefully omitted almost all the pious and moral reflections of this profound and amiable Philosopher, as inconsistent with the infidel and atheistical philosophy which then prevailed. "The retrenchments," says he "affect reflections which relate less to the sciences and philosophy, than to theology, and frequently even to the peculiar doctrines of that ecclesiastical communion in which Euler lived. *It is unnecessary to assign a reason for omissions of this description.*" These omissions were supplied, and the passages alluded to restored, by Dr. Hunter, in his English translation, but they have been again suppressed in the late edition, published in Edinburgh, in two volumes, 12mo.*

It is much to be regretted, that we have no modern Rays, Derhams, Boyles, or Nieuwentyts, to make the light of our recent discoveries in science bear upon the illustration of the perfections of the Deity, and the arrangements of his providence. Since the period when those Christian philosophers left our world, many of the sciences which they were instrumental in promoting, have advanced to a high degree of perfection, and have thrown additional light on the wisdom and intelligence of the Divine mind,

* An edition of Derham's *Physico-Theology*, in two vols. 8vo. (which is not very generally known) was published in London in 1798, which contains *additional notes* illustrative of modern discoveries, a translation of the Greek and Latin quotations of the original work, a life of the author, and sixteen copperplate engravings, illustrative of many curious subjects in the animal and vegetable kingdoms.

* As a specimen of the omissions to which we allude, the following passage may suffice :—"But the eye which the Creator has formed, is subject to no one of all the imperfections under which the imaginary construction of the freethinker labours. In this we discover the true reason why infinite wisdom has employed several transparent substances in the formation of the eye. It is thereby secured against all the defects which characterize every work of man. What a noble subject of contemplation! How pertinent that question of the Psalmist! *He who formed the eye, shall he not see? and He who planted the ear, shall he not hear?* The eye alone being a masterpiece that far transcends the human understanding, what an exalted idea must we form of Him who has bestowed this wonderful gift, and that in the highest perfection, not on man only, but on the brute creation, nay, on the vilest of insects!" The French philosopher and statesman seems to feel ashamed of the least alliance between philosophy and religion, when he is induced to discard such reflections. He seems apprehensive, as Dr. Hunter remarks, that a single drop of water from Scripture would contaminate the whole mass of philosophy. We would hope our British philosophers are not yet so deeply tinctured with the spirit of infidelity.

and the economy of the universe. Natural history has widely enlarged its boundaries; our views of the range of the planetary system have been extended; the distant regions of the starry firmament have been more minutely explored, and new objects of magnificence brought within the reach of our observation. The nature of light has been more accurately investigated, the composition of the atmosphere discovered, the properties of the different gases ascertained, the powers of electricity and galvanism detected, and chemistry—a science completely new-modelled—has opened up the secret springs of nature's operations, and thrown a new light on the economy of Divine wisdom in the various processes which are going on in the material system. Is it not unaccountable, then, that no modern system of *Physico-Theology*, embracing the whole range of modern discoveries, should have proceeded from the pens of some one or other of our most distinguished philosophers? Does this circumstance seem to indicate, that, since the early part of the last century, the piety of philosophers has been declining, and the infidel principles of the continental school gaining the ascendency? Infidelity and fatalism very generally go hand in hand. When the truths of Revelation are once discarded, a species of universal scepticism, differing little or nothing from atheism, takes possession of the mind; and hence we find, that in the writings of such men as Buffon, Diderot, and La Place, there is not the slightest reference to Final Causes, or to the agency of an All-pervading Mind that governs the universe.

That the connexion between science and theology, we have been recommending, is not a vague or enthusiastic idea, appears from the sentiments which have been expressed on this subject by the most eminent philosophers. Throughout the whole of the works of the immortal Newton, we perceive a constant attention to Final causes, or to the great purposes of the Deity. It was the firm opinion of this philosopher, "that, as we are everywhere encountered in our researches by powers and effects, which are unaccountable upon any principles of mere mechanism, or the combinations of matter and motion, we must for ever resort to a Supreme power, whose influence extends over all Nature, and who accomplishes the wisest and most benevolent ends by the best possible means." Maclaurin, the friend of Newton, and the commentator on his *Principia*, expresses the following sentiments on this subject, in his "Account of Sir I. Newton's Discoveries." "There is nothing we meet with more frequently and constantly in Nature, than the traces of an all-governing Deity. And the philosopher who overlooks these, contenting himself with the appearances of the material universe only, and the mechanical laws of motion, neglects what is most excellent; and prefers what is imperfect to what is supremely perfect, finitude to infinity, what is narrow and weak to what is unlimited and almighty, and what is perishing to what endures for ever. Such who attend not to so manifest indications of supreme wisdom and goodness, perpetually appearing before them wherever they turn their views or inquiries, too much resemble those ancient philosophers who made *Night*, *Matter*, and *Chaos*, the original of all things." Similar sentiments were expressed by the late Professor Robison, one of the most profound mathematicians and philosophers of his age. "So far from banishing the consideration of final causes from our discussions, it would look more like philosophy, more like the love of true wisdom, and it would taste less of an idle curiosity, were we to multiply our researches in those departments of nature where final causes are the chief objects of our attention—the structure and economy of organized bodies in the animal and vegetable kingdoms."—"It is not easy to account for it, and perhaps the explanation would not be very agreeable, why many naturalists so fastidiously avoid such views of nature as tend to lead the mind to the thoughts of its Author. We see them even anxious to weaken every argument for the appearance of design in the construction and operations of nature. One would think, that, on the contrary, such appearances would be most welcome, and that nothing would be more dreary and comfortless than the belief that chance or fate rules all the events of nature."—*Elements of Mechanical Philosophy*, vol. i. pp. 681-2. We know not whether such sentiments were inculcated from the chair of Natural Philosophy, which Dr. Robison so long occupied, by the distinguished philosopher who has lately deceased.

II. Besides the deductions of natural religion, to which we have now adverted—in our scientific instructions there ought to be a reference, on every proper occasion, to the leading truths of revelation. There are many scientific inquirers who would have no objections occasionally to advert to final causes, and the wisdom of the Deity, who consider it altogether irrelevant, in the discussions of science, to make the slightest reference to the facts and doctrines detailed in the Sacred Oracles. The expediency, or the impropriety of such a practice, must depend on the views we take of the nature of the communications which the Scriptures contain. If the Bible is acknowledged *as a revelation from God*, its truths must harmonize with the system of nature,—they must throw a mutual light on each other,—and the attributes of the Divinity they respectively unfold must be in perfect accordance; and therefore it can never be irrelevant, when engaged in the study of the one, to refer for illustrations to the other. On the contrary, to omit doing so, from a fastidious compliance with what has too long been the established practice, would be a piece of glaring inconsistency, either in the theologian on the one hand, or the philosopher on the other. We have too much reason to suspect, that the squeamishness of certain scientific characters, in omitting all references to the Christian system, arises either from a secret disbelief of its authority, or from a disrelish of the truths and moral principles it inculcates.

Taking for granted, then, what has never yet been disproved, that Christianity is a revelation from heaven, and recollecting, that we live in a country where this religion is professed, it follows, as a matter of *consistency* as well as of *duty*, that all our systems of instruction, whether literary or scientific, whether in colleges, academies, mechanics' institutions, or initiatory schools, ought to be founded on the basis of the Christian revelation—that, in the instructions delivered in such seminaries, its leading doctrines should be recognised, and that no dispositions or conduct be encouraged which are inconsistent with its moral principles.

More particularly, in describing the processes or phenomena of nature, an opportunity should frequently be taken of quoting the sublime and energetic sentiments of the inspired writers, and of referring to the facts they record, when they are appropriate, and illustrative of the subject in hand. This would tend to connect the operations of nature with the agency of the God of nature; and would show to the young, that their instructers felt a veneration for that Book which has God for its Author, and our present and future happiness as the great object of its revelations. Why should the Bible be almost the only book from which certain modern philosophers never condescend to borrow a quotation? They feel no hesitation—nay, they sometimes appear to pride themselves in being able to quote from Plato, Aristotle, and Zeno, or from Ovid, Virgil, and Lucretius. They would feel ashamed to be considered as unacquainted with the works of Bacon, Galileo, Newton, Halley, Huygens, Boscovich, Black, Robison, Buffon, or La Place, and unable to quote an illustrative sentiment from their writings; but they seem to feel, as if it would lessen the dignity of science to borrow an illustration of a scientific position from Moses or Isaiah, and to consider it as in nowise disrespectful to appear ignorant of the contents of the Sacred Volume. Such were not the sentiments and feelings of the philosophers to whose works I lately referred, which abound with many beautiful and appropriate sentiments from the inspired writings. Such were not the feelings of the celebrated *Euler*, whose accomplishments in science were admired by all the philosophers of Europe; nor were such the feelings of the late Dr. Robison, who was scarcely his inferior. When describing the numerous *nebulæ* in the distant regions of the heavens, he closes his remarks with the following reflection:—"The human mind is almost overpowered with such a thought. When the soul is filled with such conceptions of the extent of created nature, we can scarcely avoid exclaiming, 'Lord, what then is man, that thou art mindful of him?' Under such impressions, David shrunk into nothing, and feared that he should be forgotten among so many great objects of the Divine attention. His comfort and ground of relief from this dejecting thought are remarkable. 'But,' says he, 'thou hast made man but a little lower than the angels, and hast crowned him with glory and honour.' David corrected himself, by calling to mind how high he stood in the scale of God's works. He recognised his own divine original, and his alliance to the Author of all. Now, cheered and delighted, he cries out, 'Lord, how glorious is thy name!'"—*Elements of Mechanical Philosophy*, vol. i. p. 565.

Again, every proper opportunity should be taken of illustrating the *harmony* which subsists between the system of revelation and the system of nature—between the declarations of the inspired writers and the facts which are found to exist in the material universe. This subject presents an extensive field of investigation which has never yet been thoroughly explored, and which admits of the most extensive and diversified illustrations. The facts of *geology*—some of which were formerly set in array against the records of revelation—are now seen to be corroborative of the facts stated in the Mosaic history;* and in proportion as the system of nature is minutely explored, and the physical sciences in general approximate to perfection, the more striking appears the coincidence between the revelations of the Bible and the revelations of Nature. And one principal reason why this coincidence at present does not appear complete, is, that the Scriptures have never yet been thoroughly studied in all their references, nor the system of the material world thoroughly explored. The facts of modern science, of which many of our commentators were ignorant, have seldom been brought to bear upon the elucidation of the inspired writings, and the sentiments of the sacred writers have seldom been illustrated by an appeal to the discoveries of science.—The views which the system of nature exhibits of the plan and principles of the divine government, the reasons of the operation of those destructive agents which frequently exert their energy within the bounds of our sublunary system, and the connexion which subsists between *physical* and *moral* evil, might also form occasional subjects of investigation; as they are all deeply interesting to man considered as a moral agent, and as the subject of the moral administration of the Governor of the Universe.

† For illustrations of this position, see Dr. Ure's *Geology*, Parkinson's *Organic Remains*, &c.

In the next place we hold it as a matter of particular importance, that the instructions of science be conducted in such a manner as to make a *moral impression* upon the heart. An objection has frequently been raised by religious people against the study of science, from its tendency to produce a spirit of intellectual pride; and it can scarcely be denied that there is some ground for the objection, when the pursuits of general knowledge are entirely separated from religion. But the objects of science, *when properly exhibited, and accompanied with appropriate reflections*, have a very different tendency. When we consider the numberless multitudes of beings which exist in the universe, and the immense variety of processes incessantly going forward in every department of nature; when we consider the infinite wisdom and intelligence, far surpassing human comprehension, which they display; when we consider the immense magnitude and extent of the universal system of created beings, and the probability that man stands near the lower part of the scale of rational existence, and is only like an atom in the immensity of creation,—we perceive the most powerful motives for *humility* and self-abasement. When we consider the benevolent arrangements in the elements around us, and in the structure and functions of animated beings, and the provision made for their subsistence, it has a natural tendency to inspire the heart with *gratitude* and affection towards Him from whom all our comforts flow. And when we reflect on the grandeur of the Deity as displayed in the magnificence of his empire, and in his incessant agency throughout all its provinces, should it not inspire us with reverence and adoration, and with a lively hope, that a period will arrive when we shall behold the wonders and glories of his creation more clearly unfolded? Such sentiments and emotions, the works of God, when rightly contemplated, are fitted to produce; and to overlook them in our instruction to the young, is to deprive them of some of the purest enjoyments, and some of the greatest advantages, which flow from scientific knowledge. When their minds are deeply impressed with such emotions, they are in some measure prepared for listening with reverence to the declarations of the inspired volume, and for perceiving the force and sublimity of the description it gives of the character of God.

It would perhaps excite a smile of contempt in some, who would spurn at the idea of being ranked in the class of infidels, were I to insinuate, that our scientific meetings and lectures should be opened with prayer, and adoration of the Divine Being. It might indeed admit of a doubt, whether it would be expedient to attempt such a practice *in the present state of society*. But I have no hesitation in affirming, that, to acknowledge God in all our pursuits, and to pay Him a tribute of adoration, are dictates of natural as well as of revealed religion, and that a deist, were he to act in consistency with his avowed principles, would engage in daily prayer to the Great Author of his existence. It is expressly enjoined in the Scriptures, "In all thy ways acknowledge God, and he shall direct thy steps;" and it is declared to be one of the characteristics of the wicked man, "that God is not in all his thoughts," and that, "through the pride of his countenance he will not call upon God." If we firmly believe there is a God, we must also believe that he is present in all places, and privy to all our thoughts, that all our circumstances and wants are open to his Omniscient eye, and that "he is able to do for us above all that we can ask or think." Although we are ignorant of the precise physical connexion between prayer and the bestowment of a favour by God, yet we ought to engage in this duty, because it is accordant with the idea of a Supreme Being on whom we are every moment dependent, and has therefore been acknowledged by the untaught barbarian, as well as by the enlightened Christian; because it is positively enjoined; because there is a connexion established by the Creator between *asking* and *receiving*; because it tends to fix our thoughts on the Omnipresence of the Divine Mind, to impress our hearts with a sense of the blessings of which we stand in need, and to excite earnest desires after them; and, because it is one way in which we may hold a direct intercourse with our Creator. I would not envy the Christian feelings of that man who can habitually engage in literary compositions or scientific discussions, without acknowledging his Maker, and imploring his direction and assistance. Religion degenerates into something approaching to a mere inanity, when its spirit and principles are not carried into every department of human life and society, nor its requisitions attended to in every *secular* business in which we engage. Till the principles of Christianity be made to bear in all their force on every department of human actions, and especially on the business of education, we can scarcely expect, that its benign tendency will be generally appreciated, or that society will reap all the benefits which it is calculated to impart.

There are, however, certain descriptions of literary characters, who, although they consider it expedient to pay an occasional compliment to Christianity, would consider such remarks as bordering on superstition or fanaticism. When we talk to them about the Christian revelation in general terms, they do not choose to say any thing directly against its excellence or divine authority; but if we descend into particulars, and expatiate on any of its fundamental doctrines, or attempt to reduce to practice its holy requisitions, we are frequently met with a contemptuous sneer, or a cry of enthusiasm, and sometimes with an harangue against the follies of Methodism, or of

Bible and Missionary Societies. We are thus led to infer, with some degree of reason, that such characters have no impressive belief of the Divine origin of the Christian system ; and it would be much more honourable and consistent, at once to avow their infidelity, than to put on the mask of dissimulation and hypocrisy. No individual ought to be subjected to any civil penalties on account of the opinions he holds, as for these he is accountable only to his Maker ; nor should any opinions be attempted to be extirpated by any other weapons than the strength of reason and the force of arguments. But, at the same time, it is requisite, that society should know the leading principles of any one who proposes himself as a public instructer of his fellow-men, in order that they may judge whether it would be proper to place their relatives under the instructions of one, who might either overlook Christianity altogether, or occasionally throw out insinuations against it. To act the hypocrite, to profess a decent respect for the Christian religion, while the principles of infidelity are fixed in the mind, accompanied with a secret wish to undermine its foundations, is *mean* and *contemptible*, unworthy of the man who wishes to be designated by the title of philosopher. Yet such hypocrisy is not at all uncommon ; it was particularly displayed by the sceptical philosophers on the continent, prior to the French revolution, and avowed to their most intimate associates.

*Buffon*, the natural historian, who appears to have been an atheist, was also, according to his own confession, a consummate hypocrite. In a conversation with *M. Herault Sechelles*, in 1785, about four years before his death, and when he was in the seventy-eighth year of his age, he declared, " In my writings I have always spoken of the *creator* ; but it is easy to efface that word, and substitute in its place, the *powers of nature*, which consist in the two grand laws of attraction and repulsion. When the *Sorbonne** become troublesome to me, I never scruple to give them every satisfaction they require. It is but a *sound*, and men are foolish enough to be contented with it. Upon this account, if I were ill, and found my end approaching, I should not hesitate to receive the sacrament. *Helvetius* was my intimate friend, and has frequently visited me at Montbart. I have repeatedly advised him to use similar discretion ; and, had he followed my advice, he would have been much happier." " My first work (continued he) appeared at the same time with *L'Esprit des Lois*. *Montesquieu* and myself were tormented by the *Sorbonne*. The president was violent. '*What have you to answer for yourself?*' says he to me, in an angry tone. '*Nothing at all*,' was my answer, and he was silenced and perfectly thunderstruck at my indifference." In perfect accordance with such a system of hypocrisy, Buffon kept a father confessor almost constantly with him, to whom he was in the habit of *confessing*, in the same apartment where he had developed the *Principles of Materialism*, which, according to his system, was an abnegation of immortality. He also regularly attended mass on Sundays, unless prevented by indisposition, and communicated in the *Chapel of the Glory*, every Whitsuntide. Though he heartily despised his priestly confessor, he flattered and cajoled him with pompous promises, and condescending attentions. " I have seen this priest (says Sechelles,) in the absence of the domestics, hand over a towel to the count, set the dining table before him, and perform such-like menial services. Buffon rewards these attentions with, *I thank you my dear child*." Such was the habitual hypocrisy of this philosopher ; and, said he, " it has been observed by me in all my writings : I have published the one after the other in such a manner, that men of vulgar capacities should not be able to trace the chain of my thoughts." His intolerable *vanity* and pomposity, his breach of promises, the grossness of his conversation, and his numerous amours and intrigues, were in perfect correspondence with such principles, and the natural result of them. " His pleasantries (says Sechelles) were so void of delicacy, that the females were obliged to quit the room."* What a scene of moral anarchy would be introduced, were such principles to be universally inculcated and acted upon in society! All confidence between man and man would be shaken, and the foundations of the social system undermined and destroyed. Yet such was the morality which almost universally prevailed among the continental philosophers, in consequence of the sceptical and atheistical principles they had imbibed. Truth, sincerity, modesty, humility, and moral obligation, formed no part of the code of their morality ; and such, in all probability, would soon be the result in our own country, were the pursuits of science and philosophy to be completely dissevered from religion.

In the last place, there are several topics connected with religion, which might occasionally be made the subjects of discussion in scientific associations : such, for example, are the evidences and importance of the Christian Revelation—the physical and moral facts to which it occasionally adverts—the attributes of the Divinity—the general principles of moral action—the laws which the Creator has promulgated for preserving the order of the intelligent system, and the foundation on which they rest—the evidences for the immortality of the soul, and the eternal destiny of man. These, and similar topics might, on

* The faculty of Theology at Paris.

* See an account of some particulars in the private life of Buffon, by M. Sechelles, one of his admirers, in the Monthly Magazine for July 1797, supplementary No. vol. 3, pp. 493—501.

certain occasions, become subjects of investigation, as they can be illustrated without entering on the arena of theological controversy, or descending within the limits of sectarian opinions. I do not mean to say, that they should be discussed according to the method of Forensic disputations, by opposite parties taking different sides of a question—a mode of communicating knowledge, the tendency of which is very questionable—but that certain positions in reference to them should be proved and illustrated, in a direct manner, in the form of essays, lectures, or oral instructions. The topics now specified, and those which are intimately related to them, are subjects of the deepest interest and importance to every individual of the human race; and, therefore, no valid reason can be assigned why such subjects should not be occasionally elucidated in literary and scientific seminaries, if it be one object of such institutions to promote the happiness—and what is essentially requisite to it—the moral improvement of mankind.

For example, is it not in the highest degree important to every human being, that he should be convinced of his immortal destiny, and have his mind impressed with the realities of a future world—that he should ascertain whether, at death, he is to be reduced for ever into the same situation as the clods of the valley, or transported to a more expansive sphere of existence? Take away from man the prospect of immortality, and you throw a veil of darkness and mystery over all the scenes of creation; you reduce the moral world to a scene of confusion, and involve the ways of Providence in a dark inextricable maze; you inwrap the character of the Deity in awful obscurity, and terminate every prospect of becoming more fully acquainted with the magnificence of the universe; you reduce man to an *enigma*—to the most inexplicable phenomenon in creation, and annihilate the strongest motives to the practice of virtue. But this is not all, you remove the most powerful motives to the pursuit of scientific knowledge; for, in this case, you confine its beneficial results merely to the promotion of the comforts and conveniencies of the present transitory life; and the discoveries of the order and extent of the universe it unfolds, and the speculations to which they lead, tend only to bewilder and perplex the mind, when it is cut off from all hopes of prosecuting its inquiries beyond the grave, and of beholding the mysterious scenes of creation more fully displayed. On this ground, a man who is exhorted to cultivate an acquaintance with science, might, with some reason, exclaim, "Of what avail is it, to spend anxious days and sleepless nights in acquiring scientific knowledge, when it may be all lost before to-morrow's dawn, or, at the farthest, after the lapse of a few short years, when my intellectual faculties shall be annihilated? I can acquire but a few scattered fragments of it at most, although I were to prosecute my researches as far as the most distinguished geniuses have ever advanced; and I must quit the field of investigation before the ten thousandth part of it is half explored. Had I a prospect of enlarging my faculties and resuming my researches in a future state of being, I might engage in them with some degree of interest and vigour; but to one who is uncertain whether his connexion with the intelligent universe shall be continued for another day, it appears quite preposterous, and tends to deprive me of many sensitive gratifications which I find essential to my present enjoyment." What is affirmed of happiness, in general, may be applied to knowledge, one of its ingredients, that the expectation of its *permanency* is indispensably requisite to its perfection. It is the prospect of science being prosecuted in a future world and carried to perfection, that confers a dignity on its objects, and forms the most powerful motive to engage in its pursuits; and, in this point of view, it may be considered as forming a part of that training which is requisite to prepare us for the activities, the contemplations, and enjoyments of that higher sphere of existence. But where no such hopes are indulged, intellectual pursuits are deprived of their chief excellence and importance, and the best affections of the heart of their sublimest objects and most exalted pleasures; and the more the powers of the mind have been exercised and improved, and the more it feels itself prepared for a series of rational enjoyments, the more chagrined and disappointed must it feel when years roll away and it approaches the point where it is to sink into eternal oblivion. Without the hopes of admission to future sources of enjoyment, at the hour of dissolution, we may assume an air of composure, because we are unable to resist, or an air of fortitude from the last efforts of pride; but, in point of fact, we can await the extinction of our being only with a mournful and melancholy gloom.

This representation has frequently been realized, in the case of men of cultivated minds, who had thrown aside the obligations of religion and the idea of a future world, when they approached the confines of the tomb,—of which the following instances may suffice: *Voltaire*, when approaching his dissolution, looked back upon protracted years with remorse, and forward with dismay. He wished for annihilation, through the dread of something worse. He attempted to unburden his troubled mind by confessing to a priest; and he placed his hopes of peace with heaven, in an eager conformity to those rituals which he incessantly treated with contempt. In a previous indisposition, he insisted upon sending for a priest, contrary to the warmest remonstrances of his friends and attendants. On recovery, he was ashamed of his conduct, and ridiculed his own pusillanimity. This pusillanimity, however, returned upon a relapse; and he had again recourse to the miserable remedy. He acknowledged to *Dr. Tronchin*, his physician, the agonies of his mind, and earnestly entreated him to procure for his perusal a treatise written against *the eternity of future punishment.* These facts were communicated to Dr. Cogan, by a gentleman highly respected in the philosophical world, who received them directly from *Dr. Tronchin;* and they concur with many others, in demonstrating the impossibility of enjoying permanent felicity without the hopes and consolations of religion. M. Sechelles, to whose narrative I lately referred, relates, that, in one of his conversations with *Buffon*, the Count declared, "I hope to live two or three years longer, to indulge my habit of working in literary avocations. I am not afraid of death, and am consoled by the thought, that my name will never die. I feel myself fully recompensed for all my labours, by the respect which Europe has paid to my talents, and by the flattering letters I have received from the most exalted personages." Such were the consolations which this philosopher enjoyed in the prospect of the extinction of his being. His *name* would *live* when he himself was for ever blotted out from that creation which it was the object of his writings to describe! But, that his mind was not altogether reconciled to the idea of sinking into eternal oblivion, may be inferred from another anecdote, related by the same gentleman. "One evening I read to Buffon the verses of *Thomas* on the immortality of the soul. He smiled. '*Par dieu*,' says he, '*religion would be a valuable gift if all this were true.*'" This remark evidently implied, that the system he had adopted was not calculated to present so cheerful a prospect of futurity as the system of Revelation.

*Gibbon*, the celebrated historian of the Rise and Fall of the Roman Empire, had his mind early tinctured with the principles of infidelity; and his historical writings are distinguished by several insidious attacks on Christianity, by unfair and unmanly sneers at the religion of his country, and by the loose and disrespectful manner in which he mentions many points of morality regarded as important, even on the principles of natural religion. Such appears to have been his eagerness in this cause, that he stooped to the most despicable pun, or to the most awkward perversion of language, for the pleasure of turning the Scripture into ribaldry, or calling Jesus an impostor. Yet he appears to have been actuated by the same spirit of hypocrisy which distinguished Buffon and his philosophical associates; for, notwithstanding his aversion to Christianity, he would have felt no scruple in accepting an office in the *church*, provided it had contributed to his pecuniary interests. On the occasion of his father having been obliged to mortgage part of his estate, he thus expresses himself: "I regret that I had not embraced the lucrative pursuits of the law or of trade, the chances of civil office or India adventure, *or even the fat slumbers of the church.*" Such is too frequently the morality displayed by infidels, and there is reason to suspect that the church is not altogether purged of them even in the present day. That Gibbon's principles were not sufficient to support his mind in the prospect of dissolution, appears from many expressions in the collection of his letters published by Lord Sheffield, in which are to be traced many instances of the high value which he placed upon existence, and of the regret with which he perceived his years to be rapidly passing away. His letter on the death of Mrs. Posen, bears every mark of the despondent state of his mind at the idea, that, "*all is now lost, finally, irrecoverably lost!*" He adds, "I will agree with my lady, that *the immortality of the soul is, at some times, a very comfortable doctrine.*" The announcement of his death, in the public prints, in January 1794, was accompanied with this remark, "He left this world in gloomy despondency, without those hopes and consolations which cheer the Christian in the prospects of immortality."—Dr. A. Smith, in the account he gives of the last illness of *Hume*, the historian, seems to triumph in the fortitude which he manifested in the prospect of his dissolution, and he adduces a playfulness of expression as an evidence of it, in his jocular allusion to *Charon* and his boat. But, as Dr. Cogan, in his treatise on the passions, very properly remarks, "A moment of vivacity, upon the visit of a friend, will not conduct us to the recesses of the heart, or discover its feelings in the hours of solitude." It is, indeed, altogether unnatural for a man who set so high a value upon his literary reputation, and certainly very unsuitable to the momentous occasion, to indulge in such childish pleasantries, as Hume is represented to have done, at the moment when he considered himself as just about to be launched into non-existence; and, therefore, we have some reason to suspect, that his apparent tranquillity was partly the effect of vanity and affectation. He has confessed, says Dr. Cogan, in the most explicit terms, that his principles were not calculated to administer consolation to a thinking mind. This appears from the following passage in his treatise on Human Nature. "I am affrighted and confounded with that forlorn solitude in which I am placed by my philosophy. When I look abroad, I foresee, on every side, dispute, contradiction, and distraction. When I turn my eye inward, I find nothing but doubt and ignorance. Where am I, or what? From what causes do I derive my existence, and to what condition shall I return? I am confounded with these questions, and begin to fancy myself in the most deplorable condition imaginable, environed with the deepest darkness."*

*Diderot*, one of the French philosophists, was a man of very considerable acquirements in literature and in the physical sciences. The first publication by which he attracted public notice, was a volume written against the Christian religion, entitled *Pensées Philosophiques*. Afterwards, in company with Voltaire and D'Alembert, he conducted the publication of the *Dictionnaire Encyclopédique*, the secret object of which was to sap the foundations of all religion, while the reader, at the same time, was presented with the most splendid articles on the Belles Lettres, mathematics, and the different branches of physical science. Whilst a weak divine, to whom the theological department of the work was committed, was supporting, by the best arguments he could devise, the religion of his country, Diderot and D'Alembert were overturning those arguments under titles which properly allowed of no such disquisitions; and that the object of these digressions might not pass unnoticed by *any* class of readers, care was taken to refer to them from the articles where the question was discussed by the divine. Here was an example of that *hypocrisy* to which I have already adverted, as characteristic of the sect of infidel philosophers; and the following anecdote is illustrative of similar disingenuity, coupled with almost unparalleled impudence. In the course of his correspondence with the late Empress of Russia, Diderot mentioned his own library, as one of the most valuable in Europe, although it is supposed not to have contained above a hundred volumes. When Catharine wanted to purchase it and make him librarian, he said, that his constitution could not support the cold climate of Petersburgh. She offered to let him keep it during his lifetime at Paris; and the library was sold for an immense price. When her ambassador wanted to see it, after a year or two's payments, and the visitation could no longer be put off, he was obliged to run in a hurry, through all the booksellers' shops in Germany, to fill his empty shelves with old volumes. It was customary for Diderot and D'Alembert to frequent the coffee-houses of Paris, and to enter with keenness into religious disputes, the former attacking Christianity, and the latter, under the mask of piety, defending it, but always yielding to the arguments of his opponent. This practice was put a stop to by the police; and Diderot, when reproached by the lieutenant for preaching atheism, replied, "It is true, I am an atheist, and I glory in it." But such principles will not always support the mind, nor did they support the mind of Diderot, when his dissolution approached. When he perceived that death was at no great distance, he desired that a priest might be brought, and the Cure de St. Sulpice was introduced to him. He saw this ecclesiastic several times, and was preparing to make a public recantation of his errors, but Condorcet and the other adepts now crowded about him, persuaded him that his case was not dangerous, and that country air would restore him to health. For some time he resisted their attempts to bring him back to atheism, but they secretly hurried him to the country, where he died, and a report was spread that he died suddenly on rising from the table, without remorse, and with his atheism unshaken.

Such are the native effects of the highest intellectual accomplishments, and the most brilliant acquirements in science, when unaccompanied with the spirit of true religion and of Christian morality. They cannot improve the moral order of society; they cannot procure for their possessors substantial enjoyment, even in the present life, and they are altogether inadequate to support and tranquillize the soul in the prospect of the agonies of dissolving nature. Notwithstanding the rational gratifications such persons may have occasionally enjoyed in philosophical pursuits, they must be obliged to confess, that they have acquired no equivalent for those joys which frequently animate the hearts of the most illiterate, who are sometimes enabled to look forward to the king of terrors without dismay, and to depart in peace with hopes full of immortality,—when the philosophist is obliged to exclaim, "All is now lost, finally and irrecoverably lost." Yet such is the tendency of the principles which are now in operation in our literary and scientific seminaries, and such the result to which we must ultimately look forward, should the principles of religion be discarded from the pursuits of knowledge.

It is therefore to be hoped, that all who have a sincere regard for the promotion of science, for the interests of religion, and for the welfare of their country, will devote a portion of their attention to this important subject, and set their faces in opposition to the spirit of that sceptical philosophy which has so long debased and demoralized the continental philosophists. Were all the instructions delivered in our seminaries, from infant schools, through all the gradations of grammar and parochial establishments, mechanics' institutions, academies, and universities, judiciously amalgamated with the principles of pure and undefiled religion, it would doubtless be accompanied with a variety of pleasing and beneficial effects. It would tend to remove the prejudices which a considerable portion of the religious world still entertain against the pursuits of science,—it would lead to correct and rational views of the Christian system, and tend to dissipate those foolish and superstitious notions which have too frequently been grafted upon it,—it would promote the interests of genuine

* Treatise on Human Nature, vol i p. 458.

morality among society at large,—it would fit the inferior ranks of the community for taking a part in the elective franchise and government of their country, and the higher ranks for promoting the enactment of laws congenial to the spirit of true religion, and promotive of the best interests of the nation,—it would tend to secure the peace and tranquillity of nations by undermining the malignant passions from which wars and contentions derive their origin,—it would introduce a general spirit of philanthropy, and give efficacy to the means employed for promoting the knowledge of Christianity throughout the world, and would, ere long, usher in the period foretold in ancient prophecy, when "the knowledge of Jehovah shall cover the earth, as the waters cover the channels of the deep," and "when righteousness and praise shall spring forth before all nations."

---

# APPENDIX.

No. 1.—*Ignorance of the Dark Ages.* Page 12.

THE following facts, chiefly extracted from Dr. Robertson's history of Charles V., will show the low state of literature, and the deplorable ignorance which characterized the period to which the text refers. In the ninth century, Herbaud Comes Palatii, though supreme judge of the empire, by virtue of his office, could not subscribe his name. As late as the fourteenth century, Du Guesclin, constable of France, the greatest man in the state, could neither read nor write. Nor was this ignorance confined to laymen,—the greater part even of the clergy were not many degrees superior to them in science. Many dignified ecclesiastics could not subscribe the canons of those councils of which they sat as members. One of the questions appointed by the canons to be put to persons who were candidates for holy orders was this—"Whether they could read the Gospels and Epistles, and explain the tenor of them, at least literally?"—Alfred the Great complained, that from the Humber to the Thames, there was not a priest who understood the liturgy in his mother tongue, or who could translate the easiest piece of Latin; and that from the Thames to the sea, the ecclesiastics were still more ignorant. The ignorance of the clergy is quaintly described by Alanus, an author of the dark ages, in the following words:—"Potius dediti gulæ quam glossæ; potius colligunt libras quam legunt libros; libentius intuentur Martham quam Marcum; malunt legere in Salmone quam in Solomone," *i. e.* They gave themselves more willingly to the pleasures of gluttony than to the learning of languages; they chose rather to collect money than to read books; they looked upon *Martha* with a more affectionate eye than upon Mark, and they found more delight in reading in Salmon than in Solomon.

One of the causes of the universal ignorance which prevailed during that period, was the scarcity of books, along with their exorbitant price, and the difficulty of rendering them more common. The Romans wrote their books either on parchment, or on paper made of the Egyptian papyrus. The latter being the cheapest, was, of course, the most commonly used. But after the communication between Europe and Egypt was broken off, on account of the latter having been seized upon by the Saracens, the papyrus was no longer in use in Italy and other European countries. They were obliged, on that account, to write all their books upon parchment, and as its price was high, books became extremely rare, and of great value. We may judge of the scarcity of the materials for writing them from one circumstance. There still remain several manuscripts of the eighth, ninth, and following centuries, written on parchment, from which some former writing had been erased, in order to substitute a new composition in its place. In this manner, it is probable, several works of the ancients perished. A book of Livy, or of Tacitus might be erased, to make room for the legendary tale of a saint, or the superstitious prayers of a missal. Many circumstances prove the scarcity of books during these ages. Private persons seldom possessed any books whatever. Even monasteries of considerable note had only one missal. Lupus, abbot of Ferriers, in a letter to the Pope, A. D. 855, beseeches him to send him a copy of Cicero *De Oratore*, and Quintilian's "Institutions," "for," says he, "although we have part of those books, there is no complete copy of them in all France." The price of books became so high, that persons of a moderate fortune could not afford to purchase them. The Countess of Anjou paid for a copy of the Homilies of Haimon, bishop of Alberstadt, two hundred sheep, five quarters of wheat, and the same quantity of rye and millet. Even so late as the year 1471, when Louis XI. borrowed the works of Racis, the Arabian physician, from the faculty of medicine in Paris, he not only deposited in pledge a considerable quantity of plate, but was obliged to procure a nobleman to join with him as surety in a deed, binding himself under a great forfeiture to restore it. When any person made a present of a book to a church or monastery, in which were the only libraries during several ages, it was deemed a donative of such value, that he offered it on the altar *pro remedio animæ suæ*, in order to obtain the forgiveness of his sins. In the eleventh century, the art of making paper, in the manner now become universal, was invented; by means of which, not only the number of manuscripts increased, but the study of the sciences was wonderfully facilitated.

No. II.—*Foolish and Superstitious Opinions respecting Comets and Eclipses.* P. 18.

Aristotle held comets to be fiery exhalations, rising from the lower atmosphere to the upper or fiery region, condensing during their rapid descent, kindling on their near approach to the Empyreum, and burning until exhausted. ***Leonard Digges***, an Almanack maker of the fourteenth century, affirmed of comets—" That they signifie corruption of the ayre; they are signes of earthquake, of warres, chaunging of kingdomes, great dearth of corne, yea a common death of man and beast."—***Bodin*** supposed them spirits, which, having lived on the earth innumerable ages, and having at last completed their term of existence, celebrate their last triumphs, or are recalled to heaven in the form of shining stars. In the records of former ages, we read of a comet " coming out from an opening in the heavens, like to a dragon with blue feet, and a head covered with snakes." And we are told, that " in the year 1527, about four in the morning, not only in the Palatinate of the Rhine, but nearly over all Europe, appeared for an hour and a quarter, a most horrible comet in this sort. In its length it was of a bloody colour, inclining to saffron. From the top of its train appeared a bended arm, in the hand whereof was a huge sword, in the instant posture of striking. At the point of the sword was a star. From the star proceeded dusky rays, like a hairy tail; on the side of them other rays like javelins, or lesser swords, as if imbrued in blood; between which appeared human faces of the colour of blackish clouds, with rough hair and beards. All these moved with such terrible sparkling and brightness, that many spectators swooned with fear."—***Rosenburgi*** " *Exampla Cometarum.*"

The comet of 1454, seen at Constantinople, seemed there to be moving in the firmament, from west to east, and to present the aspect of a flaming sword. From its great magnitude, it is said even to have eclipsed the moon, and created among the Turks the utmost consternation, as it was thought to prognosticate nothing less than a crusade from all the kingdoms of Christendom, and forbode the certain overthrow of the crescent. Only two years afterwards, when, notwithstanding these direful omens, the Turkish arms had proved eminently victorious, and were spreading dismay over all Europe, Halley's comet, in 1456, with a long tail turned towards the east, created reciprocal and still greater alarms on the part of the Christians. Pope Calixtus believed it to be at once the sign and instrument of divine wrath; he ordered public prayers to be offered up, and decreed, that, in every town, the bells should be tolled at mid-day, to warn the people to supplicate the mercy and forgiveness of heaven: " ut omnes de precibus contra Turcarum tyrrannidem fundendis admonerentur. That all people may be admonished to pour out supplications against the tyranny of the Turks.—See Milne's Essay on Comets.

Even in modern times, many foolish and preposterous opinions have been entertained respecting these anomalous bodies. In a late periodical publication, the writer of an article on comets, when alluding to the comet of 1811, proceeds to state " some singular changes and circumstances," which its influence occasioned. " The winter," says he, " was very mild, the spring was wet, the summer cool, and very little appearance of the sun to ripen the produce of the earth; yet the harvest was not deficient, and some fruits were not only abundant, but deliciously ripe, such as figs, melons, and wall-fruit. Very few wasps appeared, and the flies became blind, and disappeared early in the season. No violent storms of thunder and lightning, and little or no frost and snow the ensuing winter. Venison, which has been supposed to be indebted for its flavour to a dry and parched summer, was by no means deficient in fat or in flavour. But what is very remarkable," continues this sage observer, " in the metropolis, and about it, was the number of females who produced twins; some had more; and a shoemaker's wife, in Whitechapel, produced four at one birth, all of whom," &c. &c. And all such " singular changes and circumstances," it would appear, according to the fancy of this sapient Essayist, " were occasioned by the influence of the comet which appeared in the autumn of 1811 ! !"

The poets, likewise, by their bombastic descriptions, have tended to perpetuate superstitious feelings. The following is Du Barta's description of one of these visiters.

" Here, in the night, appears a flaming spire,
There, a fierce dragon, folded all on fire;
Here, with long bloody hairs, a blazing star
Threatens the world with famine, plague, and war;
To princes death, to kingdoms many crosses;
To all estates inevitable losses;
To herdsmen rot, to ploughmen hapless seasons;
To sailors storms, to cities civil treasons."

The following extract from " Tully's *Letters from Tripoli*," contains a picturesque description of a *solar eclipse*, and the effects it produced on the inhabitants of Barbary.

" I cannot here omit describing what an extraordinary impression an eclipse makes on the uninformed part of the inhabitants of this country

Of this we had ocular proof during the great eclipse of the sun, on the 4th of this month, which was almost total, and occasioned, for some minutes, a gloomy darkness, resembling that of midnight. The beginning of the eclipse was seen at Tripoli, at half past seven in the morning; at half past eight, when it was at the height, the face of nature was changed from day to night. The screech-owl, not long retired to its rest, re-appeared, and disturbed the morning with its shrieks. Lizards and serpents were seen prowling about the terraces; and flights of evening birds, here called marabats, and held sacred by the Moors, flew about in great numbers, and increased the darkness. The noisy flitting of their wings roused the Moor, who had been stupified by fear; and, when one of these heavy birds (which often drop to the ground by coming in contact with each other) chanced to fall at his feet, the African would start aghast, look at it with horror, and set up a hideous howl. About eight o'clock, when the lustre of the morning was completely faded, the common Moors were seen assembling in clusters in the streets, gazing wildly at the sun, and conversing very earnestly. When the eclipse was at its height, they ran about distracted, in companies, firing volleys of muskets at the sun, to frighten away the monster or dragon, as they called it, by which they supposed it was being devoured. At that moment, the Moorish song of death and *walliah-woo*, or the howl they make for the dead, not only resounded from the mountains and valleys of Tripoli, but was undoubtedly re-echoed throughout the continent of Africa. The women brought into the streets all the brass pans, kettles, and iron utensils, they could collect; and, striking on them with all their force, and screaming at the same time, occasioned a horrid noise, that was heard for miles. Many of these women, owing to their exertions and fears, fell into fits, or fainted. The distress and terror of the Moors did not in the least abate, till near nine o'clock, when the sun assured them, by his refulgent beams, that all his dangers were passed.

"During the morning and the day, the atmosphere was uncommonly clear, even for a Barbary sky, which rendered the effects of this great eclipse more striking. We learned, from Hadgi Abderrahman, who paid us a visit when it was over, that the first ladies in the place had trembled at the event, and several were seriously ill. The ladies of his own family, he said had suffered much less at the appearance of the eclipse, from the circumstance of his being at home with them; for, though he considered it would be useless to enter into a philosophical account of it to them, yet he assured them that the moon went occasionally to see the sun; and when they met, by their being so close together, the moon always interrupted more or less of his light. This account, he said, the truth of which they were convinced of by his great earnestness, considerably abated their fears. To the ambassador it was a serious case, as Lilla Amnani is in a very delicate state of health; but the account he gave her of the phenomenon entirely pacified her."

The above description presents a melancholy picture of the *gross ignorance* even of the *ladies* of modern Barbary, and of the consequent shallowness of their understandings; since their fathers and husbands considered it useless to enter into a rational account of the phenomenon, and since they were pleased with such an absurd and extravagant explanation of it. And, since the higher ranks, in that country, are so grossly ignorant of the order of nature, and of the causes of so common phenomena, in what a state of mental darkness must the lower classes of society be placed! Nor is Barbary the only country in which such ignorance prevails. Among the middling and lower ranks, in many European countries, supposed to be in a moderate state of civilization, a similar degree of intellectual debasement will be found to exist. The Croatians, who inhabit a certain district of the Austrian empire, make the whole of their religion consist in the hearing of mass and the observance of Lent; and robbery or murder are considered as more venial crimes, than to eat, during Lent, with a spoon that has been dipped in broth. The Morlacchi, who occupy another district of the same empire, are described by geographers, as extremely superstitious in their religious opinions, and as firmly believing in ghosts and witches, in sorceries and enchantments, and in every species of supernatural agency, while they are ignorant of the causes of the most common phenomena of nature.

No. III.—*Absurdities of Astrology.* P. 19, &c.

Mr. Varley's "Zodiacal Physiognomy," referred to in a note, p. 19, pretends to decide, that the various signs of the zodiac create a great diversity in the features and complexions of human beings; and have, in fact, such influence over the destinies of the human race, that the system may be fairly styled, "the phrenology of the skies." The following extracts exhibit a few specimens of the positions maintained by this *profound* and *erudite* writer. "It has been discovered," says Mr. Varley, "that each sign confers a specific style of countenance, feature, and complexion, by which appearances, alone, the sign which was rising at the east, at birth, can, often without any other help, be ascertained."—"The fiery trigon, consisting of Aries, Leo, and Sagittarius, contains the spirited, generous, magnanimous, and princely natures. The earthy trigon, Taurus, Virgo, and Capricorn, contain the careful, sordid, and pernicious qualities; the aerial trigon, Gemini, Libra, and Aquarius, contain the humane, harmonious, and courteous principles; and the watery trigon, Cancer, Scorpio, and Pisces, the cold, prolific, cautious, and severe qualities." "Sagittarius, the house of Jupiter, is the only sign under which no persons are born having black or dark hair, eyes, and eye-brows." "I have always uniformly found," says the author, "those born under Sagittarius, to be very fair, with gray eyes, and, in general, of a lively, forgiving-hearted, and free dispositions." Again, "Five minutes' difference of the time of their birth, renders the members of the same family red-haired, or black-haired, blue-eyed or black-eyed, sordid or generous."—"Saturn, at any period of life, passing through the ascendant, which he does every thirty years, causes dulness or melancholy, for a few weeks, to the native, and when Jupiter passes over it, the party feels cheerful and healthy; and should a party of antiquarians, hundreds of years after a person's death, discover his grave, there must be some planet or the sun in conjunction, or some other aspect with his ascendant."—"Jupiter in the third house gives safe inland journeys, and agreeable neighbours or kindred. The moon in this house will give constant trudging from one place to another, and is often so posited in the nativities of postmen and travellers. Jupiter in the fourth, with Venus, gives fixed or landed property, and a house ornamented with matters of taste, or of the fine arts. Jupiter in the fifth, gives a family of good or clever children, and much pleasure in life and its amusements. In the sixth, he signifies good servants and assistants, good health, and that the native will be fortunate in small cattle and animals. Jupiter in the seventh, signifies a good wife or husband, and agreeable dealings with mankind in making good bargains," &c. "Children born under Mars have *well formed chins*,—under Aquarius, are fair and amiable,—under Scorpio, are dark with *aquiline noses*, and greenish or gray eyes." "Lord Byron, who was born under Scorpio, received enough of the reflected Taurus principle to prevent his nose from being aquiline, and to give to his character a degree of perverseness or eccentricity." "Persons born under Aries, with Jupiter in the first house, are likely to succeed and be appreciated in England: If he be posited in Taurus, the native is likely to succeed well in Ireland; if in Gemini, in London, of which this sign is the significator. Jupiter in Cancer will give him success in Scotland or Holland, or concerns connected with the water, unless Jupiter should be afflicted by any *malevolent planet*, or be in combustion by being too near the sun."

By this time the reader will be sufficiently satiated with the sage doctrines of Mr. John Varley, in relation to "Zodiacal Physiognomy" and the Phrenology of the heavens. If he has a desire to pick up any more of such precious fragments of wisdom, he will be abundantly gratified in perusing the work itself, where, among other unique and precious relics, he will be presented with an engraving *of the Ghost of a Flea*, together with an account of the manner in which it appeared to Mr. Blake the artist, who drew it, and of its astrological correspondency and signification. That such absurdities should be published by the first bookselling establishment in London, in the twenty-eighth year of the nineteenth century, and be purchased by hundreds, perhaps by thousands, is a proof, that strong efforts are still requisite to extirpate the superstitions of astrology from the minds of many of our countrymen.

No. IV.—*Proofs of the belief which is still attached to the doctrines of Astrology, and of the pernicious effects it produces.* P. 19,

That the predictions of astrologers are still believed by many of our countrymen in the middling ranks of life, appears from the following recent occurrences.

On the 2d September, 1829, Joseph Hyatt, a journeyman printer, was summoned before Sir Peter Laurie, at the Guildhall, London, charged with assaulting his wife, Philips, on the preceding Saturday. In his defence, Hyatt declared, that all their unhappiness proceeded from his wife (a pretty young woman of eighteen years,) continually haunting the fortune-tellers, and paying attention to their predictions. He produced a paper he had recently found, written by an astrologer, to whom his wife had applied. After laying down the position of the planets on the third of June, at the moment she applied to him, the astrologer proceeds, "The querant must not expect any thing to be very kind to her until late in this year, say October next. This day will not prove any thing kind or pleasant. The 28th day of this month also will not be friendly. July 2d, mind your phunny, and take no journey, and trust to no relative. The eighth day will not be unkind I hope. Look to it. The thirteenth day also promises you pleasure and also profit. Attend it; and avoid all dark sallow persons. (Her husband nearly answered this description.) From such your disappointments must come. August 2, 6, 23, avoid them days—may be qualified to give you vexation,—avoid them. Sept. 1, 6, will be unkind, but pray avoid 15, 20. October 4, avoid it, may be vexatious. The 20, 21, 27, 28, 29, 30, will be more kind, pray attend to them and make good use of them, they will not be unkind." The husband said, this fellow had predicted their separation for three months; what other things he had put in her head he did not know, but he led a miserable life with her.—*Morning Chronicle, Sept. 3d.* 1829.

On the same day as above stated, (Sept. 2 1829) Ann Wheeler, a servant girl, was brought to the *Mansion-house*, charged with having at tempted to enter the house of her master, at two o'clock in the morning, over the rails. She was exquisitely dressed, and wore an elegant satin bonnet, which belonged to her mistress, and put on her curls and finery, in order to attend a "*hop*" in the neighbourhood, and acknowledged that she had been walking for an hour or two up and down the streets in conversation with her friend. In the course of the investigation it was stated, that there was found in the corner of her box, wrapped up carefully, a document which might have led to those unseasonable and unfortunate assignations, which at last terminated in her being brought to the watch-house. A paper was handed to the Lord Mayor, in which was folded a card, on which was written the following words,—

"Mrs. Smith, No. 49, Wentworth Street, Dress Maker."

"Lawful questions resolved."

The paper was an answer to the question, "What sort of a husband shall I have, and how soon shall I have him?" It stated, that the "interrogator should have a nice respectable tradesman, who should be a most tender husband, and be the father of six children, of which she should be the happy mother;—*that certain planets were visible at their birth, and, in conjunction at the time, a symptom that betokened felicity, and that the union should take place as surely as he or she* (the person who wrote the paper) *had the power of predicting.*"—*Morning Chronicle, Sept. 3d,* 1829.

The above are only specimens of many similar occurrences which are occasionally recorded in the daily papers. The pernicious tendency of astrological predictions on those who are weak enough to give them credit, is sufficiently apparent in the cases now stated; having in the one case alienated the affections of a young woman from her husband, and produced contention and family discord, and in the other, tantalized a vain young female, and brought her into suspicious and disgraceful circumstances, which may lay the foundation of her ruin, and render her miserable for life.

No. V.—*Illustrations of some of the opinions and practices of our ancestors in relation to witchcraft.* P. 22.

By *witchcraft* was generally understood,—a supernatural power, of which persons were supposed to obtain the possession, by entering into a compact with the devil. They gave themselves up to him, body and soul: and he engaged that they should want for nothing, and that he would avenge them upon all their enemies. As soon as the bargain was concluded, the devil delivered to the witch an *imp*, or familiar spirit, to be ready at a call, and to do whatever it was directed. By the assistance of this imp, and of the devil together, the witch, who was almost always an old woman, was enabled to transport herself through the air, on a broomstick, or a spit, to distant places to attend the meetings of the witches. At these meetings the devil always presided. They were enabled also to transform themselves into various shapes, particularly to assume the forms of cats and hares, in which they most delighted; to inflict diseases on whomsoever they thought proper, and to punish their enemies in a variety of ways. Witchcraft was universally believed in Europe, till the sixteenth century, and maintained its ground with tolerable firmness till the middle of the seventeenth, nay, in some countries on the continent, till the middle of the eighteenth century. Vast numbers of reputed witches were convicted and condemned to be burnt every year. The methods of discovering them were various. One was to weigh the supposed criminal against the church Bible, which, if she was guilty, would preponderate; another, by making her attempt to say the Lord's Prayer,—this no witch was able to repeat entirely, but would omit some part, or sentence thereof. It is remarkable, that all witches did not hesitate at the same part,—some leaving out one part, and some another. *Teats*, through which the imps sucked, were indubitable marks of a witch; these were always raw, and also insensible, and, if squeezed, sometimes yielded a drop of blood. A witch could not weep more than three tears, and that only out of the left eye. This want of tears was, by the witch-finders, and, even by some judges, considered as a very substantial proof of guilt. Swimming a witch was another kind of popular ordeal generally practised. For this she was stripped naked, and cross-bound,—the right thumb to the left toe, and the left thumb to the right toe. Thus prepared, she was thrown into a pond or river, in which, if guilty, she could not sink; for having, by her compact with the devil, renounced the benefit of the water of baptism, that element, in its turn, renounced her, and refused to receive her into its bosom. There were two other ordeals by *fire*, by which witches were discovered; the first by burning the thatch of the house of the suspected witch,—the other, by burning any animal supposed to be bewitched by her, as a hog or an ox. These, it was held, would force a witch to confess.

The trial by the *stool* was another method used for the detection of witches. It was thus managed:—Having taken the suspected witch, she was placed in the middle of a room, upon a stool, or table, cross-legged, or in some other uneasy posture; to which, if she did not submit, she was then bound with cords,—there she was watched, and kept without meat or sleep for twenty-four hours, (for, they said, that within that time they should see her imp come and suck.) A little hole was likewise made in the door for imps to come in at, and, lest it should come in some less discernible shape, they that watched were taught to be ever and anon sweeping the room, and, if they saw any spiders or flies, to kill them,—if they could not kill them, then they might be sure they were imps. If witches, under examination or torture, would not confess, all their apparel was changed, and every hair of their body shaven off with a sharp razor, lest they should secret magical charms to prevent their confessing. It was a maxim, too, in these proceedings, that witches were most apt to confess on *Fridays*. By such trials as these, and by the accusations of children, old women, and fools, were thousands of unhappy women, condemned for witchcraft, and burned at the stake.

A work, written by *M Thoest*, was published a few years ago at Mentz, entitled, "The History of Magic, Demons, Sorcerers," &c. which contains an affecting narrative of the numbers that have suffered for the pretended crime of magic and witchcraft. The cases enumerated are proved from unequivocal authority. In these excesses of the magistrates, it appears, that female sorcerers have been the greatest sufferers. Among other curious articles in the collection, we learn, that Christopher de Runtzow, a gentleman of Holstein, whose heated imagination had misled his understanding, *consigned eighteen persons to the flames at one time*, the victims of a merciless superstition. In a village called Lindheim, containing about six hundred inhabitants, not less than *thirty* were destroyed by fire, in the narrow interval between the years 1661 and 1665, making a twentieth part of the whole population consumed in four years. In this inhuman conduct towards an unhappy class of persons, the author points out Wurtzburg as having frequently been subject to well-merited reproach. It appears from the *Acta Magica* of Naubers, that between the years 1627 and 1629, one hundred and twenty-seven individuals perished in similar instances of cruelty practised by their brother men. The principal objects of such nefarious dealings were old women, or travellers, and frequently poor children, from nine to ten years of age. Occasionally such outrages have been perpetrated on persons of some consequence,—proficients in knowledge above the general standard of the age, or such as had acquired property by their industry and genius. Among many others in these shocking details, are the respectable names of fourteen vicars, two young gentlemen, some counsellors, the largest or most corpulent man in Wurtzburg, and his wife, the handsomest woman in the city, and a student or scholar engaged in the study of foreign languages. Those innocent sufferers were frequently put to the torture. But what must our feelings and principles incline us to think of an enormity here brought to our recollection, in the instance of a poor girl, Maria Renata, who suffered so late as in the year 1749!

The extent of the judicial murders for witchcraft is far greater than most persons, who have not studied the history of demonology, can form any idea. From the period in which Pope Innocent VIII. in 1484, issued his bull against witchcraft, to the middle of the seventeenth century, if we believe the testimonies of contemporary historians, Europe was little better than a large suburb or outwork of Pandemonium, one half of the population being either bewitching or bewitched. Delrio tells us, that five hundred witches were executed in Geneva, in three months, about the year 1515. "*A thousand*," says Bartholomeus de Spina, "were executed in one year, in the diocese of Como, and they went on burning at the rate of a hundred per annum for some time after. In Lorraine, from 1580 to 1595, Remigius boasts of having burnt nine hundred. In France, the executions for the same crime were fifteen hundred and twenty. In Wurtzburg and Treves, the amount of executions in the course of the century preceding 1628, is reckoned to be 15,700. It has been calculated that in Germany alone, the number of victims that perished, from the date of Innocent's bull to the eighteenth century, considerably exceeds *one hundred thousand*. The executions were at first confined to crazed old women, or unhappy foreigners, but at length the witchcraft phrenzy rose to such a pitch, and spread so extensively, that the lives of more exalted victims were threatened. Noblemen and abbots, presidents of courts and professors, began to swell the catalogue, and no man felt secure that he might not suddenly be compelled, by torture, to bear witness against his own innocent wife and children. In the Catholic canton of *Glarus*, in Switzerland, it is said, that a witch was burnt, even so late as the year 1786! It is impossible for any rational and humane mind to peruse such a list as the above, without shuddering and horror. How dreadful the results to which ignorance and superstition have led!—and how astonishing the consideration,—that judges, lawyers, ministers of religion, nobles, and persons of all ranks should have given their sanction, without the least remorse, to such cruelties and legalized murders!

In Pitcairn's "Criminal Trials," referred to in the text, a variety of curious documents is contained, respecting the proceedings of the Justiciary Court in Scotland against witchcraft, sorcery, and incantation. One of these trials relates to a gentleman of family, Mr. Hector Monro of Fowies, who was "indytit and accusit" of "sorcerie, incantationnis, or wichecraft." This trial contains a complete specimen of the superstition of the age. Mr. Hector, it would appear, had sent for "Johne M'Connielly-gar and his wyffes, and Johne Bunes wyffe, in Lytell Alteis, thre notorious and commoune witches." They had been sent for to assist in restoring the health of Robert Monro, a brother of the said Mr.

Hector, who entertained them for five days. It is said in the indictment, that they "poillit the hair of Robert Monro, his brotheris head, and plait the naillis of his fingeris and tais," and "socht be thair develisch meanes to have cureit him of his sickness;" but it would appear, that the *weird sisters* were by no means successful, and were compelled to decamp, for "they wald haif vsit furth the rest of thair develisch craft was nocht they ferit to tarie with him (Hector Monro) be ressone of his fader, quha wald haif apprehendit thame; and they declarit to him that he was owre lang in sending for thame, swa that they cald do na guid to the said Robert Monro." Mr. Hector, however, fell sick himself, and had recourse to the hags for a cure; and as he had an eye to the patrimony of his father, to which he could not succeed as he was a younger son, he began some incantations, in concert with the hags, to deprive his elder brother, George Monro, of life, and for this he was "delatit," also of "slaughter." The indictment, which is a most remarkable document, is too long for insertion. Jonett Grant, Jonett Clark, and Bessie Roy, nurse to the "Laird of Boquhave," are the three next ladies who were called to account for being "fylit" of witchcraft. The two *Jonetts* seem to have been in partnership; and if the indictments are to be credited, they were guilty of no fewer than six "crewal murthers," by witchcraft, of the "slavchter and destructionne of saxtene heid of nolt, of raising the devil, of making men *eunuchs* by witchcraft," &c. For such hardened sinners as the two *Jonetts*, no mercy was to be expected, and accordingly they were condemned to be "tane to the Castle hill of Edinburg, and there werriet at ane staik, and their body to be burnt to assis." Bessie Roy, however, came off with flying colours, although she was also indicted as "ane commoune thief," by means of the "enchantment and slicht of the diuill."—The following is the title of a pamphlet republished by Mr. Pitcairn, containing a most extraordinary narrative. "Newes from Scotland, declaring the damnable life of *Doctor Fean*, a notable sorcerer, who was burned at Edinburg in Janurie last, 1591, which doctor was register to the deuill, that sundrie times preached at North Barricke kirk, to a number of notorious witches," &c. The poor woman who was most cruelly treated was Euphane Mackalsane, a notable witch, who appears to have been so notorious as to be "bound to ane staik, and brunt to assis, *quick* to the death." "This," says Mr. Pitcairn, "was the severest sentence ever pronounced by the court, even in the most atrocious cases," but poor Euphane died, nevertheless, with all the heroism and devotedness of a martyr. See *Edin. Lit. Gaz.* July 1829.

To attempt a serious refutation of the doctrines of witchcraft, would be altogether superfluous and even ridiculous. That there ever were witches, that is, persons endowed with such powers as are usually ascribed to witches, is what no rational and enlightened mind can for a moment admit. The actions imputed to them are either absurd or impossible. To suppose an ignorant old woman, or indeed any human being, capable of transforming herself into a cat or a hare, is to suppose her capable of counteracting the laws of nature, which is competent to none but the Supreme Ruler of the world. We might almost as soon believe that such a being is capable of creating the universe. It presents a most humiliating picture of the imbecility of the human mind, that such absurdities should ever have been believed; and certainly conveys no very favourable idea of the *humanity* of our ancestors, when they inflicted, without remorse, so many shocking cruelties, especially on the tender sex, for such fancied crimes. Yet, absurd as the doctrine of witchcraft certainly is, it is a lamentable fact, that vast multitudes of our fellow-men, both in our own country and in other lands, are still believers in sorcery and witchcraft, of which an instance or two is stated in the following note.

No. VI.—*Proofs that the belief in witchcraft is still prevalent among certain classes of society.*

Notwithstanding the degree of information which prevails in the nineteenth century, it is a melancholy consideration that superstition, and a belief in the efficacy of certain incantations, still prevail to a considerable extent, even in the most enlightened countries. The following recent occurrences will tend to corroborate this position, and at the same time show the pernicious consequences which frequently result from such a belief.

On the 2d September 1829, Laurent Raimboult, a farmer in the hamlet of Redoire, Commune of Champtre, in France, spent the day in measuring wheat at the house of Poirier, his brother-in-law. About eight o'clock in the evening, he left to go to his own house, which was about half a league from Poirier's house. He carried a bag containing the measure he had been using, and a box holding his dinner, which he had not opened; for he had stated his intention not to eat till he returned home. The next morning his corpse was found in a meadow, bordered by a wood, and not very far from his own house. His body was horribly mutilated, his clothes stained with blood, and there was a large wound on the back part of his head. All the wounds showed that he had been struck by several persons armed with contusive weapons. Near him the ground had not been trod upon; his bag and the things it contained were carefully laid by his side: all proved that he had not been robbed. Poirier, who has always had a good character in that part of the country, was on very bad terms with Raimboult, who passed for a *sorcerer*. Some time ago, the wife of Poirier had fallen sick, as well as several of his cattle. Poirier did not doubt for aninstant, that these sicknesses were the effect of sorcery. He came to Angers, and consulted a pretended diviner, a miserable victim of monomania, who gave him a full water-bottle, and told him to take it home with him, and put it in the very best place of his house. "At such an hour," said the diviner, "you should recite such and such prayers before my water-bottle, and then you will see in the water it contains, the likeness of him who has bewitched your wife and your cattle." Poirier followed these orders precisely; and it is only too probable that his imagination being pre-occupied with the idea, this wretched man fancied he saw his brother-in-law in the water-bottle of the guilty diviner, and thought he was doing a service to his country in delivering it from a being whom he regarded as the friend and favourite of the devil.—***Copied from a Paris paper, in Morning Chron. Sept.* 23, 1829.**

The following occurrence, in another Department of France, happened nearly about the same time as the preceding.

"It appears that in the department of Lot and Garonne, and particularly in some of the communes of the district of Marmande, the belief of sorcery is common among the people. John Sabathe, a peasant, with plenty of money, living in the vicinity of Clairac, had a sick daughter: medicine had failed, which is nothing extraordinary; but there remained magic, and Sabathe greatly relied upon it. He applied to Rose Peres, who enjoyed the reputation of being a witch. He stated the condition of his daughter;—the witch replied, she would go and visit her. She went the next morning to Sabathe's residence, saw the sick girl, and declared she was bewitched. [Perhaps she was not so far wrong either, for some witnesses, who were no doubt very spiteful, gave it as their opinion that love had entered a little into this affair.] Whatever was the cause of her illness, the witch promised to relieve her, and said, that the thing was not without a remedy. She told them to light a great fire, and they would see why afterwards. Little as we are initiated into the secrets of magic, we know that *odd* numbers, especially the number *three*, have singular virtues; therefore 3 multiplied by 3 must be a number prodigiously powerful. It was apparently for this reason that the witch required *nine* large pebble stones, which she put into the fire, and kept there till they were red hot: she then threw them into a kettle full of water, and the mysterious vapour that arose served to perfume the patient that was lying over it. But this was only the preamble of ceremonies much more important. She had a table brought to her; it was covered with a cloth, and two lighted candles placed on it; there was even an end of wax that had been used in the church; a hammer was placed symmetrically between the two candles, and on one side of the table the witch laid, with a grave and mysterious air, the formidable book of magic, so well known by the name of Little Albert. She still wanted one thing; it was a plate filled with water, in which a sum of 400 francs (16*l.* sterling) was to be deposited. The plate was brought;—as to the sum, we may remark, how difficult magic must be to practise, and what attention is requisite to its details. Crown pieces of six francs were about to be put into the water, when the witch called out, 'Take care what you are doing; it is crown pieces of ***five*** francs that are wanted.' She was instantly obeyed,—the crowns of five francs are at the bottom of the plate.

"Things being in this state, every body left the house. The witch remained alone for about half an hour; she then re-opened the doors, and said they might re-enter. She added, that all had succeeded, but that the malignant spirit that had appeared had carried away the 400 francs on withdrawing. The witch's husband then arrived; his wife told him that the assembly was made. 'It's all well,' said he; 'but thy sister is at thy house, and she wants to see you, and we must go there. They went accordingly; Sabathe and his family a little stupified, and the patient in the same state as before.—These were the facts which were made known to the Court by indirect evidence, for these good folks took care to make no complaint, for fear of the witches. The Court sentenced her to imprisonment for three years, and a fine of fifty francs. She had been charged before the Royal Court of Agen for swindling, under pretence of practising witchcraft.—Some years ago, the same Court sentenced to close imprisonment three or four women, living in the neighbourhood of Villereal, for having put on the fire and half-burned a pretended witch, who would not cure them of a disease she had given them."—*Gazette des Tribunaux*, as quoted in *Morn. Chron.* Sept. 28, 1829.

In both the above cases we perceive an implicit belief in the powers of divination and sorcery, a belief which appears to be general among the lower ranks of society; and it would appear that the profession of witch or sorcerer is pretty common in the principal towns in France. In the one instance this belief led to a most atrocious murder, and in the other to a dexterous robbery; and, in this latter case, it would seem, that, notwithstanding the palpable imposture that was practised on Sabathe and his family, these simple people still believed in the supernatural powers of the sorceress who had so barefacedly robbed them, for "they took care to make no complaint, *for fear of the witches*."—Nearly akin to the notions under consideration, is the following superstition relating to *bees*.

The practice of informing bees of any death that takes place in a family, is well known, and still prevails among the lower orders in England. The disastrous consequences to be apprehended from non-compliance with this strange custom is, that the bees will dwindle and die. The manner of communicating the intelligence to the little community, with due form and ceremony, is this—to take the key of the house, and knock with it three times against the hive, telling the inmates, at the same time that their master or mistress, &c. (as the case may be) is dead! Mr. Loudon says, when in Bedfordshire lately, we were informed of an old man who sung a psalm last year in front of some hives which were not doing well, but which, he said, would thrive in consequence of that ceremony.—*Magazine of Nat. Hist. for* 1828.

The *Constitutionnel* (January 1828) states, that under the influence of the Jesuits, and with the countenance of the authorities, &c. the most brutifying tales of superstition and fanaticism are printed and circulated in the provinces of France. One of the ridiculous narratives to which it alludes, details the fate of a blaspheming baker, who, being infected with the heresies of the Revolution, had addicted himself to the commission of every kind of impiety. While his oven one day was heated, and he was about to put the bread into it, he vented his usual oaths in the presence of two neighbours; when, lo! the dough miraculously refused to enter, and the baker was seized with a cold shivering, of which he died in two days. In his will he left 600 francs to the church, confessed his enormities, and besought the prayers of his friends.—In another, we are told of the discovery of a miraculous image, which will be a permanent source of ecclesiastical revenue. This image is that of a saint, which has been for the last two centuries concealed in a rock. It was discovered by means of a little white bird perched upon a brilliant crucifix, which guarded the spot. Since the discovery, the lame walk, the sick are healed, and the blind recover their sight, by resorting to the consecrated ground.

It is not above fifteen or sixteen years ago since the late Alexander Davidson, A. M., lecturer on experimental philosophy and chemistry, when in Ireland, was much annoyed by the superstitious belief in necromancy and infernal agency which still prevails among a large portion of the lower orders in that country. When delivering a course of lectures in a small town not far from Londonderry, the rumour of the experiments he performed spread among the body of the people, many of whom had listened at the outside of the hall in which he lectured, to the loud detonations produced by electrical and other experiments, particularly the explosions of hydrogen gas. The great majority of the inhabitants believed he was an astrologer and necromancer, and considered it dangerous to have the slightest intercourse with his family, even in the way of buying and selling. One morning his servant-maid was sent out for bread and groceries for breakfast. After a considerable time, she returned with a pitiful countenance and a heavy heart, and declared that not an article of any description could be obtained. "What," says Mr. D., "is there no tea, sugar, or bread in the whole village?" "O yes," replied the maid, "there is plenty of every thing we want, but nobody will sell us an article; they say we are all witches and wizards and necromancers, and *it's no canny to tak ony o' your money*." Mr. Davidson and family, in this case, might have starved, had he not bethought himself of employing the servant of an acquaintance, who was one of his auditors, to procure, in her master's name, the requisite provisions; and this plan he was obliged to adopt during the remainder of his stay in that place. At another time his boots required to be repaired; the servant took them to a shoemaker, and they were received by one of the female branches of his family; but when the shoemaker understood to whom they belonged, he stormed, and was indignant at their receiving any thing from such a dangerous individual. The servant soon after returned to inquire if the boots were repaired. "Is the *astrologer's* boots mendit?" one of the family vociferated. "No," was the reply, "they are not mendit, nor do we intend to mend them, or have any thing to do with them." The shoemaker's wife desired the servant to come in, and *lift the boots herself*; "for," said she, "I will not *touch* them;" and it appears that both the shoemaker and his family had been afraid even to put their fingers upon them, and doubtless imagined that the very circumstance of their having been received into the house would operate as an *evil omen*.—On the day previous to his leaving that place, he sent his servant to engage a chaise to carry them to the next town. The servant told the landlady of the inn (which was the only one from which a carriage could be procured) that her master wished to hire a chaise for to-morrow to carry them to N——. The landlady told her it could not be granted. "For what reason?" said the maid. "*You know very well what is the reason*," said the landlady, in a very emphatical tone. After the servant returned with this reply, Mr. Davidson himself went to the inn, when the following dialogue took place between him and the landlady:—"Well, madam, can you give me a chaise to-morrow to carry me to Newry?" "No; for our horses are very tired, as they have been out all day, and they cannot go to-morrow." "O dear, madam, is that the only reason? You know very well *I can make them go*." The landlady, putting on a grave countenance, replied with emphasis, "*We all know that very well*. We know that you could *sink the town*, if you chose to do it. But I shall give you the chaise, to carry you out of the place, and make the town rid of you: but it is more for *fear* of you than *love* to you that I consent to grant you my chaise."—Such were the absurd and superstitious notions prevalent among the lower class of the Irish in 1814 or 1815; and these were not the only instances in which they were manifested, but only specimens of what frequently occurred in other parts of that country.

However clearly persons of education and intelligence may perceive the absurdity and futility of the superstitious notions and practices to which I have now referred,—it is a fact, well known to those who have been conversant among the lower orders of society, that they still prevail to a very considerable extent among the untutored ranks, even of our own country. Nothing but a more assiduous cultivation of the rational powers, and a universal diffusion of useful knowledge among the inferior classes of society, can be expected thoroughly to undermine and eradicate such opinions, and to prevent the baneful and pernicious consequences to which they lead.

No. VII.—*Circumstances which have occasionally led to the belief of Spectres and Apparitions.* P. 23.

It is certain, that indistinct vision and optical illusions have, in many instances, been the sources of terror, and have produced a belief of supernatural appearances. When we have no other mode of judging of an unknown object but by the angle it forms in the eye, its magnitude will uniformly increase in proportion to its nearness. If it appears, when at the distance of forty or fifty paces, to be only a few feet high, its height, when within three or four feet of the eye, will appear to be above forty times greater, or many fathoms in dimension. An object of this kind, must naturally excite terror and astonishment in the spectator, till he approaches and recognises it by actual feeling; for the moment a man knows an object, the gigantic appearance it assumed in the eye, instantly diminishes, and its apparent magnitude is reduced to its real dimensions. But if, instead of approaching such an object, the spectator flies from it, he can have no other idea of it, but from the image which it formed in the eye; and in this case, he may affirm with truth, that he saw an object terrible in its aspect, and enormous in its size. Such illusions frequently occur, when persons are walking through desert and unfrequented tracts of country, surrounded with a fog, or in the dusk of the evening, when a solitary tree, a bush, an old wall, a cairn of stones, a sheep or a cow, may appear as phantoms of a monstrous size. The writer of an article in the "Encyclopædia Britannica," states, that "he was passing the Frith of Forth at Queensferry, one morning which was extremely foggy. Though the water is only two miles broad the boat did not get within sight of the southern shore, till it approached very near it he then saw to his great surprise, a large perpendicular rock, where he knew the shore was low and almost flat. As the boat advanced a little nearer, the rock seemed to split perpendicularly into portions, which separated at little distances from one another; he next saw these perpendicular divisions move, and upon approaching a little nearer, found it was a number of people standing on the beach, waiting the arrival of the ferry boat."

*Spectres are frequently occasioned by opium.* Gassendi, the philosopher, found a number of people going to put a man to death for having intercourse with the devil, a crime which the poor wretch readily acknowledged. Gassendi begged of the people, that they would permit him first to examine the wizard, before putting him to death. They did so, and Gassendi, upon examination, found, that the man firmly believed himself guilty of this impossible crime; he even offered to Gassendi to introduce him to the devil. The philosopher agreed, and when midnight came, the man gave him a pill, which he said it was necessary to swallow before setting off. Gassendi took the pill, but gave it to his dog: The man having swallowed his, fell into a profound sleep, during which he seemed much agitated by dreams; the dog was affected in a similar manner. When the man awoke he congratulated Gassendi on the favourable reception he had met with from his sable highness. It was with difficulty Gassendi convinced him that the whole was a dream, the effect of soporific medicines, and that he had never stirred from one spot during the whole night.

*Drunkenness has also the power of creating apparitions.* Drunkenness seldom or never excites fear; and, therefore, it may at first sight seem strange, that persons should imagine they see ghosts when under the influence of intoxication. But it is observable, that the ghosts which the drunkard imagines he sees, he beholds not with the same terror and alarm, as men that are sober; he is not afraid of them; he has the courage to converse with them, and even to fight them, if they give him provocation. Like Burns' "Tam o' Shanter," give him "fair play—he cares na' de'ils a bodle." A man returning home intoxicated, affirmed, that he had met with the devil; and that, after a severe encounter, he had vanquished him, and brought him to the ground, to which he had nailed him fast, by driving his staff through his body. Next morning, the staff was found stuck with great violence into a heap of turfs!

*Dreams may be considered as another source of apparitions.* While the mind is under the influence of a dream, it considers it as much a reality, as it does any particular action when awake: and, therefore, if a person of a weak superstitious mind should have a very lively dream which interests his passions, it may make so deep an impression, that he may be firmly convinced he has actually seen with his eyes, what has only passed before his imagination; especially when we consider, that there are times of slumber when we are not sensible of being asleep. On this principle, some have endeavoured to account for the spectre which is said to have appeared to Brutus. It is related, that at Philippi, the night before he gave battle to Augustus Cæsar, he saw a fearful apparition; it was in the dead of night, when the whole camp was perfectly quiet, that Brutus was employed in his tent, in reading by a lamp that was just expiring; on a sudden he thought he heard a noise as if somebody entered, and looking towards the door, he perceived it open; a gigantic figure with a frightful aspect, stood before him, and continued to gaze upon him with silent severity. At last, Brutus had courage to speak to it: "Art thou a demon or a mortal man? and why comest thou to me?" The phantom is said to have replied, "Brutus, I am thy evil genius, thou shalt see me again at Philippi." "Well then," answered Brutus, without being discomposed, "we shall meet again;" upon which the phantom vanished, and Brutus, calling to his servants, asked them if they had seen any thing; to which replying in the negative, he again resumed his studies. This circumstance is related by historians as a *vision*, but considering the circumstances, one may easily judge it to have been but a short dream; for, sitting in his tent, pensive and troubled with the horror of his late rash act, it was not hard for him, slumbering in the cold, to dream of that which most affrighted him; which fear, as by degrees it made him wake, so it must have made the apparition by degrees to vanish; and having no assurance that he slept, he could have no cause to think it a dream, or any thing else than a vision. Whatever may be said as to this solution of the case, certain it is, that vivid dreams in certain states of mind, have been mistaken for real apparitions, of which various instances could be adduced, did our limits permit.

*Fear* is another fertile source of Spectres. As partial darkness and obscurity are the most common circumstances by which the sight is deceived, so night is the season in which apparitions are most frequently said to be seen. The state of the mind at that time, especially when a person is alone, prepares it for the admission of such delusions of the imagination. The fear and caution which night naturally inspires, the opportunity it affords for ambuscades, robberies, and assassinations, the deprivation of social intercourse, and the interruption of many pleasing trains of ideas which objects in the light never fail to produce, are all circumstances of terror, and favourable to the illusions of a timid imagination; and therefore, it is by no means strange, that an ignorant person with a mind uncultivated and uninformed, and with all the prejudices of the nursery about him, should imagine he sees ghosts in those places where he believes they hover, especially at the hour of midnight, when the slightest aid of the imagination can transform a cow into a monstrous phantom, and the reflection of the beams of the moon from a little water into a ghost with a winding-sheet; or a sound which is near, such as the rustling of the leaves of a tree, the noise of falling waters, or the screams of animals, when referred to a great distance, may be magnified into horrid and unearthly voices; for, in such cases, a timid and untutored mind seldom stops to inquire into the cause of its alarms. The celebrated historian De Thou, had a very singular adventure at Saumur, in the year 1598, which shows the happy effects of a calm inquiry into the cause of any alarming or extraordinary appearance. One night, having retired to rest very much fatigued, while he was enjoying a sound sleep, he felt a very extraordinary weight upon his feet, which, having made him turn suddenly, fell down and awakened him. At first he imagined that it had been only a dream, but hearing soon after some noise in his chamber, he drew aside the curtains, and saw, by the help of the moon, which at that time shone very bright, a large white figure walking up and down, and at the same time observed upon a chair some rags, which he thought belonged to thieves who had come to rob him. The figure then approaching his bed, he had the courage to ask it what it was. "I am (said the figure) the Queen of Heaven." Had such a figure appeared to any credulous ignorant man, he would, doubtless, have trembled with fear, and frightened the whole neighbourhood with a marvellous description of it. But De Thou had too much understanding to be so imposed upon. On hearing the words which dropped from the figure, he immediately concluded that it was some mad woman, got up, called his servants, and ordered them to turn her out of doors; after which he returned to bed and fell asleep. Next morning, he found that he had not been deceived in his conjecture, and that having forgot to shut his door, this female figure had escaped from her keepers, and entered his apartment. The brave Schomberg, to whom De Thou related his adventure some days after, confessed that in such a case he would not have shown so much courage. The King likewise, who was informed of it by Schomberg, made the same acknowledgment.—See Ency. Brit., Art. *Spectre.*

The following relation contains a description of an apparition of a different kind, no less appalling. Mr. Schmidt, mathematical teacher at the school of Pforte, near Naumburg, which had formerly been a cloister, once happened to awake suddenly as the morning began to dawn. On opening his eyes, he beheld with astonishment a monk standing at the foot of his bed. Looking at him steadfastly, he appeared to be well-fed; and his head, far from small, was sunk a little

12

between a pair of very broad shoulders. The chamber was sufficiently secured; Mr. Schmidt alone slept in it; and he was very certain that no one would attempt to put a trick upon him in est. He knew also, that no part of his clothes or any thing else was hanging at his bed's foot. The figure exactly resembled that of a monk, clothed in a white surplice, the falling folds of which were very clearly to be distinguished. Had an ignorant and timid man beheld this appearance, he would probably have covered himself up with the bed clothes, and firmly maintained that the ghost of a monk had appeared to him. As the school had formerly been a cloister, many monks had been buried both in the church and church-yard, and it was currently reported among the vulgar that the place was haunted. Mr. Schmidt, however, was neither ignorant nor timid, and he immediately conjectured that his eyes were deceived, though he could not imagine in what manner. He raised himself up a little in his bed, but the apparition did not move, he only saw somewhat more of it, and the folds of the surplice were still more conspicuous. After a little while he moved towards the right, yet the apparition remained, and he seemed to have in part a side view of it; but as soon as he had moved his head so far as to have a slight glimpse of the bed's foot, the apparition retreated backward, though still with its face to the bed. Following the apparition quickly with his eyes, it retreated with speed, swelled as it retreated to a gigantic form, a rustling noise was heard, and ——at once the apparition was changed into the gothic window with white curtains which was opposite the bed's foot, and about six or seven feet distance from it. Several times after this Mr. Schmidt endeavoured when he awoke to see the same appearance, but to no purpose, the window always looking like a window only. Some weeks after, however, on awakening, as the day began to dawn, he again perceived the monk's apparition at the bed's foot. Being now aware what occasioned it, he examined it narrowly. The great arch of the window formed the monk's shoulders, a smaller arch, in the centre of this, his head, and the curtains the surplice. The folds of these appeared much stronger than they did at the same distance by day-light. Thus the figure of the monk appeared plainer, nearer, and smaller, than the window would have done. This apparition, therefore, like hundreds of others, was merely an optical deception. The reader will find a more particular description of it, with an optical and mathematical explanation of the phenomenon, in vol. i. of "The Pleasing Preceptor," translated from the German of Gerhard Ulrich Anthony Vieth.

Another cause of apparitions, and of the belief in supernatural appearances, is to be found *in the artifices and collusions of impostors, and the tricks of the waggish.* Dr Plot, in his Natural History of Oxfordshire, relates a marvellous stor which will illustrate this position. Soon after the murder of King Charles I., a commission was appointed to survey the King's house at Woodstock, with the manor, park, woods, and other demesnes belonging to that manor. One Collins, under a feigned name, hired himself as secretary to the commissioners, who, upon the 13th October 1649, met, and took up their residence in the King's own rooms. His majesty's bed-chamber they made their kitchen, the council-hall their pantry, and the presence-chamber was the place where they met for the despatch of business. His majesty's dining-room they made their wood-yard, and stored it with the wood of the famous royal oak from the High Park, which, that nothing might be left with the name of King about it, they had dug up by the roots, and split and bundled up into fagots for their firing. Things being thus prepared, they sat on the 16th for the despatch of business; and, in the midst of their first debate, there entered a large *black dog* (as they thought) which made a dreadful howling, overturned two or three of their chairs, and then crept under a bed and vanished. This gave them the greater surprise, as the doors were kept constant[illegible], so that no real dog could get in or out. The next day their surprise was increased, when sitting at dinner in a lower room, they heard plainly the noise of persons walking over their heads, though they well knew the doors were all locked, and there could be nobody there. Presently after, they heard also all the wood of the King's oak brought by parcels from the dining-room, and thrown with great violence into the presence chamber, as also all the chairs, stools, tables, and other furniture forcibly hurled about the room; their papers, containing the minutes of their transactions, were torn, and the ink-glass broken. When all this noise had ceased, Giles Sharp, their secretary, proposed to enter first into these rooms; and in presence of the commissioners, from whom he received the key, he opened the doors, and found the wood spread about the room, the chairs tossed about and broken, the papers torn, but not the least track of any human creature, nor the least reason to suspect one, as the doors were all fast, and the keys in the custody of the commissioners. It was therefore unanimously agreed that the power that did this mischief must have entered at the key-hole. The night following, Sharp, the secretary, with two of the commissioners' servants, as they were in bed in the same room, which room was contiguous to that where the commissioners lay, had their beds' feet lifted up so much higher than their heads, that they expected to have their necks broken, and then they were let fall at once with so much violence as shook the whole house, and more than ever terrified the commissioners. On the night of the 19th, as they were all [illegible]ed in the the same room for greater safety, and lights burning by them, the candles in an instant went out with a sulphurous smell, and that moment many trenchers of wood were hurled about the room, which next morning were found to be the same their honours had eaten out of the day before, which were all removed from the pantry, though not a lock was found opened in the whole house. The next night they fared still worse; the candles went out as before, the curtains of their honours' beds were rattled to and fro with great violence, they received many cruel blows and bruises by eight great pewter dishes, and a number of wooden trenchers being thrown on their beds, which, being heaved off, were heard rolling about the room, though in the morning none of these were to be seen.

The next night the keeper of the king's house and his dog lay in the commissioners' room, and then they had no disturbance. But on the night of the 22d, though the dog lay in the room as before, yet the candles went out, a number of brickbats fell from the chimney into the room, the dog howled piteously, their bed-clothes were all stripped off, and their terror increased. On the 24th they thought all the wood of the king's oak was violently thrown down by their bed-sides; they counted 64 billets that fell, and some hit and shook the beds in which they lay; but in the morning none was found there, nor had the door been opened where the billet-wood was kept. The next night the candles were put out, the curtains rattled, and a dreadful crack like thunder was heard; and one of the servants running in haste, thinking his master was killed, found three dozen of trenchers laid smoothly under the quilt by him. But all this was nothing to what succeeded afterwards. The 29th, about midnight, the candles went out, something walked majestically through the room, and opened and shut the windows; great stones were thrown violently into the room, some of which fell on the beds, others on the floor; and at about a quarter after one, a noise was heard as of forty cannon discharged together, and again repeated at about eight minutes interval. This alarmed and raised all the neighbourhood, who coming into their honours' room, gathered up the great stones, fourscore in number, and laid them by in the corner of a field, where, in Dr. Plot's time, they were to be seen. This noise, like the discharge of cannon, was heard over the country for several miles round. During these noises the commissioners and their servants gave one another over for lost and cried out for help; and Giles Sharp, snatching up a sword, had well nigh killed one of their honours, mistaking him for the spirit, as he came in his shirt from his own room to theirs. While they were together the noise was continued, and part of the tiling of the house was stripped off, and all the windows of an upper room were taken away with it. On the 30th, at midnight, something walked into the chamber treading like a bear; it walked many times about, then threw the warming-pan violently on the floor; at the same time a large quantity of broken glass, accompanied with great stones and horse bones, came pouring into the room with uncommon force. On the 1st of November the most dreadful scene of all ensued. Candles in every part of the room were lighted up, and a great fire made; at midnight, the candles all yet burning, a noise like the bursting of a cannon was heard in the room, and the burning billets were tossed about by it even into their honours' beds, who called Giles and his companions to their relief, otherwise the house had been burnt to the ground; about an hour after, the candles went out as usual, the crack as of many cannon was heard, and many pailfuls of green stinking water were thrown upon their honours' beds, great stones were also thrown in as before, the bed-curtains and bedsteads torn and broken, the windows shattered, and the whole neighbourhood alarmed with the most dreadful noises; nay, the very rabbit-stealers, that were abroad that night in the warren, were so terrified, that they fled for fear, and left their ferrets behind them. One of their honours this night spoke, and, *in the name of God, asked what it was, and why it disturbed them so?* No answer was given to this; but the noise ceased for a while, when the spirit came again; and, as they all agreed, *brought with it seven devils worse than itself.* One of the servants now lighted a large candle, and set it in the doorway between the two chambers, to see what passed; and as he watched it, he plainly saw a hoof striking the candle and candlestick into the middle of the room, and afterwards, making three scrapes over the snuff, scraped it out. Upon this the same person was so bold as to draw a sword, but he had scarce got it out when he felt another invisible hand holding it too, and pulling it from him, and at length prevailing, struck him so violently on the head with the pummel, that he fell down for dead with the blow. At this instant was heard another burst like the discharge of the broadside of a ship of war, and at the interval of a minute or two between each, no less than 19 such discharges. These shook the house so violently that they expected every moment it would fall upon their heads. The neighbours being all alarmed, flocked to the house in great numbers, and all joined in prayer and psalm-singing; during which the noise continued in the other rooms, and the discharge of cannons was heard as from without, though no visible agent was seen to discharge them. But what was the most alarming of all, and put an end to their proceedings effectually, happened the next day, as they were all at dinner, when a paper, in which they had signed a mutual agreement to reserve a part of the premises out of the general survey, and afterwards to share it equally among themselves, (which paper they had hid for the present under the earth in a pot in one corner of the room, and in which an orange tree grew,) was consumed in a wonderful manner by the earth's taking fire with which the pot was filled, and burning violently with a blue flame and an intolerable stench, so that they were all driven out of the house to which they could never be again prevailed upon to return.

This story has been somewhat abridged from the Encyclopædia Brittannica, where it is quoted from Dr. Plot's history. If I recollect right, it is embodied in the book entitled "Satan's Invisible World Discovered," and the extraordinary occurrences it relates ascribed to Satanic influence. At the time they happened, they were viewed as the effects of supernatural powers; and even Dr. Plot seems disposed to ascribe them to this cause. "Though many tricks," says the Doctor, "have been often played in affairs of this kind, many of the things above related are not reconcileable with juggling; such as the loud noises beyond the powers of man to make without such instruments as were not there; the tearing and breaking the beds; the throwing about the fire; the hoof treading out the candle; and the striving for the sword; and the blow the man received from the pummel of it." It was at length ascertained, however, that this wonderful contrivance was all the invention of the memorable Joseph Collins of Oxford, otherwise called *Funny Joe*, who, having hired himself as secretary under the name of *Giles Sharp*, by knowing the private traps belonging to the house, and by the help of *Pulvis Fulminans*, and other chemical preparations, and letting his fellow-servants into the scheme, carried on the deceit without discovery to the very last.

*Ventriloquism is another source whence a belief of apparitions has been induced.* By this art, certain persons can so modify their voice as to make it appear to the audience to proceed from any distance, and in any direction, and by which impostors have sometimes accomplished their nefarious designs, of which the following are instances.

Louis Brahant, a dexterous ventriloquist, valet-de-chambre to Francis I., had fallen desperately in love with a young, handsome, and rich heiress; but was rejected by the parents as an unsuitable match for their daughter, on account of the lowness of his circumstances. The young lady's father dying, he made a visit to the widow, who was totally ignorant of his singular talent. Suddenly, on his first appearance in open day, in her own house, and in the presence of several persons who were with her, she heard herself accosted in a voice perfectly resembling that of her dead husband, and which seemed to proceed from above, exclaiming, "Give my daughter in marriage to Louis Brahant. He is a man of great fortune and of an excellent character. I now suffer the inexpressible torments of purgatory for having refused her to him. If you obey this admonition I shall soon be delivered from this place of torment. You will at the same time provide a worthy husband for your daughter, and procure everlasting repose to the soul of your poor husband." The widow could not for a moment resist this dreadful summons, which had not the most distant appearance of proceeding from Louis Brahant, whose countenance exhibited no visible change, and whose lips were close and motionless during the delivery of it. Accordingly, she consented immediately to receive him for her son-in-law.—Louis's finances, however, were in a very low situation, and the formalities attending the marriage-contract rendered it necessary for him to exhibit some show of riches, and not to give the ghost the lie direct. He, accordingly, went to work on a fresh subject, one Cornu, an old and rich banker at Lyons, who had accumulated immense wealth by usury and extortion, and was known to be haunted by remorse of conscience, on account of the manner in which he had acquired it. Having contracted an intimate acquaintance with this man, he, one day, while they were sitting together in the usurer's little back parlour, artfully turned the conversation on religious subjects, on demons, and spectres, the pains of purgatory, and the torments of hell. During an interval of silence between them, a voice was heard, which, to the astonished banker, seemed to be that of his deceased father, complaining, as in the former case, of his dreadful situation in purgatory, and calling upon him to deliver him instantly from thence, by putting into the hands of Louis Brahant, then with him, a large sum for the redemption of Christians then in slavery with the Turks; threatening him, at the same time, with eternal damnation, if he did not take this method to expiate, likewise, his own sins. Louis Branant, of course, affected a due degree of astonishment on the occasion; and further promoted the deception by acknowledging his having devoted himself to the prosecution of the charitable design imputed to him by the ghost. An old usurer is naturally suspicious. Accordingly, the wary banker made a second appointment with the ghost's delegate for the next day: and, to render any design of imposing upon him utterly abortive, took him into the open fields, where not a house or a tree, or even a bush, or a pit were in sight, capable of screening any supposed confederate. This extraordinary caution excited the ventriloquist to exert all the powers of his art. Wherever the banker conducted him, at every step, his ears were saluted on all sides with the complaints, and groans, not only of his father, but of all his deceased relations, imploring him for the love of God, and in the name of every saint in the calender, to have mercy on his own soul and theirs, by effectually seconding with his purse the intentions of his worthy companion. Cornu could no longer resist the voice of heaven, and, accordingly, carried his guest home with him, and paid him down ten thousand crowns; with which the honest ventriloquist returned to Paris, and married his mistress. The catastrophe was fatal. The secret was afterwards blown, and reached the usurer's ears, who was so much affected by the loss of his money, and the mortifying railleries of his neighbours, that he took to his bed and died.

Another trick of a similar kind was played off about sixty or seventy years ago, on a whole community, by another French ventriloquist. "M. St. Gill, the ventriloquist, and his intimate friend, returning home from a place whither his business had carried him, sought for shelter from an approaching thunder-storm in a neighbouring convent. Finding the whole community in mourning, he inquired the cause, and was told that one of the body had died lately, who was the ornament and delight of the whole society. To pass away the time, he walked into the church, attended by some of the religious, who showed him the tomb of their deceased brother, and spoke feelingly of the scanty honours they had bestowed on his memory. Suddenly a voice was heard, apparently proceeding from the roof of the choir, lamenting the situation of the defunct in purgatory, and reproaching the brotherhood with their lukewarmness and want of zeal on his account. The friars, as soon as their astonishment gave them power to speak, consulted together, and agreed to acquaint the rest of the community with this singular event, so interesting to the whole society. M. St. Gill, who wished to carry on the joke a little farther, dissuaded them from taking this step, telling them that they would be treated by their absent brethren as a set of fools and visionaries. He recommended to them, however, the immediately calling the whole community into the church, where the ghost of their departed brother might probably reiterate his complaints. Accordingly, all the friars, novices, lay-brothers, and even the domestics of the convent, were immediately summoned and called together, In a short time the voice from the roof renewed its lamentations and reproaches, and the whole convent fell on their faces, and vowed a solemn reparation. As a first step, they chanted a *De profundis* in a full choir; during the intervals of which the ghost occasionally expressed the comfort he received from their pious exercises and ejaculations on his behalf. When all was over, the prior entered into a serious conversation with M. St. Gill; and on the strength of what had just passed, sagaciously inveighed against the absurd incredulity of our modern sceptics and pretended philosophers, on the article of ghosts or apparitions. M. St. Gill thought it high time to disabuse the good fathers. This purpose, however, he found it extremely difficult to effect, till he had prevailed upon them to return with him into the church, and there be witnesses of the manner in which he had conducted this ludicrous deception." Had not the ventriloquist, in this case, explained the cause of the deception, a whole body of men might have sworn, with a good conscience, that they had heard the ghost of a departed brother address them again and again in a supernatural voice.

It is highly probable, that many of those persons termed witches and necromancers in ancient times, who pretended to be invested with supernatural powers, performed their deceptions by the art of ventriloquism. The term literally means, *speaking from the belly*; and, in accordance with this idea, we find that the Pythoness, or witch of Endor, to whom Saul applied for advice in his perplexity, is designated in the Septuagint translation of the Old Testament, "a woman that speaks from her belly or stomach," as most magicians affected to do; and some authors have informed us, that there were women who had a demon which spake articulately from the lower part of their stomachs, in a very loud, though hoarse tone. Umbræ cum saganâ resonarent triste et acutum. Hor. Sat. viii. lib. i.

Our English translation "familiar spirit," in Hebrew, signifies "the spirit of *Ob* or *Oboth.*" The word *Ob* in its primitive sense, denotes a *bottle* or *vessel of leather*, wherein liquors were put; and it is not unlikely that this name was given to witches, because, in their fits of enthusiasm, they swelled in their bellies like a bottle. The occasion of this swelling is said by some authors to proceed from a demon's entering into the sorcerers *per partes genitales*, and so ascending to the bottom of her stomach, from whence, at that time, she uttered her predictions; and for this reason, the Latins call such persons *Ventriloqui*, and the Greeks Εγγαστρίμυθοι, that is, *people who speak out of their bellies.* Cælius Rhodiginus (Antiq. lib. 8. c. 10.) says, in reference to such cases, "While I am writing concerning ventriloquous persons, there is, in my own country, a woman of a mean extract, who has an unclean spirit in her belly, from whence may be heard a voice, not very strong indeed, but very articulate and intelligible. Multitudes of people have heard this voice, as well as myself, and all imaginable precaution has been used in examining into the truth of this fact:"—"Quando futuri avida portentus mens, sæpe accersitum ventriloquam, ac exutam amictu, ne quid fraudis occultaret, inspectare et audire concupivit." The author adds, "This demon is called *Cincinnatulus*, and when the woman calls upon him by his name, he immediately answers her."—Several ancient writers have informed us, that in the times of Paganism, evil spirits had communion with these *ventriloquæ per partes secretiores.* Chrysostom says,—"Traditur Pythia fœmina fuisse, quæ in Tripodes sedens expansa malignum spiritum per interna immissum, et per genitales partes subeuntem excipiens, furore repleretur, ipsaque resolutis crinibus baccharetur, ex ore spumam emittens, et sic furoris verba loquebatur," &c.

*Spectres have also been produced by such optical exhibitions as the phantasmagoria.* By means of this instrument, a spectre can be made apparently to start up from a white mist, and to rush forward towards the spectator with a horrific aspect. If a thin screen were placed in a dark room, and the lantern of the phantasmagoria, with its light properly concealed, the most terrific phantoms might be exhibited, which would confound and appal every one previously unacquainted with the contrivance, especially if the exhibition was suddenly made at the dead hour of night. By means of such exhibitions, combined with the art of ventriloquism, and the assistance of a confederate, almost every thing that has been recorded respecting spectres and apparitions might be realized.

I shall conclude these illustrations of apparitions, by presenting the reader with a description of the *ghost of a flea*, by Mr. Varley, formerly alluded to, as a specimen of the folly and superstition that still degrade the present age.

"With respect to the vision of the ghost of the flea, as seen by Mr. Blake, it agrees in countenance with one class of people under Gemini, which sign is the significator of the flea, whose brown colour is appropriate to the colour of the eyes, in some full-toned Gemini persons, and the neatness, elasticity, and tenseness of the flea, are significant of the elegant dancing and fencing sign Gemini. The spirit visited his imagination in such a figure as he never anticipated in an insect. As I was anxious to make the most correct investigation in my power of the truth of these visions, on hearing of this spiritual apparition of a flea, I asked him if he could draw for me the resemblance of what he saw. He instantly said, 'I see him now before me.' I therefore gave him paper and a pencil with which he drew the portrait, of which a fac-simile is given in this number. I felt convinced by his mode of proceeding, that he had a real image before him; for he left off and began on another part of the paper, to make a separate drawing of the mouth of the flea, which the spirit having opened, he was prevented from proceeding with the first sketch, till he had closed it. During the time occupied in completing the drawing, the flea told him that all fleas were inhabited by the souls of such men as were by nature blood-thirsty to excess, and were, therefore, providentially confined to the size and form of such insects; otherwise, were he himself, for instance, the size of a horse, he would depopulate a great part of the country. He added, that, 'if in attempting to leap from one island to another, he should fall into the sea, he could swim, and could not be lost.' This spirit afterwards appeared to Blake, and afforded him a view of his whole figure, an engraving of which I shall give in this work."

N. B.—Blake, who died only two or three years ago, was an ingenious artist, who illustrated Blair's Grave, and other works, and was so much of an *enthusiast*, that he imagined he could call up from the vasty deep, any spirits or corporeal forms. Were it not a fact, that a work entitled "Zodiacal Physiognomy," written by John Parley, and illustrated with engravings, was actually published in the year 1828, by Longman and Co., we should have deemed it almost impossible, that amidst the light of the present age, any man capable of writing a grammatical sentence, would *seriously* give such a description as that quoted above, and attach his belief to such absurdity and nonsense. But amidst all our boasted scientific improvements and discoveries, it appears, that the clouds of ignorance and superstition still hang over a large body of our population, and that the light of the millennial era, if it have yet dawned, is still far from its meridian splendour.

---

After what has been now stated respecting the circumstances which may have led to the popular belief of spectres and apparitions, it would be almost needless to spend time in illustrating the futility of such a belief. There is one strong objection against the probability of apparitions, and that is,—that they scarcely appear to be intelligent creatures, or at least, that they possess so small a degree of intelligence, that they are unqualified to act with prudence, or to use the means requisite to accomplish an end. Ghosts are said often to appear in order to discover some crime that had been committed; but they never appear to a magistrate, or some person of authority and intelligence, but to some illiterate clown, who happens to live near the place where the crime was committed, to some person who has no connexion at all with the affair, and who, in general, is the most improper person in the world for making the discovery. Glanville, who wrote in defence of witchcraft and apparitions, relates, for instance, the following story: "James Haddock, a farmer, was married to Elenor Welsh, by whom he had a son. After the death of Haddock, his wife married one Davis; and both agreed to defraud the son by the former marriage, of a lease bequeathed to him by his father. Upon this the ghost of Haddock appeared to one Francis Taverner, the servant of Lord Chichester, and desired him to go to Elenor Welsh, and to inform her that it was the will of her former husband that their son should enjoy the lease. Taverner did not at first execute this commission, but he was continually haunted by the apparition in the most hideous shapes, which even threatened to tear him in pieces, till at last he delivered the message." Now, had this spectre possessed the least common sense, it would have appeared first to Elenor Welsh, and her husband Davis, and frightened them into compliance at once, and not have kept poor Taverner, who had no concern in the matter, in such constant disquietude and alarm.

Another odd circumstance respecting apparitions, is, that *they have no power to speak, till they are addressed.* In Glanville's relations, we read of an old woman, that appeared often to David Hunter, a neat-herd, at the house of the Bishop of Down. Whenever she appeared, he found himself obliged to follow her; and, for three quarters of a year, poor David spent the whole of almost every night in scampering up and down through the woods after this old woman. How long this extraordinary employment might have continued, it is impossible to guess, had not David's violent fatigue made him one night exclaim, "Lord bless me!—would I were dead!—shall I never be delivered from this misery?" On which the phantom replied, "Lord bless me too!—It was happy you spoke first, for till then I had no power to speak, though I have followed you so long!" Then she gave him a message to her two sons, though David told her he remembered nothing about her. David, it seems, neglected to deliver the message, at which the old beldam was so much provoked, that she returned and hit him a hearty blow on the shoulder, which made him cry out and then speak to her. Now, if she could not speak till David addressed her, why might she not have applied this oratorial medicine, the first time she appeared to him? It would have saved both herself and him many a weary journey, and certainly David would much rather have had half a dozen blows from her choppy fists, than have wanted so many nights' sleep. To complete the story, it must be added, that when David's wife found it impossible to keep him from following the troublesome visiter, she trudged after him, but was never gratified with a sight of the enchantress.—See Ency. Brit. Art. *Spectre.*

What imaginable purpose can be served by such dumb spectres that cannot speak till they are addressed, or by sending apparitions from the invisible world that appear destitute of common sense? It is remarked by Glanville, that ghosts are generally very eager to be gone; and, indeed, they are frequently so much so, that like children and thoughtless fools, they do not stay to tell their errand. It appears altogether inconsistent with any rational or scriptural ideas of the overruling providence of the Almighty, to suppose that such beings would be selected for administering the affairs of his kingdom, and for maintaining an intercourse between the visible and invisible worlds. It is also stated to be one peculiarity of spectres that *they appear only in the night.* But if they are sent to this sublunary region on affairs of importance, why should they be afraid of the light of the sun? In the light of day their message would be delivered with as much ease, and with more chance of success. As it would excite less fear, it would be listened to with more calmness and attention; and were they to exhibit themselves before a number of intelligent witnesses in the full blaze of day, the purposes for which they were sent would be more speedily and securely accomplished. The celestial messengers whose visits are recorded in Scripture, appeared most frequently during the light of day, and communicated their messages, in many instances, to a number of individuals at once—messages, which were of the utmost importance to the individuals addressed, and even to mankind at large. To give credit, therefore, to the popular stories respecting ghosts and apparitions, embodies in it a reflection on the character of the All-wise Ruler of the world, and a libel on the administrations of his moral government.

## No. VIII.—*Explosions of Steam-Engines.* Pp. 33, 76.

As steam-engines are now applied to the purpose of impelling vessels along seas and rivers, as well as to many important manufacturing processes, and are capable of still more extensive applications, and of higher improvements than they have yet attained—it is of the utmost importance that every circumstance should be carefully guarded against, which has the remotest tendency to endanger the bursting of the boiler,—and that no person be intrusted with the direction of such engines who is not distinguished for prudence and caution, or who is unacquainted with their construction and the principle of their operation. For, to ignorance and imprudence are to be ascribed many of those accidents which have happened from the bursting of the boilers of these engines. This remark is strikingly illustrated by the following and many other tragical occurrences:—

In the month of August 1815, the following melancholy accident happened at Messrs. Nesham and Co's colliery at Newbottle. The proprietors had formed a powerful locomotive steam-engine for the purpose of drawing ten or twelve coal wagons to the staith at one time: and on the day it was to be put in motion, a great number of persons belonging to the colliery collected to see it; but, unfortunately, just as it was going off, the boiler of the machine burst. The engineman was dashed to pieces, and his mangled remains blown 114 yards. The top of the boiler, nine feet square, weighing nineteen hundred weight, was blown 100 yards, and the two cylinders 90 yards. A little boy was also thrown to a great distance. By this accident *fifty-seven persons* were killed and wounded, of whom eleven died on Sunday night; several remaining dangerously ill. The cause of the accident is accounted for as follows:—The engine-man said, "*As there are several owners and viewers here, I will make her* (the engine) *go in grand style;*" and he had scarcely got upon the boiler to loose the screw of the safety valve, but, being over-heated, it exploded.—*Monthly Magazine*, vol.40, p. 181.

From what is here stated, it appears, that this tragical accident was occasioned by a combination of vanity, ignorance, and imprudence in the person to whom the direction of the engine was committed.—The following accident which happened to the *Washington steam-boat*, belonging to *Wheeling*, N. America, is attributed to a somewhat similar cause.

"This boat started from Wheeling on Monday, June 10th, 1816, and arrived at Marietta on Tuesday evening at 7 o'clock, and came safely to anchor, where she remained till Wednesday morning. The fires had been kindled and the boilers sufficiently hot, preparatory to her departure, when the anchor was weighed and the helm put to larboard, in order to wear her in a position to start her machinery; but only having one of her rudders shipped at the time, its influence was not sufficient to have the desired effect, and she immediately shot over under the Virginia shore, where it was found expedient to throw over the kedge at the stern to effect it. This being accomplished, the crew were then required to haul it on board, and were nearly all collected in the quarter for that purpose. At this unhappy fatal moment, the end of the cylinder towards the stern exploded, and threw the whole contents of hot water among them, and spread death and torture in every direction. The captain, mate, and several seamen were knocked overboard, but were saved, with the exception of one man, by boats from the town, and by swimming to the shore. The whole town was alarmed by the explosion, and all the physicians, with a number of citizens, went immediately to their relief. On going on board, a melancholy and truly horrible scene was presented to view. Six or eight persons were nearly skinned from head to foot, and others scalded, making in the whole, seventeen. In stripping off their clothes the skin pealed off with them to a considerable depth. Added to this melancholy sight, the ears of the pitying spectators were pierced by the screams and groans of the agonizing sufferers, rendering the scene horrible beyond description.

"The cause of this melancholy catastrophe may be accounted for by the cylinder not having vent through the safety valve, which was firmly stopped by the weight which hung on the lever, having been unfortunately slipped to its extreme, without its being noticed, and the length of time occupied in wearing before her machinery could be set in motion, whereby the force of the steam would have been expended; these two causes united, confined the steam till the strength of the cylinders could no longer contain it, and gave way with great violence. Six of the unfortunate sufferers died on Wednesday night, and one or two others are not expected to survive."—*Louisiana Gazette and New Orleans Mercantile Advertiser*, July 8th, 1816.

Since the above accidents happened, many others of a similar nature have occurred, which have ultimately been ascertained to have been owing either to *ignorance*, or to carelessness and inattention, which are the natural results of ignorance. As steam-boats are now navigating all our Friths and rivers, and even ploughing the ocean itself; and as steam carriages, are likely soon to come into general use for the conveyance of passengers and goods, it is of the utmost importance to their success, and to the safety of the public, that every precaution be adopted to prevent those explosions, and disarrangements of the machinery, which might be attended with fatal effects. But, although science and art may accomplish all that seems requisite for the prevention of danger, unless persons of prudence and intelligence be obtained for the superintendence and direction of such machines, the efforts of their projectors to prevent accidents may prove abortive. And until the tone of intellect, among the middling and lower orders, be somewhat more elevated than it is at present, it may be difficult to obtain persons for this purpose of the requisite qualifications.

The following recent accidents from steam-boat explosions, in all probability originated from causes similar to those to which I have now alluded.

The boiler of the steam-boat *Caledonia*, plying on the Mississipi, exploded on the 11th April 1830, killing and wounding about fifteen of the passengers and seven of the crew,—seven or eight of whom were blown overboard and lost. It was expected that some of the wounded would recover, although badly scalded. The boiler burst in the side while the boat was under weigh, and about two hours after being wooded. There were on board about 400 deck, and sixty cabin passengers, besides the crew, being altogether about 500 souls. The hull of the boat was uninjured. It is said that the accident arose from the passengers crowding to one side of the boat, by which one side of the boiler was exposed to the direct action of the fire, and when the boat righted, a quantity of steam was suddenly generated greater than the safety valve could carry off.—The number of persons who have lost their lives by explosions in America, since the commencement of the season(1830,) is not much short of one hundred,—sixty in the *Helen Macgregor*, four in the *Huntress*, nine in the *Justice Marshall*, and fourteen in the *Caledonia*, besides those of the latter, who, it was feared would not recover from the injuries they had sustained.

In these and other instances, it is more than probable, that a want of attention to the *natural laws* of the universe, and to the obvious effects which an enlightened mind should foresee they would produce, was the chief cause of the destruction of so many human beings, and of the sufferings of those whose lives were preserved. The same remark may be applied to the circumstances connected with a late fatal accident which happened on the Liverpool and Manchester rail-road.

On Friday afternoon, February 1, 1833, as the second-class train, which leaves Liverpool at three o'clock, was proceeding over Parr Moss, a little on the other side of Newton, one of the tubes which passes longitudinally through the boiler, burst. The consequence was, that a quantity of water fell into the fire, steam was generated in abundance, and the engine stopped. Several of the passengers alighted to see what was the matter, and they incautiously got upon the line of rail-way taken by the trains in going to Liverpool,—the contrary to that on which the disabled engine stood. While they were in this situation, a train of wagons from Bolton, proceeding to Liverpool, came up. The persons who had alighted did not see the advancing train, being enveloped in a dense cloud of vapour; and, from the same cause, they were by the conductor also unseen. They accordingly came upon them with fearful violence; several were knocked down, and the wheels of the train passed over four of them. Three of the unfortunate party were killed upon the spot; their bodies being dreadfully crushed; the fourth survived, and was taken forward to the infirmary, but his recovery was considered hopeless. Two of the three killed were elderly persons, whose names were unknown; the third, an interesting young man, who had formerly been in the employ of the Company as a fireman, and who was married only three weeks before. The survivor was a boy about sixteen years of age, who was proceeding from Belfast to Halifax, where his parents reside.—The casualty, which was the occasion of this serious result, was itself but trifling, as the train went forward to Manchester after a short delay.

This shocking catastrophe was evidently caused by rashness and imprudence—by not foreseeing what might probably arise from a certain combination of circumstances—or, in other words, by inattention to certain natural laws, both on the part of those who were connected with the Liverpool train of wagons, and of those who conducted the Bolton train. In regard to the passengers in the Liverpool train, it was highly improper that they should have left their seats on the carriage. The accident which befel the unfortunate Mr. Huskisson, at the opening of the rail-way, should have operated as an impressive warning against such a practice. In the next place, it was most imprudent to venture upon the other line of rail-way, more especially when a cloud of steam prevented them from seeing what was passing around them.—In regard to the person who had the command of the Bolton train, it was incautious and imprudent in the highest degree, to urge his machinery forward, when he beheld a volume of smoke immediately before him; the least consideration must have convinced him, that some accident must have happened, and that the cloud of steam would prevent those enveloped in it from perceiving the approach of his vehicle; and, therefore, he ought immediately to have abated his speed, so as to have acquired a complete command of the engine by the time it arrived at the spot where the steam was floating. Hence the importance—in conducting steam-engines and other departments of machinery—of having as superintendents, men of prudence and of enlightened minds, capable of foreseeing the probable effects of every combination of circumstances that may happen to occur. For *Ignorance* is generally proud, obstinate, incautious, precipitate in its movements, and regardless of consequences; so that, through its heedlessness and folly, the most splendid inventions are often impeded in their progress, and their value and utility called in question.

The Liverpool and Manchester Rail-way, and the locomotive powers of the machinery and engines which move along it, constitute one of the most splendid and useful improvements of modern times. From the last half-yearly Report of the Directors, from June 30 to December 31, 1832, it it satisfactorily proved, that this rail-way is completely efficient and applicable to all the great objects for which it was designed. During the period now specified, there were carried along the rail-way 86,842 tons goods, 39,940 tons coals, and 182,823 passengers, which is 73,498 fewer than in the corresponding six months of 1831, owing to the prevalence of cholera in Dublin, and in the towns of Manchester and Liverpool. Were this rail-way continued to London, it is calculated, that the journey from Liverpool to the Metropolis, a distance of more than 200 miles, might be performed in eight or ten hours.

No. IX.—*Circumstances which led to the invention of the Safety Lamp.* Pp. 27, 81.

This lamp, by means of which hundreds of lives have been preserved, was invented in the autumn of 1815. Sir Humphry Davy, the inventor, was led to the consideration of this subject, by an application from Dr. Gray, now Bishop of Bristol, the chairman of a society established in 1813, at Bishop-Wearmouth, to consider and promote the means of preventing accidents by fire in coal-pits. Being then in Scotland, he visited the mines on his return southward, and was supplied with specimens of fire-damp, which, on reaching London, he proceeded to examine and analyze. He soon discovered that the carburretted hydrogen gas, called fire-damp by the miners, would not explode when mixed with less than six, or more than fourteen times its volume of air; and, further, that the explosive mixture could not be fired in tubes of small diameters and proportionate lengths. Gradually diminishing these, he arrived at the conclusion, that a tissue of wire in which the meshes do not exceed a certain small diameter, which may be considered as the ultimate limit of a series of such tubes, is impervious to the inflamed air; and that a lamp covered with such tissue may be used with perfect safety, even in an explosive mixture, which takes fire and burns within the cage, securely cut off from the power of doing harm. Thus, when the atmosphere is so impure that the flame of a lamp itself cannot be maintained, the Davy still supplies light to the miner, and turns his worst enemy into an obedient servant. This invention, the certain source of large profit, he presented with characteristic liberality to the public. The words are preserved in which, when pressed to secure to himself the benefit of a patent, he declined to do so, in conformity with the high-minded resolution which he formed, upon acquiring independent wealth, of never making his scientific eminence subservient to gain. "I have enough for all my views and purposes, more wealth might be troublesome, and distract my attention from those pursuits in which I delight. More wealth could not increase my fame or happiness. It might undoubtedly enable me to put four horses to my carriage, but what would it avail me to have it said, that Sir Humphry drives his carriage and four?"

*Gallery of Portraits.*

No. X.—*On the Utility of the Remarks and Observations of Mechanics and Manufacturers.* P. 81.

That the remarks of experienced artists and labourers, may frequently lead to useful discoveries, may be illustrated by the following facts:—"A soap manufacturer remarked that the residuum of his ley, when exhausted of the alkali for which he employed it, produced a corrosion of his copper boiler for which he could not account. He put it into the hands of a scientific chemist for analysis, and the result was the discovery of one of the most singular and important chemical elements, *iodine*. The properties of this, being studied, were found to occur most appositely in illustration and support of a variety of new, curious, and instructive views, then gaining ground in chemistry, and thus exercised a marked influence over the whole body of that science. Curiosity was excited; the origin of the new substance was traced to the sea-plants from whose ashes the principal ingredient of soap is obtained, and ultimately to the sea-water itself. It was thence hunted through nature, discovered in salt mines and springs, and pursued into all bodies which have a marine origin; among the rest, into sponge. A medical practitioner then called to mind a reputed remedy for the cure of one of the most grievous and unsightly disorders to which the human species is subject—the *goitre*—which infests the inhabitants of mountainous districts to an extent which in this favoured land we have happily no experience of, and which was said to have been originally cured by the ashes of burnt sponge. Led by this indication, he tried the effect of iodine on that complaint, and the result established the extraordinary fact, that this singular substance, taken as a medicine, acts with the utmost promptitude and energy on goitre, dissipating the largest and most inveterate in a short time, and acting (of course with occasional failures, like all other medicines) as a specific or natural antagonist, against that odious deformity. It is thus that any accession to our knowledge of nature is sure, sooner or later, to make itself felt in some practical application, and that a benefit conferred on science, by the casual observation or shrewd remark of even an unscientific or illiterate person, infallibly repays itself with interest, though often in a way that could never have been at first contemplated."*

Iodine was *accidentally* discovered (as above stated) in 1812, by M. De Courtois, a manufacturer of saltpetre at Paris, and derived its first illustrations from M. Clement and M. Desormes. Its name literally signifies a *violet colour*. Its specific gravity is about 4. It becomes a violet-coloured *gas* at a temperature below that of boiling water; it combines with the metals, with phosphorus and sulphur, with the alkalis and metallic oxides, and forms a detonating compound with ammonia. Dr. Coindet of Geneva first recommended the use of it, in the form of tincture, for the cure of goitres. Some readers may perhaps, require to be informed that the goitre is a large fleshy excrescence that grows from the throat, and sometimes increases to an enormous size. The inhabitants of certain parts of Switzerland, especially those in the republic of *Valais*, are particularly subject to this shocking deformity.

No. XI.—*Liberality of Religious Sectaries in America, contrasted with British bigotry.* P. 149.

The following sketches are taken from Stuart's "*Three Years in North America.*" When at Avon, a village in the north-west part of the State of New York, Mr. Stuart went to attend a church about a mile distant, of which he gives the following description.—"The horses and carriages were tied up in great sheds near the church-doors, dur

* Herschel's Prelim. Discourse to Nat. Phil.

ing the time of service. The day was hot, and the precentor, as usual, in the centre of the front gallery, opposite to the minister, officiated, not only without a gown, but without a coat upon his back. There was some sort of instrumental music—hautboys and bassoons, I think, against which there are no prejudices in this country. The clergyman, a very unaffected, sincere-looking person, delivered a plain sensible discourse, in which he introduced the names of Dr. Erskine and Dr. Chalmers, which sounded strange to us, considering where we were, on the western side of the Atlantic, not very far from the falls of Niagara. At the close of his sermon, he addressed his hearers in some such terms as these,—'My friends, the sacrament of the Lord's supper is to be dispensed here this evening. This is a free church, open to all—Presbyterians, Methodists, Baptists, and all other denominations of Christians. This is according to our belief. All are invited; the risk is theirs.' Such liberality is, we find on inquiry, not unusual among the clergymen and congregations of different sects, with the exception in general of Unitarians. I observe an example recorded in Hosack's *Life of Clinton;* and as it relates to the great Father of the United States, and is of unquestionable authority, I think it of sufficient interest for insertion. 'While the American army, under the command of Washington, lay encamped in the vicinity of Morristown, New-Jersey, it occurred that the service of the communion (then observed semi-annually only) was to be administered to the Presbyterian church in that village. In a morning of the previous week, the General, after his accustomed inspection of the camp, visited the house of the Rev. Dr. Jones, then pastor of that church, and, after the usual preliminaries, thus accosted him:—'Doctor, I understand that the Lord's supper is to be celebrated with you next Sunday. I would learn, if it accords with the canons of your church to admit communicants of another denomination.' The Doctor rejoined, 'Most certainly. Ours is not the Presbyterian table, General, but the Lord's table, and we hence give the Lord's invitation to all his followers, of whatever name.' The General replied, 'I am glad of it; that is as it ought to be, but as I was not quite sure of the fact, I thought I would ascertain it from yourself, as I propose to join with you on that occasion. Though a member of the church of England, I have no exclusive partialities.' The Doctor reassured him of a cordial welcome, and the General was found seated with the communicants the next Sabbath.

"During my residence in the United States, subsequent to this period, I was frequently witness to the good understanding which generally prevails among clergymen professing different opinions on church forms and doctrinal points, in this country; and I occasionally observed notices in the newspapers to the same purport. The two following I have preserved:—'The corner-stone of a new Baptist church was laid at Savannah in Georgia, and the ceremonial services were performed by clergymen of the Methodist, German, Lutheran, Presbyterian, Episcopal, and Baptist churches.' 'The sacrament of the Lord's supper was administered in the Rev. Mr. Post's church (Presbyterian church at Washington) and, *as usual*, all members of other churches in regular standing were invited to unite with the members of that church, in testifying their faith in, and love to, their Lord and Saviour. The invited guests assembled around the table; and it so happened that Mr. Grundy, a senator from Tennessee, and two Cherokee Indians, were seated side by side.' Nothing is more astounding in the stage-coach intercourse with the people of this country, as well as in the bar-rooms where travellers meet, than the freedom and apparent sincerity of their remarks, and the perfect feeling of equality with which the conversation is maintained, especially on religious matters. I have heard the most opposite creeds maintained, without any thing like acrimonious discussion or sarcastic remark, by persons in the same stage, professing themselves undisguisedly, Calvinists, Episcopalians, Methodists, and Unitarians," &c.

If such are the liberal views entertained in America on religious subjects, and if such dispositions are more congenial to the spirit of the Christian system, than the fiery and unhallowed zeal and unholy jealousies which many religionists display—why are they not more frequently manifested in our own country? For, the difference of localities and customs cannot alter the nature and obligation of moral principles and actions. What a striking contrast to the scenes now exhibited are such facts as the following;—"The Rev. J. T. Campbell, rector of Tilston, in the diocese of Chester, *has been suspended from his clerical function*, for twelve months, with a sequestration of his benefice, for that time, *for preaching in a methodist meeting-house* in Nantwich, and in other similar places within the diocese." "The Rev. Dr. Rice, curate of St. Lukes, London, who made himself conspicuous the other day, at Mr. Wakely's dinner, and who, in consequence of the liberal sentiments he then expressed on the subject of Church Reform, has fallen under the censure of his diocesan." Both these notices appeared in most of the newspapers in January 1833, and were never contradicted! If such conduct in the rulers of the church were *warranted* by the doctrines or precepts of the New Testament, Christianity would be unworthy of any man's attention or support. If the principles and persecuting spirit involved in such decisions, were countenanced and supported by the laws of the state, we should soon be subjected to all the burnings, hangings, maimings, tortures, and horrid cruelties, which distinguished the dark ages of Popery, and the proceedings of the Star Chamber. How long will it be ere professed Christians display *a Christian spirit!* and what is the utility of Christianity to the world, unless candour, forbearance, *love*, meekness, and other Christian virtues, be the characteristics of its professed votaries! We dare any person to bring forward a single instance of a man's being converted to the faith of our holy religion, by the display of unhallowed zeal, furious bigotry, sectarian contentions, or the manifestation of a domineering and persecuting spirit. But, thousands of instances could be produced of such dispositions being the means of recruiting the ranks of infidelity and licentiousness. The following statement, sent to the Editor of the *Liverpool Mercury*, Feb. 14th, 1833, displays the *liberality* of certain British clergymen, in the thirty-third year of the nineteenth century. "I have been recently called on by death to part with one of my children. I waited upon the Rev. ——— of——— church (where I buried a child a short time ago,) to arrange with him about its interment near the other. 'But, to what place of worship do you go?' inquired most seriously the Reverend divine. 'The Methodists, Sir, of the New Connexion,' I replied. 'As you do not attend my church, I cannot, therefore, bury your child.—Where was your child baptized?' was his second inquiry. 'At the church of which I am a member,' I answered. 'How can you think,' exclaimed the *liberal* and pious, but indignant minister, 'that I shall bury your child, which has been baptized by a Dissenter? Take your child to be buried where it was baptized.'—'But, Sir, we have no burial-ground connected with our chapel.' 'No matter; the churchwardens of my church have determined not to bury any that do not belong to the church. Go,' said the minister, 'to ———, and arrange with him.'—So saying, he turned his back and left me. *R. Emery.*"

The Duke of Newcastle—so notorious *for doing what he pleases with his own*—has the following clause introduced into certain leases in the neighbourhood of Nottingham:—"*That in none of the houses to be built, shall be held prayer-meetings, or any conventicles for the diffusion of sentiments contrary to the doctrines of the Church of England.*" A fine specimen, truly, of Christian liberality in the nineteenth century! If his Grace the Duke of Newcastle attended to his prayers as *frequently* and *fervently* as the Liturgy enjoins, he would be disposed to display a little more candour in reference to the "prayer-meetings" of his dissenting brethren. With regard to the leading *doctrines* of the Church of England, there are few dissenters disposed to find much fault with them. But what will his Grace say of the indolence and avaricious conduct of many of the ministers of that church, which have been the cause of the rapid increase of Dissenters? The Vicar of Pevensey in Sussex (as appears from a petition of the parishioners, dated February 1, 1833) derives an income from the parish of about 1200*l.* a-year, and yet has never once performed divine service, since his induction, *about seventeen years ago.* He has another living at Guestling, about fifteen miles distant, from which he derives a revenue of 400*l.* per annum. Whether he does duty there is not known; but it is not absurd to suppose, that a parson who will not so much as *read prayers* for 1200*l.* is not very likely to preach for 400*l.*—R. Hodgson, Dean of Carlisle, is also Vicar of Burg-on-Sands, Rector of St. Georges in Hanover Square, Vicar of Hellington, and yet at none of these places is he found officiating. The tithes received by the Dean and Chapter for Heshet, amount to 1000*l.* or 1500*l.* a-year; they pay the curate that does the duty 18*l.* 5*s.*, or at the rate of one shilling a-day—the wages of a bricklayer's labourer. In Wetheral and Warwick, the Dean and Chapter draw about 1000*l.* a-year for tithes, and 1000*l.* a-year from the church lands, and they pay the working minister the sum of 50*l.* a-year. The tithes of the parish of St. Cuthberts and St. Mary amount to about 1500*l.* a-year; and the two curates, who do the duty, receive each the sum of 2*l.* 13*s.* 4*d.* a-year!! Three brothers of the name of *Goodenough*, monopolize *thirteen* pieces of church preferment. One of them is Prebend of Carlisle, Westminister and York, Vicar of Wath All-Saints on Dearn, chaplain of Adwick, and chaplain of Brampton Bierlow. Those preferments produce, of course, several thousands, for which the incumbents perform absolutely nothing. And yet, one of the persons above alluded to, had lately the effrontery to come to Carlisle and preach up "the Church is in danger," because these shocking enormities are now exposed to public reprobation. See *Times* newspaper for March 7, 8, 1833. It would be no great breach of charity to suppose, that it is such doctrines and *practices* as those now stated, that the Duke of Newcastle is determined to support with such a degree of persecuting zeal—and that pure Christianity, detached from its connexions with the state, is the object of his hatred and contempt.

As a corroboration of Mr. Stuart's statements respecting the liberality of Religious Sectaries in America, the following extract of a letter, dated 18th February 1833, which the author received from the Rev. Dr. S——, a learned and pious Presbyterian minister in the State of New York, may be here inserted—

"I deeply regret to hear that so much of the spirit of sectarianism prevails among the different religious denominations of your country. We, too, have enough of it; but it is here manifestly on the decline. You may possibly think it an unreasonable stretch of liberality when I tell you, that within a few weeks, I suffered an Episcopalian to preach in my pulpit, and to use his own forms of prayer. But such is the state of feeling in my congregation, that, though such a thing had never before occurred among them, yet it met with their universal and unqualified approbation. On the other hand, I expect, in the course of a week or two, to preach a charity sermon here in one of our Episcopal churches, and to perform the whole service in my own way. This, it must be confessed, is a little uncommon even in this country; but every thing indicates, that such expressions of good will, even between Presbyterians and Episcopalians, will soon become frequent. Independents and Presbyterians here occupy nearly the same ground. They are indeed distinct denominations, but are represented in each other's public bodies." The author has perused an excellent sermon of the clergyman now alluded to, which was preached in an Independent church when introducing an *Independent* minister to his charge immediately after ordination, which shows that we have still much to learn from our transatlantic brethren, in relation to a friendly and affectionate intercourse with Christians of different denominations.

No. XII.—*On the Demoralizing Effects of Infidel Philosophy*. P. 153—156.

With the view of corroborating and illustrating more fully the statements made in the pages referred to, the following facts may be stated in relation to the moral character of the inhabitants of France, particularly those of Paris.

In the first place, the vice of *gambling* prevails in the capital of France to an extent unknown in almost any other country. The *Palais Royale* is the grand focus of this species of iniquity, which is the fertile source of licentiousness, and of almost every crime. Mr. J. Scott, who visited Paris in 1814, thus describes this sink of moral pollution. "The Palais Royale presents the most characteristic feature of Paris; it is dissolute, gay, wretched, elegant, paltry, busy, and idle—it suggests recollections of atrocity, and supplies sights of fascination—it displays virtue and vice living on easy terms, and in immediate neighbourhood of each other. Excitements, indulgences, and privations—art and vulgarity—science and ignorance—artful conspiracies and careless debaucheries—all mingle here, forming an atmosphere of various exhalations, a whirl of the most lively images—a stimulating *melange* of what is most heating, intoxicating, and subduing." Sir W. Scott, who visited Paris in 1815, gives the following description of this infamous establishment. "The Palais Royale, in whose saloons and porticoes vice has established a public and open school for gambling and licentiousness, should be levelled to the ground with all its accursed brothels and gambling houses—rendezvouses the more seductive to youth, as being free from some of those dangers which would alarm timidity in places of avowedly scandalous resort. In the *Sallon des Etrangers*, the most celebrated haunt of this Dom-Daniel, which I had the curiosity to visit, the scene was decent and silent to a degree of solemnity. An immense hall was filled with gamesters and spectators. Those who kept the bank, and managed the affairs of the establishment, were distinguished by the green shades which they wore to preserve their eyes; by their silent and grave demeanour, and by the paleness of their countenances, exhausted by their constant vigils. There was no distinction of persons, nor any passport required for entrance, save that of a decent exterior; and, on the long tables, which were covered with gold, an artisan was at liberty to hazard his week's wages, or a noble his whole estate. Youth and age were equally welcome, and any one who chose to play within the limits of a trifling sum, had only to accuse his own weakness, if he was drawn into deeper or more dangerous hazard. Every thing appeared to be conducted with perfect fairness. The only advantage possessed by the bank (which is however, enormous) is the extent of the funds, by which it is enabled to sustain any reverse of fortune; whereas, most of the individuals who play against the bank, are in circumstances to be ruined by the first succession of ill luck; so that, ultimately, the small ventures merge in the stock of the principal adventurers, as rivers run into the sea. The profits of the establishment must, indeed, be very large, to support its expenses. Besides a variety of attendants, who distribute refreshments to the players gratis, there is an elegant entertainment, with expensive wines, regularly prepared, about three o'clock in the morning, for those who choose to partake of it. With such temptations around him, and where the hazarding an insignificant sum seems at first venial or innocent, it is no wonder that thousands feel themselves gradually involved in the vortex, whose verge is so little distinguishable, until they are swallowed up, with their time, talents, fortune, and frequently also both body and soul.

"This is vice with her *fairest vizard;* but the same unhallowed precinct contains many a secret cell *for the most hideous and unheard of debaucheries;* many an open rendezvous of infamy, and many a den of usury and treason; the whole mixed with a Vanity Fair of shops for jewels, trinkets, and baubles; that bashfulness may not need a decent pretext for adventuring into the haunts of infamy. It was here that the preachers of revolution found, amidst gamblers, desperadoes, and prostitutes, ready auditors of their doctrines, and active hands to labour in their vineyard. It was here that the plots of the Buonapartists were adjusted; and from hence the seduced soldiers, inflamed with many a bumper to the health of the exile of Elba, under the mystic names of *Jean de l'Epee*, and Corporal Violet, were dismissed to spread the news of his approaching return. In short, from this central pit of Acheron, in which are openly assembled and mingled those characters and occupations which, *in all other capitals*, are driven to shroud themselves in separate and retired recesses; from this focus of vice and treason have flowed forth those waters of bitterness of which France has drunk so deeply."

The *state of marriage* in this country since the revolution is likewise the fertile source of immorality and crime. Marriage is little else than a state of legal concubinage, a mere temporary connexion, from which the parties can loose themselves when they please; and women are a species of mercantile commodity. Illicit connexions and illegitimate children, especially in Paris, are numerous beyond what is known in any other country. The following statement of the affairs of the French capital, for the year ending 22d September 1803, given by the Prefect of Police to the Grand Judge, presents a most revolting idea of the state of public morals:—During this year 490 men and 167 women committed suicide; 81 men and 69 women were murdered, of whom 55 men and 52 women were foreigners; 644 divorces; 155 murderers executed; 1210 persons condemned to the galleys, &c.; 1626 persons to hard labour, and 64 marked with hot irons; 12, 076 public women were registered; large sums were levied from these wretched creatures, who were made to pay from 5 to 10 guineas each monthly, according to their rank, beauty, or fashion; 1552 kept mistresses were noted down by the police, and 380 brothels licensed by the Prefect. Among the criminals executed were 7 fathers for poisoning their children; 10 husbands for murdering their wives; 6 wives that had murdered their husbands; and 15 children who had poisoned or otherwise destroyed their parents.

The glaring *profanation of the Sabbath* is another striking characteristic of the people of France, especially as displayed in the capital. Entering Paris on the Sabbath, a Briton is shocked at beholding all that reverence and solemnity with which that sacred day is generally kept in Christian countries, not only set aside, but ridiculed and contemned, and a whole people apparently lost to every impression of religion. The shops are all alive, the gaming-houses filled, the theatres crowded, the streets deafened with ballad-singers and mountebanks; persons of all ages, from the hoary grandsire to the child of four or five years, engaged in balls, routs, and dancings,—the house of God alone deserted, and the voice of religion alone unheard and despised. The Sabbath was the day appointed for celebrating the return of Buonaparte from Elba in 1815. In the grand square there were stationed two theatres of dancers and rope-dancers; two theatres of amusing physical experiments; six bands for dancing; a theatre of singers; a display of fire-works; a circus where Francone's troops were to exhibit; and above all, that most delectable sport called *Matts de Cocagne*. The Matts de Cocagne consists of two long poles, near the tops of which are suspended various articles of cookery, such as roast beef, fowls, ducks, &c. The poles are soaped and rendered slippery at the bottom; and the sport consists in the ludicrous failures of those who climb to reach the eatables. Two Matts de Cocagne were also erected in the square Marjury; as also four bands for dancing, a theatre of rope-dancers; a theatre of amusing experiments; a theatre of singers, &c.; and fire-works. These amusements were to commence at 2 o'clock, P. M. and to last till night. Along the avenue of the *Champ de Elysees*, there were erected 36 fountains of wine, 12 tables for the distribution of eatables, such as pies, fowls, sausages, &c. The distribution of the wine and eatables took place at three o'clock. At nine o'clock there was a grand fire-work at the Place de Concorde. Immediately afterwards a detonating balloon ascended from the Champ de Elysees. The detonation took place when the balloon was at the height of 500 toises, or above 3000 feet. In the evening all the theatres were opened gratis, and all the public edifices were illuminated. Such was the mode in which the Parisians worshipped the "goddess of Reason" on the day appointed for the Christian Sabbath.

That such profanation of the Sabbath is still continued, and that it is not confined to the city of Paris, but abounds in most of the provincial towns of France, appears from the following extract of a letter inserted in the Eevangelical Magazine for January 1833, from a gentleman who recently resided in different parts of that country:—"Could every pious reader of this letter be awakened, on the morning of that sacred day, as I have been, by the clang of the anvil, and, on his entrance into the streets and markets, observe business prosecuted or suspended according to the tastes of the tradesmen; could he mark the workmen on seasons of religious festival, erecting the triumphal arch on the Sabbath morning, and removing it on the Sabbath evening; and notice the labourers, at their option, toiling all day at the public works; could he see the card-party in the hotel, and the nine-pins before every public house, and the promenaders swarming in all the suburbs; could he be compelled to witness, on one Sunday, a grand review of a garrison; and on another be disturbed by the music of a company of strolling players· and could he find, amidst all this profanation, as I have found, no temple to which to retreat, save the barren cliff or the ocean-cave, surely he would feel and proclaim the truth, 'This people is destroyed for lack of knowledge.'" The same gentleman shows, that this profanation is chiefly occasioned by "the destitution of Scriptual information which exists in France," which the following facts, among many others that came under his own observation, tend to illustrate. "On the road to M——— on a market-day, I stopped about a dozen persons, some poor, others of the better classes, and showing them the New Testament, begged them to inform me if they possessed it. With a *single* exception, they all replied in the negative. In the town of M——— I entered, with the same inquiry, many of the most respectable shops. Only *one* individual among their occupiers was the owner of a New Testament. One gentleman, who, during a week, dined with me at my inn, and who avowed himself a deist and a materialist, said that he had not seen a Testament for many years. Indeed, I doubted whether he had *ever* read it; for, on my presenting one to him, he asked if it contained an account of the *creation*. A journeyman bookbinder, having expressed a wish to obtain this precious book, remarked, on receiving it, in perfect ignorance of its *divine* authority, that he dared to say it was 'a very fine work.' A student in a university, about 20 years of age, told me, that although he had seen the Vulgate (Latin) version of the New Testament, he had never met with it in a French translation. A young woman, who professed to have a Bible, produced instead of it a Catholic Abridgment of the Scriptures, garbled in many important portions, and interlarded with the comments of the Fathers."

Such facts afford a striking evidence of the hostility of the Roman Catholic clergy in France to the circulation of the Scriptures, and the enlightening of the minds of the community in the knowledge of Divine truths; and therefore it is no wonder that Infidelity, Materialism, and immorality, should very generally prevail. "Even among the Protestants," says the same writer, "a large number of *their* ministers are worldly men, frequenting, as a pious lady assured me, 'the chase, the dance, and the billiard table.' As to the public worship of God, the case is equally deplorable. In two large towns, and a population of 25,000, I found no Protestant sanctuary. In a third town, containing about 7000 inhabitants, there was an English Episcopal chapel for the British residents, but no French Protestant service. At a fourth, in which there was a Protestant church, the minister, who supplied four other places, preached *one* Sabbath in *five* weeks."

The mania for *dancing*, which pervades all classes and all ages, is another characteristic of the people of Paris, of which some idea may be formed from the following extract from a French public Journal, dated August 2, 1804:—"The *danso-mania* of both sexes seems rather to increase than decrease with the *warm* weather. *Sixty balls* were advertised for *last Sunday;* and for to-morrow *sixty-nine* are announced. Any person walking in the Elysian fields, or on the Boulevards, may be convinced that these temples of pleasure are not without worshippers. *Besides* these, in our own walks last Sunday, we counted no less than *twenty-two gardens* not advertised, where there was *fiddling and dancing*. Indeed, this pleasure is tempting, because it is very cheap. For a bottle of beer, which costs 6 sous (3d.,) and 2 sous (1d.,) to the fiddler, *a husband and wife, with their children, may amuse themselves from three o'clock in the afternoon till eleven o'clock at night.* As this exercise both diverts the mind and strengthens the body, and as Sunday is the only day of the week which the most numerous classes of people can dispose of, *without injury* to themselves or the state, *government encourages, as much as possible*, these *innocent amusements on that day*. In the garden of Chaumievre, on the Boulevard Neuf, we observed, in the same quadrilles, last Sunday, *four generations*, the great grandsire dancing with his great-great granddaughter, and the great-grandmamma dancing with her great-great-grandson. It was a satisfaction impossible to be expressed, to see persons of so many different ages, all enjoying the same pleasures for the present, not remembering past misfortunes, nor apprehending future ones. The *grave* seemed equally distant from the girl of ten years old, and from her great-grandmamma of seventy years, and from the boy that had not seen three lustres, as from the great grandsire reaching nearly fourscore years. In another quadrille, were four lovers dancing with their mistresses. There, again, nothing was observed but an emulation who should enjoy the present moment. Not an idea of the past, or of time to come, clouded their thoughts; in a few words, they were perfectly happy. Let those tormented by avarice or ambition frequent those places on a Sunday, and they will be cured of their vile passions, if they are not incurable."*

Such are a few sketches of the moral state and character of the people of Paris, which, there is every reason to believe, are, with a few modifications, applicable to the inhabitants of most of the other large towns in France. Among the great mass of the population of that country, there appears to be no distinct recognition of the moral attributes of the Deity, of the obligation of the Divine law, or of a future and eternal state of existence. Whirled about incessantly in the vortex of vanity and dissipation, the Creator is lost sight of, moral responsibility disregarded, and present sensual gratifications pursued with

* Several of the above sketches are extracted from the "Glasgow Geography," a work which contains an immense mass of historical, geographical, and miscellaneous information

the utmost eagerness, regardless whether death shall prove the precursor to permanent happiness or misery, or to a state of "*eternal sleep.*" Never, perhaps, in a Pagan country, was the Epicurean philosophy so systematically reduced to practice as in the country of Voltaire, Buffon, Mirabeau, Condorcet, Helvetius, and Diderot. It cannot be difficult to trace the present demoralization of France to the sceptical and atheistical principles disseminated by such writers, which were adopted in all their extent, and acted upon by the leaders of the first Revolution. Soon after that event, education was altogether proscribed. During the space of five years, from 1791 to 1796, the public instruction of the young was totally set aside, and, of course, they were left to remain entirely ignorant of the facts and doctrines of religion, and of the duties they owe to God and to man. It is easy, therefore, to conceive what must be the intellectual, the moral, and religious condition of those who were born a little before this period, and who now form a considerable portion of the population arrived at the years of manhood. A gentleman at Paris happened to possess a domestic of sense and general intelligence above his station. His master, upon some occasion, used to him the expression, "It is doing as we would be done by,"—the Christian maxim. The young man looked rather surprised: "Yes," (replied the gentleman) "I say, it is the doctrine of the Christian religion, which teaches us not only to do as we would be done by, but also to return good for evil." "It may be so Sir," (replied he) "but I had the misfortune to be born during the heat of the revolution, when it would have been death to have spoken on the subject of religion; and so soon as I was fifteen years old, I was put into the hands of the drill-serjeant, whose first lesson to me was, that as a French soldier, I was to *fear neither God nor devil.*" It is to be hoped, that the rising generation in France is now somewhat improved in intelligence and morality beyond that which sprung up during the demoralizing scenes of the first revolution; but, in spite of all the counteracting efforts that can now be used, another generation, at least, must pass away, before the immoral effects produced by infidel philosophy, and the principles which prevailed during the "reign of terror," can be nearly obliterated.

I shall conclude these sketches with the following account of the *consecration* of the "Goddess of Reason,"—one of the most profane and presumptuous mockeries of every thing that is rational or sacred, to be found in the history of mankind.

"The section of the Sans Culottes, declared at the bar of the Convention, November 10, 1793, that they would no longer have priests among them, and that they required the total suppression of all salaries paid to the ministers of religious worship. The petition was followed by a numerous procession, which filed off in the hall, accompanied by national music. Surrounded by them, appeared a young woman* of the finest figure, arrayed in the robes of liberty, and seated in a chair, ornamented with leaves and festoons. She was placed opposite the President; and Chaumette, one of the members, said, '*Fanaticism* has abandoned the place of truth; squint eyed, it could not bear the brilliant light. The people of Paris have taken possession of the temple, which they have regenerated; the Gothic arches which, till this day resounded with *lies*, now echo with the accents of truth; you see we have not taken for our festivals inanimate idols, it is a *chef d'œuvre* of nature whom we have arrayed in the habit of liberty; its sacred form has *inflamed* all hearts. The public has but one cry, "No more altars, no more priests, no other God but the God of nature." We, their magistrates, we accompany them from the temple of truth to the temple of the laws, to celebrate a new liberty, and to request that the *cidevant church of Notre Dame be changed into a temple consecrated to reason and truth.*' This proposal, being converted into a motion, was immediately decreed; and the Convention afterwards decided, that the citizens of Paris, on this day, continued to deserve well of their country. The Goddess then seated herself by the side of the President, who gave her a *fraternal kiss.* The secretaries presented themselves to share the same favour; *every one was eager to kiss the new divinity,* whom so many salutations *did not in the least disconcert.* During the ceremony, the orphans of the country, pupils of Bourdon (one of the members) *sang a hymn to reason,* composed by citizen Moline. The national music played Gosset's hymn to liberty. The Convention then mixed with the people, *to celebrate the feast of reason in her new temple.* A grand festival was accordingly held in the church of Notre Dame, in honour of this deity. In the middle of the church was erected a mount, and on it a very plain temple, the facade of which bore the following inscription—'*a la Philosophie.*' The busts of the most celebrated philosophers were placed before the gate of this temple. The torch of truth was in the summit of the mount, upon the altar of Reason, spreading light. The Convention and all the constituted authorities assisted at the ceremony. Two rows of young girls, dressed in white, each wearing a crown of oak leaves, crossed before the altar of reason, at the sound of republican music; each of the girls inclined before the torch, and ascended the summit of the mount. Liberty then came out of the temple of philosophy, towards a throne made of turf, to receive the homage of the republicans of both sexes, who sang a hymn in her praise, extending their arms at the same time towards her.

* Madame Desmoulines, who was afterwards guillotined.

Liberty ascended afterwards, to return to the temple, and, in re-entering it, she turned about, casting a look of benevolence upon her friends; when she got in, every one expressed with enthusiasm the sensations which the Goddess excited in them by songs of joy; and they swore, never, never to cease to be faithful to her."

Such were the festivities and ceremonies which were prescribed for the installation of this new divinity, and such the shameless folly and daring impiety with which they were accompanied! Such is the *Religion* of what has been presumptuously called *Philosophy*, when it has shaken off its allegiance to the Christian Revelation—a religion as inconsistent with the dictates of reason and the common sense of mankind, as it is with the religion of the Bible. Never, in any age, was Philosophy so shamefully degraded, and exposed to the contempt of every rational mind, as when it thus stooped to such absurd foolery and Heaven-daring profanity. Besides the impiety of the whole of this procedure,—which is almost without a parallel in the annals of the world—there was an imbecility and a *silliness* in it, altogether incompatible with those sublime ideas of creation and Providence, which true philosophy, when properly directed, has a tendency to inspire. And how *inconsistently*, as well as inhumanely, did these worshippers of "liberty," "reason," and "truth," conduct themselves to the representative of their goddess, when, soon after, they doomed the lady, whom they had kissed and adored in the "temple of truth," to expire under the stroke of the guillotine! Such occurrences appear evidently intended by the moral Governor of the world, to admonish us of the danger of separating science from its connexions with revealed religion, and to show us to what dreadful lengths, in impiety and crime, even men of talent will proceed, when the truths of Revelation are set aside, and the principles and moral laws of Christianity are trampled under foot.

# THE

# PHILOSOPHY

# OF A

# FUTURE STATE.

BY THOMAS DICK,

AUTHOR OF A VARIETY OF LITERARY AND SCIENTIFIC COMMUNICATIONS IN NICHOLSON'S PHILOSOPHICAL JOURNAL, THE ANNALS OF PHILOSOPHY, ETC. ETC.

HARTFORD:
PUBLISHED BY A. C. GOODMAN & CO.
1850.

TO

# THOMAS CHALMERS, D.D.

PROFESSOR OF MORAL PHILOSOPHY IN THE UNIVERSITY OF ST. ANDREWS.

---

SIR,

In dedicating to you this volume, which has for its object to exhibit a popular view of the Philosophy of a Future State, as deduced from the light of science and revelation,—a consideration of a far higher nature than the formal and customary honour of addressing a man of literary and scientific attainments, induced me to shelter it under your patronage.

In the several vocations in which Divine Providence has called you to officiate, you have proved yourself the warm and disinterested patron of all that is benevolent and good—of every thing that concerns the present and eternal welfare of mankind: and your praises have been re-echoed from one corner of the land to another, as the champion of the Christian religion,—the doctrines of which, your voice and your pen have done so much to illustrate.

Your writings furnish ample testimony to the world of your earnest, active, and unwearied solicitude for the moral and religious improvement of mankind —a solicitude which is not abated by any minor differences of opinion in those with whom you co-operate, where the great object is, to diffuse knowledge and happiness over the face of the earth.

Your kind indulgence to me, on the slight acquaintance I have of you personally, and your approbation of some of my labours, in endeavouring to connect Science and Religion, induce me to hope, that, if the views taken of the present subject in any measure correspond with your own, you will countenance my humble attempts to dispel the prejudices which many well-meaning Christians may entertain, as to the beneficial tendency of exhibiting the sciences of a *present*, as applicable to the circumstances and relations of a *future* world.

That you may long be spared as the advocate of vital Christianity—as a blessing and ornament to your country—and as a zealous instructor of those who are destined to promote its best interests; and that you may enjoy, without interruption, the pleasures arising from a consciousness of the esteem and approbation of the wise and the pious, is the sincere prayer of,

SIR,

Your much obliged,

and humble Servant,

THOMAS DICK.

*Broughty Ferry, near Dundee,*
*Dec.* 28, 1827.

# PREFACE.

THE reasonings and illustrations contained in the following pages are intended to direct the intelligent Christian in some of those trains of thought which he ought to prosecute, when looking forward to the scene of his future destination. The Author was induced to engage in the discussion of this subject, from a consideration, that many vague and erroneous conceptions are still entertained among Christians in regard to the nature of heavenly felicity, and the employments of the future world. In elucidating the train of thought which is here prosecuted, he has brought forward, without hesitation, the discoveries of modern science, particularly those which relate to the scenery of the heavens; convinced, that all the manifestations of himself which the Creator has permitted us to contemplate, are intended to throw light on the plan of his moral government in relation both to our present and our future destiny. He has carefully avoided every thing that might appear like vague or extravagant conjecture; and he trusts that the opinions he has broached, and the conclusions he has deduced, will generally be found accordant with the analogies of Nature and the dictates of Revelation. He is aware, that he has many prejudices to encounter, arising from the vague and indefinite manner in which such subjects have been hitherto treated, and from the want of those expansive views of the Divine operations which the professors of Christianity should endeavour to attain; but he feels confident that those who are best qualified to appreciate his sentiments, will treat with candour an attempt to elucidate a subject hitherto overlooked, and in which every individual in the human race is deeply interested.

It was originally intended to publish what is contained in Parts II. and III. without any dissertation on the evidences of a future state as deduced from the light of nature—taking the immortality of man for granted on the authority of Revelation. But, on second thought, it was judged expedient, for the sake of general readers, to exhibit a condensed view of those arguments which even the light of reason can produce in favour of the immortality of man. In this department of the volume, the Author has brought forward several arguments which he is not aware have been taken notice of by ethical writers, when treating on this subject. He has endeavoured to illustrate these and the other arguments here adduced, in minute detail, and in a popular manner, so as to be level to the comprehension of every reader; and he trusts, that the force of the whole combined, will be found to amount to as high a degree of moral demonstration as can be expected in relation to objects which are not cognizable by the eye of sense.

The greater portion of what is contained in Part III. having been written above eight years ago, several *apparent* repetitions of facts alluded to in the preceding Parts may perhaps be noticed by the critical reader; but, in general it will be found, that where the same facts are repeated, they are either exhibited in a new aspect, or brought forward to elucidate another subject.

The practical reflections and remarks imbodied in the last Part of this work, will not, the Author is persuaded, be considered by any of his readers, as either unnecessary, or unappropriate to the subjects treated of in the preceding parts of this volume. It is of the utmost importance that every individual be convinced, that he cannot be supposed a candidate for a blessed immortality, unless the train of his affections, and the general tenor of his conduct, in some measure correspond to the tempers and dispositions, and the moral purity which prevail in the heavenly state.

The favourable reception which the public have given to the volumes he has formerly published, induces the Author to indulge the hope, that the present volume may not be altogether unworthy of their attention. That it may tend to convince the skeptical of the reality of an immortal existence—to expand the believer's conceptions of the attributes of the Divinity, and the glory of "that inheritance which is reserved in heaven" for the faithful—and to excite in the mind of every reader an ardent desire to cultivate those dispositions and virtues which will prepare him for the enjoyment of celestial bliss—is the Author's most sincere and ardent wish, as it was the great object he had in view when engaged in its composition.

# CONTENTS.

## INTRODUCTION.



## PART I.

## CHAPTER I.

## SECTION V.



## SECTION VI.



## SECTION VII.



## SECTION VIII.



## SECTION IX.



## SECTION X.



## SECTION XI.



## CHAPTER II.

## PART II.



## PART III.



## PART IV.

## APPENDIX.

THE

# PHILOSOPHY

OF A

# FUTURE STATE.

## PART I.

### PROOFS OF A FUTURE STATE.

## INTRODUCTION.

THE sketches contained in Parts II. and III. of this work, being chiefly intended to illustrate the connexion of science with the scenes of a future world, and the aids which its discoveries afford, for enabling us to form some conception of the *perpetual improvement* of its inhabitants in knowledge and felicity—I shall endeavour, in this First Part, to exhibit a condensed view of some of those *evidences* which prove the immortality of the soul, and the eternal destination of man.

This is an inquiry far more interesting and important, to every individual of mankind, than any other which comes within the range of the human mind. Next to the being of a God, the doctrine of the immortality of man lies at the foundation of all religion, and of all the animating prospects which can cheer us in this land of our pilgrimage. Remove from the mind the belief of a future existence, and the hope of immortality, and religion becomes a shadow, life a dream, and the approach of death a scene of darkness and despair. Upon this short question, "*Is man immortal, or is he not?*" depends all that is valuable in science, in morals, and in theology, and all that is most interesting to man as a social being, and as a rational and accountable intelligence. If he is destined to an eternal existence, an immense importance must attach to all his present affections, actions, and pursuits; and it must be a matter of infinite moment, that they be directed in such a channel, as will tend to carry him forward, in safety, to the felicities of a future world. But if his whole existence be circumscribed within the circle of a few fleeting years, man appears an enigma, an inexplicable phenomenon in the universe, human life a mystery, the world a scene of confusion, virtue a mere phantom, the Creator a capricious being, and his plans and arrangements an inextricable maze.

There is too much reason to believe, that the indifference to religion which so generally prevails, especially among those who are raised a little above the vulgar throng, and the unhallowed propensities and vicious practices to which it gives rise—are owing, in a considerable degree, to the want of a *full conviction* of the reality of a future existence, or to some *doubts* which hover about the mind, in relation to this important point. There is no man, however insensible to the obligations of religion, that can fully satisfy his own mind, or the minds of others, that the idea of a future world is a mere chimera. On the contrary, the possibility, and even the probability, of the truth of man's eternal destiny, will, at certain seasons, force themselves upon the minds even of the most careless and profane. Yet, it is amazing to consider, with what ease and indifference multitudes of this description can glide down the stream of time, under the awful uncertainty whether it will land them in the shades of annihilation, the realms of bliss, or the regions of endless wo.—"Between us and these three periods or states," says a celebrated French writer, "no barrier is interposed but life, the most brittle thing in all nature; and the happiness of heaven being certainly not designed for those who doubt whether they have an immortal part to enjoy it, such persons have nothing left, but the miserable chance of annihilation, or of hell. There is not any reflection which can have more reality than this, as there is none which has greater terror. Let us set the bravest face on our condition, and play the heroes as artfully as we can, yet see here the issue which attends the goodliest life upon earth! It is in vain for men to turn aside their thoughts from this eternity which awaits them, as if they were able to destroy it, by denying it a place in their imagination. It subsists *in spite of them;* it advances unobserved; and death, which is to draw the curtain from it, will, in a short time, infallibly reduce them to the dreadful necessity of being forever nothing, or forever miserable."

To treat a subject so interesting and momentous, with levity or indifference; to exert all the energies of the soul in the pursuit of objects, which a few years, at most, will snatch forever from their embrace; and never to spend one serious hour in reflecting on what may possibly succeed the present scene of existence, or in endeavoring to find some light, to clear up the doubts that may hang over this important inquiry, and to treat with derision and scorn those who would direct them in this serious investigation, is not only foolish and preposterous, but the height of infatuation and of madness. It is contrary to every principle on which reasonable men act, in relation to the affairs of the present world. To retain the profits of a lucrative business, or to prevent the loss of fortune, or of honor, a man will sometimes strain every nerve, stretch every faculty, deprive himself of sleep, submit to numerous privations, encounter the raging elements, and brave the dangers of the ocean. Nay, he will often be overwhelmed with despondency at the slightest inconveniences, and will pass whole weeks and months in sullenness and chagrin, for an imaginary affront, or for the loss of a few pounds, while, at the same time, he remains perfectly indifferent, and without the least emotion, in regard to the unknown scenes of the eternal world, and the danger of endless misery to which he is exposed. Such a conduct, and such dispositions, which are too frequently realized in the case of thousands who occasionally mingle in our religious assemblies, are obviously inconsistent with the dictates of prudence and of common sense, and with every thing that ought to characterize a rational and an accountable creature.

When we look back into the inexplorable abyss of that eternity which is already past; when we look forward to the immeasurable extent, and the unfathomable depth of eternity to come; when we behold *Time*, and all its circling years, appearing only like a point on the surface of that vast and boundless ocean; when we consider the immense spaces of the universe with which we are surrounded, and the innumerable worlds which lie dispersed in every direction throughout the immeasurable tracts of creation; when we consider that our existence, as thinking beings, may run parallel with interminable ages; and that, in the revolutions of eternity, we may exist in regions of space immeasurably distant from our present habitation, associate with other orders of intelligent beings, and pass through new scenes and changes in distant worlds: and, when we consider that our relation to time may be dissolved, and our connexion with eternity commence, within the space of a few months or years, or even before the sun shall have described another circuit around the earth—no inquiry can appear so momentous and interesting, as that which leads to the determination of our future and eternal destiny, and of those realities which await us beyond the tomb. To remain insensible to the importance of such an inquiry, and unaffected at the prospect of the result to which it may lead; while we are feelingly alive to all the paltry concerns and little ills of life, would argue the most unaccountable stupidity, inconsistency and infatuation.

The man whose heart pants after substantial knowledge and felicity, whose affections centre on the Author of his existence, and who delights to contemplate his character and perfections, will enter, with pleasure, on every investigation which has a tendency to throw a light on the scene of his future destination. He will weigh, with impartiality, every consideration, and will seize, with delight, upon every argument by which a full conviction of his immortal destiny may be indelibly riveted upon his mind; and he will endeavor to cheer his soul amidst the sorrows of mortality, with the consideration that "when the earthly house of his tabernacle is dissolved, he has a building of God, an house not made with hands, eternal in the heavens."

In illustrating the evidences of a future state, I shall, in the *first place*, state some of those proofs which reason, or the light of nature, furnishes, of man's eternal destination; and *secondly*, those which are derived from the system of revelation.

# CHAPTER I.

## PROOFS OF A FUTURE STATE FROM THE LIGHT OF NATURE.

The evidences of a future state which the light of reason affords, though not so clear and decisive as those which are derived from divine revelation, are worthy of the serious consideration of every one in whose mind the least doubt remains on this important subject. The conviction they are calculated to produce, when attentively weighed, is sufficient to leave every one without excuse who trifles with the concerns of his future destiny, and overlooks his relation to the eternal world. Though the Deity is invisible to mortal eyes, yet his existence and perfections are clearly demonstrated by his visible operations, and he has not left himself without a witness to his beneficence, in any age, "in his giving rain from heaven, and fruitful seasons, and filling our hearts with food and gladness." In like manner, though the realities of a future world are not presented directly to the eye of sense, yet the faculties with which man is endowed, when properly exercised on all the physical and moral scenes which the universe displays, are sufficient to evince the high degree of probability, if not absolute certainty, that his duration and his sphere of action are not confined to the narrow limits of the present world, but have a relation to a future and an immortal existence.—In illustrating this topic, I shall waive the consideration of several of those metaphysical arguments which have been adduced by philosophers and divines, founded on the immateriality of the human soul, and confine myself chiefly to those popular considerations, which are level to every capacity, and, perhaps, more convincing than the subtle and refined disquisitions of metaphysical minds.

### SECTION I.

#### ON THE UNIVERSAL BELIEF WHICH THE DOCTRINE OF IMMORTALITY HAS OBTAINED IN ALL AGES.

It forms a presumptive proof of the immortality of man, that this doctrine has obtained universal belief among all nations, and in every period of time.

That the thinking principle in man is of an immortal nature, was believed by the ancient Egyptians, the Persians, the Phenicians, the Scythians, the Celts, the Druids, the Assyrians,—by the wisest and the most celebrated characters among the Greeks and Romans, and by almost every other ancient nation and tribe whose records have reached our times. The notions, indeed, which many of them entertained of the scenes of futurity were very obscure and imperfect; but they all embraced the idea, that death is not the destruction of the rational soul, but only its introduction to a new and unknown state of existence. The ancient Scythians believed that death was only a change of habitation; and the Magian sect, which prevailed in Babylonia, Media, Assyria, and Persia, admitted the doctrine of eternal rewards and punishments. The doctrines taught by the second Zoroaster, who lived in the time of Darius, were, "that there is one Supreme Being, independent and self-existent from all eternity; that under him there are two angels, one the angel of light, who is the author of all good; and the other the angel of darkness, who is the author of all evil: that they are in a perpetual struggle with each other; that where the angel of light prevails, there good reigns; and that where the angel of darkness prevails, there evil takes place; that this struggle shall continue to the end of the world: that then there shall be a general resurrection and a day of judgment, wherein all shall receive a just retribution, according to their works. After which, the angel of darkness and his disciples shall go into a world of their own, where they shall suffer, in everlasting darkness, the punishment of their evil deeds; and the angel of light and his disciples shall also go into a world of their own, where they shall receive, in everlasting light, the reward due to their good deeds; that after this they shall remain separated for ever, and light and darkness be no more mixed to all eternity."* The remains of this sect, which are scattered over Persia and India, still hold the same doctrines, without any variation, even at this day.

It is well known, that Plato, Socrates, and other Greek philosophers, held the doctrine of the soul's immortality. In his admirable dialogue, entitled, "The Phædon," Plato represents Socrates, a little before his death, encompassed with a circle of philosophers, and discoursing with them on the arguments which prove the eternal destiny of man. "When the dead," says he, "are arrived at the rendezvous of departed souls, whither their angel conducts them, they are all judged. Those who have passed their lives in a manner neither entirely criminal, nor absolutely

* Rollins' Ancient History, vol. ii.

innocent, are sent into a place where they suffer pains proportioned to their faults, till, being purged and cleansed of their guilt, and afterwards restored to liberty, they receive the reward of the good actions they have done in the body. Those who are judged to be incurable, on account of the greatness of their crimes, the fatal destiny that passes judgment upon them, hurls them into Tartarus, from whence they never depart. Those who are found guilty of crimes, great indeed, but worthy of pardon, who have committed violences, in the transports of rage, against their father or mother, or have killed some one in a like emotion, and afterwards repented—suffer the same punishment with the last, out for a time only, till by prayers and supplications, they have obtained pardon from those they have injured. But those who have passed through life with peculiar sanctity of manners, are received on high into a pure region, where they live without their bodies to all eternity, in a series of joys and delights which cannot be described." From such considerations, Socrates concludes, "if the soul be immortal, it requires to be cultivated with attention, not only for what we call the time of life, but for that which is to follow, I mean eternity; and the least neglect in this point may be attended with endless consequences. If death were the final dissolution of being, the wicked would be great gainers by it, by being delivered at once from their bodies, their souls, and their vices; but as the soul is immortal, it has no other means of being freed from its evils, nor any safety for it, but in becoming very good and very wise; for it carries nothing with it, but its good or bad deeds, its virtues and vices, which are commonly the consequences of the education it has received, and the causes of eternal happiness or misery." Having held such discourses with his friends, he kept silent for some time, and then drank off the whole of the poisonous draught which had been put into his hand, with amazing tranquillity, and an inexpressible serenity of aspect, as one who was about to exchange a short and wretched life, for a blessed and eternal existence.

The descriptions and allusions, contained in the writings of the ancient poets, are a convincing proof, that the notion of the soul's immortality was a universal opinion in the times in which they wrote, and among the nations to whom their writings were addressed. Homer's account of the descent of Ulysses into hell, and his description of Minos in the shades below, distributing justice to the dead assembled in troops around his tribunal, and pronouncing irrevocable judgments, which decide their everlasting fate, demonstrate, that they entertained the belief, that virtues are rewarded, and that crimes are punished, in another state of existence. The poems of Ovid and Virgil contain a variety of descriptions, in which the same opinions are involved. Their notions of future punishment are set forth in the descriptions they give of *Ixion*, who was fastened to a wheel, and whirled about continually with a swift and rapid motion—of *Tantalus*, who, for the loathsome banquet he made for the gods, was set in water up to the chin, with apples hanging to his very lips, yet had no power either to stoop to the one to quench his raging thirst, or to reach to the other to satisfy his craving appetite—of the *fifty daughters of Danaus*, who, for the barbarous massacre of their husbands in one night, were condemned in hell to fill a barrel full of holes with water, which ran out again as fast as it was filled—of *Sisyphus*, who, for his robberies, was set to roll a great stone up a steep hill, which, when it was just at the top, suddenly fell down again, and so renewed his labour—and of *Tityus*, who was adjudged to have a vulture to feed upon his liver and entrails, which still grew and increased as they were devoured.—Their notions of future happiness are imbodied in the descriptions they have given of the Hesperian gardens, and the Elysian fields, where the souls of the virtuous rest secure from every danger, and enjoy perpetual and uninterrupted bliss.

And as the nations of antiquity recognised the doctrine of a future state of existence, so there is scarcely a nation or tribe of mankind, presently existing, however barbarous and untutored, in which the same opinion does not prevail. The natives of the *Society Isles* believe, that after death, there is not only a state of conscious existence, but degrees of eminence and felicity, according as men have been more or less pleasing to the *Eatova*, or Deity, while upon earth. The chiefs of the *Friendly Islands* believe in the immortality of their soul, which, at death, they say is immediately conveyed in a fast-sailing canoe, to a distant country, called Doobludha, which they describe as resembling the Mahometan paradise,—that those who are conveyed thither are no more subject to death, but feast on all the favourite productions of their native soil, with which this blissful abode is plentifully furnished. The *New Zealanders* believe, that the third day after the interment of a man, the heart separates itself from the corpse, and that this separation is announced by a general breeze of wind, which gives warning of its approach, by an inferior divinity that hovers over the grave, and who carries it to the clouds. They believe that the soul of the man whose flesh is devoured by the enemy, is doomed to a perpetual fire, while the soul of the man whose body has been rescued from those that killed him, and the souls of all who die a natural death, ascend to the habitations of the gods. The inhabitants of the *Pelew Islands*, according to the account of Captain Wilson, although they have few religious rites and ceremonies, believe in one Supreme Being, and in a future state of rewards and punishments. In the religion of the *Kaumuc Tartars*, the doctrine of a future state holds a conspicuous place. They believe that hell is situated in the middle region, between heaven and earth, and their devils are represented with all sorts of frightful forms, of a black and hideous aspect, with the heads of goats, lions, and unicorns. Their holy lamas, who have obtained a victory over all their passions, are supposed to pass immediately into heaven, where they enjoy perfect rest, and exercise themselves in divine service. The *Samoiedians* of Northern Tartary believe, that there is one Supreme Being, that he is our all-merciful and common Parent, and that he will reward with a happy state hereafter, those who live virtuously in this world. The *Birmans* believe in the transmigration of souls, after which, they maintain, that the radically bad will be sentenced to lasting punishment, while the good will enjoy eternal happiness on a mountain called Meru.

The various tribes which inhabit the continent of Africa, in so far as we are acquainted with their religious opinions, appear to recognise the doctrine of a future state. "I was lately discoursing on this subject," says Mr. Addison, in one of his Spectators, "with a learned person, who has been very much conversant among the inhabitants of the most western parts of Africa. Upon his conversing with several in that country, he tells me, that their notions of heaven or of a future state of happiness, is this—that every thing we there wish for will immediately present itself to us. We find, say they, that our souls are of such a nature that they require variety, and are not capable of being always delighted with the same objects. The Supreme Being, therefore, in compliance with this state of happiness which he has implanted in the soul of man, will raise up, from time to time, say they, every gratification which it is in the human nature to be pleased with. If we wish to be in groves or bowers, among running streams or falls of water, we shall immediately find ourselves in the midst of such a scene as we desire. If we would be entertained with music, and the melody of sounds, the concert arises upon our wish, and the whole region about us is filled with harmony. In short, every desire will be followed by fruition; and whatever a man's inclination directs him to, will be present with him."—The Negroes, and other inhabitants of the interior of Africa, according to the account of Mr. Park, believe in one Supreme Ruler, and expect hereafter to enter into a state of misery or felicity. The Gallas of Abyssinia, though they reject the doctrine of future punishment, admit the reality of a future state. The Mandingoes, the Jaloffs, the Feloops, the Foulahs, the Moors, and all the other tribes who have embraced the Mahometan faith, recognise the doctrine of the immortality of the soul, and of future rewards in a celestial paradise. The natives of Dahomy entertain the same belief; and hence, it is a common practice with the sovereign of that country, to send an account to his forefathers of any remarkable event, by delivering a message to whoever may happen to be near him at the time, and then ordering his head to be chopped off immediately, that he may serve as a courier, to convey intelligence to the world of spirits.*

The Persians are said to leave one part of their graves open, from a belief that the dead will be reanimated, and visited by angels, who will appoint them to their appropriate abodes in a future state. From a similar belief, thousands of Hindoo widows annually sacrifice themselves on the funeral piles of their deceased husbands, in the hope of enjoying with them the felicities of eternal life.—The Japanese believe, that the souls of men and beasts are alike immortal; that a just distribution of rewards and punishments takes place after death; that there are different degrees of happiness, as well as of punishment, and that the souls of the wicked transmigrate, after death, into the bodies of animals, and at last, in case of amendment, are translated back again into the human form.† From a conviction of the reality of a future world, the Wahabee Arabs regard it as impious to mourn for the dead, who, they say, are enjoying felicity with Mahomet in paradise; and the Javanese make several feasts, on the decease of their friends and relations, to commemorate their entrance into a world of bliss.—The North American Indians believe that, beyond the most distant mountains of their country, there is a wide river; beyond that river a great country; on the other side of that country, a world of water; in that water are a thousand islands, full of trees and streams of water, and that a thousand buffaloes, and ten thousand deer, graze on the hills, or ruminate in the valleys. When they die, they are persuaded that the Great Spirit will conduct them to this land of souls.

Thus it appears, that not only the philosophers of antiquity, and the most civilized nations presently existing on the globe, have recognised the doctrine of the immortality of man, but that even the most savage and untutored tribes fortify their minds in the prospect of death, with the hope of a happiness commensurate to their desires, in the regions beyond the grave.

"E'en the poor Indian whose untutor'd mind
Sees God in clouds, or hears him in the wind,
Whose soul proud science never taught to stray
Far as the solar walk or milky way—
Yet simple nature to his hope has given
Behind the cloud-topt hill an humbler heaven;
Some safer world in depth of woods embraced,
Some happier island in the watery waste,
Where slaves once more their native land behold,
No fiends torment, no Christians thirst for gold,—
And thinks, admitted to yon equal sky,
His faithful dog shall bear him company."—*Pope.*

* M'Leod's Voyage to Africa, 1820, p. 64.
† Thunberg's Travels.

Among the numerous and diversified tribes that are scattered over the different regions of the earth, that agree in scarcely any other sentiment or article of religious belief, we here find the most perfect harmony, in their recognition of a Supreme Intelligence, and in their belief that the soul survives the dissolution of its mortal frame. And, as Cicero long since observed, "In every thing the consent of all nations is to be accounted the law of nature, and to resist it, is to resist the voice of God." For we can scarcely suppose, in consistency with the divine perfections, that an error, on a subject of so vast importance to mankind, should obtain the universal belief of all nations and ages, and that God himself would suffer a world of rational beings, throughout every generation, to be carried away by a delusion, and to be tantalized by a hope which has no foundation in nature, and which is contrary to the plan of his moral government. It is true, indeed, that several of the opinions to which I have now adverted, and many others which prevail among the uncivilized tribes of mankind, in regard to the *condition* of disembodied spirits, and the *nature* of future happiness, are very erroneous and imperfect; but they all recognise this grand and important truth, that death is not the destruction of the rational soul, and that man is destined to an immortal existence. Their erroneous conceptions in respect to the rewards and punishments of the future world may be easily accounted for, from a consideration of the imperfect conceptions they have formed of the Divine Being, and of the principles of his moral government; from their ignorance of those leading principles and moral laws, by which the Almighty regulates the intelligent universe; from the false ideas they have been led to entertain respecting the nature of substantial happiness; from the cruel and absurd practices connected with the system of pagan superstition; from the intellectual darkness which has brooded over the human race ever since the fall of man; and from the universal prevalence of those depraved dispositions and affections, which characterize the untutored tribes on whom the light of revelation has never shone.

To whatever cause this universal belief of a future existence is to be traced—whether to a universal tradition derived from the first parents of the human race; to an innate sentiment originally impressed on the soul of man; to a divine revelation disseminated and handed down from one generation to another, or to the deductions of human reason—it forms a strong presumption, and a powerful argument, in favour of the position we are now endeavouring to support. If it is to be traced back to the original progenitors of mankind, it must be regarded as one of those truths which were recognised by man in a state of innocence, when his affections were pure, and his understanding fortified against delusion and error. If it be a sentiment which was originally impressed on the human soul by the hand of its Creator, we do violence to the law of our nature, when we disregard its intimations, or attempt to resist the force of its evidence. If it ought to be considered as originally derived from Revelation, then it is corroborative of the truth of the Sacred Records, in which "life and immortality" are clearly exhibited. And, if it be regarded as likewise one of the deductions of natural reason, we are left without excuse, if we attempt to obscure its evidence, or to overlook the important consequences which it involves.—As the consent of all nations has been generally considered as a powerful argument for the existence of a Deity, so the universal belief of mankind in the doctrine of a future state ought to be viewed as a strong presumption that it is founded upon truth. The human mind is so constituted, that, when left to its native unbiassed energies, it necessarily infers the existence of a Supreme Intelligence, from the existence of matter, and the economy of the material world; and, from the nature of the human faculties, and the moral attributes of God, it is almost as infallibly led to conclude, that a future existence is necessary, in order to gratify the boundless desires of the human soul, and to vindicate the wisdom and rectitude of the moral Governor of the world. These two grand truths, which constitute the foundation of all religion, and of every thing that is interesting to man as an intelligent agent, are interwoven with the theological creed of all nations; and, in almost every instance, where the one is called in question, the other is undermined or denied: so that the doctrine of the immortality of man may be considered as resting on the same foundation as the existence of a Supreme Intelligence.

It must indeed be admitted, that individuals have appeared in every age, who have endeavoured to call in question, or to deny, this fundamental truth. But this circumstance forms no valid objection to the force of the argument to which I have now adverted. For the number of such persons has been extremely small, when compared with the mass of mankind; and their opinions on this subject have generally originated either from wilful ignorance; from an affectation of singularity and of appearing superior to vulgar fears; or from indulging in a course of wickedness and impiety, which has led them to wish, and if possible to believe, that there are neither punishments nor rewards beyond the grave. If it appear strange and unnatural that any man should wish his soul to be mortal, Hierocles assigns the true reason of it: "A wicked man," says he, "is afraid of his judge, and therefore wishes his soul and body may perish together by death, rather than it should appear before the tribunal of God." If a number of fools should think fit to put out their own eyes, to prevent them from feeling the effects of light, as Democritus, the ancient philosopher, was said to have done, it would form no argument to prove that all the rest of the world was blind. And, if a few sceptics and profligates endeavour to blind the eyes of their understanding by sophistry and licentiousness, it cannot prevent the light of reason, which unveils the realities of a future world, from shining on the rest of mankind, nor constitute the slightest argument to prove the fallacy of the doctrine they deny.

---

## SECTION II.

### ON THE DESIRE OF FUTURE EXISTENCE IMPLANTED IN THE HUMAN MIND.

Those strong and restless desires after future existence and enjoyment, which are implanted in the soul of man, are a strong presumptive proof that he is possessed of an immortal nature.

There is no human being who feels full satisfaction in his present enjoyments. The mind is for ever on the wing in the pursuit of new acquirements, of new objects, and, if possible, of higher degrees of felicity, than the present moment can afford. However exquisite any particular enjoyment may sometimes be found, it soon begins to lose its relish, and to pall the intellectual appetite. Hence the voracious desire, apparent among all ranks, for variety of amusements, both of a sensitive, and of an intellectual nature. Hence the keen desire for novelty, for tales of wonder, for beautiful and splendid exhibitions, and for intelligence respecting the passing occurrences of the day. Hence the eagerness with which the daily newspapers are read by all ranks who have it in their power to procure them. However novel or interesting the events which are detailed to-day, an appetite for fresh intelligence is excited before to-morrow. Amidst the numerous objects which are daily soliciting attention, amidst the variety of intelligence which newsmongers have carefully selected for the gratification of every taste, and amidst the fictitious scenes depicted by the novelist and the poet—"the eye is not satisfied with seeing, nor the ear with hearing." Hence, too, the insatiable desires of the miser in accumulating riches, and the unremitting career of ambition, in its pursuit of honours and of fame. And hence the ardour with which the philosopher prosecutes one discovery after another, without ever arriving at a resting-point, or sitting down contented with his present attainments. When Archimedes had discovered the mode of determining the relative quantities of gold and silver in Hiero's crown, did he rest satisfied with this new acquirement? No. The ecstacy he felt at the discovery, when he leaped from the bath, and ran naked through the streets of Syracuse, crying, "I have found it, I have found it"—soon subsided into indifference, and his mind pushed forward in quest of new discoveries. When Newton ascertained the law of universal gravitation, and Franklin discovered the identity of lightning and the electric fluid, and felt the transports which such discoveries must have excited, did they slacken their pace in the road of scientific discovery, or sit down contented with their past researches? No. One discovery gave a stimulus to the pursuit of another, and their career of improvement only terminated with their lives. After Alexander had led his victorious armies over Persia, Babylonia, Syria, Egypt, and India, and had conquered the greater part of the known world, did he sit down in peace, and enjoy the fruit of his conquests? No. His desires after new projects, and new expeditions, remained insatiable; his ambition rose even to madness; and when the philosopher Anaxarchus told him, there was an infinite number of worlds, he wept at the thought that his conquests were confined to *one*.

These restless and unbounded desires are to be found agitating the breasts of men of all nations, of all ranks and conditions in life. If we ascend the thrones of princes, if we enter the palaces of the great, if we walk through the mansions of courtiers and statesmen, if we pry into the abodes of poverty and indigence, if we mingle with poets or philosophers, with manufacturers, merchants, mechanics, peasants, or beggars; if we survey the busy, bustling scene of a large city, the sequestered village, or the cot which stands in the lonely desert—we shall find, in every situation, and among every class, beings animated with desires of happiness, which no present enjoyment can gratify, and which no object within the limits of time can fully satiate. Whether we choose to indulge in ignorance, or to prosecute the path of knowledge; to loiter in indolence, or to exert our active powers with unremitting energy; to mingle with social beings, or to flee to the haunts of solitude,—we feel a vacuum in the mind, which nothing around us can fill up; a longing after new objects and enjoyments, which nothing earthly can fully satisfy. Regardless of the past, and unsatisfied with the present, the soul of man feasts itself on the hope of enjoyments which it has never yet possessed

> "Hope springs eternal in the human breast;
> Man never *is*, but always *to be* blest.
> The soul uneasy, and confined from home,
> Rests and expatiates in a life to come."

That the desire of immortality is common, and natural to all men, appears from a variety of actions, which can scarcely be accounted for on any other principle, and which prove that the mind feels conscious of its immortal destiny Why, otherwise, should men be anxious about their reputation, and solicitous to secure their names from oblivion, and to perpetuate their fame, after they have descended into the grave? To accomplish such objects, and to gratify such desires, poets, orators, and historians, have been flattered and rewarded to celebrate their actions; monuments of marble and of brass have been erected to represent their persons, and inscriptions engraved in the solid rock, to convey to future generations a record of the exploits they had achieved. Lofty columns, triumphal arches, towering pyramids, magnificent temples, palaces, and mausoleums have been reared, to eternize their fame, and to make them live, as it were, in the eyes of their successors, through all the future ages of time. But, if the soul be destined to destruction at the hour of death, why should man be anxious about what shall happen, or what shall not happen hereafter, when he is reduced to a mere non-entity, and banished for ever from the universe of God? He can have no interest in any events that may befall the living world when he is cancelled from the face of creation, and when the spark of intelligence he possessed is quenched in everlasting night. If any man be fully convinced that the grave puts a final period to his existence, the only *consistent* action he can perform, when he finds his earthly wishes and expectations frustrated, is to rush into the arms of death, and rid himself at once of all the evils connected with his being. But we find the great majority of mankind, notwithstanding the numerous ills to which they are subjected, still clinging with eagerness to their mortal existence, and looking forward, with a certain degree of hope, to a termination of their sorrows.

—"They rather choose to bear those ills they have
Than fly to others that they know not of."

There is, I presume, no individual in a sound state of mind, who can entirely throw aside all concern about his posthumous reputation, and about the events that may happen in the world after his decease. And if so, it clearly demonstrates, not only that he does not *wish*, but that he does not even *suppose* that his existence will be for ever extinguished at death. The idea of the shame of being exposed naked after their death, produced such a powerful effect upon the minds of the Milesian virgins, that it deterred them from putting an end to their lives, after all other arguments had been tried in vain.* The desire of existence—and of existence, too, which has no termination, appears to be the foundation of all our desires, and of all the plans we form in life. Annihilation cannot be an object of desire to any rational being. We desire something that is *real*, something that is connected with *happiness or enjoyment*, but non-existence has no object nor concern whatever belonging to it. When a wicked man, under a consciousness of guilt, indulges a wish for annihilation after death, it is not because non-existence *is in itself an object of desire*, but he would choose it as the least of two evils: he would rather be blotted out of creation, than suffer the punishment due to his sins in the eternal world.

It may also be remarked, that the desire of immortality, however vigorous it may be in ordinary minds, becomes still more glowing and ardent in proportion as the intellect is cultivated and expanded, and in proportion as the soul rises to higher and higher degrees of virtue and moral excellence. It forms a powerful stimulus to the performance of actions which are noble, generous, public-spirited, benevolent, and humane, and which have a tendency to promote the intellectual improvement, and the happiness of future generations. Hence the most illustrious characters of the heathen world, the poets, the orators, the moralists and philosophers of antiquity, had their minds fired with the idea of immortality, and many of them were enabled to brave death without dismay, under the conviction that it was the messenger which was to waft their spirits to the realms of endless bliss. When Demosthenes had fled for shelter to an asylum from the resentment of Antipater, who had sent Archias to bring him by force, and when Archias promised upon his honour that he should not lose his life, if he would voluntarily make his personal appearance:—"God forbid," said he, "that after I have heard Xenocrates and Plato discourse so divinely on the immortality of the soul, I should prefer a life of infamy and disgrace to an honourable death." Even those who were not fully convinced of the doctrine of immortality, amidst all their doubts and perplexities on this point, *earnestly wished that it might prove true*, and few, if any of them, absolutely denied it. Hence, too, the noble and disinterested actions which Christian heroes have performed, under the influence of unseen and everlasting things. They have faced dangers and persecutions in every shape; they have endured "cruel mockings, scourgings, bonds, and imprisonments;" they have triumphed under the torments of the rack, and amidst the raging flames; they have surmounted every obstacle in their benevolent exertions to communicate blessings to their fellow-men; they have braved the fury of the raging elements, traversed sea and land, and pushed their way to distant barbarous climes, in order to point out to their benighted inhabitants the path that leads to eternal life. Nor do they think it too dear to sacrifice their lives in such services,

* "I beseech men for God's sake, (says Hale,) that if at any time there arise in them a desire or a wish that others should speak well of their death; then at that time they would seriously consider, whether those motions are not from some spirit to continue a spirit, after it leaves its earthly habitation, rather than from an earthly spirit, a vapour which cannot act, or imagine, or desire, or fear things beyond its continuance."

since "they *desire* a better country," and feel assured that death will introduce them to "an exceeding great and an eternal weight of glory."

Since, then, it appears that the desire of immortality is common to mankind, that the soul is incessantly looking forward to the enjoyment of some future good, and that this desire has been the spring of actions the most beneficent, and heroic, on what principle is it to be accounted for?

'Whence springs this pleasing hope, this fond desire,
This longing after immortality?
Or, whence this secret dread, and inward horror,
Of falling into nought?—Why shrinks the soul
Back on herself, and startles at destruction?"

Whence proceeds the want we feel amidst the variety of objects which surround us? Whence arises the disgust that so quickly succeeds every enjoyment? Wherefore can we never cease from wishing for something more exquisite than we have ever yet possessed? No satisfactory answer can be given to such questions, if our duration be circumscribed within the limits of time; and if we shall be blotted out of creation when our earthly tabernacles are laid in the dust. The desires to which I now refer appear to be an essential part of the human constitution, and, consequently, were implanted in our nature by the hand of our Creator;—and, therefore, we must suppose, either that the desire of immortality will be gratified, or that the Creator takes delight in tantalizing his creatures with hopes and expectations which will end in eternal disappointment. To admit the latter supposition, would be inconsistent with every rational idea we can form of the moral attributes of the Divinity. It would be inconsistent with his *veracity;* for to encourage hopes and desires which are never intended to be gratified, is the characteristic of a deceiver, and therefore contrary to every conception we can form of the conduct of "a God of truth." It would be inconsistent with his *rectitude;* for every such deception implies an act of injustice towards the individual who is thus tantalized. It would be inconsistent with his *wisdom;* for it would imply that he has no other means of governing the intelligent creation, than those which have a tendency to produce fallacious hopes and fears in the minds of his rational offspring. It would be inconsistent with his *benevolence;* for as "the desire accomplished is sweet to the soul," so disappointed hopes uniformly tend to produce misery. Yet the benevolence of the Deity, in every other point of view, is most strikingly displayed in all his arrangements in the material universe, and towards every species of sensitive existence.

What has been now stated in relation to desire and hope, will equally apply to those *fears* and apprehensions, which frequently arise in the mind in reference to the punishments of a future world. A Being possessed of perfect benevolence cannot be supposed to harass his intelligent creatures, and to render their lives bitter with alarming apprehensions, for which there is not the slightest foundation. But, if there is no state either of punishment or reward beyond the grave, those desires of immortal duration, which seem at first view to elevate man above the other inhabitants of this globe, actually place him below the level of the beasts, which bound through the forests and lawns, and find their chief enjoyment in browsing on the grass. They are alive to present enjoyment, but appear to have no anticipations of the future; they feel present pain, but there is no reason to believe that they are ever tormented with fears or forebodings of future punishment. They are contented with the organs with which Nature has furnished them; they appear fully satisfied with ranging the fields and feasting on the herbage; their desires need no restraint, and their wishes are completely gratified; and what pleased them yesterday will likewise give them pleasure to-morrow, without being harassed with insatiable desires after novelty and variety. They live divested of those innumerable cares and anxieties which harass and perplex the children of men, and they never wish to go beyond the boundary which nature prescribes. "The ingenious bee constructs commodious cells, but never dreams of rearing triumphal arches or obelisks to decorate her waxen city." Through ignorance of the future, they pass from life to death, with as much indifference as from watching to sleep, or from labour to repose. But man, amidst all the enjoyments and prospects which surround him, feels uneasy and unsatisfied, because he pants after happiness infinite in duration. His hopes and desires overstep the bounds of time and of every period we can affix to duration, and move onward through a boundless eternity. And if he is to be for ever cut off from existence when his body drops into the grave, how dismal the continued apprehension of an everlasting period being put to all his enjoyments after a prospect of immortality has been opened to his view!

How, then, shall we account for these anomalies? How shall we reconcile these apparent inconsistencies? In what light shall we exhibit the conduct of the Creator, so as to render it consistent with itself? There is but one conclusion we can form, in consistency with the moral attributes of God, which will completely unravel the mystery of man being animated with unbounded desires, and yet confined to a short and limited duration in the present world, and that is,—that this world is not the place of our final destination, but introductory to a more glorious and permanent state of existence, where the desires of virtuous minds will be completely gratified, and their hopes fully realized. I do not see how any other conclusion can be drawn, witnout denying both the *moral character*, and even the *very existence* of the Deity.

---

## SECTION III.

### ON THE INTELLECTUAL FACULTIES OF MAN, AND THE STRONG DESIRE OF KNOWLEDGE WHICH IS IMPLANTED IN THE HUMAN MIND.

The principle of curiosity, or the strong desire of knowledge which is implanted in the mind of man, and the noble intellectual faculties for acquiring it with which he is endowed, are evidences and proofs of his immortal destination.

Though this argument may be considered, by some, as only a branch of the preceding, it may not be inexpedient, for the sake of impression, to consider it separately, as it will admit of reasonings and illustrations distinct from those which have now been brought forward.

The desire of knowledge is natural to every rational being, and appears to be a fundamental part of the constitution of the human mind. It is perceptible even in the first stage of its progress, and has a powerful influence over the movements and the enjoyments of the young. Present to a child a beautiful landscape, as exhibited through an optical machine, and it will be highly delighted with the exhibition. Present a second and a third of a different description, in succession, and its delight will be increased; it will anxiously desire exhibitions of new and varied objects, and its curiosity will never be satisfied but with a constant succession of scenes and objects which tend to widen the circle of its knowledge, and enlarge the capacity of its mind. Hence the keen desires of the young for shows, spectacles, processions and public exhibitions of every description, and the delight which they feel in making excursions from one scene to another. Hence the delight with which travellers traverse the Alpine scenes of nature, cross seas and oceans, descend into the gloomy subterraneous cavern, or climb to the summit of the flaming volcano, notwithstanding the fatigues and perils to which they are exposed.

"For such the bounteous providence of Heaven
In every breast implanting the desire
Of objects new and strange, to urge us on
With unremitted labour to pursue
Those sacred stores that wait the ripening soul,
In Truth's exhaustless bosom.———
——————— For this the daring youth
Breaks from his weeping mother's anxious arms,
In foreign climes to rove; the pensive sage
Heedless of sleep, or midnight's harmful damp,
Hangs o'er the sickly taper; and untired
The virgin follows with enchanted step
The mazes of some wild and wondrous tale,
From morn to eve."——— *Akenside.*

If the desire of knowledge appears, in many instances, to be less ardent in after life, it is owing in a great measure to the methods of our education, and the false principles on which we attempt to convey instruction to the youthful mind. Our initiatory instructions, hitherto, present the young with little more than the *key* of knowledge, instead of *knowledge itself*. We lead them to the threshold of the temple of science without attempting to unfold its treasures. We deem it sufficient that they be taught to pronounce, like a number of puppets, a multitude of *sounds* and terms to which they attach no distinct conceptions, while we decline to communicate clear and well-defined *ideas*. We load their memories with technical phrases and propositions which they do not understand, while the objects of substantial science are carefully concealed both from the eye of sense and from the eyes of their understandings. Instead of leading them by gentle steps, in the first stage of their progress, over the grand, and beautiful, and variegated scenery of Nature and Revelation, where almost every object is calculated to arrest their attention, and to excite admiration,—we confound them with an unintelligible jargon of grammar rules, of metaphysical subtleties, and of dead languages, associated with stripes, confinement, and painful recollections, which frequently produce a disgust at every thing which has acquired the name of learning, before they are made acquainted with that in which true knowledge consists. Yet, notwithstanding the injudicious methods by which we attempt to train the youthful intellect, it is impossible to eradicate the desire of knowledge from the human mind. When substantial knowledge is presented to the mind, in a judicious and alluring manner, it will not only be relished, but prosecuted with ardour, by every one whose faculties are not altogether immersed in the mire of sensuality. Let a man, however ignorant and untutored, be made acquainted with some of the interesting details of Geography, with the wonders of the ocean, and the numerous rivers continually rolling into its abyss, with the lofty ranges of mountains which stretch along the continents, and project their summits beyond the clouds, with the volcanoes, the tornadoes, the water-spouts, and the sublime and beautiful landscapes which diversify the different climates of the earth; with the numerous tribes of animated beings which people its surface, and the manners and customs of its human inhabitants—he will feel an eager desire to know every thing else that appertains to this subject, and will prosecute his inquiries with avidity, in so far as his means and opportunities permit. Acquaint him with some of the most striking facts in ancient and modern history, and he will feel a desire to know every thing of importance that has occurred in the annals of the world since the commencement of time. Unfold to him some of the discoveries which have been made in relation to the constitution of the atmosphere, the electric, magnetic, and galvanic fluids, and the chymical changes and operations that are constantly going on in the animal, vegetable, and mineral kingdoms, and his curiosity will be strongly excited to penetrate still farther into the mysteries of nature. Direct his views to the concave of the firmament, and tell him of the vast magnitude of the sun, and the planetary globes, the amazing velocity with which they run their destined rounds, and of the immense number and distances of the stars—and he will eagerly pant after more minute information respecting the great bodies of the universe, and feel delighted at hearing of new discoveries being made in the unexplored regions of creation.

I never knew an instance in which knowledge of this description was communicated *in a rational, distinct, and alluring manner*, where it was not received with a certain degree of pleasure, and with an ardent desire to make further investigations into the wonders of creating wisdom and power. Such appears to be the original constitution of the human mind, that it is necessarily gratified with every thing that gives scope to the exercise of its faculties, and which has a tendency to extend the range of their action. It is true, indeed, that, in some men, the desire of knowledge appears to be blunted and almost annihilated, so that they appear to be little superior in their views to the lower orders of sensitive existence. But this happens only in those cases where the intellectual faculties are benumbed and stupified by *indolence* and *sensuality*. Such persons do all they can to *counteract* the original propensities of their nature; and yet even in the worst cases of this kind that can occur, the original desire is never altogether extirpated, so long as the senses are qualified to perform their functions. For the most brutish man is never found entirely divested of the principle of curiosity, when any striking or extraordinary object is presented to his view. On such an occasion, the original principles of his constitution will be roused into action, and he will feel a certain degree of wonder and delight in common with other rational minds.

And, as man has a natural desire after knowledge, and a delight in it—so, he is furnished *with noble faculties and vast capacities of intellect* for enabling him to acquire, and to treasure it up. He is furnished with *senses* calculated to convey ideas of the forms, qualities, and relations of the various objects which surround him. His sense of vision, in particular, appears to take in a wider range of objects, than that of any other sensitive being. While some of the lower animals have their vision circumscribed within a circle of a few yards or inches in diameter, the eye of man can survey, at one glance, an extensive landscape, and penetrate even to the regions of distant worlds. To this sense we are indebted for our knowledge of the sublimest objects which can occupy the mind, and for the ideas we have acquired of the boundless range of creation. And, while it is fitted to trace the motions of mighty worlds, which roll at the distance of a thousand millions of miles, it is also so constructed, as to enable him, with the assistance of art, to survey the myriads of living beings which people a drop of water. All his other senses are likewise calculated to extend the range of his knowledge, to enable him to communicate his ideas to others, and to facilitate the mutual interchanges of thought and sentiment between rational minds of a similar construction with his own.

His understanding is capable of taking in a vast variety of sentiments and ideas in relation to the immense multiplicity of objects which are perceived by his external senses. Hence the various sciences he has cultivated, the sublime discoveries he has made, and the noble inventions he has brought to light. By the powers of his understanding, he has surveyed the terraqueous globe, in all its varieties of land and water, continents, islands and oceans; determined its magnitude, its weight, its figure and motions; explored its interior recesses, descended into the bottom of its seas, arranged and classified the infinite variety of vegetables, minerals, and animals which it contains, analysed the invisible atmosphere with which it is surrounded, and determined the elementary principles of which it is composed, discovered the nature of thunder, and arrested the rapid lightnings in their course, ascertained the laws by which the planets are directed in their courses, weighed the masses of distant worlds, determined their size and distances, and explored regions of the universe invisible to the unassisted eye, whose distance exceeds all human calculation and comprehension. The sublime sciences of Geometry, Trigonometry, Conic Sections, Fluxions, Algebra, and other branches of Mathematics, evince the acuteness and perspicacity of his intellect; and their application to the purposes of Navigation and Geography, and to the determination of the laws of the celestial motions, the periods of their revolutions, their eclipses, and the distances at which they are placed from our sublunary mansion, demonstrate the vigour and comprehension of those reasoning faculties with which he is endowed.

By means of the instruments and contrivances which his inventive faculty has enabled him to form and construct, he can transport ponderous masses across the ocean, determine the exact position in which he is at any time placed upon its surface, direct his course along pathless deserts and through the billows of the mighty deep;—transform a portion of *steam* into a mechanical power for impelling waggons along roads, and large vessels with great velocity against wind and tide; and can even transport himself through the yielding air beyond the region of the clouds. He can explore the invisible worlds which are contained in a putrid lake, and bring to view their numerous and diversified inhabitants; and the next moment he can penetrate to regions of the universe immeasurably distant, and contemplate the mountains and the vales, the rocks and the plains which diversify the scenery of distant surrounding worlds. He can extract an invisible substance from a piece of coal, by which he can produce, almost in a moment, the most splendid illumination throughout every part of a large and populous city,—he can detach the element of fire from the invisible air, and cause the hardest stones, and the heaviest metals to melt like wax under its powerful agency; and he can direct the lightnings of heaven to accomplish his purposes, in splitting immense stones into a multitude of fragments. He can cause a splendid city, adorned with lofty columns, palaces, and temples, to arise, in a spot where nothing was formerly beheld but a vast desert or a putrid marsh; and can make "the wilderness and the solitary place to be glad, and the desert to bud and blossom as the rose." He can communicate his thoughts and sentiments in a few hours, to ten hundred thousands of his fellow-men; in a few weeks, to the whole civilized world; and, after his decease, he can diffuse important instructions among mankind, throughout succeeding generations.—In short, he can look back, and trace the most memorable events which have happened in the world since time began; he can survey the present aspect of the moral world among all nations;—he can penetrate beyond the limits of all that is visible in the immense canopy of heaven, and range amidst the infinity of unknown systems and worlds dispersed throughout the boundless regions of creation, and he can overleap the bounds of time, and expatiate amidst future scenes of beauty and sublimity, which "eye hath not seen," throughout the countless ages of eternity.

What an immense multitude of ideas, in relation to such subjects, must the mind of such a person as *Lord Bacon* have contained! whose mental eye surveyed the whole circle of human science, and who pointed out the path by which every branch of knowledge may be carried towards perfection! How sublime and diversified must have been the range of thought pursued by the immortal *Newton!* whose capacious intellect seemed to grasp the vast system of universal nature, who weighed the ponderous masses of the planetary globes, and unfolded the laws by which their diversified phenomena are produced, and their motions directed!

"He, while on this dim spot, where mortals toil,
Clo'ded in dust,—from Motion's simple laws
Could trace the secret hand of Providence,
Wide-working through this universal frame.
—All intellectual eye, our solar round
First gazing through, he, by the blended power
Of Gravitation and Projection, saw
The whole in silent harmony revolve.
—Then breaking hence, he took his ardent flight
Through the blue infinite, and every star
Which the clear concave of a winter's night
Pours on the eye, or astronomic tube,—
——————— at his approach
Blazed into suns, the living centre each
Of an harmonious system."———

Such minds as those of Socrates, Plato, Archimedes, Locke, Boyle, La Place, and similar illustrious characters, likewise demonstrate the vast capacity of the human intellect, the extensive range of thought it is capable of prosecuting, and the immense number of ideas it is capable of acquiring. And every man, whose faculties are in a sound state, is endowed with similar powers of thought, and is capable of being trained to similar degrees of intellectual excellence.

And as man is endued with capacious intellectual powers for the *acquisition* of knowledge, so he is furnished with a noble faculty by which he is enabled *to retain*, and *to treasure up* in his intellect the knowledge he acquires. He is endowed with the faculty of *memory*, by which the mind retains the ideas of past objects and perceptions, accompanied with a persuasion, that the objects or things remembered were formerly real and present. Without with faculty we could never advance a single step in the path of mental improvement. If the information we originally derive through the medium of the senses were to vanish the moment the objects are removed from our immediate perception, we should be left as devoid of knowledge as if we had never existed. But, by the power of memory, we can treasure up, as in a storehouse, the greater part, if not the whole of the ideas, notions, reasonings, and perceptions which we formerly acquired, and render them subservient to our future progress in intellectual attainments. And it is probable, that even a human spirit, in the vigorous exercise of the faculties with which it is now furnished, may go forward, through an interminable duration, making continual accessions to its stores of knowledge, without losing one leading idea, or portion of information which it had previously acquired.

The power of memory in retaining past impressions, and its susceptibility of improvement, are vastly greater than is generally imagined. In many individuals, both in ancient and in modern times, it has been found in such a state of perfection, as to excite astonishment, and almost to transcend belief. It is reported of Seneca, that he could repeat two thousand verses at once, in their order, and then begin at the end and rehearse them backwards, without missing a single syllable. Cyrus is said to have been able to call every individual of his numerous army by is own name. Cyneas, who was sent by Pyrrhus to the Senate at Rome, on an expedition, the very next day after his arrival, both knew and also saluted by their names, all the Senate, and the whole order of the gentlemen in Rome. Mithridates, who governed twenty-three nations, all of different languages, could converse with every one of them in their own language.* An ancient author mentions one Oritus, a Corsican boy, to whom he dictated a great number of words both sense and nonsense, and finding he could rehearse a considerable number without missing one, and in the same order in which he dictated them, increased them to the number of forty thousand, and found, to his astonishment, that he could repeat them all from beginning to end, or from the end backwards to the beginning, in the order in which they were dictated.

In modern times, there have likewise been many instances of extraordinary powers of retention. Dr. Wallis, in a paper in the Philosophical Transactions, informs us that he extracted the cube root of the number *three*, even to thirty places of decimals, by the help of his memory alone. Maglia Bethi, an Italian, had read all the books that were published in his life time, and most of those which were published before, and could not only give an account of what was contained in each author, but could likewise, from memory, quote the chapter, section, and page of any book he had read, and repeat the author's own words, in reference to any particular topic. A gentleman, in order to try his memory, lent him a long manuscript he was about to publish, and after it had been returned, called upon him soon afterwards, pretending he had lost it, and desired him to write as much of it as he could remember; when, to his surprise, he wrote it over accurately word for word, the same as in the manuscript he had lent him. M. Euler, a late celebrated mathematician and philosopher, who died in 1783, having lost his sight by too intense application to study, afterwards composed his "Elements of Algebra," and a work "On the inequalities of the planetary motions," that required immense and complicated calculations, which he performed by his memory alone, to the admiration and astonishment even of the philosophic world. His memory seemed to retain every idea that was conveyed to it, either from reading or from meditation, and his powers of reasoning and of discrimination were equally acute and capacious. He was also an excellent classical scholar, and could repeat the Æneid of Virgil from the beginning to the end, and indicate the first and last line of every page of the edition he used.† I have conversed with an individual, who was born blind, and who could repeat the whole of the Old and New Testaments from beginning to end; and not only so, but could repeat any particular chapter or *verse* that might be proposed to him, the moment after it was specified.

Thus it appears that man is not only possessed of an ardent desire after knowledge, but is endued with the most penetrating and capacious powers of intellect, both for acquiring and for treasuring it up in his mind—powers which appear susceptible of indefinite improvement in this world; and the legitimate inference that may be drawn from this, is, that they will continue to be exerted with uninterrupted activity, throughout an unceasing duration. And, is it possible to suppose, in consistency with the moral attributes of the Deity, that the exercise of such powers is intended to be confined within the narrow limits of time, and to the contracted sphere of the terraqueous globe?

————"Say, can a soul possess'd
Of such extensive, deep, tremendous powers
Enlarging still, be but a finer breath
Of spirits dancing through their tubes a while,
And then for ever lost in vacant air?"

Such a conclusion never can be admitted while we recognise the divinity as possessed of boundless goodness and unerring wisdom. It is the province of goodness to gratify those pure and ardent desires which it has implanted in the soul; and it is the part of wisdom to proportionate means to ends. But if the whole existence of human beings had been intended to be confined to a mere point in duration, is it rational to suppose, that Infinite Wisdom would have endowed the human soul with powers and capacities so marvellous and sublime, and made so many great preparations and arrangements for promoting its physical and moral perfection? To acquiesce in such a supposition, would be to degrade the divine wisdom and intelligence below the level of the wisdom of man, and to impute imperfection and folly to Him who is "the only wise God." For, in the conduct of human beings, we uniformly regard it as an evidence of folly, when they construct a complicated and an extravagant machine, which either accomplishes no end, or no end worthy of the expense and labour bestowed on its construction. And, therefore, if we would not ascribe imbecility or want of design to the adorable Creator of the universe, we must admit, that he has not formed the soul of man for this terrestrial scene *alone*, but has destined it to a state of progressive improvement, and of endless duration.

This conclusion will appear still more evident, if we consider the endless round of business and care, and the numerous hardships to which the bulk of mankind are subjected in the present state, which prevent the full and vigorous exer-

*Senec. Controvers. Lib. 1. Pliny's Nat. Hist. &c.
† Encyclopedia Britan. Art. *Euler.*

cise of the intellectual powers on those objects which are congenial to the ardent desires, and the noble faculties of the human soul. The greater part of mankind, in the present circumstances of their terrestrial existence, have their time and attention almost wholly absorbed in counteracting the evils incident to their present condition, and in making provision for the wants of their animal natures; and, consequently, the full gratification of the appetite for knowledge, is an absolute impossibility, amidst the pursuits and the turmoils connected with the present scene of things. If we likewise consider the difficulty of directing the mind in the pursuit of substantial knowledge, and the numerous obstructions which occur in our researches after truth, amidst the contradictory opinions, the jarring interests, and the wayward passions of men,—if we consider the imperfections of our senses, and the fallacies to which they are exposed—the prejudices and the passions which seduce us into error—how readily we embrace a glittering phantom for a substantial truth—and how soon our spirits faint under the pressure of intense application to mental pursuits,—we shall be convinced, that, in this sublunary sphere, there is no scope for the full exercise of the intellectual powers, and that the present world must be only *a preparatory* scene to a higher state of existence. Besides, even in those cases where every requisite for the acquisition of knowledge is possessed—where leisure, wealth, education, books, instruments, and all the assistances derived from learned associations, are conjoined with the most splendid intellectual endowments, how feeble are the efforts of the most penetrating and energetic mind, and how narrow the boundary within which its views are confined! The brightest genius, standing on the highest eminence to which science can transport him, contemplates a boundless prospect of objects and events, the knowledge of which he can never hope to attain, while he is chained down to the limits of this terrestrial ball. His mental eye beholds an unbounded and diversified scene of objects, operations, relations, changes, and revolutions, beyond the limits of all that is visible to the eye of sense: he catches an occasional glimpse of objects and of scenes which were previously involved in obscurity, he strains his mental sight, stretches forward with eagerness to grasp at new discoveries, descries some openings which direct his view into the regions of infinity and eternity—is still restless and unsatisfied—perceives all his knowledge to be mere shreds and patches, or like a few dim tapers amidst the surrounding gloom—is convinced that his present faculties are too weak and limited, and that he must be raised to a sublimer station, before he can fully grasp the magnificent objects which lie hid in the unexplored regions of immensity. All his present views and prospects are confined within a circle of a few miles, and all beyond, in the universal system, which extends through the immeasurable tracts of infinite space, is darkness and uncertainty.

Can it, then, be supposed, that a soul furnished with such noble powers and capacities, capable of traversing the realm of creation, of opening new prospects into the unbounded regions of truth that lie before it, and of appreciating the perfections of the Sovereign of the universe—a soul fired with ardent desires after knowledge, panting after new discoveries of truth and of the grandeur of the Divinity, unsatisfied with all its past attainments, and contemplating a boundless unexplored prospect before it—should be cast off from existence, and sink into eternal annihilation, at the moment when its capacities were just beginning to expand, when its desires were most ardent, and when the scenes of immensity and eternity were just opening to its view? If such a supposition could be admitted, man would be the most inexplicable phenomenon in the universe; his existence an unfathomable mystery; and there could be no conceivable mode of reconciling his condition and destination with the wisdom, the rectitude, and the benevolence of his Creator.*

## SECTION IV.

### ON THE PERPETUAL PROGRESS OF THE MIND TOWARDS PERFECTION.

As a supplement to the preceding argument, it may be stated, that *the soul of man appears to be capable of making a perpetual progress towards intellectual and moral perfection, and of enjoying felicity in every stage of its career, without the possibility of ever arriving at a boundary to its excursions.* In the present state we perceive no limits to the excursions of the intellect, but those which arise from its connexion with an unwieldy corporal frame, which is chained down, as it were, to a mere point, in the immensity of creation. Up to the latest period of its connexion with time, it is capable of acquiring new accessions of knowledge, higher attainments in virtue, and more ardent desires after

* Such considerations, as those which I have now adduced, seem to have made a powerful impression upon the minds of the philosophers of antiquity. "When I consider," says Cicero, "the wonderful activity of the mind, so great a memory of what is past, and such a capacity of penetrating into the future; when I behold such a number of arts and sciences, and such a multitude of discoveries thence arising; I believe, and am firmly persuaded, that a nature which contains so many things within itself cannot be mortal." Cicero *de Senectute*. Cap. 21 And if this argument appeared strong even in Cicero's time, it has received a vast accession of strength from the numerous arts, sciences, inventions, and discoveries, which are peculiar to the age in which we live.

moral perfection ; and the infinity of the Creator, and the immensity of that universe over which he presides, present a field in which it may for ever expatiate, and an assemblage of objects on which its powers may be incessantly exercised, without the most distant prospect of ever arriving at a boundary to interrupt its intellectual career.

As I cannot illustrate this topic in more beautiful and forcible language than has been already done by a celebrated Essayist, I shall take the liberty of quoting his words.—" How can it enter into the thoughts of man," says this elegant writer, " that the soul, which is capable of such immense perfections, and of receiving new improvements to all eternity, shall fall away into nothing almost as soon as it is created? Are such abilities made for no purpose? A brute arrives at a point of perfection which he can never pass. In a few years he has all the endowments he is capable of; and were he to live ten thousand more, would be the same thing he is at present. Were a human soul thus at a stand in her accomplishments, were her faculties to be full blown, and incapable of further enlargements, I could imagine it might fall away insensibly, and drop at once into a state of annihilation. But can we believe a thinking being, that is in a perpetual progress of improvements, and travelling on from perfection to perfection, after having just looked abroad into the works of the Creator, and made a few discoveries of his infinite goodness, wisdom and power, must perish in her first setting out, and in the very beginning of her inquiries?

" A man, considered in his present state, seems only sent into the world to propagate his kind. He provides himself with a successor, and immediately quits his post to make room for him :—

Heir urges on his predecessor heir,
Like wave impelling wave.

He does not seem born to enjoy life, but to deliver it down to others. This is not surprising to consider in animals, which are formed for our use, and can finish their business in a short life. The silk-worm, after having spun her task, lays her eggs and dies. But a man can never have taken in his full measure of knowledge, has not time to subdue his passions, esablish his soul in virtue, and come up to the perfection of his nature, before he is hurried off the stage. Would an infinitely wise Being make such glorious creatures for so mean a purpose? Can he delight in the production of such abortive intelligences, such short-lived reasonable beings? Would he give us talents that are not to be exerted? capacities that are never to be gratified? How can we find that wisdom, which shines through all his works in the formation of man, without looking on this world as a nursery for the next? and believing that the several generations of rational creatures, which rise up and disappear in such quick successions, are only to receive their first rudiments of existence here, and afterwards to be transplanted into a more friendly climate, where they may spread and flourish to all eternity?

" There is not, in my opinion, a more pleasing and triumphant consideration in religion than this, of the perpetual progress which the soul makes towards the perfection of its nature, without ever arriving at a period in it. To look upon the soul as going on from strength to strength; to consider that she is to shine for ever with new accessions of glory, and brighten to all eternity, that she will be still adding virtue to virtue, and knowledge to knowledge, carries in it something wonderfully agreeable to that ambition which is natural to the mind of man. Nay, it must be a prospect pleasing to God himself to see his creation for ever beautifying in his eyes, and drawing nearer to him by greater degrees of resemblance.

" Methinks this single consideration of the progress of a finite spirit to perfection will be sufficient to extinguish all envy in inferior natures, and all contempt in superior. That cherubim, which now appears as a god to a human soul, knows very well that the period will come about in eternity, when the human soul shall be as perfect as he himself now is: nay, when she shall look down upon that degree of perfection as much as she now falls short of it. It is true the higher nature still advances, and by that means preserves his distance and superiority in the scale of being; but he knows how high soever the station is, of which he stands possessed at present, the inferior nature will at length mount up to it, and shine forth in the same degree of glory.

" With what astonishment and veneration may we look into our own souls, where there are such hidden stores of virtue and knowledge, such inexhausted sources of perfection? We know not yet what we shall be, nor will it ever enter into the heart of man to conceive the glory that will be always in reserve for him. The soul considered with its Creator, is like one of those mathematical lines that may draw nearer to another for all eternity without a possibility of touching it: and can there be a thought so transporting, as to consider ourselves in these perpetual approaches to Him who is not only the standard of perfection but of happiness!"*

---

## SECTION V.

### ON THE UNLIMITED RANGE OF VIEW WHICH IS OPENED TO THE HUMAN FACULTIES THROUGHOUT THE IMMENSITY OF SPACE AND OF DURATION.

The unlimited range of view which is opened to the human imagination throughout the immen-

* Spectator, vol. 2.

sity of space and of duration, and the knowledge we are capable of acquiring respecting the distant regions of the universe, are strong presumptions and evidences of the eternal destination of man.

If the universe consisted solely of the globe on which we dwell, with its appendages, and were the spaces with which it is surrounded nothing more than an immense void, it would not appear surprising were the existence of man to terminate in the tomb. After having traversed this earthly ball for eighty or a hundred years, and surveyed all the varieties on its surface; after having experienced many of the physical and moral evils connected with its present constitution, and felt that "all is vanity and vexation of spirit," and that no higher prospect, and no further scope for the exercise of his faculties were presented to view; he would be ready to exclaim with Job, "I loathe it, I would not live alway; let me alone, for my days are vanity: my soul chooseth strangling and death, rather than my life." To run the same tiresome round of giddy pleasures, and to gaze perpetually on the same unvaried objects, from one century to another, without the hope of future enjoyment, would afford no gratification commensurate with the desires and capacities of the human mind. Its powers would languish, its energies would be destroyed, its progress to perfection would be for ever interrupted, and it would roam in vain amidst the surrounding void in quest of objects to stimulate its activity.

But, beyond the precincts of this earthly scene, "a wide and unbounded prospect lies before us;" and the increasing light of modern science has enabled us to penetrate into its distant regions, and to contemplate some of its sublime and glorious objects. Within the limits of the solar system of which our world forms a part, there have been discovered twenty-nine planetary bodies, which contain a mass of matter more than two thousand five hundred times greater than the earth, besides the numerous comets, which are traversing the plenetary regions in all directions, and the immense globe of the *sun*, which is like a universe in itself, and which is five hundred times larger than the earth and all the planets and comets taken together. These bodies differ from each other in their magnitude, distances and motions, and in the scenery with which their surfaces are diversified; and some of them are encircled with objects the most splendid and sublime. They appear to be furnished with every thing requisite for the accommodation of intellectual beings,—are capable of containing a population many thousands of times greater than that of our world, and are doubtless replenished with myriads of rational inhabitants. Within the limits of this system the soul of man would find full scope for the exertion of all its powers, capacities and activities, during a series of ages.

Our views of the universe, however, are not confined to the system with which we are more immediately connected. Every star which twinkles in the canopy of heaven, is, on good grounds, concluded to be a *sun*, and the centre of a magnificent system similar to our own; and perhaps surrounded with worlds more spacious and splendid than any of the planetary globes which we are permitted to contemplate. Nearly a thousand of these systems are visible to every observer, when he directs his eye, in a clear winter's night, to the vault of heaven. Beyond all that is visible to the unassisted eye, a common telescope enables us to discern several thousands more. With higher degrees of magnifying power, ten thousands more, which lie scattered at immeasurable distances beyond the former, may still be described. With the best instruments which art has hitherto constructed, many *millions* have been detected in the different regions of the sky—leaving us no room to doubt, that hundreds of millions more, which no human eye will ever discern in the present state, are dispersed throughout the illimitable tracts of creation. So that no limits appear to the scene of Creating Power, and to that vast empire over which the moral government of the Almighty extends. Amidst this boundless scene of Divine Wisdom and Omnipotence, it is evident, that the soul might expatiate in the full exercise of its energies, during ages numerous as the drops of the ocean, without ever arriving at a boundary to interrupt its excursions.

Now, it ought to be carefully remarked, in the first place, that God endowed the mind of man with those faculties by which he has been enabled to compute the bulk of the earth, to determine the size and distances of the planets, and to make all the other discoveries to which I now allude. In the course of his providence he led the human mind into that train of thought, and paved the way for those inventions by means of which the grandeur and extent of his operations in the distant regions of space have been opened to our view. It, therefore, appears to have been his *will and intention*, that the glories of his empire, in the remote spaces of creation, should be, in some measure, unveiled to the inhabitants of our world.

Again, when the soul has once got a glimpse of the magnificence and immensity of creation, it feels the most *ardent desire* to have the veil, which now interposes between us and the remote regions of the universe, withdrawn, and to contemplate at a nearer distance the splendours of those worlds whose suns we behold twinkling from afar. A thousand conjectures and inquiries are suggested to the mind, in relation to the systems and worlds which are dispersed through the immensity of space. Are all those vast globes peopled with inhabitants? Are they connected together, under the goverment of God, as parts of one vast moral system? Are their inhabitants pure moral intelligences, or are they exposed to the inroads of physical and moral evil? What are the gradations of rank or of intellect which exist among them? What correspondence do they carry on with other provinces of the Divine empire? What discoveries have they made of the perfections of Deity, of the plan of his government, and of the extent of his dominions? With what species of corporeal vehicles do they hold a correspondence with the material world? With what organs of perception, and with what powers of intellect are they furnished? What faculties and organs different from those of man do they possess, and by what laws are their social intercourses regulated? Do benignity and love for ever beam from their countenances, and does ecstatic joy perpetually enrapture their hearts? What capacities for rapid movement do they possess? Are they confined within the limits of a single globe like ours, or can they fly from one world to another, on the wings of a seraph? What magnificent landscapes adorn the places of their residence? What celestial glories are hung out for their contemplation in the canopy of heaven? What visible displays of the presence and agency of their Creator are presented to their view? By what means are they carried foward in their progress towards intellectual and moral perfection? What sciences do they cultivate,—what objects engage their chief attention—in what solemn and sublime forms of worship and adoration do they join? What changes or revolutions have taken place among them? What transactions does their history record? What scenes of glory or of terror have been displayed towards any particular system or province of this immense empire? Are sin, disease, and death altogether unknown, and do their inhabitants bask for ever in the regions of immortality? What knowledge do they possess of the character and condition of the inhabitants of our globe, and of the system of which it forms a part? What *variety* of sensitive and intellectual beings is to be found in the different systems of the universe? What *diversity* of external scenery, superior to all that the eye of man has seen or his imagination can conceive, is displayed throughout the numerous worlds which compose this vast empire? What systems exist, and what scenes of creating power are displayed in that boundless region which lies beyond the limits of human vision? At what period in duration did this mighty fabric of the universe first arise into existence? What successive creations have taken place since the first material world was launched into existence by the Omnipotent Creator? What new worlds and beings are still emerging into existence from the voids of space? Is this mighty expanse of creation to endure for ever —and to receive new accessions to its population and grandeur, while eternity rolls on? What are the grand and ultimate designs to be accomplished by this immense assemblage of material and intellectual beings, and is man never to behold this wondrous scene a little more unfolded?

Inquiries o. this description, to which no satisfactory answers can be expected in the present state, might be multiplied to an indefinite extent. The soul of man is astonished, overwhelmed, and bewildered at the immensity of the scene which is opened before it,—and at once perceives, that, in order to acquire a comprehensive knowledge of the character and attributes of the Divinity—to penetrate into the depths of his plans and operations—and to contemplate the full glory of his empire,—ages numerous as the stars of heaven are requisite, and that, if no future existence awaits it beyond the grave, its ardent desires after progressive improvement and felicity, and its hopes of becoming more fully acquainted with the universe and its Author, must end in eternal disappointment.

Again, the mind of man is not only animated with ardent desires after a more full disclosure of the wonders of this boundless scene, *but is endowed with capacities for acquiring an indefinite extent of knowledge respecting the distant regions of the universe and the perfections of its Author.* Those who have taken the most extensive excursions through the field of science, still find, that they are capable of receiving an addition to all the knowledge they have hitherto acquired on every subject, and of prosecuting inquiries beyond the range of the visible system, provided the means of investigation were placed within their reach. Were a human soul transported to a distant world, for example, to the regions of the planet *Saturn*,—were it permitted to contemplate at leisure the sublime movements of its rings, and the various phenomena of its moons; the variety of landscapes which diversify its surface, and the celestial scenery which its firmament displays,—were it to mingle with its inhabitants, to learn the laws by which their social intercourse is directed, the sciences which they cultivate, the worship in which they engage, and the leading transactions and events which their history records—it would find no more difficulty in acquiring and treasuring up such information, than it now does in acquiring, from the narrative of a traveller, a knowledge of the customs and manners of an unknown tribe of mankind, and of the nature of the geographical territory it possesses. Were angelic messengers from a thousand worlds, to be despatched, at successive intervals, to our globe, to describe the natural and moral scenery, and to narrate the train of Divine dispensations peculiar to each world—there would be ample room in the human mind for treasuring up such intelligence, notwithstanding all the stores of science which it may have previously acquired. Such information would neither annihilate the knowledge we had formerly attained, nor prevent our further progress in intellectual acquisitions. On the contrary, it would enlarge the capacity of the mind, invigorate its faculties, and add a new stimulus to its powers and energies. On the basis of such information, the soul could trace new aspects, and new displays of Divine wisdom, intelligence, and rectitude, and acquire more comprehensive views of the character of God—just as it does, in the mean time, from a contemplation of those objects and dispensations which lie within its grasp. To such researches, investigations, and intellectual progressions, no boundary can be assigned, if the soul be destined to survive the dissolution of its mortal frame. It only requires to be placed in a situation where its powers will be permitted to expatiate at large, and where the physical and moral obstructions which impede their exercise shall be completely removed.

It may be farther remarked, on the ground of what has been now stated, that all the knowledge which can be attained in the present state, is but as a drop to the ocean, when compared with "the treasures of wisdom and knowledge" that may be acquired in the eternal world. The proportion between the one and the other may bear a certain analogy to the bulk of the terraqueous globe, when compared with the immensity of the worlds and systems which compose the universe. If an *infinite variety* of designs, of objects, and of scenery, exist in the distant provinces of creation, as we have reason to believe, from the variety which abounds in our terrestrial system, —if every world be peopled with inhabitants of a different species from those of another, if its physical constitution and external scenery be peculiar to itself, if the dispensations of the Cretor towards its inhabitants be such as have not been displayed to any other world, if "the manifold wisdom of God," in the arrangement of its destinies, be displayed in a manner in which it has never been displayed to any other class of intelligences;—and, in short, if every province of creation exhibit a *peculiar manifestation* of the Deity—we may conclude, that all the knowledge of God, of his works and dispensations, which can be attained in the present life, is but as the faint glimmering of a taper when contrasted with the effulgence of the meridian sun. Those who have made the most extensive and profound investigations into the wonders of nature, are the most deeply convinced of their own ignorance, and of the boundless fields of knowledge which remain unexplored. Sir Isaac Newton had employed the greater part of his life in some of the sublimest investigations which can engage the attention of the human mind,—and yet he declared, a little before his death, "I do not know what I may appear to the world, but to myself I seem to have been only like a boy playing on the sea shore, and diverting myself in now and then finding a pebble or a prettier shell than ordinary, while the great ocean of truth lay all undiscovered before me." And is it reasonable to believe, that after a glimpse of the boundless treasures of divine science has flashed upon the mind, it is to pass only a few months or years in anxious desire and suspense, and then be extinguished for ever?

It may be farther observed, in connexion with the preceding remarks—*that the creation of such a vast universe must have been chiefly intended to display the perfections of the Deity, and to afford gratification and felicity to the intellectual beings he has formed.* The Creator stands in no need of innumerable assemblages of worlds and of inferior ranks of intelligences, in order to secure or to augment his felicity. Innumerable ages before the universe was created, he existed *alone*, independent of every other being, and infinitely happy in the contemplation of his own eternal excellences. No other reason, therefore, can be assigned for the production of the universe, but the gratification of his rational offspring, and that he might give a display of the infinite glories of his nature to innumerable orders of intelligent creatures. Ten thousand times ten thousand suns, distributed throughout the regions of immensity, with all their splendid apparatus of planets, comets, moons, and rings, can afford no spectacle of novelty to expand and entertain the Eternal Mind; since they all existed, in their prototypes, in the plans and conceptions of the Deity, during the countless ages of a past eternity. Nor did he produce these works for the improvement and information of *no being*. This amazing structure of the universe, then, with all the sensitive and intellectual enjoyments connected with it, must have been chiefly designed for the instruction and entertainment of subordinate intelligences, and to serve as a magnificent theatre on which the energies of divine power and wisdom, and the emanations of divine benevolence might be illustriously displayed. And can we suppose that the material universe will exist, while intelligent minds, for whose improvement it was reared, are suffered to sink into annihilation?

Again, *it cannot be admitted, in consistency with the attributes of God, that he will finally disappoint the rational hopes and desires of the human soul, which he himself has implanted and cherished.* If he had no ultimate design of gratifying rational beings with a more extensive display of the immensity and grandeur of his works, it is not conceivable, that he would have permitted them to make those discoveries they have already brought to light respecting the extent and the glory of his empire. Such discoveries could not have been made without his permission and direction, or without those faculties and means which he himself had imparted. And, therefore, in permitting the inhabitants of our world to take a distant glimpse of the boundless scene of his operations, he must have intended to excite those ardent desires which will be gratified in a future world, and to commence those trains of thought which will be prosecuted with increasing ardour, through eternity, till we shall be able to perceive and comprehend the contrivance and skill, the riches of divine munificence, the vast designs, and the miracles of power and intelligence which are displayed throughout every part of the universal system.—To suppose that the Creator would unfold a partial and imperfect view of the wonders of creation, and enkindle *a rational longing and desire*, merely for the purpose of *mocking and tantalizing our expectations*, would be to represent the moral character of the Deity as below the level of that of a depraved mortal. It would argue a species of *deceit*, of *envy*, and of *malignity*, which is altogether repugnant to the character of a Being of infinite benevolence. As his goodness was the principal motive which induced him to bring us into existence, his conduct must be infinitely removed from every thing that approaches to envy, malignity, or a desire to mock or disappoint the rational hopes of his creatures. His general character, as displayed in all his works, leads us to conclude, that, in so far from tantalizing the rational beings he has formed, he is both able and willing "to do to and for them exceeding abundantly above all that they can ask or think." If he had intended merely to confine our desires to sensitive enjoyments and to the present life, the habitation of man would have required no more contrivance nor decoration than what are requisite for the lion's den and the retreats of the tiger, and no farther display of the grandeur of his empire would have been unfolded to view.

Since, therefore, it appears, that the universe is replenished with innumerable systems, and is vast and unlimited in its extent—since God endued the mind of man with those faculties by which he has explored a portion of its distant regions—since the soul feels an ardent desire to obtain a more full disclosure of its grandeur and magnificence—since it is endued with faculties capable of receiving an indefinite increase of knowledge on this subject—since all the knowledge it can acquire in the present state, respecting the operations and the government of God, is as nothing when compared with the prospects which eternity may unfold—since the universe and its material glories are chiefly intended for the gratification of intelligent minds—and since it is obviously inconsistent with the moral character of the Deity, to cherish desires and expectations which he will finally frustrate and disappoint—the conclusion appears to be unavoidable, *that man is destined to an immortal existence.* During the progress of that existence, his faculties will arrive at their full expansion, and there will be ample scope for their exercise on myriads of objects and events which are just now veiled in darkness and mystery. He will be enabled to penetrate more fully into the plans and operations of the divinity—to perceive new aspects of the Eternal Mind, new evolutions of infinite wisdom and design, new displays of omnipotence, goodness, and intelligence—and to acquire a more minute and comprehensive view of all the attributes of the Deity, and of the connexions, relations, and dependencies, of that vast physical and moral system over which his government extends.

---

## SECTION VI.

### ON THE MORAL POWERS OF MAN.

The moral powers with which man is endued form a strong presumptive proof of his immortal destiny.

Man is formed for *action*, as well as for contemplation. For this purpose there are interwoven in his constitution, powers, principles, instincts, feelings, and affections, which have a reference to his improvement in virtue, and which excite him to promote the happiness of others. These powers and active principles, like the intellectual, are susceptible of vast improvement, by attention, by exercise, by trials and difficulties, and by an expansion of the intellectual views. Such are filial and fraternal affection, fortitude, temperance, justice, gratitude, generosity, love of friends and country, philanthropy, and general benevolence. Degenerate as our world has always been, many striking examples of such virtues have been displayed both in ancient and modern times, which demonstrate the vigour, expansion, and sublimity of the moral powers of man.

When we behold men animated by noble sentiments, exhibiting sublime virtues, and performing illustrious actions,—displaying generosity and beneficence in seasons of calamity, and tranquillity and fortitude in the midst of difficulties and dangers—desiring riches only for the sake of distributing them—estimating places of power and honour, only for the sake of suppressing vice, rewarding virtue, and promoting the prosperity of their country—enduring poverty and distress with a noble heroism—suffering injuries and affronts with patience and serenity—stifling resentment when they have it in their power to inflict vengeance—displaying kindness and generosity towards enemies and slanderers—vanquishing irascible passions and licentious desires in the midst of the strongest temptations—submitting to pain and disgrace in order to promote the prosperity of friends and relatives—and sacrificing repose, honour, wealth, and even life itself, for the good of their country, or for promoting the best interests of the human race,—we perceive in such examples features of the human mind, which mark its dignity and grandeur, and indicate its destination to a higher scene of action and enjoyment.

Even in the annals of the Pagan world, we find many examples of such illustrious virtues. There we read of *Regulus* exposing himself to the most cruel torments, and to death itself, rather than suffer his veracity to be impeached, or his fidelity to his country to be called in question—of *Phocion*, who exposed himself to the fury of an enraged assembly, by inveighing against the vices, and endeavouring to promote the best interests of his countrymen, and gave it as his last command to his son, when he was going to execution, "that he should forget how ill the Athenians had treated his father"—of *Cyrus*, who was possessed of wisdom, moderation, courage, magnanimity, and noble sentiments, and who employed them all to promote the happines of his people—of *Scipio*, in whose actions the virtues of generosity and liberality, goodness, gentleness, justice, magnanimity, and chastity, shone with distinguished lustre—and of *Damon* and *Pythias*, who were knit together in the bonds of a friendship which all the terrors of an ignominious death could not dissolve. But of all the characters of the heathen world, illustrious for virtue, *Aristides* appears to stand in the foremost rank. An extraordinary greatness of soul, (says Rollin) made him superior to every passion. Interest, pleasure, ambition, resentment, jealousy, were extinguished in him by the love of virtue and his country. The merit of others, instead of offending him, became his own by the approbation he gave it. He rendered the government of the Athenians amiable to their allies, by his mildness, goodness, humanity, and justice. The disinterestedness he showed in the management of the public treasure, and the love of poverty which he carried almost to an excess, are virtues so far superior to the practice of our age, that they scarce seem credible to us. His conduct and principles were always uniform, steadfast in the pursuit of whatever he thought just, and incapable of the least falsehood, or shadow of flattery, disguise, or fraud, even in jest. He had such a control over his passions, that he uniformly sacrificed his private interest, and his private resentments, to the good of the public. *Themistocles* was one of the principal actors who procured his banishment from Athens;—but, after being recalled, he assisted him on every occasion with his advice and credit, joyfully taking pains to promote the glory of his greatest enemy, through the motive of advancing the public good. And when afterwards the disgrace of Themistocles gave him a proper opportunity for revenge, instead of resenting the ill treatment he had received from him, he constantly refused to join with his enemies, being as far from secretly rejoicing over the misfortune of his adversary as he had been before from being afflicted at his good success. Such virtues reflect a dignity and grandeur on every mind in which they reside, which appear incompatible with the idea, that it is destined to retire for ever from the scene of action at the hour of death.

But the noblest examples of exalted virtue are to be found among those who have enlisted themselves in the cause of Christianity. The Apostle Paul was an illustrious example of every thing that is noble, heroic, generous, and benevolent in human conduct. His soul was inspired with a holy ardour in promoting the best interests of mankind. To accomplish this object, he parted with friends and relatives, relinquished his native country, and every thing that was dear to him either as a Jew or as a Roman citizen, and exposed himself to persecutions and dangers of every description. During the prosecution of his benevolent career, he was "in journeyings often, in perils of waters, in perils of robbers, in perils by his own countrymen, in perils by the heathen, in perils in the city, in perils in the wilderness, in perils in the sea, in perils among false brethren; in weariness and painfulness, in watchings often, in hunger and thirst, in fastings often, in stripes above measure, in cold and nakedness." Yet none of these things moved him, nor did he count his life dear to him, provided he might finish his course with joy, and be instrumental in accomplishing the present and eternal happiness of his fellow-men. In every period of the Christian era, similar characters have arisen to demonstrate the power of virtue and to bless mankind. Our own age and country have produced numerous philanthropic characters, who have shone as lights in the moral world, and have acted as benefactors to the human race. The names of Alfred, Penn, Bernard, Raikes, Neilde, Clarkson, Sharpe, Buxton, Wilberforce, Venning, and many others, are familiar to every one who is in the least acquainted with the annals of benevolence. The exertions which some of these individuals have made in the cause of liberty, in promoting the education of the young, in alleviating the distresses of the poor, in ameliorating the condition of the prisoner, and in counteracting the abominable traffic in slaves, will be felt as blessings conferred on mankind throughout succeeding generations, and will, doubtless, be held in everlasting remembrance.

But among all the philanthropic characters of the past or present age, the labours of the late Mr. Howard, stand pre-eminent. This illustrious man, from a principle of pure benevolence, devoted the greater part of his life to active beneficence, and to the alleviation of human wretchedness, in every country where he travelled,—diving into the depth of dungeons, and exposing himself to the infected atmospheres of hospitals and jails, in order to meliorate the condition of the unfortunate, and to allay the sufferings of the mournful prisoner. In prosecuting this labour of love, he travelled three times through France, four times through Germany, five times through Holland, twice through Italy, once through Spain and Portugal, and also through Denmark, Sweden, Russia, Poland, and part of the Turkish empire, surveying the haunts of misery, and distributing benefits to mankind wherever he appeared.

"From realm to realm with cross or crescent crown'd,
Where'er mankind and misery are found,
O'er burning sands, deep waves, or wilds of snow,
Mild *Howard* journeying seeks the house of woe.
Down many a winding step to dungeons dank,
Where anguish wails aloud and fetters clank,
To caves bestrewed with many a mouldering bone,
And cells whose echoes only learn to groan,
Where no kind bars a whispering friend disclose,
No sun-beam enters, and no zephyr blows;
—He treads, inemulous of fame or wealth,
Profuse of toil and prodigal of health;
Leads stern-ey'd Justice to the dark domains,
If not to sever to *relax* the chains,
Gives to her babes the self-devoted wife,
To her fond husband liberty and life.
—Onward he moves! disease and death retire;
And murmuring demons hate him and admire."
*Darwin.*

Such characters afford powerful demonstrations of the sublimity of virtue, of the activity of the human mind, and of its capacity for contributing to the happiness of fellow intelligences to an unlimited extent. We have also, in our own times, a class of men who have parted from their friends and native land, and have gone to the "uttermost ends of the earth," to distant barbarous climes, exposing themselves to the frosts of Labrador and Greenland, to the scorching heats of Africa, and to the hostile attacks of savage tribes, in order to publish the salvation of God, and to promote the happiness of men of all languages and climates. Some of these have felt their minds inspired with such a noble ardour in the cause of universal benevolence, that nothing but insurmountable physical obstructions prevented them from making the tour of the world, and imparting benefits to men of all nations, kindreds, and tongues.

Can we then imagine, that such active powers as those to which I have now alluded—powers which qualify their possessors for diffusing happiness to an indefinite extent among surrounding intelligences—will be for ever extinguished by the stroke of death? and that, after a few feeble efforts during the present transitory scene, they will never again exert their energies through all eternity? This will appear in the highest degree improbable, if we consider, 1. The limited sphere of action to which the generality of mankind are confined in the present state. Most men are confined to laborious employments, and have their attention almost entirely absorbed in providing for their families, and in anxious solicitude for their animal subsistence and success in life, so that they find no scope for their moral powers beyond the circle of the family mansion, and of their own immediate neighbourhood. 2. The period within which the most energetic powers can be exerted is extremely limited. It is not before man has arrived near the meridian of life that his moral powers begin to be fully expanded,—and it frequently happens, in the case of ardent benevolent characters, that, at the moment when their philanthropic schemes were matured, and they had just commenced their career of beneficence, death interposes, and puts a period to all their labours and designs. 3. In the present state of the world, numerous physical obstructions interpose to prevent the exertion of the moral powers, even in the most ardent philanthropic minds. The want of wealth and influence; the diseases and infirmities of an enfeebled corporeal frame; the impediments thrown in the way by malice and envy, and the political arrangements of states; the difficulty of penetrating into every region of the globe where human beings reside, and many other obstructions, prevent the full exercise of that moral energy which resides in benevolent and heroic minds, and confine its operations within a narrow span. But can we ever suppose, in consistency with Divine Wisdom and Benevolence, that God has implanted in the human constitution benevolent active powers, which are never to be fully expanded, and that those godlike characters that have occasionally appeared on the theatre of our world, are never to re-appear on the field of action, to expatiate, in the full exercise of their moral powers, in the ample career of immortality? To admit such a supposition would be in effect to call in question his Wisdom and Intelligence. It is the part of Wisdom to proportionate *means* to *ends*, and to adapt the faculties of any being to the scene in which it is to operate. But here, we behold a system of powers which can never can be brought into full operation in the present state; and, therefore, if death is to put a final termination to the activity of man, the mighty powers and energies with which he is endowed have been bestowed in vain,—and we are led to conceive of the Divine Being as deficient in Wisdom and Intelligence in his government of the intellectual beings he has formed.

This will, perhaps, appear still more obvious, if we attend to the following considerations.—Throughout the universe we perceive traces of a system of universal benevolence. This is distinctly perceptible in relation to our own globe, in the revolution of day and night; in the constitution of the atmosphere; in the beautiful and sublime scenes presented to the eye in every country; in the agencies of light and heat, and of the electrical and galvanic fluids; in the splendour of the sun, and the glories of the midnight sky; in the organization of the body of man, and the different senses with which he is endowed; in the general adaptation of the mineral and vegetable kingdoms, and of every element around us, to the wants of man and other sensitive beings; and in the abundant supply of food and drink which is annually distributed to every rank of animated existence. We perceive traces of the same benevolent agency in the arrangements connected with distant worlds—in the rotation of the planetary globes around their axes, in the assemblages of rings and moons with which they are environed, and in the diversified apparatus by which light and heat are distributed in due proportion to the several bodies which compose the solar system. And, in other systems, in the distant regions of space, we perceive that it is one great end of the Creator, to diffuse light and splendour throughout all the provinces of his immense empire, in order to unveil his glorious works to the eyes of unnumbered intelligences. But, although a system of benevolence is abundantly manifest in the mechanical fabric of the universe, yet it does not appear that happiness can be fully enjoyed *without the benevolent agency of intelligent beings*. We have abundant proofs of this position in the world in which we dwell. For although the goodness of the Creator is displayed throughout all its regions, yet the greater part of the human race is in a state of comparative misery, not owing to any deficiency in the Divine bounty, but to the selfishness, ambition, and malevolence of men. With the blessings which Heaven provides from year to year, the whole population of our globe, and a thousand millions more, would be amply supplied, and happiness extensively diffused, were *benevolence* a prominent and universal trait in the character of mankind. Even in those places where only a few energetic and benevolent individuals bestir themselves in the cause of general philanthropy, a wonderful change is rapidly produced in the condition of society. Disease, and misery, and want, fly away at their approach,—the poor are supplied, the wretched relieved, the prisoner released, the orphan provided for, and the widow's heart made to sing for joy.

Now, we have every reason to conclude, that *moral action* extends over the whole empire of God—that benevolence exerts its noblest energies among the inhabitants of distant worlds—and that it is chiefly through the medium of reciprocal kindness and affection that ecstatic joy pervades the hearts of celestial intelligences. For we cannot conceive happiness to exist in any region of space, or among any class of intellectual beings, where love to the Creator, and to one another, is not a prominent and permanent affection.

It is, therefore, reasonable to believe that those virtuous benevolent characters which have appeared in our world, have been only in the act of training for a short period, preparatory to their being transported to a nobler scene of action, and that their moral powers, which could not be brought into full exercise in this terrestrial sphere, were intended to qualify them for mingling with more exalted intelligences, and co-operating with them in carrying forward that vast system of universal benevolence, to which all the arrangements of the Creator evidently tend.

Whether then, it may be asked, does it appear most consistent with the moral powers of man, and with the wisdom and goodness of God, to suppose that such illustrious characters as Penn, G. Sharp, Clarkson, Venning, Howard, and the apostle Paul, are now for ever banished from creation, or that they are expatiating in a higher scene of action and enjoyment, where all their benevolent energies find ample scope, and where every blossom of virtue is fully expanded? If there is a God, and if wisdom, benevolence, and rectitude, form an essential part of his character, we cannot doubt for a moment that such characters are still in existence, and shall re-appear on a more splendid theatre of action in the future scenes of eternity.

I shall conclude my illustrations of the preceding arguments with the following extract from a judicious and elegant writer:—

"In tracing the nature and *destination* of any being, we form the surest judgment from his *powers of action*, and the scope and *limits* of these compared with his *state* or that field in which they are exercised. If this being passes through different states or fields of action, and we find a *succession* of powers adapted to the different periods of his progress, we conclude, that he was destined for those successive states, and reckon his nature *progressive*. If, besides the immediate set of powers which fit him for action in his present state, we observe another set which appear superfluous if he were to be confined to it, and which point to another or higher one, we naturally conclude that he is not designed to remain in his present state, but to advance to that for which those supernumerary powers are adapted. Thus, we argue, that the *insect*, which has wings forming or formed, and all the apparatus proper for flight, is not destined always to creep on the ground, or to continue in the torpid state of adhering to a wall, but is designed in its season to take its flight in air. Without this farther destination, the admirable mechanism of wings and the other apparatus, would be useless and absurd.

"The same kind of reasoning may be applied to man, while he lives only a sort of vegetative life in the womb. He is furnished even there with a beautiful apparatus of organs, eyes, ears, and other delicate senses, which derive nourishment indeed, but are in a manner folded up, and have no proper exercise or use in their present confinement. Let us suppose some intelligent spectator, who never had any connexion with man, nor the least acquaintance with human affairs, to see this odd phenomenon, a creature formed after such a manner, and placed in a situation apparently unsuitable to such various machinery, must he not be strangely puzzled about the use of his complicated structure, and reckon such a profusion of art and admirable workmanship lost on the subject: or reason by way of anticipation, that a creature endued with such various yet unexerted capacities, was destined for a more enlarged sphere of action, in which those latent capacities shall have full play? The vast variety and yet beautiful symmetry and proportions of the several parts and organs with which the creature is endued, and their apt cohesion with and dependence on the curious receptacle of their life and nourishment, would forbid his concluding the whole to be the birth of chance, or the bungling effort of an unskilful artist; at least, would make him demur a while at so harsh a sentence. But if, while he is in this state of uncertainty, we suppose him to see the babe, after a few successful struggles, throwing off his fetters, breaking loose from his little dark prison, and emerging into open day, then unfolding his recluse and dormant powers, breathing in air, gazing at light, admiring colours, sounds, and all the *fair variety* of nature; immediately his doubts clear up, the propriety and excellence of the workmanship dawn upon him with full lustre, and the whole mystery of the first period is unravelled by the opening of this new scene. Though in this *second* period the creature lives chiefly a kind of *animal* life, that is, of *sense* and *appetite*, yet by various trials and observations he gains experience, and by the gradual evolution of the powers of the *imagination* he ripens apace for an *higher* life, for exercising the arts of *design* and *imitation*, and of those in which strength or dexterity are more requisite, than acuteness or reach of judgment. In the succeeding *rational* or *intellectual* period, his *understanding*, which formerly crept in a lower, mounts into an higher sphere, canvasses the natures, judges of the relations of things, forms schemes, deduces consequences from what is past, and from present as well as past collects future events. By this succession of states, and of correspondent culture, he grows up at length into a *moral*, a *social*, and a *political* creature. This is the last period at which we perceive him to arrive in this his mortal career. Each period is introductory to the next succeeding one; each life is a field of exercise and improvement for the next higher one; the life of the *fœtus* for that of the *infant*, the life of the *infant* for that of the *child*, and all the lower for the highest and best.

"But is this the last period of nature's progression? Is this the utmost extent of her plot, where she winds up the drama, and dismisses the actor into eternal oblivion? Or does he appear to be invested with supernumerary powers, which have not full exercise and scope even in the last scene, and reach not that maturity or perfection of which they are capable, and therefore point to some higher scene, where he is to sustain another and more important character, than he has yet sustained? If any such there are, may we not conclude from analogy, or in the same way of anticipation as before, that he is destined for that after part, and is to be produced upon a more august and solemn stage, where his sublimer powers shall have proportioned action, and his nature attain its completion."*

In illustrating the preceding arguments, I have shown that man is possessed of desires which cannot be fully gratified, and of moral and intellectual powers which cannot be fully exercised in the present world, and consequently, we have the same reason to conclude, that he is destined to a higher scene of existence, as we would have, from beholding the rudiments of eyes and ears in the embryo in the womb, that it is destined to burst its confinement, and to enter into a world, where sounds, and light, and colours will afford ample scope for the exercise of these organs.

---

## SECTION VII.

### ON THE APPREHENSIONS AND FOREBODINGS OF THE MIND, WHEN UNDER THE INFLUENCE OF REMORSE.

The apprehensions of the mind, and its fearful forebodings of futurity, when under the influence of remorse, may be considered as intimations of a state of retribution in another world.

As the boundless desires of the human mind, the vast comprehension of its intellectual faculties, and the virtuous exercise of its moral powers, are indications of a future state of more enlarged enjoyment, so, those horrors of conscience which frequently torment the minds of the wicked, may be considered as the forebodings of future misery and wo. For it appears as reasonable to believe, that atrocious deeds will meet with deserved opprobrium and punishment in a future state, as that virtuous actions will be approved of and rewarded; and, consequently, we find, that all nations who have believed in a future state of happiness for the righteous, have also admitted that there are future punishments in reserve for the workers of iniquity. Every man has interwoven in his constitution a moral sense which secretly condemns

* Fordyce.

him when he has committed an atrocious action, even when the perpetration of the crime is unknown to his fellow-men, and when he is placed in circumstances which raise him above the fear of human punishment. There have been numerous individuals, both in the higher and lower ranks of life, who, without any external cause, or apprehension of punishment from men, have been seized with inward terrors, and have writhed under the agonies of an accusing conscience, which neither the charms of music, nor all the other delights of the sons of men, had the least power to assuage. Of the truth of this position, the annals of history furnish us with many impressive examples. The following may suffice as specimens :—

While *Belshazzar* was carousing at an impious banquet with his wives and concubines and a thousand of his nobles, the appearance of the fingers of a man's hand, and of the writing on an opposite wall, threw him into such consternation, that his thoughts terrified him, the girdles of his loins were loosed, and his knees smote one against another. His terror, in such circumstances, cannot be supposed to have proceeded from a fear of man; for he was surrounded by his guards and his princes, and all the delights of music, and of a splendid entertainment. Nor did it arise from the sentence of condemnation written on the wall; for he was then ignorant both of the writing and of its meaning. But he was conscious of the wickedness of which he had been guilty, and of the sacrilegious impiety in which he was then indulging, and, therefore, the extraordinary appearance on the wall, was considered as an awful foreboding of punishment from that almighty and invisible Being whom he had offended.—*Tiberius*, one of the Roman emperors, was a gloomy, treacherous, and cruel tyrant. The lives of his people became the sport of his savage disposition. Barely to take them away was not sufficient, if their death was not tormenting and atrocious. He ordered, on one occasion, a general massacre of all who were detained in prison, on account of the conspiracy of Sejanus his minister, and heaps of carcasses were piled up in the public places. His private vices and debaucheries were also incessant, and revolting to every principle of decency and virtue. Yet this tyrant, while acting in the plenitude of his power, and imagining himself beyond the control of every law, had his mind tortured with dreadful apprehensions. We are informed by *Tacitus*, that in a letter to the Senate, he opened the inward wounds of his breast, with such words of despair as might have moved pity in those who were under the continual fear of his tyranny.* Neither the splendour of his situation as an emperor, nor the solitary retreats to which he retired, could shield him from the accusations of his conscience, but he himself was forced to confess the mental agonies he endured as a punishment for his crimes.—*Antiochus Epiphanes* was another tyrant remarkable for his cruelty and impiety. He laid siege to the city of Jerusalem, exercised the most horrid cruelties upon its inhabitants, slaughtered forty thousand of them in three days, and polluted, in the most impious manner, the temple, and the worship of the God of Israel. Some time afterwards, when he was breathing out curses against the Jews for having restored their ancient worship, and threatening to destroy the whole nation, and to make Jerusalem the common place of sepulture to all the Jews, he was seized with a grievous torment in his inward parts, and excessive pangs of the colic, accompanied with such terrors as no remedies could assuage. " Worms crawled from every part of him ; his flesh fell away piece-meal, and the stench was so great that it became intolerable to the whole army; and he thus finished an impious life, by a miserable death."† During this disorder, says Polybius, he was troubled with a perpetual delirium, imagining that spectres stood continually before him, reproaching him with his crimes.—Similar relations are given by historians, of *Herod* who slaughtered the infants at Bethlehem, of Galerius Maximianus the author of the tenth persecution against the Christians, of the infamous Philip II. of Spain, and of many others whose names stand conspicuous on the rolls of impiety and crime.

It is related of Charles IX. of France, who ordered the horrible Bartholomew massacre, and assisted in his bloody tragedy, that, ever after, he had a fierceness in his looks, and a colour in his cheeks, which he never had before ;—that he slept little and never sound ; and waked frequently in great agonies, requiring soft music to compose him to rest; and at length died of a lingering disorder, after having undergone the most exquisite torments both of body and mind. D'Aubigne informs us that Henry IV. frequently told, among his most intimate friends, that eight days after the massacre of St. Bartholomew, he saw a vast number of ravens perch and croak on the pavilion of the Louvre; that the same night Charles IX. after he had been two hours in bed, started up, roused his grooms of the chamber, and sent them out to listen to a great noise of groans in the air, and among others, some furious and threatening voices, the whole resembling what was heard on the night of the massacre; that all these various cries were so striking, so remarkable, and so articulate, that Charles believing that the enemies of the Montmorencies and of their partisans had surprised and attacked them, sent a detachment of his

* Tiberium non fortuna, non solitudines protegebant, quin tormenta pectoris suasque pœnas ipse fateretur, &c.—*Tacitus*.

† Rollin's An. Hist.

guards to prevent this new massacre. It is scarcely necessary to add, that the intelligence brought from Paris proved these apprehensions to be groundless, and that the noises heard, must have been the fanciful creations of the guilty conscience of the king, countenanced by the vivid remembrance of those around him of the horrors of St. Bartholomew's day.

King Richard III. after he had murdered his innocent royal nephews, was so tormented in conscience, as Sir Thomas More reports from the gentlemen of his bed chamber, that he had no peace or quiet in himself, but always carried it as if some imminent danger was near him. His eyes were always whirling about on this side, and on that side; he wore a shirt of mail, and was always laying his hand upon his dagger, looking as furiously as if he was ready to strike. He had no quiet in his mind by day, nor could take any rest by night, but, molested with terrifying dreams, would start out of his bed, and run like a distracted man about the chamber.*

This state of mind, in reference to another case, is admirably described, in the following lines of Dryden.

"Amidst your train this unseen judge will wait,
Examine how you came by all your state;
Upbraid your impious pomp, and in your ear
Will halloo, rebel! traitor! murderer!
Your ill-got power, wan looks, and care shall bring,
Known but by discontent to be a King.
Of crowds afraid, yet anxious when alone,
You'll sit and brood your sorrows on a throne."

Bessus the Pæonian being reproached with ill nature for pulling down a nest of young sparrows and killing them, answered, that he had reason so to do, "Because these little birds never ceased falsely to accuse him of the murder of his father." This parricide had been till then concealed and unknown; but the revenging fury of conscience caused it to be discovered by himself, who was justly to suffer for it. That notorious sceptic and semi-atheist, Mr. Hobbes, author of the "Leviathan," had been the means of poisoning many young gentlemen and others, with his wicked principles, as the Earl of Rochester confessed, with extreme compunction, on his death-bed. It was remarked, by those who narrowly observed his conduct, that "though in a humour of bravado he would speak strange and unbecoming things of God; yet in his study, in the dark, and in his retired thoughts, he trembled before him." He could not endure to be left alone in an empty house. He could not, even in his old age, bear any discourse of death, and seemed to cast off all thoughts of it. He could not bear to sleep in the dark; and if his candle happened to go out in the night, he would awake in terror and amazement,—a plain indication, that he was unable to bear the dismal reflections of his dark and desolate mind, and knew not how to extinguish, nor how to bear the light of "the candle of the Lord" within him. He is said to have left the world, with great reluctance under terrible apprehensions of a dark and unknown futurity.

"Conscience, the torturer of the soul, unseen,
Does fiercely brandish a sharp scourge within.
Severe decrees may keep our tongues in awe,
But to our thoughts what edict can give law?
Even you yourself to your own breast shall tell
Your crimes, and your own conscience be your hell.

Many similar examples of the power of conscience in awakening terrible apprehensions of futurity, could be brought forward from the records of history both ancient and modern;—and there can be no question, that, at the present moment, there are thousands of gay spirits immersed in fashionable dissipation, and professing to disregard the realities of a future world, who, if they would lay open their inmost thoughts, would confess, that the secret dread of a future retribution is a spectre which frequently haunts them while running the rounds of forbidden pleasure, and embitters their most exquisite enjoyments.

Now, how are we to account for such terrors of conscience, and awful forebodings of futurity, if there be no existence beyond the grave? especially when we consider, that many of those who have been thus tormented have occupied stations of rank and power, which raised them above the fear of punishment from man? If they got their schemes accomplished, their passions gratified, and their persons and possessions secured from temporal danger, why did they feel compunction or alarm in the prospect of futurity? for every mental disquietude of this description implies a dread of something future. They had no great reason to be afraid even of the Almighty himself, if his vengeance do not extend beyond the present world. They beheld the physical and moral world moving onward according to certain fixed and immutable laws. They beheld no miracles of vengeance—no Almighty arm visibly hurling the thunderbolts of heaven against the workers of iniquity. They saw that one event happened to all, to the righteous as well as to the wicked, and that death was an evil to which they behoved sooner or later to submit. They encountered hostile armies with fortitude, and beheld all the dread apparatus of war without dismay. Yet in their secret retirements, in their fortified retreats, where no eye but the eye of God was upon them, and when no hostile incursion was apprehended, they trembled at a shadow, and felt a thousand disquietudes from the reproaches of an inward monitor which they could not escape. These things appear altogether inexplicable if there be no retribution beyond the grave.

We are, therefore, irresistibly led to the conclusion, that the voice of conscience, in such cases, is the voice of God declaring his abhor-

* Stow's Annals p. 460.

rence of wicked deeds and the punishment which they deserve, and that his providence presides over the actions of moral agents, and gives intimations of the future destiny of those haughty spirits who obstinately persist in their trespasses. And, consequently, as the peace and serenity of virtuous minds are preludes of nobler enjoyments in a future life, so those terrors which now assail the wicked may be considered as the beginnings of that misery and anguish which will be consummated in the world to come, in the case of those who add final impenitence to all their other crimes.

---

## SECTION VIII.

### ON THE DISORDERED STATE OF THE MORAL WORLD, WHEN CONTRASTED WITH THE REGULAR AND SYSTEMATICAL ORDER OF THE MATERIAL.

The disordered state of the moral world, contrasted with the regular and systematical order of the material, affords a strong presumption of another state in which the moral evils which now exist will be corrected.

When we take a general survey of the great fabric of the universe, or contemplate more minutely any of its subordinate arrangements, the marks of beauty, order and harmony, are strikingly apparent. Every thing appears in its proper place, moving onward in majestic order, and accomplishing the end for which it was intended. In the planetary system, the law of gravitation is found to operate exactly in proportion to the square of the distance, and the squares of the periodic times of the planets' revolutions round the sun are exactly proportionate to the cubes of their distances. Every body in this system finishes its respective revolution in exactly the same period of time, so as not to deviate a single minute in the course of a century. The annual revolution of the planet Jupiter was ascertained two centuries ago, to be accomplished in 4330 days, 14 hours, 27 minutes, and 11 seconds, and his rotation round his axis in 9 hours, 56 minutes, and these revolutions are still found to be performed in exactly the same times. The earth performs its diurnal revolution, from one century to another, bringing about the alternate succession of day and night, in exactly the same period of 23 hours, 56 minutes, and 4 seconds. Throughout the whole of this system, there is none of the bodies of which it is composed that stops in its motion, or deviates from the path prescribed. No one interrupts another in its course, nor interferes to prevent the beneficial influences of attractive power, or of light, and heat. Were it otherwise—were the earth to stop in its diurnal revolution, and delay to usher in the dawn at its appointed time, or were the planets to dash one against another, and to run lawlessly through the sky, the system of Nature would run into confusion, its inhabitants would be thrown into a state of anarchy, and deprived of all their enjoyments. But, in consequence of the order which now prevails, the whole presents to the eye of intelligence an admirable display of beauty and harmony, and of infinite wisdom and design.

In like manner, if we attend to the arrangements of our sublunary system—to the revolutions of the seasons, the course of the tides, the motions of the rivers, the process of evaporation, the periodical changes of the winds, and the physical economy of the animal and vegetable tribes—the same systematic order and harmony may be perceived.—In the construction and movements of the human frame, there is a striking display of systematic order and beauty. Hundreds of muscles of different forms, hundreds of bones variously articulated, thousands of lacteal and lymphatic vessels, and thousands of veins and arteries all act in unison every moment, in order to produce life and enjoyment. Every organ of sense is admirably fitted to receive impressions from its corresponding objects. The eye is adapted to receive the impression of light, and light is adapted to the peculiar construction of the eye; the ear is adapted to sound, and the constitution of the air and its various undulations are fitted to make an impression on the tympanum of the ear. Even in the construction of the meanest insect we perceive a series of adaptations, and a system of organization no less regular and admirable than those of man;—and as much care appears to be bestowed in bending a claw, articulating a joint, or clasping the filaments of a feather, to answer its intended purpose, as if it were the only object on which the Creator was employed.—And it is worthy of remark, that our views of the harmony and order of the material world become more admirable and *satisfactory*, in proportion as our knowledge of its arrangements is enlarged and extended. Whether we explore, with the telescope, the bodies which are dispersed through the boundless regions of space, or pry, by the help of the microscope, into the minutest parts of nature, we perceive traces of order, and of exquisite mechanism and design which excite admiration and wonder in every contemplative mind. Before the invention of the microscope, we might naturally have concluded, that all beyond the limits of natural vision was a scene of confusion, a chaotic mass of atoms without life, form, or order; but we now clearly perceive, that every thing is regular and systematic, that even the dust on a butterfly's wing, every distinct particle of which is invisible to the naked eye, consists of regularly organized feathers—that in the eye of a small insect, ten thousand nicely polished globules are beautifully arranged in a transparent net-work within the compass of one-twentieth of an inch—and that myriads of living beings exist, invisible to the unassisted sight, with bodies as curiously organised, and as nicely adapted to their situations as the bodies of men and of the larger animals. So that the whole frame of the material world presents a scene of infinite wisdom and intelligence, and a display of systematic order, beauty, and proportion. Every thing bears the marks of *benevolent* design, and is calculated to produce happiness in sentient beings.

On the other hand, when we take a survey of the moral world in all the periods of its history, we perceive throughout almost every part of its extent, an inextricable maze, and a scene of clashing and confusion, which are directly opposed to the harmony and order which pervade the material system. When we take a retrospective view of the moral state of mankind, during the ages that are past, what do we behold, but a revolting scene of perfidy, avarice, injustice, and revenge,—of wars, rapine, devastation, and bloodshed; nation rising against nation, one empire dashing against another, tyrants exercising the most horrid cruelties, superstition and idolatry immolating millions of victims, and a set of desperate villains, termed *heroes*, prowling over the world, turning fruitful fields into a wilderness, burning towns and villages, plundering palaces and temples, drenching the earth with human gore, and erecting thrones on the ruins of nations? *Here* we behold an *Alexander*, with his numerous armies, driving the ploughshare of destruction through surrounding nations, levelling cities with the dust, and massacring their inoffensive inhabitants in order to gratify a mad ambition, and to be eulogised as a hero,—*there* we behold a *Xerxes*, fired with pride and with the lust of dominion, leading forward an army of three millions of infatuated wretches to be slaughtered by the victorious and indignant Greeks. *Here* we behold an *Alaric*, with his barbarous hordes, ravaging the southern countries of Europe, overturning the most splendid monuments of art, pillaging the metropolis of the Roman empire, and deluging its streets and houses with the blood of the slain,—*there* we behold a *Tamerlane* overrunning Persia, India, and other regions of Asia, carrying slaughter and devastation in his train, and displaying his sportive cruelty, by pounding three or four thousand people at a time in large mortars, and building their bodies with bricks and mortar into a wall. On the one hand, we behold six millions of *Crusaders* marching in wild confusion through the eastern parts of Europe, devouring every thing before them, like an army of locusts, breathing destruction to Jews and infidels, and massacring the inhabitants of Western Asia with infernal fury. On the other hand, we behold the immense forces of *Jenghiz Kan* ravaging the kingdoms of Eastern Asia, to an extent of 15 millions* of square miles, beheading 100,000 prisoners at once, convulsing the world with terror, and utterly exterminating from the earth fourteen millions of human beings. At one period, we behold the ambition and jealousy of *Marius* and *Sylla* embroiling the Romans in all the horrors of a civil war, deluging the city of Rome for five days with the blood of her citizens, transfixing the heads of her senators with poles, and dragging their bodies to the Forum to be devoured by dogs. At another, we behold a *Nero* trampling on the laws of nature and society, plunging into the most abominable debaucheries, practising cruelties which fill the mind with horror, murdering his wife Octavia, and his mother Agrippina, insulting Heaven and mankind by offering up thanksgivings to the gods on the perpetration of these crimes, and setting fire to Rome, that he might amuse himself with the universal terror and despair which that calamity inspired. At one epoch, we behold the Goths and Vandals rushing like an overflowing torrent, from east to west, and from north to south, sweeping before them every vestige of civilization and art, butchering all within their reach without distinction of age or sex, and marking their path with rapine, desolation, and carnage. At another, we behold the emissaries of the Romish See slaughtering, without distinction or mercy, the mild and pious Albigenses, and transforming their peaceful abodes into a scene of universal consternation and horror, while the inquisition is torturing thousands of devoted victims, men of piety and virtue, and committing their bodies to the flames.

At one period of the world,† almost the whole earth appeared to be little else than one great field of battle, in which the human race seemed to be threatened with utter extermination. The Vandals, Huns, Sarmatians, Alans, and Suevi, were ravaging Gaul, Spain, Germany, and other parts of the Roman empire; the Goths were plundering Rome, and laying waste the cities of Italy; the Saxons and Angles were overrunning Britain and overturning the government of the Romans. The armies of Justinian and of the Huns and Vandals were desolating Africa, and butchering mankind by millions. The whole forces of Scythia were rushing with irresistible impulse on the Roman empire, desolating the countries, and almost exterminating the inhabitants wherever they came. The Persian armies were pillaging Hierapolis, Aleppo, and the surrounding cities, and reducing them to ashes; and were laying waste all Asia, from the Tigris to the Bosphorus. The Arabians under Mahomet

* "The conquests of Jenghiz Kan," says Millot, "were supposed to extend above eighteen hundred leagues from east to west, and a thousand from south to north."—*Modern History*, vol. 1.

† About the fifth, sixth and seventh centuries of the Christian era.

and his successors were extending their conquests over Syria, Palestine, Persia, and India, on the east, and over Egypt, Barbary, Spain, and the islands of the Mediterranean, on the west; cutting in pieces with their swords all the enemies of Islamism. In *Europe*, every kingdom was shattered to its centre; in the Mahommedan empire in *Asia*, the Caliphs, Sultans, and Emirs were waging continual wars;—new sovereignties were daily rising, and daily destroyed; and *Africa* was rapidly depopulating, and verging towards desolation and barbarism.

Amidst this universal clashing of nations, when the whole earth became one theatre of bloody revolutions,—scenes of horror were displayed, over which historians wished to draw a veil, lest they should transmit an example of inhumanity to succeeding ages—the most fertile and populous provinces were converted into deserts, overspread with the scattered ruins of villages and cities—every thing was wasted and destroyed with hostile cruelty—famine raged to such a degree that the living were constrained to feed on the dead bodies of their fellow-citizens—prisoners were tortured with the most exquisite cruelty, and the more illustrious they were, the more barbarously were they insulted—cities were left without a living inhabitant—public buildings which resisted the violence of the flames were levelled with the ground—every art and science was abandoned—the Roman empire was shattered to its centre and its power annihilated—avarice, perfidy, hatred, treachery, and malevolence reigned triumphant; and virtue, benevolence, and every moral principle were trampled under foot.

Such scenes of carnage and desolation have been displayed to a certain extent and almost without intermission, during the whole period of this world's history. For the page of the historian, whether ancient or modern, presents to our view little more than revolting details of ambitious conquerors carrying ruin and devastation in their train, of proud despots trampling on the rights of mankind, of cities turned into ruinous heaps, of countries desolated, of massacres perpetrated with infernal cruelty, of nations dashing one against another, of empires wasted and destroyed, of political and religious dissensions, and of the general progress of injustice, immorality, and crime. Compared with the details on these subjects, all the other facts which have occurred in the history of mankind are considered by the historian as *mere interludes* in the great drama of the world, and almost unworthy of being recorded.

Were we to take a survey of the moral world as it now stands, a similar prospect, on the whole, would be presented to our view. Though the shades of depravity with which it is overspread are not so thick and dark, nor its commotions so numerous and violent as in ancient times, yet the aspect of every nation under heaven presents to our view, features which are directly opposite to every thing we should expect to contemplate in a world of systematic order, harmony, and love. If we cast our eyes towards *Asia* we shall find the greater part of five hundred millions of human beings involved in political commotions, immersed in vice, ignorance, and idolatry, and groaning under the lash of tyrannical despots. In Persia, the cruelty and tyranny of its rulers have transformed many of its most fertile provinces into scenes of desolation. In Turkey, the avarice and fiend-like cruelty of the Grand Seignior and his Bashaws have drenched the shores of Greece with the blood of thousands, turned Palestine into a wilderness, and rendered Syria, Armenia, and Kurdistan scenes of injustice and rapine. In China and Japan a spirit of pride and jealousy prevents the harmonious intercourse of other branches of the human family, and infuses a cold-blooded selfishness into the breasts of their inhabitants, and a contempt of surrounding nations. Throughout Tartary, Arabia, and Siberia, numerous hostile tribes are incessantly prowling among deserts and forests in quest of plunder, so that travellers are in continual danger of being either robbed, or murdered, or dragged into captivity.—If we turn our eyes upon *Africa*, we behold human nature sunk into a state of the deepest degradation—the states of Barbary in incessant hostile commotions, and plundering neighbouring nations both by sea and land—the petty tyrants of Dahomy, Benin, Ashantee, Congo, and Angola, waging incessant wars with neighbouring tribes, masssacring their prisoners in cold blood, and decorating their palaces with their skulls—while other degraded hordes, in conjunction with civilized nations, are carrying on a traffic in man-stealing and slavery, which has stained the human character with crimes at which humanity shudders.—If we turn our eyes towards *America*, we shall find that war and hostile incursions are the principal employments of their native tribes, and that the malignity of infernal demons, is displayed in the tortures they inflict upon the prisoners taken in battle, while anarchy, intolerance, and political commotions, still agitate a great proportion of its more civilized inhabitants.—If we take a survey of the Eastern Archipelago, and of the islands which are scattered over the Pacific Ocean, we shall behold immense groups of human beings, instead of living in harmony and affection, displaying the most ferocious dispositions towards each other, hurling stones, spears and darts on every stranger who attempts to land upon their coasts; offering up human sacrifices to their infernal deities, and feasting with delight on the flesh and blood of their enemies.

If we direct our attention towards *Europe*, the most tranquil and civilized portion of the globe—even *here* we shall behold numerous symptoms of political anarchy and moral disorder. During the last thirty years, almost every nation in this quarter of the world has been convulsed to its centre, and become the scene of hostile commotions, of revolutions, and of garments rolled in blood. We have beheld France thrown from a state of aristocratical tyranny and priestly domination into a state of popular anarchy and confusion—her ancient institutions razed to the ground, her princes and nobles banished from her territories, and her most celebrated philosophers, in company with the vilest miscreants, perishing under the stroke of the guillotine. We have beheld a *Buonaparte* riding in triumph through the nations over heaps of slain, scattering "firebrands, arrows, and death," and producing universal commotion wherever he appeared; overturning governments, "changing times," undermining the thrones of emperors, and setting up kings at his pleasure. We have beheld his successors again attempting to entwine the chains of tyranny around the necks of their subjects, and to hurl back the moral world into the darkness which overspread the nations during the reign of Papal superstition. We have beheld Poland torn in pieces by the insatiable fangs of Russia, Austria, and Prussia, her fields drenched with blood, her patriots slaughtered, and her name blotted out from the list of nations. We have beheld Moscow enveloped in flames, its houses, churches, and palaces tumbled into ruins, the blackened carcases of its inhabitants blended with the fragments, and the road to Smolensko covered with the shattered remains of carriages, muskets, breast-plates, helmets, and garments strewed in every direction, and thousands of the dying and the dead heaped one upon another in horrible confusion, and swimming in blood. We have beheld the demon of war raging at Borodino, Austerlitz, the Tyrol, Wilna, Smolensko, Trafalgar, Camperdown, Eylau, Jena, La Vendee, Cadiz, Warsaw, Friedland, Talavera, Sebastian, Lutzen, Leipsic, and Waterloo, demolishing cities, desolating provinces, and blending the carcasses of horses and cattle with the mangled remains of millions of human beings. We have beheld Spain and Portugal thrown into anarchy and commotion, and become the scenes of bloody revolutions—Turkey waging war with religion and liberty—Greece overrun with blood-thirsty Mahometans, and her shores and islands the theatre of the most sanguinary contests.

And what do we *just now* behold when we cast our eyes on surrounding nations? Russia pushing forward her numerous armies into the confines of Persia for the purpose of depredation and slaughter,—the Grand Seignior ruling his subjects with a rod of iron, and decorating the gates of his palace with hundreds of the heads and ears of his enemies,* while his Janizaries are fomenting incessant insurrections,—the Greeks engaged in a contest for liberty, surrounded with blood-thirsty antagonists, and slaughtered without mercy,—Portugal the scene of intestine broils and revolutions,—Spain under the control of a silly priest-ridden tyrant, to gratify whose lust of absolute power, thousands of human beings have been sacrificed, and hundreds of eminent patriots exiled from their native land,—the Inquisition torturing its unhappy victims,—the Romish church thundering its anathemas against all who are opposed to its interests,—the various sectaries of Protestants engaged in mutual recriminations and contentions,—and the princes and sovereigns on the Continent almost all combined to oppose the progress of liberty, and to prevent the improvement of the human mind.

If we come nearer home, and take a view of the every-day scenes which meet our eye, what do we behold? A mixed scene of bustling and confusion, in which vice and malevolence are most conspicuous, and most frequently triumphant. When we contemplate the present aspect of society, and consider the prominent dispositions and principles which actuate the majority of mankind,—the boundless avaricious desires which prevail, and the base and deceitful means by which they are frequently gratified—the unnatural contentions which arise between husbands and wives, fathers and children, brothers and sisters—the jealousies which subsist between those of the same profession or employment—the bitterness and malice with which law-suits are commenced and prosecuted—the malevolence and caballing which attend electioneering contests—the brawlings, fightings, and altercations, which so frequently occur in our streets, alehouses, and taverns—and the thefts, robberies, and murders, which are daily committed,—when we contemplate the haughtiness and oppression of the great and powerful, and the insubordination of the lower ranks of society—when we see widows and orphans suffering injustice; the virtuous persecuted and oppressed; meritorious characters pining in poverty and indigence; fools, profligates, and tyrants, rioting in wealth and abundance; generous actions unrewarded; crimes unpunished; and the vilest of men raised to stations of dignity and honour—we cannot but admit, that the moral world presents a scene of discord and disorder, which mar both the sensitive and intellectual enjoyments of mankind.

Such, then, are the moral aspects of our world, and the disorders which have prevailed during

* In a communication from Odessa, dated August 8, 1824, it was stated, that the five hundred heads and twelve hundred ears of the Greeks, sent by the Captain Pacha to Constantinople, after the taking of Ipsara, were exposed on the gate of the seraglio, on the 20th of July, with the following inscription: "God has blessed the arms of the Mussulmans, and the detestable rebels of Ipsara are extirpated from the face of the world," &c. It was added, "All friendly powers have congratulated the Sublime Porte on this victory."

every period of its history. They evidently present a striking contrast to the beauty and harmony which pervade the general constitution of the material system—to the majestic movements of the planetary orbs, the regular succession of day and night, and the vicissitudes of the seasons; the changes of the moon, the ebbing and flowing of the sea; the admirable functions of the human system; and the harmonious adaptations of light and heat, air and water, and the various objects in the mineral and vegetable kingdoms to the wants and the comfort of animated beings. And can we, for a moment, suppose that this scene of moral disorder and anarchy was the ultimate end for which the material system was created? Can we suppose that the earth is every moment impelled in its annual and diurnal course by the hand of Omnipotence—that it presents new beauties every opening spring—brings forth the treasures of autumn, and displays so many sublime and variegated landscapes—that the sun diffuses his light over all its regions, that the moon cheers the shades of night, and the stars adorn the canopy of the sky, from one generation to another —merely that a set of robbers and desperadoes, and the murderers of nations, might prowl over the world for the purpose of depredation and slaughter, that tyrants might gratify their mad ambition, that vice might triumph, that virtue might be disgraced, that the laws of moral order might be trampled under foot, and that the successive generations of mankind might mingle in this bustling and discordant scene for a few years, and then sink for ever into the shades of annihilation? Yet such a conclusion we are obliged to admit, if there is no future state in which the present disorders of the moral world will be corrected, and the plan of the divine government more fully developed. And if this conclusion be admitted, how shall we be able to perceive or to vindicate the *wisdom* of the Creator in his moral administration? We account it folly in a human being when he constructs a machine, either for no purpose at all, or for no *good* purpose, or for the promotion of mischief. And how can we avoid ascribing the same imperfection to the Deity, if the present state of the moral world be the ultimate end of all his physical arrangements? But his wisdom is most strikingly displayed in the adaptations and arrangements which relate to the material system,—and a Being possessed of boundless intelligence must necessarily be supposed to act *in consistency* with himself. He cannot display wisdom in the material system, and folly in those arrangements which pertain to the world of mind. To suppose the contrary, would be to divest him of his moral attributes, and even to call in question his very existence.

We are therefore necessarily led to conclude, that the present state of the moral world is only a small part of the great plan of God's moral government—the commencement of a series of dispensations to be completed in a future scene of existence, in which his *wisdom*, as well as all his other attributes, will be fully displayed before the eyes of his intelligent offspring. If this conclusion be admitted, it is easy to conceive, how the moral disorders which now exist may be rectified in a future world, and the intelligent universe restored to harmony and happiness, and how those moral dispensations which now appear dark and mysterious, will appear illustrative of divine wisdom and intelligence, when contemplated as parts of one grand system, which is to run parallel in duration with eternity itself. But, if this be rejected, the moral world presents to our view an inextricable maze, a chaos, a scene of interminable confusion, and no prospect appears of its being ever restored to harmony and order. The conduct of the Deity appears shrouded in impenetrable darkness; and there is no resisting of the conclusion, that imperfection and folly are the characteristics of the Almighty—a conclusion from which the mind shrinks back with horror, and which can never be admitted by any rational being who recognises a supreme intelligence presiding over the affairs of the universe.

## SECTION IX.

### ON THE UNEQUAL DISTRIBUTION OF REWARDS AND PUNISHMENTS IN THE PRESENT STATE.

The unequal distribution of rewards and punishments in the present state, viewed in connexion with the justice and other attributes of the Deity, forms another powerful argument in support of the doctrine of a future state.

It is admitted, to a certain extent, that "virtue is its own reward, and vice its own punishment." The natural tendency of virtue, or an obedience to the laws of God, is to produce happiness; and were it universally practised, it would produce the greatest degree of happiness of which human nature in the present state is susceptible. In like manner, the natural tendency of vice is to produce misery; and were its prevalence universal and uncontrolled, the world would be transformed into a society of demons, and every species of happiness banished from the abodes of men. By connecting happiness with the observance of his laws, and misery with the violation of them, the Governor of the world, in the *general course* of his providence, gives a display of the rectitude of his character, and the impartiality of his allotments towards the subjects of his government.

But, although these positions hold true, in the general course of human affairs, there are innumerable cases in which the justice of God, and the impartiality of his procedure, would be liable to be impeached, if this world were the only scene of rewards and punishments. We behold a poor starving wretch, whom hunger has impelled to break open a house, in order to satisfy his craving appetite, or to relieve the wants of a helpless family, dragged with ignominy to the scaffold, to suffer death for his offence. We behold, at the same time, the very tyrant by whose order the sentence was executed, who has plundered provinces, and murdered millions of human beings, who has wounded the peace of a thousand families, and produced universal consternation and despair wherever he appeared—regaling himself in the midst of his favourites, in perfect security from human punishments. Instead of being loaded with fetters, and dragged to a dungeon, to await in hopeless agony the punishment of his crimes, he dwells amidst all the luxuries and splendours of a palace; his favour is courted by surrounding attendants; his praises are chanted by orators and poets; the story of his exploits is engraved in brass and marble; and historians stand ready to transmit his fame to future generations. How does the equity of the divine government appear, in such cases, in permitting an undue punishment to be inflicted on the least offender, and in loading the greatest miscreant with unmerited enjoyments?

Again, in almost every period of the world, we behold men of piety and virtue who have suffered the most unjust and cruel treatment from the hands of haughty tyrants and blood-thirsty persecutors. It would require volumes to describe the instruments of cruelty which have been invented by these fiend-like monsters, and the excruciating torments which have been endured by the victims of their tyranny, while justice seemed to slumber, and the perpetrators were permitted to exult in their crimes. The Waldenses, who lived retired from the rest of the world, among the bleak recesses of the Alps, were a people distinguished for piety, industry, and the practice of every moral virtue. Their incessant labour subdued the barren soil, and prepared it both for grain and pasture. In the course of two hundred and fifty years they increased to the number of eighteen thousand, occupying thirty villages, besides hamlets, the workmanship of their own hands. Regular priests they had none, nor any disputes about religion; neither had they occasion for courts of justice; for brotherly love did not suffer them to go to law. They worshipped God according to the dictates of their conscience and the rules of his word, practised the precepts of his law, and enjoyed the sweets of mutual affection and love. Yet this peaceable and interesting people became the victims of the most cruel and bloody persecution. In the year 1540, the parliament of Provence condemned nineteen of them to be burned for heresy, their trees to be rooted up, and their houses to be razed to the ground. Afterwards a violent persecution commenced against the whole of this interesting people, and an army of banditti was sent to carry the hellish purpose into effect. The soldiers began with massacring the old men, women, and children, all having fled who were able to fly; and then proceeded to burn their houses, barns, corn, and whatever else appertained to them. In the town of Cabriere sixty men and thirty women, who had surrendered upon promise of life, were butchered each of them without mercy. Some women, who had taken refuge in a church, were dragged out and burnt alive. Twenty-two villages were reduced to ashes; and that populous and flourishing district was again turned into a cheerless desert. Yet, after all these atrocities had been committed, the proud pampered priests, at whose instigation this prosecution was commenced, were permitted to live in splendour, to exult over the victims of their cruelty, to revel in palaces, and to indulge in the most shameful debaucheries.—If the present be the only state of punishments and rewards, how shall we vindicate the rectitude of the Almighty, in such dispensations?

In the reign of Louis XIV. and by the orders of that despot, the Protestants of France were treated with the most wanton and diabolical cruelty. Their houses were rifled, their wives and daughters ravished before their eyes, and their bodies forced to endure all the torments that ingenious malice could contrive. His dragoons who were employed in this infamous expedition, pulled them by the hair of their heads, plucked the nails of their fingers and toes, pricked their naked bodies with pins, smoked them in their chimneys with wisps of wet straw, threw them into fires and held them till they were almost burnt, slung them into wells of water, dipped them into ponds, took hold of them with red hot pincers, cut and slashed them with knives, and beat and tormented them to death in a most unmerciful and cruel manner. Some were hanged on the gallows, and others were broken upon wheels, and their mangled bodies were either left unburied, or cast into lakes and dunghills, with every mark of indignation and contempt. Mareschal Montrevel acted a conspicuous part in these barbarous executions. He burnt five hundred men, women, and children, who were assembled together in a mill to pray and sing psalms; he cut the throats of four hundred of the new converts at Montpelier, and drowned their wives and children in the river, near Aignes Mortes. Yet the haughty tyrant by whose orders these barbarous deeds were committed, along with his mareschals and grandees, who assisted in the execution—instead of suffering the visitations of retributive justice, continued, for thirty years after this period, to riot in all the splendours of absolute royalty, entering into solemn treaties, and breaking them when he pleased, and arrogating to himself divine honours; and his historians, instead of branding his memory with infamy, have procured for him the appellation of LOUIS THE GREAT.

A thousand examples of this description might be collected from the records even of modern history, were it necessary for the illustration of this topic. The horrible cruelties which were committed on the Protestant inhabitants in the Netherlands by the agents of Charles V. and Philip II. of Spain, where more than a hundred thousand persons of respectable characters were butchered without mercy by the Dukes of Alva and Parma, for their adherence to the religion of the Reformers,—the dreadful massacres which took place, on St. Bartholomew's day, in Paris and throughout every province of France—the persecutions of the Protestants in England, during the reign of Queen Mary, when the fires of Smithfield were kindled to consume the bodies of the most pious and venerable men—the Irish massacre in the reign of Charles I. when more than 40,000 inoffensive individuals were slaughtered without distinction of age, sex, or condition, and with every circumstance of ferocious cruelty—the persecutions endured by the Scottish Presbyterians, when they were driven from their dwellings, and hunted like wild beasts by the blood-thirsty Claverhouse and his savage dragoons—the many thousands of worthy men who have fallen victims to the flames, and the cruel tortures inflicted by the Inquisitors of Spain, while their haughty persecutors were permitted to riot on the spoils of nations—the fiend-like cruelties of the Mogul emperors in their bloody wars—the devastations and atrocities committed by the Persian despots—the massacre of the Gardiotes by Ali Pacha, and of the inhabitants of Scio by the ferocious Turks—are only a few instances out of many thousands, which the annals of history record of human beings suffering the most unjust and cruel treatment, while their tyrannical persecutors were permitted to prosecute their diabolical career without suffering the punishment due to their crimes. When the mind takes a deliberate review of all the revolting details connected with such facts, it is naturally led to exclaim, "Wherefore do the wicked live, become old, yea are mighty in power? Is there no reward for the righteous? Is there no punishment for the workers of iniquity? Is there no God that judgeth in the earth?" And, indeed, were there no retributions beyond the limits of the present life, we should be necessarily obliged to admit one or other of the following conclusions,—either that no Moral Governor of the world exists, or, that justice and judgment are not the foundation of his throne.

When we take a survey of the moral world around us, as it exists in the present day, the same conclusion forces itself upon the mind. When we behold, on the one hand, the virtuous and upright votary of religion struggling with poverty and misery, treated with scorn and contempt, persecuted on account of his integrity and piety, despoiled of his earthly enjoyments, or condemned to an ignominious death; and on the other, the profligate and oppressor, the insolent despiser of God and religion, passing his days in affluence and luxurious ease, prosecuting with impunity his unhallowed courses, and robbing the widow and the fatherless of their dearest comforts—when we behold hypocrisy successful in all its schemes, and honesty and rectitude overlooked and neglected—the destroyers of our species loaded with wealth and honours, while the benefactors of mankind are pining in obscurity and indigence—knaves and fools exalted to posts of dignity and honour, and men of uprightness and intelligence treated with scorn, and doomed to an inglorious obscurity—criminals of the deepest dye escaping with impunity, and generous actions meeting with a base reward—when we see young men of virtue and intelligence cut off in early life, when they were just beginning to bless mankind with their philanthropic labours, and tyrants and oppressors continuing the pests of society, and prolonging their lives to old age in the midst of their folly and wickedness—human beings torn from their friends and their native home, consigned to perpetual slavery, and reduced below the level of the beasts, while their oppressors set at defiance the laws of God and man, revel in luxurious abundance, and prosper in their crimes;—when we behold one nation and tribe irradiated with intellectual light, another immersed in thick darkness; one enjoying the blessings of civilization and liberty, another groaning under the lash of despotism, and doomed to slavery and bondage,—when we contemplate such facts throughout every department of the moral world, can we suppose, for a moment, that the Divine administration is bounded by the visible scene of things, that the real characters of men shall never be brought to light, that vice is to remain in eternal concealment and impunity, and that the noblest virtues are never to receive their just "recompence of reward?" To admit such conclusions would be in effect to deny the wisdom, goodness, and rectitude of the Ruler of the world, or to suppose, that his all-wise and benevolent designs may be defeated by the folly and wickedness of human beings. But such conclusions are so palpably and extravagantly absurd, that the only other alternative, the reality of a future state of existence, may be pronounced to have the force of a *moral demonstration*. So that, had we no other argument to produce in support of the doctrine of a future state of retribution, this alone would be sufficient to carry conviction to every mind that recognises the existence of a Supreme Intelligence, and entertains just views of the attributes which must necessarily be displayed in his moral administration.

When this conclusion is once admitted, it removes the perplexities, and solves all the difficulties which naturally arise in the mind, when it contemplates the present disordered state of the moral world, and the apparently capricious manner in which punishments and rewards are dispensed. Realizing this important truth, we need not be surprised at the unequal distribution of the Divine favours among the various nations and tribes of mankind; since they are all placed on the first stage of their existence, and eternity is rich in resources, to compensate for all the defects and inequalities of fortune which now exist. We need not be overwhelmed with anguish when we behold the pious and philanthropic youth cut down at the commencement at his virtuous career, since those buds of virtue which began to unfold themselves with so much beauty in the present life, will be fully expanded and bring forth nobler fruits of righteousness in that life which will never end. We need not wonder when we behold tyrants and profligates triumphing, and the excellent ones of the earth trampled under foot, since the future world will present a scene of equitable administration, in which the sorrows of the upright will be turned into joy, the triumphs of the wicked into confusion and shame, and every one rewarded according to his works. We need not harass our minds with perplexing doubts, respecting the wisdom and equity of the dispensations of Providence; since the moral government of God extends beyond the limits of this world, and all its dark and intricate mazes will be fully unravelled in the light of eternity.

———————" *The great eternal scheme*
Involving all, and in *a perfect whole*
Uniting, as the prospect wider spreads,
To Reason's eye will then clear up apace.
——————— Then shall we see the cause
Why unassuming Worth in secret liv'd,
And died neglected; why the good man's share
In life was gall and bitterness of soul;
Why the lone widow and her orphans pin'd
In starving solitude, while Luxury,
In palaces, lay straining her low thought,
To form unreal wants; why heaven-born Truth
And Moderation fair, wore the red marks
Of Superstition's scourge; why licens'd Pain,
That cruel spoiler, that imbosom'd foe,
Imbitter'd all our bliss.—Ye good distrest!
Ye noble Few! who here unbending stand
Beneath life's pressure, yet bear up awhile,
And what your bounded view, which only saw
A little part, deemed evil, is no more:
The storms of Wintry time will quickly pass,
And one unbounded Spring encircle all.—
*Thompson's Winter.*

Thus it appears, that, although God, in the general course of his providence, has connected happiness with the observance of his laws, and misery with the violation of them, in order to display the rectitude of his nature, and his hatred of moral evil; yet he has, at the same time, in numerous instances, permitted vice to triumph, and virtue to be persecuted and oppressed, to convince us, that his government of human beings is not bounded by the limits of time, but extends into the eternal world, where the system of his moral administration will be completed, his wisdom and rectitude justified, and the mysterious ways of his Providence completely unravelled.

This argument might have been farther illustrated from a consideration of those moral perceptions implanted in the human constitution, and which may be considered as having the force of moral laws proceeding from the Governor of the universe. The difference between right and wrong, virtue and vice, is founded upon the nature of things, and is perceptible by every intelligent agent whose moral feelings are not altogether blunted by vicious indulgences. Were a man to affirm that there is no difference between justice and injustice, love and hatred, truth and falsehood; that it is equally the same whether we be faithful to a friend or betray him to his enemies, whether servants act with fidelity to their masters or rob them of their property, whether rulers oppress their subjects or promote their interests, and whether parents nourish their children with tenderness, or smother them in their cradles—he would at once be denounced as a fool and a madman, and hissed out of society. The difference between such actions is eternal and unchangeable, and every moral agent is endued with a faculty which enables him to perceive it. We can choose to perform the one class of actions and to refrain from the other; we can comply with the voice of conscience which deters us from the one, and excites us to the other, or we can resist its dictates, and we can judge whether our actions deserve reward or punishment. Now, if God has endued us with such moral perceptions and capacities, is it reasonable to suppose, that it is equally indifferent to him whether we obey or disobey the laws he has prescribed? Can we ever suppose, that He who governs the universe is an unconcerned spectator of the good or evil actions that happen throughout his dominions? or that he has left man to act, with impunity, according to his inclinations, whether they be right or wrong? If such suppositions cannot be admitted, it follows that man is accountable for his actions, and that it must be an essential part of the Divine government to bring every action into judgment, and to punish or reward his creatures according to their works. And if it appear, in point of fact, that such retributions are not fully awarded in the present state, nor a visible distinction made between the righteous and the violators of his law, we must necessarily admit the conclusion, that the full and equitable distribution of punishments and rewards is reserved to a future world, when a visible and everlasting distinction will be made, and the whole intelligent creation clearly discern between him that served God and him that served him not.

---

## SECTION X.

### ON THE ABSURDITY OF SUPPOSING THAT THE THINKING PRINCIPLE IN MAN WILL EVER BE ANNIHILATED.

It is highly unreasonable, if not absurd, to suppose that the thinking principle in man will ever be annihilated.

In so far as our knowledge of the universe extends, there does not appear a single instance of annihilation throughout the material system. There is no reason to believe, that, throughout all the worlds which are dispersed through the immensity of space, a single atom has ever yet been, or ever will be annihilated. From a variety of observations, it appears highly probable, that the work of creation is still going forward in the distant regions of the universe, and that the Creator is replenishing the voids of space with new worlds and new orders of intelligent beings; and it is reasonable to believe, from the incessant agency of Divine Omnipotence, that new systems will be continually emerging into existence while eternal ages are rolling on. But no instance has yet occurred of any system or portion of matter either in heaven or earth having been reduced to annihilation. *Changes* are indeed incessantly taking place, in countless variety, throughout every department of nature. The spots of the sun, the belts of Jupiter, the surface of the moon, the rings of Saturn, and several portions of the starry heavens, are frequently changing or varying their aspects. On the earth, mountains are crumbling down, the caverns of the ocean filling up, islands are emerging from the bottom of the sea, and again sinking into the abyss; the ocean is frequently shifting its boundaries, and trees, plants, and waving grain now adorn many tracts which were once overwhelmed with the foaming billows. Earthquakes have produced frequent devastations, volcanoes have overwhelmed fruitful fields with torrents of burning lava, and even the solid strata within the bowels of the earth have been bent and disrupted by the operation of some tremendous power. The invisible atmosphere is likewise the scene of perpetual changes and revolutions, by the mixture and decomposition of gases, the respiration of animals, the process of evaporation, the action of winds, and the agencies of light, heat, and the electric and magnetic fluids. The vegetable kingdom is either progressively advancing to maturity or falling into decay. Between the plants and the seeds of vegetables there is not the most distant similarity. A small seed, only one-tenth of an inch in diameter, after rotting for a while in the earth, shoots forth a stem ten thousand times greater in size than the germ from which it sprung, the branches of which afford an ample shelter for the fowls of heaven. The tribes of animated nature are likewise in a state of progressive change, either from infancy to maturity and old age, or from one state of existence to another. The caterpillar is first an egg, next, a crawling worm, then a nymph or chrysalis, and afterwards a butterfly adorned with the most gaudy colours. The may-bug beetle burrows in the earth where it drops its egg, from which its young creeps out in the shape of a maggot, which cast its skin every year, and, in the fourth year, it bursts from the earth, unfolds its wings, and sails in rapture "through the soft air." The animal and vegetable tribes are blended, by a variety of wonderful and incessant changes. Animal productions afford food and nourishment to the vegetable tribes, and the various parts of animals are compounded of matter derived from the vegetable kingdom. The wool of the sheep, the horns of the cow, the teeth of the lion, the feathers of the peacock, and the skin of the deer—nay, even our hands and feet, our eyes and ears, with which we handle and walk, see and hear, and the crimson fluid that circulates in our veins—are derived from plants and herbs which once grew in the fields, which demonstrate the literal truth of the ancient saying, "All flesh is grass."

Still, however, amidst these various and unceasing changes and transformations, no example of annihilation has yet occurred to the eye of the most penetrating observer. When a piece of coal undergoes the process of combustion, its previous *form* disappears, and its component parts are dissolved, but the elementary particles of which it was composed still remain in existence. Part of it is changed into caloric, part into gas, and part into tar, smoke, and ashes, which are soon formed into other combinations. When vegetables die, or are decomposed by heat or cold, they are resolved into their primitive elements, caloric, light, hydrogen, oxygen, and carbon,—which immediately enter into new combinations, and assist in carrying forward the designs of Providence in other departments of nature. But such incessant changes, so far from militating against the idea of the future existence of man, are, in reality, presumptive proofs of his immortal destination. For, if amidst the perpetual transformations, changes, and revolutions that are going forward throughout universal nature in all its departments, no particle of matter is ever lost, or reduced to nothing, it is in the highest degree improbable, that the thinking principle in man will be destroyed, by the change which takes place at the moment of his dissolution. That change, however great and interesting to the individual, may be not more wonderful, nor more mysterious than the changes which take place in the different states of existence to which a caterpillar is destined. This animal, as already stated, is first an *egg*, and how different does its form appear when it comes forth a crawling worm? After living some time in the caterpillar state, it begins to languish, and apparently dies; it is incased in a tomb, and appears devoid of life and enjoyment. After a certain period it acquires new life and vigour, burst its confinement, appears in a more glorious form, mounts upward on expanded wings, and traverses the regions of the air. And, is it not reasonable, from analogy, to believe, that man, in his present state, is only the *rudiments* of what he shall be hereafter in a more expansive sphere of existence? and that, when the body is dissolved in death, the soul takes its ethereal flight into a celestial region, puts on immortality, and becomes "all eye, all ear, all ethereal and divine feeling?"

Since, then, it appears that annihilation forms no part of the plan of the Creator in the material world, is it reasonable to suppose, that a system of annihilation is in incessant operation in the world of mind? that God is every day creating thousands of minds, endued with the most capacious powers, and, at the same time, reducing to eternal destruction thousands of those which he had formerly created? Shall the material universe exist amidst all its variety of changes, and shall that noble creature, *for whose sake the universe was created*, be cut off for ever in the infancy of its being, and doomed to eternal forgetfulness? Is it consistent with the common dictates of reason to admit, that *matter* shall have a longer duration than *mind*, which gives motion and beauty to every material scene? Shall the noble structures of St. Paul and St. Peter survive the ravages of time, and display their beautiful proportions to successive generations, while Wren and Angelo, the architects that planned them, are reduced to the condition of the clods of the valley? Shall the "Novum Organum" of *Bacon*, and the "Optics" and "Principia" of *Newton*, descend to future ages, to unfold their sublime conceptions, while the illustrious minds which gave birth to these productions, are enveloped in the darkness of eternal night? There appears a palpable absurdity and inconsistency in admitting such conclusions. We might almost as soon believe that the universe would continue in its present harmony and order, were its Creator ceasing to exist. "Suppose that the Deity, through all the lapse of past ages, has supported the universe by such miracles of power and wisdom as have already been displayed—merely that he might please himself with letting it fall to pieces, and enjoy the spectacle of the fabric lying in ruins"—would such a design be worthy of infinite Wisdom, or conformable to the ideas we ought to entertain of a Being eternal and immutable in his nature, and possessed of boundless perfection? But suppose, farther, that he will *annihilate* that *rational nature* for whose sake he created the universe, while the material fabric was still permitted to remain in existence, would it not appear still more incompatible with the attributes of a Being of unbounded goodness and intelligence? To blot out from existence the rational part of his creation, and to cherish desolation and a heap of rubbish, is such an act of inconsistency, that the mind shrinks back with horror at the thought of attributing it to the All-Wise and Benevolent Creator.

We are, therefore, necessarily led to the following conclusion: "That, when the human body is dissolved, the immaterial principle by which it was animated, continues to think and act, either in a state of separation from all body, or in some material vehicle to which it is intimately united, and which goes off with it at death; or else, that it is preserved by the Father of spirits for the purpose of animating a body in some future state." The soul contains no principle of disolution within itself, since it is an immaterial uncompounded substance; and, therefore, although the material creation were to be dissolved and to fall into ruins, its energies might still remain unimpaired, and its faculties "flourish in immortal youth,

"Unhurt, amidst the war of elements,
The wrecks of matter and the crush of worlds."

And the Creator is under no necessity to annihilate the soul for want of power to support its faculties, for want of objects on which to exercise them, or for want of space to contain the innumerable intelligences that are incessantly emerging into existence; for the range of immensity is the theatre of his Omnipotence, and that powerful Energy, which has already brought millions of systems into existence, can as easily replenish the universe with ten thousand millions more. If room were wanted for new creations, ten thousand additional worlds could be comprised within the limits of the solar system, while a void space of more than a hundred and eighty thousand miles would still intervene between the orbits of the respective globes; and the immeasurable spaces which intervene between our planetary system and the nearest stars, would afford an ample range for the revolutions of millions of worlds. And, therefore, although every soul, on quitting its mortal frame, were clothed with a new material vehicle, there is ample scope in the spaces of the universe, and in the omnipotent energies of the Creator, for the full exercise of all its powers, and for every enjoyment requisite to its happiness. So that in every point of view in which we can contemplate the soul of man and the perfections of its Creator, it appears not only improbable, but even absurd in the highest degree, to suppose that the spark of intelligence in man will ever be extinguished.

---

## SECTION XI.

### ON THE GLOOMY CONSIDERATIONS AND ABSURD CONSEQUENCES INVOLVED IN THE DENIAL OF A FUTURE STATE.

The denial of the doctrine of a future state involves in it an immense variety of gloomy considerations and absurd consequences.

If the doctrine of a future existence be set aside, man appears an enigma, a rude abortion, and a monster in nature, his structure is inexplicable, and the end for which he was created an unfathomable mystery; the moral world is a scene of confusion, the ways of Providence a dark impenetrable maze, the universe a vast, mysterious, and inexplicable system, and the Deity a Being whose perfections and purposes can never be traced nor unfolded.

Let us suppose, for a few moments, that there is no state of existence beyond the grave, and consequently, that the supposed discoveries of Revelation are a mere delusion; and consider some of the gloomy prospects and absurd consequences to which such a supposition necessarily leads. I shall suppose myself standing in an attitude of serious contemplation, and of anxious inquiry respecting the various scenes and objects which surround me, and the events that pass under my review:—

I first of all look into myself, and inquire, whence I came? whither I am going? who produced me? of what my body is composed? what is the nature of my senses? of the thinking principle I feel within me? and for what purpose was I ushered into being? I perceive in my body a wonderful mechanism which I cannot comprehend: I find by experience, that my will exercises a sovereign power over my muscular system, so that my hands, feet, arms, and limbs, are disposed to obey every impulse, and, at the signal of a wish, to transport my body from one place to another. I find my thinking principle intimately connected with my corporeal frame, and both acting reciprocally on each other; but I cannot fathom the manner in which these operations are effected. I feel ardent desires after enjoyments in which I never shall participate, and capacities for knowledge and improvement which I never can attain. I feel restless and uneasy, even amidst the beauties of nature, and the pleasures of the senses. I ask whence proceeds the want I feel amidst all my enjoyments? Wherefore can I never cease from wishing for something in addition to what I now possess? Whence arises the disgust that so quickly succeeds every sensitive enjoyment, and the want I feel even in the midst of abundance? I ask why I was called into existence at this point of duration, rather than at any other period of that incomprehensible eternity which is past, or of that which is yet to come? why, amidst the vast spaces with which I am encompassed, and the innumerable globes which surround me, I was chained down to this obscure corner of creation from which I feel unable to transport myself? why I was ushered into life in Britain, and not in Papua or New Zealand? and why I was formed to walk erect and not prone, as the inferior animals? To all such inquiries I can find no satisfactory answers, —the whole train of circumstances connected with my existence appears involved in impenetrable darkness and mystery. Of one thing only I am fully assured, that my body shall, ere long, be dissolved and mingle with the dust, and my intellectual faculties, desires, and capacities for knowledge be for ever annihilated in the tomb. I shall then be reduced to nothing, and be as though I never had been, while myriads of beings, like myself, shall start into existence, and perish in like manner, in perpetual succession throughout an eternity to come.

I look backward through ages past—I behold every thing wrapped in obscurity, and perceive no traces of a beginning to the vast system around me,—I stretch forward towards futurity, and perceive no prospect of an end. All things appear to continue as they were from generation to generation, invariably subjected to the same movements, revolutions, and changes, without any distinct marks which indicate either a beginning or an end.—I look around on the scene of terrestrial nature—I perceive many beauties in the verdant landscape, and many objects the mechanism of which is extremely delicate and admirable—I inhale the balmy zephyrs, am charmed with the music of the groves, the splendour of the sun, and the variegated colouring spread over the face of creation. But I behold other scenes, which inspire melancholy and terror. The tempest, the hurricane and the tornado; the sirocco, the samiel and other poisonous winds of the desert; the appalling thundercloud, the forked lightnings, the earthquake shaking kingdoms, and the volcano pouring fiery streams around its base, which desolate villages and cities in their course.—I behold in one place a confused assemblage of the ruins of nature in the form of snow-capped mountains, precipices, chasms and caverns; in another, extensive marshes and immense deserts of barren sand; and, in another, a large proportion of the globe a scene of sterile desolation, and bound in the fetters of eternal ice. I know not what opinion to form of a world where so many beauties are blended with so much deformity, and so many pleasures mingled with so many sorrows and scenes of terror,—or what ideas to entertain of Him who formed it. But I need give myself no trouble in inquiring into such subjects; for my time on earth is short and uncertain, and when I sink into the arms of death, I shall have no more connexion with the universe.

I take a retrospective view of the moral world in past ages, in so far as authentic history serves as a guide, and perceive little else but anarchy, desolation and carnage—the strong oppressing the weak, the powerful and wealthy trampling under foot the poor and indigent—plunderers, robbers, and murderers, ravaging kingdoms, and drenching the earth with human gore. I behold the virtuous and innocent persecuted, robbed and massacred, while bloody tyrants and oppressors roll in their splendid chariots, and revel amidst the luxuries of a palace. In such scenes I perceive nothing like regularity or order, nor any traces of justice or equity in the several allotments of mankind; for since their whole existence terminates in the grave, the virtuous sufferer can never be rewarded, nor the unrighteous despot suffer the punishment due to his crimes. The great mass of human beings appear to be the sport of circumstances, the victims of oppression, and the dupes of knavery and ambition, and the moral world at large an assemblage of discordant elements tossed about like dust before the whirlwind. I hear virtue applauded, and vice denounced as odious and hateful. But what is virtue? A shadow, a phantom, an empty name! Why should I follow after virtue if she interrupts my pleasures, and why should I forsake vice if she points out the path to present enjoyment? It is my wisdom to enjoy life during the short period it continues; and if riches be conducive to my enjoyment of happiness, why should I fear to procure them either by deceit, perjury, or rapine? If sensual indulgence contribute to my pleasure, why should I refrain from drunkenness and debauchery, or any other action that suits my convenience or gratifies my passions, since present enjoyments are all I can calculate upon, and no retributions await me beyond the grave.

I feel myself subjected to a variety of sufferings, disappointments and sorrows—to poverty and reproach, loss of friends, corporeal pains and mental anguish. I am frequently tortured by the recollection of the past, the feeling of the present, and the dread of approaching sufferings. But I see no object to be attained, no end to be accomplished by my subjection to such afflictions: I suffer merely for the purpose of feeling pain, wasting my body and hastening its dissolution: I am sick only to languish under the burden of a feeble emaciated frame—perplexed and downcast only to sink into deeper perplexities and sorrows, oppressed with cares and difficulties only to enter on a new scene of danger and suffering. No drop of comfort mingles itself with the bitter cup of sorrow: no affliction is sweetened and alleviated by the prospect of a better world; for the gloomy mansions of the grave bound my views and terminate all my hopes and fears. How, then, can I be easy under my sufferings? how can I be cordially resigned to the destiny which appointed them? or how can I trace the benevolence of a superior Being in permitting me thus to be pained and tormented for no end? I will endeavour to bear them with resolute desperation, merely because I am borne down by necessity to pain and affliction, and cannot possibly avoid them.

I lift my eyes to the regions above, and contemplate the splendours of the starry frame. What an immensity of suns, and systems and worlds burst upon my view, when I apply the telescope to the spaces of the firmament! How incalculable their number! how immeasurable their distance! how immense their magnitude! how glorious their splendour! how sublime their movements! When I attempt to grasp this stupendous scene, my imagination is bewildered, and my faculties overpowered with wonder and amazement. I gaze, I ponder; I feel a longing desire to know something farther respecting the nature and destination of these distant orbs; but my vision is bounded to a general glimpse, my powers are limited, and when I would fly away to those distant regions, I find myself chained down, by an overpowering force, to the diminutive ball on which I dwell. Wherefore, then, were the heavens so beautifully adorned, and so much magnificence displayed in their structure, and why were they ever presented to my view; since I am never to become farther acquainted with the scenes they unfold? Perhaps this is the last glance I shall take of the mighty concave, before my eyes have closed in endless light. "Wherefore was light given to him that is in misery,—to a man whose way is hid, and whom God hath hedged in?" Had I been enclosed in a gloomy dungeon my situation had been tolerable, but here I stand as in a splendid palace, without comfort and without hope, expecting death every moment to terminate my prospects; and when it arrives, the glories of the heavens to me will be annihilated for ever.

I behold science enlarging its boundaries, and the arts advancing towards perfection; I see numerous institutions organizing, and hear lectures on philosophy delivered for the improvement of mankind, and I am invited to take a part in those arrangements which are calculated to produce a general diffusion of knowledge among all ranks. But of what use is knowledge to beings who are soon to lose all consciousness of existence? It requires many weary steps and sleepless nights to climb the steep ascent of science; and when we have arrived at the highest point which mortals have ever reached, we descry still loftier regions which we never can approach,—our footing fails, and down we sink into irretrievable ruin. If our progress in science here were introductory to a future scene of knowledge and enjoyment, it would be worthy of being prosecuted by every rational intelligence; but to beings who are uncertain whether they shall exist in the universe for another day, it is not only superfluous, but unfriendly to their present enjoyments. For, the less knowledge they acquire of the beauties and sublimities of nature, and the more brutish, ignorant and sottish they become, the less they will feel at the moment when they are about to be launched into non-existence. Let the mass of mankind, then, indulge themselves in whatever frivolous amusements they may choose; do not interrupt their sensual pleasures, by vainly attempting to engage them in intellectual pursuits; let them eat and drink, and revel and debauch, for to-morrow they die. All that is requisite, is, to entwine the chains of despotism around their necks, to prevent them from aspiring after the enjoyments of their superiors.

In short, I endeavour to form some conceptions of the attributes of that great unknown Cause which produced all things around me. But my thoughts become bewildered amidst a maze of unaccountable operations, of apparent contradictions and inconsistencies. I evidently perceive that the Creator of the universe is possessed of boundless *power*, but I see no good reason to conclude that he exercises unerring wisdom, unbounded goodness and impartial justice. I perceive, indeed, some traces of wisdom, in the construction of my body and its several organs of sensation; and of goodness, in the smiling day, the flowery landscape, and the fertile plains; but I know not how to reconcile these with some other parts of his operations. How can I attribute the perfection of wisdom to one who has implanted in my constitution desires which will never be gratified, and furnished me with moral and intellectual faculties which will never be fully exercised, and who has permitted the moral world in every age to exhibit a scene of disorder? I perceive no evidences of his benevolence in subjecting me to a variety of sorrows and sufferings which accomplish no end but the production of pain; in tantalizing me with hopes, and alarming me with fears of futurity which are never to be realized, and in throwing a veil of mystery over all his purposes and operations. Nor can I trace any thing like impartial justice in the bestowment of his favours, for disappointments and sorrows are equally the lot of the righteous and the wicked, and frequently it happens that the innocent are punished and disgraced, while villains and debauchees are permitted to glory in their crimes. All that I can plainly perceive, is, the operation of uncontrollable power, directed by no principle but caprice, and accomplishing nothing that can inspire ardent affection, or secure the permanent happiness of rational beings.

Such are some of the gloomy reflections of a hopeless mortal whose prospect is bounded by the grave; and such are some of the horrible consequences which the denial of a future state necessarily involves. It throws a veil of darkness over the scenes of creation, and wraps in impenetrable mystery the purposes for which man was created,—it exhibits the moral world as a chaotic mass of discordant elements, accomplishing no end, and controlled by no intelligent agency,—it represents mankind as connected with each other merely by time and place, as formed merely for sensual enjoyment, and destined to perish with the brutes,—it subverts the foundations of moral action, removes the strongest motives to the practice of virtue, and opens the flood-gates of every vice,—it removes the anchor of hope from the anxious mind, and destroys evey principle that has a tendency to support us in the midst of sufferings,—it throws a damp on every effort to raise mankind to the dignity of their moral and intellectual natures, and is calculated to obstruct the progress of useful science,—it prevents the mind from investigating and admiring the beauties of creation, and involves in a deeper gloom the ruins of nature which are scattered over the globe,—it terminates every prospect of becoming more fully acquainted with the glories of the firmament, and every hope of beholding the plans of Providence completely unfolded,—it involves the character of the Deity in awful obscurity, it deprives Him of the attributes of infinite wisdom, benevolence and rectitude, and leaves him little more than boundless omnipotence, acting at random, and controlled by no beneficent agency. In short, it obliterates every motive to the performance of noble and generous actions, damps the finest feelings and affections of humanity, leads to universal scepticism, cuts off the prospect of every thing which tends to cheer the traveller in his pilgrimage through life, and presents to his view nothing but an immense blank, overspread with the blackness of darkness for ever.

Such being the blasphemous and absurd consequences which flow from the denial of the doctrine of a future state of retribution—the man who obstinately maintains such a position, must be considered as unworthy not only of the name of a philosopher, but of that of a rational being, and as one who would believe against demonstration, and swallow any absurdity, however extravagant, which quadrates with his grovelling appetites and passions. Mathematicians frequently demonstrate a truth by showing that its contrary is impossible, or involves an absurdity. Thus, *Euclid* demonstrates the truth of the fourth proposition of the first book of his Elements, by showing that its contrary implies this obvious absurdity—"that two straight lines may enclose a space." This mode of proving the truth of a proposition is considered by every geometrician, as equally conclusive and satisfactory, as the *direct* method of demonstration; because the contrary of every falsehood must be truth, and the contrary of every truth, falsehood. And if this mode of demonstration is conclusive in mathematics, it ought to be considered as equally conclusive in moral and theological reasoning. If, for example, the denial of a future existence involves in it the idea that God is not a Being possessed of impartial justice, and of perfect wisdom and goodness—notwithstanding the striking displays of the two last-mentioned attributes in the system of nature—we must, I presume, either admit the doctrine of the immortality of man, or deny that a Supreme Intelligence presides over the affairs of the universe. For, a Being divested of these attributes, is not entitled to the name of Deity, nor calculated to inspire intelligent minds with adoration and love; but it is reduced to something like *uncontrollable fate*, or mere physical force, impelling the movements of universal nature without a plan, without discrimination, and without intelligence. On the same principle (the *reductio ad absurdum*,) we demonstrate the earth's annual revolution round the sun. The motions of the planets, as viewed from the earth, present an inexplicable maze contrary to every thing we should expect in a well arranged and orderly system. These bodies appear sometimes to move backwards, sometimes forwards, sometimes to remain stationary, and to describe looped curves, so anomalous or confused, that we cannot suppose an Infinite Intelligence the contriver of a system of such inextricable confusion. Hence the astronomer concludes, on good grounds, *that the earth is a moving body;* and no one thoroughly acquainted with the subject ever calls it in question: for when our globe is considered as revolving round the centre of the system in concert with the other planetary orbs, all the apparent irregularities in their motions are completely accounted for, and the whole system appears reduced to a beautiful and harmonious order, in accordance with every idea we ought to form of the wisdom and intelligence of its author.

In the same way, the admission of the doctrine of a future state accounts for the apparent irregularities of the moral world, and affords a key for a solution of all the difficulties that may arise in the mind respecting the equity of the Divine administration in the present state. In opposition to the desponding reflections and gloomy views of the sceptic, it inspires the virtuous mind with a lively hope, and throws a glorious radiance over the scenes of creation, and over every part of the government of the Almighty. It exhibits the Self-existent and Eternal Mind as an object of ineffable sublimity, grandeur, and loveliness, invested with unerring wisdom, impartial justice, and boundless benevolence, presiding over an endless train of intelligent minds formed after his image, governing them with just and equitable laws, controlling all things by an almighty and unerring hand, and rendering all his dispensations ultimately conducive to the happiness of the moral universe. It presents before us an unbounded scene, in which we may hope to contemplate the scheme of Providence in all its objects and bearings, where the glories of the divine perfections will be illustriously displayed, where the powers of the human mind will be perpetually expanding, and new objects of sublimity and beauty incessantly rising to the view, in boundless perspective, world without end. It dispels the clouds that hang over the present and future destiny of man, and fully accounts for those longing looks into futurity which accompany us at every turn, and those capacious powers of intellect, which cannot be fully exerted in the present life. It presents the most powerful motives to a life of virtue, to the performance of beneficent and heroic actions, to the prosecution of substantial science, and to the diffusion of useful knowledge among all ranks of mankind. It affords the strongest consolation and support, amidst the trials of life, and explains the reasons of those sufferings to which we are here exposed, as being incentives to the exercise of virtue, and as "working out for us a far more exceeding and eternal weight of glory." It affords us ground to hope that the veil which now intercepts our view of the distant regions of creation, will be withdrawn, and that the amazing structure of the universe, in all its sublime proportions and beautiful arrangements, will be more clearly unfolded to our view. It dispels the terrors which naturally surround the messenger of death, and throws a radiance over the mansions of the tomb. It cheers the gloomy vale of death, and transforms it into a passage which leads to a world of perfection and happiness, where moral evil shall be for ever abolished, where intellectual light shall beam with effulgence on the enraptured spirit, and where celestial virtue, now so frequently persecuted and contemned, shall be enthroned in undisturbed and eternal empire.

Since, then, it appears, that the denial of a future state involves in it so many difficulties, absurd consequences and blasphemous assumptions, and the admission of this doctrine throws a light over the darkness that broods over the moral world, presents a clue to unravel the mazes of the divine dispensations, and solves every difficulty in relation to the present condition of the human race—the pretended philosopher who rejects this important truth must be considered as acting in direct opposition to those principles of reasoning which he uniformly admits in his physical and mathematical investigations, and as determined to resist the force of every evidence which can be adduced in proof of his immortal destination.

---

Thus I have endeavored, in the preceding pages, to prove and illustrate the immortality of man, from a consideration of the universal belief which this doctrine has obtained among all nations—the desire of immortality implanted in the human breast—the strong desire *of knowledge*, and the *capacious intellectual powers* with which man is furnished—the capacity of making *perpetual progress* towards intellectual and moral perfection—*the unlimited range of view* which is opened to the human mind throughout the *immensity of space* and *duration*—the *moral powers* of action with which man is endued—the *forebodings* and apprehensions of the mind when under the influence of remorse—the disordered state of the *moral* world when contrasted with the systematical order of the material—the *unequal distribution of rewards and punishments*, viewed in connection with the justice of God—the *absurdity* of admitting that *the thinking principle in man will be annihilated*—and the *blasphemous and absurd consequences* which would follow if the idea of a future state of retribution were rejected.

Perhaps there are some of these arguments, *taken singly*, that would be insufficient fully to establish the truth of man's eternal destiny; but when taken in combination with each other, they carry irresistible evidence to the mind of every unbiassed inquirer. They all reflect a mutual lustre on each other; they hang together in perfect harmony; they are fully consistent with the most amiable and sublime conceptions we can form of the Deity; they are congenial to the sentiments entertained by the wisest and best of men in every age; they are connected with all the improvements and discoveries in the moral and physical worlds; and, like the radii of a circle, they all converge to the same point, and lead directly to the same conclusion. It appears next to impossible, that such a mutual harmony, consistency, and dependence, could exist among a series of propositions that had no foundation in truth; and, therefore, they ought to be considered, when taken conjunctly, as having all the force of a *moral demonstration*. They rest on the same principles and process of reasoning from which we deduce the being of a God; and I see no way of eluding their force, but by erasing from the mind every idea of a Supreme Intelligence. Hence, it has generally, I might say, uniformly been found, that all nations that have acknowledged the existence of a Divine Being, have likewise recognised the idea of a future state of retribution. These two fundamental propositions are so intimately connected, and the latter is so essentially dependent on the former, that they must stand or fall together. And, consequently, we find, that the man who obstinately rejects the doctrine of a future state, either avows himself a down-right atheist, or acts precisely in the same way as a person would do, who believes that a Supreme Moral Governor has no existence.

But even the principles of atheism itself, though frequently embraced by vicious characters to allay their fears, are not sufficient to remove all apprehensions in regard to a future existence. For, if the universe be the production merely of an eternal succession of causes and effects, produced by blind necessity impelling the atoms of matter through the voids of immensity—what should hinder, that amidst the infinite combinations arising from perpetual motion, men should be created, destroyed, and again ushered into existence, with the same faculties, reminiscences, perceptions and relations as in their former state of existence? And, although thousands or millions of years should intervene between such transformations, yet such periods might appear as short and imperceptible as the duration which passes while our faculties are absorbed in a sound repose. The idea of infinity, immensity, and an endless succession of changes, renders such a supposition not altogether impossible. But what a dreadful futurity might not the mind be left to picture to itself in such a case? If the movements of the universe were the productions of chance, directed by no intelligent agency, we should incessantly be haunted with the most dreadful anticipations. We should see the images of death, annihilation, and reproduction advancing before us in the most terrific forms, and should find it impossible to determine on what foundation the hopes and the destiny of intelligences reposed. We should be uncertain whether mankind were doomed to perish irrecoverably, or, by the operation of some unknown cause, or accident, to be reproduced, at some future period in duration, and devoted to endless torments. The comparative order and tranquillity which now subsist, or have subsisted for ages past, could afford us no ground of hope that such consequences would not take place: for all the revolutions of time to which we can look back, are but as a moment in the midst of infinite duration, and the whole earth but a point in the immensity of space. So that, during the lapse of infinite ages, changes, revolutions and transformations might be effected, which might overwhelm all the intelligent beings that ever existed, in eternal misery. Hence it appears, that even atheism itself, with all its mass of contradictions and absurdities, cannot entirely shelter its abettors from the terrors of an unknown futurity.

I shall only remark farther, on this part of my subject,—that, although the arguments now adduced in support of the immortality of man were less powerful than they really are, they ought to make a deep impression on the mind of every reflecting person, and determine the line of conduct which he ought to pursue. If they were only probable—if they possessed no greater degree of weight than simply to overbalance the opposite arguments, still, it would be every man's interest to act on the supposition, that a future world has a real existence. For, in the ordinary affairs of human life, and even in the sciences, our opinions and conduct are generally determined by a series of probabilities, and a concurrence of reasons, which supply the want of more conclusive evidence on subjects which are not susceptible of strict demonstration. A merchant, when he purchases a certain commodity, has no demonstrative evidence that the sale of it shall ultimately turn to his advantage; but, from a consideration of its price and quality, of the circumstances of trade, and of his immediate prospects, he determines on the purchase; and, by acting on the ground of similar probabilities, he conducts his affairs, so as to issue in his prosperity and success. A philosopher has no *demonstrative* arguments to support the one-half of the opinions he has formed, in relation to the phenomena of human society, and of the material world. His deductions respecting the causes of the winds, of thunder and lightning, of volcanic eruptions, of the nature of light, sound, electricity, galvanism, and other operations in the system of nature, are grounded on that species of reasoning which is termed *analogical*, and which, at best, amounts to nothing more than a high degree of probability. Notwithstanding, he feels no hesitation in prosecuting his experiments and researches, under the guidance of such reasoning, confident that it will ultimately lead him to the innermost recesses of the temple of truth; for we know, that the most splendid discoveries of modern times, have originated from inquiries and observations, conducted on the ground of analogical reasoning. In like manner, in the important subject under consideration, we ought to be determined in our views and conduct, even by *probabilities*, although the arguments adduced should leave the question at issue in some measure undetermined. For, if an eternal world has a real existence, we not only embrace an error in rejecting this idea, but, by acting in conformity with our erroneous conceptions, run the risk of exposing ourselves to the most dreadful and appalling consequences. Whereas, if there be no future state, the belief of it, accompanied with a corresponding conduct, can produce no bad effect either upon our own minds or those of others. On the contrary, it would prove a pleasing illusion during our passage, through a world of physical and moral evil, and would revive the downcast spirit, when overwhelmed with the disappointments and sorrows which are unavoidable in our present condition. So that, even in this case, we might adopt the sentiment of an ancient philosopher,* and say—"If I am wrong in believing that the souls of men are immortal, I please myself in my mistake; nor while I live will I ever choose that this opinion, with which I am so much delighted, should be wrested from me. But if, at death, I am to be annihilated, as some minute philosophers suppose, I am not afraid lest those wise men, when extinct too, should laugh at my error."

But, if the arguments we have brought forward, amount, not only to bare probability, but to *moral certainty*, or, at least, to something nearly approximating to moral demonstration—if the opposite opinion involves a train of absurdities, if it throws a dismal gloom over the destiny of man, and over the scenes of the universe, and if it robs the Almighty of the most glorious and distinguishing attributes of his nature—no words are sufficient to express the folly and inconsistency of the man, by whatever title he may be distinguished, who is determined to resist conviction, and who resolutely acts, as if the idea of a future world were a mere chimera. To pass through life with indifference and unconcern, to overlook the solemn scenes of the invisible world, and to brave the terrors of the Almighty, which may be displayed in that state—in the face of such powerful arguments as even reason can produce—is not only contrary to every prudential principle of conduct, but the height of infatuation and madness. Such persons must be left to be aroused to consideration, by the awful conviction which will flash upon their minds, when they are transported to that eternal state which they now disregard, and find themselves placed at the bar of an almighty and impartial Judge.

Among the considerations which have been adduced to prove the immortality of man, I have taken no notice of an argument, which is almost exclusively dwelt upon by some writers, namely, that which is founded on the *immateriality* of the human soul. I have declined entering upon any illustration of this topic,—1. Because the proof of the soul's immateriality involves a variety of abstract metaphysical discussions, and requires replies to various objections which have been raised against it, which would tend only to perplex readers endowed with plain common sense. 2. Because the doctrine of the immateriality of the thinking principle, however clearly it may be proved, can add nothing to the weight of the considerations already brought forward; nor, when considered by itself, can it afford any conclusive argument in favour of the soul's immortality. It simply leads us to this conclusion,

* Cicero.

—that, since the soul is an uncompounded substance, it cannot perish by a decomposition of its parts; and consequently, *may* exist, in a separate state, in the full exercise of its powers, after its corporeal tenement is dissolved. But its immortality cannot necessarily be inferred from its natural capacity of existing in a state of separation from the body; for that being who created it may, if he pleases, reduce it to annihilation, since all the works of God, whether material or immaterial, depend wholly on that power by which they were originally brought into existence. Its immortality depends solely on the will of its Creator, without whose sustaining energy the whole creation would sink into its original nothing. If it could be proved that God will employ his power to annihilate the soul, in vain should we attempt to demonstrate that it is naturally immortal. But whether God *wills* that the soul should be destroyed at death, is a very different question from that which relates to its nature as an immaterial substance. The whole train of argument illustrated in the preceding pages, affords, I presume, satisfactory evidence that the Creator will never annihilate the human soul, but has destined it to remain in the vigorous exercise of its noble faculties to all eternity.

Hence it follows, that it is a matter of trivial importance, when considering the arguments which prove our immortal destiny, whether we view the soul as a *material*, or as an *immaterial* substance. Suppose I were to yield to the sceptic, for a moment, the position, "that the soul is a material substance, and cannot exist but in connexion with a material frame," what would he gain by the concession? It would not subtract a single atom from the weight of evidence which has already been brought forward to prove the immortality of man. For, if we can prove that God has willed the immortality of the soul and, consequently, has determined to interpose his almighty power, in order to support its faculties throughout an eternal existence, in vain shall he have proved that it is not immortal *in its nature*. He who created the human soul and endued it with so many noble faculties, can continue its existence, through an unlimited extent of duration, in a thousand modes incomprehensible to us. If a material system of organical powers be necessary for the exercise of its energies, he can either clothe it with a fine ethereal vehicle, at the moment its present tenement is dissolved, or connect it, in another region of the universe, with a corporeal frame of more exquisite workmanship, analogous to that which it now animates. For any thing we know to the contrary, there may be some fine material system, with which it is essentially connected, and which goes off with it at death, and serves as a medium through which it may hold a direct communication with the visible universe. Even although its consciousness of existence were to be suspended for thousands of years, its Creator can afterwards invest it with a new organical frame, suited to the expansive sphere of action to which it is destined; and the intervening period of its repose may be made to appear no longer than the lapse of a few moments. In short, if God has sustained the material universe hitherto, and will, in all probability, continue it for ever in existence, so that not a single atom now existing, shall at any future period be annihilated—the same Power and Intelligence can, with equal ease, support the thinking principle in man, whatever may be its nature or substance, and however varied the transformations through which it may pass. If the Creator is both able and willing to perpetuate the existence of the rational spirit through an endless duration, and if his wisdom, benevolence and rectitude require that this object should be accomplished, all difficulties arising from its nature or the mode of its subsistence, must at once evanish. The preceding arguments in support of a future state, are, therefore, equally conclusive, whether we consider the soul as a pure immaterial substance, or as only a peculiar modification of matter; so that the sceptic who adopts the absurd idea of the materiality of mind, cannot, even on this ground invalidate the truth of man's eternal destination.

# CHAPTER II.

## PROOFS OF A FUTURE STATE FROM DIVINE REVELATION.

THE evidences of a future state, which we have endeavoured, in the preceding pages, to investigate on the principles of human reason, are amply confirmed and illustrated in the Revelation contained in the Sacred Scriptures. It is one of the distinguishing characteristics of that revelation, that, in every important point, it harmonizes with the deductions of sound reason, and the principles of common sense. This was naturally to be presumed; since God is the author both of the reasoning faculty, and of the declarations contained in the volume of inspiration; and this consideration forms a strong presumptive argument in support of the divine authority of the Scriptures, and should excite us to receive, with cordial veneration and esteem, a revelation which confirms the law of nature, and is congenial to the sentiments of the wisest and the best of mankind in all ages. If any serious inquirer, who had entertained doubts on this subject, has been led to a conviction of the reality of his immortal destiny, by such arguments as the preceding, he will naturally resort to the Sacred Records for more full information on this important point; and I should have no fear of any one remaining long an enemy of Revelation, when once a powerful conviction of a future state has been deeply impressed on his mind. If a man is fully convinced that he is standing every moment on the verge of an eternal state, he cannot but feel anxious to acquire the most correct information that can be obtained respecting that world which is to constitute his everlasting abode; and if he is altogether careless and insensible in this respect, it is quite clear, that he has no thorough conviction of the realities of a life to come.

The Christian Revelation has "brought life and immortality to light," not so much on account of the express assurance it gives of the reality of a future world, but chiefly, as it clearly exhibits the nature and the employments of that state, its endless duration, the ground on which we can expect happiness in it, and the dispositions and virtues which qualify us for relishing its exercises and enjoying its felicities; and particularly, as it opens to our view the glorious scene of a "*resurrection from the dead,*" and the re-union of soul and body in the mansions of bliss.

In illustrating this topic, it would be quite unnecessary to enter into any lengthened details. When the divine authority of the Scriptures is recognised, a single proposition or assertion, when it is clear and express, is sufficient to determine the reality of any fact, or the truth of any doctrine; and therefore, I shall do little more than bring forward a few passages bearing on the point under consideration, and intersperse some occasional remarks. As some have called in question the position, "that the doctrine of a future state was known to the Jews," I shall, in the first place, bring forward a few passages and considerations to show that the doctrine of immortality was recognised under the Jewish as well as under the Christian dispensations.

As the belief of a future state lies at the very foundation of religion, it is impossible to suppose, that a people whom the Almighty had chosen to be his worshippers, and the depositories of his revealed will, should have remained ignorant of this interesting and fundamental truth, and have had their views confined solely to the fleeting scenes of the present world. "Faith," says Paul, in his Epistle to the Hebrews, "is the confident expectation of things hoped for, and the conviction of things not seen."* It includes a belief in the existence of God, and of the rewards of a life to come; for, says the same apostle, "He that cometh to God must believe that he is, and that he is the rewarder of them that diligently seek him." Having stated these principles, he proceeds to show, that the ancient patriarchs were animated in all their services by their conviction of the realities of a future and invisible world. With respect to Abraham he informs us, that "he expected a city which had foundations, whose builder and maker is God." He obtained no such city in the earthly Canaan; and therefore we must necessarily suppose, that his views were directed to mansions of perpetuity beyond the confines of the present world. With respect to Moses, he says, that under all his persecutions and afflictions, "he endured as seeing Him who is invisible; for he had a respect to the recompense of reward." That *reward* did not consist in temporal grandeur, otherwise, he might have enjoyed it in much more

* Doddridge's Translation of Heb. xi. 1

splendour and security in Egypt, as the son of Pharaoh's daughter; nor did it consist in the possession of Canaan, for he was not permitted to enter into that goodly land. It must, therefore, have been the celestial inheritance to which the eye of his faith looked forward, as the object of his joyful anticipation. With regard to all the other patriarchs whose names stand high on the records of the Old-Testament Church, he declares, that "they confessed that they were strangers and pilgrims on earth," that "they declared plainly that they sought a *better country*, that is, an heavenly;" and that those who "were tortured" to induce them to renounce their religion, endured their sufferings with invincible fortitude, "not accepting deliverance" when it was offered them, "*that they might obtain a better resurrection.*"

In accordance with these declarations, the prophets, in many parts of their writings, speak decisively of their expectations of a future life, and of the consolation the prospect of it afforded them, under their sufferings. "As for me," says the Psalmist, "I shall behold thy face in righteousness; I shall be satisfied when I awake with thy likeness." "My flesh shall rest in hope; for thou wilt not leave my soul in the grave. Thou wilt show me the path of life: in thy presence is fulness of joy; at thy right hand are pleasures for evermore." "Yea, though I walk through the valley of the shadow of death, I will fear no evil; for thou art with me. Surely goodness and mercy will follow me all the days of my life, *and I shall dwell in the house of the Lord for ever.*" "God will redeem my soul from the grave; for he will receive me." "Whom have I in heaven but thee? and there is none upon earth that I desire besides thee. Thou wilt guide me with thy counsel, and afterward receive me to glory. My flesh and my heart shall fail; but God is the strength of my heart and *my portion for ever.*" Nothing can be more clear and express than such declarations. If the psalmist had no belief in a future state, and no hopes of enjoying its felicities, after the termination of his earthly pilgrimage, his language is absolutely without meaning. What rational interpretation can be given to the expressions of "dwelling in the house of God for ever," after his days on earth are numbered—of "Jehovah being his everlasting portion," after his heart had ceased to beat—and of his being "redeemed from the grave," and put in possession of "fulness of joy," and "everlasting pleasures,"—if his views were confined to the narrow limits of time, and the boundaries of the earthly Canaan? Such expressions would be a species of bombast and hyperbole altogether inconsistent with the dignity and veracity of an inspired writer.

Job, that illustrious example of patience under affliction, consoled his spirit in the midst of adversity by the hopes he entertained of a blessed immortality. "I know," says he, "that my Redeemer liveth, and that he shall stand at the latter day upon the earth: and, after I awake, though this body shall be destroyed, yet out of my flesh shall I see God." In various other passages of the prophets, not only a future state, but a resurrection from the grave and the solemnities of the day of judgment are plainly intimated. "The dead men shall live, together with my dead body shall they rise. Awake and sing, ye that dwell in dust; for thy dew is as the dew of herbs, and the earth shall cast out the dead." "Rejoice, O young man, in thy youth, and walk in the ways of thy heart, and in the sight of thine eyes: but know thou, that for all these things God will bring thee into judgment." "For God shall bring every work into judgment, with every secret thing, whether it be good, or whether it be evil." "Many of them that sleep in the dust of the earth shall awake, some to everlasting life, and some to shame and everlasting contempt. And they that be wise shall shine as the brightness of the firmament; and they that turn many to righteousness as the stars for ever and ever."

One reason, among others, why the doctrine of a future state is not frequently adverted to, and treated in detail, in the writings of the Old Testament, undoubtedly is, that it was a truth so well understood, so generally recognised, and so essential to the very idea of religion, that it would have been superfluous to have dwelt upon it in detail, or to have brought it forward as a new discovery. This doctrine is implied in the phraseology of the Old Testament, in many cases where there is no *direct* reference to a future world, as in such passages as the following: "I am the God of thy father, the God of Abraham, the God of Isaac, and the God of Jacob:" Exod. iii. 6. Our Saviour has taught us to consider this and similar passages as embodying the doctrine of a future life. "For God is not the God of the dead, but of the living." If the holy patriarchs whose names are here commemorated with so much honour, were reduced to the condition of the clods of the valley, and if their intellectual part were not in existence, Jehovah would never own the high relation of a God to those whom he has finally abandoned, and suffered to sink into non-existence. Consequently, Abraham, Isaac and Jacob were living and intelligent beings, in another state, when this declaration was made to Moses at the burning bush. The phrase, "He was gathered to his people," implies a similar sentiment. In Gen. xxv. it is said, "Abraham gave up the ghost, and was *gathered to his people.*" This expression is not to be viewed as importing that he was buried with his fathers; for the fathers of Abraham were buried several hundreds of miles from the cave of Machpelah, in which Abraham's mortal remains were deposited,—some of them in the land of Chaldea, and some of them in the country of Mesopotamia, which lay at a considerable distance from the land of Canaan. The true meaning must therefore be, that he was "gathered" to the assembly of the righteous, to the blessed society of those congenial spirits, eminent for their piety, who had passed before him into the invisible world. Hence, says the Psalmist, "*Gather* not my soul with sinners."—Hence, says Job, when describing the miseries of the wicked, "The rich man shall lie down" in the grave, "but he *shall not be gathered*;" and the prophet, when personating the Messiah, declares, "Though Israel be not *gathered*, yet shall I be glorious in the eyes of Jehovah."

These remarks may suffice to show, that the doctrine of a future state was known, and generally recognised, by the venerable patriarchs and other illustrious characters that flourished under the Jewish dispensation.

That this doctrine is exhibited in the clearest light in the *Christian* Revelation, has never been disputed, by any class of religionists, nor even by infidels themselves. In this revelation, however, the doctrine of immortality is not attempted to be proved by any laboured arguments or supernatural evidences, nor is it brought forward as a new discovery. It is evidently taken for granted, and incidentally interwoven through all the discourses of our Saviour and his apostles, as a truth which lies at the foundation of religion, and which never ought for a moment to be called in question. In elucidating this topic, it will be quite sufficient simply to quote a few passages from the New-Testament writers.

Paul, when looking forward to the dissolution of his mortal frame, declares, in his own name, and in the name of all Christians—"Our light affliction, which is but for a moment, worketh out for us a far more exceeding and eternal weight of glory; while we aim not at things which are visible, but at those which are invisible; for the things which are visible are temporary, but those which are invisible are eternal. For we know, that, if this earthly house of our tabernacle were dissolved, we have a building of God, an house not made with hands, eternal in the heavens." When the time of his departure from the body was at hand, he declared, "I have fought the good fight, I have finished my course, I have kept the faith: henceforth there is laid up for me a crown of righteousness, which the righteous Judge shall give me at that day; and not to me only, but to all them that love his appearing." The apostle Peter declares, that believers "are regenerated to the lively hope of an inheritance incorruptible, undefiled, and that fadeth not away, reserved in heaven for them." "When the chief Shepherd shall appear, we shall receive a crown of glory, which fadeth not away." Our Saviour declares, in reference to his servants, "I give unto them *eternal life*, and they shall never perish." "In my Father's house are many mansions: if it were not so I would have told you. I go to prepare a place for you. And I will come again, and receive you to myself, that where I am there you may be also." And again, "Many shall come from the east and the west, and shall sit down with Abraham, and Isaac, and Jacob, in the kingdom of heaven." "Then shall the righteous shine forth as the sun in the kingdom of their Father."

While these and similar passages clearly demonstrate the certainty of an eternal world, and the future happiness of the righteous—the apostles and evangelists are equally explicit in asserting the future misery of the wicked. "The unrighteous shall not inherit the kingdom of God," but "shall go away into everlasting punishment." "The Lord Jesus shall be revealed from heaven, with his mighty angels, in flaming fire, taking vengeance on them them that know not God, and who obey not the Gospel: who shall be punished with everlasting destruction from the presence of the Lord, and from the glory of his power." "At the end of the world, the angels shall come forth and sever the wicked from among the just, and shall cast them into a furnace of fire, where shall be weeping and gnashing of teeth." "The fearful and unbelieving, and murderers, and whoremongers, and sorcerers, and idolaters, and all liars, shall have their part in the lake which burneth with fire and brimstone. There shall in nowise enter into the heavenly Jerusalem any thing that defileth, neither whatsoever worketh abomination, or maketh a lie."

The way by which happiness in the future world may be obtained is also clearly exhibited. "Eternal life is the gift of God, through Jesus Christ our Lord." "For God so loved the world, that he gave his only begotten Son, that whosoever believeth in him should not perish but have everlasting life." "This is the record, that God hath given to us eternal life, and this life is in his son." "The God of all grace hath called us unto his eternal glory by Christ Jesus."—The dispositions of those on whom this happiness will be conferred, and the train of action which prepares us for the enjoyment of eternal bliss, are likewise distinctly described. "Whatsoever a man soweth, that shall he also reap. He that soweth to the flesh, shall of the flesh reap corruption, but he that soweth to the spirit, shall of the spirit reap life everlasting." "To them who, by patient continuance in well-doing, seek for glory, honour, and immortality, God will recompense eternal life." "The pure in heart shall see God." "He that *doeth the will of God abideth for ever.*" "*Him that overcometh* will I make a pillar in the temple of my God, and he shall go no more out." "Blessed are they that do his commandments, that they may have a right to the tree of life, and may enter through the gates into the city."

The nature of the heavenly felicity, and the employments of the future world, are likewise incidentally stated and illustrated. The foundation of happiness in that state is declared to consist in perfect freedom from moral impurity, and in the attainment of moral perfection. "No one who worketh abomination can enter the gates of he New Jerusalem." "Christ Jesus gave himself for the church, that he might sanctify and cleanse it, and that he might present it to himself a glorious church, holy, and without blemish." The honour which awaits the faithful, in the heavenly world, is designated "a crown of *righteousness*." The inheritance to which they are destined is declared to be "undefiled" with moral pollution; and it is "an inheritance *among them that are sanctified*." "When Christ, who is our life, shall appear," says the Apostle John, "*we shall be like him*," adorned with all the beauties of holiness which he displayed on earth as our pattern and exemplar. The *employments* of that world are represented as consisting in adoration of the Creator of the universe, in the celebration of his praises, in the contemplation of his works, and in those active services, flowing from the purest love, which have a tendency to promote the harmony and felicity of the intelligent creation. "I beheld," said John, when a vision of the future world was presented to his view, "and, lo, a great multitude, which no man could number, of all nations, and kindreds, and people, and tongues, stood before the throne, clothed in white robes, crying with a loud voice, Salvation to our God that sitteth upon the throne, and unto the Lamb. Blessing, and glory, and wisdom, and thanksgiving, and honour, and power, be ascribed to our God for ever and ever." That the contemplation of the works of God is one leading part of the exercises of the heavenly inhabitants, appears, from the scene presented to the same apostle, in another vision, where the same celestial choir are represented as falling down before Him that sat on the throne, and saying, "Thou art worthy, O Lord, to receive glory, and honour, and power; for thou hast created all things, and for thy pleasure they are, and were created." Such sublime adorations and ascriptions of praise, are the natural results of their profound investigations of the wonderful works of God. In accordance with the exercises of these holy intelligences, another chorus of the celestial inhabitants is exhibited as singing the song of Moses, the servant of God, and the song of the Lamb, saying, "Great and marvellous are thy works, Lord God Almighty, just and true are thy ways, thou King of saints."

The resurrection of the body to an immortal life, is also declared, in the plainest and most decisive language. This is one of the peculiar discoveries of Revelation; for, although the ancient sages of the heathen world generally admitted the immortality of the soul, they seem never to have formed the most distant conception, that the bodies of men, after putrefying in the grave, would ever be reanimated; and hence, when Paul declared this doctrine to the Atnenian philosophers, he was pronounced to be a babbler. This sublime and consoling truth, however, is put beyond all doubt by our Saviour and his apostles.—"The hour is coming," says Jesus, "when all that are in the graves shall hear the voice of the Son of God, and shall come forth: they that have done good, to the resurrection of life; and they that have done evil, to the resurrection of condemnation." "I am the resurrection and the life: he that believeth in me, though he were dead, yet shall he live." "Why should it be thought a thing incredible that God should raise the dead?" "We look for the Saviour, who shall change our vile body, that it may be fashioned like unto his glorious body, according to the energy by which he is able even to subdue all things to himself." "We shall all be changed, in a moment, in the twinkling of an eye, at the last trump; for the trumpet shall sound, and the dead shall be raised incorruptible, and we shall be changed."—The nature of this change, and the *qualities* of the resurrection-body, are likewise particularly described by Paul in the fifteenth chapter of the first epistle to the Corinthians. "It is sown," or committed to the grave "in corruption; it is raised in *incorruption*,"—liable no more to decay, disease and death, but immortal as its Creator. "It is raised in *Power*,"—endued with strength and vigour incapable of being weakened or exhausted, and fitted to accompany the mind in its most vigorous activities.—"It is raised in glory"—destined to flourish in immortal youth and beauty, and arrayed in a splendour similar to that which appeared on the body of Christ when "his face did shine as the sun, and his raiment became white and glittering."—"It is raised a *spiritual* body"—refined to the highest pitch of which matter is susceptible, capable of the most vigorous exertions and of the swiftest movements, endued with organs of perception of a more exquisite and sublime nature than those with which it is now furnished, and fitted to act as a suitable vehicle for the soul in all its celestial services and sublime investigations.

Such is a brief summary of the disclosures which the Christian Revelation has made respecting the eternal destiny of mankind—a subject of infinite importance to every rational being—a subject of ineffable sublimity and grandeur, which throws into the shade the most important transactions, and the most splendid pageantry of this sublunary scene—a subject which should be interwoven with all our plans, pursuits and social intercourses, and which ought never for a moment to be banished from our thoughts.—I shall, therefore, conclude this department of my subject with a remark or two

ON THE PRACTICAL INFLUENCE WHICH THE DOCTRINE OF A FUTURE STATE OUGHT TO HAVE UPON OUR AFFECTIONS AND CONDUCT.

When we look around us on the busy scene of human life, and especially when we contemplate the bustle and pageantry which appear in a populous city, we can scarcely help concluding, that the great majority of human beings that pass in review before us, are acting as if the present world were their everlasting abode, and as if they had no relation to an invisible state of existence. To indulge in sensual gratifications, to acquire power, wealth and fame, to gratify vanity, ambition and pride, to amuse themselves with pictures of fancy, with fantastic exhibitions, theatrical scenes and vain shows, and to endeavour to banish every thought of death and eternity from the mind, appear to be in their view the great and ultimate ends of existence. This is the case, not merely of those who openly avow themselves "men of the world," and call in question the reality of a future existence; but also of thousands who regularly frequent our worshipping assemblies, and profess their belief in the realities of an eternal state. They listen to the doctrines of eternal life, and of future punishment, without attempting to question either their reality or their importance, but as soon as they retire from "the place of the holy," and mingle in the social circle, and the bustle of business, every impression of invisible realities evanishes from their minds, as if it had been merely a dream or a vision of the night. To cultivate the intellectual faculties, to aspire after moral excellence, to devote the active powers to the glory of the Creator, and the benefit of mankind; to live as strangers and pilgrims upon earth, to consider the glories of this world as a transient scene that will soon pass away, and to keep the eye constantly fixed on the realities of an immortal life—are characteristics of only a comparatively small number of individuals scattered amidst the swarming population around us, who are frequently regarded by their fellows as a mean-spirited and ignoble race of beings. Though death is making daily havoc around them, though their friends and relatives are, year after year, dropping into the grave, though poets and orators, princes and philosophers, statesmen and stage-players, are continually disappearing from the living world; though sickness and disease are raging around and laying their victims of every age prostrate in the dust, and though they frequently walk over the solemn recesses of the burying ground, and tread upon the ashes of "the mighty man, and the man of war, the judge and the ancient, the cunning artificer, and the eloquent orator,"—yet they prosecute the path of dissipation and vanity with as much keenness and resolution, as if every thing around them were unchangeable, and as if their present enjoyments were to last for ever.

If this representation be founded on fact, we may assuredly conclude, that the great bulk of mankind have no fixed belief of the reality of a future world, and that more than the one half of those who profess an attachment to religion, are as little influenced in their general conduct by this solemn consideration, as if it were a matter of mere fancy, or of "doubtful disputation." It is somewhat strange, and even paradoxical, that, amidst the never-ceasing changes which are taking place among the living beings around us, men should so seldom look beyond the grave to which they are all advancing, and so seldom make inquiries into the certainty and the nature of that state into which the tide of time has carried all the former generations of mankind. If a young man were made fully assured that, at the end of two years, he should obtain the sovereignty of a fertile island in the Indian ocean, where he should enjoy every earthly pleasure his heart could desire,—his soul would naturally bound at the prospect, he would search his maps to ascertain the precise position of his future residence, he would make inquiries respecting it at those travellers who had either visited the spot or passed near its confines; he would peruse with avidity the descriptions which geographers have given of its natural scenery, its soil and climate, its productions and inhabitants; and, before his departure, he would be careful to provide every thing that might be requisite for his future enjoyment. If a person, when setting out on a journey which he was obliged to undertake, were informed that his road lay through a dangerous territory, where he should be exposed, on the one hand, to the risk of falling headlong into unfathomable gulfs, and, on the other, to the attacks of merciless savages,—he would walk with caution, he would look around him at every step, and he would welcome with gratitude any friendly guide that would direct his steps to the place of his destination. But, in relation to a future and invisible world, there exist, in the minds of the bulk of mankind, a most unaccountable apathy and indifference; and not only an indifference, but, in many instances, a determined resolution not to listen to any thing that may be said respecting it. To broach the subject of immortality, in certain convivial circles, would be considered as approaching to an insult; and the person who had the hardihood to do so, would be regarded as a rude, sanctimonious intruder How unaccountably foolish and preposterous is such a conduct! especially when we consider. that those very persons who seem to be entirely regardless whether they shall sink into the gulf of annihilation, or into the regions of endless perdition, will pass whole days and nights in chagrin and despair for the loss of some employment, for a slight affront, or for some imaginary reflection on their reputation and honour!

Were it necessary to bring forward additional proofs that the greater part of mankind have no belief in a future state, or, which amounts nearly to the same thing, that it has no influence whatever on the general tenor of their thoughts and actions—the prominent features of their conduct afford abundant evidence of this melancholy truth. Would a man, who firmly believes that he is destined to an everlasting state, pass fifty or sixty years of his life without spending one serious thought about that unknown futurity into which he is soon to enter, or making the least inquiry respecting its nature and employments? Would he toil from morning to night, with incessant care, to lay up a few fleeting treasures, and never spend a single hour in considering what preparations are requisite for an endless existence? Would he spurn at that book which has unveiled the glories and the terrors of eternity, and "brought life and immortality to light?" Would he sneer at the person who is inquiring the way to a blessed immortality, and count him as an enemy when he wished to direct his attention to the concerns of an unseen world? Can that man be supposed to believe that a crown of glory awaits him in the heavens, whose whole soul is absorbed in the pursuits of ambition, and who tramples on every principle of truth and justice, in order to gain possession of a post of opulence and honour? Can those parents believe that in heaven there is "a treasure that fadeth not," while they teach their children to conclude, that the acquisition of a *fortune*, and the favor of the great, are the grand objects to which they should aspire? Can that old hoary-headed votary of pleasure consider himself as standing on the verge of an eternal world, who still indulges himself in all the fashionable follies and frivolities of the age, and never casts an eye beyond the precincts of the grave? Can that hard-hearted worldling, who shuts his ears at the cry of the poor and needy, and who grasps his treasures with eagerness even amidst the agonies of dissolution—believe that "a recompense of reward" awaits the benevolent "at the resurrection of the just?" Can that man be impressed with the solemnities of the eternal world, who, the moment after he has committed the remains of a relative to the grave, violates every humane and friendly feeling, and for the sake of a few paltry pounds or shillings, deprives the widow and the orphan of every earthly enjoyment? Can that courtly sycophant, who is continually hunting after places and pensions, fawning upon his superiors, and whose whole life is a continued course of treachery, adulation and falsehood—believe that "all liars shall have their portion in the lake that burneth with fire and brimstone?" Can that thoughtless debauchee believe that future punishment awaits the workers of iniquity, who runs from one scene of dissipation to another, who wastes his time in folly and extravagance, and whose life is but one continued crime? Or can we even suppose that that clergyman, who is unremittingly aspiring after preferment, who is mercilessly fleecing his flock, yet neglecting their instruction, and engaged in incessant litigations about some paltry tythes, seriously believes, that the treasures of this world are unworthy to be compared with that "exceeding great and eternal weight of glory which is about to be revealed in the life to come?" Such conduct plainly indicates, whatever professions certain descriptions of these characters may make, that the solemn realities of the eternal world have no more practical influence on their minds than if they regarded them as unsubstantial phantoms, or as idle dreams.

The doctrine of a future state is not a mere speculative proposition, to serve as a subject of metaphysical investigation, or to be admitted merely to complete a system of philosophical or theological belief. It is a truth of the highest *practical importance*, which ought to be interwoven with the whole train of our thoughts and actions. Yet how many are there, even of those who bear the Christian name, who are incessantly engaged in boisterous disputes respecting the nature of *faith*, who have never felt the influence of that faith which is "the confident expectation of things hoped for, and the conviction of things which are not seen," and which realizes to the mind, as if actually present, the glories of the invisible world! If we really believe the doctrine of immortality, it will manifest itself in our thoughts, affections and pursuits. *It will lead us to form a just estimate of the value of all earthly enjoyments.* For, in the light of eternity, all the secular pursuits in which men now engage, appear but as vanity, and all the dazzling objects which fascinate their eyes, as fleeting shadows. A realizing view of an eternal state dissipates the illusion which the eye of sense throws over the pageantry and the splendours of this world, and teaches us that all is transitory and fading, and that our most exquisite earthly enjoyments will ere long be snatched from our embrace. For, not a single mark of our sublunary honours, not a single farthing of our boasted treasures, not a single trace of our splendid possessions, nor a single line of the beauty of our persons, can be carried along with us to the regions beyond the grave. *It will stimulate us to set our affections on things above, and to indulge in heavenly contemplations* "Where our treasure is, there will our hearts be also." Rising superior to the delights of sense, and to the narrow boundaries of time, we will expatiate at large in those boundless regions which eye hath not seen, and contemplate, in the light of reason and of revelation, those scenes of felicity and grandeur, which will burst upon the disembodied spirit, when it has dropped its earthly tabernacle in the dust. Like Seneca, when he contemplated, in imagination, the magnitude and beauty of the orbs of heaven, we will look down, with a noble indifference, on the earth as a scarcely distinguishable atom, and say, "Is it to this little spot that the great designs and vast desires of men are confined? Is it for this there is such disturbance of nations, so much carnage, and so many ruinous wars? O folly of deceived men! to imagine great kingdoms in the compass of an atom, to raise armies to divide a *point* of earth with their swords! It is just as if the *ants* should divide their mole-hills into provinces, and conceive a field to be several kingdoms, and fiercely contend to enlarge their borders, and celebrate a triumph in gaining a foot of earth, as a new province to their empire." In the light of heaven all sublunary glories fade away, and the mind is refined and ennobled, when, with the eye of faith, it penetrates within the veil, and describes the splendours of the heaven of heavens.

Again, if we believe the doctrine of immortality, we will be careful to avoid those sins which would expose us to misery in the future world, and to cultivate those dispositions and virtues which will prepare us for the enjoyment of eternal felicity. Between virtue and vice, sin and holiness, there is an essential and eternal distinction; and this distinction will be fully and visibly displayed in the eternal world. He whose life is a continued scene of vicious indulgence, and who has devoted himself to "work all manner of uncleanness with greediness," becomes, by such habits, "a vessel of wrath *fitted for destruction*;" and, from the very constitution of things, there is no possibility of escaping misery in the future state, if his existence be prolonged. Whereas, he who is devoted to the practice of holiness, who loves his Creator with supreme affection, and his neighbour as himself, who adds to his faith "virtue, knowledge, temperance, patience, brotherly-kindness, and charity," is, by such graces, rendered fit for everlasting communion with the Father of spirits, and for delightful association with all the holy intelligences that people his immense empire. Again, the belief of a future world should excite us to the exercise of *contentment*, and *reconcile our minds to whatever privations or afflictions Providence may allot* to us in the present world. "For the sufferings of the present time are not worthy to be compared with the glory which is to be revealed." If we believe that the whole train of circumstances connected with our present lot, is arranged by Infinite Wisdom and Benevolence, every thing that befalls us here must have a certain bearing on the future world, and have a tendency to prepare us for engaging in its exercises and for relishing its enjoyments. In short, if we recognise the idea of an immortal life, we will endeavour to acquire clear and comprehensive views of its nature, its pleasures, and its employments. We will not rest satisfied with vague and confused conceptions of celestial bliss; but will endeavour to form as precise and definite ideas on this subject as the circumstances of our sublunary station will permit. We will search the Oracles of Divine Revelation, and the discoveries of science, and endeavour to deduce from both the sublimest conceptions we can form of the glories of that "inheritance which is incorruptible, undefiled, and that fadeth not away, which is reserved in heaven for the faithful."

In a word, if our minds are as deeply impressed with this subject as its importance demands, we shall experience feelings similar to those which affected the mind of Hyeronymus when he contemplated the dissolution of the world, and the solemnities of the last judgment.—"Whether I eat or drink, or in whatever other action or employment I am engaged, that solemn voice always seems to sound in my ears, 'Arise ye dead and come to judgment!'—As often as I think of the day of judgment, my heart quakes, and my whole frame trembles. If I am to indulge in any of the pleasures of the present life, I am resolved to do it in such a way, that the solemn realities of the future judgment may never be banished from my recollection."*

* Sive comedam, sive bibam, sive aliquid aliud faciam, semper vox illa in auribus meus sonare videtur: Surgite Mortui, et venite ad judicium. Quotius diem judicii cogito, totus corde et corpore contremisco. Si qua enim præsentis vitæ est lætitiæ, ita agenda est, ut nunquam amaritudo futuri judicii recedat a memoria.

# PART II.

## ON THE CONNEXION OF SCIENCE WITH A FUTURE STATE.

A GREAT outcry has frequently been made, by many of those who wish to be considered as pious persons, about *the vanity of human science.* Certain divines in their writings, and various descriptions of preachers in their pulpit declamations, not unfrequently attempt to embellish their discourses, and to magnify the truths of Scripture, by contrasting them with what they are pleased to call "the perishing treasures of scientific knowledge." "T e knowledge we derive from the Scriptures," say they, "is able to make us wise unto salvation; all other knowledge is but comparative folly. The knowledge of Christ and him crucified will endure for ever; but all human knowledge is transitory, *and will perish for ever when this world comes to an end.* Men weary themselves with diving into human science, while all that results to them is vanity and vexation of spirit. Men may become the greatest philosophers, and have their understandings replenished with every kind of human knowledge, and yet perish for ever. What have we to do with the planets and the stars, and whether they be peopled with inhabitants? Our business is to attend to the salvation of our souls."

Now, although some of the above, and similar assertions, when properly modified and explained, may be admitted as true, the greater part of them, along with hundreds of similar expressions, are either ambiguous or false. But, although they were all admitted as strictly true, what effect can the frequent reiteration of such comparisons and contrasts have on the mass of the people to whom they are addressed, who are already too much disinclined to the pursuit of general knowledge—but to make them imagine, that it is useless, and in some cases dangerous, to prosecute any other kind of knowledge than what is derived *directly* from the Scriptures? And what is the knowledge which the great majority of those who attend the public services of religion have acquired of the contents of the sacred oracles? It is too often, I fear, exceedingly vague, confused and superficial; owing, in a great measure, to the want of those habits of mental exertion, which a moderate prosecution of useful science would have induced.

Such declamations as those to which I have now adverted, obviously proceed from a very limited sphere of information and a contracted range of thought. It is rather a melancholy reflection, that any persons, particularly preachers of the gospel, should endeavour to apologize for their own ignorance by endeavouring to undervalue what they acknowledge they never have acquired, and therefore, cannot be supposed to understand and appreciate. For, although several well-informed and judicious ministers of religion, have been led, from the influence of custom, and from copying the expressions of others, to use a phraseology which has a tendency to detract from the utility of scientific knowledge, yet it is generally the most ignorant, those whose reading and observation have been confined within the narrowest range, who are most forward in their bold and vague declamations on this topic. We never find, in any part of the Sacred Records, such comparisons and contrasts as those to which I allude. The inspired writers never attempt to set the *word* of God in opposition to his *works*, nor attempt to deter men from the study of the wonders of his creation, on the ground that it is of less importance than the study of his word. On the contrary, they take every proper opportunity of directing the attention to the mechanism and order, the magnificence and grandeur of the visible world; and their devotional feelings are kindled into rapture by such contemplations. When the Psalmist had finished his survey of the different departments of nature, as described in the civ. Psalm, he broke out into the following devotional strains: "How manifold are thy works, O Lord! in wisdom hast thou made them all: the earth is full of thy riches, so is the great and wide sea. The glory* of the Lord shall endure for ever, the Lord shall rejoice in all his works. I will sing unto the Lord as long as I live; I will sing praises to my God while I have my being." For the visible works of God display the same essential attributes of Deity, and of his superintending providence, as the revelations of his word; and it is one great design of that word to direct men to a rational and devout contemplation of these works in which his glory is so magnificently displayed. And, therefore, to attempt to magnify the word of God by degrading his works, or to set the one in opposition to the other, is to attempt to set the Deity in op-

*That is, the display of the Divine perfections in the material world, as the connexion of the passage plainly intimates.

position to himself, and to prevent mankind from offering a certain portion of that tribute of adoration and thanksgiving which is due to his name.

It is true, indeed, that the mere philosopher has frequently been disposed to contemplate the universe as if it were a self-acting and independent machine. He has sometimes walked through the magnificent scenes of creation, and investigated the laws which govern the motions of the celestial orbs, and the agencies which produce the various phenomena of our sublunary system, without offering up that tribute of thanksgiving and praise which is due to the great First Cause, or feeling those emotions of adoration and reverence which such studies have a tendency to inspire. But it is no less true, that the mere theologian has, likewise, not unfrequently, walked through the field of revelation, studied its doctrines, and facts and moral requisitions, written volumes in support of its heavenly origin, and defended its truths against the cavils of adversaries, without feeling that supreme love to God and affection towards his neighbour which it is the great object of the Scriptures to produce, and displaying a disposition and conduct directly repugnant to its holy precepts. An argument founded on the impiety of certain pretended philosophers, to dissuade us from the study of the material world, would, therefore, be equally powerful to deter us from the study of divine revelation, when we consider that many who profess to receive its doctrines live in open defiance of its most sacred requisitions. In both cases, such examples merely show, that man is a frail inconsistent being, and too frequently disposed to overlook his Creator, and to wander from the source of happiness.

In a work entitled, "*The Christian Philosopher*," I have endeavoured to illustrate this subject at considerable length, and to show, that the investigation of the works of creation, under the guidance of true science, has a tendency to expand our conceptions of the power, wisdom, benevolence, and superintending providence of God,—and that the various sciences and the inventions of art may be rendered subservient in promoting the objects of true religion, and diffusing its influence among the nations.—At present, I shall confine my views, in the few following remarks, to the illustration of the following position—"That science has a relation to a future state."

It is a very vague, and, in many points of view, a *false* assertion, which has so frequently been reiterated—that, what is generally termed human knowledge, or the sciences, have no connexion with an immortal existence, and that they will be of no utility whatever when this world comes to an end.—Truth, of every description, is, from its very nature, eternal and unchangeable; and. consequently, it cannot be supposed a preposterous opinion, that the established principles of several of our sciences will be the basis of reasoning and of action in a future state as well as in the present. That a whole is greater than any of its parts; that the three angles of a triangle are equal to two right angles; that the sides of a plain triangle are to one another, as the sides of the angles opposite to them: these and many similar propositions are equally true in heaven as on earth, and may probably be as useful truths there as in our present abode.

### OBJECT OF SCIENTIFIC INVESTIGATION.

In order to avoid misconception, and a confusion of thought on this subject, it may not be improper, in the first place, to define and illustrate what is meant by the term *Science*.

Science, in its most general acceptation, denotes *knowledge* of every description; in a more restricted sense, it denotes that species of knowledge which is acquired chiefly by the exercise of the human faculties; and in a still more restricted sense, it denotes that systematic species of knowledge which consists of rule and order,—such as geometry, arithmetic, algebra, natural philosophy, geography, astronomy, chymistry, mineralogy and botany.—In the observations which follow, the term may be taken in any one of these senses; but particularly in the last, which is the most common and appropriate meaning. By means of scientific investigation, the powers of the human mind have been wonderfully strengthened and expanded, and our knowledge of the operations of the Creator extensively enlarged. Science has enabled us to transport ourselves from one continent to another, to steer our course through the pathless ocean, and to survey all the variety of scenery which the terraqueous globe displays; it has taught us to mount upwards to the region of the clouds, and to penetrate into the bowels of the earth, to explore the changes which the earth has undergone since the period of its creation. It has laid open to our view the nature and constitution of the atmosphere, the principles of which it is composed, and its agency in supporting fire and flame, and vegetable and animal life. On the principles which science has established, we have been enabled to ascertain the distances of many of the heavenly bodies, to compute their magnitudes, and to determine the periods of their revolutions; and by means of the instruments it has invented, we have been enabled to take a nearer survey of distant worlds—to contemplate new wonders of creating power in regions of the sky which lie far beyond the utmost stretch of the unassisted eye,—and to explore those invisible regions, where myriads of living beings are concentrated within the compass of a visible point. —In consequence of such discoveries, we have been enabled to acquire more clear and ample conceptions of the amazing energies of omnipotence, of the inscrutable depths of infinite wisdom, of the overruling providence of the Almighty, of the benevolent care he exercises over all his creatures, and of the unlimited extent of those dominions over which he eternally presides.

The *faculties* by which man has been enabled to make the discoveries to which I have alluded, were implanted in his constitution by the hand of his Creator; and the *objects* on which these faculties are exercised, are the works of the Creator, which, the more minutely they are investigated, the more strikingly do they display the glory of his character and perfections. Consequently, it must have been the intention of the Creator that man should employ the powers he has given him in scientific researches; otherwise, he would neither have endowed him with such noble faculties, nor have opened to his view so large a portion of his empire. Scientific investigations, therefore, are to be considered as nothing less than inquiries into the plans and operations of the Eternal, in order to unfold the attributes of his nature, his providential procedure in the government of his creatures, and the laws by which he directs the movements of universal nature. It is true, indeed, that every one who calls himself a philosopher may not keep this end in view in the prosecution of scientific acquirements. He may perhaps be actuated merely by a principle of curiosity, by a love of worldly gain, or by a desire to acquire reputation among the learned by the discoveries he may bring to light, just in the same way as some theologians are actuated in prosecuting the study of the Christian system. But the discoveries which have been made by such persons, are, notwithstanding, real developements of the plans of the Deity, and open to a devout mind a more expansive view of the power, wisdom, and benevolence of Him who is "wonderful in council, and excellent in working." It is our own fault if we do not derive useful instruction from the investigations and discoveries of philosophy; it is owing to our want of intelligence to discriminate between the experiments of men, and the operations of God, and to the want of that reverence, humility, and devotion, which ought to accompany us in all our studies and contemplations of nature. Science, therefore, from whatever motives it may be prosecuted, is, in effect, and in reality, *an inquiry after God:* it is the study of angels and other superior intelligences; and we cannot suppose there is a holy being throughout the universe that is not employed, in one mode or another, in scientific research and investigation; unless we can suppose that there are moral intelligences who are insensible to the displays of the divine glory, and altogether indifferent, whether or not they make progress in the knowledge of their Creator.

### OBJECTS ON WHICH THE FACULTIES OF CELESTIAL INTELLIGENCES WILL BE EMPLOYED.

Let us now consider the objects on which the faculties of celestial intelligences will be employed in the way of scientific investigation.

The grand scene of universal nature—that august theatre on which the Almighty displays, to countless myriads, his glorious perfections—will remain substantially the same as it is at present, after all the changes in reference to our globe shall have taken place; and the clear and expansive view of its economy, its movements, and its peculiar glories, which will then be laid open to their inspection, will exercise the faculties, and form a considerable portion of the felicity of renovated moral agents.

That the general system of nature will remain materially the same, when the present fabric of our globe is dissolved, may be argued, 1. From the immense number and magnitude of the bodies of which it is composed. In every direction to which we can turn our eyes, the universe appears to be replenished with countless orbs of light, diffusing their splendours from regions immeasurably distant. Nearly one hundred millions of these globes are visible through telescopes of the greatest magnifying power; and it is more than probable, that beyond the reach of the finest glasses that art has ever constructed, thousands of millions exist in the unexplored regions of immensity, which the eye of man, while he remains in this lower world, will never be able to descry. All these luminous globes, too, are bodies of immense magnitude; compared with any one of which, the whole earth dwindles into an inconsiderable ball. It is probable that the smallest of them is at least one hundred thousand times larger than the globe on which we live.—2. All these bodies *are immensely distant from the earth.* Although we could wing our course with a swiftness equal to ten thousand miles a-day, it would require more than five millions of years before we could reach the nearest star; and the more distant of these orbs are placed in regions so immensely distant, that the imagination is bewildered and overpowered when it attempts to grasp the immeasurable extent which intervenes between us and them. This circumstance proves, that these bodies are of an immense size and splendour, since they are visible at such distances; and consequently demonstrates, that each of them is destined, in its respective sphere, to accomplish some noble purpose, worthy of the plans of a Being of infinite wisdom and goodness.—3. The whole of this vast assemblage of suns and worlds *has no immediate connexion* with the present constitution and arrangement of our globe. There are no celestial bodies that have any immediate connexion with the earth, or direct influence upon it, except the sun, the moon, and several of the planets; and therefore, those more distant orbs, to which I allude, cannot be supposed to be involved in the physical evils which the fall of man has introduced into our world; or to have the least connexion with any future change or catastrophe that may befall the terraqueous globe. Though this globe, and "all that it inherits," were dissolved; yea, although the sun himself and his surrounding planets were set in a blaze, and blotted for ever out of creation; the innumerable and vast bodies which replenish the distant regions of the universe, would still exist, and continue to illuminate the voids of creation with undiminished splendour.

### EXTENT OF THE GENERAL CONFLAGRATION.

From the considerations now stated, it is evident, that the changes which are predicted to take place at the general conflagration, will not extend beyond, the environs of our globe, or at farthest, beyond the limits of the solar system. There is, indeed, no reason to conclude, that they will extend beyond the terraqueous globe itself and its surrounding atmosphere; for since all the revelations of Scripture have a peculiar reference to the inhabitants of this globe, the predicted changes which are to take place in its physical constitution, at the close of the present economy of Providence, must be considered as limited to the same sphere. As the world was formerly destroyed by a deluge of waters, in consequence of the depravity of man, so its destruction by fire will take place, for the same reason, in order that it may be purified from all the effects of the *curse* which was originally pronounced upon the ground for man's sake, and restored to its former order and beauty. But there is not the smallest reason to conclude, either from Scripture or the general constitution of the universe, that this destruction will extend beyond that part of the frame of nature which was subjected to the curse, and is physically connected with the sin of man; and consequently, will be entirely confined to certain changes which will be effected throughout the continents, islands, and oceans, and in the higher and lower regions of the atmosphere.

This appears to be the sense in which the most judicious expositors of Scripture interpret those passages which have a particular reference to this event. Dr. Guyse, in his "Paraphrase on the New Testament," interprets 2 Peter iii. 7, 12, precisely in this sense: "When that final decisive day of the Lord Jesus shall come,—the *aerial heavens*, being all in a flame, shall be destroyed, and the constituent principles of the atmosphere, together with the earth and all things in it, shall be melted down by an intense dissolving heat into a confused chaos, like that out of which they were originally formed." And in a note on this paraphrase he remarks, "By the *heavens* is meant here the *aerial* heavens. For the heavens and the earth are here spoken of in opposition to those of the old world, which could mean nothing more than the earth and its former atmosphere, the state of which underwent a great alteration by the flood."—"By the *heavens and the earth*, in such passages as these," says the learned Dr. Mede, "is to be understood, that part of nature which was subjected to the curse, or that is inhabited by Christ's enemies, and includes in it the earth, water, and air, but not the heavenly bodies, which are not only at a vast distance from it, but it is little more than a point, if compared to them for magnitude."—Dr. Dwight, when adverting to this subject, expresses the same sentiment: "The phrase *heavens and earth* (says he) in Jewish phraseology denoted the universe. In the present case, however, (2 Peter iii. 10, 12, 13.) the words appear to be used with a meaning less extended, where it is declared, that that which is intended by both terms, shall be consumed, dissolved, and pass away. This astonishing event, we are taught, shall take place at the final judgment; *and we have no hint in the Scriptures, that the judgment will involve any other beings besides angels and men.*"

From the preceding considerations, it is obvious, that when the inspired writers use such expressions as these,—"The stars shall fall from heaven," "the powers of heaven shall be shaken," and, "the heaven departed as a scroll," they are to be understood not in a *literal*, but in a *figurative* sense, as denoting changes, convulsions, and revolutions in the moral world. And when, in reference to the dissolution of our globe and its appendages, it is said, that "the heavens shall pass away with a mighty noise," the aerial heaven, or the surrounding atmosphere is to be understood. How this appendage to our world may be dissolved, or pass away *with a mighty noise*, it is not difficult to conceive, now that we have become acquainted with the nature and energies of its constituent parts. One essential part of the atmosphere contains the principle of flame; and if this principle were not counteracted by its connexion with another ingredient, or were it let loose to exert its energies without control, instantly one immense flame would envelope the terraqueous globe, which would set on fire the foundations of the mountains, wrap the ocean in a blaze, and dissolve, not only coals, wood, and other combustibles, but the hardest substances in nature. It is more than probable, that when the last catastrophe of our globe arrives, the oxygen and nitrogen, or the two constituent principles of the atmosphere, will be separated by the interposition of Almighty power. And the moment this separation takes place, it is easy to conceive, that a tremendous concussion will ensue, and the most dreadful explosions will resound throughout the whole of the expanse which surrounds the globe, which will stun the assembled world, and shake the earth to its foundations. For, if, in chymical experiments conducted on a small scale, the separation of two gases, or their coming in contact with the principle of flame, is frequently accompanied with a loud and destructive explosion,—it is impossible to form an adequate idea of the loud and tremendous explosions which would ensue *were the whole atmosphere at once dissolved*, and its elementary principles separated from each other and left to exert their native energies. A sound as if creation had burst asunder, and accompanied the next moment with a universal blaze, extending over sea and land, would present a scene of sublimity and terror, which would more than realize all the striking descriptions given in Scripture of this solemn scene.

Again, when in reference to this tremendous event, it is said, that "the earth and the heaven fled away," (Rev. xx. 11.) we are not to imagine, that the distant bodies of the universe shall be either annihilated, or removed from the spaces they formerly occupied; but that all sublunary nature shall be thrown into confusion and disorder, and that the celestial orbs, during this universal uproar of the elements, will be eclipsed from the view, and appear as if they had fled away. The appearance of the heavens whirling with a confused and rapid motion, at this period, would be produced, were the Almighty (as will probably be the case) suddenly to put a stop to the diurnal rotation of the earth, or to increase the rate of its motion; in which case, the celestial luminaries would appear either to stop in their courses, or to be thrown into rapid and irregular agitations. And the appearance of the heavens in reality receding from the view, would be produced, were the earth to leave its present station among the planets, and to be impelled with a rapid motion towards the distant parts of the solar system, or beyond its boundaries; in which case, the sun would appear to fly off with a rapid motion to a distant part of space, till he had diminished to the size of a twinkling star, and the moon and the nearest planets would, in a short time, entirely disappear.—Whether these suppositions exactly correspond with the arrangements which Divine Wisdom has made in reference to the general conflagration, I do not take upon me positively to determine. But I have stated them in order to show, that all the descriptions contained in Scripture, of the dissolution of our globe, and of the circumstances connected with it, can be easily accounted for, and may be fully realized, without supposing any change to take place in the universe beyond the limits of the earth and its atmosphere.

To suppose, as some have done, that the whole fabric of creation will be shattered to pieces, that the stars will literally fall from their orbs, and the material universe be blotted out of existence, is a sentiment so absurd and extravagant and so contrary to the general tenor of Scripture, and the character of God, that it is astonishing it should ever have been entertained by any man, calling himself a divine or a Christian preacher.* I have already had occasion to remark, that there is no example of annihilation, or entire destruction of material substances, to be found in the universe, and that it is to the last degree improbable, that any one particle of matter which now exists will ever be completely destroyed, however numerous the changes that may take place in the universe.† We have no reason to believe, that even those changes to which our world is destined, at the general conflagration, will issue in its entire destruction. The materials of which the earth and its atmosphere are composed will still continue to exist after its present structure is deranged, and will, in all probability, be employed in the arrangement of a new system, purified from the physical evils which now exist, and which may continue to flourish as a monument of divine power and wisdom, throughout an indefinite lapse of ages.

In accordance with these sentiments, we find the inspired writers asserting the stability and perpetuity of the material universe. In a passage formerly alluded to, the Psalmist, after having contemplated the scenes of the material creation, declares, in reference to these visible manifestations of the divine perfections,—"The glory of the Lord *shall endure for ever*, the Lord shall rejoice in all his works." And the Apostle Peter, when describing the dissolution of the elementary parts of our globe, intimates, at the same time, the continued existence of the visible fabric of nature. "We look," says he, "for new heavens and a new earth, wherein dwelleth righteousness." The same truth is incidentally declared in many other portions of Scripture. In the prophecies respecting the Messiah and the duration of his kingdom, it is declared, that "His name shall endure for ever, his name shall be continued *as long as the sun*.

* As a specimen of the vague and absurd declamations on this subject, which have been published both from the pulpit and the press, the following extract from a modern and elegantly printed volume of sermons may suffice.—"The blast of the seventh trumpet thundering with terrific clangour through the sky, and echoing from world to world, shall fill the universe, and time shall be no more! The six trumpets have already sounded: when the seventh shall blow, a total change shall take place throughout the creation; the vast globe which we now inhabit shall dissolve, and mingle with yon beautoous azure firmament, with sun, and moon, and all the immense luminaries flaming there, *in one undistinguished ruin;* all shall vanish away like a fleeting vapour, a visionary phantom of the night, and *not a single trace of them be found!* Even the last enemy, Death, shall be destroyed, and time itself shall be no more!" &c. &c. When such bombastic rant is thundered in the ears of Christian people, it is no wonder that their ideas on this subject become extremely incorrect, and even extravagantly absurd.

† See Sect. x. page 44.

His seed shall endure for ever, and his throne *as the sun before me;*" which expressions evidently imply that the sun will not be blotted out of creation, but continue to hold a station in the universe as long as the Redeemer and his subjects exist. It is also stated, in reference to the same elustrious personage, "His seed will I make to endure for ever, and his throne *as the days of heaven,*" which intimates, that the heavens will endure as long as the government of Immanuel. In reference to the stability and perpetuity of the celestial luminaries, it is declared, that "Jehovah hath *prepared his* THRONE *in the heavens.*" And when the Psalmist calls upon all the beings in the universe to celebrate the praises of the Creator, he says, in reference to the orbs of heaven, "Praise ye him, sun and moon, praise him all ye stars of light—Let them praise the name of the Lord; for he commanded, and they were created. *He hath also established them for ever and ever; he hath made a decree which shall not pass;** which expressions evidently imply, that, whatever changes may happen in particular systems, the great body of the celestial orbs, which constitute some of the grandest scenes of the universe, will remain stable and permanent as the throne of the Eternal.—But, not to multiply quotations,—the following declaration of Jehovah by the prophet Jeremiah is quite decisive on this point. "Thus saith the Lord, who giveth the sun for a light by day, and the ordinances of the moon and of the stars for a light by night: The Lord of Hosts is his name. *If these ordinances depart from before me, saith the Lord,* then the seed of Israel also shall cease from being a nation before me for ever,"† which words plainly imply, that if these luminaries continue in existence, the accomplishment of the divine promise is secured to all the spiritual seed of Israel; but should they be blotted out of creation, or depart from before Jehovah, the happiness of the "ransomed of the Lord," and their relation to him as the source of their felicity, would be terminated for ever. And have not these luminaries continued in their stations, since the prediction was announced, during a period of more than two thousand years? And do they not still shine with undiminished lustre? Yes, and they will still continue to display the glory of their Creator while countless ages are rolling on. Hence it is declared, with respect to the "saints of the Most High," "They that be teachers of wisdom shall shine as the brightness of the firmament, and they that turn many to righteousness, *as the stars for ever and ever.*"

In short, when we consider the boundless extent of the starry firmament, the scenes of grandeur it displays, the new luminaries, which, in the course of ages, appear to be gradually augmenting its splendour, and the countless myriads of exalted intelligences which doubtless people its expansive regions—when we consider that it constitutes the principal portion of the empire of the Eternal, the most astonishing scene of his operations, and the most striking display of his omnipotence and wisdom,—it would be one of the most extravagant notions that can possibly be entertained, and inconsistent with every rational and Scriptural idea we can form of the goodness and intelligence of the Deity, to suppose, that these vast dominions of his, in which his perfections shine with a splendour so ineffable, will ever be suffered to fall to pieces, or to sink into non-existence. With almost equal reason might we suppose, that the Creator himself would cease to exist, and infinite space be left as a boundless blank without matter and intelligence.

If the considerations now adduced be admitted to have any force, and if the position I have endeavoured to establish, cannot be overthrown, either on Scriptural or rational grounds—many of our sermons and *poems* which profess to give a description of the scenes of the "*Last day,*" must be considered as containing a species of bombast which has a tendency to bewilder the mind, and to produce distorted views of the perfections of the Creator, and of the wise arrangements he has established in the system of the universe. A celebrated poet, when expatiating on this subject, in order to give effect to his descriptions, breaks out into the following extravagant exclamations, when alluding to the starry firmament:

"How far from east to west? The lab'ring eye
Can scarce the distant azure bounds descry—
So *vast*, this world's a grain; yet myriads grace
With golden pomp the throng'd etherial space.
How great, how firm, how sacred all appears!
How worthy an immortal round of years!
*Yet all must drop, as autumn's sickliest grain,*
*And earth and firmament be sought in vain.*
Time shall be slain, *all nature be destroy'd,*
*Nor leave an atom in the mighty void.*
One universal ruin spreads abroad,
Nothing is safe beneath the throne of God."

Again,

"The flakes aspire, and make the heavens their prey
The sun, the moon, the stars, all melt away;
All, all is lost, no monument, no sign,
Where once so proudly blaz'd the gay machine." &c.

If such descriptions were to be literally realized, *a resurrection from the dead would be an absolute impossibility*—the universe would be reduced to an immense blank—and the visible glories of the Creator, by which alone his perfections are recognised by finite intelligences, would be eclipsed in the darkness of eternal night. Poetical scraps of this description, are, however, frequently reiterated by flaming orators, in order to give effect to their turgid declamations, while they have no other tendency than

* See Psalm lxxii. 17. lxxxix. 36, &c. ciii. 19. cxlviii. 3—7.

† Jeremiah xxxi. 35, 36.

to lead their hearers into a maze of error and extravagancy, to prevent them from thinking soberly and rationally on the scenes predicted in Scripture, and to excite the sneer of philosophical infidels.

The only passage of Scripture which, at first view, seems to militate against the position I have endeavoured to establish, is that contained in Psalm cii. 25, 26. "Of old hast thou laid the foundation of the earth; and the heavens are the work of thy hands: they shall perish, but thou shalt endure; yea, all of them shall wax old like a garment; as a vesture shalt thou change them, and they shall be changed: but thou art the same," &c. Some commentators, as Mr. *Pierce* and others, suppose, that by "the earth and heavens," in this passage, are to be understood, *governments*, or *civil and ecclesiastical states*, as these words, in their figurative sense, sometimes denote. But this does not appear to be the sense in which they are here used. Taken in their literal sense, they may refer to the same objects and events alluded to by the Apostle Peter, in his Second Epistle, chap. iii. 7, 10. formerly explained; namely, to the dissolution of the earth and the *aerial* heavens, at the close of time. But, supposing that the words were taken in their most extensive sense, as denoting *the whole fabric of the material universe*, it would not in the least invalidate the proposition I am now supporting. The main design of the passage is to assert the eternity and immutability of God, in opposition to the mutable nature of created beings. All material things are liable to change; but *change* does not imply *destruction* or *annihilation*. When it is said, "the righteous *perish* and no man layeth it to heart;" and "they that are far from God shall *perish*," it is not to be understood, that either the one or the other shall be blotted out of existence. So, when it is said that the heavens and the earth *shall perish*, a change or revolution is implied, but not an entire destruction. It is farther said, "As a vesture they shall be folded up," &c. This appears to be spoken in allusion to the custom which obtains in the Eastern nations, among the grandees, of frequently changing their garments as a mark of respect; and seems to import, the *ease* and *celerity* with which the Divine Being can accomplish important changes in the universe. He can accomplish the revolutions of worlds and of systems with an ease similar to that of a prince changing his apparel, or laying aside his vestments. But his changing any particular system from its original state, implies only his opening a new scene, and varying the course of his dispensations in relation to a certain order of his creatures. Nor does the passage under consideration lead us to conclude, that the changes alluded to shall all take place throughout the whole universe *at the same period* but they may be considered as happening at different periods throughout the lapse of infinite duration, according to the designs which his wisdom has determined to accomplish.

That all material objects are subject to decomposition and changes, we have abundance of evidence in every department of nature. With respect to the earth on which we tread, we perceive the soil in the higher grounds gradually washed down by the action of winds and rains, and carried by the rivers to the bed of the ocean. Banks are accumulating at the mouths of rivers, and reefs in the midst of the seas, which are the terror of mariners and obstructions to navigation. In every pit and quarry, and on the face of every crag and broken precipice, we perceive the marks of disorder, and the effects of former changes and convulsions of nature; while around the bases of volcanic mountains, we behold cities buried under a mass of solid lava, orchards and vineyards laid waste, and fertile fields transformed into a scene of barrenness and desolation. Observation likewise demonstrates, that even the luminaries of heaven are not exempted from revolutions and changes. The law of gravitation, which extends its influence through all the celestial orbs, has a tendency, in the course of ages, to draw together all the spacious globes in the universe, and to condense them into one solid mass; and, were it not for the counteracting and sustaining hand of God, this effect, at some distant period in duration, would inevitably take place, and creation be reduced to one vast and frightful ruin. Many of the stars are ascertained to be subjected to periodical changes, varying their lustre, and appearing and disappearing at certain intervals; while others, which formerly shone with superior brilliancy, have gradually disappeared, and their place in the heavens is no longer to be found. Other stars, unknown to the ancients and to preceding observers, have made their appearance in modern times; and various nebulous spots, in the distant regions of space, appear to be increasing both in lustre and extent. These, and many other similar facts, indicate changes and revolutions as great, and even much greater than those which are predicted to befall the earth when its atmosphere shall be dissolved, its "elements melt with fervent heat," and a new world rise out of its ruins. It is probable, that, in the lapse of infinite duration, all the systems which now exist, some at one period and some at another, will undergo changes and transformations which will astonish the intelligent creation, and open new and sublimer scenes of divine operation to an admiring universe. But such changes will be altogether different from annihilation or utter destruction—altogether different from the ideas embodied in the language of poets, when they tell us that "not one atom shall be left in the mighty void," and that "earth and firmament will be sought in vain." Those stars which appeared, the one in 1572, and the other in 1604, which shone with a brightness superior to Venus, and afterwards disappeared, we have no reason to believe, are blotted out of creation. They may either have been changed, from flaming suns, to opaque globes like the planets, and may still be existing in the same region of space; or they may have been carried forward with a rapid motion, to a region of the universe altogether beyond the utmost limits of our vision, or some other transformation, beyond the reach of human conception, may have been effected. For the annihilation of matter appears to form no part of the plan of the Creator's arrangements; at least, we have no proof of it, in any one instance, and the very idea of it seems to imply an inconsistency, which is repugnant to what we already know of the divine character and operations.

Such changes, then, so far from diminishing the visible glory of the universe, will present to the view of the intelligent creation a *greater variety of sublime scenery* than if all things "continued as they were from the beginning of the creation," and will exhibit the attributes of the Almighty in all their varied aspects and diversified modes of operation. While they demonstrate the mutable nature of created beings, and the immutability of the Creator, they will enliven the scenes of the universe, and excite the admiration and praises of countless multitudes of enraptured intelligences.

From the considerations now stated, it will follow, that the various relations which now subsist among the great bodies which compose the universe, will not be materially altered by any changes or revolutions which may take place in our terrestrial sphere: nor will the general aspect of creation be sensibly altered by any changes that may occasionally happen among the celestial luminaries. Whatever may be the nature of such changes, or however important they may be to the inhabitants of the systems in which they happen, they bear no sensible proportion to the whole fabric of the universe. Though stars have, at different periods, disappeared from the visible concave of the firmament, and have, doubtless, undergone amazing revolutions, yet the general appearance of the heavens in all ages has been nearly the same, and will probably continue so for an indefinite lapse of ages yet to come. Although our earth were just now transported to a point of space a hundred thousand millions of miles beyond the sphere we presently occupy, the general aspect and the relative positions of the starry orbs, and the figures of the different constellations, would appear, on the whole, the same as they now do when we lift our eyes to the nocturnal sky. The constellations of *Orion* and *Charles's Wain*, for example, would present the same shape, the same number of stars, and the same relations to neighbouring constellations, when viewed from a region 1,000,000,000,000,000* of miles distant from the earth, as they now do from the sphere in which we are placed.†—Extension, magnitude, relative position, attraction, gravitation, central forces, rectilineal and circular motions, and other properties and relations of matter, will still subsist in the universe, after we are transported to another state and to a different region;—and, consequently the *sciences* founded on the various combinations of these properties and of the laws which govern them, will be cultivated by intelligent beings, and carried forward to that measure of perfection which they cannot attain in the present state; unless we suppose, what is evidently absurd and contrary to Scripture, that our knowledge *will be more limited* in the future, than in the present world.

For example, the laws which direct the motions of falling bodies, the appearances produced by bodies in the heavens moving with different degrees of velocity, the apparent motions of the sun and of the starry heavens, and the general principles of geography and astronomy, on the planet Jupiter, or any other similar globe, with the exception of a few local modifications, are materially the same as on the surface of the earth;—which is evident from the consideration of his spheroidal figure, his diurnal and annual motions, and from the consideration that gravitation is regulated by the same general laws on that body, and on similar globes, as on the surface of the earth or the moon.—The laws of *vision*, and the nature and properties of *light* and *colours*, are essentially the same throughout all that portion of the universe which lies within the sphere of our observation; and we have no reason to believe, that the general laws of the universe will be unhinged for the sake of man, or on account of any changes that happen in his present abode, or in reference to his future destination. For, to use the words of a late eminent Scottish philosopher, "The light by which the fixed stars are seen, is the same with that by which we behold the sun and his attending planets. It moves with the same velocity, as we observe by comparing the aberrations of the fixed stars with the eclipses of Jupiter's satellites. It is refracted and reflected by the same laws. It consists of

* That is, *a thousand billions*; a billion being equal to ten hundred thousand millions.

† This will appear quite evident to any one who considers the immense distance of the stars from the earth and from one another. We know, by experience, that a change of place equal to 190 millions of miles, or the diameter of the earth's annual orbit, produces no sensible difference in the appearance of the starry heavens, and it is certain that if this distance were multiplied by ten hundred thousand, the case would be nearly the same. The nearest star is, at least, 20 billions of miles distant, and remoter stars several thousands of billions; and therefore, the relative positions of bodies so widely dispersed from each other, would not be sensibly altered by a change of place equal in extent to a thousand billions of miles.

the same colours. No opinion therefore, can be formed of the solar light which must not also be adopted with respect to the light of the fixed stars. The medium of vision must be acted on in the same manner by both, whether we suppose it the undulations of an ether, or the emission of matter from the luminous body."—From these facts we may conclude, that the general and fundamental principles of the science of *Optics* are recognised and acted upon in the remotest regions which the telescope has explored, and from a portion of that knowledge which is possessed by the intelligences which occupy those distant provinces of the Creator's empire—always, however, making proper allowances for those local varieties and modifications, which must produce an infinite diversity of scenery throughout the universe, although the same general laws operate throughout the whole.

What has been now stated in reference to light, gravitation, and other affections of matter, might be extended to various other properties, and to the sciences which have been founded upon them; such as, the pressure and motions of fluids, the properties of gaseous bodies, the phenomena of electricity and magnetism, and all those affinities, decompositions and changes, which are the objects of *chymical* research. For, in a *material* fabric, in whatever portion of space it may be placed, there must, from the very nature of things, be a diversity of objects for the investigation of the naturalist, the chymist, and the philosopher, in which the wisdom and goodness of the Deity will always be displayed. Every system of matter, wherever existing in infinite space, has a determinate size and figure; it is composed of an infinite number of atoms, variously modified and arranged; it has certain diversities of surface and internal arrangement; it is susceptible of certain motions; it stands in certain relations to surrounding bodies, and it is destined to accomplish some wise designs corresponding to the eternal plan of the infinite Creator. There is no portion of organized matter now existing, or which may hereafter exist, but which must be considered in these and similar points of view. Now the object of every rational intelligence, whether designated by the appellations of philosopher, astronomer or chymist, when contemplating any material system, is, or ought to be, to trace the various properties and arrangements which exist in that system, in order to perceive the intelligence, wisdom and benevolence that appear in its construction, and thus to acquire a more correct and comprehensive view of the plans and perfections of his Creator. But such contemplations necessarily suppose, the cultivation of those sciences which will enable him to make such investigations with spirit and effect, without which he would be unable to trace either the qualities and relations of material objects, or to perceive the admirable designs of the all-wise Creator in the works which his almighty power has produced.

### SCIENCES WHICH WILL BE CULTIVATED IN A FUTURE STATE.

In order to illustrate this subject a little farther, I shall offer a few brief remarks on some of those sciences which will be recognised and prosecuted in a future world.

#### ARITHMETIC.

*Arithmetic*, or the knowledge of numbers, and their various powers and combinations, is a science which must be understood in a greater or less degree by all intelligent beings wherever existing; without some knowledge of which, no extensive progress could be made in the study of the works of God, and in forming just conceptions of the immense number and variety of beings which exist within the limits of his empire. By the application of the science of numbers the bulk of the earth has been ascertained; the distances and magnitudes of many of the heavenly bodies have been computed; the proportion which one part of the universe bears to another has been determined; the inconceivable minuteness of the particles of effluvia, of animalculæ, and of the atoms of light, has been brought within the limits of our contemplation; and we have been enabled to form some faint conceptions of the amazing velocities with which the celestial orbs are carried forward in their courses. The universe presents to our view an assemblage of objects, relations, and movements calculated to draw forth into exercise all the knowledge of numbers we can possibly acquire. We are presented with magnitudes so stupendous, and with spaces and distances so vast, that the mind is obliged to summon up all its powers of calculation, and all its knowledge of proportions, progressions and equations, and to add one known magnitude to another, in a long mental process, before it can approximate to any thing like a well-defined idea of such sublime and expansive objects; and, after all its mental efforts, computations and comparisons, it is frequently under the necessity of resting satisfied with ideas which are vague, inaccurate, and obscure. With regard to the *multiplicity* and *variety* of the objects which creation contains, our present knowledge of the powers of numbers is altogether inadequate to convey to the mind any thing approaching to a distinct and comprehensive conception. The *number* of systems in the heavens which lie within the range of our telescopes, is reckoned to be at least a hundred millions (100,000,000.) In the regions of infinite space, beyond the boundaries of all these, it is not improbable, that ten thousand times ten thousand millions of other systems are running their ample rounds. With each of these systems, it is probable, that at least a hundred worlds are connected.* Every one of these worlds and systems, we have reason to believe, differs from another, in its size, splendour and internal arrangements, in the peculiar beauties and sublimities with which it is adorned, and in the organization and capacities of the beings with which it is furnished. The immense multitude of rational beings and other existences with which creation is replenished, is an idea which completely overpowers the human faculties, and is beyond the power of our arithmetical notation to express. Even the multiplicity of objects in *one* world or system, is beyond our distinct conception. How very feeble and imperfect conceptions have we attained of the immensity of radiations of light incessantly emitted from the sun and falling upon our globe, and of the innumerable crossings and recrossings of these rays from every object around, in order to produce vision to every beholder! of the incalculable myriads of invisible animalculæ which swim in the waters and fly in the air, and pervade every department of nature; of the particles of vapour which float in the atmosphere, and of the drops of water contained in the caverns of the ocean! of the many millions of individuals belonging to every species of vegetables, of which 50,000 different species have already been discovered, and of the number of trees, shrubs, flowers and plants of every description which have flourished since the creation! of the countless myriads of the lower animals, and of the human species, which have been brought into existence since the commencement of time, and of those which are yet to appear in regular succession till time shall be no more! of the immense variety of movements, adjustments and adaptations connected with the structure of an animal body, of which fourteen thousand may be reckoned as belonging to the system of bones and muscles comprised in the human frame, besides a distinct variety of as numerous adaptations in each of the 60,000 different species of animals which are already known to exist! of the countless globules contained in the eyes of the numerous tribes of beetles, flies, butterflies and other insects of which 27,000 have been counted in a single eye! And, if the multiplicity of objects in one world overwhelms our powers of conception and computation, how much more the number and variety of beings and operations connected with the economy of millions of worlds! No finite intelligence, without a profound knowledge of numbers in all their various combinations, can form even a rude conception of the diversified scenes of the universe; and yet, without some faint conception at least, of such objects, the perfections of the Creator and the glories of his kingdom cannot be appreciated.

It is evident, therefore, that superior intelligences, such as angels, and redeemed men in a future state, must have their attention directed to the science of numbers, unless we suppose, what is contrary to Scripture, that their knowledge and capacities of intellect will be more limited than ours are in the present state. They may not stand in need of the aids of any thing similar to slates, pencils or numerical characters to direct them in their computations, or to give permanency to the results of their arithmetical processes. The various steps of their calculations may be carried forward with inconceivable rapidity, by a mental process which will lead to unerring certainty; but the same general principles on which we proceed in our notations and calculations, must, from the nature of things, be recognised in all their numerical processes and sublime investigations.

The Scriptures occasionally give us some intimations of objects and scenes calculated to exercise the numerical powers of the heavenly inhabitants. When Daniel beheld the vision of the "Ancient of Days" sitting on his throne, a numerous retinue of glorious beings appeared in his train to augment the grandeur of the scene. "Thousand thousands ministered unto him, and ten thousand times ten thousand stood before him." We are told in the sixty-eighth Psalm, that "the chariots of God are twenty thousand, even many thousands of angels?" and in the Epistle to the Hebrews, we read of "an innumerable company of angels." The apostle John, when narrating his visions of the celestial world, tells us, that he "beheld and heard the voice of many angels round about the throne, and the number of them was ten times ten thousand, and thousands of thousands." And again, "After this I beheld, and lo, a great multitude which no man could number, of all nations and kindreds, and people, and tongues—and all the angels stood round about the throne, and fell on their faces and worshipped God." These expressions are the strongest which the inspired writers make use of in order to express a countless multitude of objects; and they lead us to conclude, that, in the heavenly world, vast assemblages of intelligent beings will be occasionally presented to the view; and consequently, a countless variety of scenes, objects and circumstances connected with their persons, stations and employments. And, therefore, if celestial beings were not familiarized with numerical calculations and proportions, such scenes, instead of being contemplated with intelligence and rational admiration, would confound the intellect, and produce an effect similar to that which is felt by a savage when he beholds, for the first time, some of the splendid scenes of civilized life.

* With the solar system to which we belong, there are connected more than a hundred globes of different sizes, if we take into account the planets both *primary* and *secondary*, and likewise the *comets*

It is owing, in a great measure, to ignorance of the powers of numbers, and the mode of applying them, that we find it impossible to convey any distinct ideas of the velocities, distances, and magnitudes of the heavenly bodies to the illiterate ranks of mankind. We are told by travellers, that there are some untutored tribes whose knowledge of numbers is so limited, that they cannot count beyond a *hundred,* and that there are others whose notation is limited to *twenty,* or the number of fingers and toes on their hands and feet. While such ignorance of numbers exists, it is quite evident, that such persons are entirely unqualified for surveying, with an eye of intelligence, the grand and *diversified* operations of the Creator, and for appreciating their number and magnificence. Even the most cultivated minds, from an imperfect knowledge of this subject, find it difficult to form distinct conceptions of the plans of the Creator, and of the various relations which subsist in the universe. After familiarizing our minds to the classification and arrangement of numbers, we can form a tolerable notion of a *thousand,* or even of a *hundred thousand;* but it is questionable, whether we have any distinct and well-defined idea of a *million,* or ten hundred thousand. And if our conceptions of such a number be imperfect, how exceedingly vague must be our ideas of a *thousand millions,* of *billions, trillions,* and *quartillions,* when used to express the number or distances of the heavenly bodies?—It is evident, then, that beings of a superior order, or in a higher state of existence, must have a more profound and comprehensive knowledge of numbers than man: in consequence of which they are enabled to survey the universe with more intelligence, and to form more distinct and ample conceptions of the designs and operations of infinite wisdom and omnipotence.

### MATHEMATICS.

*Mathematics,* including geometry, trigonometry, conic sections, and other branches, is another department of science which will be recognised by superior beings in a future state. It is the science of *Quantity,* and treats of magnitude, or local extension, as lines, surfaces, solids, &c. The demonstrated truths of this science are eternal and unchangeable, and are applicable to the circumstances of all worlds, wherever they may exist, and in every period of duration, so long as the material fabric of the universe remains. Guided by the truths which this science unfolds and demonstrates we have been enabled to determine the figure and dimensions of the earth, to direct our course from one continent to another across the pathless deep, to ascertain the distance and magnitude of the sun and planets, and the laws which the Almighty has ordained for preserving their order and directing them in their movements; and have been led to form more correct ideas of the immense distances and the vast extent of the starry heavens. It was owing to his profound knowledge of the truths of this science that the illustrious Sir Isaac Newton determined the properties and the composition of light, the causes of the alternate movements of the ocean, and the mechanism of the planetary system; and expanded our views of the grandeur of the universe and the perfections of its Almighty Contriver.

Some of the truths of this science may appear, to a superficial thinker, as extremely trivial, and almost unworthy of regard. The properties of a *triangle,* such as, "that the square of the hypotenuse of a right-angled triangle, is equal to the squares of the other two sides"—"that the three angles of a triangle are equal to two right angles"—and, "that the sides of a plane triangle are to one another as the sines of the angles opposite to them"—may appear to some minds as more curious than useful, and scarcely deserving the least attention. Yet these truths, when applied to the relations of the universe, and traced to all their legitimate consequences, have led to the most important and sublime results. On the ground of such truths we have ascertained, that the moon is 240,000 miles distant from the earth, that the sun is thirteen hundred thousand times larger than our globe, that the planet Herschel is removed to the distance of eighteen hundred millions of miles, and that the nearest star is at least two hundred thousand times farther from us than the sun. When the length of any one side of a triangle is known, however large that triangle may be, and the quantity of its angles determined, the length of the other sides can easily be found: we know the extent of the earth's diameter; we can ascertain under what angle that diameter appears at the moon, and from these *data* we can, by an easy calculation, determine the length of any of the other two sides of this triangle, which gives the distance of the moon.

We have every reason to conclude, that angels and other superior intelligences proceed on the same general principles in estimating the distances and magnitudes of the great bodies of the universe. They may not, indeed, require to resort to the same tedious calculations, nor to the same instruments and geometrical schemes which we are obliged to use. Without such aids, *they* may arrive at the proper results with unerring precision, and their computations may be performed almost in the twinkling of an eye; and while *we* are obliged to confine our calculations to lines and triangles of only a few thousands or millions of miles in extent, *they* may be enabled to form triangles of inconceivable extent, on *base lines* of several thousands of trillions of miles in length. We are informed, in the book of Daniel, that "the angel Gabriel, being commanded to fly swiftly from the celestial regions, reached the prophet about the time of the evening sacrifice." This fact implies, not only that angelic beings are endued with powers of rapid motion, but that they are intimately acquainted with the directions, distances, and positions of the bodies which compose the material universe. This heavenly messenger, having been previously stationed far beyond the limits of our planetary system, had to shape his course in that direction, to discriminate the orbit of the earth from the orbits of the other planets, and the particular part of its orbit in which it was then moving; and having arrived at the confines of our atmosphere, he required to discriminate the particular region in which Daniel resided, and to direct his flight to the house in which he was offering up his devotions. Now, since angels are neither omniscient nor omnipresent, as they are limited beings, possessed of *rational* faculties, and as it is probable are invested with bodies, or fine material vehicles,*—they must be guided in such excursions by their reasoning powers, and the faculty of rapid motion with which they are endued. Such excursions imply the recognition of certain mathematical principles, and I have already had occasion to notice, that these principles are applicable throughout every part of the universe, and must be recognised, more or less, by all intelligent beings.

The Creator himself has laid the foundation of the mathematical sciences. His works consist of globes and spheroids of all different dimensions, and of immense concentric rings revolving with a rapid motion. These globes are carried round different centres, some of them in circles, some in ellipses, and others in long eccentric curves. Being impelled in their courses by different degrees of velocity, their real motions cannot be traced, nor the beautiful simplicity and harmony of the different systems made apparent, without the application of mathematical investigations. To an observer untutored in this science, many of the celestial motions would appear to display inextricable confusion, and lead him to conclude, that the Framer of the universe was deficient in wisdom and intelligent design.—The principles of mathematics are also exhibited in the numerous and diversified figures into which diamonds, crystals, salts, and other bodies, are formed ; in the hexagonal cells of bees, wasps and hornets, in the *polygons* and *parallel lines* which enter into the construction of a spider's web, and in many other objects in nature.—Now, since God has exhibited the elements of this science before us in his works; since he has endued us with rational faculties to appreciate and apply these elements to useful investigations; and since his wisdom and intelligence, and the beauty and order of his works, cannot be fully understood without such investigations,—it is evident, that he must have intended, that men should be occasionally exercised in such studies; in order to perceive the depths of his wisdom, and the admirable simplicity and harmony of his diversified operations. And as the applications of this science are extremely limited in the present world, its more extensive applications, like those of many other branches of knowledge, must be considered as reserved for the life to come.—To suppose, therefore, that such studies will be abandoned, and such knowledge obliterated in a future state, would be to suppose, that the works of God will not be contemplated in that state, and that redeemed men in the heavenly world will lose a part of their rational faculties, and remain inferior in their acquirements to the inhabitants of the earth, even in their present imperfect and degraded condition.

* The Author will afterwards have an opportunity of illustrating this position, in Part III. of this work.

### ASTRONOMY.

*Astronomy* is another science which will occupy the attention of pure intelligences in the future world. The object of this science is, to determine the distances and magnitudes of the heavenly bodies, the form of the orbits they describe, the laws by which their motions are directed, and the nature and destination of the various luminous and opaque globes of which the universe appears to be composed. It is the most noble and sublime of all the sciences, and presents to our view the most astonishing and magnificent objects,—whether we consider their immense magnitude, the splendour of their appearance, the vast spaces which surround them, the magnificent apparatus with which some of them are encompassed, the rapidity of their motions, or the display they afford of the omnipotent energy and intelligence of the Creator. In consequence of the cultivation of this science, our views of the extent of creation, and of the sublime scenery it unfolds, are expanded far beyond what former ages could have conceived. From the discoveries of astronomy it appears, that our earth is but as a point in the immensity of the universe—that there are worlds a thousand times larger, enlightened by the same sun which "rules our day"—that the sun himself is an immense luminous world, whose circumference would inclose more than twelve hundred thousand globes as large as ours—that the earth and its inhabitants are carried forward through the regions of space, at the rate of a thousand miles every minute—that motions exist in the great bodies of the universe, the force and rapidity of which astonish and overpower the imagination—and that beyond the sphere of the sun and planets, creation is replenished with millions of luminous globes, scattered over immense regions to which the human mind can assign no boundaries.

These objects present an immense field for the contemplation of every class of moral intelligences, and a bright mirror in which they will behold the reflection of the divine attributes. Of this vast universe, how small a portion has yet been unveiled to our view! With respect to the bodies which compose our planetary system, we know only a few general facts and relations. In regard to the fixed stars, we have acquired little more than a few rude conceptions of their immense distance and magnitudes. In relation to the *comets*, we only know that they move in long eccentric orbits, that they are impelled in their courses with immense velocity, and appear and disappear in uncertain periods of time. Of the numerous systems into which the stars are arranged, of the motions peculiar to each system, of the relations which these motions have to the whole universe as one vast machine, of the nature and arrangement of the numerous nebulæ which are scattered throughout the distant regions of space; of the worlds which are connected with the starry orbs; of the various orders of beings which people them; of the changes and revolutions which are taking place in different parts of the universe, of the new creations which are starting into existence, of the number of *opaque* globes which may exist in every region of space, of the distance to which the material world extends, and of the various dispensations of the Almighty towards the diversified orders of intelligences which people his vast empire—we remain in almost profound ignorance, and must continue in this ignorance, so long as we are chained down to this obscure corner of creation.—There will, therefore, be *ample scope* in the future world for further researches into this subject, and for enlarging our knowledge of those glorious scenes which are at present so far removed beyond the limits of natural vision, and the sphere of human investigation.

*The heavens constitute the principal part of the divine empire*—compared with which our earth is but as an atom, and " all nations are as nothing, and are accounted to Jehovah as less than nothing and vanity." Vast as this world may appear to the frail beings that inhabit it, it probably ranks among the smallest globes in the universe; but although it were twenty thousand times more spacious than it is, it would be only as a grain of sand when compared with the immensity of creation, and all the events that have passed over its inhabitants as only a few of those *ephemeral* transactions which crowd the annals of eternity. It is throughout the boundless regions of the firmament that God is chiefly seen, and his glory contemplated by unnumbered intelligences. It is there that the moral grandeur of his dispensations, and the magnificence of his works are displayed in all their variety and lustre to countless orders of his rational offspring. over which he will continue eternally to preside. Hence the numerous allusions to " the heavens," by the inspired writers, when the majesty of God and the glory of his dominions are intended to be illustrated. " All the gods of the nations are idols; but Jehovah *made the heavens.*" " The Lord hath *prepared his throne in the heavens*, and his kingdom ruleth over all." " By his Spirit he hath garnished the heavens." " The heavens declare the glory of Jehovah." " When I consider thy heavens, the work of thy fingers, the moon and the stars, which thou hast ordained—what is man, that thou art mindful of him? or the son of man, that thou visitest him?" " The heavens, even the heaven of heavens, cannot contain thee." " By the word of Jehovah were the heavens made, and *all the host of them* by the spirit of his mouth." " The heavens shall declare his righteousness." " Our God is in the heavens, he hath done whatsoever he hath pleased." " *The heavens shall declare thy wonders, O Lord!*" " I lift up mine eyes to thee, O thou that *dwellest in the heavens.*" " Thus saith God the Lord, *he that created the heavens* and stretched them out." " The heavens for height are unsearchable." " As the heaven is high above the earth, so great is his mercy toward them that fear him." He is " *the God of heaven,*—he rideth on the *heaven of heavens* which he founded of old; heaven is his *throne*, and the earth his footstool."—When the folly of idolaters is exposed, when the coming of Messiah is announced, and when motives are presented to invigorate the faith and hope of the saints, Jehovah is represented as that omnipotent Being who " meteth out the heavens with a span, who spreadeth them out as a curtain, and bringeth forth their hosts by the greatness of his might." " Thus saith God the Lord, he that created the heavens and stretched them out—I will give thee for a covenant of the people, for a light of the Gentiles."* " Thus saith the Lord that created the heavens—I said not to the seed of Jacob, seek ye me in vain," &c.† These, and hundreds of similar passages, evidently imply, that we ought to contemplate the attributes of God chiefly in relation to the display which is given of them in the firmament of his power—that the heavens are by far the most extensive portion of his dominions—and that the power and intelligence displayed in the formation and arrangement of the hosts of heaven, lay a sure foundation for the hope and joy, and the future prospects of the people of God.

In order to form just conceptions of the beauty and grandeur of the heavens, and of the intelligence of Him who arranged their numerous hosts some of the fundamental facts and principles of astronomy require to be understood and recognised. The order of the bodies which compose

* Isa. xliv 5 6 † Isa. xlv. 18, 19.

the solar system, or other systems which exist in the universe—the form of their orbits, their proportional distances and periods of revolution—their magnitudes, rotations, velocities, and the various phenomena which are observed on their surfaces—the arrangement and positions of the different clusters of stars—of the stellar and planetary *nebulæ*, of double, triple, and variable stars, and many other general facts, require to be known before the mind can receive farther information respecting the structure of the universe. It may be also necessary, even in a higher state of existence, to be acquainted with those contrivances or artificial helps by which very distant objects may be brought near to view. We know by experience, in our present state, that by means of telecsopes, millions of stars, which the unassisted eye cannot discern, are brought within the sphere of our observation, and numerous other splendid objects, which, without the aid of these instruments, would have been altogether concealed from our view. The organs of vision, indeed, of the redeemed inhabitants of our globe, after the resurrection, there is every reason to believe, will be capable of taking in a much more extensive range of view than at present. They may be endowed with qualities which will enable them to penetrate into the depths of space far beyond the reach of our most powerful telescopes, and to perceive with distinctness, objects at the distance of many billions of miles. Still, however, they may require artificial aids to their natural organs, in order to enable them to contemplate objects at still greater distances. And although such helps, to natural vision, analogous to our telescopes, may be conceived as incomparably superior to ours, yet the same general principles must be recognised in their construction. For, as has been already noticed, the light which emanates from the most distant stars consists of the same colours, and is refracted and reflected by the same laws, as the light which is emitted from the sun, and which illuminates our terrestrial abode; and, consequently, must operate on the organs of sentient beings, in those remote regions, in a manner similar to its effects on the eyes of man.

It is highly probable, that, in the future world, a considerable portion of our knowledge respecting the distant provinces of the divine empire, will be communicated by superior beings who have visited the different systems dispersed through the universe, and have acquired infortion respecting their history, and their physical and moral scenery. We learn from Scripture, that there are intelligences who can wing their way, in a short period of time, from one world to another. Such beings, in the course of a thousand centuries, must have made many extensive tours through the regions of creation, and acquired a comprehensive knowledge of the most striking scenes which the universe displays. And, since they have occasionally mingled in the society of men, and communicated intelligence from heaven to earth, it is reasonable to believe, that they will have more frequent intercourse with redeemed men in a future state, and communicate the discoveries they have made respecting the economy and grandeur of God's universal empire. But, at the same time, it ought carefully to be observed, that such communications would neither be fully understood nor appreciated, unless the mind had a previous acquaintance with the leading facts, and the grand outlines of astronomical science. To enter into the spirit of those sublime details which angels or archangels might communicate respecting other systems and worlds, the mind *must be prepared* by a knowledge of those principles which have already been ascertained, and of those discoveries which have already been made in relation to the system of the universe. Suppose a group of the native tribes of New Holland or Van Diemen's Land, were assembled for the purpose of listening to a detail of the principal discoveries which modern astronomers have made in the heavens—it would be impossible to convey to their minds a clear conception even of the prominent and leading facts of this science, from the want of those general ideas which are previously necessary in order to the right understanding of such communications. Such would be the case of men in a future state, in regard to the communications of angelic messengers from distant worlds, were their minds not imbued with a certain portion of astronomical knowledge. They might stare, and wonder at some of the facts detailed; but their ideas would be vague and confused, and they would be unable to form clear and comprehensive conceptions of the various circumstances connected with the scenes described, in all their bearings, aspects, and relations, and of the indications they afford of exquisite skill and intelligent design.

As the objects which astronomy explores are unlimited in their range, they will afford an *inexhaustible* subject of study and contemplation to superior beings, and to mankind when placed in a higher sphere of existence. Astronomical science, as having for its object to investigate and explore the facts and relations peculiar to all the great bodies in the universe, can never be exhausted; unless we suppose that finite minds will be able, at some future period in duration, to survey and to comprehend all the plans and operations of the infinite Creator. But this is evidently impossible; for " who can by searching find out God? Who can find out the Almighty to perfection?" After millions of centuries have run their rounds, new scenes of grandeur will be still bursting on the astonished mind, new regions of creation, and new displays of divine power and wisdom will still remain to be explored, and, consequently, the science of astronomy will never arrive at absolute perfection, but will be in a progressive course of improvement through all the revolutions of eternity. In the prosecution of such investigations, and in the contemplation of such objects as this science presents, the grand aim of celestial intelligences will be, to increase in the knowledge and the love of God; and, in proportion as their views of the glories of his empire are enlarged, in a similar proportion will their conceptions of his boundless attributes be expanded, and their praises and adorations ascend in sublimer strains to Him who sits upon the throne of the universe, who alone is "worthy to receive glory, honour, and power," from every order of his creatures.

Since then, it appears, that astronomy is conversant about objects the most wonderful and sublime—since these objects tend to amplify our conceptions of the divine attributes—since a clear and distinct knowledge of these objects cannot be attained without the acquisition of a certain portion of astronomical science—since the heavens constitute the principal part of God's universal empire—since our present views of the magnificence of this empire are so obscure and circumscribed—since even the information that may be communicated on this subject, by other intelligences, could not be fully understood without some acqnaintance with the principles of this science—and since the boundless scenes it unfolds present an inexhaustible subject of contemplation, and afford motives to stimulate all holy beings to incessant adoration—it would be absurd to suppose that renovated men, in a superior state of existence, will remain in ignorance of this subject, or that the study of it will ever be discontinued while eternity endures.

### NATURAL PHILOSOPHY.

*Natural Philosophy* is another subject which will doubtless engage the attention of regenerated men in a future state.

The objects of this science is to describe the phenomena of the material world, to explain their causes, to investigate the laws by which the Almighty directs the operations of nature, and to trace the exquisite skill and benevolent design which are displayed in the economy of the universe. It embraces investigations into the several powers and properties, qualities and attributes, motions and appearances, causes and effects, of all the bodies with which we are surrounded, and which are obvious to our senses,—such as light, heat, colours, air, water, sounds, echoes; the electrical and magnetical fluids; hail, rain, snow, dew, thunder, lightning, the rainbow, parhelia, winds, luminous and fiery meteors, the Aurora Borealis, and similar objects in the system of nature.

From the discoveries of experimental philosophers, we have been made acquainted with a variety of striking facts and agencies in the system of the universe, which display the amazing energies of the Creator, and which tend to excite our admiration of the depths of his wisdom and intelligence. We learn that the *light* emitted from the sun and other luminous bodies moves with a velocity equal to 200,000 miles in a *second* of time—that every ray of white light is composed of all the colours in nature, blended in certain proportions—that the immense variety of shades of colours which adorns the different landscapes of the earth, is not in the objects themselves, but in the light that falls upon them—and that thousands of millions of rays are incessantly flying off from all visible objects, crossing and recrossing each other in an infinity of directions, and yet conveying to every eye that is open to receive them, a distinct picture of the objects whence they proceed. We learn that the atmosphere which surrounds us presses our bodies with a weight equal to thirty thousand pounds, that it contains the principles of fire and flame—that, in one combination, it would raise our animal spirits to the highest pitch of ecstacy, and in another, cause our immediate destruction—that is capable of being compressed into 40,000 times less space than it naturally occupies—and that the production of sound, the lives of animals, and the growth of vegetables, depend upon its various and unceasing agencies. We learn that a certain fluid pervades all nature, which is capable of giving a *shock* to the animal frame, which shock may be communicated in an instant to a thousand individuals—that this fluid moves with inconceivable rapidity—that it can be drawn from the clouds in the form of a stream of fire—that it melts iron wire, increases the evaporation of fluids, destroys the polarity of the magnetic needle and occasionally displays its energies among the clouds in the form of fire-balls, lambent flames. and forked lightnings. We learn that the bodies of birds, fishes, quadrupeds, and insects, in relation to their eyes, feet, wings, fins, and other members, are formed with admirable skill, so as to be exactly adapted to their various necessities and modes of existence, and that they consist of an infinite number of contrivances and adaptations in order to accomplish the purpose intended—and that the beaver, the bee, the ant, and other insects, construct their habitations, and perform their operations with all the skill and precision of the nicest mathematical science. The bee, in particular, works, as if it knew the highest branches of mathematics, which required the genius of Newton to discover.—In short, the whole of nature presents a scene of wonders which, when seriously contemplated, is calculated to expand the intellectual powers, to refine the affections, and to excite admiration of the attributes of God, and the plan of his providence.

Natural Philosophy may, therefore, be considered as a branch both of the religion of nature, and of the religion of revelation. It removes, in part, the veil which is spread over the mysterious operations of nature, and discloses to our view the wonders which lie concealed from the sottish multitude, "who regard not the works of the Lord, nor consider the operations of his hands." It enables us to perceive the footsteps of the Almighty both in his majestic movements and in his most minute designs; for there is not a step we can take in the temple of nature, under the guidance of an enlightened philosophy, in which we do not behold traces of inscrutable wisdom and design, and of a benevolence which extends its kind regards to every rank of sensitive and intelligent existence. It shows us the beauty and goodness of the divine administration; and demonstrates, that the communication of happiness is the final cause of all the admirable arrangements which pervade the material system. It teaches us, that the several operations of nature are carried on by means uncontrollable by human power, and far transcending finite skill to plan or to execute. It discovers those laws by which the sovereign of the universe governs his vast dominions, and maintains them in undecaying beauty and splendour, throughout all ages. It thus enables us to consecrate the universe into one grand temple, and, from the contemplation of every object it presents, to elevate our minds, and to raise our voices in grateful praises to Him "who created all things, and for whose pleasure they are and were created."

In the future world there will be *abundant scope* for the prosecution of this subject to an indefinite extent. With respect to the state of separate spirits, after their departure from this world, the employments in which they engage, and the connection in which they stand to the material system, we can form no distinct conception, and must remain in ignorance till the period arrive when we shall be actually ushered into that mysterious scene of existence. But, we are assured, that, after the resurrection, a *material* world will be prepared for the habitation of the just, in which their connection with the visible universe will doubtless, be far more extensive than it is at present; and wherever a material system exists, it affords scope for physical investigations, and for the application of the principles of Natural Philosophy. This new world will be prepared and arranged by divine wisdom; and consequently, will exhibit scenes of beauty and grandeur, of exquisite contrivance and benevolent design. For, if the world we now inhabit, amidst all the deformities and physical derangements which sin has introduced, displays so many beautiful arrangements and marks of intelligence and skill, much more may we conclude, that the world in which "righteousness shall dwell," will abound in every thing that can charm the eye, the ear, or the imagination, and illustrate the manifold wisdom of God; and of course will present a boundless field for the most sublime investigations of science. This world, in many of its arrangements, will doubtless present a variety of objects and scenes altogether different from those we now behold, even although the same physical laws which govern our terrestrial system should still continue in operation. The inflection, refraction and reflection of light will be directed by the same general laws, and will produce effects analogous to those we now perceive in the scene around us; but the mediums through which it passes, and the various objects by which it is refracted and reflected, and many other modifications to which it may be subjected, may produce a variety of astonishing effects, surpassing every thing we now behold, and exhibit scenes of beauty and magnificence of which we can, at present, form no distinct conception. The science of optics, in unfolding to us the nature of light, and the various properties of prisms, mirrors, and lenses, has enabled us to exhibit a variety of beautiful and surprising effects, and to perceive traces of infinite intelligence in relation to this element, beyond what former ages could have believed. And, therefore, we have reason to conclude, that, in the hand of Omnipotence, when arranging other worlds, the element of light is capable of being modified in a thousand forms of which we are now ignorant, so as to produce the most glorious and transporting effects. There will probably be no such phenomena as thunder, lightning, and fiery meteors in the world to which I allude, but the electrical fluid, which is the principal agent in producing these appearances, and which pervades every part of nature, may operate in that world in a different manner, and, instead of producing effects that are terrific and appalling, may be an agent for creating scenes which will inspire the soul with admiration and delight. Some of the mechanical, pneumatical, and hydrostatical principles which enter into the construction of mills, wheel-carriages, forcing pumps, and steam-engines, may not be applied to the same purposes in the future world; but they may be applicable to a variety of other unknown purposes corresponding to the nature of that world, and the character and employments of its inhabitants.

In such cases as those now alluded to, and in thousands of others, there will be ample scope for the application of all the principles of natural science; and thousands of facts and principles, to us unknown, will doubtless be brought to light by the superior sagacity of the heavenly inhabitants. To maintain the contrary, would be, in effect, to suppose, that the inhabitants of heaven are endowed with powers of intellect *inferior* to those of the inhabitants of the earth,—that their knowledge is less extensive than ours,—that they make no progress in moral and intellectual attainments,

—and that they have no desire to explore "the works of the Lord, and to consider the operations of his hands."

What has been now stated in relation to Natural Philosophy, will equally apply to the science of *Chymistry*. This science has for its object to ascertain the first principles of all bodies, their various properties and combinations, their mode of operation, and the effects they produce in the economy of nature. Its discoveries have not only unfolded many of the admirable processes which are going forward in the animal, vegetable, and mineral kingdoms, but have opened to our view many striking displays of the wisdom and goodness of God, in producing, by the most simple means, the most astonishing and benevolent effects. The principles of this science must, therefore, be applicable, *wherever matter exists*, under whatever shape or modification it may present itself; and as all the worlds throughout the universe are composed of *matter* compounded into various forms, they must afford an ample range for the investigations and researches of chymical science.

### ANATOMY AND PHYSIOLOGY.

*Anatomy and Physiology* are subjects which we may reasonably conclude, will occasionally occupy the attention of the inhabitants of heaven. The object of these sciences is, to investigate the general structure and economy of the animal frame, and especially the parts and functions of the human body. The system of organization connected with the human frame is the most admirable piece of mechanism which the mind can contemplate—whether we consider the immense number and variety of its parts—the numerous functions they perform—the rapid movements which are incessantly going forward throughout every part of this system—the amazing force exerted by the heart and muscles—the processes of digestion and respiration—the system of veins and arteries—the articulation of the bones—the structure and course of the lymphatics—the ramifications of the nerves—the circulation of the blood—the wonderful changes, dissolutions and combinations continually going on—the chymical apparatus adapted for effecting these purposes—the organs of sense by which an intercourse is maintained with the external world—or, the harmonious correspondence of all its parts and functions with the agencies of the surrounding elements. From the researches of physiologists we learn, that there are in the human body, two hundred and forty-five bones variously articulated, each of them having above forty distinct scopes or intentions; and four hundred and forty-six muscles of various figures and magnitudes, connected with the bones, for producing the numerous movements of the animal frame—that more than a hundred of these muscles are employed every time we breathe—that there are thousands of veins and arteries distributed throughout every part of this wonderful system—that the whole mass of blood rushes with immense velocity, through these vessels, and through the heart, fourteen times every hour—that respiration is nothing else than a species of *combustion*, in which the oxygen of the atmosphere is absorbed by the blood, and diffuses heat and vigour throughout the system—that the lungs are composed of an infinite number of membranous cells or vesicles variously figured, and full of air, communicating on all sides with one another, and that their number amounts to at least 1,700,000,000—that there are above three hundred thousand millions of pores in the glands of the skin which covers the body of a middle-sized man, through which the sweat and insensible perspiration are continually issuing—that thousands of lacteal and lymphatic tubes are absorbing and conveying nutriment to the blood—that the heart, in the centre of the system, is exerting an immense muscular force, and giving ninety-six thousand strokes every twenty-four hours;—and that all this complicated system of mechanism, and hundreds of other functions of which we are ignorant, must be in constant action, in order to preserve us in existence, and secure our enjoyment.

This subject frequently engaged the attention of the pious Psalmist. With an eye of intelligence and devotion, he surveyed the curious organization of the human frame, from the rude embryo in the womb to the full developement of all its functions;—and, struck with the wisdom and goodness displayed in its formation, he raised his thoughts to God in grateful adoration. "I will praise thee," he exclaims, "for I am fearfully and wonderfully made; marvellous are thy works! How precious are thy wonderful contrivances in relation to me, O God! How great is the sum of them! If I should count them, they are more in number than the sand." This body, however, wonderful as its structure is, is liable to decay, and must soon be dissolved in the grave. But we are assured that a period is approaching, when, "all that are in their graves shall hear the voice of the Son of God, and shall come forth;" when this mortal frame "shall put on *immortality*," and when that which was sown in corruption "shall be raised in *glory*." If the human body, even in its present state of degradation, excited the pious admiration of the Psalmist, much more will it appear worthy of our highest admiration, when it emerges from darkness and corruption to participate in the glories of an *immortal* life. Its faculties will then be invigorated, its tendency to dissolution destroyed, every principle of disease annihilated, and every thing that is loathsome and deformed for ever prevented. Being "fashioned like unto Christ's glorious body," its beauty will be exquisite, its symmetry perfect, its aspect bright and refulgent, and its motions vigorous and nimble. Its sensitive organs will be refined and improved, and the sphere of their operation extended. Its auditory organs will be tuned to receive the most delightful sensations from the harmonies of celestial music, and its visual powers rendered capable of perceiving the minutest objects, and penetrating into the most distant regions. New senses and faculties of perception, and new powers of motion, fitted to transport it with rapidity from one portion of space to another, will, in all probability, be superadded to the powers with which it is now invested. And, surely, the contrivances and adaptations which must enter into the structure of such an organical frame, cannot be less curious and exquisite, nor display less wisdom and intelligence than those which we now perceive in our mortal bodies. On the contrary, we must necessarily suppose thousands of the most delicate contrivances and compensations, different from every thing we can now conceive, to be essentially requisite in the construction of an organized body intended for perpetual activity, and destined to an IMMORTAL duration.—To investigate and to contemplate the contrivances of divine wisdom, by which the elements of disease and death are for ever prevented from entering into this renovated frame, and by which it will be preserved in undecaying youth and vigour throughout the lapse of innumerable ages, we must necessarily conclude, will form a part of the studies of renovated man in the future world; —nor can we help thinking, that the knowledge of the wonders of the human frame we now acquire, may be a preparatory qualification, for enabling us to form an enlightened and comprehensive conception of the powers, qualities, and peculiar organization, of the bodies of the saints after the period of the resurrection.

### HISTORY.

Another branch of study in which the saints in heaven will engage, is ***History***. History contains a record of past facts and events; and makes us acquainted with transactions which happened hundreds or thousands of years before we were brought into existence. When viewed in its proper light, it may be considered as nothing else than a detail of the operations of Divine Providence in relation to the moral intelligences of this world. It illustrates the character of the human race, and the deep and universal depravity in which they are involved; and displays the rectitude of the character of God, and the equity of his moral administration.

History, therefore, will form a prominent object of study among the celestial inhabitants, as furnishing those materials which will illustrate the ways of Providence and display the wisdom and righteousness of Jehovah in his government of the world. At present we can contemplate only a few scattered fragments of the history of mankind. Of the history of some nations we are altogether ignorant; and of the history of others we have only a few unconnected details, blended with fabulous narrations and extravagant fictions. Of no nation whatever have we an *entire* history composed of authentic materials; and consequently, we perceive only some broken and detached links in the chain of the divine dispensations, and are unable to survey the *whole* of God's procedure towards our race, in one unbroken series, from the creation to the present time. We know nothing decisively respecting the *period* during which man remained in a state of innocence, nor of the particular transactions and events that happened previous to his fall. And how little do we know of the state of mankind, of the events which befell them, and of the civil and religious arrangements which existed, during the period of sixteen hundred years which intervened between the creation and the deluge, though the world was then more fertile and populous than it has ever since been? How little do we know of the state of mankind immediately previous to the flood, of the scenes of consternation and terror which must have been displayed over all the earth, when the fountains of the great deep were broken up, and the cataracts of heaven opened, and of the dreadful concussion of the elements of nature, when the solid strata of the earth were rent asunder, when the foundations of the mountains were overturned, and the whole surface of the globe transformed into one boundless ocean? How little do we know of the circumstances which attended the gradual rise of idolatry, and of the origin of the great empires into which the world has been divided? How little do we know even of the history of the Jewish nation, posterior to the period of the Babylonish captivity? Whither were the ten tribes of Israel scattered among the nations, what events have befallen them, and in what countries are they now to be found? Of the history of all the nations in the world (the Jews only excepted) from the time of the deluge to the days of Hezekiah, a period of nearly two thousand years, we remain in profound ignorance. And yet, during that long period, God had not forsaken the earth; his dispensations towards his rational offspring were still going forward, empires were rising and declining, one generation passing away, and another generation coming, and thousands of millions of mankind ushered into the eternal world.—Those chasms in the history of mankind, which hide from our view the greater portion of God's moral dispensations, will, doubtless, be filled up in the eternal state, so that we shall be enabled to take a full and comprehensive view of the whole of the divine procedure, in all its connections and bearings towards every nation upon earth

But the history of *man* is not the only topic in this department of knowledge, that will occupy the attention of the inhabitants of heaven. The history of *angels*—of their faculties, intercourses, and employments—of their modes of communication with each other—of their different embassies to distant worlds—of the transactions which have taken place in their society—and of the revolutions through which they may have passed—the history of *apostate* angels—the cause of their fall and the circumstances with which it was attended—the plans they have been pursuing since that period, and the means by which they have endeavoured to accomplish their infernal devices—will doubtless form a portion of the history of divine dispensations, which "the saints in light" will be permitted to contemplate. Over this part of the divine economy a veil of darkness is spread, which, we have reason to believe, will be withdrawn, when that which is perfect is come, and, "when we shall know even as also we are known."—It is also probable, that the leading facts in relation to the history of other worlds will be disclosed to their view. The history of the different planets in the solar system, and of those which are connected with other systems in the universe—the periods of their creation, the character of their inhabitants, the changes through which they have passed, the peculiar dispensations of Providence towards them, and many other particulars, may be gradually laid open to the "redeemed from among men," for enlarging their views of the divine government. By means of such communications they will acquire a clearer and more distinct conception of the moral character and attributes of God, of the rectitude of his administrations, and of "his manifold wisdom" in the various modes by which he governs the different provinces of his vast empire. Under the impressions which such views will produce, they will rejoice in the divine government, and join with rapture in the song of Moses, the servant of God, and the song of the Lamb, saying, "Great and marvellous are thy works, Lord God Almighty! *Just and true are thy ways, thou King of saints!*"

Thus I have briefly stated, in the preceding pages, some of those branches of science which will be recognised by the righteous in a future state. Several other departments of scientific knowledge might have been specified; but my intention simply was, to present to the view of the reader, a few specimens as illustrations of my general position, "that science must be considered as having a relation to a future world." If it be admitted that any one science will be cultivated in heaven, it will follow, that the greater part if not the whole, of those sciences which bring to light the treasures of useful knowledge, will likewise be prosecuted by superior intelligences. For all the useful sciences have an intimate connexion with each other; so that an acquaintance with one department of knowledge is essentially requisite to a clear and comprehensive view of another. Astronomy supposes a knowledge of arithmetic, geometry, trigonometry, conic sections, and other parts of mathematics; experimental philosophy supposes a previous acquaintance with natural history and physiology, and is intimately connected with chymistry, mineralogy and botany; and anatomy and physiology suppose a knowledge of the leading principles of hydrostatics, pneumatics, and optics. The principles of one science run into another, and reflect a mutual lustre on each other, so that all the sciences, when properly conducted, and viewed in their true light, have but one object in view, namely, to ascertain the facts existing in the universe, their connexions and relations, the laws by which they are governed, and the illustrations they afford of the power, wisdom and benevolence of the Creator.

In order to elucidate this topic a little farther, the following brief remarks may be stated.—It is admitted, by every believer in Revelation,* that, at the close of the present arrangements respecting our world, "All that are in their graves shall be raised to life;" and that, however different the constitution of these new-modelled bodies may be from their present state of organization, they will still be *material* vehicles, furnished with organs of sensation as the medium of perception to the immaterial spirit. In what manner the disembodied spirit views material objects and relations, and applies the knowledge of them which it acquired while united to an organical structure, we can have no conception whatever, till we be actually ushered into the separate state; and therefore, the observations already made, or which may yet be thrown out on this subject, are not intended to apply to the intermediate state of the spirits of good men. That state, whatever may be the *modus* of perception and enjoyment in it, is a state of imperfection, and, in some respects, an *unnatural* state, if we suppose that the spirit is not connected with any material vehicle.—Now, if it be admitted, that the spirits of the just, at the general resurrection, are to be reunited to *material* organical structures, it must also be admitted, that those structures must have some material *substratum* on which to rest, or, in other words, a material world or habitation in which they may reside. This last position is also as evident, from the declarations of Scripture, as the first. For, while we are informed that the elementary parts of our globe shall be dissolved, we are at the same time assured, that "*new heavens and a new earth*" shall be prepared, "wherein the righteous shall dwell;"—that is, a world purified from physical and moral

* The followers of Baron Swedenberg only excepted.

evil, and fitted to the renovated faculties of the redeemed, will be prepared in some part of the universe, for the residence of the just.

In reference to the *locality*, and the circumstances of our future destination, there appear to be only four or five suppositions that can be formed. Either, 1. The world we now inhabit will be new-modelled, after the general conflagration, and furnished as a proper place of residence for its renovated inhabitants;—or, 2. Some of the globes now existing in other regions of space, to which the holy inhabitants of our world will be transported, may be allotted as the more permanent habitation of the just;—or, 3. Some new globe or world will be immediately created, adapted to the circumstances of redeemed men, and adorned with scenery fitted to call forth into exercise their renovated powers;—or, 4. The redeemed inhabitants of heaven may be permitted to transport themselves from one region or world to another, and be furnished with faculties and vehicles for this purpose;—or, 5. After remaining for a certain lapse of ages in that particular world to which they shall be introduced immediately after the resurrection, they may be transported to another region of the universe, to contemplate a new scene of creating power and intelligence, and afterwards pass, at distant intervals, through a successive series of transportations, in order to obtain more ample prospects of the riches and glory of God's universal kingdom.

In all these cases, whatever supposition we may adopt as most probable, the general laws which now govern the universe, and the general relations of the great bodies in the universe to each other will remain, on the whole, unchanged; unless we adopt the unreasonable and extravagant supposition, that the whole frame of Jehovah's empire will be unhinged and overturned, for the sake of our world, which, when compared with the whole system of nature, is but an undistinguishable atom amidst the immensity of God's works. With equal reason might we suppose, that the conduct of the inhabitants of a planet which revolves around the star *Sirius*, or the catastrophe which may have befallen the planets Ceres, Pallas, Juno, and Vesta, must necessarily involve in them the destruction of the terraqueous globe.

Let us suppose, for a moment, that the globe we now inhabit, with its surrounding atmosphere, shall be cleared from the physical evils which now exist, and undergo a new arrangement to render it fit for being the abode of holy intelligences in a future state. On this supposition, would not the *general relation of things* in the universe remain materially the same as at present? The wide expanse of the firmament, and all the orbs it contains, would present the same general arrangement and relation to each other which they now do. Supposing this new-modelled world to be of a spherical or spheroidal figure—which appears to be the general from of all the great bodies in the universe with which we are acquainted—there would then exist certain properties and relations between circles cutting each other at right angles, or in any other direction; or, in other words, between an equator and poles, parallels and meridians, &c. as at present. The direction of its motion, the inclination of its axis, the component parts of its surface and atmosphere, and other circumstances might be changed, which would produce an immense variety of phenomena, different from what now takes place; but the same general principles of geography, astronomy, arithmetic, geometry, chymistry and mechanics, which apply to all the various relations of material objects wherever existing, would also be applicable in the present case; and, consequently, such sciences would be recognised and cultivated, and the principles on which they are built, reasoned and acted upon, though in a more perfect manner than at present, in this new world and new order of things. Such sciences, therefore, as flow from the natural and necessary relations of material objects, and which tend to direct us in our conceptions of the wisdom and power of the great Architect of nature, must be known and cultivated in a future world, where rational spirits are united to an organical structure, and related to a material system; and consequently, if the elementary and fundamental principles of such sciences be not acquired now, they will remain to be acquired hereafter.

The remarks now stated, with a few modifications, will apply to any of the other suppositions which may be made in reference to the place and circumstances of our future destination.—Even although the relations of external objects and their various properties, in the future world, were altogether different from those which obtain in the present state of things, still, it would be useful and highly gratifying to the mind, to be enabled to compare the one with the other, and to perceive how the divine wisdom is displayed in every mode and variety of existence. No possible mode of material existence, however, can be conceived to exist, to which some of the elementary principles of scientific knowledge do not apply.

There are, indeed, several arts and sciences which more immediately respect the present world, and our relations in it, which cannot be supposed to be subjects of investigation in a future state of happy existence. The study of *languages*—which forms a prominent object of attention with many of those who declaim on the vanity of human science—the study of medicine as a practical art; the study of civil and municipal law; the study of political economy, heraldry and fortification, the arts of war, farriery, falconry, hunting and fishing; the arts of the manufacturer, clothier, dyer, &c.—in short, all those arts and sciences which have their foundation in the moral depravity of our nature, will, of course, pass away, as exercises which were peculiar to the deranged state of our terrestrial habitation, and the degraded condition of its inhabitants; and which, therefore, can have no place in a scene of moral perfection. But the principles of the mathematics, and the axioms on which they are built, the truths of natural philosophy, astronomy, geography, mechanics, and similar sciences, will be recognised, and form the basis of reasoning and of action, so long as we are sentient beings, and have a relation to the material system of the universe. Many truths, indeed, which now require much study, and long and intricate trains of reasoning before they can be acquired, may be perceived by simple intuition, or, at least, be more easily and rapidly apprehended than at present. If a genius like that of Sir Isaac Newton, could perceive at a glance, the truth of Euclid's propositions in geometry, without attending to every part of the process requisite for ordinary minds, we may reasonably conclude, that, in a world where the physical and moral obstructions to intellectual energy are removed, every science, and every relation subsisting among corporeal and intellectual beings, will be more clearly, rapidly, and comprehensively perceived and understood.

Many striking instances have occasionly occurred, of the capacity and vigour of the human mind, even amidst the obscurities, and the obstructions to mental activity which exist in the present state of things. The illustrious *Pascal*, no less celebrated for his piety than for his intellectual acquirements, when under the age of twelve years, and while immersed in the study of languages, without books, and without an instructor, discovered and demonstrated most of the propositions in the first book of Euclid, before he knew that such a book was in existence—to the astonishment of every mathematician; so that, at that early age, he was an inventor of geometrical science. He afterwards made some experiments and discoveries on the nature of sound, and on the weight of the air, and demonstrated the pressure of the atmosphere: and, at the age of sixteen, composed a treatise on *Conic Sections*, which in the judgment of men of the greatest abilities, was viewed as an astonishing effort of the human mind. At nineteen years of age, he invented an arithmetical machine by which calculations are made, not only without the help of a pen, but even without a person's knowing a single rule in arithmetic; and by the age of twenty-four, he had acquired a proficiency in almost every branch of human knowledge, when his mind became entirely absorbed in the exercises of religion.—The celebrated *Grotius*, at the age of thirteen, only a year after his arrival at the university of Leyden, maintained public theses in mathematics, philosophy and law, with universal applause. At the age of fourteen, he ventured to form literary plans which required an amazing extent of knowledge; and he executed them in such perfection, that the literary world was struck with astonishment. At this early age he published an edition of *Martianus Capella*, and acquitted himself of the task in a manner which would have done honour to the greatest scholars of the age. At the age of seventeen he entered on the profession of an advocate, and pleaded his first cause at Delf, with the greatest reputation, having previously made an extraordinary progress in the knowledge of the sciences.—The *Admirable Crichton*, who received his education at Perth and St. Andrews, by the time he had reached his twentieth year, was master of ten languages, and had gone through the whole circle of the sciences as they were then understood. At Paris he one day engaged in a disputation, which lasted nine hours, in the presence of three thousand auditors, against four doctors of the church and fifty masters, on every subject they could propose, and having silenced all his antagonists, he came off amidst the loudest acclamations, though he had spent no time in previous preparation for the contest.—*Gassendi*, a celebrated philosopher of France, at the age of four, declaimed little sermons of his own composition; at the age of seven, spent whole nights in observing the motions of the heavenly bodies, of which he acquired a considerable knowledge at sixteen, he was appointed professor of rhetoric at Digne, and at the age of nineteen, he was elected professor of philosophy in the university of Aix. His vast knowledge of philosophy and mathematics was ornamented by a sincere attachment to the Christian religion, and a life formed upon its principles and precepts.—*Jeremiah Horrox*, a name celebrated in the annals of astronomy, before he attained the age of seventeen, had acquired, solely by his own industry, and the help of a few Latin authors, a most extensive and accurate knowledge of astronomy, and of the branches of mathematical learning connected with it. He composed astronomical tables for himself, and corrected the errors of the most celebrated astronomers of his time. He calculated a transit of the planet Venus across the sun's disk, and was the first of mortals who beheld this singular phenomenon, which is now considered of so much importance in astronomical science. Sir Isaac Newton, the fame of whose genius has extended over the whole civilized world, made his great discoveries in geometry and fluxions, and laid the foundation of his two celebrated works, his "*Principia*" and "*Optics*," by the time he was twenty-four years of age; and yet these works contain so many abstract profound and sublime truths, that only the first rate mathematicians are qualified to understand and appreciate them. In learning mathematics, he did not study the geometry of Euclid, who seemed to him too plain and simple, and unworthy of taking up his time. He understood him almost before he read him; and a cast of his eye upon the contents of his theorems, was sufficient to make him master of their demonstrations.—Amidst all the sublime investigations of physical and mathematical science in which he engaged, and amidst the variety of books he had constantly before him, the *Bible* was that which he studied with the greatest application; and his meekness and *modesty* were no less admirable than the variety and extent of his intellectual acquirements.—*J. Philip Barratier*, who died at Halle in 1740, in the twentieth year of his age, was endowed with extraordinary powers of memory and comprehension of mind. At the age of five, he understood the Greek, Latin, German and French languages; at the age of nine he could translate any part of the Hebrew Scriptures into Latin, and could repeat the whole Hebrew Psalter; and before he had completed his tenth year, he drew up a Hebrew lexicon of uncommon and difficult words, to which he added many curious critical remarks. In his thirteenth year he published, in two volumes octavo, a translation from the Hebrew of Rabbi Benjamin's "Travels in Europe, Asia and Africa," with historical and critical notes and dissertations; the whole of which he completed in four months. In the midst of these studies, he prosecuted philosophical and mathematical pursuits, and in his fourteenth year invented a method of discovering the longitude at sea, which exhibited the strongest marks of superior abilities. In one winter he read twenty great folios, with all the attention of a vast comprehensive mind.

Such rapid progress in intellectual acquirements strikingly evinces the vigour and comprehension of the human faculties; and if such varied and extensive acquisitions in knowledge can be attained, even amidst the frailties and physical impediments of this mortal state, it is easy to conceive, with what energy and rapidity the most sublime investigations may be prosecuted in the future world, when the spirit is connected with an incorruptible body, fitted to accompany it in all its movements; and when every moral obstruction which now impedes its activity shall be completely removed. The flights of the loftiest genius that ever appeared on earth, when compared with the rapid movements and comprehensive views of the heavenly inhabitants, may be no more than as the flutterings of a microscopic insect, to the sublime flights of the soaring eagle. When endowed with new and vigorous senses, and full scope is afforded for exerting all the energies of their renovated faculties, they may be enabled to trace out the hidden springs of nature's operations, to pursue the courses of the heavenly bodies, in their most distant and rapid career, and to survey the whole chain of moral dispensations in reference not only to the human race, but to the inhabitants of numerous worlds

I shall conclude this part of my subject with an observation or two, which may tend to illustrate and corroborate the preceding remarks.

In the first place, it may be remarked, that our knowledge in the future world, will not be diminished, but increased to an indefinite extent. This is expressly declared in the Sacred Records. "Now we see through a glass darkly, but then face to face. Now we know in part, but then shall we know, even as also we are known," 1 Cor. xiii. 12. This passage intimates, not only that our knowledge in a future state shall be enlarged, but that it shall be increased to an extent to which we can, at present, affix no limits. And if our intellectual views shall be immensely expanded in the realms of light, we may rest assured that all those branches of useful science which assist us in exploring the operations of the Almighty, will not only be cultivated, but carried to their highest pitch of perfection. For the faculties we now possess will not only remain in action, but will be strengthened and invigorated; and the range of objects on which they will be employed will be indefinitely extended. To suppose otherwise, would be to suppose man to be deprived of his intellectual powers, and of the faculty of reasoning, as soon as he entered the confines of the eternal world.* When we enter that world we carry with us the moral and intellectual faculties, of which we are now conscious, and, along with them, all those ideas and all that knowledge which we acquired in the present state. To imagine that our present faculties will be *essentially* changed, and the ideas we have hitherto acquired totally lost, would be nearly the same as to suppose that, on entering the invisible state, men will be transformed into a new order of beings, or be altogether annihilated. And, if our present knowledge shall not be destroyed at death, it must form the groundwork of all the future improvements we may make, and of all the discoveries that may be unfolded to our view in the eternal state.

Again, the superior intellectual views which some individuals shall possess beyond others, will constitute the principal distinction between redeemed men in the heavenly state. The principal preparation for heaven will consist in renewed dispositions of mind—in the full exercise

* An old Welch minister, while one day pursuing his studies, his wife being in the room, was suddenly interrupted by her asking him a question, which has not always been so satisfactorily answered—"John Evans, do you think we shall be known to each other in heaven?" Without hesitation he replied,—"To be sure we shall,—do you think we shall be *greater fools* there, than we are here."—If the reader keep in mind that our knowledge in heaven will be *increased*, and not diminished; or, in other words, that we shall not be "greater fools there than we are here," he will be at no loss to appreciate all that I have hitherto stated on this subject.

of love to God, and love to all subordinate holy intelligences, and in all the diversified ramifications of action into which these grand principles necessarily diverge. When arrived at that happy world the saints will feel themselves to be all equal,—as they were once "children of disobedience even as others," as they were all redeemed "by the precious blood of Christ," as they were renewed by the influence of the Spirit of grace, —as they stand in the relation of brethren in Christ, and "sons and daughters of the Lord God Almighty," as they are the companions of angels, and kings and priests to the God and Father of all. Without the exercise of holy dispositions, heaven could not exist, although its inhabitants had reached the highest pitch of intellectual improvement;—and all who shall ultimately be admitted into that happy state, will feel that they are eternally indebted for the privileges and the felicity they enjoy, to "Him that sits upon the throne, and to the Lamb who was slain, and redeemed them to God by his blood." But, notwithstanding, there will be a considerable difference, at least in the first instance, in regard to the *expansion of their intellectual views*. In this point of view, it is impossible to suppose that they can be all equal. Suppose a Negro slave, who had been recently converted to Christianity, and a profound Christian philosopher, to enter the eternal world at the same time, is it reasonable to believe, that there would be no difference in the amplitude of their intellectual views? They would both feel themselves delivered from sin and sorrow, they would be filled with admiration and wonder at the new scenes which opened to their view, and would be inspired with the most lively emotions of humility and reverence; but if each of them carried along with him that portion of knowledge which he acquired in the present life, there behoved to be a considerable difference in the comprehension of their views and the range of their intellectual faculties; unless we suppose that a change amounting to a miracle was effected in the mind of the Negro, whose mental views were previously circumscribed within the narrowest limits. And, to suppose such a miracle wrought in every individual case, would not only be contrary to every thing we know of the general plan of the divine procedure, but would destroy almost every motive that should now induce us to make progress "in the knowledge of our Lord and Saviour Jesus Christ," and in our views of the works and dispensations of the Almighty. In the course of ages, indeed, the Negro may equal the philosopher in the extent of his intellectual acquisitions; but, in the first instance, both Scripture* and reason declare, that a difference must exist, unless the laws which govern the intellectual world be entirely subverted. Can we suppose, for a moment, that an ignorant profligate, who has been brought to repentance, and to "the knowledge of the truth," only a few hours before his entrance into the world of spirits, shall, at the moment he has arrived in the world of bliss, acquire those enlarged conceptions of divine truth, which an Owen, a Watts, a Doddridge, or a Dwight, attained at the same stage of their existence? or that a Hottentot, who had been brought to the knowledge of Christianity only during the last month of his life, shall enter into heaven with the expansive views of a Newton or a Boyle? Such a supposition would involve a reflection on the *wisdom* of the divine administration, and would lead us to conclude, that all the labour bestowed by the illustrious characters now alluded to, in order to improve in the knowledge of divine subjects, was quite unnecessary, and even somewhat approaching to egregious trifling.

Not only will the views of the saints in heaven be different in point of expansion and extent, but their love to God, and the virtues and graces which flow from this principle, will be diminished or increased, or, at least, somewhat modified by the narrowness or expansion of their intellectual views. If it be admitted, that the more we know of God the more ardently shall we love him,—it will follow, that, in proportion as we acquire a comprehensive and enlightened view of the operations of God in the works of creation, in the scheme of providence, and in the plan of redemption, in a similar proportion will our love and adoration of his excellencies be ardent and expansive. In this point of view, "the saints in light" will make improvement in holiness throughout all the ages of eternity, though, at every stage of their existence, they will enjoy pure and unmingled bliss. Every science they cultivate, and every stage to which they advance in intellectual improvement, will enable them to discover new glories in the divine character, which will raise their affections to God still higher, and render their conformity to his moral image more complete.

It has frequently been a subject of discussion among theologians, "Whether there shall be degrees of glory in heaven." This question may be easily settled, if there be any weight in the remarks and considerations now stated. In so far as there is a difference in the vigour and expansion of the intellectual powers, and in the amplitude of objects they are enabled to embrace, in so far may there be said to be "degrees of glory:" and a superiority, in this respect, may be considered as the natural reward which accompanies the diligent improvement of our time and faculties upon earth, though such a distinction can never be supposed to produce any disposition approaching to envy, as so frequently happens in the present state. On the contrary, it may be supposed to produce a holy emulation to improve

* See Dan. xii. 3. 1 Cor. xv. 41, 42. Matt. xxv. 14, &c.

every faculty, to cultivate every branch of celestial science, and to increase in the knowledge of God. In corroboration of these views, we are told in Scripture, that the reward bestowed on those servants to whom talents were intrusted, was in proportion to the improvement they had made; and that, at the close of time, the saints will present an appearance analogous to that of the spangled firmament; for "as one star differeth from another star in glory, so also is the resurrection from the dead." And the reason of this difference is intimated by the prophet Daniel, "They that excel in wisdom shall shine as the brightness of the firmament; and they that turn many to righteousness as the stars for ever and ever."

If the remarks now stated have any solid foundation, it will follow, that what is generally termed *human science*, ought not to be indiscriminately considered as having a relation merely to the present world. Such an idea would tend to damp our ardour in the prosecution of scientific knowledge, and immensely to lessen its value. He who prosecutes science as a subject of speculation merely in reference to the contracted span of human life, acts from very mean and narrow views, and may be considered, in some points of view, as little superior to the avaricious man whose mind is completely absorbed in the acquisition of the perishing treasures of this world. The Christian philosopher, who traces the perfections and the agency of God in every object of his investigation, ought to consider his present pursuits as the commencement of a course of improvement which will have no termination—as introductory to the employments and the pleasures of a higher state of existence—and as affording him a more advantageous outset into that better world than happens to those who are destitute of his enlarged views. For the more we know at present of the wonders of infinite power, wisdom, and goodness, in the material works of the Almighty, it is obvious, that the better prepared we shall be for more enlarged contemplations of them at a future period, and the greater pleasure shall we feel in beholding those objects and operations, which are now hid in obscurity, unveiled to view.

In throwing out the preceding reflections, I am far from pretending to determine the particular arrangements which the Almighty has formed in relation to our future destination, or the particular circumstances which may exist in other worlds. These things lie altogether beyond the range of our investigation, and must, therefore, remain inscrutable in our present state. But there are certain general principles or relations which necessarily flow from the nature of things, which must be considered as included within any particular arrangements which may be formed; and, it is such general principles only to which I refer.—Nor should it be considered as presumption, to endeavour to ascertain these general principles or necessary relations of things. The Creator evidently intended we should know them; since he has exhibited such an immense variety of his works before us, and has bestowed upon us faculties adequate to explore their magnitude and arrangement, to investigate the laws which direct their motions, and to perceive their connection and dependency, and some of the grand designs for which they were intended.

To every thing that has just now been stated in relation to the prosecution of science in the celestial world, I am aware it will be objected by some, that such knowledge, if it be requisite in a future state, will be acquired by immediate intuition, or communicated in a direct maner by the Creator himself.—For such an assumption, however, though frequently reiterated, there is no foundation in any passage of Scripture when rationally interpreted; and it is repugnant to the clearest dictates of reason. It is contrary to every regular mode with which we are acquainted, by which rational beings are conducted to knowledge and happiness; it would imply a continued miracle—it would supersede the use of the intellectual faculty—and it would ultimately detract from the felicity of intelligent agents. For, a great part of the happiness of finite intelligences arise from the gradual evolution of truth, in consequence of the exercise of their rational powers. Were all our knowledge in a future state to be acquired by immediate intuition, or by direct supernatural communications from the Deity, our rational faculties would, in many respects, be bestowed in vain. It appears to be one of the main designs for which these faculties were bestowed, that we might be directed in the prosecution of knowledge, and led to deduce, from the scenes of the visible universe, those conclusions which will gradually expand our views of the plans and perfections of its Almighty Author. Adam, when in a state of innocence, (and his condition in that state, as a moral agent was precisely similar to the state of good men in a future world, except his liability to fall) was not acquainted, in the first instance, with every object in the world in which he was placed, and their various relations to each other. He could not know, for example, the peculiar scenery of nature which existed on the side of the globe opposite to that on which he was placed. He must have exercised his senses, his locomotive faculties, and his reasoning powers, and made observations and experimental researches of various kinds, before he became thoroughly acquainted with the structure, the order and beauty of his terrestrial habitation.—For to suppose man, in any state, a mere passive subject of intellectual and external impressions, would be, to reduce him to something like a mere machine; and would imply a subversion of all the established laws which regulate the operations of matter and intellect throughout the universe.

We know, likewise, that truth is gradually developed even to superior intelligences. The manifold wisdom of God in reference to the church, and the plans of his grace in relation to the Gentile world, were, in some measure, veiled to the angels, till the facts of the death and resurrection of Christ, and the preaching and miracles of the Apostles were exhibited to their view;* and hence they are represented as "desiring to look into," or prying with avidity into the mysteries of redemption; which evidently implies, the active exertion of their powers of reason and intelligence, and their gradual advancement in the knowledge of the purposes and plans of the Almighty. And, if beings far superior to man in intellectual capacity, acquire their knowledge in a *gradual* manner, by reflection on the divine dispensations, and the exercise of their mental powers, it is unreasonable to suppose, that man, even in a higher sphere of existence, will acquire all his knowledge at once, or without the exertion of those intellectual energies with which he is endowed.

In short, were the saints in heaven to acquire all their knowledge as soon as they entered on that scene of happiness, we must suppose them endowed with capacities, not only superior to the most exalted seraphim, but even approximating to the infinite comprehension of the Deity himself. For the range of investigation presented to intelligent beings is boundless, extending to all the objects and moral dispensations of God, throughout the immensity of his empire. And could we suppose finite minds capable of embracing the whole of this range of objects at one comprehensive grasp, their mental energy would soon be destroyed, and their felicity terminate; for they could look forward to no farther expansion of their views, nor to a succession of a new range of objects and operations through all the future ages of eternity.

* Ephes. iii. 5—11.

# PART III.

## ON THE AIDS WHICH THE DISCOVERIES OF SCIENCE AFFORD, FOR ENABLING US TO FORM A CONCEPTION OF THE PERPETUAL IMPROVEMENT OF THE CELESTIAL INHABITANTS IN KNOWLEDGE AND FELICITY.

On the subject of a future world, and the exercises and enjoyments of its inhabitants, many foolish and inaccurate conceptions have prevailed, even in the Christian world. We are assured, that the foundation of the felicity to be enjoyed in that world, rests on the absence of every evil, and the attainment of moral perfection—that the principle of depravity must be destroyed, and the affections purified and refined, before we can enjoy "the inheritance of the saints in light." These are principles which are clearly exhibited in the Scriptures, which are accordant to the dictates of sound reason, and which are generally recognised by the various sections of the religious world. But the greater part of Christians rest contented with the most vague and incorrect ideas of the felicity of heaven, and talk and write about it in so loose and figurative a manner, as can convey no rational nor definite conception of the sublime contemplations and employments of celestial intelligences. Instead of eliciting, from the metaphorical language of Scripture, the *ideas* intended to be conveyed, they endeavour to expand and ramify the figures employed by the sacred writers still farther, heaping metaphor upon metaphor, and epithet upon epithet, and blending a number of discordant ideas, till the image or picture presented to the mind assumes the semblance of a splendid chaotic mass, or of a dazzling but undefined meteor. The term *Glory*, and its kindred epithets, have been reiterated a thousand times in descriptions of the heavenly state;—the redeemed have been represented as assembled in one vast crowd above the visible concave of the sky, adorned with "starry crowns," drinking at "crystal fountains," and making "the vault of heaven ring" with their loud acclamations. The Redeemer himself has been exhibited as suspended like a statue in the heavens above this immense crowd, crowned with diadems, and encircled with a refulgent splendour, while the assembly of the heavenly inhabitants were *incessantly* gazing on this object, like a crowd of spectators gazing at the motion of an air balloon, or of a splendid meteor. Such representations are repugnant to the *ideas intended to be conveyed* by the metaphorical language of Inspiration, when stripped of its drapery. They can convey nothing but a meagre and distorted conception of the employments of the celestial state, and tend only to bewilder the imagination, and to "darken counsel by words without knowledge."

Hence it has happened, that certain infidel scoffers have been led to conclude, that the Christian Heaven is not an object to be desired; and have frequently declared, that "they could feel no pleasure in being suspended for ever in an ethereal region, and perpetually singing psalms and hymns to the Eternal"—an idea of heaven which is too frequently conveyed, by the vague and distorted descriptions which have been given of the exercises and entertainments of the future world.

There is an intimate connection between the word and the works of God: they reflect a mutual lustre on each other; and the discoveries made in the latter, are calculated to expand our conceptions and to direct our views, of the revelations contained in the former. Without taking into account the sublime manifestations of the Deity, exhibited in his visible creation, our ideas of celestial bliss must be very vague and confused, and our hopes of full and *perpetual* enjoyment in the future state, extremely feeble and languid. From the very constitution of the human mind, it appears, that in order to enjoy uninterrupted happiness, without satiety or disgust, it is requisite that *new* objects and new trains of thought be continually opening to view. A perpetual recurrence of the same objects and perceptions, however sublime in themselves, and however interesting and delightful they may have been felt at one period, cannot afford uninterrupted gratification to minds endowed with capacious powers, and capable of ranging through the depths of immensity. But all the objects in this sublunary world and its environs, and all the events recorded in sacred and profane history, are not sufficient to occupy the expansive minds of renovated intelligences for a million of ages, much less throughout an endless duration of existence. A series of objects and of moral dispensations, more extensive than those immediately connected with the globe we inhabit, must, therefore, be supposed to engage the attention of "the spirits of just men made perfect," during the revolutions of eternal ages; in order that their faculties may be gratified and expanded—that new views of the divine character may be unfolded—and that in the contemplation of his perfections, they may enjoy a perpetuity of bliss.

It has been, indeed, asserted by some, that "the mysteries of redemption will be sufficient to afford scope for the delightful investigation of the saints to all eternity." It is readily admitted, that contemplations of the divine perfections, as displayed in human redemption, and of the stupendous facts which relate to that economy, will blend themselves with all the other exercises of redeemed intelligences. While their intellectual faculties are taking the most extensive range through the dominions of Him who sits upon the throne of universal nature, they will never forget that love "which brought them from darkness to light," and from the depths of misery to the splendours of eternal day. Their grateful and triumphant praises will ascend to the Father of glory, and to the Lamb who was slain, *for ever and ever*. But, at the same time, the range of objects comprised within the scheme of redemption, in its reference to human beings, cannot be supposed, without the aid of other objects of contemplation, to afford full and uninterrupted scope to the faculties of the saints in heaven, throughout an unlimited duration.—This will appear, if we endeavour to analyze some of the objects presented to our view in the economy of redemption.

In the first place, it may be noticed, that a veil of mystery surrounds several parts of the plan of redemption. "God manifested in the flesh," the intimate union of the eternal self-existent Deity with "the man Christ Jesus,"—is a mystery impenetrable to finite minds. But the eternity, the omnipresence, and the omniscience of the Deity, are equally mysterious; for they are equally incomprehensible, and must for ever remain incomprehensible to all limited intelligences. It is equally incomprehensible, that a sensitive being should exist, furnished with all the organs and functions requisite for animal life, and yet of a size ten thousand times less than a mite. These are facts which must be admitted on the evidence of sense and of reason, but they lie altogether beyond the sphere of our comprehension.—Now, an object which involves a mystery cannot be supposed to exercise and entertain the mind through eternity, considered simply as *incomprehensible*, without being associated with other objects which lie within the range of finite comprehension; otherwise, reflections on the eternity and omnipresence of God, considered purely as abstractions of the mind, might gratify the intellectual faculties, in the future world, in as high a degree as any thing that is mysterious in the scheme of redemption. But it is quite evident, that perpetual reflection on infinite space and eternal duration, abstractly considered, cannot produce a very high degree of mental enjoyment, unless when considered in their relation to objects more definite and comprehensible. Such contemplations, however, will, doubtless, be mingled with all the other views and investigations of the saints in the heavenly world. In proportion as they advance through myriads of ages in the course of unlimited duration, and in proportion to the enlarged views they will acquire, of the distances and magnitudes of the numerous bodies which diversify the regions of the universe, their ideas of infinite space, and of eternal duration, will be greatly expanded. For we can acquire ideas of the extent of space, only by comparing the distances and bulks of material objects with one another,—and of duration by the trains of thought, derived from sensible objects, which pass through our minds, and, from the periodical revolutions of material objects around us.—The same things may be affirmed in relation to all that is mysterious in the economy of human redemption; and, if what has been now said be admitted, it will follow that such mysteries, considered merely as incomprehensible realities, could not afford a rapturous train of thought to entertain the mind throughout the ages of eternity. It is definite and tangible objects, and not abstract mysteries, that constitute the proper subject of contemplation to a rational mind. For although we were to ponder on what is incomprehensible, such as the eternity of God, for millions of years, we should be as far from comprehending it, or acquiring any new ideas respecting it, at the end of such a period, as at the present moment.

In the next place, redemption may be considered in reference to the important *facts* connected with it, in which point of view, chiefly, it becomes a tangible object for the exercise of the moral and intellectual powers of man. These facts relate either to the "man Christ Jesus, the Mediator between God and man," or to the saints whose redemption he procured. The general facts which relate to Christ, while he sojourned in our world, are recorded in the New Testament by the Evangelists. These comprehend his miraculous conception, and the circumstances which attended his birth; his private residence in Nazareth; his journies as a public teacher through the land of Judea; his miracles, sufferings, crucifixion, resurrection, and ascension to heaven. There is doubtless a variety of interesting facts, besides those recorded in the Gospels, with which it would be highly gratifying to become acquainted: such as, the manner in which he spent his life, from the period of the first dawnings of reason, to the time of his commencing his public administrations—the various trains of thought that passed through his mind—the mental and corporeal exercises in which he engaged—the social intercourses in which he mingled—the topics of conversation he suggested—the amusements (if any) in which he indulged—the pious exercises and sublime contemplations in which he engaged, when retired from the haunts and the society of men;—and particularly those grand and important transactions in which he has been employed, since that moment when a cloud interposed between his glorified body, and the eyes of his disciples, after his ascent from Mount Olivet—What regions of the material universe he passed through in his triumphant ascent—what intelligence of his achievements he conveyed to other worlds—what portion of the immensity of space, or what globe or material fabric is the scene of his more immediate residence—what are the external splendours and peculiarities of that glorious world—what intercourse he has with the spirits of just men made perfect; with Enoch and Elijah, who are already furnished with bodies, and with other orders of celestial intelligences—what scenes and movements will take place in that world, when he is about to return to our terrestrial sphere, to summon all the tribes of men to the general judgment? The facts in relation to these, and similar circumstances, still remain to be disclosed, and the future details which may be given of such interesting particulars, cannot fail to be highly gratifying to every one of the "redeemed from among men." But still, it must be admitted, that although the details respecting each of the facts to which I allude, were to occupy the period of a thousand years, the subject would soon be exhausted, if other events and circumstances, and another train of divine dispensations were not at the same time presented to view; and the future periods of eternal duration would be destitute of that *variety* and *novelty* of prospect which are requisite to secure perpetual enjoyment.

The other class of facts relates to the redeemed themselves, and comprehends those diversified circumstances in the course of providence, by means of which they were brought to the knowledge of salvation, and conducted through the scenes of mortality to the enjoyment of endless felicity. These will, no doubt, afford topics of interesting discourse, to diversify and enliven the exercises of the saints in heaven. But the remark now made in reference to the other facts alluded to above, is equally applicable here. The series of divine dispensations towards every individual, though different in a few subordinate particulars, partakes of the same character, and wears the same general aspect. But although the dispensations of Providence towards every one of the redeemed were as different from another as it is possible to conceive, and although a hundred years were devoted to the details furnished by every saint, eternity would not be exhausted by such themes alone.

Again, it has been frequently asserted, that the saints in heaven will enjoy perpetual rapture in continually gazing on the glorified humanity of Christ Jesus. The descriptions sometimes given of this circumstance, convey the idea of a vast concourse of spectators gazing upon a resplendent figure placed upon an eminence in the midst of them,—which, surely, must convey a very imperfect and distorted idea of the sublime employments of the saints in light. The august splendours of the "man Christ Jesus," the exalted station he holds in the upper world, the occasional intercourse which all his saints will hold with him, the lectures on the plans and operations of Deity with which he may entertain them—the splendid scenes to which he may guide them—and many other circumstances—will excite the most rapturous admiration of Him who is "the brightness of the Father's glory."—But, since the glorified body of Christ is *a material substance*, and, consequently, limited to a certain portion of space, it cannot be supposed to be at all times within the view of every inhabitant of heaven; and although it were, the material splendours of that body, however august and astonishing, cannot be supposed to afford new and varied gratification, throughout an endless succession of duration. He will be chiefly recognised as the *Head* of the redeemed family of man, "in whom are hid all the treasures of wisdom and knowledge," who will gradually reveal the secret counsels of God, and direct his saints to those displays of divine glory which will enlighten and entertain their mental powers. This seems to be intimated in such representations as the following,—"The Lamb that is in the midst of the throne shall feed them, and shall lead them to living fountains of water." By directing their attention to those objects in which they may behold the most august displays of divine perfection, and teaching them in what points of view they ought to be contemplated, and what conclusions they ought to deduce from them, "he will feed" the minds of his people with divine knowledge, and "lead them" to those sublime and transporting trains of thought, which will fill them with "joy unspeakable and full of glory."

Thus it appears, that neither the mysteries, nor the leading facts connected with the plan of redemption, when considered merely in relation to human beings—can be supposed to be the principal subjects of contemplation in the heavenly state, nor sufficient to produce those diversified gratifications which are requisite to insure perpetual enjoyment to the expanded intellects of redeemed men in the future world—though such contemplations will undoubtedly be intermingled with all the other intellectual surveys of the saints in glory.

I now proceed to the principal object in view, namely, to inquire, what other objects will employ the attention of good men in the world to come, and what light the material works of God, which have been unfolded to our view, tend to throw upon this subject.

The foundation of the happiness of heavenly intelligences being laid in the destruction of every principle of moral evil,—in the enjoyment of moral perfection—and in the removal of every physical impediment to the exercise of their intellectual powers—they will be fitted for the most profound investigations, and for the most enlarged contemplations. And one of their chief employments, of course, will be, to investigate, contemplate, and admire the glory of the divine perfections. Hence it is declared in Scripture as one of the privileges of the saints in light, that "*they shall see God as he is*"—that "they shall see his face"—and that "they shall behold his glory,"—which expressions, and others of similar import, plainly intimate, that they shall enjoy a clearer vision of the divine glory than in the present state. But how is this vision to be obtained? The Deity, being a spiritual uncompounded substance, having no visible form, nor sensible quantities, "inhabiting eternity," and filling immensity with his presence—his essential glory cannot form an object for the *direct contemplation* of any finite intelligence. His *glory*, or, in other words, the grandeur of his perfections, can be traced only in the external manifestation which he gives of himself in the material creation which his power has brought into existence—in the various orders of intelligences with which he has peopled it—and in his moral dispensations towards all worlds and beings which now exist, or may hereafter exist, throughout his boundless empire.

It is in this point of view, that our knowledge of the material universe assists our conceptions of the scenes of a future state, and throws a refulgence of light on the employments, and the uninterrupted pleasures of the redeemed in heaven. By the discoveries of modern science, in the distant regions of space, we are fully assured, that the attributes of the Deity have not been exercised solely in the construction of our sublunary sphere, and of the aerial heavens with which it is encompassed, nor his providential regards confined to the transactions of the frail beings that dwell upon its surface, but extend to the remotest spaces of the universe. We know, that far beyond the limits of our terrestrial abode, the Almighty has displayed his omnipotence in framing worlds which, in magnitude, and in splendour of accompaniments, far surpass this globe on which we dwell. The eleven planetary bodies which, in common with the earth, revolve about the sun, contain a mass of matter two thousand five hundred times greater, and an extent of surface sufficient to support an assemblage of inhabitants three hundred times more numerous than in the world which we inhabit. The divine *wisdom* is also displayed in reference to these vast globes,—in directing their motions, so as to produce a *diversity of seasons*, and a regular succession of *day and night*—in surrounding some of them with *moons*, and with luminous rings of a magnificent size, to adorn their nocturnal heavens, and to reflect a mild radiance in the absence of the sun—in encompassing them with *atmospheres*, and diversifying their surface with *mountains and plains*. These and other arrangements, which indicate special contrivance and design, show, that those bodies are destined by the Creator to be the abodes of intellectual beings, who partake of his bounty, and offer to him a tribute of adoration and praise.

Although no other objects were presented to our view, except those to which I now allude, and which are contained within the limits of our system, yet even here—within this small province of the kingdom of Jehovah—a grand and diversified scene is displayed for the future contemplation of heavenly intelligences. But it is a fact which cannot be disputed, that the sun and all his attendant planets form but a small speck in the map of the universe. How great soever this earth, with its vast continents and mighty oceans, may appear to our eye,—how stupendous soever the great globe of Jupiter, which would contain within its bowels a thousand worlds as large as ours—and overwhelming as the conception is, that the sun is more than a thousand times larger than both,—yet, were they this moment detached from their spheres, and blotted out of existence, there are worlds within the range of the Almighty's empire where such an awful catastrophe would be altogether unknown. Nay, were the whole cubical space occupied by the solar system—a space 3,600,000,000 miles in diameter—to be formed into a solid globe, containing 24,000,000,000,000,000,000,000,000,000 cubical miles, and overspread with a brilliancy superior to that of the sun, to continue during the space of a thousand years in this splendid state, and then to be extinguished and annihilated—there are beings, who reside in spaces within the range of our telescopes, to whom its creation and destruction would be equally unknown: and to an eye which could take in the whole compass of nature, it might be altogether unheeded, or, at most, be regarded as the appearance and disappearance of a lucid point in an obscure corner of the universe—just as the detachment of a drop of water from the ocean, or a grain of sand from the sea shore is unheeded by a common observer.

At immeasurable distances from our earth and system immense assemblages of shining orbs display their radiance. The amazing extent of that space which intervenes between our habitation and these resplendent globes, proves their immense magnitude, and that they shine not with borrowed but with native splendour. From what we know of the wisdom and intelligence of the divine Being, we may safely conclude, that he has created nothing in vain; and consequently, that these enormous globes of light were not dispersed through the universe, merely as so many splendid tapers to illuminate the voids of infinite space. To admit, for a moment, such a supposition, would be inconsistent with the marks of intelligence and design which are displayed in all the other scenes of nature which lie within the sphere of our investigation. It would represent the Almighty as amusing himself with splendid toys,—an idea altogether incompatible with the adorable Majesty of heaven, and which would tend to lessen our reverence of his character, as the only wise God.—If every part of nature in our sublunary system is destined to some particular use in reference to sentient beings—if even the muddy waters of a stagnant pool are replenished with myriads of inhabitants, should we for a moment doubt, that so many thousands of magnificent globes have a relation to the accommodation and happiness of intelligent beings; since in every part of the material system which lies open to our minute inspection, it appears, that matter exists solely for the purpose of sentient and intelligent creatures. As the Creator is consistent in all his plans and operations, it is beyond dispute, that those great globes which are suspended throughout the vast spaces of the universe are destined to some noble purposes worthy of the infinite power, wisdom, and intelligence, which produced them. And what may these purposes be? Since most of these bodies are of a size equal, if not superior, to our sun, and shine by their own native light, we are led by analogy to conclude, that they are destined to subserve a similar purpose in the system of nature—to pour a flood of radiance on surrounding worlds, and to regulate their motions by their attractive influence. So that each of these luminaries may be considered, not merely as a world, but as the centre of thirty, sixty, or a hundred worlds, among which they distribute light, and heat, and comfort.*

If, now, we attend to the *vast number* of those stupendous globes, we shall perceive what an extensive field of sublime investigation lies open to all the holy intelligences that exist in creation. When we lift our eyes to the nocturnal sky, we behold several hundreds of these majestic orbs, arranged in a kind of magnificent confusion, glimmering from afar on this obscure corner of the universe. But the number of stars, visible to the vulgar eye, is extremely small, compared with the number which has been descried by means of optical instruments. In a small portion of the sky, not larger than the apparent breadth of the moon, a greater number of stars has been discovered than the naked eye can discern throughout the whole vault of heaven. In proportion as the magnifying powers of the telescope are increased, in a similar proportion do the stars increase upon our view. They seem ranged behind one another in boundless perspective, as far as the assisted eye can reach, leaving us no room to doubt, that, were the powers of our telescopes increased a thousand times more than they now are, millions beyond millions, in addition to what we now behold, would start up before the astonished sight. Sir William Herschel informs us, that, when viewing a certain portion of the *Milky Way*, in the course of seven minutes, more than fifty thousand stars passed

*The Author will have an opportunity of illustrating this subject, in minute detail, in a work entitled, *The scenery of the heavens displayed,* with the view of proving and illustrating the doctrine of a *plurality of worlds;*" in which the positions here assumed will be shown to have the force of a moral demonstration, on the same general principles by which we prove the being of a God, and the immortality of man. In this work, all the known facts in relation to *descriptive astronomy*, and the structure of the heavens, will be particularly detailed, and accompanied with original remarks and moral and religious reflections, so as to form a comprehensive compend of popular astronomy

across the field of his telescope,—and it has been calculated, that within the range of such an instrument, applied to all the different portions of the firmament, more than *eighty millions* of stars would be rendered visible.

Here, then, within the limits of that circle which human vision has explored, the mind perceives, not merely eighty millions of worlds, but, at least *thirty* times that number; for every star, considered as a sun, may be conceived to be surrounded by at least thirty planetary globes;* so that the *visible system* of the universe may be stated, at the lowest computation, as comprehending within its vast circumference, 2,400,000,000 of worlds! This celestial scene presents an idea so august and overwhelming, that the mind is confounded, and shrinks back at the attempt of forming any definite conception of a multitude and a magnitude so far beyond the limits of its ordinary excursions. If we can form no adequate idea of the magnitude, the variety, and economy of *one* world, how can we form a just conception of *thousands?* If a *single million* of objects of any description presents an image too vast and complex to be taken in at one grasp, how shall we ever attempt to comprehend an object so vast as two thousand four hundred millions of worlds! None but that Eternal Mind which counts the number of the stars, which called them from nothing into existence, and arranged them in the respective stations they occupy, and whose eyes run to and fro through the unlimited extent of creation—can form a clear and comprehensive conception of the number, the order, and the economy of this vast portion of the system of nature.

But here, even the very feebleness and obscurity of our conceptions tend to throw a radiance on the subject we are attempting to illustrate. The magnitude and incomprehensibility of the object, show us, how many diversified views of the divine glory remain to be displayed; what an infinite variety of sublime scenes may be afforded for the mind to expatiate upon; and what rapturous trains of thought, ever various, and ever new, may succeed each other without interruption, throughout an unlimited duration.

Let us now endeavour to analyze some of the objects presented to our mental sight, in this vast assemblage of systems and worlds, which lie within the sphere of human vision.

The first idea that suggests itself, is, that they are all *material structures*—in the formation of which, infinite wisdom and goodness have been employed; and consequently, they must exhibit scenes of sublimity and of exquisite contrivance worthy of the contemplation of every rational being. If this earth, which is an abode of apostate men, and a scene of moral depravity, and which, here and there, has the appearance of being the ruins of a former world—presents the variegated prospect of lofty mountains, romantic dells, and fertile plains; meandering rivers, transparent lakes, and spacious oceans; verdant landscapes, adorned with fruits and flowers, and a rich variety of the finest colours, and a thousand other beauties and sublimities that are strewed over the face of nature—how grand and magnificent a scenery may we suppose, must be presented to the view, in those worlds where moral evil has never entered to derange the harmony of the Creator's works—where love to the Supreme, and to one another, fires the bosoms of all their inhabitants, and produces a rapturous exultation, and an incessant adoration of the Source of happiness! In such worlds, we may justly conceive, that the sensitive enjoyments, and the objects of beauty and grandeur which are displayed to their view, as far exceed the scenery and enjoyments of this world, as their moral and intellectual qualities excel those of the sons of men.

In the next place, it is highly reasonable to believe, that *an infinite diversity of scenery exists* throughout all the worlds which compose the universe; that no one of all the millions of systems to which I have now adverted, exactly resembles another in its construction, motions, order, and decorations. There appear, indeed, to be certain laws and phenomena which are common to all the systems which exist within the limits of human vision. It is highly probable that the laws of gravitation extend their influence through every region of space occupied by material substances; and, it is beyond a doubt, that the phenomena of vision, and the laws by which light is reflected and refracted, exist in the remotest regions which the telescope has explored. For the light which radiates from the most distant stars (as formerly stated) is found to be of the same nature, to move with the same velocity, to be refracted by the same laws, and to exhibit the same colours as the light which proceeds from the sun, and is reflected from surrounding objects. The medium of vision must, therefore, be acted upon, and the organs of sight perform their functions, in those distant regions, in the same manner as takes place in the system of which we form a part, or, at least, in a manner somewhat analogous to it. And this circumstance shows, that the Creator evidently intended we should form some faint ideas, at least, of the general procedure of nature in distant worlds, in order to direct our conceptions of the sublime scenery of the universe, even while we remain in this obscure corner of creation. But, although the visible systems of the universe

* The solar system consists of eleven primary and eighteen secondary planets; in all twenty-nine, besides more than a hundred comets; and it is probable that several planetary bodies exist within the limits of our system which have not yet been discovered. Other systems may probably contain a more numerous retinue of worlds, and perhaps of a larger size than those belonging to the system of the sun

appear to be connected by certain general principles and laws which operate throughout the whole, yet the indefinite modifications which these laws may receive in each particular system, may produce an almost infinite diversity of phenomena in different worlds, so that no one department of the material universe may resemble another. Nor is it difficult to conceive how such a diversity of scenery may be produced. With regard to the terraqueous globe,—were its axis to be shifted, so as to point to a different quarter of the heavens, or were the angle which it forms with the ecliptic to be greater or less than it now is, the general appearance of the firmament would be changed, the apparent motions of the sun and stars, the days and nights, the seasons of the year, and an immense variety of phenomena in the earth and heavens would assume a very different aspect from what they now wear. Were the component parts of the atmosphere materially altered, were its refractive power much increased, or were a greater portion of *caloric* or of *electricity* introduced into its constitution, the objects which diversify the landscape of the earth, and the luminaries of heaven, would assume such a variety of new and uncommon appearances, as would warrant the application of the Scripture expression, "a new heaven and a new earth." It is, therefore, easy to conceive, that, when infinite power and wisdom are exerted for this purpose, every globe in the universe, with its appendages, may be constructed and arranged in such a manner as to present a variety of beauties and sublimities peculiar to itself.

That the Creator has actually produced this effect, is rendered in the highest degree probable, from the infinite variety presented to our view in those departments of nature which lie open to our particular investigation. In the *animal kingdom* we find more than a hundred thousand different species of living creatures, and about the same variety in the productions of *vegetable* nature; the *mineral* kingdom presents to us an immense variety of earths, stones, rocks, metals, fossils, gems, and precious stones, which are strewed in rich profusion along the surface, and throughout the interior parts of the globe. Of the individuals which compose every distinct species of animated beings, there is no one which bears an exact resemblance to another. Although the eight hundred millions of men that now people the globe, and all the other millions that have existed since the world began, were to be compared, no two individuals would be found to present exactly the same aspect in every point of view in which they might be contemplated. In like manner, no two horses, cows, dogs, lions, elephants, or other terrestrial animals will be found bearing a perfect resemblance. The same observation will apply to the scenery of lakes, rivers, grottos, and mountains, and to all the diversified landscapes which the surface of the earth and waters presents to the traveller, and the student of nature.

If, from the earth, we direct our views to the other bodies which compose our planetary system, we shall find a similar diversity, so far as our observations extend. From the surface of one of the planets, the sun will appear seven times *larger*, and from the surface of another, three hundred and sixty times *smaller* than he does to us. One of those bodies is destitute of a moon; but from its ruddy aspect, either its surface or its atmosphere appears to be endowed with a phosphorescent quality, to supply it with light in the absence of the sun. Another is surrounded by *four* resplendent moons, much larger than ours; a third is supplied with *six*, and a fourth, with seven moons, and two magnificent rings to reflect the light of the sun, and diversify the scenery of its sky. One of these globes revolves round its axis in *ten*, and another in *twenty-three hours* and a half. One of them revolves round the sun in eighty-eight, another in two hundred and twenty-four days; a third in twelve years, a fourth in thirty, and a fifth in eighty-two years. From all which, and many other circumstances that have been observed, an admirable *variety* of phenomena is produced, of which each planetary globe has its own peculiarity. Even our moon, which is among the smallest of the celestial bodies, which is the nearest to us, and which accompanies the earth during its revolution round the sun, exhibits a curious variety of aspect, different from what is found on the terraqueous globe. The altitude of its mountains, the depths of its vales, the conical form of its insulated rocks, the circular ridges of hills which encompass its plains, and the celestial phenomena which are displayed in its firmament—present a scenery which though in some points resembling our own, is yet remarkably different, on the whole, from the general aspect of nature in our terrestrial habitation.

If, therefore, the Author of nature act on the same general principles, in other systems, as he has done in ours—which there is every reason to believe, when we consider his infinite wisdom and intelligence—we may rest assured, that every one of the two thousand four hundred millions of worlds which are comprehended within the range of human vision, has a magnificence and glory peculiar to itself, by which it is distinguished from all the surrounding provinces of Jehovah's empire. In this view, we may consider the language of the Apostle Paul as expressing not only an *apparent*, but a *real* fact. "There is one glory of the sun, and another glory of the moon, and another glory of the stars; "*for one star differeth from another star in glory.*" To suppose that the Almighty has exhausted his omnipotent energies, and exhibited all the manifestations of his glory which his perfections can produce, in one system, or even in one million of systems, would be to set limits to the resources of his wisdom and intelligence which are infinite and incomprehensible. Hence we find the sacred writers, when contemplating the numerous objects which creation exhibits, breaking out into such exclamations as these, "*How manifold*, O Jehovah, are thy works! In *wisdom* hast thou made them all."

In the next place,—Besides the magnificence and variety of the material structures which exist throughout the universe, *the organized and intelligent beings with which they are peopled*, present a vast field of delightful contemplation. On this general topic, the following ideas may be taken into consideration:—

1. The *gradations of intellect* or the *various orders* of intelligences which may people the universal system. That there is a vast diversity in the scale of intellectual existence, may be proved by considerations similar to those which I have already stated. Among sentient beings, in this world, we find a regular gradation of intellect, from the muscle, through all the orders of the aquatic and insect tribes, till we arrive at the dog, the monkey, the beaver and the elephant, and last of all, to *man*, who stands at the top of the intellectual scale, as the lord of this lower world. We perceive, too, in the individuals which compose the human species, a wonderful diversity in their powers and capacities of intellect, arising partly from their original constitution of mind, partly from the conformation of their corporeal organs, and partly from the degree of cultivation they have received. But it would be highly unreasonable to admit, that the most accomplished genius that ever adorned our race, was placed at the summit of intellectual perfection. On the other hand, we have reason to believe, that man, with all his noble powers, stands nearly at the bottom of the scale of the intelligent creation. For a being much inferior to man, in the powers of abstraction, conception, and reasoning, could scarcely be denominated a rational creature, or supposed capable of being qualified for the high destination to which man is appointed. As to the number of species which diversify the ranks of superior intellectual natures, and the degrees of perfection which distinguish their different orders, we have no *data*, afforded by the contemplation of the visible universe, sufficient to enable us to form a definite conception. The intellectual faculties, even of finite beings, may be carried to so high a pitch of perfection, as to baffle all our conceptions and powers of description.—The following description in the words of a celebrated Swiss naturalist, may perhaps convey some faint idea of the powers of some of the highest order of intelligences:—

"To convey one's self from one place to another with a swiftness equal or superior to that of light; to preserve one's self by the mere force of nature, and without the assistance of any other created being; to be absolutely exempted from every kind of change; to be endowed with the most exquisite and extensive senses; to have distinct perceptions of all the attributes of matter, and of all its modifications; to discover effects in their causes; to raise one's self by a most rapid flight to the most general principles; to see in the twinkling of an eye these principles;—to have at the same time, without confusion, an almost infinite number of ideas; to see the past as distinctly as the present, and to penetrate into the remotest futurity; to be able to exercise all these faculties without weariness: these are the various outlines from which we may draw a portrait of the perfections of superior natures." *

A being possessed of faculties such as these, is raised as far above the limited powers of man, as man is raised above the insect tribes. The Scriptures assure us, that beings, approximating, in their powers and perfections, to those now stated, actually exist, and perform important offices under the government of the Almighty. The perfections of the angelic tribes, as represented in Scripture, are incomparably superior to those of men. They are represented as possessed of powers capable of enabling them to wing their flight with amazing rapidity from world to world. For the angel Gabriel, being commanded to fly swiftly, while the prophet Daniel was engaged in supplication, approached to him, before he had made an end of presenting his requests. During the few minutes employed in uttering his prayer, this angelic messenger descended from the celestial regions to the country of Babylonia. This was a rapidity of motion surpassing the comprehension of the most vigorous imagination, and far exceeding even the amazing velocity of *light*.—They have power over the objects of inanimate nature; for one of them "rolled away the stone from the door of the sepulchre," at the time of Christ's resurrection. They are intimately acquainted with the springs of life, and the avenues by which they may be interrupted; for an angel slew, in one night, 185,000 of the Assyrian army.—They are perfectly acquainted with all the relations which subsist among mankind, and can distinguish the age and character of every individual throughout all the families of the earth. For one of these powerful beings recognised all the first-born in the land of Egypt, distinguished the Egyptians from

* This writer, in addition to these, states the following properties:—"To be invested with a power capable of displacing the heavenly bodies, or of changing the course of nature, and to be possessed of a power and skill capable of organizing matter, of forming a plant, an animal, a world."—But I can scarcely think that such perfections are competent to any being but the Supreme.

the children of Israel, and exerted his powers in their destruction. And as they are "ministering spirits to the heirs of salvation," they must have a clear perception of the persons and characters of those who are the objects of the Divine favour, and to whom they are occasionally sent on embassies of mercy.—They are endowed with great physical powers and energies; hence they are said "*to excel in strength*:" and the phrase, "a *strong* angel," and "a *mighty* angel," which are sometimes applied to them, are expressive of the same perfection. Hence they are represented, in the book of the Revelation, as "holding the four winds of heaven," as executing the judgments of God upon the proud despisers of his government, as "throwing mountains into the sea," and binding the prince of darkness with chains, and "casting him into the bottomless pit."

They are endowed with unfading and immortal youth, and experience no decay in the vigour of their powers. For the angels who appeared to Mary at the tomb of our Saviour, appeared as *young men*, though they were then more than four thousand years old. During the long succession of ages that had passed since their creation, their vigour and animation had suffered no diminution, nor decay,—they are possessed of *vast powers of intelligence*. Hence they are exhibited in the book of Revelation, as being "*full of eyes*," that is, endowed with "all sense, all intellect, all consciousness; turning their attention every way; beholding at once all things within the reach of their understandings; and discerning them with the utmost clearness of conception." The various other qualities now stated, necessarily suppose a vast comprehension of intellect; and the place of their residence, and the offices in which they have been employed, have afforded full scope to their superior powers. They dwell in a world where *truth* reigns triumphant, where moral evil has never entered, where substantial knowledge irradiates the mind of every inhabitant, where the mysteries which involve the character of the Eternal are continually disclosing, and where the plans of his providence are rapidly unfolded. They have ranged through the innumerable regions of the heavens, and visited distant worlds, for thousands of years; they have beheld the unceasing variety, and the endless multitude of the works of creation and providence, and are, doubtless, enabled to compare systems of worlds, with more accuracy and comprehension than we are capable of surveying villages, cities and provinces. Thus, their original powers and capacities have been expanded, and their vigour and activity strengthened; and, consequently, in the progress of duration, their acquisitions of wisdom and knowledge must indefinitely surpass every thing that the mind of man can conceive.—We have likewise certain intimations, that, among these celestial beings, there are *gradations of nature and of office*; since there are among them, "seraphim and cherubim, archangels, thrones, dominions, principalities and powers," which designations are evidently expressive of their respective endowments, of the stations they occupy, and of the employments for which they are qualified.

Hence it appears, that although we know but little in the mean time of the nature of that diversity of intellect which prevails among the higher orders of created beings—the intimations given in the sacred volume, and the general analogy of nature, lead us to form the most exalted ideas of that amazing progression and variety which reign throughout the intellectual universe.

2. Not only is there a gradation of intellect among superior beings, but it is highly probable, that a similar gradation or variety obtains, in the form, the organization, and the movements of their corporeal vehicles.

The human form, especially in the vigour of youth, is the most beautiful and symmetrical of all the forms of organized beings with which we are acquainted; and, in these respects, may probably bear some analogy to the organical structures of other intelligences. But, in other worlds, there may exist an indefinite variety, as to the general form of the body or vehicle with which their inhabitants are invested, the size, the number, and quality of their organs, the functions they perform, the splendour and beauty of their aspect, and particularly, in the number and perfection of their senses. Though there are more than a hundred thousand species of sensitive beings, which traverse the earth, the waters, and the air, yet they all exhibit a marked difference in their corporeal forms and organization. Quadrupeds exhibit a very different structure from fishes, and birds from reptiles; and every distinct species of quadrupeds, birds, fishes, and insects, differs from another in its conformation and functions. It is highly probable, that a similar variety exists, in regard to the corporeal vehicles of superior intelligences—accommodated to the regions in which they respectively reside, the functions they have to perform, and the employments in which they are engaged; and this we find to be actually the case, so far as our information extends. When any of the angelic tribes were sent on embassies to our world, we find, that, though they generally appeared in a shape somewhat resembling a beautiful human form, yet, in every instance, there appeared a marked difference between them and human beings. The angel who appeared at the tomb of our Saviour, exhibited a bright and resplendent form: "His countenance was like the brightness of lightning, and his raiment as white as snow," glittering with an extraordinary lustre beyond what mortal eyes could bear. The angel who delivered Peter from the prison to which he had been confined by the tyranny of Herod, was arrayed in such splendour, that a glorious light shone through the whole apartment where the apostle was bound, dark and gloomy as it was. That these beings have organs of speech, capable of forming articulate sounds and of joining in musical strains, appears form the words they uttered on these and other occasions, and from the song they sung in the plains of Bethlehem, when they announced the birth of the Saviour. They appear to possess the property of rendering themselves *invisible* at pleasure; for the angel that appeared to Zacharias in the sanctuary of the temple, was invisible to the surrounding multitudes without, both at the time of his entrance into, and his exit from the "holy place."*

In particular, there is every reason to conclude, that there is a wonderful variety in the number and acuteness of their organs of sensation. We find a considerable variety, in these respects, among the sensitive beings which inhabit our globe. Some animals appear to have only *one* sense, as the *muscle*, and the *zoophytes;* many have but *two* senses; some have *three;* and man, the most perfect animal, has only *five*. These senses, too, in different species, differ very considerably, in point of vigour and acuteness. The dog has a keener scent, the stag a quicker perception of sounds, and the eagle and the lynx more acute visual organs than mankind. The same diversity is observable in the form and the number of sensitive organs. In man, the ear is short and erect, and scarcely susceptible of motion; in the horse and the ass, it is long and flexible; and in the mole, it consists simply of a hole which perforates the skull. In man there are *two* eyes; in the scorpion and spider, *eight;* and in a fly, more than *five thousand.*

That superior beings, connected with other worlds, have additional senses to those which we possess, is highly probable, especially when we consider the general analogy of nature, and the gradations which exist among organized beings in our world. It forms no reason why we should deny that such senses exist, because we can form no distinct conceptions of any senses besides those which we possess. If we had been deprived of the senses of *sight* and *hearing*, and left to derive all our information merely through the medium of feeling, tasting and smelling, we could have had no more conception of articulate language, of musical harmony and melody, of the beauties of the earth, and of the glories of the sky, than a muscle, a vegetable, or a stone. To limit the number of senses which intelligent organized beings may possess to the five which

* To what is stated in this paragraph respecting angels, it will doubtless be objected, "that these intelligences are *pure spirits*, and assume corporeal forms only on particular occasions." This is an opinion almost universally prevalent; but it is a mere assumption, destitute of any rational or scriptural argument to substantiate its truth. There is no passage in Scripture, with which I am acquainted, that makes such an assertion. The passage in Psalm civ. 4, "Who maketh his angels spirits, and his ministers a flaming fire," has frequently been quoted for this purpose; but it has no reference to any opinion that may be formed on this point; as the passage should be rendered, "Who maketh the winds his messengers, and a flaming fire his ministers." Even although the passage were taken as it stands in our translation, and considered as referring to the angels, it would not prove, that they are pure immaterial substances; for, while they are designated *spirits*, which is equally applicable to *men* as well as to angels—they are also said to be "a flaming fire," which is a *material* substance. This passage seems to have no particular reference to either opinion; but, if considered as expressing the attributes of angels, its meaning plainly is,—that they are endowed with *wonderful activity*—that they move with the swiftness of the winds, and operate with the force and energy of flaming fire;—or, in other words, that He, in whose service they are, and who directs their movements, employs them "with the strength of winds, and the rapidity of lightnings."

In every instance in which angels have been sent on embassies to mankind, they have displayed *sensible* qualities. They exhibited a *definite form* somewhat analogous to that of man, and *colour and splendour*, which were perceptible by the organs of vision—they emitted *sounds* which struck the organ of hearing—they produced the harmonies of *music*, and sung sublime sentiments which were uttered in articulate words, that were distinctly heard and recognized by the persons to whom they were sent, Luke ii. 14.—and they exerted their power over the sense of *feeling;* for the angel who appeared to Peter in the prison, "*smote* him on the side, and *raised him up*." In these instances, angels manifested themselves to men, through the medium of three principal senses by which we recognize the properties of material objects; and why, then, should we consider them as purely immaterial substances, having no connection with the visible universe? We have no knowledge of angels but from revelation; and all the descriptions it gives of these beings leads us to conclude, that they are connected with the world of matter, as well as with the world of mind, and are furnished with organical vehicles, composed of some refined material substance suitable to their nature and employments

When Christ shall appear the second time, we are told that he is to come, not only in the glory of his Father, but also in "the glory of his holy angels," who will minister to him and increase the splendour of his appearance. Now, the glory which the angels will display, must be *visible*, and, consequently, material; otherwise it could not be contemplated by the assembled inhabitants of our world, and could present no glory or lustre to their view. An assemblage of purely spiritual beings, however numerous and however exalted in point of intelligence, would be a mere inanity, in a scene intended to exhibit *a visible* display of the divine supremacy and grandeur.—The vehicles or bodies of angels are doubtless of a much finer mould than the bodies of men; but, although they were at all times invisible through such organs of vision as we possess, it would form no proof that they were destitute of such corporeal frames. The air we breathe is a *material* substance, yet it is *invisible;* and there are substances whose rarity is more than ten times greater than that of the air of our atmosphere. Hydrogen gas is more than twelves times lighter than common atmospheric air. If, therefore, an organized body were formed of a material substance similar to air, or to hydrogen gas, it would in general be invisible; but, in certain circumstances, might reflect the rays of light, and become visible, as certain of the lighter gaseous bodies are found to do. This is, in some measure, exemplified in the case of *animalculæ*, whose bodies are imperceptible to the naked eye, and yet, are regularly organized material substances, endowed with all the functions requisite to life, motion, and enjoyment.

have been bestowed upon man, would be to set bounds to the infinite wisdom and skill of the Creator, who, in all his works, has displayed an endless variety in the manner of accomplishing his designs. While, in the terrestrial sphere in which we move, our views are limited to the *external* aspects of plants and animals—organized beings, in other spheres, may have the faculty of penetrating into their *internal* (and to us, invisible) movements—of tracing an animal from its embryo-state, through all its gradations and evolutions, till it arrive at maturity—of perceiving, at a glance, and, as it were, through a transparent medium, the interior structure of an animal, the complicated movements of its curious machinery, the minute and diversified ramifications of its vessels, and the mode in which its several functions are performed—of discerning the fine and delicate machinery which enters into the construction, and produces the various motions of a microscopic animalculum, and the curious vessels, and the circulation of juices which exist in the body of a plant—of tracing the secret processes which are going on in the mineral kingdom, and the operation of chymical affinities among the minute particles of matter, which produce the diversified phenomena of the universe. And, in fine, those senses which the inhabitants of other worlds enjoy in common with us, may be possessed by them in a state of greater acuteness and perfection. While our visual organs can perceive objects distinctly, only within the limits of a few yards or miles around us, *their* organs may be so modified and adjusted, as to enable them to perceive objects with the same distinctness, at the distance of a hundred miles—or even to descry the scenery of distant worlds. If our powers of vision had been confined within the range to which a worm or a mite is circumscribed, we could have formed no conception of the amplitude of our present range of view; and it is by no means improbable, that organized beings exist, whose extent of vision as far exceeds ours, as ours exceeds that of the smallest insect, and that they may be able to perceive the diversified landscapes which exist in other worlds, and the movements of their inhabitants, as distinctly as we perceive the objects on the opposite side of a river, or of a narrow arm of the sea.

After Stephen had delivered his defence before the Sanhedrim, we are told "he looked up steadfastly into heaven, and saw the glory of God, and Jesus standing at the right hand of God; and said, Behold I see the heavens opened, and the Son of man standing on the right hand of God." Some have supposed that the eyes of Stephen, on this occasion were so modified or strengthened, that he was enabled to penetrate into that particular region where the glorified body of Christ more immediately resides. But whether his opinion be tenable or not, certain it is, that angels are endowed with senses or faculties which enable them to take a minute survey of the solar system, and of the greater part of our globe, even when at a vast distance from our terrestrial sphere; otherwise, they could not distinguish the particular position of our earth in its annual course round the sun, in their descent from more distant regions, nor direct their course to that particular country, city, or village, whither they are sent on any special embassy.

What has been now said in reference to the organs of vision, is equally applicable to the organs of *hearing*, and to several of the other senses; and since faculties or senses, such as those I have now supposed, would tend to unveil more extensively the wonderful operations of the Almighty, and to excite incessant admiration of his wisdom and beneficence, it is reasonable to believe that he has bestowed them on various orders of his creatures for this purpose—and that man may be endowed with similar senses, when he arrives at moral perfection, and is placed in a higher sphere of existence.

Besides the topics to which I have now adverted, namely, the gradation of intellect, and the diversity of corporeal organization—a still more ample and interesting field of contemplation will be opened in the HISTORY *of the numerous worlds dispersed throughout the universe*,—including the grand and delightful, or the awful and disastrous events which have taken place in the several regions of intellectual existence.

The particulars under this head which may be supposed to gratify the enlightened curiosity of holy intelligences, are such as the following:—the *different periods* in duration at which the various habitable globes emerged from nothing into existence—the *changes and previous arrangements* through which they passed before they were replenished with inhabitants—the distinguishing *characteristic features* of every species of intellectual beings—their *modes of existence*, of improvement, and of social intercourse—the solemn *forms of worship* and adoration that prevail among them—the *laws of social, and of moral order* peculiar to each province of the divine empire*—*the progress they have made*

* There are certain general laws which are common to all the orders of intellectual beings throughout the universe. The two principles which form the basis of our *moral law* are of this nature:—"Thou shalt love the Lord thy God with all thine heart, and with all thine understanding," and "thou shalt love thy neighbour as thyself." For we cannot suppose the Deity, in consistency with the sanctity and rectitude of his nature, *to reverse these laws*, in relation to any class of intelligences, or to exempt them from an obligation to obey them; and, therefore, they may be considered as the two grand moral principles which direct the affections and conduct of all holy beings throughout the immensity of God's empire, and which unite them to one another, and to their common Creator. But, in subordination to these principles or laws, there may be a variety of special moral laws, adapted to the

*in knowledge*, and the discoveries they have brought to light, respecting the works and the ways of God—the *peculiar manifestations* of himself which the Divine Being may have made to them, "at sundry times and in divers manners"—the most remarkable *civil and moral events* which have happened since the period of their creation—the *visible emblems of the Divine Presence* and glory which are displayed before them—the information they have obtained respecting *the transactions and the moral government of other worlds*—the various stages of improvement through which they are appointed to pass—the different regions of the universe to which they may be transported, and the final destination to which they are appointed.

In particular, the facts connected with their *moral history*, in so far as they may be unfolded, will form an interesting subject of discourse and of contemplation. It is highly probable, when we consider the general benignity of the Divine Nature, and the numerous evidences of it which appear throughout the whole kingdom of animated nature—that the inhabitants of the greatest portion of the universal system, have retained the moral rectitude in which they were created, and are, consequently, in a state of perfect happiness. But, since we know, from painful experience, that *one* world has swerved from its allegiance to the Creator, and been plunged into the depths of physical and moral evil, it is not at all improbable, that the inhabitants of several other worlds have been permitted to fall into a similar calamity,—for this purpose among others—that the importance of moral order might be demonstrated, that the awful consequences of a violation of the eternal laws of heaven might be clearly manifested, and that a field might be laid open for the display of the rectitude and *mercy* of God as the moral Governor of the universe. In reference to such cases (if any exist) the points of inquiry would naturally be—What is the ultimate destination of those beings who, in other regions of creation, have acted the part of rebellious man? Has their Creator interposed for their deliverance in a manner analogous to that in which he has accomplished the redemption of mankind? If so, wherein do such schemes of mercy differ, and wherein do they agree with the plan of salvation by Jesus Christ? What scenes of moral evil have been displayed, and how have the moral disorders in those worlds been overruled and counteracted by the providential dispensations of the Almighty? Here, a thousand questions would crowd upon the mind, a variety of emotions of opposite kinds would be excited, and a most interesting field of investigation would be laid open to the contemplation of the redeemed inhabitants of such a world as ours. And, it is easy to conceive, with what kindred emotions and sympathetic feelings, and with what transporting gratulations, the renovated inhabitants of such worlds, would recognise each other, should they ever be brought into contact, and permitted to mingle their ascriptions of praise to the Creator and Redeemer of worlds.

Even in those worlds where the inhabitants have retained their primeval innocence, there may be an almost infinite variety in the divine dispensations, both in a moral, and intellectual point of view.—As finite intelligences, from their very nature, are *progressive* beings, and, therefore, cannot be supposed to acquire all the treasures of wisdom and knowledge, and to comprehend all the multifarious displays of divine perfection, during the first stages of their existence—there may be an admirable diversity of modes, corresponding to their peculiar circumstances and stages of improvement, by which the Creator may gradually unfold to them the glory of his nature, and enable them to take a more extensive survey of the magnitude and order of his dominions. Some may be only emerging from the first principles of science, like Adam soon after his creation, and may have arrived but a few degrees beyond the sphere of knowledge which bounds the view of man; others may have arrived at a point where they can take a more expansive survey of the order, economy, and relations of material and intellectual existences,—while others after having contemplated, for ages, a wide extent of creation, in *one* district of the empire of God, may be transported to a new and a distant province of the universe, to contemplate the perfections of Deity in another point of view, and to investigate and admire a new scene of wonders.—If every individual of the human race, from his birth to his death, passes through a train of providences peculiar to himself, it appears at least highly probable, reasoning from the analogies to which we have already adverted, and from the variety that every where appears in the natural and moral world, that the divine dispensations towards every distinct class of intelligent beings, have some striking peculiarities, which do not exactly coincide with those of any other.

That some portion, at least, of the natural and moral history of other worlds will be laid open to the inspection of redeemed men in the future world, may be argued from this consideration,—that such views will tend *to unfold the moral character of the Deity*, and to display more fully his intelligence, wisdom, and rectitude, in the diver-

peculiar economy, circumstances, and relations, which exist in each distinct world. As we have certain special laws, in our moral code, such as the *fifth* and *seventh* precepts of the Decalogue, which, in all probability, do not apply to the inhabitants of some other worlds, so they may have various specific regulations or laws, which cannot apply to us in our present state. The reader will find a particular illustration of the two fundamental laws to which I have now adverted, and of their application to the inhabitants of all worlds, in a work which I lately published, entitled, "*The Philosophy of Religion*; or, an Illustration of the Moral Laws of the Universe."

sified modes of his administration, as the Governor of the universe. We have reason to believe that the material creation exists solely for the sake of sentient and intelligent beings; and that it has been arranged into distinct departments, and peopled with various ranks of intellectual natures, chiefly for the purpose of giving a display of the moral attributes of God, and of demonstrating the indispensable necessity and the eternal obligation of the moral laws he has enacted, in order to secure the happiness of the whole intelligent system. And, if so, we may reasonably conclude, that a certain portion of the divine dispensations towards other classes of the intelligent creation, will ultimately be displayed to our view.—This position may likewise be argued from the fact that other intelligences have been made acquainted with the affairs of our world, and the tenor of the dispensations of God towards our race. The angelic tribes have been frequently sent on embassages to our terrestrial sphere. On such occasions they have indicated an intimate acquaintance with the most interesting transactions which have taken place among us; and we are informed, that they still "desire to pry into" the scheme of redemption, and "to learn" from the divine dispensations towards the church "the manifold wisdom of God."* Some notices of the history, the employments, and the destination, of these celestial beings have likewise been conveyed to us. We know that they hold an elevated station in the kingdom of Providence; that they are possessed of great power and wisdom, of wonderful activity, of superior intellectual faculties, and of consummate holiness and rectitude of nature; that they are employed on certain occasions as ambassadors from God to man, in executing his judgments upon the wicked, and ministering to the heirs of salvation; and that a certain number of them fell from the high station in which they were originally placed, and plunged themselves into a state of sin and perdition. We have therefore reason to believe, that it is one part of the plan of the government of God, to disclose the history of one species of intellectual beings to another, in such portions, and at such seasons, as may seem most proper to Infinite Wisdom, and best suited to the state and character, and the gradual improvement of his intelligent offspring.

In conformity to what has been now advanced, we find the saints in heaven represented as uttering a song of praise to God, in consequence of the survey they had taken of his moral administration, and of the admiration it excited. "They sing the song of Moses, and the song of the Lamb, saying, *Just and true are thy ways, thou King of saints.*" And, in proportion as the dispensations of Providence towards other worlds are unfolded, in the same proportion will their views of Jehovah's "eternal righteousness" be expanded, and a new note of admiration and rapture added to their song of praise.—The knowledge of the saints in heaven is represented as being very accurate and comprehensive. Hence it is declared, that, in that state of perfection, "they shall know, even as also they are known." This expression certainly denotes a very high degree of knowledge respecting the works and the ways of God; and, therefore, most commentators explain it as consisting in such an intuitive and comprehensive knowledge "as shall bear some fair resemblance to that of the Divine Being, which penetrates to the very centre of every object, and sees through the soul, and all things, as at one single glance;" or, at least, that "their knowledge of heavenly objects shall be as certain, immediate and familiar, as any of their immediate friends and acquaintances now have of them."* And, if such interpretations be admitted, this knowledge must include a minute and comprehensive view of the dispensations of the Creator towards other worlds, and other orders of moral and intelligent agents.

In regard to the *manner* in which information respecting the structure, the inhabitants, and the history of other worlds may be communicated, our limited knowledge affords no certain *data* on which to ground a definite opinion. We may, however, reasonably suppose, that an intercourse and correspondence will be occasionally opened up, by means of celestial beings endowed with faculties of rapid motion, who may communicate particular details of the intelligence they acquire in the regions they are accustomed to visit. Such correspondence has already partially taken place in our world, by means of those beings termed, in Scripture, "the angels," or "the *messengers* of Jehovah;" and, it is highly probable, had man continued in his state of original integrity, that such angelic embassies would have been much more frequent than they have ever been, and we might have been made acquainted, in this way, with some outlines of the physical and moral scenery of other worlds, particularly of those which belong to our own system—of which we must now be contented to remain in ignorance; and must have recourse to the aids of reason, and science, and observation, in order to trace some very general outlines of their physical economy. This is, doubtless, one deplorable effect, among others, of the apostacy of man—that intelligences endowed with moral perfection can no longer hold familiar intercourse with the race of Adam, but in so far as they are employed by their Creator in communicating occasional messages, which have a respect merely to their moral renovation.†—We may likewise,

* See Ephes. iii. 10. 1 Peter i. 12.

* See Doddridge's and Guyse's paraphrase on I Cor. xiii. 12.

† It is probable that the celestial beings who have occasionally held a communication with our race, are not all of the same species, or inhabit the same regions; since they are distinguished in Scripture by different names, as Seraphim, Cherubim, Thrones, Dominions, Angels, Archangels, &c.

with some degree of probability, suppose, that every distinct order of holy intelligences, after having resided for a certain number of ages, in one region of the universe, may be conveyed to another province of creation, to investigate the new scenes of wisdom and omnipotence there unfolded,—and so on, in a continued series of transportations, throughout the ages of eternity. We know that man is destined to undergo such a change of locality; and although sin has made the passage from one world to another, assume a gloomy and alarming aspect, it may nevertheless be an example, (though in a different manner) of those removals which take place with respect to other beings, from one province of creation to another. Nor have we any reason to believe, that the locality in which we shall be placed, after the general resurrection, will form our permanent and everlasting abode; otherwise, we should be eternally chained down, as we are at present to a small corner of creation.

In regard to the redeemed inhabitants of our world, there is every reason to believe, that the *Redeemer* himself, he, "in whom dwell all the treasures of wisdom and knowledge," will be one grand medium through which information will be communicated respecting the distant glories of Jehovah's empire. This seems to be directly intimated, though in metaphorical language, in the following passage from the book of Revelation: "The Lamb who is in the midst of the throne shall feed them, and shall lead them to fountains of living water." Knowledge is the food of the mind; and in this sense the term is frequently applied in the Scriptures:—"I will give them pastors (saith God) after mine own heart, who shall *feed them* with *knowledge* and *understanding*." "Feed the church of God," says the apostle Peter; that is, instruct them in the knowledge of the truths of religion. Therefore, by imparting to his saints a knowledge of the plans and operations of God, and information respecting the magnificence of his works in the regions around, "the Lamb in the midst of the throne *will feed them*," by gratifying their intellectual powers, and their desires after knowledge; and the noble and transporting trains of thought which such discoveries will inspire, (and which may be aptly compared to the effect produced by "fountains of living water" on a parched traveller,) will arrest all the faculties of their souls, and fill them "with joy unspeakable and full of glory."

Perhaps, it may not be beyond the bounds of probability to suppose, that, at certain seasons, during a grand convocation of the redeemed with Jesus their exalted head president among them —that glorious personage may impart to them knowledge of the most exalted kind, direct their views to some bright manifestations of Deity, and deliver most interesting lectures on the works and the ways of God. This would be quite accordant with his office as the "Mediator between God and man," and to his character as the "Messenger of Jehovah," and the "Revealer" of the divine dispensations.

Pointing to some distant world, (which, even to the acute visual organs of heavenly beings, may appear only as a small lucid speck in their sky,) we may suppose him giving such a descant as the following:—"That world presents a very different aspect from what yours once did, owing, chiefly to the moral purity and perfection of its inhabitants. *There*, the most grand and variegated objects adorn their celestial canopy; and the scenes around their habitations are intermingled with every thing that is beautiful to the eye, and gratifying to the senses and the imagination. Neither scorching heats, nor piercing colds, nor raging storms, ever disturb the tranquillity of those happy mansions. The fine etherial fluid which they breathe produces a perpetual flow of pleasing emotions, and sharpens and invigorates their intellectual powers for every investigation. The peculiar refractive and reflective powers possessed by the atmospheric fluid which surrounds them, produce a variety of grand and beautiful effects, sometimes exhibiting aerial landscapes, and scenes emblematical of moral harmony and perfection,—sometimes a magnificent display of the riches and most variegated colouring, and sometimes reflecting the images of the celestial orbs in various aspects and degrees of magnitude. Their vegetable kingdom is enriched with a variety of productions unknown in your former world, diversified with thousands of different forms, shades, colours, and perfumes, which shed a delicious fragrance all around. The inferior sentient beings are likewise different, and exhibit such ingenious, mild, and affectionate dispositions, as contribute, in no inconsiderable degree, to the pleasure and entertainment of the more intelligent order of the inhabitants. The organs of vision of these intelligences are so acute, that they are enabled to perceive, as through a transparent medium, the various chymical and mechanical processes that are incessantly going on in the numberless ramifications of the vegetable tribes, and in the more curious and complicated structure of animal bodies; for the Creator has ordained, as one part of their mental enjoyments, that they shall be furnished with the means of tracing the mode of his operations, and the designs they are intended to accomplish in the different departments of nature.

"They are likewise extensively acquainted with moral science—with the moral relations of intelligent beings to their Creator, and to one another, and with the outlines of the history of several other worlds; for the leading facts in the history of your world, respecting the fall of man, its dismal consequences, and your subsequent redemption and renovation, have been communicated to them, for the purpose of enlarging their views of God's moral dispensations, and illustrating the rectitude and benevolence of his government.—In their intercourses and associations, no discordant voice is ever heard, no symptom of disaffection ever appears, no boisterous passions ever disturb their tranquillity; but all is harmony and order, peace and love. Their progress in the knowledge of God, and of his works, is rapid and sure, for they see clearly the first principles of all reasoning and science; and, without once making a false step, or deducing an erroneous conclusion, they trace them with rapidity and certainty, to all their legitimate consequences. Their acquaintance with natural and moral facts is extensive and minute. For the most sacred regard is attached to truth, which was never once violated in that happy society; and, therefore, every discovery, every new doctrine and fact which is brought to light by any individual, is regarded by all others as an established truth which is never called in question, and which serves to direct and facilitate all their other researches. Unlike the exaggerations and falsehoods which were once propagated by lying travellers and sceptical philosophers, in your former world, which tended to bewilder the anxious inquirer, and to obscure the radiance of truth; in yonder world truth is regarded as a most sacred and invaluable treasure, as the basis of the happiness of the moral universe, and the foundation on which rests the throne of the eternal; and, therefore, being never violated by any individual, every testimony and assertion is received with unhesitating confidence. By a rapid mode of communication which has been established, their intercourses with each other are frequent and delightful, and the discoveries which are made of the operations of infinite wisdom and benevolence, are quickly circulated through all the intelligent ranks of that abode of felicity and love. Beings from other worlds occasionally visit them, and convey interesting intelligence, and affectionate congratulations from the regions whence they came; and a glorious symbol of the divine Majesty was lately displayed in their firmament, from which was announced, in majestic but mild and transporting language—the approbation of their Creator, and his purpose of translating them, as a reward of their obedience, to another region of his empire, to behold new displays of his beneficence and power.

"This is a specimen of the moral order and happiness which prevail among the greater part of those worlds which shine from afar in yonder firmament, but which are distinguished by a variety of peculiar circumstances, which shall be unfolded on another occasion."

Directing their view to another distant orb, which appears like a dim ruddy speck in an obscure quarter of the firmament, he may thus proceed:—"That, too, is a world on a different scale, and in a different condition. It is a thousand times larger than the globe you once inhabited, and was originally arrayed with all that magnificence and beauty which characterize the works of the Creator. During a considerable period its inhabitants retained their allegiance to their Maker, and their affection for each other. But certain individuals, whom a principle of pride and ambition had led to desire stations of pre-eminence, having dared to violate some of the fundamental laws of their Creator,—the moral turpitude which this disposition and conduct produced, gradually spread from one rank to another, till the whole mass of its inhabitants was completely contaminated, and plunged into a gulph of misery. To such a dreadful length has this depravity proceeded, that even the external aspect of that world, which was once fair as Eden, has assumed the appearance of a gloomy waste, and a barren wilderness. The rivers have been turned out of their course, by these infatuated beings, that they might overflow and change into a marsh the once fertile plains. The earth has been dug into immense pits and chasms, and the vegetable tribes have been torn from their roots and stripped of their verdure, in order to deface the primeval beauty of creation. By these, and other horrible devastations, the ethereal fluid in which they breathed, which formerly diffused a delightful fragrance, has now become the receptacle of noisome exhalations, which nauseate and irritate every species of sensitive existence. Its brilliancy has thereby become obscured, so that their sun appears lowering through its dense vapours, like a dusky ball; and their nocturnal sky, which once presented a splendid assemblage of shining orbs, is now covered with blackness, and darkness, and tempest, through which no celestial orb ever transmits the least glimmering ray. For the almighty Contriver of all worlds has so arranged, proportioned, and adjusted every circumstance in the constitution of nature, that the smallest derangement, by malevolent beings, of the order he has established, is always productive of disastrous effects.

"Instead of being animated with love to their Creator, and to one another, which is the first duty of all intelligent creatures, they hate their Maker, and curse him on account of the existence he has given them; and they hate each other, with a perfect hatred. There exists among them no peace, justice, sympathy, friendship, or confidence. Every one beholds and recognises another with the countenance of a fiend, and is ever intent upon annoying him to the utmost of his power. And, were it not that their bodies are constructed on an *immortal* principle, so that no power less than infinite can completely destroy them,—their ferocious passions would, long ere now, have effected the utter extermination of every individual in that populous but miserable world. Their bodies, which were once fair and glorious, are now covered with every mark of vileness and deformity. They have no delight in contemplating the glories of their Creator's workmanship, for they have defaced every beauty which creation displayed, when it came fresh and fair from the hand of its Maker; and the intelligence and wisdom they formerly possessed, are now obliterated, and changed into ignorance and folly.

"At the commencement of this affecting scene of depravity, a messenger was despatched by their Almighty Sovereign to warn them of their danger, and to urge them to reformation; but, as they had not then felt the full effects of that wretchedness into which they were plunging—after a few temporary pangs of remorse, 'they returned every one to his evil ways.' Holy intelligences, from other worlds, have occasionally been sent, to contemplate the gloomy aspect, and the sad desolations of this wretched world; in order that they might bring back intelligence to the worlds with which they are more immediately connected, of the dismal effects produced by the violation of those eternal laws of rectitude which the Governor of the universe has ordained. The Creator has, for many ages, permitted those physical and moral disorders to exist—not because he delights in the misery of any of his creatures, but because he has a regard to the ultimate happiness of the whole intelligent system. He leaves them, in the mean time, 'to eat of the fruit of their own ways,' that they may feel the full effects of their apostacy and wickedness. He has permitted them to proceed thus far in their rebellion and depravity, in order that surrounding worlds may be fully apprised of the dismal effects that must inevitably ensue on every infringement of moral order. This desolated world and its wretched inhabitants are doomed to remain in their present deplorable state, for ages yet to come, till an extensive and indelible impression be made on the inhabitants of every province of God's empire, of their eternal obligation to conform to those laws and principles of moral order which his infinite wisdom has established for the regulation of the intelligent universe; and also, that those miserable beings themselves may be aroused to consideration, led to humble themselves in his presence, and made to feel some emotions of contrition for their impiety and ingratitude. When these ends are accomplished, a bright effulgence shall suddenly illume the darkness of their night, their atmosphere shall be cleared of its vapours, and the glorious orbs of heaven shall once more burst upon their view; the astonished inhabitants shall lift up their eyes with amazement at the wondrous and unlooked-for spectacle, and a divine messenger, arrayed in splendid majesty, shall proclaim, 'Peace from heaven—Good-will from Jehovah to this guilty world.' In both hemispheres of this globe, shall the joyful message be proclaimed. This sudden and unexpected announcement will arrest the attention of every inhabitant, and rekindle in his breast those sparks of gratitude, which had been so long extinguished. To prove the sincerity of this annunciation, the 'Power of the Highest' will be interposed to purify the atmosphere, to restore the desolations which had been produced, and to renew the face of nature. A series of moral instructions will commence, and be carried on with vigour, till all be fully convinced of the folly and impiety of their conduct. Order will be gradually re-established; affectionate intercourses will commence; an indelible impression of their ingratitude and wickedness, and of the justice and benevolence of God, will be for ever fixed in their minds, which will secure them, at all future periods, from a similar apostacy; and peace, truth, and happiness shall finally reign triumphant."

On such topics as these, may we suppose our Redeemer, in the character of Mediator, occasionally to expatiate, with irresistible eloquence, when presiding in the assemblies of his redeemed; and the emotions produced by such communications, will doubtless excite them to join in unison in celebrating the divine character and administration, in such strains as these:—"Halleluia! the Lord God omnipotent reigneth. True and righteous are his judgments. Salvation, and glory, and honour, and power, unto the Lord our God. Thou art worthy to receive glory, honour, and power; for thou hast created all things, and for thy pleasure they are and were created."*

Thus I have endeavoured to show, that even that portion of the universe which lies within

* I hope none of my readers will consider the supposition of the Redeemer occasionally delivering lectures on divine subjects to an assembly of his saints, as either improbable, extravagant, or romantic. Since writing the above, I find, that the pious and philosophic *Dr. I. Watts* entertained a similar opinion. In his sermon, "On the happiness of separate spirits," when describing the employments of the upper world, he thus expresses his sentiments on this topic;—"Perhaps you will suppose there is no such service as hearing sermons, that there is no attendance upon the word of God there. But are we sure there are no such entertainments? Are there no lectures of divine wisdom and grace given to the younger spirits there, by spirits of a more exalted station? Or, may not our Lord Jesus Christ himself be the everlasting Teacher of his church? May he not at solemn seasons summon all heaven to hear him publish some new and surprising discoveries which have never yet been made known to the ages of nature or of grace, and are reserved to entertain the attention, and to exalt the pleasure of spirits advanced to glory? Must we learn all by the mere contemplation of Christ's person? Does he never make use of speech to the instruction and joy of saints above.—Or, it may be, that our blessed Lord (even as he is man) has some noble and unknown way of communicating a long discourse, or a long train of ideas and discoveries to millions of blessed spirits at once, without the formalities of voice and language, and at some peculiar seasons he may thus instruct and delight his saints in heaven."

the reach of our assisted vision, comprehends within its capacious sphere, at least two thousand four hundred millions of worlds—that each of these worlds, being constructed by infinite wisdom, must exhibit, even in its external aspect, a scene worthy of the contemplation of every rational being—that it is highly probable, from ascertained facts, from analogy, and from revelation, that each of these worlds has a peculiarity of scenery, and of appendages, which distinguish it from every other—that there is a gradation of intellect, and beings of different orders among the inhabitants of these worlds—that it is probable their corporeal forms and their organs of sensation are likewise wonderfully diversified—and that the natural and moral history of each presents scenes and transactions different from those which are found in any other world. So that when the mind endeavours to grasp the immense number of worlds, here presented to our mental view, and considers the variety of aspect in which each of them requires to be contemplated—there appears, to such limited intellects as ours, no prospect of a termination to the survey of a scene so extensive and overwhelming; but, on the contrary, a rational presumption, that one scene of glory will be followed by another, in perpetual succession, while ages roll away.

If it would require, even to beings endowed with mental powers superior to those of man, several hundred of years, to survey the diversified landscapes which our globe displays, to investigate the numerous chymical processes going on in the animal, the vegetable, and the mineral kingdoms, throughout the surface of the earth, the recesses of the ocean, and the subterraneous regions, and to trace the history of every tribe of its inhabitants during a period of six thousand years,—if it would require thousands of years to explore the plantery system, which presents a field of inquiry two thousand times more extensive—how many hundreds of thousands of millions of years would be requisite to study and investigate the visible universe in all that variety of aspect to which I have now adverted!—To explore the diversified structure and arrangements of the bodies which compose the solar system, and the moral events which have taken place among its inhabitants, would require a long series of ages. The system of bodies connected with the planet Saturn, would, of itself, require several hundreds of years of study and research, in order to acquire a *general* view of its physical, moral, and intellectual aspects and relations. Here we have presented to view,—1. A globe of vast dimensions capable of containing a population of sentient and intelligent beings more than a hundred times greater than that of the earth. 2. Two immense rings, the one of them containing, on both its sides an area of *eight thousand millions* of square miles, and the other an area of *twenty thousand millions* of miles, and sufficient to contain a population, *one hundred and forty times* larger that of our globe, although they were as thinly peopled as the earth is at present. 3. Seven satellites, or moons, each of which is undoubtedly as large as the globe on which we live, and some of them, probably, of much greater dimensions. The magnificent and astonishing scenery displayed in this planet, so very different from any thing that is beheld in our terrestrial sphere—the stupendous luminous arches which stretch across its firmament, like pillars of cloud by day and pillars of fire by night—the diversified shadows they occasionally cast on the surrounding landscape—the appearance and disappearance of its moons, their eclipses, and diversified aspects in respect to each other, and to the inhabitants of the planet itself,—the novel scenes which would appear in the animal, vegetable, and mineral kingdoms—the customs, manners, and employments of the inhabitants—the series of events which have happened among them and the tenor of the divine dispensations in relation to their past history and their future destination—these, and a thousand other particulars, of which we can form no distinct conception—could not fail to afford a sublime and delightful gratification to a rational intelligence for a series of ages.

"It is probable, too, that even within the boundaries of our solar system, important physical and moral revolutions have happened since its creation, besides those which have agitated the world in which we dwell. On the surface of the planet Jupiter, changes are occasionally taking place, visible at the remote distance at which we are placed. The diversity of appearance that has been observed in the substances termed its *belts*, in whatever they may consist, or from whatever cause this diversity may originate,—indicates change as great, as if the whole mass of clouds which overhang Europe, and the northern parts of Asia and America, were to be completely swept away, and suspended in dense strata over the Pacific and the Indian oceans,—or as if the waters of the Atlantic ocean were to overflow the continent of America, and leave its deepest caverns exposed to view.—There were lately discovered, between the orbits of Mars and Jupiter, four small planetary bodies; and, on grounds which are highly probable, astronomers have concluded, that they once formed a larger body which moved in the same region, and which had burst asunder by some immense eruptive force proceeding from its central parts. This probable circumstance, together with a variety of singular phenomena exhibited by these planets, naturally lead us to conclude, that some important moral revolutions had taken place, in relation to the beings with which it was peopled; and suggest to the mind a variety of sublime and interesting reflections

which may hereafter be disclosed.—The planet Mars, in several respects, bears a striking resemblance to our earth. Its rotation round its axis is accomplished in nearly the same time as the earth, namely, in 24 hours and 40 minutes. The inclination of its axis to the plane of its orbit is 28 degrees and 42 minutes, that of the earth being 23 degrees 28 minutes. Consequently, it experiences a diversity of seasons, and different lengths of days and nights, as we do in our sublunary sphere. Hence Sir William Herschel informs us, that he observed a luminous zone about the poles of this planet, which is subject to periodical changes, and is of opinion, that this phenomenon is produced by the reflection of the sun's light upon its polar regions, and that the variation in the magnitude and appearance of this zone is owing to the melting of these masses of polar ice. Its atmosphere is likewise found to be very dense and obscure; which is the cause of that *ruddy* appearance which this orb uniformly exhibits. These circumstances indicate a striking similarity, in its *physical* constitution, to that of the earth. Whether the *moral* state of its inhabitants bears any resemblance to the present condition of mankind, is a question which naturally suggests itself, and which may possibly be solved in the future state to which we are destined. Frost and snow, the accumulation and melting of vast masses of polar ice, long nights, and wintry storms, scenes of darkness and desolation, stormy clouds, and a dense hazy atmosphere surcharged with wintry exhalations, do not appear to be the characteristics of a world where perfect happiness is enjoyed. The Sun which is the centre of our system, and which enlightens surrounding worlds with his beams, is five hundred times larger than all the planets and moons taken together. And, since we perceive frequent changes taking place in his surface and luminous atmosphere, there is doubtless a variety of astonishing processes and transformations going on, both in the exterior and interior parts of this immense luminary, on a scale of magnitude and grandeur, which it would be highly gratifying to behold and investigate, and which would raise to the highest pitch, our conceptions of the magnificence and glory of Him "who dwells in light unapproachable."

If, then, the planetary system, which occupies no larger a portion of space than one of the smallest stars that twinkle in our sky, would afford such a vast multiplicity of objects for the contemplation of intelligent beings, during a lapse of ages,—what an immense assemblage of august objects and astonishing events is presented before us in the physical arangements, and the moral history of the myriads of systems and worlds to which I have alluded, and what an immense duration would be requisite for finite minds to survey the wondrous scene! This consideration suggests an idea of duration, which to limited intellects such as ours, seems to approximate to the idea of eternity itself. Even although it could be shown, that creation extended no farther than the utmost bounds which the ingenuity of man has enabled him to penetrate, —still, the vast assemblage of glorious objects contained within the range of our assisted vision, shows what an infinite variety of mental gratification the Creator may bestow on his intelligent offspring; and we are assured, that "no good thing will he withhold from them that walk uprightly."

But, would it be reasonable to admit, that the dominions of the universal Sovereign terminate at the boundaries of human vision? Can we believe, that puny man, who occupies so diminutive a speck among the works of God, has penetrated to the utmost limits of the empire of Him who fills the immensity of space with his presence? As soon might we suppose, that a snail could penetrate to the utmost extremity of the ocean, and, with one glance, survey its deepest caverns; or, that a microscopic animalcula, which is confined to a drop of water, in the crevice of a small stone, could explore at one comprehensive view, the regions of Europe, Asia, Africa, and America. Shall we consider the *visible* system of nature,—magnificent and extensive as it is,—a palace sufficient for the habitation of the Deity? No: this would be, to circumscribe the Almighty within the limits of our imperfect vision, and within the sphere of our comprehension. "Behold, the heavens, and the heaven of heavens, cannot contain him!" This declaration implies, that, beyond all that the inhabitants of this world can explore in the visible firmament, there is a "*heaven of heavens*"—a region which contains unnumbered firmaments, as glorious and extensive as that which we behold,—throughout the vast extent of which, the Deity is eternally and essentially present. With regard to all that is visible by the unassisted eye, or by the telescope, in the vault of heaven, we may say with the poet:—

"Vast concave! ample dome! wast thou design'd
A meet apartment for the Deity?
Not so: that thought alone thy state impairs,
Thy *lofty* sinks, and shallows thy *profound*,
And straitens thy diffusive; dwarfs the whole,
And makes an universe an *orrery*."

Beyond the wide circumference of that sphere which terminates the view of mortals, a boundless region exists, which no human eye can penetrate, and which no finite intelligence can explore. To suppose that the infinitely extended region which surrounds all that is visible in creation, is a mere void, would be as unreasonable, as to have affirmed, prior to the invention of the telescope, that no stars existed beyond those which are visible to the naked eye. When we consider the limited faculties of man, and the infinite attributes of the Eternal Mind, we have the highest reason to conclude, that it is but a very small portion of the works of God which has been disclosed to our view. "Could you soar beyond the moon, (says a well-known writer) and pass through all the planetary choir; could you wing your way to the highest apparent star, and take your stand on one of those loftiest pinnacles of heaven, you would there see other skies expanded, another sun distributing his beams by day, other stars that gild the alternate night, and other, perhaps nobler systems established in unknown profusion through the boundless dimensions of space. Nor would the dominion of the universal Sovereign terminate *there*. Even at the end of this vast tour, you would find yourself advanced no farther than the suburbs of creation,—arrived only at the frontiers of the great Jehovah's kingdom."

It is highly probable, that, were all the two thousand four hundred millions of worlds to which we have adverted, with all the eighty millions of suns around which they revolve, to be suddenly extinguished and annihilated, it would not cause so great a blank in creation, to an eye that could take in the whole immensity of nature, as the extinction of the *pleiades*, or seven stars, would cause in our visible firmament. The range of material existence may, indeed, have certain limits assigned to it; but such limits can be perceived only by that *Eye* which beholds, at one glance, the whole of infinite space. To the view of every *finite* mind, it must always appear boundless and incomprehensible. Were it possible that we could ever arrive at the outskirts of creation, after having surveyed all that exists in the material universe, we might be said, in some measure, to comprehend the Creator himself; having perceived the utmost limits to which his power and intelligence have been extended. For, although we admit, that the perfections of the Creator are *infinite;* yet we have no tangible measure of these perfections, but what appears in the immense variety and extent of material and intellectual existence. And we may hence conclude, that the highest order of created intellects, after spending myriads of ages in their research, will never come to a period in their investigations of the works and the ways of God.

Even although we could conceive certain limits to the material universe, and that, after the lapse of millions of ages, a holy intelligence had finished his excursions, and made the tour of the universal system which now exists,—yet, who can set bounds to the active energies of the Eternal Mind, or say, that new systems of creation, different from all that have hitherto been constructed, shall not be perpetually emerging into existence? By the time a finite being had explored every object which now exists, and acquired a knowledge of all the moral and physical revolutions which have happened among the worlds which, at present, diversify the voids of space—a new region of infinite space might be replenished with new orders of material and intellectual existence: and, were he to return to the point from which he at first set out, after numerous ages had elapsed, he would, doubtless, behold new changes and revolutions in many provinces of the Creator's dominions—new heavens and new earths—and new species of sentient and intellectual beings, different from all those he at first contemplated.

That such is the plan of the Creator's operations, is not a mere conjecture or surmise, but is warranted from observations which have been made on the phenomena of the celestial bodies. New stars have, at different periods, appeared in the heavens; which are plain indications of the continued exertion of creating power. Some planets have burst asunder into different fragments, and stars which had shone for ages have disappeared, and their existence, in their former state, cannot now be traced.* Such facts evidently show, that some important revolutions have taken place in relation to the bodies which have thus been withdrawn from our view. Having for ages run their destined course, either their constitution has undergone an essential change, or they have been removed to another region of immensity, to subserve other purposes in the magnificent arrangements of the Sovereign Intelligence. The observations made by Sir William Herschel on the *nebulous* appearances in the heavens, and on the changes and modifications which they undergo, lead to the conclusion, that new systems are gradually forming in the distant regions of the universe. And, if the creating energy of the Omnipotent is at present in constant operation, and has been so for ages past, who shall dare to affirm, that it shall ever cease its exertion through all the ages of eternity?

Here, then, we have presented to our contemplation, an assemblage of material and intellectual existence, to which the human mind can affix no boundaries,—which is continually increasing, and still an infinity of space remaining for perpetual accessions, during the lapse of endless ages,—an assemblage of beings, which, in point of number, of magnitude, and of extent, seems to correspond with a boundless duration. So that, we have no reason to doubt, that "the saints in light" will be perpetually acquiring new discoveries of the divine glory, new prospects into the immensity of God's operations, new views of the rectitude and grandeur of his moral government, new accessions to their felicity, and new and transporting trains of thought, without the least interruption, as long as eternity endures.

* Stars which are marked in ancient catalogues, are not now to be found, and others are now visible which were not known to the ancients. Some have gradually increased in brilliancy. Some that were formerly *variable*, now shine with a steady lustre, while others have been constantly diminishing in brightness.

### THRONE OF GOD.

There is just one idea more that may be suggested, in addition to the several views exhibited above, in order to raise to a higher pitch of sublimity, our views of the grandeur of the Divine Being, and of the magnificence of his works.

The Scriptures frequently refer to a particular place, circumstance, or manifestation, termed *the throne of God;* as in the following passages:—"Heaven is my *throne*, and the earth is my footstool." "The Lord hath prepared *his throne in the heavens.*" "A *glorious high throne*, from the beginning, is the place of thy sanctuary." "Therefore are they before the throne of God, and serve him day and night in his temple." "Blessing, and honour, and glory, and power, be unto Him that sits upon the throne."—These, and similar expressions and representations, must be considered, either as merely metaphorical, or as referring to some particular region of the universe, where the Divine glory is reflected, in some peculiarly magnificent manner, from material objects; and where the manifestations of the Divine character are most illustriously displayed. If there be a reference to the splendour and magnitude of a particular portion of creation, there is an astronomical idea, which may help us to form some conception of this "glorious high throne," which is the peculiar residence of the Eternal. It is now considered by astronomers, as highly probable, if not certain,—from late observations, from the nature of gravitation, and other circumstances, that all the systems of the universe revolve round one common centre,—and that this centre may bear as great a proportion, in point of magnitude, to the universal assemblage of systems as the sun does to his surrounding planets. And, since our sun is five hundred times larger than the earth, and all the other planets and their satellites taken together,—on the same scale, such a central body would be five hundred times larger than all the systems and worlds in the universe. Here, then, may be a vast universe of itself—an example of material creation, exceeding all the rest in magnitude and splendour, and in which are blended the glories of every other system. If this is in reality the case, it may, with the most emphatic propriety, be termed, THE THRONE OF GOD.

This is the most sublime and magnificent idea that can possibly enter into the mind of man We feel oppressed and overwhelmed in endeavouring to form even a faint representation of it. But, however much it may overpower our feeble conceptions, we ought not to revolt at the idea of so glorious an extension of the works of God; since nothing less magnificent seems suitable to a being of infinite perfections.—This grand central body may be considered as the *Capital* of the universe. From this glorious centre, embassies may be occasionally despatched to all surrounding worlds, in every region of space. Here, too, deputations from all the different provinces of creation, may occasionally assemble, and the inhabitants of different worlds mingle with each other, and learn the grand outlines of those physical operations and moral transactions, which have taken place in their respective spheres. Here, may be exhibited to the view of unnumbered multitudes, objects of sublimity and glory, which are no where else to be found within the wide extent of creation. Here, intelligences of the highest order, who have attained the most sublime heights of knowledge and virtue, may form the principal part of the population of this magnificent region. Here, the glorified body of the Redeemer may have taken its principal station, as "the head of all principalities and powers:" and here likewise, Enoch and Elijah may reside, in the mean time, in order to learn the history of the magnificent plans and operations of Deity, that they may be enabled to communicate intelligence respecting them to their brethren of the race of Adam, when they shall again mingle with them in the world allotted for their abode, after the general resurrection. Here, the GRANDEUR of the Deity, the glory of his physical and moral perfections, and the immensity of his empire, may strike the mind with more bright effulgence, and excite more elavated emotions of admiration and rapture, than in any other province of universal nature. In fine, this vast and splendid central universe may constitute that august mansion referred to in Scripture, under the the designation of the THIRD HEAVENS—THE THRONE OF THE ETERNAL—the HEAVEN OF HEAVENS—THE HIGH AND HOLY PLACE—and THE LIGHT THAT IS INACCESSIBLE AND FULL OF GLORY.*

* Within the limits of the last 150 years, it has been found, that the principal fixed stars have a certain apparent motion, which is nearly uniform and regular, and is quite perceptible in the course of thirty or forty years. The star *Arcturus*, for example, has been observed to move three minutes and three seconds in the course of seventy-eight years. Most of the stars have moved toward the south. The stars in the northern quarter of the heavens seem to widen their relative positions, while those in the southern appear to contract their distances. These motions seem evidently to indicate, that the earth, and all the other bodies of the solar system, are moving in a direction from the stars, in the southern part of the sky, toward those in the northern. Dr. Herschel thinks, that a comparison of the changes now alluded to, indicates a motion of our sun with his attending planets towards the constellation *Hercules*. This progressive movement which our system makes in absolute space is justly supposed to be a portion of that curve, which the sun describes around the *centre* of that *nebula* to which he belongs; and, that all the other stars belonging to the same nebula, describe similar curves. And since the universe appears to be composed of thousands of *nebulæ*, or starry systems, detached from each other, it is reasonable to conclude, that all the starry systems of the universe revolve round one common centre, whose bulk and attractive influence are proportionable to the size and the number of the bodies which perform their revolutions around it. We know, that the law of gravitation extends its influ-

Perhaps some whose minds are not accustomed to such bold excursions through the regions of material existence, may be apt to consider the grand idea which has now been suggested, and many of the preceding details as too improbable and extravagant to claim our serious attention. In reply to such an insinuation, let it be considered, in the *first place*, that nothing has been stated but what corresponds to the whole analogy of nature, and to several sublime intimations contained in the system of divine Revelation. It is a fact, which, in the present day, cannot be denied by any one acquainted with the subject, that the material universe, as far as our eye and our glasses can carry us, consists of a countless multitude of vast bodies, which completely baffle our feeble powers in attempting to form any adequate conception of them. This amazing fact, placed within the evidence of our senses, shows us, that it is impossible for the human mind to form too extravagant ideas of the universe, or to conceive its structure to be more glorious and magnificent than it really is.†

Again, nothing short of such sublime and magnificent conceptions seems at all suitable to the idea of *a Being of infinite perfection and of eternal duration.* If we admit, that the divine Being is *infinite*, pervading the immensity of space with his presence, why should we be reluctant to admit the idea, that his *almighty energy is exerted* throughout the boundless regions of space? for it is just such a conclusion as the notion of an infinite intelligence should naturally lead us to deduce. Whether does it appear to correspond more with the notion of an infinite Being, to believe, that his creative power has been confined to this small globe of earth, and a few sparkling studs fixed in the canopy of the sky, or to admit, on the ground of observation and analogy, that he has launched into existence millions of worlds—that all the millions of systems within the reach of our vision, are but as a particle of vapour to the ocean, when compared with the myriads which exist in the unexplored regions of immensity—that the whole of this vast assemblage of suns and worlds revolves around the grand centre of the universe—and that this centre where the throne of God is placed, is superior to all the other provinces of creation in magnitude, beauty, and magnificence? Who would dare to *prove* that such conceptions are erroneous, or impossible, or unworthy of that *Being* who sits on the throne of the universe? To attempt such a proof would be nothing less than to set bounds to Omnipotence—to prescribe limits to the operations of him "whose ways are past finding out.'

"Can man *conceive beyond* what God *can do?*
Nothing but *quite impossible* is *hard.*
He summons into being with like ease
A *whole creation*, and a *single grain.*
Speaks he the word? a thousand worlds are born!
A thousand worlds? There's space for millions more;
And in what space can his great Fiat fail?
Condemn me not, cold critic! but indulge
The warm imagination; why condemn?
Why not *indulge* such thoughts as swell our hearts
With fuller admiration of that *Power*
Which gives our hearts with such high thoughts to swell?
Why not indulge in his augmented praise?
Darts not his glory a still brighter ray,
The less is left to chaos, and the realms
Of hideous night?"

These views and reasonings are fully corroborated by the sublime descriptions of Deity contained in the Holy Scriptures.—"Canst thou by searching find out God? canst thou find out the Almighty to perfection?" "He is the high and lofty One who inhabiteth eternity"—"He is glorious in power"—"He dwells in light unapproachable and full of glory"—"Great is our Lord and of great power, his greatness is unsearchable; his understanding is infinite"—"Can any thing be too hard for Jehovah? "The everlasting God the Lord, the Creator of the ends of the earth, fainteth not, neither is weary, there is no searching of his understanding"—"He doeth great things, past finding out, and wonders without number." "He meteth out the heavens with a span, and comprehendeth the dust of the

ence from the sun to the planet *Herschel*, at the distance of eighteen hundred millions of miles, and to the remotest parts of the orbits of the comets, which stretch far beyond this limit; and there is the strongest reason to believe, that it forms a connecting bond between all the bodies of the universe, however distant from each other. This being admitted,—the *motion* of the different systems now alluded to, and the *immensity* of the central body, from which motion of every kind originates, to produce the order and harmony of the universe,—appear to be necessary, in order to preserve the balance of the universal system, and to prevent the numerous globes in the universe from gradually approaching each other, in the course of ages, and becoming one universal wreck.—We are mechanically connected with the most distant stars visible through our telescopes, by means of *light*, which radiates from those distant luminaries, mingles with the solar rays, penetrates our atmosphere, and effects our optic nerves with the sensation of colours, similar to those produced by the rays of the sun. And we have equal reason to conclude, that we are likewise mechanically connected with these bodies by the law of gravitation. So that the idea thrown out above, however grand and overwhelming to our feeble powers, is not a mere conjecture, but is founded on observation, and on the general analogies of the universe.

† In descending to the minute parts of nature, we obtain *ocular demonstration* of facts which overpower our faculties, and which would be altogether incredible, were they not placed within the evidence of the senses. In a drop of water, in which certain vegetable substances have been infused, *millions* of living creatures have been seen, and, in some instances where the animalculæ are transparent, their eyes, and the peristaltic motion of their bowels have been perceived. The *minuteness* of the blood-vessel, and other parts of the structure of such creatures, is as wonderful, and as incomprehensible, on the one hand, as the magnitude and immensity of the universe are on the other,—demonstrating, that, in the works of the Creator, there is an infinity on either hand, which limited intellects will never be able fully to comprehend.

earth in a measure." "By the word of the Lord were the heavens made, and all the host of them by the Spirit of his mouth." "He spake, and it was done;—He commanded, and it stood fast." "He stretched forth the heavens alone, and bringeth forth their hosts by number." "Lo these are *parts* of his ways, but how little a portion is heard of him; and the thunder of his power who can understand? Behold the heaven, and the heaven of heavens cannot contain him!" "The heavens declare the glory of God, and the firmament showeth forth his handy-work." "Thine, O Lord! is the greatness, and the glory, and the majesty, for all in heaven and earth is thine, and thou art exalted above all." "Behold the heaven and the heaven of heavens is the Lord's." "Jehovah *hath prepared his throne in the heavens*, and his kingdom ruleth over all." "I will speak of *the glorious honour of thy majesty*, and of *thy wondrous works*." "Blessed be thy glorious name who art exalted above all blessing and praise." "Thou, even thou, art Lord alone; thou hast made heaven, the heaven of heavens, with all their host, thou preservest them all, and the host of heaven worshippeth thee." "Who can utter the mighty acts of the Lord? who can show forth *all* his praise?" "Touching the Almighty, we cannot find him out." "He is excellent in power, and his glory is above the earth and heavens."

Such sublime descriptions of the Divine Being, which are interspersed throughout various parts of Revelation, lead us to form the most august conceptions of his creative energy; and plainly indicate, that it is impossible for the highest created intellect to form a more magnificent idea of his designs and operations than what in reality exists.

In short, though some of the preceding views may not precisely correspond to the facts which shall ultimately be found to exist in the universe,—they ought, nevertheless, to be entertained and rendered familiar to the mind, since they open a sublime and interesting train of thinking; and since they cannot go beyond the magnificence of Jehovah's kingdom, nor be very different from what actually exists in the universe. They form a kind of sensible *substratum* of thought for the mind to fix upon, when it attempts to frame the loftiest conceptions of the object of our adoration.—It may be laid down as a principle which ought never to be overlooked in Theology,—that, *our conceptions of the grandeur of God are precisely, or, at least, nearly commensurate with our conceptions of the grandeur and extent of his operations throughout the universe.* We all admit, that the Deity is infinite, both in respect of space and of duration. But, an infinity of empty space, and an infinity of duration, abstractly considered, convey no precise or tangible ideas to the mind, to guide it in forming distinct conceptions of the Deity or of any other beings. It is only when the immensity of space is considered as diversified with an immense variety and multiplicity of objects, and when eternal duration is contemplated as connected with a constant succession of glorious scenes and transactions, that the soul of man can expand its views and elevate its conceptions of the incomprehensible Jehovah.

If these sentiments be admitted, it will follow, that the man whose ideas are confined within limits of a few hundred miles, or even within the range of the globe we inhabit, must have his views of Deity confined within nearly the same sphere. For we have no sensible measures of the attributes of God, but those which are derived from the number and extent of his actual operations. When we attempt to think of Him, without the assistance of his visible works, our thoughts instantly run into confusion, and sink into inanity. And, since we find, that the material works of God are so "great above all measure," so widely extended, and so magnificent in the scale of their operation, it is of the utmost importance, in a religious point of view, that the mind accustom itself to range at large through the wide extent of creation—to trace, by analogy, from what is known, the probable magnitude, arrangement, and grandeur of what is removed beyond the limits of our vision—to add magnitude to magnitude, system to system, and motion to motion, till our thoughts are overwhelmed with the mighty idea. And, though we may occasionally frame some erroneous or inadequate notions, when forming our conceptions of certain subordinate particulars, yet, we need not fear, that in point of number, magnitude, and variety, our conceptions can ever go beyond the realities which exist within the range of universal nature, unless we suppose, that "man can conceive *beyond* what God can do." Such trains of thought will tend to expand and elevate the mind, and give it a sublime turn of thinking; and will naturally produce an ardent desire of beholding a brighter display of the magnificence of the Creator in the eternal world.

From what has been now detailed respecting the numerous and august objects that may be presented to the contemplation of celestial intelligences, we may conclude, that the chief subjects of study in the heavenly world will be *History* and *Philosophy*. Under the department of history, may be comprehended all the details which will be exhibited to them respecting the origin, progress, and consummation of the redemption of man, and the information they may receive respecting the natural and moral scenery, and the prominent providential occurrences and arrangements of other worlds.

As it is evident, that matter exists chiefly for the sake of sensitive and intelligent beings, so, it is highly probable, if not demonstratively certain, that the peopling of worlds with rational creatures is intended chiefly to display the *moral character* of the Creator in his providential dispensations, and in the whole series of his moral administration towards the numerous worlds and orders of creatures which exist throughout his dominions. All his other perfections, particularly his power and intelligence, appear to be exerted in subserviency to this grand object, and to the distribution of happiness throughout the universe. In so far, then, as the facts respecting his moral government, in other worlds, are made known to the redeemed in heaven, in so far will their views of his moral attributes, and of the principles of his administration in the universe, be enlarged and expanded. In the disclosures which, in the course of ages, may be made on this subject, displays of the *eternal righteousness* of Jehovah, of his *retributive justice*, of his "*tender mercy*," and of his *boundless benevolence*, may be exhibited, which will astonish and enrapture the mind more highly than even the magnificence and grandeur of his physical operations, and fill it with admiration of the amiable and adorable excellencies of the Sovereign Ruler of the universe. If we account it a pleasant study to investigate the habits and economy of some of the insect tribes;—if we should reckon it highly gratifying to learn the history of all the events which have befallen every nation and tribe of mankind since the world began, particularly those which relate to our first parents in paradise, and after their expulsion from it,—to the antediluvians, to the ten tribes of Israel, to the Christians in the first centuries, to the Waldenses, to the Assyrians, Babylonians and American Indians,—how delightful and gratifying must it be, to learn the history of angels, principalities and powers, and to become acquainted with the leading transactions which have occurred among beings of a higher order and of different species, dispersed among ten thousands of worlds! Great and marvellous as the history of our world, and of human redemption appears, it may be far surpassed by the events which eternity will unfold. "The day is coming," (to use the words of a celebrated modern writer *) when the whole of this wondrous history shall be looked back upon by the eye of remembrance, and be regarded as one incident in the extended annals of creation, and with all the illustration, and all the glory it has thrown on the character of the Deity, will it be seen as a single step in the evolution of his designs; and as long as the time may appear, from the first act of our redemption to its final accomplishment, and close and exclusive as we may think the attentions of God upon it, it will be found that it has left him him room enough for all his concerns, and that on the high scale of eternity, it is but one of those passing and ephemeral transactions, which crowd the history of a never-ending administration."

Under the department of *Philosophy* may be included all those magnificent displays which will be exhibited of the extent, the magnitude, the motions, the mechanism, the scenery, the inhabitants, and the general constitution of other systems, and the general arrangement and order of the universal system comprehended under the government of the Almighty. On these topics, with all their subordinate and infinitely diversified ramifications, the minds of redeemed intelligences from this world will find ample scope for the exercise of all their powers, and will derive from their investigations of them perpetual and uninterrupted enjoyment, throughout an endless existence.

That the subjects of contemplation now stated, will, in reality, form the chief employments of renovated men and other intellectual beings, in a future state, may also be proved from the representations given in the word of God of the present exercises of these intelligences. In the book of Revelation, the angels, under the figure of "living creatures full of eyes," and the "elders," or representatives of the church of the redeemed, are represented as falling down before the throne of the Eternal, saying, "Thou art worthy, O Lord, to receive glory, honour, and power, *for thou hast created all things, and for thy pleasure they are and were created.*" Here, the material works of God are represented as the *foundation* or *reason* of the thanksgiving and adorations of the heavenly host; and the language evidently implies, that these works are the subject of their contemplation—that they have beheld a bright display of divine perfection in their structure and arrangement—that they are enraptured with the enlarged views of the divine glory which these works exhibit—and that their hearts, full of gratitude and admiration, are ever ready to burst forth in ascriptions of "glory, honour, and power to him" who called the vast assemblage of created beings into existence.—In another scene, exhibited in the same book, the saints who had come out of great tribulation, and had gotten the victory over all enemies, are represented with the harps of God in their hands, celebrating the divine praises in this triumphant song, "Great and marvellous are thy works, Lord God Almighty—just and true are thy ways, thou King of saints."—The first part of this song may be considered as the result of their contemplations of the magnificent fabric of the universe, and the omnipotent energies which its movements display; and the last part of it as the result of their study and investigation of the moral government of God in his providential arrangements towards men and angels, and towards all the worlds whose moral economy may be opened

* Dr. Chalmers.

to their view. For the words of the song plainly imply, that they have acquired such an expansive view of the works of God as constrains them to declare, that they are "great and marvellous;" and that they have attained such an intimate knowledge of the divine dispensations towards the intelligent universe, a senables them to perceive that all the ways of the King of heaven are "righteous and true."

From the preecding details we may also learn, what will form one constituent part of the misery of the wicked in the future world. As one part of the happiness of the righteous will consist in "seeing God as he is," that is, in beholding the divine glory as displayed in the physical and moral economy of the universe,—so, it will, in all probability, form one bitter ingredient in the future lot of the unrighteous, that they shall be deprived of the transporting view of the Creator's glory, as displayed in the magnificent arrangements he has made in the system of nature. Confined to one dreary corner of the universe, surrounded by a dense atmosphere, or a congeries of sable clouds, they will be cut off from all intercourse with the regions of moral perfection, and prevented from contemplating the sublime scenery of the Creator's empire. This idea is corroborated by the declarations of Scripture, where they are represented "as banished from the new Jerusalem," "thrust out into outer darkness," and reserved for "the blackness ot darkness for ages of ages." And, nothing can be more tormenting to minds endowed with capacious powers, than the thought of being for ever deprived of the opportunity of exercising them on the glorious objects which they know to exist, but which they can never contemplate, and about which they never expect to hear any transporting information.

If it be one end of future punishment to make wicked men sensible of their folly and ingratitude, and of the mercy and favours they have abused, it is probable, that, in that future world or region to which they shall be confined, every thing will be so arranged, as to bring to their recollection, the comforts they had abused, and the divine goodness they had despised, and to make them feel sensations opposite to those which were produced by the benevolent arrangements which exist in the present state.—For example, in the present economy of nature, every one of our senses, every part of our bodily structure, every movement of which our animal frame is susceptible, and the influence which the sun, the atmosphere, and other parts of nature, produce on our structure and feelings, have a direct tendency to communicate pleasing sensations. But, in that world, every agency of this kind may be reversed, as to the effect it may produce upon percipient beings. Our sense of *touch* is at present accompanied with a thousand modifications of feelings which are accompanied with pleasure; but *there*, every thing that comes in contract with the organs of feeling may produce the most *painful* sensations. *Here*, the variety of colours which adorn the face of nature, delights the eye and the imagination,—*there*, the most gloomy and haggard objects may at all times produce a dismal and alarming aspect over every part of the surrounding scene. *Here*, the most enchanting *music* frequently cheers, and enraptures the human heart, *there*, nothing is heard but the dismal sounds "weeping, and wailing, and gnashing of teeth." Ungrateful for the manifold blessings they received in this world from the bountiful Giver of all good, the inhabitants of that dreary region will behold their sin in their punishment, in being deprived of every thing which can administer to their sensitive enjoyment.

With regard to their *moral state*, similar effects will be produced. *Here*, they hated the society of the righteous, and loved to mingle with evil doers in their follies and their crimes; *there* they will be for ever banished from the company of the wise and the benevolent, and will feel the bitter effects of being perpetually chained to the society of those malignant associates who will be their everlasting tormentors. *Here* they delighted to give full scope to their depraved appetites and passions, *there*, they will feel the bitter and horrible effects of the full operation of such lusts and passions, when unrestrained by the dictates of reason, and the authority of the divine law. If, to these sources of sorrow and bitter deprivations, be added the consideration, that, in such minds, the principles of malice, envy, hatred, revenge, and every other element of evil, which pervaded their souls while in this life, will rage without control, we may form such a conception of future misery as will warrant all the metaphorical descriptions of it which are given in Divine Revelation, without supposing any farther interposition of the Deity, in the *direct* infliction of punishment. While he leaves them simply to "*eat of the fruit of their own ways, and to be filled with their own devices*," their punishment must be dreadful, and far surpassing every species of misery connected with the present state of the moral world.

On the other hand, a consideration of the infinitely diversified sources of bliss to which our attention has been directed, has a powerful tendency to impress the minds of the saints with a lively perception of the *unbounded* nature of divine benignity, and of "the love of God which is in Christ Jesus our Lord." It is chiefly in connection with such expansive views of the attributes and the government of the Deity, that the love of God towards the redeemed appears "boundless," and "passing comprehension;" for it introduces them into a scene which is not only commensurate with infinite duration, but is boundless in its prospects of knowledge, of felicity, and of glory. And, therefore, amidst all the other employments of the heavenly state, they will never forget their obligation to that unmerited grace and mercy which rescued their souls from destruction, but will mingle with all their sublime investigations,—ascriptions of "blessing, and honour, and glory, and power, to Him that sits upon the throne, and to the Lamb, for ever and ever."

The substance of what has been detailed in this department of my subject may be now briefly stated in the following summary:

The redeemed in heaven will enjoy perpetual and uninterrupted felicity—the foundation of this felicity will be laid in their complete freedom from sin, and their attainment of moral perfection—their renovated faculties will be employed in contemplating the divine glory—the divine glory consists in the manifestation of the divine perfections—the sensible display of these perfections will be given, (and can only be given) in the works of creation, in the intelligences which people the material world, their orders, gradations, history, and present state—in the variety of scenery which the abodes of intelligence exhibit—in the economy and moral order which prevail among them,—and in the various dispensations of Divine Providence in reference to all worlds and orders of beings.

With regard to the happiness of heaven, the Scriptures convey to us, in general propositions, certain intimations of its nature, qualities, and objects, and of the qualifications which are requisite in order to its enjoyment. The discoveries which science has made in the visible creation form so many illustrations of the scriptural declarations on this subject; and it is undoubtedly our duty to direct our trains of thought, and to expand our conceptions of the felicities of the future world, by every illustrative circumstance which can be traced in the scene of nature which the Almighty has presented to our view. For the word and the works of God must always harmonize, and reflect a mutual lustre on each other. What we find to be actually existing within the visible scene of the universe, can never contradict any of the statements of Revelation; but, on the contrary, must tend to elucidate some one or other of its interesting communications. And since we find, in our survey of the system of nature, an assemblage of astonishing objects which tend to raise our conceptions of the Supreme Being, and of the sublime and diversified nature of future felicity,—it becomes us to prosecute those trains of thought which the analogies of Nature and of Revelation suggest, in order to enlarge the capacities of our minds, to exalt our ideas of celestial bliss, and to prepare us for more expansive and sublime contemplations, in that world where the physical and moral obstructions which now impede our progress, and obscure our intellectual views, shall be completely and for ever removed.

From the whole of what we have stated on this department of our subject, we may learn *the value of the human soul*, and *the importance which ought to be attached to our immortal destination.* What a shadow does human life appear when contrasted with the scenes of futurity! What a small point in duration do the revolutions of time present when compared with a boundless eternity! What a limited scene does this world, with all its glories, exhibit, when set in competition with the extent, and the splendours of that empire which stretches out into immensity, and shall endure for ever! And is man to be transported to other regions of the universe, to mingle with the inhabitants of other worlds, and to exist throughout an endless duration? What a noble principle does the human mind appear, when we consider it as qualified to prosecute so many diversified trains of thought, to engage in so sublime investigations, to attain the summit of moral perfection, and to expatiate at large, through the unlimited dominions of the Almighty, while eternal ages are rolling on! How important, then, ought every thing to be considered which is connected with the scene of our eternal destination! If these truths be admitted, reason and common sense declare, that a more interesting and *momentous* subject cannot possibly occupy the mind of man. It is so profoundly interesting, and connected with so many awful and glorious consequences, that we must be utterly dead to every noble and refined feeling, if we be altogether indifferent about it.

If there were only a bare *probability* for the opinion, that man is immortal, and that the scenes to which I have alluded might possibly be realized, it ought to stimulate the most anxious inquiries, and awaken all the powers and energies of our souls. For it is both our duty and our highest interest to obtain light and satisfaction, on a point on which our present comfort and our ultimate happiness must depend. But, if the light of nature, and the dictates of revelation both conspire to *demonstrate* the eternal destiny of mankind, nothing can exceed the folly and the infatuation of those who trifle with their everlasting interests, and even try every scheme, and prosecute every trivial object, that may have a tendency to turn aside their thoughts from this important subject. Yet, how often do we find, in the conduct of the various classes of mankind, the merest trifles set in competition with the scenes of happiness or of misery that lie beyond the grave. The grovelling pleasures derived from hounding and horse-racing, balls, masquerades, and theatrical amusements; the acquisition of a few paltry pounds or shillings, the rattling of dice, or the shuffling of a pack of yards, will absorb the minds of thousands who profess to be rational beings, while they refuse to spend *one serious hour* in reflecting on the fate of their immortal spirits, when their bodies shall have dropped into the tomb. Nay, such is the indifference, and even *antipathy* with which this subject is treated by certain classes of society, that it is considered as unfashionable, and in certain cases, would be regarded as a species of insult, to introduce, in conversation, a sentiment or a reflection on the eternal destiny of man. "The carelessness which they betray in a matter which involves their existence, their eternity, their all, (says an energetic French writer) awakes my indignation, rather than my pity. It is astonishing. It is horrifying. It is monstrous. I speak not this from the pious zeal of a blind devotion. On the contrary, I affirm, that self-love, that self-interest, that the simplest light of reason, should inspire these sentiments; and, in fact, for this we need but the perceptions of ordinary men.—It requires but little elevation of soul to discover, that here there is no substantial delight; that our pleasures are but vanity, that the ills of life are innumerable; and that, after all, death, which threatens us every moment, must, in a few years, perhaps in a few days, place us in the eternal condition of happiness, or misery, or nothingness."

It is, therefore, the imperative duty of every man who makes any pretensions to prudence and rationality, to endeavour to have his mind impressed with a conviction of the reality of a future and invisible world, to consider its importance, and to contemplate, in the light of reason and of revelation, the grand and solemn scenes which it displays. While the least doubt hovers upon his mind in relation to this subject, he should give himself no rest till it be dispelled. He should explore every avenue where light and information may be obtained; he should prosecute his researches with the same earnestness and avidity as the miser digs for hidden treasures; and above all things, he should study, with deep attention and humility, the revelation contained in the Holy Scriptures, with earnest prayer to God for light and direction. And if such inquiries be conducted with reverence, with a devotional and contrite spirit, and with perseverance, every doubt and difficulty that may have formerly brooded over his mind will gradually evanish, as the shades of night before the orient sun. "If thou criest after knowledge, and liftest up thy voice for understanding; if thou seekest her as silver, and searchest for her as for hid treasures—then shalt thou understand the fear of the Lord, and find the knowledge of God. For the Lord giveth wisdom, out of his mouth cometh knowledge and understanding. In all thy ways acknowledge him, and he shall direct thy paths. Then shall thy light break forth in obscurity, and thy darkness shall be as the noon-day."

In fine, if we are thoroughly convinced of our relation to an eternal world, it will be our constant endeavour to cultivate those heavenly dispositions and virtues, and to prosecute that course of action which will prepare us for the enjoyments of the heavenly state. "For without holiness no man can see the Lord; and we are assured that "no unclean thing can enter the gates of the New Jerusalem," and that neither "thieves, nor extortioners, nor the covetous, nor the effeminate, nor drunkards, nor revilers, nor idolaters shall inherit the Kingdom of God."

---

# PART IV.

## ON THE MORAL QUALIFICATIONS REQUISITE TO THE ENJOYMENTS OF THE FELICITY OF THE FUTURE WORLD.

There is scarcely an individual who admits the doctrine of the immortality of man, who does not indulge a certain degree of hope, that he shall be admitted into a happier world, when his spirit wings its way from this earthly scene. Even the man of the world, the profligate and the debauchee, notwithstanding their consciousness of guilt, and of the opposition of their affections to the Divine Law, and the duties of the Christian life, are frequently found buoying themselves up, in the midst of their unhallowed courses, with the vain expectation, that an All-Merciful Creator will not suffer them ultimately to sink into perdition, but will pity their weakness and follies, and receive them, when they die, into the joys of heaven. Such hopes arise from ignorance of the divine character, and of that in which true happiness consists, and from fallacious views of the exercises of a future state and the nature of its enjoyments. For, in order to enjoy happiness in any state, or in any region of the universe, the mind must be imbued with a relish for the society, the contemplations, and the employments peculiar to that region or state, and feel an ardent desire to participate in its enjoyments.

What pleasure would a miser whose mind is wholly absorbed in the acquisition of riches, feel in a world where neither gold nor silver, nor any other object of avarice is to be found? What entertainment would a man whose chief enjoyment consists in hounding, horse-racing, routes, and masquerades, derive in a scene where such amusements are for ever abolished? Could it be supposed that those who now find their highest intellectual pleasures in Novels and Romances, and in listening to tales of scandal, would experience any high degree of enjoyment in a world where there is nothing but substantial realities, and where the inhabitants are united in bonds of the purest affection?—or, that those whose minds never rise beyond the pleasures of gambling, card-playing, and gossipping chit-chat, would feel any relish for the refined enjoyments, the sublime contemplations, and the enraptured praises of the heavenly inhabitants? All the arrangements of the celestial state, behoved to be changed and overturned, and angels, archangels, and redeemed men, banished from its abodes, before such characters could find entertainments agreeable to their former habits and desires. Although they were admitted into the mansions of bliss, they would be miserably disappointed; and would feel themselves in a situation similar to that of a rude savage or a Russian boor, were he to be introduced into an assembly of princes and nobles. They would perceive nothing congenial to their former pursuits; they would feel an inward reluctance to the pure and holy exercises of the place, and they would anxiously desire to fly away to regions and to companions more adapted to their grovelling views and affections. For, it is the decree of Heaven—a decree founded on the moral laws which govern the intelligent universe, and which, like the law of the Medes and Persians, cannot be changed,—that "*Without holiness no man can see the Lord,*" and that "no impure person that worketh abomination, or maketh a lie, can enter within the gates of the Heavenly Jerusalem."

The foundation of felicity in the future state, is substantially the same as that which forms the basis of happiness in the present world. However elevated the station in which an individual may be placed, however much wealth he may possess, and however splendid his rank and equipage, he can enjoy no *substantial* felicity, while he remains the slave of grovelling appetites and affections, and while pride and envy, ambition and revenge, exercise a sovereign control over his mind. While destitute of supreme love to God, and benevolent affections towards man, and of the Christian virtues which flow from these fundamental principles of moral action, the mind must remain a stranger to true happiness, and to all those expansive views, and delightful feelings, which raise the soul above the pleasures of sense, and the trivial vexations and disappointments of the present life.

These positions could be demonstrated, were it necessary, by numerous facts connected with the moral scenery of human society. Whence proceeds that *ennui*, which is felt in the fashionable world, in the absence of balls, parties, operas, and theatrical entertainments? Whence arise those domestic broils, those family feuds and contentions, which are so common in the higher, as well as in the lower ranks of life, and which embitter every enjoyment? Whence does it happen, that, in order to obtain gratification, and to render existence tolerable, so many thousands of rational beings condescend to indulge in the most childish, foolish, and brutal diversions? Even in the most polished circles of society, many who pride themselves on their superiority to the vulgar throng, are found deriving their chief gratification, not only in scattering destruction among the brutal and the feathered tribes but in mingling among the motley rabble of a *cock-pit*, and in witnessing a couple of *boxers* encountering like furious fiends, and covering each other with wounds and gore. Whence arise the torments that are felt from wounded pride and disappointed ambition? and how does it happen that social parties cannot enjoy themselves for a couple of hours, without resorting to cards and dice, gambling and gossipping, and the circulation of tales of scandal? How is it to be accounted for, that suicide is so frequently committed by persons in the higher circles, who are surrounded with luxuries and splendour; and that murmuring, discontentment, and ingratitude, mark the dispositions and conduct of the lower ranks of society? All these effects proceed from the absence of Christian principles and dispositions, and from the narrow range of objects to which the intellectual powers are confined. The man who is actuated by Christian views and affections, looks down with indifference and contempt, on the degrading pursuits to which I have alluded; his soul aspires after objects more congenial to his rational and immortal nature; and in the pursuit of these, and the exercise of the virtues which religion inculcates, he enjoys a refined pleasure which the smiles of the world cannot produce, and which its frowns cannot destroy.

As in the present life there are certain mental endowments necessary for securing substantial happiness, so, there are certain *moral* qualifications *indispensably* requisite in order to prepare us for relishing the entertainments and the employments of the life to come. The foundation of future felicity must be laid in "repentance towards God, and faith towards our Lord Jesus Christ." We must be convinced of our sin and depravity as descendants of the first Adam, of the demerit of our offences, of the spotless purity and eternal rectitude of that Being whom we have offended, and of the danger to which we are exposed as the violators of his law. We must receive, with humility and gratitude, the salvation exhibited in the Gospel, and "behold," with the eye of faith, "the Lamb of God who taketh away the sins of the world." We must depend on the aid of the Spirit of God to enable us to counteract the evil propensities of our nature, to renew our souls after the divine image, and to inspire us with ardent desires to abound all in those "fruit-of righteousness which are to the praise and glory of God." We must "add to our faith, fortitude and resolution, and to fortitude knowledge, and to knowledge, temperance, and to temperance, patience, and to patience, godliness, and to godliness, brotherly kindness and charity. For, if these things be in us and abound, they will permit us to be neither barren nor unfruitful in the knowledge of our Lord Jesus Christ;—and so an entrance shall be abundantly administered unto us into the everlasting kingdom of our Lord and Saviour."*

The foundation of Religion being thus laid in the exercise of such Christian graces, the following dispositions and virtues, among many others, will be cherished and cultivated, and will form substantial qualifications for enabling us to participate in "the inheritance of the saints in light."

1. Supreme love to God, the original source of happiness. This is the first duty of every rational creature, and the most sublime affection that can pervade the human mind. It glows in the breasts of angels and archangels, of cheruhim and seraphim, yea, there is not an inhabitant of any world in the universe who has retained his primitive integrity, in whose heart it does not reign triumphant. It unites all holy intelligences to their Creator and to one another; and consequently, it must qualify us for holding a delightful intercourse with such beings, wherever they exist, and in whatever region of the universe our future residence may be appointed. It enlivens the adorations of the angelic tribes, when they exclaim, "Thou art worthy, O Lord, to receive glory, and honour, and thanksgiving, and power." It animates them in all their celestial services; it inspires them with a noble ardour in executing the commands of their Sovereign, and it qualifies its possessor, to whatever world he may belong, for co-operating with them, in carrying forward that scheme of universal benevolence, towards the accomplishment of which all the arrangements of the Creator ultimately tend.

This holy affection is congenial to every view we can take of the character and operations of the Deity, and its obligation is deduced from the clearest principles of *Reason*, as well as from the dictates of Revelation. It is founded on every attribute of the Divinity, and on every part of his physical and moral administration. His omnipotence is every moment exerted in supporting the frame of the universe, in bringing about the alternate succession of day and night, summer and winter, seed-time and harvest, and in directing the operation of the elements of nature, in such a way as to contribute to the happiness of man. His wisdom and intelligence are displayed in proportionating and arranging every object in the system of nature, in such a manner, that every thing is preserved in order and harmony and in organizing the bodies of men and other creatures, so as to prevent pain, and to produce a combination of pleasurable sensations. His goodness extends over all his works, and is displayed towards every rank of sensitive and intelligent existence. It appears in the splendours of the sun, in the radiance of the moon, in the glories of the starry firmament, in the beautiful assemblage of colours which diversify the face of Nature, in the plants and flowers, which adorn the fields, in the gentle zephyrs, in the rains and dews that fertilize the soil, in the provision made for the sustenance of the innumerable beings that inhabit the air, the waters, and the earth, and "in filling the hearts of men with food and gladness." His mercy and forbearance are exercised towards all men, even to the most profligate and abandoned, in supporting them in existence and loading them with his benefits, even when they are engaged in acts of rebellion against him. For he commandeth his sun to arise on the *evil* as well as on the good, and sendeth rain both on the just and on the *unjust*. He displays his long-suffering, for many years, towards the thoughtless prodigal, and the violators of his law, to demonstrate, that "he desires not that any should perish, but that all should come to repentance."

A Being possessed of such attributes, and incessantly displaying such beneficence throughout creation, demands the highest affection and veneration of all his intelligent offspring; so that it is the dictate of enlightened reason as well as of revelation, "Thou shalt love the Lord thy God with all thy heart, with all thy soul, and with all thy strength." For, it is from him as the original source of felicity, that all our sensitive and intellectual enjoyments proceed, and on him we depend for all the blessings that shall accompany us in every future stage of our existence. Love to God, is therefore, the most reasonable and amiable affection that can glow in the human heart, and the spring of every virtuous action, and of every pleasing and rapturous emotion. If we are possessed of this divine principle, we shall delight in his worship, and bow with reverence at his footstool; we shall feel complacency in his character and administration; we shall contemplate with *admiration*, the incomprehensible knowledge, the omnipotent power, and the boundless beneficence displayed in the mighty movements of creation and providence; we shall feel the most lively emotions of gratitude for the numerous blessings he bestows; we shall be resigned to his will under every providential arrangement, and we shall long for that happy world where the glories of his nature, and the "kindness of his love" shall be more illustriously displayed. But the man who is destitute of this amiable affection, is incapable of those sublime and rapturous emotions which animate the minds of celestial intelligences, and

*2 Peter i. 5, 6, 7, 8, 11 Doddridge's Translation.

altogether unqualified for mingling in their society. He is a rebel against the divine government, a nuisance in the universe of God, the slave of grovelling appetites and passions, and consequently, unfit for participating in the exercises and enjoyments of the saints in glory.

2. *Love to mankind* is another affection which is indispensably requisite to qualify us for participating in the joys of heaven. This distinguishing characteristic of the saints naturally and necessarily flows from love to the Supreme Being. "For (says the apostle John) every one that loveth him who begat, loveth them also who are begotten of him. If God loved us we ought also to love one another. If a man say, I love God, and hateth his brother, he is a liar; for he who loveth not his brother whom he hath seen, how can he love God whom he hath not seen." As the spring flows from the fountain and partakes of its qualities, and as the shadow always accompanies the substance, and is produced by it, so love to man uniformly accompanies the love of God, and is produced by the powerful influence which this governing principle exerts over the mind.

This affection is accordant with the dictates of reason, and congenial to the best feelings of the human heart. When we consider that our fellow-men derived their origin from the same almighty Being who brought *us* into existence—that they are endowed with the same physical functions as ourselves, and the same moral and intellectual powers,—that they relish the same pleasures and enjoyments, possess the same feelings, and are subjected to the same wants and afflictions—that they are involved in the same general depravity, and liable to the same temptations and disasters—that they are journeying along with us to the tomb, and that our dust must soon mingle with theirs—when we consider the numerous relations in which we stand to our brethren around us, and to all the inhabitants of the globe—our dependence upon all ranks and descriptions of men, and upon almost every nation under heaven for our sensitive and intellectual enjoyments,—and that thousands of them are traversing sea and land, and exposing themselves to innumerable dangers, in order to supply us with the comforts and the luxuries of life—when we consider, that they are all destined to an immortal existence, and shall survive the dissolution of this globe, and bear a part in the solemn scenes which shall open to view when time shall be no more—in short, when we consider, that the Great Father of all, without respect of persons, makes the same vital air to give play to their lungs, the same water to cleanse and refresh them, the same rains and dews to fructify their fields, the same sun to enlighten their day, and the same moon to cheer the darkness of their night—we must be convinced, that love to our brethren of mankind is the law of the Creator, and the most rational and amiable affection that can animate the human heart in relation to subordinate intelligences. He who is destitute of this affection is a pest in society, a rebel and a nuisance in the kingdom of God, and, of course, unqualified for the enjoyment of celestial bliss. "For he who hateth his brother, is a *murderer;* and we know that no murderer hath eternal life abiding in him."*

But, our love is not to be confined to our brethren of the race of Adam. It must take a loftier flight, and comprehend within its expansive grasp, all the holy intelligences in the universe, in so far as their nature and qualities have been made known to us. We must love the angelic tribes. They are beings who stand near the summit of the scale of intellectual existence; they are endowed with faculties superior to man; they dwell in the glorious presence of God, and are employed as his ministers in superintending the affairs of his government. They are possessed of wonderful activity, invested with powers of rapid motion, and flourish in immortal youth. They are adorned with consummate holiness and rectitude, and with peculiar loveliness of character. Pride and vanity, envy and malice, wrath and revenge, never rankle in their breasts. They never indulge in impiety, never insult the Redeemer, nor bring a railing accusation against their brethren. They glow with an intense and immortal flame of love to their Creator; they are incessantly employed in acts of benevolence; they occasionally descend to our world on embassies of mercy, and are ministering spirits to the heirs of salvation. On all these accounts they demand our esteem, our approbation, and our affectionate regard. And, although they are at present placed beyond the reach of our beneficence, and we have no opportunity of expressing our benevolent wishes, yet we may afterwards be joined to their society, and co-operate with them in their labours of love.

The indispensable necessity of love to mankind, and to every class of holy intelligences, as a preparation for heaven, will appear, when we consider, that we shall mingle in their society, and hold intimate fellowship with them in the eternal world. For the inhabitants of our world who are admitted into heaven, are represented in Scripture, as joining "the general assembly and church of the first-born, the spirits of just men made perfect and the innumerable company of angels;" and hence they are exhibited, in the book of Revelation, as joining with one heart and one mind in contemplating the divine operations, and in celebrating the praises of their common Lord. In the society of that blessed world, love pervades every bosom, it reigns for ever triumphant; and therefore, every exercise and

* 1 John iii. 15.

intercourse is conducted with affection, harmony, and peace. Among the other evils which shall be banished from the New Jerusalem, it is declared in the book of Revelation, that "there shall be no more *crying*," or, as the words should be rendered, "there shall be no more *clamour*, *broils*, or *contentions*," arising from the operation of malignant principles. No jarring affection is ever felt, no malevolent wish is ever uttered, and no discordant voice is ever heard, among all the myriads of those exalted intelligences. Kindness and benignity expansive, benevolence, condescension and humility, are the characteristics of all the inhabitants of heaven. Without these qualities the celestial world would become a scene of eternal confusion, and happiness would be banished from its abodes. If, therefore, we would be qualified to associate with those glorious beings and to participate in their enjoyments, we must cultivate the same virtues, and be animated by similar dispositions, otherwise, we could experience no delight in the society of angels, and of "the spirits of the just made perfect." Were an individual whose heart is full of rancour and envy, who delights in broils and contentions, and in the exercise of revenge, to be admitted into that society, he would find no associates actuated by congenial feelings, he would disturb the harmony of the celestial choir, and would be instantly expelled, with every mark of indignation and horror, from those blessed abodes. "For what fellowship hath righteousness with unrighteousness? what communion hath light with darkness? and what concord hath Christ with Belial?" By a law which pervades the whole moral universe wherever it extends, which can never be rescinded, and which, like the law of gravitation in the material world, connects all the individuals of which it is composed in one harmonious system; such characters must, of necessity, be for ever excluded from the mansions of the blessed. On the other hand, the man whose heart glows with love to his Creator, and with expansive affection to mankind, and towards all holy beings, is secured of eternal happiness, as *the necessary result* of the possession of such divine principles; and must enjoy felicity, while such principles remain in exercise, during all the future periods of his existence, and in every region of the universe to which he may be transported.

3. *Humility* is another essential qualification for enjoying the felicity of the future world. There is nothing that appears more prominent in the character of the bulk of mankind, than *pride*, which displays itself in a thousand different modes in the intercourses of society. It is uniformly accompanied with haughtiness of demeanour, self-conceit, obstinacy, arrogance, and a whole train of malignant passions and affections. It is the pest of general society, the source of domestic broils and contentions, and the greatest curse that can fall on a Christian church, when it insinuates itself into the minds of those who "love to have the pre-eminence." It is a source of torment to its possessor, and to all around him; and of all the malignant passions which rankle in the human breast, it is the most inconsistent with the present character and condition of man. It is peculiar to fallen and depraved intelligences, for it is certain, from the very constitution of the moral system, that no emotions of pride or haughtiness are ever felt in the breasts of angels, or any other holy beings; because such affections are incompatible with the principle of love to God and to our fellow-creatures.

In opposition to this principle, which predominates in the minds of fallen man, and apostate angels,—*humility* is a distinguishing characteristic of the sons of God, whether on earth or in heaven. Hence, we are told that "God resisteth the proud, but giveth grace to the humble"—that even "a proud look is an abomination in his sight," while he beholds with complacency "the humble and the contrite spirit." Hence, we are exhorted "to clothe ourselves with humility;" and "to forbear one another in all lowliness and meekness of mind, and to esteem others better than ourselves." Humility consists in a just sense of our character and condition, both as depending beings and as apostate creatures, accompanied with a correspondent train of dispositions and affections. However much this disposition has been disrelished by Hume and other infidels, who consider it as both vicious and contemptible,—when viewed in its true light, it appears congenial to the best feelings of our nature, and to the plainest deductions of reason.—When we consider our condition as *creatures*, dependent every moment on a Superior Being "for life, and breath, and all things," when we reflect on the curious organization of our corporeal frame, the thousands of veins, arteries, muscles, bones, lacteals, and lymphatics, which are interwoven through its constitution; the incessant pulsation of the heart in the centre of the system and the numerous other functions and movements over which we have no control, —when we reflect on our *character* as guilty and depraved creatures, in the presence of Him "who is of purer eyes than to behold iniquity;" and on the numerous diseases, pains, sorrows, and physical evils from the war of the elements, to which we are subjected,—when we consider, that, ere long, our bodies must crumble into dust, and become the prey of noisome reptiles;—when we reflect on *the low station in which we are placed in the scale of intelligent existence*—that we are only like so many atoms, or microscopic animalculæ when contrasted with the innumerable myriads of bright intelligences that people the empire of God—and that the globe on which we dwell is but as "the drop of a bucket," when compared with the millions of more resplendent worlds that roll through the vast spaces of creation;—and, in short, when we consider the grandeur of that Omnipotent Being whose presence pervades every region of immensity, and in whose sight "all the inhabitants of the world, are as grasshoppers, and are counted to him as less than nothing and vanity," there is no disposition that appears more conformable to the character and condition of man, than "lowliness of mind," and none more unreasonable and inconsistent with the rank and circumstances in which he is placed, than pride, haughtiness and arrogance.

This amiable disposition forms a peculiar trait in the character of angels and other pure intelligences. It is poor, puny, sinful man, alone, who dares to be proud and arrogant. It is that rebellious worm of the dust *alone*, (if we except the angels of darkness,) that looks down with supercilious contempt on his fellow-creatures, and attempts to exalt himself above the throne of God. No such affections are ever felt in the breast of superior beings who have kept their first estate. In proportion to the enlarged capacity of their minds; in proportion to the expansive views they have acquired of the dominions of Jehovah, in proportion to the elevated conceptions they have attained of the character and attributes of their Creator, in a similar proportion are their minds inspired with *humility*, reverence and lowly adoration. Having taken an extensive survey of the operations of Omnipotence, having winged their way to numerous worlds, and beheld scenes of wisdom and benevolence, which the eye of man hath not yet seen, nor his imagination conceived, and having contemplated displays of intelligence and power, which are beyond the reach even of their own superior faculties to comprehend—they see themselves as finite and imperfect creatures, and even as it were *fools*,* in the presence of Him whose glory is ineffable and whose ways are past finding out.—Hence, they are represented as "covering their faces with their wings," in the presence of their Sovereign;† and, in the Book of Revelation, they are exhibited as "casting their crowns before the throne, and saying thou art worthy, O Lord, to receive glory, and honour, and power."‡ What a striking contrast does such a scene present to the haughty airs, and the arrogant conduct of the proud beings that dwell on this terrestrial ball, who are at the same time immersed in ignorance and folly, immorality and crime!

In their intercourses with the inhabitants of our world, and the offices they perform as ministering spirits to the heirs of salvation, the same humble and condescending demeanor is displayed. One of the highest order of these celestial messengers—"Gabriel, who stands in the presence of God,"—winged his flight from his heavenly mansion to our wretched world, and, directing his course to one of the most despicable villages of Galilee, entered into the hovel of a poor virgin, and delivered a message of joy, with the most affectionate and condescending gratulations. Another of these benevolent beings entered the dungeon in which Peter was bound with chains, knocked off his fetters, addressed him in the language of kindness, and delivered him from the hands of his furious persecutors. When Paul was tossing in a storm, on the billows of the Adriatic, a forlorn exile from his native land, and a poor despised prisoner, on whom the grandees of this world looked down with contempt,—another of these angelic beings, "stood by him," during the darkness of the night and the war of the elements, and consoled his mind with the assurance of the divine favour and protection. Lazarus was a poor despised individual, in abject poverty and distress, and dependent on charity for his subsistence. He lay at the gate of a rich man, without friends or attendants, desiring to be fed with the crumbs that fell from his table. His body was covered with boils and ulcers, which were exposed without covering to the open air; for the "dogs came and licked his sores." What nobleman or grandee would have condescended to make a companion of a fellow-creature in such loathsome and abject circumstances? Who, even of the common people, would have received such a person into their houses, or desired his friendship? Who would have accounted it an honour, when he died, to attend his funeral? Celestial beings, however, view the circumstances, and the characters of men in a very different light, from that in which they appear to "the children of pride." Poor and despised as Lazarus was, a choir of angels descended from their mansions of glory, attended him on his dying couch, and wafted his disembodied spirit to the realms of bliss.

Since, then, it appears, that angelic beings, notwithstanding their exalted stations, and the superior glories of their character, are "clothed with humility,"—it must form a distinguishing trait in our moral characters, if we expect to be admitted into their society in the world to come For how could we enter into harmonious fellowship with these pure intelligences, if we were actuated with dispositions diametrically opposite to theirs, and what happiness would result from such an association, were it possible to be effected? A proud man, were he admitted into heaven, could feel no permanent enjoyment. The external glory of the place might dazzle his eyes for a little, but he would feel no relish for the society and the employments of that world. The peculiar honour conferred on patriarchs, pro-

* In the book of Job, Eliphaz, when describing the perfections of the Almighty, declares, that "the heavens are not clean in his sight," and that even his angels he chargeth with *folly*." Job iv. 18. xv.15.

† Isaiah vi. 2.

‡ Rev. iv. 10, 11

phets, and apostles, and the noble army of martyrs, and the exalted stations of the cherubim and seraphim, would excite his envy and ambition, and, ere long, he would attempt to sow the seeds of discord, and to introduce anarchy and confusion among the hosts of heaven. So that the passion of pride, when cherished in the soul as the governing principle of action, is utterly incompatible with our admission into the regions of harmony and love.

Let me ask the man in whose heart pride and haughtiness predominate, if he really imagines that he can be a candidate for a glorious and immortal existence? Does he not at once perceive the inconsistency of such a thought with the dictates of reason, and the nature of future felicity? —Of what has he any reason to be proud? Is he proud of his *birth?* of his *ancestors?* of his *wealth?* of his *station?* of his *beauty?* of his personal *accomplishments?* of his *gallantry?* of his *debaucheries?* of his military *prowess?* or of *the thousands of human beings he has slain in battle?* Is he proud of his skill in music, in dancing, in fencing, in fox-hunting, and in gambling? of his knowledge in languages, in literature, in arts and sciences? Or is he proud that he is subjected to the asthma, the gravel, the dropsy, and the gout, that his funeral will be attended by a train of mourners, and that a monument of marble will be erected to his memory, when his carcass is putrefying with the reptiles of the dust? Suppose he were admitted into the celestial mansions--which of all these topics would he choose for the theme of his conversation, and the ground of his boasting? Would he attempt to entertain the cherubim and the seraphim, by telling them how many rude chieftains he was descended from, how many ancient families he was connected with, and how many acres of land he possessed as a patrimony in that wretched world which is soon to be wrapt in flames? Would he tell them of his expertness as a marksman, of his dexterity as a horse-racer, of his adroitness as a boxer, of his skill in manœuvring an army, of the villages he had burned, of the towns he had pillaged, or of the thousands he had butchered in storming a city?—He would be overwhelmed with shouts of indignation, and instantly hissed from their abodes.—Would he boast of his skill in languages and antiquities, or of his knowledge in arts and sciences? What a poor *ignoramus*, (if I may use the expression) would he appear in the presence of Gabriel, the angel of God, who has so frequently winged his way, in a few hours, from heaven to earth, and surveyed the regions of unnumbered worlds! Would a poor worm of the earth, whose view is confined within a few miles around it, boast of its knowledge in the presence of beings endowed with such capacious powers, and who have ranged over so vast a portion of the universe of God? And, if he has nothing else to boast of, why is he proud? What a pitiful figure he would make among the *intelligent* and adoring hosts of heaven? While such a disposition, therefore, predominates in the mind, its possessor can enjoy no substantial felicity either in this life or in the life to come.

On the other hand, the man, who, like his Redeemer, is "meek and lowly in heart," has "the witness in himself," that he has obtained the approbation of his God, that he is assimilated to angelic beings in his temper and affections, that he has the principle of eternal life implanted in his soul, and that he is in some measure qualified for joining in the exercises, and enjoying the felicity of the heavenly state. "For thus saith the high and lofty One that inhabiteth eternity, whose name is holy; I dwell in the high and holy place,—*with him also that is of a contrite and humble spirit*, to revive the spirit of the humble, and to revive the heart of the contrite ones."

4. *Active Beneficence*, with all its accompanying virtues, is another characteristic of the man who is training for the heavenly inheritance. Wherever the principle of love to God and man, and the grace of humility are in exercise, they will uniformly lead the individual who is under their influence to "abound in the fruits of righteousness, and to use every active endeavour to promote the comfort and happiness of mankind. He will endeavour, as far as his power and influence extend, to relieve the wants of the poor, the fatherless and the widow, to soothe the disconsolate, to comfort the afflicted, to shelter the houseless and benighted traveller, to instruct the ignorant, and to meliorate the moral and physical condition of every rank of society. He will patronize every scheme which has for its object to remove the evils which exist in the social state—to increase the comforts of mankind—to improve the soil—to facilitate human labour—to clear away nuisances from the habitations of men—to promote order, cleanliness, and domestic enjoyment—to train the minds of the young to knowledge and virtue—to introduce improvement in the mechanical arts, and to diffuse useful science among all ranks. Above all things he will endeavour, in so far as his station and opportunities permit, to promote the spiritual improvement and the *eternal happiness* of mankind, and will study to render all his other exertions subservient to the attainment of this most interesting and momentous object. In contributing to the accomplishment of this end, he will give his countenance and support to every institution, and to every rational scheme which is calculated to promote the knowledge of the scriptures of truth, throughout our own country, and in other lands, and to make known "the salvation of God" over all the earth.—In such benevolent exertions he will persevere, even in the face of every species of opposition, obloquy, and reproach, through the whole course of his existence in this world, till death

transport him to a nobler sphere of action and enjoyment.

The necessity of acquiring habits of active beneficence, in order to our preparation for the felicity of the future world, will appear, if we consider, that heaven is a *social state*, and that a considerable portion of its happiness will consist in the mutual interchange of benevolent affections and beneficent actions. There will, indeed, be no poor and distressed objects to be relieved and comforted, no sorrows to be alleviated, and no physical nor moral evils to be counteracted; for, in the New Jerusalem "there shall be no more death, neither sorrow nor crying, neither shall there be any more pain, for the former things shall have passed away, and God shall wipe away all tears from their eyes." But its inhabitants will be for ever employed in acts of beneficence towards each other, corresponding to their dignified stations, and the circumstances in which they are placed. This is evident from the very nature of *Love*, which pervades the hearts of the whole of that "multitude which no man can number." Love can be manifested only by its *effects*, or by those external acts of kindness and benignity which tend to communicate happiness to others; and, there can be no doubt, that, in a thousand ways incomprehensible to us, the inhabitants of the upper world will be the means of diffusing ecstatic delight through the bosoms of surrounding intelligences, which will form a part of that joy which is "unspeakable and full of glory." The sympathetic feelings they will express for each other, both in respect to their former and their present condition, the interest they will take in listening to each other's history, the scenes of felicity to which they will conduct each other, the noble and enrapturing subjects of conversation with which they will entertain one another, the objects of beauty and sublimity to which they will direct each other's attention, the lectures on divine subjects, which the more capacious and exalted spirits among them may deliver to their younger brethren of "the church of the first-born," and the intelligence from distant worlds which the seraphim may communicate, on returning from their embassies of love to other regions—may form a part of those beneficent services, into which every inhabitant of that world will engage with peculiar pleasure. To communicate happiness in every possible mode, to make surrounding associates exult with joy, and to stimulate them to celebrate the praises of the "Giver of all Good," will be their unceasing desire and their everlasting delight.

We have every reason to believe, that a vast system of universal Benevolence is going on throughout the universe of God, and that it is the grand object of his moral government to distribute happiness among unnumbered worlds. In prosecuting this object, he employs created intelligences, as his ministers in accomplishing his designs, and for communicating enjoyment to each other. With respect to the angels, we are informed by Paul, that "they are all *ministering spirits*, sent forth to minister to them who shall be heirs of salvation." Hence we learn from sacred history, that they delivered Peter from the fury of Herod and the Jewish rulers,—Daniel from the ravenous lions—Lot from the destruction of Sodom, and Jacob from the hands of Esau; that they strengthened and refreshed Elijah in the wilderness, comforted Daniel when covered with sackcloth and ashes, directed Joseph and Mary in their journey to Egypt, and Cornelius to Peter, to receive the knowledge of salvation; that they communicated "good tidings of great joy" to Zacharias the father of John the Baptist, to the Virgin Mary, and to the shepherds in the plains of Bethlehem, and consoled the hearts of the disconsolate disciples, by proclaiming the resurrection of their Lord and Master;—and we have reason to conclude, that such ministrations are appointed to be continued throughout all the periods of time.

It is not improbable that the spirits of just men made perfect are likewise occasionally employed in similar services. When the vision of the New Jerusalem was exhibited to John by a celestial messenger, he "fell down to worship before the feet of the messenger, who showed him these things." But the messenger forbade him, saying,—"See thou do it not; for *I am thy fellow-servant, and of thy brethren the prophets*, and of them that keep (or are interested in) the sayings of this book." These words would naturally lead us to conclude, that this messenger was a departed saint, since he designates himself a *brother*, a *prophet*, and a *fellow-servant*. Perhaps it was the spirit of Moses, of David, of Isaiah, of Jeremiah, or of Daniel, who would account it an honour to be employed in such a service by their exalted Lord. But whether or not such a supposition may be admitted, certain it is, that the saints will hereafter be employed in active beneficent services, in concert with other holy beings, so long as their existence endures. For they are constituted "Kings and Priests to the God and Father of our Lord Jesus Christ," and are "workers together with God," in carrying forward the plans of his government.

Since, then, it appears, that the inhabitants of heaven are incessantly employed in acts of beneficence, the habit of beneficence which is acquired in this world, along with its accompanying virtues, may be considered as a preparation and a qualification for that more extensive sphere of moral action into which the saints shall be introduced, when they wing their way from this earthly ball to the regions above. And, consequently, those who never engage in "works of faith and labours of love," and who are governed by a principle of *selfishness* in the general tenor of their conduct, must be considered as unqualified for taking a part in the benevolent employments of the celestial world.*

Let us now consider for a little, the happiness which must flow from an association with intelligent beings animated with the sublime principles and holy dispositions to which I have now adverted.

In the present world, one of the principal sources of misery, arises from the malevolent dispositions, and immoral conduct of its inhabitants. Pride, ambition, malignant passions, falsehood, deceit, envy, and revenge, which exercise a sovereign sway over the hearts of the majority of mankind—have produced more misery and devastation among the human race, than the hurricane and the tempest, the earthquake and the volcano, and all the other concussions of the elements of nature. The lust of *ambition* has covered kingdoms with sackcloth and ashes, levelled cities with the ground, turned villages into heaps of smoking ruins, transformed fertile fields into a wilderness, polluted the earth with human gore, slaughtered thousands and millions of human beings, and filled the once cheerful abodes of domestic life, with the sounds of weeping, lamentation, and woe. *Injustice* and violence have robbed society of its rights and privileges, and the widow and fatherless of their dearest enjoyments. Superstition and revenge have immolated their millions of victims, banished peace from the world, and subverted the order of society. The violation of truth in contracts, affirmations, and promises, has involved nations in destruction, undermined the foundations of public prosperity, blasted the good name and the comfort of families, perplexed and agitated the minds of thousands and millions, and thrown contempt on the revelations of heaven, and the discoveries of science. Malice, envy, hatred, and similar affections, have stirred up strifes and contentions, which have invaded the peace of individuals, families, and societies, and imbittered all their enjoyments. It is scarcely too much to affirm, that more than nine-tenths of all the evils, perplexities, and sorrows, which are the lot of suffering humanity, are owing to the wide and extensive operation of such diabolical principles and passions.

What a happiness, then, must it be, to mingle in a society where such malignant affections shall never more shed their baleful influence, and where love, peace, and harmony, mutual esteem, brotherly-kindness and charity, are for ever triumphant! To depart from a world where selfishness and malignity, strife and dissensions, wars and devastations so generally prevail, and to enter upon a scene of enjoyment where the smiles of benevolence beam from the countenances of unnumbered glorious intelligences, must raise in the soul the most ecstatic rapture, and be the ground-work of all those other "pleasures which are at God's right hand for evermore."—Even in this world, amidst the physical evils which now exist, what a scene of felicity would be produced, were all the illustrious philanthropic characters now living, or which have adorned our race in the ages that are past, to be collected into one society, and to associate exclusively, without annoyance from "the world that lieth in wickedness!" Let us suppose a vast society composed of such characters as Moses, Elijah, Jeremiah, Daniel, Paul, James and John, the Evangelists, men who accounted it their highest honour to glorify God and to promote the salvation of mankind,—such philanthropists as Howard, Clarkson, Venning, and Sharpe, who displayed the most benignant affections, and spent their mortal existence in unwearied efforts to meliorate the condition of the prisoner, and relieve the distresses of the wretched in every land—to deliver the captive from his oppressors—to unloose the shackles of slavery—to pour light and vital air into the noisome dungeon, and to diffuse blessings among mankind wherever they were found;—such profound philosophers as Locke, Newton, and Boyle, whose capacious intellects seemed to embrace the worlds both of matter and of mind, and who joined to their mental accomplishments, modesty, humility, equanimity of temper, and general benevolence;—such amiable divines as Watts, Doddridge, Bates, Hervey, Edwards, Lardner, and Dwight, whose hearts burned with zeal to promote the glory of their Divine Master, and to advance the present and everlasting interest of their fellowmen. To associate perpetually with such characters, even with the imperfections and infirmities which cleaved to them in this sublunary region, would form something approaching to a paradise on earth.

But, let us suppose such characters divested of every moral and mental imperfection, endowed with every holy principle and virtue that can adorn a created intelligence, and with capacious intellectual powers in vigorous and incessant exercise, dwelling in a world where every natural evil is removed, where scenes of glory meet the eye at every step, and where boundless prospects stretch before the view of the enraptured mind. Let us further suppose, intelligences invested with faculties far more energetic and sublime—who have ranged through the immen-

* This subject might have been illustrated at greater length; but as the author has already had occasion to enter into a minute discussion of the principles of moral action, and their relation to the inhabitants of all worlds, in his work on "The Philosophy of Religion,"—he refers his readers to that treatise, for a more ample elucidation of the several topics, to which he has briefly adverted in the preceding pages—particularly to Chap. I. throughout, Chap. II. Section 3, 4, 5, 6, 8, and the *General Conclusions*.

sity of creation, who have mingled with the inhabitants of ten thousand worlds, who have learned the history of the divine dispensations in relation to them all, and who are inspired with every amiable and benignant feeling, and with humility, love and condescension;—let us suppose ambassadors of this description, from numerous worlds, occasionally joining this celestial society, and "rehearsing the mighty acts of Jehovah," as displayed in the regions from whence they came,—let us suppose, "the man Christ Jesus" president among them, in the effulgence of his glory, and unfolding his peerless excellences to every eye,—let us suppose these glorious beings engaged in conversations, contemplations, investigations, thanksgivings, adorations, and beneficent services, corresponding to the magnificence of the region in which they reside, and to the dignity of their natures—and we have a faint picture of the social enjoyments of the celestial world. This is the society of heaven, the general assembly of the church triumphant, for which we must now be inspired with a divine relish and for which we must now be prepared in the temper and disposition of our minds, if we expect to be hereafter admitted into that "house not made with hands which is eternal in the heavens."

O blessed and glorious society! where no contentions ever arise, where no malignant spirit interrupts the universal harmony, where no malevolent affection is ever displayed, where no provocation disturbs the serenity of the mind, where not one revengeful thought arises against the most depraved inhabitant of the universe, where a single falsehood is never uttered, where folly, impertinence and error never intrude, where no frown sits lowering on the countenance, and no cloud ever intercepts the sunshine of benevolence!—where "Holiness to the Lord" is inscribed on every heart, where every member is knit to another by the indissoluble bonds of affection and esteem, where a friendship is commenced which shall never be dissolved, where love glows in every bosom, and benignity beams from every countenance, where moral excellence is displayed in its most sublime, and diversified, and transporting forms, where "a multitude which no man can number, from all nations, and kindreds, and people, and tongues," join in unison with angels and archangels, principalities and powers, in swelling the song of salvation to Him that sits upon the throne, and to the Lamb that was slain, for ever and ever!—ye glorious hosts of heaven, who minister to the heirs of salvation on earth! Ye redeemed inhabitants from our world, "who came out of great tribulation, and are now before the throne of God, and serve him day and night in his temple!" we long to join your blessed society. You dwell amidst scenes of magnificence and the splendours of eternal day;—you are for ever secure from sin and sorrow, and every evil annoyance;—your joys are uninterrupted, ever increasing, and ever new;—your prospects are boundless as the universe, and your duration permanent as the throne of the Eternal!—We dwell "in houses of clay whose foundation is in the dust:" we sojourn in "a land of pits and snares," and within "the region of the shadow of death:" we walk amidst scenes of sorrow and suffering, surrounded by "the tents of strife," and exposed to the malice of "lying lips and deceitful tongues!" From our earthly prison, to which we are now chained as "prisoners of hope," we lift up our eyes to your happy mansions, with longing desires, and exclaim, "O that we had the wings of a seraph, that we might fly away to your blissful seats and be at rest!" We long to join "the general assembly and church of the first-born, which are written in heaven—the spirits of just men made perfect—the innumerable company of angels—Jesus the Mediator of the new covenant, and God the Judge of all."

May the Father of all mercies, who hath begotten us to the lively hope of an incorruptible inheritance, grant that we may persevere in the Christian course, be kept from falling, be "guarded by his almighty power, through faith unto salvation," and that in due time, an entrance may be abundantly administered to us into the everlasting kingdom of our Lord and Saviour Jesus Christ." To whom be glory for ever and ever. Amen.

From the subject to which our attention has now been directed, we may learn, what will constitute one bitter ingredient in the punishment that awaits the wicked in the future world. As the principle of love, which pervades the minds of the inhabitants of heaven, with the diversified ramifications into which it diverges, forms the groundwork of all the other enjoyments of the celestial world,—so the principle of malignity which predominates in the hearts of the wicked, will be the source of the greater part of that misery they are doomed to suffer in the eternal state.—"We cannot form a more dreadful picture of future punishment than by conceiving the principles of falsehood, deceit, and malignity, and the passions of pride, hatred, malice, and revenge, raging with uncontrolled and perpetual violence. We need represent to ourselves nothing more horrible in the place of punishment, than by supposing the Almighty simply permitting wicked men to give full scope to their malevolent dispositions; leaving them 'to eat of the fruit of their own ways, and to be filled with their own devices.' The effects produced by the uncontrolled operation of such principles and passions, would be such as may be fitly represented by the emblems of the worm that never dies, of 'devouring fire,' and of their necessary concomitants, 'weeping and wailing and gnashing of teeth.'"*

* Philosophy of Religion, pp. 55. 58.

In order to illustrate this sentiment, and to impress it more deeply upon the mind of the reader, I shall select two or three facts in relation to certain characters whose names stand conspicuous in the annals of history.

Every reader of history is acquainted with the character and actions of *Antiochus Epiphanes*, whose name stands so high on the rolls of impiety and crime. Having besieged the city of Jerusalem, he took it by storm, and, during the three days it was abandoned to the fury of the soldiers, he caused forty thousand* men to be inhumanly butchered: he exercised every species of cruelty upon the citizens, and unmercifully put to death all those who fell into his hands, and whom he considered as his enemies. He despatched Appollonius at the head of 22,000 men, with orders to plunder *all the cities of Judea*, to murder all the men, and sell the women and children for slaves. He accordingly came with his army, and to outward appearance, with a peaceable intention; neither was he suspected by the Jews, as he was superintendent of the tribute in Palestine. He kept himself inactive till the next Sabbath, when they were all in a profound quiet, and then, on a sudden, began the work of slaughter. He sent a portion of his men to the temple and synagogues, with orders to cut to pieces all who were found in these places of resort; whilst the rest going through the streets of the city, massacred all who came in their way. He next ordered the city to be plundered and set on fire, pulled down all their stately buildings, and carried away captive ten thousand of those who had escaped the slaughter. Not yet satisfied with the blood of the Jews, Antiochus resolved either totally to abolish their religion, or to destroy their whole race. He issued a decree that all nations within his dominions should forsake their old religion and gods, and worship those of the king, under the most severe penalties. He dedicated the temple at Jerusalem to Jupiter Olympus, and set up his own statue on the altar of burnt-offering; and all who refused to come and worship this idol were either massacred or put to some cruel tortures, till they either complied or expired under the hands of the executioners. He put to death Eleazar, one of the most illustrious of the Jews, a venerable old man, ninety years of age, and a doctor of the law, "whose life had been one continued series of spotless innocence," and his execution was accompanied with the most cruel torments. He seized the *seven brothers* commonly called the *Maccabees*, along with their mother, and caused them to be scourged in a most inhuman manner, in order to compel them to swallow swine's flesh, which their law forbade, and when they refused, he was so exasperated that he ordered brazen pans and cauldrons to be heated; and, when they were red, he caused the tongue of the eldest to be cut off—had the skin torn from his head, and the extremities of his hands and feet cut off, before his mother and his brethren. After being mutilated, he was brought close to the fire, and fried in the pan. The second brother was then taken, and, after the hair of his head, with the skin, was torn away, he was tortured in the same manner as his elder brother; and in like manner were the other five brethren put to death,—the last of whom, who was the youngest, he caused to be tortured more grievously than the rest. Last of all the mother also suffered death.†

Hearing, some time afterwards, that the Jews had revolted, he assembled all his troops, which formed a mighty army, and determind to destroy the whole Jewish nation, and to settle other people in their country. He commanded Lysias, one of his generals, to extirpate them root and branch, so as not to leave one Hebrew in the country. When in Persia advice was brought him of the defeat of Lysias, and that the Jews had retaken the temple, thrown down the altars and idols which he had set up, and re-established their ancient worship. At this news his fury rose to madness. In the violence of his rage, he set out with all possible expedition, like an infernal fiend, venting nothing but menaces on his march, and breathing only final ruin and destruction to every inhabitant of Judea, and to all that appertained to them. He commanded his coachman to drive with the utmost speed, that no time might be lost for fully satiating his vengeance, threatening at the same time, with horrid imprecations, to make Jerusalem the burying place of the whole Jewish nation, and not to leave one single inhabitant within its confines. But the Almighty, against whose providence he was raging, interposed, and stopped him in his wild career. "He was seized," says Rollin, "with incredible pains in his bowels, and the most excessive pangs of the colic." Still, his pride and fury were not abated: he suffered himself to be hurried away by the wild transport of his rage, and breathing nothing but vengeance against the land of Judea and its inhabitants, he gave orders to proceed with still greater celerity in his journey. But as his horses were running forward impetuously, he fell from his chariot, and bruised every part of his body in so dreadful a manner, that he suffered inexpressible torments; and soon after finished an impious life by a miserable death.

The Turks, in their wars with neighbouring states, both in former and present times, have been proverbial for the malevolence they have displayed, and the cruelties they have exercised towards their enemies. The following is only one instance out of a thousand which might be produced, of the desperate length to which human beings will proceed in treachery and in the in-

* Rollin states the number at 80,000.

† The details of these shocking cruelties may be seen in Rollin's Ancient History, vol. 7.

fliction of torment, when under the influence of a principle of malignity.

In the war with Turkey and the states of Venice, about the year 1571, the Venetians were besieged by the Turks in the city of Famagosta in the island of Cyprus. Through famine and want of ammunition, the Venetian garrison was compelled to enter upon terms of capitulation. A treaty was accordingly set on foot, and hostages exchanged. The following terms were agreed to by both parties:—That the officers and soldiers should march out with all the honours of war, drums beating, colours flying, five pieces of cannon, all their baggage, and be conveyed in safety to Candia, under an escort of three Turkish gallies; and that the inhabitants should remain in the free use of their religion, untouched in their property, and in full possession of their freedom. Next day *Bragadino*, the Venetian commander, went to pay his compliments to *Mustapha*, the Turkish general, attended by some of his chief officers. At first they met with a civil reception, Mustapha ordering a seat to be placed for Bragadino on his own right hand.

They soon entered into discourse about the prisoners, and Mustapha taxing Bragadino with some violences committed by the garrison during the suspension granted for settling a capitulation, Bragadino, with a generous disdain, denied the charge. Upon which Mustapha, rising up in a fury, ordered him to be bound hand and foot, and the others to be massacred before his face, without regard to hospitality, their bravery, the treaty subsisting, or their being unarmed.

Bragadino was reserved for a more cruel treatment: after being insulted with the most vilifying and opprobrious language; after undergoing the most excrutiating tortures; after having his ears, nose, and lips slit, his neck was stretched upon a block, and trampled upon by the dastardly Mustapha, who asked him where was now that *Christ* whom he worshipped, and why he did not deliver him out of his hands? At the same time the soldiers on board the fleet were despoiled of every thing, and lashed to the oars. This day's work being finished, Mustapha entered the city, where he gave immediate orders, that Tiepolo, a person of high rank and authority, should be hanged upon a gibbet. A few days after, before Bragadino had recovered from the wounds he had received, he was carried in derision to all the breaches made in the walls, loaded with buckets filled with earth and mortar, and ordered to kiss the ground as often as he passed by Mustapha, a spectacle that raised pangs of pity in the callous hearts of the meanest Turkish soldiers, but could not move compassion in the obdurate breast of Mustapha. Afterwards, the brave Bragadino was cooped up in a cage, and ignominiously hung to a sail-yard in one of the gallies, where his intrepid soldiers were chained to the oars. This sight rendered them almost furious: they exclaimed against the baseness, the treachery of Mustapha; they called aloud for revenge, and desired to be set at liberty, that they might, even without arms, rescue their brave general, and inflict the deserved punishment upon their mean, dastardly, and cowardly foes. Their request was answered with cruel lashes Bragadino was taken down, conducted to the market-place, amidst the din of trumpets, drums, and other warlike instruments, where *he was flayed alive*, and a period put to his glorious life. His skin was hung, by way of trophy, to the sail-yard of a galley sent round all the coasts to insult the Venetians. His head, with those of Andrea Bragadino, his brother, Lodovico Martinenga, and the brave Quirino, were sent as presents to Selim the Turkish Emperor.*

Could an infernal fiend have devised more excruciating tortures, or have acted with greater baseness and malignity than this treacherous and cruel monster? What a horrible thing would it be to be subjected to the caprice and under the control of such a proud and vindictive spirit every day, only for a year, much more for hundreds and thousands of years! A group of such spirits giving vent to their malevolent passions without control, are sufficient to produce a degree of misery among surrounding intelligences, surpassing every thing that the human mind, in the present state, can possibly conceive.

When the Norman barons and chevaliers, under William the Conqueror, had obtained possession of England, they displayed the most cruel and malignant dispositions towards the native inhabitants. They afflicted and harassed them in every state, forcing them to work at the building of their castles; and when the castles were finished, they placed on them a garrison of wicked and diabolical men. They seized all whom they thought to possess any thing—men and women—by day and night; they carried them off; imprisoned them; and, to obtain from them gold or silver, inflicted on them tortures such as no martyrs ever underwent. Some they suspended by their feet, with their heads hanging in smoke; others were hung by the thumb, with fire under their feet. They pressed the heads of some by a leathern thong, so as to break the bones, and crush the brain; others were thrown into ditches full of snakes, toads, and other reptiles; others were put in the *chambre à crucit*. This was the name given in the Norman tongue to a sort of chest, short, strait, and shallow, lined with sharp stones, into which the sufferer was crammed to the dislocation of his limbs.—In most of the castles was a horrible and frightful engine used for putting to the torture. This was a bundle of chains so heavy that two or three men could hardly lift them. The unfortunate person upon whom

* See "Modern Universal History," vol. 27, pp. 405, 406.

they were laid, was kept on his feet by an iron collar fixed in a post, and could neither sit, nor lie, nor sleep. They made many thousands die of hunger. They laid tribute upon tribute on the towns and villages. When the towns-people had no longer any thing to give, they plundered and burned the town. You might have travelled a whole day without finding one soul in the towns, or in the country one cultivated field. The poor died of hunger, and they who had formerly possessed something, now begged their bread from door to door. Never were more griefs and woes poured upon any land;—nay the Pagans in their invasions caused fewer than the men of whom I now speak. They spared neither the church-yards, nor the churches; they took all that could be taken, and then set fire to the church. To till the ground had been as vain as to till the sand on the sea-shore.*

What scenes of wretchedness do such proud and malignant demons produce even in the present world! Can such spirits be supposed qualified for joining the general assembly and church of the first-born, and for taking a part in the beneficent operations of heaven? If they exist at all in a future world, they must exist in misery; and so long as such diabolical passions continue to rage, they must produce "lamentation and wo" among all the associates with which they are surrounded.—Even within the confines of mortality, the man who is under the despotic sway of pride, ambition, and similar malevolent passions, imbitters every enjoyment he might otherwise possess, produces pain in the minds of others, and experiences in his own soul pangs similar in kind to those which are felt in the place of punishment. I shall illustrate this position by the spirit and temper displayed by two illustrious individuals who have lately departed to the invisible state;—the one renowned in the political, the other in the literary world.

The first character to which I allude is that of *Napoleon Buonaparte.* This extraordinary man, who for nearly twenty years dazzled the whole Eastern hemisphere, like a blazing meteor, appears to have been actuated by the most extravagant and restless *ambition.* Though he exercised many cruelties in the midst of his career, as at Jaffa and other places, yet delight in deeds of atrocity formed no part of his ruling passion, and were only occasionally resorted to, in order to accomplish his ambitious projects. The agitated state of mind into which he was thrown by his love of conquest, and the daring enterprises in which he embarked, is strikingly depicted by M. Segur, in his "History of Napoleon's Expedition to Russia." When at Vitepsk, on his way to Moscow, M. Segur says—"He at first hardly appeared bold enough to confess to himself a project of such great temerity—[the marching against Moscow.] But by degrees he assumed courage to look it in the face. He then began to deliberate, and the state of great irresolution which tormented his mind, affected his whole frame. He was observed to wander about his apartments, as if pursued by some dangerous temptation: nothing could rivet his attention; he every moment began, quitted, and resumed his labour; he walked about without any object; inquired the hour, and looked at his watch;—completely absorbed, he stopped, hummed a tune with an absent air, and again began walking about. In the midst of his perplexity, he occasionally addressed the persons whom he met with such half sentences as 'Well —What shall we do!—Shall we stay where we are, or advance?—How is it possible to stop short in the midst of so glorious a career?' He did not wait for their reply, but still kept wandering about, as if he was looking for something, or somebody, to terminate his indecision.—At length, quite overwhelmed with the weight of such an important consideration, and oppressed with so great an uncertainty, he would throw himself on one of the beds which he had caused to be laid on the floor of his apartments. His frame, exhausted by the heat and the struggles of his mind, could only bear a covering of the slightest texture. It was in that state that he passed a portion of his day at Vitepsk."

The same restless agitations seemed to have accompanied him at every step in this daring expedition. "At Borodino," says the same writer, "his anxiety was so great as to prevent him from sleeping. He kept calling incessantly to know the hour, inquiring if any noise was heard, and sending persons to ascertain if the enemy was still before him,—Tranquillized for a few moments, anxiety of an opposite description again seized him. He became frightened at the destitute state of the soldiers, &c. He sent for Bessieres, that one of his marshals in whom he had the greatest confidence:—he called him back several times, and repeated his pressing questions, &c. Dreading that his orders had not been obeyed, he got up once more, and questioned the grenadiers on guard at the entrance of his tent, if they had received their provisions. Satisfied with the answer, he went in, and soon fell into a doze. Shortly after he called once more. His aid-de-camp found him now supporting his head with both his hands; he seemed, by what was overheard, to be meditating on the *vanities of glory.*—'*What is war? A trade of barbarians, the whole art of which consists in being the strongest on a given point.*' He then complained of the fickleness of fortune, which he now began to experience. He again tried to take some rest. But the marches he had just made with the army, the fatigues of the preceding days and nights, so many cares, and his

* Thierry's "History of the Norman Conquest," 3 vols. 1825.

intense and anxious expectations, had worn him out. An irritating fever, a dry cough, and excessive thirst consumed him. During the remainder of the night he made vain attempts to quench the burning thirst that consumed him."

What man that ever enjoyed the pleasures of tranquillity, would envy such a state of mind as that which has now been described, although the individual were surrounded with every earthly glory? Such mad ambition as that which raged in the breast of this singular personage, must be a perpetual torment to its possessor, in whatever region of the universe he exists, and must produce baleful effects on every one within the sphere of its influence.—The coolness with which such characters calculate on the destruction of human life, and the miseries which their lawless passions produce on their fellow-creatures, appears in the following extract.

"He asked Rapp, if he thought we should gain the victory? 'No doubt,' was the reply, 'but it will be sanguinary.' 'I know it,' resumed Napoleon, 'but I have 80,000 men; I shall lose 20,000; I shall enter Moscow with 60,000; the stragglers will then rejoin us, and afterwards the battalions on the march; and we shall be stronger than we were before the battle.'"

The other personage to whom I alluded is Lord Byron.

The following sketches of his character are taken from "Recollections of the life of Lord Byron, from the year 1808 to the year 1818. Taken from authentic documents, &c. by R. C. Dallas, Esq."

"He reduced his palate," says Mr. Dallas, "to a diet the most simple and abstemious—but the passions of his heart were too mighty; nor did it ever enter his mind to overcome *them*. Resentment, anger, and hatred, held full sway over him; and his greatest gratification at that time, was in overcharging his pen with gall, which flowed in every direction, against individuals, his country, the world, the universe, creation, and the Creator.—Misanthropy, disgust of life, leading to skepticism and impiety, prevailed in his heart, and imbittered his existence. Unaccustomed to female society, he at once dreaded and abhorred it. As for domestic happiness he had no idea of it. 'A large family,' he said, 'appeared like opposite ingredients, mixed *per* force in the same salad, and I never relished the composition.' He was so completely disgusted with his relations, especially the female part of them, that he completely avoided them. 'I consider,' said he, 'collaterial ties as the work of prejudice, and not the bond of the heart, which must choose for itself unshackled.'—In correspondence with such dispositions and sentiments, "he talked of his relation to the Earl of Carlisle with indignation." Having received from him a frigid letter, "he determined to lash his relation with all the gall he could throw into satire."—He declaimed against the ties of consanguinity, and abjured even the society of his sister, from which he entirely withdrew himself, until after the publication of "Childe Harold," when at length he yielded to my persuasions, and made advances to a friendly correspondence."

Here we have a picture of an individual, in whom "resentment, anger, and hatred," reigned without control: who could vent his rage even against the Creator, and the universe he had formed, who hated his fellow-creatures, and even his own existence; who spurned at the ties of relationship, and "abjured even the society of his sister." What horrible mischiefs and miseries would a character of this description produce, were such malevolent passions to rage with unbounded violence, without being checked by those restraints, which human laws impose in the present state!

I shall state only another example of this description, taken from Captain Cochrane's "Travels in Russia."—On arriving at the Prussian frontiers, says the captain, "My passport demanded, myself interrogated by a set of whiskered ruffians, obliged to move from one guard to another, the object of sarcasm and official tyranny, I wanted no inducement, fatigued as I was, to proceed on my journey, but even this was not permitted me. A large public room, full of military rubbish, and two long benches serving as chairs, to an equally long table, were the place and furniture allotted me. I asked the landlord for supper; he laughed at me; and to my demand of a bed, *grinningly* pointed to the floor, and refused me even a portion of the straw which had been brought in for the soldiers. Of all the demons that ever existed, or have been imagined in human shape, I thought the landlord of the inn the blackest. The figure of Gil Peres occurred to me, but it sunk in the comparison with the wretch then before me for ill nature, malignity, and personal hideousness. His face half covered with a black beard, and large bristly whiskers, his stature below the common, his head sunk between his shoulders to make room for the protuberance of his back; his eyes buried in the ragged locks of his lank grisly hair;—added to this a club foot, and a voice which, on every attempt to speak, was like the shrieking of a screech-owl,—and you have some faint idea of this mockery of a man."—Here, we have presented to view a human being, who, in the malignity of his mind, and in the conformation of his body, bears a certain resemblance to those wretched beings in whose or--ts benevolence never glows, and in whose dwellings nothing is seen but the most haggard and deformed objects, and nothing heard but horrid imprecations, and the sounds of wo.

Let us now suppose, for a moment, a vast

assemblage of beings of the description to which I have adverted, collected in a dark and dreary region. Let us suppose many thousands of millions of such characters as *Nero*, who set fire to Rome, that he might amuse himself with the wailings and lamentations which this calamity inspired, and insulted Heaven by offering thanksgivings to the gods, after murdering his wife and his mother,—*Tiberius* who delighted in torturing his subjects, and massacring them in the most tormenting and cruel manner,—*Caligula*, celebrated in the annals of folly, cruelty, and impiety, who murdered many of his subjects with his own hand, and caused thousands who were guilty of no crimes to be cruelly butchered, —*Antiochus Epiphanes*, who butchered forty thousand of the inhabitants of Jerusalem in cold blood, and rushed forward, like an infernal demon, with the intention of destroying every inhabitant of Judea,—*Hamilcar*, who threw all the prisoners that came into his hand, to be devoured by wild beasts,—*Asdrubal*, who put out the eyes of all the Roman captives he had taken during two years, cut off their noses, fingers, legs, and arms, tore their skin to pieces with iron rakes and harrows, and threw them headlong from the top of his battlements,—*Jenghiz Khan*, who caused seventy chiefs to be thrown into as many caldrons of boiling water, and took pleasure in beholding his army beheading a hundred thousand prisoners at once,—*Tamerlane*, who displayed his sportive cruelty in pounding three or four thousand people in large mortars, or building them among bricks and mortar into a wall,—*Mustapha*, who treacherously murdered the Venetian officers, after having entered into a treaty with them, and who beheld with delight the noble-minded Bragadino, whom he had cruelly tortured, flayed alive,—*Buonaparte*, whose mad ambition sacrificed so many millions of human beings, and Lord Byron,* in whose breast " resentment, anger, and hatred," raged with violence, and who made his gall flow out " against individuals, his country, the world, the universe, creation, and the Creator;"—let us suppose such characters associated together in a world where no pleasing objects meet the eye, or cheer the heart and imagination; and let us likewise suppose, that the malignant principles and boisterous passions which reigned in their minds during the present state, still continue to rage with uncontrolled and perpetual violence against all surrounding associates; it is evident, that, in such a case, a scene of misery would be produced, beyond the power of the human mind either to conceive or to describe. If so dreadful effects have been produced, by such diabolical passions, even in the present world, where Providence " sets restraining bounds to the wrath of man," and where benignant dispositions are blended with the evil principles which so generally prevail, what must be the effects where *pure malignity*, without any mixture of benevolent feelings, reigns *universally*, is perpetually tormenting its objects, is ever increasing in its fury, and is never controlled by physical obstructions or by moral considerations! This is the society of hell: this is the essence of future misery: this is " the worm that never dies, and the fire that is never quenched;" and the natural effects produced by it is universal anguish and despair,—" weeping, and wailing, and gnashing of teeth."—If such be the end of the ungodly, and the malignant despiser of God's law, and the riches of his mercy as manifested in Christ Jesus,—how careful should we be to counteract every evil propensity and passion, and how fervently ought we to join in the prayer of the Psalmist, and in the resolution of Jacob: " Gather not my soul with sinners, nor my life with bloody men." " O my soul, come not thou into their secret; unto their assembly, mine honour, be not thou united!"

Let none imagine, because I have selected some of the more atrocious characters recorded in history, as illustrations of the effects of depravity—that only such are " vessels of wrath, fitted for destruction." The principle of malevolence is substantially the same in every heart where it is predominant, however much it may be varnished over by hypocrisy, dissimulation, and the various forms of politeness which prevail in the world; and it requires only a certain stimulus to excite it to action, and full scope to exert its energies, in order to produce the most horrible and extensive effects. Several of the atrocious characters to which I have alluded, appeared, in the commencement of their career, to be possessed of a certain portion of benevolence, and of other amiable qualities. Nero, in the beginning of his reign, showed several marks o of the greatest kindness and condescension, affability, complaisance, and popularity. When he was desired to sign his name to a list of malefactors that were to be executed, he exclaimed, " *Would to Heaven I could not write!*"—Caligula began his reign with every promising appearance of becoming the real father of his people. Tiberius at first concealed his thoughts under the mask of an impenetrable dissimulation. He governed with moderation, and even appeared to excel in modesty. But afterwards, when these individuals became intoxicated with power,

* The Author trusts, that none of his readers will for a moment suppose, that, in bringing forward the above-mentioned characters as examples of malignity, he presumes to decide on their eternal destiny. His object merely is to show, that such malignant principles and passions as they displayed in the general tenor of their conduct, *if resolutely persisted in*, necessarily led to misery. With regard to Buonaparte and Lord Byron, he is disposed to indulge a hope, that their malevolent dispositions were in some measure counteracted, before they passed into the eternal world. The grounds of his hope, on this point, are stated in the Appendix.

and had thrown aside all considerations of morality and decorum, the latent principles of malignity burst forth in all their violence, till they became a scourge and an execration to mankind. So will it happen with those who now harbour malicious and vindictive passions, under a cloak of dissimulation and fashionable politeness, when they enter the invisible world under the dominion of such affections. When the restraints of society, of common decorum, and of human laws, are completely removed; when they have lost all hopes of the divine mercy; when they find themselves surrounded by none but malignant associates, and when they feel the effects of their infernal malice and revenge—those passions, which sometimes lay dormant in this life, will be roused into action, and rage with ungovernable fury against every one around, against themselves, "against the universe, and against the Creator."

Nor let it be imagined, that God will interpose at the hour of death, and, by an exertion of his power and benevolence, destroy the principles of sin, and prepare such characters for the joys of heaven. Such an interference, in every individual case, would imply a continued miracle, and would be inconsistent with the established order of the divine government; as it would supersede the use of all those instructions, admonitions, and moral preparations which God hath appointed for rendering his people "*meet* for the inheritance of the saints in light;" and would prevent the moral renovation of the world, which is now gradually effecting by the exertions of those who are "renewed in the spirit of their minds." It is true, indeed, that the mercy of God is infinite, and that so long as there is life, there is hope;—so that the most abandoned sinner has no reason to despair, while he remains within the confines of the present state. But as for those who pass from time into eternity, evidently under the power of revengeful and depraved passions, we have but slender grounds on which to hope that they shall ever afterwards be prepared for the felicity of heaven.

From the whole of what I have stated in this department of my subject, it is evident, that there are *two different states* in the future world; or, in other words, *a heaven* and *a hell;* a state of happiness, and a state of misery. If human beings are to exist at all in another region of creation, and throughout an unlimited duration, it is necessary that there be a separation effected, on the ground of their leading dispositions and characters. The nature of things, the moral constitution of the universe, and the happiness of the intelligent creation, as well as the decree of the Creator, require, that such an arrangement should take place. For it is altogether incompatible with the laws of moral order, that pride, hatred, malignity, and revenge, should dwell in the same abode with humility, benevolence, friendship, and love; or, that beings, actuated by principles and affections diametrically opposite to each other, could engage with harmony in the same employments, and relish the same pleasures. Were such an incongruous association permitted, the moral universe would soon become a scene of universal anarchy, and happiness be banished from all worlds. So that the two states of immortality revealed in Scripture, are equally accordant with the dictates of reason, and with the declaration of our Saviour, who has solemnly assured us, that "the wicked shall depart into everlasting punishment, and the righteous into life eternal."

# APPENDIX.

The following facts and documents, in relation to Lord Byron, lead us to indulge the hope, that, prior to his dissolution, he was actuated by sentiments and dispositions, different from those which are stated at page 122.

The lady of Mr. John Shepherd of Frome, having died some time ago, leaving amongst her papers, a prayer which her husband believed to have been composed on behalf of the noble poet, Mr. Shepherd addressed it to his Lordship, which called forth the reply which is here subjoined.

*Frome, Somerset, Nov. 21st,* 1821.

*To the Right Honourable Lord Byron, Pisa.*

My Lord,—More than two years since, a lovely and beloved wife was taken from me, by lingering disease, after a very short union. She possessed unvarying gentleness and fortitude, and a piety so retiring, as rarely to disclose itself in words, but so influential, as to produce uniform benevolence of conduct. In the last hour of life, after a farewell look on a lately born and only infant, for whom she had evinced inexpressible affection, her last whispers were, "God's happiness! God's happiness!" Since the second anniversary of her decease, I have read some papers which no one had seen during her life, and which contained her most secret thoughts. I am induced to communicate to your Lordship a passage from these papers, which, there is no doubt, refers to yourself; as I have more than once heard the writer mention your agility on the rocks at Hastings:—

"O my God, I take encouragement from the assurance of thy word, to pray to Thee in behalf of one for whom I have lately been much interested. May the person to whom I allude, (and who is now, we fear, as much distinguished for his neglect of Thee, as for the transcendent talents Thou hast bestowed on him) be awakened to a sense of his own danger, and led to seek that peace of mind in a proper sense of religion, which he has found this world's enjoyments unable to procure. Do thou grant that his future example may be productive of far more extensive benefit, than his past conduct and writings have been of evil; and may the Sun of Righteousness, which, we trust, will, at some future period, arise upon him, be bright in proportion to the darkness of those clouds which guilt has raised, and soothing in proportion to the keenness of that agony which the punishment of his vices has inflicted on him! May the hope, that the sincerity of my own efforts for the attainment of holiness, and the approval of my own love to the great Author of religion, will render this prayer, and every other for the welfare of mankind, more efficacious—cheer me in the path of duty; but let me not forget, that, while we are permitted to animate ourselves to exertion, by every innocent motive, these are but the lesser streams which may serve to increase the current, but which, deprived of the grand fountain of good, (a deep conviction of inborn sin, and firm belief in the efficacy of Christ's death, for the salvation of those who trust in him, and really seek to serve him) would soon dry up, and leave us as barren of every virtue as before.—*Hastings, July 31st,* 1814."

There is nothing, my Lord, in this extract, which, in a literary sense, can at all interest you; but it may, perhaps, appear to you worthy of reflection, how deep and expansive a concern for the happiness of others, a Christian faith can awaken in the midst of youth and prosperity.—Here is nothing poetical and splendid, as in the expostulatory homage of M. Delamartine; but here is the *sublime,* my Lord; for this intercession was offered on your account, to the supreme Source of happiness. It sprang from a faith more confirmed than that of the French poet, and from a charity, which, in combination with faith, showed its power unimpaired amidst the languors and pains of approaching dissolution. I will hope, that a prayer, which, I am sure, was deeply sincere, may not be always unavailing.

It would add nothing, my Lord, to the fame with which your genius has surrounded you, for an unknown and obscure individual to express his admiration of it. I had rather be numbered with those who wish and pray, that "wisdom from above," and "peace," and "joy," may enter such a mind.

THE ANSWER.

*Pisa, Dec. 8th,* 1821.

Sir,—I have received your letter. I need not say that the extract which it contains has affected me, because it would imply a want of all feeling to have read it with indifference. Though I am not quite sure that it was intended by the writer for me, yet the date, the place where it was written, with some other circumstances, which you mention, render the allusion probable. But, for whomsoever it was meant, I have read it with all the pleasure which can arise from so melancholy a topic. I say, *pleasure*, because your brief and simple picture of the life and demeanor of the excellent person whom I trust that you will again meet, cannot be contemplated without the admiration due to her virtues, and her pure and unpretending piety. Her last moments were particularly striking; and I do not know, that in the course of reading the story of mankind, and still less in my observations upon the existing portion, I ever met with any thing so unostentatiously beautiful. Indisputably, the firm believers in the gospel have a great advantage over all others—for this simple reason, that if true, they will have their reward hereafter; and if there be no hereafter, they can be but with the infidel in his eternal sleep, having had the assistance of an exalted hope through life, without subsequent disappointment, since (at the worst of them) "out of nothing, nothing can arise," not even sorrow. But a man's creed does not depend upon *himself; who* can say, I *will* believe this, that, or the other? and least of all that which he least can comprehend? I have, however, observed, that those who have begun with extreme faith, have in the end greatly narrowed it, as Chillingworth, Clark, (who ended as an Arian,) and some others; while on the other hand, nothing is more common, than for the early skeptic to end in a firm belief, like Maupertius and Henry Kirke White. But my business is to acknowledge your letter, and not to make a dissertation. I am obliged to you for your good wishes, and more obliged by the extract from the papers of the beloved object whose qualities you have so well described in a few words. I can assure you, that all the fame which ever cheated humanity into higher notions of its own importance, would never weigh on my mind against the pure and pious interest which a virtuous being may be pleased to take in my welfare. In this point of view, I would not exchange the prayer of the deceased in my behalf, for the united glory of Homer, Cæsar, and Napoleon, could such be accumulated upon a living head. Do me the justice to suppose, that "video meliora proboque," however the "deteriora sequor" may have been applied to my conduct. I have the honour to be your obliged and obedient servant, Byron.

P. S. I do not know that I am addressing a clergyman; but I presume that you will not be affronted by the mistake (if it is one) on the address of this letter. One who has so well explained, and deeply felt, the doctrines of religion, will excuse the error which led me to believe him its minister.

This letter, every one will admit, exhibits Lord Byron in a much more amiable point of view than the traits of his character sketched by Mr. Dallas, prior to the year 1818. The following account of his death-bed sentiments is extracted from "Last days of Lord Byron."

A very few days before his Lordship's death, Mr. Parry relates:—"It was seven o'clock in the evening when I saw him, and then I took a chair at his request, and sat down by his bedside, and remained till ten o'clock. He sat up in his bed, and was then calm and collected. He talked with me on a variety of subjects, connected with himself and his family. He spake of death also with great composure, and though he did not believe his end was so very near, there was something about him so serious and so firm, so resigned and composed, so different from any thing I had ever before seen in him, that my mind misgave, and at times foreboded his speedy dissolution. 'Parry,' he said, when I first went to him, 'I have much wished to see you today. I have had most strange feelings, but my head is now better. I have no gloomy thoughts, and no idea but I shall recover. I am perfectly collected—I am sure I am in my senses—but a melancholy will creep over me at times.' The mention of the subject brought the melancholy topics back, and a few exclamations showed what occupied Lord Byron's mind when he was left in silence and solitude. 'My wife! my Ada! my country! the situation of this place—my removal impossible, and perhaps death—all combine to make me sad. I am convinced of the happiness of domestic life. No man on earth respects a virtuous woman more than I do; and the prospect of retirement in England, with my wife and Ada, gives me an idea of happiness I have never experienced before. Retirement will be every thing to me, for heretofore to me life has been like the ocean in a storm. You have no conception of the unaccountable thoughts which come into my mind when the fever attacks me.—Eternity and space are before me, but on this subject, thank God, I am happy and at ease. The thought of living eternally, of again reviving, is a great pleasure. Christianity is the purest and most liberal religion in the world, but the numerous teachers who are continually worrying mankind with their denunciations and their doctrines, are the greatest enemies of religion. I have read with more attention than half of them the Book of Christianity, and I admire the liberal and truly charitable principles which Christ has laid down. There are questions connected with this subject which none but Almighty God can solve. Time and space who can conceive? None but God—on him I rely.'"

Who knows but the prayer of the amiable young lady, inserted above, was the mean of leading his Lordship to indulge such sentiments, and of ultimately securing his eternal happiness! "The effectual fervent prayer of a righteous man availeth much." This consideration should not only excite us to offer up intercessions in behalf of particular individuals, but also to use every prudent and delicate mean—by conversation, epistolary correspondence, or otherwise, to rouse the attention of those, especially in the higher circles of life, who appear unconcerned about "the things which relate to their everlasting peace."

The following lines, written by Lord Byron, are said to have been found in his Bible:—

"Within this awful volume lies
The mystery of mysteries.
Oh! happiest they of human race,
To whom our God has given grace,
To hear, to read, to fear, to pray,
To lift the latch, and force the way;
But better had they ne'er been born,
Who read to doubt, or read to scorn."

With regard to *Buonaparte*, we have nothing so satisfactory as in the case of Byron, that might lead us to conclude that his moral and religious sentiments were changed for the better. In his solitude at St. Helena, however, it appears that the subject of religion occasionally occupied his attention. The following anecdote, extracted from La Casas' Journal, will show the opinion which he entertained of the morality of the New Testament:—

In a conversation on the subject of religion, which he had with his friends at St. Helena, he said, among many other things, "'How is it possible that conviction can find its way to our hearts, when we hear the absurd language, and witness the acts of iniquity of the greatest number of those whose business it is to preach to us? I am surrounded with priests who preach incessantly that their reign is not of this world, and yet they lay hands upon every thing they can get. The Pope is the head of that religion from heaven, and he thinks only of this world,' &c. The Emperor ended the conversation by desiring my son to bring him the New Testament, and taking it from the beginning, he read as far as the conclusion of the speech of Jesus on the mountain. *He expressed himself struck with the highest admiration at the purity, the sublimity, the beauty of the morality it contained*, and we all experienced the same feeling."

# THE PHILOSOPHY OF RELIGION;

OR,

## AN ILLUSTRATION

OF THE

## MORAL LAWS OF THE UNIVERSE.

---

BY THOMAS DICK,

AUTHOR OF A VARIETY OF LITERARY AND SCIENTIFIC COMMUNICATIONS
IN NICHOLSON'S PHILOSOPHICAL JOURNAL, THE ANNALS
OF PHILOSOPHY, ETC. ETC.

---

"Knowledge is power."—*Lord Bacon.*
"Love is the fulfilling of the law."—*Paul*

HARTFORD:
PUBLISHED BY A. C. GOODMAN & CO.
1850.

# PREFACE.

To delineate the moral bearings of the Christian Revelation, — to display the reasonableness and the excellence of its precepts, and the physical and rational grounds on which they rest, — and to exhibit a few prominent features in the moral aspect of the world, — were some of the principal objects which the author had in view in the composition of the following work. He is not aware that a similar train of thought has been prosecuted, to the same extent, by any preceding writer; and is therefore disposed to indulge the hope that it may prove both entertaining and instructive to the general reader, and to the intelligent Christian.

It may not be improper to remind the reader that the author's object simply is, to *illustrate* the topics he has selected as the subject of this volume. As he has taken his fundamental principles from the system of revelation, he was under no necessity, as most ethical writers are, to enter into any laboured metaphysical discussions on the *foundation* of morality, and the motives from which moral actions should proceed. — The truth of revelation is, of course, taken for granted; and all who acknowledge its divine authority, will readily admit the principles which form the basis of the system here illustrated. But, although it formed no particular part of the author's plan to illustrate the *evidences* of the Christian revelation, he trusts that the view which is here given of the benignant tendency of its moral requisitions, will form a powerful presumptive argument in support of its celestial origin.

The Christian reader may also be reminded, that it is only the *philosophy* of religion which the author has attempted to illustrate. It formed no part of his plan to enter into any particular discussion on the *doctrines* of revelation, or on those topics which have so frequently been the subject of controversy in the Christian church. It is not to support the tenets of Calvinism, Arminianism, Baxterianism, Arianism, or any other *ism* which distinguishes the various denominations of the religious world, that these illustrations are presented to public view; but to elucidate an object which it appears to be the grand design of revelation to accomplish, and in the promotion of which every section of the Christian church is equally interested, and to which they would do well to "take heed." — In his illustration of this subject, the author has kept his eye solely on the two revelations which the Almighty has given to mankind, — THE SYSTEM OF NATURE, and the SACRED RECORDS *just as they stand*, — without any regard to the theories of philosophers, the opinions of commentators, or the systems of theologians. He is disposed to view the revelations of the Bible rather as a series of important *facts*, from which moral instructions are to be deduced, than as a system of metaphysical opinions for the exercise of the intellect.

PREFACE.

On the leading topics which have divided the Christian world, the author has formed his own opinion, and has adopted those which he has judged, on the whole, to be most correct; but it is of no importance to the reader what these opinions are, or of what system of speculative theology he is inclined, on the whole, to support. He sets very little value upon purely speculative opinions, except in so far as they tend to promote the grand moral objects of Christianity; and while he assumes the unalienable right of thinking for himself on the subject of religion, he is disposed to allow the same privilege to others. He believes, on the authority of Scripture, that "God is the Creator of heaven and earth;"—that "he is righteous in all his ways, and holy in all his works;"—that "he is good to all, and that his tender mercies are over all his works;"—that "he so loved the world, that he gave his only begotten Son, that whosoever believeth on him might not perish, but have everlasting life;"—that "Christ died for our sins, that he was buried, and that he rose again from the dead according to the Scriptures;"—that "he is the propitiation for our sins, and that he ever lives to make intercession;"—together with all the other facts and doctrines with which these are essentially connected. But he views the recognition of such doctrines and facts not as the *end* of religion, but only as the *means* by which the great moral objects of Christianity are to be promoted and accomplished.

In illustrating the moral state of the world, the author is sorry that he was obliged to compress his details within so narrow limits. Few readers, however, will appreciate the labour and research he was under the necessity of bestowing, in order to select and arrange the facts which he has detailed. He has occasionally had to condense a long history or narrative, and even a whole volume, into the compass of two or three pages; and to search through more than twenty volumes, in order to find materials to fill a couple of pages. With the same degree of research, (excepting the mechanical labour of transcription,) he might have filled several volumes with similar illustrations; and he is convinced that a work of this description, judiciously executed, would prove highly instructive, as well as entertaining, not only to the Christian world, but to readers of every description.

Various topics connected with the philosophy of religion still remain to be illustrated. These shall form the subject of discussion in a future volume, should the present work be received with general approbation.

PERTH, *January*, 1826.

# CONTENTS.

## INTRODUCTION.



## CHAPTER I.



### SECTION I.



### SECTION II.



### SECTION III.



### SECTION IV.



### SECTION V.

## SECTION VI.



## SECTION VII.



# CHAPTER II.



## SECTION I.



## SECTION II.



## SECTION III.



## SECTION IV.



## SECTION V.



## SECTION VI.



## SECTION VII.

## SECTION VIII.



## CHAPTER III.



## CHAPTER IV.



## SECTION I.



## SECTION II.



## SECTION III.

## SECTION IV.

THE

# PHILOSOPHY OF RELIGION.

## INTRODUCTION.

THE objects of human knowledge may be reduced to two classes—the relations of *matter* and the relations of *mind;* or, in other words, the *material* and the *intellectual* universe. Of these two departments of science, the intellectual universe is, in many respects, the most interesting and important. For, in so far as our knowledge and researches extend, it appears highly probable, if not absolutely certain, that the material universe exists solely for the sake of sentient and intelligent beings—in order to afford a sensible manifestation of the attributes of the great First Cause, and to serve as a vehicle of thought and a medium of enjoyment to subordinate intelligences. So intimately related, however, are these two objects of human investigation, that a knowledge of the one cannot be obtained but through the medium of the other. The operations of mind cannot be carried on without the intervention of external objects; for if the material universe had never existed, we could never have prosecuted a train of thought;* and the beauties and sublimities of external nature can be perceived only by thinking beings, without the existence of which, the material universe would remain like a mighty blank, and might be said to have been created in vain. Hence it appears, that, previous to our inquiries into the nature and relations of mind, it is necessary, in the first place, to study the phenomena of the material world, and the external actions of all those percipient beings with which it is peopled; for the knowledge of the facts we acquire in relation to these objects must form the ground-work of all our investigations.

We are surrounded, on every hand, with minds of various descriptions, which evince the faculties of which they are possessed, by the various senses and active powers with which they are furnished. These minds are of various gradations, in point of intellectual capacity and acumen, from man downwards through all the animated tribes which traverse the regions of earth, air, and sea. We have the strongest reason to believe, that the distant regions of the material world are also replenished with intellectual beings, of various orders, in which there may be a *gradation* upwards, in the scale of intellect above that of a man, as diversified as that which we perceive in the descending scale, from man downwards to the immaterial principle which animates a muscle, a snail, or a microscopic animalcula. When we consider the variety of original forms and of intellectual capacities which abounds in our terrestrial system, and that there is an infinite gap in the scale of being between the human mind and the Supreme Intelligence, it appears quite conformable to the magnificent harmony of the universe, and to the wisdom and benevolence of its Almighty Author, to suppose, that there are beings within the range of his dominions as far superior to man in the comprehension and extent of mental and corporeal powers, as man is, in these respects, superior to the most despicable insect; and that these beings, in point of number, may exceed all human calculation and comprehension. This idea is corroborated by several intimations contained in the records of revelation, where we have presented to our view a class of intelligences endowed with physical energies, powers of rapid motion, and a grasp of intellect, incomparably superior to those which are possessed by any of the beings which belong to our sublunary system.

* The whole train of ideas which passes through our minds on any subject may be considered as the images of external objects variously modified and combined. These images we receive through the medium of our senses, by which we hold a communication with the material world. All our ideas of God, and of the objects of religion, are derived from the same source. The illustrations of the attributes of the Deity, and of his moral administration, contained in Scripture, are derived from the external scenes of creation, and from the relations of human society; consequently, had the material world never existed, we could have formed no conceptions of the divine perfections similar to those which we now entertain, nor have prosecuted a train of thought on any other subject; for the material universe is the basis of all the knowledge we have hitherto acquired, or can acquire, respecting ourselves, our Creator or other intelligences. Any person who is disposed to call in question this position must be prepared to point out, distinctly and specifically, those ideas or trains of thought which are not derived through the medium of the external senses, and from the objects on which they are exercised.

To contemplate the various orders of intelligences which people the material universe, and the relations which subsist among them—the arrangements of the different worlds to which they respectively belong—the corporeal vehicles by which they hold a correspondence with the material system—the relation in which they stand to other worlds and beings, from which they are separated by the voids of space—and the excursions they occasionally make to different regions of that vast empire of which they form a part—to trace the superior intellectual faculties and the sensitive organs with which they are endowed—the profound investigations they have made into the economy of the universe—the trains of thought which they pursue, and the magnificent objects on which their faculties are employed—the emotions with which they view the scenes and transactions of such a world as ours—the means by which they have been carried forward in the career of moral and intellectual improvement—the history of their transactions since the period at which they were brought into existence—the peculiar dispensations of the Creator, and the revolutions that may have taken place among them—the progressions they have made from one stage of improvement to another—the views they have acquired of the perfections and the plans of their Almighty Sovereign—the transporting emotions of delight which pervade all their faculties—and the sublime adorations they offer up to the Fountain of all their felicity—would constitute a source of the most exquisite gratification to every holy, intelligent, and inquiring mind. But, since we are at present confined to a small corner of the universe of God, and surrounded by immeasurable voids of space, which intervene between our habitation and the celestial worlds, through which no human power can enable us to penetrate, we must remain ignorant of the nature and economy of those intellectual beings, till our souls take their flight from these "tabernacles of clay," to join their kindred spirits in the invisible world. While we remain in our sublunary mansion, our investigations into the world of mind must, therefore, of necessity, be confined to the nature and attributes of the Uncreated Spirit, and to the faculties of our own minds and those of the sensitive beings with which we are surrounded. These faculties, as they constitute the instruments by which all our knowledge, both human and divine, is acquired, have employed the attention of philosophers in every age, and have been the theme of many subtle and ingenuous speculations; and they, doubtless, form an interesting subject of investigation to the student of intellectual science.

But, of all the views we can take of the world of mind, the *moral relations* of intelligent beings, and the laws founded on these relations, are topics by far the most interesting and important. This subject may be treated in a more definite and tangible manner than the theories which have been formed respecting the nature and operations of the intellectual powers. Illustrations level to every capacity, and which come home to every one's bosom, may be derived both from reason and experience, from the annals of history, and the records of revelation. It is not involved in the same difficulties and obscurity which have perplexed the philosophy of the intellect; and there are certain principles which may be traced in relation to this subject, which apply to all the rational intelligences that God has formed, however diversified in respect of the regions of the universe which they occupy, and in the extent of their intellectual powers. Above all, this subject is more intimately connected with the present and future happiness of man than any other which comes within the range of human investigation; and therefore, forms a prominent and legitimate branch of what may be termed "The Philosophy of Religion."

That the moral relations of intelligent minds, and the temper and conduct corresponding with these relations, are essentially connected with the happiness of every rational agent, might be made to appear from a variety of cases, in which the reversing of certain moral laws or principles would inevitably lead to disorder and misery. I shall content myself with stating the following illustration:—We dwell in an obscure corner of God's empire; but the light of modern science has shown us, that worlds, a thousand times larger than ours, and adorned with more refulgent splendours, exist within the range of that system of which we form a part. It has also unfolded to our view other systems dispersed throughout the voids of space, at immeasurable distances, and in such vast profusion, that our minds are unable to grasp their number and their magnitude. Reason and revelation lead us to conclude, that all these worlds and systems are adorned with displays of divine wisdom, and peopled with myriads of rational inhabitants. The human mind, after it has received notices of such stupendous scenes, naturally longs for a nearer and more intimate inspection of the grandeur and economy of those distant provinces of the Creator's empire; and is apt to imagine, that it would never weary, but would feel unmingled enjoyment, while it winged its flight from one magnificent scene of creation to another. But although an inhabitant of our world were divested of the quality of gravitation endowed with powers of rapid motion adequate to carry him along "to the suburbs of creation," and permitted by his Creator to survey all the wonders of the universe, if a principle of love and kindly affection towards fellow-intelligences did not animate his mind, if rage and revenge pride and ambition, hatred and envy, were incessantly rankling in his breast, he could feel no transporting emotions, nor taste the sweets of true enjoyment. The vast universe, through which he roamed, would be transformed into a *spacious hell*; its beauties and sublimities could not prevent misery from taking possession of his soul; and, at every stage of his excursion, he could not fail to meet with the indications of his Creator's frown. For there appears, from reason and experience, as well as from the dictates of revelation, an absolute impossibility of enjoying happiness so long as malevolent affections retain their ascendancy in the heart of a moral intelligence, in whatever region of universal nature his residence may be found.

Hence we may learn, that the highest attainments in science to which any one can arrive, though they may expand the range of his intellectual views, will not ensure to their possessor substantial and unmingled enjoyment, while his heart is devoid of benevolent affections, and while he is subjected to the influence of degrading and immoral passions. If it be possible that any one now exists in the literary world, who has devoted his life to the sublimest investigations of science, and has taken the most extensive views of the arrangements of the material world, and yet who remains doubtful as to the existence of a Supreme Intelligence, and of an eternal state of destination; who is elated with pride at the splendour of his scientific acquirements; who treats his equals with a spirit of arrogance; who looks down with a haughty and sullen scowl on the inferior ranks of his fellow-men; who is haughty, overbearing, and revengeful in his general deportment, and who is altogether indifferent as to the moral principles he displays,—I would envy neither his happiness nor his intellectual attainments. He can enjoy none of those delightful emotions which flow from the exercise of Christian benevolence, nor any of those consolations which the good man feels amidst the various ills of life; and, beyond the short span of mortal existence, he can look forward to no brighter displays of the grandeur of the material and intellectual universe, but to an eternal deprivation of his powers of intelligence in the shades of annihilation.

It must, therefore, be a matter deeply interesting to every intelligent agent, to acquire correct notions of the fundamental principles of moral action, and to form those habits which will fit him for the enjoyment of true felicity, to whatever region of the universe he may afterwards be transported.—In the illustration of this subject, I shall pursue a train of thought which I am not aware has been prosecuted by any previous writers on the subject of morality, and shall endeavour to confirm and illustrate the views which may be exhibited, by an appeal to the discoveries of revelation.

We have an abundance of ponderous volumes on the subject of moral philosophy; but the different theories which have been proposed and discussed, and the metaphysical mode in which the subject has been generally treated, have seldom led to any beneficial practical results. To attempt to treat the subject of morals without a reference to divine revelation, as most of our celebrated moral writers have done, seems to be little short of egregious trifling. It cannot serve the purpose of an *experiment*, to ascertain how far the unassisted faculties of man can go in acquiring a knowledge of the foundation and the rules of moral action; for the prominent principles of Christian morality are so interwoven into the opinions, intercourses, and practices of modern civilized society, and so familiar to the mind of every man who has been educated in a Christian land, that it is impossible to eradicate the idea of them from the mind, when it attempts to trace the duty of man solely on the principles of reason. When the true principles of morality are once communicated through the medium of revelation, reason can demonstrate their utility, and their conformity to the character of God, to the order of the universe, and to the relations which subsist among intelligent agents. But we are by no means in a situation to determine whether they could ever have been discovered by the investigations and efforts of the unassisted powers of the human mind. The only persons who could fairly try such an experiment were the Greeks and Romans, and other civilized nations, in ancient times, to whom the light of revelation was not imparted. And what was the result of all their researches on this most important of all subjects? What were the practical effects of all the fine-spun theories and subtle speculations which originated in the schools of ancient philosophy, under the tuition of Plato and Socrates, of Aristotle and Zeno? The result is recorded in the annals of history, and in the writings of the apostles. "They became vain in their imaginations, and their foolish hearts were darkened. They were filled with all unrighteousness, fornication, wickedness, covetousness, maliciousness, envy, murder, deceit, malignity; they were backbiters, haters of God, despiteful, proud, inventors of evil things, disobedient to parents, without natural affection, implacable, and unmerciful." Their general conduct was characterized by pride, lasciviousness, and revenge; they indulged in the commission of unnatural crimes; they were actuated by restless ambition, and they gloried in covering the earth with devastation and carnage.

It is true, indeed, that some of the sects of philosophers propounded several maxims and moral precepts, the propriety of which cannot be questioned; but none of them could agree respecting either the foundation of virtue, or the ultimate object toward which it should be directed, or that in which the chief happiness of man consists; and hence it happened, that the precepts delivered by the teachers of philosophy had little influence on their own conduct, and far less on that of the unthinking multitude. Where do we find, in any of the philosophical schools of Greece and Rome, a recommendation of such precepts as these, "Love your enemies; do good to them who hate you; and pray for them who despitefully use you and persecute you?" In opposition to such divine injunctions, we can trace, in the maxims and conduct of the ancient sages, a principle of pride insinuating itself into the train of their most virtuous actions. It has been reckoned by some a wise and a witty answer which one of the philosophers returned to his friend, who had advised him to revenge an injury he had suffered; "What, (says he) if an ass kicks me, must I needs kick him again?" Some may be disposed to consider such a reply as indicating a manly spirit, and true greatness of soul; but it carries in it a proud and supercilious contempt of human nature, and a haughtiness of mind, which are altogether inconsistent with the mild and benevolent precepts of Him, who, in the midst of his severest sufferings from men, exclaimed, "Father, forgive them, for they know not what they do."

It appears somewhat preposterous to waste our time, and the energies of our minds, in laboured metaphysical disquisitions, to ascertain the foundations of virtue, and the motives from which it is to be pursued; whether it consists in *utility*, in the *fitness of things*, or in the regulations of states and political associations, and whether it is to be prosecuted from a principle of self-love or of benevolence, when every useful question that can be started on this subject may be immediately solved by a direct application to the revelations of heaven, and an infallible rule derived for the direction of our conduct in all the circumstances and relations in which we may be placed. Even although the moral philosopher were to reject the Bible, *as a revelation from God*, it would form no reason why its annunciations should be altogether overlooked or rejected. As an impartial investigator of the history of man, of the moral constitution of the human mind, and of the circumstances of our present condition, he is bound to take into view every fact and every circumstance which may have a bearing on the important question which he undertakes to decide. Now, it is a *fact*, that such a book as the Bible actually exists—that, amidst the wreck of thousands of volumes which the stream of time has carried into oblivion, it has survived for several thousands of years—that its announcements have directed the opinions and the conduct of myriads of mankind—that many of the most illustrious characters that have adorned our race have submitted to its dictates, and governed their tempers and their actions by its moral precepts—that those who have been governed by its maxims have been distinguished by uprightness of conduct, and been most earnest and successful in promoting the happiness of mankind—that this book declares, that a moral revulsion has taken place in the constitution of man since he was placed upon this globe—and that the whole train of its moral precepts proceeds on the ground of his being considered as a depraved intelligence. These are facts which even the infidel philosopher must admit; and, instead of throwing them into the shade, or keeping them entirely out of view, he is bound, as an unbiassed inquirer, to take them all into account in his researches into the moral economy of the human race. In particular, he is bound to inquire into the probability of the alleged fact of the depravity of man, and to consider, whether the general train of human actions, the leading facts of history in reference to all ages and nations, and the destructive effects of several operations in the system of nature, have not a tendency to corroborate this important point. For the fact, that man is a fallen intelligence, must materially modify every system of ethics that takes it into account. Should this fact be entirely overlooked, and yet ultimately be found to rest on a solid foundation, then, all the speculations and theories of those moralists who profess to be guided solely by the dictates of unassisted reason, may prove to be nothing more than the reveries of a vain imagination, and to be built on "the baseless fabric of a vision."

# CHAPTER I.

## ON THE MORAL RELATIONS OF INTELLIGENT BEINGS TO THEIR CREATOR.

### SECTION I.

#### ON THE PRIMARY OR MOST GENERAL IDEA OF MORALITY.

I CONCEIVE, that the first or most general idea of morality is, ORDER,—or, that harmonious disposition and arrangement of intelligent beings, which is founded on the nature of things, and which tends to produce the greatest sum of happiness.

*Physical Order*, or the order of the material universe, is that by which every part is made to harmonize to the other part, and all individually to the whole collectively. Thus, the adaptation of light to the eye, and of the eye to light; the adaptation of the structure of the ear and of the lungs to the constitution of the atmosphere, and its various undulations; the adaptation of the waters, the vegetable productions of the field, the minerals in the bowels of the earth, the colours produced by the solar rays, and all the other parts and agencies of external nature, to the wants and the happiness of sentient beings; the adaptation of day and night to the labour and rest appointed for man; and the regularity of the motions of the planetary bodies in their circuits round the sun—constitute the *physical* order, or harmony of the visible world; and it is this which constitutes its principal beauty, and which evinces the wisdom of its Almighty Author.

*Moral Order* is the harmony of intelligent beings in respect to one another, and to their Creator, and is founded upon those relations in which they respectively stand to each other.—Thus, reverence, adoration, and gratitude, from creatures, correspond or harmonize with the idea of a self-existent, omnipotent, and benevolent Being, on whom they depend, and from whom they derive every enjoyment,—and love, and good will, and a desire to promote each other's happiness, harmonize with the idea of intelligences of the same species mingling together in social intercourses. For, it will at once be admitted, that affections directly opposite to these, and universally prevalent, would tend to destroy the moral harmony of the intelligent universe, and to introduce anarchy and confusion, and consequently *misery*, among all the rational inhabitants of the material world.

The following brief illustration, by way of contrast, may, perhaps, have a tendency more particularly to impress the mind with the idea of order intended to be conveyed in the above stated definitions.

Suppose the principle which unites the planetary globes in one harmonious system, to be dissolved, and the planets to run lawlessly through the sky—suppose the planet Jupiter to forsake his orbit, and in his course to the distant regions of space, to impinge against the planet Saturn, and to convulse the solid crust of that globe from its surface to its centre, to disarrange the order of its satellites, to shatter its rings into pieces, and to carry the fragments of them along with him in his lawless career,—suppose the sun to attract his nearest planets to his surface with a force that would shake them to their centres, and dissolve their present constitution,—suppose the moon to fly from her orbit, and rush towards the planet Venus,—the earth to be divested of its atmosphere, the foundations of its mountains to be overturned, and to be hurled into the plains, and into the ocean; its seas and rivers to forsake their ancient channels, and to overflow the land, and its human inhabitants swept promiscuously along with the inferior animals into dens and caves, and crevices of the earth, and into the bottom of the ocean:—in such a scene, we should have presented to our view a specimen of physical confusion and disorder; and it would form an impressive emblem of the state of rational beings, whose moral order is completely subverted.

Again, suppose the rational inhabitants of our globe to be universally set against each other, in order to accomplish their misery and destruction—suppose the child rising in opposition to his parents, the wife plotting the destruction of her husband, the brother insnaring his sister, and decoying her to ruin,—teachers of all descriptions inculcating the arts of deception, of revenge, and of destruction, and representing every principle and fact as contrary to what it really is—falsehoods of every description industriously forged and circulated as facts through every rank of society—rulers setting themselves in opposition to the populace, and plotting their destruction, while they are at the same time actuated by a principle of pride, of envy, and malice against each other—the populace setting themselves in opposition to their rulers, exterminating them from the earth, subverting every principle of law and order, gratifying, without control, every principle of revenge, avarice, lasciviousness and sensual indulgence, and enjoying diabolical satisfaction in contemplating the scenes of misery they have created:—in short, every one beholding in his neighbour the malevolence of a fiend armed with instruments of destruction, and devising schemes to secure his misery and ruin. Suppose the lower animals, impelled by revenge, to rise up in indignation against man, and to swell the horrors of this general anarchy—suppose the superior orders of intelligences to mingle in this scene of confusion, to exert their high physical and intellectual powers in adding fuel to these malevolent principles and operations, and in attempting to drag other intelligences of a still higher order from their seats of bliss—suppose all these intelligences actuated by an implacable hatred of their Creator, combined to deface the beauties of the material creation, and then to engage in a war of universal extermination throughout the whole intelligent system in every region of the universe: such a state of things, if it could exist in the universe, would form a perfect contrast to *moral order;* it would present a scene in which existence could not be desirable to any intelligent mind, and in which happiness could not possibly be enjoyed by any rational being, but by Him who is eternally happy independently of his creatures. Moral order, then, is completely opposed to such a state of things as has now been represented; it consists in every being holding its proper station in the universe, acting according to the nature of that station, and using its powers and faculties for the purposes for which they were originally intended; and the grand object intended to be accomplished by this order, is, the happiness of the whole,—without which misery would reign uncontrolled throughout all the ranks of intelligent existence.

This state of the moral world is most frequently designated in scripture by the term *holiness.* Of the ideas included under this term, and several of its kindred epithets, very vague and imperfect conceptions are frequently entertained. Its leading or generic idea, from what has been now stated, will evidently appear to be, *a conformity to order*, founded on the relations of intelligent beings to each other; or, in other words, it consists in a complete conformity to the law of God, (which is founded on those relations) including both the *action* and the *principle* from which it flows. In reference to created beings, holiness may, therefore, be defined to be *a conformity to the moral order of the universe*,—and, in relation to the Creator, it is *that perfection of his nature, which leads him to promote the moral order and happiness of intelligent beings, and to counteract every thing which stands in opposition to this object.*

That the leading ideas and definitions now stated are correct, will, perhaps, more distinctly appear in the course of the following discussions and illustrations; but should any one be disposed to call in question the statements now given in reference to the primary idea of morality, his difference of opinion on this point will not materially affect the leading train of sentiment prosecuted in the further elucidation of this subject.

---

## SECTION II.

### ON THE FUNDAMENTAL PRINCIPLES OF MORALITY.

The leading idea of morality or holiness, as now stated, resolves itself into the two following principles—*love to God the Creator, and love to fellow intelligences.* These are the two grand springs on which the whole moral machine of the universe depends. All the diversified actions by which happiness is diffused among intelligent agents, are only so many ramifications of these two simple and sublime principles, which connect all holy beings throughout the wide empire of God, in one harmonious union. This we are not left to infer merely from the nature of things, but have the authority of the supreme Legislator, as our warrant for placing these principles as the foundation of all moral virtue among every class of moral agents. For thus saith our Saviour, "THOU SHALT LOVE THE LORD THY GOD WITH ALL THY HEART, AND WITH ALL THY MIND, AND WITH ALL THY STRENGTH. *This is the first and great commandment. The second is like unto it:* THOU SHALT LOVE THY NEIGHBOUR AS THYSELF. *On these two principles hang all the law and the prophets.*"

These principles, now that they are communicated, and sanctioned by divine authority, appear quite accordant to the dictates of enlightened reason, and calculated to promote the happiness of the intelligent creation; yet we never find that the moral systems of pagan philosophers, in any country, were built on this foundation, or that they assumed them as indispensable axioms to guide them in their speculations on the subject of ethics.

In elucidating this topic, I shall endeavour to show the reasonableness and the utility of these principles of moral action, from a consideration of the nature of God, and the relations in which intelligent beings stand to him as the source of their existence and felicity—from the nature of subordinate intelligences, and the relations in which they stand to one another—from the misery which must inevitably follow, where such principles are violated or reversed—from the happiness that would necessarily flow from their full operation—and, lastly, that they apply to the circumstances of all created intelligences wherever existing, throughout the boundless universe —I have used the plural term *principles*, to express the foundation of moral action, because our Saviour has arranged them under two distinct heads, in the passage just now quoted; but strictly speaking, there is but *one* principle, namely, *Love*, which divides itself, as it were, into two great streams, one directing its course towards the supreme Source of all felicity, and the other towards all the subordinate intelligences He has created.

*First Principle*—LOVE TO GOD.

Love, considered in reference to the Supreme Being, may be viewed as dividing itself into a variety of streams or kindred emotions, all flowing from one source. The most prominent of these emotions are the following—*Admiration*, which consists in a delightful emotion, arising from a contemplation of the wonderful works of God, and of the wisdom and goodness which they unfold—*Reverence*, which is nearly allied to admiration, is a solemn emotion, mingled with awe and delight, excited in the mind, when it contemplates the perfections, and the grand operations of the Eternal Mind—*Gratitude*, which consists in affection to the Supreme Being, on account of the various benefits he has conferred upon us —*Humility*, which consists in a just sense of our own character and condition, especially when we compare ourselves with the purity and perfection of the divine character. To these emotions may be added *Complacency* and delight in the character and operations of God—*Adoration* of his excellencies, and an unlimited *Dependence* upon him in reference to our present concerns, and to our future destination. I have stated these different modifications of the first principle of morality, because, in the following illustrations, they may all occasionally be taken into account, when an allusion is made to the affections, which the character and operations of the divine Being have a tendency to excite.

Love is that noble affection which is excited by amiable objects; and therefore, in order to its being rational, permanent, and delightful, it must be founded on the perception of certain amiable qualities or attributes connected with its object. In order to demonstrate the reasonableness of this affection in reference to God, it is only requisite to consider his character and perfections, and the relation in which he stands to us as the Author of our existence and enjoyments. But, as a comprehensive view of this subject would require volumes for its illustration, I shall confine myself to the illustration of only two or three lineaments of the divine character.

## SECTION III.

### ON THE OMNIPOTENCE OF GOD.

We naturally venerate and admire a character in which physical energy is combined with high intellectual powers, when these powers are uniformly exerted in the counteraction of vice and misery, and in the promotion of happiness. On this ground, the *Omnipotence* of God is calculated to affect the mind with that particular modification of love, which is designated by the term *Reverence*. Were it possible that any human being could construct a machine, by means of which, in combination with his own physical powers, he could transport himself and his treasures from one region of the globe to another, at the rate of 200 miles in an hour, and were he, at the same time, to devote his treasures, and his moral and intellectual energies to the improvement and melioration of the various tribes of mankind in every clime through which he passed, such an object could not fail of exciting in our minds a sentiment of admiration and reverence. Were one of the highest orders of created intelligences to descend from his celestial mansion, and to display himself to our view in all the bright radiance of his native heaven—were he to take his station over the regions of Thibet or Hindostan, and, after having excited the attention of a wondering populace, were he to detach the huge masses of the Himalaya mountains from their foundations, and toss them into the depths of the Indian Ocean, and, in the course of a few hours, transform the barren wastes of that dreary region into a scene of beauty and luxuriant vegetation, and cause splendid cities to arise, where formerly nothing was presented to the view but a bleak and frightful wilderness—at such a display of physical power, combined with benevolent design, we could not withhold a feeling of awe, and a sentiment of reverence, almost approaching to religious adoration.

If, then, the contemplation of physical and mental energies, with which even created beings may possibly be invested, would excite our admiration and reverence, what powerful emotions of this description must the energies of the Uncreated Mind be calculated to produce, when they are contemplated by the eye of enlightened reason, and in the light of divine revelation! When this huge globe on which we dwell existed in the state of a shapeless and unformed mass; when land, and water, and air, were blended in wild confusion, and chaos and darkness extended their dominion over all its gloomy regions, at His command "light sprung out of darkness, and order out of confusion;" the mountains reared their projecting summits, the valleys were depressed, the caverns of the ocean were hollowed out, and the waters retired to the places which He had appointed for them. The fields were clothed with luxuriant verdure; Eden appeared in all its beauty, the inferior tribes of animated existence took possession of the air, the waters, and the earth, and man was formed in the image of his Maker, to complete this wondrous scene. At this period, too, the earth received such a powerful impulse from the hand of its Creator, as has carried it along through the voids of space, with all its furniture and inhabitants, in the most rapid career, for six thousand years; having already moved through a space of 3,480,000,000,000 miles, and will still continue its unremitting course for thousands of years to come, till the "mystery of Providence be finished."

Would we be struck with admiration and astonishment, at beholding a superior created intelligence tossing a mountain into the sea? What strong emotions of reverence and awe, then, ought to pervade our minds, when we behold the Almighty every moment producing effects infinitely more powerful and astonishing! What would be our astonishment, were we to behold, from a distance, a globe as large as the earth tossed from the hand of Omnipotence, and flying at the rate of a thousand miles every minute! Yet this is nothing more than what is every day produced by the unceasing energies of that Power which first called us into existence. That impulse which was first given to the earth at its creation is still continued, by which it is carried round every day from west to east, along with its vast population, and at the same time impelled forward through the regions of space at the rate of sixty-eight thousand miles in an hour. Nor is this among the most wonderful effects of divine power: it is only one comparatively small specimen of that omnipotent energy which resides in the Eternal Mind. When we lift our eyes towards the sky, we behold bodies a thousand times larger than this world of ours, impelled with similar velocities through the mighty expanse of the universe. We behold the planetary globes wheeling their rapid courses around the sun, with unremitting velocity—the comets returning from their long excursions in the distant regions of space, and flying towards the centre of our system with a velocity of hundreds of thousands of miles an hour—the sun himself impelled toward some distant region of space, and carrying along with him all his attendant planets—and, in a word, we have the strongest reason to conclude, that all the vast systems of the universe, which are more numerous than language can express, are in rapid and incessant motion around the throne of the Eternal, carrying forward the grand designs of infinite wisdom which they are destined to accomplish.*

It must, however, be admitted, that the manifestation of power, or great physical energy, abstractly considered, is not of itself calculated to produce that emotion of reverence which flows from love, unless the being in whom it resides exerts it for the purposes of benevolence. A superior being, endowed with great physical and intellectual energies, which were exerted solely for the purpose of destruction, could inspire no feelings but those of dread and alarm: and were it possible to conceive an *omnipotent* being divested of the attribute of benevolence, or possessed of a capricious character, he would form the most *terrible* object which the human mind could contemplate. But the attribute of infinite power, when conjoined with infinite wisdom and goodness, conveys an idea the most glorious and transporting. Every display of divine power to which I have now alluded, has the communication of happiness for its object. The motion of the earth around its axis every twenty-four hours, is intended to distribute light and darkness, in regular proportions, to all the inhabitants of the earth, and to correspond to the labour and rest appointed for man. It produces a variety which is highly gratifying to the rational mind; for, while our fellow-men on the opposite side of the globe are enjoying the splendours of the noonday sun, the shades of night, which at that time envelope our hemisphere, are the means of disclosing to our view the magnificent glories of the starry frame. Were this motion to cease, this world and all its inhabitants would be thrown into a state of confusion and misery. While the inhabitants of one hemisphere enjoyed the splendours of perpetual day, the glories of the nocturnal heavens would be for ever veiled from their view, and the inhabitants of the other hemisphere would be enveloped in the shades of eternal night. While the one class was suffering under the scorching effects of excessive heat, the other would be frozen to death amidst the rigours of insufferable cold—vegetable nature, in both cases, would languish, and the animal tribes would be gradually extinguished.

The same benevolent intention may be perceived in that exertion of power by which the earth is carried forward in its *annual* course around the sun. From this motion we derive all the pleasures we enjoy from the vicissitude of the seasons; without which the variety of nature that appears in the beauties of spring, the luxuriance of summer, the fruits of autumn, and the repose of winter, would be completely destroyed. And, it is worthy of notice, that all this variety is enjoyed every moment by some one tribe or other of the human family; for while it is summer in one region, it is winter in another; and while one class of our fellow-men is contemplating the opening beauties of spring, another is gathering in the fruits of harvest. The same benevolent designs, we have every reason to believe, are displayed in those more magnificent exertions of divine power which appear among all the rolling worlds on high; for, in so far as our observations extend, all the arrangements of the planetary globes appear calculated to promote the happiness of sentient and intellectual beings.

* See a more comprehensive illustration of this subject in "The Christian Philosopher," pp. 8—29.

While, therefore, we contemplate the operations of divine power, either in the earth or in the heavens, we perceive every thing which is calculated to inspire us with love, admiration, and reverence. When we lie down on our pillows in the evening, how pleasing it is to reflect, that the power of our Almighty Father will be exerted in carrying us round in safety several thousands of miles, during our repose in sleep, in order that our eyes may be again cheered with the morning light? When, amid the gloom and storms of winter, we look forward to the reviving scenes of spring, we know that we must be carried forward more than a hundred millions of miles, before we can enjoy the pleasures of that delightful season; and when spring arrives, we must be carried through the voids of space a hundred millions of miles farther, before we can reap the fruits of summer and harvest. How delightful, then, is the thought, that the omnipotent energy of our heavenly Father is incessantly exerted in producing such a wonderful effect, accompanied by such a variety of beneficent changes, all contributing to our enjoyment!*

What is the reason, then, why we feel so little admiration and reverence at the beneficent operations of divine power? If we should be struck with veneration and wonder at beholding a superior created intelligence tossing a range of mountains into the sea, why do we behold, with so much apathy, effects ten thousand times more energetic and astonishing? One general reason, among others, undoubtedly is, that the moral constitution of man has suffered a melancholy derangement; in consequence of which, the train of his thoughts and affections has been turned out of its original channel. The Scriptures are clear and explicit on this point; they declare, in the most positive terms, that "the carnal mind is *enmity against God*," and that, in consequence of this depraved principle, the wicked "walk in the vanity of their minds, being alienated from the life of God. They say to the Almighty, Depart from us, for we desire not the knowledge of thy ways. God is not in all their thoughts, and through pride of their countenances they will not call upon God."—Another reason is, that the almighty Agent who produces so stupendous effects remains invisible to mortal eyes. Were a celestial intelligence to appear in a splendid and definite form, and to produce such effects as I have supposed, the connexion between the agent and the effects produced, would forcibly strike the senses and the imagination. But he who sits on the throne of the universe, and conducts all its movements, is a being "who dwells in light unapproachable, whom no man hath seen, or can see." He can be contemplated only through the *sensible* manifestations he gives of his perfections; and, were the train of our thoughts properly directed, we would perceive him operating in every object and in every movement. We would hear his voice in the wind and the thunder, in the earthquake, the storm, and the tempest; we would see him in the beauties and sublimities of sublunary nature, in the splendours of the sun, and the glories of the nocturnal sky; and, in whatever situation we might be placed, we would feel ourselves surrounded with the omnipotent energies of an ever-present Deity.

The contemplation of God as an omnipotent being, is calculated to inspire the mind with love and confidence in the prospect of futurity. The promises addressed to us by a wise and benevolent being can excite in us trust and dependence, only in so far as we are convinced of his ability to secure their fulfilment. If almighty power were not an attribute of the Eternal Mind, or were we unable to trace its operations in visible existing facts, then all the promises and delineations of revelation, in reference to unseen and eternal objects, might prove to be nothing more than imaginary scenes, that could never be realized. But the good man, who perceives omnipotent energy in incessant operation throughout all the scenes of the universe which surround him, feels the most perfect security in looking forward to the scene of his future destination, and to those changes and revolutions which shall succeed the period of his present existence. He knows that, in a few years at most, that immortal principle which now animates his frame, will take its flight from its earthly mansion to a world unknown. To what regions it will direct its course; what scenes and prospects will be unfolded to its view; what intercourse it may have with the spirits of departed men, or with other intelligences; in what state it shall pass its existence till the consummation of the present plan of Providence—whether it shall remain as a naked spirit entirely disconnected with the visible universe, or be clothed with some etherial vehicle, to enable it to hold a correspondence with other regions of the material creation—he is at present unable to determine. He knows that his body, too, shall disappear from the living world, and be reduced to corruption and ashes. In what manner the essential particles of this body shall be preserved distinct from those of all other human bodies, after they have been tossed about by the winds, and blended with the other elements of nature; by what means they shall be reunited into a more glorious form; and how

*In this, and other places of this work, the truth of the annual and diurnal motions of the earth is taken for granted, because I conceive it is susceptible of the clearest demonstration—(See "Christian Philosopher," pp. 23, 83, 147, 149.) But, should the truth of this position be called in question or denied, it will not materially affect the propriety of such moral reflections as are here stated; for, in this case, a similar, or even a much greater display of omnipotence must be admitted in reference to the motions of the heavenly bodies, in bringing about the succession of day and night, and the changes of the seasons.

the separate spirit shall be enabled to recognize its renovated and long-lost partner at the resurrection of the just—he can form no conception.

He knows, that the globe on which he now resides is doomed to be dissolved amidst devouring flames, when "the elements shall melt with fervent heat, and the earth, and the works that are therein, shall be burnt up"—that the ashes of all the myriads of the race of Adam shall issue from the caverns of the ocean, and from the charnel houses, in every region of the land—that they shall be moulded into new organical structures, united with their kindred spirits, and be convened in one grand assembly before God, the Judge of all. He knows, that "new heavens and a new earth" will be arranged for the residence of the "redeemed from among men;" but in what region of the universe this abode may be prepared, what scenes it will unfold, and by what means the innumerable company of the righteous shall be transported from amidst the ruins of this globe to that celestial habitation—he is at present at a loss to form even a conjecture. He knows, that after these solemn changes have been effected, ages numerous as the drops of the ocean will roll over him—that worlds numerous as the stars of heaven will still run their destined rounds—that other systems may undergo important changes and revolutions—that new systems of creation may be gradually emerging into existence, and that scenes of magnificence and glory, different from all that ever preceded them, may incessantly rise to view, throughout the lapse of unceasing duration. But, in the prospect of all these solemn and important events, he beholds—in that almighty energy which wheels our globe around from day to day, and impels it in its annual course, and which directs, at the same time, the movements of all the hosts of heaven—the exertion of a benevolent power, which is calculated to inspire him with love and confidence, and which is able to secure his happiness amidst the revolutions of worlds, and amidst all the scenes through which he may pass during an immortal existence. Under this impression, he can adopt the affectionate and triumphant language of the psalmist—"Whom have I in heaven but thee, and there is none upon earth that I desire beside thee! My heart and my flesh shall fail, but God is the strength of my heart, and *my portion for ever.*"

Thus it appears, that the omnipotence of God is one of those attributes of his nature which is particularly calculated to fill the mind with sentiments of love and confidence, admiration and reverence. And, if such emotions be at all excited in the mind, they must rise to the highest pitch of elevation to which we can carry them; for there is no other object or being that possesses the same perfection, or can claim the same degree of affection and love. If we love God at all, it must be "with all our heart, with all our understanding, and with all our strength." The considerations to which I have now adverted, have been too seldom taken into view in moral and religious discussions on this topic. The omnipotence of the Deity is seldom exhibited as a ground and an excitement of veneration and love, and yet it stands, as it were, on the forefront of the divine character, giving beauty and efficiency to all his other perfections: without which wisdom, benevolence, faithfulness, mercy, and patience, would degenerate into empty names, and form no solid foundation for the exercise of confidence and hope. And, therefore, it is the duty of every Christian to endeavour, by every proper means, to enlarge his conceptions of the operations of omnipotence, and to familiarize his mind to contemplations of the magnitude, motions, grandeur, and immensity of God's works, in order that his love to God may be elevated and expanded, and his faith and hope strengthened and invigorated. To this attribute of Jehovah the inspired writers uniformly direct our views, as a source of joy and confidence. "Praise ye the Lord,—praise him, ye servants of the Lord; for I know that Jehovah is *great*, and that our Lord is above all gods. Whatever the Lord pleased, that did he, in heaven, and in earth, in the seas, and all deep places. Great is the Lord, and greatly to be praised; his greatness is unsearchable. I will speak of the glorious honour of thy majesty, and of thy *wondrous works.* I will speak of the might of thy terrible acts, and will declare thy greatness; to make known to the sons of men thy mighty operations, and the glorious majesty of thy kingdom. Happy is he who hath the God of Jacob for his help, whose hope is in the Lord his God, who made heaven and earth, the sea, and all that in them is, who keepeth truth for ever."

---

## SECTION IV.

### ON THE WISDOM AND GOODNESS OF GOD.

Another feature in the divine character, which is calculated to excite our most ardent affection, is, the *Wisdom* and *Goodness* of God. These two attributes may be considered under one head, since they are always inseparable in their operation. *Goodness* proposes the *end*, namely, the happiness of the sensitive and intelligent creation; and *Wisdom* selects the most proper *means* for its accomplishment.

Wherever genius appears combined with benevolent intentions and beneficent operations, we cannot withhold a certain portion of affection and regard.

When we behold a man like *Howard*, devoting his wealth, his knowledge, his intellectua and active powers, to alleviate the sorrows, and to promote the happiness of his fellow-men—when we behold him in retirement at his native mansion, a universal blessing to his neighbours around him, furnishing employment for the poor, erecting schools for the instruction of their children, watching over the morals of his neighbourhood, visiting the abodes of affliction, acting the part of a physician to their bodies, imparting spiritual instruction to their souls, promoting the knowledge and practice of religion, and extending his benevolent regards to persons of all religious persuasions—when we behold him leaving his native country and the friends of his youth, on a tour of benevolence over all Europe and the East; hazarding his health and his life in the service of humanity, diving into the depths of dungeons, plunging into the infected atmospheres of hospitals and jails, visiting the lonely and squalid prisoner, entering the wretched hovels of sorrow and affliction, administering consolation and relief, and surveying the dimensions of misery and distress among men of all nations, for the purpose of devising schemes for the relief of the distresses of suffering humanity, and for promoting the comforts of mankind—when such a character appears on the stage of life, there is no class of the human race, whose powers are not completely vitiated, but must feel towards it strong emotions of esteem and affectionate regard.

But what are all the wise and beneficent designs of a fellow-mortal, when compared with the numerous and diversified streams of benevolence which are incessantly flowing from the uncreated source of felicity! They are but as a drop to the ocean, or as an atom when compared with the immensity of the universe. On him all beings depend, from the archangel to the worm; from Him they derive their comforts; to Him they are indebted for all their powers and faculties; and on him their eternal felicity depends. Were we to prosecute this subject to any extent, it would lead us into a field on which volumes might be written, and yet the greater part of the displays of divine beneficence would remain unrecorded. I shall therefore confine myself to the selection of only a few instances of the wisdom and goodness of God.

Wherever we turn our eyes in the world around us, we behold innumerable instances of our Creator's beneficence. In order that the *eye* and the *imagination* may be gratified and charmed, he has spread over the surface of our terrestrial habitation an assemblage of the richest colours, which beautify and adorn the landscape of the earth, and present to our view a picturesque and diversified scenery, which is highly gratifying to the principle of novelty implanted in the human mind. On all sides we behold a rich variety of beauty and magnificence. Here, spread the wide plains and fertile fields, adorned with fruits and verdure; there, the hills rise in gentle slopes, and the mountains rear their snowy tops to the clouds, distilling from their sides the brooks and rivers, which enliven and fertilize the plains through which they flow. Here, the lake stretches into a smooth expanse in the bosom of the mountains; there, the rivers meander through the forests and the flowery fields, diversifying the rural scene, and distributing health and fertility in their train. Here, we behold the rugged cliffs and the stately port of the forest; there, we are charmed with the verdure of the meadow, the enamel of flowers, the azure of the sky, and the gay colouring of the morning and evening clouds. In order that this scene of beauty and magnificence might be rendered visible, He formed the element of light, without which the expanse of the universe would be a boundless desert, and its beauties for ever veiled from our sight. It opens to our view the mountains, the hills, the vales, the woods, the lawns, the flocks and herds, the wonders of the mighty deep, and the radiant orbs of heaven. It paints a thousand different hues on the objects around us, and promotes a cheerful and extensive intercourse among all the inhabitants of the globe.

Again, in order to gratify the sense of *hearing*, He formed the atmosphere, and endowed it with an undulating quality, that it might waft to our ears the pleasures of sound, and all the charms of music. The murmuring of the brooks, the whispers of the gentle breeze, the soothing sound of the rivulet, the noise of the waterfall, the hum of bees, the buzz of insects, the chirping of birds, the soft notes of the nightingale, and the melody of thousands of the feathered songsters, which fill the groves with their warblings, produce a pleasant variety of delightful emotions;—the numerous modulations of the human voice, the articulate sounds peculiar to the human species, by which the interchanges of thought and affection are promoted, the soft notes of the piano forte, the solemn sounds of the organ—and even the roaring of the stormy ocean, the dashings of the mighty cataract, and the rolling thunders which elevate the soul to sentiments of sublimity and awe—are all productive of a mingled variety of pleasures; and demonstrate that the distribution of happiness is one grand end of the operations of our bountiful Creator.

To gratify the sense of *smelling*, he has perfumed the air with a variety of delicious odours, which are incessantly exhaled from a thousand plants and flowers. Countless millions of these odoriferous particles, which elude the penetrating power of the finest microscope to discover, are continually wafted about by the air, and floating around us, impervious to the sight, the hearing, and the touch, but calculated to convey pleasure to the soul, through the medium of the olfactory nerves, and to enable us to "banquet on the invisible dainties of nature."

To gratify the sense of *feeling*, he has connected pleasure with the contact of almost every thing we have occasion to touch, and has rendered it subservient for warning us of whatever may be disagreeable or dangerous. Had a malevolent being constructed the body of man, and formed the arrangements of external nature, he might have rendered the contact of every object of touch as acutely painful as when we clasp a prickly shrub, or thrust our fingers against the point of a needle.

To gratify the sense of *taste*, and to nourish our bodies, he has furnished us with a rich variety of aliments, distributed not with a niggardly and a sparing hand, but with a luxuriant profusion, suited to the tastes of every sentient being, and to the circumstances of the inhabitants of every clime. He has not confined his bounty merely to the relief of our necessities, by confining us to the use of a few tasteless herbs and roots, but has covered the surface of the earth with an admirable profusion of plants, herbs, grains, and delicious fruits of a thousand different qualities and tastes, which contribute to the sensitive enjoyment and comfort of man. In almost every region of the earth, corn is to be found in the valleys surrounded by the snowy mountains of the North, as well as in the verdant plains of the Torrid Zone. In warm regions, cool and delicious fruits are provided for the refreshment of the inhabitants, and the trees are covered with luxuriant foliage to screen them from the intensity of the solar heat!* Every season presents us with a variety of fruits peculiar to itself, distributed by the munificent hand of the "Giver of all good." The month of June presents us with cabbages, cauliflowers, and cherries; July, with gooseberries, raspberries, peaches, and apricots; August and September scatter before us, in luxuriant abundance, plums, figs, apples, pears, turnips, carrots, cresses, potatoes, and, above all, wheat, oats, rye, and barley, which constitute the "staff of bread" for the support of man and beast; and although we are indebted chiefly to the summer and autumn for these rich presents, yet, by the assistance of human art, we can preserve and enjoy the greater part during winter and spring. The soil which produces these dainties has never yet lost its fertility, though it has brought forth the harvests of six thousand years, but still repays our labour with its annual treasures;—and, were selfish man animated with the same liberal and generous views as his munificent Creator, every individual of the human family would be plentifully supplied with a share of these rich and delicious bounties of nature.

In fine, the happiness of man appears to be the object of the divine care, every returning season, every moment, by day and by night. By *day*, He cheers us with the enlivening beams of the sun, which unfolds to us the beauty and the verdure of the fields; and lest the constant efflux of his light and heat should enfeeble our bodies, and wither the tender herbs, he commands the clouds to interpose as so many magnificent screens, to ward off the intensity of the solar rays. When the earth is drained of its moisture, and parched with heat, he bids the clouds condense their watery treasures, and fly from other regions on the wings of the wind, to pour their waters upon the fields, not in overwhelming and destructive torrents, but in small drops and gentle showers, to refresh the thirsty soil, and revive the vegetable tribes. He has spread under our feet a carpet of lovely green richer than all the productions of the Persian loom, and has thrown around our habitation an azure canopy, which directs our view to the distant regions of infinite space.—By *night*, he draws a veil of darkness over the mountains and the plains, that we may be enabled to penetrate to the regions of distant worlds, and behold the moon walking in brightness, the aspects of the planetary globes, the long trains of comets, and the innumerable host of stars. At this season, too, all nature is still, that we may enjoy in quiet the refreshments of sleep, to invigorate our mental and corporeal powers. "As a mother stills every little noise, that her infant be not disturbed; as she draws the curtain around its bed, and shuts out the light from its tender eyes: so God draws the curtains of darkness around us, so he makes all things to be hushed and still, that his large family may sleep in peace."—In a word, if we look around us to the forests which cover the mountains, or if we look downwards to the quarries and mines in the bowels of the earth, we behold abundance of materials for constructing our habitations, for embellishing the abodes of civilized life, and for carrying forward improvements in the arts and sciences. And, if we consider the surrounding atmosphere, we shall find it to contain the principle of life, and the element of *fire*, by means of which our winter evenings are cheered and illuminated in the absence of the sun.—Contemplating all these benign agencies as flowing from the care and

* The manner in which the Creator has contrived a supply for the thirst of man, in sultry places, is worthy of admiration.—He has placed amidst the burning sands of Africa, a plant, whose leaf, twisted round like a cruet, is always filled with a large glass full of fresh water; the gullet of this cruet is shut by the extremity of the leaf itself so as to prevent the water from evaporating. He has planted in some other districts of the same country, a great tree, called by the negroes *boa*, the trunk of which, of a prodigious bulk, is naturally hollowed like a cistern. In the rainy season, it receives its fill of water, which continues fresh and cool in the greatest heats, by means of the tufted foliage which crowns its summit. In some of the parched, rocky islands in the West Indies, there is found a tree called the *water lianne*, so full of sap, that if you cut a single branch of it, as much water is immediately discharged as a man can drink at a draught, and it is perfectly pure and limpid. See Pierre's "*Studies of Nature.*"

benevolence of our Almighty Parent, the pious mind may adopt the beautiful language of the poet, though in a sense somewhat different from what he intended:

"For me kind Nature wakes her genial power,
Suckles each herb, and spreads out every flower;
Annual for me, the grape, the rose renew
The juice nectareous, and the balmy dew;
For me the mine a thousand treasures brings;
For me health gushes from a thousand springs;
Seas roll to waft me, suns to light me, rise;
My footstool earth, my canopy the skies." *Pope.*

Viewing the various scenes and harmonies of nature, in relation to man, and to the gratification of his different senses, we may also say, in the language of Akenside, in his poem "On the Pleasures of Imagination," that

——— Not a breeze
Flies o'er the meadow, not a cloud imbibes
The setting sun's effulgence; not a strain
From all the tenants of the warbling shade
Ascends, but whence his bosom can partake
Fresh pleasure and delight.———
The rolling waves, the sun's unwearied course,
The elements and seasons, all declare
For what the Eternal Maker has ordain'd
The powers of man: we feel within ourselves
His energy divine: He tells the heart
He meant, He made us to behold and love
What He beholds and loves, the general orb
Of life and being: to be great like Him,
Beneficent and active."

Let us now consider, for a few moments, the wisdom which is displayed in the harmonious adjustment of the organs of sense to the scenes of external nature. All the scenes of beauty, grandeur, and benignity, which surround us, in the earth and heavens, would remain as one mighty blank, unproductive of enjoyment, unless our bodies were "fearfully and wonderfully" framed, and endowed with organs fitted for enabling us to hold a correspondence with the material world. Ten thousands of vessels, tubes, bones, muscles, ligaments, membranes, motions, contrivances, and adaptations, beyond the reach of the human understanding fully to investigate or to comprehend, must be arranged, and act in harmonious concert, before any one sense belonging to man can perceive and enjoy its objects.

Before the *eye* can behold a landscape, and be charmed with its beauties, it was requisite that three humours should be formed, of different sizes, different densities, and different refractive powers—three coats, or delicate membranes, with some parts opaque, and some transparent, some black, and some white, some of them formed of *radial*, and some with *circular* fibres, composed of threads finer than those of the spider's web. The *crystalline* humour required to be composed of two thousand very thin spherical lamina, or scales, lying one upon another, every one of these scales made up of one single fibre, or finest thread, wound in a most stupendous manner, this way, and that way, so as to run several courses, and to meet in as many centres. This curious and delicate piece of organization required to be compressed into the size of a ball of only half an inch in diameter, and a socket composed of a number of small bones, to be hollowed out and exactly fitted for its reception. A bed of loose fat for this ball to rest upon, a lid or curtain to secure it from danger, a variety of muscles to enable it to move upwards and downwards, to the right and to the left, and a numerous assemblage of minute veins, arteries, nerves, lymphatics, glands, and other delicate pieces of animal machinery, of which we have no distinct conception, were still requisite to complete this admirable organ. Even in this state it would be of no use for the purpose of vision, unless it were connected with the brain by the optic nerve, through the medium of which the impressions of visible objects are conveyed to the soul. Still, in addition to all these contrivances, a wonderful machinery requires to be in action, and an admirable effect produced, before a landscape can be contemplated. Ten thousand millions of rays, compounded of a thousand different shades of colour, must fly off in every direction from the objects which compose the surrounding scene, and be compressed into the space of one-eighth of an inch, in order to enter the eye, and must paint every object in its true colour, form, and proportion, on a space not exceeding half an inch in diameter. Were any one of the parts which compose this complicated machine either wanting or deranged; were it changed into a different form, or placed in a different position; were even a single muscle to lose its capacity of acting, we might be for ever deprived of all the enchanting prospects of the earth and heavens, and enveloped in the darkness of eternal night. Such is the skill and intelligence requisite for accomplishing, even in a single organ, the purpsoes of divine benevolence.

Again, before we could enjoy the harmony of sounds, the charms of music, and the pleasures of conversation, an instrument no less wonderful than the eye required to be constructed. In the *ear*, which is the organ of hearing, it was requisite, that there should be an outward porch for collecting the vibrations of the air, constructed, not of fleshy substances, which might fall down upon the orifice, or absorb the sounds, nor of solid bones, which would occasion pain and inconvenience when we repose ourselves—but composed of a cartilaginous substance, covered with a smooth membrane, endowed with elasticity, and bent into a variety of circular folds, or hollows, for the reflection of sound. It was farther requisite, that there should be a tube, or passage, composed partly of cartilage, and partly of bone, lined with a skin or membrane, and moistened with a glutinous matter, to form a communication with the internal machinery of this organ, where the principal wonders of hearing are performed. This machinery consists, first, of the *tympanum*, or *drum* of the ear, which consists of a dry, thin, and round membrane, stretched upon a bony ring, so as actually to resemble the instrument we call a drum. Under this membrane is a small nerve, or string, stretched tight, for the purpose of stretching or relaxing the drum, and increasing or diminishing its vibrations, so as to render it capable of reflecting every possible tone. Behind it is a cavity, hewn out of the temporal bone, the hardest one in the body, in which there seems to be an echo, by which the sound is reflected with the utmost precision. This cavity contains four very small, but remarkable bones, denominated the *hammer*, the *anvil*, the *orbicular bone*, and the *stirrup*, all connected together, and necessary for contributing to the extension and vibration of the tympanum. In this cavity are also formed various windings or cavities filled with air; and, in order that the air may be renewed, there is an opening which communicates with the back part of the mouth, called the Eustachian tube.

The next apparatus belonging to this curious machine, is the *labyrinth*, which is composed of three parts, the *vestibule* or porch, *three semicircular canals*, and the *cochlea*. This last is a canal, which takes a spiral course, like the shell of a snail, and is divided by a very thin lamina, or septum of cords, which keeps decreasing from the base to the top. The air acting on either side of these diminutive cords, produces a motion, nearly in the same manner as the sound of one musical instrument excites a tremulous motion in the cords of another. All these tubes, and winding canals, may be considered as so many sounding galleries, for augmenting the smallest tremours, and conveying their impressions to the auditory nerves, which conduct them to the brain. Besides the several parts now mentioned, a number of arteries, veins, lymphatics, glands, and a variety of other contrivances, which the human mind can neither trace nor comprehend, are connected with the mechanism of this admirable organ.

All this curious and complicated apparatus, however, would have been of no avail for the purpose of hearing, had not the atmosphere been formed, and its particles endowed with a tremulous motion. But, this medium being prepared, a sounding body communicates an undulatory motion to the air, as a stone thrown into a pond produces circular waves in the water; the air, thus put in motion, shakes the drum of the ear; the tremours, thus excited, produce vibrations in the air within the drum; this air shakes the handle of the hammer; the hammer strikes the anvil, with which it is articulated; the anvil transmits the motion to the stirrup, to which its longer leg is fastened; the stirrup transmits the motion it has received to the nerves; and the nerves, vibrating like the strings of a violin, or lyre, and the motion being still further augmented in the *labyrinth*,—the soul, in a manner altogether incomprehensible to us, receives an impression proportioned to the weakness or intensity of the vibration produced by the sounding body. Such is the exquisite and complicated machinery which required to be constructed, and preserved in action every moment, before we could enjoy the benefits of sound, and the pleasures of articulate conversation.

Again, before we could enjoy the pleasures of *feeling*, an extensive system of organization required to be arranged. A system of nerves, originating in the brain and spinal marrow, and distributed, in numberless minute ramifications, through the heart, lungs, bowels, blood-vessels, hands, feet, and every other part of the body, was requisite to be interwoven through the whole constitution of the animal frame, before this sense, which is the foundation of all the other sensations, and the source of so many pleasures, could be produced. Wherever there are nerves, there are also sensations; and wherever any particular part of the body requires to exert a peculiar feeling, there the nerves are arranged and distributed in a peculiar manner, to produce the intended effect. And how nicely is every thing arranged and attempered, in this respect, to contribute to our comfort! If the points of the fingers require to be endowed with a more delicate sensation than several other parts, they are furnished with a corresponding number of nervous ramifications; if the heel require to be more callous, the nerves are more sparingly distributed. If feelings were equally distributed over the whole body, and as acutely sensible as in the membranes of the eye, our very clothes would become galling and insupportable, and we should be exposed to continual pain; and if every part were as insensible as the callus of the heel, the body would be benumbed, the pleasures we derive from this sense would be destroyed, and the other organs of sensation could not perform their functions in the manner in which they now operate. So that in this, as well as in all the other sensitive organs, infinite wisdom is admirably displayed in executing the designs of benevolence.

In order that we might derive enjoyment from the various aliments and delicious fruits which the earth produces, a peculiar organization, different from all the other senses, was requisite to be devised. Before we could relish the peculiar flavour of the pear, the apple, the peach, the plumb, or the grape, the *tongue*, the principal organ of *taste*, required to be formed, and its surface covered with an infinite number of nervous *papillæ*, curiously divaricated over its surface, to receive and convey to the soul the impressions of every flavour. These nerves required to be guarded with a firm and proper tegument or covering, to defend them from danger, and enable them to perform their functions so long as life continues; and at the same time, to be perforated in such a manner, with a multitude of pores, in the papillary eminences, as to give a free admission to every variety of taste. It was likewise necessary, that these papillary nerves should be distributed in the greatest number, in those parts of the organ to which the objects of taste are most frequently applied; and hence we find, that they are more numerous on the upper than on the lower parts of the tongue; and, therefore, when we apply highly-flavoured substances to the under part, we are not so sensible of the taste, till we remove them to the upper surface. A variety of veins, arteries, glands, tendons, and other parts with which we are unacquainted. are also connected with this useful organ. When we consider how frequently these delicate organs are used, during a length of years, it is matter of admiration how well they wear. While our clothes wear out in the course of a year or two, while the hairs of our heads turn gray, and are nipped asunder at the roots, and while age shrivels the most beautiful skin, these delicate nervous papillæ last longer than instruments of iron or steel; for the sense of taste is generally the last that decays. For the bestowment of this sense, therefore, and the pleasures it conveys, we have abundant reason to admire and adore the wisdom and goodness of our Almighty Creator.

Finally, that we might be regaled with the scent of flowers, and the aromatic perfumes of spring and summer, and that none of the pleasures of nature might be lost, the organ of *smelling* was constructed to catch the invisible odoriferous effluvia which are continually wafted through the air. For this purpose it was requisite that bones, nerves, muscles, arteries, veins, cartilages, and membranes, peculiarly adapted to produce this effect, should be arranged, and placed in a certain part of the body. As the bones of the head are too hard for this purpose, the nerves of smelling required to have a bone of a peculiar texture, of a spongy nature, full of little holes, like a sieve, through which they might transmit their slender threads or branches to the papillous membrane which lines the cavities of the bone and the top of the nostrils. The nostrils required to be cartilaginous and not fleshy, in order to be kept open, and to be furnished with appropriate muscles to dilate or contract them as the occasion might require. It was likewise requisite, that they should be wide at the bottom, to collect a large quantity of effluvia, and narrow at the top, where the olfactory nerves are condensed, that the effluvia might act with the greatest vigour, and convey the sensation to the brain. By means of these and numerous other contrivances, connected with this organ, we are enabled to distinguish the qualities of our food, and to regale ourselves on those invisible effluvia which are incessantly flying off from the vegetable tribes, and wafted in every direction through the atmosphere.

Of all the senses with which we are furnished, the sense of smelling is that which we are apt to consider as of the least importance; and some have even been ready to imagine, that our enjoyments would scarcely have been diminished, although its organs had never existed. But, it is presumptuous in man to hazard such an opinion in reference to any of the beneficent designs of the Creator. We know not what relation the minutest operations, within us or around us, mny bear to the whole economy of nature, or what disastrous effects might be produced, were a single pin of the machinery of our bodies broken or destroyed. The exhalations which are, at this moment, rising from a putrid marsh in the centre of New Holland, and hovering in an invisible form, over that desolate region, may be forming those identical clouds which, the next month, shall water our fields and gardens, and draw forth from the flowers their aromatic perfumes. The sense of smelling may be essentially requisite to the perfection of several of the other senses; as we know that the sense of feeling is inseperably connected with the senses of seeing, hearing, and tasting. Let us consider, for a moment, some of the agencies whieh require to be exerted when this sense is exercised and gratified. Before we could derive pleasure from the fragrance of a flower, it was requisite that a system of the finest tubes, filaments, and membranes should be organized, endowed with powers of absorption and perspiration, furnished with hundreds of vessels for conveying the sap through all its parts, and perforated with thousands of pores to give passage to myriads of odoriferous particles, secreted from the internal juices. It was also requisite that the atmosphere should be formed, for the purpose of affording nourishment to the plant, and for conveying its odoriferous effluvia to the olfactory nerves. The rains, the dews, the principle of heat, the revolution of the seasons, the succession of day and night, the principle of evaporation, the agitation of the air by winds, and the *solar light*,—all combine their influence and their agencies in producing the grateful sensation we feel from the smell of a *rose*. So that the sense of smelling is not only connected with the agency of all the terrestrial elements around us, but bears a relation to the vast globe of the sun himself; for an energy exerted at the distance of ninety-five millions of miles, and a motion of 200,000 miles every second, in the particles of light, are necessary to its existence; and consequently, it forms one of the subordinate ends for which that luminary was created:—and, being related to the sun, it may bear a certain relation to similar agencies which that central globe is producing among the inhabitants of surrounding worlds.

Thus it appears, that the various senses of man, as well as the external objects which contribute to their gratification, are the results of infinite wisdom and goodness, and calculated to promote the happiness of sensitive and intelligent beings.

But, before any one of these senses could perform its functions, it required to be united with a most wonderful system of organization. The heart required to be endowed with an immense degree of muscular power, and to be set in action in the centre of this complicated system—hundreds of arteries required to be bored, and ramified, and arranged, to convey the blood to its remotest extremities, and hundreds of veins to bring it back again to its reservoir—thousands of lacteal and lymphatic tubes to absorb nutriment from the food, and convey it to the circulating fluid—thousands of glands to secrete humours that are noxious or redundant from the mass of blood, and emunctories to throw them off from the system—hundreds of muscles for moving the different members of the body, and for conveying the whole corporeal frame from place to place—hundreds of fine cords infinitely ramified over the whole body, to convey sensation to all its parts; and thousands of millions of perforations to be made in the skin, through which the insensible perspiration might continually flow. To support this fine and delicate system of vessels, hundreds of bones of diversified forms, and different sizes, and connected together by various modes of articulation, required to be constructed and arranged, and nicely adapted to their peculiar functions; and hundreds of tendons and ligaments, to connect these bones with the muscles, and with every other part of the animal frame. This machine required to be preserved in constant action, whether we be sleeping or waking, sitting or standing, in motion or at rest. The heart required to give ninety-six thousand strokes every twenty-four hours, to send off streams of the vital fluid through hundreds of tubes, and to impel the whole mass of blood through every part of the body every four minutes. The lungs required to be in constant play, expanding and contracting their thousand vesicles, at least twenty times every minute, to imbibe the oxygen of the atmosphere, and to transmit its enlivening influence to the circulating fluids—the stomach to be dissolving the food, and preparing it for the nourishment of the body—the liver and kidneys to be drawing off their secretions—the lacteals to be extracting nutritious particles, to be conveyed, by the absorbent vessels, into the mass of blood—and the perspiration, which might otherwise clog the wheels of the whole machine, to be thrown off incessantly through millions of pores. All this curious and delicate machinery, constructed of the most flabby substances, required to be put in motion, and to be preserved in action every moment, before we could contemplate the beauties of a landscape, be delighted with the sounds of music, or inhale the fragrance of a rose.

It is worthy of notice, that, in the construction and arrangement of these numerous and complicated parts and functions, there is not a single instance, that any physiologist can produce, in which *pain* is the *object* of the contrivance. Of all the thousands of adaptations which infinite Wisdom has contrived, there is not *one* but what has for its object the communication of pleasure to the sentient being in which it is found. If a number of small muscles are connected with the eye, it is for the purpose of rendering that organ susceptible of a quick and easy motion in every direction, to meet every exigence. If the arteries are furnished with numerous valves, opening only in one direction, it is intended to prevent the blood from returning by a wrong course, and endangering the whole structure of the animal machine. If a joint is formed to move only in one direction, as the joints of the fingers, it is intended to prevent those inconveniences which would inevitably have been felt, had it been capable of moving in every direction. If another kind of joint is constructed so as to move in every direction, it is intended to enable us to perform, with facility, those movements and operations which would otherwise have been either impossible, or have been attended with the greatest inconvenience and pain. There are certain parts connected with the human frame, whose precise use cannot be accurately determined, but this is owing to our limited knowledge of the various functions which are requisite to be performed in this complicated machine. In no instance whatever can it be shown, that the infliction of pain is the object of any one part or function of whose use we are uncertain;—and it is conformable to the dictates of the soundest reason to conclude, that, since every part, whose use we can ascertain, is adapted to communicate pleasure, every other part, throughout every branch of the animal system, is calculated to produce a similar effect.

It is true, indeed, that pain is frequently felt in the different members which compose our corporeal system; but this is not owing to its original construction, but to the derangement which its parts receive, either from internal disease or from external violence: and such consequences are the effects either of the folly of man, in exposing his body to danger, or in using its members for improper purposes,—or of the physical changes which have happened in the system of nature since man was created,—or of those depraved and immoral passions which so frequently agitate and convulse his corporeal frame.

Let us now endeavour, if we can, to sum up a few of the blessings which we enjoy from these wise arrangements of our beneficent Creator. In our bodies there are reckoned 245 *bones*, each of them having forty distinct scopes or intentions, and 446 muscles for the purpose of motion, each having at least ten several intentions. All these are ready every moment to perform their functions; and every breath we draw, whether we be in motion or at rest, asleep or awake, a hundred muscles at least are in constant action. In the act of breathing, we respire at least twenty times every minute; the heart exerts its muscular force in propelling the blood into the arteries sixty times every minute; the stomach and abdominal muscles are every moment in action, and the curious little bones of the ear are ever ready to convey sensations of the softest whisper to the brain. So that, without an hyperbole, or the least extravagance of expression, it may truly and literally be said, that we enjoy *a thousand blessings every minute*, and, consequently, sixty thousand every hour, and one million four hundred and forty thousand every day. For, if any one of these numerous functions were to stop, or to be interrupted, pain, and even death itself might be induced. Let us ask the man who is gasping for breath, under an incurable asthma, or him who is smarting under the pain of a toothache, or him who has wounded a nerve, an artery, or a vein, or him who has dislocated his shoulder-blade, if he would not consider it as a peculiar blessing to have the functions of nature restored to their original action? And if one member out of joint, or one function out of order, produces so much pain and uneasiness, how grateful ought we to feel for the thousands of blessings we enjoy every moment, while the wheels of the animal machine are moving on with smoothness and harmony! If we consider the number of years during which these blessings have been continued,—if we consider the mercies received in childhood, which have been long overlooked or forgotten,—if we count the many nights which we have passed in sound repose, and the many days we have enjoyed without bodily pain,—if we reflect on the numerous objects of sublimity and beauty with which our eyes have been delighted, the numerous sounds which have charmed our ears and cheered our hearts, and the numerous gratifications which our other senses have received; if we consider how often food has been provided and administered for the nourishment of our bodies, and from how many visible and invisible dangers we have been delivered—and, if we view all these countless blessings as proceeding every moment from Him, "whose hands have made and fashioned us," and who "breathed into our nostrils the breath of life," can we forbear to recognise our Almighty Benefactor as worthy of our supreme affection and our most lively gratitude?

"For me, when I forget the darling theme,—
Be my tongue mute, my fancy paint no more,
And, dead to joy, forget my heart to beat."

Under an impression of the diversified agencies of Divine Wisdom which are incessantly contributing to our enjoyment, and of the vast profusion of our Creator's beneficence which we behold around us, and experience every passing hour, can we forbear exclaiming with the enraptured poet:—

"When all thy mercies, O my God!
My rising soul surveys,
Transported with the view, I'm lost
In wonder, love, and praise.
Through every period of my life
Thy goodness I'll proclaim;
And, after death, in distant worlds,
Renew the glorious theme.
Through all eternity to Thee
A joyful song I'll raise;
For, oh! eternity 's too short
To utter all thy praise."

If, then, the construction of our bodies, and the terrestrial scene in which we are placed, present so many striking displays of wisdom and benevolence, what an astonishing and transporting scene of divine benignity would burst upon the view, were we permitted to explore those more extensive provinces of the empire of Omnipotence, where physical and moral evil have never shed their baleful influence to interrupt the happiness of intellectual natures! Could we soar beyond the regions of the planetary system; could we penetrate into that immensity of worlds and beings which are scattered in magnificent profusion through the boundless fields of ether; could we draw aside the veil which now conceals the grandeur and beauty of their physical economy and arrangements; could we behold their inhabitants arrayed in robes of beauty, with ecstatic joy beaming from their countenances, basking perpetually in the regions of bliss, united to one another by indissoluble bands of love and affection, without the least apprehension of evil, or of an interruption to their enjoyments; and looking forward with confidence to an interminable succession of delighted existence; could we retrace the history of their Creator's dispensations towards them since the first moment of their existence, and the peculiar displays of divine glory and benignity, that may occasionally be exhibited to their view,—it is more than probable, that all the displays of wisdom and benevolence which we now behold, numerous as they are, would be thrown completely into the shade, and that this world would appear only as a Lazar-house, when compared with the bright and transporting scenes of the celestial worlds. This we are infallibly led to conclude, in regard to a certain class of intelligences in the future state, by the express declarations of Scripture. For thus it is written, "Eye hath not seen, nor ear heard, neither have entered into the heart of man, the things which God hath prepared for them that love him." And if renovated men shall experience such superior enjoyments in the eternal world, there can be no doubt that all those intelligences, in every region, who have retained their primitive integrity, are at this moment in the possession of similar transporting enjoyments. It must, therefore, have an additional tendency to elevate our affections to the Supreme Intelligence, when we view Him not only communicating happiness to the various tribes of beings which people our globe, but also distributing streams of felicity in boundless profusion, among the inhabitants of unnumbered worlds

I shall now conclude my illustrations of this topic, by exhibiting a few instances of the wisdom and goodness of God as delineated in the Sacred Scriptures.

"The Lord is good to all, and his tender mercies are over all his works He stretched forth the heavens, and laid the foundation of the earth, and formeth the spirit of man within him. He planted the ear, and formed the eye; and he breathed into our nostrils the breath of life. In his hand is the soul of every living thing, and the breath of all mankind. With him is wisdom and strength, and his understanding is infinite. He is wonderful in counsel, and excellent in working. He hath established the world by his wisdom, and stretched out the heavens by his understanding. O the depth of the riches both of the wisdom and the knowledge of God! how unsearchable are his operations, and his ways past finding out! He causeth the vapours to ascend from the ends of the earth; he bindeth up the waters in his thick clouds, and the cloud is not rent under them. He hath compassed the waters with bounds, until the day and night come to an end. He visiteth the earth and watereth it, he greatly enricheth it with rivers; he prepareth corn for its inhabitants; he watereth the ridges thereof abundantly; he settleth the furrows thereof; he maketh it soft with showers; he blesseth the springing thereof; he crowneth the year with his goodness, and his paths drop fatness. The pastures are clothed with flocks; the valleys are covered over with corn, and the little hills are encircled with joy.*

"He sendeth the springs into the valleys which run among the hills; they give drink to every beast of the field. Beside these springs the fowls of heaven have their habitation, which sing among the branches. He causeth the grass to grow for the cattle, and herb for the service of man; and wine that maketh glad the heart of man, and oil that maketh his face to shine, and bread that strengtheneth his heart. He planted the tall trees and the cedars of Lebanon, where the birds make their nests, and the storks their dwellings. The high hills are a refuge for the wild goats, and the rocks for the conies. He appointed the moon for seasons, and the sun to enlighten the world; he makes darkness a curtain for the night, till the sun arise, when man goeth forth to his work and to his labour till the evening. How manifold are thy works, O Lord! In *wisdom* hast thou made them all; the earth is full of thy riches; so is the great and wide sea, wherein are things creeping innumerable, both small and great beasts. These all wait upon thee, that thou mayest give them their meat in due season. Thou givest them—they gather; thou openest thine hand—they are filled with good. Thou hidest thy face—they are troubled; thou sendest forth thy spirit—they are created; and thou renewest the face of the earth. The glory of the Lord shall endure for ever; Jehovah shall rejoice in all his works. He is Lord of heaven and earth; he giveth to all, life, and breath, and all things; he hath made of one blood all nations of men, to dwell on all the face of the earth; and hath determined the times before appointed, and the bounds of their habitation. For in him we live, and move, and have our being. I will sing unto Jehovah as long as I live; I will sing praises to my God, while I have my being; I will utter abundantly the memory of his great goodness, and speak of all his wondrous works."

The inspired writers rise to still higher strains when they celebrate the Divine Goodness in reference to our eternal salvation.

"Praise ye Jehovah, for Jehovah is good; he remembered us in our low estate; for his mercy endureth for ever. I will praise thee, O Lord, my God, *with all my heart*, and I will glorify thy name for evermore; for great is thy mercy toward me, and thou hast delivered my soul from the lowest hell. God so loved the world, that he gave his only-begotten Son, that whosoever believeth on him should not perish, but have everlasting life. He sent an angel from the celestial glory to announce his birth; and a multitude of the heavenly host to proclaim, Glory to God in the highest, peace on earth, and good will to men. He spared not his own Son, but delivered him up for us all—and shall he not with him also freely give us all things? Blessed be the God and Father of our Lord Jesus Christ, who hath blessed us with all spiritual blessings in heavenly things in Christ; in whom we have redemption through his blood, the forgiveness of sins, according to the riches of his grace.—Bless the Lord, O my soul, and all that is within me bless his holy name; who forgiveth all thine iniquities, who healeth all thy diseases; who redeemeth thy life from destruction, and crowneth thee with loving kindness and tender mercies. As the heaven is high above the earth, so great is his mercy toward them that fear him. The mercy of Jehovah is from everlasting to everlasting, upon

* In this, and several other quotations from the Scriptures, the literal rendering from the Hebrew is substituted in place of the common translation, and the *supplements* are frequently omitted.

them that fear him; and his righteousness unto children's children. Many, O Lord, my God, are thy wonderful works, which thou hast done, and thy thoughts to us ward; they cannot be reckoned up in order unto thee; if I would declare and speak of them, they are more than can be numbered.—I will praise thee, for I am fearfully and wonderfully made: marvellous are thy works. How precious are thy thoughts (or designs) towards me, O God! how great is the sum of them! If I should count them, they are more in number than the sand."

Thus it appears, that both the system of nature, and the system of revelation, concur in exhibiting the wisdom and benevolence of the Deity as calculated to excite the highest degree of ardent affection in the minds of the whole intelligent creation. If an atom of gratitude is due to an earthly benefactor, it is impossible to set bounds to that affection and gratitude which ought incessantly to rise in our hearts towards the Creator of the universe, who is the "Father of mercies, and the God of all consolation." And, therefore, we need not wonder, that "holy men of old," whose minds were overpowered with this sacred emotion, broke out into language which would be deemed extravagant, by the frigid moralists of the present age. Under a sense of the unbounded love and goodness of God, the psalmist felt his heart elated, and formed these pious resolutions: "Seven times a day will I praise thee, O Lord! At midnight will I rise to give thanks to thee, because of thy righteous precepts, I will rejoice in the way of thy precepts, as much as in all riches. The law of thy mouth is better unto me than thousands of gold and silver. Oh, how I love thy law! it is my meditation all the day. I will speak of thy testimonies before kings, and will not be ashamed of thy commandments. Whom have I in heaven but thee? and there is none upon earth that I desire beside thee. As the hart panteth after the brooks of water, so panteth my soul after thee, O God!" Under similar emotions, the Apostle Paul exclaims, "I am persuaded that neither death, nor life, nor angels, nor principalities, nor powers, nor things present, nor things to come, shall be able to separate us from the love of God, which is in Christ Jesus our Lord."

---

## SECTION V.

### ON THE MERCY AND PATIENCE OF GOD.

Another feature in the divine character, which is peculiarly calculated to excite admiration, affection, and gratitude, is the *mercy and patience of God.*

Mercy has its source in the divine goodness, and may be considered as a particular modification of the benevolence of the Deity. Goodness is the *genus*, mercy the *species*. The goodness of God extends to all the creatures he has formed, of whatever description or character,—to the fowls of the air, the fishes of the sea, the microscopic animalcula, and the most wicked class of human beings, as well as to angels, archangels, and other superior intelligences. Mercy can have a reference only to those who have sinned against their Maker, and rendered themselves unworthy of his favours. It consists in the bestowment of blessings upon those who have forfeited every claim to them, and have rendered themselves obnoxious to punishment. It cannot be exercised toward "the angels who have kept their first estate," or towards any other class of holy intelligences, because they do not stand in need of its exercise.—The *patience* or *forbearance* of God, is that attribute of his nature which consists in his bearing long with sinners, and refraining from inflicting deserved punishment, notwithstanding their impenitence, and long-continued provocations.

These attributes are seldom displayed, in our world, by one man, or class of men, towards another. Instead of clemency, mercy, and forbearance, we find in the character of mankind, as delineated in the page of history, the principle of *revenge* operating more powerfully than almost any other disposition; and, therefore, when any striking instance of mercy and long-suffering is exhibited in human conduct, we are disposed to wonder at it, and to admire it as an extraordinary moral phenomenon. When we behold a personage who is possessed of every degree of moral and physical power for crushing his enemies—yet remaining calm and tranquil, and forbearing to execute deserved punishment, notwithstanding repeated insults and injuries, we are led to admire such qualities, as indicating a certain degree of greatness and benevolence of mind. On this principle, we admire the forbearance of David, the anointed king of Israel, towards Saul, his bitterest enemy, when he had an opportunity of slaying him at the cave of Engedi; and afterwards, when he was sleeping in a trench at Hachila;—and at the clemency which he exercised tawards Shimei, who had cursed and insulted him, and treated him most reproachfully. On the same principle, we admire the conduct of Sir Walter Raleigh, a man of known courage and honour, towards a certain rash, hot-headed youth. Being very injuriously treated by this impertinent mortal, who next proceeded to *challenge* him, and, on his refusal, spit on him, and that too in public;—the knight taking out his handkerchief, with great calmness, made him only this reply: "Young man, if I could as easily wipe your blood from my conscience, as I can this injury from my face, I would this moment take away your life."

In order to exhibit the mercy and long-suffering of the Deity in their true light, let us consider, for a moment, some of the leading features in the conduct and the character of mankind.—Whether we go back to the remote ages of antiquity, or review the present moral state of the inhabitants of our globe, we shall find the following, among other similar traits, in the character of the great mass of this world's population; —*An utter forgetfulness of God, and the prevalence of abominable idolatries.* Though an invisible and omnipotent energy may be clearly perceived in that majestic machinery by which the vault of heaven appears to be whirled round our globe from day to day; and though every returning season proclaims the exuberant goodness of that Being who arranged our terrestrial habitation,—yet, of the great majority of human beings that have hitherto existed, or now exist, it may with truth be said, that "God is not in all their thoughts, and the fear of God is not before their eyes." And how grovelling have been the conceptions of those who have professed to offer their adorations to a superior Intelligence! They have changed the glory of the incorruptible God into an image made like to corruptible man, and have invested with the attributes of divinity a block of marble, the stock of a tree, a stupid ox, and a crawling reptile: to which they have paid that worship and homage which were due to the Almighty Maker of heaven and earth.—*Blasphemy and impiety* is another characteristic of the majority of our species. How many have there been of our wretched race in all ages, and how many are there in the present age, who "set their mouths against the heavens in their blasphemous talk," and "dare defy the Omnipotent to arms!" They say to God, "Depart from us, for we desire not the knowledge of thy ways: What is the Almighty, that we should serve him? and what profit should we have, if we pray unto him?" While his hand is making their pulse to beat, and their lungs to play, and while he is distributing to them corn, and wine, and fruits in rich abundance, they are blaspheming his venerable Majesty, and prostituting these very blessings for the purpose of pouring dishonour on his name.

The *diabolical passions* which men have displayed towards one another, is another striking trait in their character. War has been their employment and their delight in every age. Thousands of rational beings of the same species have set themselves in array against thousands, and have levelled at each other spears, and arrows, and darts, and musquetry, and cannon, and every other instrument of destruction, till legs and arms, and skulls, and brains, were mingled with the dust—till the earth was drenched with human gore—till cities, and towns, and villages, were tumbled into ruins, or given up as a prey to the devouring flames—and till the bounties of Providence, which God had provided for man and beast, were destroyed, and trampled down as the mire of the streets. And, what adds to the enormity of such dreadful passions, they have often had the effrontery to implore the assistance of the God of mercy in this work of horror and destruction. When, to all these abominable dispositions and practices, we add, the the numerous other acts of atrocity, that are daily committed in every quarter of the world,—the oppression and injustice which the poor, the widow, and the fatherless have suffered from the overwhelming hand of power; the persecutions which tyranny has inflicted on the select few, who have raised their voices against such abominations; the falsehood, and treachery, and perjury, which are rampant in every land, the lewd and unnatural crimes that are daily committed; the thefts, and murders, and assassinations, that are incessantly perpetrating in some one region of the world or another; the haughty pride and arrogance which so many of the puny sons of men assume; the murmurings and complainings at the dispensations of Providence, and the base ingratitude with which the majority of mankind receive the bounties of heaven;—and when we consider, for how many thousands of years these abominable dispositions have been displayed, we have reason to wonder that condign punishment is not speedily executed, and that the Almighty does not interpose his omnipotence, to shatter this globe to atoms, and to bury its inhabitants in the gulf of everlasting oblivion.

Yet, notwithstanding these depraved and ungrateful dispositions; notwithstanding that this spacious world, which was erected for a temple to the Deity, has been turned into a temple of idols, its seas and rivers stained, and its fields drenched with the blood of millions of human beings, and its cities transformed into a sink of moral pollution; in spite of all these innumerable and aggravated provocations, the God of heaven still exercises his mercy, long-suffering, and forbearance. He impels the earth in its annual and diurnal course, to bring about the interchanges of day and night, and the vicissitudes of the seasons; he makes his sun to arise on the world, to cheer the nations with his light and heat; he sends his rains, to refresh the fields, both of "the just, and of the *unjust*;" he causes the trees, the herbs, and the flowers, to bud and blossom every returning spring; he ripens the fields in harvest; he crowns the year with his bounty, and encircles the little hills with rejoicing. Instead of "sending forth his mighty winds," in incessant storms and hurricanes, to tear up whole forests by their roots, and to lay waste the productions of the soil, he fans the groves and the lawns with gentle breezes, and odoriferous gales. Instead of opening the cataracts of heaven, and dashing down overwhelming torrents, to deluge the plains, and frustrate the hopes of man, he refreshes the parched ground with gentle showers, as if they proceeded from a watering-pot. Instead of confining our sensitive enjoyments to bread and water, as if we were the tenants of a jail, he has strewed our gardens and fields with every variety of luxuriant delicacies, to gratify every appetite. Instead of directing the lightnings to set on fire the mountains, and to level our cities to the ground, and the thunders to roll incessantly around us, he commands this terrific meteor to visit us only at distant intervals, and in its gentler operations, just to remind us what tremendous instruments of destruction he is capable of wielding, and that we ought to "be still and know that He is God," and that "he has punished us less than our iniquities deserve." O that man would praise the Lord for his mercy, and for his long-suffering towards the children of men!

This character of God is *peculiar to himself*, and cannot be supposed to belong, unless in a very inferior degree, to any created intelligence. Were the meekest man that ever appeared on the theatre of our world—or were even one of the highest intelligences in heaven to be invested with a portion of the attribute of omniscience; could he penetrate, at one glance, over all that hemisphere of our globe on which the sun shines, and, at the next glance, survey the other hemisphere which is enveloped in darkness; could his eye pierce into the secret chambers of every habitation of human beings, in every city, and town, and village, and especially into those haunts where crimes are veiled by the shades of night from every human eye; could he behold at one glance all the abominations that are hourly perpetrating in every region of the world—the pagan worshippers in Thibet and Hindostan, performing their cruel and execrable rites—the wheels of Juggernaut crushing to death its wretched devotees—the human victims which are tortured and sacrificed, to gratify the ferocity of some barbarous chief—the savage hordes of New Zealand, feasting on the flesh of their fellow-men, whom they have cruelly butchered, and drinking their blood out of human skulls—the Indians of America, tearing with pincers the flesh of their prisoners, and enjoying a diabolical pleasure in beholding their torments—the haughty inquisitors of Spain insulting their devoted victims, in the name of the merciful Saviour, and preparing tortures, and stakes, and flames for their destruction—the assassin plunging his dagger into his neighbour's bosom—the midnight robber entering into the abode of honest industry, strangling its inmates, and carrying off their treasures—the kidnapper tearing the poor African from his wife and children, and native land—the unfeeling planter and overseer lashing his degraded slaves—tyrants and persecutors dragging "the excellent ones of the earth" to prisons, to dungeons, and to gibbets—the malevolent and envious man devising schemes for the ruin and destruction of his neighbour—the mutinous crew, in the midst of the ocean, rising up against their superiors, slashing them with their sabres, and plunging their bodies into the deep—the gamester ruining a whole family by a throw of the dice—the skeptic sporting with the most sacred truths—the atheist attempting to defy the Omnipotent—the prostitute wallowing in the mire of uncleanness—the drunkard blaspheming the God of heaven in his midnight revels—numerous tribes of human beings, in every quarter of the globe, dashing out each other's brains in mutual combat—hypocritical professors of religion, harbouring malice and revenge against their brethren—and thousands of other iniquitous scenes which are daily presented before the pure eyes of Omniscience; could he behold all the abominable acts of this description which are perpetrated on the surface of our globe, in the course of *a single day*, and were the elements under his control, for executing condign punishment on transgressors,—it is more than probable, that, before another day dawned upon the world, the great globe we inhabit would be shattered to its centre, and enveloped in devouring flames. For no finite intelligence could refrain his indignation for a length of years, or could penetrate into all the reasons, why "sentence against an evil work should not be *speedily* executed;" why the murderer should not be arrested by death before his hand is lifted up to strike; why the tyrant should not be cut off before his victims are secured; and why the slave should be doomed to drag out so many long years under the rod of a relentless master. But God beholds all these actions in all their bearings and relations to the plan of his government, and in all their eternal consequences; and beholding them, he "keeps silence," and refrains from executing immediate and deserved punishment.

This part of the divine character, when seriously considered, is calculated to excite strong emotions of admiration and wonder; and these emotions must be raised to their highest pitch, when we consider the many instruments of vengeance which are every moment wielded by the hand of the Almighty. If forbearance were owing to *impotence*, or a want of means for the infliction of retributive justice, our admiration would cease. But all the elements of nature are under the immediate control of the Governor of the universe; and, in a thousand modes incomprehensible by us, He could make them the instruments of his vengeance to chastise a guilty world. "For in his hand is the soul of every living thing, and the breath of all mankind." Let us consider, for a little, some of those agents which lie within the sphere of our knowledge in the system of nature.

Of all the elements of nature, there is none more delightful and beautiful in its effects than *light.* "Truly the light is sweet, and a pleasant thing it is for the eyes to behold the sun." It diffuses a thousand shades of colouring over the hills, the vales, the rivers, and the boundless deep, and opens to our view the glorious host of heaven. Yet this delightful visitant, by a slight modification, from the hand of Omnipotence, is capable of being transformed into the most destructive element in nature. Light flies from the sun at the rate of 200,000 miles in a second of time; and it is owing to its particles being almost infinitely small, that we feel no inconvenience from their rapid velocity. But, were the Creator to condense several millions of these particles into one, or impel them with a still greater velocity, the solid crust of our globe would be perforated and shattered in every point by this celestial artillery, and its inhabitants would soon be battered to atoms.

Again, the *atmosphere* which surrounds us, and in which we live and breathe; which contains the principles of life; which fans us with its gentle gales, and wafts to our ears the harmonies of music—is capable of being converted into an instrument of terror and destruction. It is composed chiefly of two different ingredients; one of these is the principle of flame,—and if the other ingredient were extracted from the atmosphere, and this principle left to exert its native energy without control, instantly the forests would be in a blaze; the hardest metals, and the most solid rocks, would melt like wax; the waters of the ocean would add fuel to the raging element; and, in a few minutes, the whole expanse of our globe would be enveloped in one devouring flame.

Again, the globe on which we reside is whirling round its axis every twenty-four hours, and is carried round the sun with a still greater velocity. Should that Almighty arm which first impelled it in its career, cause these motions suddenly to cease, mountains would be tumbled into the sea, forests torn up by their roots, cities overthrown and demolished, all nature would be thrown into confusion, and terror and destruction would overwhelm the inhabitants of the world. Not only the stopping of the earth's motions, but even a new direction given to its axis of rotation, would be productive of the most fatal effects. The earth's axis at present is directed to certain points of the heavens, from which it never deviates, but in a very small degree; but were the hand of Omnipotence to bend it so as to make it point in a different direction, the ocean would abandon its present bed, and overflow the land; and a second universal deluge would overwhelm all the monuments of human grandeur, and sweep the earth's inhabitants into a watery grave.

Again, not only the elements which immediately surround us, but even celestial bodies which are just now, invisible to our sight, and removed to the distance of a thousand millions of miles might be employed as ministers of vengeance. There are at least a hundred *comets* connected with the solar system, which are moving in all directions, and crossing the orbits of the earth, and the other planets. Were the orbit of one of these bodies, in its approach to the sun, to be bent in a direction to that of the earth, the most alarming phenomena would be exhibited in the heavens. A ruddy globe, larger in appearance than the moon, would first announce terror to the inhabitants of the earth—every day this terrific object would increase in size, till it appeared to fill the celestial hemisphere with its tremendous disk;—the light of the sun would be eclipsed—the stars would disappear—the ocean would be thrown into violent agitation, and toss its billows to the clouds—the earth would "reel to and fro, like a drunkard"—and universal alarm and confusion would seize upon all the tribes of the living world. At length, this tremendous orb would approach with accelerated velocity, and, striking the earth with a *crash,* as if heaven and earth had burst asunder, would shiver the globe into fragments, and for ever exterminate the race of man.

It will at once be admitted, by every one who acknowledges the incessant agency of a Supreme Being in the movements of the universe, that any one, or all of these effects combined, are within the compass of Omnipotence; and not only so, but they might all be accomplished with terrific energy in the course of a few moments. If puny man, by his mechanical dexterity, can suddenly stop a stupendous machine which he has put in motion—if he can impel red-hot balls at the rate of 500 miles an hour—if he can extract the oxygen from a small portion of the atmosphere, and cause it to set on fire the hardest metallic substances—we cannot doubt for a moment, that, with infinitely greater ease, the Almighty could stop the earth in its career, separate the component parts of the atmosphere, set on fire the foundations of the mountains, or impel the blazing comet towards the earth, to crush it to atoms. That God has been a constant spectator of the wickedness of man for four thousand years; that he has, during all that period, wielded in his hands so many terrific ministers of vengeance; and that he has hitherto refrained from executing deserved punishment on the workers of iniquity—is, therefore, a striking evidence that his mercy is infinite, and that he is "long-suffering and slow to anger, not willing that any should perish, but that all should come to repentance."

It would, however, be a most unwarrantable conclusion, from this circumstance, to imagine that God beholds with indifference the scenes of iniquity that are hourly presented before him. In order to show that he is not an unconcerned spectator of the ways of men, and that the instruments of punishment are always in his hand, he sometimes "cometh out of his place, to punish the inhabitants of the earth for their iniquity," and displays the holiness of his nature, by "terrible things in righteousness." In such visitations, "his way is in the whirlwind and the storm; clouds and darkness are round about him; a fire goeth before him, and burneth up his enemies round about; the stormy winds are his messengers, and flames of fire his ministers; the clouds pour out their waters; the sky sends forth a sound; the voice of his thunder is in the heavens; his lightnings enlighten the world; the earth quakes and the people tremble." The *hurricane*, which tears up whole forests by the roots, and tosses them about as stubble, which levels the loftiest spires with the ground, and dashes the stateliest ships against each other, till they are broken into shivers, and plunged into the deep; the *lightnings*, which fill the atmosphere with their blaze, which shatter the strongest buildings, and strike whole herds of cattle into a lifeless group; the *pestilence*, "which walketh in darkness," and cuts off thousands of its victims in a day; the *volcano*, belching forth rivers of fire, causing surrounding cities to tremble, and sending forth its bellowings over a circuit of a thousand miles;—these, and many other agents which are in operation in the system of nature, are experimental proofs of the dreadful energy of those ministers of destruction, which are constantly under the superintendence of the Almighty, and of his occasionally using them for the purpose of chastising the nations for their iniquities.

In particular, the *earthquake* is one of the most terrible and destructive instruments of vengeance. In the year 1755, the shock of an earthquake was felt at Lisbon, which levelled to the ground more than half of that populous city, and buried fifty thousand of its inhabitants in the ruins. The shock extended its influence over an extent of four millions of square miles; and therefore, it is easy to conceive, that, had a little greater impulse been given to the physical agents which produced this terrible effect, the solid globe on which we stand might have been convulsed to its centre, and all its inhabitants crushed to death, amidst the universal ruin.

We have also an experimental proof, that there are physical principles in the constitution of our globe, sufficient to give it a shock throughout every part of its solid mass, and that such a shock, at one period, it actually received. When the wickedness of man became great upon the earth, "when every imagination of the thoughts of his heart was only evil continually," the fountains of the great deep were broken up, the cataracts of heaven were opened, and the whole solid crust of our globe received such a shock as rent the mountains asunder, and hurled them into the plains; the effects of which are still visible, in every Alpine district, and in the subterraneous caverns of the earth. Of all the millions of the race of Adam that then existed, only eight individuals, after having been tossed for seven months on the tremendous billows of a boundless ocean, survived, to tell to their posterity the tidings of this universal wreck. The dreadful scenes of horror and consternation which must have been presented at this awful crisis; the stupendous forces which must have been in operation in the atmosphere above, and in the foundations of the earth beneath, and the tremendous clash of elemental war which must have ensued, throughout every region of earth, air, and sea,—it is beyond the power of the human imagination to depict, in all their terrific grandeur. But we have every reason to conclude, that the bottom of the ocean was lifted up to the level of the loftiest mountains, that disruptions of the mountains and of the densest rocks ensued, that dreadful explosions resounded throughout the whole expanse of nature, and that the mighty waters hurled their billows with resistless fury in every direction, rolling immense rocks and forests from one continent to another, and whirling the wrecks of different regions to the opposite extremities of the globe.

Were it at any time the intention of the Almighty to inflict deserved punishment on a particular district, or class of men, without deranging the whole structure of our globe, we have also an experimental proof how easily this could be effected, even without infringing the established laws of nature. He has only to condense the powerful energies of the electrical fluid in a large cloud, and to despatch it on the wings of the wind, to discharge its thunderbolts on any particular city, or mountain, or plain,—and the work of destruction is instantly accomplished. A striking instance of this kind happened, in the year 1772, in the island of Java, in the East Indies. On the 11th of August, at the dead hour of night, a bright cloud was observed covering a mountain in the district of *Cheribon*, and at the same moment several reports were heard, like those of a cannon. The people who dwelt on the upper parts of the mountain not being able to fly with sufficient swiftness, a great part of the cloud, about nine miles in circumference, detached itself under them, and was seen at a distance, rising and falling like the waves of the sea, and emitting globes of fire so luminous, that the night became as clear as day. The effects of this dreadful explosion were astonishing. Every thing was destroyed for twenty miles around. The houses were demolished; the plantations were buried in the earth; vast numbers of goats, sheep, and horses, and 1500 head of cattle were destroyed; and above two thousand human beings were in a moment plunged into the gulf of eternity.* "With God is terri-

* In this, and the other illustrations of this subject stated above, I consider the Divine Being as the grand agent in directing the operations of the ele-

ble majesty. Who can stand before his indignation? who can abide in the fierceness of his anger? The mountains quake before him; the hills melt, and the earth is burned at his presence."—"Let all the earth fear the Lord; let all the inhabitants of the world stand in awe of him."

Thus it appears, that God is not an unconcerned spectator of the ways of men—that he has every moment at his command the most destructive elements of nature—and that we have abundant proofs that these destructive elements have been occasionally used, for inflicting condign punishment on the workers of iniquity. Notwithstanding these resources of vengeance, we find, by experience, that his mercy is exercised, from year to year, and from century to century, towards a world, the majority of whose inhabitants are daily trampling under foot his sacred institutions, and his holy laws. The instances which occur, of the devastations of the hurricane, the thunder, the volcano, the earthquake, and the pestilence, are comparatively few, and seem intended chiefly to arouse the attention of thoughtless and ungrateful man; to prevent him from running to the extreme of wickedness; and to convince him that the Most High ruleth in the kingdoms of men," and that "verily there is a God who judgeth in the earth." Hence we may perceive the striking emphasis of the language of the inspired writers: "The Lord is *slow to anger*," and yet "*great in power*."

This display of the exercise of perfect self-command in the Divine Mind, is, therefore, calculated, as well as his wisdom and goodness, to inspire us with emotions of reverence, admiration, and love. "The Lord is merciful and gracious, slow to anger, and plenteous in mercy As the heaven is high above the earth, so great is his mercy toward them that fear him. Bless the Lord, O my soul, and forget not all his benefits."

ments, but without infringing those general laws which are found to operate with undeviating constancy in the system of the universe. To explore the *manner* in which those general laws are directed to produce certain specific effects, in reference to particular regions and tribes of mankind, must obviously be beyond the limits of our faculties; unless we could enter into all the designs of the Eternal Mind, when he gave birth to the universe, and arranged its elementary parts; and unless we could take a comprehensive view of the remotest tendencies of the elements of nature, and the times and circumstances in which they shall produce a specific and extraordinary effect. All these tendencies and circumstances were before the mind of the Eternal Jehovah, when he established the plan of his moral government; and, therefore, whatever events may occur in the physical system, must be considered as the accomplishment of his moral purposes, in reference to the moral agents he has created. It would be presumptuous in so limited a being as man, to determine, in every case, what is the precise moral reason of the extraordinary destructive effects of physical agents. We can only say, in general, that they are connected with the sin and depravity of man. But, at that solemn day, when the reasons of the divine dispensations shall be laid open, it will perhaps be found, that such uncommon and alarming effects were the punishment of aggravated transgressions, the peculiar malignity and tendency of which were removed, in a great measure, beyond the sphere of general observation.

---

## SECTION VI.

### OF THE RECTITUDE OF THE DIVINE CHARACTER.

Another perfection in the character of God, which is calculated to inspire confidence and affection, is his *Justice*, or, the *Rectitude* of his nature.

The rectitude of the Divine Being, in its most extensive sense, consists in doing that which, in all cases, is *right*, upon the whole; or, in other words, that which will have the greatest tendency to promote the order and happiness of his universal empire. It includes under it, the idea of *distributive* justice, which consists in rewarding the good, and punishing the bad, according to equitable laws, calculated to produce harmony and happiness throughout the whole intelligent system. This perfection of the Deity may be considered as a branch of his general *benevolence*, which appears to be the source of all his moral attributes, and the spring of all his actions. The display of his natural and moral perfections, and the general happiness of the intelligences which exist throughout his immense and eternal empire, appear to be the great objects in view, in his moral government of the universe: and, in order to secure these objects, it is requisite that justice be impartially administered, according to the eternal rules of rectitude, and that "every one be rewarded according to his works."

That this attribute is possessed by the Divine Being, in the highest degree, appears from the following considerations. He exists, and has always existed, completely *independent* of all his creatures; he is in the actual possession of boundless felicity, which no other being can interrupt; and is consequently liable to no evil, nor diminution of enjoyment. He is *omnipotent*, and therefore can accomplish whatever he pleases, and can effectually prevent whatever might detract from his happiness, or disturb the order of his government. He has, therefore, nothing to fear from any other being, and can desire nothing from his creatures to increase his felicity. Consequently, *no possible motive or temptation can exist*, to induce him to inflict an act of injustice on any of the intellectual beings he has formed. Injustice, among men, proceeds either from want of intelligence to discriminate between what is right and wrong; from want of power to bring their purposes into effect; from the fear of some evil or disadvantage which may arise from the impartial distribution of justice; from the idea of some imaginary good of which they might be deprived; from some mental defect incident to the present state of humanity; from some prejudice against the individuals towards whom justice ought to be administered; or from the indulgence of some cruel and depraved dispositions. But none of these causes or motives can exist in the mind of the All-perfect and infinite Creator. His comprehensive eye takes in, at one glance, all the circumstances, even the most minute, on which a righteous decision depends; he is no "respecter of persons;" he can indulge no malevolent dispositions; he can expect no accession of enjoyment from an act of injustice; he has nothing to fear from the execution of his decisions; his power is all-sufficient to bring them into full effect, at the time, and in the manner, which is most conducive to the happiness of the universe; and his benevolence, which is displayed throughout all his works, effectually prevents him from withholding good, or inflicting evil, beyond the desert of the subjects of his government.

This character of the Deity is amply exhibited and confirmed in the declarations of Sacred Scripture, where it is asserted, that "He is a God of truth, and without iniquity; just and right is he." "Thou art just," says Nehemiah, "in all that is brought upon us; for thou hast done right, but we have done wickedly." "Shall mortal man be more just than God? Surely God will not do wickedly, neither will the Almighty pervert judgment. Wilt thou condemn Him that is most just? Is it fit to say to a king, Thou art wicked; or to princes, Ye are ungodly? How much less to him who accepteth not the persons of princes, nor regardeth the rich more than the poor?"—"The righteous Lord loveth righteousness; he shall judge the world in righteousness; he shall minister judgment to the people in uprightness. Justice and judgment are the foundation of his throne. The Lord our God is righteous in all his works which he doth." "I am the Lord who exercise judgment and righteousness in the earth." "God is not unrighteous to forget your work and labour of love which ye have showed towards his name.—Great and marvellous are thy works, Lord God Almighty; *just and true* are thy ways, thou King of saints." The equitable laws which he has promulgated to his creatures; the justice he requires to be exercised by one man to another; his promises of reward, and his threatenings of punishment; and the impressive judgments which he has executed on individuals, on nations, and on the world at large, all bear testimony to the existence of perfect rectitude in the divine character.

But, although Scripture and Reason combine in attesting the immutable justice of God, we are unable, in many instances, to trace the display of this perfection in his dispensations towards the inhabitants of our world. This is owing, in part, to the false maxims by which we form a judgment of his procedure; to the limited views we are obliged to take of the objects of his government; to the want of a comprehensive knowledge of the whole plan of his dispensations, and the ends to be effected by them; to the limited views we have acquired of the whole range of his universal dominions; and to our ignorance of the relations which may subsist between our world and the inhabitants of other provinces of the divine Empire. We behold many of "the excellent of the earth," pining in the abodes of poverty, and almost unnoticed by their fellow-men; while we behold the wicked elevated to stations of power, and encircled with riches and splendour. From a false estimate of true enjoyment, we are apt to imagine, that misery surrounds the one, and that happiness encircles the other; and that there is an apparent act of injustice in these different allotments; whereas, God may have placed the one in the midst of worldly prosperity as a punishment for his sins, and the other in obscurity, as a stimulus to the exercise of virtue. We behold a man of piety and benevolence falling before the dagger of an assassin, who escapes with impunity: we are startled at the dispensation, and confounded at the mystery of providence, and are apt to exclaim, "Is there not a God that judgeth in the earth?" But, we are ignorant of the relation which such an event bears to the general plan of the divine government—of the links in the chain of events which preceded it, and of those which shall follow in its train. We are ignorant of the relation it bears to particular families and societies, or to the nation at large in which it happened, and even to all the nations of the earth. An event apparently trivial, or mysterious, or, according to our views, unjust, may, for aught we know, form an essential link in that chain of events which extends from the commencement of time to its consummation, which runs through a thousand worlds, and stretches into the depths of eternity. We all know, that some of the most appalling scenes of terror and destruction have often proceeded from an apparently trivial accident, and that events of the greatest importance have originated from causes so inconsiderable as to be almost overlooked. The British and Foreign Bible Society, which now engages the attention of the whole mass of the Christian world, and whose beneficent effects will soon extend to the remotest corners of the world, derived its origin from a casual conversation between a few obscure individuals, on the subject of distributing the Scriptures. And the apparently trivial circumstance, of observing that a certain mineral substance, when left free to move itself, uniformly points towards the north, has been the means, not only of the knowledge we have acquired of the different regions of our globe, but of imparting to millions of mankind incalculable blessings, which will descend to their posterity to the latest generations.

Hence it appears, that, in our present circumstances, we are altogether incompetent to form a correct judgment of what is just or unjust in the present dispensations of the Almighty, unless we could survey, with the eye of a seraph, the ample plan of the divine government,—the whole chain of God's dispensations towards our race,—the numerous worlds and beings over which his moral government extends,—the relation which the events now passing among us bear to other moral intelligences, either as subjects of contemplation, as warnings of the danger of apostacy from God, or as motives to universal subjection and obedience,—and the connexions, bearings, and dependencies of the whole of that moral system which embraces unnumbered worlds, and constitutes one grand and boundless empire, under the government of the Creator.—Even then, with the eye and the mind of a finite intelligence, we should occasionally meet with events which would surpass our comprehension, and be altogether inexplicable, on the grounds of the knowledge we had previously acquired, and should still be constrained to exclaim, "O the depth of the riches both of the wisdom and the knowledge of God! How unsearchable are his judgments, and his ways past finding out!"

But although "clouds and darkness" at present hang over the ways of the Almighty, so that we cannot, in every instance, perceive the rectitude of his procedure, we may rest satisfied that "justice and judgment are for ever the foundation of his throne;" and we are assured, by the Sacred Oracles, that a period is approaching, when the mystery of Providence will be unfolded, and when all its dark and perplexing events, in reference to this world, will be explained to the full conviction of all its assembled inhabitants. For "God hath appointed a day in which he will judge the world *in righteousness* by that man whom he hath ordained; whereof he hath given assurance unto all men, in that he hath raised him from the dead." Then "the secrets of all hearts" shall be disclosed, and every man rewarded "according to his works;" for, "God shall bring every work into judgment, with every secret thing, whether it be good, or whether it be evil." Then it will be clearly perceived, that "verily there is a reward for the righteous, and that there is a God that judgeth in the earth." Then the rectitude of Jehovah, in every part of his moral administration, will shine forth in all its lustre; a visible and everlasting distinction will be made between the righteous and the wicked, and the whole intelligent creation will plainly discern between "him that served God, and him that served him not."

In the mean time, God has not left himself without a witness to the impartiality of his justice in his allotments towards men, in that he has invariably connected *misery* with *the violation of his laws*, and *happiness* with *the observance of them.* However different the allotments of mankind may be, in regard to wealth, honour, or station, it holds invariably true, that "there is no peace," or substantial happiness, "to the wicked;" and that "the man is *blessed* who fears the Lord, and delights in his commandments."* Place a man on the highest pinnacle of earthly grandeur, and let him indulge in schemes of ambition, avarice, pride, revenge, cruelty, and other violations of the divine law, and he may as soon attempt to stop the sun in his course, as to expect substantial enjoyment while he continues in the indulgence of such malevolent passions. Place another in the most obscure abode of human life, and let him exercise piety, benevolence, humility, and every other Christian temper; and he will enjoy a peace, an equanimity, and a portion of happiness, which the wicked can never possess, and which the wealth of the world can neither give nor take away. Hence it is, that we behold so many instances of disgust at life, and of self-destruction, among those who are elevated to stations of power, and surrounded with every kind of sensitive enjoyment.—This consideration, of itself, should silence every murmur that is apt to arise at the dispensations of God's providence, and convince us that "he is righteous in all his ways, and holy in all his works."

On the whole, then, it appears, that the justice of God has a tendency to inspire us with confidence, and love, and joy, no less than his mercy and benevolence. Were it not for this perfection of the divine character, omnipotence might become a most terrific and tremendous attribute of the Deity. We should have no motive but that of *fear* to stimulate us to obedience; we should feel no security against danger, and distress, and the perpetual recurrence of spectacles of vengeance, and, in the course of ages, the spacious universe might be transformed into an immense region of "lamentation, and mourning, and wo." Were it not for this perfection, the benevolence of the Deity would degenerate into weakness and imbecility. Wicked men, and other depraved intelligences, presuming on freedom from impunity, and their diabolical passions acquiring strength and vigour, by long exercise, would carry misery and destruction in their train, wherever they exerted their energies; and would interrupt, and ultimately destroy the harmony and felicity of the intelligent universe. But, while we recognize the rectitude of the divine character as an immutable attribute of Deity, we can look forward with confidence through all the revolu-

*Psal. cxii. 1.

tions of time, and to all those eternal scenes which shall succeed the demolition of the present system of things, fully assured, that God is the universal Protector of his unnumbered offspring—that his power will never be interposed to inflict an act of injustice—that no intelligent being will ever suffer a punishment beyond his desert—and that no happiness which his benevolence has devised, and his word has promised, will ever be withheld from those "who put their trust in his name, and hearken to the voice of his commandments."

Thus I have endeavoured to show, that *love to God*, which is the first principle of the moral law, is founded upon the natural and moral perfections of the Deity—that the attributes of *omnipotence, wisdom, goodness, mercy, forbearance*, and *justice*, are calculated to excite this noble affection to the highest degree in the minds of all holy intelligences. I might also have illustrated this subject from considerations drawn from the infinity, the eternity, the immutability, the holiness, and veracity of God. But the illustrations already stated, will, I presume, be sufficient to demonstrate, that this affection, in conjunction with all its kindred emotions, ought to occupy the highest place in the human heart, and in the minds of all created intelligences.

It may, perhaps, be insinuated by some, that the preceding illustrations have been carried to a greater length than the nature of the subject required—and it is readily admitted, that the mere logical argument did not require so extended illustrations. Every person who knows the meaning of the terms made use of, will at once admit, that, since God is a Being possessed of almighty power, infinite wisdom, boundless benevolence, mercy, forbearance, and perfect rectitude—he ought to be loved affectionately and supremely. But such general and metaphysical reasoning, though perfectly conclusive and incontrovertible, possesses but a slender influence over the mind, in exciting it to the cultivation of holy affections. For the sake of *impression*, it is essentially requisite, that the various *manifestations* of divine perfection should be presented to the view, in order that the mind may have a tangible train of thought before it, to stimulate its activities, and its religious emotions. General views and reasonings on any subject, and especially on the subject of religion, produce a very slight impression on the majority of mankind. It is not owing so much to the want of conviction of the truth of certain important propositions in religion, that divine truths take so slender a hold of the mind, as to the want of those *definite* and *impressive* conceptions which can be acquired only by a minute and attentive survey of the works and the dispensations of God. And, in this point of view, the preceding illustrations, had the limited nature of the present work permitted, might have been prosecuted to a much greater extent.

I might also have illustrated this subject from a consideration of *the relations* in which God stands to us, and to all his creatures. He is our *Creator*, and we are the workmanship of his hands. He formed our bodies, and he sustains our spirits. His physical energy is felt by us every moment, in making our hearts to beat, and our lungs to play, and in impelling the crimson fluid which circulates in our bodies, through a thousand different tubes. To him we are indebted for life, and all its comforts; and for all the powers, capacities, and privileges, which dignify our nature, and exalt us above the lower ranks of existence. He is our *Preserver* and bountiful *Benefactor*, who "sustains our souls in life," who supports the course of nature, in its diversified movements, and "daily loads us with his benefits." To his superintending providence we are indebted for the food we eat, the water we drink, the clothes we wear, the air we breathe, the light which cheers us, the splendours of the sun, the milder radiance of the moon, the magnificence of the starry sky, the rains and dews which fertilize the soil; the earth, with its riches and abundance; the trees, plants, and waving grain, which enrich our fields; the flowers which deck the meadows, the beautiful and magnificent colouring which is spread over the terrestrial landscape, the succession of day and night, and the vicissitude of the seasons. In short, to him we are indebted for all the objects and movements around us, which render our abode on earth convenient, desirable, and productive of enjoyment.

He is our *Father*, and we are his children. He watches over us with a tender care; and, "as a father pitieth his children, so the Lord pitieth them that fear him." This tender and indissoluble relation binds us to him by the strongest ties, and is calculated to excite the most ardent filial affection and gratitude. He is our *Sovereign* and *Lawgiver*, and we are his subjects; and all his laws are framed on the principles of eternal and immutable rectitude, and are calculated to promote the harmony and happiness of the whole intelligent creation. He is our *Master*, and we are his servants, and "his commandments are not grievous." He is our *Friend* in adversity, our *Protector* in danger and in distress; our *Instructor*, who has imparted to us knowledge and understanding; and our *Redeemer*, who "spared not his own Son, but delivered him up for us all," that we might be rescued from the gulf of depravity and ruin, and exalted to a state of consummate felicity. In fine, he is that being who is the inexhaustible fountain of light, of life, and of joy to all beings—on whom depend all our future prospects in this world, and all the transporting scenes to which we look forward in an interminable state of existence.—All these, and many other relations, in which we stand to the God of heaven, demonstrate, that supreme love to this beneficent Being, is the first and highest duty of every rational creature; and they present the most powerful motives to stimulate us to its exercise. But, to illustrate these topics, in minute detail, would be inconsistent with the limited plan of the present work; and it is the less necessary, as several of them have already been brought into view, in the course of the preceding illustrations.

---

## SECTION VII.

### MODES IN WHICH LOVE TO GOD IS DISPLAYED.

I shall now offer a remark or two on the *nature* of this sublime affection, and the manner in which it ought to be manifested. Love to God is not a single and solitary affection in the human breast, which evaporates in a few transient and undefined emotions; but is the spring of every holy activity, and is intimately connected with every virtuous emotion, with every pious sentiment, with every religious requirement, with every sensitive enjoyment, with our present comforts, and our future and eternal prospects.

It includes in it, *complacency, or delight in the character and administration of God.* Viewing him as a self-existent and eternal Being,—filling immensity with his presence, launching innumerable worlds into existence, upholding them all by the "word of his power," and superintending the minutest concerns of all his offspring, from the loftiest seraph, through all the inferior gradations of existence, to the smallest animalcula,—the mind feels the most delightful emotions, in regarding the happiness of the universe as *perfectly secure* under his physical and moral administration. Contemplating his bounty to angels and to men, to the birds of the air, the fishes of the sea, and the numerous tribes which traverse the surface of the land,—his mercy towards our fallen race,—his long-suffering and forbearance towards wicked nations and individuals,—his faithfulness in the accomplishment of his promises and threatenings,—and the unerring rectitude of his dispensations towards all his creatures,—the mind feels supreme approbation and complacency in his attributes, purposes, and administrations; beholding in his character an excellence and amiableness, a moral dignity and grandeur which is not to be found in any created intelligence. Even in reference to those acts of his government which appear dreadful and appalling—in the volcano, the earthquake, the thunders, the hurricane, the tempest, and the doom of the impenitent, its approbation and complacency are not withheld, convinced that perfect rectitude is the rule of his procedure, and that his righteousness will one day be brought to light before an assembled world.

Love to God includes *admiration of his wonderful works.* The man whose affections are directed to the Supreme Intelligence is not an indifferent spectator of the manifestations of Deity. He beholds the magnificent canopy of heaven daily moving around him in silent grandeur; his eye penetrates beyond the apparent aspects of the twinkling luminaries which adorn it, and surveys the hand of the Almighty wheeling stupendous globes through the immeasurable regions of space, and extending his operations throughout unnumbered systems, dispersed over the boundless expanse of the universe. He beholds the great globe on which he is placed, impelled by the same omnipotent arm, prosecuting its course through the depths of space, and circling around the sun, to bring about the revolutions of the seasons. He contemplates the vast ranges of mountains that stretch around it—the mass of waters in the mighty ocean, and its numerous tribes of animated beings—the "dry land," with all its furniture and inhabitants—the vast caverns, chasms, and shattered strata which appear in its interior recesses—and the atmosphere with which it is surrounded, with the clouds, the lightnings, and the tempests which diversify its aspect. He traces the footsteps of the Almighty in his moral administration—in the deluge which swept away the inhabitants of the antediluvian world—in the burning of Sodom, the dividing of the Red sea, the thunders and lightnings of Sinai—the manifestation of the Son of God in human flesh; his sufferings, death, resurrection, and triumphant ascension—in the propagation of the gospel in the face of every opposition, in the rise and fall of empires, the dethronement of kings, the battles of warriors, and the convulsions of nations. And, while he contemplates such objects and operations, his *admiration* is excited by the incomprehensible knowledge displayed in the contrivance of the universe, the boundless benevolence which extends over all these works, and the omnipotent power by which all the mighty movements of Creation and Providence are effected. And, while he admires, he is filled with strong emotions of *reverence* of the glorious perfections of that Being, whose mighty hand conducts those stupendous movements, and he feels the full force of the impressive exhortation of the psalmist, "Let all the earth fear the Lord; let all the inhabitants of the world stand in awe of him: for he spake, and it was done; he commanded, and it stood fast." Even the abstract conceptions we have of the *immensity* of the Divine Being, by which he is present in every part of infinite space—the *eternity* of his duration, and the range of his *omniscience* which embraces an intimate knowledge of the thoughts, the purposes, and the actions of all creatures; are calculated to overpower the mind with emotions of veneration and awe, blended with feelings of affection and delight at the recollection of the relation in which we stand to this glorious Intelligence.

Again, Love to God includes *Humility* and self-abasement in the divine presence. There is no disposition which appears more incompatible with supreme affection for the Creator than pride, haughtiness, and arrogance. "God resisteth the proud." Even "a proud look" is declared to be an "abomination" in his sight. And, if the indulgence of pride be inconsistent with the love of God, humility must be regarded as one of its essential and distinguishing accompaniments. When a man who loves God reflects on his *condition and character*—that he is a creature who derived his existence from a superior Being, to whom he is indebted for all his powers and faculties, and by whose power and mercy he is every moment preserved in existence; when he considers his *station in the universe*—that he is only like an atom in the immensity of creation, when compared with the innumerable beings which people its wide domains—that he stands near the lowest part of the scale of intelligent existence, and that "all the inhabitants of the earth are as grasshoppers" before Him who sits on the throne of the heavens; when he recollects that he has apostatized from the God who made him, that he is guilty of innumerable violations of his righteous laws, and stands condemned at the bar of Him "who is of purer eyes than to behold iniquity;" when he contemplates the circumstances in which he is now placed in consequence of his transgressions—the pains, diseases, poverty, bereavements, and reproaches, to which he is subjected; the storms, and tempests, and elemental war to which he is exposed; the degradation which awaits his body at the hour of dissolution and in the mansions of the tomb; and the ignorance, the errors, and follies into which he has fallen;—when he considers that "lowliness of mind" is a characteristic of the most exalted of created intelligences, who "veil their faces" in the divine presence, and cheerfully extend their benevolent regards to the meanest human being who is an "heir of salvation;" and, above all, when he reflects on the ineffable grandeur of that Being before whom "all nations are as the drop of a bucket," he is convinced that pride is the most unreasonable principle that can exist in the human breast, and that the most profound *humility* ought for ever to characterize his thoughts and actions, both in the presence of God, and before the eyes of men. On such a character only will "the High and Lofty One who inhabits eternity," look with complacency, and in such a heart alone can the love of God be expected to reside in all its generous and noble exercises. Such a disposition, mingling with all the other benevolent affections, will render them sweet and delightful; it will render us amiable in the eyes of our fellow-men; it will secure us against all the wretched effects and boisterous passions which flow from haughtiness and pride; it will mitigate the sorrows, the perplexities, and anxieties to which we are subjected in our earthly pilgrimage; it will enable us to preserve our minds tranquil and serene amidst the provocations, the affronts, and the contentions to which we are exposed in our intercourses with general society, and will prepare us for associating with the inhabitants of that happier world, where seraphic love, profound reverence of the Divine Majesty, and profound humility, mingle with all their intercourses and employments.

*Resignation* to the providential dispensations of the Almighty is another manifestation and accompaniment of love to God. To be habitually discontented, and to murmur and repine under the allotments of his providence, must obviously appear to be inconsistent with sincere and ardent affection for the Supreme Disposer of events.—Resignation to the will of God is the duty of every intelligent creature towards the Creator; and in proportion to the degree in which this principle exists, will be the happiness of the intellectual being that exercises it. Angels are perfectly happy, because they are perfectly submissive to the will of their Creator—being fully contented with the station allotted them in the universe, and completely resigned to all the future services and allotments which Infinite Wisdom has ordained. Wherever pure affection towards God actuates the mind among the inhabitants of our world, it produces a disposition similar in kind, though inferior in degree, to that which animates the breasts of the cherubim and the seraphim in the regions of bliss.

He, who is actuated by this noble principle, regards every providential event as the appointment of his Father in heaven. The devouring flames may consume his habitation to ashes, and scatter his treasures to "the four winds of heaven;" the ship in which his wealth is embarked may be dashed against the rocks, and sink "as lead in the mighty waters;" his friends may forsake him in the season of his deepest anxiety and distress; the wife of his bosom, whom he tenderly loved, may be snatched from his embrace by the cold hand of death; his children, dearer to him than his own soul, may fall victims, one after another, to some pestilential disease, and be for ever removed from his sight to the "land of deep forgetfulness;" his familiar friend in whom he trusted may "lift up his heel against him," and load him with unmerited reproaches, his own body may be chastened with sore pain and loathsome disease; a fall from a horse may break the bones of his leg, and render him lame for life; a random blow may bruise his eye-balls, and deprive him of all the entertainments of vision; he may be stretched for many long years on the bed of languishing; his country may either be ravaged and laid waste by destroying armies, or rains and inundations may sweep away the produce of his fields. But under all such calamities, he bows with submission to the will of Him "who rules in the whirlwind and directs the storm;" not because he has fortified his mind with a stoical apathy and indifference towards the evils of life; not because he is incapable of feeling the evils he is doomed to suffer; for he may feel them in the acutest degree, even while he exercises full resignation; but he is resigned, because he feels assured that they are the appointment of his Almighty Friend—that they are parts of the plan of unerring wisdom—that they are intimately connected with the whole chain of providence that runs through his present existence—that they are intended, in the scheme of infinite benevolence, to promote his happiness in a way which his limited faculties are unable at present to comprehend—and that they have a bearing on the scenes and enjoyments of the eternal world. And therefore, under the pressure of his most painful feelings, he is enabled to adopt the triumphant language of the prophet, "Although the fig-tree shall not blossom, neither fruit be in the vine; the labour of the olive fail, and the fields yield no meat; the flock be cut off from the fold, and there be no herd in the stall; yet will I rejoice in the Lord, I will be glad in the God of my salvation." While others murmur and rage, and toss themselves like a wild bull in a net, and curse the supposed authors of their calamities, he is enabled to "possess his soul in patience," convinced of the rectitude of the divine dispensations; and thus displays a nobleness of mind, and a heroism which is "above all Greek, above all Roman fame."

Again, Love to God comprehends *Gratitude* for the benefits he bestows. Gratitude is that particular modification of love which flows out towards God, considered as the Author and Bestower of all felicity: it is love excited by kindness communicated from benevolent motives. It is one of the most natural and obvious manifestations of that general principle which I have been hitherto illustrating; for ingratitude is altogether inconsistent with love to a benefactor. In order to kindle this amiable affection into a lively flame, the person in whose bosom it glows endeavours to take a minute and expansive survey of the "loving-kindness of God," and of the countless variety of benefits he is continually receiving. He feels grateful to God for his existence, for the powers and capacities with which he is endowed, for the rank which he holds in the scale of terrestrial existence; in being raised above the clods of the valley, and furnished with faculties superior to the beasts of the forest and the fowls of heaven. He feels grateful that he was brought into existence in a Christian land, and in civilized society; that the "glad tidings of salvation" have reached his ears; that "God so loved the world, that He gave his only begotten Son, that whosoever believeth on him might not perish, but have everlasting life," and that every enjoyment requisite for his present and future happiness is secured through this plan of divine benevolence. But he does not rest satisfied with vague and general views of these important benefits; he contemplates the degradation into which sin had plunged him, the greatness of the misery from which the love of God has delivered him, the moral perfection of his nature to which he is now training, the serenity of mind he experiences in the practice of the divine precepts, the security he feels for his present and future safety under the protection of Omnipotence, the "strong consolation" under the evils of life which the promises of God lead him to expect, the victory over death of which he is secured "through Christ Jesus his Lord," the resurrection of his body at the close of time, the "new heavens and the new earth" to which he is destined at the dissolution of this sublunary system, the alliance into which he is brought to the angelic tribes and other pure intelligences, his moral capacity for associating with every holy being in the universe, and the endless succession of transporting scences which will burst upon his view through the ages of eternity. While contemplating these high privileges, in all their bearings and varied ramifications, emotions of affection and gratitude arise in his breast which can only be expressed in the language of elevated devotion.

"O How shall words with equal warmth  
The gratitude declare  
That glows within my ravish'd heart!  
But Thou canst read it there."

"Bless the Lord, O my soul! and all that is within me bless his holy name. Give thanks to the Lord, and forget not all his benefits; who forgiveth all thine iniquities, who healeth all thy diseases; who redeemeth thy life from destruction, and crowneth thee with loving-kindness and tender mercies."

Nor does he feel less grateful to God for his kindness as displayed in the material world, and in the ordinary course of his providence. He feels grateful for these scenes of sublimity and beauty with which the visible universe is adorned—for the sun when he ascends the vault of heaven, and diffuses his radiance over the mountains and the vales—for the moon, when she "walks in brightness" through the heavens, and cheers the shades of night—for the planets, while they run their ample rounds, and evince, by their magnitude and motions, the eternal omnipotence of their Maker—for the innumera-

the host of stars, which unite their splendours to adorn the canopy of the sky, and display the riches, and grandeur, and boundless extent of God's universal kingdom—for the light, which darts with unconceivable rapidity from the celestial luminaries, and diffuses a thousand shades of colour on the terrestrial landscape—for the surrounding atmosphere, which supports the element of fire, conveys the clouds over every region, and sustains and invigorates the functions of animal life—for the variety of beautiful and majestic scenery which diversifies our terrestrial system—for the towering cliffs, the lofty mountains, and the expansive vales—for the meandering river, gliding through the fields, and diffusing health and fertility wherever it flows—for the riches which abound in the gardens, the forests, and the fields, and the mineral treasures contained in the bowels of the mountains—for the harmony of musical sounds, the mellifluous notes of the nightingale and the lark, and the melodious warblings which resound from the vales, the mountains, and the groves—for the flowers which enamel the meadows, the trees, the shrubs, and the waving grain which adorn the earth with picturesque beauty—for the animated beings which contribute to our comfort, the bee which collects for us honey from every opening flower, the sheep which yields its fleeces for our clothing, and thousands of other creatures which contribute to supply us with food, raiment, furniture, and innumerable enjoyments. In all these, and similar objects, he perceives ample reasons for elevating his soul in lively gratitude to his bountiful Benefactor.

When he turns his eyes upon himself, and considers the wonderful machinery which gives life and motion to his frame, he perceives the strongest reason for the exercise of incessant admiration and gratitude. He feels grateful for every joint of his fingers, and for every movement of his wrist, by which he is enabled with the utmost ease to perform a countless variety of manual operations essential to his comfort—for the hundreds of bones which support his animal system, with their various articulations, and the hundreds of muscles and tendons which are interwoven with every part of the machine, which enable it to perform without the least obstruction, a thousand varied movements subservient to his health, convenience, and pleasure. He cannot walk through his apartment, nor lift his eyes to the heavens, nor move a joint of his finger, nor draw a single breath, without perceiving an evidence of the wisdom and intelligence of his Almighty Maker. He perceives, that if only one joint were wanting, or one muscle out of action, or one movement out of a thousand interrupted, he would instantly be subjected to a thousand painful sensations which would throw a gloom on every earthly enjoyment. But especially, when he reflects on the wonders of vision—the thousands of millions of rays that are every moment darting from the objects around him, crossing each other in an infinity of directions, and yet conveying to every eye a distinct perception of their colours, motions, and diversified aspects; when he reflects on the facility with which he can turn his eye in every direction, upwards and downwards, to the right hand and to the left, and in a moment take in the landscape of the earth and the heavens "at a small inlet which a grain might close;" when he considers the numerous and complicated movements continually going on within him—the heart, like a powerful engine in perpetual motion, impelling, with prodigious force, streams of blood through a thousand different tubes—the numerous lacteal and lymphatic vessels absorbing nutriment from the food, and conveying it through every part of this wonderful machine. when he considers that these incessant motions are, as it were, the immediate hand of the Divinity within him, over which he can exercise no control, and which are all intended to preserve his existence and minister to his enjoyment,—he cannot forbear exclaiming, in the language of grateful admiration, "How precious are thy wonderful contrivances concerning me, O God! how great is the sum of them! If I should count them, they are more in number than the sand. I will praise thee, for I am fearfully and wonderfully made!"

He does not overlook such instances of "the loving-kindness of God," because, to some, they may appear minute and trivial. He does not contrast them with what are reckoned spiritual and more important blessings; nor attempt to institute comparisons between the beneficent operations of Omnipotence, in order to throw a certain portion of them into the shade. He considers all the operations of God from the plan of redemption for guilty men, and the mission of his Son into our world, to the minutest muscle that moves the joint of a finger, or the ray of light that darts from a flower of the field, as parts of one vast system of boundless benevolence, as essentially connected together as the links of a chain; and, in regard to himself, he views all the variety of blessings now alluded to, as one undivided stream of unbounded beneficence, commencing with the first moment of his existence, running through all the scenes and circumstances of his terrestrial existence, and expanding into the unfathomable ocean of eternity. In the whole series of contrivances and events which relate to his present and future existence, both in what we consider the minutest and the most magnificent works of the Deity, he perceives the stamp of *infinite perfection*, and a connexion of plan and of operation, which excludes all attempts at comparisons and contrasts. Under such impressions, and with such views of the concatenation of every part of the scheme of divine benevolence, he is led to contemplate the kindness of God at every step, and in every object, and is ever ready to exclaim, "What shall I render to the Lord for *all* his benefits toward me?"

In fine, supreme love to God includes in its exercise, a delight in the public and private exercises of his worship, a constant endeavour to yield a willing and unreserved obedience to all the institutions he has appointed, and to all the laws he has issued forth for counteracting the depravity of our natures, and for raising us to a state of moral perfection; an active and enlightened zeal for the honour of his name, and for promoting those institutions which have a tendency to advance his kingdom in the earth; a sincere and disinterested affection to all our fellow-men, and particularly to every class of holy intelligences; a cordial approbation of all his plans and movements in creation and providence; and devout aspirations after that higher state of existence, where the glories of his nature and "the kindness of his love" shall be more clearly unfolded, and where love shall glow in one uninterrupted and perpetual emotion.

Thus, it appears that love to God consists in complacency in his character and administration, and is inseparably connected with admiration of his wonderful works, with humility, resignation, and gratitude.

I cannot conclude my remarks on this topic without adverting, for a little, to the nobleness and sublimity of this first and fundamental spring of all moral action. From what has been already stated, it appears that love to God is the most reasonable and amiable affection that can animate the human mind; for that Being who is the object of it is the sum of all perfection, the standard of all moral and physical excellence, and the source of all the felicity enjoyed by every rank of existence throughout the boundless universe. It is also the most *sublime and expansive affection* that can pervade the mind of any created intelligence. It excites the most rapturous emotions when we contemplate the harmonies, the beauties, and the sublimities of the universe; for it recognizes them as the displays of boundless wisdom and boundless goodness; as the production of that Almighty Being who stands in the relation of our *Father* and our *Friend;* and leads us to conclude, that that power and intelligence which gave birth to all that is grand and beautiful in heaven and on earth, will be for ever exercised in contributing to our eternal enjoyment. Without such a recognition, creation appears only like an immense desert, and is apt to fill the mind with apprehension and terror; for it can feel no pleasurable emotions in contemplating the operations of a Being for whom it entertains no affectionate regard. But, in our solitary walks in the fields and the gardens, amidst the emanations of divine munificence; in our journeys through the fertile plains; in our excursions through the Alpine scenes of nature; in our investigations into the structure of the animal and vegetable tribes; and in our contemplations on the wonders of the starry sky—love throws a radiance on all these objects, and excites an interest which cannot be appreciated by that mind which has never felt the force of this sacred emotion.

It renders us superior to the ills of life, while, under its influence, we bow, in cordial submission, to the divine dispensations, as the result of perfect wisdom, rectitude, and benevolence. It enables us to recognize the hand of a Divine Benefactor in every enjoyment, and the rod of an affectionate Father, in every trial and affliction to which we are subjected. It raises the soul above the carking cares and degrading pursuits of the world, and enables it to look down with heroic indifference on all those trivial incidents and fancied insults which irritate, and inflame, and torment "the children of pride." It preserves the mind in calm serenity amidst the raging of the tempest, the rolling thunders, the whirlwind, and the hurricane, the eruptions of the volcano, and the convulsions of the earthquake; while it recognizes the Ruler of the storm, who presides amidst the crash of warring elements, as its omnipotent Protector and its eternal refuge.* It enables the man in whose bosom it resides, to contemplate with composure the downfall of kings and the revolutions of nations, to anticipate the hour of his dissolution without dismay, and to look forward with fortitude to the ruins of dissolving nature, when "the elements shall melt with fervent heat," and the earth, with all its magnificence, shall be wrapt in flames; confident that, under "the shadow of the wings of the Almighty," he shall remain in perfect security, amidst "the wreck of matter and the crush of worlds."

This divine principle assimilates us to angels, and to every other class of holy intelligences. It renders us qualified for associating with these superior intellectual natures—for entering into their vast and comprehensive views—for conversing with them on the sublime topics which occupy their attention—for bearing a part in their extensive schemes of universal benevo-

* The celebrated *Kircher*, in his relation of the dreadful earthquake in Calabria, in 1638, which overthrew the city of Euphemia, of which he was a spectator, expresses his feelings on that occasion in the following words:—"The universal ruin around me, the crash of falling houses, the tottering of towers, and the groans of the dying, all contributed to raise terror and despair. On every side of me, I saw nothing but a scene of ruin and danger threatening wherever I should fly. I commended myself to God, as my last great refuge. At that hour, O how vain was every sublunary happiness. wealth, honour, empire, wisdom, all mere useless sounds, and as empty as the bubbles of the deep Just standing on the threshold of eternity, nothing but God was my pleasure; and the nearer I approached, I only loved him the more."

lence—and for contributing, along with them, to the order and prosperity of God's everlasting kingdom. It secures to us the friendship and affection of all the virtuous inhabitants of the universe, and renders us fit for affectionate intercourse with them, wherever we may afterwards exist, throughout the boundless expanse of creation. Should we ever be permitted, during the lapse of eternal duration, to wing our flight from world to world, in order to enlarge our views of God's unbounded empire, the exercise of this holy affection would secure to us a friendly reception and an affectionate intercourse among all the pure intelligences within the range of his moral administration: for, as this principle is founded on the nature of God, who is eternal and unchangeable, it must pervade the minds of the inhabitants of all worlds that have retained their primitive integrity. It is this divine affection which excites the rapturous flame that glows in the breasts of the angelic tribes, which enlivens the songs and the adorations of the cherubim and the seraphim, which inspires them with a noble ardour in executing the commands of their Creator, and which animates them in their flight from the celestial regions to this obscure corner of creation, when they minister to the heirs of salvation. It was this noble principle which impelled the angel Gabriel in his rapid flight through the celestial spaces, when he descended to announce to Daniel the answer to his supplications, and to Zacharias and Mary the birth of the Saviour; which animated the angels who unbarred the prison doors to Peter, and gave assurance to Paul of the divine protection, while he was tossing on the tempestuous billows of the Adriatic sea; and which fanned the flame of devotion in the heavenly host, when they sung, in the plains of Bethlehem, "Glory to God in the highest, peace on earth, and good will towards men."

In fine, this sublime affection assimilates us to God, who is benevolence itself, who supremely loves his own character, and who is incessantly displaying his benevolence, in all its infinitely diversified effects, throughout the intelligent universe. It assimilates us to Jesus the Son of the Highest, who is "the brightness of the Father's glory, and the express image of his person," and who is for ever actuated with fervent zeal for the honour of God, and for the happiness of man. It constitutes the foundation of all felicity; it opens the gates to perpetual enjoyment; it secures its possessor of eternal happiness, *as its natural and necessary result*, and prepares him for mingling in the employments of the "innumerable company of angels and the spirits of just men made perfect:" for all the transporting scenes of glory, and all the avenues to felicity, which will be opened to the immortal spirit, while ages, numerous as the sand, are rolling on, while mighty worlds are emerging out of nothing, and innumerable orders of beings are starting into existence, may be considered as so many infinitely diversified streams flowing from supreme affection to the blessed God, as the spring of every rapturous enjoyment. Possessed of this divine principle, we secure the most honourable connexions, become benefactors to the intelligent universe, participators of the enjoyments of seraphic natures, agents for carrying forward the plans of Infinite Benevolence, and "workers together with God," in accomplishing his eternal designs. Without it, we become nuisances in the kingdom of God, rebels against his government, pests to fellow intelligences, destitute of the noblest of all affections, deprived of substantial enjoyment in the present world, and exposed to misery, without interruption, in the world to come.

If such be the native effects of supreme love to God, and if this principle lie at the foundation of all genuine morality, how foolish and preposterous is it for Christian moralists to wander through the dark labyrinths of Greek and Roman literature, and the intricate mazes of modern skeptical philosophy, in search of any other principles of moral action? It is like groping for the light of the sun in the windings of a subterraneous grotto, and preferring the glimmering of a taper to the full blaze of the orb of day. It is, to forsake "the fountain of living waters, and to hew out to themselves broken and empty cisterns, that can hold no water."

In order to invigorate and expand this affection in the mind, it is requisite that we take a comprehensive view of all the manifestations of that Being towards whom it is directed, as exhibited in the history of his operations recorded in the volume of inspiration; in the details of his moral government among the nations, both in ancient and in modern times, which may be collected from the writings of historians, voyagers, travellers, and missionaries; in the economy of the inferior tribes of animated beings; in the diversified scenery of nature around us in our terrestrial system; and in the sublime movements that are going forward, among distant worlds, in the firmament of his power; for, the more we know of the manifestations of the Creator, the more acquaintance shall we have of the Creator himself; and, in proportion as our knowledge of his character is enlarged, in a similar proportion will our love be ardent and expansive. Such extensive views and contemplations are indispensably requisite, in order to a full recognition of the divine injunction "*Thou shalt love the Lord thy God with all thy heart, and with all thy strength, and with all thine understanding.*" This is the first and the great commandment.

# CHAPTER II.

## SECOND PRINCIPLE OF MORAL ACTION—LOVE TO ALL SUBORDINATE INTELLIGENCES.

IN the commencement of the last chapter, I had occasion to remark that, strictly speaking, the fundamental principle or affection which gives birth to all the ramifications of moral action, is but one, namely, *Love.* This noble affection may be considered as dividing itself into two great streams, one directing its course towards the Creator, as the supreme source of all felicity, and the other expanding itself towards all the intellectual beings which he has formed.

Having, in the preceding pages, endeavoured to illustrate the foundation and the reasonableness of the principle of love to God, from a consideration of his perfections, character, and relations, and having described some of those kindred affections by which its existence in the minds of moral agents is manifested,—I shall now endeavour to exhibit the foundation, and the reasonableness, of that modification of love which is directed towards created intelligences, and which may be termed the *second principle of moral action*—THOU SHALT LOVE THY NEIGHBOUR AS THYSELF. Taking it for granted that this is the fundamental law prescribed by the Creator for regulating the conduct of intelligent beings towards each other—because the Supreme Lawgiver has proclaimed it as such in the revelation which he has given us of his will—I shall endeavour to exhibit the reasonableness and the beauty of this amiable principle—from the nature of man, and the relations in which all the individuals of the human race stand to each other—from the happiness which would flow from the uniform operation of this principle—and from the misery which would inevitably ensue were it completely eradicated from the minds of moral agents.

Before proceeding to the illustration of these particulars, it may be proper to remark, that by "*our neighbour*" is to be understood *men of every nation and of every clime, whether they avow hemselves as our friends or our enemies, and whatever may be their language, their religion, their rank, or station.* The inhabitants of New Zealand, of Patagonia, of New Holland, of the Ladrones, of Kamtschatka, or of Greenland, are our neighbours, in the sense intended in the divine injunction above quoted, as well as those who reside in our own nation and in our more immediate neighbourhood. For with all these, and other tribes of mankind, we may happen to have intercourses, either directly or indirectly, and towards them all we ought to exercise an affection analogous to that which every man exercises towards himself. This we are decisively taught by our Saviour in the parable of the good Samaritan, in which it is clearly shown, that under the designation of *neighbour*, we are to include even our bitterest enemies. His apostles avowed the same sentiment, and taught, that in the bonds of Christian love, no distinction should exist between "Jews and Greeks, Barbarians, Scythians, bond, or free." For they are all members of the great family of God, and recognized as children by the universal parent.

---

### SECTION I.

#### THE NATURAL EQUALITY OF MANKIND CONSIDERED AS THE BASIS OF LOVE TO OUR NEIGHBOUR.

I SHALL now exhibit a few considerations founded on the Natural Equality of Mankind, in order to evince the reasonableness and the necessity of the operation of the principle of love towards all our fellow-men.

In the first place, Men, of whatever rank, kindred, or tribe, are the offspring of the great Parent of the universe. They were all created by the same Almighty Being, and to him they are indebted for all the members and functions of their animal frames, and for those powers, capacities, and endowments, which render them superior to the clods of the valley and to the beasts of the forest. They derived their origin too, as to their bodies, from the same physical principles and from the same earthly parent. "Of the dust of the ground" the body of the first man was formed; and from Adam, the primogenitor of the human race, have descended all the generations of men which now exist, or will hereafter exist till the close of time. This is equally true of the prince and of his subjects; of the monarch arrayed in purple, and seated on a throne, and of the beggar, who is clothed in rags, and embraces a dunghill; of the proud nobleman, who boasts of a long line of illustrious ancestors, and of the obscure peasant, whose progenitors were unnoticed and unknown. All derived their origin from the dust, and all return to the dust again. This consideration, on which it is unnecessary to dwell, shows the reasonableness of union and affection among men, on the same grounds from which we conclude that brothers and sisters belonging to the same family ought to manifest a friendly affection for each other.

Secondly, Men of all nations and ranks are equal in respect to the mechanism of their bodies and the mental faculties with which they are endowed. Whether their bodies be rudely covered with the skins of beasts, or adorned with the splendours of royalty; whether they be exposed naked to the scorching heats and piercing colds, or arrayed in robes of silk and crimson—in their construction and symmetry they equally bear the impress of infinite wisdom and omnipotence. The body of the meanest peasant, who earns his scanty subsistence from day to day by the sweat of his brow, is equally admirable, in the motions of its fingers, the structure of its limbs, and the connexion and uses of its several functions, as the body of the mightiest and the proudest baron who looks down upon him with contempt. The organs of vision comprise as many coats and humours, muscular fibres, and lymphatic ducts, and form as delicate pictures upon the retina—the bones are equally numerous, and as accurately articulated—the muscles perform their functions with as great precision and facility—the lymphatic and absorbent vessels are as numerous and incessant in their operations—and the heart impels the blood through a thousand veins and arteries with as great a degree of rapidity and of *purity* in the corporeal frame of a poor African slave, who is daily smarting under the lash of an unfeeling planter, as in the body of the Emperor of China, who sways his sceptre over half the inhabitants of the globe. All the external trappings which fascinate the vulgar eye, and by which the various ranks of mankind are distinguished, are merely adventitious, and have no necessary connexion with the intrinsic dignity of man. They are part of the consequences of the depravity of our species: in most instances they are the results of vanity, folly, pride, and frivolity; and they constitute no essential distinction between man and man; for a few paltry guineas would suffice to deck the son of a peasant with all the ornaments of a peer.

Men are also nearly on a level in respect to the mental faculties which they possess. Every man, however low his station in the present world, is endowed with a spiritual principle which he received by "the inspiration of the Almighty," which is superior to all the mechanism and modifications of matter, and by which he is allied to beings of a superior order. The faculties of consciousness, perception, memory, conception, imagination, judgment, reasoning, and moral feeling, are common to men of all casts and nations. The power of recollecting the past, and of anticipating the future—of deducing conclusions from premises previously demonstrated—of representing to the mind objects and scenes which have long ceased to exist; of forming in the imagination new combinations of the objects of sense; of perceiving the qualities of moral actions, and distinguishing between right and wrong; of recognizing a supreme intelligent Agent in the movements of the universe, and of making perpetual advances in knowledge and felicity; faculties which distinguish man from all the other tribes which people the earth, air, or sea; are possessed by the dwarfish Laplander and the untutored peasant, as well as by the ruler of kingdoms, the enlightened statesman, and the man of science. It is true, indeed, that there is a mighty difference among men in the direction of these faculties, in the objects towards which they are directed, in the cultivation they have received, and in the degree of perfection to which they have attained. There are innumerable gradations in the improvement and the energies of intellect, from the narrow range of thought possessed by a Greenlander or an Esquimaux, to the sublime and expansive views of a *Bacon*, or a *Newton*. But, this difference depends more on the physical and moral circumstances in which they are placed than on any intrinsic difference in the faculties themselves. Place the son of a boor or of a Laplander in circumstances favourable to the developement of his mental powers, and afford him the requisite means for directing and increasing their activity, and he will display powers of intelligence equal to those which are found in the highest ranks of civilized life. A sound understanding, a correct judgment, vigour of mind, control over the irascible passions, and other mental endowments, though destitute of polish, will as frequently be found in the lower walks of life as in the elevated ranks of opulence and power.

The philosopher, however, as well as the man of rank, is apt to look down with a contemptuous sneer on the narrow conceptions of the husbandman, the mechanic, and the peasant; and is disposed to treat them as if they were an inferior species of intelligent beings. He does not always consider that the profound and the subtle speculations, which are dignified with the title of *philosophy*, are frequently of less importance to the progress of the human mind, and to the enjoyment of substantial comfort, than the deductions of common sense and the dictates of a sound though plain understanding; that they torment him with feelings, doubts, and perplexities, which sometimes shake the whole fabric of his knowledge, and lead him into labyrinths, out of which he can scarcely extricate his way; while the man of plain understanding, guided by a few certain and important points of truth, prosecutes the path of virtue with safety and success. For it may be considered as an established maxim, that the most interesting and salutary truths connected with the happiness of man are neither numerous nor difficult to be acquired, and are level to the comprehension of men of every nation and of every rank. But however grovelling may be the affections, and however limited the intellectual views of the untutored ranks of society, *they are capable of being trained* to the knowledge and the practice of every thing which regards their present comfort and their future happiness; and to devise and execute the means by which this object may be accomplished, is one way among many others by which our love to mankind should be displayed and demonstrated. We have no reason to complain of the want of mental energy, or of the ignorance and folly of the lower orders of mankind, and to despise them on this account, while we sit still in criminal apathy, and refuse to apply those means which are requisite to raise them from their state of moral and intellectual degradation.

Thirdly, Mankind are on an equality, in respect of that moral depravity with which they are all infected. From whatever cause it may be conceived to have originated, the fact is certain, that a moral disease has spread itself through all the branches of the human family, in whatever station, or in whatever regions of the globe they may be placed. Whether we look back on the "generations of old," or survey the moral state of the nations in modern times; whether we turn our eyes to the abodes of savage or of civilized life; whether we contemplate the characters of the higher orders of society, or the practices which abound among the inferior ranks of social life; the stamp of depravity, in one shape or another, appears impressed upon the general conduct of mankind. In the case of *nations*, this depravity has manifested itself in those wars, dissensions, devastations, and contentions for territory and power, which have in all ages convulsed the human race and disturbed the peace of the world. Among lesser societies, families, and individuals, it is displayed in the operation of the principles of pride, ambition, tyranny, persecution, revenge, malice, envy, falsehood, deceit, covetousness, anger, and other malignant passions, which have infested all ranks and conditions of men. This depravity infects the higher ranks of mankind equally with the lower, though among the former it is sometimes varnished over with a fairer exterior; and therefore, there is no rank or order of men that have any valid reason on this ground for despising their fellow-creatures, or withholding from them the exercise of love and affection. For "there is none righteous, no, not one: for all have sinned, and come short of the glory of God." And in this point of view, love ought to exercise its beneficent energies, in endeavouring to counteract the stream of human corruption, and in disseminating those divine principles which are calculated to raise mankind to the moral dignity of their nature.

Fourthly, Mankind possess substantially the same pleasures and enjoyments. It is a trite saying, but it is nevertheless a true and important one, that happiness does not depend upon the rank and stations we occupy in life, nor upon the quantity of wealth or riches we possess. The pleasures which flow from the movements of the system of nature, and from the beauties which adorn the heavens and the earth, are common and open to all the inhabitants of the globe. The rising sun, the smiling day, the flowery landscape, the purling streams, the lofty mountains, the fertile vales, the verdure of the meadows, the ruddy hues of the evening clouds, the rainbow adorned with all the colours of light, the coruscations of the northern lights, the music of the groves, the songs of the nightingale and the lark, the breath of spring, the fruits of harvest, the azure sky, the blazing comet, the planets in their courses, the moon walking in brightness, and the radiant host of stars, convey to the mind thousands of delightful images and sensations, which charm the cottager and the mechanic no less than the sons of opulence and fame. The pleasures of the senses, of eating and drinking, of affectionate friendship, of social and domestic intercourse, of a cheerful contented mind, of fervent piety towards God, and of the hope of immortality beyond the grave, may be enjoyed by men of every colour, and rank, and condition in life; by the inhabitants of the cottage, as well as by the potentate who sways his sceptre over kingdoms. Nor does it materially detract from these enjoyments in the case of the peasant, that his body is frequently hung with rags, that he subsists on the coarsest fare, and reposes under the thatch of a miserable hut. For *habit* is the great leveller of mankind; it reconciles us to innumerable inconveniences and privations, and blunts the edge of the keenest pleasures. The owner of a princely mansion frequently loathes the most delicious dainties on his table, and walks through his magnificent apartments, surrounded with paintings and decorations, with as much apathy and indifference as if he were in an Indian wigwam or a clay-built cottage. So that, in the pleasures of sense, of affection, and sentiment, there is no essential distinction between the high and the low, the rich and the poor. But should it be insinuated that the poor and the ignoble have fewer enjoyments than the rich, then it will follow, that towards them in a particular manner our benevolent affections ought to be directed, in order that they may enjoy a competent portion of those physical and intellectual pleasures which the Creator has provided for all his creatures.

Fifthly, Men in every condition and in every clime have the same wants, and are exposed to the same disasters and afflictions. Hunger and thirst, cold and heat, motion and rest, are common to all orders and conditions of men; and in order to supply and alleviate such wants, the aid of our fellow-men is indispensably requisite, to enable us to obtain food, raiment, light, warmth, comfortable accommodation, and shelter from the blasts of the tempest. We all stand in need of comfort and advice in the hour of difficulty and danger; we all long for the love, and friendship, and good offices of those around us; and we all thirst for an increase of knowledge, happiness, and joy. And those wants and desires can be supplied and gratified only by the kindly intercourse and affection of kindred spirits.

All are exposed to the same sorrows and afflictions. Disappointments, anxiety, disgrace, accidents, pain, sickness, disease, loss of health, fortune, and honour, bereavement of children, friends, and relatives, are equally the lot of the prince and the peasant. The prince in the cradle is a being as weak and feeble, as dependent on his nurse, has as many wants to be supplied, is liable to as many diseases and accidents, and requires as many exertions to learn to lisp, to speak, and to walk, as the new-born babe of his meanest subject. Nay, the rich and the powerful are frequently exposed to miseries and vexations from fancied insults, affronts, and provocations, from frustrated hopes, from pride, vanity, and ill-humour, from abortive projects and disconcerted plans, to which the poor are generally strangers. If we enter into one of the abodes of poverty, where one of the victims of disease is reclining, we may behold a poor emaciated mortal, with haggard looks and a heaving breast, reposing on a pillow of straw, surrounded by ragged children and an affectionate wife, all eager to sooth his sorrows and alleviate his distress. If we pass through a crowd of domestics and courtly attendants into the mansion of opulence, where disease or the harbinger of death has seized one of its victims, we may also behold a wretch, pale, blotched, and distorted, agonizing under the pain of the asthma, the gravel, or the gout, and trembling under the apprehensions of the solemnity of a future judgment, without one sincere friend to afford him a drop of consolation. Neither the splendour of his apartment, nor the costly crimson with which his couch is hung, nor the attentions of his physicians, nor the number of his attendants, can prevent the bitter taste of nauseous medicines, the intolerable pains, the misgivings of heart, and the pangs of conscience which he feels in common with the meanest wretch who is expiring on a dunghill.

Lastly, All ranks come to the same termination of their mortal existence. "Dust thou art, and unto dust thou shalt return," is a decree which has gone forth against every inhabitant of our globe, of whatever kindred, rank, or nation. The tombs of mighty princes, of intrepid generals, of illustrious statesmen, may be adorned with lofty columns, with sculptured marble, and flattering inscriptions; but within these varnished monuments their bodies present putrid carcasses, as loathsome, and as much the prey of worms and corruption, as the corpse of their meanest vassal. Their eyes are equally impenetrable to the light of day, their ears are equally deaf to the charms of music, and their tongues are equally silent in this land of deep forgetfulness. This consideration of itself fully demonstrates, if any demonstration be necessary, the *natural equality* of mankind, and that there is no essential difference between the noble and the ignoble, the emperor, and the slave. And since mankind are all equally liable to afflictions and distresses, and are all journeying to the tomb, nothing can be more reasonable than the exercise of love, with all its kindred affections, towards every class of our fellow-men, in order to alleviate their sorrows, and to cheer them on their passage through this region of mortality.

Thus it appears, that there is a natural equality subsisting among mankind, in respect of their origin, their corporeal organization, their intellectual powers, their moral depravity, their wants, their afflictions, their pleasures, and enjoyments, and the state to which they are reduced after they have finished the career of their mortal existence. The illustration of such circumstances would be quite unnecessary, were it not that a certain proportion of mankind, under the influence of pride and other malignant passions, are still disposed to look down on certain classes of their fellow-mortals as if they were a species of beings of an inferior order in the scale of existence. To the propriety of the sentiments now stated, the sacred Scriptures bear ample testimony. "The rich and the poor meet together; the Lord is the maker of them all."* "Did not he that made me in the womb make my servant, and did he not fashion us alike?"† "God hath made of one blood all nations of men for to dwell on all the face of the earth, and hath determined the times before appointed, and the bounds of their habitation."‡

Since, therefore, it appears, that mankind are equal in every thing that is essential to the human character, this equality lays a broad foundation for the exercise of universal love towards men of all nations, tribes, conditions, and ranks. It must obviously appear contrary to every principle of reason, repugnant to every amiable feeling, and inconsistent with the general happiness of the species, that intelligent beings, who are all children of the same Almighty Parent, members of the same great family, and linked together by so many fraternal ties, should "bite and devour one another," engage in hostile enterprises against each other, look down with scorn and

* Prov. xxii. 2. † Job xxxi. 15. ‡ Acts xvii. 26.

contempt on each other, or even behold with indifference the condition of the meanest member of the family to which they belong. On the other hand, it is consistent with the dictates of enlightened reason, congenial to the best feelings of human nature, and indispensably requisite to the promotion of universal happiness, that such beings should be united in the bonds of affection and harmony, that they should sympathize with the distressed, delight in beholding the happiness of all, "rejoice with them that do rejoice, and weep with them that weep;"—that every one, whether he be near or far off, whether he be rich or poor, whether he be learned or unlearned, whether he belong to this or the other civil or religious society, whether his colour be black or white, whether he be blind, or deaf, or lame, whether he be an inhabitant of Greenland, Iceland, Barbary, Germany, France, or Spain, whatever may be his language, manners, or customs, should be recognized, wherever he may be found, as a friend and brother; and a cordial interest felt in every thing that concerns his welfare and comfort. Such a recognition of man as man, is a duty which necessarily flows from the natural equality of mankind, and is congenial to the conduct of the Universal Parent towards all his human offspring. For, in his love to his numerous family, and without respect of persons, he makes the same vital air to give play to their lungs, the same sun to cheer and enlighten them, and the same rains and dews to refresh their fields, and to ripen the fruits of harvest.

Let it not, however, be inferred, from what has been now stated, that we mean to sap the foundations of that subordination of ranks which exists in this world. This gradation in society is the appointment of God, and necessarily flows from the circumstances and relations in which man is placed in this first stage of his existence; and, were it completely overthrown, society would be plunged into a scene of anarchy and confusion; and the greater part of the individuals which compose it, would become a lawless banditti. Whether or not there exists a subordination of office and rank among *superior* intelligences of the same species, or among the inhabitants of other globes, we are unable at present to determine; but in the actual condition of society in the world in which we dwell, a state of complete independence, and a perfect equality of wealth, station, and rank, are impossible, so long as there exists a diversity in the capacities, tempers, and pursuits of men. On the diversity of rank, and the relations which subsist between the different classes of society, as parents and children, masters and servants, princes and subjects, is founded a great proportion of those moral laws which God hath promulgated in his word, for regulating the inclinations and the conduct of mankind.

Diversity of fortune and station appears absolutely inevitable in a world where moral evil exists, and where its inhabitants are exposed to dangers, difficulties, and distress. Whether the inhabitants of a world, where moral perfection reigns triumphant, can exist in a state of perfect felicity, and move forward in progressive improvement, without a subordination of rank, it is not for us to determine. But in such a world as ours, it is a wise and gracious appointment of the Creator, and is attended with many and important advantages. Were there no diversity of wealth and station, we should be deprived of many of the comforts, conveniences, and assistances which we now enjoy. Every one would be obliged to provide for himself food, drink, clothing, furniture, shelter, medicines, and recreations; and in the season of sickness, danger, and distress, he would have few or none to alleviate his affliction, and contribute to his comfort. But, in consequence of the diversity which now exists, an opportunity is afforded of employing the several capacities and endowments of mankind in those lines of active exertion, for which they are respectively fitted, and of rendering them subservient for the improvement and happiness of general society. One exercises the trade of a weaver, another that of a baker; one is a shoemaker, another a tailor; one is an architect, another a farmer; one is a teacher of science or religion; others have their minds entertained and improved by his instructions. One is appointed a ruler over a city, another over a kingdom; one is employed in writing for the amusement and instruction of mankind, another is employed in printing and publishing his writings. By this arrangement, the powers and capacities in which individuals excel, are gradually carried to the highest degree of attainable perfection; and the exertions of a single individual are rendered subservient to the ease, the convenience, and the mental improvement of thousands.

It is not to the diversity of rank and station, that the evils which exist among the various classes of society are to be attributed; but to the influence of a spirit of pride, on the one hand, and a spirit of insubordination on the other—to the want of a disposition to discharge the duties peculiar to each station, and to the deficiency of those kindly affections which ought to be manifested towards every human being, by men in all the ranks and departments of life. If love, in all its benevolent ramifications, were to pervade the various ranks of social life, kings would never oppress their subjects, nor masters act unjustly towards their servants; nor would subjects and servants refuse to submit to just laws, and equitable regulations. All would act their parts with harmony and delight in this great moral machine, and every station and rank would contribute, in its sphere, to the prosperity and happiness of another. For the poor cannot do without the rich, nor the rich without the poor; the prince without his subjects, nor subjects without wise and enlightened rulers, and equitable laws. All are linked together by innumerable ties; and the recognition of these ties, and the practice of the reciprocal duties which arise out of them, form the source of individual happiness, and the bonds of social enjoyment

---

## SECTION II.

### THE CONNEXIONS AND RELATIONS WHICH SUBSIST AMONG MANKIND CONSIDERED AS ESTABLISHING THE BASIS OF LOVE TO OUR NEIGHBOUR.

THE relations which subsist among mankind lay a foundation for the exercise of the benevolent affections, and for the various duties of social life; and these relations are far more numerous and extensive than the generality of mankind are disposed to admit. The relations of parents and children, of husbands and wives, of brethren and sisters, of masters and servants, of rulers and subjects, of teachers and scholars, of buyers and sellers, &c. are recognized by all as involving an obligation to the exercise of certain corresponding duties and affections. The moment we contemplate the relation of a parent and a child, we at once perceive the obligation of love on the part of the parent, and of reverence and obedience on the part of the child; and, in every other relation, a corresponding duty is involved, resulting from the nature of that relation, and founded on the principle of love. But as these relations, and their corresponding duties and affections have been frequently illustrated, I shall advert to a variety of circumstances, generally overlooked, which demonstrate the universal connexion of human beings with each other, and the reasonableness of the exercise of love towards all mankind.

Wherever we turn our eyes towards the great family of mankind—whether we look around on the land of our nativity, or to distant continents, and the oceans which surround them, we behold thousands of human beings toiling for our ease, our convenience, our pleasure, and improvement.—Here, we behold the ploughman turning up the furrows of the soil, and the sower casting in the seed which is to produce the fruits of harvest:—there, we behold the reaper cutting down the corn which is to serve for our nourishment. On the one hand, we behold the cow-herd tending his cattle, which are to afford us milk, butter, and cheese; on the other, we behold the shepherd tending his flocks, whose wool is to provide us with warm and comfortable clothing. One is preparing leather from the hides of oxen, another is shaping it into shoes and boots. One is spinning flax and cotton into yarn, another is weaving it into linen and muslin, to cover and adorn us. One is dressing the vine, whose juice is to cheer and refresh us; another is treading the wine-press, and preparing the wine for our use. Here, we behold the blacksmith toiling and sweating at the anvil, preparing tongs, and shovels, and grates, for our apartments; there, we behold the carpenter, with his hammer, and plane, and saw, fitting up beds, and tables, and chairs, for our ease and accommodation. Here, one is preparing our food, and another our clothing; there, one is preparing our drink, and another our medicines. In one chamber, the student of nature and of science is preparing, at the midnight lamp, those compositions which are to convey entertainment and instruction to the minds of the public; in another, the herald of salvation is meditating on those divine subjects, which he is about to proclaim for the illumination and comfort of assembled multitudes. In short, to whatever department of human society we direct our attention, and to whatever quarter we turn our eyes, in the busy scene around us, we behold thousands of our fellow-men exerting their corporeal and intellectual powers in those employments which will ultimately contribute either to our ease, our entertainment, our security, our accommodation, our subsistence, or our moral and intellectual improvement.

But our connexions with human beings are not confined to our immediate neighbourhood, nor even to the nation in which we reside. There is scarcely a region of the globe towards which we can direct our view, in which we do not behold innumerable links which connect us with the great family of mankind. Let us turn our eyes to the West India islands, and we shall behold the poor African slave toiling under the scorching heat of a tropical sun, and smarting under the cruel lash of an unfeeling overseer, in order to provide for us sugar, molasses, and rice, to mingle with our dainties, and to regale our appetites. If we direct our view to the empire of China, on the opposite side of the globe, twelve thousand miles distant from the former region, we shall behold thousands and tens of thousands of our brethren of the human family busily employed in planting the *tea* tree, in plucking its leaves, in exposing them to the steam of boiling water, in spreading them out to dry, in assorting them into different parcels, in packing and shipping them off for distant shores, that we, at a distance of nine thousand miles, may enjoy a delicious beverage for our morning and evening meals.* If we turn our eyes on India and Persia,



* For a portion of this beverage we are indebted even to some of the monkey tribe. As the tea shrub often grows on the rugged banks of steep mountains, access to which is dangerous, and sometimes impracticable, the Chinese, in order to come at the leaves, make use of a singular stratagem. These

we shall find multitudes of men, women, and children assiduously employed in cultivating the mulberry plant, in hatching and rearing silk-worms, in winding and twisting the delicate threads which proceed from these insects, and preparing them for the loom, in order that our ladies may be adorned with this finest production of nature and art. Let us pass in imagination to the frozen regions of Siberia and Kamtschatka, to the inhospitable shores of Onalaska and the Aleutian isles, and we shall behold numbers of weather-beaten wretches exposed to innumerable dangers by sea and land, traversing snowy mountains, forests, marches, and deserts, suffering frequent shipwrecks on the coasts of unknown islands inhabited by savage tribes, and exposed, night and day, to the chilling frosts of the polar region, and the attacks of ravenous wolves, in order to collect the skins of otters, and furs of various descriptions, to adorn the dress of our female friends, and to shelter them from the winter's cold. Let us pass to the forests of Norway, Sweden, Canada, and Jamaica, and hundreds of hardy, weather-beaten peasants, exposed to many accidents and privations, will be seen cutting down the tall firs, larches, and mahogany, sawing them into planks and logs, and conveying them in floats along rapid rivers towards the sea, to be shipped for our country, for the purpose of being formed into floors and roofs for our buildings, and into elegant furniture to decorate our apartments.

Not only in distant islands and continents, but even in the midst of the vast ocean, multitudes of our brethren are toiling for our pleasure, convenience, and comfort. See yonder vessel in the Southern Atlantic ocean, which has just weathered the storms on the southern cape of Africa, and narrowly escaped the dangers of shipwreck on a rocky shore. For several weeks the hardy mariners have been beating against the wind in the midst of thunders, lightnings, and tempests, with mountainous waves continually breaking over them, darkness surrounding them for many sleepless nights, and the dread of impending destruction filling them with trembling and horror. And why have they been exposed to danger so dreadful and appalling? That they might convey to our shores, from China and Hindostan, stores of tea, coffee, sugar, porcelain, silks, carpets, and precious stones, to supply luxuries to our tables, and ornaments to our dress. See yonder vessel, too, which is tossing in the midst of the Northern ocean, passing between shoals and icebergs, and liable every moment to be crushed to pieces between mountains of ice. Her mariners have long been exposed to the rigours of an arctic sky, and have narrowly escaped being plunged into the deep by the stroke of an enormous whale, in order that we might be supplied with seal-skins, whalebone, and oil for our lamps.

Even in the bowels of the ocean thousands of poor wretches, on the coasts of Califonia, Ceylon, Persia, and China, are diving amidst its waves, remaining whole half hours, at sixty feet below the surface of its waters, exposed to the danger of being devoured by sharks and other monsters of the deep, in order to collect *pearls* for ornaments to the ladies of Europe, Asia, Africa, and America.—In short, wherever we turn our eyes on the surface of the mighty deep, we contemplate a busy scene of human beings ploughing the ocean in every direction, and toiling, in the midst of dangers, storms, and tempests, in order to promote the accommodation of their fellow-mortals, who dwell on opposite regions of the globe. On the one hand, we behold thousands of hardy Russians, Swedes, and Norwegians, steering their vessels along the Baltic and the German sea, to convey to our shores copper, timber, pitch, skins, hemp, and tallow; on the other, we behold the Americans ploughing the waves of the Atlantic, with stores of mahogany, sugar, rice, flour, tobacco, rum, and brandy. Along the vast Pacific ocean, the Spanish galleons are conveying to Europe, gold, silver, pearls, precious stones, and all the other riches of Peru. Even from the southern icy ocean, where nature appears bound in the fetters of eternal ice, the adventurous mariner is conveying to our shores furs of various kinds, with the products of seals and whales. And, in return for the supply we receive from foreign regions, our British sailors are traversing every sea and ocean, and distributing to the inhabitants of every clime the productions of our arts, sciences, and manufactures.

Even in the subterraneous apartments of the globe, as well as upon its surface, many thousands of human beings are labouring, in confined and gloomy regions, to promote our comforts and enjoyments. The copper mines in Sweden are situated at more than a thousand feet below the surface of the ground, and contain a vast number of subterraneous apartments, branching in all directions. In these dreary abodes, twelve hundred wretched beings are doomed to pass their existence, deprived of the cheerful light of day—toiling, almost naked, in the midst of hot and sulphureous vapours, and under severe task-masters, in order that we may be supplied with the best species of copper, for forming our kettles, cauldrons, and copper-plate engravings. The salt mines of Hungary and Poland, the gold and silver mines of Potosi and Peru, and hundreds of similar subterraneous mansions, in various parts of the earth, present to our view numerous groups of our fellow-men, all engaged

steep places are generally frequented by great numbers of monkeys, which, being irritated and provoked, to avenge themselves, tear off the branches, and shower them down upon those who have insulted them. The Chinese immediately collect these branches and strip off their leaves.—*Ency. Brit. Art. Tea.*

in similar toils and labours, in order that we may enjoy the riches, the elegancies, and the conveniences of life. In our own country, how many thousands of our brethren are labouring in the dark recesses of the earth, far beneath its surface, exposed to the suffocation of the *choke-damp* and the explosions of the *fire-damp*, in procuring for us that invaluable fossil, which warms and cheers our winter apartments, which cooks our victuals, and enables us to carry on the various processes of our arts and manufactories!

Thus it appears, that we are connected with our fellow-men, in every quarter of the world, by thousands of ties;—that millions of human beings, whom we have never seen, nor never will see on this side the grave, are labouring to promote our interests, without whose exertions we should be deprived of the greatest proportion of our accomodations and enjoyments. While we are sitting in our comfortable apartments, feasting on the bounties of Providence, thousands, and ten thousands of our brethren of mankind, in different regions of the globe, are assiduously labouring to procure for us supplies for some future entertainment. One is sowing the seed, another gathering in the fruits of harvest; one is providing fuel, and another furs and flannel, to guard us from the winter's cold; one is conveying home the luxuries and necessaries of life, another is bringing intelligence from our friends in distant lands; one is carrying grain to the mill, another is grinding it, and another is conveying it along the road to our habitations; one is in search of medicines to assuage our pains, and another is in search of consolation to sooth our wounded spirits. In the midst of these never-ceasing exertions, some are crossing deep and dangerous rivers, some are traversing a vast howling wilderness; some are wandering amidst swampy moors, and trackless heaths; some are parched with thirst in sandy deserts; some are shivering and benumbed amidst the blasts of winter; some are toiling along steep and dangerous roads, and others are tossing in the midst of the ocean, buffeted by the winds and raging billows.

And, since we are connected with our fellow-creatures by so many links, is it not reasonable, is it not congenial to the nature of man, that we should be connected with them by the ties of sympathy and benevolent affections? It is true, indeed, that the various classes of mankind in every country, who are toiling for our ease and gratification, seldom or never think of us in the midst of their difficulties and labours. Perhaps they have no other end in view than to earn their daily subsistence, and provide food and clothing for their families; perhaps they are actuated by the most selfish motives, and by principles of vanity and avarice; and some of them, perhaps, under the influence of that depravity which is common to the species, may be secretly cursing and reproaching us as individuals, or as a nation. But, from whatever motives their labours and exertions proceed, it is a fact which cannot be denied, and which they cannot prevent, that we actually enjoy the benefit of them; and, that, without them, we should be deprived of the greater part of those comforts and enjoyments which render existence desirable, and which cheer us in our pilgrimage to the grave.

We have, therefore, in almost every artificial object that surrounds us, and in every enjoyment we possess from day to day, so many sensible emblems of our connexion with every branch of the great family of mankind. When we sit down to a dish of tea, we are reminded of the crowded and busy population of China, where this plant is produced, and of the poor African slave, through whose sorrows and toils the sugar we mix with it is prepared. And shall we not feel a kindly affection for those whose labours procure us such a refreshing beverage? And should not our love prompt us to every active exertion by which their miseries may be alleviated, and their intellectual and religious improvement promoted? When we look at the pearls which adorn us, we are reminded of the poor wretch who has plunged to the bottom of the deep, and scrambled among projecting rocks, to the danger of his life, in order to procure them. When we look at a copper-plate engraving, we are reminded of the dark and cheerless recesses of the copper mines, where hundreds are employed in digging for this useful metal. When we enjoy the comfort of a cheerful fire, we are reminded of the gloomy subterraneous regions to which so many of our countrymen are confined, and the toils and dangers to which they are exposed, before our coals can be dragged from the bowels of the earth. And while we feel delighted with the diversified enjoyment which flows from the labour and industry of every class of mankind, is it reasonable that we should look with indifference on any one of them? Is it not accordant with the dictates of enlightened reason, and with every thing that we consider as amiable in the nature of man, that we should embrace them all in the arms of kindness and brotherly affection, and that our active powers, so far as our influence extends, should be employed in endeavouring to promote their present and everlasting happiness? At present, they seldom think about the benefits they are procuring for us and others by their useful labours; but were their circumstances meliorated, were their miseries relieved, were their minds expanded by instruction, were their moral powers cultivated and improved, were they to behold the various branches of the human family for whom they are labouring, exerting every nerve to promote their moral improvement and domestic enjoyment, it would produce many pleasing emotions in their breasts, in the midst of all their toilsome labours, to reflect that their exertions are the means of distributing numerous comforts and conveniences among men of different nations, ranks, kindreds, and languages. Their minds would take a more extensive range among the various tribes of mankind with which they are connected, as intelligences of the same species; they would learn to trace the remotest consequences of every branch of labour, and of every mechanical operation in which they are engaged, and they would thus feel themselves more intimately related to every individual of the great family to which they belong.

That it is the intention of the Creator that an extensive and affectionate intercourse should be carried on between the remotest tribes of mankind, appears even from the physical constitution and arrangement of our globe. The surface of the earth is every where indented with rivers of various dimensions, winding in every direction through the continents and the larger islands, and some of them running a course of several thousands of miles. In the eastern continent, above four hundred rivers of large dimensions are rolling from the mountains towards the sea; and in the western continent, more than one hundred and forty majestic streams are to be found, connecting the highest and the remotest parts of the land with the ocean, besides thousands of streams of smaller dimensions. The water of the sea is formed of such a consistency, or specific gravity, that it is capable of supporting large floating edifices; while, at the same time, its parts are so yielding as to permit such vehicles to move with rapidity along its surface, through its waves and billows. In virtue of this arrangement, the ocean, instead of standing as an everlasting barrier between the nations, has become a medium for the most speedy intercourse between distant lands. The atmosphere which surrounds the globe, contributes likewise by its agency to promote the same important end. By the impulsion of its different masses in various directions, our ships are wafted with considerable velocity along the surface of rivers, seas, and oceans, to the remotest extremities of the globe. By means of these arrangements which the Creator has established, the treasures of the mountains, and of the inland parts of the continents and islands, are conveyed towards the sea, and transported from one island and continent to another; and thus the various tribes of mankind have an opportunity of visiting each other, of cultivating an affectionate intercourse, and of contributing to their mutual enjoyment. And as it is probable that there exist in nature certain powers or principles not yet discovered, the agency of which may be applied to the propelling of machines and vehicles over land and water, and through the regions of the atmosphere, with a velocity much superior to what has hitherto been effected;—it appears evident, that the Creator, in forming such principles, and in permitting man to discover their nature and energies, intended that they should be applied for promoting a rapid and endearing intercourse among all the branches of that large family which he has placed upon the globe. And I have no doubt, that in the future ages of the world, by means of improvements in art and science, such intercourse will be carried on in the spirit of benevolence, to an extent and with a rapidity of which we cannot at present form any adequate conception.

It appears, then to be one great design of the Creator, in connecting mankind by so many links, and in rendering them dependent upon each other, though placed in opposite regions of the globe, to lay a broad foundation for the exercise of the benevolent affections between men of all nations, and ultimately to unite the whole human race in one harmonious and affectionate society. And it is obviously the duty of every human being to cultivate those dispositions, and to prosecute that train of action which have a tendency to accomplish the plans of the Universal Parent, and to promote the happiness of his intelligent offspring. In so doing, he contributes to his own individual happiness, and at the same time to that of all the moral intelligences in heaven and earth with which he is connected.

---

## SECTION III.

### THE ULTIMATE DESTINATION OF MANKIND CONSIDERED AS A BASIS FOR LOVE TO OUR NEIGHBOUR, AND AS A MOTIVE TO ITS EXERCISE.

THE present world is not the ultimate destination of mankind. It is only a passing scene through which they are now travelling to that immortal existence which will have no termination. Man is at present in the infancy of his being; his faculties are only beginning to expand, his moral powers are feeble and depraved, his intellectual views are circumscribed within a narrow range, and all the relations in which he stands demonstrate that the present scene is connected with the future, and is introductory to a higher sphere of action and enjoyment. "We know," says the Apostle Paul, "that if this earthly house of our tabernacle were dissolved, we have a building of God, an house not made with hands, eternal in the heavens." And our Saviour declares, that "the hour is coming, in which all that are in their graves shall hear his voice, and shall come forth," and that "our vile bodies shall be changed, and fashioned like unto his glorious body," and shall enter into the enjoyment of a new world, "which is incorruptible, undefiled, and which fadeth not away."

The capacity of making perpetual advances in knowledge and moral improvement in a future state of existence, is that in which the true dignity of man consists; and in this capacity, and the high destination with which it is connected, there is no difference between the high and the low, the slave who is chained to a galley, and the sovereign at whose nod the nations tremble. They are equally destined to immortality, and will exist in a future world, when time and all the arrangements of the present state shall come to a close. If man were only the creature of a day, whose prospects are bounded by this terrestrial scene, and whose hopes terminate in the tomb, it might appear a matter of comparatively little importance whether or not our benevolent regards were extended to our fellow-men, except in so far as our self-interest and avarice were concerned. The happiness of a fellow-creature might then be considered as a matter of indifference, and his dissolution, at death, a circumstance as trivial as the falling of a leaf in autumn, or the sinking of a stone to the bottom of the ocean. Even in this case, however, it would still be conducive to human happiness during the short and uncertain span of our existence, that all the branches of the human family were cemented together in union and affection. But when we reflect that all the intelligent beings around us, with whom we more immediately associate, and all those in distant lands with whom we are connected by the ties of one common nature, and on whom we depend for many of our comforts, are destined along with ourselves to an eternal world, in another region of the Creator's empire; and that the affections we now cultivate, and the conduct we pursue in reference to our brethren, have an intimate relation to that immortal existence;—this consideration stamps an importance on the exercise of brotherly affection which is beyond the power of human language to express. It shows us, that the dispositions which we now indulge, and the manner in which we treat the meanest of our fellow-creatures, may be recognised and attended with the most important effects a thousand millions of years hence, and may run parallel in their consequences even with eternity itself.

We may, perhaps, view it as a matter of trivial moment in what manner we now conduct ourselves towards a servant or a slave; whether we render his life miserable by hard labour, cruel insults, and contemptuous treatment, or study to promote his comfort and domestic enjoyment; whether we neglect to instruct him in the knowledge of his duty to his God and to his fellow men, or labour to promote his moral and religious improvement. We may view with indifference or contempt the person and the family of a poor pious neighbour, who has earned a scanty subsistence by the sweat of his brow, and may behold his body laid in the grave with as much apathy as we behold the carcass of a dog thrown into a pond. But could we follow the pious man beyond the precincts of the tomb, into that immortal scene which has burst upon his disencumbered spirit; could we trace the gradual expansion of his faculties towards objects which lie beyond the grasp of mortals, and the perfection of his moral powers; could we behold his mouldered frame starting up to new life at "the resurrection of the just," and arrayed in new splendour and beauty; could we contemplate him placed in a station of dignity and honour among the sons of God," in that glorious residence to which he is destined; his intellectual powers expanding, grasping the most sublime objects, and pushing forward in the career of perpetual improvement, without the least stain of moral imperfection;—would we now treat such a one with malevolence, or even with indifference or neglect? And were we placed by his side in such a dignified station, what would our feelings be when we recollected the apathy, the indifference, and even the contempt with which he was treated in this sublunary scene? On the other hand, could we follow the poor wretched slave to the future world, and contemplate the degradation and misery to which he is there reduced in consequence of our malevolence and neglect, what emotions of horror and indignation should we not feel at the recollection of that pride and disaffection which led us to act so basely towards a fellow-immortal, whom it was in our power to have trained to wisdom, to excellence, and to a happy immortality? When, therefore, we behold individuals withholding their benevolent regard from their brethren of mankind, and treating them with haughtiness and contempt, we must conclude that such persons overlook the true dignity of man, and secretly disbelieve the reality of an immortal state of existence, whatever professions they may make to the contrary. For the consideration of the eternal destiny of mankind reflects a dignity on the meanest human being, and attaches an importance to all our affections and actions in relation to him, unspeakably greater than if his existence were circumscribed within the narrow limits of time, and throws completely into the shade all the degrading circumstances with which he is now surrounded.

When we consider our brethren of the human family in the light of *immortal* intelligences, and look forward to the scenes of the eternal world, a crowd of interesting reflections naturally arises in the mind. A wide and unbounded prospect opens before us. Amidst new creations and the revolutions of systems and worlds, new displays of the Creator's power and providence burst upon the view. We behold ourselves placed on a theatre of action and enjoyment, and passing through "scenes and changes" which bear no resemblance to the transactions and events of this sublunary world. We behold ourselves mingling with beings of a superior order, cultivating nobler affections, and engaged in more sublime employments than those which now occupy our attention. We behold ourselves associated with men of all nations and kindreds, and with those who lived in the remotest periods of time. Millions of years roll on after millions, our capacities and powers of intellect are still expanding, and new scenes of beauty and magnificence are perpetually bursting on the astonished mind, without any prospect of a termination.—Amidst those eternal scenes, we shall doubtless enter into the most intimate connexions with persons whom we have never seen, from whom we are now separated by continents and oceans, with those whose bodies are now mouldering in the dust, with those who have not yet entered on the stage of existence, and with those with whom we now refuse to associate on account of their rank, and station, and religious opinions. That man, into whose dwelling we would not at present deign to enter, and with whom we would abhor to mingle in the public services of religion, may then be one of our chief companions in the regions of bliss, in directing and expanding our views of the glory and magnificence of God. The man whom we now hate and despise, and whose offers of assistance we would treat with disdain, may in that happier world be a principal agent in opening to our view new sources of contemplation and delight. That servant whom we now treat as a being of inferior species, at whom we frown and scold with feelings of proud superiority, may be our instructor and director, and every way our superior, in that region where earthly distinctions are unknown. That humble instructor whom we now despise, and whose sentiments we treat with contempt, may, in that world of intelligence and love, be our teacher and our guide to direct our views of the attributes of the Deity, of the arrangements of his providence, and of the glories of his empire. There the prince may yield precedence to his subjects, the master to the slave, and the peer to the humblest peasant. For no pre-eminence of birth, fortune, or learning, no excellence but that which is founded on holiness and virtue, on moral and intellectual endowments, will have any place in the arrangements of that world where human distinctions are for ever abolished and unknown. And shall we now refuse to acknowledge those who are to be our friends and companions in that future world? Is it not agreeable to the dictates of reason and to the voice of God that we should regard them with complacency and affection, whatever be the garb they now wear, whatever be their colour or features, and in whatever island or continent they may now reside?

It must, indeed, be admitted, that all the inhabitants of our world will not be exalted to dignity and happiness in the future state. A great proportion of them, in their present state of depravity and degradation, are altogether unqualified for participating in the exercises and enjoyments of celestial intelligences. Whole nations are still overspread with intellectual darkness, ignorant of their eternal destination, and immersed in immoralities and vile abominations. And, even in those countries where the light of revelation has dispelled the gloom of heathenism, a vast mass of human beings are to be found, "having their understandings darkened, alienated from the life of God," and sunk into the mire of every moral pollution. Still, we have no reason, on this account, to overlook their native dignity, and their high destination. Every human being we see around us, however low in rank, or degraded by vice, *is endowed with an immortal nature, and is capable of being raised to the dignity of an inhabitant of heaven;* and there is not a single individual to whom we can point, either in our own country or in other lands, in relation to whom we are authorized to affirm, that he will not be a participator in immortal bliss. And, therefore, every man with whom we associate, and whom we recognize in the circle of society around us, ought to be viewed as one with whom we may associate in the world to come. And as to those who appear to be partially enlightened and renovated in their minds, we ought not to withhold our affection and complacency on account of their ignorance, their contracted views, or erroneous opinions. We should view them, not as they are in their present state of infancy and weakness, but as they will be when arrived at maturity and manhood; not as they appear in the first weak essays of their intellectual powers, and in the lowest step of their existence, but as they will appear in their career of improvement after a lapse of millions of ages. Carrying forward our views to those eternal scenes, and accompanying our brethren of the human family through all the gradations of their existence in future worlds, we behold their faculties in progressive expansion, their minds approximating nearer to the source of eternal wisdom, their views of the empire of Omnipotence continually enlarging, their knowledge of the plan of redemption, and its numerous bearings, for ever increasing; their love and affection to God and to fellow intelligences waxing into a more ardent flame; every evil propensity corrected, every imperfection removed, every blossom of virtue fully expanded, and "joy unspeakable and full of glory" pervading every faculty of their souls. And can we behold intelligent minds, capable of so high and dignified attainments, and the companions of our future destiny, with indifference or contempt? Is there not here a broad foundation laid for the most expansive emanations of love towards every member of the great family of mankind, however much he may be obscured, and sullied by folly and sin in this first stage of his existence?

In the mean time, while the greater part of mankind are immersed in ignorance and vice, while the image of their Maker is defaced, and their immortal powers prostituted to the vilest passions, the most noble and honourable operation in which love can be engaged, is to devise and execute schemes by which our degraded brethren may be raised to intellectual and moral excellence: to train up young immortals in religion and virtue; to diffuse the principles of useful knowledge among all ranks; to counteract the diabolical spirit of war and contention; to abolish slavery in every shape; to meliorate the social and domestic condition of the lower orders of society; to publish the revelation of God in every language, and to send forth the messengers of salvation to every land, to instruct men of all nations and kindreds and tongues in the knowledge of the true God, and of the path which leads to a blessed immortality. Thus shall we be enabled to manifest our love towards all our brethren of the human family; thus shall we contribute to render them worthy of our highest affection, and to prepare them for the exalted exercises and employments of the life to come.

---

## SECTION IV.

LOVE TO GOD AND OUR NEIGHBOUR ENFORCED AND ILLUSTRATED, FROM A CONSIDERATION OF THE MISERABLE EFFECTS WHICH WOULD ENSUE WERE THESE PRINCIPLES REVERSED, AND WERE RATIONAL BEINGS TO ACT ACCORDINGLY.

THE two leading principles which I have endeavoured to illustrate, in the preceding pages, form the basis of the moral order of the intelligent universe. Consequently, were these principles reversed, and were moral agents to act accordingly, the moral world would soon be transformed into a scene of the most dismal anarchy and confusion. Every action would be dictated by feelings of pure *malevolence*, and misery in every shape would be the great object which human beings would exert their powers to accomplish. Could we suppose for a moment, that society could subsist for any length of time under the unrestrained operation of such a principle, the following, among many thousands of similar effects, would be the natural and necessary results.

Every individual would exhibit, in every action, the character of a fiend; and every family would display a miniature picture of hell.—Between the husband and wife there would be nothing but incessant brawling, dissension, and execration. Whatever was ardently desired by the one would be as resolutely and obstinately opposed by the other; and the fury and resentment excited by unsatisfied desires, and disappointed hopes, would destroy every vestige of peace and tranquillity, and stimulate a host of infernal passions to rage without control. Their children would be actuated by the same diabolical tempers. The son would take an infernal pleasure in cursing, insulting, and reproaching "the father that begat him," and in trampling with scorn and indignation on the mother who gave him birth.—Brothers and sisters would live under the continual influence of malice and envy, "hateful, and hating one another." Whatever actions tended to irritate, to torment, and to enrage the passions of each other, and to frustrate their desires and expectations, would be performed with a grin of infernal delight. Mutual scuffles and execrations would ensue. One would have his eye-ball bruised, or knocked out of its socket, another would have his teeth driven out of his jaws; one would have his hair torn from its roots, another his skull fractured with repeated blows; the legs of one would be full of bruises and putrifying sores, and the face of another all over covered with blotches and scars, most hideous to behold; and, in the progress of contention, the hand of a brother would plunge his dagger into a brother's heart. In larger societies, fraud, falsehood, deceit, seduction, quarrels, oppression, plunder, rapine, murder, and assassination, would be the common occurrences of every day and every hour. The seller would uniformly endeavour to cheat the buyer, and the buyer would endeavour, by every kind of fraud, or open force, to deprive the seller of the value of his commodities. Poison would be sold for medicine, and deleterious mixtures and poisonous drugs would be mixed up with the common articles of food, that the venders might enjoy the diabolical pleasure of hearing of the pains, the agonies, and the dying groans of the victims of their villany. The debauchee would triumph in the number of victims he had rendered wretched and forlorn by his wiles and depraved passions; the strong would oppress the weak, and rejoice in depriving them of every comfort, and the powerful would exult in trampling under their feet the persons and the property of the poor, and in beholding the extent of the miseries they had created.

In the common intercourse of life, every one would be maltreated, insulted, and reproached, as he walked along the street; the lip would be shot out with a diabolical grin at every passenger, which would be returned with the frown and the scowl of a demon. Every passenger that met another on the highway would be encountered with blows, execrations, and reproaches; and he who met his neighbour unawares in the recesses of a forest, would receive a dagger in his breast before he was aware of his danger. Words would be exchanged between man and man that would cut each other's hearts "like the piercings of a sword," and horrible contentions, accompanied with rage and fury, and wounds and bruises would be presented to the view in every city, and village, and rural scene. When one had finished a house to shelter him from the storm, a number of desperadoes, in horrid combination, would overturn the mansion, and crush him among the ruins. When one had planted vines and fruit-frees, others would seize the opportunity, when they were beginning to bud and blossom, to tear them up by the roots; persons who sowed the seed in spring could have no confidence that they would ever reap the fruits in autumn; and no one could have the least security that the wealth and property he possessed to-day would be his to-morrow. No one could feel secure for a single hour, that his life was not in danger from the sword of the murderer or the assassin; every man would live in continual fear and alarm; no pleasing prospects nor hopes of future enjoyment would ever calm the tumultuous passions, or cheer the distracted mind; all confidence between man and man would be completely destroyed: falsehood in every shape would walk triumphant; the mind would be distracted amidst its ignorance of the scenes and events that were happening around it; for no intelligence could be believed, and no one could certainly know the reality of any object or event, unless he beheld it with his own eyes. Schools, seminaries of learning, universities, and academies would have no existence, and no one could gain an acquaintance with any principle or fact in the universe around him, except in so far as he had made the investigation by means of his own senses and powers. Tormented by tumultuous passions raging within, in continual alarm from desperadoes, plunderers, and assassins raging around, looking back on the past with horrible recollections, and contemplating the future with terror and dismay, the mind would feel itself fixed in a scene of misery and wretchedness, which no words could describe nor pencil delineate.

If we could suppose a number of such beings leagued together for the purpose of carrying the schemes of malevolence more completely into effect, one of their employments would be to set fire to houses and villages, in order that they might enjoy the infernal pleasure of seeing their fellow-creatures deprived of every shelter, and of beholding men, women, and children roasting in the flames. Another employment would be to poison the springs of water, that they might behold one after another, from the sucking child to the hoary head, seized with excruciating pains, and sinking into the agonies of death. Another gratification of malevolence would be to dam up the rivers in their rapid course, that they might overflow the circumjacent plains, in order that they might feast their eyes on the scenes of devastation and ruin that would thus be created, and on the terror and destruction of the wretched inhabitants. The conflagration of a city, with all its accompaniments, the crash of falling houses, and of palaces tumbling into ruin; the terror and confusion of its inhabitants, the wailings of women and children, and the groans of the burning victims, would be a feast to the eyes and music to the ears of such malignant beings, as they once were to *Nero*, when, from the top of a high tower, he beheld Rome wrapt in the flames which he himself had kindled, and sung on his lyre the destruction of Troy. Even in the midst of the ocean such revolting scenes would be frequently realized. When two ships descried each other, a diabolical onset would ensue. To set on flames the respective vessels, to sink them in the deep, or to cause them to burst with a horrid explosion, would be the object of both the crews; that they might feast their malevolence on the spectacle of wounds and carnage, of drowning wretches covered with blood and scars, fighting with the billows, and scrambling for safety among the shattered fragments of the wreck.

Were it possible that discoveries in art and science could be made by intelligences actuated by such malignant passions, they would be all applied to subserve the purposes of malevolence. The force of gunpowder would be employed to blow ships and houses to atoms, to shake populous cities to their foundations, and to create among their inhabitants universal horror and alarm; the force of steam would be employed in producing destructive explosions, and in propelling the instruments of death and devastation among a surrounding populace. Air balloons would be employed for enabling them to carry their malignant schemes, in relation to distant tribes, more speedily into effect; for hurling down upon towns and villages stones, and bullets, and darts; and for enabling them to escape in safety when they had finished the work of destruction. The discovery of the nature of lightning, and its identity to the electrical fluid, instead of being applied for the protection of persons and of buildings from the stroke of that terrific meteor, would be destined to the purpose of devastation and destruction. The electricity of the atmosphere and the lightnings from the clouds would be conducted and directed so as to set on fire stacks of corn, to shatter lofty buildings, and lay groups of men and cattle prostrate with the dust. Every mechanical power, and all the combinations of physical forces which art can produce, would be applied to the framing of engines for torture, devastation, and massacre; and on the front of every new invention would be displayed, as if engraved in legible characters —TERROR, MISERY, AND DESTRUCTION.

Could we suppose for a moment such beings occasionally combining together on a large scale, for the purpose of more extensively glutting their malevolence, their conduct towards each other *as nations*, and the contests in which they would be engaged in this capacity, would be tremendous and horrible beyond the power of description. Every malevolent affection would be brought into action; every infernal passion would be raised to its highest pitch of fury; every one, stimulated by his associates, would breathe nothing but revenge, execrations, slaughter, and utter extermination against opposing armies; every engine of human destruction which ingenuity could invent would be brought into the scene of action; the yell of demons would accompany the fierce and sanguinary onset; and a scene of horror would ensue beyond the power of imagination to conceive, which would not terminate till the one class of combatants had exterminated the other; till they had trampled down and destroyed the fruits of their ground, and turned their land into a wilderness; till they had burned their villages to ashes, and tumbled their cities into a heap of ruins; till they had drenched their fields with blood, and strewed them with skulls, and limbs, and the mangled carcasses of thousands and ten thousands of men, women, and children, thrown together in horrible confusion. But it is needless to dwell on such scenes; since the history of all nations—since even the history of modern Europe presents us with spectacles of horror, scarcely inferior to those I have now described, and with moral agents who bear too striking a resemblance to those whose actions are completely subversive of the second commandment of the law, "*Thou shalt love thy neighbour as thyself.*"

Such, then, would be some of the dreadful effects which would flow from a subversion of the second principle of the moral law, if we could suppose that organical intelligences, *not endowed with immortal bodies*, could exist for any length of time amidst such scenes of depravity and wretchedness. But it is more than probable that such a state of society could not long subsist in such a world as we now inhabit, and among rational beings, whose corporeal organization is constructed after the model of the human frame. The whole mass of society in every land would soon be transformed into one boundless scene of anarchy and confusion; every one would flee from his neighbour as from an infernal fiend; a war of universal extermination would commence; nothing would be beheld over all the regions of the globe but spectacles of rapine, devastation, and destruction; and nothing would be heard among all the eight hundred millions of its inhabitants but the voice of execration, and the yells of lamentation, and mourning, and wo, till at length every beauty which now adorns the face of nature would be effaced, every fertile field transformed into a desert, every human habitation overturned, and every inhabitant of the earth sunk into oblivion.* This is one of the most terrible representations we can form of the horrors of the future state of punishment, where malevolent passions rage without control; and the considerations now stated demonstrate, that the man who is actuated by a principle of hostility towards his neighbour, is training and preparing himself for becoming an inhabitant of that miserable and dreary region, "where the worm dieth not, and the fire" of malevolence and revenge "is never quenched." We are thus instructed, that if there be a future state at all, it *must*, from the very nature and constitution of things, be a state of misery and horror to every man whose mind is under the unrestrained dominion of depraved affections and malignant passions; so that there is no possibility, in such a case, of escaping the "wrath to come," unless the moral constitution of the intelligent universe were entirely subverted.

If, then, it appears that such dismal consequences would flow from the subversion of this principle or law, it is obvious that the law itself must be "holy, just, and good," and calculated to promote the perfection and happiness of all created intelligences, among whom it is found in full operation. And in a world such as ours, where this law is partially violated, the consequent misery which is suffered will be nearly in proportion to the extent to which this violation is carried, and to the number of individuals who are actuated by a principle of opposition to its requirements.

In like manner, it might be shown, that the most dismal effects would be produced, were the first principle of the moral law reversed, and the malevolence of intelligent beings directed towards their Creator. In this case, instead of assembled multitudes joining in solemn adorations of the divine character and perfections, the God of heaven would be blasphemed, and his name abhorred in every land. Instead of reverence and profound humility in the presence of Jehovah, a spirit of pride and independence, and an impatience of control, would pervade every mind. Instead of thanksgivings for the bounties of his providence, the basest ingratitude would be manifested, and the most marked contempt of all his favours. Instead of cordial submission to his wise arrangements, nothing but murmurings and repinings would be heard, and the most presumptuous decisions uttered against all the dis-

* Whether such scenes as some of them now described may be realized in the future state of punishment, or whether the principles of the moral law will be entirely subverted among the miserable beings who are subjected to that punishment, it becomes not us positively to determine. But we can scarcely conceive a more horrible idea than that of intelligent beings acting uniformly from principles of pure malevolence, and at the same time endowed with *immortal bodies*, capable of sensations similar to those we now feel. In this case, every accumulated wound received from malignant associates would be an additional source of pain and misery which would continually increase, without any prospect of relief from the stroke of death.

pensations of his providence. Instead of complacency and delight in his character and operations, insults and reproaches would burst forth at every display of his wisdom, justice, and omnipotence. Instead of admiration of the beauty and grandeur of his wonderful works in heaven and earth, feelings of contempt and disdain would be mingled with all their surveys of the operations of nature. His omnipotence would be disregarded, his benevolence called in question or despised, and his wisdom and intelligence arraigned. Like Alphonso, king of Castile, they would not hesitate to affirm, "If we had been of God's privy council when he made the world, we would have advised him better." Under the influence of such diabolical dispositions, the harmony of the visible creation would be attempted to be deranged, and its beauties defaced, in so far as their limited powers would be able to effect. The fields would be stripped of their verdure; the forests would be torn up by the roots, and strewed in shapeless masses along the plains; the vegetable beauties which now diversify the rural landscape would be effaced; the rivers would be turned out of their courses to overflow the adjacent plains, and to transform them into stagnant marshes and standing pools; the air would be impregnated with pestilential vapours; and the grand, and beautiful, and picturesque scenes of nature would be stripped of their glory, leaving nothing but naked rocks and barren deserts, covered with the wrecks of nature, to mark the operations of malevolence.

Such would be the dispositions and the conduct of intelligent beings were the first principle of the moral law reversed, and their actions regulated by a principle of malevolence: and such, in a greater or less degree, are the dispositions of every man in whose heart the love of God has never taken up its residence. Revolting as the scenes now supposed must appear to every mind possessed of moral feeling, they must be admitted to be the necessary results of malignant passions raging without control. And if there be any region of creation in which pure malevolence actuates its inhabitants, we must suppose the restraining influence of the Almighty interposed, to preserve their malignant operations within those bounds which are consistent with the plans of his moral government and the general happiness of the intelligent universe. That principles and practices have existed among mankind, which, if left to operate without restraint, would produce all the effects now supposed, appears from the description which the apostle Paul gives of the character of the Gentile world, and even of that portion of it which had been brought into a civilized state. He declares that "they did not like to retain God in their knowledge, but changed the glory of the incorruptible God into an image made like to corruptible man, and to birds, and four-footed beasts, and creeping things," that they were "filled with all unrighteousness, fornication, wickedness, covetousness, *maliciousness*;" that they were "full of envy, murder, deceit, malignity, backbiters, *haters of God*, despiteful, proud, boasters, inventors of evil things, disobedient to parents; without understanding, *without natural affection*, *implacable*, *unmerciful*. Who, knowing the judgment of God, that they who commit such things are worthy of death, not only do the same, but have pleasure in them that do them." Were practices and passions of this description, which are all directly opposed to the principle of benevolence, to operate without control, the universe would soon be transformed into a boundless scene of devastation and sterility, of misery and horror, of lamentation and wo.

Turning our eyes from such revolting scenes, I shall now direct the attention of my readers to a more pleasing picture, and endeavour to delineate some of the happy effects which would naturally result from a complete conformity in thought and action to the principles of the divine law.

---

## SECTION V.

### EFFECTS WHICH WOULD FLOW FROM THE FULL OPERATION OF THE PRINCIPLE OF LOVE TO GOD AND TO MAN.

Were this divine principle in full operation among the intelligences that people our globe, this world would be transformed into a paradise, the moral desert would be changed into a fruitful field, and "blossom as the rose," and Eden would again appear in all its beauty and delight. Fraud, deceit, and artifice, with all their concomitant train of evils, would no longer walk rampant in every land. Prosecutions, lawsuits, and all the innumerable vexatious litigations which now disturb the peace of society, would cease from among men. Every debt would be punctually paid; every commodity sold at its just value; every article of merchandise exhibited in its true character; every promise faithfully performed; every dispute amicably adjusted; every man's character held in estimation; every rogue and cheat banished from society; and every jail, bridewell, and house of correction, would either be swept away, or transformed into the abodes of honesty, industry, and peace. Injustice and oppression would no longer walk triumphant through the world, while the poor, the widow, and the fatherless were groaning under the iron rod of those who had deprived them of every comfort. No longer would the captive be chained to a dungeon, and doomed to count, in sorrow and solitude, the many long days and years he has been banished from the light of day and the society of his dearest friends. No longer should we see a hard-hearted creditor doom a poor unfortunate man, for the sake of a few shillings or pounds, to rot in a jail, while his family, deprived of his industry, were pining away in wretchedness and want. No longer should we hear the harsh creaking of iron doors, ponderous bolts, and the clanking of the chains of criminals; nor the sighs and groans of the poor slave, fainting under the lash, and the reproaches of a cruel master. The bands of the oppressed would be loosed, the captives would be set at liberty, the iron fetters would be burst asunder, and a universal jubilee proclaimed throughout every land. The haunts of riot and debauchery would be forsaken, and their inmates hissed from the abodes of men. The victims of seduction would no longer crowd our streets at the dead hour of night, to entice the "simple ones" into the paths of vice and destruction; but purity, righteousness, and peace would "run down our streets like a river," distributing safety, happiness, and repose.

The tongue of the slanderer and the whisperings of the backbiter would no longer be heard in their malicious attempts to sow the seeds of discord and contention among brethren. Falsehood in all its ramifications, with the numerous train of evils it now produces, would be banished from the intercourses of society; nor would treachery prove the ruin of families and societies, and interrupt the harmony of the commercial and the moral world. No longer should we hear of the embezzling of property by unfaithful servants, nor the blasted hopes, the cruel disappointments, and the ruin of credit and of reputation now produced by the votaries of falsehood. "The lips of truth would be established for ever," and the liar and deceiver would be hissed to the shades of hell. Our property would remain sacred and secure from the thief and the midnight robber, and our persons from the attacks of the murderer and the assassin. We should no longer hesitate to prosecute our journeys by day or by night for fear of the foot-pad or the highwayman, but should recognize every passenger as a friend and protector. Plunder and devastation would cease from the earth; "violence would no more be heard in our land; nor wasting nor destruction in all our borders." Execrations and malicious insults would never harrow up the feelings of our fellow-men, nor would a single instance of revenge be heard of among all the inhabitants of the earth.

Pride, which now stalks about with stately steps and lofty looks, surveying surrounding intelligences with feelings of contempt, would be for ever banished from the world. Ambition would no longer wade through slaughter to a throne, nor trample on the rights of an injured people. Wars would cease to the ends of the earth, and the instruments of human destruction would be beaten into ploughshares and pruning-hooks. That scourge which has drenched the earth with human gore—which has convulsed every nation under heaven—which has produced tenfold more misery than all the destructive elements of nature, and which has swept from existence so many millions of mankind—would be regarded as the eternal disgrace of the human character, and the most shocking display of depravity in the annals of our race. No longer should we hear "the sound of the trumpet and the alarm of war," the confused noise of "the horseman and the bowman," and of the mighty armies encamping around "the city of the innocent," to hurl against its walls the instruments of destruction. No longer should we behold the fires blazing on the mountain tops, to spread the alarm of invading armies; nor the city, which was once full of inhabitants, "sitting solitary," without a voice being heard within its dwellings but the sighs of the disconsolate and the groans of the dying. Human wolves thirsting for the blood of nations, would cease to prowl among men. Nation would not lift up sword against nation, neither would they learn war any more. The instruments of cruelty, the stake, the rack, the knout, and the lash, would no longer lacerate and torture the wretched culprit; cannons, and guns, and swords, and darts would be forged no more; but the influence of reason and affection would preserve order and harmony throughout every department of society. The traveller, when landing on distant shores, and on the islands of the ocean, would no longer be assailed with stones, spears, arrows, and other instruments of death, and be obliged to flee from the haunts of his own species, to take refuge in the lion's den, or on the bosom of the deep; but would be welcomed as a friend and a messenger of peace. The animosities which now prevail among religious bodies would cease; the nicknames by which the different sects of religionists have been distinguished, would be erased from the vocabulary of every language; Christians would feel ashamed of those jealousies and evil surmisings which they have so long manifested towards each other, and an affectionate and harmonious intercourse would be established among all the churches of the saints.

These, and a thousand other evils, which now render this world a vast wilderness of perturbation, wretchedness, and sorrow, would be completely eradicated, were the principle of holy love in incessant operation; and in their place a scene of loveliness and moral beauty would burst upon the view, which would diffuse joy and ecstatic delight through every bosom.

Every family would become a mansion of peace and love—a temple consecrated to the God of heaven, from which the incense of prayer, and praise, and pious aspirations, would daily ascend in sweet memorial to the throne above.

Domestic broils and contentions would cease; brothers and sisters would be cemented in the closest bonds of holy affection; the law of kindness would swell their hearts and dwell upon their tongues; serenity and joy, and a desire to please, would appear on every countenance; a mutual exchange of sentiment and generous affections would circulate joy from father to son, and from children to parents; and all the members of the family circle, animated by the same benevolent spirit, would "dwell together in unity." To communicate useful knowledge, to train each other to piety and virtue, to point out the different spheres in which benevolence should act, to assist in every kindly office, to sooth each other in distress, and to direct each other in the path to an endless life, would be the unceasing desire and endeavour of every inmate of the family mansion. From every such mansion, the radiations of love would fly from family to family, from one hamlet and village to another, from one town and city to another, from one nation to another, and from one continent to another, till all the families of the earth were converted into "the dwellings of the God of Jacob."

In larger communities the principle of love would effectuate a mighty change. That spirit of jealousy and selfishness, of avarice and monopoly, which now produces so many jarrings, contentions, and collisions of interests among town councils, corporations, and other smaller associations, would cease to operate. Every one would see and *feel*, that the prosperity of the whole is also the prosperity of every portion of the general community. Boisterous disputations, sneers, hisses, reproaches, and angry passions, would be banished from the deliberations of every society; and candour, good-will, and kindly affections would animate the minds of all its members. Righteous laws would be enacted, and distributive justice equitably administered. Every nation would form one great and harmonious family; all its members being linked together by the ties of kindness and reciprocal affection. Its magistrates would become "nursing fathers" to the whole body of the people, to promote their peace, their domestic comfort, their knowledge, and their general improvement; and throughout all ranks of the community nothing would appear but submission, obedience, reverence, and respect.

The mutual intercourse of nations would be established on the principles of friendship and affection, and on the basis of immutable justice and eternal truth. Raised above petty jealousies, secure from the alarms of war, and viewing each other as branches of the same great family, and as children of the same Almighty Parent,—every nation and empire would feel an interest in promoting the prosperity of another, and would rejoice in beholding its happiness and improvement. Commerce would be free and unshackled, and the productions of nature and of art would quickly be transported into every nation from every clime. Travellers and navigators would visit foreign shores without danger or alarm from insidious or hostile tribes, and would land on the most obscure island of the ocean, fully assured of protection and comfort, and the welcome of friendship and affection. Every vessel that ploughed the deep would become a floating temple, from which incense and a pure offering would daily ascend to the Ruler of the skies; and its mariners would join, with one heart and one mind, in imploring upon each other the blessing and protection of the God of heaven. The beams of love and affection would gladden every land, and add a new lustre to the natural beauties of its landscape. The inhabitants of China and Japan would be hailed as benefactors when they arrived on our coasts with their cargoes of tea, sugar, silk, and porcelain; and the natives of France and Great Britain, when they transported their manufactures to these distant empires, would be welcomed as friends, and conducted, without the least jealousy or suspicion, through all their cities and rural scenes, to survey the beauties of nature and art with which those countries are adorned. The natives of Papua and New-Zealand would land on our shores without spears, or darts, or other hostile weapons, and be recognized as friends and brethren; and our countrymen, when traversing the different regions of the globe, would always meet with a cordial reception when landing on their coasts. For national jealousies and antipathies would cease; and instead of selfish and revengeful passions, reason would be cultivated, and its powers expanded; the smile of benevolence and the hand of beneficence would gladden the inhabitants of every clime, and "righteousness and praise would spring forth before all the nations."

Under the benignant influence of the spirit of love, useful intelligence of every description would be rapidly and extensively communicated; the sciences would be improved, and carried forward to perfection; the jealousies which now exist among scientific men would cease to operate, and every fact on which science is built would be impartially investigated, and exhibited in its true aspect; the arts would flourish, and be carried to the highest pitch of improvement; no secrets in arts or trades would be locked up in the breast of the discoverer; but every useful hint would at once be communicated to the public; every invention would uniformly be applied to the promotion of a benevolent object, and the arts of destruction would cease to be cultivated, and be held in universal detestation. Under the hand of art, the habitations of men would be beautified and adorned, to correspond with the purity and improvement of their moral feelings, and a new lustre would be thrown over the face of nature. Towns and villages would be built on spacious plans, divested of all that gloom and filth which now disgrace the abodes of millions of human beings, and which form an emblem of their physical and moral wretchedness; and the landscape of every country would present a scene of grandeur, fertility, and picturesque beauty. Those immense treasures which have been so long expended in the arts of war and devastation would be employed in turning immense deserts into fruitful fields, in beautifying the aspect of rural nature, in planting orchards and vineyards, in forming spacious roads, in establishing seminaries of instruction, in erecting comfortable habitations for the lower orders of society, and promoting their domestic enjoyment. What an immense variety of objects of this description would be accomplished within the limits of Great Britain by means of a thousand millions of pounds, which we all know have been lately expended within the space of twenty-four years, in carrying forward the work of destruction!

Under the influence of the reign of love, the instruction of all ranks, in every department of useful knowledge, would be rapidly promoted; ignorance and error, with all their attendant evils, would soon evanish from the minds even of the lowest orders of society; seminaries would be erected and established on a liberal basis, for instructing every class of mankind in all those branches of science which tend to expand the capacity of the human mind, and to extend the range of its contemplations; the hours of active labour would be abridged, in order that they might have leisure for the cultivation of their understanding and the exercise of their moral powers. To add to their stock of knowledge, and to increase the sum of happiness around them, would be considered as interesting and as delightful as it now is to the sons of Mammon to "add house to house, and field to field," and to riot on the gains of avarice. Societies would be formed for mutual improvement in knowledge and virtue; lectures delivered on every interesting and useful subject; experiments performed to illustrate the order and mechanism of nature; and instruments of every description procured for exhibiting the wisdom and omnipotence of the Creator and the glories of the universe. The revelation of heaven would be studied with intelligence in all its aspects and bearings, and every passion, affection, and active exertion would be directed by its moral requisitions. The human mind, thus trained and carried forward in wisdom and holiness, would shed a moral radiance around it, and be gradually prepared for entering on a higher scene of contemplation and enjoyment.

Among all ranks of men, a spirit of selfishness and avarice would be extinguished, and in its stead a spirit of noble generosity and beneficence would pervade the whole mass of society. That divine maxim inculcated by our Saviour, "*It is more blessed to give than to receive*," would be engraven on every heart, and appear in every action. This sublime principle forms a prominent trait in the character of God, and in all his arrangements towards his creatures; and it animates the minds of superior intelligences in their associations with each other, and in their occasional intercourses with the inhabitants of our world. In imitation of these glorious beings, the human race would consider it as the grand end of their existence, not merely to acquire wealth, knowledge, or power, but to employ themselves in the unceasing diffusion of beneficence to all around. To communicate happiness throughout all the ranks of their fellow-men with whom they mingle, to sooth the disconsolate and the desponding, to relieve the distressed, to instruct the ignorant, to expand the intellect, to animate and direct the benevolent affections, to increase the enjoyments of the lower orders of the community, to direct the opening minds of the young, to lead them by gentle steps into the paths of wisdom and holiness, and to promote every scheme which has a relation to the public good, would form the constant aim of all conditions of men from the highest to the lowest. Every house would be open to the weary and benighted traveller, every heart would welcome him to the refreshments and repose it afforded, every countenance would beam benignity, every comfort would be afforded, every wish anticipated, and every stranger thus entertained would "bless the mansion," and implore the benediction of heaven on all its inmates. The houseless child of want would no longer wander amidst scenes of plenty, tattered and forlorn, pinched with poverty, exposed to the piercing blasts, and obliged to repose under the open canopy of heaven, for want of more comfortable shelter; the poor would soon cease out of the land, every one would be active and industrious, and every one would enjoy a comfortable portion of the bounties of Providence. And what a happy world would it be were *kindness* and affection the characteristic of all its inhabitants! The face of nature would wear a more cheering aspect, "the desert would rejoice and blossom as the rose," the flowers would look more gay, the "little hills" would be encircled with joy, the light of heaven would appear more glorious and transporting, a thousand delightful emotions would spring up in the mind amidst every rural scene, and every social intercourse would be a source of unmingled bliss. Paradise would be restored, heaven would descend to earth, and an emblem would be presented of the joys of the blessed above.

O blissful and auspicious era! When wilt thou arrive to still the restless agitation of malignant passions, to promote peace on earth and good will among men? When will the benevolence of angels and archangels descend to dwell with man upon earth, to expel selfishness from the human breast, to hush every disordered affection, and to restore tranquillity and order among the bewildered race of Adam? When will the spirit of love, in all its beneficent energies, descend from the Father of light to arrest the convulsions of nations, to heal the wounds of suffering humanity, to transform fields of slaughter into regions of tranquillity, to soften the ferocious tempers of "the people who delight in war," to unite in one holy and harmonious society men of every language and of every tribe? Not till Christianity shall have shed its benign influence on every land; not till "the knowledge of the Lord shall cover the earth," and the cannons, and swords, and spears, and battle-axes of the warrior shall be broken to shivers, and forged into ploughshares and pruning-hooks. "Then shall the wolf dwell with the lamb, and the leopard shall lie down with the kid, and the calf, and the young lion, and the fatling together, and a little child shall lead them." "Then judgment shall dwell in the wilderness, and righteousness in the fruitful field. And the work of righteousness shall be peace, and the effect of righteousness, quietness and assurance for ever. And all people shall dwell in peaceable habitations, and in sure dwellings, and in quiet resting-places."

In fine, under the reign of love, most of the evils, both physical and moral, under which men are now doomed to suffer, would be either greatly mitigated or completely abolished. It is scarcely too much to affirm, that nine-tenths of all the evils that affect humanity are the result of the malice and unkindness of mankind towards each other. If all the sorrow and wretchedness produced by fraud, falsehood, avarice, extortion, injustice, oppression, perjury, seduction, treachery, litigations, slander, pride, ambition, revenge, robbery, murder, plunder, and devastation, were extirpated, little would remain besides the incidental evils which occasionally flow from the elements of nature. And even these would be greatly mitigated by the benevolent operations of art, directed by the discoveries of science. By clearing the surface of the globe of immense forests, by draining stagnant marshes, and by the universal cultivation and improvement of the soil, the seasons would be meliorated, and storms and tempests would be deprived of their wonted violence and fury; and the partial physical evils which still remained would be almost annihilated to the sufferer, by the sympathy, and tenderness, and the kind and fostering hand of universal benevolence. Where virtue, temperance, serenity of mind, and social joy reigned triumphant, and where none of the ghastly phantoms of skepticism and superstition haunted the mind, disease would seldom invade the human frame; the span of mortal existence would be extended; death would become calm and tranquil, and every one would "come to his grave, like as a shock of corn cometh in his season." In short, under the influence of the emanations of love, malignity would be transformed into benevolence, vice into virtue, oppression into justice, cruelty into sympathy and tenderness, selfishness into beneficence, contention into unity and friendship, fraud into honesty, avarice into generosity, pride into humility, wretchedness into comfort, sorrow into joy, war into peace, and this spacious globe, now the receptacle of misery and vice, would be transformed into the temple of concord, happiness, and peace.

Such are some of the beneficial effects which would be experienced in the social state of the human race, were a principle of benevolence to pervade the minds of mankind. The immense mass of moral evils, under which the earth now groans, would be removed; the moral aspect of society, in every nation, would assume a new lustre of loveliness and excellence; and nature herself would be arrayed in new robes of gracefulness and beauty. For it would be easy to show, were it at all necessary, that every particular now stated, and a thousand similar effects, would be the *natural* and *necessary* results of *love*, when it becomes the mainspring of human actions

I shall now shortly trace some of the effects of love, considered as directed more immediately towards God.

Supreme love to God would excite complacency in his character and perfections; and piety, in all its fervent and delightful emotions, would naturally flow upwards to the fountain of all purity. His glorious character would be venerated, and his name revered over all the earth; trophies would be erected to his honour, and temples consecrated to his worship in every land. Crowds of worshippers, beaming benignity and devotion, would be held in every region, converging towards the "dwelling-place" of the Most High, and encouraging one another in such language as this: "Come ye and let us go up to the mountain of the Lord, to the house of the God of Jacob, and he will teach us of his ways, and we will walk in his paths." With enlightened views of the attributes of Jehovah, with glowing affections, and with profound reverence, would they join in the sublime exercises of the sanctuary, and listen to the intimations of his will. All voices would be tuned to melodious strains, and the solemn organ, and those instruments of music which are now devoted to the gratification of the sons of fashionable folly and dissipation, would harmonize in exciting devotional affections, and in swelling the song of salvation "to Him who sits upon the throne, and to the Lamb who hath redeemed us to God by his blood." Every landscape, in every point of view, would present a noble edifice devoted to the worship of the God of heaven, adorned with every majestic decoration suitable to its sanctity, and rearing its spacious dome above all the surrounding habitations of men. Its gates "would be open continually; they would not be shut day nor night," that men might have access at all seasons to bring "incense and a pure offering" to the shrine of Jehovah. The whole earth would soon be converted into one universal temple, sacred to the God and Father of our Lord Jesus Christ, from which, thanksgiving, and the voice of melody, and the holy aspirations of gratitude and love, would ascend to heaven without intermission, and in every direction, from the regions of the north to the regions of the south, and "from the rising of the sun to the going down of the same." Solemn seasons would be appointed, and spacious plains consecrated for the assembling of ten thousands of "the sons of God," not for carnage and devastation, as when the warrior "mustereth the armies to the battle," but "to rehearse the mighty acts of the Lord," to exchange sentiments and feelings of affectionate regard, and to swell the song of triumph over sin and misery, with the harmony of human voices and musical instruments, in one loud chorus to the skies. Then the name of Jehovah would be One throughout all the earth. "All his works would praise him, and his saints would bless him. They would abundantly utter the memory of his great goodness, they would speak of the glorious honour of his majesty, and sing of his righteousness."

Among all ranks of men cordial submission to the will of God, and contentment under the arrangements of his providence would be uniformly manifested. Every one would consider the situation in which Providence had placed him as the best possible for promoting his present improvement and his future felicity, viewing it as the allotment of infinite wisdom and benevolence. In adversity he would sustain his afflictions with patience, and derive from them "the peaceable fruits of righteousness." In prosperity he would acknowledge God as the source of all his enjoyments, and devote the wealth and influence he possessed to the promotion of religion, and the best interests of his fellow-men. By day, and by night, and at every returning season, the overflowings of gratitude, in every heart, would burst forth in songs of thanksgiving to the Giver of all good. Every comfort would be recognized as "coming down from the Father of lights," and every pleasing sensation produced by the scenery of nature, as the result of his wisdom and beneficence. His wonderful works, which are now overlooked, or gazed at with apathy by nine-tenths of the inhabitants of the globe, would be contemplated with enlightened understandings, and with emotions of reverence, admiration, and delight. The majestic movements of the planetary orbs, the glories of the starry sky, the light beaming from a thousand suns through the immeasurable voids of space, the mighty ocean with all its wonders, the numerous rivers rolling into its abyss, the lofty ranges of mountains which encircle the earth, the treasures of the fields, the riches of the mines, the beauties which adorn the hills and plains, the wonders of the atmosphere, the admirable structure and economy of the numerous tribes of animated beings,—these, and thousands of other objects, considered as manifestations of the attributes of Deity, would supply topics of conversation in every social circle, on which every heart would dwell with increasing delight. "They would speak of the glory of his kingdom, and talk of his power, to make known to the sons of men his mighty acts, and the glorious majesty of his kingdom." The work of human redemption, in its origin and progress, in its connexions and bearings, in the lustre it reflects on the perfections of the Deity, in its relation to the angelic tribes, and in its glorious and happy consequences on thousands of millions of human beings throughout an eternal round of existence—the person of the Redeemer, his amiable character, his grace and condescension, and the glories of his exalted state—the joys of departed saints, the general resurrection, with all its solemn and transporting scenes, the new heavens and the new earth, and the boundless scene of grandeur and felicity which will open to the view when death shall be swallowed up in victory, and all things subjected to the moral order of the universe, would afford subjects of sublime contemplation, and themes for social converse, on which enlightened and renovated minds would expatiate with ever-growing improvement and ever-growing pleasures.

The providential dispensations of God towards the human race, would form another subject of investigation, which would be prosecuted with feelings of astonishment, admiration, and reverence. The history of all nations would be carefully perused—not for the purpose of admiring the exploits of mighty conquerors and barbarous heroes, and feasting the imagination on spectacles of human slaughter and devastation—but for exciting abhorrence of those depraved passions which had drenched the earth with blood—for drawing forth the tear of pity over the graves of slaughtered nations—for stimulating the exercise of those holy affections which restored peace and tranquillity to the world—for acquiring a display of the rectitude of the moral character of God, and the equity of his administration among the nations—for tracing the accomplishment of divine predictions—for illustrating the long-suffering and forbearance of God, and for exciting admiration of that inscrutable wisdom by which the whole train of events was conducted, so as to set restraining bounds to the wrath of man, and to make it subservient to the introduction of the reign of happiness and peace. In all the revolutions of past ages, and in all the events that daily passed in review before them, they would uniformly recognize the agency and the purposes of that Almighty Being "who doth according to his will in the armies of heaven, and among the inhabitants of the earth," and who is carrying forward all the plans of his government to a glorious consummation.

Every useful invention, every new instrument for investigating the operations of nature, every new discovery in the earth, or in the heavens, every exploration of an unknown region of the globe, every branch of commerce and manufacture, every new mode of facilitating labour and improving the productions of the soil; every improvement in the ease and rapidity of travelling, and of conveying intelligence from one region to another, and every art and science, would be consecrated, in some form or other, to the service of God, and to the accomplishment of the objects of general benevolence. One grand diffusive principle, manifesting itself in numberless ramifications, would pervade the whole mass of society; and one grand aim, the honour and glory of the Creator, and the universal diffusion of happiness in every direction, and among every rank of sentient and intelligent beings, would be the unceasing endeavour of men of all nations, and kindreds, and languages. The whole mass of this world's inhabitants would appear like one vast celestial army marching forward in harmony to the regions of bliss, every one, in his appointed order, passing in peace and tranquillity through the gates of death, to join the general assembly above, and to augment and enliven the congregation of the heavens.

On such a world the God of heaven would look down with complacency, and his providential care would be exercised in averting those physical evils which now increase the moral wretchedness of mankind. His eye would be continually upon them for good, and his ear would be ever open to their requests. Then that glorious scene presented to the view of the apostle John, would be fully realized,—"Behold the tabernacle of God is with men, and he will dwell with them; and they shall be his people, and God himself shall be with them, and be their God. And God shall wipe away all tears from their eyes, and there shall be no more curse, neither sorrow nor crying, neither shall there be any more pain; for the former things have passed away." To such a world celestial messengers would rejoice to wing their downward flight, on messages of love. Their visits, which have been "few, and far between," and which have been long interrupted by the malevolence of men, would be again resumed; and those "morning stars" that shouted for joy when this fair creation arose into existence, would be filled with unutterable delight when they beheld moral order restored, and the smiles of universal love irradiating the inhabitants of our globe, and would shout even with more ecstatic joy than they did before, "Glory to God in the highest, peace on earth, and good will among men!"

Alas! such a picture as that which we have now faintly sketched, has never yet been realized in the moral aspect of the inhabitants of this world. To the eye of an angelic intelligence, while he hovers over our globe in his flight through the planetary regions, nothing appears but a vast cloud of moral darkness and depravity, with here and there only a few faint radiations of truth and love emerging from the general gloom. He beholds throughout the whole extent of Africa, from the shores of Barbary and Egypt to the Cape of Good Hope—throughout the vast regions of Asia and its numerous islands, and throughout four-fifths of the continent of America, little else than one wide scene of moral desolation, where idolatry and superstition, tyranny and ambition, treachery and cruelty, war and dissension, reign triumphant among almost every tribe; and where scarcely a ray of divine light and divine love gilds the horizon, from the one end of these extensive regions to the other. Even in Europe, where the light of science and of revelation is converged to a focus, what an immense cloud of moral darkness still appears enveloping its population? The fields of Waterloo, of Leipsic, of Borodina, and of Smolensko, where so many thousands of human beings were sacrificed to the demon of war—the vales of Switzerland and Hungary, the plains of France and Italy, the anarchy and commotions of Spain and Portugal, and the ensanguined shores of Turkey and Greece, where massacres have been perpetrated with the rage and fury of infernal demons, bear witness to the melancholy fact, that hatred and malignity still hold the ascendency over the nations of Europe, and over all the efforts of benevolence and love.

But, we trust, that the period is fast approaching, when the breath of a new spirit shall pervade the inhabitants of every clime, and when holy love shall unite all the tribes of mankind in one harmonious society. When the messengers of the Prince of Peace "shall run to and fro" from the north to the south, and from the rising to the setting sun: when the sound of the gospel-trumpet shall re-echo throughout every land; when the light of divine revelation shall diffuse its radiance on the benighted nations; when its sublime doctrines and moral requisitions shall be fully understood and recognized in all their practical bearings, and when the energy of that Almighty spirit which reduced to light and order the dark and shapeless chaos, shall be exerted on the depraved and benighted minds of the mass of this world's population—then the death-like slumber which has seized upon the race of Adam shall be broken; the dead in trespasses and sins shall awake to new life and activity; this bedlam of the universe will be restored to reason and intellectual freedom, and to the society of angelic messengers, and the face of the moral creation will be renewed after the image of its maker. Then wars shall cease to the ends of the earth, and anarchy and dissension shall convulse the nations no more; violence will no more be heard in any land, "liberty will be proclaimed to the captives, and the opening of the prison-doors to them that are bound." The spirit of malevolence will be vanquished, its power will be broken, and its operations demolished. The order and beauty of the celestial system will be restored. "Holiness to the Lord" will be inscribed on all the implements and employments of mankind. Kindness and compassion will form the amiable characteristic of every rank of social life. Love will spread her benignant wings over the globe, and reign uncontrolled in the hearts of all its inhabitants. For thus saith the voice of Him who sits on the throne of the universe, "Behold I make all things new—I create new heavens and a new earth, and the former shall not be remembered, nor come into mind. Be ye glad, and rejoice for ever in that which I create; for behold, I create Jerusalem a rejoicing, and her people a joy, and the voice of weeping shall be no more heard in her, nor the voice of crying."

---

## SECTION VI.

### UNIVERSALITY OF THE PRINCIPLES OF LOVE TO GOD, AND TO FELLOW-INTELLIGENCES.

The grand principles of morality to which I have now adverted, are not to be viewed as confined merely to the inhabitants of our globe, but as extending to all intellectual beings. They form the basis of the moral laws, which govern all intelligences throughout the vast universe, in whatever world or region of infinite space they may have their physical residence; and they constitute the bond which unites to the supreme intelligence, and to one another, all holy beings, wherever existing in the wide empire of Omnipotence. This will at once appear, if we reflect for a moment, on what has been stated in the preceding sections. We have seen, that, if those laws or principles were reversed, and were the moral agents of our world to act accordingly, nothing would ensue, but anarchy, wretchedness, horror, and devastation, and ultimately a complete extermination of the race of mankind. And by parity of reason, it will follow, that were the same principles to operate in any other world, however different the capacities, relations, and physical circumstances of its inhabitants might be, similar disastrous effects would be the inevitable result; and were they to pervade all worlds, disorder and misery would reign uncontrolled throughout the whole intelligent system.

When the Creator brought any particular world into existence, and peopled it with inhabitants, we must suppose, that the laws to which I am now adverting, were either formally addressed to them by some external revelation, or so powerfully impressed upon their moral constitution, as to become the main-spring of all their actions, so long as they might retain the original principles implanted in their minds by the Author of their existence. Any other supposition would be fraught with the most absurd and horrible consequences. It would be subversive of every idea we are led to form of the character of the Divine Being, inconsistent with the perfect benevolence and rectitude of his nature, and incompatible with the relations in which rational beings stand to Him and to one another, and with the harmony and happiness of the universe, to suppose, that any creatures now exist, or ever can exist, to whom such commands as these would be given,—"Thou shalt *hate* thy Creator, who is the source of thine existence;" and "Thou shalt *hate* all thy fellow-intelligences with whom thou mayst associate." And if the mind would recoil with horror, at the idea of such laws issuing forth from the throne of the Eternal to any class of moral agents, it must necessarily be admitted, that the opposite principles or laws, to which I allude, are promulgated to all intelligences, and are obligatory on every inhabitant of all the worlds which lie between the range o Jehovah's empire. The natural scenery with which the inhabitants of other worlds are surrounded, the organization of their corporeal frames, the intellectual capacities with which they are endowed, the stated employments in which they engage, and the relations in which they stand to each other, may be very different from those which obtain in our terrestrial sphere, but the grand principles to which I refer, must necessarily pervade every faculty of their minds, every active exertion, and every relation that subsists among them, by whatever character it may be distinguished, if they be found existing in a state of happiness.

The moral code of laws in other worlds may be somewhat differently modified from ours, according to the circumstances in which the inhabitants of each respective world are placed, and the relations which obtain among them; but the same general principles will run through every ramification of their moral precepts, and appear in the minutes actions they perform, as the sap which proceeds from the trunk of a tree diffuses itself among the minutest and the most distant branches. The *seventh* commandment of our moral code can have no place in a world where the inhabitants "neither marry nor are given in marriage;" where the succession of intelligent beings is not carried on by any process analogous to human generation, where death is unknown, and where rational agents have a fixed and permanent abode. The *fifth* precept of our law cannot be recognized in a world where the relations of parents and children, princes and subjects, superiors and inferiors, have no existence. And in those worlds where the bounties of Divine Providence are equally enjoyed by all, or where external comforts are not necessary for the happiness of the individual, as in our world, or where the slightest temptation to interfere with the property of another does not exist, there will be no necessity for a distinct moral regulation corresponding to the *eighth* commandment of our moral code.—But in every world where happiness exists, and where the inhabitants have retained their original integrity, love to God, and love to all subordinate intelligences with which they are connected, will animate every heart, regulate every desire, and run through every action. And in those worlds (if any such exist besides our own) where these principles are counteracted, or not recognized as the foundation of moral action, misery and disorder, in a greater or less degree, must be the inevitable consequence.

The greater part, however, of the precepts comprised in the moral law given to man, must be considered as obligatory upon all the rational inhabitants of the universe. The *first* commandment, which forbids the recognition of any object of adoration, or of supreme affection, besides the eternal Jehovah—the *second*, which forbids the representation of this incomprehensible Being by any visible or material objects—the *third*, which enjoins reverence of the name or attributes of God—and the spirit of the *fourth*, which enjoins a certain portion of duration to be set apart for solemn acts of worship and adoration, are applicable to all the moral agents that Jehovah has created. The *sixth* commandment, which forbids malice, revenge, and injurious actions of every description—the *ninth*, which forbids falsehood, and inculcates *truth*, which is the basis of the moral universe—and the *tenth*, which forbids envy, and every unhallowed desire to deprive our neighbour of any portion of his happiness—are also binding upon every class of moral intelligences, wherever existing, throughout the unlimited empire of God. For, if we suppose any one of these precepts to be reversed, and moral agents to act on the principle of this subversion, their moral order and harmony would be interrupted, and consequently, their happiness destroyed.—For example, let the law, which inculcates truth, be supposed to be universally violated among any class of rational beings, and instantly all improvement in wisdom and knowledge would cease; nothing could be depended upon as fact but what was obvious to the senses of every individual; social compacts would be dissolved; a mutual repulsion would ensue, and every social affection and enjoyment would be unhinged and destroyed.

By overlooking considerations of this kind, the celebrated Dr. Chalmers, in his "Discourses on the Christian Revelation viewed in connexion with Modern Astronomy," deprived himself of an important argument to prove that Christianity is not confined to this sublunary region. For, as it is the great object of the Christian Revelation to bring into full effect, in all their practical bearings, the principles I have been endeavouring to illustrate, and as these principles must be interwoven with the moral code of all worlds—it follows, that the spirit and essence of our religion must be common to all the holy inhabitants of the universe.

From what has been now stated respecting the universality of the principle of love, the following conclusions may be deduced:—

1. That the man in whose heart this principle is predominant, and whose actions are directed by its influence, is qualified for associating with the pure intelligences of all worlds. Were we transported to the surface of the planet Jupiter, and had we access to mingle with its vast population; or were we conveyed to one of the planets which revolve around the star *Sirius*—if the inhabitants of these globes have retained the primeval purity of their natures, and if the principle of love reigned supreme in *our* hearts, we should be assured of a welcome reception from those distant intelligences, and be qualified to mingle with them in their adorations of our common Creator, and in all their affectionate and harmonious intercourses. We should only have to learn the mode by which they communicate to each other their ideas and emotions. Love would form the basis of every union, and amalgamate us with every department of their society. With pleasure, and with the most endearing affection, would they point out to us the peculiar glories of the world they inhabit, and rehearse the history of the Creator's dispensations in that portion of his empire; and with equal pleasure should we listen to the instructions which flow from the lips of Benevolence, and survey those transporting objects and arrangements which decorate a world where love pervades the breasts of all its inhabitants. To visit a distant world, although it were in our power, where the inhabitants were of an opposite description, could afford no gratification to an intelligent and benevolent mind, but would overwhelm it with anguish and dismay. What enjoyment would the capacious mind of a pure intelligence from the regions of the constellation *Orion*, derive from visiting a world inhabited by such beings as the inhabitants of Nootka Sound, New Guinea, or New Zealand, where the moral and intellectual principle is completely debased, and where the beauties of Nature are defaced with interminable forests and marshes, and the haunts of beasts of prey? He

would be filled with disappointment and horror—he might drop a tear of pity over the wretched inhabitants; but he would soon wing his flight back to a more delectable region. A similar disappointment would be felt, were an inhabitant of our world, in whose mind hatred and cruelty, avarice and ambition, reigned without control—to be conveyed to a world of happiness and love. The novel scenes of beauty and grandeur, which would burst upon his sight, might captivate his senses for a little: but he would feel no enjoyment in the exercise of virtuous affections and rapturous adorations, to which he was never accustomed; he would find no objects on which to gratify his cruel and ambitious desires, and he would be glad to escape from the abodes of affection and bliss, to the depraved society from whence he came. Hence we may learn, that, however expansive views we may have acquired of the range of the Creator's operations, and of the immensity of worlds which are diffused through boundless space, and however ardent desires we may indulge of visiting the distant regions of creation, we never can indulge a rational hope of enjoying such a privilege, were it possible, unless love to God and to man become the predominant disposition of our minds. For, although we were invested by the Almighty with corporeal vehicles, capable of transporting us from one region of creation to another, with the most rapid motion, we could enjoy no solid satisfaction, while we remained unqualified for relishing the exercises, and mingling in the associations of holy intelligences. In every happy world on which we alighted, we should feel ourselves in a situation similar to that of a rude and ignorant boor, were he conveyed to a palace, and introduced into an assembly of courtiers and princes.

2. Another conclusion deducible from this subject is, that by virtue of this grand and governing principle, man is connected with the highest order of intelligences, and with the inhabitants of the most distant worlds; and his happiness perpetually secured. When we take a view of the universe by the light of modern science, our minds are overpowered and confounded at the idea of its vast and unlimited range. When we consider that it would require several millions of years for a cannon ball, flying at the rate of five hundred miles an hour, to reach the nearest stars—when we consider that there are stars visible to the naked eye, at least fifty times farther distant than these—when we consider that there are stars visible by the telescope a thousand times farther distant than any of the former—and when we consider that all the suns and worlds which lie within this unfathomable range are, in all probability, only as a grain of sand to the whole earth, when compared with the immensity of systems which lie beyond them in the unexplored abyss of infinite space,—we are lost in the immensity of creation, and can set no bounds to the empire of the Almighty Sovereign. When we look forward to that eternal state to which we are destined—when we consider that after thousands of millions of centuries have run their rounds, eternity will be no nearer to a termination, and that ages, numerous as the drops of the ocean, will still roll on in interminable succession,—we behold a lapse of duration, and a succession of events stretching out before us, which correspond with the immeasurable spaces of the universe, and the number and magnitude of the worlds with which it is stored. When we view ourselves as thus connected with the immensity of creation on the one hand, and with infinite duration on the other; and when we reflect on the numerous changes that have happened, both in the physical and moral aspect of our globe, within the period of six thousand years, we cannot but conclude that we are destined to pass through new scenes and changes in that eternity which lies before us, of which at present we can form no conception. After remaining for thousands of millions of years in that world which will be prepared for the righteous at the general resurrection, we may be transported to another system as far distant from that abode as we now are from the most distant stars visible to our sight, in order to contemplate new displays of the attributes of God, in another province of his empire. We may afterwards be conveyed to an unoccupied region of immensity, where new creations, displaying new objects of glory and magnificence, are starting into existence. We may afterwards be invested with the wings of a seraph, and be enabled to wing our way, in company with angels, from world to world, and to visit the most distant regions of that immense universe over which Omnipotence presides. In short, the imagination can set no limits to its excursions, when it attempts to survey the revolutions and changes that may take place, and the new scenes of glory which may burst upon the view, throughout the lapse of duration which will have no end.

Now, in whatever relation man may stand to any portion of the universal system, throughout every future period of his existence, and during all the revolutions of eternity, love will unite him to all other holy beings with whom he may associate, however distant their abode from the spot he now occupies, however different its scenery and arrangements, and however superior they may be in point of corporeal organization and intellectual capacity. For no intelligence, in any region of the universe, in whom the principle of love predominates, can ever be supposed to disdain to associate with another, of whatever rank or order, who is actuated by a similar affection; otherwise his love would degenerate into malevolence. This principle will unite him to angels and archangels, to cherubim and seraphim, to thrones, dominions, principalities, and powers, from whose discourses he will learn the history of the divine dispensations, the wonders of Almighty power, and the "manifold wisdom of God." So long as it reigns uncontrolled in his heart, it will secure his happiness in all places, and in every period of his existence, by a law established by the Almighty, and founded on his perfections; a law which binds together the whole intelligent system, and forms the basis of the felicity of the moral universe. So that his future blessedness is for ever secure, beyond the reach of danger, and rests upon a foundation stable and permanent as the throne of the Eternal.

3. From what has been now stated, we may learn that *there is but one religion throughout the universe*, however vast its magnitude and boundless its extension. In this world, numerous systems of religion prevail, and thousands of different opinions in relation to its ceremonies and objects; but experience has demonstrated, that all of them, except *one*, are insufficient to guide rational beings to substantial felicity. And of this one system, how many foolish and inaccurate, and even contradictory opinions, have been formed, through the ignorance and perversity of the human mind! Though all its parts have a direct reference to the *actions* of intelligent agents, and to the cultivation of *benevolent affections*, yet it has been represented, even by its professed abetters, as a congeries of metaphysical dogmas and speculative opinions; and in this point of view it has been the source of perpetual wrangling and contentions. Though it is calculated to expand the understanding, to warm the heart, and to elevate the soul to God, yet it has been reduced, by the cunning artifice of man, to a mass of mere quibbles and unmeaning ceremonies. And though it breathes nothing but peace and good-will to man, it has been employed as an engine of persecution and of human destruction. It is only in proportion as our religion approximates to the character of the religion which is common to all holy beings, that it is worthy of our veneration and our ardent pursuit. And therefore, in order to determine the truth and importance of any particular system of religious opinions, the best test we can apply to it is, to ascertain what bearings it has upon the grand principles to which we have been adverting. "Do all the sentiments and tenets which it strenuously supports, like the lines from the circumference to the centre of a circle, converge towards the promotion of *love* in all its practical ramifications? Are the opinions we now so fiercely maintain of such a nature, that we shall probably recognize them as important practical principles a million of years hence, in the regions of distant worlds?" If such a test were applied to hundreds of opinions which have agitated the religious world, and obstructed the operations of the benevolent affections, they would be driven away from the Christian system as chaff before the whirlwind; and Christians would feel ashamed of the importance they attached to their "mint, and anise, and cummin," while they neglected the weightier matters of the law, "judgment, mercy, and the love of God." How many false and foolish opinions shall we leave behind us in this region of darkness and contention, when we enter within the confines of the eternal state? How sublime, how lovely, and how beautifying will religion appear in that world, where it will be contemplated in its native simplicity, and stripped of all the foreign and adventitious circumstances which now obscure its brightness and glory! I need scarcely say, that the one religion to which I allude is *Christianity*, considered, not so much in the scheme of mediation which it unfolds, which may have a relation solely to man viewed in his character as a sinner, but in the *leading dispositions and virtues* it inculcates, and in the *great objects* which all its doctrines, facts, and supernatural communications have a tendency to accomplish. In these points of view, it must be considered as imbodying principles and laws which pervade the religious systems of all worlds.

Finally, Love is a principle in the moral and intelligent system which bears a striking analogy to the principle of *attraction* in the material world. Each of them unites, in its respective sphere, all the beings which compose it in one grand and harmonious system; and both of them combined give birth to all the moral and physical phenomena which diversify the intellectual and the material universe. By the principle of attraction, the inhabitants of the earth, along with their habitations, are retained to its surface, and prevented from flying off in wild confusion through the voids of space. By the same power the mountains rest on a solid basis, the rivers flow from the mountains to the plains, and the ocean is confined within its appointed channels. It produces the various phenomena which arise from the meandering rill, the majestic river, and the roaring cataract. It produces the descent of rain and dew, and the alternate flux and reflux of the tides. It prevents the waters of the great deep from covering the mountain-tops, and mingling in confusion with the clouds of heaven. It binds together the infinity of atoms which constitute the globe on which we tread; it regulates the various movements of men and other animated beings; it forms mechanical powers, and gives impulsion to numerous machines and engines. It rolls the moon in regular succession around the earth, and prevents her from running lawlessly through the sky. It extends its influence from the sun to the remotest planets, conducting revolving worlds, with all their satellites, in their ample circuits, and preserving them all in one harmonious system. It connects the earth and the planetary globes with other systems in the distant regions of space; and carries the sun, with all his attendant orbs, around the centre of that *nebula* to which it belongs, and all the systems and nebulæ of the universe around the throne of God.

In like manner, love unites all holy intelligences, wherever dispersed through the amplitudes of creation, in one amiable and harmonious system. It unites man to God, and God to man. It unites the renovated inhabitants of our globe to angels and archangels, and qualifies them for entering into the closest bonds of friendship and affection with superior intelligences that people the regions of distant worlds. It produces an expansive and harmonious spirit, and an ardent desire to diffuse happiness among all surrounding beings. It gives birth to those sublime emotions which flow out towards the Creator in the various forms of adoration, complacency, hope, confidence, humility, joy, submission, and reverence; and it is the spring of all those virtuous dispositions which flow out towards our fellow-creatures in the form of mercy, compassion, sincerity, candour, sympathy, kindness, long-suffering, gentleness, meekness, charity, generosity, justice, and active beneficence. It impels its possessor to run to the assistance of the distressed, to support the weak, to console the desponding, to comfort the dying, to diffuse the rays of heavenly light over the benighted mind, and to rejoice in the prosperity of all around. It is "the bond of perfection" which unites the members of an affectionate family, and preserves the union of the faithful in all the churches of the saints. It unites man to man by the closest ties, however different in language, customs, colour, and complexion, and however far removed from each other in point of place. It enables the Greenlander, the Icelander, the African, the inhabitant of Hindostan, and the inhabitant of the British Isles, in whose hearts it resides, to recognize each other as "the sons of God," and as "brethren in Christ Jesus." It sends forth the imagination over every quarter of the globe, carrying benevolent wishes, fervent prayers, and intercessions for men of all kindreds and ranks; and employs every active endeavour to promote the present enjoyment and the eternal felicity of the family of mankind. It inspires the soul with emotions of delight, when it becomes the instrument of communicating happiness to all within the sphere of its influence. It unites the host of seraphim and cherubim in one vast and harmonious association; so that no jarring affection is ever felt, and no discordant voice is ever heard, among the thousands and ten thousands of these exalted intelligences. It preserves every member of the holy and intelligent system in the rank and orbit prescribed by Infinite Wisdom, and leads them all to rejoice in accomplishing the plans of their benevolent Creator. Around him, as the sun of the moral system—the centre of light, and love, and joy—they all revolve in their appointed order; cheered by the emanation of his love, enlightened by his beams, and reflecting a radiance upon all the beings with which they are surrounded. Though one orb differs from another in motion, in magnitude, and in glory, yet no one interferes with another to impede its progress, or to intercept the emanations of light and joy from the Uncreated Source and Centre of all enjoyment.

Were the principle of attraction which binds together the atoms of our globe, and connects the planetary orbs with the sun, to be completely dissolved, the earth would be shattered to its centre; the waters of the ocean would fly upwards, and be dispersed through the highest regions of the atmosphere; rocks and mountains would be detached from their bases, and raised aloft above the clouds; forests would be torn up from their roots, and tossed about in confusion through the sky; the moon would forsake her ancient course; the planets would run lawlessly through the immensity of space, and mighty worlds would be seen dashing against each other, till they were shattered to pieces, and their fragments tossed about in disorder throughout surrounding systems. Effects equally disastrous to the intelligent system would be produced, were the influence of love, in all its varied emanations, to be completely suspended or annihilated. War would be proclaimed in heaven, and myriads of angels hurled from their seats of bliss. The rapturous songs and adorations of seraphs would be changed into the howlings and execrations of demons. The population of the universe would be transformed into one vast assemblage of fiends; its regions of beauty and fertility would become one wide scene of desolation and horror, and the voice of lamentation and misery would be heard resounding throughout all worlds. On earth kingdoms would be shaken and convulsed; governments overturned; societies dissolved; families dispersed; the bonds of friendship burst asunder; husbands torn from their wives, and parents from their children; the intercourse of nations suspended; the pursuits of science and religion abandoned; every rank and relation overturned, end virtue banished from the abodes of men. Deserting all social beings, and forsaken by all, man would become a solitary monster, wandering without plan or object, an enemy to himself and to his species. Anarchy and disorder would reign triumphant over the whole race of human beings, and the howlings of wretchedness and despair would re-echo from every land.

Such a scene of moral desolation *selfishness* and *malignity* have a natural *tendency* to create; and such a scene they have actually created in our world, *in so far as their influence has extended*. The power of attraction has never been completely suspended in relation to our globe, nor has the moral Governor of the universe suffered the principle of love to be entirely eradicated from the minds of its inhabitants. But, as when the law of gravitation is counteracted in case of earthquakes and volcanoes, the most destructive and desolating convulsions ensue,—so it happens in the moral world, when the law of benevolence is trampled under foot. "Nation rises against nation, and kingdom against kingdom;" hostile armies encounter like tigers rushing on their prey; "firebrands, arrows, and death" are scattered in every direction; a confused noise of chariots, and horsemen, and of engines of destruction, is wafted on every breeze; garments are rolled in blood, and whole plains drenched with human gore, and covered with the carcasses of the slain. But wherever love diffuses its powerful and benign influence, there harmony, happiness, and peace are enjoyed by every rank of sensitive and intellectual existence. In every world where it reigns supreme, the intellectual faculty is irradiated, the affections are purified and expanded, transporting joys are felt, and, like the planetary orbs and their train of satellites, all shine with a steady lustre, and move onward in harmonious order, around the Supreme Source of intelligence, and the Eternal Centre of all felicity.

---

## SECTION VII.

### THE PRECEDING VIEWS CORROBORATED BY DIVINE REVELATION.

In the preceding sections I have endeavoured to illustrate the two grand principles of the Moral Law, and to demonstrate their reasonableness, and the necessity of their universal operation, in order to the promotion of the happiness of the intelligent system. I have proceeded all along on the ground of revelation, as well as of reason, and the nature of things. But since these important principles form the basis of the system of religion, and of all the practical conclusions I may afterwards deduce in the remaining part of this work, it may be expedient to advert a little more explicitly to the declarations of Scripture on this subject. And here I propose very briefly to show, that it is the great end of Divine Revelation to illustrate these principles in all their various bearings, and to bring them into practical operation.

This position is expressly stated by our Saviour himself, in his reply to the scribe, who proposed the question, "Which is the great commandment in the law?" "Thou shalt love the Lord thy God with all thy heart, and with all thy soul, and with all thy mind." This is the first and great commandment. And the second is like unto it; Thou shalt love thy neighbour as thyself. ON THESE TWO COMMANDMENTS HANG ALL THE LAW AND THE PROPHETS." This declaration evidently implies, that it is the design of the whole of the Old Testament Revelation, to illustrate and enforce these laws, and to produce all those holy tempers which are comprised in the love of God, and of our neighbour. This appears to be the grand object of all the historica facts, religious institutions, devotional exercises, moral maxims, prophecies, exhortations, promises, and threatenings, which it records. The history of the formation of the universe, and of the beautiful arrangement of our globe, as detailed in the Book of Genesis, is calculated to display the wisdom and goodness of the Creator, and to draw forth our affections towards Him who is the Author of our enjoyments, and who pronounced every thing he had made to be "very good." The history of the wickedness of the antediluvian world, of the dreadful effects it produced in the state of society, and of the awful catastrophe by which its inhabitants were swept from existence, and buried in the waters of the deluge, is calculated to illustrate, in the most striking manner, the guilt and the danger of withdrawing the affections from God, and of indulging a principle of malevolence towards man. The history of the crimes of Sodom, and of the fate of its wretched inhabitants; the destruction of Pharaoh and his armies at the Red Sea; the history of the idolatrous practices of the Israelites, of their murmurings in the wilderness, and of the punishments inflicted for their rebellion; the fate of Korah, Dathan, and Abiram, and of the worshippers of Baal: The destruction of the nations of Canaan; the judgments which pursued the Jewish nation, during the whole period of their history, on account of their defection from God, and the calamities which befell them at the period of the Babylonish captivity—together with all the other facts connected with the history of that people and of the surrounding nations, are intended to exhibit the dismal consequences, and the moral wretchedness which inevitably follow, when the affections of mankind are withdrawn from the God of Heaven, and left to grovel in the mire of depravity and vice.

The institutions of the Jewish Church were appointed for promoting the knowledge and the love of God, and for exciting an abhorrence of every thing which is contrary to the rectitude and purity of his nature. Among the tribes that inhabited the land of Canaan, prior to the entrance of the Israelites, and among all the surrounding natioes, the worship of false gods, the grossest superstitions, and the most abominable vices universally prevailed. It was one great end of the laws and ceremonies enjoined upon Israel, to excite the highest degree of abhorrence at every thing which was connected with idolatry, to portray its wickedness and folly, to rivet the affections of the people to the worship of the true God, to preserve them uncontaminated from the malignant disposition, and the vile practices of the neighbouring nations, and to instruct them in the nature and attributes of the Deity; that they might be "a *peculiar* people to Jehovah, separated from all the people that were on the face of the earth." Hence, the following intimation and injunction are placed on the front of the moral code of laws delivered to that nation, "Hear, O Israel, the Lord our God is one Lord Thou shalt have no other gods before me." To promote harmony and affection between man and man; to enforce the exercise of justice and equity in all their dealings; to inculcate chastity and purity of affection, kindness to strangers, compassion, tenderness, and sympathy; obedience to parents, charitable dispositions towards the poor and needy, and tenderness and mercy towards the inferior animals, were the great objects of the various laws and regulations comprised in their moral and political code.

The devotional portions of the Old Testament, particularly those contained in the book of Psalms, have the same general tendency. The descriptions of the work of creation and providence, the adorations of the majesty of the God of Israel, the celebration of the divine character and excellences, and the ascriptions of thanksgiving and praise for the mercy, long-suffering, and goodness of God, with which these divine compositions abound, are calculated to raise the affections to Jehovah as the source of every blessing, and to inspire the soul with love, admiration, and reverence. In many of these sublime odes, particularly in the 119th Psalm, the mind of the Psalmist is absorbed in meditation on the excellency of the divine precepts, and the happiness which the observance of them is calculated to convey to the soul. "O how I love thy law!" says David; "it is my meditation all the day. The law of thy mouth is better unto me than thousands of of gold and silver. I have rejoiced in thy testimonies as much as in all riches." The moral maxims contained in the writings of Solomon are likewise intended to draw forth the desires after God, to counteract the influence of the depraved passions of the human heart, and to promote the exercise of candour, sincerity, justice, and benevolence among mankind. The exhortations, remonstrances, and denunciations of the prophets, were also intended to recall the affections of the people of Israel to the God from whom they had revolted, to show the unreasonableness of their conduct in "forsaking the fountain" of their happiness; to display the purity, the excellence, and the eternal obligation of the divine precepts, and to warn them of the inevitable misery and ruin which will overtake the workers of iniquity. In short, all the promises and threatenings of the word of God, all the considerations addressed to the hopes and the fears of men, all the providential dispensations of God, all the manifestations of the divine character and perfections, and all the descriptions of the glories of heaven, and of the terrors of hell, have a tendency to illustrate the indispensable obligation of love to God, and love to all mankind, in order to secure our present comfort and eternal felicity.

And, as it was the main design of the Old Testament economy to illustrate and enforce the principle of love to God and to man, so it is, in a particular manner, the great object of the Christian Revelation, to exhibit the law of love in all its bearings and practical applications. In one of the first sermons delivered by our Saviour, and the longest one recorded in the Evangelical History, the Sermon on the Mount, the main design is to explain and enforce these principles, in relation both to God and to man, and to sweep away all the false glosses which Ignorance and Prejudice had mingled with their interpretations of the Divine Law. In one part of this discourse, our Lord declares, that we may as soon expect to see "heaven and earth pass away," or the whole frame of the universe dissolved, as that "one jot or one tittle shall pass from the law." For, as it is a law founded on the nature of God, it must be of eternal obligation, and can never be abrogated with regard to any class of rational beings, in consistency with the perfections of the divine nature. As it is a law absolutely perfect, comprehending within its range every disposition and affection, and every duty which is requisite for promoting the order and happiness of intelligent agents, nothing can be taken from it without destroying its perfection; and nothing can be added to it without supposing that it was originally imperfect. And as it was intended to preserve the harmony and to secure the felicity of the intellectual beings that people the earth and the heavens, the fabric of universal nature must be destroyed, before this law can be set aside or cancelled. For we have already seen, (Sect. IV.) that, were it reversed, the whole intelligent system would be transformed into a scene of confusion, misery, and horror. For the purpose of affording an immense theatre, on which the operations of this law might be displayed, the earth with all its furniture and decorations, and the heavens, with all their hosts, were called into existence; and, therefore, were it either cancelled or reversed, neither the glory of the Creator would be displayed, nor the happiness of his intelligent creation secured. The mighty expanse of the universe, enclosing so many spacious worlds, would become one boundless moral desert, in which no "fruits of righteousness" would appear, nor any trace of the beauty and benevolence of the Eternal Mind. —In the same discourse, our Saviour enforces the duty of love towards even our most bitter enemies and most furious persecutors. "Ye have heard that it hath been said, Thou shalt love thy neighbour, and hate thine enemy. But I say unto you, Love your enemies; bless them that curse you; do good to them that hate you; and pray for them that despitefully use you, and persecute you; that you may be the children of your Father who is in heaven; for he maketh his sun to arise on the evil and on the good, and sendeth rain on the just and on the unjust." This is one of the most sublime exercises of the principle of love, in reference to our fellow-men; and it is enforced from the most sublime motive and consideration—the conduct of Benevolence itself towards a race of rebellious and ungrateful creatures.

All the other instructions of this Divine Teacher—his parables, exhortations, admonitions, warnings, and consolatory addresses, though referring to particular cases and circumstances—had the same general object in view. When his disciples would have called for fire from heaven, to consume the Samaritans, he kindly, but with energy and decision, reminded them, that a principle of malignity was imbodied in their unhallowed desires, which is directly opposed to the law of love. "Ye know not what manner of spirit ye are of; for the Son of man is not come to destroy men's lives, but to save them." Among his last instructions to his followers, when he was about to depart from the scene of his earthly pilgrimage, love was the grand theme on which he repeatedly expatiated. "A new commandment give I unto you, that ye love one another; as I have loved you, that ye also love one another. By this shall all men know that ye are my disciples, if ye have love one to another." "These things I command you, that ye love one another."

And, as the promotion of the spirit of love was the great object of his instructions, so his whole life was an uninterrupted exemplification of the purest *benevolence*, both towards friends and towards enemies. Never did that holy affection which unites the angelic tribes, and diffuses joy among the poor inhabitants of all worlds, appear within the confines of *our* world, so amiable, so disinterested, and so ardent, as during the period of the public ministry of Jesus, and particularly towards the close of his earthly career. In the immediate prospect of sufferings, dreadful beyond our conceptions, his love to mankind was "strong as death," which the many waters of affliction which surrounded him were unable to quench. His whole soul seemed to be absorbed in affection towards his disconsolate disciples, and in a desire to cheer and animate their drooping spirits. His last addresses, as recorded by the Evangelist John, breathe a spirit of tenderness and compassion, and of Divine benignity, of which we have no parallel in the annals of our race."

To display his kindness and condescension, and to teach his disciples to peform with cheerfulness the humblest offices of friendship, he rose from supper; he laid aside his garments; he took a towel; he girded himself; he poured water into a bason; he began to wash the disciples' feet; and he wiped them with the towel wherewith he was girded. He then addressed them in such language as this:—"Let not your heart be troubled; in my Father's house are many mansions; I go to prepare a place for you. And, if I go and prepare a place for you, I will come again and receive you to myself; that where I am there ye may be also. I will not leave you comfortless; I will pray the Father, and he shall give you another comforter, even the Spirit of truth, which shall abide with you for ever. Whatsoever ye shall ask in my name, I will do it. Peace I leave with you; my peace I give unto you; not as the world giveth, give I unto you. Let not your heart be troubled, neither let it be afraid." In his last prayer, which accompanied these benedictions, the same ardent flow of affection burst from his benevolent heart—"Holy Father! keep, through thine own name, those whom thou hast given me, that they may be one as we are." But his love was not confined to the select few with whom he was surrounded at this interesting hour. His mental eye surveyed the various tribes which people this department of creation—it pierced through all the succeding generations of mankind—and he embraced in his expansive affections the whole race of the faithful till the close of time. "Neither pray I for these alone; but for them also who shall believe on me through their word; that they all may be one, as thou, Father, art in me, and I in thee; that they also may be one in us." Even towards his bitterest enemies his benevolent emotions flowed out, in earnest supplications for their forgiveness. Neither "the floods of ungodly men," which compassed him, nor the torrents of abuse which were poured upon him while he was nailing to the cross, could overpower that heavenly flame which burned in his holy breast. In the midst of all the mockeries, insults, and indignities which he endured, when he was made "a spectacle to angels and to men," his affectionate desires ascended, with the smoke of the evening sacrifice, to the throne of God, in behalf of his murderers—"Father, forgive them; for they know not what they do." O, what a striking contrast is here presented, to those scenes of pride, malignity, and revenge, which have so long disgraced the race of Adam, and spread lamentation, and mourning, and terror, among families, societies, and nations! What a happy world would this become, were it peopled with such amiable characters, and were all who profess to be followers of Jesus, instead of contending about "questions which gender strife," to vie with each other in imitating his mild and benevolent spirit! Then Christianity would appear in its native lustre, and receive the homage due to its divine character: and the name of Jenovah would soon be proclaimed throughout all the earth, and the joys of his salvation felt in every clime.

Again, it is one great end of the death of Christ to destroy the principle of malignity in the human heart, and to promote the operation of the law of love. "While we were enemies, (says the Apostle Paul,) we were reconciled to God by the death of his Son." "We are sanctified through the offering of the body of Jesus Christ once for all." "He loved us, and washed us from our sins in his own blood." "They who were enemies in their mind, and by wicked works, he reconciled in the body of his flesh through death, to present them holy and unblameable, and unreprovable in his sight." Love to his heavenly Father, and love to mankind, impelled him to "humble himself, and to become obedient to death, even the death of the cross." And, in order that this divine principle might be kept alive, and form a bond of union among all his followers, he appointed an ordinance, consisting of sensible signs, in commemoration of his death, to be observed in all ages as a memorial of his love, and to remind his friends of the indispensible obligation under which they are laid to love one another. To promote the same benevolent design, he arose from the dead, ascended to heaven, sent down the Spirit of Holiness to abide in the Church, and now presides in the celestial world as "a Prince and a Saviour, to give repentance and the remission of sins."

And, as the instructions and the example of Jesus Christ were calculated to exhibit the principle of love in all its interesting aspects, and to promote its practical influence, so the preaching and the writings of his Apostles had the same important object in view, as the ultimate scope of all their ministrations. The one half of every epistle to the Christian churches is occupied in delineating the practical bearings of this holy affection. Like the lines which proceed from the centre to the circumference of a circle, the various radiations of Christian affection are traced from love, as the grand central point, and exhibited in all their benign influence on individuals, families, churches, and the diversified relations which subsist in civil and Christian society. "Above all things," says the Apostle, "put on *love*, which is the bond of perfection. Though we speak with the tongues of men and angels, and have not love, we are become as sounding brass, or a tinkling cymbal. And though we understand all mysteries, and all knowledge, and bestow all our goods to feed the poor, and have not love, it profiteth nothing. Love suffereth long, and is kind; love envieth not, vaunteth not itself, doth not behave itself unseemly, seeketh not her own, is not easily provoked, thinketh no evil. Prophecies shall fail, languages shall cease, earthly knowledge shall vanish away, but love *never faileth.*" "Love worketh no ill to his neighbour; therefore, love is the fulfilling of the law. All the law is comprehended in this saying, namely, Thou shalt love thy neighbour as thyself. The works of the flesh," or those which flow from a principle of malignity, "are these: fornication, uncleanness, idolatry, hatred, variance, emulations, wrath, strife, seditions, envyings, murders, revellings, and such like. But the fruit of the spirit is love, joy, peace, long-suffering, gentleness, goodness, fidelity, meekness, and temperance." "Let love be without dissimulation, and walk in love as Christ also hath loved us. Be kindly affectioned one toward another with brotherly love, in honour preferring one another. Distributing to the necessity of saints; given to hospitality. Bless them that persecute you? bless, and curse not. Rejoice with them that do rejoice, and weep with them that weep. Husbands, love your wives, even as Christ also loved the church; children, obey your parents in the Lord; fathers, provoke not your children to wrath, but bring them up in the nurture and admonition of the Lo d. Servants, be obedient to your masters, with good will doing service as to the Lord, and not unto men; and ye masters, do the same thing unto them, forbearing threatening, knowing that your master also is in heaven." "Put on, as the elect of God, holy and beloved, bowels of mercies, kindness, humbleness of mind, meekness, long-suffering; forbearing one another in love, and forgiving one another, if any man have a quarrel against any; even as Christ forgave you, so also do ye."

Such is the general scope of the instructions which the apostles delivered, in all their communications to the Christian churches, whether composed of Jews or Gentiles. And, had it not been for the strong prejudices of the Jews, and the erroneous conceptions of the Gentiles, which the apostles had to combat, it is probable, that the whole of their epistles would have been solely occupied in delineating the practical effects of love to God, and to our brethren of mankind, and its glorious consequences in the future world. And, as it was the great aim of the apostles themselves, in their writings and personal administrations, to illustrate the numerous bearings of Christian love, so they gave solemn charges to their successors in the work of the ministry, to make all their instructions subservient to the promotion of the same important object. Almost the whole of the epistles addressed to Timothy and Titus, which relate to the duties and the objects of the Christian ministry, has a reference, not to the discussion of metaphysical questions in theology, which "are unprofitable and vain," but to the illustration and the inculcating of those practical duties which flow from the spirit of love, and to the counteracting of those proud, malignant, and speculative dispositions which are opposed to the meekness and benignity of the gospel of peace.

I might also have shown, by numerous quotations, that, in the *general* epistles of Peter, James, and John, the same grand object to which I have been adverting is steadily and uniformly kept in view. The first epistle of John is almost exclusively devoted to the illustration of the love of God and of man; and on this theme, in which his soul appears to be almost entirely absorbed, he expatiates with peculiar energy and delight: "We know that we have passed from death to life, because we love the brethren. He that loveth not his brother abideth in death. Whosoever hateth his brother is a murderer; and ye know that no murderer hath (the principle of) eternal life abiding in him. Behold, what manner of love the Father hath bestowed on us, that we should be called the sons of God! Beloved, let us love one another; for love is of God: and every one that loveth is born of God, and knoweth God. He that loveth not knoweth not God; for God is love. No man hath seen God at any time. If we love one another, God dwelleth in us, and his love is perfected in us. If any man say, I love God, and hateth his brother, he is a liar; for he that loveth not his brother, whom he hath seen, how can he love God, whom he hath not seen?" It is recorded, by some ancient authors, that when this apostle was grown old, and unable to preach, he used to be led to the church at Ephesus, and only to say these words to the people, *Little children, love one another*." Such was the importance which this venerable apostle attached to *love*, as the grand and governing principle in the Christian system.

Finally, The procedure of the last judgment will be conducted on evidence, deduced from the manifestations of love. At that solemn period, when the present economy of Divine Providence shall come to a termination; when the elements shall melt with fervent heat, and the great globe on which we tread shall be wrapt in flames; when the archangel shall descend, and sound an alarm with "the trump of God;" when the graves shall open, and give forth their dead; and when all the generations of men, "both small and great," shall stand before the throne of God; the eternal destiny of all the millions of mankind will be unalterably determined, on the ground of the manifestations which have been given of the existence and the operation of the principle of love, and of the affections and conduct to which it is opposed. "When the Son of man shall come in his glory, and all the holy angels with him, then shall he sit upon the throne of his glory. And before him shall be assembled all nations. Then shall he say to them on his right hand, Come ye blessed of my Father, inherit the kingdom prepared for you from the foundation of the world. For I was an hungered, and ye gave me meat; I was thirsty, and ye gave me drink; I was a stranger, and ye took me in; naked, and ye clothed me; I was sick, and ye visited me; I was in prison, and ye came unto me." And, though ye had no opportunity of performing these offices to me in person, yet, "inasmuch as ye did it to one of the least of these my brethren, ye did it unto me." "Then shall he also say to them on the left hand, Depart from me, ye cursed; for I was an hungered, and ye gave me no meat; I was thirsty, and ye gave me no drink; I was a stranger and ye took me not in; naked, and ye clothed me not; sick, and in prison, and ye visited me not. Verily, I say unto you, inasmuch as ye did it not to one of the least of these, ye did it not to me. And these shall go away into everlasting punishment, but the righteous into life eternal." For every one shall be rewarded according to his works.—Such is the importance which will be attached to the influence of this holy affection over the human mind, at that "day of dread, decision, and despair;" for it is quite obvious, that every action here specified in relation to the righteous, is an effect of the love of God and of man presiding in the heart, and, therefore, if we shall ultimately be found destitute of this holy principle, we cannot expect the reward of the faithful, nor "have boldness in the day of judgment."

Thus it appears that it is the great end of all the historical facts, the religious institutions, the devotional writings, the moral maxims, the instructions of the prophets, the warnings, exhortations, promises, and threatenings, comprised in the Jewish revelation, to illustrate and enforce the law of love in its references both to God and to man—that it is explained and illustrated in the various instructions delivered by our blessed Saviour, and enforced by his example—that its numerous bearings and modifications are displayed in the writings of all the apostles, and in their instructions to Christian teachers—and, that its existence in the heart, and its operation in active life, will form the decisive test of our character at the final judgment.

---

## SECTION VIII.

### ON THE PRACTICAL OPERATION OF LOVE, AND THE VARIOUS MODES IN WHICH IT SHOULD BE DISPLAYED TOWARDS MANKIND.

We have already seen, that love is a most noble and expansive affection. It is not like a blazing meteor which dazzles the eye for a few moments, and then vanishes from the sight. It does not consist merely in a few transient emotions, and fruitless wishes for the good of others. It does not waste its energies in eloquent harangues on the beauty of virtue, in theorizing speculations on the principles of morals, in framing Quixotic schemes of philanthropy, or in weeping over tales of fictitious wo. It is a substantial and an ever *active* principle; its energies are exerted for the purpose of communicating happiness to every rank of sensitive and intellectual beings; and the moral world, as it actually exists, is the grand theatre of its operations. I have already endeavoured to illustrate some of the modifications of this affection, in its relation to God;* and, in the preceding sections of this chapter, have occasionally adverted to some of its benignant effects in reference to man. It may, however, be expedient, in this place, to enter a little more explicitly into the practical operations of benevolence, and the various modes by which its influence may be manifested in relation to our brethren of mankind.

The grand object which love proposes to accomplish is the communication of happiness. And, in order to stimulate and direct us in its operations, the character and agency of God are set before us as our examplar. There is not a more amiable, attractive, nor comprehensive idea of the Divine Being any where to be found than that which is exhibited by the Apostle John, in three words—GOD IS LOVE. He is the eternal, uncreated Source of felicity, from which flow all those streams of joy which gladden the hearts of angels and archangels, cherubim and seraphim; and whatever portion of happiness, sensitive or intellectual, is enjoyed by man on earth, and by all the subordinate tribes of animated nature, is derived from the same inexhaustible fountain. For the purpose of communicating happiness, he called the material universe into existence, to serve as an immense theatre, on which his benevolence might be displayed to countless orders of sensitive and intelligent creatures; and all the perfections of his nature may be considered as so many agents employed for the execution of this noble design. Impelled, as it were, by this essential and characteristic affection of the Divine Mind, all the attributes of Deity are incessantly operating throughout the immensity of creation in the view of the inhabitants of all worlds. His *Omnipotence* is employed in supporting the worlds already created, and in bringing new systems, and new orders of beings into existence; and his *Wisdom*, in devising, selecting, and arranging those means which are requisite for accomplishing the plans of benevolence. Towards those wretched beings who have abused his goodness, and wandered from happiness, his *Mercy* is proclaimed; and his *Patience* and forbearance are long exercised, in order to lead them to repentance, and to the paths of felicity. His *Justice*, conjoined with his power, is exercised for the purpose of restraining the efforts of malevolence, for preventing the inroads of anarchy and confusion, and for preserving the order and happiness of the intelligent creation. In this view, all the judgments, however dreadful and appalling, which have been inflicted on the workers of iniquity in every age, have had a tendency to accomplish the purposes of benevolence, in reference to the universal system. For, the general good of God's universal empire, *considered as one whole*, must be viewed as the great end which benevolence is accomplishing, and the partial exclusions from happiness, which now happen in the case of certain classes of moral agents, must be regarded as necessary arrangements subservient to this important end. His infinite *Knowledge*, extending to all events, past, present, and to come; and his *Omniscient* eye, piercing into the secret purposes of every heart, surveying the various tribes of men, and the circumstances of all the worlds which float in the immensity of space, and comprehending the remotest consequences of all actions throughout infinite duration, enable Him, in every instance, to form those arrangements by which the objects of benevolence may be accomplished on the most extensive scale, and by which the everlasting happiness of the holy and intelligent system may be most effectually secured.

For the purpose of displaying his love to the moral intelligences of our world, he has given us a revelation of his character and will; he has exhibited his law as a law of love; he has promised the agency of his holy Spirit, to produce in us those dispositions which his law requires; and he has given the most affecting display of his love, in the mission of his Son into the world. "In this," says the Apostle John, "was manifested the love of God towards us; because that God sent his only-begotten Son into the world, that we might live though him. Herein is love; not that we loved God, but that he loved us, and sent his Son to be a propitiation for our sins. Beloved, if God so loved us, how ought we to love one another?"

Now, we are commanded in the Sacred Scriptures to be imitators of God in his benevolent operations, and especially in those cases in which love requires to surmount every obstacle, and to exert all its powers in opposition to hatred, enmity, and ingratitude. "Be ye perfect," says our Saviour, "as your Father who is in heaven is perfect. Love your enemies; bless them who curse you; do good to them who hate you; and pray for them who despitefully use you and persecute you. That you may be the children of your Father who is in heaven: for he maketh his sun to rise on the *evil* and on the good; and sendeth rain on the just and on the *unjust*." So that his enemies subsist on his bounty, and are cheered and refreshed by his providential care. In like manner, the operation of love on the part of man may be consideredas the whole energy of an intelligent, mind, directing its faculties of perception, judgment, reasoning, and imagination, along with its physical powers, to the production of happiness both among friends and enemies, so far as its influence can extend. In the prosecution of this noble end, man

* See pages 40—51

becomes "a worker together with God," a subordinate agent in carrying forward those plans of Infinite Benevolence which will issue in the ultimate happiness of the moral universe. And as the Almighty, in his benevolent operations, preserves the harmony of the universe by certain laws of order which he has established, as is apparent in the arrangement of the planetary system, and in the physical and moral economy of our terrestrial sphere; so it is the duty of man, in all the movements to which love impels him, to imitate his Creator in this respect, and to employ the intellectual faculties with which he is endued, for regulating the exercise of the benevolent principle, for adapting and proportioning means to ends, and for discriminating between rational and enthusiastic schemes of exertion; so that order may facilitate his movements, and that the greatest sum of happiness may result from his active endeavours.

We may now attend more particularly to the practical operations of love, and the objects towards which it should be directed.

The principal objects towards which our benevolence should be directed are, *intelligent beings;* and in the sphere of action to which we are at present confined, *man* is the chief object whom we have it in our power to benefit by our benevolent exertions. Our benevolent affections, indeed, ought to expand towards all the holy intelligences of which we have any intimation; and, in another stage of our existence, we may have an opportunity of mingling with other orders of intellectual beings, and of co-operating with them in diffusing happiness throughout the universe; but while we continue in this sublunary region, the improvement and happiness of our fellow-men is the chief object to which our exertions must necessarily be confined; and when we view the present state of the moral world in all nations and climates, we behold a field of exertion sufficiently ample to employ all the energies of benevolence that have ever yet been displayed, or perhaps ever will be displayed during the existing economy of our world.

Man may be considered in two points of view: as possessed of a *body*, which is susceptible of agreeable or disagreeable sensations and feelings; and, as endued with a *mind*, or spiritual principle which is capable of perpetual improvement in knowledge and virtue, and which is destined an endless existence. In both these respects, love will exert its powers in meliorating the condition and promoting the enjoyments of mankind. In regard to his *corporeal system*, man has various *wants*, which require to be supplied, and he is subjected to various *sufferings* which require to be soothed and alleviated. He stands in need of food, raiment, shelter from the blasts of the tempests, comfortable lodging and accommodation, light to cheer and enable him to prosecute his employments, pure atmospheric air to invigorate his animal system, and water to cleanse and refresh him. He is exposed to corporeal weakness and to mental imbecility; to pain, sickness, and disease; to the loss of sight, of hearing, and of bodily feelings; to the decrepitude of old age and to all those lingering disorders which terminate in dissolution. He is also exposed to the afflictions occasioned by the loss of friends and relatives; to dejection of mind, to remorse of conscience, to doubt, despondency, and despair, and to a long train of anxieties, vexations, perplexities, and troubles of various kinds. Now, in reference to the wants of mankind, love, when genuine and ardent, will endeavour to supply them wherever a deficiency is known to exist, and in reference to their calamities and sorrows, it will use its utmost exertions to relieve and assuage them, in as far its powers and influence can extend. In this respect, every one, however low his situation in life, however limited the range of his knowledge, and how ever contracted the sphere of his influence may be, has it in his power, in a greater or less degree, to communicate blessings to his brethren of mankind. He can visit the sick bed of an afflicted neighbour; he can supply a cup of cold water to cool his parched tongue; he can wipe the sweat from his forehead; he can smooth his pillow; he can turn him round on his bed of languishing, that he may enjoy a more comfortable repose; and he can cheer him with those expressions of tenderness and affection, which have a tendency above all other acts of kindness to sooth and revive the downcast spirit. He can assist his neighbour by his strength, or by his skill, by his counsel and advice, and by taking a lively interest in his concerns; he can promote his joy by rejoicing in his prosperity and success, by assisting him in his employment, by rescuing him from danger, by forgiving the injuries he may have received, by acknowledging the worth of the skill, virtues, and endowments of which he is possessed, and by listening with patience and complacency to his sentiments, complaints, or grievances. He can even promote the happiness of his neighbour in a *negative* way, by not injuring him in his character or reputation; by not standing in the way of his prosperity or advancement; by not thwarting him in his schemes and enterprises; by not interrupting him in his innocent amusements; and by refraining from every thing that would tend unnecessarily to injure him in his trade or profession. Such friendly attentions to promote the comfort of his fellow-men, every one has it in his power to bestow: and upon such apparently trivial actions the happiness of mankind in general more immediately depends, than on many of those legislative arrangements which arrest the attention of a whole empire. For, were they universally performed, the greater par of the miseries which afflict humanity would disappear from the world.

But, in cases where a high degree of intellectual talent, of wealth, and of influence is possessed, love is enabled to take a wider range in its beneficent operations, by endeavouring to counteract public evils, and to promote rational schemes of general philanthropy. When we take a survey of the condition of the great mass of the lower orders of society, we find them labouring under many physical evils and inconveniences, which have a tendency to injure their health and their comfort, and to obstruct their moral and intellectual improvement. In their private habitations, we find multitudes of them residing in places where they are almost deprived of light and of pure air, and surrounded with noxious effluvia, putrid smells, and every thing that is insalubrious and offensive to the senses. We find whole families packed into a narrow apartment of twelve feet square, in a narrow lane, where the rays of the sun never penetrate, where the refreshing breeze is seldom felt, and where the beauties of nature are never beheld. In public manufactories we find hundreds of men, women, and children, with pale faces and emaciated looks, breathing a polluted atmosphere half-poisoned with deleterious fumes, steam, smoke, or noxious gases. In large cities, we find numbers of children, through the carelessness and unprincipled disposition of their parents, left to wallow in filth and wretchedness, without even rags to cover their nakedness, and encouraged in the haibits of pilfering, and of every other vice which can debase their minds and render them pests to society; and we behold others doomed to the degrading employment of chimney-sweeping, deprived of the attentions which flow from the tender affection of parents, and subjected to the harsh treatment of unfeeling masters. We behold multitudes of human beings torn from their families and their native land, cooped up in an infernal floating dungeon, carried to a foreign land, sold like cattle to an avaricious planter, and held in the chains of perpetual slavery. In reference to all these and similar evils which exist in human society, love will exert its energies, either to alleviate or to remove them. It will induce one individual to investigate their causes, to point out the proper means of remedy, and to publish to the world the result of his deliberations and researches. It will induce another to apply the discoveries of natural science and the inventions of art to the purpose of improving the physical condition of mankind. It will induce a third individual, in conjunction with others, to form rational plans of melioration, and to organize societies to carry them into effect; and it will impel others to come forward with their wealth and influence to provide the means for carrying forward on the most extensive scale the plans of general beneficence. In short, the whole machinery of nature and art, of mind and matter, of religion and literature, of science and legislation, would be set in motion to promote the external enjoyments of mankind, were love a predominant principle in human society. Cottages on commodious and healthy plans would be reared for the industrious poor; streets would be formed and gardens allotted them for their pleasure and accommodation; public manufactories would be arranged and regulated in such a manner as to contribute to health, to comfort, and to rational improvement;* the children of the poor would be fed and clothed, and trained up to habits of industry and virtue; employment would be provided for all classes of labourers and mechanics, and subsistence furnished when employment could not be procured; idleness would be universally discouraged, and honourable industry would be rewarded in such a manner as to afford not only the comforts, but even many of the luxuries of life; slavery in every shape, with all its injustice and cruelties, would be abolished, and rational liberty would be proclaimed among all ranks and in every clime.

Thus the man in whose heart love presides, takes a lively and sincere interest in every thing that has a tendency to promote the external comfort and welfare of his neighbour. He is compassionate and merciful, gentle and indulgent, kind and tender-hearted, generous and humane; he feels for the sorrows of suffering humanity, and his wealth and activity are directed to relieve the distresses of the poor and the afflicted, to feed the hungry, to clothe the naked, to protect the widow and the orphan, to encourage honest industry, to meliorate the condition of the useful mechanic, and to increase and extend his comforts and enjoyments. Of such a one it may be said, in the language of Job, "He is eyes to the blind, feet to the lame, and a father to the poor. When the ear hears him, then it blesses him, and when the eyes sees him, it gives witness to him; because he delivers the poor that cries, and the fatherless, and him that hath none to help

*Some may be disposed to insinuate, that such attempts would be altogether visionary, and could never be realized. But I would ask such persons, Have such schemes ever been attempted to be realized on an extensive scale? Has the promotion of the health and comfort of the industrious poor ever become *a particular object of attention* to the legislature, to men of rank and influence, and to the whole class of opulent manufacturers? Is it not a fact, that while the acquisition of wealth is made the main object of attention, the melioration of the condition of the industrious labourer and mechanic is either altogether overlooked, or viewed as a very subordinate object of attention? He is generally left to shift for himself the best way he can, and left to breathe in an impure atmosphere without any *particular sacrifice* being made to remedy the evil. I venture to affirm, that were the comfort of the lower orders of society made as particular an object of attention as is the acquisition of wealth, every obstacle to its accomplishment would soon be removed.

him. The blessing of him that was ready to perish comes upon him, and he causes the widow's heart to sing for joy."

But the activities of benevolence are not confined to the communication of sensitive enjoyments. Man is a rational and immortal, as well as a sensitive being; and the operations of genuine love will have for their ultimate object the promotion of his best interests as a moral and intellectual agent, and as an heir of immortality.

When we consider man as an intellectual being, standing in various important relations to his God and to his fellow-creatures, we behold numerous evils which require to be remedied, as well as in the circumstances of his physical condition. Though the human mind is capable of vast expansion, of acquiring an immense number of sublime and interesting ideas, and of enjoying the purest pleasure in contemplating the objects which lie within its range, yet it is a melancholy fact, that in all ages, mental darkness has enveloped the great majority of our race; and that the grossest ignorance of the most important truths, accompanied with the most degrading affections, still prevails among the greater part of the population of every region of the globe. We need not go to the frozen climes of Lapland and Labrador, to the filthy huts of the Greenlander and the Esquimaux, to the rude savages of Nootka Sound, to the degraded tribes of New-Holland and Van Dieman's Land, to the wild and wretched Boshemen and Caffres, or to the swarthy sons of Central Africa, in order to be convinced of this lamentable truth. We need only to look around us among the various ranks of our own population, and we shall not fail to see ignorance, in all its diversified forms, exerting its malign influence over the minds of men, accompanied with superstition, enthusiasm, bigotry, intolerance, and every grovelling affection that can debase the human mind. Multitudes of the young, both in the city and in the country, are suffered to shoot up from infancy to manhood, as if they were mere animal existences, ignorant of the character and operations of God, of the duties they owe to their Creator and to one another, and of the eternal state of existence to which they are destined. Even in many of those places where instruction is attempted to be communicated, what a pitiful picture is exhibited of the results of education, and of the folly which attaches itself to the character of man! The pronunciation of a number of unmeaning words, the reciting of passages which the young cannot understand, the repetition of a few propositions in religion to which no ideas are attached, and the casting of a few accounts, are considered as sufficient to lead them forward in the path of knowledge and virtue; and are substituted in the place of those definite and luminous instructions which are requisite to expand the opening intellect, to convey distinct ideas to the mind, to unfold the scenes of creation and providence, to display the character of God, and to train up the youthful mind to glory and immortality.

Now, in reference to the ignorance which prevails in the world, love to man, as an intellectual being, will excite to active endeavours in order to counteract its influence. It will prove an excitement to the erection of seminaries of instruction wherever they are deficient; it will patronize every scheme and every exertion by which knowledge may be increased; and will diffuse mental illumination as far as the sphere of its influence extends. It will not rest satisfied with the form of instruction, without the substance; with the elements of language, without the elements of thought; with the key of knowledge, without knowledge itself; but will devise rational plans for conveying *substantial* information to the minds of the young, so as to win their affections, arrest their attention, and carry them forward with pleasure in the paths of improvement. It will not offer them stones and ashes instead of bread, but will spread before them an intellectual feast, and "feed them with knowledge and understanding." It will not confine its attention merely to the instruction of the young, but will endeavour, by writing, by conversation, by lectures, by lending and circulating books, by establishing public libraries, and by organizing rational and scientific institutions, to diffuse the rays of intellectual light among men of all ages, ranks, and professions; and will never cease its exertions till ignorance, with all its degrading accompaniments, be banished from society, and till the light of truth illuminate the inhabitants of every land. In a word, it will endeavour to render every branch of knowledge subservient to the illustration of the character and the revelation of God, and to the preparing of mankind for the employments of that nobler state of existence to which they are destined.

Again, as man is possessed of an immortal nature, and in his present state of sin and degradation is exposed to misery in the future world, so it is one of the highest offices of love to endeavour to promote the eternal salvation of mankind. For the accomplishment of this important object, all its activities are concentrated, and all its other labours are rendered subservient. To improve the physical condition of man as a sensitive being, and to enlarge his knowledge as an intellectual, while we overlook his eternal interests, is to neglect one of the most important duties of Christian philanthropy. The sensitive enjoyments of man are conducive to his happiness so long as they continue; and "knowledge is pleasant to the soul." But what are all the acquisitions and enjoyments of time, when compared with the concerns of eternity! and what will they avail, if their possessor be found *unqualified* for the employments of an endless life! If the soul of man be an immortal principle, and if the least danger exists of its being deprived, though ignorance and guilt, of happiness in the future world, no words can express the importance which ought to be attached to this "labour of love." "What will it profit a man if he shall gain the whole world, and lose his own soul? or what shall a man give in exchange for his soul?" And therefore, the man in whose breast true benevolence resides, will consider the *eternal* happiness of his fellow-immortals as the grand and ultimate object which ought always to be kept in view, and will exert all his faculties, powers, and influence, in order to its accomplishment. He will not rest satisfied with prayers and wishes for the salvation of men; he will not wait for any extraordinary afflatus of the Divine Spirit; but will prosecute with judgment and perseverance that course of active duty, which has a tendency to produce the desired effect. So far as the circle of his influence extends, he will endeavour to instruct the ignorant, to arouse the careless, to reclaim the dissipated, to convince the skeptic, to train up the young in the knowledge of God and in the paths of virtue, and to encourage and animate every one who is inquiring the way to eternal life. He will exhibit religion in its most amiable, and attractive, and sublime aspects; and will endeavour to fix the attention on the lovely tempers, and the beneficial effects which the observance of its precepts has a tendency to produce. He will not make it his chief object to convert men to the belief of certain metaphysical dogmas in religion, nor to gain them over to embrace the peculiarities of a party; but to produce in their minds a cordial acquiescence in the plan of salvation which the Gospel exhibits, a reverence of the divine character and perfections, a desire to cultivate holy tempers, and a fixed determination to walkin the paths of God's commandments.

Such a character will give every due encouragement by his advice and by his wealth to Christian churches, and to faithful and intelligent ministers of religion. He will patronize every rational scheme which has for its object to propagate the Gospel of peace among all nations. He will encourage the translation of the Scriptures into the languages of all kindreds and tribes; he will give countenance to societies formed for circulating the Bible in foreign lands; and he will assist in sending forth intelligent and philanthropic missionaries to barbarous and unenlightened tribes, for the purpose of diffusing the blessings of knowledge, civilization, and religion; and he will rejoice to co-operate in such benevolent schemes with all who sincerely wish to promote the best interests of their fellow men, by whatever name they are distinguished, and to whatever section of the Christian church they may belong.

In short, love, when genuine and ardent, will set itself in opposition to every species of bigotry and intolerance, and to all those petty jealousies and bitter animosities which have so long distracted the Christian church, which have thrown an odium on its character, and prevented the harmonious intercourse of the followers of Jesus. It will make every sacrifice consistent with the great objects of Christianity, and will use every appropriate mean to heal the unhappy divisions which exist in the religious world, and to promote an affectionate union of "all who love our Lord Jesus in sincerity;" in order that the church of Christ may form one compact harmonious body, in opposition to atheists, skeptics, and the men of the world, and in order that every plan and effort to diffuse the knowledge and influence of the Christian religion may be carried more speedily and more extensively into effect.

With regard to all the other branches of Christian morality, and to all the virtues which can adorn the human character, in every station and relation in life, they will be found to flow from the exercise of the principle I have now been illustrating, as naturally as the sap flows from the trunk of the remotest ramifications of a tree, or as the gas which now illuminates our streets and churches flows from the main gasometer, through hundreds of pipes, to all the different burners. Sincerity and veracity in our words and actions, honesty and fair dealing in trade and commerce, fidelity to compacts and engagements, a regard to public liberty, an equitable administration of justice, condescension and kindness to inferiors, reverence and respect to superiors, submission to just laws and regulations, friendship, and a cordial interchange of friendly sentiments and affections; courtesy, civility, affability, harmony, and good neigbourhood; modesty, chastity, and discretion; forgiveness of injuries, hospitality to strangers, humanity to servants and dependants, compassion to the distressed; parental, filial, and fraternal affection, sympathy, generosity, temperance, and fortitude, together with all the other social virtues which unite man to man, will as naturally flow from the fountain of love, when it exists in the human breast, as water flows from a reservoir, through all the pipes which distribute it to the inhabitants of a large city. For he who withholds the exercise of such virtues, or acts in direct opposition to them, can never be supposed to be sincerely attached to his fellow-creatures, or to consult their happiness; and the meaning of language must be inverted before we can apply to him the epithet *benevolent;* and the order of the moral system deranged, before we can expect happiness to flow from such a conduct.

• The cardinal virtues have been arranged by some moralists under the heads of ***Prudence Temperance***, ***Fortitude***, and ***Justice***. ***Prudence*** consists in judging what is best, in the choice both of ends and means, particularly in reference to our own interests, and to the good or evil which may result from our choice. *Temperance* is that virtue which moderates and restrains the sensual appetites. *Fortitude* is that calm and steady habit of the mind which either enables us bravely to encounter the prospect of ill, or renders us serene and invincible under its immediate pressure. *Justice* is that virtue which impels us to give to every person what is his due. Now, it could easily be shown, that love is the impelling principle which excites to the exercise of all these virtues. It will lead us to pay a due regard to our own comfort and interest, but not so as to interfere with the interests or to obstruct the happiness of others. It will teach us to preserve the dominion of the soul over sense and passion, and to restrain the influence of the sensual appetites, from considerations drawn from our own happiness, and from the good of others. For, as intemperance kindles the fire of resentment and the flames of lust, excites to boisterous words and to lawless actions, wastes the substance and reduces families to wretchedness and ruin, it must be directly opposed to the principle of benevolence. It will inspire us with a generous and heroic indifference to the precarious possessions of this mortal scene, and will excite to activity and perseverance in promoting human happiness, in the face of every difficulty and obstruction, and in spite of obstinacy and ingratitude, and of all the sneers and reproaches that may be thrown out upon us on account of the singularity of our conduct. And as *Justice* is nothing else than the *measure of benevolence*, it will uniformly direct us to give to every one his due, and restrain us from withholding from our neighbour any thing to which he is entitled by equity or by law. And in cases where the division of property is concerned, it will in many instances be induced to relinquish its right when only a few paltry pounds or shillings are at stake, rather than run the risk of dissolving the bonds of affection and friendship.

The duties of morality have by other moralists, particularly by the moderns, been arranged into *the duties we owe to God*, as piety, reverence, and confidence; *the duties we owe to other men*, as fidelity, loyalty, humanity, and justice; and *the duties we owe to ourselves*, as chastity, sobriety, and temperance. From what has been already stated, both in this and in several of the preceding sections, it will obviously appear, that all these classes of duties necessarily flow from the operation of that primary, diffusive, and ever active principle, which resides originally in the Eternal Mind, and which pervades the minds of all holy intelligences.

Finally, The man who is animated by the noble principle of benevolence, will endeavour to discharge with fidelity every social and relative duty, and will feel an interest in the domestic comfort and the moral and religious improvement of all around him. He will display the activities of this holy affection more immediately in the family in which he resides, as a friend, a father, a husband, a son, or a brother; performing with punctuality all the duties which such relations include; promoting unity, harmony, affection, and a reciprocal interchange of all those offices of kindness, which tend to secure mutual confidence, pleasure, and improvement. From the family, his affections will be diffused to the neighbourhood around, in all the forms of kindness, compassion, faithfulness, forgiveness, charity, generosity, humanity, and justice. He will contemplate every member of society as a kinsman and a brother; he will feel a fraternal attachment; he will delight in his success and prosperity, and will endeavour to encourage the social virtues, and to multiply the sources of enjoyment wherever his influence extends. From the circle of his immediate neighbourhood, his affections will extend over all the nation to which he belongs. Its prosperity and advancement in arts, sciences, and legislation, its peace and tranquillity, and the wisdom and rectitude of its rulers, will be the object of his fervent prayers to the God of heaven. To watch over its interests, to promote the improvement of its constitution and its laws, to expose the intrigues of bribery and corruption, to resist the efforts of tyranny and ambition, and to defeat every encroachment on its rights and liberties, in a manly and Christian manner, he will consider as a duty which he owes to his fellow-subjects, to his rulers, and to succeeding generations. It will be his chief aim, not so much to prevent men from becoming thieves, and robbers, and murderers, as to make them pious, virtuous, and useful members of the general community; that every one may live " a quiet and peaceable life, in all godliness and honesty."

Nor will his benevolence be confined within the limits of a narrow-minded and selfish patriotism:—his affections will expand to surrounding nations, and embrace the interests of every people, and will excite him to co-operate in every scheme by which civilization and science, liberty and Christianity, may be promoted among all the tribes and kindreds of the earth. He will occasionally transport himself in imagination to distant climes, and to the islands scattered over the face of the ocean,—and the joy or sorrow which is felt in the hut of the Greenlander, in the Indian wigwam, or among the tents of the Tartars, will find access to his feeling heart. An inundation, an earthquake, the eruption of a volcano, a destroying pestilence, or the horrors of war, happening in Persia, China, or Japan, will not be viewed with apathy or indifference, because those countries are placed thousands of miles beyond the boundaries of his own; but he will sympathise in the sorrows of those distant sufferers, as well as in the calamities which befall his brethren in his native land. Nor will his affections be confined to the men of the present age, but will stretch forward to embrace the sons and daughters of future times, who are destined to appear on the theatre of this world, in successive generations, till time shall be no longer. The plans which he now forms, the ground-works of the improvements which he is now establishing, and the diversified operations of benevolence in which he is now engaged, will have, for their ultimate object, the diffusion of the light of science and of religion, and the communication of happiness, in various forms, to unnumbered multitudes of the human race, after his spirit shall have taken its flight beyond the bounds of this terrestrial sphere. Nor will the current of his love towards fellow-intelligences be bounded by the limits of time, and the range of this sublunary system, but will run forward into those interminable ages, which shall succeed the dissolution of our globe, and will rise upward to the inhabitants of those glorious worlds which roll in the distant regions of creation. Contemplating the diversified scenes in which he may hereafter be placed, and the various orders of intellectual beings with which he may mingle, his soul will be transported at the prospect of entering upon a more extensive field for the range of his benevolent affections, and of being qualified to receive and to communicate happiness on a more enlarged scale, in company with other holy intelligences,—where the field of benevolence will be continually expanding, and the most exquisite delight springing up in his bosom, and ever increasing, as eternal ages are rolling on.

Thus, it appears, that Benevolence is an expansive and an ever active principle, diffusing happiness in its train wherever it extends. Were an extensive moral machinery to be set in action by this powerful principle, it is impossible to describe what a variety of blessings would soon be distributed among mankind, and what a mighty change would be effected in the social state of human beings, and on the whole aspect of the moral world. And from what has been already stated, it is evident, that, although intellectual talent, wealth, and influence, have most in their power, as the prime directors of the moral machine,—yet there is no individual in whom this principle resides, however limited his faculties, and his sphere of action, but has it in his power to communicate happiness to his fellow creatures, and to become at least a subordinate agent in promoting the plans of universal benevolence.

From what has been stated above, and in several of the preceding parts of this work, we may learn, that, in order to acquire a knowledge of our duty, and of the motives which should stimulate us to its performance, there is no need to engage in the study of voluminous systems of ethical science, or to perplex the mind with laboured disquisitions on the principles of morals. The general path of duty is plain to every one who is inclined to walk in it; and whoever wishes to be assisted and directed in his progress towards moral perfection, will find, in the Proverbs of Solomon, the sermons of Jesus Christ, and the practical parts of the apostolic epistles, maxims, and precepts, and motives inculcated, infinitely superior in regard both to their authority and their excellence, to those of all other systems of moral philosophy, whether in ancient or in modern times. This seems to be partly admitted even by moral philosophers themselves. The celebrated Dr. Reid, in his "Essays on the Active Powers of Man," after a variety of learned and abstract discussions on active power, and the principles of human action, when treating on the theory of morals, says, "This is an intricate subject, and there have been various theories and much controversy about it in ancient and in modern times. But it has little connexion with the knowledge of our duty, and those who differ most in the theory of our moral powers, agree in the practical rules of morals which they dictate. As a man may be a good judge of colours, and of the other visible qualities of objects, without any knowledge of the anatomy of the eye, and of the theory of vision; so a man may have a very clear and comprehensive knowledge of what is right and of what is wrong in human conduct, who never studied the structure of our moral powers. A good ear in music may be much improved by attention and practice in that art; but very little by studying the anatomy of the ear, and the theory of sound. In order to acquire a good eye, or a good ear, in the arts that require them, the theory of vision, and the theory of sound, are by no means necessary, and indeed of very little use. *Of as little necessity or use is what we call the theory of morals, in order to improve our moral judgment.*"—Reid, "*On the Active Powers,*" Essay v. chap. 2.

To a man who is familiar with the Scriptures, and whose mind has acquired a relish for the simplicity and excellence of the Christian code of morals, how cold, and frigid, and uninteresting, do the laboured disquisitions of our most celebrated ethical writers appear! There is little to be found in such writings to kindle the fire of holy love, and to inspire the soul with a noble ardour, in carrying forward the plan of divine benevolence. What powerful stimulus to exalted virtue can be expected from abstract discussions on active power, on liberty and necessity, on theories of moral action, on the reason and fitness of things, on self-love, on public and private interest, on the law of honour, and the like; and of how little practical utility are the results of such disquisitions; since every principle of action, every motive, and every duty conducive to the happiness of the intelligent system, is laid down in the Scriptures, with a plainness and perspicuity, which render them level to the meanest understanding? And what shall we say of those moralists who teach us, that "modesty, humility, and forgiveness of injuries," belong to the class of vices;* and, by consequence, that pride, imprudence, and revenge, are to be ranked among the *virtues!* Such virtue, alas! has too long prevailed in our degenerate world; but were it universally to prevail, it would transform creation into a chaos, and banish happiness from the universe. What beneficial practical effects have ever yet been produced by all the systems of ethics which have hitherto been published to the world? Let us look back on the nations of antiquity, on the schools of Plato, Socrates, Epicurus, and Zeno; let us survey the conduct of our modern skeptical philosophers, and the practices of our youths who attend courses of ethical lectures in our universities and academies, and say, whether the general depravity of human nature has been counteracted, and a spirit of universal benevolence has been cherished and promoted by such instructions. I venture to affirm, that we are far more indebted to our Saviour's sermon on the mount, and to the practical writings of the apostle Paul, for that portion of morality which has given a polish to the manners of modern society, than to all the systems of ethics, detached from Christianity, which have ever been published by the philosophers either of Greece or Rome, or of the British empire: and that it is only by following out the instructions of these divine teachers that we can expect to see the world regenerated, and vice and iniquity banished from our streets.

In throwing out the preceding hints, I have confined my attention chiefly to the intelligent creation. But it is evident, that where a principle of genuine love actuates the mind, it will extend its benevolent regards even to the lower orders of animated existence. Towards them the Creator has displayed his benevolence, as well as towards man. He has framed their bodies in as curious and admirable a manner, as the bodies of mankind. He has bestowed upon them organs of sensation exactly adapted to the situations they occupy, and to their various modes of subsistence. He has formed them with instincts which enable them to construct their habitations, to select their food, to protect themselves from danger, and to choose the fittest places for bringing forth their young. He has provided, in the different departments of nature, all that variety of food which is requisite to supply the wants of the whole of that immense assemblage of living beings which traverse the air, the waters, and the earth. "These all wait upon Him, and he giveth them their meat in due season."

* This sentiment is taught by Mr. Hume, and his followers.

Their sportive motions, their varied movements, and the delight with which they seem to exercise their faculties, testify, that they are the objects of the beneficence of their Almighty though unknown Maker. So that God not only takes care of men, but of the fishes of the sea, the creeping insects, and the fowls of heaven, for "a sparrow cannot fall to the ground" without his providential permission.

This benevolent care of the Creator, which extends to the lowest order of his creatures, instructs us, that our benevolence also should be displayed towards the inferior ranks of sensitive existence—that we should not only abstain from vexing, and torturing, and unnecessarily depriving them of existence; but should endeavour to promote their comfort and enjoyment. It was the object of several of the laws delivered to the Jews, to inculcate compassion and humanity towards their domestic animals: and Solomon lays it down as a moral maxim, that "the righteous man regardeth the life of his beast." Benevolence will display itself, in the shape of tenderness and humanity towards every creature that is endowed with feeling and sensation; but it cannot be supposed to have a powerful influence over that man who can wantonly torture a poor fly, lash a feeble old horse, wound a bird or a hare for mere sport, twirl a cockchaffer on a crooked pin, or even intentionally trample under foot a snail or a worm, that is doing him no injury. The benevolent man rejoices in the happiness of all creation around him; and, were this disposition universally prevalent, not only should we see cock-fighting, dog-fighting, bull-baiting, and other cruel and degrading sports for ever abolished, but should form a more delightful intercourse with many of the lower animals than we have ever yet enjoyed.—The Arabians never beat their horses; they never cut their tails; they treat them gently; they speak to them, and seem to hold a discourse; they use them as friends; they never attempt to increase their speed by the whip, nor spur them but in cases of great necessity. They never fix them to a stake in the fields, but suffer them to pasture at large around their habitations; and they come running the moment they hear the sound of their master's voice. In consequence of such treatment, these animals become docile and tractable in the highest degree. They resort at night to their tents, and lie down in the midst of the children, without ever hurting them in the slightest degree. The little boys and girls are often seen upon the body or the neck of the mare, while the beasts continue inoffensive and harmless, permitting them to play with and caress them without injury.—Several species of birds have a natural attachment to the habitations of man; but his malevolence prevents them from entering into any intimate and friendly association; for they seem to be fully aware of his guns, and snares, and other arts of destruction, which make them shy, even in cases of necessity, of trusting themselves to his generosity and protection. How many amusing and instructive associations might be formed with this class of animals, if the kindness and benevolence of man were to secure their confidence! Even the beasts of the forest, the elephant, the lion, and the tiger,* have had their ferocious dispositions softened by kindness and attention, and have become the protectors and the friends of man.

Although the lower animals seem to be incapable of making improvements when left to themselves, yet experience has proved, that, under the tuition of man, they are capable of making considerable advancement in knowledge, and in the exercise of the benevolent affections. Kindness and affection will frequently soften the most savage and obdurate dispositions among mankind; and it is not improbable, that a judicious and universal display of friendly attentions towards those animals which occasionally associate with man, would go far to counteract their malevolent propensities, and to promote their harmony and affection. I never was more delighted with an exhibition of animals than on a late occasion, when I beheld a *cat*, a *bird*, and a *mouse* living in the same cage, in the most cordial harmony and peace—a fact which demonstrates that the strongest antipathies of the animal tribes may be overcome by the care and attention of man. And as such an experiment could not have been attempted with success, except when these animals were very young, it shows us the immense importance of an *early* attention to the training of our youth in habits of kindness and affection towards each other, and of humanity towards every sensitive being; and that it ought to be the great care of parents, nurses, and servants, to counteract the *first appearance* of malevolent dispositions in very early life, however trivial the circumstances in which such dispositions are manifested.

The famous Baron Trenck, when confined in his dungeon in Magdeburg, had so tamed a mouse, that it would play round him, and, eat round him, and eat from his mouth. When he whistled, it would come and jump upon his shoulder. After his cruel keepers had given orders that he should be deprived of its society, and had actually taken it away blindfolded, it found its way back again to the door of his dungeon, waited the hour of visitation, when the door would be opened, and immediately testified its joy, by its antic leaping between his legs. This mouse was afterwards carried off, and put into a cage, where it pined, refused all sustenance, and, in a few days, was found dead. "In this small animal," says the Baron, "I discovered proofs of intelligence too great to easily gain belief. Were I to write them, such philosphers as suppose man alone endowed with the power of thought, allowing nothing but what they call instinct in animals, would proclaim me a fabulous writer, and my opinions heterodox to what they suppose sound philosophy."—A nobleman of France, a Count Lauzun, was condemned to a rigid imprisonment. Cut off from all human society, and allowed no means of diverting his solitude, he made a companion of a *spider*, who had spun her web in the corner of his cell. He at length familiarized her so far, that she would come upon his hand, and eat from it a portion of his food which he gave her. The jailer, totally devoid of feeling, thought this too great an indulgence for the unfortunate prisoner, and crushed the spider to death.

Many such instances could be brought forward to illustrate the affection of the inferior tribes, and their capability of improvement. But although they were entirely destitute of mental qualities and affections, as they are sensitive beings, susceptible of pleasure and pain, the truly benevolent man will never intentionally inflict upon them unnecessary pain, and far less will he ever enjoy a savage delight, like some monsters in human shape, in beholding them writhing under the agonies occasioned by barbarous treatment. He will feel a joy in their comfort, and will endeavour to counteract their malignant propensities, and to train them up in those habits by which they may be rendered useful to man, and pleasing to ach other. Were such a kind and humane disposition towards the lower animals generally to prevail, we might ultimately expect the literal accomplishment of those predictions recorded in ancient prophecy:—"In that day will I make a covenant for them with the beasts of the field, and with the fowls of heaven, and with the creeping things of the ground; and I will break the bow and the sword, and the battle out of the earth, and will make them to lie down safely." "I will cause the evil beasts to cease out of the land, and they shall dwell safely in the wilderness, and sleep in the woods." "The wolf shall dwell with the lamb: the cow and the bear shall feed in one pasture, and their young ones shall lie down together; the sucking child shall play on the hole of the asp, and the weaned child shall put his hand on the adder's den. They shall not hurt nor destroy in all my holy mountain, saith the Lord."

The remarks which have been stated in this section, in reference to the practical influence of the principle of benevolence, are intended merely as a few insulated hints in regard to some of the modes in which it may be made to ope-

* An experiment was lately exhibited, by the keeper of the animals in the Tower of London, which demonstrates, that even the *tiger* is capable of being tamed, and rendered susceptible of friendly feelings towards man.

rate. To illustrate its operation in *detail*, and to trace its progress in all its diversified bearings and ramifications, would be, to write a Body of Practical Morality, which would fill several volumes—a work which is still a desideratum in Christian literature. I cannot conclude this chapter more appropriately than with the following excellent passage, extracted from Dr. Dwight's "System of Theology."

"The divine law is wholly included in two precepts: *Thou shalt love the Lord thy God with all thy heart; and thy neighbour as thyself.* These are so *short*, as to be necessarily included in a very short sentence; so *intelligible*, as to be understood by every moral being who is capable of comprehending the meaning of the words God and neighbour; so *easily remembered* as to render it impossible for them to escape from our memory, unless by wanton, criminal negligence of ours; and so *easily applicable to every case of moral action*, as not to be mistaken unless through indisposition to obey. At the same time, *obedience to them is rendered perfectly obvious and perfectly easy* to every mind which is not indisposed to obey them. The very disposition itself, if sincere and entire, is either entire obedience, or the unfailing means of that external conduct by which the obedience is in some cases completed. *The disposition to obey is also confined to a single affection of the heart*, easily distinguished from all other affections, viz. *love. Love*, saith St. Paul, *is the fulfilling of the law.* The humblest and most ignorant moral creatures, therefore, are in this manner efficaciously preserved from mistaking their duty.

"In the mean time, *these two precepts*, notwithstanding their brevity, *are so comprehensive* as to include every possible action. The archangel is not raised above their control, nor can any action of his exceed that bound which they prescribe. The child who has passed the verge of moral agency, is not placed beneath their regulation: and whatever virtue he may exercise, is no other than a fulfilling of their requisitions. All the duties which we immediately owe to God, to our fellow-creatures, and to ourselves, are, by these precepts, alike comprehended and required. In a word, endlessly varied as moral action may be, it exists in no form or instance in which he who perfectly obeys these precepts will not have done his duty, and will not find himself justified and accepted by God."

---

# CHAPTER III.

## ON THE MORAL LAW AND THE RATIONAL GROUNDS ON WHICH ITS PRECEPTS ARE FORMED.

In the preceding chapters, I have endeavoured to illustrate the foundation of love to God, from a consideration of his attributes, and the relations in which he stands to his creatures. I have also illustrated the rational grounds of love to our neighbour, from a consideration of the natural equality of mankind, of the various relations in which they stand to one another, and of their eternal destination. The dismal consequences which would result from a total subversion of these laws, the beneficial effects which would flow from their universal operation, their application to the inhabitants of other worlds, the declarations of Scripture on this subject, and the various modes in which benevolence should display its activities, have also been the subject of consideration.

The two principles now illustrated, may be considered as two branches proceeding from the same trunk, and spreading into different ramifications. The first *four* commandments of the moral law may be viewed as flowing from the principle of love to God, and the remaining *six* as ramifications of the principle of benevolence, or love to man. In the following brief illustrations, I shall endeavour to show the *reasonableness* of these moral laws in relation to man, from a consideration of the misery which would necessarily result from their universal violation, and of the happiness which would flow from universal obedience to their requisitions.

These laws were published in the most solemn manner, to the assembled tribes of Israel in the wilderness of Horeb. While Mount Sinai was shaking to its centre, and smoking like a furnace; while flames of fire were ascending from its summit, and thick darkness surrounding its base; while thunders were rolling in clouds above, and lightnings flashing amidst the surrounding gloom; and while the earth was quaking all around, and the voice of a trumpet waxing louder and louder,—in the midst of this solemn and terrific scene, God spake the commandments with an audible articulate voice, in the hearing of the trembling multitude assembled round the mountain. A combination of objects and events more awful and impressive, the human mind can scarcely conceive; compared with which, the pretended pomp of Pagan deities, and Jupiter shaking Olympus with his imperial rod, are lame, ridiculous, and profane; and never, perhaps, since the commencement of time, was such a striking scene presented to the view of any of the inhabitants of this world. The most solemn preparations, were made for this divine manifestation; the people of Israel were commanded to purify themselves from every mental and corporeal pollution, and strictly enjoined to keep within the boundaries marked out for them, and not to rush within the limits assigned to these awful symbols of the Deity. An assemblage of celestial beings, from another region of creation, was present on this occasion, to perform important services, to swell the grandeur of the scene, and to be witness of the impressive transactions of that solemn day.* Moses was appointed as a temporary mediator between God and the people, to explain to them in milder terms the words of the law, and the further intimations of the divine will. Yet so terrible were the symbols of the present Deity, that even Moses was appalled, and said, "I exceedingly fear and quake." In order that the impressive words which were uttered on that day might not be forgotten in future generations, they were written on tables of stone with the finger of God. They were not simply *drawn* on a plane, like the strokes of writing upon paper, but the characters were *engraved*, or cut out of the solid stone, so that they could not be erased. They were not written on paper or parchment, or even on wood, but on *stone*, which is a much more durable material. "The tables were written upon *both their sides*, on the one side, and on the other were they written; and the tables were the work of God, and the writing was the writing of God, graven upon the tables."† This was intended to prevent the possibility of any thing being added to the law, or taken from it. The tables were *two* in number, the one containing the precepts which inculcate love to God, and the other containing those which enjoin the love of our neighbour. These laws, thus engraven on the most durable materials, were deposited in the most sacred part of the tabernacle, in the ark of the covenant under the mercy-seat. All the striking circumstances, now mentioned, were evidently intended to proclaim the Majesty and Grandeur of the Supreme Legislator—the excellency and perfection of his law—that it is the eternal and unalterable rule of rectitude—that it is of perpetual obligation on all the inhabitants of the earth—that it is the rule of action to angels and archangels, and to all other moral intelligences, as well as to the human race—and that the most dreadful consequences must ensue on all those who persist in violating its righteous precepts.

The proclamation of this law was prefaced by these words, "I am Jehovah thy God," which contain a ground and reason for our obedience. They evidently imply, that he is the Self-existent and Eternal Being who brought the vast universe into existence, who "garnished the heavens, and laid the foundations of the earth," and peopled all worlds with their inhabitants—that he has sovereign authority to prescribe a rule of action to his creatures—that he knows best what laws are requisite to preserve the order of his vast empire, and to secure the happiness of the intelligent creation—that he is the former of our bodies, the Father of our spirits, and the director of all the movements of nature and providence, from whose unceasing agency every joy proceeds—and that all his regulations and arrangements are calculated to promote the present and everlasting felicity of all rational agents that submit to his authority.—That these laws are not mere acts of Divine Sovereignty, but founded on the nature of things, and are calculated to preserve the harmony and order of the intelligent universe, will appear from the following illustrations and remarks.

### THE FIRST COMMANDMENT.

*Thou shalt have no other gods before me.*

All the commandments, except the fourth and fifth, are expressed in a *negative* form: But it is obvious, that every negative command includes a requisition of the duty which is opposed to the sin forbidden; and those which are *positive* include a prohibition of the conduct which is opposed to the duty required. This first commandment, therefore, though expressed in the negative form, must be considered as including a positive injunction to love God with all our hearts, to offer a tribute of supreme adoration to his perfections, and to exercise the graces of hope, gratitude, submission, and reverence. Having already considered the precept in this point of view, (pp. 85—95) it is only necessary, in this place, to attend for a little, to the *negative* form of the command. The prohibition contained in this precept must be considered as extending not only to Polytheism, and the various objects of worship which have prevailed in the heathen world, but to every thing which is the object of our supreme affection and regard.

It is a dictate of enlightened and unprejudiced reason, that the Being to whom we are indebted for our existence, on whom we every moment

* Stephen says, that the Jews "received the law by the disposition of angels." Grotius observes, on this passage, that the Greek preposition *(eis)* here signifies *amidst*, and that *(diatagas agelon,)* denotes *troops* of angels ranged in military order; and that there is a reference to Deut. xxxiii. 2. "The Lord came from Sinai, and rose up from Seir unto them; he shined forth from Mount Paran, and he came with ten thousands of his holy ones; from his right hand went a fiery law for them."

† Exod. xxxii. 16.

depend, who directs the movements of the system of nature, who daily loads us with his benefits, and on whom our hopes of eternal felicity entirely depend—should be contemplated with the most ardent affection and gratitude, regarded as the most excellent and venerable of all beings, and recognised as the Supreme Legislator, whose laws we are bound, by every tie of gratitude, to obey. Wherever such sentiments and affections pervade the mind, they constitute the first principles of piety, the source of all holy obedience, and the foundation of all true happiness. Were they universally felt, and acted upon by human beings, the Most High God, would be adored in every land, his image would be impressed on every heart, his righteous law would never be violated, grovelling desires and affections would be eradicated, and our world would be transformed into an abode of felicity, where joys similar to those of angels would succeed to scenes of wretchedness and wo.

On the other hand, where the unity and the attributes of the divine Being are not recognised, and where other objects are substituted in his place, the foundations of religion, and of moral order are completely subverted, and a door opened for the introduction of every absurdity, immorality, and vile abomination, that can degrade a rational intelligence. The command under consideration is placed on the front of the divine law as the foundation of all the other precepts; and, therefore, wherever it is violated, or not recognised, a regular obedience to the other subordinate injunctions of religion is not, in the nature of things, to be expected. Were its violation, in our world, complete and universal, it is impossible to say what would be the miserable condition of human beings in their social capacity. To its general violation, may be traced all the evils under which humanity has groaned in every age, and all the depraved passions, and shocking immoralities which now disfigure the aspect of the moral world.

There is nothing that appears more prominent in the history and the character of almost every nation under heaven, than an infringement of this first and fundamental law of the Creator. A rational and enlightened mind, on the first consideration of this subject, would be apt to surmise, that such a law is almost superfluous and unnecessary. There is such an immense disproportion between a block of marble, or a crawling reptile, and that Being who supports the system of universal nature, that it appears, at first view, next to impossible, that a reasonable being should ever become so stupid and degraded, as to substitute the one for the other, and to offer his adorations to an object completely devoid of life, power, and intelligence. Yet experience teaches us, that there is no disposition to which the human mind is more prone than "to depart from the living God," and to multiply objects of idolatrous worship. This will appear, if we take but the slightest glance of the objects of adoration which have prevailed, and which still prevail in the pagan world.

At one period of the world, with the single exception of the small nation of the Jews, idolatry overspread the face of the whole earth. And how numerous and degrading were the objects which the blinded nations adored! We are informed, by Hesiod, Varro, and other ancient authors, that no less than *thirty thousand* subordinate divinities were comprised within that system of idolatry which prevailed among the Greeks and Romans. They had both celestial and terrestrial deities. They assigned peculiar gods to the fountains, the rivers, the hills, the mountains, the lawns, the groves, the sea, and even to hell itself. To cities, fields, houses, edifices, families, gates, nuptial chambers, marriages, births, deaths, sepulchres, trees, and gardens, they also appropriated distinct and peculiar deities. Their principal *celestial* deities were Jupiter, Mars, Mercury, Apollo, Bacchus, Venus, Juno, and Minerva—their *terrestrial*, Saturn, Ceres, Diana, Neptune, Cybele, Proserpine, and Pluto. Their chief idol was Jupiter, whom they called the father of gods and men; and under his authority, Neptune had the jurisdiction of the *sea*, Juno, of the *air*, Cybele, of the *earth*, and Pluto, of the *realms below*. Instead of worshipping the *living* and immortal God, they deified a host of *dead men*, called heroes, distinguished for nothing so much, as for murder, adultery, sodomy, rapine, cruelty, drunkenness, and all kinds of debauchery. To such contemptible divinities, splendid temples were erected,* adorations addressed, costly offerings presented, and rites and ceremonies performed, subversive of every principle of decency and morality, and degrading to the reason and the character of man.—A system of idolatry of a similar kind, though under a different form, prevailed among the Egyptians. The meanest and the most contemptible objects—sheep, cats, bulls, dogs, cows, storks, apes, vultures, and other birds of prey; wolves, and several sorts of oxen, were exalted as objects of adoration. "If you go into Egypt," says Lucian, "you will see Jupiter with the face of a *ram*, Mercury as a fine *dog*, Pan, is become a *goat*; another god is *Ibis*, another the crocodile, and another the ape. There, many shaven priests gravely tell us, that the gods being afraid of the rebellion of the giants, assumed these shapes." Each city and district in Egypt entertained a peculiar devotion for

* The temple of *Diana* at *Ephesus*, has been always admired as one of the noblest pieces of architecture that the world ever produced. It was 425 feet long, 200 feet broad, and supported by 127 columns of marble 60 feet high; 27 of which were beautifully carved. Diodorus Siculus mentions, that the rich presents made to the temple of *Apollo* at Delphos, amounted to one million three hundred and thirty three thousand pounds.

some animal or other, as the object of its adoration. The city of Lentopolis worshipped a lion; the city of Mendez, a goat; Memphis, the Apis; and the people at the lake *Myris*, adored the crocodile. These animals were maintained, in or near their temples, with delicate meats; were bathed, anointed, perfumed, had beds prepared for them; and when any of them happened to die, sumptuous funerals were prepared in honour of the god. Of all these animals, the bull, *Apis*, was held in the greatest veneration. Honours of an extraordinary kind were conferred on him while he lived, and his death gave rise to a general mourning.

Such was the abominable idolatry that prevailed even among the most enlightened nations of antiquity. They changed the glory of the incorruptible God into "the similitude of an ox that eateth grass," and into images made like to corruptible man and to birds, and to four-footed beasts, and creeping things. And if the Egyptians, the Greeks, and the Romans, who are distinguished from the rest of the world for their improvements in literature, science, and the arts, had so far renounced their allegiance to the God of heaven, we may rest assured that the surrounding nations were sunk still farther into the pollutions of idolatry and of mental debasement. The Phenicians, the Syrians, the Canaanites, the Chaldeans and Babylonians, the Arabians, the Scythians, the Ethiopians, and the Carthaginians, the ancient Gauls, Germans, and Britons, were, if possible, more deeply debased; and mingled with their idolatrous rites, many cruel, obscene, and vile abominations.—Such is still the moral and religious debasement, even in modern times, of the greater part of the nations which dwell upon the earth. Even the Hindoos, the Birmans, the Chinese, the Persians, and the Japanese, though ranked among the most polished nations of the heathen world, are sunk into the grossest ignorance of the true God, and are found perpetrating, in their religious worship, deeds revolting to humanity, and stained with horrid cruelty and injustice.

The *moral effects* which were produced by a departure from this fundamental law of the Créator, were such as correspond with the abominations of that religious system which was adopted. Man is an imitative being; and he generally imitates the actions of those whom he conceives to be placed in a superior rank and station. When, therefore, the gods were introduced to his view, as swollen with pride, mad with rage, fired with revenge, inflamed with lust, engaged in wars, battles, and contests, delighting in scenes of blood and rapine, in hatred and mutual contentions, and in all kinds of riot and debauchery, it was natural to suppose that such passions and crimes would be imitated by their blinded votaries. Accordingly we find, that such vices universally prevailed, even among the politest nations of antiquity; and some of their sacred rites, solemnized in honour of their gods, were so bestial and shocking, as to excite horror in every mind possessed of the least sense of decency and virtue. They gloried in the desolation and destruction of neighbouring nations. To conquer, and oppress, and enslave their fellowmen, and to aggrandize themselves by slaughter and rapine, was the great object of their ambition. The law of kindness and of universal benevolence was trampled under foot, and even the common dictates of humanity, equity, and justice, were set at defiance. But this was not all—Idolatry soon began to instigate its votaries to the perpetration of the most revolting and unnatural *cruelties*. Dreadful tortures were inflicted on their bodies, to appease their offended deities; human victims, in vast numbers, were sacrificed, and even their infants and little children were thrown into the flames, as an offering to the idol which they adored.

The Mexicans were accustomed to treat themselves with the most inhuman austerities, thinking that the diabolical rage of their deities would be appeased by human blood. "It makes one shudder," says Clavigero, "to read the austerities which they practised upon themselves, either in atonement for their transgressions, or in preparation for their festivals. They mangled their flesh as if it had been insensible, and let their blood run in such profusion, as if it had been a superfluous fluid in the body. They pierced themselves with the sharpest spines of the aloe, and bored several parts of their bodies, particularly their ears, lips, tongues, and the fat of their arms and legs." The priests of Baal, we are told, in the book of Kings, "cut themselves with knives and lancets, till the blood gushed out upon them." When the Carthaginians were vanquished by Agathocles, king of Sicily, they conceived that their god, Jupiter Latialis was displeased with their conduct. In order to appease him, and propitiate his favour, they sacrificed to him, at once, *two hundred* sons of the first noblemen of their state. On the altars of Mexico, *twenty thousand* human beings are said to have been sacrificed every year; and *fifty thousand* were annually offered up in the various parts of that empire, accompanied with circumstances of such dreadful cruelty and horror, as makes us shudder at the recital. In Hindostan, even at the present day, several thousands of women are annually burned on the funeral piles of their deceased husbands, as victims to the religion they profess; besides multitudes of other human victims, which are crushed to death under the wheels of that infernal engine which supports the idol Juggernaut. Were the one hundredth part of the abominations which have been perpetrated under the system of idolatry, in those countries where it has prevailed, to be fully detailed, it would exhibit a picture of depravity and of infernal agency, at which the human mind would shrink back with horror; and would form a striking commentary on the divine declaration, that "the dark places of the earth are full of the habitations of horrid cruelty."

It appears, then, that a violation of the first precept of the moral law is the greatest crime of which a rational creature can be guilty; for it is the source of all the other crimes which have entailed wretchedness on mankind, and strewed the earth with devastation and carnage. It is a comprehensive summary of wickedness; which includes pride, falsehood, blasphemy, malignity, rebellion, hatred of moral excellence, and the basest ingratitude towards Him from whom we derived our being, and on whom we depend for all our enjoyments. It is a crime which, above all others, has a tendency to *degrade* the character of man; for where it abounds, the human mind is sunk into the lowest state, both of moral and of intellectual debasement. What a pitiful and humiliating sight is it, and what emotions of astonishment must it excite in the mind of an archangel, to behold a rational and immortal intelligence cutting down an oak in the forest, burning part of it in the fire, baking bread, and roasting flesh upon its embers, and forming the residue of it into an idol, falling down and worshipping it, and saying, "Deliver me, for thou art my God!"* And when we behold the same degraded mortal sacrificing the children of his own bowels before this stump of a tree, can we refrain from exclaiming, in the language of the prophet, "Be astonished, O ye heavens, at this; and be ye horribly afraid!" Were idolatry to become *universal* in the world, there is no crime, no species of cruelty, no moral abomination within the compass of the human heart to devise, but would soon be perpetrated without a blush, in the open face of day. Had not God, in his mercy, communicated a revelation of his will, in order to counteract the influence of Pagan theology,—instead of cultivating the powers of our minds, and expanding our conception of the Almighty, by a contemplation of his word and works, we might, at this moment, have been sunk into the lowest depths of moral degradation, been prostrating ourselves, in adoration, before a stupid ox or a block of marble, and sacrificing our sons and daughters to an infernal Moloch. It is one of the glories of Revelation, and a strong proof of its divine origin, that all its promises and threatenings, its admonitions and reproofs, its doctrines, its laws and ordinances, are directly opposed to every idolatrous practice; and that there is not a single instance in which the least countenance is given to any of the abominations of the Pagan world.

In the present age, and in the country in which we reside, we are in little danger of relapsing into the practices to which I have now adverted. But idolatry is not confined to the adoration of Pagan divinities: it has it seat in every heart where God is banished from the thoughts, and where pride, ambition, and avarice occupy the highest place. "*Covetousness*," or an inordinate love of wealth, is declared by the Apostle Paul to be "*idolatry*;" and such mental idolatry, though more refined than that of the heathen world, is almost equally abhorrent to the Divine Being, and equally subversive of the grand principles of Christian morality. If the acquisition of wealth and riches be the constant and *supreme* aim of any individual, Mammon is the god whom he regularly worships, and the God of heaven is dethroned from his seat in the affections. Such moral effects as the following are the natural results of this species of idolatry: It steels the heart against every benevolent and generous emotion; it shuts the ears to the cries of the poor and needy; it engenders cheating, falsehood, and deceit; it prevents the man in whom it predominates from exerting his active powers, and from contributing of his wealth to promote the happiness of mankind; it chains down his noble faculties to the objects of time and sense; it leads him to love and to serve himself more than the Creator; it wraps him up in selfishness, and an indifference to the concerns of all other beings; it destroys the principles of equity and justice; it blunts the feelings of humanity and compassion; and prevents him from attending to the salvation of his soul, and from looking at those things which are unseen and eternal. And in every other case where a similar principle holds the supreme seat in the affections, similar effects will be produced.

### THE SECOND COMMANDMENT.

*Thou shalt not make unto thee any graven image, nor any likeness of any thing that is in heaven above, or that is in the earth beneath, or that is in the waters under the earth: thou shalt not bow down thyself to them, nor serve them.*

The *first* commandment, which I have illustrated above, respects the *object* of our worship; forbidding us to substitute any other being in the room of God, or to offer it that homage which is due to the eternal Jehovah. This second commandment respects the *manner* in which he is to be worshipped. And in regard to the manner in which the Divine Being is to be contemplated and adored, it is expressly declared, that no *image* nor *representation* of this incomprehensible Being is at any time, or on any account, to be formed. This command, like the former, might at first sight appear to be unnecessary, if the almost universal practice of mankind had not taught us that there is no disposition which the

* See Isaiah xlv. 9—21.

human mind is more apt to indulge, than to endeavour to bring the invisible Divinity within the range of our senses, and to contemplate him as such a one as ourselves. The necessity of this injunction, its reasonableness, and the folly and absurdity of the practice against which it is directed, will appear from the following considerations.

The Divine Being fills the immensity of space with his presence, and to his essence we can set no bounds. He inhabited eternity, before the earth or the heavens were brought into existence, rejoicing in the contemplation of his own excellences, and in the future effects of his power and benevolence. He is a spiritual uncompounded substance, and consequently invisible to mortal eyes, and impalpable to every other organ of sensation. His omnipotence neither man nor angel can scan, nor can they explore the depths of his wisdom and intelligence. When universal silence and solitude reigned throughout the infinite void—when not a sound was heard nor an object seen within the immeasurable extent of boundless space—at his command, worlds, numerous as the sand, started into being. Thousands of suns diffused their splendours through the regions of immensity; the ponderous masses of the planetary globes were launched into existence, and impelled in their rapid courses through the sky; their surfaces were adorned with resplendent beauties, and replenished with myriads of delighted inhabitants. The seraphim and the cherubim began to chant their hymns of praise, and "shouted for joy" when they beheld new worlds emerging from the voids of space. Life, motion, activity, beauty, grandeur, splendid illumination, and rapturous joy, among unnumbered intelligences, burst upon the view, where a little before nothing appeared but one immense, dark, and cheerless void. And ever since duration began to be measured, either in heaven or on earth, by the revolutions of celestial orbs, the same omnipotent energy has been incessantly exerted in directing the movements of all worlds and systems, and in upholding them in their vast career. Of a being invested with attributes so glorious and incomprehensible, with power so astonishing in its effects, with goodness so boundless, and with wisdom so unsearchable, what image or representation can possibly be formed which will not tend to contract our conceptions, and to debase the character of the infinite and eternal Mind! "To whom will ye liken me, or shall I be equal, saith the HOLY ONE."

When a person of dignity and of respectability of character is *caricatured*, and associated with objects and circumstances that are mean, ridiculous, and grotesque, it has a tendency to degrade his character, and to lessen our veneration. For the respect we entertain for any individual is founded on the view we take of him in all the aspects in which he may be contemplated. For a similar reason, every attempt to represent the Divine Majesty by sensible images, must have a tendency to narrow our conceptions of his glory, to debase his character, and to lessen our reverence and esteem. What possible similitude can there be between that mighty being, who by his word lighted up the sun, and diffused ten thousands of such immense luminaries through the regions of creation, whose hand wields the planets, and rolls them through the tracts of immensity; between him who "meteth out the heavens with a span, and holds the ocean in the hollow of his hand," and the most resplendent image that was ever formed by human hands! Even the sun himself, with all his immensity of splendour, although our minds were expanded to comprehend his vast magnificence, would form but a poor and pitiful image of Him, whose breath has kindled ten thousand times ten thousand suns. How much less can a block of marble or a stupid ox adumbrate the glories of the King eternal, immortal, and invisible! It will doubtless redound to the eternal disgrace of the human character, in every region of the universe where it is known, that ever such an impious attempt was made by the inhabitants of our degenerate world, as to compare the glory of the incorruptible God to an image made like to corruptible man. Wherever such attempts have been made, there we behold human nature in its lowest state of debasement; the intellectual faculties darkened, bewildered, and degraded; the moral powers perverted and depraved; grovelling affections predominating over the dictates of reason, and diabolical passions raging without control. Hence, too, the debasing tendency of all those attempts which have been made to introduce into the Christian church, pictures and images, to represent "The invisible things of God," and the sufferings of the Redeemer. For, wherever such practices prevail, the minds of men will generally be found to entertain the grossest conceptions of the Divine Being, and of the solemn realities of religion.

But the principal reason why any representation of God is expressly forbidden in this commandment, is, that whenever such a practice commences, it infallibly ends in adoring the *image itself*, instead of the *object* it was intended to represent. Or, in other words, the breach of this commandment necessarily and uniformly leads to a breach of the first. Notwithstanding the shock which the human mind appears to have received by the fall, it is altogether inconceivable, that any tribe of mankind should have been so debased and brutalized, as, in the first instance, to mistake a crocodile, or the stump of a tree, however beautifully carved, for the Creator of heaven and earth. Such objects appear to have been first used as *symbols* or representations of the Deity, in order to assist the mind in forming a conception of his invisible attributes. But as they had a direct tendency to debase the mind, and to obscure the glory of the Divinity, in process of time they began to be regarded by the ignorant multitude as the very gods themselves, which they were at first intended to represent; and that tribute of adoration was paid to the *symbol* itself, which was originally intended to be given to the invisible God, through this sensible medium. And, when we contemplate kings and princes, poets and philosophers, heroes and sages, "young men and virgins, old men and children," whole provinces, nations, and continents, prostrating themselves before the shrine of such despicable and abominable idols, and the idea of the true God almost banished from the world, we have reason to feel ashamed, and to be deeply humbled, that we belong to a race of intelligences that have thus so grossly prostituted their rational and moral powers.

The only *natural* image or representation of God which is set before us for our contemplation, is, the boundless universe which his hands have formed; and his *moral* image is displayed in the laws which he has published, in the movements of his providence, and in the face of Jesus Christ his Son, who is "the image of the invisible God, and the brightness of his glory." All these exhibitions of the Divine Majesty, we are commanded to study, to contemplate, and admire; and it is essentially requisite in order to our acquiring correct and comprehensive views of the object of our adoration, that no one of these displays of the Divinity should be overlooked, or thrown into the shade. There are some Christians, who imagine they may acquire a competent knowledge of the character of God, although they should never spend a single moment in contemplating his perfections as displayed in his visible works. In regard to such, I hesitate not to affirm, that they are, to a certain extent, *idolaters*, and remain wilful idolaters, contented with the most inadequate and grovelling conceptions of the Deity, so long as they refuse to contemplate, with fixed attention, and with intelligence, the operations of his hands. If a man's ideas never extend beyond the bounds of his visible horizon, or beyond the limits of the country in which he resides, and if, at the same time, he has overlooked the most striking displays of divine wisdom and goodness within these bounds—his conceptions of the Divine Being himself, will nearly correspond with the conceptions he forms of his works. If his views be even confined within the limits of the globe on which he dwells, his conceptions of God will still be grovelling, distorted, and imperfect. And, therefore, the idea which such an individual forms to himself of God, may be inferior to that which is due to one of the higher orders of created intelligences. And, if so, he has only an image of a creature in his mind, instead of a comprehensive conception of the Great Creator. We have too much reason to believe, that there are multitudes in the religious world, who pass for enlightened Christians, whose ideas of the Supreme Ruler of the universe do not rise beyond the conceptions we ought to form of the powers and capacities of Gabriel the archangel, or of one of the highest order of the seraphim.

We can never expect, from the very nature of things, to be able to explore the depths of Jehovah's essence, or to comprehend the whole range of his dominions and government. But, a large portion of his operations lies open to our inspection; and it is from an enlightened contemplation of what is presented to our view in the visible universe, that we are to form our conceptions of the grandeur of the Eternal Mind. For, it may be admitted as an axiom, both in natural and revealed theology, that *our conceptions of God will nearly correspond with the conceptions we acquire of the nature and extent of his operations.* In the universe around us, we perceive an image of his infinity, in so far as a finite and material existence can adumbrate the attributes of an Infinite and Invisible Existence. When we lift our eyes towards the midnight sky, we behold a thousand suns diffusing their splendours from regions of space immeasurably distant. When we apply a telescope to any portion of this vast concave, we perceive thousands more which the unasisted eye cannot discern. When we increase the magnifying powers of the instrument, we descry numerous orbs of light, stretching still farther into the unfathomable depths of space; so that there appear no limits to the scene of creating power. When the eye of reason penetrates beyond all that is visible through the most powerful telescopes, it contemplates a boundless region teeming with other resplendent suns and systems, whose number and magnificence overwhelm the imagination; so that no limit can be set to the excursions of the intellect when it wings its flight over the wide empire of Jehovah. Over all this vast assemblage of material splendour, over its movements, and over all the diversified ranks of intelligence it supports, God eternally and unchangeably presides. He is an *Infinite* Being;—and in this immense universe which he has opened to our view, he has given us an image of his infinity, which corresponds with the perfections which the inspired writers ascribe to him—and without a contemplation of which, the mind must have a very unworthy and circumscribed idea of the attributes of the Eternal Mind. Even in many of the objects which surround us in this lower world, we perceive an image of the infinity of the Creator—particularly in those living worlds which are contained in a few drops of water, some of the inhabitants of which are several hundreds of thousands of times smaller than the least grain of sand.—To the contemplation of such objects we are directed by God himself, in order to acquire an impressive view of his character and operations. "Lift up your eyes on high, and behold who hath created these orbs, that bringeth out their host by number: he calleth them all by names, by the greatness of his might, for that he is strong in power."—And, the prophets, when reasoning against idolatry, present us with a train of thought similar to that to which I have now adverted. They describe the Almighty as "sitting on the circle of the heavens, and the inhabitants of the earth as grasshoppers in his sight." They represent him as "measuring the waters in the hollow of his hand, weighing the mountains in scales, and *meting out the heavens with a span*—before whom all nations are as the drop of a bucket, and are counted to him less than nothing and vanity."

It is strange, indeed, that the duty of contemplating the image of God as impressed upon his works, should be so much overlooked by the great body of the Christian world, notwithstanding the obvious reasonableness of this duty, and the pointed injunctions in relation to it which are reiterated in every department of the word of God. It is still more strange, that the instructions of many religious teachers have a tendency to dissuade Christians from engaging in this duty, by the foolish contrasts they attempt to draw between the word and the works of God; so that the great mass of Christians are left to remain half idolaters for want of those expansive conceptions of God which a knowledge of his works is calculated to produce.

It is also most unaccountable, on every principle of reason, and of Revelation, that the wilful neglect of this duty should never be accounted either as a sin, or as a want of that respect which is due to the Majesty of heaven. We have known persons rebuked, and even excluded from a Christian Church, for holding a metaphysical sentiment different from their brethren respecting the divine plans and decrees; but we never heard of an individual being either reproved or admonished by a Christian society, for neglecting to contemplate the character of God as displayed in his works, although he had lived fifty years amidst the magnificence of creation, and had acquired little more knowledge of his Creator, from this source, than the ox which browses on the grass. Yet, to this neglect is to be imputed a great proportion of those grovelling conceptions, superstitious notions, and distorted views of the doctrines of religion which still disgrace the Christian world. This fact is still more unaccountable, when we consider that a knowledge of the abstrusities and technicalities of science is not requisite in order to the performance of this duty. It requires only the eye of sense, of reason, and of devotion to be directed to the scene of divine operation within us, and around us, and to be occasionally fixed on the object we contemplate, in order to appreciate the perfections and the glory of the ever present Deity. Although there were no other striking objects around us, the single fact of the apparent revolution of the celestial concave, with all its magnificent orbs, around the earth every twenty-four hours, is sufficient to overpower the mind of every rational observer with admiration and wonder, if his attention were seriously directed to it only for a single hour. The ideas of majesty, of grandeur, and of omnipotent energy which this single circumstance is calculated to inspire, are such as irresistibly to lead the mind to the contemplation of a Being whose perfections are incomprehensible, and whose ways are past finding out. Yet, I believe, it may be affirmed with truth, that more than one half of the Christian world are ignorant that such a fact exists;* such is the indifference and the apathy with which many religionists view the wonderful works of God.

It was chiefly owing to such criminal inattention to the displays of the Divine Character in the works of creation, that the inhabitants of the Pagan world plunged themselves into all the absurdities and abominations of idolatry. "For the invisible things of God, even his eternal power and godhead, are clearly seen in the things that are made," if men would but open their eyes, and exercise their powers of intelligence. "The heavens declare the glory of Jehovah," they declare it to all the inhabitants of the earth. "There is no speech nor language where their voice is not heard: their line is gone out through all the earth, and their words to the end of the world."

"In reason's ear they all rejoice,
And utter forth a glorious voice;
For ever singing, as they shine,
'The hand that made us is divine.'"

But the Heathen world did not listen to the instructions thus conveyed, nor did they apply their understandings, as they ought to have done, to trace the invisible things of God, from the visible displays of his character and perfections, in the universe around them. "They became vain in their imaginations, and their foolish hearts were darkened; and professing themselves to be wise, they became fools." While "the harp and the viol, the tabret, the pipe, and the wine were in their feasts, they regarded not the works of the Lord, nor considered the operations of his hands." "Wherefore they were given up by God to indulge" in vile affections, and "to worship and serve the creature rather than the Creator, who is blessed for ever." And, even under the

* Here I refer simply to the *apparent* motion of the heavens—leaving every one to form his own opinion as to the other alternative—the motion of the earth. In either case the mind is overpowered with ideas of grandeur and of Almighty power. See this topic more particularly illustrated in "Christ. Philosopher,"

Christian dispensation, we have too much reason to fear, that effects somewhat analogous to these have been produced, and a species of mental idolatry practised by thousands who have professed the religion of Jesus; owing to their inattention to the visible operations of Jehovah, and to their not connecting them with the displays of his character and agency as exhibited in the revelations of his word.

### THE THIRD COMMANDMENT.

*Thou shalt not take the name of the Lord thy God in vain.*

The *name* of any person is that which distinguishes him from other individuals. Whatever word is employed to distinguish any object, whether animate or inanimate, is its name. In like manner, the *Name* of God is that by which he is distinguished from all other beings. It includes those *terms* which express his nature and character, as *Jehovah*—those *titles* by which his relation to his creation is designated, as "The Creator of the ends of the earth,—The Father of mercies,—The God of salvation," &c.—the *attributes* of which he is possessed, as his Eternity, Omnipotence, Holiness, Justice, &c.—the *works* which he has exhibited in heaven and on earth—the movements of his *Providence*, and the *Revelations* of his word. By every one of these, the character of God is distinguished from that of all other beings in the universe. In relation to this name or character of the Divine Being, it is solemnly commanded that "we are not to take it in vain,"—that is, we are not to use any of the titles or designations of the Divine Majesty, for trifling, vain, or evil purposes; nor are we to treat any displays of his character with levity, profaneness, or irreverence.

We violate this command, when we use the name of God, in common discourse, in a light and irreverent manner, when we interlard our conversations with unnecessary oaths and asseverations in which this name is introduced; when we swear to what we know to be false, or when we multiply oaths in reference to vain and trifling concerns; when we imprecate curses and damnation on our fellow-creatures; when we approach God in prayer, without those feelings of reverence and awe, which his perfections demand; when we swear by any object in heaven or in earth, or by the false deities of the heathen world; when we treat his wonderful works with indifference or contempt; when we endeavour to caricature, and misrepresent them, or attempt to throw a veil over their glory; when we insinuate that his most glorious and magnificient works were made for no end, or for no end worthy of that infinite wisdom and intelligence by which they were contrived; when we overlook or deny the Divine Agency, which is displayed in the operations of nature; when we murmur and repine at his moral dispensations, or treat the mighty movements of his providence, whether in ancient or in modern times, with a spirit of levity, with ridicule, or with contempt; when we treat the revelations of the Bible with indifference or with scorn; when we make the declarations of that book, which unfolds to us the sublime and adorable character of Jehovah, the subject of merriment and jest; when we endeavour to throw upon them contempt and ridicule, with the view of undermining their divine authority; and when we sneer at the public and private worship of God, and at the ordinances which he hath appointed. —In all these and many other ways, the name of God is profaned, his character reproached, and that *reverence* of the Divine Being, which is the foundation of all religion and moral order, undermined and subverted.

When the name or the titles by which a fellow-mortal is distinguished, are made the subject of banter and ridicule in every company, when they are brought forward for the purpose of giving an edge to a sarcastic sneer; and when his employments and the works he has constructed are contemned, and associated with every thing that is mean and degrading; it is an evidence of the low estimation in which he is held by the individual who does so, and has a tendency to debase his character in the eyes of others. On the same principle, the profanation of the name of God, has an evident tendency to lessen our admiration of the Majesty of Heaven, and to banish from the mind every sentiment of veneration and reverence. The man who can deliberately violate this command, from day to day,—thus offering a continual insult to his Maker—proclaims to all around, that he has no emotions of reverence and affection towards that Almighty Being, whose power upholds the fabric of heaven and earth, and who dispenses life and death to whomsoever he pleases. "He stretcheth out his hand against God, and strengtheneth himself against the Almighty." He proclaims to every reflecting mind, that pride, enmity, rebellion, and irreverence, are deeply seated in his heart, and that "the fear of God," and the solemnities of a future judgment "are not before his eyes."

Were the violation of this law to become *universal* among men—the name of God, among all ranks, ages, and conditions of life, would be associated, not only with every trifling discourse and altercation, but with every species of ribaldry and obscenity. The lisping babe would be taught to insult that Mighty Being, from whom it so lately derived its existence; and the man of hoary hairs, even in the agonies of death, would pass into the eternal state, imprecating the vengeance of his Maker. All reverence for Jehovah would, of course, be banished from society; no temples would be erected to his honour; no silent adorations of the heart would ascend to his throne; no vows would be paid; no forms of worship appointed; no tribute of thanksgiving and gratitude would be offered to his name,—but the voice of profanity and of execration, among high and low, rich and poor, the young and the old, in every social intercourse, and in every transaction, would resound throughout all lands. No motives to excite to moral action, would be derived from the authority and the omnipresence of God, and from a consideration of his future retributions; for his character would be reproached, and his authority trampled under foot by all people. "They would set their mouths against the heavens in their blasphemous talk," and they would say, "How doth God know, and is there knowledge in the Most High?" "What is the Almighty that we should serve him, and what profit shall we have, if we pray unto him?" "The Lord doth not see, neither doth the God of Jacob regard us." His wonderful works would either be overlooked, or treated with contempt, or ascribed to the blind operation of chance or of fate. They would be represented as accomplishing no end, as displaying no wisdom, and as controlled by no intelligent agency. Their *apparent* irregularities and defects would be magnified, and expatiated upon with diabolical delight; while the glorious evidences they exhibit of infinite wisdom and beneficence would be thrown completely into the shade. The dispensations of his providence would be viewed as an inextricable maze, without order or design, directed by chance, and by the ever-varying caprice of human beings. His venerable word would universally become the subject of merriment and laughter,—a topic for the exercise of ribaldry and ridicule, and a theme for enlivening the unhallowed song of the drunkard. The most solemn scenes which it displays, and its most joyful and alarming declarations, would be equally treated with levity and contempt.—Such are some of the impious practices, and horrible effects which would follow, if the name of Jehovah were universally profaned. The very name of religion would be blotted out from the earth, its forms abolished, its sanctions disregarded, its laws violated, virtue and piety annihilated, the flood-gates of every evil burst open, and moral order entirely subverted.

On the other hand, universal reverence of the name and character of God would lead to the practice of all the duties of piety and morality. The Most High would be recognised with sentiments of veneration at all times; and the silent adorations of the heart would flow out towards him in all places; in the house, and in the street, in the bosom of the forest, and in the fertile plain, in the city, and in the wilderness, under the shades of night, and amidst the splendours of day. In every place, temples would be erected for his worship, hallelujahs of praise would ascend, and "incense and a pure offering" be presented to his name. With reverence and godly fear, with expansive views of his magnificence and glory, with emotions of affection and of awe would his worshippers approach him in prayer, in praise, in contemplation, and in all the services of his sanctuary. The whole earth would be consecrated as one grand temple, from which a grateful homage would ascend from the hearts and from the lips of millions of devout worshippers, in all places, from the rising to the setting sun. In the domestic circle, in the social club, in the convivial meeting, in the streets, in "the high places of the city," in the public walks, in the councils of the nations, and in every other intercourse of human beings, the name of God would never be mentioned nor his character alluded to, but with feelings of profound and reverential awe. His works would be contemplated with admiration, with reverence, and with gratitude, as proclaiming the glory of his kingdom, the depths of his wisdom, and the extent of his power. His mighty movements among the nations would be regarded with submission and reverence, as accomplishing the eternal purposes of his will, and his holy word would be perused by all classes of men with affection and delight, as the oracle which proclaims the glories of his nature and the excellence of his laws, the blessings of his salvation, and the path which conducts to eternal felicity in the life to come. Such are some of the delightful effects which would follow, were a sentiment of profound reverence to pervade the whole mass of human beings;—and corresponding sentiments of love and affection for each other, would be the necessary and unceasing accompaniments of respect and veneration for their common Parent.

### THE FOURTH COMMANDMENT.

"*Remember the Sabbath day, to keep it holy. Six days shalt thou labour, and do all thy work; but the seventh day is the Sabbath of the Lord thy God,*" *&c.*

This commandment obviously enjoins the setting apart of one day in seven, as a day of rest from worldly labour, and as a portion of time to be devoted to the devotional exercises of religion, and particularly to the public worship of God. It was given forth, not merely to display the Sovereignty of the Lawgiver; but to promote both the sensitive and the intellectual enjoyment of man. "The Sabbath," says our Saviour, "was made *for man*, and not man for the Sabbath."

It was made for man, in the *first* place, as *a day of rest*. In this point of view, it is a most wise and merciful appointment, especially when we consider the present condition of mankind, as doomed to labour, and toil, and to the endurance of many sorrows. When we reflect on the tyrannical dispositions which prevail among mankind, on the powerful influence of avarice over the human mind, and on the almost total absence of benevolence and compassion towards suffering humanity, wherever such dispositions predominate, we cannot but admire the wisdom and benevolence of the Creator, in the appointment of a weekly jubilee for the rest and refreshment of labourers spent with toil. On this day, the master has an opportunity of divesting his mind of worldly cares and anxieties, the servant of obtaining liberty and respite from his toilsome employments; and labourers of every class, of enjoying repose in the bosom of their families. Such, however, are the avaricious dispositions, and the contracted views of a great proportion of mankind, that they are apt to regard the institution of the Sabbath as an obstruction to the advancement of their worldly interests. They will calculate how much labour has been lost by the rest of one day in seven, and how much wealth might have been gained, had the Sabbath not intervened to interrupt their employments. But all such selfish calculations, even in a worldly point of view, proceed on the principles of a narrow and short-sighted policy. We know by experience, that, on the six days out of seven appointed for labour, all the operations requisite for the cultivation of the fields, and for the manufacture of every useful article for the comfort of mankind, can be performed with ease, and without the least injury to any class of men. And what more could be accomplished, although the Sabbath were converted into a day of labour? Were this violation of the divine command to become universal, it might be shown that, instead of producing an increase of wealth, it would infallibly produce an increase of toil and misery in relation to the great mass of mankind, without any corresponding pecuniary compensation. The labouring class at present receive little more wages than is barely sufficient to procure the necessaries of life. If their physical strength would permit them to work eighteen hours a day, instead of twelve, it is beyond a doubt, that, in a very short time, the work of eighteen hours would be demanded by their employers for the price of twelve—particularly in all cases where a sufficient number of labourers can be easily obtained. In like manner, were the Sabbath to be used as a day of labour, the wages of seven days would soon be reduced to what is now given for the labour of six. In the first instance, indeed, before such a change was thoroughly effected, the labouring part of the community would acquire a seventh part more wages every week than they did before; and men unaccustomed to reflection, and who never look beyond a present temporary advantage, would imagine that they had acquired a new resource for increasing their worldly gain. But, in a very short time, when the affairs of the social state were brought to a certain equilibrium, they would be miserably undeceived; and the abolition of the Sabbath, instead of bringing along with it an increase of wealth, would carry in its train an increase of labour,—a continued series of toilsome and unremitting exertions, which would waste their animal powers, cut short the years of their mortal existences, "make their lives bitter with hard bondage," and deprive them of some of the sweetest enjoyments which they now possess.

And as the sabbath was appointed for the rest of *man*, so it was also intended as a season of repose for the *inferior animals* which labour for our profit. "The seventh day is the Sabbath of the Lord thy God; in it thou shalt not do any work, thou, nor thy son, nor thy daughter, thy man-servant, nor thy maid-servant, *nor thy cattle*, nor the stranger that is within thy gates." This injunction exhibits the compassionate care and tenderness of the Creator in a very amiable and impressive point of view. It shows us, that the enjoyments of the lowest ranks of sensitive existence are not beneath his notice and regard. As he knew what degree of relaxation was necessary for the comfort of the labouring animals, and as he foresaw that the avarice and cruelty of man would endeavour to deprive them of their due repose, so he has secured to them, by a law which is to continue in force so long as the earth endures, the rest of one day in seven in common with their proprietors and superiors. And this privilege they will undoubtedly enjoy hereafter, in a more eminent degree than they have yet done, when man himself shall be induced to pay a more cordial and unreserved obedience to this divine precept,—when "he shall call the Sabbath a delight, and the holy of the Lord honourable."

Again, the Sabbath was appointed for man, as *a season for pious recollection, and religious contemplation*. "Remember the Sabbath day, *to keep it holy*." Amidst the numerous cares and laborious employments of human life, it is impossible to fix the mind, for any length of time, on the divine glory, as displayed in the works of creation, on the important facts and doctrines of revealed religion, and on the grand realities of the life to come. And, therefore, if the labouring classes enjoyed no regular season of repose for serious reflection, and religious instruction, the objects of religion would soon be entirly neglected, and the impression of a future world evanish from the mind. But in the wise arrangements of the beneficent Creator, an opportunity is afforded to all ranks of men for cultivating their moral and intellectual powers, and for directing them to the study and contemplation of the most glorious and interesting objects. As the Sabbath was originally instituted as a sacred memorial of the finishing of the work of creation, so it is obvious that the contemplation of the fabric of the universe, and of the perfections of its Almighty Author therein displayed, ought to form one part of the exercises of this holy day; and, consequently, that illustrations of this subject ought to be frequently brought before the view of the mind in those discourses which are delivered in the assemblies of the saints. Since the references to this subject, throughout the whole of divine revelation, are so frequent and so explicit, it is evident, that the Creator intended that this amazing work of his should be contemplated with admiration, and make a deep and reverential impression upon every mind. To call to remembrance a period when there was no terraqueous globe, no sun, nor moon, nor planets, nor starry firmament, when darkness and inanity reigned throughout the infinite void—to listen to the voice of God resounding through the regions of boundless space, "LET THERE BE LIGHT; and light was"—to behold ten thousands of spacious suns instantly lighted up at his command—to trace the mighty masses of the planetary worlds projected from the hand of Omnipotence, and running their ample circuits with a rapidity which overwhelms our conceptions—to contemplate the globe on which we stand emerging from darkness and confusion to light and order; adorned with diversified scenes of beauty and of sublimity, with mountains, and plains, with rivers, and seas, and oceans; and with every variety of shade and colour; cheered with the melody of the feathered songsters, and with the voice of man, the image of his Maker, where a little before eternal silence had prevailed,—to reflect on the Almighty energy, the boundless intelligence, and the overflowing beneficence displayed in this amazing scene—has a tendency to elevate and expand the faculties of the human mind, and to excite emotions of reverence and adoration of the omnipotent Creator. This is a work which the eternal Jehovah evidently intended to be held in everlasting remembrance, by man on earth, and by all the inhabitants of the heavenly regions. It is the mirror of the Deity, and the natural image of the invisible God; and it forms the *groundwork* of all those moral dispensations towards his intelligent offspring, which will run parallel with eternity itself. And, therefore, to overlook this subject in the exercises of the Sabbath, is to throw a veil over the glories of the Deity, to disregard the admonitions of his word, and to contemn one of the most magnificent and astonishing displays of Divine perfection. "By the word of Jehovah were the heavens made, and all the host of them, by the breath of his mouth. He gathereth the waters of the sea together as an heap, he layeth up the depth in storehouses. Let all the earth fear the Lord; let all the inhabitants of the world stand in awe of him. For he spake, and it was done, he commanded, and it stood fast."

This is a command which never was abrogated, and which never can be abrogated in relation to any intelligent beings, so long as the Creator exists, and so long as the universe remains as a memorial of his power and intelligence. Those sacred songs which are recorded in scripture for directing the train of our devotional exercises, are full of this subject, and contain specimens of elevated sentiments, of sublime devotion, incomparably superior to what is to be found in any other record, whether ancient or modern.* But man, whose unhallowed hand pollutes and degrades every portion of revelation which he attempts to improve, has either endeavoured to set aside the literal and sublime references of these divine compositions, or to substitute in their place the vague and extravagant fancies of weak and injudicious minds, for directing the devotional exercises of Christian churches.† As the book of God is the only correct standard of religious worship, so our devotional exercises both in public and in private, ought to be chiefly, if not solely, directed by the examples of devotion contained in the inspired writings, which are calculated to regulate and enliven the pious exercises of men of every age and of every clime.

But, the celebration of the work of creation is not the only, nor the principal exercise to which we are called on the Christian sabbath. Had man continued in primeval innocence, this would probably have constituted his chief employment. But he is now called to celebrate, in conjunction with this exercise, a most glorious deliverance from sin and misery, effected by the Redeemer of mankind. And, for this reason, the Sabbath has been changed from the seventh to the *first* day of the week, in memorial of the resurrection of Christ, when he was "declared to be the Son

* See particularly Psalms 8, 18, 19, 29, 33, 65, 66, 68, 74, 89, 92, 93, 94, 95, 96, 100, 104, 107, 111, 135, 136, 139, 145, 146, 147, 148, &c. &c.

† I here allude to several collections of *Hymns* which have been introduced into the public worship of Christian societies—many of which, contain a number of vague and injudicious sentiments, and extravagant fancies, while they entirely omit many of those subjects on which the inspired writers delight to expatiate. This position could easily be illustrated by abundance of examples, were it expedient in this place. I am firmly of opinion, that the praises of the Christian church ought to be celebrated in *Scripture-language*—that selections for this purpose should be made from the book of Psalms, the Prophets, and the New Testament writers, which shall embody every sentiment expressed in the original, without gloss or comment, and be as nearly as possible in the very words of Scripture. This has been partly effected in many of the Psalms contained in metrical version, used in the Scottish Church, in which simplicity, and sublimity, and a strict adherence to the original, are beautifully exemplified. In this case there would be no need for a separate hymn-book for Baptists, Methodists, Independents, Presbyterians, and Episcopalians. But, when a poet takes an insulated passage of Scripture, and spins out a dozen stanzas about it, he may interweave, and most frequently does, as many fancies of his own as he pleases. Were the ideas contained in certain hymns to be painted on canvass, they would represent, either a congeries of clouds and mists, or a group of distorted and unnatural objects. And why should such vague fancies, and injudicious representations, be imposed on a Christian assembly? What a disgrace is thrown upon Christianity, when the different sects of Christians cannot cordially join together in the *same songs* of thanksgiving and praise to their common Father and Lord!

of God with power." In this deliverance, as in the first creation, a variety of the grandest and most interesting objects is presented to our view:—The Son of God manifested in the flesh—the *moral* image of the invisible Creator embodied in a human form, displaying every heavenly disposition, and every divine virtue, performing a series of the most astonishing and beneficent miracles, giving sight to the blind, and hearing to the deaf, making the lame man leap as a hart, and the tongue of the dumb to sing, restoring the infuriated maniac to the exercise of reason, commanding diseases to fly at the signal of a touch, recalling departed spirits from the invisible world, raising the dead to life, and, on every occasion, imparting heavenly instructions to attending multitudes. We behold this illustrious personage suspended on the cross, encompassed with the waters of affliction, and with the agonies of death; the veil of the temple rent in twain, from the top to the bottom—the rocks of mount Calvary rent asunder—the sun covered with blackness—darkness surrounding the whole land of Judea—the graves opening—the dead arising, and the Prince of Life consigned to the mansions of the tomb. On the third morning after this solemn scene, "a great earthquake" having shaken the sepulchre of the Saviour, we behold him bursting the prison-doors of the tomb, and awakening to a new life, which shall never end—we behold celestial messengers, in resplendent forms, descending from the ethereal regions to announce to his disconsolate disciples, that he who was dead "is alive, and lives for evermore;" we behold him, at length, bestowing his last benediction on his faithful followers, rising above the confines of this earthly ball, winging his way on a resplendent cloud, attended by myriads of angels, through distant regions which "eye hath not seen;" and entering "into heaven itself, there to appear in the presence of God for us." In the redemption achieved by this glorious person, we are directed to look back on that scene of misery in which sin has involved the human race, and to those "regions of sorrow and doleful shades," from which his mercy has delivered us; and to look forward to a complete deliverance from moral evil, to a resurrection from the grave, to a general assembly of the whole race of Adam—to the destruction and renovation of this vast globe on which we dwell, and to the enjoyment of uninterrupted felicity, in brighter regions, while countless ages roll away.—Such are some of the sublime and interesting objects which we are called upon to contemplate and to celebrate on the day appointed for the Christian sabbath—objects which have a tendency to inspire the mind with sacred joy, and with an anticipation of noble employments in the life to come.

Again, the Sabbath was appointed as a stated season *for the public worship of God*. As mankind are connected by innumerable ties, as they are subject to the same wants and infirmities, are exposed to the same sorrows and afflictions, and stand in need of the same blessings from God,—it is highly reasonable and becoming, that they should frequently meet together, to offer up in unison their thanksgiving and praise to their common Benefactor, and to supplicate the throne of his mercy. These exercises are connected with a variety of interesting and important associations. In the public assemblies where religious worship is performed, "the rich and the poor meet together." Within the same walls, those who would never have met in any other circumstances, are placed exactly in the same situation before Him in whose presence all earthly distinctions evanish, and who is the Lord, and "the Maker of them all." Here, pride and haughtiness are abased; all are placed on the same level as sinners before Him "who is of purer eyes than to behold iniquity; the loftiness of man is humbled, the poor are raised from the dust, and the Lord alone is exalted in the courts of his holiness. Here, cleanliness and decency of apparel are to be seen, and human nature appears, both in its physical and its moral grandeur.* Here, civility of deportment, and kindly affections are generally displayed. Here, we feel ourselves in the immediate presence of Him before whom all nations are as the drop of a bucket; we feel our guilty and dependant character, and stand, as suppliants, for mercy to pardon, and for grace to help us in the time of need. Here, knowledge of the most important kind is communicated to assembled multitudes, almost "without money and without price." Here, the poorest beggar, the youth, and the man of hoary hairs, may learn the character of the true God, and of Jesus Christ whom he hath sent—the way to eternal happiness—the sources of consolation under the afflictions of life—and the duties they owe to their Creator, and to all mankind. In a word, here the sinner, in the midst of his unhallowed courses, is aroused to consideration; and here the saint is animated and encouraged in his Christian journey, and enjoys a foretaste of the blessedness of heaven, and an earnest of the delightful intercourses and employments of "the saints in light."

Let us now suppose, for a moment, that the Sabbath, and its exercises, were *universally abolished* from the civilized world. What would be the consequences? The knowledge of the true God, which the institution of the Sabbath, more than any other mean, has tended to perpetuate, would soon be lost, his worship abandoned, and religion and moral principle buried in the dust. In Pagan countries, where the Sabbath is un-

* What a striking contrast, even in a physical point of view, is presented between a modern assembly of Christian worshippers, and the hideous and filthy group of human beings that are to be seen in the kraal of a Hottentot, or in the cave of a New Hollander.

known, the true God is never adored, the soul of man is debased, and prostrates itself before the sun and moon, and even before demons, monsters, insects, reptiles, and blocks of wood and stone. In France, where the Sabbath was for a season abolished, an impious phantom, called the Goddess of Reason, was substituted in the room of the Omnipotent and Eternal God; the Bible was held up to ridicule, and committed to the flames; man was degraded to the level of the brutes; his mind was assimilated to a piece of clay, and the cheering prospects of immortality were transformed into the shades of an eternal night. Atheism, Scepticism, and Fatalism, almost universally prevailed; the laws of morality were trampled under foot; and anarchy, plots, assassinations, massacres, and legalized plunder, became "the order of the day."—With the loss of the knowledge of God, all impressions of the Divine presence, and all sense of accountableness for human actions, would be destroyed. The restraints of religion, and the prospect of a future judgment, would no longer deter from the commission of crimes; and nothing but the dread of the dungeon, the gibbet, or the rack, would restrain mankind from the constant perpetration of cruelty, injustice, and deeds of violence. No social prayers, from assembled multitudes, would be offered up to the Father of mercies; no voice of thanksgiving and praise would ascend to the Ruler of the skies; the work of creation, as displaying the perfections of the Deity, would cease to be admired and commemorated; and the movements of Providence, and the glories of redemption, would be overlooked and disregarded. The pursuit of the objects of time and sense, which can be enjoyed only for a few fleeting years, would absorb every faculty of the soul; and the realities of the eternal world would either be forgotten, or regarded as idle dreams. In short, were the Sabbath abolished, or, were the law which enforces its observance to be reversed, man would be doomed to spend his mortal existence in an unbroken series of incessant labour and toil; his mental powers would languish, and his bodily strength would be speedily wasted. Habits of cleanliness, civility of deportment, and decency of apparel, would be disregarded; and the persons, and the habitations of the labouring classes, would soon resemble the filthiness and the wretched objects which are seen in the kraal of a Hottentot. Their minds would neither be cheered with the prospect of seasons of stated repose in this world, nor with the hope of eternal rest and joy in the world to come.

### THE FIFTH COMMANDMENT.

"*Honour thy Father and thy Mother.*"

The four preceding commandments, whose importance I have endeavoured to illustrate, were written on a separate tablet from those that follow, and have been generally considered as enjoining the practice of *piety*, or those duties which more immediately respect God as their object. But they also include the duties we owe to *ourselves;* for in yielding obedience to these requirements, we promote our best interests in this world, and are gradually prepared for participating in the enjoyments of the world to come. These laws are binding upon angels and archangels, and upon every class of intelligent beings, in whatever quarter of the universe their local residence may be found, as well as upon the inhabitants of the earth. The fourth commandment, indeed, in so far as regards the *particular portion of time* to be set apart for the worship of God, may possibly be peculiar to the inhabitants of our world. Even although the inhabitants of such a world as the planet Jupiter were commanded to set apart every seventh natural day for the stated public worship of God, the proportion of absolute time allotted for this purpose, would not be the same as ours; for the natural day in that world is equal to only ten hours of our time. But the spirit of this precept, or, the principle on which it is founded, must be common to all worlds. For we can conceive of no class of intelligent creatures, on whom it is not obligatory to devote a certain portion of time for the social worship and adoration of their Creator, and for commemorating the displays of his Power and Benevolence; and all holy intelligences will cheerfully join in such exercises, and will consider it as a most ennobling and delightful privilege, to engage at stated seasons, along with their fellow-worshippers, in admiring and extolling the Uncreated Source of their enjoyments. But the stated seasons appointed by the Creator for such solemn acts of worship, the manner and circumstances in which they shall be performed, and the number of worshippers that may assemble on such occasions, may be different in different worlds, according to the situations in which they are placed.

The fifth commandment, to which I am now to advert, is one of those moral regulations which may possibly be peculiar to the relations which exist in our world; at least, it cannot be supposed to apply to the inhabitants of any world where the relations of parents and children, of superiors and inferiors, are altogether unknown. But, in the circumstances in which man is placed, it is a law indispensably requisite for preserving the order and happiness of the social system.—It requires the exercise of those dispositions, and the performance of those duties, which are incumbent upon mankind, *in the various relations in which they stand to each other.* It, consequently, includes within its spirit and references, the duties which children owe to their parents, and parents to their children; the duties of husbands and wives, of masters and servants, of teachers and scholars, of brothers and sisters, of the young and the old, and of governors and their subjects; together with all those dispositions of reverence, submission, affection, gratitude, and respect, with which the performance of these duties ought to be accompanied. It must also be considered as forbidding every thing that is opposed to these dispositions, and to the obedience required; as contumacy, rebellion, and want of respect, on the part of children towards their parents; disobedience of servants to the reasonable commands of their masters; and every principle of disaffection and of insubordination among the various ranks of society. That all this is included within the range of this precept, might be proved from the principles on which our Saviour explains the *sixth* and *seventh* commandments, in his Sermon on the Mount, and from the illustrations of these duties which are given in the Apostolic epistles, and in other parts of Scripture.

As it forms no part of my plan, to enter into any particular explanations of the duties required in the Decalogue, which have frequently been expounded by many respectable writers, in works particularly appropriated to this object,—I shall simply illustrate, in a few words, the reasonableness of this, and the following precepts, from a consideration of the effects which would follow, were these laws either universally observed, or universally violated.

Were this law to be reversed, or universally violated, it is impossible to form an adequate conception of the dreadful scene of anarchy and confusion which would immediately ensue. Every social tie would be torn asunder, every relation inverted, every principle of subordination destroyed, every government overturned, every rank and order of mankind annihilated, and the whole assembly of human beings converted into a discordant mass of lawless banditti. Every family would present a scene of riot, confusion, insubordination, contention, hatred, tumult, and incessant execration. Instead of love, peace, unity, and obedience, the son would rise in rebellion against his father, and the father would insult and trample under foot his son. To use the words of our Saviour, "The brother would deliver up the brother to death, and the father the child; and the children would rise up against their parents, and cause them to be put to death; the daughter would be set at variance against her mother, and the daughter-in-law against her mother-in-law; and a man's foes would be they of his own household." Children would be unprovided with proper food, clothing, and instruction, and left to wander, houseless and forlorn, as vagabonds on the face of the earth; and parents, abandoned by their children, in sickness, poverty, and old age, would sink into the grave in wretchedness and despair. The young, instead of "rising up before the hoary head, and honouring the face of the old man," would treat the aged and infirm with every mark of scorn, derision, and contempt; and would feel a diabolical delight in vexing, thwarting, and overpowering their superiors in age and station. No instructions could be communicated by teachers and guardians to the rising generation; for riot, insolence, insult, derision, and contempt, would frustrate every effort to communicate knowledge to a youthful group. No building nor other work of art could be commenced with the certain prospect of being ever finished; for its progress would depend upon the whims and humours of the workmen employed, who, of course, would rejoice in endeavouring to frustrate the plans and wishes of their employers. No regular government nor subordination in a large community, could possibly exist; for the great mass of society would endeavour to protect every delinquent, and would form themselves into a league to prevent the execution of the laws. These effects would inevitably follow, even although the requisition contained in this precept, were to be viewed as confined solely to the reverence and obedience which children owe to their parents. For, were this obedience withdrawn, and an opposite disposition and conduct uniformly manifested, the young would carry the same dispositions which they displayed towards their parents, into all the other scenes and relations of life, and fill the world with anarchy and confusion. But it would be needless to expatiate on this topic, as it appears obvious to the least reflecting mind, that a universal violation of this law would quite unhinge the whole fabric of society, and would soon put an end to the harmonious intercourse of human beings.

On the other hand, a constant and universal obedience to this precept would produce such effects on the deformed aspect of our world as would transform it into a paradise of moral beauty, of happiness and love. Every family would exhibit a picture of peace and concord, of harmony and affection. No harsh and bitter language, no strifes, nor jars, nor contentions would ever interrupt the delightful flow of reciprocal affection between parents and children. No longer should we behold the little perverse members of the domestic circle, indulging their sulky humours, and endeavouring to thwart the wishes of their superiors, nor the infuriated parent stamping and raging at the obstinacy of his children; nor should we hear the grating sounds of discord, and insubordination which now so frequently issue from the family mansion. Every parental command would be cheerfully and promptly obeyed. Reverence and filial affection would glow in every youthful breast towards the father that begat him, and towards the mother that gave him birth. Their persons, and their characters would be regarded with veneration and respect, and their admonitions submitted tc without a murmur or complaint. To gladden the hearts of their parents, to run at the least signal of their will, to share in their benignant smile or approbation, and to avoid every species of conduct that would produce the least uneasiness or pain—would be the unceasing aim of all the youthful members of the family circle. In sickness, they would smooth their pillows, and alleviate their sorrows, watch like guardian angels around their bed, drop the tear of affection, and pour the balm of consolation into their wounded spirits. In the decline of life, they would minister with tenderness to their support and enjoyment, guide their feeble steps, sympathize with them in their infirmities, cheer and animate their dejected spirits, and render their passage to the tomb smooth and comfortable. And how delighted would every parent feel amidst such displays of tenderness and affection! There is perhaps nothing in the whole range of human enjoyment that creates a higher and more unmingled gratification to parents, than the dutiful and affectionate conduct of their offspring. It sweetens all the bitter ingredients of human life, and adds a relish to all its other comforts and enjoyments. It imparts a continual satisfaction and serenity to the parental breast; it smooths the wrinkles of age; it cheers the spirits under the infirmities of declining nature, and makes the dying bed of old age comfortable and easy. And the joy and satisfaction thus felt by parents would be reflected into the bosom of their children; which would produce a union of interests, a cordiality of affection, and a peace and tranquillity of mind in every member of the family, which no adverse occurrence in future life could ever effectually destroy.

From the family circle the emanations of filial piety would spread and diffuse themselves through all the other departments of society. The same spirit of love and dutiful respect which united and endeared parents to children, and children to parents, would unite one family to another, one village to another, one city to another, one province to another, one kingdom and empire to another, till all the tribes of the human race were united in kindness and affection, as one great and harmonious family. Every dutiful child would become a faithful and obedient servant, a docile scholar, and a loyal and submissive subject, when placed in those relations; and would prove a blessing and an ornament to every society of which he was a member. And every dutiful and affectionate parent, when placed in the station of a king, or a subordinate ruler, would display a parental affection towards every member of the community over which he was appointed. Hence it might easily be shown, that an uninterrupted and universal observance of this single precept, viewed in all its connexions and bearings, would completely regenerate the world—and that the peace, the harmony, and the prosperity of all the nations of the earth, will ultimately depend on the spirit of filial piety being infused into every family. "Honour thy father and thy mother," says the Apostle, "which is the first commandment with promise; *that it may be well with thee, and that thou mayest live long upon the earth.*" These words, which are frequently repeated in Scripture, are not empty sounds; nor ought they to be deprived, even under the Christian dispensation, of their obvious and literal meaning. Filial piety has a natural tendency to produce health, long life, and prosperity; and could we trace the whole of the secret history of Providence in reference to this precept, we should, doubtless, find this position abundantly exemplified. At any rate, were it universally practised, it would carry along with it a train of blessings which would convert the tumults and convulsions of nations into peace and tranquillity, and transform the moral wilderness of this world into a scene of verdure, beauty, and loveliness, which would enrapture the mind of every moral intelligence; and among its other benefits, "length of days, and long life and peace," would undoubtedly "be added" to the other enjoyments of mankind.

### THE SIXTH COMMANDMENT.

"*Thou shalt not kill.*"

This precept forbids the taking away of the life of sensitive or intelligent existence. The command is *absolute*, without the least exception, as it stands in the Decalogue; and it is *universal*, extending to every rational and moral agent. It implies that, as every sensitive and every intelligent being derived its existence from the omnipotent Creator of heaven and earth, no one has a right to deprive it of that existence, except that Being by whom it was bestowed. And, whatever exceptions to the universality of this law may be admitted, they can be admitted only on the authority of the Lawgiver himself, who is the Original Fountain of existence to all his creatures. The principal exceptions to this law are the following:—1. The man who has violently taken away the life of another is commanded, by the authority of God, to be put to death. "Whoso sheddeth man's blood, by man shall his blood be shed." This is the dictate of reason as well as of revelation; for no human power can recall the departed spirit or re-animate the lifeless corpse, and no adequate compensation can ever be given for such a crime.* 2. The life of the lower animals is permitted by the same

* Notwithstanding the considerations here stated, the Author is doubtful whether the Creator has conceded to man the right of taking away the life of another, even in case of murder. If the passage here quoted ought to be considered as a *prediction* rather than a law, as is most probable, it will afford no warrant for the destruction of human life; and there is no other injunction of this kind which has any relation to the New Testament dispensation.

authority to be taken away *when these animals are necessary for our food, or when they endanger our existence.* This permission was first granted, immediately after the flood, to Noah and his descendants. "God said to Noah and his sons; every thing that moveth shall be meat for you; even as the green herb have I given you all things." Without such a positive grant from the Creator, man could have had no more right to take away the life of an ox or a sheep, than he has to imbrue his hands in the blood, or to feast on the flesh of his fellow-men. To take the life of any sensitive being, and to feed on its flesh, appears incompatible with a state of innocence; and, therefore, no such grant was given to Adam in paradise; nor does it appear that the Antedeluvians, notwithstanding their enormous crimes, ever feasted on the flesh of animals. It appears to have been a grant suited only to the degraded state of man after the deluge; and, it is probable, that as he advances in the scale of moral perfection, in the future ages of the world, the use of animal food will be gradually laid aside, and he will return again to the productions of the vegetable kingdom, as the original food of man, and as that which is best suited to the rank of rational and moral intelligence. And, perhaps, it may have an influence, in combination with other favourable circumstances, in promoting health and longevity. —But, although the inferior animals are, in the mean time, subjected to our use, no permission is granted to treat them with harshness or cruelty, or to kill them for the sake of sport and amusement. And, therefore, the man who wantonly takes away the lives of birds, hares, fishes, and other animals, for the mere gratification of a taste for hunting or fishing, can scarcely be exculpated from the charge of a breach of this commandment.

The above are the principal exceptions which the Creator has made in reference to the law under consideration. And it may not be improper to remark, that, besides the direct act of murder, every thing that leads to it, or that has a tendency to endanger life, is to be considered as forbidden in this commandment. All unkindness and harsh treatment exercised towards servants, dependants, and brute animals, by which life may be shortened or rendered intolerable—all furious and revengeful passions, which may lead to acts of violence—all quarrelling, fighting, and boxing, either for bets, or for the gratification of hatred or revenge—all wishes for the death of others, and all contrivances either direct or indirect to compass the destruction of our neighbour—all criminal negligence by which our own life or the life of others may be endangered or destroyed—and all those actions by which murder may be committed as a probable effect, as the burning of inhabited houses, and the throwing of the instruments of death into the midst of a crowd—are to be regarded as involving the principle of murder, as well as the direct acts of suicide, duelling, and assassination; and, consequently, as violations of that law which extends to the secret purposes of the heart, as well as to the external actions. Even unreasonable anger, malice, and scurrility are declared by our Saviour to be a species of murder: "Whosoever is angry with his brother without a cause, shall be in danger of the judgment, and whosoever shall say to his brother, *Raca*," that is, thou worthless empty fellow, "shall be in danger of the council."* Life is desirable only as it is connected with enjoyment, and, therefore, when a man treats his brother with such a degree of hatred and scurrility, as to render his existence either unpleasant or intolerable, he ought to be ranked among the class of murderers. For the apostle John declares, without the least limitation, that "whosoever hateth his brother is a murderer, and he that loveth not his brother abideth in death." And, if this criterion be admitted, a train of murderers will be found existing in society far more numerous than is generally supposed.

It would be needless to attempt an illustration of the consequences which would ensue, were the breach of this law to become universal. It is obvious, on the slightest reflection, that were this to happen, human society would soon cease to exist. That prophecy which was given forth respecting Ishmael would then receive a most terrible and extensive accomplishment, in the case of every human agent: "His hand shall be against every man, and every man's hand against him." Every man would assume the character of an infernal fiend; every lethal weapon would be prepared and furnished for slaughter; every peaceful pursuit and employment would be instantly abandoned; the voice of wailing and the yells of fury and despair, would be heard in every family, in every village, in every city, in every field, in every kingdom, and in every clime. Every house, every street, every valley, every forest, every river, every mountain, and every continent would be strewed with fearful devastation, and with the mangled carcasses of the slain. The work of destruction would go on with dreadful rapidity, till the whole race of man were extirpated from the earth, leaving this vast globe a scene of solitude and desolation, an immense sepulchre, and a spectacle of horror to all superior intelligences.—And, let it be remembered, that such a picture, horrible and revolting as it is, is nothing more than what would be the na-

*Math. v. 22. Christ, in this passage, refers to a court among the Jews, composed of *twenty-three men*, wherein capital sentences might be passed on which a malefactor might be strangled or be headed: this was called *the Judgment*. But the Sanhedrim, or *Council*, was the supreme Jewish court, consisting of *seventy-two*; in which the highest crimes were tried, which they, and they alone, punished with *stoning*, which was considered a more terrible death than the former.

*tural result* of the principle of *hatred*, were it left to its native energies, and were it not controlled, in the course of providence, by Him who sets restraining bounds to the wrath of man.

In order to counteract the tendencies of this baleful principle, it is of the utmost importance that youth be trained up in habits of kindness, tenderness, and compassion, both towards human beings, and towards the inferior animals; that an abhorrence should be excited in their minds of quarrelling, fighting, and all mischievous tricks and actions; that they be restrained from the indulgence of malicious and resentful passions; that every indication of a cruel and unfeeling disposition be carefully counteracted; and that every tendency of the heart towards the benevolent affections, and every principle of active beneficence be cultivated and cherished with the most sedulous care and attention. For, in youth, the foundation has generally been laid of those malevolent principles and passions which have led to robbery, assassination, and deeds of violence,—which have filled the earth with blood and carnage; and which have displayed their diabolical energy in so dreadful a manner amidst the contests of communities and nations.

Were the disposition to indulge hatred, which leads to every species of murder, completely counteracted, the greatest proportion of those evils which now afflict our world, would cease to exist. Human sacrifices would no longer bleed upon Pagan altars; the American Indians would no longer torture to death their prisoners taken in war, nor the New Zealanders feast upon the flesh and the blood of their enemies. The widows of Hindostan would no longer be urged to burn themselves alive on the corpses of their deceased husbands; nor would the mothers of China imbrue their hands in the blood of their infant offspring. The practice of *Duelling* would forever cease, and would be universally execrated as an outrage on common sense, and on every generous and humane feeling, and as the silly attempt of a puny mortal to gratify wounded pride or disappointed ambition, at the expense of the life of his fellow-creature. Despotism would throw aside its iron sceptre, and the nations would be ruled with the law of love; and plots, conspiracies, treasons, and massacres would be attempted no more. The fires of the Inquisition would cease to be kindled, the supposed heretic would no longer be consigned to the horrors of a gloomy dungeon, racks and gibbets and guillotines would be shivered to pieces and thrown into the flames, and the spirit of cruelty and persecution would be extirpated from the earth. Riot, tumult, and contention would be banished from our streets, and harmony and concord would prevail throughout all our borders. War would forever cease to desolate the nations; the confused noise of invading armies, the sounds of martial music, the groans of dying victims, and the hoarse shouts of conquerors, would be heard no more. Peace would descend from heaven to dwell with man on earth; prosperity would follow in her train, science would enlarge its boundaries and shed its benign influence upon all ranks; the useful arts would flourish and advance towards perfection; philanthrophy would diffuse its thousand blessings in every direction, and every man would sit "under his vine and fig-tree" in perfect security from all danger or annoyance.

### SEVENTH COMMANDMENT.

"*Thou shalt not commit adultery.*"

This commandment is to be viewed as comprehending within its prohibition, every species of lewdness, both in thought, word, and action; as adultery, fornication, incest, polygamy, &c.; and likewise all those licentious desires and affections from which such actions proceed. In this comprehensive sense it is explained by our Saviour, in his Sermon on the Mount, and by the Apostles, in their letters to the Christian Churches. It is founded on the distinction of sexes which exists among mankind, and on the law of Marriage, which was promulgated immediately after the creation of the first pair—a law which was intended to limit, and to regulate the intercourse of the sexes; and to promote purity, affection, and order, among the several generations of mankind. By this law the marriage union is limited to two individuals. He who made mankind at the beginning, says Christ, made them male and female, and said, "For this cause shall a *man* leave father and mother and shall cleave to his *wife*; and they twain shall be one flesh." And, it might easily be shown, from an induction of facts, and from a consideration of the present circumstances of the human race, that this law, and this alone, is calculated to promote the mutual affection of the married pair, and to secure the peace and happiness of families, and the harmony of general society. By this law the union is made *permanent*, so long as the parties exist in this world. "What God hath joined, let no man put asunder." This regulation has a tendency to promote union of affection and interests, and to induce the parties to bear with patience the occasional inconveniences and contentions which may arise. Were divorces generally permitted, on the ground of unsuitableness of temper, or occasional jars, society would soon be shaken to its centre. Every real or supposed insult, or provocation, would be followed out, till it terminated in the separation of the parties; families would thus be torn into shreds; the education of the young would be neglected; parental authority disregarded; and a door opened for the prevalence of unbounded licentiousness. Soon after the commencement of the Revolution in France, a law, permitting divorces, was passed by the National Assembly; and, in less than three months from its date, nearly as many divorces as marriages were registered in the city of Paris. In the whole kingdom, within the space of eighteen months, upwards of twenty thousand divorces were effected; and the nation sunk into a state of moral degradation, from the effects of which it has never yet recovered. This is one of the many practical proofs presented before us, of the danger of infringing on any of the moral arrangements which the Creator has established.

The precept under consideration is to be considered as directly opposed to all promiscuous and licentious intercourse between the sexes. And the reasonableness of this prohibition will appear, if we consider, for a moment, what would be the consequences which would inevitably follow were this law to be set aside, or universally violated. A scene of unbounded licentiousness would ensue, which would degrade the human character, which would destroy almost all the existing relations of society, and unhinge the whole fabric of the moral world.—One end of the institution of marriage was, to "replenish the earth" with inhabitants, to perpetuate the successive generations of men, and to train up a virtuous and intelligent race to people the congregation of the heavens. But this end would be ultimately frustrated, were a promiscuous and unlimited intercourse to become either general or universal. For, it has been found, that, wherever such intercourse partially prevails, it strikes at the root of human existence, and has a tendency to prevent the operation of that law which the Creator impressed on all living beings, "Increase and multiply." In the haunts of licentiousness, in large cities, and in all such societies as those which formerly existed in Otaheite, under the name of *Arreoy*, the laws of nature are violated, the course of generation obstructed, and numbers of human beings strangled at the very porch of existence. So that were mankind at large to relapse into such licentious practices, the human race instead of increasing in number, to replenish the desolate wastes of our globe, according to the Creator's intention, would rapidly decrease every succeeding generation, till after the lapse of a few centuries, human beings would be entirely extirpated, and the earth, barren and uncultivated, would be left to the dominion of the beasts of the forest.

But, although such a distant event were to be altogether disregarded, the immediate consequences of such unhallowed courses would be dismal in the extreme. That union of heart, affection, and of interests, which subsists between the great majority of married pairs, and those reciprocal sympathies and endearments which flow from this union, would be altogether unknown. The female sex, (as already happens in some nations,) with minds uncultivated and unpolished, would be degraded into mere instruments of sensitive enjoyment, into household slaves, or into something analogous to beasts of burden, and would be bought and sold like cattle and horses. The minds of all would be degraded to the level of brutes, and would be incapable of prosecuting either rational or religious pursuits. Their bodies would be wasted and enfeebled with squalid disease: the infirmities of a premature old age would seize upon them; and before they had "lived half their days," they would sink into the grave in hopelessness and sorrow. A universal sottishness, and disregard of every thing except present sensual enjoyment, would seize upon the whole mass of society, and benumb the human faculties: the God of heaven would be overlooked, and the important realities of an immortal existence completely banished from their thoughts and affections. Thousands, and ten thousands of infants would be strangled at their entrance into life; and the greater part of those who were spared, would be doomed to a wretched and precarious existence. The training up of the youthful mind to knowledge and virtue would be quite neglected; and all that civility and softness of manners, which are now acquired under the eye of parental authority and affection, would be unknown in society. The endearing relations of father and mother, of brothers and sisters, of uncles, aunts, and cousins, and all the other ramifications of kindred, which now produce so many interesting and delightful associations, would fail to be recognised among men; for in such a state of society, the natural relations of mankind would be either disregarded, or blended in undistinguishable confusion.

Children, neglected or abandoned by their mothers, would be left to the full influence of their own wayward and impetuous passions; they would depend for subsistence, either on accident, on pilfering, or on the tender mercies of general society; they would wander about as vagabonds, tattered and forlorn; their hearts shrivelled with unkindness, their bodies chilled with the rains and biting frosts, and deformed with filthiness and disease. They would be left to perish in the open fields, without a friend to close their eyes; and their bodies, unnoticed and unknown, would remain as a prey, to be devoured by the fowls of heaven. In every land would be seen multitudes of houseless and shivering females, set adrift by their seducers, wandering with their hungry and half famished offspring, the objects of derision and contempt; and imploring, in vain, the comforts of food, of shelter, and protection. For, among human beings, in such a degraded state, the kindly and benevolent affections would seldom be exercised; cold-blooded selfishness and apathy, in relation to the sufferings of others, would supplant all the finer feelings of humanity; which would dispose them to view the wretched objects around them with perfect indifference, and even with contempt. "However it may be accounted for," says Dr. Paley, "the criminal commerce of the sexes corrupts and depraves the mind, and the moral character, more than any single species of vice whatsoever. That ready perception of guilt, that prompt and decisive resolution against it, which constitutes a virtuous character, is seldom found in persons addicted to these indulgences. They prepare an easy admission for every sin that seeks it; are, in low life, usually the first stage in men's progress to the most desperate villanies; and, in high life, to that lamented dissoluteness of principle which manifests itself in a profligacy of public conduct, and a contempt of the obligations of religion and of moral probity. Add to this that habits of libertinism incapacitate and indispose the mind for all intellectual, moral, and religious pleasures."*

In short, in such a state of society as would inevitably accompany a general violation of the seventh precept of the moral law, all the softness and loveliness of filial piety, of parental affection, of brotherly attachment, and of the intercourse of kindred, would forever cease; science and literature would be neglected; and churches, colleges, schools, and academies would crumble into ruins: a sufficient stimulus would be wanting to the exercise of industry and economy; a lazy apathy would seize upon the mass of society; the earth would cease to be cultivated, and would soon be covered with briers and thorns, or changed into the barren wastes of an African desert. The foundation of all regular government would be undermined; for it is chiefly in those habits of submission and obedience which are acquired under the domestic roof, that the foundations are laid of that subordination which is necessary to secure the peace and order of mankind. Society would, consequently, be thrown into a state of disorder, and would speedily sink into oblivion, in the mire of its own pollution.

The positions now stated could be illustrated, were it expedient, by a variety of melancholy facts, borrowed from the history and the present state, both of savage and of civilized nations. The annals of Turkey, of Persia, of Hindostan, of China, of Japan, of the Society Isles, and even of the civilized nations of Europe and America, would furnish abundance of impressive facts, to demonstrate the demoralizing, and brutalizing, and miserable effects which would flow from a spirit of universal licentiousness.—What revolting scenes would open to view, were we to survey the haunts of licentiousness which abound in Algiers, in Constantinople, in Teheran, in Pekin, in Canton, in Jeddo, and other populous cities, where the restraints of Christianity are altogether unknown! In such receptacles of impurity, every moral feeling is blunted, and every moral principle abandoned. Impiety, profanity, falsehood, treachery, perjury, and drunkenness, rear their unblushing fronts, and thefts, robberies, and murders, follow in their train. The unhappy female who enters these antechambers of hell, is, for the most part, cut off from all hopes of retreat. From that moment, the shades of moral darkness begin to close around her; she bids a last adieu to the smiles of tenderness and sympathy, to the kind embraces of father and mother, of sisters and brothers, to the house of God, to the instructions of his word, and to the society of the faithful. Instead of the cheering sounds of the Gospel of peace, her ears become accustomed to oaths, and curses, and horrid imprecations; the voice of conscience is hushed amidst the din of revelry and riot; every generous feeling is shrunk and withered; she stalks abroad like a painted corpse, to fill with horror the virtuous mind, and to allure the unwary to the shades of death; till at length, wasted with consumption and loathsome disease, she is stretched upon the bed of languishing, abandoned by her former associates, deprived of the least drop of consolation, haunted with the ghastly apparitions of departed joys, and the forebodings of futurity, and sinks, "in the midst of her days," into the chambers of the grave, without the least hope of a glorious resurrection. —And if we consider, that this is a picture of the wretchedness, not only of a few individuals, but of thousands, of tens of thousands, and of millions of human beings, it is impossible to describe the accumulated mass of misery which impurity has created, or to form any adequate conception of the horrible and revolting scenes of wretchedness which would be displayed, were the law under consideration to be set aside by all the inhabitants of our globe.

There is a certain levity and flippancy of speech in relation to this subject, which prevails among many who wish to be considered as respectable characters, which proceeds from a contracted view of the consequences of human actions. They conceive, that no great harm can be done to society, by a few insulated actions of the kind alluded to, especially if they be concealed from general observation; and that the Creator will be disposed to make every allowance for human frailty. But let such remember that, if it were right to violate this, or any other law of the Creator, in one instance, it would be right in a hundred, in a thousand, in a million, and in eight hundred millions of instances: and then all the revolting scenes now described, and thousands of similar effects, of which we cannot at present form a distinct conception, would inevitably take place. And, therefore, every man who, from levity and thoughtlessness, or from a disregard to the laws of heaven, persists in the occasional

* Principles of Moral and Political Philosophy, Book III. Part III. chap 2.

indulgence of such unhallowed gratifications, indulges in a practice which, were it universally to prevail, would sap the foundations of all moral order, exterminate the most endearing relations of society, prostrate man below the level of the brute, open the flood-gates of all iniquity, diffuse misery over the whole mass of human beings, and, at length, empty the world of its inhabitants.

The precept which we have now been considering, is one which, in all probability, is confined, in its references, to the inhabitants of our globe. At any rate, it would be quite nugatory, and therefore can have no place, in the moral code of a world where the distinction of sexes does not exist. And even in those worlds where a similar distinction may exist, the very different circumstances in which their inhabitants are placed, may render the promulgation of such a law altogether unnecessary. It appears to be a temporary regulation, to remain in force only during the limited period of the present economy of Providence; for, in the future destination of the righteous, we are told, that "they neither marry nor are given in marriage, but are as the angels of God in heaven." And, therefore, it is probable, that the recognition of such a law will not be necessary, in the intercourses which take place among redeemed men in the eternal world; but the principle on which it is founded, and from which it flows, will run through all the other new relations and circumstances in which they may be placed. In the existing circumstances of mankind, however, the operation of this law is essentially necessary to the stability and the happiness of the moral world; and, were its requisitions universally observed, the melancholy scenes to which I have alluded would no longer exist; the present and everlasting ruin of thousands, and of millions, would be prevented; and a scene of happiness and love, such as the world has never yet witnessed, would be displayed among all the families of the earth.

### THE EIGHTH COMMANDMENT.

"*Thou shalt not steal.*"

When the Creator had arranged our globe in the form in which we now behold it, he furnished it with every thing requisite for the sustenance and accommodation of living beings, and bestowed the whole of its riches and decorations as a free grant to the sons of men. To man he said, "Behold, I have given you every herb bearing seed, which is upon the face of all the earth, and every tree in the which is the fruit of a tree yielding seed; to you it shall be for meat." Ever since the period when this grant was made, God has not left himself without a witness to his benignity, in that he has unceasingly bestowed on mankind "rain from heaven, and fruitful seasons, filling their hearts with food and gladness." The earth has, in every age, brought forth abundance to supply the wants of all the living beings it contains; and there is still ample room on its surface, for the accommodation and support of thousands of millions of the human race, in addition to those which now exist. But mankind have never yet agreed about the division and allotment of this free and ample gift of the Creator; for every one is disposed to think that his share in it is too small, and is continually attempting to make inroads upon the allotment of his neighbours. And to this disposition is to be ascribed more than one half of all the evils which have afflicted the world in every age since the fall of man. To counteract such a propensity in mankind, and to regulate their dispositions and conduct in relation to property, is the great object of this command, "Thou shalt not steal."

*To steal*, is to take the property of others, without their knowledge or consent, and to apply it to our own use. The most flagrant and violent breaches of the law, consist in robbery, housebreaking, pilfering, plunder, and pillage. But it may be violated in a thousand different ways of which human laws seldom take any cognizance. It is violated by every species of fraud by which our neighbour may be injured in his wealth or property. It is violated in the ordinary commerce of mankind, by the use of false weights and measures; by selling deteriorated commodities as if they were sound and good; by depreciating the value of what we wish to buy, and concealing the defects of what we wish to sell; by contracting debts which we have no prospect of discharging, and neglecting to pay them when they are due; by breaches of trust, in the case of servants, guardians, executors, or public officers, embezzling and squandering away the substance of others, or applying it to their own use.—It is also violated by trespassing on the property of others, so as to injure fences, gardens, orchards, plantations or cornfields; and by that disposition to vulgar mischief which delights in breaking lamps, windows, and fences; in injuring and defacing public buildings, walks, and ornamental improvements; in hacking and carving walls, wainscottings, doors, and balustrades; and in cutting down trees and shrubs planted for use or for ornament.—It is violated when we retain borrowed articles beyond a reasonable time, when we suffer them to be injured through negligence, when we circulate them from one person to another, without the knowledge or consent of the proprietors, and when we apply them to purposes for which they were never intended, and which the lender never contemplated.—In short, this law is violated by every species of idleness, pride, vanity, gaming, and prodigality, which has a tendency to injure the external prosperity, either of our own family, or of the families of others.

Were the law which forbids those actions to be entirely set aside, or universally violated, it is easy to foresee, that, in a very short time, the whole assemblage of human beings would be transformed into a set of lawless banditti. Peace, harmony, and good neighbourhood, would be unknown among men; the strong would plunder the possessions of the weak, and deprive them of every enjoyment; children would rob their parents, and parents their children; brothers would plunder brothers, and servants their masters; buying and selling would cease, and all regular trade and commerce would be destroyed: every man's covetous eye would be directed to the wealth and property of his neighbour, with a view of depriving him of his enjoyments; and a thousand schemes, either of treachery or of open violence, would be contrived to effectuate his purpose. Murders would be daily contrived and perpetrated, for the purpose of more easily obtaining possession of the wealth and estates of the powerful and the opulent; and every man's life and happiness would be at the mercy of his covetous neighbour. The inhabitants of one province would rise up against those of another, and, by force of arms, plunder them of all their earthly treasures. One nation would invade the territories of another, for the purpose of ravaging its cities and provinces, and of appropriating its wealth and riches; and, in the midst of such lawless depredations, towns would be demolished, villages consumed to ashes, the fruits of the earth destroyed, men, women, and children, trampled under foot, and crushed to death, and every city and fertile field would present a scene of carnage and desolation. In such a state of society, no man could have confidence in his brother; fear would be on every side; uncertainty would attend every pursuit and possession; of the wealth which any one had acquired, and of the enjoyments which he possessed to-day, he might be deprived before to-morrow; and if, by means of circumspection and vigilance, and the strong arm of power, he were enabled to maintain possession of his property for one year, he could have no rational ground to expect, that he would enjoy it in security for another. And, as no one would think of engaging in regular labour, while he could subsist in plundering his weaker neighbours —the earth would soon be left uncultivated, the useful arts would be abandoned, agricultural industry and improvement would cease, and a universal famine would overspread every land, which would thin the human race, and gradually exterminate them from the face of the earth.

Such scenes of plunder and depredation, have in fact been partially realized in every age and nation of the world, and are still realized, to a certain extent, even in nations which boast of their progress in religion, in civilization, and in science. The annals of the human race contain little more than a number of melancholy records of wholesale robbery, committed by one tribe of human beings upon another. One public robber and desperado has arisen after another, in constant succession, and, at the head of numerous armies, has violated the territories of peaceful industry, demolished the habitations of their unoffending inhabitants, broken down their furniture, and consigned it to the flames; wasted and devoured the fruits of their ground, and plundered them of every thing which could render existence desirable. And the inferior ranks of mankind, stimulated by the same principles which actuate their superiors, have supported a system of peculation, of cheating, of litigation, of injustice, and oppression, which, were it left solely to its own native energies, would soon undermine the foundations of the moral world. That such principles and practices have never yet become universal in their operation, is not owing so much to any deficiency in their malignant tendency, as to the over-ruling providence of the Moral Governor of the world, who has, by his influence, and his physical arrangements, confined the lawless passions of men within certain bounds, beyond which they cannot pass.

Were a principle of honesty and of justice, in regard to property, to pervade the mind of every human being; or, in other words, were the law to which I am now adverting universally recognised, a new scene would open upon the moral world, altogether different from what has hitherto been displayed in the transactions of mankind. The iron rod of oppression would be shivered to atoms, and destroying armies would no longer ravage the habitations of men. The crowds of sharpers, cheats, and jockeys, that now stalk through the world, with unblushing fronts, to entrap the unwary, would forever disappear from the world; and impartial justice would reign triumphant over every department of society. No malignant purpose would ever be formed to injure any one in his wealth and property; and all the harassing law-suits and prosecutions, which now distress so many thousands of families, would be swept away. Every loan of money, books, furniture, or utensils, would be returned without injury, and without unnecessary delay; and every debt punctually discharged, according to the nature of the obligation, and at the period at which it was due: Every bargain would be transacted on the principles of immutable justice, and the conditions of every contract faithfully performed: No suspicions of knavery would ever harbour in the breast, nor the least alarm at the possible consequences of any mercantile transaction. Public buildings would be secure from the inroads of the genius of mischief, and gardens and orchards from every wanton depredation. Locks, and bars, and bolts, would no longer be required for securing our substance from the pilferer and the robber; and the iron gratings of a bridewell or a jail, would never again remind us of the dishonesty and the depravity of man. Servants would be universally honest and trustworthy, and the property of their masters would be regarded as a sacred deposit.

And what a happy change would such a state of society introduce among mankind! What a host of cares, anxieties, suspicions, vexations, and perplexities, would be chased away! and what a world of conveniences, and of delightful associations, would thus be created! Every merchant, by marking the price and the quality of each commodity, might leave his goods open to the inspection of the public, and enjoy himself in the bosom of his family, or in active services for the good of the community, without the east risk of loss or of depredations; and every purchaser might depend upon procuring the articles he wanted at their just value. Every traveller would prosecute his journey, either by day or by night, without the least apprehension from sharpers or robbers, and without being harassed by the impositions of inn-keepers, coachmen, carriers, and porters. Every one's mind would be at perfect ease, in regard to his property, whether he were at home or abroad, in health or in sickness; being firmly persuaded that every trust would be faithfully discharged, and every commercial concern fairly and honourably transacted. Selfishness and rapacity would give place to a spirit of justice, equity, and benevolence; contentions, jockeyings, and altercations would cease; peace and concord would prevail, and righteousness and truth would shed their benign influence over the whole brotherhood of mankind.

### THE NINTH COMMANDMENT.

"*Thou shalt not bear false witness against thy neighbour.*"

This command, like most of the others, is expressed in a *negative* form. It is directed against every species of falsehood, and, consequently, must be viewed as inculcating a sacred and universal adherence to truth, in all our thoughts, words, and actions. In the remarks I may throw out in relation to this precept, I shall consider it chiefly in its *positive* form, as commanding an inviolable attachment to *truth*. Truth may be considered in *two* different points of view—*logical* truth, which consists in *the conformity of a proposition or assertion with the actual state of things*; and *moral* truth, which consists in *the agreement of our words and actions with our thoughts*. Logical truth belongs to the *thing* or the fact asserted; moral truth, or what is termed, *veracity*, has a reference to the *person* who utters it. In both these respects, truth is of immense importance to all intelligent beings.—The importance of truth and veracity will appear from the following considerations.

In the first place, it is the bond of society, and the foundation of all that confidence and intercourse which subsist among rational beings. By far the greater part of all the knowledge we possess, has been derived from the testimony of others. It is from the communication of others, and from a reliance on their veracity, that those who were never beyond the limits of Great Britain, know that there are such cities as Paris, Vienna, Constantinople, and Cairo; and that there are such countries as Canada, Nova Scotia, Brazil, Peru, Persia, China, and Hindostan. It is from the same source that we have learned the facts of ancient and modern history, and that there once existed such empires as the Greek and Roman, the Persian, Assyrian, and Babylonian. On the same ground, the veracity of others, we confide in all the domestic relations and intercourses of life; and on this ground all the transactions of commercial society, and all the arrangements and operations of government are conducted. On the implied veracity of others, we retire from our employments at certain hours, and sit down to breakfast or dinner; and, on the first day of the week, we assemble in a certain place, at an appointed hour, for religious worship. On this ground, the pupil confides in his teacher, for instruction—the child in his parents, for sustenance, clothing and protection, the master in his servant, for the execution of his orders, and the wife in her husband for provision and support. We confide every moment in the *faithfulness* of the Almighty for the regular returns of day and night, of summer and winter, of seed-time and harvest. Could the veracity of God be impeached or rendered liable to suspicion, we should remain in awful suspense, whether another day would again dawn upon the world, or whether the earth would be shattered to pieces, and its fragments dispersed throughout surrounding worlds, before the sun again appeared in the horizon. A Being possessed of boundless knowledge and omnipotence, without veracity, would be the terror of the whole intelligent universe, and would fill them with universal agitation and alarm.

Again, truth is the foundation of our present comfort and of our future prospects. On the veracity of those illustrious characters that have gone before us, whose declarations were confirmed by signs and miracles, we depend for the hope of forgiveness and acceptance with God, and for those rich sources of consolation which are calculated to support the mind under the afflictions of mortality, and to cheer and animate us in the prospect of a future world. Our hopes of happiness beyond the grave, of the resurrection of our bodies at the termination of the present plan of providence—of the renovation of the physical system of our globe—of a complete restoration to holiness and virtue—of a re-union with departed friends—of associating with virtuous beings of a superior order—of mingling in a happier world with all those illustrious saints who have gone before us—of contemplating the manifestations of Deity on a more extensive scale; and of enjoying unmixed felicity without interruption and without end; depend upon the testimony of the inspired writers, and the light in which we view the truths or declarations which they have recorded. And, therefore, the man who endeavours to undermine the authority of the sacred records, or to distort or misrepresent their meaning by sophistical reasonings, ought to be viewed as a deceiver, and as an enemy to his species, who wishes to deprive his fellow-men of their most substantial enjoyments, and of their most cheering prospects.

Again, truth and veracity are of the utmost importance in relation to the views we ought to take of the character of God. The moral character of the Deity is delineated in the Scriptures, and we are enabled to contemplate this character, in its true light, in so far as we understand and appreciate the delineations of the sacred writers. But his character is also exhibited in the works of creation and providence. Every physical law of nature, every arrangement in the material system, every movement which exists in the boundless universe; every apparent deviation from the general course of nature, as in the case of earthquakes and volcanoes; every event in the history of nations, every fact in relation to the physical and moral condition of the different tribes of the human race, and every arrangement in reference to the lower ranks of animated beings—embodies in it an exhibition of certain aspects of the divine character; and these aspects, if fairly represented, ought to harmonize with the delineations contained in the sacred records. To ascertain such facts as those to which I now allude, requires, in many instances, the exercise of profound reasoning, and of accurate investigation, and that the mind should be free from the influence of prejudice and of every improper bias, and that the facts, when ascertained, be fairly represented, and accurately recorded; otherwise, nothing but a *distorted* view of the divine character will be exhibited to the mind. For example, if the earth be represented as among the largest bodies in nature, and as placed at rest in the centre of the universe, and that the sun, moon, and all the other celestial orbs revolve around it every day, and consequently, that the planetary bodies move in orbits which display inextricable confusion—such a representation is not a true exhibition of the God of heaven, but a phantom of our own imagination; and, if carried out to all its legitimate consequences, would involve an impeachment of the wisdom and intelligence of the Deity, and of the sublime simplicity and order, which characterize his operations in the universe. If the planet Saturn be represented as a globe 900 times larger than the earth, and surrounded with a ring 600,000 miles in circumference, it conveys a very different idea of the majesty of the divine Being who formed it, from what we are led to entertain, when we consider it as only a taper, or a brilliant stud, fixed in the vault of heaven. If the eye of a fly be exhibited as containing ten thousand polished transparent globes, nicely adjusted for the purpose of vision, it displays the character of its Maker in a different light from that in which we might be disposed to view it, when this animal is represented as a nuisance in creation, and designed only to be mangled and tortured by a cruel and unthinking schoolboy.

In some instances the inaccurate statement of a physical fact, or the false colouring put upon it, may have a tendency to endanger the eternal interests of mankind. Mr. Brydone, in his "Tour through Sicily," states, on the authority of a priest, named Recupero, that, in sinking a pit near Jaci, in the neighbourhood of Mount Ætna "they pierced through seven distinct lavas, one under the other, the surfaces of which were parallel, and most of them covered with a bed of thick earth." From suppositions founded on questionable data, he concluded, that "it requires 2000 years or upwards to form but a scanty soil on the surface of a lava," and, consequently, that "the eruption which formed the lowest of these lavas, must have flowed from the mountain at least 14000 years ago. This pretended fact was, for a while, triumphantly exhibited by sceptics, as an unanswerable argument against the truth of the Mosaic history; and its publication has, no doubt, tended to stagger weak minds, and to confirm the infidel in his prejudices against the truth of Revelation. But it has been shown by eminent geologists, that the facts alluded to are grossly mis-stated, and that no vegetable mould exists between these beds of lava; and, consequently, the argument founded upon them goes for nothing. Mr. Brydone himself, in the very same volume in which these pretended facts are stated, before he had advanced twenty pages farther in his account of the regions about Mount Ætna, states a fact which completely overturns all his preceding reasonings and calculations. In describing the country near Hybla, as having been "overwhelmed by the lava of Ætna, and having then become totally barren," he adds, "in a second eruption, by a shower of ashes from the mountain, *it soon resumed its ancient beauty and fertility*." So that it is here admitted, that, instead of requiring a period of 2000 years, a bed of lava may *speedily* be transformed into a beautiful and fertile region. But even although such facts were fairly represented,—yea, although Mr. Brydone and the Canon Recupero could have proved, to a demonstration, that the strata of the earth is not only fourteen thousand, but fourteen hundred thousand years old, it would not in the least invalidate a single assertion contained in the Mosaic history; for Moses describes only the *arrangement* of the earth into its present form, but no where asserts, that the *materials* of which our globe is composed were *created*, or brought out of nothing, at the period at which his history commences. The circumstance, however, to which I have now adverted, shows us of how much importance it is, in many cases, that even a physical fact be fairly stated, as well as the moral facts and the doctrines contained in the Scriptures. For, since every fact in the economy of nature, and in the history of providence, exhibits a certain portion of the divine character, a very different view of this character will be exhibited, according to the different lights in which we view the divine operations. And therefore, every one who wilfully misrepresents a physical fact or law of nature, is a deceiver, who endeavours to exhibit a distorted view of the character of the Deity. It is nothing less than a man "bearing false witness" against his Maker.

Again, veracity is of infinite importance in reference to our future improvement in the eternal world. In that world, we have every reason to believe our knowledge of the attributes of God will be enlarged, and our views of the range of his operations in creation and providence extended far beyond the limits to which they are now confined. But the Divine Being himself, from the immateriality and immensity of his nature, will remain forever invisible to all finite intelligences; and hence he is described by the Apostle, as "the King Eternal, Immortal, and *Invisible*, whom no man hath seen or can see." It is, therefore, not only probable, but absolutely certain, that a great portion, perhaps the greatest portion of our knowledge in that state, will be derived from the communications of other intelligences. With intellectual beings of a higher order we shall hold the most intimate converse; for we are informed, that "just men made perfect" will join "the innumerable company of angels." These beings are endued with capacious powers of intellect, and have long been exercising them on the most exalted objects. As messengers from the King of heaven to the inhabitants of the earth, they have frequently winged their way through the celestial regions, and surveyed many of those glorious systems which lie hid from the view of mortals. We have every reason to believe, that they have acquired expansive views of the dispensations of the Almighty, not only in relation to man, but in relation to numerous worlds and intelligences in different provinces of the empire of God. And, therefore, they must be admirably qualified to impart ample stores of information on the sublimest subjects, to the redeemed inhabitants from our world. From the communications of these intelligences we may derive information of the order and arrangements of other systems; of the natural scenery of other worlds; of the different orders of intellectual beings who people them; of the means by which they are carried forward in moral and intellectual improvement; of the most remarkable events which have happened in the course of their history; of the peculiar displays of divine glory that may be made to them, and of the various changes through which they may have passed in the course of the divine dispensations.

But the utility of all such sublime communications, and the delightful transports with which they will be accompanied, will entirely depend upon the immutable *veracity* of these moral intelligences who shall be employed in conveying information respecting the divine plans and operations. No *fictitious* scenes and narrations will be invented, as in our degenerate world, to astonish a gaping crowd; nothing but unvarnished truth will be displayed in that world of light; and the *real scenes* which will be displayed, will infinitely transcend, in beauty, in grandeur, and in interest, all that the most fertile imagination can conceive. Were a single falsehood to be told in heaven, were the tongue of an archangel to misrepresent a single fact in the divine economy, or were the least suspicion to exist that truth might be violated in such communications, the mutual confidence of celestial intelligences would instantly be shaken; and, from that moment, their intercourse and their happiness would be destroyed. Hence, we are repeatedly told, in the book of Revelation, that, "Whosoever loveth, or maketh a lie, shall in no wise enter within the gates of the new Jerusalem." And, therefore, every one who expects to be an inhabitant of that happy world, ought now to cultivate a strict regard to truth and veracity in all its researches, intercourses, and communications; otherwise he cannot be admitted, from the very constitution of things, to the society of saints and angels in the realms of bliss.

Thus it appears, that truth is of the utmost importance to all rational beings, as it forms the source of our knowledge, the foundation of all social intercourse, the ground of our present comfort and future prospects, the basis of all the views we can take of the Divine character and operations, and of all our prospects of future improvement in the eternal world. It is the bond of union among all the inhabitants of heaven; it is the chain which connects the whole moral universe; and it constitutes the immutable basis on which rests the throne of the Eternal.

In the depraved society of our world, truth is violated in ten thousand different ways. It is violated in thoughts, in words, in conversation, in oral discourses, in writings, in printed books, by gestures and by signs, by speaking, and by remaining silent. It is violated in reference to *the character of our neighbour*, when we invent tales of falsehood respecting him; when we listen with pleasure to such tales when told by others; when we sit mute, and refuse to vindicate his character when it is unjustly aspersed; when we endeavour to aggravate the circumstances which may have accompanied any criminal action; when we make no allowances for the force of temptation, and the peculiar circumstances in which the criminal may have been placed; when we fix upon an insulated act of vice or folly, and apply it to our neighbour as a general character; when we rake up, with a malevolent design, an action which he has long since reprobated and repented of; when his character is made the subject of jest or merriment, and when, by smiles, and noddings, and gestures, we insinuate any thing injurious to his reputation. It is violated in *promises*—when we promise, either what we have no intention of performing, or what we had no right to promise, or what is out of our power to perform, or what would be unlawful for us to execute. It is violated in *threatenings*, when we neglect to put them in execution, or we threaten to inflict what would be either cruel or unjust. It is violated in *history*, when the principal facts are blended with doubtful or fictitious circumstances; when the conduct of liars and intriguers, of public robbers and murderers, is varnished over with the false glare of heroism and of glory; and when the actions of upright men are, without sufficient evidence, attributed to knavery, or to the influence of fanaticism; when the writer construes actions and events, and attributes to the actors motives and designs, in accordance with his own prejudices and passions, and interweaves his opinions and deductions, as if they were a portion of the authenticated records of historical fact. —It is violated in the invention of *fictitious* narratives, and in the relation of marvellous stories, when the system of nature is distorted, historical facts caricatured, misrepresented, and blended with the vagaries of a romantic imagination; when scenes, events, and circumstances, "which never did nor can take place," are presented to the view, merely to convey a transient gratification to trifling and indolent minds.

It is violated by *men of science* when they give an inaccurate statement of the results of their observations and experiments; when, either through carelessness or design, they give an unfair representation of the facts and principles in nature, in order to support a favourite system or hypothesis; and when they studiously keep out of view the various circumstances in which every fact should be contemplated.—It is violated in the *literary world*, when the editor of a magazine or a review writes an article, and addresses it to himself, as if it came from the pen of another; when, for the sake of "filthy lucre," or to gratify a friend, he bestows encomiums on a work which is unworthy of the attention of the public; or when, to gratify a mean, or revengeful passion, he misrepresents or abuses the literary productions of his opponents; or when an author writes a review of his own work, and imposes it on the public, as if it were the decision of an impartial critic. —It is violated by *controversialists*, when they bring forward arguments in support of any position which they are conscious are either weak or unsound; when they appear more anxious to display their skill and dexterity, and to obtain a victory over their adversaries, than to vindicate the cause of truth; when sneers, and sarcasms, and personal reproaches, are substituted in the room of substantial arguments; when they misrepresent the sentiments of their opponents, by stating them in terms which materially alter their meaning; and when they palm upon them the doctrines and opinions which they entirely disavow.

It is violated in *commercial transactions*, when deteriorated goods are varnished over with a fair outside, and puffed off as if they were saleable and sound; when a merchant asks more than he is willing to take for any commodity; when he depreciates the commodities of his neighbour; when he undervalues whatever he is purchasing, and makes an overcharge for the articles of which he is disposing; when he denies the goods he has in his possession, when there is the prospect of an advancing price,—and in a thousand other ways, best known to the nefarious trader.—It is violated by persons in every department of life, not only when they utter what they know to be false, but when they profess to declare the whole truth, and keep back part of it with an intention to deceive; when they make use of a proposition that is literally true, in order to convey a falsehood;* when they flatter the vanity of weak minds; when they ascribe to their friends or to others good qualities which do not belong to them, or refuse to acknowledge those accomplishments of which they are possessed; when they endeavour to cajole children into obedience, by promising what they never intend to perform, and threatening what they never intend to inflict; and when they indulge in a habit of exaggeration, in the account they give of their adventures, and of the things which they have seen or heard.

Truth is violated by *signs*, as well as by words, —as, when we point with our finger in a wrong direction, when a traveller is inquiring about the road he should take; when a British ship hoists

* The following fact will illustrate this and similar pieces of falsehood:—A person, when selling a watch, was asked by the purchaser if it kept time correctly? He was told by the owner, that neither the hour nor the minute hand had required to be altered for more than a twelve-month. This was *literally* true; but the watch was, nevertheless, a very bad regulator of time. When hung in a perpendicular position, it went too slow, and, when laid in a horizontal position, it went too fast: but by alternately shifting these positions, and thus modifying the rates of motion, the hands did not require to be altered. Such assertions, however, are to be considered as direct lies, when they are intended to convey a false or erroneous conception, as in the instance now stated.

Spanish colours; when flags of truce are violated; when spies insinuate themselves into society as upright men, for the purpose of entrapping the unwary; when false intelligence is communicated to an enemy; when fires are lighted, or put out, in order to deceive mariners at sea; and when signals of distress are counterfeited by ships sea, for the purpose of decoying into their power the ships of an enemy.

Truth is violated in relation to God, when we conceal from those whom we are bound to instruct, the grandeur and immensity of his works, and the displays of divine intelligence and skill which are exhibited in his visible operations; when we exhibit a diminutive view of the extent and glory of his kingdom; when we give an inaccurate and distorted representation of the laws of nature, and of the order and the economy of the universe; when we misrepresent the facts which exist in the system of nature, and which occur in the truth of providence; when we call in question the history of that revelation which he has confirmed by signs and miracles, and by the accomplishment of numerous predictions; when we misrepresent its facts, its doctrines, and its moral requisitions; when we transform its historical narrations into a series of parables and allegories; when we distort its literal meaning by vague and injudicious *spiritualizing* comments; when we fix our attention solely on its doctrines, and neglect to investigate its moral precepts; and when we confine our views to a few points in the system of revelation, and neglect to contemplate its whole range, in all its aspects and bearings.

In the above, and in ten thousand other modes, is the law of truth violated by the degenerate inhabitants of our world. The mischiefs and the miseries which have followed its violation, in reference to the affairs of nations, to the private interests of societies, families, and individuals, and to the everlasting concerns of mankind, are incalculable, and dreadful beyond description. It is one of the principal sources from which have sprung the numerous abominations and cruelties connected with the system of Pagan idolatry, the delusions and the persecuting spirit of the votaries of Mahomet, and the pretended miracles, and "the lying wonders," of that church which is denominated "the mother of harlots and abominations of the earth." It has been chiefly owing to the violation of this law, that the thrones of tyrants have been supported, that liberty has been destroyed, that public safety and happiness have been endangered, that empires have been overturned, that nations have been dashed one against another, and that war has produced among the human race so many overwhelming desolations. By the pernicious influence of falsehood, the peace of families has been invaded, their comforts blasted, their good name dishonoured, their wealth destroyed, their hopes disappointed, and their bright prospects of happiness involved in a cloud of darkness and despair. By the sophistry of unprincipled men, literature and science have been perverted, and the avenues to substantial knowledge rendered difficult and dangerous; litigations have been multiplied without number; human beings have been agitated, perplexed, and bewildered; and the widow and the fatherless oppressed and robbed of their dearest enjoyments. Could we search the private records of ancient kings, princes, and legislators, and trace the deceitful plans which have been laid in palaces and cabinets—or could we, at this moment, penetrate into all the intrigues, deceptions, treacheries, plots, and machinations, which are going forward in the cabinets of despots, the mansions of princes, and the courts of law, throughout Europe, Africa, and Asia; such a host of falsehoods and "lying abominations," like an army of spectres from the infernal regions, would stare us in the face, as would make us shrink back with horror and amazement, and fill us with astonishment that the patience of the God of heaven has been so long exercised towards the inhabitants of such a depraved and polluted world.

Let us now consider, for a little, some of the effects which would inevitably follow were the law of truth *universally* violated. In this case a scene of horror and confusion would ensue, of which it is difficult for the mind to form any distinct conception. It is obvious, in the first place, that rational beings could never improve in knowledge, beyond the range of the sensitive objects that happened to be placed within the sphere of their personal observation. For, by far the greater part of our knowledge is derived from the communications of others, and from the stimulus to intellectual exertion which such communications produce.—Let us suppose a human being trained up, from infancy, in a wilderness, by a bear or a wolf, as history records to have been the case of several individuals in the forests of France, Germany, and Lithuania,—what knowledge could such a being acquire beyond that of a brute? He might distinguish a horse from a cow, and a man from a dog, and know that such objects as trees, shrubs, grass, flowers, and water, existed around him; but knowledge, strictly so called, and the proper exercise of his rational faculties, he could not acquire, so long as he remained detached from other rational beings. Such would be our situation, were falsehood universal among men. We could acquire a knowledge of nothing but what was obvious to our senses in the objects with which we were surrounded. We could not know whether the earth were twenty miles, or twenty thousand miles in extent, and whether oceans, seas, rivers, and ranges of mountains, existed on its surface, unless we had made the tour of it in person, and, with our own eyes, surveyed the various objects it contains. Of course, we should remain in ab solute ignorance of the existence and the attributes of God, of the moral relations of intelligent beings to their Creator, and to one another, and of the realities of a future state. For it is only, or chiefly, through the medium of *testimony*, combined with the evidence of our senses, that we acquire a knowledge of such truths and objects.

In the next place, all confidence among intelligent beings, would be completely destroyed. Disappointment would *invariably* attend every purpose and resolution, and every scheme we wished to execute, if it depended in the least degree upon the direction or assistance of others. We durst not taste an article of food which we received from another, lest it should contain poison; nor could we ever construct a house to shelter us from the storm, unless our own physical powers were adequate to the work. Were we living in Edinburgh, we could never go to Musselburgh or Dalkeith, if we were previously ignorant of the situation of these places; or were we residing in London, it would be impossible for us ever to find our way to Hommerton or Hampstead, unless, after a thousand attempts, *chance* should happen to direct us; and when we arrived at either of these villages, we should still be in as much uncertainty as ever whether it was the place to which we intended to direct our steps. Confidence being destroyed, there could be no friendship, no union of hearts, no affectionate intercourse, no social converse, no consolation or comfort in the hour of distress, no hopes of deliverance in the midst of danger, and no prospect of the least enjoyment from any being around us. In such a case, the mind would feel itself as in a wilderness, even when surrounded by fellow intelligences, and wherever it roamed over the vast expanse of nature, or among the mass of living beings around it, it would meet with no affectionate interchange of feelings and sentiments, and no object on which it could rest for solace and enjoyment. Every one would feel as if he were placed in the midst of an infinite void, and as if he were the only being residing in the universe. In such a case we would flee from the society of men as we would do from a lion or a tiger when rushing on his prey; and hide ourselves in dens, and forests, and caverns of the earth, till death should put a period to a cheerless and miserable existence.

All social intercourses and relations would cease;—families could not possibly exist; nor any affectionate intercourse between the sexes; for truth, and the confidence which is founded upon it, are implied in all the intercourses of husbands and wives, of brothers and sisters, and of parents and children;—and consequently, the human race, dropping into the grave, one after another, like the leaves of autumn, without any successors, would, in a short time, be extirpated from the earth. In such a state, kindness and affection would never be exercised; trade and commerce, buying and selling, social compacts and agreements would be annihilated; science, literature, and the arts, could not exist; and consequently, universities, colleges, churches, academies, schools, and every other seminary of instruction would be unknown. No villages, towns, nor cities would be built; no fields cultivated; no orchards, vineyards, nor gardens planted; no intercourse would exist between different regions of the globe; and nothing but one dreary barren waste would be presented to the eye, throughout the whole expanse of nature. So that were truth completely banished from the earth, it would present a picture of that dark and dismal region where "all liars have their portion!" where all are deceivers and deceived, and where the hopeless mind roams amidst innumerable false intelligences, for one ray of comfort, or one confidential spirit in which it may confide, but roams in vain.

In short, were truth banished not only from this world, but from the universe at large, creation would be transformed into a chaos; the bond which now connects angels and archangels, cherubim and seraphim, in one harmonious union, would be forever dissolved; the inhabitants of all worlds would be thrown into a state of universal anarchy, they would shun each other's society, and remain as so many cheerless and insulated wretches, amidst the gloom and desolations of universal nature; all improvements in knowledge, and all progressive advances towards moral perfection, would be forever interrupted; and happiness would be banished from the whole intelligent system. Every mind would become the seat of terror and suspense, and would be haunted with frightful spectres and dreadful expectations. The government of the Eternal would be subverted, the moral order of the intelligent system overturned; all subordination would cease, and misery would reign uncontrolled throughout every region of intellectual existence. For *truth* is implied in the principle of *love*; it is essential to its existence; so that the one cannot operate except on the basis of the other: and we have already shown, that the destruction of love would be the destruction of all order, and of all happiness among intelligent beings.

Such are some of the dreadful effects which would inevitably follow, were the law under consideration reversed or universally violated. In our world this law has, hitherto, been only *partially* violated; yet what dreadful mischiefs, beyond calculation, and even beyond conception, has its frequent violation created! Ever since that moment when "the father of lies" deceived the first human pair, how many thousands of millions of liars have trodden in his footsteps! and what a host of falsehoods has followed in their train, which have destroyed the harmony of the moral system, and robbed the world of happiness and repose! Yet how little are we affected by the frequent violations of this law? and how seldom do we reflect, that every falsehood we unadvisedly utter, is an infringement of that law on which rest the throne of the Almighty and the eternal happiness of the universe? For if one lie may be palliated or vindicated, on the same principle we might vindicate a thousand, and a million, and millions of millions, till falsehood became universal among all ranks of beings and till the moral order of the intelligent creation was completely subverted. Of how much importance is it then, that an inviolable attachment to truth, in its minutest ramifications, be early impressed upon the minds of the young, by persuasion, by precept, by example, by reasoning, and by a vivid representation of its importance, and of its inestimable benefits? and how careful should we be to preserve them from all incentives to the practice of lying, and especially from the company of those "whose mouth speaketh vanity, and their right hand is a right hand of falsehood."

Were falsehood universally detested, and the love of truth universally cherished; were a single lie never more to be uttered by any inhabitant of this globe, what a mighty change would be effected in the condition of mankind, and what a glorious radiance would be diffused over all the movements of the intelligent system? The whole host of liars, perjurers, sharpers, seducers, slanderers, tale-bearers, quacks, thieves, swindlers, harpies, fraudulent dealers, false friends, flatterers, corrupt judges, despots, sophists, hypocrites, and religious impostors, with the countless multitude of frauds, treacheries, impositions, falsehoods, and distresses which have followed in their train, would instantly disappear from among men. The beams of truth, penetrating through the mists of ignorance, error, and perplexity, produced by sophists, sceptics, and deceivers, which have so long enveloped the human mind, would diffuse a lustre and a cheerfulness on the face of the moral world, like the mild radiance of the morning after a dark and tempestuous night. Confidence would be restored throughout every department of social life; jealousy, suspicion, and distrust would no longer rankle in the human breast; and unfeigned affection, fidelity, and friendship, would unite the whole brotherhood of mankind. With what a beautiful simplicity, and with what smoothness and harmony would the world of trade move onward in all its transactions! How many cares and anxieties would vanish! how many perplexities would cease! and how many ruinous litigations would be prevented? For the violation of truth may be considered as the chief cause of all those disputes respecting property, which have plunged so many families into suspense and wretchedness. The tribunals of justice would be purified from every species of sophistry and deceit; and the promises of kings, and the leagues of nations, would be held sacred and inviolate. Science would rapidly advance towards perfection; for, as all its principles and doctrines are founded upon facts, when truth is universally held inviolable, the facts on which it is built will always be fairly represented. Every fact asserted by voyagers and travellers, in relation to the physical or the moral world, and every detail of experiments made by the chemist and the philosopher, would form a sure ground-work for the development of truth, and the detection of error; without the least suspicion arising in the mind respecting the veracity of the persons on whose testimony we rely. For want of this confidence the mind has been perplexed and distracted by the jarring statements of travellers, naturalists, and historians; false theories have been framed; systems have been reared on the baseless fabric of a vision; the foundations of science have been shaken; its utility called in question, and its most sublime discoveries overlooked and disregarded.

In fine, the clouds which now obscure many of the sublime objects of religion, and the realities of a future world, would be dispelled, were falsehood unknown, and truth beheld in its native light; and religion, purified from every mixture of error and delusion, would appear arrayed in its own heavenly radiance, and attract the love and the admiration of men. When exhibited in its native grandeur and simplicity, all doubts respecting its divine origin would soon evanish from the mind—the beauty and sublimity of its doctrines would be recognised as worthy of its Author; and all its moral requisitions would be perceived to be "holy, just, and good," and calculated to promote the order, and the ever lasting happiness of the intelligent universe. Divine truth irradiating every mind, and accompanied with the emanations of heavenly love, would dispel the gloom which now hangs over many sincere and pious minds; would unite man to man, and man to God; and the inhabitants of this world, freed from every doubt, error, and perplexity, would move forward in harmony and peace, to join "the innumerable company of angels, and the general assembly of the spirits of just men made perfect, whose names are written in heaven."

## THE TENTH COMMANDMENT.

"*Thou shalt not covet* thy neighbour's house, thou shalt not covet thy neighbour's wife, nor his man-servant, nor his maid-servant, nor his ox, nor his ass, nor *any thing that is thy neighbour's.*"

Every precept of the law to which I have hitherto adverted, has a reference not only to the *external conduct* of moral agents, but also to the *internal motives* or *principles* from which that conduct proceeds. This is evident from the considerations already stated, and from the whole tenor of Divine Revelation;—and it is in unison with reason, and with the common sense of mankind, that the merit or demerit of any action is to be estimated, according to the intention of the actor, and the disposition from which it flows. That no doubt may remain on this point, the Supreme Legislator closes the decalogue with a command, which has a reference solely to the desires and dispositions of the mind: "Thou shalt not covet." Covetousness consists in an *inordinate* desire of earthly objects and enjoyments. This desire, when uniformly indulged, leads to a breach of almost every other precept of the Divine law; and is the source of more than one half of all the evils which afflict the human race. It leads to a breach of the eighth command, by exciting either to fraudulent dealings, or to direct acts of theft and robbery.—It leads to a breach of the ninth command, by cherishing the principle of falsehood which is implied in every fraudulent transaction.—It leads to a violation of the sixth command, by engendering a spirit of revenge against those who stand in the way of its gratification; and by exciting the covetous man to the commission of murder, in order to accomplish his avaricious desires.—It also leads to a violation of the seventh command; for, when one "covets his neighbour's wife," the next step is to endeavour to withdraw her affection from her husband, and to plunge a family into misery and distress.—It also leads to a violation of the fifth precept of the law, not only as it steels the heart against those kindly filial affections which children ought to exercise towards their parents, but as it excites them to withhold from their parents, when in old age and distress, those external comforts which are requisite to their happiness, and which it is the duty of affectionate children to provide. And, when covetousness has thus led to the breach of every other precept of the second table of the law, it follows, that all the precepts of the first table are also virtually violated. For all the commandments of the first table are briefly summed up in this comprehensive precept, "Thou shalt love the Lord thy God with all thy heart:" but it is obviously impossible, nay, it would be a contradiction in terms, to suppose, that supreme love to the Creator can reside in the same breast in which an *inordinate* desire of worldly enjoyments reigns uncontrolled, and in which love to man has no existence. So that covetousness may be considered as the great barrier which separates between man and his Maker, and also as the polluted fountain from whence flow all the moral abominations and the miseries of mankind.

The more obvious and direct manifestation of this principle is generally distinguished by the name of *Avarice*, or an inordinate desire of riches. And what a countless host of evils has flowed from this unhallowed passion, both in relation to individuals, to families, to nations, and to the world at large! In relation to the avaricious man himself, could we trace all the eager desires, anxieties, perplexities, and cares, which harass his soul; the fraudulent schemes he is obliged to contrive, in order to accomplish his object; the miserable shifts to which he is reduced, in order to keep up the appearance of common honesty; the mass of contradictions, and the medley of falsehoods, to which he is always obliged to have recourse; the numerous disappointments to which his eager pursuit of wealth continually exposes him, and by which his soul is pierced as with so many daggers—we should behold a wretched being, the prey of restless and contending passions, with a mind full of falsehoods, deceitful schemes, and grovelling affections, like a cage-full of every unclean and hateful bird,—a mind incapable of any rational enjoyment in this life, and entirely incapacitated for relishing the nobler enjoyments of the life to come. Such a man is not only miserable himself, but becomes a moral nuisance to the neighbourhood around him; stinting his own family of its necessary comforts; oppressing the widow and the fatherless; grasping with insatiable fangs every house, tenement, and patch of land within his reach; hurrying poor unfortunate debtors to jail; setting adrift the poor and needy from their long-accustomed dwellings; and presenting to the young and thoughtless a picture, which is too frequently copied, of an immortal mind immersed in the mire of the most degrading passions, and worshipping and serving the creature more than the Creator, who is blessed forever.

In relation to large communities and nations, this grovelling passion has produced, on an extensive scale, the most mischievous and destructive effects. It has plundered palaces, churches, seats of learning, and repositories of art; it has polluted the courts of judicature, and the tribunals of justice; it has corrupted magistrates, judges, and legislators; and has transformed many even of the ministers of religion, into courtly sycophants, and hunters after places and pensions. It has ground whole nations to poverty, under the load of taxation; it has levelled spacious cities with the dust; turned fruitful fields into a wilderness; spread misery over whole empires; drenched the earth with human gore; and waded through fields of blood in order to satiate its ungovernable desires. What has led to most of the wars which have desolated the earth, in every age, but the insatiable cravings of this restless and grovelling passion? It was the cursed love of gold that excited the Spaniards to ravage the territories of Mexico and Peru, to violate every principle of justice and humanity, to massacre, and to perpetrate the most horrid cruelties on their unoffending inhabitants. It is the same principle, blended with the lust of power, which still actuates the infatuated rulers of that unhappy nation, in their vain attempts to overthrow the independence of their former colonies. The same principle commenced, and still carries on, that abominable traffic, the *slave trade*,—a traffic which has entailed misery on millions of the sons of Africa; which has excited wars, and feuds, and massacres, among her numerous tribes; which has forever separated from each other brothers and sisters, parents and children; which has suffocated thousands of human beings in the cells of a floating dungeon, and plunged ten thousands into a watery grave;—a traffic which is a disgrace to the human species; which has transformed civilized men into infernal fiends; which has trampled on every principle of justice; which has defaced the image of God in man, and extinguished every spark of humanity from the minds of the ferocious banditti which avarice has employed for accomplishing her nefarious designs.*

*Ambition*, or, an inordinate desire of power, superiority, and distinction, is another modification of this malignant principle. This passion is manifested, in a greater or less degree, by men of all ranks and characters, and in every situation in life. It is displayed in the *school-room* by the boy who is always eager to stand foremost in his class; in the *ball-room*, by the lady who is proud of her beauty, and of her splendid attire; in the *corporation-hall*, by the citizen who struts with an air of conscious dignity, and is ever and anon aiming at pompous harangues; on *the bench*, by the haughty and overbearing judge; in the *church*, by those rulers who, like Diotrephes, "Love to have the pre-eminence;" in the *pulpit*, by the preacher whose main object it is to excite the admiration and applause of a surrounding audience; in the *streets*, by the pompous airs of the proud dame, the coxcomb, and the dashing squire; in the *village*, by him who has a better house, and a longer purse, than his neighbours; in the *hamlet*, by the peasant who can lift the heaviest stone, or fight and wrestle with the greatest strength or agility; and in *the city*, by the nobleman who endeavours to rival all his compeers in the magnificence of his mansion, and the splendour of his equipage; among the *learned*, by their eager desire to spread their name to the world, and to extend their fame to succeeding generations; and among all classes who assume airs of importance, on account of the antiquity of their families, their wealth, their exploits of heroism, and their patrimonial possessions.

But it is chiefly on the great theatre of the world that ambition has displayed its most dreadful energies, and its most overwhelming devastations. In order to gain possession of a throne, it has thrown whole nations into a state of convulsion and alarm. The road to political power and pre-eminence, has been prepared by the overflow of truth and justice, by fomenting feuds and contentions, by bribery, murder, and assassinations, by sanguinary battles, by the plunder of whole provinces, the desolation of cities and villages, and by the sighs, the groans, and lamentations of unnumbered widows and orphans. In order to raise a silly mortal to despotic power on the throne of Spain, how many human victims have been sacrificed at the altar of ambition! how many families have been rent asunder, and plunged into irremediable ruin! and how many illustrious patriots have been immured in dungeons, and have expired under the axe of the executioner! At the present moment, the fertile vales of Mexico, the mountains and plains of South America, the forests of the Burmese, and the shores of Turkey and of Greece, are every where covered with the ravages of this fell destroyer, whose path is always marked with desolation and bloodshed. To recount all the evils which ambition has produced over this vast globe, would be to write a history of the struggles and contests of nations, and of the sorrows and sufferings of mankind. So insatiable is this ungovernable passion, that the whole earth appears a field too small for its malignant operations. Alexander the Great, after having conquered the greater part of the known world, wept, because he had not another world to conquer. Were there no physical impediments to obstruct the course of this detestable passion, it would ravage, not only the globe on which we dwell, but the whole of the planetary worlds; it would range from system to system, carrying ruin and devastation in its train, till the material universe was involved in misery and desolation; and it would attempt to subvert even the foundations of the throne of the Eternal.

Such are some of the dismal and destructive effects of *covetousness*, when prosecuting the paths of avarice and ambition: and when we consider that it is uniformly accompanied in its progress, with pride, envy, discontentment, and restless desires,—it is easy to perceive, that, were it left to reign without control over the human mind, it would soon desolate every region of the earth, and produce all the destructive effects which, as we have already shown, would flow from a universal violation of the other precepts of God's law.

On the other hand, ***Contentment***,—the duty implied in this command, would draw along with

* That this accursed traffic is still carried on, with unabated vigour, by the civilized powers of Europe, appears from the following statement:—"The boats of a British Frigate, the Maidstone, boarded, in eleven days of June, 1824, no less than ten French vessels, at a single spot upon the coast of Africa; the measurement of which vessels was between 1400 and 1600 tons, while they were destined for the incarceration—we might say, the living burial—of 3000 human beings!" The report to Government says—"The schooner La Louisa, Capt. Armand, arrived at Gaudaloupe, during the first days of April, 1824, with a cargo of 200 negroes, the *remainder* of a complement of 375, which the vessel had on board. The vessel not being large enough to accommodate so great a number of men, *the overplus were consigned* ALIVE *to the waves by the Captain!*"

it an unnumbered train of blessings, and would restore tranquillity and repose to our distracted world. To be contented under the allotments of the providence of God, is one of the first and fundamental duties of every rational creature. By contentment and resignation to the divine disposal, we recognise God as the supreme Governor of the universe ; as directed by infinite wisdom, in the distribution of his bounty among the children of men ; as proceeding on the basis of eternal and immutable justice, in all his providential arrangements ; and as actuated by a principle of unbounded benevolence, which has a regard to the ultimate happiness of his creatures. Under the government of such a Being, we have abundant reason, not only to be contented and resigned, but to be glad and to rejoice. "The Lord reigneth, let the earth be glad, let the multitude of the isles thereof rejoice." However scanty may be the portion of earthly good measured out to us at present, and however perplexing and mysterious the external circumstances in which we may now be involved, we may rest assured, that, under the government of unerring wisdom, rectitude, and benevolence, all such dispensations shall ultimately be found to have been, not only consistent with justice, but conducive to our present and everlasting interests. Were such sentiments and affections to pervade the minds of all human beings, what a host of malignant passions would be chased away from the hearts and from the habitations of men? Restless cares, and boundless and unsatisfied desires, which constitute the source and the essence of misery, would no longer agitate and torment the human mind. Voluptuousness would no longer riot at the table of luxury on dainties, wrung from the sweat of thousands ;—nor avarice glut its insatiable desires with the spoils of the widow and the orphan ;—nor ambition ride in triumph over the miseries of a suffering world. Every one, submissive to the allotments of his Creator, and grateful for that portion of his bounty which he has been pleased to bestow, would view the wealth and enjoyments of his neighbour with a kind and benignant eye, and rejoice in the prosperity of all around him. Benevolence and peace would diffuse their benign influence over the nations, and mankind, delivered from the fear of every thing that might "hurt or destroy," would march forward in harmony and affection, to that happier world where every wish will be crowned, and every holy desire satisfied in God "their exceeding great reward."

Thus it appears, that, on the observance of this law, which closes the Decalogue, and which has a reference to a single affection of the mind —the order and happiness of the intelligent system almost entirely depends. Let the floodgates of *Covetousness* be burst open, and let it flow in every direction without control,—in a short period the world is desolated, and overwhelmed with a deluge of miseries. Let the current of every passion and desire be restrained within its legitimate boundary, and let contentment take up its residence in every heart, and this deluge will soon be dried up, and a new world will appear, arrayed in all the loveliness, and verdure, and beauty of Eden. May Jehovah hasten it in his time!

Thus I have endeavoured, in the preceding sketches, to illustrate the *reasonableness* of those laws which God has promulgated for regulating the moral conduct of the intelligent creation. If the propriety of these illustrations be admitted, they may be considered as a commentary on the words of the Apostle Paul: "*The law is holy, and the commandment is holy and just and good.*" In like manner it might have been shown, that all the Apostolic injunctions, and other precepts recorded in the volume of inspiration, are accordant with the dictates of reason, and with the relations of moral agents ; for they are all so many subordinate ramifications of the principles and laws, which I have already illustrated.

### *General Conclusions and Remarks, founded on the preceding illustrations.*

I shall now conclude this chapter with the statement of a few remarks in relation to the moral law, founded on the illustrations which have been given in the preceding pages; which may be considered as so many inferences deduced from the general subject which has now occupied our attention.

I. In the *first place*, one obvious conclusion from the preceding illustrations is, That the laws of God are not the commands of an arbitrary Sovereign, but are founded on the nature of things, and on the relations which exist in the intelligent system. Many divines, especially those of the supralapsarian school, have been disposed to ascribe every regulation of the Deity to the Divine Sovereignty. I have been told that, in one of the Latin treatises of Mr. Samuel Rutherford, Professor of Divinity, in St. Andrews, there is a sentiment to the following purpose: "That such is the absolute sovereignty of God, that had it so pleased him, he might have made every precept of the moral law given to man exactly the reverse of what we now find it." A sentiment more directly repugnant to the scriptural character of God, and to every view we can take of the divine attributes, it is scarcely possible for the human mind to entertain ; and it shows us the dangerous consequences to which we are exposed, when we attempt to push certain theological dogmas to an extreme. If it were possible to suppose the Deity capable of such an act, it would overturn all the grounds on which we are led to contemplate him as glorious, amiable, and adorable. At some future period in the revolutions of eternity, his love, his rectitude and his faithfulness, might be changed into malevolence, injustice, and falsehood. If the requisitions of the moral law depended solely on the Divine Sovereignty, then there is no inherent excellence in virtue; and theft, falsehood, murder, idolatry, profanity, cruelty, wars, devastations, and the malevolence of infernal demons, might become equally amiable and excellent as truth, justice, benevolence, and the songs and adorations of angels; provided the Deity *willed* the change to take place. But this is impossible; and it is evident, I trust, from the preceding illustrations, that, were moral laws, directly opposite to those contained in the scriptural code, to be prescribed to men, or to any other class of moral agents, not only would misery reign uncontrolled through the universe, but, in a short time, the operation of such laws would annihilate the whole intelligent creation.

It is evident, then, that the moral law is not founded on the *will* of God, but on the relations of intelligent beings, and on its own intrinsic excellence; or, in other words, on its tendency to produce happiness throughout the intelligent system. This idea nearly coincides with that of some of our modern moralists, who maintain "that virtue is founded on utility,"—if, by *utility*, is meant a tendency to promote happiness. But it by no means follows, from this position, as some moralists have concluded, that utility is the guide, or the rule by which we are to be directed in our moral conduct. This may be considered as the rule which directs the conduct of the Divine Being, whose eye takes in the whole system of creation, whose knowledge extends from eternity past, to eternity to come, and who perceives, at one glance, the remotest consequences of every action. But it cannot be a rule for subordinate intelligences, and especially for man, who stands near the lowest degree of the scale of intellectual existence. From the limited range of view to which he is confined, he cannot trace the remote consequences of any particular action, the bearings it may have on unnumbered individuals, and the relation in which it may stand to the concerns of the eternal world. An action which, to our limited view, may appear either beneficial or indifferent, may involve a principle which, if traced to its remotest consequences, would lead to the destruction of the moral universe. It might appear, at first view, on the whole, beneficial to society, that an old unfeeling miser should be gently suffocated, and his treasures applied for the purpose of rearing asylums for the aged poor, and seminaries of instruction for the young. But the principle which would sanction such an action, if generally acted upon, would lead to universal plunder, robbery, and bloodshed. To tell a lie to a child, in order to induce it to take a nauseous medicine which is essential to its recovery from disease, may appear, in such a case, to have a benevolent tendency; but we have already shown, that were such a principle universally admitted, it would introduce anarchy and misery through the universe, and would ultimately annihilate the intelligent creation. Man, in his present state, can be directed only by *positive laws* proceding from the Almighty, whose comprehensive mind alone can trace all their consequences to the remotest corners of the universe, and through all the ages of eternity. These laws are contained in the Scriptures—a comprehensive summary of which has been the subject of the preceding illustrations. And we know, in point of fact, that in every country where these laws are either unknown, or not recognised, there is no fixed standard of morals: and vice, in its various ramifications, almost universally prevails.

From what has been now stated we may infer —that a *full and unreserved obedience to the Divine law is a most reasonable requisition*. Men are too frequently disposed to view the commands of God as the dictates of an arbitrary Sovereign. There is a secret thought that occasionally lodges in the heart of every human being, that the law of God is too extensive and rigorous in its demands, accompanied with a secret wish, that the severity of its requisitions could be a little modified or relaxed. Every man is subject to some "besetting sin," and he is apt to say within himself—"If I were allowed but a little license with regard to *one* precept of the law, I would endeavour to do what I could to comply with the requisitions of the rest." But, it would be inconsistent both with the *benevolence* of the Deity, and with the happiness of his moral creation, either to modify or to relax any one requirement of his law; for it is a *perfect* law, from which nothing can be taken without impairing its excellence and utility. Were he to do so, it would be in effect, to shut up the path to happiness, and to open the flood-gates of misery upon the universe. Although it is impossible for man in his present degraded condition, to yield a *perfect* obedience to this law, yet nothing short of perfect obedience ought to be his aim. For in as far as we fall short of it, in so far do we fall short of happiness; and consequently, till that period arrives when our obedience shall reach the summit of perfection, our happiness must remain incomplete, and a certain portion of misery must be expected to mingle itself with all our enjoyments.

II. *There is so intimate a connexion between all the parts of the Divine law, that the habitual violation of any one precept necessarily includes the violation of the greater part, if not the whole of the other precepts.* This is evident from the general tenor of the preceding illustrations. It has been shown that a breach of the first commandment includes pride, falsehood, blasphemy, ingratitude, and hatred of moral excellence, and that it leads to injustice, cruelty, murder, obscenity, and the most revolting abominations. A breach of the fifth involves a principle which would sap the foundations of all government and moral order, and transform society into a rabble of lawless banditti. The violation of the eighth is connected with falsehood, treachery, and covetousness, and leads to oppression, robbery, plunder, murders, and the devastation of empires; and the violation of the tenth, though consisting only in the indulgence of an irregular desire, is the origin of almost every other species of moral turpitude, in relation either to God or to man. In like manner it might be shown, that the strict and regular observance of any one precept is necessarily connected with a regard for all the other requirements of God's law.

III. It appears, from the preceding illustrations, that a universal violation of any one of the six precepts of the second table of the law, would lead to the entire destruction of the human race. In the case of the sixth commandment being supposed to be reversed, or universally violated, this effect would be most rapidly produced; but the destruction and complete extirpation of human beings from the earth would be as certainly effected, in the course of two or three generations, by the universal violation of any one of the other five precepts. Some of the circumstances which would necessarily produce this effect, are alluded to, in the preceding illustration of these precepts. And as the first principle of the moral law, love to God, is the foundation of the precepts contained in the second table, it is obvious, that the same effect would ultimately follow from a universal violation of the first four precepts of the Decalogue.

IV. It follows from what has hitherto been stated, That the moral law has never yet been universally violated, nor has any one of its precepts been completely reversed in the conduct of the inhabitants of our globe. Every individual, of all the millions of mankind that have existed since the fall of Adam, has, indeed, in one shape or another, broken every one of the commandments of God; but such breaches have not been constant and uniform, and running through every action he performed. Falsehood has always been mingled with a portion of truth, theft with honesty, cruelty with clemency and mercy, anarchy with subordination, and licentiousness with chastity and purity. It is owing to this partial obedience to the dictates of the law of nature, impressed upon every human heart, that the world of mankind has hitherto been preserved in existence. The partial violation, however, of the divine law, which has characterized the actions of mankind, in all ages, has been the source of all the calamities, miseries, and moral abominations, under which the earth has groaned from generation to generation; and, in proportion to the extent of this violation, will be the extent of wretchedness and misery entailed on the human race.—That a universal violation of God's law has never yet taken place in any region of the earth, is not owing so much to any want of energy, or of malignity in the principle of disobedience which is seated in the hearts of men as to the restraining influence of the moral Governor of the world, and to the physical impediments which he has placed to prevent the diabolical passions of men from raging without control. Whether it be possible for any class of intelligent organized beings to subsist for any length of time, under a complete violation of the moral law, it is not for us positively to determine; but it is evident to a demonstration, that in the present physical condition of the human race, such a violation would unhinge the whole fabric of society, and, in a short time, exterminate the race of Adam from the earth.

V. The greater part of the precepts of the Decalogue is binding upon superior intelligences, and upon the inhabitants of all worlds, as well as upon man. For any thing we know to the contrary, there may be worlds in different regions of the universe, and even within the bounds of our planetary system, where their inhabitants are placed in circumstances similar to those in which man was placed in his paradisiacal state; and, consequently, where the precepts which compose their moral code may be exactly the same as ours. But, it is highly probable that, in general, the inhabitants of the various globes, which float in the immensity of space, differ as much in their moral circumstances and relations, as the globes themselves do in their size, their physical constitution, and their natural scenery. I have already shown, (p. 78, &c.) that there are seven precepts of our moral law which are common to the inhabitants of all worlds, namely, the *first*, *second*, *third*, *fourth*, (see p. 114,) the *sixth*, the *ninth*, and the *tenth*. And, if there be no portion of the intelligent system in which *subordination*, in a greater or less degree, does not exist, then, the fifth precept of our code must also be a law common to all intelligences. It was formerly stated, (p. 102,) that the seventh precept is in all probability, a law peculiar to the inhabitants of the earth, during the present economy of Providence; and, perhaps it is the only one which is not applicable to the other inhabitants of the universe. So that the moral laws given to man may be considered as substantially the same with those which govern all the other parts of the universal system.

VI. From the preceding illustrations, we may infer, the excellency and the divine origin of the Christian Revelation. The Scriptures contain the most impressive evidence of their heavenly original in their own bosom. The wide range of objects they embrace, extending from the commencement of our earthly system, through all the revolutions of time, to the period of its termination · and from the countless ages of eternity past, to the more grand and diversified scenes of eternity to come—the plan of Providence which they unfold, and the views they exhibit of the moral principles of the Divine government, and of the subordination of all events to the accomplishment of a glorious design—the character and attributes of the Creator, which they illustrate by the most impressive delineations, and the most lofty and sublime descriptions—the views they exhibit of the existence, the powers, the capacities, the virtues, and the employments of superior orders of intellectual beings—the demonstrations they afford of the dignified station, and of the high destination of man—and the sublime and awful scenes they unfold, when the earth "shall melt like wax at the presence of the Lord," when the throne of judgment shall be set, and the unnumbered millions of the race of Adam shall be assembled before the Judge of all—infinitely surpass every thing which the unassisted imaginations of men could have devised, and every thing which had ever been attempted by the greatest sages of antiquity, either in prose or in rhyme; and, consequently prove, to a moral demonstration, that a Power and Intelligence, superior to the human mind, must have suggested such sublime conceptions, and such astonishing ideas; since there are no prototypes of such objects to be found within the ordinary range of the human mind.

But the subject to which we have been hitherto adverting, when properly considered, suggests an evidence of the truth and divinity of the Scriptures, as striking, and, perhaps, more convincing than any other. They unfold to us the moral laws of the universe—they present to us a summary of moral principles and precepts, which is applicable to all the tribes and generations of men, to all the orders of angelic beings, and to all the moral intelligences that people the amplitudes of creation—to man, during his temporary abode on earth, and to man, when placed in heaven, so long as eternity endures—precepts, which, if universally observed, would banish misery from the creation, and distribute happiness, without alloy, among all the intellectual beings that exist throughout the empire of God. Can these things be affirmed of any other system of religion or of morals that was ever published to the world? The Greek and Roman moralists, after all their laboured investigations, could never arrive at any certain determination with regard to the nature of happiness, and the means of attaining it. We are told by Varro, one of the most learned writers of the Augustan age, that, the heathen philosophers had embraced more than two hundred and eighty different opinions respecting the supreme good. Some of them taught that it consisted in sensual enjoyments, and in freedom from pain; others considered it as placed in study and contemplation, in military glory, in riches, honours, wealth, and fame. Some of their moral maxims, separately considered, were rational and excellent; but they were connected with other maxims, which completely neutralized all their virtue, and their tendency to produce happiness. Pride, falsehood, injustice, impurity, revenge, and an unfeeling apathy to the distresses of their fellow-creatures, were considered as quite consistent with their system of morality; and such malignant principles and practices were blended with their most virtuous actions. But we have already shown, that the uniform operation of such principles would necessarily lead to the destruction of all happiness, and to the overthrow of all order throughout the intelligent creation.

Now, can it be supposed, for a moment, that a *Jew*, who had spent forty years of his life as a shepherd in a desert country, who lived in a rude age of the world, who had never studied a system of ethics, and whose mind was altogether incapable of tracing the various relations which subsists between intelligent beings and their Creator, could have investigated those moral principles and laws which form the foundation of the moral universe, and the basis of the divine government in all worlds; unless they had been communicated immediately by Him, who, at one glance, beholds all the physical and moral relations which exist throughout creation, and who can trace the bearings and the eternal consequences of every moral law? Or can we suppose, that, throughout the whole period of the Jewish economy, and during the first ages of the Christian dispensation, a multitude of writers should appear, many of them unknown to each other, all of whom should uniformly recognise those laws in their minutest bearings and ramifications, unless their minds had been enlightened and directed by the same powerful and unerring Intelligence? If these laws are distinguished by their extreme *simplicity*, they are the more characteristic of their divine Author, who, from the general operation of a few simple principles and laws in the system of nature, produces all the variety we perceive in the material world, and all the harmonies, the contrasts, the beauties, and the sublimities of the universe. If it be asked why these laws, which are so extremely simple and comprehensive, were not discovered nor recognised by the ancient sages? It might be answered, by asking why the laws of gravitation, which are also simple and comprehensive, were not discovered, till Newton arose to investigate the agencies of nature, and to pour a flood of light on the system of the universe? But the true reasons are—the unassisted powers of the human mind were inadequate to the task of surveying all the moral relations which subsist throughout the intelligent system, and of tracing those moral principles which would apply to the whole assemblage of moral agents, so as to secure the happiness of each individual, and of the system as one great whole—that the laws of God were almost directly contrary to the leading maxims of morality which prevailed in the world—and that they struck at the root of all those principles of pride, ambition, revenge, and impurity, which almost universally directed the conduct of individuals and of nations.

If, then, we find in a book which professes to be a revelation from heaven, a system of moral laws which can clearly be shown to be the basis of the moral order of the universe, and which are calculated to secure the eternal happiness of all intellectual beings—it forms a strong presumptive proof, if not an unanswerable argument, that the contents of that book are of a celestial origin, and were dictated by Him who gave birth to the whole system of created beings.

VII. From this subject we may learn the absurdity and pernicious tendency of Antinomianism. Of all the absurdities and abominations which have assumed the name of Religion, I know none more pernicious and atheistical in its tendency, than the sentiment which is tenaciously maintained by modern Antinomians, "That Christians are set free from the law of God as a rule of conduct." That in the nineteenth century of the Christian era, amidst the rapid progress of physical and moral science, under the mask of a Christian profession, and with the moral precepts and injunctions of the prophets of Jesus Christ, and of his apostles, lying open before them, a set of men, calling themselves rational beings, should arise to maintain, that there is such a thing as "imputed sanctification," that the moral law is not obligatory upon Christians, and that "whoever talks of progressive sanctification is guilty of high treason against the majesty of heaven"*—is a moral phenomenon truly humbling and astonishing; and affords an additional proof, to the many other evidences which lie before us, of the folly and perversity of the human mind, and of its readiness to embrace the most wild and glaring absurdities! If the leading train of sentiment which has been prosecuted in the preceding illustrations be admitted, there appears nothing else requisite in order to show the gross absurdity and the deadly malignity of the Antinomian system. If any system of religion be founded on the cancellation of every moral tie which connects man with man, and man with God—if its fundamental and distinguishing principles, when carried out to their legitimate consequences, would lead men to *hate* their Creator and to *hate* one another—if it can be shown, that the operation of such principles constitutes the chief ingredient of the misery which arises from "the worm that never dies, and the fire which is never quenched;" and that, if universally acted upon, they would overthrow all order in the intelligent system, and banish every species of happiness from the universe—it necessarily follows, that such a system cannot be the religion prescribed by the All-wise and benevolent Creator, nor any part of that revelation which proclaims "peace on earth and good-will among men," and which enjoins us to "love the Lord our God with all our hearts, and our neighbour as ourselves."

The Antinomian, in following out his own principles, if no human laws or prudential considerations were to deter him, might run to every excess of profligacy and debauchery—might indulge in impiety, falsehood, and profanity—might commit theft, robbery, adultery, fraud, cruelty, injustice, and even murder, without considering himself as acting contrary to the spirit of his religious system. On his principles, the idea of *heaven*, or a state of perfect happiness, is a physical and moral impossibility; and the idea of *hell* a mere bugbear to frighten children and fools. For, wherever the moral law is generally observed, there can be no great portion of misery experienced under the arrangements of a benevolent Creator; and if this law be set aside, or its observance considered as a matter of indifference, the foundation of all the happiness of saints and angels is necessarily subverted. A heaven without love pervading the breasts of all its inhabitants, would be a contradiction in terms; but love, as we have already seen, is the foundation of every moral precept.

I trust the moral conduct of the deluded mortals who have embraced this system is more respectable than that to which their principles naturally lead;—but the consideration, that such absurd and dangerous opinions have been deduced from the Christian revelation, should act as a powerful stimulus on the Christian world, for directing their attention to a more minute and comprehensive illustration than has hitherto been given, of the *practical bearings* of the Christian system, and of the eternal and immutable obligation of the law of God, which it is the great end of the gospel of Christ to enforce and demonstrate. For it is lamentable to reflect how many thousands of religionists, both in North and in South Britain, even in the present day, have their minds tinctured, in a greater or less degree, with the poison of Antinomianism, in consequence of the general strain of many of the doctrinal sermons they are accustomed to hear, and of the injudicious sentiments they have imbibed from the writings of the supralapsarian divines of the seventeenth century.

VIII. Faith and repentance, as required in the Gospel, are absolutely necessary, in the present condition of man, in order to acceptable obedience to the divine law. "Without faith it is impossible to please God; for he that cometh

* See Cottle's "Strictures on the Plymouth Antinomians."

to God must believe that he is, and that he is the rewarder of them that diligently seek him."— Faith, as the term is used in scripture, denotes *confidence* in the moral character of God, founded on the belief we attach to the declarations of his word. It is defined, by the Apostle Paul, in the eleventh chapter of the epistle to the Hebrews, to be "the confident expectation of things hoped for," and "the conviction of things which are not seen."* Faith substantiates and realizes those objects which are invisible to the eye of sense, and which lie beyond the reach of our present comprehension. It recognises the existence and the omnipresence of an invisible Being, by whose agency the visible operations of nature are conducted; and views him as possessed of infinite wisdom, power, benevolence, faithfulness, rectitude, and eternal duration. It realizes the scenes of an invisible and eternal world—the destruction of the present fabric of our globe, the resurrection of the dead, the solemnities of the last judgment, the new heavens, and the new earth, the innumerable company of angels, and the grandeur and felicity of the heavenly world. These invisible realities it recognises, on the testimony of God exhibited in his word; and without a recognition of such objects, religion can have no existence in the mind.—In a particular manner, faith recognises the declarations of God in relation to the character and the condition of men as violators of his law, and as exposed to misery; and the exhibition which is made of the way of reconciliation, through the mediation of Jesus Christ, who is "set forth as a propitiation to declare the righteousness of God in the remission of sins." The man in whose heart the principle of faith operates, convinced that he is guilty before God, and exposed to misery on account of sin, *confides* in the declarations of God respecting "the remission of sins through the redemption that is in Christ Jesus;"—he confides in the goodness, mercy, faithfulness, and power of God, which secure the accomplishment of his promises, and the supply of all requisite strength and consolation to support him amidst the dangers and afflictions of life; he confides in the wisdom and excellence of those precepts which are prescribed as the rule of his conduct, and which are fitted to guide him to the regions of happiness;—and in the exercise of this confidence, he "adds to his faith, fortitude and resolution, knowledge, temperance, patience, godliness, brotherly kindness, and charity;" and prosecutes with courage this course of obedience, till at length "an entrance is abundantly administered to him into the everlasting kingdom of our Lord and Saviour, Jesus Christ." But, without a recognition of such objects, and an unshaken confidence in the declarations of God respecting them, it is obvious, from the nature of things, that we "cannot please God," nor yield to him an acceptable and "reasonable service."

In like manner it might be shown, that *repentance* is essentially requisite in order to acceptable obedience. Sin is directly opposed to the character of God, and is the great nuisance of the moral universe. While the love of it predominates in any mind, it leads to every species of moral turpitude and depravity; and, consequently, completely unfits such a mind for yielding a cheerful obedience to the divine law. But repentance, which consists in hatred of sin, and sorrow for having committed it, naturally fits and prepares the mind for the practice of universal holiness. It tends to withdraw the soul from the practice of sin, and warns it of the danger of turning again to folly. It is the commencement of every course of virtuous conduct, and the avenue which ultimately leads to solid peace and tranquillity of mind. It is intimately connected with humility and self-denial, and is directly opposed to pride, vanity, and self-gratulation. It must, therefore, be indispensably requisite to prepare us for conformity to the moral character of God, for universal obedience to his law, and for the enjoyment of substantial and never-ending felicity. Hence the importance which is attached to the exercise of repentance by our Saviour and his Apostles. In connexion with faith, it is uniformly represented as the first duty of a sinner, and the commencement of the Christian life. Repentance was the great duty to which the forerunner of the Messiah called the multitudes who flocked to his baptism, and on which the Messiah himself expatiated during the period of his public ministry. "Repent ye, for the kingdom of heaven is at hand." "Except ye repent, ye shall all likewise perish." And the apostles, in their instructions to every nation and to every class of men, laid down the following positions as the foundation of every moral duty. "Repentance towards God, and faith towards our Lord Jesus Christ."

IX. From the preceding illustrations we may learn, that no *merit*, in the sense in which that term is sometimes used, can be attached to human actions in the sight of God; and that the salvation, or ultimate happiness of sinners, is the effect of the grace or benevolence of God.— That the good works of men are *meritorious* in the sight of God, is a notion, as unphilosophical and absurd, as it is impious and unscriptural. They are requisite, and *indispensably* requisite, as *qualifications*, or *preparations* for the enjoyment of felicity, without which the attainment of true happiness either here or hereafter, is an absolute impossibility; but the actions of no created being, not even the sublimest services and adorations of the angelic hosts, can have the least merit in the eyes of the Creator. "Thy wickedness may hurt a man as thou art, and thy righteousness may profit the son of man;" but "if thou

* Doddridge's translation of Heb. xi. 1.

sinnest, what dost thou against God; or, if thou be righteous, what givest thou him? and what receiveth he of thine hand?"* "Thy goodness extendeth not unto him," and he that sinneth against him wrongeth his own soul."—What merit can there be in the exercise of love, and in the cultivation of benevolent affections, when we consider, that these affections are essentially requisite to our happiness, and that the very exercise of them is a privilege conferred by God, and one of the principal ingredients of bliss? What merit can be attached, in the presence of the Most High, to the noblest services we can perform, when we reflect, that we derived all the corporeal and intellectual faculties by which we perform these services, and all the *means* by which they are excited and directed, from our bountiful Creator? What merit can there be in obedience to his law, when disobedience must infallibly lead to destruction and misery? Is it considered as meritorious in a traveller, when he is properly directed, furnished with strength of body and mind, and provided with every necessary for his journey,—to move forward to the place of his wished for destination? Our benevolent affections, and the active services to which they lead, may be meritorious in the eyes of our fellow-men, in so far as they are the means of contributing to their enjoyment; but in the presence of Him who sits on the throne of the universe, dispensing blessings to all his offspring, we shall always have to acknowledge, that "we are unprofitable servants." It is probable, that, if the great object of religion were represented in its native simplicity, if the nature of salvation were clearly understood, and if less were said on the subject of human merit in sermons, and systems of divinity, the idea which I am now combating, would seldom be entertained by any mind possessed of the least share of Christian knowledge, or of common sense.

That the eternal salvation of men, is the effect of the love and the grace of God, is also a necessary consequence from what has been now stated. For every power, capacity, and privilege we possess, was derived from God. "What have we that we have not received?" Even our very existence in the world of life, is *an act of grace.* We exerted no power in ushering ourselves into existence: We had no control over the events which determined that we should be born in Britain, and not in Africa; which determined the particular family with which we should be connected; the education we should receive; the particular objects towards which our minds should be directed, and the privileges we should enjoy. And, when we arrive at the close of our earthly career, when the spirit is hovering on the verge of life, and about to take its flight from this mortal scene, can it direct its course, by its own energies, through the world unknown? can it wing its way over a region it has never explored, to its kindred spirits in the mansions of bliss? can it furnish these mansions with the scenes and objects from which its happiness is to be derived? can it re-animate the body after it has long mouldered in the dust? can it re-unite itself with its long-lost partner? can it transport the resurrection-body, to that distant world where it is destined to spend an endless existence? or can it create those scenes of glory and magnificence, and those ecstatic joys which will fill it with transport while eternity endures? If it cannot be supposed to accomplish such glorious objects by its own inherent powers, then, it must be indebted for every entertainment in the future world to the unbounded and unmerited love and mercy of God. To Him, therefore, who sits upon the throne of the heavens, and to the Lamb who was slain and hath redeemed us to God by his blood, let all praise, honour, dominion, and power, be ascribed now and forever. Amen.

Having now finished what I proposed in the illustration of the principles of love to God and to man, and of the precepts of the Decalogue,—in the following chapter, I shall take a bird's eye view of the moral state of the world; and endeavour to ascertain, to what extent these principles and laws have been recognised and observed by the inhabitants of our globe.

* Job xxxv. 6, 8. Psalm xvi. 2 &c.

# CHAPTER IV.

## A BRIEF SURVEY OF THE MORAL STATE OF THE WORLD; OR, AN EXAMINATION OF THE GENERAL TRAIN OF HUMAN ACTIONS, IN REFERENCE TO ITS CONFORMITY WITH THE PRINCIPLES AND LAWS NOW ILLUSTRATED.

THE discoveries of modern astronomy have led us infallibly to conclude, that the universe consists of an immense number of systems and worlds dispersed, at immeasurable distances from each other, throughout the regions of infinite space. When we take into consideration the *Benevolence* of the Deity, and that the happiness of the intelligent creation is the great object which his Wisdom and Omnipotence are employed to accomplish—it appears highly probable, that the inhabitants of the whole, or at least of the greater part, of those worlds whose suns we behold twinkling from afar, are in a state of moral perfection, and consequently, in a state of happiness. At any rate, it is reasonable to conclude, that the exceptions which exist are not numerous. Perhaps this earth is the only material world where physical evil exists, where misery prevails, and where moral order is subverted; and these dismal effects may have been permitted to happen, under the government of God, in order to exhibit to other intelligences, a specimen of the terrible and destructive consequences of *moral* evil, as a warning of the danger of infringing, in the least degree, on those moral principles which form the bond of union among the intelligent system.

Could we trace the series of events which have occurred, in any one of those happy worlds, where moral perfection prevails, ever since the period when it was replenished with inhabitants, and the objects to which their physical and rational powers have been directed, we should, doubtless, be highly delighted and enraptured with the moral scenery which the history of such a world would display. Its annals would uniformly record the transactions of *benevolence*. We should hear nothing of the pomp of hostile armies, of the shouts of victory, of the exploits of heroes, of the conflagration of cities, of the storming of fortifications, of the avarice of merchants and courtiers, of the burning of heretics, or of the ambition of princes. The train of events, presented to our view, would be directly opposed to every object of this description, and to every thing which forms a *prominent* feature in the history of mankind. To beautify and adorn the scenery of nature around them, to extend their views of the operations of the Almighty, to explore the depths of his wisdom and intelligence, to admire the exuberance of his goodness, to celebrate, in unison the praises of the "King Eternal," the Author of all their enjoyments, to make progressive advances in moral and intellectual attainments, to circulate joy from heart to heart, to exert their ingenuity in the invention of instruments by which their physical powers may be improved, and the wonders of creation more minutely explored; to widen the range of delightful contemplation, to expand their views of the Divine perfections, and to increase the sum of happiness among all their fellow-intelligences, will doubtless form a part of the employments of the inhabitants of a world where moral purity universally prevails. One circumstance which may probably diversify the annals of such a world, and form so many eras in its history, may be the occasional visits of angelic or other messengers, from distant regions of creation, to announce the will of the Almighty on particular emergencies, to relate the progress of new creations in other parts of the Divine Empire, and to convey intelligence respecting the physical aspects, the moral arrangements, and the history of other worlds, and of other orders of intellectual beings. Such visits and occasional intercourses with celestial beings, would, undoubtedly, have been more frequent in our world, had not man rendered himself unqualified for such associations, by his grovelling affections, and by the moral pollutions with which his character is now stained.

When we turn our eyes from the transactions of such a world, to the world in which we live, how very different a scene is presented to the view! The history of all nations embraces little more than

### A RECORD OF THE OPERATIONS OF MALEVOLENCE.

Every occurrence has been considered as tame and insipid, and scarcely worthy of being recorded, unles it has been associated with the confused noise of warriors, the shouts of conquerors, the plunder of provinces, the devastation of empires, the groans of mangled victims, the cries of widows and orphans, and with garments rolled in blood. When such malevolent operations cease for a little, in any part of the world, and the tumultuous passions which produced them, subside into a temporary calm, the historian is presented with a *blank* in the annals of the human race, the short interlude of peace and of apparent tranquillity is passed over as unworthy of notice, till the restless passions of avarice and ambition be again roused into fury, and a new set of desperadoes arise, to carry slaughter and desolation through the nations. For, during the short temporary periods of repose from the din of war, which the world has occasionally enjoyed, the malignant passions, which were only smothered, but not extinguished, prevented the operation of the benevolent affections; and, of course, no extensive plans for the counteraction of evil, and the improvement of mankind, worthy of being recorded by the annalist and the historian, were carried into effect.

In order to produce a definite impression of the moral state of the world, I shall endeavour, in this chapter, to give a rapid sketch of the prominent dispositions of mankind, as displayed in the general train of human actions—that we may be enabled to form a rude estimate of the degree in which the law of God has been recognised, and of the extent to which its violation has been carried, on the great theatre of the world, and in the ordinary transactions of general society.

I shall, in the first place, take a rapid view of the moral state of the world in ancient times, and then take a more particular survey of the present state of morals, among savage and civilized nations—in the Christian world—and among the various ranks and orders of society.

---

## SECTION I.

### STATE OF MORALS IN THE ANCIENT WORLD.

MAN was originally formed after the moral image of his Maker. His understanding was quick and vigorous in its perceptions; his will subject to the divine law, and to the dictates of his reason; his passions serene and uncontaminated with evil; his affections dignified and pure; his love supremely fixed upon his Creator; and his joy unmingled with those sorrows which have so long been the bitter portion of his degenerate race. But the primogenitor of the human race did not long continue in the holy and dignified station in which he was placed. Though he was placed in "a garden of delights," surrounded with every thing that was delicious to the taste and pleasant to the eye, yet he dared to violate a positive command of his Maker, and to stretch forth his impious hand to pluck and to taste the fruit of the forbidden tree—a picture and a prelude of the conduct of millions of his degraded offspring who despise the lawful enjoyments which lie within their reach, and obstinately rush on forbidden pleasures, which terminate in wretchedness and sorrow. The dismal effects of the depraved dispositions thus introduced among the human species, soon became apparent. Cain, the first-born son of Adam, had no sooner reached to the years of maturity, than he gave vent to his revengeful passions, and imbrued his hands in his brother's blood. And ever since the perpetration of this horrid and unnatural deed, the earth has been drenched with the blood of thousands and of millions of human beings, and the stream of corruption has flowed without intermission, and in every direction around the globe.

Of the state of mankind in the ages before the flood, the sacred history furnishes us with only a few brief and general descriptions. But those descriptions, short and general as they are, present to us a most dreadful and revolting picture of the pitch of depravity and wickedness to which the human race had arrived. We have the testimony of God himself to assure us, that, within 1600 years from the creation of the world, "the wickedness of man had become great upon the earth—that the earth was filled with violence"—yea, that "every imagination of the thoughts of man's heart was only evil continually,"—or, as it may more literally be rendered from the Hebrew, "the whole imagination, comprehending all the purposes and desires of the mind, was only evil from day to day."—"God looked upon the earth; and behold it was corrupt; for all flesh had corrupted their way upon the earth." A more comprehensive summary of the greatness and the extent of human wickedness it is scarcely possible to conceive. The mind is left to fill up the outline of this horrid picture with every thing that is degrading to the human character, with every thing that is profligate and abominable in manners, with every thing that is base, false, deceitful, licentious, and profane, and with every thing that is horrible and destructive in war, and ruinous to the interests of human happiness.

The description now quoted, contains the following intimations:—1. That, previous to the deluge, wickedness had become universal. It was not merely the majority of mankind that had thus given unbounded scope to their licentious desires, while smaller societies were to be found in which the worship of the true God, and the precepts of his law were observed. For "*all flesh* had corrupted their ways." And, at this period the world is reckoned to have been much more populous than it has been in any succeeding age, and to have contained at least ten billions of inhabitants, or many thousands of times the amount of its present population. So that universal wickedness must have produced misery among human beings to an extent of which we can form no adequate conception. 2. The description implies, that every invention, and every purpose and scheme devised both by individuals and by communities, *was of a malevolent nature.* "The imagination of every man's heart was *only evil* continually." The dreadful spectacles of misery and horror which the universal prevalence of such principles and practices which then existed, must have produced, are beyond the power of human imagination either to conceive or to delineate. Some faint idea, however, may be formed of some of these spectacles, from the descriptions I have already given of the effects which would inevitably follow, were the principle of *benevolence* to be eradicated from the mind, or were any one of the precepts of the divine law to be universally violated—(see ch. ii. sect. iv. and ch. iii. throughout.) 3. The *effects* produced by this universal depravity are forcibly expressed in the words, "The earth was filled with violence." From this declaration we are necessarily led to conceive a scene in which universal anarchy and disorder, devastation and wretchedness, every where prevailed—the strong and powerful forcibly seizing upon the wealth and possessions of the weak, violating the persons of the female sex, oppressing the poor, the widow, and the fatherless, overturning the established order of families and societies, plundering cities, demolishing temples and palaces, desolating fields, orchards, and vineyards, setting fire to towns and villages, and carrying bloodshed and devastation through every land—a scene in which cruelty, injustice, and outrages of every kind, obscenity, revelry, riot, and debauchery of every description, triumphed over every principle of decency and virtue—a scene in which the earth was strewed with smoking ruins, with the fragments of human habitations, with mangled human beings in a state of wretchedness and despair, and with the unburied carcasses of the slain.

Such appears to have been the state of general society at the time when Noah was commanded to build an ark of refuge—a state of society which could not have long continued, but must inevitably, in the course of a few generations, have thinned the race of mankind, and ultimately have extirpated the race of Adam from the earth, even although the deluge had never been poured upon the world. Wickedness appears to have come to such a height, that no interposition of Providence could be supposed available to produce a reformation among mankind, without destroying their freedom of will; and, therefore, it was an act of *mercy*, as well as of judgment, to sweep them away at once by the waters of the flood, after having given them warnings of their danger; in order to convince such obstinate and abandoned characters, that "there is a God that judgeth in the earth;" and in order to prevent the misery which would otherwise have been entailed on succeeding generations.

Not only the Sacred, but also the Pagan writers, when alluding to the antediluvians, uniformly represent them as abandoned to uncleanness, and all kinds of wickedness. Eutychus, in his *Annals*, when speaking of the posterity of Cain, says, "that they were guilty of all manner of filthy crimes with one another, and, meeting together in public places for that purpose, two or three men were concerned with the same woman the ancient women, if possible, being more lustfu and brutish than the young. Nay, fathers lived promiscuously with their daughters, and the young men with their mothers, so that neither the children could distinguish their own parents, nor the parents know their own children."—Lucian, a native of Samosata, a town situated on the Euphrates, a spot where memorials of the deluge were carefully preserved, gives the following account of the antediluvians:—"The present race of mankind," says he, "are different from those who first existed; for those of the antediluvian world were all destroyed. The present world is peopled from the sons of Deucalion [or Noah;] having increased to so great a number from one person. In respect of the former brood, they were men of violence, and lawless in their dealings. They were contentious, and did many unrighteous things; they regarded not oaths, nor observed the rights of hospitality, nor showed mercy to those who sued for it. On this account they were doomed to destruction: and for this purpose there was a mighty eruption of waters from the earth, attended with heavy showers from above; so that the rivers swelled, and the sea overflowed, till the whole earth was covered with a flood, and all flesh drowned. Deucalion alone was preserved to re-people the world. This mercy was shown to him on account of his piety and justice. His preservation was effected in this manner:—He put all his family, both his sons and their wives, into a vast ark which he had provided, and he went into it himself. At the same time animals of every species—boars, horses, lions, serpents, whatever kind lived upon the face of the earth—followed him by pairs; all which he received into the ark, and experienced no evil from them; for there prevailed a wonderful harmony throughout, by the immediate influence of the Deity. Thus were they wafted with him as long as the flood endured."

Such is the account which Lucian gives of the antediluvian world, and of the preservation of the human race, as he received it from the traditions of the inhabitants of Hierapolis, in Syria, where the natives pretended to have very particular memorials of the deluge. It corroborates the facts stated in the sacred history, and bears a very near resemblance to the authentic account which has been transmitted to us by Moses.—These facts, respecting the depravity of the antediluvians, present to us a striking example, and a demonstrative evidence of the dreadful effects to which a general violation of the divine law necessarily leads; and of the extensive confusion and misery which are inevitably produced, when the law of love is set aside, and when malevolence exerts, without control, its diabolical energies. All order in society is subverted, every species of rational happiness is destroyed, and the existence of intelligent beings, in such a state, becomes a curse to themselves, and to all around them. Had not this been the case in the primeval world, we cannot suppose that the Deity would have exerted his Omnipotence in shattering the crust of the terraqueous globe, and burying its inhabitants under the waters of a deluge.

After the deluge had subsided, and the race of Noah had begun to multiply on the earth, it was not long before the depravity of man began to show itself by its malignant effects; though human wickedness has never arrived to such a pitch as in the times before the flood; for this reason, among others, that the life of man has been reduced to a narrow span, which prevents him from carrying his malevolent schemes to such an extent as did the inhabitants of the world before the flood, whose lives were prolonged to the period of nearly a thousand years. The lust of *ambition* soon began to exert its baleful influence over the mind; and an inordinate desire after wealth, distinctions, and aggrandizement, paved the way for the establishment of despotism, and for encroachments on the rights and the enjoyments of mankind. Among the heroes and despots of antiquity, *Nimrod*, the founder of the Babylonish empire, holds a distinguished place. He was the grandson of *Ham*, the son of Noah, and is the first one mentioned in Scripture who appears to have made invasions on the territories of his neighbours. Having distinguished himself, by driving from his country the beasts of prey, and by engaging in other valorous exploits, he appears to have aspired after regal dignity and power, and to have assumed the reins of absolute government. He was the first that subverted the patriarchal government; and is supposed to have introduced, among his subjects, the *Zabian* idolatry, or the worship of the heavenly host. "The beginning of his kingdom," we are told, "was Babylon, and Erech, and Accad, and Calneh, in the land of Shinar." In the footsteps of this proud and ambitious despot, has followed a train of Alexanders, Cæsars, Hannibals, Jenghiz-Kans, Attilas, Alaric, Tamerlanes, Marlboroughs, Fredericks, and Bonapartes, who have driven the plough-share of devastation through the world, erected thrones over the graves of slaughtered nations, decorated their palaces with trophies dyed in blood, and made the earth to resound with the groans and shrieks of dying victims, and the voice of mourning, lamentation, and wo.

To delineate all the scenes of desolation and horror which have been produced by such desperadoes, and the atrocious crimes and immoralities which have followed in their train, would be to transcribe the whole records of ancient and modern history, which contain little else than a register of human folly, avarice, ambition, and cruelty; and of the daring villanies with which they have been accompanied. Even then, we should acquire but a very limited conception of the extent of moral evil, and of the immense variety of shapes which it has assumed; for the one tenth of the crimes of mankind has never been recorded; and it is to the public transactions of only a small portion of the world that the page of the historian directs our attention. I shall, therefore, content myself with stating a few insulated facts, as specimens of the train of actions which have generally prevailed in the world.

### WARLIKE DISPOSITIONS OF MANKIND.

*War*, as already noticed, has been the delight and the employment of man in every age; and, under this term may be included every thing that is base and execrable in moral conduct, every thing that is subversive of the principle of benevolence, every thing that is destructive of human enjoyment, every thing that rouses the passions into diabolical fury, every thing that adds to the sum of human wretchedness, every thing that is oppressive, cruel, and unjust, and every thing that is dreadful and appalling to mankind.—As an exemplification of the destructive effects of war, I shall, in the first place, state a few facts in relation to the Carthaginians.

Carthage was originally a small colony of Phenicians, who, about 800 years before the Christian era, settled on the northern coast of Africa, on a small peninsula, adjacent to the bay of Tunis. Having increased in wealth and power, by means of their extensive commerce, like most other nations, they attempted to make inroads on the territories of neighbouring tribes, and to plunder them of their treasures. By degrees they extended their power over all the islands in the Mediterranean, Sicily only excepted. For the entire conquest of this island, about 480 years before Christ, they made vast preparations, which lasted for three years. Their army consisted of 300,000 men; their fleet was composed of upwards of 2000 men of war, and 3000 transports. With such an immense armament, they made no doubt of conquering the whole island in a single campaign. But they found themselves miserably deceived. Hamilcar, the most experienced captain of the age, sailed from Carthage with this formidable army, and invested the city of Hymera. The besieged were much straitened and dismayed by the operations of this powerful armament; but Gelon, the tyrant of Syracuse, flew immediately to their relief, with 50,000 foot and 5000 horse. A dreadful slaughter ensued: an hundred and fifty thousand of the Carthaginians were killed in the battle and pursuit, and all the rest taken prisoners; so that not a single person escaped of this mighty army. Of the 2000 ships of war, and the 3000 transports of which the fleet consisted, *eight* ships only, which then happened to be out at sea, made their escape: these immediately set sail for Carthage, but were all cast away, and every soul perished, except a few who were saved in a small boat, and at last reached Carthage with the dismal tidings of the total loss of the fleet and army.—Here we have presented to our view, in one short struggle, the entire destruction of more than *two hundred thousand* human beings, if we take into account the number which must necessarily have fallen in the Sicilian army. And, if we take into consideration the many thousands of mangled wretches, whose existence, from that moment, would be rendered miserable; the destruction of property in the besieged city; the victims crushed to death amidst the ruins of falling houses; the cries, and shrieks, and lamentations of women and children; the diseases and the misery induced by terror and alarm, and the loss of friends; the terrific and appalling spectacle of 5000 ships all on a blaze, of ten thousands of burning and drowning wretches, supplicating in vain for mercy, and the oaths, execrations, and furious yells which would be mingled with this work of destruction, we shall find it difficult to form an adequate conception of the miseries and horrors of such a scene. And what was the cause of this dreadful slaughter and devastation? That a proud and opulent city, whose inhabitants were rioting in every species of luxury, might gratify its ambition, by tyrannizing over neighbouring tribes, and by plundering them of that wealth of which it did not stand in need. And this is but *one* instance out of ten hundred thousand of the miseries of war,—one *faint shade* in the picture of human wo!

One would have thought, that, after such a signal loss and discomfiture, the Carthaginians would have contented themselves with their own territory, and refrained from aggressive war. This, however, was not the case. Where benevolence is banished from the mind, and *revenge* occupies its place in the affections, it will hurry unprincipled men to the most wild and atrocious actions, although they should terminate in destruction to themselves and to all around them. It was not long after this period, when preparations were again made for the invasion of Sicily. Hannibal, the grandson of Hamilcar, landed on the coast of Sicily, and laid siege to Selinus. The besieged made a vigorous defence; but at last the city was taken by storm, and the inhabitants were treated with the utmost cruelty. All were massacred by the savage conquerors, except the women, who fled to the temples;—and these escaped, not through the merciful dispositions of the Carthaginians, but because they were afraid, that, if driven to despair, they would set fire to the temples, and by that means consume the treasure they expected to find in those places. Sixteen thousand were massacred; the women and children, about 5000 in number, were carried away captive; the temples were plundered of all their treasures, and the city razed to the ground. Hymera was next besieged by Hannibal, and razed to its foundations. He forced three thousand prisoners to undergo all kinds of ignominy and punishments, and at last murdered them, on the very spot where his grandfather had been killed by Gelon's cavalry, to appease and satisfy his *manes*, by the blood of these unhappy victims. such is the *humanity* and the *justice* of those men, whom we are accustomed to distinguish by the names of *Patriots* and *Heroes!*—Elated with these partial victories, the Carthaginians meditated the reduction of the whole of Sicily. They marched against the city of Agrigentum, and battered its walls with dreadful fury. The besieged defended themselves with incredible resolution. In a sally, they burned all the battering machines raised against their city, and repulsed the enemy with immense slaughter. Again the Carthaginians rallied their forces, beat down the walls of the city, plundered it of an immense booty, and with their usual cruelty, put all its inhabitants to the sword, not excepting even those who had fled to the temples. The Carthaginians were soon after forced to retire from Sicily. Again they renewed their expeditions; again they were repulsed; and again they plunged into the horrors of war; while thousands and ten thousands were slaughtered at every onset; men, women, and children massacred in cold blood and the pestilence produced by the unburied carcasses of the slain, proved more fatal to myriads, than even the sword of the warrior.

In this manner did these infatuated mortals carry on a series of sanguinary contests for several centuries, with the Sicilians, Greeks, and other nations; till, at length, they dared to encounter the power, and the formidable forces of the Romans, and commenced those dreadful and long-continued conflicts, distinguished in History by the name of *The Punic Wars.* The first Punic war lasted twenty-four years; the second, seventeen years; and the third, four years and some months. In this last contest, the ploughshare of destruction was literally driven through their devoted city, by the Romans. It was delivered up to be plundered by their soldiers; its gold, silver, statues, and other treasures amounting to 4,470,000 pounds weight of silver, were carried off to Rome; its towers, ramparts, walls, and all the works which the Carthaginians had raised in the course of many ages, were levelled to the ground. Fire was set to the edifices of this proud metropolis, which consumed them all, not a single house escaping the fury of the flames. And though the fire began in all quarters at the same time, and burned with incredible violence, it continued for *seventeen* days before all the buildings were consumed.—Thus perished Carthage—a city which contained 700,000 inhabitants, and which had waged so many ferocious wars with neighbouring nations—a terrible example of the destructive effects produced by malevolent passions, and of the retributive justice of the Governor of the world. The destruction of human life in the numerous wars in which it was engaged, is beyond all specific calculation. During the space of sixteen years, Hannibal, the Carthaginian general, plundered no less than four hundred towns, and destroyed 300,000 of his enemies; and we may safely reckon, that nearly an equal number of his own men must have been cut off by the opposing armies; so that several millions of human victims must have been sacrificed in these bloody and cruel wars.

The following is a summary statement of the number of human beings that were slain in several of the battles recorded in history.—In the year 101 before Christ, in an engagement between Marius, the Roman Consul, and the Ambrones and the Teutones, in Transalpine Gaul, there were slain of these barbarians, besides what fell in the Roman army, 200,000, some historians say, 290,000. And it is related, that the inhabitants of the neighbouring country made fences for vineyards of their bones. In the following year, the Romans, under the command of the same general, slaughtered 140,000 of the Cimbri, and took 60,000 prisoners. In the year 105, B. C. the Romans, in a single engagement with the Cimbri and the Teutones, lost upwards of 80,000 men. In the battle of Cannæ, the Romans were surrounded by the forces of Hannibal, and cut to pieces. After an engagement of only *three hours*, the carnage became so dreadful, that even the Carthaginian general cried out, to spare the conquered. Above 40,000 Romans lay dead on the field, and six thousand of the Carthaginian army. What a dreadful display of the rage and fury of diabolical passions must have been exhibited on this occasion! and what a horrible scene must have been presented on the field of battle, when we consider, that, in the mode of ancient warfare, the slain were literally mangled, and cut to pieces!—In the battle of Issus, between Alexander and Darius, were slain 110,000; in the battle of Arbela, two years afterwards, between the same two despots, 300,000; in the battle between Pyrrhus and the Romans, 25,000; in the battle between Scipio and Asdrubal, 40,000; in the battle between Suetonius and Boadicea, 80,000. In the siege of Jerusalem by Vespasian, according to the account of Josephus, there were destroyed, in the most terrible manner, 1,100,000; and there were slaughtered in Jerusalem, in 170, B. C. by Antiochus, 40,000. At Cyrene, there were slain of Romans and Greeks, by the Jews, 220,000; in Egypt and Cyprus, in the reign of Trajan, 240,000; and in the reign of Adrian, 580,000 Jews. After Julius Cæsar had carried his arms into the territories of Usipetes in Germany, he defeated them with such slaughter, that 400,000 are said to have perished in one battle. At the defeat of Attila, King of the Huns, at Chalons, there perished about 300,000. In the year 631, there were slain by the Saracens in Syria, 60,000; in the invasion of Milan by the Goths, no less than 300,000; and in A. D. 734, by the Saracens in Spain, 370,000. In the battle of Fontenay, were slaughtered 100,000; in the battle of Yermouk, 150,000; and in the battle between Charles Martel and the Mahometans, 350,000. In the battle of Muret, in A. D. 1213, between the Catholics and the Albigenses, were slain 32,000; in the battle of Cressy, in 1346, 50,000; in the battle of Halidon-hill, in 1333, 20,000; in the battle of Agincourt, in 1415, 20,000; in the battle of Towton, in 1461, 37,000; in the battle of Lepanto, in 1571, 25,000; at the siege of Vienna, in 1683, 70,000; and in a battle in Persia, in 1734, 60,000.*

The most numerous army of which we have any account in the annals of history, was that of Xerxes. According to the statement of Rollin, which is founded on the statements of Herodotus, Isocrates, and Plutarch, this army consisted of 1,700,000 foot, 80,000 horse, and 20,000 men for conducting the carriages and camels. On passing the Hellespont, an addition was made to it from other nations, of 300,000, which made his land forces amount to 2,100,000. His fleet consisted of 1207 vessels, each carrying 230 men; in all 277,610 men, which was augmented by the European nations, with 1200 vessels carrying 240,000 men. Besides this fleet the small galleys, transport ships, &c. amounted to 3000, containing about 240,000 men. Including servants, eunuchs, women, sutlers, and others, who usually follow an army, it is reckoned, that the whole number of souls that followed Xerxes into Greece, amounted to 5,283,220; which is more than the whole of the male population of Great Britian and Ireland, above twenty years of age, and nearly triple the whole population of Scotland. After remaining some time in Greece, nearly the whole of this immense army, along with the fleet, was routed and destroyed. Mardonius, one of his ablest commanders, with an army of 300,000, was finally defeated and slain at the battle of Platea, and only three thousand of this vast army, with difficulty escaped destruction.

The destruction of human life in the wars which accompanied and followed the incursions of the barbarians, who overthrew the Roman empire, is beyond all calculation or conception. It forms an era in history most degrading to the human species. In the war which was waged in Africa, in the days of Justinian, Procopius remarks, "It is no exaggeration to say, that five

* The above statements are collected from the facts stated in Rollin's Ancient History, Millot's Elements, Mavor's Universal History, the historical Articles in the Encyclopedia Britannica, from a list of battles contained in the "Pictures of War," &c.

millions perished by the sword, and famine, and pestilence." The same author states that, during the twenty years' war which Justinian carried on with the Gothic conquerors of Italy, the loss of the Goths amounted to above 15 millions; nor will this appear incredible, when we find, that in one campaign, 50,000 labourers died of hunger. About the beginning of the 13th century arose that cruel and bloody tyrant Jenghiz-Khan. With immense armies, some of them amounting to more than a million in number, he overran and subdued the kingdom of Hya in China, Tangut, Kitay, Turkestan, Karazum, Great Buckaria, Persia, and part of India, committing the most dreadful cruelties and devastations. It is computed, that, during the last 22 years of his reign, no fewer than 14,470,000 persons were butchered by this scourge of the human race. He appeared like an infernal fiend, breathing destruction to the nations of the East, and the principle which he adopted, after conquest, was *utter extermination.*

Nearly about the same period when this monster was ravaging and slaughtering the eastern world, those mad expeditions, distinguished by the name of the *Crusades*, were going forward in the west. Six millions of infatuated wretches, raging with hatred, and thursting for blood, assumed the image of the cross, and marched in wild disorder to the confines of the Holy land, in order to recover the city of Jerusalem from the hands of the infidels. In these *holy wars*, as they were impiously termed, more than 850,000 Europeans were sacrificed before they obtained possession of Nice, Antioch, and Edessa. At the siege of Acre, 300,000 were slain; and at the taking of Jerusalem, in 1099, about seventy thousand. For 196 years, these wild expeditions continued in vogue, and were urged forward by proclamations issued from the throne, and by fanatical sermons thundered from the pulpit, till several millions of deluded mortals perished from the earth; for by far the greater part of those who engaged in the crusades, were either slain or taken prisoners. About this period, and several centuries before it, the whole earth exhibited little else than one great field of battle, in which nations were dashing against each other, conquerors ravaging kingdoms, tyrants exercising the most horrid cruelties; superstition and revenge immolating their millions of victims; and tumults, insurrections, slaughter, and universal alarm, banishing peace and tranquillity from the world, and subverting the moral order of society. "In Europe, Germany and Italy were distracted by incessant contests between the pope and the emperors; the interior of every European kingdom was torn in pieces by the contending ambition of the powerful barons; in the Mahomedan empire, the caliphs, sultans, emirs, &c. waged continual war; new sovereignties were daily arising, and daily destroyed; and amidst this universal slaughter and devastation, the whole earth seemed in danger of being laid waste, and the human race to suffer a total annihilation."*

Such is the bird's eye view of the destruction of the human species, which war has produced in different periods. The instances I have brought forward present only a few detached circumstances in the annals of warfare, and relate only to a few limited periods in the history of man: and yet in the four instances above stated, we are presented with a scene of horror, which includes the destruction of nearly 50 millions of human beings. What a vast and horrific picture, then, would be presented to the eye, could we take in at one view *all the scenes* of slaughter, which have been realized in every period, in every nation, and among every tribe! If we take into consideration not only the number of those who have fallen in the field of battle, but of those who have perished through the natural consequences of war, by the famine and the pestilence, which war has produced; by disease, fatigue, terror, and melancholy; and by the oppression, injustice, and cruelty of savage conquerors,—it will not, perhaps, be overrating the destruction of human life, if we affirm, that *one tenth* of the human race has been destroyed by the ravages of war. And if this estimate be admitted, it will follow, that more than *fourteen thousand millions* of human beings have been slaughtered in war, since the beginning of the world—which is about *eighteen times* the number of inhabitants which, at the present, exist on the globe; or, in other words, it is equivalent to the destruction of the inhabitants of eighteen worlds of the same population as ours.† That this conclusion is rather within than beyond the bounds of truth, will appear, from what has been stated above respecting the destruction of the Goths, in the time of Justinian. In the course of 20 years, 15 millions of persons perished in the wars. Now, if the population of the countries of Europe, in which these wars took place, did not exceed 60 millions, the proportion of the slaughtred to the whole population was as *one* to *four*, and, if 20 years be reckoned as only half the period of a generation, the proportion was as *one* to *two*; in other words, at the rate of one half of a whole generation in the course of 40 years. What a horrible and tremendous consideration?—to reflect, that 14,000,000,000 of beings, endowed with intellectual faculties, and furnished with bodies curiously organized by divine wisdom—that the inhabitants of eighteen worlds should have been massacred, mangled, and cut to pieces, by those

* Mavor's Universal History, Robertson's Charles V. &c.

† This calculation proceeds on the ground, that 145 thousand millions of men have existed since the Mosaic creation. See Christian philosopher, Art. *Geography.*

who were partakers of the same common nature, as if they had been created merely for the work of destruction! Language is destitute of words sufficiently strong to express the emotions of the mind, when it seriously contemplates the horrible scene. And how melancholy is it to reflect, that in the present age, which boasts of its improvements in science, in civilization, and in religion, neither reason, nor benevolence, nor humanity, nor Christianity, has yet availed to arrest the progress of destroying armies, and to set a mark of ignominy on "the people who delight in war!"

### ATROCITIES CONNECTED WITH WAR.

However numerous may have been the victims that have been sacrificed in war, it is not so much the mere extinction of human life that renders the scene of warfare so horrible, as the cruelties with which it has always been accompanied, and the infernal passions which it has engendered and carried into operation. It extirpates every principle of compassion, humanity, and justice; it blunts the feelings, and hardens the heart; it invents instruments of torture, and perpetrates, without a blush, cruelties revolting to every principle of virtue and benevolence.

When Jerusalem was taken by Antiochus Epiphanes, in the year 168, B. C. he gave orders to one division of his army to cut in pieces all who were found in the temple and synagogues; while another party, going through the streets of the city, massacred all that came in their way. He next ordered the city to be plundered and set on fire; pulled down all their stately buildings, caused the walls to be demolished, and carried away captive ten thousand of those who had escaped the slaughter. He set up the statue of Jupiter Olympus on the altar of burnt-offerings, and all who refused to come and worship this idol were either massacred, or put to some cruel tortures, till they either complied or expired under the hands of the executioners. In the war which the Carthaginians waged with the Mercenaries, Hamilcar, the Carthaginian general, threw all the prisoners that fell into his hands to be devoured by wild beasts. Asdrubal, another Carthaginian general, when engaged in war against the Romans, in revenge for a defeat he had sustained, brought all the Roman prisoners he had taken during two years, upon the walls, in the sight of the whole Roman army. There he put them to the most exquisite tortures, putting out their eyes, cutting off their noses, ears, and fingers, legs and arms, tearing their skin to pieces with iron rakes or harrows; and then threw them headlong from the top of the battlements.* He was of a temper remarkably inhuman, and it is said that he even took pleasure in seeing some of these unhappy men flayed alive.—In the year 1201, when Jenghiz-Khan had reduced the rebels who had seized upon his paternal possessions, as a specimen of his lenity, he caused seventy of their chiefs to be thrown into as many cauldrons of boiling water. The plan on which this tyrant conducted his expeditions, as already stated, was that of total extermination. For some time he utterly extirpated the inhabitants of those places which he conquered, designing to people them anew with his Moguls; and, in consequence of this resolution, he would employ his army in beheading 100,000 prisoners at once.—Tamerlane, one of his successors, who followed in his footsteps, is said to have been more humane than this cruel despot. Historians inform us that "his sportive cruelty seldom went farther than the pounding of three or four thousand people in large mortars, or building them among bricks and mortar into a wall." If such be the "tender mercies of the wicked," how dreadful beyond description must their cruelties be!

We are accustomed to hear Alexander the Great eulogized as a virtuous and magnanimous hero; and even the celebrated Montesquieu, in his "Spirit of Laws," has written a panegyric on his character. Yet we find him guilty of the most abominable vices, and perpetrating the most atrocious crimes. At the instigation of the strumpet Thais, during a drunken banquet, he set on fire the beautiful city of Persepolis, and consumed it to ashes. Clitus, one of his captains, and brother of Helenice who had nursed Alexander, and saved his life at the battle of the Granicus, at the imminent danger of his own. Yet this man, to whom he was so highly indebted, he thrust through with a javelin, at an entertainment to which he had invited him; on account of his uttering some strong expressions, which were intended to moderate Alexander's vanity. His treatment of the Branchidæ furnishes an example of the most brutal and frantic cruelty which history records. These people received Alexander, while pursuing his conquests, with the highest demonstrations of joy, and surrendered to him, both themselves and their city. The next day, he commanded his phalanx to surround the city, and, a signal being given, they were ordered to plunder it, and to put every one of its inhabitants to the sword, which inhuman order was executed with the same barbarity with which it had been given. All the citizens, at the very time they were going to pay homage to Alexander, were murdered in the streets and in their houses; no manner of regard being had to their cries and tears, nor the least distinction made of age or sex. They even pulled up the very foundations of the walls, in order that not the least traces of that city might remain. And why were these ill-fated citizens punished in so summary and inhuman a manner? Merely because their forefathers, upwards of one hundred and fifty years before, had

* Rollin's Ancient History, Vol. I

delivered up to Xerxes the treasure of the temple of Didymaon, with which they had been intrusted !*—When he entered the city of Tyre, after a siege of seven months, he gave orders to kill all the inhabitants, except those who had fled to the temples, and set fire to every part of the city. Eight thousand men were barbarously slaughtered; and two thousand more remaining, after the soldiers had been glutted with slaughter, he fixed two thousand crosses along the seashore,† and caused them all to be crucified.

War has given rise to the most shocking and unnatural crimes, the idea of which might never otherwise have entered into the human mind. Lathyrus, after an engagement with Alexander, king of the Jews, on the banks of the river Jordan,—the same evening he gained the battle, in going to take up his quarters in the neighbouring villages, he found them full of women and children, and caused them all to be put to the sword, and their bodies to be cut to pieces, and put into cauldrons in order to their being dressed, as if he intended to make his army sup upon them. His design was to have it believed, that his troops ate human flesh, to spread the greater terror throughout the surrounding country.‡

Even under the pretext of religion, and of the *Christian* religion too, the most shocking barbarities have been committed. Under the pretence of vindicating the cause of Him who, in the midst of cruel sufferings from men, prayed, "Father, forgive them, for they know not what they do," the crusaders hurried forward towards Jerusalem, wading through seas of blood. When their banners were hoisted on a principal eminence of Antioch, they commenced their butchery of the sleeping inhabitants. The dignity of age, the helplessness of youth, and the beauty of the weaker sex, were disregarded by these sanctimonious savages. Houses were no sanctuaries; and the sight of a mosque added new virulence to cruelty. The number of Turks massacred, on this night of frantic fury, was at least ten thousand. After every species of habitation, from the marble palace to the meanest hovel, had been converted into a scene of slaughter; when the narrow streets and the spacious squares were all alike disfigured with human gore, and crowded with mangled carcasses, then the assassins turned robbers, and became as mercenary as they had been merciless. When Jerusalem was taken by these furious fanatics, they suffered none to escape the slaughter: "Yet, after they had glutted themselves with blood and carnage, they immediately became devout pilgrims, and in religious transports, ran barefooted to visit the holy sepulchre."§ In what light must that religion appear to Eastern Infidels which is supposed to lead to the perpetration of such enormities? And how woefully are the mild precepts and doctrines of Christianity misrepresented, when desperadoes of this description dare assume the Christian name!

Even the finer feelings of the female sex have been blunted, and, in many instances, quite extirpated by the mad schemes of ambition, and the practices connected with war. Towards the beginning of the thirteenth century, a Queen of Hungary took the sign of the cross, and embarked in the mad expeditions of the crusaders, as did likewise fifty thousand children and a crowd of priests; because, according to the Scripture, "God has made children the instruments of his glory."‖—Cleopatra, daughter of Ptolemy Philometer, in order to gratify her restless ambition of reigning alone and uncontrolled in her dominions, killed her son Seleucus, with her own hand, by plunging a dagger into his breast. She had been the wife of three Kings of Syria and the mother of four, and had occasioned the death of two of her husbands. She prepared a poisoned draught to destroy Grypus another of her sons; but her intention having been suspected, she was compelled to swallow the deadly potion she had prepared, which took immediate effect, and delivered the world from this female monster. The Carthaginians were in the practice of offering human sacrifices to their god Saturn, when they were defeated in war, in order to propitiate the wrath of this deity. At first, children were inhumanly burned, either in a fiery furnace, like those in the valley of Hinnom, so frequently mentioned in Scripture, or in a flaming statue of Saturn.—The cries of these unhappy victims were drowned by the uninterrupted noise of drums and trumpets. Mothers made it a merit, and a part of their religion, to view the barbarous spectacle with dry eyes, and without so much as a groan; and if a tear or sigh stole from them, the sacrifice was considered as less acceptable to the deity. This savage disposition was carried to such excess, that even mothers would endeavour, with embraces and kisses to hush the cries of their children, lest they should anger the god.¶ When Carthage was taken by the Romans, the wife of Asdrubal, the Carthaginian general, who had submitted to the Romans, mounted to the upper part of one of the temples which had been set on fire; and, placing herself, with her two children, in sight of her husband, uttered the most bitter imprecations against him. "Base coward (said she) the mean things thou hast done to save thy life shall not avail thee; thou shalt die this instant, at least in thy two children." Having thus spoken, she stabbed both the infants with a dagger, and while they were yet struggling for life, threw them both from the top of the temple, and then leaped down after them into the flames!**

* Rollin's Ancient Hist. † Ibid. ‡ Ibid.
§ Millot's Elements of Gen. Hist.

‖ Millot's Elem. ¶ Rollin's An. Hist.
** Ency. Brit. Art. *Carthage*.

Such are only a few insulated pictures of the atrocities of war, and of the unnatural and infernal passions which uniformly follow in its train, which may be considered as specimens of many thousands of similar instances, which the records of history furnish of the malignity and depravity of mankind. I have selected my examples chiefly from the history of ancient warfare: but were we to search the annals of *modern* warfare, and confine our attention solely to the battles of Alexandria, of the Pyramids, of Borodina, of Smolensko, of Austerlitz, of Leipsic, of Jena, of Eylan, of Waterloo, and other warlike events which have happened within the last thirty years, we should meet with atrocities and scenes of slaughter, no less horrible than those which I have now related. I shall content myself with stating only two or three instances.

After the taking of Alexandria by Bonaparte, "We were under the necessity," says the relator, "of putting the whole of them to death at the breach. But the slaughter did not cease with the resistance. The Turks and inhabitants fled to their mosques, seeking protection from God and their prophet; and then, *men and women, old and young, and infants at the breast, were slaughtered.* This butchery continued for *four hours;* after which the remaining part of the inhabitants were much astonished at not having their throats cut." Be it remembered that all this bloodshed was premeditated. "We might have spared the men whom we lost," says General Boyer, "by only summoning the town; but it was necessary to begin by confounding our enemy."* After the battle of the Pyramids, it is remarked by an eye-wintess, that "the whole way through the desert, was tracked with the bones and bodies of men and animals who had perished in these dreadful wastes.—In order to warm themselves at night, they gathered together the dry bones and bodies of the dead, which the vultures had spared, and *it was by a fire composed of this fuel that Bonaparte lay down to sleep in the desert.*"† A more revolting and infernal scene it is scarcely possible for the imagination to depict.

Miot gives the following description in relation to a scene at Jaffa:—"The soldier abandons himself to all the fury which an assault authorizes. He strikes, he slays, nothing can impede him. All the horrors which accompany the capture of a town by storm, are repeated in every street, in every house. You hear the cries of violated females calling in vain for help to those relatives whom they are butchering. No asylum is respected. The blood streams on every side; at every step you meet with human beings groaning and expiring," &c.—Sir Robert Wilson, when describing the campaigns in Poland relates, that "the ground between the wood and the Russian batteries, about a quarter of mile, was *a sheet of naked human bodies*, which friends and foes had during the night mutually stripped, not leaving the worst rag upon them, although numbers of these bodies *still retained consciousness* of their situation. It was a sight which the eye loathed, but from which it could not remove."—In Labaume's "Narrative of the Campaign in Russia," we are presented with the most horrible details of palaces, churches, and streets, enveloped in flames,—houses tumbling into ruins,—hundreds of blackened carcasses of the wretched inhabitants, whom the fire had consumed, blended with the fragments,—hospitals containing 20,000 wounded Russians on fire, and consuming the miserable victims,—numbers of half-burned wretches crawling among the smoking ruins,—females violated and massacred,—parents and children half naked, shivering with cold, flying in consteration with the wrecks of their half-consumed funiture,—horses falling in thousands, and writhing in the agonies of death,—the fragments of carriages, muskets, helmets, breast-plates, portmanteaus, and garments strewed in every direction,—roads covered for miles with thousands of the dying and the dead heaped one upon another, and swimming in blood,—and these dreadful scenes rendered still more horrific by the shrieks of young females, of mothers and children, and the piercing cries of the wounded and the dying, invoking death to put an end to their agonies.

But I will not dwell longer on such revolting details. It is probable, that the feelings of some of my readers have been harrowed up by the descriptions already given, and that they have turned away their eyes in disgust from such spectacles of depravity and horror. Every mind susceptible of virtuous emotions, and of the common feelings of humanity, must, indeed, feel pained and even agonized, when it reflects on the depravity of mankind, and on the atrocious crimes they are capable of committing, and have actually perpetrated. A serious retrospect of the moral state of the world in past ages, is calculated to excite emotions, similar to those which overpowered the mourning prophet when he exclaimed, "O that my head were waters, and mine eyes a fountain of tears, that I might weep day and night, for the slain of the daughters of my people!" But, however painful the sight, we ought not to turn away our eyes, with fastidious affectation, from the spectacles of misery and devastation which the authentic records of history present before us. They form traits in the character of man, which ought to be contemplated,—they are *facts* in the history of mankind, and not the mere pictures of fancy which are exhibited in poetry, in novels, and romances,—facts which forcibly exemplify the operations of the malevolent principle, and from which we ought to deduce important instructions, in reference

* Miot's Memoirs. † Ibid.

to the evil of sin, and the malignancy of pride, covetousness, ambition, and revenge. We think nothing, in the common intercourse of life, of indulging a selfish disposition, of feeling proud and indignant at a real or supposed affront, of looking with a covetous eye at the possessions of our neighbours, of viewing the success and prosperity of our rivals with discontentment and jealousy, or of feeling a secret satisfaction at the distress or humiliation of our enemies; and we seldom reflect on the malignant effects which such passions and dispositions would produce, were they suffered to rage without control. But, in the scenes and contentions of warfare which have been realized on the great theatre of the world, we contemplate the nature and effects of such malignant dispositions in their true light; we perceive the ultimate tendency of every malevolent affection, when no physical obstruction impedes its progress; we discern that it is only the same dispositions which we daily indulge, operating on a more extensive scale; and we learn the necessity of mortifying such dispositions, and counteracting their influence, if we expect to enjoy substantial felicity either here or hereafter; and if we wish to see the world restored to order, to happiness and repose.

I shall only observe farther on this part of my subject, that, besides the atrocities already noticed, war has been *the nurse of every vicious disposition*, and of every immoral practice. The Carthaginians, who were almost incessantly engaged in war, were knavish, vicious, cruel, and superstitious; distinguished for craft and cunning, lying and hypocrisy, and for the basest frauds and the most perfidious actions. The Goths and Vandals are uniformly characterized, as not only barbarous and cruel, but avaricious, perfidious, and disregardful of the most solemn promises. It was ever a sufficient reason for them to make an attack, that they thought their enemies could not resist them. Their only reason for making peace, or for keeping it, was because their enemies were too strong; and their only reason for committing the most horrible massacres, rapes, and all manner of crimes, was because they had gained a victory. The Greeks and Romans, it is well known, notwithstanding their superior civilization, were distinguished for the most degrading and immoral practices. They gloried in being proud, haughty, and revengeful; and even their amusements were characterized by a spirit of ferocity, and by the barbarisms of war.—It is almost needless to say that war blunts the finer feelings of humanity, and engenders a spirit of selfishness, and of indifference even towards friends and companions. Of this many shocking instances could be given.

Miot in his Memoirs of the War in Egypt, relates the case of a soldier who was seized with the plague, and with the delirium which sometimes accompanies the disease. He took up his knapsack, upon which his head was resting, and placing it upon his shoulders, made an effort to rise, and to follow the army. The venom of the dreadful malady deprived him of strength, and after three steps, he fell again upon the sand, headlong. The fall increased his terror of being left by the regiment, and he rose a second time, but with no better fortune. In his third effort, he sunk, and, falling near the sea, remained upon that spot which fate had destined for his grave. The sight of this soldier was frightful: the disorder which reigned in his senseless speech—his figure, which represented whatever is mournful—his eyes staring and fixed—his clothes in rags—presented whatever is most hideous in death. The reader may perhaps believe that his comrades would be concerned for him; that they would stop to help him; that they would hasten to support him, and direct his tottering steps. Far from it: the poor wretch was only an object of horror and *derision*. They ran from him, and they burst into *loud laughter* at his motions, which resembled those of a drunken man, "He has got his account," cried one; "He will not march far," said another; and, when the wretch fell for the last time, some of them added, "See, he has taken up his quarters!" This terrible truth, says the narrator, which I cannot help repeating, must be acknowledged—*Indifference and selfishness are the predominant feelings of an army.*

Rocca, in his "Memoirs of the War in Spain," remarks, "The habit of danger made us look upon death as one of the most ordinary circumstances of life; when our comrades had once ceased to live, the indifference which was shown them amounted almost to irony. When the soldiers, as they passed by, recognised one of their companions stretched among the dead, they just said, 'He is in want of nothing, he will not have his horse to abuse again, he has got drunk for the last time,' or something similar, which only worked, in the speaker, a stoical contempt of existence. Such were the funeral orations pronounced in honour of those who fell in our battles."—Simpson, in his "Visit to Flanders," in 1815, remarks, "Nothing is more frightful than the want of feeling which characterizes the French soldiery. Their prisoners who were lying wounded in the hospitals of Antwerp, were often seen *mimicking the contortions of countenance which were produced by the agonies of death, in one of their own comrades in the next bed.* There is no curse to be compared with the power of fiends like these."

Thus, it appears, that wars have prevailed in every period, during the ages that are past, and have almost extirpated the principle of *benevolence* from the world; and, therefore, it is obvious, that, before the prevailing propensity to warfare be counteracted and destroyed, the happiness which flows from the operation of the benevolent affections cannot be enjoyed by mankind at large. To counteract this irrational and most deplorable propensity, by every energetic mean which reason, humanity, and Christianity can suggest, must be the duty of every one who is desirous to promote the present and everlasting happiness of his species.*

---

## SECTION II.

### STATE OF MORALS IN MODERN TIMES.

### *Moral state of Savage Nations.*

I shall now take a very brief survey of the state of morals in modern times, and of the prevailing dispositions which are displayed by the existing inhabitants of our globe. Were I to enter into those minute and circumstantial details which the illustration of this subject would require, several volumes would be filled with the detail of facts, and with the sketches of moral scenery which might be brought forward. And such a work, if judiciously executed, might be rendered highly interesting, and might produce a variety of benignant effects both on Christian and on general society. But the narrow limits within which the present work must be comprised, compels me to confine my attention to a few prominent features in the characters of mankind, and, to a few insulated facts by which they may be illustrated.—I shall consider, in the first place, some of the

### *Prominent dispositions which appear among Savage and Half Civilized Nations.*

It is not to be disputed, that numerous individuals among the uncivilized tribes of mankind, have occasionally displayed the exercise of many of the social virtues,—that they have been brave and magnanimous, faithful to their promises, strong in their attachments, and generous and affectionate to their friends and relatives. But their virtues, for the most part, proceed from a principle of selfishness, and are confined to the clan or tribe to which they belong. Towards their enemies, and towards all who have injured them in the slightest degree, they almost uniformly display cruel, perfidious, and revengeful dispositions. The following facts and descriptions, selected from the authentic records of voyagers and travellers, will tend to corroborate these positions.

The most prominent feature which appears in the character of savage nations, is, their disposition for *war*, and to inflict *revenge* for real or supposed injuries. With respect to the NORTH AMERICAN Indians, it is the uniform description given of them by all travellers, that, if we except hunting, *war is the only employment of the men*, and every other concern is left to the women. Their most common motive for entering into war, is, either to revenge themselves for the death of some lost friends, or to acquire prisoners, who may assist them in their hunting, and whom they adopt into their society. In these wars, they are cruel and savage, to an incredible degree. They enter unawares, the villages of their foes, and, while the flower of the nation are engaged in hunting, massacre all the children, women, and helpless old men, or make prisoners of as many as they can manage. But when the enemy is apprized of their design, and coming on in arms against them, they throw themselves flat on the ground, among the withered herbs and leaves, which their faces are painted to resemble. They then allow a part to pass unmolested; when, all at once, with a tremendous shout, rising up from their ambush, they pour a storm of musket-balls on their foes. If the force on each side continues nearly equal, the fierce spirits of these savages, inflamed by the loss of friends, can no longer be restrained. They abandon their distant war, they rush upon one another with clubs and hatchets in their hands, magnifying their own courage, and insulting their enemies. A cruel combat ensues; death appears in a thousand hideous forms, which would congeal the blood of civilized nations to behold, but which rouse the fury of these savages. They trample, they insult over the dead bodies, tearing the scalp from the head, wallowing in their blood like wild beasts, and sometimes devouring their flesh. The flame rages on till it meets with no resistance; then the prisoners are secured, whose fate is a thousand times more dreadful than theirs who have died in the field. The conquerors set up a hideous howling, to lament the friends they have lost. They approach to their own village; the women, with frightful shrieks, come out to mourn their dead brothers, or their husbands. An orator proclaims aloud a circumstantial account of every particular of the expedition; and as he mentions the names of those who have fallen, the shrieks of the women are redoubled. The last ceremony is the proclamation of victory: each individual then forgets his private misfortune, and joins in the triumph of his nation; all tears are wiped from their eyes, and, by an unaccountable transition, they pass in a moment from the bitterness of sorrow, to an extravagance of joy.*

As they feel nothing but revenge for the enemies of their nation, their prisoners are treated with cruelty in the extreme. The cruelties in-

* The Author intended, had his limits permitted, to state some additional considerations to show the folly and wickedness of war. In the mean time, he refers his readers to "Letters addressed to Caleb Strong, Esq.," which contain a series of energetic and impressive reasonings on the subject.—"Pictures of War," by Irenicus, and a duodecimo volume, lately published, entitled, "An Inquiry into the accordancy of War with the principles of Christianity," &c.

* See Ency. Brit. Art. *America*.

flicted on those prisoners who are doomed to death, are too shocking and horrible to be exhibited in detail: one plucks out the nails of the prisoner by the roots; another takes a finger into his mouth, and tears off the flesh with his teeth; a third thrusts the finger, mangled as it is, into the bowl of a pipe made red hot, which he smokes like tobacco: they then pound his toes and fingers to pieces between two stones; they apply red hot irons to every part of his mangled body; they pull off his flesh, thus mangled and roasted, and devour it with greediness;—and thus they continue for several hours, and sometimes for a whole day, till they penetrate to the vital parts, and completely exhaust the springs of life. Even the women, forgetting the human, as well as the female nature, and transformed into something worse than furies, frequently outdo the men in this scene of horror; while the principal persons of the country sit round the stake to which the prisoner is fixed, smoking, and looking on without the least emotion. What is most remarkable, the prisoner himself endeavours to brave his torments with a stoical apathy. "I do not fear death, (he exclaims in the face of his tormentors,) nor any kind of tortures; those that fear them are cowards, they are less than women. May my enemies be confounded with despair and rage! Oh, that I could devour them, and drink their blood to the last drop!"

Such is a faint picture of the ferocious disposition of the Indians of America, which, with a few slight modifications, will apply to almost the whole of the original natives of that vast continent. Instead of the exercise of benevolent affections, and of forgiving dispositions; instead of humane feelings, and compassion for the sufferings of fellow-mortals, we here behold them transported into *an extravagance of joy*, over the sufferings they had produced, the carnage they had created, the children whom they had deprived of their parents, and the widows whose husbands they had mangled and slain; because they had glutted their revenge, and obtained a victory. Nothing can appear more directly opposed to the precepts of Christ, and to the benevolence of heaven.

If, from America, we cross the Atlantic, and land on the shores of Africa, we shall find the existing inhabitants of that continent displaying dispositions no less cruel and ferocious.—Bosman relates the following instances of cruelties practised by the Adomese Negroes, inhabiting the banks of the Praa or Chamah river.

"Anqua, the king, having in an engagement taken five of his principal Antese enemies prisoners, he wounded them all over; after which, with a more than brutal fury, he satiated, though not tired himself, by sucking their blood at the gaping wounds; but, bearing a more than ordinary grudge against one of them, he caused him to be laid bound at his feet, and his body to be pierced with hot irons, gathering his blood that issued from him in a vessel, one half of which he drank, and offered up the rest to his god. On another occasion, he put to death one of his wives and a slave, drinking their blood also, as was his usual practice with his enemies."*—Dispositions and practices no less abominable, are regularly exhibited in the kingdom of *Dahomy*, near the Gulf of Guinea. An immolation of human victims, for the purpose of watering the graves of the king's ancestors, and of supplying them with servants of various descriptions in the other world, takes place every year, at a grand festival which is held generally in April and May, about the period, possibly, when the Bible and Missionary Societies of this country are holding their anniversaries. The victims are generally prisoners of war, reserved for the purpose; but, should there be lack of these, the number (between sixty and seventy) is made up from the most convenient of his own subjects. The immolation of victims is not confined to this particular period; for at any time, should it be necessary to send an account to his forefathers of any remarkable event, the king despatches a courier to the shades, by delivering a message to whoever may happen to be near him, and then ordering his head to be chopped off immediately. It is considered an honour where his majesty personally condescends to become the executioner in these cases; an office in which the king prides himself in being expert. The governor was present on one occasion, when a poor fellow, whose fear of death outweighing the sense of the honour conferred upon him, on being desired to carry some message to his father, humbly declared on his knees, that he was unacquainted with the way. On which the tyrant vociferated, "I'll show you the way," and, with one blow, made his head fly many yards from his body, highly indignant that there should have been the least expression of reluctance.† On the thatched roofs of the guard-houses which surround the palace of this tyrant, are ranged, on wooden stakes, numbers of human skulls; the top of the wall which encloses an area before it, is stuck full of human jaw-bones, and the path leading to the door is paved with the skulls.

In the kingdom of Ashantee, similar practices uniformly prevail. "When the king of this country (says Dupuis) was about to open the campaign in Gaman, he collected together his priests, to invoke the royal *Fetische*, and perform the necessary orgies to ensure success. These ministers of superstition sacrificed thirty-two male, and eighteen female victims as an expiatory offering to the gods; but the answers from the priests being deemed by the council as still devoid of inspiration, the king was induced to *make a custom*, at the sepulchres of his ancestors, where many hundreds bled. This, it is af-

* Dupuis' Journal in Ashantee.
† M'Leod's voyage to Africa.

formed, propitiated the wrath of the adverse god." The same king, when he returned, having discovered a conspiracy, decreed, that seventeen of his wives, along with his own sister, should be strangled and beheaded. "His sister's paramour, and all those of his party, were doomed to the most cruel deaths, at the grave of the king's mother. While these butcheries were transacting, the king prepared to enter the palace; and in the act of crossing the threshold of the outer gate, was met by several of his wives, whose anxiety to embrace their sovereign lord impelled them thus to overstep the boundary of female decorum in Ashantee; for it happened that the king was accompanied by a number of his captains, who, accordingly, were compelled to cover their faces with both their hands, and fly from the spot. This is said to have angered the monarch, although his resentment proceeded no farther than words, and he returned the embraces of his wives. But another cause of anger soon after occurred, and he was inflamed to the highest pitch of indignation, and, in a paroxysm of anger, caused these unhappy beings to be cut in pieces before his face, giving orders, at the same time, to cast the fragments into the forest, to be devoured by birds and beasts of prey. Nor did the atonement rest here; for six more unhappy females were impeached of inconstancy, and they also expiated their faults with their lives. Like another Ulysses, his majesty then devoted himself to the purification of his palace, when, to sum up the full horrors of these bloody deeds, two thousand wretches, selected from the Gaman prisoners of war, were slaughtered over the royal death-stool, in honour of the shades of departed kings and heroes."*

Such are a few specimens of the ferocious dispositions of the petty tyrants of Africa. But we are not to imagine, that such dispositions are confined to kings, and to the higher ranks of society. Wherever such malevolent passions are displayed among barbarous chieftains, they pervade, in a greater or less degree, the whole mass of the people, and almost every one, in proportion to the power with which he is invested, perpetrates similar barbarities. The following instance will corroborate this position, and, at the same time, show, for how many cruelties and acts of injustice the abettors of the infamous traffic in slaves, are accountable. It is extracted from Major Gray's "Travels in Africa, in 1824."

The Kaartan force which the Major accompanied, had made 107 prisoners, chiefly women and children, in a predatory excursion into Bondoo, for the purpose of supplying themselves with slaves. The following is an account of the manner in which they were dragged along. "The men were tied in pairs by the necks, their hands secured behind their backs; the women by the necks only; but their hands were not left free, from any sense of feeling for them, but in order to enable them to balance the immense loads of corn or rice which they were obliged to carry on their heads, and their children on their backs." —"I had an opportunity," says Major Gray, "of witnessing, during this short march, the new-made slaves, and the sufferings to which they are subjected in their first state of bondage. They were hurried along (*tied*) at a pace little short of running, to enable them to keep up with the horsemen, who drove them on, as Smithfield drovers do fatigued bullocks. Many of the women were old, and by no means able to endure such treatment. One, in particular, would not have failed to excite the tenderest feelings of compassion in the breast of any, save a savage African. She was at least sixty years old, in the most miserable state of emaciation and debility, nearly doubled together, and with difficulty dragging her tottering limbs along. To crown the heart-rending picture, she was naked, save from her waist, to about half way to the knees. All this did not prevent her inhuman captor from making her carry a heavy load of water, while, with a rope about her neck, he drove her before his horse; and whenever she showed the least inclination to stop, he beat her in the most unmerciful manner with a stick."

Were we to travel through the whole interior of Africa, and round its northern, eastern, and western coasts, we should find, among almost every tribe, numerous displays of the most inhuman and depraved dispositions. The *Algerines* are characterized as the most cruel and dangerous pirates—base, perfidious, and rapacious, to the last degree. No oaths, nor ties, human or divine, will avail to bind them, when their interest interferes. Whatever respect they may pretend to pay to their prophet Mahomet, gold is the only true idol which they worship. The emperors of Morocco are well known as a set of rapacious and blood-thirsty tyrants, who have lived in a state of habitual warfare with Christian nations, and in the perpetration of deeds of injustice and cruelty. The *Gallas*, on the borders of Abyssinia, are a barbarous and warlike nation. They are hardy, and of a ferocious disposition; they are trained to the love of desperate achievements, taught to believe that conquest entitles them to the possession of whatever they desire, and to look upon death with the utmost contempt; and, therefore, in their wars, they fight with the most desperate resolution, and neither give nor take any quarter. The inhabitants of *Adel*, too, are of a warlike disposition, and most frequently live in enmity and hostility with those around them. The *Feloops* are gloomy and unforgiving in their tempers, thirsting for vengeance even in the hour of dissolution, and leaving their children to avenge their quarrels. The inhabitants of the *Grain*

* Dupuis' Mission to Ashantee, in 1823

*Coast*, especially the Mulattoes, are said to be a most abandoned set of people. The men are drunkards, lewd, thievish, and treacherous, and the women are the most abandoned prostitutes, sacrificing themselves at all times, and to all sorts of men, without the least degree of restraint.* The natives of *Ansico*, which borders on Angola, live by plundering all who happen to fall in their way, some of whom they kill, and others they keep as slaves.† "The *Boshemen* are land pirates, who live without laws and without discipline; who lurk in thickets, to watch the passage of travellers, and shoot them with poisoned arrows, in order to seize their cattle."‡ "The negroes of Congo, (says M. de la Brosse in his Travels along the coast of Angola, in 1738,) are extremely treacherous and vindictive. They daily demanded of us some brandy for the use of the king and the chief men of the town. One day this request was denied and we had soon reason to repent it; for all the English and French officers having gone to fish on a small lake near the sea-coast, they erected a tent for the purpose of dressing and eating the fishes they had caught. When amusing themselves after their repast, seven or eight negroes, who were the chiefs of Loango, arrived in sedans, and presented their hands according to the custom of the country. These negroes privately rubbed the hands of the officers with a subtle poison, which acts instantaneously; and, accordingly, five captains and three surgeons died on the spot."

The *Moors* are characterized by Mr. Park as having cruelty and low cunning pictured on their countenances. Their treachery and malevolence are manifested in their plundering excursions against the Negro villages. Without the smallest provocation, and sometimes under the fairest professions of friendship, they will seize upon the Negroes' cattle, and even on the inhabitants themselves. The *Bedouins* are plunderers of the cultivated lands, and robbers on the high roads; they watch every opportunity of revenging their enemies, and their animosities are transmitted as an inheritance from father to children. Even the *Egyptians*, who are more civilized than the tribes to which I have now alluded, are characterized by excessive pride, vindictive tempers, inordinate passions, and various species of moral turpitude. There is a trait in the character of the women of this country, pointedly adverted to by Sonini, in his "Travels in Egypt," which is particularly odious and horrible. On discovering any partiality in their husbands for other females, they are transported into an unbounded and jealous fury. Such are their deceit and cruelty on these occasions, that they instil into the blood of their faithless husband, a slow and mortal poison. Their revenge is meditated in silence, and they indulge the diabolical satisfaction of taking off an unhappy being by a lingering death. It is said, with confidence, that their own persons supply the horrid means of perpetrating their malicious designs on their husbands, and that they mix with their aliment a certain portion of an ingredient of a poisonous nature, which infallibly induces a slow langour and consumption, and in time brings the wretched victims to the grave. The symptoms are dreadful. The body desicates, the limbs become excessively weak, the gums rot, the teeth loosen, the hair falls off, and, at length, after having dragged a miserable and tortured existence, for a whole year or more, the unhappy beings die in the most extreme torment.

If we pass from Africa to the regions of Asia, we shall find similar depraved principles and practices pervading its several tribes, and the various ranks of its population. Here, tyranny, in all its degrading and cruel forms, reigns supreme and uncontrolled over a superstitious, a deluded, and an idolatrous race of mankind,—of which the following recent instances, in relation to a petty despot of Persia, may serve as a specimen. "The governor Zulfecar Khun is pronounced to be a cruel and unprincipled tyrant; unfortunately for the people, he has the ear of the sovereign, and they have no resource against his rapacity. He pays to the crown 7000 tomauns a year, but it is asserted, that he collects from the district 100,000. His oppression was so grievous, that the inhabitants, wearied out, went in a body to the king to complain; but his majesty only referred them back to their tyrant, who, exasperated at their boldness, wreaked upon them a cruel vengeance. It is said, that he maimed and put to death upwards of a thousand of both sexes, cutting off the hands, putting out the eyes, and otherwise mutilating the men, and cutting off the noses, ears, and breasts of the women. The people, desponding and brokenhearted after this, paid, in as far as they were able, the rapacious demands of their oppressor, and the natural consequence, ruin and desolation has ensued."§

Sir John Chardin gives us the following account of the inhabitants of Mingrelia, particularly of the women. "The people are generally handsome, the men strong and well-made, and the women very beautiful; but both sexes are very vicious and debauched. The women, though lively, civil, and affectionate, are very perfidious; for there is no wickedness which they will not perpetrate, in order to procure, to preserve, or to get rid of their gallants. The men likewise possess many bad qualities. All of them are trained to robbery, which they study both as a business, and as an amusement. With great satisfaction they relate the depredations

* Cooke's Universal Geography, Vol. I. p. 447.

† Ibid

‡ Vaillant's Travels.

§ Frazer's Journey to Khorasan, 1823

they have committed; and, from this polluted source, they derive their greatest praise and honour. In Mingrelia, falsehood, assassination, and theft, are good actions; and whoredom, bigamy, and incest, are esteemed as virtuous habits. The men marry two or three wives at a time, and keep as many concubines as they choose. They not only make a common practice of selling their children, either for gold, or in exchange for wares and provisions, but even murder them, or bury them alive, when they find it difficult to bring them up."

The *Tartars*, who occupy vast regions of the Asiatic continent, are uniformly described by travellers, as a rude, plundering, and uncultivated race of men. "There is something frightful," says Smellie, "in the countenances of the Calmuck Tartars. All of them are wandering vagabonds, and live in tents made of cloth or of skins. They eat the flesh of horses, either raw, or a little softened by putrifying under their saddles. No marks of religion, or of decency in their manners, are to be found among most of these tribes. They are fierce, warlike, hardy, and brutally gross, They are all robbers; and the Tartars of Daghestan, who border on civilized nations, have a great trade in slaves, whom they carry off by force, and sell to the Persians and Turks."*

The *Arabians*, like the Tartars, live mostly without government, without law, and almost without any social intercourse. They still continue in a state of rudeness and of lawless independency. Their chiefs authorize rape, theft, and robbery. They have no estimation for virtue, and glory in almost every species of vice. They roam about in the deserts, and attack caravans and travellers of every description, whom they frequently murder, and plunder of their property.—The *Chinese*, though more highly civilized than the tribes now mentioned, and though they merit great applause for their ingenuity, industry, and perseverance, are as despicable in their moral characters, and as destitute of true benevolence, as almost any nation upon earth. Avarice is their leading passion; and in order to gratify it, they practise every species of duplicity and fraud. They cannot be influenced by motives either of honesty or of humanity; and they surpass every nation on the globe in private cheating. Captain Cook observes, that (the danger of being hanged for any crime being excepted) "there is nothing, however infamous, which the Chinese will refuse to do for gain." In this opinion he concurs with every preceding and subsequent writer, and confirms it by a variety of striking proofs, of which an additional number may be seen in the accounts which have been published of our late embassies to that empire.

* Smellie's Philosophy of Natural History.

The *Birmans* are a lively inquisitive race, active, irascible, and impatient. While in peace, they give proofs of a certain degree of gentleness and civilization; in war, they display the ferocity of savages.—The *Malays*, though inhabiting a country beautiful and delightful in the extreme, where refreshing gales and cooling streams assuage the heat, where the soil teems with delicious fruits, where the trees are clothed with a continual verdure, and the flowers breathe their fragrant odours, are remarkably ferocious in their manners. They go always armed (except the slaves,) and would think themselves disgraced, if they went abroad without their poignards. The inland inhabitants of Malacca, called *Monucaboes*, are a barbarous savage people, delighting in doing continual mischief to their neighbours; on which account, no grain is sown about Malacca, but what is enclosed in gardens, with the thickest hedges, or deep ditches; for when the grain is ripe in the open plains, the Monucaboes never fail to set fire to it. The *Persians*, in their dispositions, says Mr. Franklin, are much inclined to sudden anger, are quick, fiery, and very sensible of affronts, which they resent on the spot. Chardin describes them as "warlike, vain, and ambitious of praise; exceedingly luxurious, prodigal, voluptuous, and addicted to gallantry." It is well known that the wars and fiend-like cruelties in which the despots of this country have been engaged, have transformed many of its provinces into scenes of sterility and desolation.—The *Hindoos* are effeminate, luxurious, and early initiated into the arts of dissimulation. They can caress those whom they hate, and behave with the utmost affability and kindness to such as they intend to deprive of existence, by the most sanguinary means. Though they seldom scold or wrangle, they often stab each other insidiously, and, without any public quarrel, gratify a private revenge. The destruction of infants, the immolation of widows, the drowning of aged parents, which prevail among them, and the cruel and idolatrous rites which distinguish their religious services, are too well known to require description.—The *Turks*, though grave, sedate, and rather hypocondriac, yet when agitated by passion, are furious, raging, ungovernable, fraught with dissimulation, jealous, suspicious, and vindictive beyond conception. They are superstitious, and obstinately tenacious in matters of religion, and are incapable of exercising benevolence or even humanity towards Christians, or towards Jews. Interest is their supreme good, and when that comes in competition, all ties of religion, consanguinity, or friendship, are with the generality, speedily dissolved. They have deprived of their liberty, and of their wealth, all who have been subjected to their iron sceptre, and have plunged them into the depths of moral and of mental debasement. The page of history is filled with details of their devastations and cruelties, and the deeds of injustice and of horror which they have perpetrated, even in our own times, are scarcely equalled by the atrocities of the most savage hordes of mankind.

If we take a survey of the numerous tribes which inhabit the Islands of the Indian and the Pacific Oceans, we shall find similar depraved and malevolent passions, raging without control, and producing all those malignant and desolating effects which have counteracted the benevolence of the Creator, and entailed misery on the human race. The dismal effects of the principle of hatred directed towards human beings, the disposition to engage in continual warfare, and the savage ferocity of the human mind, when unrestrained by moral and prudential considerations, are nowhere so strikingly displayed, as in the isles which are scattered throughout the wide expanse of the Pacific Ocean. Of the truth of these positions we have abundance of melancholy examples, in the reports of missionaries, and in the journals which have been published by late navigators, from which I shall select only two or three examples..

The first instance I shall produce, has a relation chiefly to the inhabitants of *New Zealand.* With respect to these islanders Captain Cook remarks, "Their public contentions are frequent, or rather perpetual; for, it appears from their number of weapons, and dexterity in using them, that war is their principal profession."— "The war-dance consists of a great variety of violent motions, and hideous contortions of the limbs, during which the countenance also performs a part; the tongue is frequently thrust out to an incredible length, and the eye-lid so forcibly drawn up, that the white appears both above and below, as well as on each side of the iris, so as to form a circle around it; nor is any thing neglected so as to render the human shape frightful and deformed. To such as have not been accustomed to such a practice, they appear more like demons than men, and would almost chill the boldest with fear; at the same time they brandish their spears, shake their darts, and cleave the air with their patoo-patoos. To this succeeds a circumstance almost foretold in their fierce demeanour, horrid and disgraceful to human nature, which is, cutting to pieces, even before being perfectly dead, the bodies of their enemies; and, after dressing them on a fire, devouring the flesh, not only without reluctance, but with peculiar satisfaction." There is perhaps nothing that can convey a more striking idea of the actions of pure malevolence, and of the horrible rage and fury of infernal fiends, than the picture here presented of these savage islanders.

These people live under perpetual apprehensions of being destroyed by each other; there being few of their tribes that have not, as they think, sustained wrongs from some other tribe, which they are continually on the watch to avenge and the desire of a good meal is no small incitement. Many years will sometimes elapse before a favourable opportunity happens, yet the son never loses sight of an injury that has been done to his father.—"Their method of executing their horrible designs is by stealing upon the adverse party in the night, and if they find them unguarded (which is very seldom the case) they kill every one indiscriminately, not even sparing the women and children. When the massacre is completed, they either feast and gorge themselves on the spot, or carry off as many of the dead bodies as they can, and devour them at home, with acts of brutality too shocking to be described. If they are discovered before they execute their bloody purpose, they generally steal off again; and sometimes are pursued and attacked by the other party in their turn. To give quarter, or to take prisoners, makes no part of their military law; so that the vanquished can save their lives only by flight. This perpetual state of war, and destructive method of conducting it, operates so strongly in producing habits of circumspection, that one hardly ever finds a New Zealander off his guard, either by night or by day."* While the mind is kept in such a state of incessant anxiety and alarm, it must be impossible for human beings to taste the sweets of rational, or even of sensitive enjoyment. A melancholy gloom must hang over these wretched beings, and the dark suspicions, and the revengeful passions which agitate their minds, can only fit them for those regions of darkness where the radiations of benevolence are completely extinguished.

The implacable *hatred* which these savages entertain towards each other, is illustrated, in the following short narrative from Captain Cook.— "Among our occasional visiters was a chief named Kahoora, who, as I was informed, headed the party that cut off Captain Furneaux's people, and himself killed Mr. Rowe, the officer who commanded. To judge of the character of Kahoora, by what I had heard from many of his countrymen, he seemed to be more feared than beloved among them. Not satisfied with telling me that he was a very bad man, some of them even importuned me *to kill him:* and, I believe, they were not a little surprised that I did not listen to them; for according to their ideas of equity, this ought to have been done. But if I had followed the advice of all our pretended friends, I might have extirpated the whole race; *for the people of each hamlet or village, by turns, applied to me, to destroy the other.* One would have almost thought it impossible, that so striking a proof of the divided state in which this people live, could have been assigned."

Similar dispositions are displayed throughout

* Cooke's Voyages.

almost all the other islands of the Southern Ocean. The following description is given by M. de la Perouse, of the inhabitants of *Maouna Oyolava*, and the other islands in the *Navigator's Archipelago*. "Their native ferocity of countenance always expresses either surprise or anger. The least dispute between them is followed by blows of sticks, clubs, or paddles, and often, without doubt, costs the combatants their lives." With regard to the women, he remarks: "The gross effrontery of their conduct, the indecency of their motions, and the disgusting offers which they made of their favours, rendered them fit mothers and wives for the ferocious beings that surrounded us." The treachery and ferocity of these savages were strikingly displayed in massacring M. de Langle, the astronomer, and eleven of the crew that belonged to Perouse's vessel, and such was their fierce barbarity, that, after having killed them, they still continued to wreak their fury upon the inanimate bodies with their clubs. The natives of *New Caledonia* are a race of a similar description. Though Captain Cook describes them as apparently a good natured sort of people, yet subsequent navigators have found them to be almost the very reverse of what he described; as ferocious in the extreme, addicted to cannibalism, and to every barbarity shocking to human nature. The French navigator, Admiral D'Entrecasteaux, in his intercourse with these people, received undoubted proofs of their savage disposition, and of their being accustomed to feed on human flesh. Speaking of one of the natives, who had visited his ship, and had described the various practices connected with cannibalism, he says,—"It is difficult to depict the ferocious avidity with which he expressed to us, that the flesh of their unfortunate victims was devoured by them after they had broiled it on the coals. This cannibal also let us know, that the flesh of the arms and legs was cut into slices, and that they considered the most muscular parts a very agreeable dish. It was then easy for us to explain, why they frequently felt our arms and legs, manifesting a violent longing; they then uttered a faint whistling, which they produced by closing their teeth, and applying to them the tip of the tongue; afterwards opening their mouth, they smacked their lips several times in succession."

The characters of the islanders now described, may be considered as common to the inhabitants of the New Hebrides, the Friendly Islands, the Marquesas, the Sandwich, New Guinea, New Britain, the Ladrones, and almost all the islands which are dispersed over the vast expanse of the Pacific Ocean. Captain Cook, when describing the natives of New Zealand, remarks, that, "the inhabitants of the other parts of the South Seas have not even the idea of indecency with respect to any object, or to any action." The inhabitants even of the Society and of the Sandwich Isles, prior to the state of moral and religious improvement to which they have lately advanced, though their dispositions were somewhat milder than those of the other islands were almost equally low in point of moral debasement. Captain Cook, speaking of the natives of Otaheite, declares, "They are all arrant thieves, and can pick pockets with the dexterity of the most expert London blackguard."* When describing the societies distinguished by the name of *Arreoy*, he declares, as a characteristic of the female part of the community, "If any of the women happen to be with child, which in this manner of life, happens less frequently than in ordinary cases, the poor infant is smothered the moment it is born, that it may be no incumbrance to the father, nor interrupt the mother in the pleasures of her diabolical prostitution."† Another circumstance, stated by the same navigator, exhibits their former moral character in a still more shocking point of view. On the approach of war with any of the neighbouring islands, or on other interesting occasions, human sacrifices were a universal practice. "When I described," says this illustrious voyager, "the Natibe at Tongabatoo, I mentioned, that, on the approaching sequel of that festival, we had been told that ten men were to be sacrificed. This may give us an idea of the extent of this religious massacre on that island. And though we should suppose, that never more than one person is sacrificed on any single occasion at Otaheite, it is more than probable, that these occasions happened so frequently, as to make a shocking waste of the human race; for I counted no less than forty-nine skulls of former victims, lying before the Morai, where we saw one more added to the number. And, as none of these skulls had, as yet, suffered any considerable change from the weather, it may hence be inferred, that no great length of time had elapsed, since this considerable number of unhappy wretches had been offered on this altar of blood."‡ He also informs us, that human sacrifices were more frequent in the Sandwich, than in any of the other islands. "These horrid rites," says he, "are not only had recourse to upon the commencement of war, and preceding great battles, and other signal enterprises; but the death of any considerable chief calls for a sacrifice of one or more *Towtows*, (that is, vulgar or low persons,) according to his rank; and we were told that *ten* men were destined to suffer on the death of *Terreeoboo*, one of their great chiefs.§

Such are a few specimens of the moral dispositions—the hatred, the horrid warfare, and the abominable practices, which are displayed over

* Hawkesworth's Narrative of Cook's Voyages, vol. II.

† Ibid. ‡ Ibid.

§ Hawkesworth's Narrative of Cook's Voyages, Vol. II.

the greater portion of the Eastern and Western Continents, and among the thousands of islands which diversify the surface of the Ocean—dispositions and practices, which, if permitted to extend their influence universally, and without control, would soon extirpate the intelligent creation, and banish happiness from the empire of God.

### WARLIKE ATTITUDE OF NATIONS.

Were benevolence a characteristic of the inhabitants of our globe, every traveller would be secure from danger from his fellow-men; he might land on every shore without the least suspicion or alarm, and confidently expect that his distresses would be relieved, and his wants supplied, by every tribe of the human race among whom he might occasionally sojourn. No hostile weapons would be lifted up to repel a stranger, when gratifying his curiosity in visiting distant lands, and contemplating foreign scenes; and no instruments of destruction would require to be forged, to preserve a nation from the inroads of destroyers. But when we survey the actual state of mankind, we find almost every nation under heaven, if not actually engaged in war, at least in a warlike attitude, and one of their chief employments consists in divising schemes, either of conquest or revenge, and in furbishing the instruments of death. The following instances may suffice, as illustrations of this position.

The armies of ASHANTEE, says Dupuis, amount to upwards of eighty thousand men, armed with tomahawks, lances, knives, javelins, bows, and arrows; and forty thousand, who can occasionally be put in possession of muskets and blunderbusses.—The opposing armies of MOSLEM and DINHERU, amounted at times to 140,000 men.—The King of DAHOMY, and his auxiliaries, can raise about 50,000 men, armed with bows and arrows, sabres, and iron maces.—The king of BENIN can arm 200,000, upon an emergency, and furnish 10,000 of them with muskets. In those countries of Africa, where fire-arms and gunpowder are unknown, they wield the following kinds of arms with great dexterity and execution. These are, very strong supple lances, which are barbed and poisoned, targets, bows and arrows, tomahawks, and iron maces; the former of which they are in the practice of poisoning with a venom more deadly than that which is used by any other nation, as its operation is said to be sometimes instantaneous, and its wound, though ever so slight, usually produces death within the lapse of a few minutes.*

Such is the warlike disposition displayed by a few comparatively insignificant tribes in Africa, and similar dispositions are manifested, and similar attitudes assumed, by almost all the tribes which inhabit that vast continent. Their time, and their physical and mental exertions, seem to be spent much in war, and in the preparation of warlike instruments, as if these were the great ends for which the Creator had brought them into existence. If the ingenuity and the energies displayed in such preparations and pursuits, were employed in operations calculated to promote the benefit of mankind, what an immense proportion of happiness would be distributed among numerous tribes which are just now sunk into depravity, and into the depths of wretchedness and wo!

Pallas, in his description of the nations inhabiting the *Caucasus*, when speaking of the CIRCASSIANS, says, "Persons of wealth and rank never leave the house without a sabre, nor do they venture beyond the limits of the village without being completely arrayed, and having their breast pockets supplied with ball cartridges." In regard to the lower class, "when they do not carry a sabre, with other arms, they provide themselves with a strong staff, two arshines long, on the top of which is fixed a large iron head, and the lower end is furnished with a sharp iron pike, about eighteen inches long, which they are accustomed to throw expertly, like a dart. The princes and knights pursue no other business or recreation than war, pillage, and the amusements of the chase; they live a lordly life, wander about, meet at drinking parties and undertake military excursions." Among these people, "the desire of revenge, for injuries received, is hereditary in the successors, and in the whole tribe. It remains, as it were, rooted with so much rancour, that the hostile princes or nobles of two different tribes, when they meet each other on the road, or accidentally in another place, are compelled to fight for their lives; unless they have given previous notice to each other, and bound themselves to pursue a different route. Unless pardon be purchased, or obtained by intermarriage between the two families, the principle of revenge is propagated to all succeeding generations."*

It is well known, that in almost all the islands in the Indian and the Southern Oceans, when navigators attempt to land, in order to procure water and provisions, they are almost uniformly opposed by crowds of ferocious savages, armed with long spears, clubs, lances, bows and arrows and, with horrid yells, brandishing them in the most hostile attitudes. In some instances, these warlike attitudes might be accounted for, from a fear of the depredations and murders which might be committed by strangers, with whose dispositions and characters they are unacquainted. But the implacable hatred which they manifest towards even the neighbouring tribes, with which they are acquainted, and of which I have already

* Dupuis' "Mission to Ashantee, in 1823"

* Pallas' "Travels through the Southern Provinces of the Russian Empire," Vol II. pp. 401 405.

stated several instances, shows, that war, revenge, and the preparation of the instruments of death, are both their employment, and their delight. Yea, not only savage and half-civilized tribes, but almost every civilized nation on the face of the earth, is found in a hostile attitude with respect to surrounding nations—either actually engaged in a deadly warfare with a foreign power, or preparing for an attack, or keeping up fleets and standing armies, and forging cannons, and balls, and swords, in the prospect of a rupture with neighbouring states. And in such deadly preparations and employments, a great proportion of those treasures is expended, which, if directed by the hand of benevolence, would be the means of transforming the wilderness into a fruitful field, of distributing intelligence and moral principle among all ranks, and of making the hearts of the poor, the widow, and the orphan, "to leap for joy." What a pitiful picture is here presented of Man, who was originally formed after the image of his Maker, for the purpose of displaying benevolent affections towards his fellows,—now divided into hostile tribes, and brandishing, with infernal fury, at all around, the instruments of destruction! How art thou fallen, O man, from thy original station of dignity and honour! "How is the gold become dim, and the most fine gold changed! The crown is fallen from our heads; wo unto us, for we have sinned!"

### INHUMANITY OF UNCIVILIZED TRIBES TO UNFORTUNATE TRAVELLERS.

In passing through the scene of his earthly pilgrimage, Man is exposed to a variety of distresses and dangers. Sometimes he is exposed to "the pestilence that walketh in darkness," and to the fever "that wasteth at noon-day." Sometimes he is exposed to the desolations of the earthquake and the volcano; the blasts of the tempest, the hurricane, and the tornado, and the billows of the stormy ocean; and, at other times, he is exposed to the attacks of the lion, the tiger, and the hyena, in the dark recesses of the forest. It would be well, however, with man, were these the only evils and enemies which he had to encounter. But the greatest enemy which man has to encounter, is *Man* himself—those who are partakers of the same nature, and destined to the same immortal existence; and from these kindred beings, he is exposed to evils and distresses, incomparably greater and more numerous, than all the evils which he suffers from the ravenous beasts of the forest, or from the fury of the raging elements. It is a most melancholy reflection, that, throughout the greater part of the habitable world, no traveller can prosecute his journey, without being in hazard either of being dragged into captivity, or insulted and maltreated, or plundered of his treasures, or deprived of his life, by those who ought to be his friends and protectors. After he has eluded the pursuit of the lion or the wolf, or after he has escaped, with difficulty, from the jaws of the devouring deep, he is frequently exposed to the fury of demons in human shape, who insult over his misfortunes, instead of relieving the wants of his body, and soothing the anguish of his mind. The following relations, among a numerous series which might be presented to the view of the reader, will tend to illustrate these remarks.

My first example shall be taken from the "Narrative of the Loss of the Grosvenor Indiaman." This vessel sailed from Trincomalee, June 13th, 1782, on her homeward-bound voyage, and was wrecked on the coast of Caffraria, on the 4th of August following. It is needless to dwell on the circumstances which attended the shipwreck, and on the consternation, distraction, and despair, which seized upon the passengers and the crew, when they became alive to all the terrors of the scene. Shipwreck, even in its mildest form, is a calamity which never fails to fill the mind with horror; but what is instant death, considered as a temporary evil, compared with the situation of those who had hunger, and thirst, and nakedness, to contend with; who only escaped the fury of the waves, to enter into conflicts with the savages of the forest, or the still greater savages of the human race; who were cut off from all civilized society, and felt the prolongation of life to be only the lengthened pains of death?

After losing about twenty men, in their first attempts to land, the remaining part of the crew and the passengers, in number about a hundred, after encountering many difficulties and dangers, reached the shore. Next morning a thousand uneasy sensations were produced, from the natives having come down to the shore, and, without ceremony, carried off whatever suited their fancy. They were at this time about 447 leagues from the Cape of Good Hope, and 226 beyond the limits of any Christian habitation. Their only resource appeared to be, to direct their course by land to the Cape, or to the nearest Dutch settlement. As they moved forward, they were followed by some of the natives, who, instead of showing compassion to this wretched group, plundered them from time to time, of what they liked, and sometimes pelted them with stones. In this way they pursued their journey for four or five days; during which the natives constantly surrounded them in the day, taking from them whatever they pleased, but invariably retired in the night. As they proceeded, they saw many villages, which they carefully avoided, that they might be less exposed to the insults of the natives. At last, they came to a deep gully, where three of the Caffres met them, armed with lances, which they held several times to the captain's throat. Next day, on coming to a large village, they found these three men, with three or four hundred of their countrymen, all armed with lances and targets, who stopped the English, and began to pilfer and insult them, and at last fell upon them and beat them. With these inhuman wretches they had to engage in a kind of running fight for upwards of two hours; after which, they cut the buttons from their coats, and presented them to the natives, on which, they went away and returned no more. The following night they were terrified with the noise of the wild beasts, and kept constant watch for fear both of them and the natives. How dreadful a situation, especially for those delicate ladies and children, who had so lately been accustomed to all the delicacies of the East! Next day, as they were advancing, a party of natives came down upon them, and plundered them, among other things, of their tinder-box, flint and steel, which proved an irreparable loss. Every man was now obliged to travel, by turns, with a fire-brand in his hand; and before the natives retired, they showed more insolence than ever, robbing the gentlemen of their watches, and the ladies of their jewels, which they had secreted in their hair. Opposition was vain; the attempt only brought fresh insults or blows.

This group of wretched wanderers now separated into different parties, and took different directions; their provisions were nearly exhausted; and the delay occasioned by travelling with the women and children was very great. Their difficulties increased, as they proceeded on their journey; they had numerous rivers, sometimes nearly two miles in breadth, to swim across in the course of their route, while the women and children were conveyed across on floating stages, at the imminent hazard of their lives, and of being carried down by the impetuous current into the sea. Whole days were spent in tracing the rivers towards their source, in order to obtain a ford. They traversed vast plains of sand, and bleak and barren deserts, where nothing could be found to alleviate their hunger, nor the least drop of water to quench their raging thirst. They passed through deep forests, where human feet had never trod, where nothing was heard but the dreadful howlings of wild beasts, which filled them with alarm and despair. Wild sorrel, berries which the birds had picked at, and a few shell-fish which they occasionally picked up on the shore, were the only food which they had to subsist on for several days; and on some occasions the dead body of a seal, or the putrid carcass of a whale, was hailed as a delicious treat to their craving appetites. One person fell after another into the arms of death, through hunger, fatigue, and despair, and were sometimes obliged to be left in the agonies of dissolution, as a prey to ravenous beasts, or to the fowls of heaven. The following circumstance shows the dreadful situation to which they were reduced for want of food. "It appeared that the captain's steward had been buried in the sand of the last desert they had passed, and that the survivors were reduced to such extremity, that, after he had been interred, they sent back two of their companions to cut off part of his flesh; but while they proceeded in this horrid business, they had the good fortune to discover a young seal, newly driven on shore, which proved a most seasonable relief."

Imagination cannot form a scene of deeper distress than what the tender sex, and the little children must, in such a case, have experienced. It harrows up the very soul to think what pangs those delicate females who had so lately been inured to all the pleasures and luxuries of India, must have endured, when they were fain to appease their craving appetites on the putrid carcass of a whale, and were obliged to repose on the bare ground, amidst the howlings of the tempest, and the more dismal yells of the beasts of prey. But, amidst this heart-rending scene, their fellow-men, who ought to have been their soothers and protectors, and who had it in their power to have alleviated their distresses, were the greatest enemies they had to encounter; and their appearance filled their minds with greater alarm than if they had beheld a roaring lion, or a raging bear. The following are some specimens of the perfidy and inhumanity of the natives. In passing through a village, one of the company observing, "that a traffic would not be unacceptable, offered them the inside of his watch for a calf; but though they assented to the terms, no sooner had they obtained the price, than they withheld the calf, and drove the English from their village." In the same manner were they used on many other occasions. One time, when resting at a village, where the natives offered no particular resistance, "they produced two bowls of milk, which they seemed willing to barter, but as our wretched countrymen had nothing to give in exchange, they denied them this humble boon without an equivalent, and ate it up themselves." At the same place, they implored in the most impressive terms, to partake with the natives of the spoils of a deer, which they had just killed, but they turned a deaf ear to their solicitations, and insisted, moreover, on their quitting the kraal. On another occasion, "on coming to a large village, the inhabitants set upon them with such fury, that several were severely wounded, and one of them died soon after."

In this manner, did the wretched remains of these hapless wanderers traverse the wilds of Africa, during the space of one hundred and seventeen days, till they accidentally met with some Dutch settlers, when within 400 miles of the Cape. Here they were treated with the kindest attention, and their wants relieved. But, by this time, only 15 or 20 emaciated beings survived, out of more than 120 persons who were on board the Grosvenor. What became of the captain and his party is still unknown. Some are supposed to have perished from hunger, some through grief and fatigue, and others to have been killed by the inhospitable natives.—Now, all the accumulated miseries endured by these unfortunate travellers, and the premature death of nearly a hundred persons, are to be attributed to that spirit of selfishness, inhumanity, and hostility, which, in all ages, has prevented enjoyment, and entailed misery on the human race. Had a principle of love to mankind pervaded the hearts of the wretched Caffres, or had even the common feelings of humanity been exercised towards their fellow-creatures in distress, the whole of the unfortunate individuals that perished in Africa's inhospitable clime, might have been conducted in safety to their friends and their native land.

My next example is taken from M. De Brisson's "Narrative of his shipwreck, and captivity among the Moors."

M. Brisson was shipwrecked on the coast of Barbary, on the 10th July, 1785, and, after much difficulty and danger, he, along with the crew, escaped safe to land. No sooner had they reached the shore, than they were surrounded by a crowd of savages, and seized by the collars. 'The Arabs," says M. Brisson, "armed with cutlasses and large clubs, fell upon my companions with incredible ferocity; and I had the mortification of soon seeing some of them wounded, whilst others, stripped and naked, lay stretched out and expiring on the sand. The news of our shipwreck being spread abroad through the country, we saw the savages running with the greatest eagerness from all quarters. The *women*, enraged that they could not pillage the ship, threw themselves upon us, and tore from us the few articles of dress which we had left. While they went to the shore to obtain more plunder, a company of Ouadelims discovered and pillaged our retreat, and beat us in the most unmerciful manner, till I was almost at the last gasp. My mind was so much affected that I could not refrain from tears: and some of the women having observed it, instead of being moved with compassion, *threw sand in my eyes*, 'to dry up my tears,' as they expressed it." M. Brisson was forced, by these rude barbarians, into the interior of the country, as a captive. "After passing," says he, "mountains of a prodigious height, which were covered with small sharp flints, I found that the soles of my feet were entirely covered with blood. I was permitted to get up behind my master on his camel; but as I was naked, I could not secure myself from the friction of the animal's hair, so that in a very little time my skin was entirely rubbed off. My blood trickled down over the animal's sides, and this sight, instead of moving the pity of these barbarians, *afforded them a subject of diversion.* They sported with my sufferings; and that their enjoyments might be still higher, they spurred on their camels." After travelling for sixteen days, during which they were exposed to the greatest fatigue, and the most dreadful miseries, they at length reached the place of their destination, in a most wretched and exhausted condition. And what was the manner of their reception? The women having satisfied their curiosity in inquiries about the strangers, immediately began to load them with abuse. "They even spat in our faces," says M. B. "and pelted us with stones. The children, too, copying their example, pinched us, pulled our hair, and scratched us with their nails, whilst their cruel mothers ordered them to attack sometimes one and sometimes another, and took pleasure in causing them to torment us."

They were compelled to work at the most fatiguing and menial employments, and beaten with severity when they did not exert themselves far beyond their strength, while they were denied a single morsel of wholesome food. "As we were Christians," says the narrator, "the dogs fared better than we, and it was in the basins destined for their use that we received our allowance: our food was raw snails, and herbs and plants trodden under foot by the multitude." In this manner did these unfortunate travellers drag out the period of their captivity; some died of the blows and harsh treatment they received, and others died of hunger and despair. M. Brisson one day found the captain of the vessel in a neighbouring hamlet, stretched out lifeless upon the sand, and scarcely distinguishable but by the colour of his body. In his mouth he held one of his hands, which his great weakness had no doubt prevented him from devouring. He was so changed by hunger, that his body exhibited the most disgusting appearance; all his features being absolutely effaced. A few days after, the second captain, having fallen down through weakness below an old gum tree, became a prey to the attacks of a monstrous serpent. Some famished crows, by their cries, frightened away the venomous animal, and, alighting on the body of the dying man, were tearing him to pieces, while four savage monsters, in human shape, still more cruel than the furious reptile, beheld this scene without offering him the least assistance. "I attempted to run towards him," says M. Brisson, "and to save his life, if possible, but the barbarians stopped me, and after insulting me, said, 'This Christian will soon become a prey to the flames.'" The bad state of health of this unfortunate man would not permit him to labour, and his master and mistress would not allow him the milk necessary for his subsistence. —Such were the scenes of inhumanity and cruelty which M. Brisson witnessed, during the whole period he remained in the territories of these barbarous tribes. They present to our view so many pictures of abominable *selfishness* and even of pure *malevolence*. And it is a most melancholy reflection, that numerous tribes of a similar description are spread over a very large portion of the habitable world. It makes one feel degraded when he reflects that he is related, by the ties of a common nature, to beings possessing a character so malignant and depraved.

I shall select only another example, illustrative of this topic, extracted from the travels of Mr. Park. This enterprising traveller prosecuted a journey of many hundred miles in the interior of Africa, for the most part on foot, and alone. Sometimes, his way lay over a burning sandy wilderness, where he found little to alleviate either his hunger or his thirst; and sometimes he travelled among woods and thickets, and across rivers and marshes, exposed to the wild beasts, and without any path to guide him. Though the negroes of that country frequently relieved his wants and distresses, yet the Moors used him with great cruelty and inhumanity, so that he hardly escaped with life. The chiefs through whose territories he passed, generally exacted a tribute from him, so long as he had any thing to give, and, under that plea, they often robbed him of all the articles which he had it not in his power to conceal. When he passed through the town of Deena, the Moors insulted him in every form which malignity could invent. A crowd of them surrounded the hut in which he lodged, and, besides hissing and shouting, uttered much abusive language. Their aim seemed to be to provoke Park to make retaliation, that they might have some pretence to proceed to greater outrages, and to rob him of his property. Suspecting their intentions he bore all with the greatest patience, and, though they even spit in his face, he showed no marks of resentment. Disappointed in their aim, they had recourse to an argument common among Mahometans, to convince themselves that they had a right to whatever the stranger might have in his possession. He was a *Christian*. They opened his bundles, and took whatever they thought might be of use, and whatever suited their fancy.

Having been kept for some time in captivity by a Moorish tribe, they not only robbed him of the few articles which were still in his possession, but insulted and oppressed him with the most wanton cruelty. The day was passed in hunger and thirst; to hunger and thirst were added the malignant insults of the Moors, of whom many visited him, whose only business seemed to be to torment him. He always saw the approach of the evening with pleasure; it terminated another day of his miserable existence, and removed from him his troublesome visitants. A scanty allowance of kouskous,* and of salt and water, was brought him generally about midnight. This scanty allowance was all that he and his two attendants were to expect during the whole of the ensuing day. "I was a stranger," says he, "I was unprotected, and I was a Christian; each of these circumstances is sufficient to drive every spark of humanity from the heart of a Moor. Anxious, however, to conciliate favour, and, if possible, to afford the Moors no pretence for ill-treating me, I readily complied with every command, and patiently bore every insult. But never did any period of my life pass away so heavily. From sun-rise to sun-set, was I obliged to bear, with an unruffled countenance, the insults of the rudest savages upon earth." Having, at length, made his escape from these barbarians, he declares, "It is impossible to describe the joy that arose in my mind, when I looked around, and concluded that I was out of danger. I felt like one recovered from sickness. I breathed freer; I found unusual lightness in my limbs; even the desert looked pleasant; and I dreaded nothing so much as falling in with some wandering parties of the Moors, who might convey me back to the land of thieves and murderers from which I had just escaped."—Alas! what a load of sorrow and of misery have the selfishness and inhumanity of man accumulated upon the heads of forlorn and unfortunate sufferers! While our disconsolate traveller, after his escape, was wandering in an unknown desert, fainting with hunger, and parched with thirst, surrounded with pitchy darkness, which was only relieved by the flashes of the lightnings; where no sounds were heard but the howlings of wild beasts, and the rolling thunders:—"About two in the morning," says he, "my horse started at something, and, looking round, I was not a little surprised to see a light, at a short distance among the trees, and supposing it to be a town, I groped along the sand, in hopes of finding corn stalks, cotton, or other appearances of cultivation, but found none. As I approached, I perceived a number of lights in other places, and, leading my horse cautiously towards the light, I heard, by the lowing of the cattle, and the clamorous tongues of the herdsmen, that it was a watering place, and most likely belonged to the Moors. Delightful as the sound of the human voice was to me, I resolved once more to strike into the woods, and rather run the risk of perishing with hunger, than trust myself again into their hands."—It is a most affecting consideration, and shows to what a degree of malignity human beings have arrived, when a hungry, houseless, and benighted traveller prefers to flee for protection to the haunts of the beasts of prey, rather than commit himself to the tender mercies of those who are partakers of the same common nature, and who have it in their power to alleviate his distresses.

Mr. Park, when among the Moors, was forced to pass many days, almost without drink, under

* A species of food somewhat resembling *Scotch porridge.*

a burning climate, where, to a European, the heat is almost insufferable. His raging thirst induced him to run every risk, and to burst through every restraint. He sent his boy to the wells to fill the skin which he had for holding water; but the Moors were exasperated that a Christian should presume to fill his vessel at wells consecrated to the use of the followers of Mahomet. Instead, therefore, of permitting the boy to carry away water, they gave him many severe blows; and this mode of treatment was repeated as often as an attempt was made.—On another occasion, when awaking from a dream, in which, during his broken slumbers, his fancy had transported him to his native country, and placed him on the verdant brink of a transparent rivulet, and perceiving that his raging thirst had exposed him to a kind of fever, he resolved to expose himself to the insults of the Moors at the wells, in hopes that he might procure a small supply. When he arrived at them he found the Moors drawing water. He desired permission to drink, but was driven from well to well with reiterated outrage. At length he found one well where only an old man and two boys drew for their cattle. He earnestly begged a small quantity. The old man drew the bucket from the well, and held it out. Park was about eagerly to seize it, when the Moor, recollecting that the stranger was a Christian, instantly threw the water into the trough, where the cows were already drinking, and told Park to drink thence. He hesitated not for a moment. His sufferings made even this offer acceptable. He thrust his head between those of two cows, and, with feelings of pleasure which can be experienced only by those who have been reduced to a similar state of wretchedness, he continued to quench his thirst till the water was exhausted, and "till the cows began to contend with each other for the last mouthful."

In this instance, we can partly account for the barbarity of the action, from the inveterate prejudices which all Mahometans entertain against Christians; but it still remains to be accounted for, why any one should refuse to a suffering fellow-creature the common bounties of Providence, which he has in his power to bestow, however different he may be in complexion, in national character, or in the religion he professes. A religion which encourages such prejudices, and which leads to such inhumanity, must be an abomination in the sight of Him who has a special regard to the wants of all his creatures, and who "sendeth rain to refresh the fields of the just and of the *unjust*." The prevalence of such characters and dispositions over so large a portion of the world, shows that the moral constitution of man has suffered a sad derangement since the period when he proceeded as a pure intelligence from the hands of his Creator.

Such incidents as those to which I have now adverted, when properly considered, are calculated to inspire us with contentment, and to excite to gratitude for the common blessings which we enjoy without the least fear of danger or annoyance. How often do we enjoy the refreshment of a delicious beverage, without thinking of the parched tongues of the African pilgrims; and how often do we spurn at a wholesome dish, which would be hailed with transports of gratitude by the houseless and hungry wanderer of the desert! Yea, how many are there, even in our civilized country, who enjoy, in luxurious abundance, all the blessings which nature and art can furnish, who never once acknowledge, with heart-felt gratitude, the goodness of Him "who daily loads them with his benefits," nor reflect on the wants and the sufferings of their fellow-men! Mr. Park, when oppressed with hunger and fatigue, applied, at the chief magistrate's house, in a village named Shrilla, for some relief, but was denied admittance. He passed slowly through the village till he came without the walls, where he saw an old motherly-looking woman at the door of a mean hut. She set before him a dish of boiled corn, that had been left the preceding night, on which he made a tolerable meal. "Overcome with joy," says Park, "at so unexpected a deliverance, I lifted up my eyes to heaven, and, while my heart swelled with gratitude, I returned thanks to that gracious and bountiful Being, whose power had supported me under so many dangers, and had now spread for me a table in the wilderness."

When Mr. Park was returning from the interior of Africa, he was encountered by a party of armed negroes, who led him into a dark place of the forest through which he was passing, and stripped him entirely naked, taking from him every thing which he possessed, except an old shirt and a pair of trowsers. He begged them to return his pocket compass; but, instead of complying with his request, one of them assured him, that, if he attempted to touch that, or any other article, he would immediately shoot him dead on the spot. He was thus left in the midst of a vast wilderness, in the depth of the rainy season, naked and alone, without food, and without the means of procuring it; surrounded by savage animals, and by men still more savage, and 500 miles from the nearest European settlement. "All these circumstances," says this intrepid traveller, "crowded at once on my recollection, and, I confess, my spirits began to fail me. I considered that I had no other alternative, but to lie down and die. The influence of religion, however, aided and supported me. At this moment, painful as my reflections were, the extraordinary beauty of a small moss irresistibly caught my eye. Can that Being, thought I, who planted, watered, and brought to perfection, in this obscure part of the world, a thing which appears of so small importance, look with unconcern on the situation and sufferings of creatures formed after his own image? Surely not. Reflections like these would not allow me to despair. I started up, and, disregarding both hunger and fatigue, travelled forwards, assured that relief was at hand, and I was not disappointed." Thus was this unfortunate adventurer delivered, by the care of Providence, from those accumulated distresses which had been brought upon him by the malignity and inhumanity of man.

Such are a few specimens of the inhumanity displayed by uncivilized tribes towards strangers, and unfortunate voyagers and travellers. They exhibit dispositions and conduct directly repugnant to every principle of benevolence, and present to our view a gloomy prospect of the difficulties and dangers to be surmounted by philanthropic missionaries, before the habitable world can be thoroughly explored, and before the blessings of knowledge, civilization, and religion can be communicated to the benighted and depraved tribes of mankind.

### MALEVOLENT DISPOSITIONS, AS DISPLAYED IN DISFIGURING THE HUMAN BODY.

The human frame, when preserved in its original state, is one of the finest pieces of mechanism which the mind can contemplate. In beauty, in symmetry, in the harmony and proportion of all its parts and functions, it is superior to the organical structures of all the other ranks of sensitive existence. There is no part imperfect or deformed, no part defective, and no part useless or redundant. All its members are so constructed and arranged as to contribute to the beauty and perfection of the whole, and to the happiness of the intelligent mind by which it is governed and directed. In combination with the power of thought and volition, and when unstained by malignant passions, it is a visible representative of the Creator, having been formed after his image; and it displays, in a most striking manner, the wisdom and the goodness of its Almighty Maker. But, notwithstanding the acknowledged excellence of the human frame, it has been the practice of the degraded tribes of mankind, in almost every country, and in every age, to disfigure its structure, and to deface its beauty; as if the Creator, when he formed it, had been deficient in intelligence and in benevolent design. Such practices, I am disposed to think, imply a principle of malevolence directed towards the Creator, and a disposition to find fault with his wise contrivances and arrangements. At any rate, they display a degree of ignorance and folly, a vitiated taste, and a degradation of mind, inconsistent with the dignity of a rational intelligence. The following facts will, perhaps, tend to illustrate these remarks:—

Condamine, when describing the natives of South America, informs us, that the Omaguas, and some other savages, flatten the faces of their children, by lacing their heads between two boards; that others pierce the nostrils, lips, or cheeks, and place in them feathers, the bones of fishes, and similar ornaments;—and that the savages of Brazil pull the hair out of their beards, their eye-brows, and all parts of their bodies, which make them have an uncommon, and a ferocious appearance. Their under-lip they pierce, and, as an ornament, insert into it a green stone, or a small polished bone. Immediately after birth the mothers flatten the noses of their children. The whole of them go absolutely naked, and paint their bodies of different colours.—Captain Cook informs us, that, in New Zealand, both sexes mark their faces and bodies with black stains, similar to the tattooing in Otaheite. The men, particularly, add new stains every year, so that, in an advanced period of life, they are almost covered from head to foot. Besides this, they have marks impressed, by a method unknown to us, of a very extraordinary kind. They are furrows of about a line deep, and a line broad, such as appear upon the bark of a tree which has been cut through after a year's growth. The edges of these furrows are afterwards indented by the same method, and, being perfectly black, they make a most frightful appearance. Both sexes bore their ears: they gradually stretch the holes till they are so large as to admit a finger. Into these holes they put feathers, coloured cloth, bones of birds, twigs of wood, and frequently the nails which they received from the ships.—The same voyager, when describing the New Hollanders, tells us,—"Their chief ornament is a bone, which is thrust through a hole bored in the cartilage which divides the nostrils. This bone is as thick as a man's finger, and six inches in length. It reaches quite across the face, and so effectually stops up both nostrils, that they are forced to keep their mouths wide open for breath, and snuffle so when they attempt to speak, that they are scarcely intelligible to each other. Our seamen with some humour, called it their *sprit-sail yard;* and indeed it had so ludicrous an appearance, that, till we were used to it, we found it difficult to restrain from laughter." He also describes a custom of a peculiar nature which prevails in the Friendly Islands. "The greater part of the inhabitants, both male and female, were observed to have lost one or both of their little fingers. This custom seemed not to be characteristic of rank, of age, or of sex; for, with the exception of some young children, very few people were discovered in whom both hands were perfect. They likewise burn or make incisions in their cheeks."

All the eastern nations are said to have a predilection for long ears. Some draw the lobe of the ear, in order to stretch it to a greater length, and pierce it so as to allow the admission of an ordinary pendant. The natives of *Laos* so prodigiously widen the holes in their ears, that a man's hand may be thrust through them. Hence, the ears of these people often descend to the tops of their shoulders.* Gentil assures us, that the women, in the northern parts of China, employ every art in order to diminish their eyes. For this purpose, the girls, instructed by their mothers, extend their eye-lids continually, with the view of making their eyes oblong and small. These properties, in the estimation of the Chinese, when joined to a flat nose, and large, open, pendulous ears, constitute the perfection of beauty.—We are informed by Struys, that the women of Siam wear so large and heavy pendants in their ears, that the holes gradually become wide enough to admit a man's thumb. The natives of New Holland pull out the two fore-teeth of the upper jaw. In Calicut, there is a band of nobles called *Naires*, who lengthen their ears to such a degree, that they hang down to their shoulders, and sometimes even lower.† The Arabs paint their lips, arms, and the most conspicuous parts of their bodies, with a deep blue colour. This paint, which they lay on in little dots, and make it penetrate the flesh, by puncturing the skin with needles, can never be effaced. Some of the Asiatics paint their eye-brows of a black colour, and others eradicate the hairs with *rusma*, and paint artificial eye-brows, in the form of a black crescent, which gives them an uncommon and ugly appearance. The inhabitants of Prince William's Sound, paint their faces and hands, bore their ears and noses, and slit their under lips. In the holes made in their noses, they hang pieces of bone or ivory, which are often two or three inches long; and, in the slit of the lip, they place a bone or ivory instrument with holes in it, from which they suspend beads that reach below the chin. These holes in the lip disfigure them greatly, for some of them are as large as their mouths.‡

Such distortions of the beautiful structure of the human frame, are not peculiar to the savage tribes of the human race, but are practised by nations which have made considerable advances in science and civilization. It is well known that, in China, a ridiculous custom prevails, of rendering the feet of their females so small, that they can with difficulty support their bodies. This is deemed a principal part of their beauty; and no swathing nor compression is omitted, when they are young, to give them this fancied accomplishment. Every woman of fashion, and every woman who wishes to be reckoned handsome, must have her feet so small, that they could easily enter the shoe of a child of six years of age. The great toe is the only one left to act with freedom; the rest are doubled down under the foot, in their tenderest infancy, and restrained by tight bandages, till they unite with, and are buried in the sole. I have inspected a model of a Chinese lady's foot, exactly of this description, which, I was assured, was taken from life. The length was only two inches and three-fourths; the breadth of the base of the heel, seven eighths of an inch; the breadth of the broadest part of the foot, one and one fourth of an inch; and the diameter of the ankle, three inches above the heel, one and seven eighths of an inch. With feet of this description the Chinese ladies may be said rather to totter than to walk; and, by such practices, they evidently frustrate the benevolent intentions of the Creator, and put themselves to unnecessary inconvenience and pain. Yet such is the powerful influence of fashion, however absurd and ridiculous, that women of the middling and inferior classes frequently suffer their feet to be thus maimed and distorted, in order to ape the unnatural customs of their superiors.

We have every reason to believe that the harsh and ugly features, and the ferocious aspect, by which numerous tribes of mankind are distinguished, are owing to such voluntary distortions of the human frame, and to the filthy and abominable practices in which they indulge. Father Tertre assures us, that the flat noses of the negroes are occasioned by a general practice of mothers, who depress the noses of their new-born infants, and squeeze their lips, in order to thicken them; and that those children who escape these operations have elevated noses, thin lips, and fine features.—It is somewhat unaccountable, and it shows the perversity of the human mind, in its present degraded state, that such practices should be so general, and so obstinately persisted in, when we consider the pain and inconvenience with which they are attended. —To pull the hairs of the chin or eye-brows from the roots; to slit the under lip, till the incision be as large as one's mouth; to pierce the nostrils, till a bone as large as a man's finger can be thurst through them; and to cover the body with black streaks, which make the blood to flow at every stroke of the instrument by which they are produced, must be attended with excruciating pain. Sir Joseph Banks, who accompanied Captain Cook in his first voyage, was present, in the island of Otaheite, at the operation of tattooing, performed on the back of a girl of thirteen years of age. The instrument used had twenty teeth; and at each stroke, which was repeated every moment, issued an ichor or serum, tinged with blood. The girl bore the pain with great resolution, for some minutes, till, at length, it became so intolerable, that she burst out into violent exclamations; but the operator, notwithstanding the most earnest entreaties to desist, was inexorable, while two women, who attended upon the occasion, both chid and beat her for struggling.

* Smellie's Philosophy of Natural History, vol. II.
† Ibid. ‡ Portlock's Voyage round the World.

I am therefore disposed to view such absurd and barbarous practices, as intimately connected with the operation of a principle of malevolence, as an attempt to frustrate the wise designs of divine benevolence, and as directly repugnant to the spirit of Christianity, and to the benevolent precepts of the gospel of peace. And it becomes some of the ladies, and the dandies of modern Europe to consider, whether some of their awkward attempts to improve the symmetry of the human frame ought not to be viewed in the same light. Not many years ago, it was considered, in the higher circles of society, as an admirable improvement of the female form, to give the lower half of the body the appearance of the frustum of a large tun, as if it had been ten times the capacity of its natural size, by supporting their robes with enormous *hoops*;—and, about the same period, the lower ranks of female society considered it as the perfection of proportion and beauty, to have their waists compressed into the smallest possible space, till the vital functions, in many instances, were deranged, and ultimately destroyed. Were the dictates of sound reason universally attended to, and were the influence of Christianity fully felt among all nations, the preposterous and savage practices to which I have now adverted, would not only be discontinued, but held in abhorrence. And were such customs completely abolished, we might soon expect to behold, among all the tribes of mankind, every distortion of the features or the countenance removed, and the human form restored to its original beauty and perfection. Instead of a warlike visage, and a ferocious aspect, and the frightful appearance of naked savages, streaked with colours of black and blue, we should behold, in every land, every countenance beaming with the radiations of benevolence, and reflecting the moral image of the Creator.

### MALEVOLENCE AS IT APPEARS IN THE RELIGION OF SAVAGE TRIBES.

There is scarcely a nation on the surface of the globe but what appears to have some impressions of the existence of a Superior Power, and to have formed a system of religious worship. But, it is a striking fact, that, among the greater portion of human beings, their religious notions, and their sacred rites, instead of breathing a spirit of kindness and benevolence towards their fellow-creatures, are blended with a principle of hatred and revenge. This might be illustrated by an induction of a great variety of instances, in reference to almost every uncivilized portion of the human race. I shall content myself, however, with stating only one instance, in reference to the *Nesserie*, a tribe not much known in Europe, and which may serve as an example of many others.

The territory of this people extends from Antioch nearly to Tripoli. They occupy almost all the mountains to the east of Latakia, and a great part of the plain. Among them is perceived a mixture of the religious usages of Paganism of the Jewish law, of that of Mahomet and Ali, and of some dogmas of the Christian Religion. —The women are considered as a part of the domestic animals of the house, and treated as slaves. They have no idea of religion, and when they are bold enough to inquire of their masters concerning it, the latter answer them that their religion is, to be charged with the reproduction of the species, and to be subject to the will of their husbands.—The Nesseric say their prayers at midnight, and before sun-set. They may say them either sitting, standing, or walking; but they are obliged to begin again repeating their ablution, if they speak to a person not of their religion,—if they perceive, either near or at a distance, a camel, a pig, a hare, or a negro. In their prayers, they curse the man who shaves below the chin, him who is impotent, and the two Caliphs, Omar and Abou-Bekr. They detest the Turks, to whom they are sworn enemies. This warlike people of mountaineers would be strong enough to shake off the yoke of the Turks, and live independently, if they were not divided by interested motives, almost all occasioned by implacable family hatreds. They are *vindictive*, and cherish their rancour for a length of time: even the death of the guilty person cannot assuage their fury; their vengeance is incomplete, if it does not fall besides on one or several members of his family. They are so obstinately superstitious in their attachment to their peculiar system, that no threats nor punishments can extort from them the secrets of their religion.*

Here, then, we are presented with a system of religion which appears to be founded on malevolence,—which directs its devotees to curse their fellow-men—which leads them to keep their women in profound ignorance of every thing which they hold sacred—which induces them to conceal its mysteries from all the rest of the world—and which, in so far from producing any beneficial effects on their own conduct, leads to "implacable family hatreds." A religion, unless it be founded on a principle of benevolence, is unworthy of the name; it must be an abhorrence in the sight of God, and can never communicate happiness to man. And were we to examine the various religious systems which prevail in the numerous islands of the Indian and Pacific Oceans, in Cabul, Thibet, and Hindostan, and among the uncivilized tribes which are scattered over a large portion of Asia and of Africa, we should find them, not only blended with malevolent principles and maxims, but sanctioning the perpetration of deeds of cruelty, obscenity, and horror.

In the preceding pages, I have endeavoured to

* See Dupont's "Memoirs of the Manners and Religious Ceremonies of the Nesserie," a work lately published.

illustrate some of the prominent features in the moral character of the savage and uncivilized tribes of the human race. The examples I have selected have not been taken from the records of missionaries, or of professed religionists, who might be suspected by some to give an exaggerated description of the depravity of the Pagan world—but from the unvarnished statements of respectable voyagers and travellers, who could have no motives for misrepresenting the facts which they have recorded. These illustrations might have been extended to a much greater length, had it been consistent with the limited nature of the present work. Instead of occupying only forty or fifty pages, they might have been extended so as to have filled as many volumes; for every book of travels, as well as every historical document, contains a record of the operations of malignity, and of the diversified modes in which human depravity is displayed. The dispositions which I have illustrated, it will be readily admitted, are all of a *malignant* character, directly repugnant to that benevolent principle which forms the basis of the moral laws of the universe. And when we consider, that such malevolent dispositions are displayed by a mass of human beings, amounting to more than three fourths of the population of the globe, and that true happiness cannot be experienced where malignant passions reign uncontrolled, a benevolent mind cannot refrain from indulging a thousand melancholy reflections, when it casts its eye over the desolations of the moral world, and from forming an anxious wish, that the period may soon arrive, when the darkness which covers the nations shall be dispelled, and when benevolence and peace shall reign triumphant over all the earth.

I shall now endeavour to present a few facts and sketches which may have a tendency to illustrate the present state, and the moral character and aspect of the *civilized* world.

---

## SECTION III.

### MORAL STATE OF CIVILIZED NATIONS.

The present population of the globe may be estimated at about 800 millions. Of these, if we except the empires of China and **Hindostan**, we cannot reckon above 180 millions as existing in a state of enlightened civilization; a number which is less than the fourth part of the human race. Were even this small portion of mankind uniformly distinguished for intelligence, and for the practice of benevolence, it would form a glorious picture for the philanthropist to contemplate; and would be a sure prelude of the near approach of that happy period, when "*all the ends* of the earth shall remember and turn to the Lord, when *all the kindreds of the nations* shall do homage unto him, and when there shall be nothing to hurt nor destroy" among all the families of mankind. But alas! when we investigate the moral state even of this portion of human beings, we find the principle of malignity distinctly visible in its operations, and interwoven, in numerous and minute ramifications, through all the ranks and gradations of society. Though its shades are less dark and gloomy, they are no less real than among the hordes of Africa and Tartary, and the other abodes of savage life. To illustrate this position is the object of the following sketches; in which I shall chiefly refer to the state of society among the nations of Europe, and the United States of America, and particularly to the moral character and aspect of the British empire.

I shall, in the first place, consider the operation of the malevolent principle as it appears in the actions and dispositions of the young, and in the modes of tuition by which they are trained.

In many thousands of instances, it may be observed, that, even before a child has been weaned from its mother's breasts, malignant dispositions are not only fostered, but are regularly taught both by precept and example. Does a child happen to hit its head accidentally against the corner of a table—it is taught by its nurse, and even by its mother, to avenge the injury on the inanimate object which caused it, and to exhibit its prowess and its revenge by beating the table with all its might. Does it cry, through peevishness or pain—it is immediately threatened with being thrown into the ditch, tossed out of the window, or committed to the charge of some frightful spectre. Is it expedient to repress its murmurings, and to cajole it into obedience—it is then inspired with fallacious hopes, and allured with deceitful promises of objects and of pleasures which are never intended to be realized. Does it require to have its physical powers exercised—a wooden sword or a whip is put into its hands; and it is encouraged to display its energies in inflicting strokes on a dog, a cat, or any of its play-fellows or companions. I have seen a little urchin of this description, three or four years of age, brandishing its wooden sword with all the ardour of a warrior, and repeating its strokes on every person around, while the foolish parents were exulting in the prowess displayed by their little darling, and encouraging it in all its movements. By these and similar practices, revenge, falsehood, superstition, and the elements of war, are fostered in the youthful mind; and is it to be wondered at, that such malignant principles and passions should "grow with their growth, and strengthen with their strength," till they burst forth in all those hideous forms which they assume amidst the contests of communities and of nations?—The false maxims by which children are frequently trained under the domestic roof, and the foolish indulgence with which they are treated by injudicious parents, in too many instances lay the foundation of those petulant and malignant tempers, which are a pest both to Christian and to general society. Indulgence often leads to an opposite extreme; and produces such a degree of insubordination among the young, that nothing is to be seen and heard but a perpetual round of scolding and beating, and the contest of angry passions. "Among the lower ranks of people," says Dr. Witherspoon, "who are under no restraint from decency, you may sometimes see a father or mother running out into the street, after a child who has fled from them, with looks of fury and words of execration, and they are often stupid enough to imagine that neighbours or passengers will approve them in this conduct." Wherever parental authority is thus undermined, and such conduct uniformly pursued, a sure foundation is laid for an extensive display, in after life, of the malignant passions of the human heart.

If we follow our youth from the nursery to the *school-room*, we shall find the same malevolent affections developing themselves on a larger scale, and indirectly cherished, by the books they read, the discipline by which they are trained, and the amusements in which they indulge. Here we may behold one little fellow taking a malicious pleasure in pinching his neighbour, another in kicking him, a third in boxing him, a fourth in tearing his book, a fifth in pilfering his property, and a sixth in endeavouring to hold him up to scorn and ridicule; and all of them combined to frustrate, if possible, the exertions of their teacher, and to prevent their own improvement.—If we look into the majority of the *books* which are read in schools, we shall find them full of encomiums upon *war*, and upon *warriors*. The Cæsars, the Alexanders, and the Bonapartes, whose restless ambition has transformed the earth into scenes of desolation and carnage, are represented as patterns of every thing that is brave, noble, generous, and heroic. The descriptive powers of the poet are also called in, in order to inflame the youthful mind with warlike dispositions, and to excite an ardent desire for mingling in scenes of contention, and for the acquisition of false glory and of military renown. Hence, there is no part of their school exercises in which the young so much delight, and in which they so much excel, as in that in which they are called upon to recite such speeches as "Sempronius's speech for war," or to ape the revengeful encounter of Norval and Glenalvon. While the spirit of war is thus virtually cherished, the counteraction of vicious propensities, and the cultivation of the moral powers of the young, are considered as a matter of inferior importance, and, in many seminaries of instruction, are altogether overlooked. Many of the school collections to which I allude—instead of exhibiting, in simple language, the beauties and sublimities of the works of nature, the displays of the natural and moral character of the Deity, the facts of Sacred History, the morality of the Gospel, the scenes of rural and domestic life, and the operations of philanthrophy—are filled with extracts from metaphysical writers, from parliamentary debates, and from old plays, novels, and farces, which are frequently interlarded with oaths, obscenity, and the slang of Billingsgate, which can have no other tendency than to pollute and demoralize the youthful mind. It needs, therefore, excite no surprise, that the great body of mankind is still so deficient in rational information and substantial knowledge, and that a warlike spirit is afloat, and exerting its baleful influence among the nations.

If we follow the young from the school-room to the *play-ground*, or to the streets and the highways, we shall find the spirit of malignity displaying itself in a vast diversity of forms. *Here*, we may behold one mischievous little boy slapping his neighbour in the face, another tearing his neighbour's clothes, another tossing his cap into a dirty ditch, another chalking his back in order to hold him up to ridicule, and another pouring out upon him a torrent of nicknames, and of scurrilous epithets. *There*, we may behold a crowd of boys pelting a poor beggar or an unfortunate maniac with stones and dirt for their diversion; mocking the lame, the deformed, and the aged, and insulting the passing traveller. And, when such objects do not happen to occur, we may see them assailing, with a shower of stones, a cat, a dog, a hare, or a fowl, that happens to cross the path, and enjoying a diabolical pleasure in witnessing the sufferings of these unfortunate animals. *Here*, we may behold an insolent boy insulting a timid girl, overturning her pitcher, and besmearing her with mire;—there we behold another saluting his fellow with a malignant scowl, and a third brandishing his whip, and lashing a horse or a cow, for his amusement. On the one hand, we may sometimes behold a ring of boys, in the centre of which two little demons are engaged in mutual combat, with eyes glaring with fury and revenge, exerting their physical powers to the utmost stretch, in order to wound and lacerate, and cover with blood and gore, the faces of each other: on the other hand, we may behold an unfortunate boy, whom a natural temperament, or a virtuous principle, prevents from engaging in similar combats, assailed with opprobrious epithets, and made a laughing-stock, and an object of derision and scorn, because he will not be persuaded to declare war against his neighbour. And, what is still more atrocious and disgusting, we may behold *children* of thirty or forty years of age, encouraging such malevolent dispositions, and stimulating such combatants in their diabolical exertions!* Such infernal

* The practice of boxing, among boys, which so generally prevails, especially in England, is a disgrace to the boasted civilization and Christianity o

practices, among creatures originally formed after the divine image, if they were not so common, would be viewed by every one in whose breast the least spark of virtue resides, with feelings of indignation and horror.

The great body of our youth, habituated to such dispositions and practices, after having left school at the age of fourteen or fifteen—a period when head-strong passions and vicious propensities begin to operate with still greater violence—have access to no other seminaries, in which their lawless passions may be counteracted and controlled, and in which they may be carried forward in the path of moral and intellectual improvement. Throughout the whole of the civilized world, I am not aware that there exist any regular institutions exclusively appropriated for the instruction of young persons, from the age of fifteen to the age of twenty-five or upwards, on moral, religious, and scientific subjects; in order to expand their intellectual capacities, and to direct their moral powers in the path of universal benevolence. Yet, without such institutions, all the knowledge and instructions they may have previously acquired, in the great majority of instances, are rendered almost useless and inefficient for promoting the great end of their existence. From the age of fifteen to the age of twenty-five, is the most important period of human life; and, for want of proper instruction and direction, during this period, and of rational objects to employ the attention at leisure hours, many a hopeful young man has been left to glide insensibly into the mire of vice and corruption, and to become a pest to his friends, and to general society. Our streets and highways are infested, and our jails and bridewells filled with young persons of this age, who, by means of rational and religious training, might have been rendered a comfort to their friends, blessings to society, and ornaments of the Christian Church.

It would be inconsistent with the limited plan of this work, to attempt to trace the principle of malignity through all the scenes of social, commercial, and domestic life. Were I to enter into details of filial impiety, ingratitude, and rebellion—of faithless friendships—of the alienations of affection, and of the unnatural contentions between brothers and sisters—of the abominable *selfishness* which appears in the general conduct and transactions of mankind—of the bitterness, the fraud, and the perjury, with which law-suits are commenced and prosecuted—of the hatred, malice, and resentment, manifested for injuries real or supposed—of the frauds daily committed in every department of the commercial world—of the shufflings and base deceptions which are practised in cases of bankruptcy—of the slanders, the caballing, and the falsehood, which attend electioneering contests—of the envy, malice, and resentment displayed between competitors for office and power—of the haughtiness and insolence displayed by petty tyrants both in church and state—of the selfishness and injustice of corporate bodies, and the little regard they show for the interests of those who are oppressed, and deprived of their rewards—of the gluttony, drunkenness, and prodigality, which so generally prevail—of the brawlings, fightings, and contentions, which are daily presented to the view in taverns, ale-houses, and dram-shops, and the low slang and vulgar abuse with which such scenes are intermingled—of the seductions accomplished by insidious artfulness and outrageous perjury—of the multiplied falsehoods of all descriptions which are uttered in courts, in camps, and in private dwellings—of the unblushing lies of public newspapers, and the perjuries of office—of the systematic frauds and robberies by which a large portion of the community are cheated out of their property and their rights—of the pride, haughtiness, and oppression of the rich, and of the malice, envy, and discontentment of the poor—such pictures of malignity might be presented to the view, as would fill the mind of the reader with astonishment and horror, and which would require a series of volumes to record the revolting details.

There is one very general characteristic of civilized, and even of Christian society, that bears the stamp of malignity, which may particularly be noticed; and that is, the pleasure with which men expatiate on the faults and delinquencies of their neighbours, and the eagerness with which they circulate scandalous reports through every portion of the community. Almost

that country, and to the superintendents of its public seminaries. That pugilistic contests between grown-up *savages* in a civilized shape, should be publicly advertised, and described in our newspapers, and the arena of such contests resorted to by so many thousands of the middling and higher classes of society, is a striking proof that the spirit of folly and of malignity still prevails to a great extent, and that the spirit of Christianity has made little progress, even within the limits of the British empire.—The following late occurrence shows the fatal effects with which such practices are sometimes attended. "On Monday, February 28, 1825, two of the scholars at Eton, the Hon. F. A. Cooper, the son of the Earl of Shaftesbury, and Mr. Wood, the son of Colonel Wood, and nephew to the Marquis of Londonderry, in consequence of a very warm altercation on the play-ground, on the preceding day, met, for the purpose of settling the unhappy quarrel by a pugilistia encounter—*a prevalent practice at Eton and all our public schools*. Almost the whole school assembled to witness the spectacle The inexperienced youth commenced fighting at four o'clock, and partly by their own energy, and partly by the criminal excitement of others, continued the fatal contest till within a little of six, when, mournful to relate, the Earl of Shaftesbury's son fell very heavily upon his head, and never spoke afterwards. He was carried off to his lodgings, where he expired in a few hours. On the coroner's inquest it came out, that brandy had been administered very freely, and that no decisive effort had been made to discontinue a contest prolonged beyond all due limits.—About forty years ago a similar cause led to a similar result at the same establishment. The survivor is a clergyman of great respectability."—*See the Public Prints for Feb. and Evan. Mag. for April*, 1825.

the one half of the conversation of *civilized* men, when strictly analyzed, will be found to consist of malignant insinuations, and of tales of scandal and detraction, the one half of which is destitute of any solid foundation. How comes it to pass, that the slightest deviation from propriety or rectitude, in the case of one of a generally respectable character, is dwelt upon with a fiend-like pleasure, and aggravated beyond measure, while all his good qualities are overlooked and thrown completely into the shade? What is the reason why we are not as anxious to bring forward the good qualities and actions of our fellow-men, and to bestow upon them their due tribute of praise, as we are to blaze abroad their errors and infirmities? How often does it happen, that a single evil action committed by an individual, contrary to the general tenor of his life, will be trumpeted about by the tongue of malice, even to the end of his life, while all his virtuous deeds and praiseworthy actions will be overlooked and forgotten, and attempted to be buried in oblivion! If benevolence were the prevailing characteristic of mankind, such dispositions would seldom be displayed in the intercourses of human beings. If benevolence pervaded every heart, we would rejoice to expatiate on the *excellences* of others;—these would form the chief topics of conversation in our personal remarks on others; we would endeavour to throw a veil over the infirmities of our brethren, and would be always disposed to exercise that candour and charity "which covers a multitude of sins."

If we now turn our eyes for a moment, to the *amusements* of civilized society, we shall find many of them distinguished by a malignant character and tendency. What an appropriate exhibition for rational and immortal beings do the scenes of a *cockpit* display! to behold a motley group of *bipeds*, of all sorts and sizes, from the peer to the chimney-sweep, and from the man of hoary hairs to the lisping infant, betting, blustering, swearing, and feasting their eyes with a savage delight on the sufferings of their fellow-bipeds, whom they have taught to wound, to torment, and to destroy each other! There is scarcely any thing that appears so congenial to the spirit which pervades the infernal regions, as the attempt to inspire the lower animals with the same malignant dispositions which characterize the most degraded of the human species. That such a cruel and disgusting practice still prevails in England, and that it formed, until lately, a part of the amusements of almost all the schools in Scotland, is a reproach to the civilization, the humanity, and the Christianity of our country. And what a fine spectacle to a humane and civilized mind is the amusement of *bull-baiting!* an amusement in which the strength and courage of this animal are made the means of torturing him with the most exquisite agonies! Can benevolence, can even the common feelings of humanity, reside in the breast of that man who can find enjoyment in encouraging and in witnessing such barbarous sports? And what a dignified amusement is the *horse race!* where crowds of the nobility, gentry, and of the most polished classes of society, as well as the ignoble rabble, assemble from all quarters, to behold two noble animals panting, and heaving, and endeavourin to outstrip each other on the course! What scene of bullying, and jockeying, and betting and cheating, and cursing, and swearing, an fighting, is generally presented on such occasions! What a wonderful degree of importance is attached, by the most dignified rank of society, to the issue of the race; as if the fate of an empire, or the salvation of an immortal spirit, were depending on the circumstance of one horse getting a start of another! I do not mean to decry, indiscriminately, public amusements; nor to call in question the propriety of improving the locomotive powers of the horse; but, surely, it would require no great stretch of invention, to devise spectacles and entertainments, much more dignified and congenial to the noble powers, and to the high destination of the human mind, and which might be exhibited with as little expense either of time or of money.

And what shall we say of *lion fights*, and *dog fights*, and *boxing matches* between animals in the shape of men, which have been lately advertised in the public prints with so much impudence and effrontery? Are the patrons of such revolting exhibitions, and the crowds which resort to them, to be considered as patterns of taste, of humanity, and of refined benevolence? And what shall we think of the amusements of one half of our gentry, country squires, gentlemen farmers, and the whole tribe of the sporting community, who derive more exquisite enjoyment in maiming a hare, a partridge, or a moorfowl, than in relieving the wants of the friendless poor, in meliorating the condition of their dependants, or in patronising the diffusion of useful knowledge? If one of our best moral poets declared, that "he would not enter, on his list of friends, though graced with polished manners and fine sense, the man who needlessly sets foot upon a worm," what would be his estimate of the man who derived one of his chief gratifications, day after day, from making havoc among the feathered tribes, and from lacerating and maiming a timid hare, for the sole purpose of indulging a sporting humour, and proving himself an excellent marksman? Can we suppose that the benevolent Creator so curiously organized the beasts of the earth and the fowls of heaven, and endowed them with exquisite feelings and sensibility, merely that tyrannical man might torture and destroy them for his *amusement?* For the persons to whom I allude cannot plead *necessity* for such conduct, as if they were dependant for subsistence on their carcasses. Such is still the mania for these cruel arguments, that the butchery of the brutal and the winged tribes, it is likely, will soon be reduced to a regular system, and enrolled among the number of the *fine arts*. For, an octavo volume, of 470 pages, which has already passed through three editions, has been lately published, entitled, "Instructions to young Sportsmen in all that relates to Game and Shooting:" by Lieut. Colonel Hawker. The author, after having stated that he has now lost his eyes and nerves for a good shot, says "The greatest pleasure that can possibly remain for me, is to resign the little I have learned for the benefit of young sportsmen. The rising generation of shooters might otherwise be left for many years, to find out all these little matters." And a most important loss, doubtless, the rising generation would have sustained, had not the worthy Colonel condescended to communicate his discoveries! I was lately making an excursion in a steam-boat, through one of the Scottish lakes. Among the passengers were several of the sporting gentry, furnished with all their requisite accoutrements, who seemed to enjoy a higher gratification in disturbing the happiness of the feathered tribes, than in contemplating the natural beauties of the surrounding scene. When any of these hapless animals appeared in view, a hue and cry commenced, a shot was prepared, and a musket levelled at the unoffending creatures, which created among them universal agitation and alarm. Some of them were killed; and others, doubtless, maimed, and rendered miserable for life; while no human being could enjoy the least benefit from such wanton cruelty. To kill, or even to maim any living creature that is doing us no harm, and when there is no possibility, nor even a desire, to procure its carcass for food, cannot, I should think, by any sophistry of reasoning, be construed into an act of benevolence.*

I cannot, here, forbear inserting a passage from "Salt's Travels in Abyssinia," which exhibits a very different spirit in one whom some would be disposed to rank among the class of semi-barbarians. "In the evening, Baharnegash Yasons, a servant of the Ras (of Abyssinia) who had attended me during my whole stay in the country, took his leave. Among all the men with whom I have been intimately acquainted, I consider this old man as one of the most perfect and blameless characters. His mind seemed to be formed upon the purest principles of the Christian religion; his every thought and action appeared to be the result of its dictates. He would often, to ease his mule, walk more than half the day; and as he journeyed by my side, continually recited prayers for our welfare and future prosperity. On all occasions he sought to repress in those around him, every improper feeling of anger; conciliated them by the kindest words, and excited them, by his example, to an active performance of their duties. If a man were weary, he would assist him in carrying his burden; if he perceived any of the mules' backs to be hurt, he would beg me to have them relieved; and, constantly, when he saw me engaged in shooting partridges, or other birds, he would call out to them to fly out of the way, shaking his head, and begging me, in a mournful accent, not to kill them. I have remarked, in my former journal, that, with all this refined feeling of humanity, he was far from being devoid of courage; and, I had an opportunity, subsequently, of witnessing several instances of his bravery, though he appeared on all occasions peculiarly anxious to avoid a quarrrel. We parted, I believe, with mutual regret; at least for my own part, I can truly say, that I have seldom felt more respect for an individual than I did for this worthy man."

As a contrast to the benevolent dispositions displayed by this worthy Abyssinian,—I shall give a short description of a *bull-fight*, in Madrid, extracted from a work, the author of which was a spectator (in 1803) of the scene he describes. "The Spanish bull-fights are certainly the most extraordinary exhibition in Europe: we were present at one of them this morning. The places in the amphitheatre were nearly all filled at half past nine, and at ten, the corregidor came into his box; upon which the trumpet sounded, and the people rose and shouted, from the delight that the show was to begin immediately. Four men in black gowns then came forward, and read a proclamation, enjoining all persons to remain in their seats. On their going out of the arena, the six bulls which were to be fought this morning, were driven across, led on by a cow, with a bell round her neck. The two *Picadores* (the men who were appointed to fight the furious animals) now appeared, dressed in leathern gaiters, thick leathern breeches, silk jackets covered with spangles, and caps surmounted by broad brimmed white hats; each rode a miserable hack, and carried in his hand a long pole, with a goad at the end. As soon as they were prepared, a door was opened, and the first bull rushed in. In the course of the contest, I felt first alarmed for the men, and then for the horses. Soon the accidents of the men withdrew my pity from the beasts; and, latterly, by a natural, and dreadful

* In throwing out these reflections, the author by no means wishes to insinuate, that it is improper, in every instance, to kill any of the inferior animals; his remarks being directed solely against the practice of wantonly maiming or destroying them for the sake of mere sport or amusement. Even in those cases where it may appear expedient or necessary, to extirpate a portion of the animal tribes, it appears somewhat strange, that *gentlemen* should be the voluntary agents employed in this work of destruction, and that their minds should be so much absorbed in the satisfaction which it creates. One would have thought that the very lowest class of the community would have been selected for this purpose, as there is something naturally revolting in the employment of destroying the life of any sensitive being.

operation of the mind, I began to look without horror on the calamities of both. The manner of the fight is thus:—the bull rushes in, and makes an attack severally upon the picadores, who repulse him; he being always, upon these occasions, wounded in the neck; after a few rencounters, he becomes somewhat shy; but at the same time, when he does rush on, he is doubly dangerous. He follows up the attack, and frequently succeeds in overthrowing both horse and rider. As long as the horse has strength to bear the picadore, he is obliged to ride him. This morning one of these wretched animals was forced to charge, *with his guts hanging in festoons between his legs!* His belly was again ripped open by the bull, and he fell for dead; but the attendants obliged him to rise and crawl out! This seems the cruellest part of the business; for the men almost always escape; but *the blood and sufferings of thirteen horses were exhibited in the short space of two hours.* Four men were hurt; one who was entirely overturned with his horse upon him, was carried out like a corpse; but the spectators, *totally disregarding this melancholy sight, shouted for his companion to renew the attack.* The bull after his first rage and subsequent fury during many rounds, begins to feel weakness, and declines further attacks on the horsemen. Upon this, a loud shout re-echoes through the theatre, and some of the attendants advance and stick his gored neck full of arrows which cause him to *writhe about in great torment.* When the efforts he makes under these sufferings have considerably spent his strength, the corregidor makes a motion with his hand, and the trumpets sound as a signal to the matador to despatch him. This is a service which requires great skill and bravery; for the madness of the bull, and the torture he endures, prompt him to destroy every one around. The matador advances with a red cloak in one hand, and a sword in the other. He enrages the bull with the cloak, till, at length getting opposite to him, he rushes forward, and the sword pierces his spinal marrow, or what is more common, is buried to the hilt in his neck; upon which he turns aside, at first moaning, but a torrent of blood gushes from his mouth; and he staggers round the arena, and falls. The trumpets sound; three mules, ornamented with ribbons and flags, appear, to drag the wretched victim out by the horns, and the horsemen to prepare for the attack of a fresh animal."

"In the evening the show began at half-past four, and ten bulls were brought forward. To tame them before the matador approached, a new expedient was resorted to, most infamously cruel, namely, the covering of the darts with sulphur and fireworks. The torments of these were so dreadful, that the animals whose strength was fresh, raged about terribly, so that the assistants were forced to use great agility to get from them. There were many hair-breadth escapes, one of the animals in pursuit of a man, leaped the barrier of the arena, which is about eight feet high. A second bull was still more furious, and made more tremendous attacks. In one of these he pinned the man and horse against the barriers, got his horns under the horse, and lacerated him dreadfully; in a moment afterwards, he lifted him up, and threw the man with such force through one of the apertures, as to kill him on the spot. He was borne past the box in which we were with his teeth set, and his side covered with blood; the horse staggered out spouting a stream of gore from his chest. The remaining picador renewed the charge, and *another came in with shouts to take the dead man's place.* One of these had his horse's skin dreadfully ripped off his side, and when he breathed, *the entrails swelled out of the hole;* to prevent which, the rider got off and stuffed in his pocket handkerchief," &c.*—"I have seen," says Bourgoing, "eight or ten horses torn, and their bellies ripped open, fall and expire in the field of battle. Sometimes these horses, affecting models of patience, of courage, of docility—present a spectacle, at which it may be allowable to shudder. You see them tread under their feet, their own bloody entrails, hanging out of their open sides, and still obey, for some time the hand that guides them."

Such are the amusements which, in Spain fascinate all ranks of the community, from the prince to the peasant. Young ladies, old men, servant girls, and people of all ages and all characters are present. The art of killing a bull, which seems exclusively to be the business of a butcher, is gravely discussed and exalted with transport, not only by the rabble, but by men of sense, and by women of delicacy. The day of a bull-fight is a day of solemnity for the whole canton. "The people come," says Bourgoing, "from ten and twelve leagues distance. The artisan who can with difficulty earn enough for his subsistence, has always sufficient to pay for the bull-fight. Wo be to the chastity of a young girl whose poverty excludes her! The man who pays for her admittance, will be her first seducer. It is indeed a very striking sight, to see all the inhabitants assemble round the circus, waiting the signal for the fight, *and wearing in their exterior every sign of impatience.*" There is not a town in Spain, but what has a large square for the purpose of exhibiting bull-fights; and it is said, that even the poorest inhabitants of the smallest villages will often club together, in order to procure a cow or an ox, and fight them riding upon asses for want of horses.† Can a spirit of pure bene-

* Travels through Spain and part of Portugal in 1803, Vol. 2. pp. 35—45. A more circumstantial account of these fights, and in perfect accordance with the above description, may be seen in Bourgoing's "Modern State of Spain," vol. II. pp. 346—360.

† It is said that these fights were prohibited in 1805 *to the deep regret of the most numerous part of the*

volence be general among a people addicted to such cruel and savage amusements! And, need we wonder to find, that troops of lawless banditti are continually prowling among the mountains and forests of that country, committing murders and depredations? One of the authors just now quoted, when alluding to banditti, and detailing the incidents which occurred on his route to Madrid, says, "In this country it is impossible to distinguish friends from foes, as all travellers go well armed. We met just here half a dozen horsemen, many of whom had swords and pistols, and we afterwards saw peasants riding on asses, armed in the same way. A few leagues further on, we met a strong detachment of cavalry patroling the road, in consequence of a daring robbery, which had just been committed on a nobleman who was bringing his bride to court from Bacrelona. He had a numerous retinue; the banditti were twelve in number, and completely armed."

If we now take a cursory glance at our POPULAR LITERARY WORKS, and at several of our publications intended for the *nursery*, we shall find that a goodly portion of them is stamped with the character of frivolity and of *malignity*. When the young mind is just beginning to expand, instead of being irradiated with the beams of unadulterated truth, a group of distorted and unsubstantial images, which have no prototypes in nature, is presented to the view of the intellect, as the groundwork of its future progress in wisdom and knowledge. Instead of the simple and sublime precepts of Christian benevolence, the wild and romantic notions connected with chivalry, the superstitions of the dark ages, and the love of false heroism, and of military glory, are attempted to be indelibly riveted on the minds of the young. What else can be expected, when such legends and romances as the following, occupy the principal part of the nursery library?—*Blue Beard*; Cinderella; Tom Thumb; *Jack the Giant-Killer*; Valentine and Orson; *The Seven Champions of Christendom*; Robin Hood; Goody Two-Shoes; Puss in Boots; Sinbad the Sailor; Aladdin, or, the Wonderful Lamp; Thalaba, or, the Destroyer; The Blood-Red Knight; The Maid and the Magpie; *Fairy Tales*, and a long list of similar tales and romances, equally improving and important! Such works are published, even at the present time, not only in a Lilliputian size, to suit the lower ranks of the community, but in a style of splendour and elegance, calculated to fascinate the highest circles of society. Ten thousands of copies of such publications, are presently in circulation throughout every part of the British empire:—and what is the great object they are calculated to accomplish? To exhibit distorted views of the scenes of nature, and of human society; to foster superstitious notions; to inspire the minds of the young with an inordinate desire after worldly honour and distinction; to set before them, as an ultimate object, the splendour and felicity of "riding in a coach and six;" and to familiarize their minds to chivalrous exploits, and to scenes of butchery and revenge.

If we glance at the popular literary works of the present day, intended for the amusement of children of a larger growth, we shall find many of them imbued with a similar spirit, and having a similar tendency. What is it that just now fascinates our literary loungers, our polished gentry, our educated females, nay, all ranks of the community, from the dignified clergyman to the humble weaver, and which threatens to destroy all relish for plain unvarnished facts, and for substantial knowledge? The novels of Waverley, Guy Mannering, Rob Roy, Tales of my Landlord, The Fortunes of Nigel, St. Ronan's Well, Marmion, The Corsair, Childe Harold, and a shoal of similar publications, which are daily issuing from the press. And what is the general tendency of the great majority of such works? To distort and caricature the facts of real history; to gratify a romantic imagination; to pamper a depraved mental appetite; to excite a disrelish for the existing scenes of nature, and for the authenticated facts which have occurred in the history of mankind; to hold up venerable characters to derision and contempt; to excite admiration of the exploits and the malignant principles of those rude chieftains and barbarous heroes, whose names ought to descend into everlasting oblivion; to revive the revengeful spirit of the dark ages; to undermine a sacred regard for *truth* and moral principle, which are the basis of the happiness of the intelligent universe; and to throw a false glory over scenes of rapine, of bloodshed, and of devastation.—To such works, and to their admirers, we might apply the words of the ancient Prophet: "He feedeth on *ashes*; a deceived heart hath turned him aside, that he cannot say, Is there not a lie in my right hand?"

"For, sure, to hug a fancied case,
That never did, nor can take place,
And for the pleasures it can give,
Neglect the 'facts of real life,'
Is madness in its greatest height,
Or I mistake the matter quite."—*Wilkie.*

To affirm, that it is necessary for the entertainment of the human mind, to have recouse to fictitious scenes and narratives, and to the wild vagaries of an unbridled imagination, is, in effect, to throw a reflection upon the plans and the conduct of the Creator. It implies, that, in the scenes of nature which surround us, both in the heavens and on the earth, and in the administrations of his moral government among men, God

*nation*; but another entertainment, called *fiesta de novillos*, which is an image of the bull-fight, is still retained and it is not improbable, that, by this time, the true bull-fight has been again revived.

has not produced a sufficient variety of interesting objects for the contemplation, the instruction, and the entertainment of the human race—and that the system of the moral and physical world must be distorted and deranged, and its economy misrepresented and blended with the creations of human folly, before its scenery be rendered fit to gratify the depraved and fastidious tastes of mankind.* And is it indeed true, that there is not a sufficient *variety* to gratify a *rational* mind in the *existing scenes* of creation and providence? If we survey the Alpine scenes of nature; if we explore the wonders of the ocean; if we penetrate into the subterraneous recesses of the globe; if we direct our view to the numerous objects of sublimity and of beauty to be found in every country; if we investigate the structure and economy of the animal and the vegetable tribes; if we raise our eyes to the rolling orbs of heaven; if we look back to the generations of old, and trace the history of ancient nations; if we contemplate the present state of civilized and of savage tribes, and the moral scenery which is every where displayed around us—shall we not find a sufficient variety of every thing which is calculated to interest, to instruct, and to *entertain* a rational mind? I am bold to affirm, that were a proper selection made of the *facts* connected with the system of nature, and with the history and the present state of human society, and were the sketches of such facts executed by the hand of a master, and interspersed with rational and moral reflections—volumes might be presented to the public, no less entertaining, and certainly far more instructive, than all the novels and romances which the human imagination has ever produced; and that, too, without distorting a single fact in the system of nature or of human society, or exciting a sentiment of admiration or of approbation of the exploits of warriors. If we wish to be amused with entertaining narrations and novel scenes, the narratives of adventurous voyagers and travellers, when written with spirit and animation, will supply us with entertainment scarcely inferior to that of the best writen novel; and it is the reader's own fault, if he do not, from such sources, derive moral instruction. Such adventures as those of Mungo Park in Africa, and Captain Cochrane in Siberia, and such narratives as those of Byron, Brisson, Pierre Viaud, Anson, Cook, Bligh, Perouse, and others, abound with so many striking and affecting incidents, that the reader's attention is kept alive, and he feels as lively an interest in the fate of the adventurers, as is usually felt in that of the fictitious hero of a novel, or a romance.

If man were only the creature of a day, whose whole existence was confined within the limits of this sublunary scene, he might amuse himself either with facts or with fictions, or with any toys or gewgaws that happened to strike his fancy while he glided down the stream of time to the gulf of oblivion. But if he is a being destined for eternity, the train of his thoughts ought to be directed to objects corresponding to his high destination, and all his amusements blended with those moral instructions which have an ultimate reference to the scene of his immortal existence. When I read one of our modern novels, I enjoy, for a few hours, a transitory amusement, in contemplating the scenes of fancy it displays, and in following the hero through his numerous adventures; I admire the force and brilliancy of the imagination of the writer (for I am by no means disposed to underrate the intellectual talent which has produced some of the works to which I allude,) but when I have finished the perusal, and reflect, that all the scenes which passed before my mental eye, were only so many unsubstantial images, the fictions of a lively imagination—I cannot indulge in rational or religious reflections on the subject, nor derive a single moral instruction, any more than I can do from a dream or a vision of the night. When I survey the scenes of creation; when I read the history of ancient nations; when I peruse the authentic narratives of the voyager and traveller; when I search the records of revelation; and when I contemplate the present state of society around me,—I learn something of the character, the attributes, and the providence of God, and of the moral and physical state of mankind. From almost every scene, and every incident, I can deduce instructions calculated to promote the exercise of humility, meekness, gratitude, and resignation—to lead the mind to God as the source of felicity, and as the righteous governor of the world—and to impress the heart with a sense of the folly and depravity of man. But it is obvious, that no distinct moral instructions can be fairly deduced from scenes, circumstances, and events "which never did nor can take place."—Such however is, at present the tide of public opinion on this subject that we

* The following sketch of Sir Walter Scott, the supposed author of some of the works alluded to, is given in Hazlitt's "Spirit of the Age, or Contemporary Portraits" "His mind receives and treasures up every thing brought to it by tradition or custom—it does not project itself beyond this into the world unknown, but mechanically shrinks back as from the edge of a precipice. The land of *pure reason* is to his apprehension like *Van Dieman's Land*, barren, miserable, distant, a place of exile, the dreary abode of savages, convicts, and adventurers. Sir Walter would make a bad hand of a description of the *millennium*, unless he would lay the scene in Scotland 500 years ago; and then he would want facts and worm-eaten parchments to support his drooping style. Our historical novelist firmly thinks, that nothing *is* but what *has been*—that the moral world stands still, as the material one was supposed to do of old—and that we can never get beyond the point where we actually are, without utter destruction, though every thing changes and will change, from what it was 300 years ago and what it is now; from what it is now, to all that the bigoted admirer of the good old times most dreads and hates."

might as soon attempt to stem a mountain torrent by a breath of wind, or to interrupt the dashings of a mighty cataract by the waving of our hand, as to expect to counteract, by any considerations that can be adduced, the current of popular feeling in favour of novels, and tales of knights, and of tournaments; of warlike chieftains, and military encounters. Such a state of feeling, I presume, never can exist in a world where moral evil has never shed its malign influence.

Again, if we consider the sentiments and the conduct of many of our *Literary and Scientific characters*, we shall find that even philosophy has had very little influence, in counteracting the stream of malignity, and promoting the exercise of benevolence. Do not many of our literary characters in their disputes frequently display as keen resentments, and as malevolent dispositions, as the professed warrior, and the man of the world? and have they not some times resorted even to horsewhips and to pistols to decide their contests? In proof of this, need I refer to the gentlemen now or formerly connected with the "Edinburgh Magazine," "Blackwood's Magazine," the "London Magazine," the "Quarterly Review," and other periodical works—and to the mean jealousies and contentions which have been displayed, and the scurrilous paragraphs which have been written by various descriptions of competitors for literary fame? Such a display of temper and conduct in men of professed erudition, is not only inconsistent with moral principle, and the dignity of true science, but has a tendency to hold up philosophy and substantial knowledge to the scorn and contempt both of the Christian and of the political world.

Again, is it an evidence that benevolence forms a prominent character of modern civilized society, when philanthropists, who have devoted their substance and their mental activities to the promotion of the best interests of mankind; and when men of science, who have enlarged the sphere of our knowledge, and improved the useful arts, are suffered to pine away in penury and neglect, and to descend into the grave, without even a "frail memorial" to mark the spot where their mortal remains are deposited; while, on the warrior, who has driven the ploughshare of destruction through the world, and wounded the peace of a thousand families, enormous pensions are bestowed, and trophies erected to perpetuate his memory to future generations? And how comes it to pass, if benevolence and justice be distinguishing features of our age and nation, that authors, whose writings afford instruction and entertainment to a numerous public, are frequently suffered to pine away in anxiety and distress, and to remain in hopeless indigence, while publishers and booksellers are fattening on the fruit of their labours? Yet, while we leave them to remain in abject penury, during life,—no sooner have their spirits taken their flight into the world unknown, than subscriptions are set on foot, statues and mausoleums are erected, flattering inscriptions are engraved on their tombs, and anniversary dinners are appointed to celebrate their memories. Such displays of liberality might have been of essential benefit to the individuals, while they sojourned within the limits of this sublunary sphere; but they are altogether futile and superfluous in relation to the separate spirits, which are now placed forever beyond the reach of such vain pageantry and posthumous honours.

If we now attend, for a little, to the *Penal Codes* of civilized nations, we shall find them, not only glaringly deficient in a spirit of benevolence, but deeply imbued with a spirit of cruelty and revenge. The great object of all civil punishments ought to be, not only the prevention of crimes, but also the reformation of the criminal, in order that a conviction of the evil of his conduct may be impressed upon his mind, and that he may be restored to society as a renovated character. When punishments are inflicted with a degree of severity beyond what is necessary to accomplish these ends, the code which sanctions them, becomes an engine of cruelty and of injustice. But, the reformation, and the ultimate happiness of the criminal, never seem to have been once taken into consideration, in the construction of the criminal codes of any nation in Europe. The infliction of *pain*, and even of *torture*, and of every thing that is degrading and horrible, to a degree far beyond what is necessary for the security of the public, and which has no other tendency than to harden the culprit, seems to have been the great object of the framers of our penal statutes. If a man has committed an offence against society, he is either confined to a jail, thrown into a dungeon, loaded with irons, whipped through the streets, banished to a distant land, hung upon a gallows, or broken on the wheel. No system of moral regimen, calculated to counteract his criminal habits, to impart instruction to his mind, and to induce habits of industry and temperance, (except in a few insulated cases) has yet been arranged by our legislators, so as to render punishment a blessing to the criminal, and to the community which he has injured.

The following circumstances, in relation to punishments, manifest a principle both of folly and of malignity in the arrangements of our criminal jurisprudence.—In the first place, the present system of our prison discipline, instead of operating to prevent the increase of crime, has a direct and inevitable tendency to produce vice and wretchedness, and to render our jails the nurseries of every depraved propensity, and of every species of moral turpitude. From the indiscriminate association of the young and the old, and of persons charged with every degree of criminality, the youthful and inexperienced culprit is soon tutored in all the arts of fraud, deception, and robbery, and prepared for acting a more conspicuous and atrocious part on the theatre of crime. "I make no scruple to affirm," says Mr. Howard, "that if it were the aim and wish of magistrates to effect the destruction, present and future, of young delinquents, they could not desire a more effectual method than to confine them in our prisons." Of the truth of this position, the reader will find an ample and impressive proof in the Honourable T. F. Buxton's "Inquiry whether crime and misery are produced or prevented by our present system of Prison Discipline."

In the second place, the disproportion between crimes and punishments, and the sanguinary character of every civilized code of penal statutes, are directly repugnant to every principle of justice and benevolence. The punishment assigned by the law to the man who steals a sheep, or pilfers a petty article of merchandise, is the same as that which it inflicts on the miscreant who has imbrued his hands in his father's blood. In France, prior to the revolution, the punishment of robbery, either with or without murder, was the same; and hence it happened, that robbery was seldom or never perpetrated without murder. For, when men see no distinction made in the nature and gradations of punishment, they will be generally led to conclude, that there is no distinction in the guilt. In our own country, it is a melancholy truth, that, among the variety of actions which men are daily liable to commit, no less than *one hundred and sixty* have been declared, by act of parliament, to be felonies, without benefit of clergy; or, in other words, to be worthy of instant death.* It is an indelible disgrace to an age which boasts of its being enlightened with the beams of science and of religion, that laws, framed in an ignorant and barbarous age, and intended to apply to temporary or fortuitous occurrences, should still be acted upon, and stand unrepealed in the criminal codes of the nations of Europe, in the 19th century of the Christian era, when so many distinguished writers have demonstrated their futility, their injustice, and their inadequacy for the prevention of crime. For, instead of diminishing the number of offenders, experience proves, that crimes are almost uniformly increased by an undue severity of punishment. This was strikingly exemplified in the reign of Henry VIII. remarkable for the abundance of its crimes, which certainly did not arise from the mildness of punishment. In that reign alone, says his historian, *seventy-two thousand executions* took place, for robberies alone, exclusive of the religious murders which are known to have been numerous, —amounting, on an average, to *six executions a day*, Sundays included, during the whole reign of that monarch.

* Ency Brit. Art. Crime

In the next place, *the shocking and unnecessary cruelties* which are frequently inflicted upon criminals, are inconsistent with every principle of reason and of justice, and revolting to every feeling of humanity. If the forfeiture of life ought, in any case, to be resorted to as the punishment of certain crimes, humanity dictates, that it should be accompanied with as little pain as possible to the unfortunate criminal. But man, even *civilized man*, has glutted his savage disposition by inventing tortures to agonize his fellow man, at which humanity shudders. It is not enough that a poor unfortunate wretch, in the prime of life, whom depravity has hurried to the commission of crime, should be deprived of his mortal existence,—his soul must be harrowed up at the prospect of the prolonged torments which he must endure, before his spirit is permitted to take its flight to the world unknown. Instead of simply strangling or beheading the unhappy criminal, his flesh must be torn with pincers, his bones dislocated, his hands chopped off, or his body left to pine away in exquisite torments, amidst devouring flames. In Sweden, murder is punished by beheading and quartering, after having previously chopped off the hand. In Germany, Poland, Italy, and other parts of the continent, it was customary, and, I believe, still is, in some places, to put criminals to death, by breaking them alive on the wheel. The following account is given, by a traveller, who was in Berlin, in 1819, of the execution of a man for murder, which shows that the execution of criminals, in Prussia, is frequently distinguished by a species of cruelty worthy of the worst days of the inquisition. Amidst the parade of executioners, officers of police, and other judicial authorities, the beating of drums, and the waving of flags and colours, the criminal mounted the scaffold. No ministers of religion appeared to gild the the horrors of eternity, and to sooth the agonies of the criminal; and no repentant prayer closed his quivering lips. "Never," says the narrator, "shall I forget the one bitter look of imploring agony that he threw around him, as immediately on stepping on the scaffold, his coat was rudely torn from off his shoulders. He was then thrown down, the cords fixed round his neck, which were drawn until strangulation almost commenced. Another executioner then approached, bearing in his hands a heavy wheel, bound with iron, with which he violently struck the legs, arms, and chest, and lastly the head of the criminal. I was unfortunately near enough to witness his mangled and bleeding body still convulsed. It was then carried down for interment, and, in less than a quarter of an hour from the beginning of his torture, the corpse was completely covered with earth. Several large stones, which were thrown upon him, hastened his last gasp; *he was mangled into eternity!*"

In Russia, the severest punishments are frequently inflicted for the most trivial offences. The *knout* is one of the most common punishments in that country. This instrument is a thong made of the skin of an elk or of a wild ass, so hard that a single stroke is capable of cutting the flesh to the bone. The following description is given by *Olearius* of the manner in which he saw the knout inflicted on eight men, and one *woman*, only for selling brandy and tobacco without a license. "The executioner's man, after stripping them down to the wast, tied their feet, and took one at a time on his back. The executioner stood at three paces distance, and, springing forward with the knout in his hand,—whenever he struck, the blood gushed out at every blow. The men had each twenty-five or twenty-six lashes; the woman, though only sixteen, fainted away. After their backs were thus dreadfully mangled, they were tied together two and two; and those who sold tobacco having a little of it, and those who sold brandy a little bottle put about their necks; they were then whipped through the city of Petersburgh for about a mile and a half, and then brought back to the place of their punishment, and dismissed." That is what is termed the *moderate* knout; for when it is given with the utmost severity, the executioner, striking the flank under the ribs, cuts the flesh to the bowels; and, therefore, it is no wonder that many die of this inhuman punishment.—The punishment of the pirates and robbers who infest the banks of the Wolga, is another act of savage cruelty common to Russia. A float is built, whereon a gallows is erected, on which is fastened a number of iron hooks, and on these the wretched criminals are hung alive by the ribs. The float is then launched into the stream, and orders are given to all the towns and villages on the borders of the river, that none, upon pain of death, shall afford the least relief to any of these wretches. These malefactors sometimes hang, in this manner, three, four, and even five days alive. The pain produces a raging fever, in which they utter the most horrid imprecations, imploring the relief of water and other liquors.* During the reign of Peter the Great, the robbers who infested various parts of his dominions, particularly the banks of the Wolga, were hung up in this manner by hundreds and thousands, and left to perish in the most dreadful manner. Even yet, the boring of the tongue, and the cutting of it out, are practised in this country as an inferior species of punishment. Such cruel punishments, publicly inflicted, can have no other tendency than to demoralize the minds of the populace, to blunt their natural feelings, and to render criminal characters still more desperate: and hence we need not wonder at what travellers affirm respecting the Russians, that they are very indifferent as to life or death, and undergo capital punishments with unparalleled apathy and indolence.

Even among European nations more civilized than the Russians, similar tortures have been inflicted upon criminals. The execution of *Damiens*, in 1757, for attempting to assassinate Louis XV. King of France, was accompanied with tortures, the description of which is sufficient to harrow up the feelings of the most callous mind—tortures, which could scarcely have been exceeded in intensity and variety, although they had been devised and executed by the ingenuity of an infernal fiend. And yet, they were beheld with a certain degree of apathy by a surrounding populace; and even counsellors and physicians could talk together about the best mode of tearing asunder the limbs of the wretched victim, with as much composure as if they had been dissecting a dead subject, or carving a pullet. Even in Britain, at no distant period, similar cruelties were practised. Those who are guilty of high treason are condemned, by our law, "to be hanged on a gallows for some minutes; then cut down, *while yet alive*, the heart to be taken out and exposed to view, and the entrails burned." Though the most cruel part of this sentence has never been actually inflicted in our times, yet it is a disgrace to Britons that such a statute should still stand unrepealed in our penal code.—The practice, too, of *torturing* supposed criminals for the purpose of extorting a confession of guilt, was, till a late period, common over all the countries of Europe; and if I am not mistaken, is still resorted to, in several parts of the continent. Hence, Baron Bielfeld, in his "Elements of Universal Erudition," published in 1770, lays down as one of the branches of criminal jurisprudence, "*The different kinds of tortures for the discovery of truth.*" Such a practice is not only cruel and unjust, but absurd in the highest degree, and repugnant to every principle of reason. For, as the Marquis Beccaria has well observed, "It is confounding all relations to expect that a man should be both the accuser and the accused, and *that pain shouled be the test of truth*; as if truth resided in the muscles and fibres of a wretch in torture. By this method, the robust will escape, and the feeble be condemned.—To discover truth by this method, is a problem which may be better resolved by a mathematician than a judge, and may be thus stated: *The force of the muscles and the sensibility of the nerves of an innocent person being given, it is required to find the degree of pain necessary to make him confess himself guilty of a given crime.*"*

* See Hanway's "Travels through Russia and Persia"—Salmon's "Present State of all Nations," vol. 6. Guthrie's Geography, &c

* See Beccaria's "Essay on Crimes and Punishments," p. 52. 56. The following is a brief summary of the principal punishments that have been adopted by men, in different countries, for tormenting and destroying each other. *Capital* punishments—be

If the confined limits of the present work had admitted, I might have prosecuted these illustrations to a much greater extent. I might have traced the operations of malevolence in the practice of that most shocking and abominable traffic, the *Slave Trade*— the eternal disgrace of individuals and of nations calling themselves *civilized*. This is an abomination which has been encouraged by almost every nation in Europe, and even by the enlightened states of America. And although Great Britain has formally prohibited, by a law, the importation of slaves from Africa; yet, in all her West Indian colonies, slavery in its most cruel and degrading forms still exists; and every proposition, and every plan for restoring the negroes to their natural liberty, and to the rank which they hold in the scale of existence, is pertinaciously resisted by *gentlemen* planters, who would spurn at the idea of being considered as either infidels or barbarians. They even attempt to deprive these degraded beings of the chance of obtaining a happier existence in a future world, by endeavouring to withhold from them the means of instruction, and by persecuting their instructers. "In *Demerara* alone there are 76,000 immortal souls linked to sable bodies, while there are but 3,500 whites; and yet, for the sake of these three thousand whites, the seventy-six thousand, with all their descendants, are to be kept in ignorance of the way of salvation, for no other purpose than to procure a precarious fortune for a very few individuals out of their sweat and blood." Is such conduct consistent with the spirit of benevolence, or even with the common feelings of humanity? I might have traced the same malignant principle, in the practice of a set of men denominated *wreckers*, who, by setting up false lights, allure mariners to destruction, that they may enrich themselves by plundering the wrecks—in the *warlike dispositions* of all the governments of Europe, and the enormous sums which have been expended in the work of devastation, and of human destruction, while they have refused to give the least *direct* encouragement to philanthropic institutions, and to the improvement of the community in knowledge and virtue—and in that spirit of tyranny, and thirst for despotic power, which have led them to crush the rising intelligence of the people, and to lend a deaf ear to their most reasonable demands. For, there is no government on this side of the Atlantic, so far as I know, that has ever yet formed an institution for promoting the objects of general benevolence, for counteracting the baleful effects of depravity and ignorance, and for enlightening the minds of the people in useful knowledge; or which has even contributed a single mite to encourage such institutions after they were set on foot by the people themselves. Knowledge is simply *permitted* to be diffused; it is never directly encouraged; its progress is frequently obstructed; and, in some instances, it is positively interdicted, as appears from the following barbarous edict, published in the year 1825.—"A royal Sardinian edict directs, that henceforth no person shall learn to read or write who cannot prove the possession of property above the value of 1500 livres, (or about 60*l*. sterling.) The qualification for a student is the possession of an income to the same amount."* Such is the firm determination of many of the kings and princes of Europe to hold their subjects in abject slavery and ignorance; and such is the desperate tendency of proud ambition, that they will rather suffer their thrones to shake and totter beneath them, than give encouragement to liberal opinions, and to the general diffusion of knowledge.—But, instead of illustrating such topics in minute detail, I shall conclude this section by presenting a few miscellaneous facts, tending to corroborate several of the preceding statements, and to illustrate the moral state of the civilized world.

The following statement, extracted from "Neale's Travels through Germany, Poland, Moldavia, and Turkey," exhibits a faint picture of the state of morals in Poland. "If ever there was a country," says Mr. Neale, "where 'might constitutes right,' that country was Poland, prior to its partition." The most dreadful oppression, the most execrable tyranny, the most wanton cruelties were daily exercised by the nobles upon the unfortunate peasants.—Let us quote a few facts; they will speak volumes. A

heading, strangling, crucifixion, drowning, burning, roasting, hanging by the neck, the arm, or the leg; starving, sawing, exposing to wild beasts, rending asunder by horses drawing opposite ways, shooting, burying alive, blowing from the mouth of a cannon, compulsory deprivation of sleep, rolling on a barrel stuck with nails, cutting to pieces, hanging by the ribs, poisoning, pressing slowly to death by a weight laid on the breast; casting headlong from a rock, tearing out the bowels, pulling to pieces with red hot pincers, stretching on the rack, breaking on the wheel, impaling, flaying alive, cutting out the heart, &c. &c. &c. Punishments short of death have been such as the following. Fine, pillory, imprisonment, compulsory labour at the mines, galleys, highways, or correction-house; whipping, bastinading; mutilation by cutting away the ears, the nose, the tongue, the breasts of women, the foot, the hand; squeezing the marrow from the bones with screws or wedges, castration, putting out the eyes; banishment, running the gauntlet, drumming, shaving off the hair, burning on the hand or forehead; and many others of a similar nature. Could the ingenuity of the inhabitants of *Tophet* have invented punishments more cruel and revolting? Has any one of these modes of punishment a tendency to reform the criminal, and promote his happiness? On the contrary, have they not all a direct tendency to irritate, to harden, and to excite feelings of revenge? Nothing shows the malevolent dispositions of a great portion of the human race, in so striking a light, as the punishments they have inflicted on one another; for these are characteristic, not of insulated individuals only, but of *nations*, in their collective capacity.

* Hamburgh Paper, August, 1825

Polish peasant's life was held of the same value with one of his horned cattle; if his lord slew him, he was fined only 100 Polish florins, or 2*l.* 16*s.* sterling. If, on the other hand, a man of ignoble birth dared to raise his hand against a nobleman, death was the inevitable punishment. If any one presumed to question the nobility of a magnate, he was forced to prove his assertion, or suffer death; nay, if a powerful man chose to take a fancy to the field of his humbler neighbour, and to erect a landmark upon it, and if that landmark remained for three days, the poor man lost his possession. The atrocious cruelties that were habitually exercised, are hardly credible. A Masalki caused his hounds to devour a peasant who happened to frighten his horse. A Radzivil had the belly of one of his subjects ripped open, to thrust his feet into it, hoping thereby to be cured of a malady that had tormented him.

One of the most infallible signs of a degraded state of morals in any country, is the corrupt administration of justice. As specimens of Polish justice, Mr. Neale mentions the case of a merchant of Warsaw, whom it cost 1400 ducats to procure the conviction and execution of two robbers who had plundered him; and another case, still more flagrant, that of a peasant who had apprehended an assassin, and who, on taking him to the Staroste, was coolly dismissed with the prisoner, and the corpse of the murdered person which he had brought in his wagon; because he had not ten ducats—the fee demanded by the magistrate for his interference.—"During the reign of Stanislaus Poniatowsky, a petty noble having refused to resign to Count Thisenhaus his small estate, the Count invited him to dinner, as if desirous of amicably adjusting the affair; and whilst the knight, in the pride of his heart at such unexpected honour, assiduously plied the bottle, the Count despatched some hundreds of peasants with axes, ploughs, and wagons, ordering the village, which consisted only of a few wooden buildings, to be pulled down, the materials carried away, and the plough to be passed over the ground which the village had occupied. This was accordingly done. The nobleman, on his return home in the evening, could find neither road, house, nor village. The master and his servant were alike bewildered, and knew not whether they were dreaming or had lost the power of discrimination; but their surprise and agony were deemed so truly humorous, that the whole court was delighted with the joke!" How depraved must be the state of moral feeling, when the injustice inflicted upon fellow-creatures, and the miseries they endure, become the subjects of merriment and derision!—"The morals of the people of Poland," says Mr. Neale, "were, and continue to be, nearly at the lowest point of debasement. Female chastity is a phenomenon; while the male sex are proportionally profligate. Drunkenness, gluttony, and sensuality, prevail to a degree unknown in other countries in Europe."



The following extract from Mr. Howison's "Foreign Scenes and Travelling Recreations," will convey some idea of the state of morals in the island of Cuba. "Nothing can be worse," says Mr. H., "than the state of society in Havana. The lower classes are all alike dissolute and unprincipled. Assassinations are so frequent that they excite little attention; and assault and robbery are matters of course, when a man passes alone and at night through a solitary quarter of the town. Several assassinations take place in the streets every week." This depraved and lawless state of things may be ascribed to three causes: the inefficiency of the police; the love of gaming and dissipation which prevails among the lower orders; and the facility with which absolution of the greatest crimes may be obtained from the priests. In fact, the Catholic religion, as it now exists in Cuba, tends to encourage rather than to check vice. We shall suppose, for example, that a man makes himself master of 100 dollars by robbing or by murdering another; and that the church grants him absolution for half the sum thus lawlessly obtained; it is evident that he will gain 50 dollars by the whole transaction, and think himself as innocent as he was before he committed the crime. No man need mount the Havana scaffold, whatever be his crime, if he has the means of ministering to the rapacity of the church, and of bribing the civil authorities. A poor friendless criminal is executed in a few days after sentence is pronounced upon him; but a person of wealth and influence generally manages to put off capital punishment for a series of years, and at last get it commuted to fine and imprisonment. Of these depraved practices, Mr. Hewison states several striking examples.—Those statements of Mr. H. in reference to the moral state of Cuba, I find corroborated by a short account of this island in the Monthly Magazine for March, 1820, page 120. "They act here very frequently those sacred mysteries which so delighted our good forefathers. I have witnessed (says the writer) the triumph of the *Ave Maria*, a tragicomedy, which closes with the sudden appearance, in the midst of a theatre, of a chivalrous worthy, mounted on a real horse, shaking at the end of a lance the bloody head of an infidel. This horrid exhibition excited a titter of enjoyment in all the spectators. The *ladies*, in particular, seemed to be highly entertained,—no fainting fits, no nervous attacks. How could a mere fiction agonize the blunt feelings of women, hardened by the spectacle of bull-fights, and almost every day meeting with the dead body of some human being who has been assassinated?"

There is no situation in which human beings can be placed, where we should more naturally expect the manifestation of benevolent affections, than in those scenes of danger where all are equally exposed to deep distress, and where the exercise of sympathy and kindness is the only thing that can alleviate the anguish of the mind. When the prospect of immediate death, or of prolonged agonies even more dreadful than the simple pain of dissolution, is full before the mind, one should think that ferocious dispositions would be instantly curbed, and kindly affections begin to appear. Yet, even in such situations, it frequently happens, that feelings of malevolence and revenge, and all the depraved passions, are most powerfully excited to action. The following facts will tend to illustrate this remark. Mr. Byron was shipwrecked, in a violent storm on the coast of South America. A mountainous sea broke over the ship; she was laid on her beam ends; darkness surrounded them; nothing was to be seen but breakers all around; and every soul on board looked upon the present minute as his last. "So terrible was the scene of foaming breakers around us," says Mr. B. "that one of the bravest men we had could not help expressing his dismay at it, saying it was too shocking a sight to bear." Even in this dreadful situation, malignant passions began to appear; and, like the dashing waves around, to rage with unbounded violence. No sooner had the morning thrown a ray of light over the dismal gloom, and a faint glimpse of land was perceived, than many of the crew who, but a few minutes before, had shown the strongest signs of despair, and were on their knees praying for mercy, "grew extremely riotous, broke open every chest and box that was at hand, stove in the heads of casks of brandy and wine, and got so drunk that some of them were drowned on board, and lay floating about the decks for some days after." After the greater part, to the number of 150 persons, had got to shore—"the boatswain and some of the people would not leave the ship so long as there was any liquor to be got at; they fell to beating every thing to pieces that came in their way, and carrying their intemperance to the greatest excess, broke open chests and cabins for plunder that could be of no use to them. So earnest were they in this wantonness of theft, that one man had evidently been murdered on account of some division of the spoil, or for the sake of the share that fell to him, having all the marks of a strangled corpse." The same malignant dispositions were displayed, in numerous instances, during their abode on the desolate and barren island on which they had been thrown, notwithstanding the hunger, the rains, the cold, and the attacks of wild beasts to which they were all equally exposed.*

There is, perhaps, no occurrence that has happened in modern times, which so strikingly displays the desperate malignity of human beings in the midst of danger, as the conduct of the crew of the Medusa Frigate, while tossing on the *raft* by which they endeavoured to save themselves, after that vessel had been shipwrecked. The Medusa was stranded, in the month of June, 1816, on the bank of Arguin, near the western coast of Africa. A raft was hastily constructed, which was but scantily supplied with provisions. There were five boats, which contained in all about 240 persons; and upon the raft, there embarked about 150 individuals. The boats pushed off in a line, towing the raft, and assuring the people on board that they would conduct them safely to land. They had not proceeded, however, above two leagues from the wreck, when they, one by one, cast off the tow lines, and abandoned the raft to its fate. By this time the raft had sunk below the surface of the water to the depth of three feet and a half, and the people were so squeezed one against another, that it was found impossible to move; fore and aft they were up to the middle in water. Night at length came on; the wind freshened; the sea began to swell; about midnight the weather became very stormy, and the waves broke over them in every direction. Tossed by the waves from one end to the other, and sometimes precipitated into the sea; floating between life and death; mourning over their own misfortunes; certain of perishing, yet contending for the remains of existence with that cruel element which menaced to swallow them up—such was their situation till break of day, when a dreadful spectacle presented itself. Ten or twelve unhappy men, having their extremities jammed between the spars of the raft, had perished in that situation, and others had been swept away by the violence of the waves.—All this, however, was nothing to the dreadful scene which took place the following night. "Already," says the narrator, "was the moral character of the people greatly changed. A spirit of sedition spread from man to man, and manifested itself by the most furious shouts." Night came on; the heavens were obscured with thick clouds; the wind rose, and with it the sea; the waves broke over them every moment; numbers were swept away, and several poor wretches were smothered by the pressure of their comrades. Both soldiers and sailors resolved to sooth their last moments by drinking to excess; they became deaf to the voice of reason; boldly declared their intention of murdering their officers; and, cutting the ropes which held the rafts together, one of them seizing an axe, actually began the dreadful work. The officers rushed forward to quell the tumult, and the man with the hatchet was the first that fell—the stroke of a sabre terminated his existence. One fellow was detected secretly cutting the ropes, and was immediately thrown overboard; others destroyed the shrouds

* See Byron's "Narrative of the Loss of the Wager Man of War."

and haulyards; and the mast, destitute of support, immediately fell on a captain of infantry, and broke his thigh; he was instantly seized by the soldiers and thrown into the sea, but was saved by the opposite party. About an hour after midnight the insurrection burst forth anew. They rushed upon the officers like desperate men, each having a knife or a sabre in his hand; and such was the fury of the assailants, that they tore their flesh, and even their clothes with their teeth. There was no time for hesitation; a general slaughter took place, and the raft was strewed with dead bodies. On the return of day, it was found that, in the course of the preceding night of horror, *sixty-five* of the mutineers had perished, and two of the small party attached to the officers. A third night of horror approached, distinguished by the piercing cries of those whom hunger and thirst devoured; and the morning's sun showed them a dozen unfortunate creatures stretched lifeless on the raft. The fourth night was marked by another massacre. Some Spaniards and Italians conspired to throw the rest into the sea. A Spaniard was the first to advance with a drawn knife; the sailors seized him and threw him into the sea. The Italian seeing this, jumped overboard; the rest were mastered, and order was restored. But, before the ship Argus came to their relief, of the 150 that embarked on the raft, 15 unhappy creatures only remained, covered with wounds and bruises, almost naked, stripped of their skin, shrivelled with the rays of the sun, their eyes hollow, and their countenances savage.—Such are the dreadful effects of *malignity*, which produces more sufferings and fatal effects, than the most tremendous elements of nature!

A certain portion of the same spirit was lately displayed by several individuals on board of the Kent East Indiaman. In the midst of a most violent gale, in the Bay of Biscay, when the sea was running mountains high, this vessel, containing about 600 persons, took fire, in consequence of the spirits from a stoved cask having communicated with a lamp; and all hopes of safety became extinguished, till the ship Cambria, Captain Cooke, hove in sight. But the danger of passing from one ship to the other, in boats, in such a tempestuous sea, rendered the preservation of the passengers and crew in a degree doubtful. Yet, in the midst of the danger, the alarm and the anguish which accompanied this tremendous scene, we are told by the narrator, page 24, that "it is suspected that one or two of those who perished, must have sunk under the weight of their spoils; the same individuals having been seen eagerly plundering the cuddy cabins." And, a little afterwards, page 31, he adds: "Some time after the shades of night had enveloped us, I descended to the cuddy in quest of a blanket to shelter me from the increasing cold, and the scene of desolation that there presented itself was melancholy in the extreme. The place, which only a few short hours before had been the seat of kindly intercourse, and of social gayety, was now entirely deserted, save by a few miserable wretches, who were either stretched in irrecoverable intoxication on the floor, or prowling about, like beasts of prey, in search of plunder."*

The following is a short description of the moral character of the inhabitants of Carolina, and of one of the *amusements* of a people who boast of their liberty and their civilization,—as it is found in "Morse's American Geography." "The citizens of North Carolina who are not better employed, spend their time in drinking, or gaming at cards or dice, in cock-fighting, or horse-racing. Many of the interludes are filled up with a boxing match; and these matches frequently become memorable by feats of *gouging*. This *delicate* and *entertaining* diversion is thus performed: When two boxers are worried with fighting and bruising each other, they come, as it is called, to close quarters; and each endeavours to twist his fore-fingers in the ear-locks of his antagonist. When these are fast clenched, the thumbs are extended each way to the nose, and *the eyes gently twined out of their sockets*. The victor, for his expertness, *receives shouts of applause* from the sporting throng, *while his poor eyeless antagonist is laughed at for his misfortune*. In a country that pretends to any degree of civilization, one would hardly expect to find a prevailing custom of putting out the eyes of each other. Yet this more than barbarous custom is prevalent in both the Carolinas, and in Georgia among the lower class of people."—"Lord, what is man!" In a savage and a civilized state—in infancy and in manhood—in his games and diversions—in the instructions by which he is trained—in the remarks he makes upon his neighbours—in the sports and amusements in which he indulges—in his literary pursuits and lucubrations—in his system of rewards and

* See a "Narrative of the Loss of the Kent East Indiaman, by fire, in the Bay of Biscay, on the 1st of March, 1825, by a Passenger," supposed to be Major Macgregor.—The humanity and intrepidity displayed, amidst the heart-rending scene which this narrative describes—by Captain Cobb of the Kent; by Messrs. Thompson, Fearon, Macgregor, and the other officers, and many of the soldiers; by Captain Cooke of the Cambria, his crew, and the Cornish miners—is above all praise. Their benevolent and heroic conduct at that alarming crisis, is far more deserving of a public monument being raised for its commemoration, than that of many of our military heroes, in honour of whom so many trophies have been erected. If men, who have been instrumental in destroying the lives and the happiness of hundreds and of thousands, have pensions bestowed on them, and are exalted to posts of honour, surely those who have exerted their energies in preserving the lives of hundreds, and in preventing the anguish of thousands, ought not to be suffered to sink into oblivion, or to pass unrewarded. It is, I presume, *one* reason among others, why virtue is so little practised, that it is seldom rewarded according to its merit.

punishments—in his intercourses and contests with communities and nations—in his commercial transactions—in his judicial administrations—in the height of prosperity—and in scenes of danger, and of the deepest distress,—a principle of malignity is forever operating to destroy his comforts, and to undermine the foundation of his happiness!

The above sketches may suffice, in the mean time, as specimens of some of the prominent dispositions of that portion of the human race who have assumed to themselves the character of *civilized nations.* It will readily be admitted, by most of my readers, that the dispositions displayed in the instances I have selected, are all directly repugnant to the principle of benevolence recognised in the divine law, and tend to undermine the happiness of intelligent beings.—I shall now conclude with a very brief sketch of the conduct of Christians, and of Christian societies towards each other, and of the leading traits of character which appear in the religious world.

## SECTION IV.

### MORAL STATE OF THE PROFESSING CHRISTIAN WORLD.

I have already endeavoured to show, that Christianity is a religion of *love;* that its facts, its doctrines, and its moral precepts, are all calculated to promote "peace on earth," and to form mankind into one affectionate and harmonious society. This glorious and happy effect, in the first instance, it actually produced. We are told, in the history of the Apostles, that the multitudes who were converted to the Christian faith, by the powerful sermons delivered by Peter on the day of Pentecost, had their malignant propensities subdued, and their minds animated with an ardent affection for each other; and, as a practical proof of the operation of this noble principle, "they had all things common, and sold their possessions and goods, and parted them to all, as every man had need." During the early ages of Christianity, a goodly portion of the same spirit was manifested by the greater part of those who had enrolled themselves as the disciples of Christ. Even in the midst of the reproaches, and the severe persecutions to which they were subjected during the two first centuries of the Christian era, a meek and forgiving disposition, and a spirit of benevolence towards one another, and towards all men, distinguished them from the heathen around, and constrained even their enemies to exclaim, "Behold how these Christians love one another!"—But no sooner was the Christian Church amalgamated with the kingdoms of this world, in the reign of Constantine, than its native purity began to be tainted, and Pagan maxims, and worldly ambition began to be blended with the pure precepts and the sublime doctrines of the Gospel. Many of its professed adherents, overlooking the grand practical bearings of the Christian system, began to indulge in vain speculations on its mysterious doctrines; to substitute a number of unmeaning rites and ceremonies in the room of love to God and to man; and even to prosecute and destroy all those who refused to submit to their opinions and decisions. Pride, and a desire of domination, usurped the place of meekness and humility; and the foolish mummeries of monastic superstition, and the austerities of the *Ascetics,* were substituted in the room of the active duties of justice and benevolence. Saints were deified; the power of the clergy was augmented; celibacy was extolled; religious processions were appointed; pilgrimages were undertaken to the tombs of the martyrs; monasteries and nunneries, without number, were erected; prayers were offered up to departed saints; the Virgin Mary was recognised as a species of inferior deity; the sign of the cross was venerated as capable of securing victory in all kinds of trials and calamities, and as the surest defence against the influence of malignant spirits; the bishops aspired after wealth, magnificence, and splendour; errors in religion were punished with civil penalties and bodily tortures; and the most violent disputes and contentions convulsed every section of the Christian world; while the mild and beneficent virtues of the religion of Jesus were either discarded, or thrown into the shade.

Of these, and similar dispositions and practices, details might be exhibited which would fill many volumes, and which would carry conviction to every impartial mind, that the true glory of Christianity was sadly tarnished and obscured, and its heavenly spirit almost extinguished amidst the mass of superstitious observances, of vain speculations, and of angry feuds and contentions. Millot, when adverting to the state of the Church in the days of Constantine and the succeeding emperors, justly remarks: "The disciples of Christ were inspired with mutual feuds, still more implacable and destructive than the factions which were formed for or against different emperors. The spirit of contention condemned by St. Paul became almost universal. New sects sprung up incessantly, and combated each other. Each boasted its apostles, gave its sophisms for divine oracles, pretended to be the depository of the faith, and used every effort to draw the multitude to its standard. The church was filled with discord; bishops anathematized bishops; violence was called in to the aid of argument, and the folly of princes fanned the flame which spread with so destructive rage. They played the theologists, attempted to command opinions, and punished those whom they could not convince. The laws against idolaters were soon extended to heretics; but what one emperor proscribed as heretical, was to another sound doctrine. What was the consequence? The clergy, whose influence was already great at court, and still greater among the people, began to withdraw from the sovereign authority that respect which religion inspires. The popular ferments being heightened by the animosity of the clergy, prince, country, law, and duty, were no longer regarded. Men were Arians, Donatists, Priscillianists, Nestorians, Eutychians, Monotholites, &c., but no longer citizens; or rather, every man became the mortal enemy of those citizens whose opinions he condemned.—This unheard-of madness, for irreconcilable quarrels on subjects that ought to have been referred to the judgment of the Church, *never abated amidst the most dreadful disasters*. Every sect formed a different party in the state, and their mutual animosities conspired to sap its foundations."*

At the period to which these observations refer, it appears that two erroneous maxims generally prevailed, which tended to undermine the moral system of revelation, and which were productive of almost all the tumults, massacres, and disasters, which distinguished that era of the Christian church. These were, 1. That religion consists chiefly in the belief of certain abstract and incomprehensible dogmas, and in the performance of a multitude of external rites and ceremonies: and, 2. That all heresies or differences of opinion on religious points, ought to be extirpated by the strong arm of the civil power. Than such maxims, nothing can be more repugnant to reason, more subversive of genuine morality, or more inconsistent with the spirit and genius of the Christian religion. And yet, to this very hour, they are recognised and acted upon by more than three fourths of the Christian world, notwithstanding the melancholy examples which history has furnished of their futility, and their pernicious tendency.—The narrow limits to which I am confined will permit me to state only two or three instances in reference to the period to which I allude.

Theodosius, one of the emperors, who commenced his reign in the year 379, and who received baptism during a dangerous distemper, in the second year of it, professed great zeal in favour of religion. By a law addressed to the people of Constantinople, he enacted, "That all subjects shall profess the catholic faith with regard to the articles of the Trinity; and that they who do not conform shall ignominiously be called heretics, until they shall feel the vengeance of God and our own, according as it shall please Divine providence to inspire us." He declared apostates and Manicheans incapable of making a will, or receiving any legacy; and having pronounced them worthy of death, the people thought they had a right to kill them as proscribed persons. He enacted a law, condemning to the flames *cousins german* who married without a special license from the emperor. He established *inquisitors* for the discovery of heretics. He drove the Manicheans* from Rome as infamous persons, and, on their death, ordered their goods to be distributed among the people. Yet, with all this religious zeal, he, on one occasion, gave orders for a universal massacre at Thessalonica, because some persons of distinction had been killed in a sedition at the time of the races. The inhabitants were caused to assemble in the circus, under the pretence of an exhibition of games, and slaughtered without distinction of age. Seven thousand, according to some, and fifteen thousand according to others, the greatest part unquestionably innocent, were thus sacrificed to atrocious revenge.† Leo, another emperor, "commanded every person to be baptized, under pain of banishment, and made it capital to relapse into idolatry, after the performance of the ceremony;" just as if Christians could be made by a forced baptism, or by a law of the state. Such edicts clearly showed, that, whatever zeal princes or the clergy might manifest in favour of the Christian religion, they were grossly ignorant of its true spirit, and of the means by which its benevolent objects were to be accomplished.

As a specimen of the manner in which such edicts were sometimes carried into effect, the following instance may be stated. Hypatia, daughter of the celebrated Geometrician, Theon of Alexandria, exceeded her father in learning, and gave public lectures in Philosophy, with the greatest applause; nor was she less admirable for the purity of her virtue, joined to an uncommon beauty, and every accomplishment that could adorn human nature. But this excellent woman, *because she was a Pagan*, trusted by the magistrates and *suspected* to be active against St. Cyril, the bishop, became an object of detestation to the *Christian* multitude. A set of monks and desperadoes, headed by a priest, seized her in the open street, hurried her into a church, where they stripped her naked, tore her body with whips, cut her in pieces, and publicly burned her mangled limbs in the market place.‡ St. Cyril, who was suspected of having fomented this tragedy, had previously attacked the synagogues, and driven out the Jews; their goods were pillaged, and several persons perished in the tumult. Such conduct plainly demonstrates the tendency of the human mind, in every situation, to abuse power and authority, for the purposes of persecution and revenge; and shows us what false ideas the Christians of that period must have entertained of the God of Mercy: and how

* Millot's Modern History, vol. 1

* The distinguishing characteristic of the Manicheans was, their recognising the doctrine of two independent and eternal principles, the one the author of all good, and the other the author of all evil.

† Millot's Ancient History, vol. ii.

‡ Millot's Ancient Hist. vol. ii.

soon they had forgotten the sufferings which their fathers had so lately endured, under the reign of the heathen emperors.

About this period, too, vain speculations about abstruse and incomprehensible subjects, occupied the attention of theologians, and engendered religious quarrels and disputes, which burst asunder the bonds of affection and concord. A play of words and vain subtleties, were substituted in place of clear conceptions and substantial knowledge, which, instead of directing the faculties of the human mind to their proper objects, tended only to darken the light of reason, and to introduce the long night of ignorance which soon succeeded. It was a prevailing madness among the Greek theologians, who were intractable in their opinions,—and it is too much the case with certain modern divines,—to dispute about incomprehensible mysteries, to render them more obscure by their attempts to explain them, and perpetually to revive the most dangerous contentions. The Arians rejected the Divinity of the Word, in order to maintain the unity of God;—the Nestorians denied that Mary is the mother of God, and gave two persons to Jesus Christ, to support the opinon of his having two natures;—the Eutychians, to maintain the unity of the person, confounded the two natures into one. This heresy became divided into ten or twelve branches; some of the sections maintaining that Jesus Christ was merely a phantom, or appearance of flesh, but no real flesh. The Monotholites maintained, that there was only one will in Christ, as they could not conceive two free wills to exist in the same person. Another sect maintained, that the body of Christ was *incorruptible*, and that from the moment of his conception, he was incapable of change, and of suffering. This chimera Justinian attempted to establish by an edict. He banished the Patriarch Eutychius, and several other prelates, who opposed his sentiments; and was proceeding to tyrannize over the consciences of men with more violence than ever, when death interposed, and transported him to another scene of existence.—In such vain and preposterous disputes as these, were the minds of professed Christians occupied, notwithstanding the perils with which they were then environed. Councils were held, to determine the orthodox side of a question; anathemas were thundered against those who refused to acquiesce in their decisions; princes interposed their authority, and the civil sword was unsheathed to compel men to believe what they could not understand;—while the substantial truths of religion were overlooked, and its morality disregarded.—"Religion," says Millot, "inspires us with a contempt of earthly vanities, a detestation of vice, and indulgence for the frailties of our neighbour; invincible patience in misfortunes, and compassion for the unhappy; it inspires us with charity and heroic courage; and tends to sanctity every action in common and social life. How sublime and comforting the idea it gives of the Divinity! What confidence in his justice and infinite mercy! What encouragement for the exercise of every virtue! Wherefore, then, such errors and excesses on religious pretences? It is because heresy, shooting up under a thousand different forms, incessantly startles the faith by subtleness and sophistry, by which almost the whole energy of men's minds is absorbed in the contest Disputes engender hatred; from hatred springs every excess; and virtue, exhausted with words and cabals, loses her whole power."—How happy would it be, and how glorious for the cause of genuine Christianity, were the present generation of Christians to profit by the sad experience of the past!

As we advance in the history of the Christian church, through the middle ages, the prospect appears still more dark and gloomy. The human mind, at that period, appeared to have lost its usual energy, and its powers of discrimination; the light of reason seemed almost extinguished; sophisms, and absurdities of all kinds, were greedily swallowed; and superstition displayed itself in a thousand diversified forms. Morality was in a manner smothered under a heap of ceremonies and arbitrary observances, which acquired the name of devotion. Relics, pilgrimages, offerings, and pious legacies, were thought capable of opening the gate of heaven to the most wicked of men. The virgin Mary, and the souls of departed saints, were invoked; splendid churches were erected to their honour; their assistance was entreated with many fervent prayers: while the mediation of Jesus Christ was thrown into the shade, and almost disregarded. An irresistible efficacy was attributed to the bones of martyrs, and to the figure of the cross, in defeating the attempts of Satan, in removing all sorts of calamities, and in healing the diseases both of the body and of the mind. Works of piety and benevolence were viewed as consisting chiefly in building and embellishing churches and chapels in endowing monasteries; in hunting after the relics of martyrs; in procuring the intercession of saints, by rich oblations; in worshipping images, in pilgrimages to holy places; in voluntary acts of mortification; in solitary masses; and in a variety of similar services, which could easily be reconciled with the commission of the most abominable crimes. So that the worship of "the God and Father of our Lord Jesus Christ," was exchanged for the worship of bones, hair, fragments of fingers and toes, tattered rags, images of saints, and bits of rotten wood, supposed to be the relics of the cross. The dubbing of saints became a fruitful source of frauds and abuses throughout the Christian world; lying wonders were invented, and fabulous histories composed, to celebrate exploits that were never performed, and to glorify persons that never had a being.

and absolution from the greatest crimes could easily be procured, either by penance, or by money.

The absurd principle, that Religion consists in *acts of austerity*, produced the most extravagant behaviour in certain devotees, and reputed saints. They lived among the wild beasts; they ran naked through the lonely deserts, with a furious aspect, and with all the agitations of madness and frenzy; they prolonged their wretched lives, by grass and wild herbs; avoided the sight and conversation of men, and remained almost motionless for several years, exposed to the rigour and inclemency of the seasons;—and all this was considered as an acceptable method of worshipping the Deity, and of attaining a share in his favour.—But of all the instances of superstitious frenzy, which disgraced those times, none was held in higher veneration than that of a certain order of men, who obtained the name of *Pillar saints*. These were persons of a most singular and extravagant turn of mind, who stood motionless on the tops of pillars, expressly raised for this exercise of their patience, and remained there for several years, amidst the admiration and applause of a stupid and wondering populace. This strange superstitious practice began in the fifth century, and continued in the East for more than six hundred years.—To the same principle are to be attributed the revolting practices of the *Flagellants*, a sect of fanatics who chastised themselves with whips in public places. Numbers of persons of this description, of all ages and sexes, made processions, walking two by two, with their shoulders bare, which they whipped till the blood ran down in streamlets; in order to obtain mercy from God, and appease his indignation against the wickedness of the age. They held, among other things, that flagellation was of equal virtue with baptism, and the other sacraments; that the forgiveness of all sins was to be obtained by it, without the merits of Jesus Christ; that the old law of Christ was soon to be abolished, and that a new law, enjoining the baptism of blood, to be administered by whipping, was to be substituted in its place.

The *enormous power conferred on the ministers of religion* was another source of immorality and of the greatest excesses. The pope and the clergy reigned over mankind without control, and made themselves masters of almost all the wealth of every country in Europe. They were immersed in crimes of the deepest dye; and the laity, imagining themselves able to purchase the pardon of their sins for money, followed the example of their pastors without remorse. The most violent contentions, animosities, and hatred, reigned among the different orders of monks, and between the clergy of all ranks and degrees. "Instead of consecrating ecclesiastical censures solely to spiritual purposes, they converted them into a weapon for defending their privileges, and supporting their pretensions. The priesthood, which was principally designed to bless, was most frequently employed in *cursing*. Excommunication was made the instrument of *damning*, instead of *saving* souls, and was inflicted according to the dictates of policy or of revenge." The great and the noble, and even kings and emperors, were excommunicated, when it was designed to rob, or to enslave them; and this invisible engine, which they wielded with a powerful and a sovereign hand, was used to foment dissensions between the nearest relatives, and to kindle the most bloody wars. The generality of priests and monks kept wives and concubines, without shame or scruple, and even the papal throne was the seat of debauchery and vice. The possessions of the church were either sold to the highest bidder, or turned into a patrimony for the bastards of the incumbents. Marriages, wills, contracts, the interests of families and of courts, the state of the living and the dead, were all converted into instruments for promoting their credit, and increasing their riches. It was, therefore, a necessary result from such a state of things, that vices of every description abounded, that morals were ruined, and that the benevolence of the divine law was trampled under foot.

The *theological speculations* in which they indulged, corresponded to the degrading practices to which I have adverted, and tended to withdraw the mind from the substantial realities both of science and of religion. Sophisms and falsehoods were held forth as demonstrations. They attempted to argue after they had lost the rules of common sense. The cultivation of letters was neglected; eloquence consisted in futile declamations; and philosophy was lost in the abyss of scholastic and sophistical theology. "They attempted to penetrate into mysteries, and to decide questions which the limited faculties of the human mind are unable to comprehend or to resolve;" and such vain speculations they endeavoured to incorporate into the system of religion, and to render theology a subject of metaphysical refinement, and of endless controversy. A false logic was introduced, which subtilized upon *words*, but gave no idea of *things*; which employed itself in nice and refined distinctions concerning objects and operations which lie beyond the reach of human understanding, which confounded every thing by attempting to analyze every thing, and which opened an arena for men of fiery zeal to kindle the flame of controversy, and to give birth to numerous heresies. The following are a few instances, out of many, which might be produced, of the questions and controversies which occupied the attention of bishops and seraphical doctors, and gave rise to furious contentions:—Whether the conception of the Blessed Virgin was immaculate? Whether Mary should be denominated the Mother of God, or the Mother of Christ? Whether the bread and wine used in the eucharist were digested?

In what manner the *will* of Christ operated, and whether he had *one* will or *two?* Whether the Holy Ghost proceeded from the Father and Son, or only from the Father? Whether leavened or unleavened bread ought to be used in the eucharist? Whether souls in their intermediate state see God, or only the human nature of Christ? It was disputed between the Dominicans and the Franciscans, *Whether Christ had any property?* The Pope pronounced the negative proposition to be a pestilential and blasphemous doctrine, subversive of catholic faith. Many councils were held at Constantinople, to determine what sort of light it was the disciples saw on Mount Tabor: it was solemnly pronounced to be the eternal light with which God is encircled; and which may be termed his energy or operation, but is distinct from his nature and essence. The disputes respecting the real presence of Christ in the eucharist, led to this absurd conclusion, which came to be universally admitted—"That the substance of the bread and wine used in that ordinance is changed into the real body and blood of Christ;" and consequently, when a man eats what has the appearance of a wafer, he really and truly *eats the body and blood, the soul and divinity of Jesus Christ;* and when he afterwards drinks what has the appearance of wine, he drinks the very same body and blood, soul and divinity, which, perhaps, not a minute before, he had *wholly and entirely eaten!*—At the period to which I now allude, the *authenticity of a suspected relic* was proved by bulls—councils assembled and decided upon the authority of forged acts with regard to *the antiquity of a saint*, or the place where his body was deposited; and a bold impostor needed only to open his mouth, to persuade the multitude to believe whatever he pleased. To feed upon animals strangled or unclean, to eat flesh on Tuesday, eggs and cheese on Friday, to fast on Saturday, or to use unleavened bread in the service of the mass—were, by some, considered as indispensable duties, and by others, as vile abominations. In short, the history of this period is a reproach to the human understanding; an insult offered to the majesty of reason and of science, and a libel on the benevolent spirit which breathes through the whole of the Christian system.*

Nothing can be conceived more directly repugnant to the benevolence which the religion of Jesus inculcates, than the temper and conduct of those who arrogated to themselves the character of being God's vicegerents on earth, and who assumed the supreme direction and control of the Christian church. In persons who laid claim to functions so sacred and divine, it might have been expected, that the appearance at least, of piety, humility, and benevolence, would have been exhibited before the eyes of the Christian world. But the history of the popes and their satellites, displays almost every thing which is directly opposed to such heavenly virtues. Their avarice, extortion, and licentiousness, became intolerable and excessive almost to a proverb. To extend their power over the kingdoms of this world, to increase their wealth and revenues, to live in opulence and splendour, to humble kings, to alienate the affections of their subjects, and

* As a striking instance of the folly and imbecility of the human mind at this period, it may be noticed, that in several churches in France they celebrated a festival in commemoration of the Virgin Mary's flight into Egypt, which was called the *Feast of the ass.* A young girl richly dressed, with a child in her arms, was set upon an ass richly caparisoned. The ass was led to the altar in solemn procession. High mass was said with great pomp. The ass was taught to kneel at proper places; a hymn, no less childish than impious, was sung in his praise; and when the ceremony was ended, the priest, instead of the usual words with which he dismissed the people, *brayed three times like an ass*, and the people, instead of the usual response, "We bless the Lord," *brayed* in the same manner. This ridiculous ceremony was not a mere farcical entertainment; but *an act of devotion*, performed by the ministers of religion, and *by the authority of the church.*—Robertson's History of Charles V. vol. I. —In accordance with such ceremonies were the ideas which prevailed of the foolish qualifications requisite to constitute a good Christian. "He is a good Christian," says St. Eloy, a canonized saint of the Romish church, "who comes frequently to church; who presents the oblation offered to God upon the altar; who doth not taste of the fruits of his own industry until he has consecrated a part of them to God; who when the holy festivals approach, lives chastely even with his own wife during several days, that with a safe conscience he may draw near to the altar of God; and who, in the last place, can repeat the Creed and the Lord's prayer. Redeem, then, your souls from destruction, while you have the means in your power; offer presents and tithes to churchmen; come more frequently to church; humbly implore the patronage of the saints; for if you observe these things, you may come with security in the day of retribution to the tribunal of the eternal Judge, and say, 'Give to us, O Lord, for we have given unto thee.'"—Here we have an ample description of a good Christian, in which there is not the least mention of the love of God, of resignation to his will, obedience to his laws, or of justice, benevolence, or charity towards men.—*Mosheim's Church History.*

The following are the terms in which Tetzel and his associates describe the benefit of *indulgences*, about the beginning of the 16th century, a little before the era of the reformation. "If any man," said they, "purchase letters of indulgence, his soul may rest secure with respect to its salvation. The souls confined in purgatory, for whose redemption indulgences are purchased, as soon as the money tinkles in the chest, instantly escape from that place of torment, and ascend into heaven. The efficacy of indulgences were so great, that the most heinous sins, even if one should violate (which was impossible) the Mother of God, would be remitted and expiated by them, and the person be free both from punishment and guilt. That this was the unspeakable gift of God, in order to reconcile men to himself. That the cross erected by the preachers of indulgences, was as efficacious as the cross of Christ itself. Lo! the heavens are open, if you enter not now, when will you enter? For twelve pence you may redeem the soul of your father out of purgatory: and are you so ungrateful that you will not rescue your parent from torment? If you had but one coat, you ought to strip yourself instantly and sell it, in order to purchase such benefits," &c.—*Robertson's Charles V* vol. ii.

to riot in the lap of luxury and debauchery, seemed to be the great objects of their ambition. Instead of acting as the heralds of mercy, and the ministers of peace, they thundered anathemas against all who called in question their authority, kindled the flames of discord and of civil wars, armed subjects against their sovereigns, led forth hostile armies to the battle, and filled Europe with confusion, devastation, and carnage. Instead of applying the mild precepts of Christianity, and interposing the authority they had acquired for reconciling enemies, and subduing the jealousies of rival monarchs, they delighted to widen the breach of friendship, and to fan the flame of animosity and discord. Dr. Robertson, when adverting to the personal jealousies of Francis I. and Charles V. remarks, "If it had been in the power of the Pope to engage them in hostilities, without rendering Lombardy the theatre of war, nothing would have been more agreeable to him than to see them waste each other's strength in endless quarrels."* The Son of man came into the world, not to *destroy* men's lives, but to *save* them; but, in such instances, we behold his pretended vicars, preparing and arranging the elements of discord, laying a train for the destruction of thousands and tens of thousands, and taking a diabolical delight in contemplating the feuds, the massacres, and the miseries which their infernal policy had created. The decrees of the papal throne, instead of breathing the mildness and benevolence of Jesus, became thundering curses, and sanguinary laws, and a set of frantic enthusiasts, or a lawless banditti, were frequently appointed to carry them into effect.

Not contented with the insurrections and the desolations they had produced among the European nations, they planned an expedition for the purpose of massacring the inhabitants of Asia, and ravaging their country. Urban II. about A. D. 1095, travelled from province to province, levying troops, even without the consent of their princes; preaching up the doctrine of "destruction to the infidels;" and commanding the people, in the name of God, to join in the *holy war*. St. Bernard ran from town to town haranguing the multitude, performing pretended miracles, and inducing all ranks, from the emperor to the peasant, to enrol themselves under the banners of the cross. Peter the Hermit, a man of a hideous figure and aspect, covered with rags, walking barefooted, and speaking as a prophet, inspired the people every where with an enthusiasm similar to his own. Thousands of wicked and abandoned debauchees were thus collected; bishops, priests, monks, women and children, were all enrolled in the holy army. A plenary absolution of all their sins was promised: and if they died in the contest, they were assured of a crown of martyrdom in the world to come. With hearts burning with ury and revenge, this army of banditti, without discipline or provisions, marched in wild confusion through the eastern parts of Europe, and, at every step of their progress, committed the most dreadful outrages. So inveterate was their zeal against the Jews, wherever they were found, that many of those unfortunate beings, both men and women, murdered their own children, in the midst of the despair to which they were driven by these infuriated madmen; and when they arrived at Jerusalem, and had taken that city by assault, they suffered none of the infidels to escape the slaughter. Such was the way in which the successors of the Apostle Peter displayed their general benevolence, and their love to the souls and bodies of men.

The establishment of the *Inquisition*, is another mode in which the tyranny and cruelty of the Romish church has been displayed. This court was founded in the 12th century, by Father Dominic, and his followers, who were sent by Pope Innocent III. with orders to excite the Catholic princes and people to extirpate heretics. It is scarcely possible to conceive any institution more directly opposed to the dictates of justice and humanity, to the genius of Christianity, and to the meekness and gentleness of Christ, than this infernal tribunal. The proceedings against the unhappy victims of this court, are conducted with the greatest secrecy. The person granted them as counsel is not permitted to converse with them, except in the presence of the Inquisitors; and, when they communicate the evidence to the accused persons, *they carefully conceal from them the names of the authors*. The prisoners are kept for a long time, till they themselves, through the application of the *torture*, turn their own accusers; for they are neither told their crime, nor confronted with witnesses. When there is no shadow of proof against the pretended criminal, he is discharged, after suffering the most cruel tortures, a tedious and dreadful imprisonment, and the loss of the greatest part of his effects. When he is convicted and condemned, he is led in procession, with other unfortunate beings, on the festival of the *Auto da fe*, to the place of execution. He is clothed with a garment, painted with flames, and with his own figure, surrounded with dogs, serpents, and devils, all open-mouthed, as if ready to devour him. Such of the prisoners as declare that they die in the communion of the church of Rome, are first strangled, and then burned to ashes. Those who die in any other faith, are burned *alive*. The priests tell them, that they leave them to the devil, who is standing at their elbow, to receive their souls, and carry them with him into the flames of hell. Flaming furzes, fastened to long poles, are then thrust against their faces, till their faces are burned to a coal, which is accompanied with the loudest acclamations of joy, among the thousands of spectators. At last fire is set to the furze at the bottom of the

* Robertson's Charles V. vol. ii.

stake, over which the criminals are chained so high, that the top of the flame seldom reaches higher than the seat they sit on; so that they seem to be *roasted* rather than burned. There cannot be a more lamentable spectacle; the sufferers continually cry out, while they are able, "Pity, for the love of God;" yet it is beheld by all sexes and ages, with transports of joy and satisfaction; and even the monarch, surrounded by his courtiers, has sometimes graced the scene with his presence, imagining that he was performing an act highly acceptable to the Deity!!*

And what are the heinous crimes for which such dreadful punishments are prepared? Perhaps nothing more than reading a book which has been denounced as heretical by the holy office, such as "Raynal's History of the Indies,"—assuming the title of a freemason—irritating a priest or mendicant friar—uttering the language of freethinkers—declaiming against the celibacy of the clergy—insinuating hints or suspicions respecting their amours and debaucheries—or throwing out a joke to the dishonour of the Virgin Mary,†—or, at most, holding the sentiments of a Mahometan, of a Jew, or the followers of Calvin or Luther. In the year 1725, the Inquisition discovered a family of Moors at Grenada, peaceably employed in manufacturing silks, and possessing superior skill in the exercise of this profession. The ancient laws, supposed to have fallen into disuse, were enforced in all their rigour, and *the wretched family was burnt alive.*‡ On the entry of the French into Toledo, during the late Peninsular war, General Lasalle visited the palace of the Inquisition. The great number of instruments of torture, especially the instruments to stretch the limbs, and the drop-baths, which cause a lingering death, excited horror, even in the minds of soldiers hardened in the field of battle. One of these instruments, singular in its kind for refined torture, and disgraceful to humanity and religion, deserves particular description. In a subterraneous vault adjoining to the audience chamber, stood, in a recess in the wall, a wooden statue made by the hands of monks, representing the Virgin Mary. A gilded glory beamed round her head, and she held a standard in her right hand. Notwithstanding the ample folds of the silk garment which fell from her shoulders on both sides, it appeared that she wore a breastplate; and, upon a closer examination, it was found, that the whole front of the body was covered with extremely sharp nails, and small daggers, or blades of knives, with the points projecting outwards. The arms and hands had joints, and their motions were directed by machinery, placed behind the partition. One of the servants of the Inquisition was ordered to make the machine manœuvre. As the statue extended its arms, and gradually drew them back, as if she would affectionately embrace, and press some one to her heart, the well-filled knapsack of a Polish grenadier supplied for this time the place of the poor victim. The statue pressed it closer and closer; and when the director of the machinery made it open its arms and return to its first position, the knapsack was pierced two or three inches deep, and remained hanging upon the nails and daggers of the murderous instrument.

This infamous tribunal is said to have caused, between the years 1481 and 1759, 34,658 persons to be burnt alive; and between 1481 and 1808, to have sentenced 288,214 to the galleys, or to perpetual imprisonment.* In the *Auto* of Toledo, in February, 1501, 67 women were delivered over to the flames for Jewish practices. The same punishment was inflicted on 900 females for being *witches*, in the Dutchy of Lorraine, by one Inquisitor alone. Under this accusation, upwards of *thirty thousand women* have perished by the hands of the Inquisition.† Torquemada, that infernal inquisitor of Spain, brought into the Inquisition, in the space of 14 years, no fewer than 80,000 persons; of whom 6000 were condemned to the flames, and burned alive with the greatest pomp and exultation; and, of that vast number, there was perhaps not a single person who was not more pure in religion, as well as morals, than their outrageous persecutors.‡—Has the Deity, then, whom the Inquisition professes to serve, such a voracious appetite for the blood of human victims? Has that benevolent Being, who maketh his sun to cheer the habitations of the *wicked* as well as of the righteous, and whose "tender mercies are over all his works"—commissioned such bloodthirsty monsters to act as his ministers of vengeance, and to torment and destroy the rational creatures he has formed? The very thought is absurd and *blasphemous* in the highest degree. All his beneficent operations in creation around us, and all the gracious promises and declarations of his word, stand directly opposed to such hellish practices, and condemn the perpetrators as audacious rebels against the divine government, and as nuisances in the universe of God.

The numerous ***Massacres*** which, in different ages, have taken place, on account of religious

* See Ency. Brit. Art. *Act of faith*, and *Inquisition*, and Bourgoing's "Modern state of Spain," Vol. I. The "Instructions for the office of the holy Inquisition given at Tobda in 1561," may be seen in the *Appendix* to "Peyron's Essays on Spain," which forms the fourth volume of Bourgoing's work.

† The Chevalier de St. Gervais, was imprisoned in the Inquisition on the following occasion.—A mendicant having come to his chamber, with a purse, begged him to contribute something for the lights or tapers to be lighted in honour of the Virgin, he replied, "My good father, the Virgin has no need of lights, she need only go to bed at an earlier hour."

‡ Bourgoing's State of Spain, Vol. I. p. 349.

* Histoire Abregée de l'Inquisition.

† "The Inquisition Unmasked." By Antonio Puigblanch.

‡ Kaim's Sketches, Vol. IV.

opinions, is another revolting and melancholy trait in the character of the professed votaries of the Christian cause. Of these, the massacre of the Protestants in France on the feast of St. Bartholomew, on the 24th August, 1572, was perhaps, one of the most diabolical acts of perfidy, injustice, and cruelty, which have stained the character of our race. Every thing was atrocious and horrible in this unexampled conspiracy and assassination; feelings of the most sacred nature were annihilated; religious zeal was changed into an impious frenzy; and filial piety degenerated into sanguinary fury. Under the direction of the infamous Duke of Guise, the soldiers and the populace *en masse*, at the signal of the tolling of a bell, flew to arms, seizing every weapon that presented itself; and then rushing in crowds to every quarter of the city of Paris,—no sound was heard but the horrible cry, *Kill the Huguenots!* Every one suspected of being a Calvinist, without any distinction of rank, age, or sex, was indiscriminately massacred. The air resounded with the horrid cries and blasphemous imprecations, of the murderers, the piercing shrieks of the wounded, and the groans of the dying. Headless trunks were every instant precipitated from the windows into the court-yards, or the streets; the gate-ways were choked up with the bodies of the dead and dying, and the streets presented a spectacle of mangled limbs, and of human bodies, dragged by their butchers in order to be thrown into the Seine. Palaces, hotels, and public buildings, were reeking with blood; the image of death and desolation reigned on every side, and under the most hideous appearances; and in all quarters, carts were seen loaded with dead bodies, destined to be cast into the river, whose waters were for several days sullied by tides of human gore. The infuriated assassins, urged on by the cry, that "It was the king's will that the very last of this race of vipers should be crushed and killed," became furious in the slaughter; in proof of which, one Cruce, a jeweller, displaying his naked and bloody arm, vaunted aloud, that he had cut the throats of more than 400 Huguenots in one day. During this horrid period, every species of the most refined cruelty became exhausted; the weakness of infancy proved no impediment to the impulse of ferocity; children of ten years, exercising the first homicidal deed, were seen committing the most barbarous acts, and cutting the throats of infants in their swaddling clothes! the number of victims thus slaughtered in the city of Paris, amounted to above six thousand; and, in the provinces, at the same time, there perished about sixty thousand souls. And, what is still more shocking, the news of this massacre was welcomed at Rome with the most lively transports of joy. The Cardinal of Lorraine gave a large reward to the courier: and interrogated him upon the subject, in a manner that demonstrated he had been previously aware of the intended catastrophe. The cannons were fired, bonfires were kindled, and a solemn mass was celebrated, at which Pope Gregory XIII. assisted, with all the splendour which that court is accustomed to display on events of the most glorious and important consequence!*

The horrid practice of *Dragooning*, which was used by Papists, for converting supposed heretics, was another melancholy example of religious cruelty and frenzy. In the reign of Louis XIV. of France, his troopers, soldiers, and dragoons, entered into the houses of the Protestants, where they marred and defaced their household stuff, broke their looking-glasses, let their wine run about their cellars, threw about and trampled under foot their provisions, turned their dining-rooms into stables for their horses, and treated the owners with the highest indignity and cruelty. They bound to posts mothers that gave suck, and let their sucking infants lie languishing in their sight for several days and nights, crying, mourning, and gasping for life. Some they bound before a great fire, and after they were half roasted, let them go. Some they hung up by the hair, and some by the feet, in chimneys, and smoked them with wisps of wet hay till they were suffocated. Women and maids were hung up by their feet, or by their arm-pits, and exposed stark naked to public view. Some they cut and slashed with knives, and after stripping them naked, stuck their bodies with pins and needles from head to foot; and, with red hot pincers, took hold of them by the nose and other parts of the body, and dragged them about the rooms till they made them promise to be *Catholics*, or till the cries of these miserable wretches, calling upon God for help, induced them to let them go. If any, to escape these barbarities, endeavoured to save themselves by flight, they pursued them into the fields and woods, where they shot at them, as if they had been wild beasts; and prohibited them from departing the kingdom, upon pain of the galleys, the lash, and perpetual imprisonment. On such scenes of desolation and horror, the Popish clergy feasted their eyes, and made them only a matter of laughter and of sport.† —What a striking contrast to the benevolence of the Deity, whom they impiously pretend to serve! Could a savage American have devised more barbarous and infernal cruelties?

In the civil wars, on account of religion, which happened in France, in the beginning of the 17th century, above a million of men lost their lives, and nine cities, 400 villages, 2000 churches, 2000 monasteries, and 10,000 houses were burn-

* See a late publication entitled "Memoirs of Henry the Great, and of the Court of France during his reign," 2 vols. 8vo, in which is contained the fullest description of this massacre which has appeared in our language.

† For a more particular account of such scenes, see Ency. Brit. Article Dragooning.

ed or destroyed, during their continuance; besides the many thousands of men, women, and children, that were cruelly butchered: and 150,000,000 of livres were spent in carrying forward these slaughters and devastations. It is said of Louis XIII. who carried on these wars, by one of his biographers and panegyrists, Madame de Motteville that, "what gave him *the greatest pleasure*, was his thought of *driving heretics out of the kingdom*, and thereby purging the different religions which corrupt and infect the church of God."* In the Netherlands alone, from the time that the edict of Charles V. was promulgated against the reformers, more than 100,000 persons were hanged, beheaded, buried alive, or burned on account of religion. The prisons were crowded with supposed heretics; and the gibbet, the scaffold, and the stake, filled every heart with horror. The Duke of Alva, and his bloody tribunal, spread universal consternation through these provinces; and, though the blood of eighteen thousand persons, who, in five years, had been given up to the executioner for heresy, cried for vengeance on this persecutor, and his adherents, yet they gloried in their cruelty. Philip II. in whose reign these atrocities were committed, hearing one day, that thirty persons at least had a little before been burned at an *auto da fe*, requested that a like execution might be performed in his presence; and he beheld with joy forty victims devoted to torments and to death. One of them, a man of distinction, requesting a pardon, "No," replied he, coldly, "were it my own son I would give him up to the flames, if he obstinately persisted in heresy."†

Even in our own island, the flames of religious persection have sometimes raged with unrelenting fury. During two or three years of the short reign of Queen Mary, it was computed that 277 persons were committed to the flames, besides those who were punished by fines, confiscations, and imprisonments. Among those who suffered by fires were five bishops, twenty-one clergymen, eight lay gentlemen, and eighty-four tradesmen; one hundred husbandmen, fifty-five women, and four children. And, a century and a half has scarcely elapsed, since the Presbyterians in Scotland were hunted across moors and mosses, like partridges of the wilderness, slaughtered by bands of ruffian dragoons, and forced to seek their spiritual food in dens, and mountains, and forests, at the peril of their lives. Hunter, a young man about nineteen years of age, was one of the unhappy victims to the zeal for Papacy of Mary queen of England. Having been inadvertently betrayed by a priest, to deny the doctrine of transubstantiation, he absconded to keep out of harm's way. Bonner, that arch-hangman of Popery, threatened ruin to the father if he did not deliver up the young man. Hunter, hearing of his father's danger, made his appearance, and was burned alive, instead of being rewarded for his filial piety. A woman of Guernsey was brought to the stake, without regard to her advanced pregnancy, and she was delivered in the midst of the flames. One of the guards snatched the infant from the fire; but the magistrate, who attended the execution, ordered it to be thrown back, being resolved, he said, that nothing should survive which sprung from a parent so obstinately heretical.*

What a dreadful picture would it present of the malignity of persons who have professed the religion of Christ, were we to collect into one point of view, all the persecutions, tortures, burnings, massacres, and horrid cruelties, which, in Europe, and Asia, and even in the West Indies and America, have been inflicted on conscientious men for their firm adherence to what they considered as the truths of religion! When we consider, on the one hand, the purity of morals, and the purity of faith which generally distinguished the victims of persecution; and, on the other, the proud pampered priests, abandoned without shame to every species of wickedness, we can scarcely find words sufficiently strong to express the indignation and horror which arise in the mind, when it views this striking contrast, and contemplates such scenes of impiety and crime. Could a religion, which breathes peace and good will from heaven towards men, be more basely misrepresented? or can the annals of our race present a more striking display of the perversity and depravity of mankind? To represent religion as consisting in the belief of certain incomprehensible dogmas, and to attempt to convert men to Christianity, and to inspire them with benevolence, by fire, and racks, and tortures, is as absurd as it is impious and profane and represents the Divine Being as delighting in the torments and the death of sinners, rather than that they should return and live.—But, without dwelling longer on such reflections and details, I shall just present an example or two of the moral state of Roman Catholic countries, as a specimen of the effects to which their system of religion naturally leads.

"By their fruits shall ye know them," says our Saviour. Wherever religion is viewed as consisting chiefly in the observance of a number of absurd and unmeaning ceremonies, it is natural to expect that the pure morality of the Bible will seldom be exemplified in human conduct. This is strikingly the case in those countries, both in Europe and America, where the Catholic religion reigns triumphant.—Mr. Howison, whose work, entitled "Foreign Scenes," I formerly quoted, when speaking of the priesthood in the island of Cuba, says, "The number of priests in Havana exceeds four hundred. With a few excep-

* Motteville's Memoirs of Anne of Austria, Vol. I. p. 98.

† Millot's Modern History, vol. ii. p. 190.

* Kaim's Sketches, vol. iv.

tions, they neither deserve nor enjoy the respect of the community. However no one dares openly to speak against them. In Havana, the church is nearly omnipotent, and every man feels himself under its immediate jurisdiction. Most people, therefore, attend mass regularly, make confession, uncover, when passing a religious establishment of any kind, and stand still in the streets, or stop their volantos, the moment the vesper-bell begins ringing. But they go no further; and the priests do not seem at all anxious that the practice of such individuals should correspond to their profession. The priests show, by their external appearance, that they do not practice those austerities which are generally believed to be necessary concomitants of a monastic life. The sensual and unmeaning countenances that encircle the altars of the churches, and the levity and indifference with which the most sacred partsof the service are hurried through, would shock and surprise a Protestant, were he to attend mass with the expectation of finding the monks, those solemn and awe-inspiring persons, which people, who have never visited Catholic countries, often imagine them to be.

The following extract, from a late writer, exhibits a specimen of the religion and of the moral feelings of the NEAPOLITANS. "When Vesuvius thunders aloud, or when an earthquake threatens them with destruction—when fiery streams vomited from the roaring mouth of the volcano roll on, carrying desolation over the plains below—when the air is darkened by clouds of smoke, and showers of ashes, the Neapolitans will fall on their knees, fast, do penance, and follow the processions barefooted; but as soon as the roar has ceased, the flame has disappeared, and the atmosphere has recovered its wonted serenity, they return to their usual mode of life, they sink again to their former level, and the tinkling sounds of the tumburella call them again to the lascivious dance of the tarentella."*—As an evidence of the litigious dispositions of the Neapolitans, the same author informs us, "That there is scarcely a landholder but has two or three causes pending before the courts—that a lawyer, and a suit, are indispensable appendages of property;—and that some of the principal families have suits which have been carried on for a century, and for which a certain sum is yearly appropriated, although the business never advances; and, at last the expenses swallow up the whole capital."—"The infinite number of churches," says a late writer, "is one of the most efficient causes of the decline of the religion of Rome, whose maxims and practice are diametrically opposite to those of the Gospel. The Gospel is the friend of the people, the consoler of the poor. The religion of Rome, on the contrary, considers all nations as great flocks, made to be shorn or eaten according to the good pleasure of the shepherds: for her the golden lever is the lever of Archimedes. The favours of the church are only showered on those who pay; with money we may purchase the right to commit perjury and murder, and be the greatest villains at so much per crime; according to the famous Tariff printed at Rome, entitled, "Taxes of the Apostolic Chancery."*

M. Jouy, in his late publication, "The Hermit in Italy," presents the following picture of the religion and the practical morality of the Tuscans. The greediness after profit is such, among the lower classes of shop-keepers, that they adulterate their merchandise so much as to render it almost intolerable. Milk, cheese, and butter, are always in peril under the hands of a Florentine shop-keeper. It is impossible to meet with good butter, except at the dairies. The grocers are not exempt from the imputation of these illicit mixtures, and adulterations of their goods. I bought, from one of them, some brown sugar, which would not dissolve in the mouth; and, on examination, I found, that nearly one third part consisted of powdered marble, which had been mixed up with it. Yet they are excessively punctual in the outward ceremonies of religion; and whenever they remove from one place to another, a large cross, or a madonna, is always stuck up at full length in the cart."

In a conversation which Bonaparte had with his friends at St. Helena, on the subject of religion, as related by Las Casas, in his Journal, he said, among many other things, "'How is it possible that conviction can find its way to our hearts, when we hear the absurd language, and witness the acts of iniquity of the greatest number of those whose business it is to preach to us? I am surrounded with priests, who preach incessantly that their reign is not of this world, and yet they lay hands upon every thing they can get. The Pope is the head of that religion from heaven, and he thinks only of this world,' &c. The Emperor ended the conversation, by desiring my son to bring him the New Testament, and taking it from the beginning, he read as far as the conclusion of the speech of Jesus on the mountain. He expressed himself struck with the highest admiration at the purity, the sublimity, the beauty of the morality it contained, and we all experienced the same feeling."

Such facts may suffice as specimens of the benevolence and morality which exist in Roman Catholic countries.

### MORAL STATE OF THE PROTESTANT CHURCH, AND OF THE DISPOSITIONS GENERALLY MANIFESTED AMONG CHRISTIANS IN OUR OWN COUNTRY.

This is a topic which would admit of a very extended illustration; but my present limits will

* Vieusseux's "Italy in the 19th century," 1824.

* "Picture of Modern Rome," by M. Santo Domingo. 1824.

permit me to do little more than simply to allude to a few prominent dispositions displayed by the different sections of the Protestant church.—We have already seen some of the pernicious effects which flowed from the divisive and contentious spirit of Christians, under the reign of the Christian emperors, and during the middle ages, when ignorance and intolerance so extensively prevailed.

The present state of the Christian world affords abundant proofs that this spirit is far from being extinguished. Christians are at present distinguished by the peculiarity of their opinions respecting—the person of Christ, and the attributes of which he is possessed—the means by which salvation is to be obtained—the measure and extent of divine benevolence—the Government of the Christian church—and the ceremonies connected with the administration of the ordinances of religion. Hence the religious world appears arranged into such sects and parties as the following:—Arians, Socinians, Unitarians, Sabellians, Necessarians, and Trinitarians;—Baxterians, Antinomians, Arminians, Calvinists, Lutherans, Sub-lapsarians, Supra-lapsarians, Sandemanians, Swedenborgians, and Moravians;—Roman Catholics, Protestants, Huguenots, Episcopalians, Presbyterians, Independents, Seceders, Brownists, Pædo-Baptists, Anti-Pædo-Baptists, Keilamites, Methodists, Jumpers, Universalists, Sabbatarians, Millennarians, Destructionists, Dunkers, Shakers, Mystics, Hutchinsonians, Muggletonians, the followers of Joanna Southcott, &c. &c.—Most of these sectaries *profess their belief* in the existence of One Eternal, Almighty, Wise, Benevolent, and Righteous Being, the Creator and Preserver of all things;—in the Divine authority of the Holy Scriptures;—that God is the alone object of religious worship;—that Jesus of Nazareth is the true Messiah, and the Son of God;—"that he died for our offences, and was raised again for our justification;"—that there is a future state of rewards and punishments;—that there will be a resurrection from the dead;—that it is our duty to love God with all our hearts, and our neighbour as ourselves;—that the Divine law is obligatory on the consciences of all men;—that virtue and piety will be rewarded, and vice and immorality punished, in the world to come.

Yet, though agreeing in these important articles of the Christian system, how many boisterous and malignant disputes have taken place between Calvinists and Arminians, Episcopalians, Presbyterians, Independents, and Methodists, respecting the speculative points in which they disagree! While controversies among philosophers have frequently been conducted with a certain degree of candour and politeness, the temper with which religious disputants have encountered the opinions of each other, has generally been opposed to the spirit of Christian love, to the meekness and gentleness of Christ, and even to common civility and decorum. The haughty and magisterial tone which theological controversialists frequently assume,—the indignant sneers, the bitter sarcasms, the malignant insinuations, the personal reproaches, they throw out against their opponents,—the harsh and unfair conclusions they charge upon them,—the general asperity of their language,—and the bold and unhallowed spirit with which they apply the denunciations of Scripture to those whom they consider as erroneous, are not only inconsistent with every thing that is amiable and Christian, but tend to rivet more powerfully in the minds of their opponents, those very opinions which it was their object to subvert. To gain a victory over his adversary, to hold up his sentiments to ridicule, to wound his feelings, and to bespatter the religious body with which he is connected, is more frequently the object of the disputant, than the promotion of truth, and the manifestation of that "character which is the bond of perfection." And what are some of the important doctrines which frequently rouse such furious zeal? Perhaps nothing more than a metaphysical dogma respecting the sonship of Christ, absolute or conditional election, the mode of baptism, the manner of sitting at a communion-table, an unmeaning ceremony, or a circumstantial punctilio in relation to the government of the church! While the peculiar notions of each party, on such topics, are supported with all the fierceness of unhallowed zeal, the grand *moral* objects which Christianity was intended to accomplish are overlooked, and the law of meekness, humility, and love, is trampled under foot.

The following are some of the ideas entertained respecting the *rights* of religious disputants, as assumed by the disputants themselves:—"The Controversialist," says Mr. Vaughan, in his "Defence of Calvinism," "is a wrestler; and is at full liberty to do all he can, in the fair and honest exercise of his art, to supplant his antagonist. He must not only be dexterous to put in his blow forcibly; but must have a readiness *to menace with scorn*, and *to tease with derision*, if haply he may, by these means, unnerve or unman his competitor. I know not that he is under any obligation to withhold a particle of his skill and strength, whether offensive, or defensive, in this truly Spartan conflict." In perfect accordance with these maxims, he thus addresses his adversary: "Why, Sir, I will *fight you* upon this theme, as the Greeks did for the recovery of their dead Patroclus; as Michael the archangel, when, contending with the Devil, he disputed about the body of Moses; as the famed Athenian, who *grasped his ship with his teeth*, when he had no longer a hand to hold it by. It shall be with a loss not less than life, that I resign this splendid attestation (Rom. viii. 28-

30.) to the triumphal origin, procession, and coronation, of grace in the redeemed."

Wo to religion, when it meets with such boisterous "wrestlers!" Its true glory will be obscured, its beauty defaced, its interests betrayed, and its benevolent spirit smothered, amidst the smoke and dust raised by the onsets of such angry combatants. Do such controversialists really imagine, that "the wrath of man worketh the righteousness of God?" or, that the religion of Heaven stands in need of such warlike arts, and unhallowed passions, for its vindication and defence? If it did, it would be a religion unworthy of our reception and support. What a contrast to the mild and gentle spirit of Christianity, to behold one zealot dipping his pen in wormwood and gall, when he sits down to defend the Religion of Love! and another, standing up in a Synod or Assembly, with eyes sparkling with indignation, a mouth foaming with rage, and a torrent of anathemas and abusive epithets bursting from his lips, against the supposed abettors of an erroneous opinion! while at the same time, they imagine that they are fired with holy zeal for the honour of the Lord God of Sabaoth. Such disputants seem not to be aware, that they are grossly misrepresenting the genius of the Christian system, and bidding defiance to its most distinguishing principles and laws.—There are heresies in *conduct*, as well as heresies in doctrine; and of all heresies, the former are the most pestilential and pernicious. And why do not Controversialists and Religious Societies manifest as much zeal against heresies in temper and morality, which are nursed among the members of every church, as they do against heresies in theology? If these heresies were more particularly investigated and subverted, and a greater latitude allowed for the exercise of private judgment, the church of Christ would present a very different moral aspect from what she has hitherto done.

Again, there is nothing which so strikingly marks the character of the Christian world in general, as the want of candour, the spirit of jealousy, and the evil surmisings which the different denominations of religionists manifest towards each other. There is a prevailing disposition in one religious party to speak evil of another; and it appears, in many instances, to afford a high degree of satisfaction, when one party can lay hold of the inadvertencies of another denomination, or even of the imprudence of a single individual, in order to asperse the character of the whole body, and to hold it up to general derision and contempt. Episcopalians look down with feelings of scorn and contempt on Methodists and Dissenters; Independents sneer at Methodists, and Methodists at Independents; Presbyterians are disposed to revile Independents, as self-conceited, sanctimonious pretenders, and Independents, to treat with unbecoming levity, and even with ridicule, the opinions and practices of Presbyterians; while the different classes of Baptists, distinguishable only by the slightest shades of opinion, stand aloof from each other, in a warlike attitude, and refuse to join with cordiality in the ordinances of Divine worship. I have seldom been in company with individuals of any particular party, in which I have not found, when allusions were made to another denomination, innuendoes thrown out to their prejudice; and that the detail of any error or imperfection which attached to them, was generally relished, and even received with a high degree of satisfaction. Hence it happens, that the rules of common civility are every day violated by the different sectaries. If a person belonging to a particular denomination be accidently introduced into a company composed of persons belonging to another religious party, he is frequently treated with reserve, and with a spirit of jealousy and suspicion, even although he may be viewed, on the whole, as a Christian at bottom. I have known individuals of respectable character and attainments, who, from conscientious motives, had forsaken the denomination to which they formerly belonged, have, merely on this account, been treated with scorn and neglect, been banished from the intimacies of social and friendly intercourse, and been regarded nearly in the same light as a Turk or an infidel; and that, too, by men who pretended to liberality, and to literary accomplishments.

There is certainly neither heresy nor orthodoxy inherent in stone or lime, in a church-pew, or a pulpit cushion:—yet one denomination will rudely refuse to another, the liberty of preaching in their place of worship, when it can conveniently be spared, although nothing but the fundamental doctrines acknowledged by both are intended to be proclaimed; just as if the walls, the pews, and the pulpit of a church, would receive a stain of pollution from the presence of another sectary. Even in those cases where the common interests of Christianity are to be supported,—as in vindicating the cause of Missionary, and other Philanthropic institutions,—if the preacher belongs to a dissenting body, he is shut out from the spacious churches of the Establishment, where he might address a numerous audience, and obtain a large collection; and is obliged to confine his exertions within the narrow walls of any public hall, or meeting-house, that he can procure. We account it no more than a piece of common civility, to accommodate a neighbour with a barn, a parlour, or even a dining-room, for the entertainment of his friends at a wedding or a funeral; but such is the little progress that professed Christians have made in the exercise of a noble and generous liberality, that, when we ask the use of a church, or meeting-house, only for a couple of hours, we are spurned away with rudeness and indignation.—The Christian world is unhappily divided into sects and parties; and these divisions must still continue for a time; but what should hinder Christian ministers of different parties from, occasionally at least, officiating for each other, in order to show to the world, that they entertain no malignant jealousies, and that they are united in the bonds of a common Religion? Yet, do we ever behold an Episcopalian officiating for a Methodist, an Independent preaching in an Established church, or a Baptist leading the devotional exercises of a society of Presbyterians? If such a case occasionally occur, it is so far from being a matter of course, that it is considered a phenomenon in the religious world. Yet all these different parties recognise the leading doctrines and duties exhibited in the Christian Revelation; and the points in which they differ are "trifles light as air," when compared with those important truths in which they all agree.*

Even among Christians belonging to the same religious society how often do we behold a display of "bitter envyings," contentious dispositions, and malignant passions! Perhaps a mere punctilio respecting a certain mode of worship, or a difference in opinion about the choice of a pastor, will throw the whole society into a flame. Evil passions will be engendered; backbitings, whisperings, tumults, and dissensions, will arise; harsh and unfounded conclusions, respecting the motives and characters of individuals, will be drawn; alienations of affection will be induced; friendly intercourse interrupted; an attitude of hostility assumed; and even the rules of common civility violated;—so that a calm and impartial spectator will plainly discern, that the spirit of Christianity has never been thoroughly imbibed, and that they have never learned the apostolic precept, "to forbear one another in love," however high pretensions they may have previously made to spirituality of affection and deportment. Among Christians of every name, we find dispositions and practices daily prevailing, which are altogether inconsistent with the genius of the religion of Christ, and directly repugnant to its precepts. Slander, dishonesty, falsehood, cheating, swindling, and vexatious litigations, are far from being uncommon among those who profess to be united in the bonds of a common Christianity. How little dependence can we have, in social and commercial transactions, on the promise or the declaration of a man, merely on the ground of his being a Christian in profession! If written engagements, and civil laws, did not secure our property, and the performance of promises and contracts, our reliance on Christian principle, abstractly considered, in the present state of the religious world, would prove like that of a person who leans upon a broken reed. How few would fulfil their promises and engagements, when they interfered with their ambitious schemes, and their pecuniary interests! How many instances of fraudulent bankruptcy happen among the professors of religion! And in cases of common bankruptcy, where a legal settlement has been obtained, is there one out of a hundred that ever thinks of performing an act of natural justice, in restoring to his creditors the loss they had sustained, when he afterwards has it in his power?

Finally, the degree in which the spirit of *intolerance* and *persecution* still prevails, shows a lamentable deficiency of benevolence and of Christian spirit in the religious world. Notwithstanding the unjust and cruel sufferings which English Protestants endured from Popish priests and rulers, a short period only elapsed, after they had risen to power, before they began in their turn, to harass their Dissenting brethren, with vexations and cruel prosecutions, and fines and imprisonments, till they were forced to seek for shelter in a distant land. And no sooner had the English Independents settled in America, than they set on foot a persecution against the Quakers, no less furious than that which they themselves had suffered in the country from which they had fled. A number of these worthy persons they threw into prison, and seized upon the books they had brought from England, and committed them to the flames. In virtue of a law which had been made against heretics in general, sentence of banishment was passed upon them all; and another law punished with *death*, "all Quakers who should return into the jurisdiction after banishment;" and it is a fact, that *four* persons actually suffered death, under this impolitic and unjust law.* Nor did the Reformed clergy in Scotland lose sight of that

* The following recent facts will illustrate some of the positions contained in this paragraph.—It appears that the minister of the parish of Annan has been in the habit of allowing Dissenters occasionally to preach in the parish church. His Assistant brought this heavy offence before a late meeting of the Presbytery; and, by that body, it was declared, that no Dissenter should, in future, *pollute* the said pulpit. They, at the same time, voted thanks to the Assistant, for his manly and *liberal* conduct in making the complaint.—*Public Prints, April*, 1824.

"Lately, the minister of a parish, a few miles to the westward of Cupar, hearing that, at the request of some of his parishioners, a sermon was to be preached to them, by a Dissenting clergyman from Cupar, and knowing that the school-room was the only place where that could be conveniently done, he called upon the teacher and *commanded* him not to allow the school-room to be used for such a purpose. In a few days, a company of strolling players visited the parish; whereupon the worthy pastor, calling on the schoolmaster, ordered the school-room to be at their service, to perform in"—*Dundee Courier April* 1825.

* Morse's American Geography.—The following severe laws, among others, were enacted against the Quakers. "Any Quaker, after the first conviction, if a man, was to lose one *ear*,—and for the second offence, the other:—a woman, to be each time severely whipped;—and the third time, whether man or woman, *to have their tongues bored through with a red hot iron.*

magisterial authority which had been assumed by the Romish church. Upon a representation, in 1646, from the commission of the Kirk of Scotland, James Bell, and Colin Champbell, baillies of Glasgow, were committed to prison by the Parliament, merely for having said, that "Kirkmen meddled too much in civil matters."* Even so late as the middle of the eighteenth century, when Whitefield, Wesley, and other pious men, began to address the ignorant villagers of England on the most important subjects, "a multitude has rushed together, shouting and howling, raving, and cursing, and acccompanying their ferocious cries and yells with loathsome or dangerous missiles, dragging or driving the preacher from his humble stand, forcing him, and the few who wished to hear him, to flee for their lives, sometimes not without serious injury before they could escape. And these savage tumults have, in many cases, been well understood to be instigated by persons, whose advantage of superior condition in life, or even express vocation to instruct the people better, has been infamously lent in defence of the perpetrators, against shame or remorse, or legal punishment for the outrage. And there would be no hazard in affirming, that, since Wesley and Whitefield began to conflict with the heathenism of the country, there have been in it hundreds of instances answering in substance to this description.—Yet the good and zealous men who were thus set upon by a furious rabble of many hundreds, the foremost of whom active in direct violence, and the rest venting their ferocious delight, in a hideous blending of ribaldry and execration, of joking and cursing,—were taxed with a canting hypocrisy, or a fanatical madness, for speaking of the prevailing ignorance, in terms equivalent to those of the prophet, 'The people are destroyed for lack of knowledge.'"†

But we need not go back even to the distance of half a century in order to find instances of religious intolerance among Protestant communities and churches; our own times unhappily furnish too many examples of a bigoted, intolerant, and persecuting spirit. Little more than two years have elapsed since the Methodist chapel in Barbadoes was thrown down and demolished by the *mob-gentry*, and with the connivance of the public authorities of that slave trafficking island, and Mr. Shrewsbury, a worthy and respected pastor and missionary, obliged to flee for his life. Previous to this outrage, he suffered every species of insult, contumely, and reproach. He was abused as a villain, and hissed at in the streets, not by mere rabble, but by the *great vulgar;* by merchants from their stores, and individuals in the garb of gentlemen. By such characters his chapel was surrounded, and partly filled, on Sunday the 5th October, 1823. Thin glass bottles had been previously prepared and filled with a mixture of oil and assafœtida, and all of a sudden, they were thrown with great violence in the midst of the people, and one was aimed at the head of the preacher; and during the whole service, stones were rattling against the chapel from every quarter. On the next Sabbath an immense concourse of people assembled, "breathing out threatenings and slaughter;" and from 20 to 30 of the *gentlemen-mob* planted themselves around the pulpit apparently ready for any mischief. Men wearing masks, and having swords and pistols, came galloping down the street and presenting their pistols, fired them at the door; and it was originally designed to have fire crackers among the females, to set their clothes on fire. At length, on Sabbath, the 19th, this execrable mob, consisting of nearly 200 *gentlemen*, and others, again assembled, with hammers, saws, hatchets, crows, and every other necessary implement; and in the course of a few hours, the lamps, benches, pews, pulpit, and even the walls, were completely demolished. They entered the dwelling-house broke the windows and doors, threw out the crockery ware, chopped up tables, chairs, and every article of furniture; tore the manuscripts of the preacher, and destroyed a library of more than 300 volumes. All this was done under the light of the full moon, in the presence of an immense crowd of spectators, without the least attempt being made to check them either by the civil or military authorities—while the unfortunate preacher, with his wife in an advanced state of pregnancy, had to flee to a neighbouring island to save his life! Such is the tolerant and humane conduct of *gentlemen* Protestants of the nineteenth century! gentlemen who would, no doubt, consider it very unhandsome were they to be compared to Goths and Vandals, or to the rude and barbarous savages of Papua or New Holland.*

About the same period, the authorities of Demerara set on foot a persecution against Mr. Smith, Missionary from the London Society, under various pretexts: but his real crime in the eyes of his persecutors, was, his unwearied zeal in instructing the negroes in the knowledge of religion. He was condemned to death by a court-martial, in the face of every principle of justice: he died in prison, was refused the privilege of a Christian burial, and his friends were prohibited from erecting a stone to mark the spot where his body was laid. The whole details of this transaction present a scene of savage barbarity, created by the lust of gain, scarcely to be paralleled in the history of Europe.

In Switzerland, which was formerly the head

* Kaim's Sketches.

† Foster's "Essay on Popular Ignorance.

* For a more particular detail of these execrable transactions, see "Report of the Wesleyan Missionary Society for 1824:" and the debates in Parliament in 1825.

quarters of Protestantism, the demon of religious persecution has again reared its head. The council of state of the Pays de Vaud, at the instigation of the clergy, on January 15, 1825, published a decree, "prohibiting, under the penalty of severe fines and imprisonments, all meetings for religious worship or instruction, other than those of the Established Church:" and in the following May, another decree was issued, which denounces "fines, imprisonment, or banishment, upon the most private kind of religious assembly, or even the admission of a single visiter to family worship." In pursuance of these disgraceful laws, several ministers and private Christians of high character for piety and acquirements, have been banished from the Canton, some for one and some for two years—cut off from all means of subsistence, unless possessed of independent fortunes, and left perhaps to starve and perish in foreign lands. If they returned before the expiration of their sentence, it is said that *death* is the punishment to be inflicted. One poor man, a school-master, in the principality of Neufchatel, has been condemned to *ten* years' banishment. He was brought out from prison, tied with cords, and compelled to kneel in the snow in the public square to hear his sentence read. His crime was, gathering together a few fellow Christians in his own house, and there having the Lord's supper administered by a regularly ordained minister!*

And is England pure from the spirit of persecution and intolerance? Let us see.—At Kenneridge in Dorsetshire a worthy and excellent individual, belonging to the Wesleyan denomination, had attended on a green, where 20 or 30 persons usually congregated, on a Sunday afternoon, to listen to the truths he thought it important to declare. The clergyman of the parish approached with a retinue of servants, and *commanded* him to desist. The preacher took no notice of the command and proceeded to read his text. The clergyman then commanded the tithing-man to seize him. He was directed to be conveyed to Wareham jail; and to every question the preacher put, as to the ground of his being seized upon, the *reverend* and *worthy* clergyman only replied by the brandishing of his stick.—Instances have occurred in which clergymen of the establishment have refused *to bury the dead.* At Chidds Ercal, in Shropshire, the child of a poor man was refused interment, and the father was obliged to carry it six miles, before it could be laid at rest in its mother earth. —At Catsfield, in Sussex, a similar act of infamy was committed.—At the moment when the bell had tolled, when the earth was to fall heavily upon the coffin, containing the only remains of the being that affection had endeared, and when those who stood by needed all the consolations that religion can supply—at this moment the clergyman appeared, but advanced only to give pain to the mourners, and to agonize a parent's heart, by saying, "Now that you have waited an hour till it suited me to come, I will not inter your child! I did not know that you were Dissenters—take your child some where else—take it where you please—but here it shall not lie in consecrated ground." And, in fact, they were compelled to carry the child away eleven miles from the abode of its parents, and from the place that gave it birth, before it could find repose in its kindred dust.—At Mevagissey, in the county of Cornwall, the vicar refused to allow the corpse of a Dissenter to be brought within the church, and, therefore, read the burial service in the open air; but, in consequence of which, he read only a part of that service, and omitted the most beautiful portion.—Such a power appears to be conceded to the clergy by the laws of the church; but the spirit which gave it existence is deeply to be deplored, as the spirit of bigotry and intolerance. At Wellingborough, a clergyman, in opposition to a custom which had been established for sixty years, issued orders, that no bell should toll when a Dissenter expired. He boldly avowed, "that he never would permit the passing bell to be rung for a Dissenter, even in the event of an interment in the church-yard; that whilst he held the curacy, no bell of his church should ever toll for a Dissenter; and that he would not even permit the bells to ring for a marriage where the parties were Dissenters." In reference to this case, an appeal was made to the Bishop of Peterborough, who wrote a long letter on the subject, and defended the conduct of this Wellingborough curate.—At Newport Pagnel, two persons of decent appearance, teachers of Baptist Societies, were collecting subscriptions for the erection of a new place of worship.—After arriving at the residence of the parish clergyman, they were taken before a clerical magistrate, who upon the oath of the other clergyman, that they were rogues and vagrants, committed them to Aylesbury jail; where they were confined for three weeks in common with the basest felons; among convicted thieves of the most abandoned character;—nay, more, they were sentenced to the tread-mill, and kept at hard labour there, though, during the whole time, one of them was afflicted with spitting of blood. Their papers were seized upon; their money was taken from them; and by means of it the expense of sending them to prison was defrayed.*

All the above-stated instances, and many others of a similar description, occured within the limits of the year 1824; and every year since

* See a pamphlet on this subject by Dr. PyeSmith. See also Cong. Mag. for June, 1825, and other periodical works of that date.

* The reader will find a more particular detail of these cases, in the "Address of John Wilks, Esq at the Fourteenth Anniversary of the Protestant Society for the Protection of religious Liberty, in May, 1825.

the "Society for the Protection of Religious Liberty" was formed, similar instances, some of them of a more barbarous nature, have been brought forth to public view. And, were it not for the protection which this Society affords to the victims of intolerance, it is highly probable, that vexatious persecutions, insults, fines, and imprisonments, on account of differences in religious opinions, would be much more common than they now are. Were such individuals as those to whom we have now alluded, permitted, by the laws of our country, to carry their intolerant spirit to its utmost extent, Dissenters would have no security either for their property or their lives; and the fires of Smithfield would again be kindled, to torture the souls, and to consume the bodies, of all who refused to conform to the dogmas of a national church.

After what has been stated in the preceding part of this work, it is almost needless to say, that such an intolerant and persecuting spirit is diametrically opposite to every principle that pervades the Christian system; and there cannot be a grosser misrepresentation of its spirit and tendency, than to ascribe such dispositions and conduct to the genius of that religion which INTOLERANCE has thought proper to assume. Can a single instance be produced of a persecuting spirit in the conduct of Jesus Christ, or in that of any one of his apostles! When he "was reviled, he reviled not again; and when he suffered, he threatened not; and he solemnly rebuked his followers when the least symptom of intolerance or revenge was displayed. Can a religion, which commands us to love our neighbours as ourselves —to be kindly affectionate one towards another —to love our enemies—to do good to them that hate us—to bless them that curse us—and to pray for them that despitefully use us,"—can such a religion be supposed to give the least countenance to actions that are both intolerant and inhumane? If the religion of Christ have any one prominent object which distinguishes it from all others, it is this—to unite mankind in one harmonious and affectionate society; and such an object is altogether incompatible with resentment, intolerance, or persecution in any shape. "By this shall all men know," says Jesus, "that you are my disciples, if ye love one another."

---

Here I must close the illustration of the moral state of mankind, though they might have been carried to a much greater extent. They present to every benevolent mind a *gloomy* picture of the moral aspect of the human race, and of the depravity which the principle of malevolence carries in its train. It is a picture which shows us that those moral principles and laws which the Creator intended to promote, the felicity of all worlds, have never yet been brought into full effect in the world in which we live. It is a picture, however, from which we ought not to turn away our eyes. It sets before us the evils which require to be counteracted, and the obstacles which must be surmounted, before the principles of malignity be extirpated, and the moral principles of the Christian system take root in the world. But such views of the existing state of the moral world, so far from operating as sedatives, ought to stimulate us to exert every energy, and to use every judicious and powerful mean, which has a tendency to promote the accomplishment of this important object.

It would have given me pleasure to have presented before the eye of the reader a more cheerful and alluring picture; but "facts are stubborn things," and there is no resisting the force of the evidence which they adduce,—I intend to relieve some of the dark shades of this picture, by exhibiting some faint radiations of truth and benevolence which are still visible amidst the surrounding gloom. For, amidst the moral darkness which has so long covered the earth, some streaks of celestial light have always been visible; and the dawning of a brighter day now begins to gild our horizon. Substantial knowledge is now beginning to diffuse its benign influence on all ranks; the shackles of despotism are bursting asunder; the darkness of superstition is gradually dispelling; the spirit of persecution is borne down and powerfully opposed by the force of truth and of common sense, and the rights of conscience are beginning to be generally recognised. Philanthropic institutions of various descriptions have been established, education is extending its beneficial effects; the instruction of the young is becoming an object of more general attention; philosophical institutions, village libraries, and associations for intellectual improvement, are rapidly organizing; Bible and missionary societies are extending their influence through every portion of the religious world, and Christianity is now beginning to display its beneficent energies on distant continents, and the islands of the ocean.—But, instead of entering into details in the illustration of these and similar effects which have always, in a greater or less degree, accompanied the progress of the Christian religion, I shall, in the mean time, refer the reader to the excellent work of Dr. Ryan, "On the History of the effects of Religion on Mankind."

Here a question may be proposed by some of my readers,—Is it possible to bring the inhabitants of this world, in their present depraved state, to a general observance of the laws of benevolence which have been illustrated in the preceding part of this work? To such a question I would reply,—*Whatever man has done, man may do.* Amidst the depravity and the darkness with which the earth has been generally enveloped, individuals have occasionally arisen who have shone as lights in the moral world, and exhibited bright patterns of Christian temper and of active beneficence. The Apostle Paul had his mind imbued with a large portion of the spirit of love. He voluntarily embarked in a tour of benevolence through the nations; and in spite of reproaches, persecutions, stripes and imprisonments; in the midst of "perils in the waters, perils of robbers, perils by his own countrymen, perils in the city, and perils in the wilderness;" and in the face of every danger, and of death itself, he prosecuted, with a noble heroism, his labour of love, purely for the sake of promoting the best interests of mankind. All the Apostles engaged in the same benevolent undertaking; they sacrificed every private interest, every selfish consideration; "neither counted they their lives dear unto themselves, so that they might finish their course with joy," and be the means of accomplishing the salvation of their fellow-men.

Even in our own times, many distinguished individuals have arisen, who have reflected honour on our species. The name of *Howard* is familiar to every one who is in the least acquainted with the annals of philanthropy, (see p. 20.) This excellent man, and truly philanthropic character, devoted his time, his strength, his genius, his literary acquisitions, and his fortune, and finally sacrificed his life, in the pursuits of humanity, and in the unwearied prosecution of active benevolence. He travelled over every country in Europe and in the adjacent regions of Asia, impelled by the spirit of Christian love, in order to survey the mansions of sorrow and of pain, and to devise schemes for the relief of human wretchedness wherever it existed; and, in the execution of this scheme of benevolence, the energies of his mind were so completely absorbed, that "he never suffered himself, for a moment, to be diverted from carrying it into effect, even by the most attractive of those objects which formerly possessed all their most powerful influence upon his curiosity and his taste."*

The late Walter Venning, Esq., who has been denominated, by Prince Galitzin, the *second Howard*, walked in the steps of his illustrious predecessor, and with the most fervent Christian zeal, devoted his short, but useful life, to the alleviation of human misery, and to the promotion of the best interests of thousands of wretched individuals who "were ready to perish." He withdrew himself from the ordinary round of genteel society, and declined all commercial business, that he might devote the whole energies of his soul to benevolent occupations. He commenced his philanthropic career, by co-operating in the formation of the "Society for improvement of Prison discipline," which was formed in London in 1816; and afterwards visited the prisons in Petersburgh, Novogorod, Tver, Moscow, and other cities in the Russian empire. The prisons, hospitals, work-houses, mad houses, houses of correction, and the abodes of misery of every description in Petersburgh, were visited by him, day after day: "and many a prisoner, bowed down with affliction and iron, was cheered, instructed, and saved by his ministrations;" for his philanthropy extended both to the bodies and to the souls of men."*

Many other examples might be produced from the annals of our times, and of illustrious characters, presently existing, to demonstrate, that a noble and disinterested benevolence is a principle, capable of being exercised even in the present degenerated state of the inhabitants of our world. We find parents some times displaying a high degree of benevolent feeling towards their offspring, and sacrificing their ease, and their personal interests, in order to secure their health, their happiness, and enjoyments. We find bosom friends like David and Jonathan, and like Damon and Pythias, rejoicing in the welfare of each other, and encountering difficulties and dangers in promoting the interests of the objects of their friendship. What, then, should hinder such dispositions from becoming universal? What should hinder them from being transferred to all the sensitive and intellectual beings, with whom we may have occasion to correspond, or to associate? Would not the universal exercise of such dispositions be *highly desirable?* would it not tend to banish war and discord from the world, and promote peace on the earth, and good will among men? Why, then, are such dispositions so seldom displayed? Not because the universal exercise of them is a thing impossible; but because men, actuated by selfishness, are *unwilling* to give full scope to the benevolent affections; because they have never yet employed all the requisite means for bringing them into full operation. If all the energies of the intellect, and all the treasures which have been expended in fostering malignant passions, and in promoting contentions and warfare, had been devoted to the great object of cultivating the principle of benevolence, and distributing happiness among men; the moral and physical aspect of our world would long ago have assumed a very different appearance from what it now wears.

The philanthropic individuals, to whom I have alluded, were men, whose actions were sometimes blended with the failings and imperfections incident to degenerated humanity; but the principle of benevolence ruled supreme over all the subordinate affections; and if the world were peopled with such men, notwithstanding the imperfections which attached to them, society, in every land, would present the appearance of a moral paradise, and form an image of the har-

* For a particular account of the labours of this eminent philanthropist, see Brown's "Memoirs of the public and private life of John Howard."

* Mr. Venning died in Petersburgh, in 1821, in the fortieth year of his age.

mony and felicity of "the saints in light." Every one who believes in the existence of a future state, fondly imagines that he shall enjoy happiness in that state. But, whence is his happiness to arise in the future world, but from the exercise of those dispositions which the law of God requires? And if the exercise of benevolent dispositions be essentially requisite for securing supreme felicity in the eternal state, their cultivation, even in the present world, must be an *indispensable* duty, in order to our *preparation* for the employments of the celestial world. For it is a law of the Creator, which is eternal and immutable, that "without holiness, no man can see the Lord." And whenever the requisite means are employed for the cultivation of holy and beneficent dispositions, we may rest assured, that our labour will be crowned with success. For the energy of the divine Spirit, from whom proceedeth every good and perfect gift, is promised to accompany the use of every proper mean, so as to render it effectual for counteracting the effects of moral evil, and for promoting the renovation of the world.

We have examples before us, not only of a few insulated individuals, but of societies, where the principle of benevolence, in a greater or less degree, pervades the whole mass. The people who have been denominated *Quakers*, have always been distinguished by their humane and peaceable dispositions, their probity and hospitality to each other, the cheerfulness of their manners, their opposition to war, and the active zeal which they have displayed in contributing to the good of mankind. The *Moravians* are also distinguished for their affectionate intercourse with each other, the liberality of their dispositions, the peaceableness of their tempers, the purity and simplicity of their lives, and their missionary efforts for evangelizing the heathen world.* Would to God that the whole world were Quakers and Moravians, notwithstanding their peculiarities of opinion! With all their foibles and imperfections, society would then wear a more beautiful and alluring aspect than it has ever yet done; peace and industry would be promoted: the fires of persecution would be quenched; philanthropy would go forth among the nations, distributing a thousand blessings, and the people would learn war, no more.

---

I intend in this place, to inquire into the MEANS BY WHICH THE PRACTICE OF CHRISTIAN MORALITY MIGHT BE PROMOTED. But I find that this is a subject which would require a distinct volume for its illustration. At present, I can suggest only two or three hints.

In the first place, The *intellectual* instruction of the young, should be an object of universal attention, both in public and private. For true knowledge is the spring of all religious emotions, and of all virtuous actions. By intellectual instruction, I do not mean merely a series of exercises in spelling, pronouncing, parsing, construing, writing, and figuring; but a communication of the elements of thought, and of clear and extensive conceptions of the physical and moral relations of the universe.—2. The moral instruction of the young should be an object of particular and incessant attention. Moral instruction should be inculcated, not merely by a reiteration of dry precepts, maxims, and abstract doctrines, or by a reference to the details and flimsy sentiments contained in fictitious narratives; but by a pointed and pacific reference to real facts; as exhibited in the Sacred History, the annals of nations, and in the scenes of the family, and of general society. I would expect no greater assistance in the work of moral instruction from the religious novels with which the Christian world is now deluged, than I would do from a circulation of the Pious Frauds which were so common in the first ages of the church. In schools, and in families, every thing which has a tendency, either directly or indirectly to foster pride, envy, contention, revenge, and other malignant affections, should be firmly and sedulously discouraged and counteracted; and higher rewards (if rewards be expedient) should in every instance, be bestowed on the individual who cultivates and displays benevolent affections,

* The following anecdote, is illustrative of the character of many of the Moravians, or Hernhutters as they are sometimes called.—In a late war in Germany, a captain of cavalry was ordered out on a foraging party. He put himself at the head of his troop, and marched to the quarter assigned him. It was a solitary valley, in which hardly any thing but woods was to be seen. In the midst stood a little cottage; on perceiving it he rode up, and knocked at the door; out comes an ancient Hernhutter with a beard silvered by age. "Father," says the officer, "show me a field where I can set my troopers a foraging." "Presently," replied the Hernhutter. The good old man walked before, and conducted them out of the valley. After a quarter of an hour's march, they found a field of barley. "There is the very thing we want," says the captain.—"Have patience for a very few minutes," replied the guide, "and you shall be satisfied." They went on, and about the distance of a quarter of a league farther, they arrived at another field of barley. The troop immediately dismounted, cut down the grain, trussed it up, and remounted. The officer upon this, says to his conductor, "Father, you have given yourself and us unnecessary trouble; the first field was much better than this." "Very true, Sir," replied the good old man. "*But it was not mine.*"—Here we have a beatiful *practical* exhibition of *love to our neighbour*, and of calm resignation to the providential dispensations of God. How few professed Christians have been found acting in this manner? And yet I doubt not, that this good man would experience more true satisfaction in the temper and conduct he displayed, than if he had offered resistance, practised dissimulation, or set them to plunder his neighbour's field. A number of disinterested actions such as this, would contribute more powerfully to the support of the Christian cause than a thousand theological disputes, imbued with the spirit and temper with which they have been most frequently conducted.

than on him who is distinguished merely for intellectual acquirements. Hitherto, a more decided preference seems to have been given to what is termed *genius* than to moral accomplishments.—3. Institutions should be formed for communicating literary and scientific knowledge, blended with moral and religious instructions, to persons of both sexes, and of every rank and age, from fifteen years and upwards, particularly to apprentices, journeymen, clerks, shop-keepers, and others, for the purpose of calling forth into action the energies of their minds, and for preventing the growth of habits of dissipation. In such institutions, the manifestation of benevolent affections, and propriety of moral conduct, should be made the conditions of enjoying the instructions and privileges of the association.—4. In connexion with these and other means, the cause of practical morality would be powerfully promoted, were the ministers of religion, among all parties, to direct their energies to the discussion of moral subjects, on Christian principles, instead of confining their attention almost exclusively to doctrinal discussions. Religion is not a system merely of speculative and metaphysical truths, nor does it consist in the contemplation of mysterious facts, or incomprehensible dogmas; but it is a rational and tangible subject, addressed to the reason, the hopes, and fears, and the common sense of mankind; and therefore, its illustrations should be chiefly derived from the facts of Sacred History, the system of nature, and from the existing objects, scenes, and associations with which we are connected.—A much greater degree of animation, and of energy, than is now displayed in instructions from the pulpit, is also requisite for arresting the attention, and riveting impressions of moral and religious truths upon the mind. If fewer sermons were delivered, and a greater portion of intellectual energy concentrated in each discourse, and if preachers, particularly among Dissenters, had fewer discourses to compose, and more time for taking an ample intellectual range through the system of nature, of Providence, and of revelation, a more powerful effect would undoubtedly be produced on the Christian world, and upon all who occasionally attend on the ministrations of religion.

I need scarcely add, that all such means ought to be accompanied with fervent prayer to the "Father of lights," and dependence on the promised aid of the Spirit of holiness. But without the application of all the energetic means which reason and revelation suggest, we have no reason to conclude, and it would be presumption to expect, that the influences of heaven will descend upon the moral world. For it appears, in point of fact, to be one part of the plan of the divine procedure, that human agents shall be the means of enlightening each other, and of promoting the renovation of the world, as "workers together with God."

## CONCLUSIONS FROM THE GENERAL PRINCIPLES ILLUSTRATED IN THIS VOLUME.

If the general train of sentiment which runs through the preceding discussions and illustrations be admitted, the following conclusions may be deduced respecting,

I. The subject of preaching, and the grand aim which the ministers of religion, in their discourses, ought always to have in view.* We have already seen, that it is the great object of revelation to bring into practical operation the principles of love to God and to man: and, it is obvious, that, what is the main object of Christianity to accomplish, ought to be the ultimate aim of every Christian preacher. It is not merely to convert men to the belief of certain *opinions*, or to induce them to embrace the peculiarities of a party. It is, that they may "be renewed in the spirit of their minds," and, "made meet for the inheritance of the saints in light"—it is, that they may "deny ungodliness and worldly lusts, and live soberly, righteously, and godly, in the present evil world;" and be "united together in *love*, which is the bond of perfection."—Metaphysical disquisitions, respecting dogmas in religion, have very little tendency to meliorate the heart, and to promote benevolent dispositions and affections. On the contrary, they have frequently produced a temper of mind directly opposite to the spirit of Christianity. They have led multitudes to pique themselves on the supposed purity of their profession, and the orthodoxy of their creed, and to point at others as heretics, and subverters of the gospel, on account of some slight differences in sentiment about a particular doctrine; while they themselves have never attempted to cultivate heavenly dispositions, and to display that charity which "suffereth long, and is kind, which is not easily provoked, and thinketh no evil." There are certain doctrines and facts, which we ought always to recognise, and to keep in view as fundamental axioms in the Christian system;—such as, that "there is one God, and one Mediator between God and man, the man Christ Jesus;" that "he died for our offences, and rose again for our justification;" that "all have sinned and come short of the glory of God;" and that "we are justified freely by his grace, through the redemption that is in Christ Jesus." But, there is no necessity for expatiating almost exclusively on these and similar doctrines, as is frequently done, to the exclusion of practical morality; since they ought to be regarded in the light rather of first principles in religion, than as topics which require to

* The Author originally intended to illustrate this, and the following conclusions, at considerable length, and to enter into a variety of circumstantial details; but, as the intended illustrations would occupy more than a hundred pages, and as the work has already swelled to a considerable size, he is under the necessity of postponing them for the present.

so proved by laboured and diffused arguments. Yet, it is a fact, that such doctrines, which are only the means of religion, have been expatiated upon without intermission, as if the simple belief of them were the end of religion; while the great moral object of Christianity has been either entirely overlooked, or thrown into the shade. What should we think of the instructer of youth, who confined the attention of his pupil solely to the characters of the alphabet, and to the pronunciation of a few elementary sounds, and then dismissed him with a general exhortation, to apply them to all the combinations of letters and syllables he might find in every book? Could we ever expect, that, in ordinary cases, such a pupil would either make progress in the art of reading, or use it as the medium of acquiring knowledge? And what shall we think of those who do little more than attempt to explain the axioms of the Christian system, but never show their bearings on the scenery of real life, nor endeavour to extend our views of the providential operations of God, and of the glory of his kingdom? If Christianity consisted merely in abstract disquisitions, and metaphysical dogmas, such a practice might be, in some measure, defensible; but since it is, in every sense of the word, a *practical* system, it is next to trifling with its prominent objects, to confine the range of religious discussions within so narrow bounds as is generally done by many of those who are designated by the term *evangelical;* and argues a complete forgetfulness of the apostle's exhortation, "Therefore, leaving the first principles of the doctrine of Christ, let us go on to perfection," tracing first principles through all their diversified bearings on mortal action, and on Christian contemplation.

One of the great objects of preaching ought, undoubtedly, to be, to investigate the numerous and minute ramifications of human conduct; to explore every avenue of corruption; to endeavour to draw forth from its hiding-place every immoral principle and action, which exerts its pernicious influence in Christian or in general society; and with all the powers of graphical description we can command, to portray them before the eyes of men, in all their repulsive features, and in all their abominations. At the same time, we ought to apply the touch-stone of the divine law to every unchristian propensity and practice; to exhibit its contrariety to the spirit of our holy religion; to show how the principle of love ought to operate in every given case and circumstance, and in the minutest actions of human life; and how very different effects would be produced, were the principles laid down by our Saviour and his apostles, to operate with full effect throughout every department of the moral world. Unless such objects be generally aimed at, and steadily kept in view, in the course of public instruction, religion will be apt to degenerate into a mere figment, or, at most, into a subject of wrangling, or a matter of curious speculation.

Let no class of religionists presume to tell us, that, if the fundamental doctrines of religion be simply declared, Christian morality will follow as a matter of course; and that, to expatiate on any particular branch of social conduct, is to degenerate into *legal preaching.* If this principle were to be admitted, then all the expostulations and denunciations of the prophets, all the reproofs and exhortations of the apostles, all the moral sermons of our Saviour, and all the minute directions in reference to moral conduct, detailed in every epistle to the Christian churches, may be regarded as egregious trifling. If it be one grand design of revelation to restore mankind from the ruins of the fall, and to reinstate them in that integrity which they at first possessed;—if it was the chief design of "the law and the prophets" to bring forth into action, on the theatre of the world, the two fundamental principles of the moral law, as the Lawgiver himself has expressly stated; (Matt. xxii. 37—40;)—if the sweet singer of Israel devoted a large portion of his inspired strains to the celebration of the divine precepts, (Psalm cxix. &c.;)—if most of the sermons and parables of our Saviour have a direct bearing on the same important subject;—if the apostle Paul, in his instructions to a Christian minister, enlarged particularly on the duties which should be inculcated on the various ranks and relations of men, (Titus ii. iii.;)—if all the apostolic letters to the Christian churches are full of minute directions, in relation to every branch of moral duty;—if heaven be the scene of perfect moral rectitude, where ardent affection towards God, and towards fellow-intelligences, ever reigns—where love, peace, and harmony, eternally prevail;—if the happiness of that world depend upon the absence of moral evil, and the attainment of moral perfection;—if the present world be a state of preparation for the enjoyments of that happier region;—if this preparation consist in having the principles of love to God and to man interwoven through the whole constitution of the mind, and brought forth into action in the diversified scenes of civil and religious intercourse;—if such important effects cannot be produced, unless by laying open to view the latent abominations of the heart, by impelling the moral principles of the gospel through all the avenues and windings of the human passions and affections; and by illustrating, with minute particularity, every subordinate branch of Christian duty;—if these positions be admitted, it will follow, that the duties of Christian morality, so far from being thrown into an obscure corner, ought to occupy a *prominent place* in the range of the ministration of every Christian minister, who is desirous to promote the improvement of society, and the renovation of the world.

In short, we expect no grand moral reformation to be achieved—no commencement of the millennial era of the church, till "the watchmen upon Mount Sion," with more energy than they have yet displayed, "shall lift up their voice like a trumpet, and show to the house of Jacob their transgressions"—till they "lift it up with strength, and not be afraid" of any suspicions that may be thrown out against their orthodoxy, when they show unto men the path of duty in all its bearings on the relations of time, and on the employments of eternity—till they make the moral principles of Revelation bear, in all their force, not only on the prominent features of social life, but upon every minute ramification of human conduct till every lurking principle of jealousy, envy, avarice, and revenge be made to feel their energy—till even the very *amusements* of public and domestic life be made to bend to the eternal laws of rectitude, and to carry on their fronts that noble inscription, "HOLINESS TO THE LORD."

II. If the preceding train of sentiments be admitted, we may be directed in our views of the *nature* and *ends* of church discipline, and the persons on whom it ought to be exercised.

In a great majority of Christian churches, censures are inflicted chiefly, or solely, on persons guilty of an *external* breach of one or two precepts of the decalogue—only one or two species of violation of the moral law are considered as worthy of cognizance; while the systematic operations of slander, revenge, envy, and avarice—the indications of harsh, sour, and ungovernable tempers, and the absence of Christian candour and affection—circumstances which display the real characters of men far more distinctly than any *insulated* acts of immorality can do—are either wholly overlooked, or considered as characteristics of very trivial import. The censures to which I allude, are likewise accompanied, in many instances, with a degree of magisterial haughtiness, severity, and unchristian feeling, which is directly repugnant to every amiable, candid, and generous principle. A person guilty, in a single instance, of a breach of the seventh or eight commandments, will lie under the frown of a religious society for years, and even to the close of his life, notwithstanding every evidence he can give of the sincerity of his repentance, and even be deprived of the means of earning his subsistence; while another may habitually violate almost all the other precepts of the decalogue, and be screened from the discipline of the church. He may be avaricious, cunning, and deceitful; harsh and unfeeling in his conduct; uncandid and uncharitable in his dispositions towards others; proud, selfish, and obstinate in his temper; addicted to slander and to incessant litigations; impatient of control; and boisterous and contentious in his general deportment—and yet be considered as no proper object of censure; and, though never manifesting the least symptom of penitence, will be viewed as a tolerably fair character in religious society, especially if he has acquired a considerable share of wealth and of influence in general society.—Of such cases and practices, the author had selected a number of striking examples, which the narrow limits to which he is confined in the present work, constrain him, in the mean time, to postpone.

Now, if the general sentiments already thrown out be founded on truth, and on the nature of things, such a practice as that to which we allude, must be absurd, unchristian, and inconsistent with the preservation of the moral purity of religious society. It has this pernicious tendency, among others, that it leads multitudes to imagine, that, if they can keep clear of two or three acts of moral delinquency, they may trample on every divine principle and law with impunity. A poor wretch, under the pressure of poverty, steals a hen or a pocket handkerchief, and, notwithstanding his subsequent repentance, is banished from social intercourse, and held up to execration; while a sanctimonious hypocrite will swindle his neighbour out of a hundred pounds, if no criminal law can take hold of him, and will retain his station in the church, and hold up his face without a blush in the presence of general society. It is obvious, if there be any truth in what we have hitherto stated, that the general tenor of the conduct, and the uniform manifestation of benevelent affections, ought, in every case, to form the grand criterion of a man's being entitled to the character of a Christian; and, that dispositions of an opposite nature habitually displayed, however much overlooked in the general intercourse of life, ought to form a ground of exclusion from the society of the faithful.

III. This subject has a particular bearing upon the *divisions* which subsist in the religious world, and the grand principles which ought to form a *bond of union* among all who acknowledge the truth of the Christian Revelation.—If the train of thought illustrated in the preceding pages be correct, it will follow, that a cordial union of the various sections of the Christian church is to be expected from the cultivation of the Spirit of Love, more than from any attempt to produce an exact coincidence of opinion on these theological points in which they now differ Wherever this spirit is found expanding the soul, and governing the affections, it will lead its possessors to view the peculiar opinions of others with candour; to respect their persons; to allow them liberty of thought on all the subordinate ramifications of theological sentiment; and to set a higher value on moral qualifications, and the manifestation of benevolent affections, than on those circumstantial opinions which do not enter into the essence of the Christian scheme. If the professing Christian world were thoroughly investigated, it would be found, that it is owing more to the absence of this spirit, that Christians stand so much aloof from each other, than to the speculative opinions which they respectively maintain. The prevalent disposition for sneering at other denominations, and the pleasure that seems to be felt in laying open their sores, will generally be found to proceed from a principle of pride, and of self-conceit in regard to our own favourite opinions, some of which, when probed to the bottom, will be found as rotten as our neighbour's. Why are men not as much disposed to pass encomiums on what is sound in the opinions, and laudable in the conduct, of other parties, as they are to censure them for minor peculiarities of sentiment? Why? Because it appears, that many professed Christians take more delight in the exercise of malevolent feelings than of benevolent affections; and are like flies, that pass over the sound parts of a man's body, and fix upon his sores. Till such unchristian dispositions be undermined, and tempers of an opposite description pervade the ranks of Christian society, we can expect no cordial nor lasting union in the visible church, however many ingenious schemes may be formed, to bring about this desirable event. For every effect must have an adequate cause: this cause will be found to consist more in the affection than in opinion; and a union formed on an apparent coincidence of sentiment, unmingled with ardent love and affection, would be unworthy of the name, and would soon be dissolved.

It can form no decisive mark of a man's Christianity, that he recognises the *peculiar opinions* of the Baptists or Pædo-Baptists, of Presbyterians, Episcopalians, or Independents; it is a matter, comparatively of little importance, whether a man believes that Christ was an actual or a virtual Mediator under the Old Testament; whether he be designated the *Son of God* in virtue of his office, or of his nature; whether or not we be guilty of Adam's first sin; whether the transaction which passed between him and his Creator, should be viewed as a law, or as a covenant; whether the ordinance of baptism should be administered by dipping, or by sprinkling, &c. &c.—But it is, unquestionably, a matter of the highest moment, both to the person himself, and to Christian society, that his temper, affections, and conduct, should be in unison with the holy law of God, and that he should display the love which it requires, in all his social, commercial, domestic, and Christian intercourses;—and if such dispositions and conduct were universally to prevail among the various denominations of the religious world, union would soon follow, as a matter of course.—If, therefore, we wish to behold the unhappy divisions of the church cemented, let us cultivate, with ardour, those amiable and affectionate dispositions which our benevolent religion inculcates, and be more anxious to correct our own mental and moral aberrations, than to magnify the errors and the faults of others. Let us make every allowance for the effects which education, habit, temper local circumstances, and particular associations, may have produced on the opinions of our supposed erring brethren; and let us consider, that we ourselves, had we been placed in the same circumstances, might have imbibed the same sentiments. Let us endeavour to acquire clear and well-defined ideas on every subject connected with religion; that we may not contend about trifles, about mere abstract ideas, or the application of particular terms or phrases. Let us keep our eyes fixed on the great and prominent objects of revelation, and on all the subordinate active means by which they may be promoted. Let us consider religion as consisting more in action, than in speculation. Let our love to Christian brethren be founded, not so much on a general coincidence of opinion, as on the resemblance they bear to the Divine image; and then we may confidently expect, that that period will soon approach, when the saints of God "shall see eye to eye," in reference to all the grand bearings of the Gospel scheme, and when the name of Jehovah shall be ONE throughout all the earth.

IV. We may learn from the subject we have been illustrating, what notions we ought to form of *the* NATURE *of a future state of happiness, and of the* PREPARATION *requisite to enable us to engage in its employments.*—The felicity of the future world will not consist simply in a *change of place;* nor will it consist chiefly in change of sentiment or opinion. Its foundation must be laid in the principle of *Love*, and in the complete renovation of the moral powers of the human mind, without which no celestial scene could produce permanent enjoyment. Although all the theologians who now exist were united in opinion about every article of the system of Divinity; and although they were transported to the most splendid world that revolves around the star *Arcturus;* after the first transports, arising from the novelty and the grandeur of the scene had subsided, they would enjoy little more happiness in that orb, than they do in this terrestrial sphere, unless they were actuated with moral dispositions and affections very different from those which many of them now display. For, not only rancour and malice, but even coldness and indifference to the welfare of others, would prevent happiness from being enjoyed in any region of the material universe. All who believe in the reality of a future world, indulge in anxious wishes to be made happy when they pass from this mortal scene to the world of spirits. Even wicked men, whose consciences frequently forebode evil to them in the other world, indulge the hope that God will ultimately be merciful to them, and admit them to the joys of heaven. But this is impossible, in the very nature of things, unless they be "renewed in the spirit of their minds," and endowed with those holy dispositions which alone can qualify them for relishing substantial happiness, and for participating in "the inheritance of the saints of light." How could Malignity associate with Benevolence, Contention with Friendship, or War with Peace? How could the sons of discord dwell in unity, in an assembly where all is harmony and love? How could the malicious and revengeful spirit find delight in the employments of kindness and pure benignity? How could the man who now finds his chief pleasure in hounding and horse-racing, in brawling and fighting, have any relish for the sublime adorations, the enraptured praises, and the lofty and refined contemplations, of the celestial inhabitants? The thing is impossible, unless the moral order of all worlds were completly subverted. Such characters will be banished from the abodes of bliss; not by any arbitrary decree of the Almighty, but in virtue of the moral constitution of the intelligent universe.

It is, therefore, evident, that the happiness of heaven must be founded upon the exercise of love, affection, harmony, perfect good-will to fellow-intelligences, and the infinite variety of ramifications into which such principles may diverge; combined with profound, enlightened, and venerable views and affections, in relation to the God and Father of our Lord Jesus Christ. When these and similar dispositions are uniformly exercised, without the least mixture of any one ingredient of moral evil, it is easy to conceive, with what transports of delight the inhabitants of heaven will contemplate the displays of Divine Power, Wisdom, and Goodness, and investigate the history of his dispensations in the moral government of our world, and in the arrangements of all the other worlds whose physical and moral economy may be laid open to their view.*

Such views are in perfect accordance with the representations of Scripture.—"Without holiness, no man shall see the Lord." "The pure in heart (and they alone) shall see God." "Nothing that worketh abomination, can enter within the gates of the heavenly city." "As we have borne the image of the earthly, (says the Apostle,) so shall we bear the image of the heavenly." "Christ Jesus gave himself for the church, that he might sanctify and cleanse it, and that he might present it to himself a glorious church, holy, and without blemish." The crown of glory, reserved in heaven for the faithful, is designated "a crown of righteousness." "The spirits of just men," in the future world, "are made perfect," freed from every taint of moral pollution, and unrestrained in the exercise of their moral powers. The inheritance to which they are destined, is "undefiled" with the least stain of corruption, or with the example of impure and malignant spirits. "When Christ, who is our life, shall appear, we shall be like him;" transformed into his moral image, and animated with those Divine principles and virtues, which he displayed in his conduct, when he tabernacled among men. The saints "shall walk with him in white," an emblem of their perfect moral purity; "they shall receive an inheritance among them that are sanctified," and "there shall be no more death, neither sorrow, nor crying; for the former things shall have passed away."

V. From the preceding illustrations we may learn something *of the nature and essence of future punishment.* If the exercise of love, in all its diversified modifications, constitutes the foundation and the essence of happiness, the unrestrained operations of malevolence must be the source and the sum of misery. We cannot form a more dreadful picture of future punishment, than by conceiving the principles of falsehood, deceit, and malignity, and the passions of pride, hatred, malice, and revenge, raging with uncontrolled and perpetual violence. We need represent to ourselves nothing more horrible in the place of punishment, than by supposing the Almighty simply to permit wicked men to give full scope to their malevolent dispositions; leaving them "to eat of the fruit of their own ways, and to be filled with their own devices." The effects produced by the uncontrolled operation of such principles and passions would be such, as may be fitly represented by the emblems of "the worm that never dies," of "devouring fire," and of their necessary concomitants, "weeping, and wailing, and gnashing of teeth." (See Chap. II. Sect. iv. pp. 55. 58.) What other ingredients of misery, arising either from local circumstances, from the recollection of the past, or the anticipation of the future, may be mingled with the cup of future wo, it becomes not us particularly to determine. And, whether this scene of misery will ever come to a termination, must be determined by the consideration, whether the effects produced by such a punishment will have a tendency to produce repentance and reformation on the minds of the sufferers. If, after a lapse of ages, the principles of hatred to God, and to surrounding intelligences, continue to operate with increasing violence, without producing the least desire of returning to their allegiance to God, or the least symptom of reformation,—then, we may conclude, that the misery of wicked intelligences will continue so long as they remain in existence.

* The Author will have an opportunity of illustrating this topic in more minute detail, in a work entitled, "*The Philosophy of a Future state*; or, an Illustration of the Connexion of Science with the Eternal World,—and of the Aids which its discoveries afford, for enabling us to form a conception of the *perpetual improvement* of the celestial inhabitants in knowledge and felicity."

THE

# CHRISTIAN PHILOSOPHER,

OR,

THE CONNEXION OF

## SCIENCE AND PHILOSOPHY

WITH

## RELIGION.

---

BY THOMAS DICK,

AUTHOR OF A VARIETY OF LITERARY AND SCIENTIFIC COMMUNICATIONS
IN NICHOLSON'S PHILOSOPHICAL JOURNAL, THE ANNALS
OF PHILOSOPHY, ETC. ETC.

---

HARTFORD:
PUBLISHED BY A. C. GOODMAN & CO.
1850.

# PREFACE TO THIS EDITION.

---

THE following pages were written under the impression that the visible manifestations of the attributes of the Deity are too frequently overlooked by Christians in their views of the great objects of Religion, and in the worship they offer to the Father of their spirits; and are intended to show, that the Teachers of Religion, in imparting instruction either to the old or to the young, ought to embrace a wider range of illustration, in reference to Divine subjects, than that to which they are usually confined.

Throughout the whole of the discussions contained in this work, the Author has pursued his own train of thought; and, in so doing, he trusts that he has been enabled to render some of his illustrations more interesting to the young and untutored mind than if he had adhered rigidly to the sentiments of others, and to the technical language of science. The sketches of the different sciences are not mere extracts, or compilations, but are, for the most part, original composition—in which it has been his main object to imbody as many facts as his limits would permit—in order to excite the inquiring mind to farther investigations into the different departments of physical science.

It is presumed, that no Christian reader will for once imagine, that the views illustrated in this work are intended to be *substituted* in place of the peculiar revelations of the Bible. The object of the volume is to illustrate the harmony which subsists between the system of Nature and the system of Revelation; and to show, that the manifestations of God in the material universe ought to be blended with our views of the facts and doctrines recorded in the volume of Inspiration.

It is taken for granted, throughout the whole range of the following illustrations, that the Scriptures contain a Revelation from Heaven; and, under a firm belief of this important truth, the Author has embellished his work with frequent quotations from the energetic and sublime language of this Sacred Book. It would, therefore, be unfair in any critic, who entertains doubts on this point, to find fault with such quotations, or with the allusions to Bible phraseology which occur, unless they can be shown to be introduced without judgment or discrimination.

The Author has carefully revised every portion of the present edition, and introduced a variety of corrections and modifications. He has likewise introduced additional matter, to the extent of between 20 and 30 pages, and also several illustrative engravings. In its present form, the Author trusts, that independently of the moral reflections it contains, it will be found to comprise popular descriptions of a greater number of scientific facts than is to be found in any other volume of the same size.

Various topics, originally intended to be illustrated, have been unavoidably omitted. Some of these are stated in the last paragraph of Chapter IV. the illustration of which, in combination with other kindred topics, would fill a volume of nearly the same size as the present. This subject (for which the author has abundance of materials) will be prosecuted in another volume, under the title of THE PHILOSOPHY OF RELIGION; and will comprise, among many other objects of discussion, illustrations of the moral relation of intelligent beings to their Creator, and to one another—the physical and rational grounds of those moral laws which the Deity has promulgated—the views which science affords of the incessant energies of Creating Power, and of the grand and multifarious objects over which Divine Providence presides—the relation of science to a future state, and of the aids which the discoveries of science afford, for enabling us to form a conception of the perpetual improvement of the celestial inhabitants in knowledge and felicity. These subjects will be illustrated by a variety of interesting details of facts, in relation to the system of nature, the history of nations, and the moral state of Christian and general society

# CONTENTS.



## CHAPTER I.

### OF THE NATURAL ATTRIBUTES OF THE DEITY.

### SECTION I.



### SECTION II.



### SECTION III.

## SECTION IV.



# CHAPTER II.

## A CURSORY VIEW OF SOME OF THE SCIENCES WHICH ARE RELATED TO RELIGION AND CHRISTIAN THEOLOGY.

CONTENTS.

## CHAPTER III.

### THE RELATION WHICH THE INVENTIONS OF ART BEAR TO THE OBJECTS OF RELIGION.



## CHAPTER IV.

### SCRIPTURAL FACTS ILLUSTRATED FROM THE SYSTEM OF NATURE.



## CHAPTER V.

### BENEFICIAL EFFECTS WHICH WOULD RESULT FROM CONNECTING SCIENCE WITH RELIGION.

## APPENDIX.

THE

# CHRISTIAN PHILOSOPHER.

## INTRODUCTION.

On the subject of RELIGION, mankind have, in all ages, been prone to run into extremes. While some have been disposed to attach too much importance to the mere exertions of the human intellect, and to imagine that man, by the light of unassisted reason, is able to explore the path to true wisdom and happiness,—the greater part of religionists, on the other hand, have been disposed to treat scientific knowledge, in its relation to religion, with a degree of indifference bordering upon contempt. Both these dispositions are equally foolish and preposterous. For he who exalts human reason, as the only sure guide to wisdom and felicity, forgets, that man, in his present state, is a *depraved* intelligence, and, consequently, liable to err; and that all those who have been left solely to its dictates, have uniformly failed in attaining these desirable objects. During a period of more than 5,800 years, the greater part of the human race have been left solely to the guidance of their rational powers, in order to grope their way to the Tempe of Knowledge, and the Portals of Immortality; but what has been the result of all their anxious researches? Instead of acquiring correct notions of the Great Author of their existence, and of the nature of that homage which is due to his perfections, "they have become vain in their imaginations, and their foolish hearts have been darkened. Professing themselves to be wise, they have become fools; and have changed the glory of the Incorruptible God into an image made like to corruptible man, and to four-footed beasts, and creeping things." Instead of acquiring correct views of the principles of moral action, and conducting themselves according to the eternal rules of rectitude, they have displayed the operation of the most diabolical passions, indulged in continual warfare, and desolated the earth with rapine and horrid carnage; so that the history of the world presents to our view little more than a series of revolting details of the depravity of our species, and of the wrongs which one tribe of human beings has wilfully inflicted upon another.

This has been the case, not only among a few uncultivated hordes on the coasts of Africa, in the plains of Tartary, and the wilds of America, but even among those nations which stood highest in the ranks of civilization, and of science.— The ancient Greeks and Romans, who boasted of their attainments in philosophy, and their progress in the arts, entertained the most foolish, contradictory, and unworthy notions of the Object of Divine worship, of the requirements of religion, and of the eternal destiny of man. They adored a host of divinities characterized by impiety, fraud, injustice, falsehood, lewdness, treachery, revenge, murder, and every other vice which can debase the human mind, instead of offering a tribute of rational homage to that Supreme Intelligence who made and who governs the universe. Even their priests and philosophers indulged in the most degrading and abominable practices, and entertained the most irrational notions in regard to the origin of the universe, and the moral government of the world. Most of them denied a future state of retribution, and all of them had their doubts respecting the reality of an immortal existence: and as to the doctrine of a resurrection from the dead, they never dreamed of such an event, and scouted the idea, when proposed to them, as the climax of absurdity. The glory to which their princes and generals aspired, was, to spread death and destruction among their fellow-men—to carry fire and sword, terror and dismay, and all the engines of destruction, through surrounding nations—to fill their fields with heaps of slain—to plunder the survivors of every earthly comfort, and to drag captive kings at their chariot wheels—that they might enjoy the splendour and the honours of a triumph. What has been now stated, with regard to the most enlightened nations of antiquity, will equally apply to the present inhabitants of China, of Hindostan, of the Japanese Islands, of the Birman Empire, and of every other civilized nation on which the light of revelation has never shone—with this additional consideration, That they have enjoyed an additional period of 1800 years for making further investigations; and are, at this moment, as far from the object of their pursuit as when they first commenced their researches; and not only so, but some of these nations, in modern times, have mingled with their abominable superstitions and idolatries many absurdities and horrid cruelties, which were altogether unknown among the Greek and Roman population.

Such are the melancholy results to which men have been led, when left to the guidance of unassisted reason, in the most interesting and important of all investigations. They have wandered in the mazes of error and delusion; and their researches, instead of directing and expanding our religious views, have tended only to bewilder the human mind, and to throw a deeper shade of intellectual gloom over our apostate world. After a period of six thousand years has been spent in anxious inquiries after the path to true knowledge and happiness—Ignorance, Superstition, Idolatry, Vice, and Misery still continue to sway their sceptre over the great majority of the human race; and, if we be allowed to reason from the past to the future, we may rest assured, that while mankind are destitute of a Guide superior to the glimmerings of depraved reason, they would be no nearer the object of their pursuit, after the lapse of *sixty thousand years*, than at the present moment. It is only in connection with the discoveries of Revelation, that we can expect that the efforts of human reason and activity will be successful in abolishing the reign of Ignorance and degrading Superstition—in illuminating the benighted tribes of the Pagan World—and in causing "Righteousness, and Order, and Peace, to spring forth before all the nations." Though the Christian Religion has never yet been fully understood and recognised in all its aspects and bearings, nor its requirements been cordially complied with, by the great body of those who profess to believe in its Divine origin, yet it is only in those nations who have acknowledged its authority, and in some measure submitted to its dictates, that any thing approximating to just conceptions of the Supreme Intelligence, and of his moral government, is found to prevail.

But, on the other hand, though the light of Nature is of itself a feeble and insufficient guide, to direct us in our views of the Supreme Intelligence, and of our eternal destination, yet it is a most dangerous and delusive error to imagine, that Reason, and the study of the material world, ought to be discarded from the science of religion. The man who would discard the efforts of the human intellect and the science of Nature from Religion, forgets—that He who is the Author of human redemption, is also the Creator and Governor of the whole system of the material universe—that it is one end of that moral renovation which the Gospel effects, to qualify us for contemplating aright the displays of Divine Perfection which the works of creation exhibit—that the visible works of God are the principal medium by which he displays the attributes of his nature to intelligent beings—that the study and contemplation of these works employ the faculties of intelligences of a superior order*—that man, had he remained in primeval innocence, would have been chiefly employed in such contemplations—that it is one main design of Divine Revelation to illustrate the operations of Providence, and the agency of God in the formation and preservation of all things—and that the Scriptures are full of sublime descriptions of the visible creation, and of interesting references to the various objects which adorn the scenery of Nature. Without the cultivation of our reasoning powers, and an investigation of the laws and economy of Nature, we could not appreciate many of the excellent characters, the interesting aspects, and the sublime references of revealed religion: we should lose the full evidence of those arguments by which the existence of God and his attributes of Wisdom and Omnipotence are most powerfully demonstrated: we should remain destitute of those sublime conceptions of the perfections and agency of Jehovah which the grandeur and immensity of his works are calculated to inspire. we should never perceive, in its full force, the evidence of those proofs on which the Divine authority of Revelation is founded: we could not give a rational interpretation of the spirit and meaning of many parts of the Sacred Oracles: nor could we comply with those positive commands of God which enjoin us to contemplate the wonder of his power, to "meditate on all his works, and to talk of all his doings."

Notwithstanding these and many other considerations, which show the folly of overlooking the visible manifestations of Deity in the exercises of Religion, it has long been the practice of certain theologians to depreciate the wonderful works of Jehovah, and to attempt to throw them into the shade, as if they were unworthy of our serious contemplation. In their view, to be a bad philosopher is the surest way to become a good Christian, and to expand the views of the human mind, is to endanger Christianity, and to render the design of religion abortive. They seem to consider it as a most noble triumph to the Christian cause, to degrade the material world, and to trample under foot, not only the earth, but the visible heavens. as an old, shattered, and corrupted fabric, which no longer demands our study or admiration. Their expressions, in a variety of instances, would lead us almost to conclude, that they considered the economy of Nature as set in opposition to the economy of Redemption, and that it is not the same God that contrived the system of Nature, who is also the "Author of eternal salvation to all them that obey him."

It is, unquestionably, both foolish and impious to overlook or to undervalue any of the modes by which the Divine Being has been pleased to make known his nature and perfections to mankind. Since he has given a display of his "Eternal Power and Godhead" in the grand theatre of nature, which forms the subject of scientific investigation, it was surely never intended, and would ill comport with reverence for its adorable Author, that such magnificent dis-

* Rev. iv. 11 xv 3, &c.

plays of his Power, Wisdom, and Beneficence, as the material universe exhibits, should be treated, by his intelligent offspring, with indifference or neglect. It becomes us to contemplate, with adoring gratitude, every ray of our Creator's glory, whether as emanating from the light of Revelation, or as reflected from the scenery of nature around us, or as descending from those regions where stars unnumbered shine, and planets and comets run their solemn rounds. Instead of contrasting the one department of knowledge with the other, with a view of depreciating the science of nature, our duty is, to derive from both as much information and instruction as they are calculated to afford; to mark the harmony of the revelations they respectively unfold; and to use the revelations of nature for the purpose of confirming and amplifying, and carrying forward our views of the revelation contained in the Sacred Scriptures.

With regard to the revelation derived from the Sacred Records, it has been imagined by some, that it has little or no reference to the operations of the material system, and that, therefore, the study of the visible works of God can be of little importance in promoting religious knowledge and holy affections. In the sequel of this volume, I shall endeavour to show, that this sentiment is extremely fallacious, and destitute of a foundation. But, in the mean time, although it were taken for granted, it would form no argument against the combination of science with religion. For it ought to be carefully remarked, that Divine Revelation is chiefly intended to intruct us in the knowledge of those truths which interest us as subjects of the *moral administration* of the Governor of the world,—or, in other words, as apostate creatures, and as moral agents. Its grand object is to develop the openings and bearings of the plan of Divine Mercy; to counteract those evil propensities and passions which sin has introduced; to inculcate those holy principles and moral laws which tend to unite mankind in harmony and love; and to produce those amiable tempers and dispositions of mind, which alone can fit us for enjoying happiness either in this world, or in the world to come. For this reason, doubtless, it is, that the *moral* attributes of Deity are brought more prominently into view in the Sacred Volume, than his *natural* perfections; and that those special arrangements of his Providence, which regard the *moral* renovation of our species, are particularly detailed; while the immense extent of his universal kingdom, the existence of other worlds, and their moral economy, are but slightly hinted at, or veiled in obscurity. Of such a Revelation we stood in need; and had it chiefly embraced subjects of a very different nature, it would have failed in supplying the remedies requisite for correcting the disorders which sin has introduced among mankind.—But, surely, it was never intended, even in a religious point of view, that the powers of the human mind, in their contemplations and researches, should be bounded by the range of subjects comprised in that revelation, which is purely, or chiefly, of a *moral* nature, since the Almighty has exibited so magnificent a spectacle in the universe around us, and endowed us with faculties adequate to the survey of a considerable portion of its structure, and capable of deducing from it the most noble and sublime results. To walk in the midst of this "wide extended theatre," and to overlook, or to gaze with indifference on those striking marks of Divine omnipotence and skill, which every where appear, is to overlook the Creator himself, and to contemn the most illustrious displays he has given of his eternal power and glory. That man's religious devotions are much to be suspected, whatever show of piety he may affect, who derives no assistance, in attempting to form some adequate conceptions of the object of his worship, from the sublime discoveries of astronomical science; from those myriads of suns and systems which form but a small portion of the Creator's immense empire!* The professing Christian, whose devotional exercises are not invigorated, and whose conceptions of Deity are not extended, by a contemplation of the magnitude and variety of his works, may be considered as equally a stranger to the more elevated strains of piety, and to the noble emotions excited by a perception of the beautiful and the sublime.

"The works of the Lord," says an inspired writer, "are *great*, and are sought out by all those who have pleasure therein." They all bear the stamp of Infinite Perfection, and serve as so many sensible mediums to exalt and expand our conceptions of him, whose invisible glories they represent and adumbrate. When contemplated in connection with the prospects opened by Divine Revelation, they tend to excite the most ardent desires after that state of enlarged vision, where the plans and operations of Deity will be more clearly unfolded—and to prepare us for bearing a part in the immortal hymn of the church triumphant:—"Great and marvellous are thy works, Lord God Almighty, just and true are thy ways, thou King of Saints." The most illustrious characters that have adorned our race in all ages, have been struck with the beauty and magnificence of the visible creation, and have devoted a certain portion of their

* As some readers seem to have mistaken the Author's meaning, in this and similar passages, it may be proper to state, that his meaning is not—that a knowledge of natural science is *essential* to genuine piety; but, that the person *who has an opportunity of making himself acquainted with the science of nature*, and of contemplating the wonders of the heavens in their true light, and who does not find his views of the Creator expanded, and his religious emotions elevated, by such studies, has reason to call in question the nature and the sincerity of his devotional feelings.

time and attention in investigating its admirable economy and arrangement: and there can be no question, that a portion of our thoughts devoted to the study of the wondrous works of the Most High, must ultimately be conducive to the improvement of our intellectual powers, to our advancement in the Christian life, and to our preparation for the exalted employments of the eternal world.

In fine, since the researches of modern times have greatly enlarged our views of the System of Universal Nature, and of the vast extent to which the operations of the Creator are carried on in the distant regions of space,—since the late discoveries of Naturalists and Experimental Philosophers, with respect to the constitution of the atmosphere, water, light, heat, the gases, the electric, galvanic and magnetic fluids, and the economy and instincts of animated beings, have opened to our view a bright display of Divine Wisdom, in the contrivance and arrangement of the different parts of our terrestrial habitation,—since improvements in the useful arts have kept pace with the progress of science, and have been applied to many beneficial purposes, which have ultimately a bearing on the interests and the progress of religion—since a general desire to propagate the truths of Christianity in Heathen lands now animates the mass of the religious world—since the nations of both Continents are now aroused to burst asunder the shackles of despotism, and to inquire after rational liberty and mental improvement,—and since all these discoveries, inventions, and movements, and the energies of the human mind, from which they spring, are under the direction and control of that Omnipotent Being who made and who governs the world—they ought to be considered as parts of those Providential arrangements, in the progress of which He will ultimately accomplish the illumination of our benighted race, and make the cause of righteousness and truth to triumph among all nations. And, therefore, the enlightened Christian ought thankfully to appreciate every exhibition, and every discovery, by which his conceptions of the attributes of God, and of the grandeur of his works, may be directed and enlarged, in order that he may be qualified to "speak of the honour of his majesty, and talk of his power; to make known to the sons of men his mighty acts, and the glorious majesty of his kingdom."

# CHAPTER I.

## OF THE NATURAL ATTRIBUTES OF THE DEITY, WITH PARTICULAR ILLUSTRATIONS OF HIS OMNIPOTENCE AND WISDOM.

### SECTION I.

*On the Relation of the Natural Attributes of* DEITY *to* RELIGION.

A FIRM conviction of the existence of God, and a competent knowledge of his natural perfections, lie at the foundation of all religion, both natural and revealed. In proportion as our views of the perfections of Deity are limited and obscure, in a similar proportion will be our conceptions of all the relations in which he stands to his creatures, of every part of his providential procedure, and of all the doctrines and requirements of revealed religion.

By the natural or essential attributes of God, we understand such perfections as the following:—His Eternity, Omnipresence, Infinite Knowledge, Infinite Wisdom, Omnipotence, and Boundless Beneficence. These are the characters and attributes of Deity, which, we must suppose, form the chief subjects of contemplation to angels, and to all other pure intelligences—and in investigating the displays of which, the sons of Adam would have been chiefly employed, had they continued in primeval innocence. These attributes form the ground-work of all those gracious relations in which the God of salvation stands to his redeemed people in the economy of redemption—they lie at the foundation of the whole Christian superstructure—and were they not recognized as the corner-stones of that sacred edifice, the whole system of the Scripture Revelation would remain a baseless fabric. The full display of these perfections will be exhibited in the future world—the contemplation of this display will form one of the sublime employments "of the saints in light"—and to prepare us for engaging in such noble exercises, is one of the chief designs of the salvation proclaimed in the Gospel.

The Christian Revelation ought not to be considered as superseding the Religion of Nature, but as carrying it forward to perfection. It introduces the Deity to us under *new* relations, corresponding to the degraded state into which we have fallen. It is superadded to our natural relations to God, and takes it for granted, that these natural relations must for ever subsist. It is true, indeed, that the essential attributes of God, and the principles of Natural Religion, cannot be fully discovered without the light of Revelation, as appears from the past experience of mankind in every generation; but it is equally true, that, when discovered by the aid of this celestial light, they are of the utmost importance in the Christian system, and are as essentially connected with it, as the foundation of a building is with the superstructure. Many professed Christians, however, seem to think, and to act, as if the Christian Revelation had annulled the natural relations which subsist between man and the Deity; and hence the zealous outcry against every discussion from the pulpit, that has not a *direct* relation to what are termed the doctrines of grace. But nothing, surely, can be more absurd than to carry out such a principle to all its legitimate consequences. Can God ever cease to be Omnipotent, or can man ever cease to be dependent for existence on his infinite power? Can the Divine Being ever cease to be Omnipresent and Omniscient, or can man ever cease to be the object of his knowledge and superintendence? Can Infinite Wisdom ever be detached from the Almighty, or can man ever be in a situation where he will not experience the effects of his wise arrangements? Can Goodness ever fail of being an attribute of Jehovah, or can any sentient or intelligent beings exist that do not experience the effects of his bounty? In short, can the relation of *Creature* and of *Creator* ever cease between the human race, in whatever moral or physical situation they may be placed, and that almighty Being, "who giveth to all, life and breath, and all things?" If none of these things can possibly happen, then the relations to which we refer must be eternal and unchangeable, and must form the basis of all the other relations in which we can possibly stand to the Divine Being, either as apostate or as redeemed creatures; and, therefore, they ought to be exhibited as subjects for our frequent and serious contemplation, as religious and moral agents. But, unless we make such topics a distinct subject of attention, and endeavour to acquire a clear and comprehensive conception of our natural relations to God, we can never form a clear conception of those new and interesting relations into which we have been brought by the mediation of Jesus Christ.

If man had continued in his primitive state of integrity, he would have been for ever exercised in tracing the Power, the Beneficence, and other attributes of Deity, in the visible creation alone. Now that his fallen state has rendered additional revelations necessary, in order to secure his happiness—is he completely to throw aside those contemplations and exercises which constituted his chief employment, while he remained a pure moral intelligence? Surely not. One great end of his moral renovation, by means of the Gospel, must be, to enable him *to resume his primitive exercises*, and to qualify him for more enlarged views and contemplations of a similar nature, in that future world, where the physical and moral impediments which now obstruct his progress will be completely removed.

It appears highly unreasonable, and indicates a selfish disposition of mind, to magnify one class of the Divine attributes at the expense of another, to extol, for example, the Mercy of God, and neglect to celebrate his Power and Wisdom—those glorious perfections, the display of which, at the formation of our globe, excited the rapture and admiration of angels, and of innocent man. All the attributes of God are *equal*, because all of them are *infinite;* and, therefore, to talk of *darling* attributes in the Divine Nature, as some have done, is inconsistent with reason, unwarranted by Scripture, and tends to exhibit a distorted view of the Divine character. The Divine mercy ought to be celebrated with rapture by every individual of our fallen race; but with no less rapture should we extol the Divine Omnipotence; for the designs of mercy cannot be accomplished without the intervention of Infinite Power. All that we hope for, in consequence of the promises of God, and of the redemption accomplished by Jesus Christ, must be founded on the conception we form of the operations of Omnipotence. An example or two may not be unnecessary for illustrating this position.

We are warranted, by the sacred oracles, to entertain the hope, that these mortal bodies of ours, after they have mouldered in the dust, been dissolved into their primary elementary parts, and become the prey of devouring reptiles, during a lapse of generations or of centuries,—shall spring forth from the tomb to new life and beauty, and be arrayed in more glorious forms than they now wear; yea, that all the inhabitants of our globe, from Adam to the end of time, though the bodies of thousands of them have been devoured by cannibals, have become the food of fishes and of beasts of prey, and have been burnt to cinders, and their ashes scattered by the winds, over the different regions of sea and land,—shall be reanimated by the voice of the Son of God, and shall appear, each in his proper person and identical body, before God, the Judge of all. Now, the firmness of our hope of so astonishing an event, which seems to contradict all experience, and appears involved in such a mass of difficulties and apparent contradictions, must be in proportion to the sentiments we entertain of the Divine Intelligence, Wisdom, and Omnipotence. And where are we to find the most striking visible displays of these perfections, except in the actual operations of the Creator, within the range of our view in the material world?

Again, we are informed, in the same Divine records, that, at some future period, the earth on which we now dwell shall be wrapt up in devouring flames, and its present form and constitution for ever destroyed; and its redeemed inhabitants, after being released from the grave, shall be transported to a more glorious region; and that "new heavens and a new earth shall appear, wherein dwelleth righteousness." The Divine mercy having given to the faithful the promise of these astonishing revolutions, and most magnificent events, our hopes of their being fully realized must rest on the infinite wisdom and omnipotence of Jehovah; and, consequently, if our views of these perfections be limited and obscure, our hope in relation to our future destiny will be proportionably feeble and languid; and will scarcely perform its office "as an anchor to the soul, both sure and steadfast." It is not merely by telling a person that God is All-wise, and All-powerful, that a full conviction of the accomplishment of such grand events will be produced. He must be made to see with his own eyes what the Almighty *has already done*, and what he is now doing in all the regions of universal nature which lie open to our inspection; and this cannot be effected without directing his contemplations to those displays of intelligence and power which are exhibited in the structure, the economy, and the revolutions of the material world.

If the propriety of these sentiments be admitted, it will follow that the more we are accustomed to contemplate the wonders of Divine intelligence and power, in the objects with which we are surrounded, the more deeply shall we be impressed with a conviction, and a confident hope, that all the purposes of divine mercy will ultimately be accomplished in our eternal felicity. It will also follow, that, in proportion as the mind acquires a clear, an extensive, and a reverential view of the essential attributes of the Deity, and of those truths in connection with them, which are objects of contemplation common to all holy beings, in a similar proportion will it be impressed, and its attention arrested, by every other divine subject connected with them. And it is, doubtless, owing to the want of such clear and impressive conceptions of the essential character of Jehovah, and of the first truths of religion, that the bulk of mankind are so little impressed and influenced by the leading doctrines and duties connected with the plan of the Gospel salvation, and that they entertain so many vague and untenable notions respecting the character and the objects of a superintending Providence. How often, for example, have we witnessed expressions of the foolish and limited notions which are frequently entertained respecting the operations of Omnipotence? When it has been asserted that the earth with all its load of continents and oceans, is in rapid motion through the voids of space—that the sun is ten hundred thousand times larger than the terraqueous globe—and that millions of such globes are dispersed throughout the immensity of nature—some who have viewed themselves as enlightened Christians, have exclaimed at the impossibility of such facts, as if they were beyond the limits of Divine Power, and as if such representations were intended to turn away the mind from God and religion; while, at the same time, they have yielded a firm assent to all the vulgar notions respecting omens, apparitions, and hobgoblins, and to the supposed extraordinary powers of the professors of divination and witchcraft. How can such persons assent, with intelligence and rational conviction, to the dictates of Revelation respecting the energies of Omnipotence which will be exerted at "the consummation of all things," and in those arrangements which are to succeed the dissolution of our sublunary system? A firm belief in the Almighty Power and unsearchable wisdom of God, as displayed in the constitution and movements of the material world, is of the utmost importance, to confirm our faith, and enliven our hopes, of such grand and interesting events.

Notwithstanding the considerations now stated, which plainly evince the connection of the natural perfections of God with the objects of the Christian Revelation, it appears somewhat strange, that, when certain religious instructers happen to come in contact with this topic, they seem as if they were beginning to tread upon forbidden ground; and, as if it were unsuitable to their office as Christian teachers, to bring forward the stupendous works of the Almighty to illustrate his nature and attributes. Instead of expatiating on the numerous sources of illustration, of which the subject admits, till the minds of their hearers are thoroughly affected with a view of the essential glory of Jehovah—they despatch the subject with two or three vague propositions, which, though logically true, make no impression upon the heart; as if they believed that such contemplations were suited only to carnal men, and mere philosophers; and as if they were afraid, lest the sanctity of the pulpit should be polluted by particular descriptions of those operations of the Deity which are perceived through the medium of the corporeal senses. We do not mean to insinuate, that the essential attributes of God, and the illustrations of them derived from the material world, should form the sole, or the chief topics of discussion, in the business of religious instruction—but, if the Scriptures frequently direct our attention to these subjects—if they lie at the foundation of all accurate and extensive views of the Christian Revelation—if they be the chief subjects of contemplation to angels, and all other pure intelligences, in every region of the universe—and if they have a tendency to expand the minds of professed Christians, to correct their vague and erroneous conceptions, and to promote their conformity to the moral character of God—we cannot find out the shadow of a reason, why such topics should be almost, if not altogether, overlooked, in the writings and the discourses of those who profess to instruct mankind in the knowledge of God, and the duties of his worship.

We are informed by our Saviour himself, that "this is life eternal, to know thee the living and true God," as well as "Jesus Christ whom he hath sent." The knowledge of God, in the sense here intended, must include in it the knowledge of the natural and essential attributes of the Deity, or those properties of his nature by which he is distinguished from all "the idols of the nations." Such are, his Self-existence, his All-perfect knowledge, his Omnipresence, his Infinite Wisdom, his Boundless Goodness, and Almighty Power—attributes, which, as we have just now seen, lie at the foundation of all the other characters and relations of Deity revealed in the Scriptures. The acquisition of just and comprehensive conceptions of these perfections, must, therefore, lie at the foundation of all profound veneration of the Divine Being, and of all that is valuable in religion. Destitute of such conceptions, we can neither feel that habitual *humility*, and that *reverence* of the majesty of Jehovah, which his essential glory is calculated to inspire, nor pay him that tribute of adoration and gratitude which is due to his name. Devoid of such views, we cannot exercise that cordial acquiescence in the plan of his redemption, in the arrangements of his providence, and in the requirements of his law, which the Scriptures enjoin. Yet, how often do we find persons who pretend to speculate about the mysteries of the Gospel, displaying—by their flippancy of speech respecting the eternal counsels of the Majesty of Heaven—by their dogmatical assertions respecting the Divine character, and the dispensations of providence—and by their pertinacious opinions respecting the laws by which God *must* regulate his own actions—that they have never felt impressive emotions of the grandeur of that Being, whose "operations are unsearchable, and his ways past finding out?" Though they do not call in question his immensity and power, his wisdom and goodness, as so many abstract properties of his nature, yet the unbecoming familiarity with which they approach this august Being, and talk about him, shows that they have never associated in their minds, the stupendous displays which have been given of these perfections, in the works of his hands; and that their religion (if it may be so called) consists merely in a farrago of abstract opinions, or in an empty name.

If, then, it be admitted, that it is essentially requisite, as the foundation of religion, to have the mind deeply impressed with a clear and comprehensive view of the natural perfections of the Deity, it will follow, that the ministers of religion, and all others whose province it is to communicate religious instruction, ought frequently to dwell, with particularity, on those proofs and illustrations with tend to convey the most definite and impressive conceptions of the glory of that Being whom we profess to adore. But from what sources are such illustrations to be derived? Is it from abstract reasonings and metaphysical distinctions and definitions, or from a survey of those objects and movements which lie open to the inspection of every observer? There can be no difficulty in coming to a decision on this point. We might affirm, with the schoolmen, that "God is a Being whose centre is every where, and his circumference no where;" that "he comprehends infinite duration in every moment;" and that "infinite space may be considered as the *sensorium* of the Godhead;" but such fanciful illustrations, when strictly analyzed, will be found to consist merely of *words* without *ideas*. We might also affirm with truth, that God is a Being of infinite perfection, glory, and blessedness—that he is without all bounds or limits either actual or possible—that he is possessed of power sufficient to perform all things which do not imply a contradiction—that he is independent and self-sufficient—that his wisdom is unerring, and that he infinitely exceeds all other beings. But these, and other expressions of a similar kind, are *mere technical terms*, which convey no adequate, nor even tolerable, notion of what they import. Beings, constituted like man, whose rational spirits are connected with an organical structure, and who derive all their knowledge through the medium of corporeal organs, can derive their clearest and most affecting notions of the Divinity, chiefly through the same medium, namely, by contemplating the *effects* of his perfections, as displayed through the ample range of the visible creation. And to this source of illustration, the inspired writers uniformly direct our views—"Lift up your eyes on high, and behold! who hath created these orbs? who bringeth forth their host by number, and calleth them all by their names? The everlasting God, the Lord, by the greatness of his might, for that he is strong in power."—"He hath made the earth by his power; he hath established the world by his wisdom; he hath stretched out the heavens by his understanding." These writers do not perplex our minds by a multitude of technical terms and subtle reasonings but lead us directly to the source whence our most ample conceptions of Deity are to be derived, that, from a steady and enlightened contemplation of the effects, we may learn the greatness of the Cause; and their example, in this respect, ought, doubtless, to be a pattern for evey religious instructer.

---

## SECTION II.

### *Illustrations of the Omnipotence of the* Deity.

In order to elucidate more distinctly what has been now stated, I shall select a few illustrations of some of the natural attributes of the Deity. And, in the first place, I shall offer a few considerations which have a tendency to direct and to amplify our conceptions of Divine Power.

Omnipotence is that attribute of the Divine Being, by which he can accomplish every thing that does not imply a contradiction—however far it may transcend the comprehension of finite minds. By his power the vast system of universal nature was called from nothing into existence, and is continually supported, in all its movements, from age to age. In elucidating this perfection of God, we might derive some striking illustrations from the records of his dispensations towards man, in the early ages of the world—when he overwhelmed the earth with the deluge, which covered the tops of the highest mountains, and swept the crowded population of the ancient world into a watery grave—when he demolished Sodom and Gomorrah, and the cities around them, with fire from heaven—when he slew all the first-born of Egypt, and turned their rivers into blood—when he divided the Red Sea and the waters of Jordan before the tribes of Israel—when he made the earth to open its jaws and swallow up Korah and all his company—and when he caused Mount Sinai to smoke and tremble at his presence. But these and similar events, however awful, astonishing, and worthy of remembrance, were only *transitory* exertions of Divine Power, and are not calculated, and were never intended, to impress the mind in so powerful a manner as those displays of Omnipotence which are exhibited in the ordinary movements of the material universe. We have no hesitation in asserting, that, with regard to this attribute of the Divinity, there is a more grand and impressive display in the works of Nature, than in all the events recorded in the Sacred History. Nor ought this remark to be considered as throwing the least reflection on the fulness and sufficiency of the Scripture revelation; for that revelation, as having a special reference to a *moral* economy, has for its object to give a more particular display of the *moral* than of the *natural* perfections of God. The miracles to which we have now referred, and every other supernatural fact recorded in the Bible, were not intended so much to display the *plenitude* of the power of Deity, as to bear testimony to the Divine mission of particular messengers, and to confirm the truths they declared. It was not, for example, merely to display the energies of Almighty power, that the waters of the Red Sea were dried up before the thousands of Israel, but to give a solemn and striking attestation to all concerned, that the Most High God had taken this people under his peculiar protection—that he had appointed Moses as their leader and legislator—and that they were bound to receive and obey the statutes he delivered. The most appropriate and impressive illustrations of Omnipotence, are those which are taken from the *permanent* operations of Deity, which are visible every moment in the universe around us; or, in other words, those which are derived from a detail of the facts which have been observed in the material world, respecting *magnitude* and *motion*.

In the first place *the immense quantity of matter* contained in the universe, presents a most striking display of Almighty power.

In endeavouring to form a definite notion on this subject, the mind is bewildered in its conceptions, and is at a loss where to begin or to end its excursions. In order to form something approximating to a well-defined idea, we must pursue a train of thought commencing with those magnitudes which the mind can easily grasp, proceeding through all the intermediate gradations of magnitude, and fixing the attention on every portion of the chain, till we arrive at the object or magnitude of which we wish to form a conception. We must endeavour, in the first place, to form a conception of the bulk of the world in which we dwell, which, though only a point in comparison of the whole material universe, is in reality a most astonishing magnitude, which the mind cannot grasp, without a laborious effort. We can form some definite idea of those protuberate masses we denominate *hills*, which arise above the surface of our plains; but were we transported to the mountainous scenery of Switzerland, to the stupendous range of the Andes in South America, or to the Himmalayan mountains in India, where masses of earth and rocks, in every variety of shape, extend several hundreds of miles in different directions, and rear their projecting summits beyond the region of the clouds—we should find some difficulty in forming an adequate conception of the objects of our contemplation. For, (to use the words of one who had been a spectator of such scenes,) "Amidst those trackless regions of intense silence and solitude, we cannot contemplate, but with feelings of awe and admiration, the enormous masses of variegated matter which lie around, beneath, and above us. The mind labours, as it were, to form a definite idea of those objects of oppressive grandeur, and feels unable to grasp the august objects which compose the surrounding scene." But what are all these mountainous masses, however variegated and sublime, when compared with the bulk of the whole earth? Were they hurled from their bases, and precipitated into the vast Pacific Ocean, they would all disappear in a moment, except perhaps a few projecting tops, which, like a number of small islands, might be seen rising a few fathoms above the surface of the waters.

The earth is a globe whose diameter is nearly 8,000 miles, and its circumference about 25,000, and, consequently, its surface contains nearly two hundred millions of square miles—a magnitude too great for the mind to take in at *one* conception. In order to form a tolerable conception of the whole, we must endeavour to take a leisurely survey of its different parts. Were we to take our station on the top of a mountain, of a moderate size, and survey the surrounding landscape. we, should perceive an extent of view stretching 40 miles in every direction, forming a circle 80 miles in diameter, and 250 in circumference and comprehending an area of 5,000 square miles. In such a situation the terrestrial scene around and beneath us—consisting of hills and plains, towns and villages, rivers and lakes—would form one of the largest objects which the eye, and even the imagination, can steadily grasp at one time. But such an object, grand and extensive as it is, forms no more than the *forty-thousandth part* of the terraqueous globe; so that before we can acquire an adequate conception of the magnitude of our own world, we must conceive 40,000 landscapes of a similar extent, to pass in review before us: and were a scene, of the magnitude now stated, to pass before us every hour, till all the diversified scenery of the earth were brought under our view, and were 12 hours a day allotted for the observation, it would require 9 years and 48 days before the whole surface of the globe could be contemplated, even in this *general* and *rapid* manner. But, such a variety of successive landscapes passing before the eye, even although it were possible to be realized, would convey only a very vague and imperfect conception of the scenery of our world; for objects at the distance of 40 miles cannot be distinctly perceived; the only view which would be satisfactory would be, that which is comprehended within the range of 3 or 4 miles from the spectator.

Again, I have already stated, that the surface of the earth contains nearly 200,000,000 of square miles. Now, were a person to set out on a minute survey of the terraqueous globe, and to travel till he passed along every square mile on its surface, and to continue his route without intermission, at the rate of 30 miles every day, it would require 18,264 years before he could finish his tour, and complete the survey of "this huge rotundity on which we tread:" so that, had he commenced his excursion on the day in which Adam was created, and continued it to the present hour, he would not have accomplished one third part of this vast tour.

In estimating the size and extent of the earth, we ought also to take into consideration the vast variety of objects with which it is diversified, and the numerous animated beings with which it is stored; the great divisions of land and water, the continents, seas, and islands into which it is distributed; the lofty ranges of mountains which rear their heads to the clouds; the unfathomed abysses of the ocean; its vast subterraneous caverns and burning mountains; and the lakes, rivers, and stately forests with which it is so magnificently adorned;—the many millions of animals, of every size and form, from the elephant to the mite, which traverse its surface; the numerous tribes of fishes, from the enormous whale to the diminutive shrimp, which "play" in the mighty ocean; the aerial tribes which sport in the regions above us, and the vast mass of the surrounding atmosphere, which encloses the earth and all its inhabitants as "with a swaddling band." The immense variety of beings with which our terrestrial habitation is furnished, conspires with every other consideration, to exalt our conceptions to that power by which our globe, and all that it contains, were brought into existence.

The preceding illustrations, however, exhibit the vast extent of the earth, considered only as a mere superficies. But we know that the earth is a solid globe, whose specific gravity is nearly five times denser than water, or about twice as dense as the mass of earth and rocks which compose its surface. Though we cannot dig into its bowels beyond a mile in perpendicular depth, to explore its hidden wonders, yet we may easily conceive what a vast and indescribable mass of matter must be contained between the two opposite portions of its external circumference, reaching 8000 miles in every direction. The solid contents of this ponderous ball is no less than 263,858,149,-120 cubical miles—a mass of material substance of which we can form but a very faint and imperfect conception—in proportion to which all the lofty mountains which rise above its surface are less than a few grains of sand, when compared with the largest artificial globe. Were the earth a hollow sphere surrounded merely with an external shell of earth and water, 10 miles thick, its internal cavity would be sufficient to contain a quantity of materials *one hundred and thirty-three times* greater than the whole mass of continents, islands and oceans, on its surface, and the foundations on which they are supported. We have the strongest reasons, however, to conclude, that the earth, in its general structure, is one solid mass, from the surface to the centre, excepting, perhaps, a few caverns scattered here and there amidst its subterraneous recesses: and that its density gradually increases from its surface to its central regions. What an enormous mass of materials, then, is comprehended within the limits of the globe on which we tread! The mind labours, as it were, to comprehend the mighty idea, and after all its exertion, feels itself unable to take in such an astonishing magnitude at *one* comprehensive grasp. How great must be the power of that Being who commanded it to spring from nothing into existence, who "measureth the ocean in the hollow of his hand, who weigheth the mountains in scales, and hangeth the earth upon nothing!"

It is essentially requisite, before proceeding to the survey of objects and magnitudes of a superior order, that we should endeavour, by such a train of thought as the preceding, to form some tolerable and clear conception of the bulk of the globe we inhabit; for it is the only body we can use as a standard of comparison to guide the mind in its conceptions, when it roams abroad to other regions of material existence. And, from what has been now stated, it appears, that we have no *adequate* conception of a magnitude of so vast an extent; or, at least, that the mind cannot, in any one instant, form to itself a distinct and comprehensive idea of it, in any measure corresponding to the reality.

Hitherto, then, we have fixed only on a determinate magnitude—on a scale of a few inches, as it were, in order to assist us in our measurement and conception of magnitudes still more august and astonishing. When we contemplate, by the light of science, those magnificent globes which float around us, in the concave of the sky, the earth with all its sublime scenery, stupendous as it is, dwindles into an inconsiderable ball. If we pass from our globe to some of the other bodies of the planetary system, we shall find that one of these stupendous orbs is more than 900 times the size of our world, and encircled with a ring 200,000 miles in diameter, which would nearly reach from the earth to the moon, and would enclose within its vast circumference several hundreds of worlds as large as ours. Another of these planetary bodies, which appears to the vulgar eye only as a brilliant speck on the vault of heaven, is found to be of such a size, that it would require 1,400 globes of the bulk of the earth to form one equal to it in dimensions. The whole of the bodies which compose the solar system, (without taking the sun and the comets into account,) contain a mass of matter 2,500 times greater than that of the earth. The sun himself is 520 times larger than all the planetary globes taken together; and one million three hundred thousand times larger than the terraqueous globe. This is one of the most glorious and magnificent visible objects, which either the eye or the imagination can contemplate; especially when we consider, what perpetual and incomprehensible and powerful influence he exerts, what warmth and beauty and activity he diffuses, not only on the globe we inhabit, but over the more extensive regions of surrounding worlds. His energy extends to the utmost limits of the planetary system—to the planet Herschel, which revolves at the distance of 1,800 millions of miles from his surface, and there he dispenses light, and colour, and comfort, to all the beings connected with that far-distant orb, and to all the moons which roll around it.

Here the imagination begins to be overpowered and bewildered in its conceptions of magnitude, when it has advanced scarcely a single step in its excursions through the material world: For it is highly probable that all the matter contained within the limits of the solar system, incomprehensible as its magnitude appears, bears a smaller proportion to the whole mass of the material universe, than a single grain of sand to all the particles of matter contained in the body of the sun and his attending planets.

If we extend our views from the solar system to the starry heavens, we have to penetrate, in our imagination, a space which the swiftest ball that was ever projected, though in perpetual motion, would not traverse in ten hundred thousand years. In those trackless regions of immensity, we behold an assemblage of resplendent globes, similar to the sun in size and in glory, and, doubtless, accompanied with a retinue of worlds, revolving, like our own, around their attractive influence. The immense distance at which the nearest stars are known to be placed, proves that they are bodies of a prodigious size, not inferior to our sun, and that they shine, not by reflected rays, but by their own native light. But bodies encircled with such refulgent splendour would be of little use in the economy of Jehovah's empire, unless surrounding worlds were cheered by their benign influence, and enlightened by their beams. Every star is, therefore, with good reason, concluded to be a sun, no less spacious than ours, surrounded by a host of planetary globes, which revolve around it as a centre, and derive from it light, and heat, and comfort. Nearly a thousand of these luminaries may be seen in a clear winter night, by the naked eye; so that a mass of matter equal to a thousand solar systems, or to *thirteen hundred and twenty millions of globes of the size of the earth*, may be perceived, by every common observer, in the canopy of heaven. But all the celestial orbs which are perceived by the unassisted sight, do not form the eighty-thousandth part of those which may be descried by the help of optical instruments. The telescope has enabled us to descry, in certain spaces of the heavens, thousands of stars where the naked eye could scarcely discern twenty. The late celebrated astronomer, Dr. Herschel, has informed us, that, in the most crowded parts of the Milky-way, when exploring that region with his best glasses, he has had fields of view which contained no less than 588 stars, and these were continued for many minutes: so that "in one quarter of an hour's time there passed no less than *one hundred and sixteen thousand stars* through the field of view of his telescope."

It has been computed, that nearly *one hundred millions* of stars might be perceived by the most perfect instruments, were all the regions of the sky thoroughly explored. And yet, all this vast assemblage of suns and worlds, when compared with what lies beyond the utmost boundaries of human vision, in the immeasurable spaces of creation, may be no more than as the smallest particle of vapour to the immense ocean. Immeasurable regions of space lie beyond the utmost limits of mortal view, into which even imagination itself can scarcely penetrate, and which are, doubtless, replenished with the operations of Divine Wisdom and Omnipotence. For, it cannot be supposed, that a being so diminutive as man, whose stature scarcely exceeds six feet—who vanishes from the sight at the distance of a league—whose whole habitation is invisible from the nearest star—whose powers of vision are so imperfect, and whose mental faculties are so limitted—it cannot be supposed that man, who "dwells in tabernacles of clay, who is crushed before the moth," and chained down, by the force of gravitation, to the surface of a small planet,—should be able to descry the utmost boundaries of the empire of Him who fills immensity, and dwells in "light unapproachable." That portion of his dominions, however which lies within the range of our view, presents such a scene of magnificence and grandeur, as must fill the mind of every reflecting person with astonishment and reverence, and constrain him to exclaim, "Great is our Lord, and of great power, his understanding is infinite."—"When I consider the heavens, the work of thy fingers, the moon and the stars which thou hast ordained—what is man that thou art mindful of him!"—"I have heard of thee by hearing of the ear;" I have listened to subtle disquisitions on thy character and perfections, and have been but little affected, "but now the eye *seeth* thee; wherefore I humble myself, and repent in dust and ashes."

In order to feel the full force of the impression made by such contemplations, the mind must pause at every step, in its excursions through the boundless regions of material existence: for it is not by a mere attention to the figures and numbers by which the magnitudes of the great bodies of the universe are expressed, that we arrive at the most distinct and ample conceptions of objects so grand and overwhelming. The mind, in its intellectual range, must dwell on every individual scene it contemplates, and on the various objects of which it is composed,

It must add scene to scene, magnitude to magnitude, and compare smaller objects with greater—a range of mountains with the whole earth, the earth with the planet Jupiter, Jupiter with the sun, the sun with a thousand stars, a thousand stars with 80 millions, and 80 millions with all the boundless extent which lies beyond the limits of mortal vision; and, at every step of this mental process, sufficient time must be allowed for the imagination to expatiate on the objects before it, till the ideas approximate, as near as possible, to the reality. In order to form a comprehensive conception of the extent of the terraqueous globe, the mind must dwell on an extensive landscape, and the objects with which it is adorned; it must endeavour to survey the many thousands of diversified landscapes which the earth exhibits—the hills and plains, the lakes and rivers and mountains, which stretch in endless variety over its surface—it must dive into the vast caverns of the ocean—penetrate into the subterraneous regions of the globe, and wing its way amidst clouds and tempests, through the surrounding atmosphere. It must next extend its flight through the most expansive regions of the solar system, realizing, in imagination, those magnificent scenes which can be described neither by the naked eye nor by the telescope, and comparing the extent of our sublunary world with the more magnificent globes that roll around us. Leaving the sun and all his attendant planets behind, till they have diminished to the size of a small twinkling star, it must next wing its way to the starry regions, and pass from one system of worlds to another, from one Nebulæ* to another, from one region of Nebulæ to another, till it arrive at the utmost boundaries of creation which human genius has explored. It must also endeavour to extend its flight beyond all that is visible by the best telescopes, and expatiate at large in that boundless expanse into which no human eye has yet penetrated, and which is, doubtless, replenished with other worlds, and systems, and firmaments, where the operations of infinite power and beneficence are displayed in endless variety, throughout the illimitable regions of space.

Here, then, with reverence, let us pause, and wonder! Over all this vast assemblage of material existence, God presides. Amidst the diversified objects and intelligences it contains, he is eternally and essentially present. By his unerring wisdom, all its complicated movements are directed. By his Almighty fiat, it emerged from nothing into existence, and is continually supported from age to age. "HE SPAKE AND IT WAS DONE; HE COMMANDED AND IT STOOD FAST."—"By the word of the Lord were the heavens made, and all the host of them by the spirit of his mouth." What an astonishing display of Divine power is here exhibited to our view! How far transcending all finite comprehension must be the energies of Him who only "spake and it was done;" who only gave the command, and this mighty system of the universe, with all its magnificence, started into being! The infinite ease with which this vast fabric was reared, leads us irresistibly to conclude, that there are powers and energies in the Divine mind which have never yet been exerted, and which may unfold themselves to intelligent beings, in the production of still more astonishing and magnificent effects, during an endless succession of existence. That man who is not impressed with a venerable and overwhelming sense of the power and majesty of Jehovah, by such contemplations, must have a mind incapable of ardent religious emotions, and unqualified for appreciating the grandeur of that Being "whose kingdom ruleth over all." And shall such ennobling views be completely withheld from a Christian audience? Shall it be considered as a matter of mere indifference, whether their views of the Creator's works be limited to the sphere of a few miles around them, or extended to ten thousand worlds?—whether they shall be left to view the operations of the Almighty throughout eternity past and to come, as confined to a small globe placed in the immensity of space, with a number of brilliant studs fixed in the arch of heaven, at a few miles distance; or as extending through the boundless dimensions of space?—whether they shall be left to entertain no higher idea of the Divine majesty than what may be due to one of the superior orders of the seraphim or cherubim,—or whether they shall be directed to form the most august conceptions of the King eternal, immortal, and invisible, corresponding to the displays he has given of his glory in his visible works? If it be not, both reason and piety require, that such illustrations of the Divine perfections should occasionally be exhibited to their view.

In the next place, the *rapid motions* of the great bodies of the universe, no less than their magnitudes, display the Infinite Power of the Creator.

We can acquire accurate ideas of the relative velocities of moving bodies, only by comparing the motions with which we are familiar, with one another, and with those which lie beyond the general range of our minute inspection. We can acquire a pretty accurate conception of the velocity of a ship impelled by the wind—of a steamboat—of a race-horse—of a bird darting through the air—of an arrow flying from a bow—and of the clouds when impelled by a stormy wind. The velocity of a ship is from 8 to 12 miles an hour—of a race-horse, from 20 to 30 miles—of a bird, say from 50 to 60 miles, and of the clouds, in a violent hurricane, from 80 to 100 miles an hour. The motion of a ball from a

* For an account of the *Nebulæ*, see Ch. II. Art. *Astronomy*.

loaded cannon is incomparably swifter then any of the motions now stated; but of the velocity of such a body we have a less accurate idea; because, its rapidity being so great, we cannot trace it distinctly by the eye through its whole range, from the mouth of the cannon to the object against which it is impelled. By experiments, it has been found, that its rate of motion is from 480 to 800 miles in an hour, but it is retarded every moment, by the resistance of the air and the attraction of the earth. This velocity, however, great as it is, bears no sensible proportion to the rate of motion which is found among the celestial orbs. That such enormous masses of matter should move at all, is wonderful; but when we consider the amazing velocity with which they are impelled, we are lost in astonishment. The planet Jupiter, in describing his circuit round the sun, moves at the rate of 29,000 miles an hour. The planet Venus, one of the nearest and most brilliant of the celestial bodies, and about the same size as the earth, is found to move through the spaces of the firmament at the rate of 76,000 miles an hour, and the planet Mercury with a velocity of no less than 150,000 miles an hour, or 1750 miles in a minute—a motion two hundred times swifter than that of a cannon ball.

These velocities will appear still more astonishing, if we consider the magnitude of the bodies which are thus impelled, and the immense forces which are requisite to carry them along in their courses. However rapidly a ball flies from the mouth of a cannon, it is the flight of a body only a *few inches* in diameter; but one of the bodies, whose motion has been just now stated, is *eighty-nine thousand miles* in diameter, and would comprehend, within its vast circumference, more than a thousand globes as large as the earth. Could we contemplate such motions, from a fixed point, at the distance of only a few hundreds of miles from the bodies thus impelled—it would raise our admiration to its highest pitch, it would overwhelm all our faculties, and, in our present state, would produce an impression of awe, and even of terror, beyond the power of language to express. The earth contains a mass of matter equal in weight to at least 2,200,000,000,000,000,000,000 tons, supposing its mean density to be only about 2½ times greater than water. To move this ponderous mass a single inch beyond its position, were it fixed in a quiescent state, would require a mechanical force almost beyond the power of numbers to express. The physical force of all the myriads of intelligences within the bounds of the planetary system, though their powers were far superior to those of men, would be altogether inadequate to the production of such a motion. How much more must be the force requisite to impel it with a velocity one hundred and forty times swifter than a cannon ball, or 68,000 miles an hour, the actual rate of its motion, in its course round the sun! But whatever degree of mechanical power would be requisite to produce such a stupendous effect, it would require a force one hundred and fifty times greater to impel the planet Jupiter, in his actual course through the heavens! Even the planet Saturn, one of the slowest moving bodies of our system, a globe 900 times larger than the earth, is impelled through the regions of space at the rate of 22,000 miles an hour, carrying along with him two stupendous rings, and seven moons larger than ours, through his whole course round the central luminary. Were we placed within a thousand miles of this stupendous globe, (a station which superior beings may occasionally occupy,) where its hemisphere, encompassed by its magnificent rings, would fill the whole extent of our vision—the view of such a ponderous and glorious object, flying with such amazing velocity before us, would infinitely exceed every idea of grandeur we can derive from terrestrial scenes, and overwhelm our powers with astonishment and awe. Under such an emotion, we could only exclaim, "GREAT AND MARVELLOUS ARE THY WORKS, LORD GOD ALMIGHTY!" The ideas of *strength* and *power* implied in the impulsion of such enormous masses of matter through the illimitable tracts of space, are forced upon the mind with irresistible energy, far surpassing what any abstract propositions or reasonings can convey; and constrain us to exclaim, "Who is a strong Lord like unto thee! Thy right hand is become glorious in power! the Lord God omnipotent reigneth!"

If we consider the *immense number* of bodies thus impelled through the vast spaces of the universe—the rapidity with which the *comets*, when near the sun, are carried through the regions they traverse,—if we consider the high probability, if not absolute certainty, that the sun, with all his attendant planets and comets, is impelled with a still greater degree of velocity towards some distant region of space, or around some wide circumference—that all the thousands of systems of that nebulæ to which the sun belongs, are moving in a similar manner—that all the nebulæ in the heavens are moving around some magnificent central body—in short, that all the suns and worlds in the universe are in rapid and perpetual motion, as constituent portions of one grand and boundless empire, of which Jehovah is the Sovereign—and, if we consider still further, that all these mighty movements have been going on, without intermission, during the course of many centuries, and some of them, perhaps, for myriads of ages before the foundations of our world were laid—it is impossible for the human mind to form any adequate idea of the stupendous forces which are in incessant operation thoughout the unlimited empire of the Almighty. To estimate such mechanical force even in a single instance, completely baffles the mathematician's skill, and sets the power of numbers at defiance. "Language," and figures, and comparisons, are "lost in wonders so sublime," and the mind, overpowered with such reflections, is irresistibly led upwards, to search for the cause in that OMNIPOTENT BEING who upholds the pillars of the universe—the thunder of whose power none can comprehend. While contemplating such august objects, how emphatic and impressive appears the language of the sacred oracles, "Canst thou by searching find out God? Canst thou find out the Almighty to perfection? Great things doth he, which we cannot comprehend. Thine, O Lord, is the greatness, and the glory, and the majesty; for all that is in heaven and earth is thine. Among the gods there is none like unto thee, O Lord, neither are there any works like unto thy works. Thou art great, and dost wondrous things; thou art God alone. Hast thou not known, hast thou not heard, that the everlasting God, the Lord, the Creator of all things, fainteth not, neither is weary? there is no searching of his understanding. Let all the earth fear the Lord, let all the inhabitants of the world stand in awe of him; for, he *spake*, and *it was done;* he commanded, and it stood fast."

Again, the *immense spaces* which surround the heavenly bodies, and in which they perform their revolutions, tend to expand our conceptions on this subject, and to illustrate the magnificence of the Divine operations. In whatever point of view we contemplate the scenery of the heavens, an idea of grandeur irresistibly bursts upon the mind; and, if empty space can, in any sense, be considered as an object of sublimity, nothing can fill the mind with a grander idea of magnitude and extension, than the amplitude of the scale on which planetary systems are constructed. Around the body of the sun there is allotted a cubical space, 3,600 millions of miles in diameter, in which eleven planetary globes revolve—every one being separated from another, by intervals of many millions of miles. The space which surrounds the utmost limits of our system, extending in every direction, to the nearest fixed stars, is, at least, 40,000,000,000,000 miles in diameter; and, it is highly probable, that every star is surrounded by a space of equal, or even of greater extent. A body impelled with the greatest velocity which art can produce, a cannon ball, for instance would require twenty years to pass through the space that intervenes between the earth and the sun, and four millions, seven hundred thousand years, ere it could reach the nearest star. Though the stars seem to be crowded together in clusters, and some of them almost to touch one another, yet the distance between any two stars which seem to make the nearest approach, is such as neither words can express, nor imagination fathom. These immense spaces are as unfathomable on the one hand, as the magnitude of the bodies which move in them, and their prodigious velocities, are incomprehensible on the other; and they form a part of those magnificent proportions according to which the fabric of universal nature was arranged—all corresponding to the majesty of that infinite and incomprehensible Being, "who measures the ocean in the hollow of his hand, and meteth out the heavens with a span." How wonderful that bodies at such prodigious distances should exert a mutual influence on one another! that the moon at the distance of 240,000 miles should raise tides in the ocean, and currents in the atmosphere! that the sun, at the distance of ninety-five millions of miles, should raise the vapours, move the ocean, direct the course of the winds, fructify the earth, and distribute light, and heat, and colour, through every region of the globe; yea, that his attractive influence, and fructifying energy, should extend even to the planet Herschel, at the distance of eighteen hundred millions of miles! So that, in every point of view in which the universe is contemplated, we perceive the same *grand scale* of operation by which the Almighty has arranged the provinces of his universal kingdom.

We would now ask, in the name of all that is sacred, whether such magnificent manifestations of Deity ought to be considered as irrelevant in the business of religion, and whether they ought to be thrown completely into the shade, in the discussions which take place in religious topics, in "the assemblies of the saints?" If religion consists in the intellectual apprehension of the perfections of God, and in the moral effects produced by such an apprehension—if all the rays of glory emitted by the luminaries of heaven, are only so many reflections of the grandeur of Him who dwells in light unapproachable—if they have a tendency to assist the mind in forming its conceptions of that ineffable Being, whose uncreated glory cannot be directly contemplated—and if they are calculated to produce a sublime and awful impression on all created intelligences,—shall we rest contented with a less glorious idea of God than his works are calculated to afford? Shall we disregard the works of the Lord, and contemn "the operations of his hands," and that, too, in the face of all the invitations on this subject, addressed to us from heaven? For thus saith Jehovah: "Lift up your eyes on high, and behold, who hath created these things, who bringeth forth their host by number. I, the Lord, who maketh all things, who stretcheth forth the heavens alone, and spread abroad the earth by himself; all their host have I commanded." And, if, at the command of God, we lift up our eyes to the "firmament of his power," surely we ought to do it, not with a brute, unconscious gaze," not with the vacant stare of a savage, not as if we were still enveloped with the mists and prejudices of the dark ages—but as surrounded by that blaze of light which modern science has thrown upon the scenery of the sky, in order that we may contemplate, with fixed attention, all that enlightened reason, aided by the nicest observations, has ascertained respecting the magnificence of the celestial orbs. To overlook the sublime discoveries of modern times, to despise them, or to call in question their reality, as some religionists have done, because they bring to our ears such astonishing reports of the "eternal power" and majesty of Jehovah—is to act as if we were afraid lest the Deity should be represented as more grand and magnificent than he really is, and as if we would be better pleased to pay him a less share of homage and adoration than is due to his name.

Perhaps some may be disposed to insinuate, that the views now stated are above the level of ordinary comprehension, and founded too much on scientific considerations, to be stated in detail to a common audience. To any insinuations of this kind, it may be replied, that such illustrations as those to which we have referred, are more easily comprehended than many of those abstract discussions to which they are frequently accustomed; since they are definite and tangible, being derived from those objects which strike the senses and the imagination. Any person of common understanding may be made to comprehend the leading ideas of extended space, magnitude, and motion, which have been stated above, provided the descriptions be sufficiently simple, clear, and well-defined; and should they be at a loss to comprehend the principles on which the conclusions rest, or the mode by which the magnificence of the works of God has been ascertained, an occasional reference to such topics would excite them to inquiry and investigation, and to the exercise of their powers of observation and reasoning on such subjects—which are too frequently directed to far less important objects. The following illustration, however, stands clear of every objection of this kind, and is level to the comprehension of every man of common sense: Either the earth moves round its axis once in twenty-four hours—or, the sun, moon, planets, comets, stars, and the whole frame of the universe move round the earth, in the same time. There is no alternative, or third opinion, that can be formed on this point. If the earth revolve on its axis every 24 hours, to produce the alternate succession of day and night, the portions of its surface about the equator must move at a rate of more than a thousand miles an hour, since the earth is more than twenty-four thousand miles in circumference. This view of the fact, when attentively considered, furnishes a most sublime and astonishing idea. That a globe of so vast dimensions, with all its load of mountains, continents, and oceans, comprising within its circumference a mass of two hundred and sixty-four thousand million of cubical miles, should whirl around with so amazing velocity, gives us a most august and impressive conception of the greatness of that Power which first set it in motion, and continues the rapid whirl from age to age! Though the huge masses of the Alpine mountains were in a moment detached from their foundations, carried aloft through the regions of the air, and tossed into the Mediterranean sea, it would convey no idea of a force equal to that which is every moment exerted, if the earth revolve on its axis. But should the motion of our earth be called in question, or denied, the idea of force, or power, will be indefinitely increased. For, in this case, it must necessarily be admitted, that the heavens, with all the innumerable host of stars, have a diurnal motion around the globe; which motion must be inconceivably more rapid than that of the earth, on the supposition of its motion. For, in proportion as the celestial bodies are distant from the earth, in the same proportion would be the rapidity of their movements. The sun, on this supposition, would move at the rate of 414,000 miles in a minute; the nearest stars, at the rate of fourteen hundred millions of miles in a *second:* and the most distant luminaries, with a degree of swiftness which no numbers could express.* Such velocities, too, would be the rate of motion, not merely of a single globe like the earth, but of all the ten thousand times ten thousand spacious globes that exist within the boundaries of creation. This view conveys an idea of power still more august and overwhelming than any of the views already stated, and we dare not presume to assert, that such a degree of physical force is beyond the limits of infinite perfection; but on the supposition it existed, it would confound all our ideas of the wisdom and intelligence of the Divine mind, and would appear altogether inconsistent with the character which the scripture gives us of the Deity as "the only wise God." For, it would exhibit a stupendous system of means altogether disproportioned to the end intended—namely, to produce the alternate succession of day and night to the inhabitants of our globe, which is more beautifully and harmoniously effected by a simple rotation on its axis, as is the case with the other globes which compose the planetary system. Such considerations, however, show us, that, on whatever hypothesis, whether on the vulgar or the scientific, or in whatever other point of view, the frame of nature may be contemplated, the mind is irresistibly impressed with ideas of power, grandeur, and magnificence. And, therefore, when an inquiring mind is directed to contemplate the works of God, on any hypothesis it may choose, it has a tendency to rouse reflection, and to stimulate the exercise of the moral and intellectual faculties, on objects which are worthy of the dignity of immortal minds.

* See Appendix, No. 1.

We may now be, in some measure, prepared to decide, whether illustrations of the omnipotence of the Deity, derived from the system of the material world, or those vague and metaphysical disquisitions which are generally given in theological systems, be most calculated to impress the mind, and to inspire it with reverence and adoration. The following is a description, given of this attribute of God, by a well-known systematic writer, who has generally been considered as a judicious and orthodox divine :—

"God is almighty, Rev. i. 18, chap. iv. 8. This will evidently appear, in that, if he be infinite in all his other perfections, he must be so in power: thus, if he be omniscient, he knows what is possible or expedient to be done ; and if he be an infinite sovereign, he wills whatever shall come to pass. Now this knowledge would be insignificant, and his power inefficacious, were he not infinite in power, or almighty. Again, this might be argued from his justice, either in rewarding or punishing : for if he were not infinite in power, he could do neither of these, at least so far as to render him the object of that desire or fear, which is agreeable to the nature of these perfections ; neither could infinite faithfulness accomplish all the promises which he hath made, so as to excite that trust and dependence which is a part of religious worship ; nor could he say without limitation, as he does, *I have spoken it, I will also bring it to pass ; I have purposed it, I will also do it ;* Isa. xlvi. 11. But since power is visible in, and demonstrated by its effect, and infinite power by those effects which cannot be produced by a creature, we may observe the almighty power of God in all his works, both of nature and grace : thus his eternal power is understood, as the apostle says, *By the things that are made*, Rom. i. 20, not that there was an eternal production of things, but the exerting this power in time proves it to be infinite and truly divine ; for no creature can produce the smallest particle of matter out of nothing, much less furnish the various species of creatures with those endowments in which they excel one another, and set forth their Creator's glory. And the glory of his power is no less visible in the works of providence, whereby he upholds all things, disposes of them according to his pleasure, and brings about events which only he who has an almighty arm can effect."—*Ridgley's Body of Divinity*, p. 39.

This is the whole that Dr. Ridgley judges it necessary to state, in illustration of the attribute of Omnipotence, except what he says in relation to its operation "in the work of grace," in "the propagation and success of the Gospel," &c. subjects, to which the idea of power, or physical energy, does not properly apply. Such, however, are the meager and abstract disquisitions generally given by most systematic writers. There is a continual play on the term "infinite," which to most minds conveys no idea at all, unless it be associated with ample conceptions of motion, magnitude, and extension ; and it is constantly applied to subjects to which it was never intended to apply, such as "infinite faithfulness, infinite justice, infinite truth," &c. an application of the term which is never sanctioned by Scripture, and which has a tendency to introduce confusion into our conceptions of the perfections of God. Granting that the statements and reasonings in such an extract as the above were unquestionable, yet what impression can they make upon the mind ? Would an ignorant person feel his conceptions of the Divinity much enlarged, or his moral powers aroused, by such vague and general statements ? And, if not, it appears somewhat unaccountable, that those sources of illustration, which would convey the most ample and definite views of the "eternal power" and glory of God, should be studiously concealed from the view. Vague descriptions and general views of any object will never be effectual in awakening the attention, and arresting the faculties of the mind. The heart will always remain unimpressed, and the understanding will never be thoroughly excited in its exercise, unless the intellect have presented before it a well-defined and interesting object, and be enabled to survey it in its various aspects · and this object must always have a relation to the material world, whether it be viewed in connexion with religion, or with any other subject.

---

Thus I have endeavoured, in the preceding sketches, to present a few detached illustrations of the omnipotence and grandeur of the Deity, as displayed in the vast magnitude of the material universe—the stupendous velocities of the celestial bodies—and in the immeasurable regions of space which surround them, and in which their motions are performed. Such a magnificent spectacle as the fabric of the universe presents—so majestic, God-like, and overwhelming, to beings who dwell "in tabernacles of clay"—was surely never intended to be overlooked, or to be gazed at with indifference, by creatures endowed with reason and intelligence, and destined to an immortal existence. In forming a universe composed of so many immense systems and worlds, and replenished with such a variety of sensitive and intelligent existences, the Creator doubtless intended that it should make a sublime and reverential impression on the minds of all the intellectual beings to whom it might be displayed, and that it should convey some *palpable* idea of the infinite glories of his nature, in so far as material objects can be supposed to adumbrate the perfections of a spiritual and uncreated Essence. Dwelling in "light inaccessible" to mortals, and for ever veiled from the highest created being, by the pure spirituality and immensity of his natu there is no conceivable mode by which the infinite grandeur of Deity could be exhibited to finite intelligences, but through the medium of those magnificent operations which are incessantly going forward throughout the boundless regions of space. Concealed from the gaze of all the "principalities and powers" in heaven, in the unfathomable depths of his Essence, he displays his presence in the universe he has created, and the glory of his power, by launching magnificent worlds into existence, by adorning them with diversified splendours, by peopling them with various ranks of intelligent existence, and by impelling them in their movements through the illimitable tracts of creation.

It will readily be admitted by every enlightened Christian, that it must be a highly desirable attainment, to acquire the most glorious idea of the Divine Being which the limited capacity of our minds is capable of receiving. This is one of the grand difficulties in religion. The idea of a Being purely IMMATERIAL, yet pervading infinite space, and possessed of no sensible qualities, confounds and bewilders the human intellect, so that its conceptions, on the one hand, are apt to verge towards extravagancy, while, on the other, they are apt to degenerate into something approaching to inanity. Mere abstract ideas and reasonings respecting infinity, eternity, and absolute perfection, however sublime we may conceive them to be, completely fail in arresting the understanding, and affecting the heart; our conceptions become vague, empty, and confused, for want of a material vehicle to give them order, stability, and expansion. Something of the nature of vast extension, of splendid and variegated objects, and of mighty movements, is absolutely necessary, in order to convey to spirits dwelling in bodies of clay, a definite conception of the invisible glories of the Eternal Mind; and, therefore, in the immense variety of material existence with which the universe is adorned, we find every requisite assistance of this kind to direct and expand our views of the great object of our adoration. When the mind is perplexed and overwhelmed with its conceptions, when it labours, as it were, to form some well-defined conceptions of an Infinite Being, it here finds some tangible objects on which to fix, some sensible *substratum* for its thoughts to rest upon for a little, while it attempts to penetrate, in its excursions, into those distant regions which eye hath not seen, and to connect the whole of its mental survey with the energies of the "King, Eternal, Immortal, and Invisible.

To such a train of thought we are uniformly directed in the sacred oracles, where Jehovah is represented as describing himself by the *effects* which his power and wisdom have produced. "Israel shall be saved in the Lord with an everlasting salvation. For thus saith Jehovah that created the heavens; God himself that formed the earth and made it; he hath established it, he created it not in vain, he formed it to be inhabited; I am the Lord, and there is none else."—"I have made the earth and created man upon it, my hands have stretched out the heavens, and all their host have I commanded."—"Hearken unto me, O Israel: I am the first, I also am the last. Mine hand also hath laid the foundation of the earth, and my right hand hath spanned the heavens: when I call unto them, they stand up together."—"Who hath measured the waters in the hollow of his hand, and meted out heaven with the span, and weighed the mountains in scales? He who sitteth upon the circle of the earth, and the inhabitants thereof are as grasshoppers; that stretched out the heavens as a curtain, that fainteth not, neither is weary."—"The Lord made the heavens, the heaven of heavens, with all their hosts; honour and majesty are before him, and his kingdom ruleth over all."* Such sublime descriptions of Jehovah, and references to his material works, are reiterated in every portion of the sacred volume; and the import and sublimity of such expressions cannot be fully appreciated, unless we take into view all the magnificent objects which science has unveiled in the distant regions of creation.

This subject is calculated not merely to overpower the intellect with ideas of sublimity and grandeur, but also to produce a deep *moral* impression upon the heart; and a Christian philosopher would be deficient in his duty, were he to overlook this tendency of the objects of his contemplation.

One important moral effect which this subject has a natural tendency to produce, is, profound HUMILITY. What an insignificant being does man appear, when he compares himself with the magnificence of creation, and with the myriads of exalted intelligences with which it is peopled! What are all the honours and splendours of this earthly ball, of which mortals are so proud, when placed in competition with the resplendent glories of the skies? Such a display as the Almighty has given of himself, in the magnitude and variety of his works, was evidently intended "to stain the pride" of all human grandeur, that "no flesh should glory in his presence." Yet, there is no disposition that appears so prominent among puny mortals, as pride, ambition, and vainglory —the very opposite of humility, and of all those tempers which become those "who dwell in tabernacles of clay, and whose foundation is in the dust." Even without taking into account the state of man as a *depraved* intelligence, what is there in his situation that should inspire him with "lofty looks," and induce him to look down on his fellow-men with supercilious contempt? He derived his origin from the dust, he is allied with the beasts that perish, and he is fast hastening to the grave, where his carcass

* Isa. xlv 10, 12. xlviii, 12, 13. xl. 12, 22, &c.

will become the food for noisome reptiles. He is every moment dependent on a Superior Being for every pulse that beats, and every breath he draws, and for all that he possesses; he is dependent even on the meanest of his species for his accommodations and comforts. He holds every enjoyment on the most precarious tenure,—his friends may be snatched in a moment from his embrace; his riches may take to themselves wings and fly away; and his health and beauty may be blasted in an hour, by a breath of wind. Hunger and thirst, cold and heat, poverty and disgrace, sorrow and disappointment, pain and disease, mingle themselves with all his pursuits and enjoyments. His knowledge is circumscribed within the narrowest limits, his errors and follies are glaring and innumerable; and he stands as an almost undistinguishable atom, amidst the immensity of God's works. Still, with all these powerful inducements to the exercise of humility, man dares to be proud and arrogant.

——— ———" Man, proud Man,
Dressed in a little brief authority,
Plays such fantastic tricks before high Heaven,
As make the angels weep."

How affecting to contemplate the warrior, flushed with diabolical pride, pursuing his conquests through heaps of slain, in order to obtain possession of "a poor pitiable speck of perishing earth;" exclaiming in his rage, "I will pursue, I will overtake, I will divide the spoil, my lust shall be satisfied upon them, I will draw my sword, my hand shall destroy them"—to behold the man of rank glorying in his wealth, and his empty titles, and looking around upon the inferior orders of his fellow-mortals as the worms of the dust—to behold the man of ambition pushing his way through bribery, and treachery, and slaughter, to gain possession of a throne, that he may look down with proud pre-eminence upon his fellows—to behold the haughty airs of the noble dame, inflated with the idea of her beauty, and her high birth, as she struts along, surveying the ignoble crowd as if they were the dust beneath her feet—to behold the smatterer in learning, puffed up with a vain conceit of his superficial acquirements, when he has scarcely entered the porch of knowledge—in fine, to behold all ranks, from the highest to the lowest, big with an idea of their own importance, and fired with pride and revenge at the least provocation, whether imaginary or real! How inconsistent the manifestations of such tempers, with the many humiliating circumstances of our present condition, and with the low rank which we hold in the scale of Universal Being?

It is not improbable, that there are in the universe intelligences of a superior order, in whose breasts pride never found a place—to whom this globe of ours, and all its inhabitants, appear as inconsiderable as a drop of water filled with microscopic animalculæ, does to the proud lords of this earthly region. There is at least *one* Being to whom this sentiment is applicable, in its utmost extent:—" Before Him all nations are as a drop of a bucket, and the inhabitants of the earth as grasshoppers; yea, they are as nothing, and are counted to him less than nothing, and vanity." Could we wing our way, with the swiftness of a seraph, from sun to sun, and from world to world, till we had surveyed all the systems visible to the naked eye, which are only as a mere speck in the map of the universe—could we, at the same time, contemplate the glorious landscapes and scenes of grandeur they exhibit—could we also mingle with the pure and exalted intelligences which people those resplendent abodes, and behold their humble and ardent adorations of their Almighty Maker, their benign and condescending deportment towards one another; "each esteeming another better than himself," and all united in the bonds of the purest affection, without one haughty or discordant feeling—what indignation and astonishment would seize us, on our return to this obscure corner of creation, to behold beings enveloped in the mist of ignorance, immersed in depravity and wickedness, liable to a thousand accidents, exposed to the ravages of the earthquake, the volcano and the storm; yet proud as Lucifer, and glorying in their shame! We should be apt to view them, as we now do those bedlamites, who fancy themselves to be kings, surrounded by their nobles, while they are chained to the walls of a noisome dungeon. "Sure pride was never made for man." How abhorrent, then, must it appear in the eyes of superior beings, who have taken an expansive range through the field of creation? How abhorrent it is in the sight of the Almighty, and how amiable is the opposite virtue, we learn from his word:—" Every one that is proud in heart is an abomination to the Lord."—" God resisteth the proud, but giveth grace to the humble."—" Thus saith the High and Lofty One who inhabiteth eternity, I dwell in the high and holy place; with him also that is of an humble and contrite spirit; to revive the spirit of the humble, and the heart of the contrite ones."—While, therefore, we contemplate the omnipotence of God, in the immensity of creation, let us learn to cultivate humility and self-abasement. This was one of the lessons which the pious Psalmist deduced from his survey of the nocturnal heavens. When he beheld the moon walking in the brightness, and the innumerable host of stars, overpowered with a sense of his own insignificance, and the greatness of divine condescension, he exclaimed, "O Lord! what is man, that thou art mindful of him, or the son of man, that thou shouldest visit him!"

Again, this subject is also calculated to inspire us with REVERENCE and VENERATION of God. Profound veneration of the Divine Being lies at the foundation of all religious worship and obedience. But, in order to venerate God aright, we must know him; and, in order to acquire the true knowledge of him, we must contemplate him throught the medium of those works and dispensations, by which he displays the glories of his nature to the inhabitants of our world. I have already exhibited a few specimens of the stupendous operations of his power, in that portion of the system of the universe which lies open to our inspection; and there is surely no mind in which the least spark of piety exists, but must feel strong emotions of reverence and awe, at the thought of that Almighty and Incomprehensible Being, who impels the huge masses of the planetary globes with so amazing a rapidity through the sky, and who has diversified the voids of space with so vast an assemblage of magnificent worlds. Even those manifestations of Deity which are confined to the globe we inhabit, when attentively considered, are calculated to rouse even the unthinking mind, to astonishment and awe. The lofty mountains, and expansive plains, the mass of water in the mighty ocean, the thunders rolling along the sky, the lightnings flashing from cloud to cloud, the hurricane and the tempest, the volcano vomiting rivers of fire, and the earthquake shaking kingdoms, and levelling cities with the ground—all proclaim the Majesty of Him, by whom the elements of nature are arranged and directed, and seem to address the sons of men in language like this: "The Lord reigneth, he is clothed with majesty; at his wrath the earth trembles; a fire goeth before him, and burneth up his enemies."—"Let all the earth fear the Lord, let all the inhabitants of the world stand in awe of him."

There is one reason, among others, why the bulk of mankind feel so little veneration of God, and that is, that they seldom contemplate, with fixed attention, "the operations of his hands." If we wish to cherish this sublime sentiment in our hearts, we must familiarize our minds to frequent excursions over all those scenes of Creation and Providence, which the volume of nature, and the volume of inspiration unfold to view. We must endeavour to assist our conceptions of the grandeur of these objects, by every discovery which has been or may yet be made, and by every mode of illustration by which a sublime and comprehensive idea of the particular object of contemplation may be obtained. If we would wish to acquire some definite, though imperfect, conception of the physical extent of the universe, our minds might be assisted by such illustrations as the following:—Light flies from the sun with a velocity of nearly two hundred thousand miles in a moment of time, or, about 1,400,000 times swifter than the motion of a cannon ball: Suppose that one of the highest order of intelligences is endowed with a power of rapid motion superior to that of light, and with a corresponding degree of intellectual energy; that he has been flying without intermission, from one province of creation to another, for six thousand years, and will continue the same rapid course for a thousand millions of years to come; it is highly probable, if not absolutely certain, that, at the end of this vast tour, he would have advanced no further than "the suburbs of creation"—and that all the magnificent systems of material and intellectual beings he had surveyed, during his rapid flight, and for such a length of ages, bear no more proportion to the whole Empire of Omnipotence, than the smallest grain of sand does to all the particles of matter of the same size contained in ten thousand worlds. Nor need we entertain the least fear, that the idea of the extent of the Creator's power, conveyed by such a representation, exceeds the bounds of reality. On the other hand, it must fall almost infinitely short of it. For, as the poet has justly observed—

"Can man *conceive beyond what* God can *do*?"

Were a seraph, in prosecuting the tour of creation in the manner now stated, ever to arrive at a limit beyond which no farther displays of the Divinity could be perceived, the thought would overwhelm his faculties with unutterable anguish and horror: he would feel, that he had now, in some measure, comprehended all the plans and operations of Omnipotence, and that no farther manifestation of the Divine glory remained to be explored. But we may rest assured, that this can never happen in the case of any created intelligence. We have every reason to believe, both from the nature of an Infinite Being, and from the vast extent of creation already explored, that the immense mass of material existence, and the endless variety of sensitive and intellectual beings with which the universe is replenished, are intended by Jehovah to present to his rational offspring a *shadow*, an *emblem*, or a *representation*, (in so far as finite extended existence can be a representation,) of the *Infinite Perfections* of his nature, which would otherwise have remained for ever impalpable to all subordinate intelligence.

In this manner, then, might we occasionally exercise our minds on the grand and diversified objects which the universe exhibits; and in proportion as we enlarge the sphere of our contemplations, in a similar proportion will our views of God himself be extended, and a corresponding sentiment of veneration impressed upon the mind. For the soul of man cannot venerate a mere abstract being, that was never manifested through a sensible medium, however many lofty terms may be used to describe his perfections. It venerates that Ineffable Being, who conceals himself behind the scenes of Creation, through the medium of the visible displays he exhibits of his Power, Wisdom, and Beneficence, in the Economy of Nature, and in the Records of Revelation. Before the universe was formed Jehovah existed alone, possessed of every attribute which he now displays. But, had only one solitary intelligence been created, and placed in the infinite void, without a material substratum beneath and around him, he could never have been animated with a sentiment of profound veneration for his Creator; because no objects existed to excite it, or to show that his Invisible Maker was invested with those attributes which he is now known to possess. Accordingly, we find, in the sacred writings, that, when a sentiment of reverence is demanded from the sons of men, those sensible objects which are calculated to excite the emotion, are uniformly exhibited. "Fear ye not me? saith the Lord. Will ye not tremble at my presence? who have placed the sand for the bound of the sea, by a perpetual decree, that it cannot pass it; and though the waves thereof toss themselves, yet they cannot prevail; though they roar, yet can they not pass over it." "Who would not fear thee, O King of nations? Thou art the true God, and an everlasting King. Thou hast made the earth by thy power, thou hast established the world by thy wisdom, thou hast stretched out the heavens by thy discretion. When thou utterest thy voice, there is a noise of waters in the heavens, thou causest the vapours to ascend from the ends of the earth, thou makest lightnings with rain, and bringest forth the winds out of thy treasures."*

But, however enlarged and venerable conceptions of God we may derive from the manifestations of his power, they must fall infinitely short of what is due to a being of boundless perfection. For there may be attributes in the Divine Essence, of which we cannot possibly form the least conception—attributes which cannot be shadowed forth or represented by any portion of the material or intellectual world yet discovered by us, or by all the mighty achievements by which human redemption was effected—attributes which have not been yet displayed, in their effects, to the highest orders of intelligent existence. And, therefore, as that excellent philosopher and divine, the honourable Mr. Boyle, has well observed—"Our ideas of God, however so great, will rather express the greatness of our veneration, then the Immensity of his perfections; and the notions worthy of the most intelligent men are far short of being worthy the incomprehensible God—the brightest idea we can frame of God being infinitely inferior, and no more than a *Parhelion*† in respect of the sun; for though that meteor is splendid, and resembles the sun, yet it resides in a cloud, and is not only much beneath the sun in distance, but inferior in bigness and splendour."

* Jerem. x. 7—13.

† A *Parhelion* or *Mock-Sun*, is a meteor in the form of a very bright light, appearing on one side of the sun, and somewhat resembling the appearance of that luminary. This phenomenon is supposed to be produced by the refraction and reflection of the sun's rays from a watery cloud. Sometimes three or four of these parhelia, all of them bearing a certain resemblance to the real sun, have been seen at one time.

In short, were we habitually to cherish that profound veneration of God which his works are calculated to inspire, with what humility would we approach the presence of this august Being! with what emotions of awe would we present our adorations! and with what reverence would we talk of his inscrutable purposes, and incomprehensible operations! We would not talk about him, as some writers have done, with the same ease and indifference, as a mathematician would talk about the properties of a triangle, or a philosopher about the effects of a mechanical engine; nor would we treat, with a spirit of levity, any of the solemn declarations of his word, or the mighty movements of his providence. We would be ever ready to join with ardour in the sublime devotions of the inspired writers, "Great and marvellous are thy works, Lord God Almighty, just and true are thy ways, thou King of saints. Who would not fear thee, O Lord, and glorify thy name? Let all the earth fear the Lord, let all the inhabitants of the world stand in awe of him."

Lastly, the views we have taken of the omnipotence and grandeur of the Deity are calculated to *inspire us with* HOPE *and* CONFIDENCE *in the prospect of that eternal existence which lies before us.* The period of our existence in this terrestrial scene will soon terminate, and those bodies through which we now hold a correspondence with the visible creation, be crumbled into dust. The gradual decay, and the ultimate dissolution of human bodies, present a scene at which reason stands aghast; and, on a cursory survey of the chambers of the dead, it is apt to exclaim, in the language of despair, "Can these dry bones live?" A thousand difficulties crowd upon the mind, which appear repugnant to the idea that "beauty shall again spring out of the ashes, and life out of the dust." But, when we look abroad to the displays of Divine power and intelligence, in the wide expanse of Creation, we perceive that

——————"Almighty God
Has done much more; nor is his arm impaired
Through length of days. And what he can, he will
His faithfulness stands bound to see it done."

We perceive that he has created systems in such vast profusion, that no man can number them. The worlds every moment under his superintendence and direction, are unquestionably far more numerous than all the human beings who have hitherto existed, or will yet exist till the close of time. And, if he has not only arranged the general features of each of these worlds, and established the physical laws, by which its economy is regulated, but has also arranged the diversified circumstances, and directs the minutest movements of the myriads of sensitive and intellectual existences it contains, we ought never for a moment to doubt, that the minutest particles of every human body, however widely separated from each other and mingled with other extraneous substances, are known to him whose presence pervades all space; and that all the atoms requisite for the construction of the Resurrection body will be reassembled for this purpose "by the energy of that mighty power, whereby he is able to subdue all things to himself." If we suppose that a number of human beings, amounting to three hundred thousand millions, shall start from the grave into new life, at the general resurrection, and that the atoms of each of these bodies are just now under the special superintendence of the Almighty—and that at least an equal number of worlds are under his particular care and direction—the exertion of power and intelligence, in the former case, cannot be supposed to be greater that what is requisite in the latter. To a Being possessed of infinite Power, conjoined with boundless Intelligence, the superintendence of countless atoms, and of countless worlds, is equally easy, where no contradiction is implied. For as the poet has well observed,—

> "He summons into being, with like ease,
> A whole creation, and a single grain."

And since this subject tends to strengthen our hope of a resurrection from the dead, it is also calculated to inspire us with confidence in the prospect of those eternal scenes which will burst upon the view, at the dissolution of all terrestrial things. Beyond the period fixed for the conflagration of this world, "a wide and unbounded prospect lies before us;" and though, at present, "shadows, clouds, and darkness rest upon it," yet the boundless magnificence of the Divine empire which science has unfolded, throws a radiance over the scenes of futurity, which is fraught with consolation in the view of "the wreck of matter and the crush of worlds." It opens to us a prospect of perpetual improvement in knowledge and felicity; it presents a field in which the human faculties may be for ever expanding, for ever contemplating new scenes of grandeur rising to the view, in boundless perspective, through an interminable succession of existence. It convinces us that the happiness of the eternal state will not consist in an unvaried repetition of the same perceptions and enjoyments, but that new displays of the Creator's glory will be continually bursting on the astonished mind, world without end. And as we know the same beneficence and care which are displayed in the arrangement of systems of worlds, are also displayed in supporting and providing for the smallest microscopic animalculæ, we have no reason to harbour the least fear, lest we should be overlooked in the immensity of creation, or lost amidst the multiplicity of those works among which the Deity is incessantly employed; for, as he is Omnipresent and Omniscient, his care and influence must extend to every creature he has formed. Therefore, though "the elements shall melt with fervent heat, and the earth, and all the works therein be dissolved, yet we, according to his promise, look for new heavens and a new earth, wherein dwelleth righteousness."

---

## SECTION III.

*On the Wisdom and Intelligence of the* Deity.

In surveying the system of nature with a Christian and a Philosophic eye, it may be considered in different points of view. It may be viewed either as displaying the power and magnificence of the Deity in the immense quantity of materials of which it is composed, and in the august machinery and movements by which its economy is directed;—or, as manifesting his Wisdom in the nice adaptation of every minute circumstance to the end it was intended to accomplish;—or as illustrating his unbounded beneficence in the provision which is made for the accommodation and happiness of the numerous tribes of sentient and intelligent beings it contains. Having, in the preceding section, endeavured to exhibit some of those objects which evince the Omnipotence of Deity, and the pious emotions they are calculated to excite, I shall now offer a few popular illustrations of Divine Wisdom, as displayed in the arrangements of the material world—which shall chiefly be confined to those objects which are most prominent and obvious to the vulgar eye.

*Wisdom* is that perfection of an intelligent agent, by which he is enabled to select and employ the most proper means in order to accomplish a good and important end. It includes the idea of knowledge or intelligence, but may be distinguished from it. Knowledge is opposed to ignorance, wisdom is opposed to folly or error in conduct. As applied to God, it may be considered as comprehending the operations of his Omniscience and benevolence, or, in other words, his knowledge to discern, and his disposition to choose those means and ends which are calculated to promote the order and the happiness of the universe.

The Wisdom of God is, doubtless, displayed in every arrangement he has made throughout all the provinces of his immense and eternal kingdom, however far they may be removed from the sphere of human observation. But it is only in those parts of the system of nature which lie open to our particular investigation, that the traces of this perfection can be distinctly perceived. The *Heavens* declare the glory of God's Wisdom, as well as of his Power. The planetary system—that portion of the heavens with which we are best acquainted—displays both the magnificence and the skill of its Divine Author, in the magnitudes, distances, revolutions, proportions, and uses of the various globes of which it is composed, and in the diversified apparatus by which light and darkness are alternately distributed. The sun, an immense luminous world, by far the largest body in the system, is placed in the centre. No other position would have suited for an equable distribution of illumination and heat through the different parts of the system. Around him, at different distances, eleven primary planets revolve, accompanied with eighteen secondaries, or moons, —all in majestic order and harmony, no one interrupting the movements of another, but invariably keeping the paths prescribed them, and performing their revolutions in their appointed times. To all these revolving globes, the sun dispenses motion, light, heat, fertility, and other unceasing energies, for the comfort and happiness of their respective inhabitants—without which, perpetual sterility, eternal winter, and eternal night, would reign over every region of our globe, and throughout surrounding worlds.

The distance at which the heavenly bodies, particularly the sun, are placed from the earth, is a manifest evidence of Divine Wisdom. If the sun were much nearer us than he is at present, the earth, as now constituted, would be wasted and parched with excessive heat; the waters would be turned into vapour, and the rivers, seas, and oceans, would soon disappear, leaving nothing behind them but frightful barren dells and gloomy caverns; vegetation would completely cease, and the tribes of animated nature languish and die. On the other hand, were the sun much farther distant than he now is, or were his bulk, or the influence of his rays, diminished one half of what they now are, the land and the ocean would soon become one frozen mass, and universal desolation and sterility would overspread the fair face of nature, and, instead of a pleasant and comfortable abode, our globe would become a frightful desert, a state of misery and perpetual punishment.* But herein is the wisdom of God displayed, that he has formed the sun of such a determinate size, and placed it at such a convenient distance, as not to annoy, but to refresh and cheer us, and to enliven the soil with its genial influence; so that we plainly perceive, to use the language of the prophet, that "He hath established the world by his wisdom, and stretched out the heavens by his understanding."

* It forms no objection to these remarks, that *caloric*, or the matter of *heat*, does not altogether depend upon the direct influence of the solar rays. The substance of caloric may be chiefly connected with the constitution of the globe we inhabit. But still, it is quite certain that the earth, *as presently constituted*, would suffer effects most disastrous to sentient beings, were it removed much nearer to, or much farther from the central luminary. Those planets which are removed several hundreds of millions of miles farther from the sun than our globe, may possibly experience a degree of heat much greater then ours; but, in this case, the constitution of the solid parts of these globes, and of their surrounding atmospheres, must be very different from what obtains in the physical arrangements of our globe.

The rotation of the several planetary globes around their axis, to produce the alternate succession of day and night, strikingly demonstrates the wisdom and benevolence of their great Author. Were the earth and the other planetary worlds destitute of a diurnal motion, only one half of their surfaces could be inhabited, and the other half would remain a dark and cheerless desert. The sun woud be the only heavenly orb which would be recognized by the inhabitants of each respective world, as existing in the universe; and that scene of grandeur which night unfolds in the boundless expanse of the sky, would be for ever veiled from their view. For, it appears to be one grand design of the Creator, in giving these bodies a diurnal motion, not only to cheer their inhabitants with light and warmth, and the gay colouring produced by the solar rays, but also to open to them a prospect of other portions of his vast dominions, which are dispersed in endless variety throughout the illimitable regions of space; in order that they may acquire a more sublime impression of the glory of his kingdom, and of his eternal Power and Godhead. But, were perpetual day to irradiate the planets, it would throw an eternal and impenetrable veil over the glories of the sky, behind which, the magnificent operations of Jehovah's power would be, in a great measure, concealed. It is this circumstance which we should consider as the principal reason why a rotatory motion has been impressed on the planetary globes; and not merely that a curtain of darkness might be thrown around their inhabitants, during the repose of sleep, as in the world in which we dwell. For in some of the other planetary worlds belonging to our system, the intelligent beings with which they are peopled may stand in no need of that nocturnal repose which is necessary for man; their physical powers may be incapable of being impaired, and their mental energies may be in perpetual exercise. And in some of those bodies which are surrounded with an assemblage of rings and moons, as the planet Saturn, the diversified grandeur of their celestial phenomena, in the absence of the sun, may present a scene of contempation and enjoyment, far more interesting than all the splendours of their noon-day. Besides, had the planets no motion round their axis, and were both their hemispheres supposed to be peopled with inhabitants, their physical state and enjoyments would be as opposite to each other, as if they lived under the government of two distinct independent beings. While the one class was basking under the splendours of perpetual day, the other would be involved in all the horrors of an everlasting night. While the one hemisphere would be parched with excessive heat the other would be bound in the fetters of eternal ice; and, in such a globe as ours, the motion of the tides, the ascent of the vapours, the currents of the atmosphere, the course of the winds, the benign influences of the rains and dews, and a thousand other movements which produce so many salutary and beneficial effects, would be completely deranged. Hence we find that in all the planetary bodies on which observations can conveniently be made, a rotatory motion actually exists, in the secondary, as well as in the primary planets, and even in the sun himself, the centre, and the mover of the whole: in which arrangement of the Almighty Creator, the evidences of wisdom and design are strikingly apparent.

This amazing scene of Divine workmanship and skill, which the planetary system exhibits, we nave reason to believe, is multiplied, and diversified, to an indefinite extent, throughout all the other systems of creation, displaying to the intelligences of every region, "the manifold wisdom of God." For there can be no question, that every star we now behold, either by the naked eye, or by the help of a telescope, is the centre of a system of planetary worlds, where the agency of God, and his unsearchable wisdom, may be endlessly varied, and, perhaps, more strikingly displayed than even in the system to which we belong. These vast globes of light could never have been designed merely to shed a few glimmering rays on our far-distant world; for the ten-thousandth part of them has never yet been seen by the inhabitants of the earth, since the Mosaic creation, except by a few astronomers of the past and the present age; and the light of many of them, in all probability, has never yet reached us; and perhaps never will, till the period of "the consummation of all terrestrial things." They were not made in vain; for such a supposition would be inconsistent with every idea we can form of the attributes of a Being of infinite perfection. They were not intended merely to diversify the voids of infinite space with a useless splendour, which has no relation to intellectual natures; for this would give us a most distorted and inconsistent idea of the character of Him who is "the only-wise God;" and we are told, by an authority which cannot be questioned, that "by his wisdom he made the heavens, and stretched them out by his understanding." The only rational conclusion, therefore, which can be deduced, is that they are destined to distribute illumination and splendour, vivifying influence, and happiness, among incalculable numbers of intelligent beings, of various degrees of physical, moral, and intellectual excellence. And, wherever the Creator has exerted his Almighty energies in the production of sensitive and intellectual natures, we may rest assured, that there also his infinite wisdom and intelligence, in an endless variety of arrangements, contrivances, and adaptations, are unceasingly displayed.

But, after all, whatever evidences of contrivance and design the celestial globes may exhibit, it is not in the heavens that the most striking displays of Divine *wisdom* can be traced by the inhabitants of our world. It is only a few *general relations* and adaptations that can be distinctly perceived among the orbs of the firmament; though, in so far as we are able to trace the purposes which they subserve, the marks of beauty, order, and design are uniformly apparent. But we are placed at too great a distance from the orbs of heaven, to be able to investigate the particular arrangements which enter into the physical and moral economy of the celestial worlds. Were we transported to the surface of the planet Jupiter, and had an opportunity of surveying, at leisure, the regions of that vast globe, and the tribes of sensitive and intellectual existence which compose its population—of contemplating the relations of its moons to the pleasure and comfort of its inhabitants—the constitution of its atmosphere as to its reflective and refractive powers, in producing a degree of illumination to compensate for the great distance of that planet from the sun—its adaptation to the functions of animal life—the construction of the visual organs of its inhabitants, and the degree of sensibility they possess corresponding to the quantity of light received from the sun—the temperature of the surface and atmosphere of this globe corresponding to its distance from the central source of heat, and to the physical constitution of sensitive beings—in short, could we investigate the relations which inanimate nature, in all its varieties and sublimities, bears to the necessities and the happiness of the animated existences that traverse its different regions, we should, doubtless, behold a scene of Divine Wisdom and intelligence, far more admirable and astonishing that even that which is exhibited in our sublunary world. But since it is impossible for us to investigate the economy of other worlds, while we are chained down to this terrestrial sphere, we must direct our attention to those arrangements and contrivances in the constitution of our own globe, which lie open to our particular inspection, in order to perceive more distinctly the benevolent designs of Him "in whom we live and move, and have our being." And here an attentive observer will find, in almost every object, when minutely examined, a display of goodness and intelligence, which will constrain him to exclaim, "Oh the depth of the riches both of the wisdom and the knowledge of God."

Wisdom, considered as consisting in contrivance, or the selection of the most proper means in order to accomplish an important end, may be exemplified and illustrated in a variety of familiar objects in the scene of nature.

The *earth* on which we tread was evidently intended by the Creator to support man and other animals, along with their habitations, and to furnish those vegetable productions which are necessary for their subsistence; and, accordingly, he has given it that exact degree of consistency which is requisite for these purposes. Were it much harder than it now is; were it, for example, as dense as a rock, it would be incapable of cultivation, and vegetables could not be produced from its surface. Were it softer, it would be insufficient to support us, and we should sink at every step, like a person walking in a quagmire. Had this circumstance not been attended to in its formation, the earth would have been rendered useless as a habitable world, for all those animated beings which now traverse its surface. The exact adjustment of the solid parts of our globe to the nature and necessities of the beings which inhabit it, is, therefore, an instance and an evidence of *Wisdom*.

The *diversity of surface* which it every where presents, in the mountains and vales with which it is variegated, indicates the same benevolent contrivance and design. If the earth were divested of its mountains, and its surface every where uniformly smooth, there would be no rivers, springs, or fountains; for water can flow only from a higher to a lower place; the vegetable tribes would droop and languish; man and other animals would be deprived of what is necessary for their existence and comfort; we should be destitute of many useful stones, minerals, plants, and trees, which are now produced on the surface, and in the interior of mountains; the sea itself would become a stagnant marsh, or overflow the land; and the whole surface of nature in our terrestrial sphere would present an unvaried scene of dull uniformity. Those picturesque and sublime scenes which fire the imagination of the poet, and which render mountainous districts so pleasing to the philosophic traveller, would be completely withdrawn; and all around, when compared with such diversified landscapes, would appear as fatiguing to the eye as the vast solitudes of the Arabian deserts, or the dull monotony of the ocean. But in consequence of the admirable distribution of hills and mountains over the surface of our globe, a variety of useful and ornamental effects is produced. Their lofty summits are destined by providence to arrest the vapours which float in the regions of the air; their internal cavities form so many spacious basins for the reception of waters distilled from the clouds; they are the original sources of springs and rivers, which water and fertilize the earth; they form immense magazines, in which are deposited stones, metals, and minerals, which are of so essential service in the arts that promote the comfort of human life; they serve for the production of a vast variety of herbs and trees; they arrest the progress of storms and tempests; they afford shelter and entertainment to various animals which minister to the wants of mankind: in a word, they adorn and embellish the face of nature—they form thousands of sublime and beautiful landscapes, and afford from their summits the most delightful prospects of the plains below. All these circumstances demonstrate the consummate wisdom of the Great Architect of nature, and lead us to conclude, that mountains, so far from being rude excrescences of nature, as some have asserted, form an essential part in the constitution, not only of our globe, but of all habitable worlds. And this conclusion is confirmed, so far as our observation extends, with regard to the moon, and several of the planetary bodies which belong to our system, whose surfaces are found to be diversified by sublime ramifications of mountain scenery; which circumstance forms one collateral proof, among many others, that they are the abodes of sentient and intellectual beings.

Again, the *colouring* which is spread over the face of nature indicates the wisdom of the Deity. It is essential to the present mode of our existence, and it was evidently intended by the Creator, that we should be enabled easily to recognize the forms and properties of the various objects with which we are surrounded. But were the objects of nature destitute of colour, or were the same unvaried hue spread over the face of creation, we should be destitute of all the entertainments of vision, and be at a loss to distinguish one object from another. We should be unable to distinguish rugged precipices from fruitful hills; naked rocks from human habitations; the trees from the hills that bear them, and the tilled from the untilled lands. "We should hesitate to pronounce whether an adjacent enclosure contained a piece of pasturage, a plot of arable land, or a field of corn; and it would require a little journey, and a minute investigation, to determine such a point. We could not determine whether the first person we met were a solder in his regimentals, or a swain in his Sunday suit; a bride in her ornaments, or a widow in her weeds." Such would have been the aspect of nature, and such the inconveniences to which we should have been subjected, had God allowed us light, without the distinction of colours. We could have distinguished objects only by intricate trains of reasoning, and by circumstances of time, place, and relative position. And, to what delays and perplexities should we have been reduced, had we been obliged every moment to distinguish one thing from another by reasoning! Our whole life must then have been employed rather in study than in action; and, after all, we must have remained in eternal uncertainty as to many things which are now quite obvious to every one as soon as he opens his eyes. We could neither have communicated our thoughts by writing, nor have derived instruction from others through the medium of books: so that we should now have been almost as ignorant of the transactions of past ages, as we are of the events which are passing in the planetary worlds; and, consequently, we could never have enjoyed a written revelation from heaven, nor any other infallible guide to direct us in the path to happiness, is the Almighty had not distinguished the rays of light, and painted the objects around us with a diversity of colours,—so essentially connected are the minutest, and the most magnificent works of Deity. But now, in the present constitution of things, colour characterizes the class to which every individual belongs, and indicates, upon the first inspection, its respective quality. Every object wears its peculiar livery, and has a distinguishing mark by which it is characterized.

The different hues which are spread over the scenery of the world, are also highly ornamental to the face of nature, and afford a variety of pleasures to the eye and the imagination. It is this circumstance which adds a charm to the fields, the valleys, and the hills, the lofty mountain, the winding river, and the expansive lake; and which gives a splendour and sublimity to the capacious vault of heaven. Colour is, therefore, an essential requisite to every world inhabited by sensitive beings; and we know, that provision has been made for diffusing it throughout all the globes which may exist in the distant regions which our telescopes have penetrated; for the light which radiates from the most distant stars is capable of being separated into the prismatic colours, similar to those which are produced by the solar rays; which furnishes a presumptive proof that thay are intended to accomplish designs in their respective spheres analogous to those which light subserves in our terrestrial habitation—or, in other words, that they are destined to convey to the minds of sentient beings, impressions of light and colour, and consequently, beings susceptible of such impressions must reside within the sphere, or more immediate influence of these far-distant orbs.

The same benevolent design is apparent in the *general colour which prevails throughout the scene of sublunary nature.* Had the fields been clothed with hues of a deep red, or a brilliant white, the eye would have been dazzled with the splendour of their aspect. Had a dark-blue or a black colour generally prevailed, it would have cast a universal gloom over the face of nature. But an agreeable green holds the medium between these two extremes, equally remote from a dismal gloom and excessive splendour, and bears such a relation to the structure of the eye, that it refreshes, instead of tiring it, and supports, instead of diminishing its force. At the same time, though one general colour prevails over the landscape of the earth, it is diversified by an admirable variety of shades, so that every individual object in the vegetable world can be accurately distinguished from another; thus producing a beautiful and variegated appearance over the whole scenery of nature. "Who sees not in all these things that the hand of the Lord hath wrought this?"

If from the earth we turn our attention to the *waters*, we shall perceive similar traces of the exquisite wisdom and skill of the Author of nature. Water is one of the most essential elementary parts in the constitution of our globe, without which the various tribes of beings which now people it could not exist. It supplies a necessary beverage to man, and to all the animals that people the earth and the air. It forms a solvent for a great variety of solid bodies; it is the element in which an infinitude of organized beings pass their existence; it acts an important part in conveying life and nourishment to all the tribes of the vegetable kingdom, and gives salubrity to the atmospherical regions. Collected in immense masses in the basins of the sea, it serves as a vehicle for ships, and as a medium of communication between people of the most distant lands. Carried along with a progressive motion over the beds of streams and of rivers, it gives a brisk impulse to the air, and prevents the unwholesome stagnation of vapours; it receives the filth of populous cities, and rids them of a thousand nuisances. By its impulsion it becomes the mover of a multitude of machines; and, when rarefied into steam, it is transformed into one of the most powerful and useful agents under the dominion of man. All which beneficial effects entirely depend on the exact degree of density, or specific gravity, which the Creator has given to its constituent parts. Had it been much more rarified than it is, it would have been altogether unfit to answer the purposes now specified; the whole face of the earth would have been a dry and barren waste; vegetable nature could not have been nourished; our floating edifices could not have been supported; the lightest bodies would have sunk, and all regular intercourse with distant nations would have been prevented. On the other hand, had its parts been much denser than they are; for example, had they been of the consistency of a thin jelly, similar disastrous effects would have inevitably followed; no ships could have ploughed the ocean; no refreshing beverage would have been supplied to the animal tribes; the absorbent vessels of trees, herbs, and flowers would have been unable to imbibe, the moisture requisite for their nourishment; and we should thus have been deprived of all the beneficial effects we now derive from the use of that liquid element, and of all the diversified scenery of the vegetable world. But the configuration and consistency of its parts are so nicely adjusted to the constitution of the other elements, and to the wants of the sensitive and vegetable tribes, as exactly to subserve the ends intended in the system of nature.

Water has been ascertained to be a compound body formed by the union of two different kinds of air—oxygen and hydrogen. It has the property of becoming, in certain cases, much lighter than air; though, in its natural liquid state, it is 800 times heavier than that fluid; and has also the property of afterwards resuming its natural weight. Were it not for this property, evaporation could not be produced; and, consequently, no clouds, rain, nor dew, could be formed, to water and fertilize the different regions of the earth. But, in consequence of this wonderful property, the ocean becomes an inexhaustible cistern to our world. From its expansive surface are exhaled those vapours which supply the rivers, and nourish the vegetable productions of every land. "The air and the sun," says an elegant writer, "constitute the mighty engine which works without intermission to raise the liquid treasure; while the clouds serve as so many aqueducts to convey them along the atmosphere, and distribute them, at seasonable periods, and in regular proportions, through all the regions of the globe."

Notwithstanding the properties now stated, *motion was still requisite*, to ensure all the advantages we now derive from the liquid element. Had the whole mass of waters been in a stagnant state, a thousand inconveniences and disastrous consequences would have inevitably ensued. But the All-wise Creator has impressed upon its various masses a circulating motion, which preserves its purity, and widely extends its beneficial influence. The rills pour their liquid stores into the rivers; the rivers roll their watery treasures into the ocean; the waters of the ocean, by a libratory motion, roll backwards and forwards every twelve hours, and, by means of currents, and the force of winds, are kept in constant agitation. By the solar heat, a portion of these waters is carried up into the atmosphere, and, in the form of clouds, is conveyed by the winds over various regions; till, at last, it descends in rain and dew, to supply the springs "which run among the hills." So that there is a constant motion and circulation of the watery element, that it may serve as an agent for carrying forward the various processes of nature, and for ministering to the wants of man and beast.

In fine, were the waters in a state of perpetual stagnation, the filth of populous cities would be accumulated to a most unwholesome degree; the air would be filled with putrid exhalations; and the vegetable tribes would languish and die. Were they deprived of the property of being evaporated, (in which state they occupy a space 1400 times greater than in their liquid state,) rain and dew could never be produced, and the earth would be turned into "a dry and parched wilderness;" neither grass nor corn could be sufficiently dried to lay up for use; *our clothes, when washed, could never be dried*; and a variety of common operations, which now conduce to our convenience and comfort, could never be carried on. But the infinite wisdom of the Creator, foreseeing all the effects which can possibly arise from these principles of nature, has effectually provided against such disasters, by arranging all things, in number, weight and measure, to subserve the beneficial ends for which they were ordained. "He causeth the vapours to ascend from the ends of the earth; he sendeth the springs into the valleys, which run among the hills. They give drink to every beast of the field; the wild asses quench their thirst. By them the fowls of heaven are refreshed, which sing among the branches. He watereth the hills from his chambers, and the earth is satisfied with the the fruit of his works."

Let us now attend to the *atmosphere*, in the constitution of which the wisdom of God is no less conspicuous than in the other departments of nature.

The atmosphere is one of the most essential appendages to the globe we inhabit, and exhibits a most striking scene of Divine skill and omnipotence. The term *atmosphere* is applied to the whole mass of fluids, consisting of air, vapours, electric fluid, and other matters, which surround the earth to a certain height. This mass of fluid matter gravitates to the earth, revolves with it in its diurnal rotation, and is carried along with it in its course round the sun every year. It has been computed to extend about 45 miles above the earth's surface, and it presses on the earth with a force proportioned to its height and density. From experiments made by the barometer, it has been ascertained, that it presses with a weight of about 15 pounds on every square inch of the earth's surface; and, therefore, its pressure on the body of a middle-sized man, is equal to about 32,000 lbs. or 14 tons avoirdupois, a pressure which would be insupportable, and even fatal, were it not equal in every part, and counterbalanced by the spring of the air within us. The pressure of the whole atmosphere upon the earth, is computed to be equivalent to that of a globe of lead 60 miles in diameter, or about 5,000,000,000,000,000 tons; that is, the whole mass of air which surrounds the globe, compresses the earth with a force or power equal to that of *five thousand millions of millions of tons.* * This amazing pressure is however, essentially necessary for the preservation of the present constitution of our globe, and of the animated beings which dwell on its surface. It prevents the heat of the sun from converting water, and all other fluids on the face of the earth, into vapour; and preserves the vessels of all organized beings in due tone and vigour. Were the atmospherical pressure entirely removed, the elastic fluids contained in the finer vessels of men and other animals, would inevitably burst them, and life would become extinct;† and most

* See Appendix, No. II.

† The necessity of the atmospherical pressure, for the comfort and preservation of animal life, might be illustrated by the effects experienced by those who have ascended to the summits of very high mountains, or who have been carried to a great height above the surface of the earth in balloons

of the substances on the face of the earth, particularly liquids, would be dissipated into vapour.

The atmosphere is now ascertained to be a compound substance, formed of two very different ingredients, termed *oxygen* and *nitrogen gas*. Of 100 measures of atmospheric air, 21 are oxygen, and 79 nitrogen. The one, namely, oxygen, is the principle of combustion, and the vehicle of heat, and is absolutely necessary for the support of animal life, and is the most powerful and energetic agent in nature. The other is altogether incapable of supporting either flame or animal life. Were we to breathe oxygen air, without any mixture or alloy, our animal spirits would be raised, and the fluids in our bodies would circulate with greater rapidity; but we should soon infallibly perish by the rapid and unnatural accumulation of heat in the animal frame. If the nitrogen were extracted from the air, and the whole atmosphere contained nothing but oxygen, or vital air, combustion would not proceed in that gradual manner which it now does, but with the most dreadful and irresistible rapidity: not only wood and coals, and other substances now used for fuel, but even stones, iron, and other metallic substances, would blaze with a rapidity which would carry destruction through the whole expanse of nature. If even the proportions of the two airs were materially altered, a variety of pernicious effects would instantly be produced. If the oxygen were less in quantity then it now is, fire would lose its strength, candles would not diffuse a sufficient light, and animals would perform their vital functions with the utmost difficulty and pain. On the other hand, ware the nitrogen diminished, and the oxygen increased, the air taken in by respiration would be more stimulant, and the circulation of the animal fluids would become accelerated; but the tone of the vessels thus stimulated to increased action would be destroyed by too great an excitement, and the body would inevitably waste and decay. Again, were the oxygen completely extracted from the atmosphere, and nothing but nitrogen remained, fire and flame would be extinguished, and instant destruction would be carried throughout all the departments of vegetable and animated nature. For a lighted taper will not burn for a single moment in nitrogen gas, and if an animal be plunged into it, it is instantly suffocated.

Again, not only the extraction of any one of the component parts of the atmosphere, or the alteration of their respective proportions, but even the slightest increase or diminution of their *specific gravity*, would be attended with the most disastrous effects. The nitrogen is found to be a little lighter than common air, which enables it to rise towards the higher regions of the atmosphere. In breathing, the air which is evolved from the lungs, at every expiration, consists chiefly of nitrogen, which is entirely unfit to be breathed again, and therefore rises above our heads before the next inspiration.—Now, had nitrogen, instead of being a little lighter, been a slight degree heavier than common air, or of the same specific gravity, it would have accumulated on the surface of the earth, and particularly in our apartments, to such a degree as to have produced diseases, pestilence, and death, in rapid succession. But being a little lighter than the surrounding air, it flies upwards, and we never breathe it again, till it enters into new and salutary combinations. Such is the benevolent skill which the Author of Nature has displayed, for promoting the comfort and preservation of every thing that lives.*

Farther, *were the air coloured*, or were its particles much larger than they are, we could never obtain a distinct view of any other object. The exhalations which rise from the earth, being rendered visible, would disfigure the rich landscape of the universe, and render life disagreeable. But the Almighty, by rendering the air invisible, has enabled us not only to take a delightful and distinct survey of the objects that surround us, but has veiled from our view the gross humours incessantly perspired from animal bodies, the filth exhaled from kitchens, streets, and sewers, and every other object that would excite disgust. Again, *were the different portions of the atmosphere completely stationary*, and not susceptible of agitation,

Acosta, in his relation of a journey among the mountains of Peru, states, that "he and his companions were surprised with such extreme pangs of straining and vomiting, not without casting up of blood too, and with so violent a distemper, that they would undoubtedly have died had they remained two or three hours longer in that elevated situation." Count Zambeccari, and his companions, who ascended in a balloon, on the 7th of November, 1783, to a great height, found their hands and feet so swelled, that it was necessary for a surgeon to make incisions in the skin. In both the cases now stated, the persons ascended to so great a height that the pressure of the atmosphere was not sufficient to counterbalance the pressure of the fluids of the body.

* The necessity of atmospherical air for the support of life, was strikingly exemplified in the fate of the unhappy men who died in the *Black-hole* of Calcutta. On the 20th of June, 1756, about 8 o'clock in the evening, 146 men were forced, at the point of the bayonet, into a dungeon only 18 feet square. They had been but a few minutes confined in this infernal prison, before every one fell into a perspiration so profuse, that no idea can be formed of it. This brought on a raging thirst, the most difficult respiration, and an outrageous delirium. Such was the horror of their situation, that every insult that could be devised against the guard without, and all the opprobrious names that the Viceroy and his officers could be loaded with, were repeated, to provoke the guard to fire upon them, and terminate their sufferings. Before 11 o'clock the same evening, one-third of the men were dead; and before 6 next morning, only 23 came out alive, but most of them in a high putrid fever. All these dreadful effects were occasioned by the want of atmospheric air, and by their breathing a superabundant quantity of the nitrogen emitted from their lungs.

all nature would soon be thrown into confusion. The vapours which are exhaled from the sea by the heat of the sun would be suspended, and remain for ever fixed over those places from whence they arose. For want of this agitation of the air, which now scatters and disperses the clouds over every region, the sun would constantly scorch some districts, and be for ever hid from others; the balance of nature would be destroyed; navigation would be useless, and we could no longer enjoy the productions of different climates. In fine, were the atmosphere capable of being frozen, or converted into a solid mass, as all other fluids are, (and we know no reason why it should not be subject to congelation, but the will of the Creator,) the lives of every animal in the air, the waters, and the earth, would, in a few moments, be completely extinguished. But the admirable adjustment of every circumstance, in relation to this useful element, produces all the beneficial effects which we now experience, and strikingly demonstrates, that the intelligent Contriver of all things is "wonderful in counsel, and excellent in working."

From the instances now stated, we may plainly perceive, that if the Almighty had not a particular regard to the happiness of his intelligent offspring, and to the comfort of every animated existence; or, if he wished to inflict summary punishment on a wicked world, he could easily effect, by a very slight change in the constitution of the atmosphere, the entire destruction of the human race, and the entire conflagration of the great globe they inhabit,—throughout all its elementary regions. He has only to extract one of its constituent parts, and the grand catastrophe is at once accomplished. With what a striking propriety and emphasis, then, do the inspired writers declare, that, "In Him we live, and move, and have our being;" and that "in His hand is the soul of every living thing, and the breath of all mankind!"

A great variety of other admirable properties is possessed by the atmosphere, of which I shall briefly notice only the following:—It is the vehicle of *smells*, by which we become acquainted with the qualities of the food which is set before us, and learn to avoid those places which are damp, unwholesome, and dangerous. It is the medium of *sounds*, by means of which knowledge is conveyed to our minds. Its undulations, like so many couriers, run for ever backwards and forwards, to convey our thoughts to others, and theirs to us; and to bring news of transactions which frequently occur at a considerable distance. A few strokes on a large bell, through the ministration of the air, will convey signals of distress, or of joy, in a quarter of a minute, to the population of a city containing a hundred thousand inhabitants. So that the air may be considered as the conveyer of the thoughts of mankind, which are the cement of society. It transmits to our ears all the harmonies of music, and expresses every passion of the soul: it swells the notes of the nightingale, and distributes alike to every ear the pleasures which arise from the harmonious sounds of a concert. It produces the blue colour of the sky, and is the cause of the morning and evening twilight, by its property of bending the rays of light, and reflecting them in all directions. It forms an essential requisite for carrying on all the processes of the vegetable kingdom, and serves for the production of clouds, rain, and dew, which nourish and fertilize the earth. In short, it would be impossible to enumerate all the advantages we derive from this noble appendage to our world. Were the earth divested of its atmosphere, or were only two or three of its properties changed or destroyed, it would be left altogether unfit for the habitation of sentient beings. Were it divested of its undulating quality, we should be deprived of all the advantages of speech and conversation—of all the melody of the feathered songsters, and of all the pleasures of music; and, like the deaf and dumb, we could have no power of communicating our thoughts but by visible signs. Were it deprived of its reflective powers, the sun would appear in one part of the sky of a dazzling brightness, while all around would appear as dark as midnight, and the stars would be visible at noon-day. Were it deprived of its refractive powers, instead of the gradual approach of the day and the night which we now experience, at sunrise, we should be transported all at once from midnight darkness to the splendour of noon-day and, at sunset, should make a sudden transition from the splendours of day to all the horrors of midnight, which would bewilder the traveller in his journey, and strike the creation with amazement. In fine, were the oxygen of the atmosphere completely extracted, destruction would seize on all the tribes of the living world, throughout every region of earth, air, and sea.

Omitting at present the consideration of an indefinite variety of other particulars, which suggest themselves on this subject, I shall just notice one circumstance more, which has a relation both to the waters and to the atmosphere. It is a well-known law of nature, that all bodies are expanded by heat, and contracted by cold. There is only one exception to this law which exists in the economy of our globe, and that is, *the expansion of water, in the act of freezing.* While the parts of every other body are reduced in bulk, and their specific gravity increased by the application of cold; water, on the contrary, when congealed into ice, is increased in bulk, and becomes of a less specific gravity than the surrounding water, and, therefore, swims upon its surface. Now, had the case been otherwise: had water, when deprived of a portion of its heat, followed the general law of nature, and, like all other bodies, become specifically heavier than it was before, the present constitution of nature would have been materially deranged, and many of our present comforts, and even our very existence, would have been endangered. At whatever time the temperature of the atmosphere became reduced to 32° of the common thermometer, or to what is called the freezing point, the water on the surface of our rivers and lakes would have been converted into a layer of ice; this layer would have sunk to the bottom as it froze; another layer of ice would have been immediately produced, which would also have sunk to the former layer, and so on in succession, till, in the course of time, all our rivers from the surface to the bottom, and every other portion of water, capable of being frozen, would have been converted into solid masses of ice, which all the heat of summer could never have melted. We should have been deprived of most of the advantages we now derive from the liquid element, and, in a short time, the face of nature would have been transformed into a frozen chaos. But in the existing constitution of things, all such dismal effects are prevented, in consequence of the Creator having subjected the waters to a law contrary to that of other fluids, by means of which the frozen water swims upon the surface, and prevents the cold from penetrating to any great depth in the subjacent fluid; and when the heat of the atmosphere is increased, is exposed to its genial influence, and is quickly changed into its former liquid state. How admirably, then, does this *exception* to the general law of nature display the infinite intelligence of the Great Contriver of all things, and his providential care for the comfort of his creatures, when he arranged and established the economy of nature!

### *Variety of Nature.*

As a striking evidence of Divine Intelligence, we may next consider the *immense variety which the Creator has introduced into every department of the material world.*

In every region on the surface of the globe, an endless multiplicity of objects, all differing from one another in shape, colour, and motion, present themselves to the view of the beholder Mountains covered with forests, hills clothed with verdure, spacious plains adorned with vineyards, orchards, and waving grain; naked rocks, abrupt precipices, extended vales, deep dells, meandering rivers, roaring cataracts, brooks and rills; lakes and gulfs, bays and promontories, seas and oceans, caverns and grottoes—meet the eye of the student of Nature, in every country, with a variety which is at once beautiful and majestic. Nothing can exceed the variety of the *vegetable kingdom*, which pervades all climates, and almost every portion of the dry land, and of the bed of the ocean. The immense collections of Natural History which are to be seen in the Museum at Paris, show, that botanists are already acquainted with nearly fifty-six thousand different species of plants.* And yet, it is probable, that these form but a very small portion of what actually exist, and that several hundreds of thousands of species remain to be explored by the industry of future ages. For, by far the greater part of the vegetable world still remains to be surveyed by the scientific botanist. Of the numerous tribes of vegetable nature which flourish in the interior of Africa and America, in the immense islands of New Holland, New Guinea, Borneo, Sumatra, Java, Ceylon, Madagascar, and Japan; in the vast regions of Tartary, Thibet, Siberia, and the Burman empire; in the Philippines, the Moluccas, the Ladronas, the Carolinas, the Marquesas, the Society, the Georgian, and in thousands of other islands which are scattered over the Indian and Pacific oceans—little or nothing is known by the naturalists of Europe, and yet it is a fact which admits of no dispute, that every country hitherto explored produces a variety of species of plants peculiar to itself; and those districts in Europe which have been frequently surveyed, present to every succeeding explorer a new field of investigation, and reward his industry with new discoveries of the beauties and varieties of the vegetable kingdom. It has been conjectured by some naturalists, on the ground of a multitude of observations, that "there is not a square league of earth, but what presents some one plant peculiar to itself, or, at least, which thrives there better, or appears more beautiful than in any other part of the world." This would make the number of species of vegetables to amount to as many millions as there are of square leagues on the surface of the earth.

Now, every one of these species of plants differs from another, in its size, structure, form, flowers, leaves, fruits, mode of propagation, colour, medicinal virtues, nutritious qualities, internal vessels, and the odours it exhales. They are of all sizes, from the microscopic mushroom, invisible to the naked eye, to the sturdy oak, and the cedar of Lebanon, and from the slender willow to the banian tree, under whose shade 7000 persons may find ample room to repose. A thousand different shades of colour distinguish the different species. Every one wears its peculiar livery, and is distinguished by its own native hues; and many of their inherent beauties can be distinguished only by the help of the microscope. Some grow upright, others creep along in a serpentine form. Some flourish for ages, others wither and decay in a few months; some spring up in moist, others in dry soils; some turn towards the sun, others shrink and

* Edinburgh Philosophical Journal, July, 1822. p. 48.

contract when we approach to touch them. Not only are the different species of plants and flowers distinguished from each other, by their different forms, but even the different individuals of the same species. In a bed of tulips or carnations, for example, there is scarcely a flower in which some difference may not be observed in its structure, size, or assemblage of colours; nor can any two flowers be found in which the shape and shades are exactly similar. Of all the hundred thousand millions of plants, trees, herbs, and flowers, with which our globe is variegated, there are not, perhaps, two individuals precisely alike, in every point of view in which they may be contemplated; yea, there is not, perhaps, a single leaf in the forest, when minutely examined, that will not be found to differ, in certain aspects, from its fellows. Such is the wonderful and infinite diversity with which the Creator has adorned the vegetable kingdom.

His wisdom is also evidently displayed in this vast profusion of vegetable nature—in adapting each plant to the soil and situation in which it is destined to flourish—in furnishing it with those vessels by which it absorbs the air and moisture on which it feeds—and in adapting it to the nature and necessities of animated beings. As the earth teems with animated existence, and as the different tribes of animals depend chiefly on the productions of the vegetable kingdom for their subsistence, so there is an abundance and a variety of plants adapted to the peculiar constitutions of every individual species. This circumstance demonstrates, that there is a precontrived relation and fitness between the internal *constitution* of the animal, and the *nature of the plants* which afford it nourishment; and shows us, that the animal and vegetable kingdoms are the workmanship of *one* and the same Almighty Being, and that, in his arrangements with regard to the one, he had in view the necessities of the other.

When we direct our attention to the tribes of *animated nature*, we behold a scene no less variegated and astonishing. Above fifty thousand species of animals have been detected and described by naturalists, besides several thousands of species which the naked eye cannot discern, and which people the invisible regions of the waters and the air. And, as the greater part of the globe has never yet been thoroughly explored, several hundreds, if not thousands, of species unknown to the scientific world may exist in the depths of the ocean, and in the unexplored regions of the land. All these species differ from one another in colour, size, and shape; in the internal structure of their bodies, in the number of their sensitive organs, limbs, feet, joints, claws, wings, and fins; in their dispositions, faculties, movements, and modes of subsistence. They are of all sizes, from the mite and the gnat, up to the elephant and the whale, and from the mite downwards to those invisible animalculæ, a hundred thousand of which would not equal a grain of sand. Some fly through the atmosphere, some glide through the waters, others traverse the solid land. Some walk on two, some on four, some on twenty, and some on a hundred feet. Some have eyes furnished with two, some with eight, some with a hundred, and some with eight thousand distinct transparent globes, for the purpose of vision.*

Our astonishment at the variety which appears in the animal kingdom is still farther increased when we consider not only the diversities which are apparent in their external aspect, but also in their internal structure and organization. When we reflect on the thousands of movements, adjustments, adaptations, and compensations, which are requisite in order to the construction of an animal system, for enabling it to perform its intended functions;—when we consider, that every species of animals has a system of organization peculiar to itself, consisting of bones, joints, blood-vessels, and muscular motions, differing in a variety of respects from those of any other species, and exactly adapted to its various necessities and modes of existence; and when we consider, still farther, the incomprehensibly delicate contrivances, and exquisite borings, polishings, claspings, and adaptations, which enter into the organization of an animated being ten thousand

* The *eyes* of beetles, silk-worms, flies, and several other kinds of insects, are among the most curious and wonderful productions of the God of Nature. On the head of a fly are two large protuberances, one on each side; these constitute its organs of vision. The whole surface of these protuberances is covered with a multitude of small hemispheres placed with the utmost regularity, in rows, crossing each other in a kind of lattice work. These little hemispheres have each of them a minute transparent convex lens in the middle, each of which has a distinct branch of the optic nerve ministering to it; so that the different lenses may be considered as so many distinct eyes. Mr. Leeuwenhoek counted 6236 in the two eyes of a silk-worm, when in its *fly* state; 3180 in each eye of the beetle; and 8000 in the two eyes of a *common fly*. Mr. Hook reckoned 14,000 in the eyes of a *drone fly*; and, in one of the eyes of a *dragon fly* there have been reckoned 13,500 of these lenses, and, consequently, in both eyes, 27,000, every one of which is capable of forming a distinct image of any object, in the same manner as a common convex glass; so that there are 27,000 images formed on the retina of this little animal. Mr. Leeuwenhoek having prepared the eye of a fly for the purpose, placed it a little farther from his microscope than when he would examine an object, so as to leave a proper local distance between it and the lens of his microscope; and then looked through both, in the manner of a telescope, at the steeple of the church, which was 299 feet high, and 750 feet distant, and could plainly see through every little lens, the whole steeple inverted, though not larger than the point of a fine needle: and then directing it to a neighbouring house, saw through many of these little hemispheres, not only the front of the house, but also the doors and windows, and could discern distinctly whether the windows were open or shut. Such an exquisite piece of Divine mechanism transcends all human comprehension.

times less than a mite; and that the different species of those animals are likewise all differently organized from one another,—we cannot but be struck with reverence and astonishment, at the *Intelligence* of that Incomprehensible Being who arranged the organs of all the tribes of animated nature, who "breathed into them the breath of life," and who continually upholds them in all their movements!

Could we descend into the subterraneous apartments of the globe, and penetrate into those unknown recesses which lie towards its centre, we should, doubtless, behold a variegated scene of wonders, even in those dark and impenetrable regions. But all the labour and industry of man have not hitherto enabled him to penetrate farther into the bowels of the earth than the six thousandth part of its diameter; so that we must remain for ever ignorant of the immense caverns and masses of matter that may exist, and of the processes that may be going on, about its central regions. In those regions, however, near the surface, which lie within the sphere of human inspection, we perceive a variety analogous to that which is displayed in the other departments of nature. Here we find substances of various kinds formed into strata, or layers, of different depths—earths, sand, gravel, marl, clay, sandstone, freestone, marble, limestone, fossils, coals, peat, and similar materials. In these strata are found metals and minerals of various descriptions—salt, nitrate of potash, ammonia, sulphur, bitumen, platina, gold, silver, mercury, iron, lead, tin, copper, zinc, nickel, manganese, cobalt, antimony, the diamond, rubies, sapphires, jaspers, emeralds, and a countless variety of other substances, of incalculable benefit to mankind. Some of these substances are so essentially requisite for the comfort of man, that, without them, he would soon degenerate into the savage state, and be deprived of all those arts which extend his knowledge, and which cheer and embellish the abodes of civilized life.

If we turn our eyes upward to the regions of the atmosphere, we may also behold a spectacle of variegated magnificence. Sometimes the sky is covered with sable clouds, or obscured with mists; at other times it is tinged with a variety of hues, by the rays of the rising or the setting sun. Sometimes it presents a pure azure, at other times it is diversified with strata of dappled clouds. At one time we behold the rainbow rearing its majestic arch, adorned with all the colours of light; at another, the Aurora Borealis illuminating the sky with its fantastic coruscations. At one time we behold the fiery meteor sweeping through the air; at another, we perceive the forked lightning darting from the clouds, and hear the thunders rolling through the sky. Sometimes the vault of heaven appears like a boundless desert, and at other times adorned with an innumerable host of stars, and with the moon "walking in brightness." In short, whether we direct our view to the vegetable or the animal tribes, to the atmosphere, the ocean, the mountains, the plains, or the subterranean recesses of the globe, we behold a scene of beauty, order, and *variety*, which astonishes and enraptures the contemplative mind, and constrains us to join in the devout exclamations of the Psalmist, "*How manifold are thy works,* O Lord! In wisdom hast thou made them all, the earth is full of thy riches; so is the great and wide sea, wherein are things creeping, *innumerable*, both small and great beasts."

This countless variety of objects which appears throughout every department of our sublunary system, not only displays the depths of Divine wisdom, but also presents us with a faint idea of the *infinity* of the Creator, and of the *immense multiplicity of ideas and conceptions* which must have existed in the Eternal Mind, when the fabric of our globe, and its numerous tribes of inhabitants, were arranged and brought into existence. And, if every other world which floats in the immensity of space be diversified with a similar variety of existence, altogether different from ours, (as we have reason to believe, from the variety we already perceive, and from the boundless plans and conceptions of the Creator,) the human mind is lost and confounded, when it attempts to form an idea of those endlessly diversified plans, conceptions, and views, which must have existed during an eternity past, in the Divine mind. When we would attempt to enter into the conception of so vast and varied operations, we feel our own littleness, and the narrow limits of our feeble powers, and can only exclaim, with the Apostle Paul, "Oh the depth of the riches both of the wisdom and knowledge of God! how unsearchable are his counsels, and his ways of creation and providence past finding out."

This characteristic of variety, which is stamped on all the works of Omnipotence, is doubtless intended to gratify the principle of curiosity and the love of novelty, which are implanted in the human breast; and thus to excite rational beings to the study and investigation of the works of the Creator; that therein they may behold the glory of the Divine character, and be stimulated to the exercise of love, admiration, and reverence. For as the records of revelation, and the dispensations of providence, display to us the various aspects of the moral character of Deity, so, the diversified phenomena, and the multiplicity of objects and operations which the scenery of nature exhibits, present to us a specimen *of the ideas*, as it were, of the Eternal Mind, in so far as they can be adumbrated by material objects, and exhibited to mortals, through the medium of corporeal organs.

To convey an adequate conception of the *number* of these ideas, as exhibited on the globe in which we live, would baffle the arithmetician's skill, and set his numbers at defiance. We may, however, assist our conceptions a little, by confining our attention to one department of nature, for example, the ANIMAL KINGDOM. The number of the different species of animals, taking into account those which are hitherto undiscovered, and those which are invisible to the naked eye, cannot be estimated at less than 300,000. In a human body there are reckoned about 446 muscles, in each of which according to anatomists, there are at least 10 several intentions, or due qualifications to be observed—its proper figure, its just magnitude, the right disposition of its several ends, upper and lower, the position of the whole, the insertion of its proper nerves, veins, arteries, &c. so that in the muscular system alone there are 4,460 several ends or aims to be attended to. The bones are reckoned to be in number about 245, and the distinct scopes or intentions of each of these are above 40; in all, about 9,800; so that the system of bones and muscles alone, without taking any other parts into consideration, amounts to about 14,000 different intentions or adaptations. If now, we suppose, that all the species of animals above stated are differently constructed, and, taken one with another, contain at an average a system of bones and muscles as numerous as in the human body—the number of species must be multiplied by the number of different aims or adaptations, and the product will amount to 4,200,000,000. If we were next to attend to the many thousands of blood vessels in an animal body, and the numerous ligaments, membranes, humours, and fluids of various descriptions —the skin, with its millions of pores, and every other part of an organical system, with the aims and intentions of each, we should have another sum of many hundreds of millions to be multiplied by the former product, in order to express the diversified ideas which enter into the construction of the animal world. And, if we still farther consider, that of the hundreds of millions of individuals belonging to each species, no two individuals exactly resemble each other—that all the myriads of vegetables with which the earth is covered, are distinguished from each other, by some one characteristic or another, and that every grain of sand contained in the mountains, and in the bed of the ocean, as shown by the microscope, discovers a different form and configuration from another—we are here presented with an *image* of the *infinity* of the *conceptions* of Him in whose incomprehensible mind they all existed, during countless ages, before the universe was formed.

To overlook this amazing scene of Divine Intelligence, or to consider it as beneath our notice as some have done—if it be not the characteristic of impiety, is, at least, the mark of a weak and undiscriminating mind. The man who disregards the visible displays of Infinite Wisdom, or who neglects to investigate them, when opportunity offers, acts as if he considered himself already possessed of a sufficient portion of intelligence, and stood in no need of sensible assistances to direct his conceptions of the Creator. Pride, and false conceptions of the nature and design of true religion, frequently lie at the foundation of all that indifference and neglect with which the visible works of God are treated, by those who make pretensions to a high degree of spiritual attainments. The truly pious man will trace, with wonder and delight, the footsteps of his Father and his God, wherever they appear in the variegated scene of creation around him, and will be filled with sorrow, and contrition of heart, that, amidst his excursions and solitary walks, he has so often disregarded "the works of the Lord, and the operation of his hands."

In fine, the variety which appears on the face of nature, not only enlarges our conceptions of Infinite Wisdom, but is also the foundation of all our discriminations and judgments as rational beings, and is of the most essential utility in the affairs of human society. Such is the variety of which the features of the human countenance are susceptible, that it is probable that no two individuals, of all the millions of the race of Adam that have existed since the beginning of time, would be found to resemble each other. We know no two human beings presently existing, however similar to each other, but may be distinguished either by their stature, their forms, or the features of their faces; and on the ground of this dissimilarity, the various wheels of the machine of society move onward, without clashing or confusion. Had it been otherwise—had the faces of men and their organs of speech been cast exactly in the same mould, as would have been the case, had the world been framed according to the Epicurean system, by blind chance directing a concourse of atoms, it might have been as difficult to distinguish one human countenance from another, as to distinguish the eggs laid by the same hen, or the drops of water which trickle from the same orifice; and consequently, society would have been thrown into a state of universal anarchy and confusion. Friends would not have been distinguished from enemies, villains from the good and honest, fathers from sons, the culprit from the innocent person, nor the branches of the same family from one another. And what a scene of perpetual confusion and disturbance would thus have been created! Frauds, thefts, robberies, murders, assassinations, forgeries, and injustice of all kinds, might have been daily committed without the least possibility of detection. Nay, were even the *variety of tones* in the human voice, peculiar to each person, to cease, and the *handwriting* of all men to become perfectly uniform, a multitude of distressing deceptions and perplexities would be produced in the domestic, civil, and commercial transactions of mankind. But the All-wise and Beneficent Creator has prevented all such evils and inconveniences, by the character of *variety* which he has impressed on the human species; and on all his works. By the peculiar features of his countenance every man may be distinguished in the light; by the tones of his voice he may be recognized in the dark, or when he is separated from his fellows by an impenetrable partition; and his handwriting can attest his existence and individuality, when continents and oceans interpose between him and his relations, and be a witness of his sentiments and purposes to future generations.

---

Thus, I have taken a very cursory view of some evidences of Divine Wisdom, which appear in the general constitution of the *earth*, the *waters*, and the *atmosphere*, and in the characteristic of *variety*, which is impressed on all the objects of the visible creation. When these and other admirable arrangements, in our sublunary system, are seriously contemplated, every rational and pious mind will be disposed to exclaim with the Psalmist—" There is none like unto thee, O Lord, neither are there any works like unto thy works."—" Thou art great, and dost wondrous things, thou art God alone."—" O that men would praise the Lord for his goodness, and for his wonderful works towards the children of men!"

When we consider not only the *utility*, but the *beauty* and *grandeur* of the wise arrangements of nature, what reason have we to admire and adore the goodness of the great Author of our existence! Were all the diversities of shape and colour, of mountains and vales, of rivers and lakes, of light and shade, which now embellish the various landscapes of the world, to disappear, and were one unvaried scene perpetually to present itself to the eye, how dull and wearisome, and uninteresting, would the aspect of the universe appear to an intelligent mind! Although the variegated beauties which adorn the surface of our globe, and the vault of heaven, are not essential to our existence, as sensitive beings, yet, were they completely withdrawn, and nothing presented to the eye but a boundless expanse of barren sands, the mind would recoil upon itself, its activity would be destroyed, its powers would be confined, as it were, to a prison, and it would roam in vain amidst the surrounding waste, in search of enjoyment. Even the luxuries of a palace, were it possible to procure them amidst such a scene of desolation, would become stale and insipid, and would leave the rational soul, almost destitute of ideas and of mental energy, to the tiresome round of a cheerless existence. But in the actual state of the world we live in, there is no landscape in nature, from the icebergs of Greenland to the verdant scenes of the torrid zone, in which objects, either of sublimity or of beauty, in boundless variety, are not presented to the view; in order to stimulate the mind to activity, to gratify its desire of novelty, and to elevate its conceptions of the Beneficent Creator.

And, if the present constitution of our world displays so evident marks of beauty and benevolent design, now that it is inhabited by an assemblage of depraved intelligences, and its physical aspect deformed, in consequence of " the wickedness of man"—what transporting beauties and sublimities must it have presented, when it appeared fresh from the hand of its Almighty Maker, and when all things were pronounced by him to be *very good?* After a deluge of waters has swept away many of its primeval beauties, and has broken and deranged even its subterraneous strata, this terrestrial world still presents to the eye a striking scene of beauty, order, and beneficence. But we have the strongest reason to believe, that before sin had disfigured the aspect of this lower world, all was " beauty to the eye, and music to the ear"—that " immortality breathed in the winds, flowed in the rivers," and exhaled from every plant and flower. No storms disturbed the tranquillity of nature, nor created the least alarm in the breasts of its holy inhabitants. No earthquakes shook the ground, nor rent the foundations of nature. No volcanoes vomited their rivers of lava, nor overwhelmed the plains with deluges of fire. No barren deserts of heath and sand disfigured the rich landscape of the world—no tempests nor hurricanes tossed the ocean, nor scorching heats, nor piercing colds, nor pestilence, nor disease, annoyed the human frame. In the paradisaical state of the world, we may reasonably suppose, that all the elements of nature contributed directly to the pleasure and enjoyment of man, and of the other tribes of animated nature; and that they were not subjected, as they now are, to the operation of those natural agents which so frequently spread destruction and ruin among the abodes of men. To suppose the contrary to have happened, would be inconsistent with the state of pure and happy intelligences, and with the benignity of the Creator; and would imply, that God was either unwilling or unable to remove such physical evils. But we cannot suppose it beyond the limits of Infinite Wisdom and Omnipotence, to create and arrange a world entirely free from those evils and inconveniences which now flow from the operation of certain physical agents; without, at the same time, supposing that his power and intelligence are confined within certain bounds, beyond which they cannot pass. And, therefore, if, in the existing constitution of things, the harmony of nature is occasionally disturbed, and its beauty defaced, by earthquakes, storms, and tempests—we must remember, that the inhabitants of the earth are now a depraved race of mortals, no longer adorned with primeval purity and innocence; and that the physical economy of our globe has undergone a certain derangement, corresponding to the *moral state* of its present occupants. But since this earth, even in its present state of degradation and derangement, presents to the view of every beholder so many objects of beauty and magnificence, and so numerous traces of Divine Beneficence—we may reasonably conclude, that scenes of Divine Wisdom and Goodness, far more glorious and transporting, must be displayed in those worlds where moral evil has never shed its malign influence, and where the inhabitants—superior to disease and death—bask for ever in the regions of immortality. And, therefore, however admirable the displays of Divine Wisdom may appear in the sublunary scene around us, they must be considered as inferior to those which are exhibited in many other provinces of Jehovah's empire, in so far as they are blended with those physical derangements which indicate his displeasure against the sins of men.

---

Were we now to direct our attention to the mechanism of animated beings, and to consider the numberless contrivances and adaptations in their organical structure and functions, a thousand instances of exquisite wisdom and design, still more striking and admirable, would crowd upon our view. For, although the general fabric of the world, and the immense variety of objects it contains, are evident proofs of a Wise and Intelligent Contriver, yet it is chiefly in the minute and delicate contrivances of organical structures, their adaptation to the purposes of life, motion, and enjoyment, and their relation and correspondence to the surrounding elements, that the consummate skill of the Great Architect of nature is most strikingly perceived. But as it forms no part of my present plan to enter on so extensive a field of illustration, on which volumes might be written, I shall content myself with merely stating an example or two. My first example shall be taken from

### *The Structure of the Human Eye.*

The eye is one of the nicest pieces of mechanism which the human understanding can contemplate; but as it requires a knowledge of its anatomical structure, and of the principles of optics, to enable us to appreciate its admirable functions, I shall confine myself to a few *general* descriptions and remarks.

The eye is nearly of a globular form. It consists chiefly of three *coats*, and three *humours*. The first or outer coat, is termed *sclerotica*; it is every where white and opaque, and is joined at its anterior edge to another which has more convexity than any other part of the globe of the eye, and, being exceedingly transparent, is called the *cornea*. These two parts are perfectly different in their structure, and are supposed, by some anatomists, to be as distinct from each other as the glass of a watch is from the case into which it is fixed. Next within this coat is that called the *choroides*, on account of its being furnished with a great number of vessels. It serves, as it were, for a lining to the other, and is joined with that part of the eye termed *iris*. The *iris* is an opaque membrane like the choroides, but of different colours in different eyes, as gray, black, or hazel. It is composed of two sets of muscular fibres, the one of a circular form, which contracts the hole in the middle, called the *pupil*, when the light is too strong for the eye; and the other, of radial fibres, tends every where from the circumference of the iris towards the middle of the pupil; which fibres, by their contractions, dilate and enlarge the pupil, when the light is weak, in order to let in more of its rays. The third coat is called the *retina*, upon which are painted the images of all visible objects, by the rays of light which flow from them. It spreads like net-work all over the inside of the choroides, and is nothing more than a fine expansion of the optic nerve; by which nerve the impressions of visible objects are conveyed to the brain.

The inside of the globe of the eye, within these tunics or coats, is filled with three humours, called the aqueous, the crystalline, and the vitreous. The *aqueous* humour lies at the fore part of the eye, and occupies all the space between the crystalline and the prominent cornea. It has the same specific gravity and refractive power as water, and seems chiefly of use to prevent the crystalline from being easily bruised by rubbing, or by a blow —and perhaps it serves for the crystalline humour to move forward in, while we view near objects, and backward for remoter objects; without which, or some other mechanism effecting the same purpose, we could not, according to the laws of optics, perceive objects distinctly, when placed at different distances. Behind the aqueous lies the *crystalline* humour, which is shaped like a double convex glass, and is a little more convex on the back than on the fore part. This humour is transparent like crystal, is nearly of the consistence of hard jelly, and converges the rays which pass through it, from visible objects, to its focus at the bottom or back part of the eye. The *vitreous* humour lies behind the crystalline, and fills up the greatest part of the orb of the eye, giving it a globular shape. It is nearly of the consistence of the white of an egg, and very transparent; its fore part is concave, for the crystalline humour to lodge in, and its back part being convex, the retina is spread over it. It serves as a medium to keep the crystalline humour and the retina at due distance. From what has now been stated, it is obvious, that the images of external objects are depicted in the retina, in an inverted position, in the same manner as the images formed by a common convex lens; but how the mind, in this case, perceives objects erect, is a question, about which the learned have divided in their opinions.*

* An idea of the relative positions of the *coats* and *humours* described above, may be obtained by a simple inspection of the Plate, Fig. 6.—Fig. 5, represents a *front view* of the human eye, as it ap-

The ball of the eye, as now described, is situated in a bony cavity, called its orbit, composed by the junction of seven different bones, hollowed out at their edges. This cavity is in all the vacant spaces filled with a loose fat, which serves as a proper medium for the eye to rest in, and as a socket in which it may move. It is sheltered by the eyebrows, which are provided with hair, to prevent the descending sweat of the forehead from running down into it. As a still farther protection to this delicate organ, it is furnished with the eyelid, which, like a curtain, is drawn over it with inconceivable swiftness, for its security, on the approach of danger. It also serves to wipe it from superfluous moisture, and to cover it during sleep. In the upper part of its orbit, it is furnished with a gland, to supply it with water sufficient to wash off dust, and to keep its outer surface moist, without which the cornea would be less transparent, and the rays of light would be disturbed in their passage; and the superfluous water is conveyed to the nose through a perforation in the bone.

For the purpose of enabling the eye to move in its socket, *six muscles* are provided. These are admirably contrived to move it in every direction, upwards or downwards, to the right or to the left, or in whatever direction the occasion may require; and thus we are spared the trouble of turning our heads continually towards the objects we wish to inspect. If we want to look upward, one of these muscles lifts up the orb of the eye; if we would cast our eyes to the ground, another muscle pulls them down. A third muscle moves the globe outwards towards the temples, and a fourth draws it towards the nose. A fifth, which slides within a cartilaginous ring, like a cord over a pulley, and is fastened to the globe of the eye in two points, makes it roll about at pleasure. A sixth lies under the eye, and is designed to temper and restrain, within proper bounds, the action of the rest, to keep it steadily fixed on the object it beholds, and to prevent those frightful contortions which otherwise might take place. By these, and a multitude of other mechanical contrivances, all acting in harmonious combination, the eye, as a natural telescope and microscope, is made to advance, to recede, to move to the right and to the left, and in every other direction; and to view near and distant objects with equal distinctness; so that a single eye, by the variety of positions it may assume, performs the office of a thousand.*

The utility of these several movements, and the pain and inconvenience which would be suffered, were any of them wanting, can scarcely be conceived, by any one whose eyes have always remained in a sound state. We are so much accustomed to the regular exercise of our visual organs, that we seldom reflect on the numerous delicate springs which must be set in action, before the functions of vision can, with ease, be performed. But were any one of the muscular organs, now described, to fail in its functions, we should soon experience so many inconveniences, as would throw a gloom on all the other comforts of life; and convince us, how much we are indebted, every moment, to the provident care and goodness of our Beneficent Creator, for thousands of enjoyments which we seldom think of, and for which we are never sufficiently grateful.—"With much compassion, as well as astonishment at the goodness of our loving Creator," says Dr. Nieuwentyt, "have I considered the sad state of a certain gentleman, who, as to the rest, was in pretty good health, but only wanted the use of those two little muscles that serve to lift up the eyelid, and so had almost lost the use of his sight—being forced, as long as this defect lasted, to shove up his eyelids every moment, with his own hands."†

How admirable, then, is the formation of the eye, and how grateful ought we to feel at the consideration, that we are permitted to enjoy all the transporting pleasures of vision, without the least perplexity or effort on our part! If the loss of action in a single muscle produces so many distressing sensations and efforts, what would be the consequence if all the muscles of the eye were wanting or deranged? And is it man that governs these nice and intricate movements? or is it the eye itself, as a self-directing machine, that thus turns around, seasonably and significantly, towards every visible object? Man knows neither the organs of vision, nor the functions they ought to perform. The eye is only an unconscious machine, in the hands of a Superior Intelligence, as a watch, or a steam engine, is in the hands of a mechanic. It is God alone who constantly performs its movements, according to certain laws, which he has submitted to our inclinations and desires; "*for in him we live and move.*" We are *desirous* to see certain objects around us: this is all the share we have in the operations of our eyes; and without perplexing our understanding, without the least care or management, in regard to any of the functions, we can, in a few moments, take a survey of the beauties and sublimities of an extensive landscape, and of the glories of the vault of heaven. Thus, the Divine Being operates not only in this, but in a thousand different ways, in the various senses and contrivances which belong to our animal system; and yet, thoughtless and ungrateful man often inquires, in the language of doubt

pears in its natural state, and exhibits the relative positions of the *Cornea*, *Iris*, and *Pupil*.

* Flies, and other insects, whose eyes are immoveable, have several thousands of distinct globes in each eye. See note page 38.

† Nieuwentyt's Religious Philospher, vol. 1, p. 282.

and hesitation, "Where is God my Maker?" He is in us, and around us, directing every movement in our animal frame to act in harmony with the surrounding elements, and to minister to our enjoyments; and it is only when his exquisite operations are deranged by external violence, that we feel inconvenience or pain.

Such are only a few general outlines of the structure of the eye: for no notice has been taken of the numerous minute veins, arteries, nerves, lymphatics, glands, and many other particulars which are connected with this organ. But all this delicate and complicated apparatus, in the structure of the eye, would have been of no use whatever for the purpose of vision, had not a distinct substance been created to act upon it, exactly adapted to its nature and functions. In order that the eye might serve as the medium of our perceptions of visible objects, *light* was formed, and made to travel from its source at the rate of 195,000 miles in a second of time. This prodigious velocity of light is, doubtless, essential to the nature of vision; since it actually exists, and since we find that it radiates with the same swiftness from the most distant visible star, as from the sun which enlightens our system. To abate the force of this amazing velocity, its particles have been formed almost infinitely small—a circumstance which alone prevents this delightful visitant from becoming the most tremendous and destructive element in nature. Dr. Nieuwentyt has computed, that, in one second of time, there flows 418,660,000,000,000,000,000,000,000,000,000,000,000,000,000* particles of light out of a burning candle, which number contains at least 6,337,242,000,000 times the number of grains of sand in the whole earth, supposing every cubic inch of the earth to contain a million of grains. It has been justly remarked, by Mr. Ferguson and other authors, that "if the particles of light were so large, that a million of them were equal in bulk to an ordinary grain of sand, we durst no more open our eyes to the light, than suffer sand to be shot point blank against them, from the mouth of a cannon." It may also be remarked, that the property which all bodies possess, of *reflecting* light, is essential to the purpose of vision, without which, the splendid and variegated scene of nature would be changed into a dreadful gloom; and were the rays of light of one uniform colour, and not compounded of various hues, one object could not be distinguished from another, and the beautiful aspect of our globe would instantly disappear.

Thus we see, that the eye is adapted to light, and light to the eye; and in this admirable adaptation the wisdom of the Creator is strikingly displayed. For light has no effect upon the ear, or upon any other organ of sensation; so as to produce a perception of visible objects; as, on the other hand, the undulations of the air have no effect upon the eye, so as to produce the sensation of *sound*. The eye did not produce the light, nor did the light form the eye; they are perfectly distinct from each other, yet so nicely adapted in every particular, that had any one quality or circumstance been wanting in either, the functions of vision could not have been performed in the manner in which they now operate, which strikingly demonstrates, that one and the same Intelligent Being, possessed of a wisdom beyond our comprehension, formed the curious structure of the eye, and endued the rays of light with those properties of colour, motion, and minuteness, which are calculated, through the medium of this organ, to produce, in sentient beings, the ideas of visible objects. And, surely, he never intended that such exquisite skill and contrivance should be altogether overlooked by rational beings, for whose pleasure and enjoyment all this benevolent care is exercised.

### *Manner in which vision is performed.*

Let us now attend a little to the manner in which vision is performed, by the medium of light acting on the organs of sight. If we take a common convex glass—a reading glass for example—and hold it at some distance from a candle or a window sash, placing a piece of white paper behind the glass, at the distance of its focus, the image of the candle or sash will be painted on the paper, in an inverted position. This experiment may be performed, with a better effect, by darkening a room, and placing the convex glass in a hole cut out of the window shutter, when the rays of light flowing from the objects without, and passing through the glass, will form a picture of the objects opposite the window, on the white paper, adorned with the most beautiful colours. In a manner similar to this, are the images of external objects depicted on the back part of the inner coat or membrane of the eye. The rays of light, proceeding in all directions, from surrounding objects, and falling on the eye, are transmitted through the pupil; and being refracted by the different humours, (particularly by the *crystalline* humour, which acts the part of a convex lens,) they converge to a focus on the *retina*, where the images of visible objects are painted in an inverted position; and, by means of the optic nerve, these images are conveyed to the mind.

The following figure will perhaps more distinctly illustrate this point. Let *a*, *b*, *c*, *x*, *y*, represent the globe of the eye, and A, B, C, an object at a certain distance from it. Now, it is well known that every point of a visible object sends out rays of light in all directions; and, therefore, a certain portion of the rays which flow from the object A B C, will fall upon the *cornea*, between *x* and *y*, and, passing through the

* See Appendix, No. V

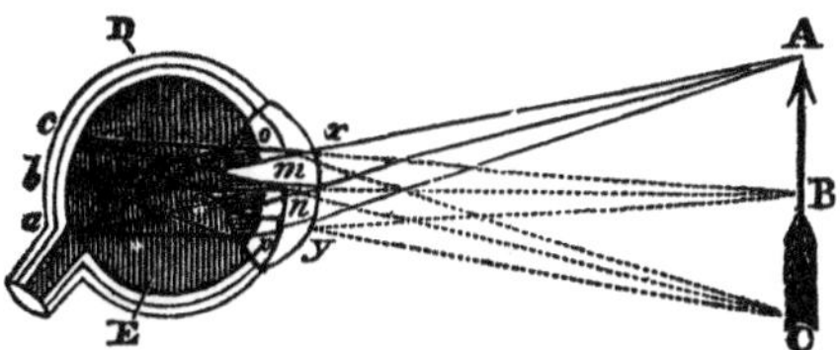


aqueous humour, m, n, and the *crystalline* humour o, p, and the *vitreous* humour, D, E, will be converged to a focus on the retina, and paint a distinct picture, *a b c*, of the object A B C, in an inverted position. The rays from the point A of the object, after being refracted by the different humours, will be brought to a point at *a*; those from B will be converged at *b*; and those from C at *c*; and, of course, the intermediate rays between A B, and B C, will be formed between *a b*, and *b c*, and the object will become visible by means of its image or representation being painted on the retina, in all the colours and proportions which belong to it. If we take a bullock's eye, and cut off the three coats from the back part, and put a piece of thin white paper over that part, and hold the eye towards the window or any bright object, we shall see the image of the object depicted upon the paper, and in an inverted position, as stated above.

In order that we may more distinctly perceive the wonders of vision, and the numerous circumstances on which it depends, let us suppose ourselves placed on an eminence, which commands a view of a variegated and extensive landscape. Let us suppose ourselves stationed on Arthur's seat, or on the top of Salisbury Crags, in the vicinity of Edinburgh. Turning our face to the north-west, the city, with its castles, spires, and stately edifices, presents itself to our view. Beyond it, on the north and west, a beautiful country, adorned with villas, plantations, and fertile fields, stretches as far as the eye can reach, till the view is bounded by the castle of Stirling, at the distance of more than thirty miles. On the right hand, we behold the port of Leith, the shipping in the roads, the coast of Fife, the isles of Inchkeith and of May, and the Frith of Forth, gradually losing itself in the German ocean. If we suppose the length of this landscape to be forty miles, and its breadth twenty-five, it will, of course, comprehend an area of a thousand square miles.

The first circumstance which strikes the mind, is *the immense multitude of rays of reflected light* which flow, in all directions, from the myriads of objects which compose the surrounding scene. In order to form a rude idea of this infinity of radiations, I fix my attention on a single object—I direct my eye to Nelson's monument, o the Calton hill. From the parapet at the top, a thousand different points send forth a thousand different cones of rays, which, entering my eye, render the different parts of it distinctly visible, besides myriads of rays from the same points, which flow in every other direction through the open spaces of the atmosphere which surround them. How many thousands of millions, then, of different radiations, must be issuing forth every moment from the whole mass of the monument! And if one object pours forth such a flood of rays, how immense must be the number of radiations which are issuing from all the objects which compose this extensive landscape! Myriads of rays, from myriads of objects, must be crossing each other in an infinity of directions, so that the mind is confounded at the apparent confusion which seems to exist in this immensity of radiations; yet every ray passes forward in the crowd, in the most perfect order, and without being blended or confused with any other ray, produces its specific effect on every eye that is open to receive it. But this is not all: these millions of rays which flow from the minutest points of the surrounding scene, before they can produce the sensation of vision, and form a picture of the landscape on the retina, must be compressed into a space little more than one-eighth of an inch in diameter, before they can enter the pupil of the eye; yet they all pass through this small aperture without the least confusion, and paint the images of their respective objects in exactly the same order in which these objects are arranged. Another circumstance demands attention. The rays which proceed from the objects before me are not all directed to the spot where I stand, but are diffused throughout every point of the surrounding space, ready to produce the same effect, wherever sentient beings are present to receive them. Were the whole inhabitants of Edinburgh placed on the sloping declivity of Arthur's seat, and along the top of Salisbury Crags, and were millions of other spectators suspended in the surrounding atmosphere, similar sensations would be produced, and a scene similar to that which I now behold, would be depicted in every eye. Amidst the infinity of cones of light, crossing each other in an infinity of directions, no confusion would ensue, but every spectator, whose eyes were in a sound state, would obtain a correct view of the scene before him; and hence it happens, that, whenever I shift my position to the right hand or to the left, other streams of light enter my eye, and produce the same effect Yet me now attend to another circumstance, no less admirable than the preceding, and that is, the *distinct impression* which I have of the shape, colour, and motion, of the multiplicity of objects I am now contemplating, and the *small space* within which their images are depicted at the bottom of my eye. Could a painter, after a long series of ingenious efforts, delineate the extensive landscape now before me, on a piece of paper not exceeding the size of a silver sixpence, so that every object might be distinctly seen, in its proper shape and colour, as it now appears when I survey the scene around me, he would be incomparably superior to all the masters of his art that ever went before him. This effect, which far transcends the utmost efforts of human genius, is accomplished in a moment, in millions of instances, by the hand of nature, or, in other words, by "the finger of God." All the objects I am now surveying, comprehending an extent of a thousand square miles, are accurately delineated in the bottom of my eye, on a space *less than half an inch* in diameter. How delicate, then, must be the strokes of that Divine pencil, which has formed such a picture! I turn my eyes to the castle of Edinburgh, which appears one of the most conspicuous objects in my field of view. Supposing that portion of it which strikes my eye to be 500 feet long, and 90 in height, I find, by calculation, that it occupies only the six hundred thousandth part of the whole landscape, and, consequently, fills in my eye no more than the twelve hundred thousandth part of an inch. I next direct my eye towards the Frith of Forth, and perceive a steamboat sailing between Queensferry and Newhaven,—I distinctly trace its motion for the space of 40 minutes, at the end of which it reaches the chain pier at Newhaven, having passed over a space of five miles in length, which is but the eighth part of the *lineal* extent of the landscape in that direction; and, consequently, occupies, in the picture formed on my retina, a lineal space of only one-sixteenth of an inch in extent. And, if the boat be reckoned about 88 feet in length, its image is only the three hundredth part of this extent; and of course, fills a space in the eye of only the four thousand eight hundredth part of a *lineal* inch. Yet, my perception of the motion of the vessel could be produced only by a corresponding motion of its image in my eye; that is, by the *gradual* motion of a point one 4,800th of an inch in diameter, over a space one-sixteenth of an inch in length. How inconceiveably fine and accurate, then, must be the impression of those strokes which the rays of light, from visible objects, produce on the retina of the eye! The mind is lost in wonder when it attempts to trace so exquisite and admirable an effect.

I take a reflecting telescope, and, through it, view some of the distant parts of the landscape. My wonder is still increased, when I consider the new direction into which the rays of light are bent—the crossings and recrossings, and refractions, and reflections, that take place between the mirrors and the lenses of the instrument, and the successive images that are formed—so that, instead of a scene of confusion, which, previous to experience, might have been expected from the numerous additional bendings and intersections of the rays—I now perceive hundreds of objects, with the most perfect distinctness, which were before invisible. Rays of light from distant and minute objects, which a moment before made no sensible impression on my eye, being collected and variously modified by the telescope, now paint a vivid representation of their objects, in their true figures, colours, and positions.

From a consideration of the innumerable modifications of the rays of light, and of the immense variety of effects they produce in every region of the earth—I am led to investigate *what proportion of the solar light falls upon our globe*, in order to produce so diversified a scene of sublimity and beauty. Supposing the sun's rays to be chiefly confined, in their effects, within the limits of the planetary system, since they diverge in every direction, they must fill a cubical space of 3,600,000,000 miles in diameter; which, consequently, will contain about 24,000,000,000,000,000,000,000,000 cubical miles; so that an eye, placed in any point of this vast space, would receive a distinct impression from the solar rays. The solidity of the earth is about 264,000,000,000 cubical miles, and, therefore, it receives only the $\frac{1}{90,000,000,000,000,000}$th part of the light which fills the sphere of the solar system. So that the light which cheers all the inhabitants of the world, and unveils such a variety of beautiful and magnificent objects, is nothing more than *a single stream* of celestial radiance out of ninety thousand billions of similar streams which the great source of light is every moment diffusing throughout the surrounding worlds. But the solar rays are not confined within the bounds of the planetary system; their influence extends, in every direction, as far as the nearest stars, filling a cubical space at least 40,000,000,000,000 miles in diameter, and which contains 33,500,000,000,000,000,000,000,000,000,000,000,000,000,000, or thirty-three thousand, five hundred sextillions of cubical miles. And, were we to institute comparisons and calculations, with respect to the possible variety of effects they might produce throughout this immense region, whole pages might be filled with figures, cyphers, and computations. We might compute how many globes similar to the earth, or any of the larger planets, might be contained within this vast space, allowing several hundreds of cubical miles of empty space around each globe —how many myriads of refractions and reflections the rays of light would suffer, in regard to the peculiar objects connected with every one of these globes—how many eyes of sentient beings might be affected by the diversities of colour, shape, and motion, which would thus be produced—and what a variety of shades of light and colour, and what a diversity of scenery, would be produced, according to the distances of the respective globes from the central luminary. After what we have just now stated, however, we may rest satisfied with joining in the pious exclamation of one who had just finished a devout survey of the structure of the human frame: "Marvellous are thy works, and that my soul knoweth right well. How precious are thy thoughts unto me, O God!" (or, as the words might be rendered,) "How precious are thy wonderful contrivances concerning me, O God! how great is the sum of them! If I should count them, they are more in number than the sand." In what direction soever I turn mine eyes, whatever portion of thy works I investigate, "*I am still with thee.*"* Thine infinity and unsearchable wisdom are impressed on every object, so that I feel myself every moment encompassed by thine immensity, and am irresistibly led to wonder and adore.

I shall now conclude these reflections on vision, with two or three additional remarks. It is worthy of notice, in the first place, that the eye has the power of adapting itself to objects placed at different distances. By means of some delicate pieces of mechanism, not hitherto satisfactorily explained, it can perceive, with distinctness, a large object, at the distance of six miles, and the next moment it can adjust itself to the distinct perception of an object at the distance of six inches; so that it acts the part both of a telescope and a microscope, and can be instantaneously adjusted to perform either as the one instrument or as the other. This necessarily supposes a corresponding alteration in the state of the organ, every time we lift our eye from a near, to look at a distant object. Either the cornea is somewhat flattened, or the crystalline humour is pushed backwards, or both these changes, in combination with others, may concur in causing the rays from distant objects to unite exactly on the retina, without which distinct vision cannot be produced. This contrivance, in whatever kind of mechanism it may consist, is one which art would vainly attempt to imitate. We can see objects that are near us, with a microscope, and those that are distant, with a telescope; but we would in vain attempt to see distant objects with the former, or those that are only a few inches from us with the latter, without a variety of changes being made in the apertures and positions of the glasses belonging to the respective instruments. In this respect, therefore, as well as in every other, the eye is an optical instrument, incomparably superior to any instrument or imitation that art can produce. and, were it not for the peculiar property now described, it would be almost unfit for the purpose of vision, notwithstanding all the other delicate contrivances which enter into its construction. If it were adjusted only for the distinct perception of distant objects, every object within the limits of an ordinary apartment would appear a mass of confusion; and were it adjusted solely for viewing objects within the limits of a few feet or inches, the glories of the heavens, and the beautiful landscape of the earth, would be veiled from our sight as if they were enveloped in a mist.

Another circumstance worthy of attention, is, the power which the pupil of the eye possesses of contracting or enlarging the aperture or hole through which the light is admitted. When the light is too weak, the pupil is enlarged; when it is too strong, it is again contracted. Accordingly, we find, that when we enter a darksome apartment, though, at first, nothing can be accurately distinguished, yet, in the course of a minute or two, when the pupil has had time to dilate, we can perceive most objects with considerable distinctness. And, on the other hand, when we pass from a dark room to an apartment lighted up with a number of lustres, we feel uneasy at the sudden glare, till the pupil has contracted itself, and excluded a portion of the superfluous rays. Were it not for this property, we should for the most part either be surrounded with a disagreeable gloom or oppressed with an excessive splendour. It is for this reason, that we are unable to look upon the sun without being dazzled, and are under the necessity of closing the eyelids, or of turning away the head, when a strong light suddenly succeeds to darkness.

Again, it may not be improper to observe, how wisely the Author of nature has fixed the distance at which we ordinarily see near objects most distinctly. This distance is generally from five to eight inches from the eye. But had the eye been formed for distinct vision at the distance of only one inch, the object would have obstructed the light, and room would have been wanting for the performance of many necessary operations, which require the hand to intervene between the eye and the object. And had the limits of distinct vision for near objects been beyond two or three feet, sufficient light would not have been afforded for the inspection of minute objects, and we could neither have written a letter, nor have read a book, with the same convenience and ease we are now enabled to do.

From the preceding descriptions and remarks, it will evidently appear, with what admirable skill the different parts of the organs of vision are constructed, and how nicely they are adapted to the several ends they were intended to subserve. Were any one of these parts wanting, or obstructed in its functions, vision would either be impeded, or rendered painful and distressing, or

* Psalm cxxxix. 14, 17, 18.

completely destroyed. If any of the *humours* of the eye were wanting—if they were less transparent—if they were of a different refractive power—or if they were of a greater or less convexity than they now are, however minute the alteration might be, vision would inevitably be obstucted, and every object would appear confused and indistinct. If the retina, on which the images of objects are painted, were flat, instead of being concave, while objects in the middle of the view appeared distinct, every object towards the sides would appear dim and confused. If the *cornea* were as opaque as the sclerotica, to which it is joined, or if the retina were not connected with the optic nerve, no visible object could possibly be perceived. If one of the six muscles of the eye were wanting, or impeded in its functions, we could not turn it to the right; if a second were deficient, we could not turn it to the left; if a third, we could not lift it upwards; if a fourth, we could not move it downwards; and if it were deprived of the other two muscles, it would be apt to roll about in frightful contortions. If the eyes were placed in any other part of the body than the head—if they were much more prominent than they now are—if they were not surrounded by the bony socket in which they are lodged—and if they were not frequently covered by the eyelid—they would be exposed to a thousand accidents from which they are now protected. If they wanted moisture, and if they were not frequently wiped by the eyelids, they would become less transparent, and more liable to be inflamed; and if they were not sheltered by the eyebrows, the sweat and moisture of the forehead would frequently annoy them. Were the light which acts upon them devoid of colour—were it not reflected from objects in every direction—were its motion less swift, or its particles much larger than they now are—in short, were any one circumstance connected with the structure of this organ, and with the modification of the rays of light, materially different from its present arrangement, we should either be subjected to the hourly recurrence of a thousand painful sensations, or be altogether deprived of the entertainments of vision.

How admirable an organ, then, is the eye, and how nicely adapted to unveil to our view the glories of the universe! Without the application of any skill or laborious efforts, on our part, it turns in every direction, transports us to every surrounding object, depicts the nicest shades and colours on its delicate membranes, and

"Takes in, at once, the landscape of the world,
*At a small inlet, which a grain might close,*
And half creates the wond'rous world we see."
*Young.*

—How strikingly does it display, in every part of its structure and adaptations, the marks of benevolent design, and of Infinite Intelligence! However common it is to open our eyes, and to behold, in an instant, the beauties of an extensive landscape, and however little we may be accustomed to admire this wonderful effect,—there is not a doctrine in Religion, nor a fact recorded in Revelation, more mysterious and incomprehensible. An excellent French writer has wel observed—"The sight of a tree and of the sun, which God shows me, is as real and as immediate a revelation as that which led Moses towards the burning bush. The only difference between both these actions of God on Moses and me, is, that the first is out of the common order and economy; whereas the other is occasioned by the sequel and connexion of those laws which God has established for the regulation both of man and nature."

If, then, the eye of man (who is a depraved inhabitant of a world lying partly in ruins) is an organ so admirably fitted for extending our prospects of the visible creation—we may reasonably conclude, that organized beings, of superior intelligence and moral purity, possess the sense of vision in a much greater degree of perfection than man, in his present state of degradation—and that they may be enabled, by their *natural* organs, to penetrate into regions of the universe far beyond what man, by the aid of artificial helps, will ever be able to descry. It may not be altogether extravagant, nor even beyond the reality of existing facts, to suppose, that there are intelligences in the regions of Jupiter or Saturn, whose visual organs are in so perfect a state, that they can descry the mountains of our moon, and the continents, islands, and oceans which diversify our globe, and are able to delineate a map of its surface, to mark the period of its diurnal rotation, and even to distinguish its cities, rivers, and volcanoes. It is quite evident, that it must be equally easy to Divine Wisdom and Omnipotence, to form organs with powers of vision far surpassing what I have now supposed, as to form an organ in which the magnificent scene of heaven and earth is depicted, in a moment, within the compass of half an inch. There are animals whose range of vision is circumscribed within the limits of a few feet or inches; and, had we never perceived objects through an organ in the same state of perfection as that with which we are furnished, we could have formed as little conception of the sublimity and extent of our present range of sight, as we can now do of those powers of vision, which would enable us to descry the inhabitants of distant worlds. The invention of the telescope shows, that the penetrating power of the eye may be indefinitely increased; and since the art of man can extend the limits of natural vision, it is easy to conceive, that, in the hand of Omnipotence, a slight modification of the human eye might enable it, with the utmost distinctness, to penetrate into regions to which the imagination can set no bounds. And, therefore, it is not unreasonable to believe, that, in the future world, this will be one property, among others, of the *resurrection-body*, that it will be furnished with organs of vision far superior to the present, in order to qualify its intelligent inhabitant for taking an ample survey of the "riches and glory" of the empire of God.

I have dwelt somewhat particularly on the functions of the eye, in order to show, that it is only when we take a *minute* inspection of the operations of the Creator, that his Infinite Wisdom and Intelligence are most distinctly perceived. The greater part of Christians will readily admit that the Wisdom of God is manifested in every object, but few of them take the trouble to inquire *in what particular contrivances and adaptations* this wisdom is displayed; and, therefore, rest satisfied with vague and general views, which seldom produce any deep impression on the mind. "The works of the Lord," which are "great" and admirable, "*must be sought out* by all those who have pleasure therein;" and the more minutely they are inspected, the more exquisite and admirable do all his arrangements appear.

Were we to enter into an investigation of the *visual organs of the lower animals*, and to consider the numerous varieties which occur in their structure, position, and movements, and how nicely the peculiar organization of the eye is adapted to the general structure of the animal, and to its various necessities and modes of existence—the operation of the same inscrutable Wisdom and Intelligence would meet our eye at every step. *Birds*, for example, which procure their food by their beak, have the power of seeing distinctly at a very small distance; and, as their rapid motion through the air renders it necessary that they should descry objects at a considerable distance, they have two *peculiar* mechanical contrivances, connected with their organs of vision, for producing both these effects. One of these contrivances consists in a flexible rim formed of bone, which surrounds the broadest part of the eye, and by occasionally pressing upon its orb, shortens its focal distance, and thus enables it to inspect very near objects. The other consists of a peculiar muscle, which draws back, as occasion requires, the crystalline humour, by which means it can take a distinct view of a distant landscape; and can pass from the sight of a very near, to the sight of a distant object, with rapidity and ease. In *fishes*, which live in a medium of a different refractive power from that of air, the crystalline humour has a greater degree of convexity, and more nearly approaches to a globular form than that of land animals—which conformation is essentially requisite to distinctness of vision in the watery element. A fish of course cannot see distinctly in air, nor a quadruped under water; and every person who has dived into the water with his eyes open, knows, that though he may perceive the general forms and colours of objects, his vision is obscure and indistinct. In *hares* and *rabbits* the eyes are very convex and prominent, so that they can see nearly quite round them; whereas, in *dogs*, which pursue these animals, the visual organs are placed more in the front of the head, to look rather before than behind them. Some animals, as *cats* and *owls* which pursue their prey in the dark, have the pupil of their eye so formed as to be capable of great expansion, so that a few rays of light may make a lively impression on their retina; while the *eagle*, which is able to look directly at the sun, has its pupil capable of being contracted almost to a point. Insects, such as the *beetle*, the *fly*, and the *butterfly*, whose eyes are incapable of motion, have several thousands of small transparent globes set in a convex hemisphere, every one of which is capable of forming an image of an object; so that they are enabled to view the objects around them without moving their heads. But, it would be beyond the limits of my plan to prosecute this subject any farther; enough has already been stated, to show, that the eyes of men and other animals are master-pieces of art, which far transcend the human understanding; and that they demonstrate the consummate wisdom of Him who planned and constructed the organical functions of the various tribes of animated existence.

I shall now conclude this branch of my subject, by presenting an instance or two of the *mechanism* of the *bones*, and the movements it is fitted to produce.

The bones of the human frame are *articulated*, or connected together, in different ways, but most frequently in the following manner. Either, 1. a bone with a round head is articulated with a cavity, and plays in it as a ball in a socket; or, 2. they are connected together by a hinge-like articulation, which enables a bone to move up or down, backwards or forwards, like a door upon its hinges. An idea of these two motions, and the purposes they serve, may be obtained, by considering the construction of the pedestal of a telescope, and the joints on which it moves. One of the joints is of the nature of a hinge, by which a vertical motion, or a motion upwards and downwards is produced. A horizontal motion, or a motion towards the right hand or the left, is produced by a pivot moving in a socket; so that, by these two motions, the telescope can be made to point in any direction. Such is the nature of the articulations of the bones, and the movements they produce; and wherever one or other of these motions, or both of them combined, are requisite for the comfort and convenience of the individual, such a power of motion is uniformly found to exist. If the movement of a joint in every direction would, in any particular case, be found inconvenient, the hinge-like articulation is fixed upon; but if a motion in every direction is required for the convenient use of particular members, and for the variety of evolutions which a sentient being may have occasion to make, the ball and socket articulation is combined with the former.

For example, let any person, for a moment, consider the joints of his fingers, and compare them with the joint at his *wrist*, where the hand is connected with the fore arm. If he hold the back of his hand upwards, he will find that he can move his fingers upwards, or downwards; but he cannot turn them to the right hand, or to the left, so as to make them describe a circular motion. He will also find that his *wrist* is capable of a similar movement, so that the hand may be bent in a vertical direction. But, in addition to this motion, it is also capable of being turned in a horizontal direction, or from one side to another. In the former case, we have an example of the hinge articulation; in the latter, it is combined with an articulation which produces nearly the same effect as a pivot moving in a socket. Now, had the joints of the fingers been capable of the same motions as the wrist, the hand would have lost its firmness, and been incapable of performing a variety of mechanical operations which require objects to be held with a steady grasp. On the other hand, if the joint of the wrist had been formed in the same manner as the joints of the fingers, and confined to a vertical motion, the hand would have been incapable of one out of a hundred varied movements, which it can now perform with the greatest ease. In this case, we could not have bored a hole with a gimblet, cut down corn with a sickle, digged the earth with a spade, sewed clothes with a needle, tossed up a ball, or turned up the palm of the hand, for any of the useful purposes for which that motion was ordained. In short, without the rotatory motion of the wrist, the greater part of the operations connected with gardening, agriculture, cookery, washing, spinning, weaving, painting, carving, engraving, building, and other mechanical arts, could not be performed; and such of them as could be effected, would be accomplished only with the greatest inconvenience and labour. Any person may convince himself of this, by holding his hand in a horizontal position, and preventing his wrist joint from turning round, and then by trying what operations he can easily perform without the rotatory motion; and he will soon perceive with what exquisite skill the numerous movements of our animal frames have been contrived by the great Author of our existence. In each hand there are 27 bones, all of which are essential to the different motions we wish to perform. Every finger is composed of three bones, connected together by articulations, muscles, and ligaments. If, instead of three, each finger were composed of only one bone, it would be quite impossible for us to grasp a single object.

The same admirable contrivance may be perceived in the movements of which the *head* is susceptible. It was requisite, in order to our convenience and comfort, that we should be enabled to move our head backwards or forwards—to look up towards the heavens, or downwards to the ground. It was also expedient, that it should have a power of turning to the right, or to the left, so as to take in a considerable portion of a circle, without being under the necessity of turning round the whole body. Accordingly we find, that both these motions are provided for, in the manner in which the head is connected with the *vertebræ*. The head rests upon the uppermost of these bones, to which it is connected by a hinge joint, similar to those in the fingers, which allows it to move backwards and forwards; and, by means of a round, longish process, or projection, which moves in a socket, it is enabled to move horizontally, as upon an axis. Had the first motion been wanting, we could not have looked up to the zenith, without laying flat on our back; nor could we have looked to the ground, without placing our bodies in a prone position, and, in such a case, we could never have seen our own feet, unless when they were bent considerably forward. Had the second motion been wanting, we could have looked to nothing except the objects directly before us, without the trouble of turning round the whole body, either to the right, or to the left. But in the construction of our corporeal system, every thing is so arranged and adapted to another, as at once to contribute to ease, and facility of motion, in all the varied operations and movements we have occasion to perform; which circumstance forcibly demonstrates both the benevolent intentions, and the admirable wisdom of Him "whose hands have made and fashioned us," and who "breathed into our nostrils the breath of life."

The above are only two or three out of a hundred of similar instances, which might be produced to show the benevolent care which has been exercised in arranging and articulating the system of bones, of which the prop-work of the human frame is composed. Were we to enter into an investigation of the actions and uses of the various muscles, the wonderful system of veins and arteries, the action of the heart, stomach, and bowels; the process of respiration, and insensible perspiration, and the system of nerves, glands, lymphatics, and lacteals—a thousand instances of Divine wisdom and beneficence would crowd upon our view, which could not fail to excite the pious and contemplative mind to join in the devotions of the "sweet singer of Israel," "I will praise thee; for I am fearfully and wonderfully made; marvellous are thy works, and that my soul knoweth right well."—But as I intended to present only a few *specimens* of the Wisdom of God, as displayed in the construction of the material world, I shall conclude this department of my subject with a single reflection.*

*How foolish and ungrateful is it for rational beings to overlook the wise and benevolent arrangements of the Creator, in the material universe!* How many thousands of human beings pass their existence without once reflecting on the numerous evidences of Divine Wisdom and Beneficence, which appear around them, or feeling the least spark of gratitude for their preservation and comforts, to that Being "in whose hand their breath is, and whose are all their ways!" Yea, how many are there who consider themselves as standing high in the ranks of the Christian profession, who affect to look down, with a certain degree of contempt, on the study of the material works of God, as if it were too gross a subject for their spiritual attainments! They profess to trace the wisdom of God in the Scriptures, and to feel gratitude for his pardoning mercy; but they seldom feel that gratitude which they ought to do for those admirable arrangements in their own bodies, and the elements around them, by which their lives are preserved, and their happiness promoted; and even seem to insinuate, that they have little or nothing to do with the contrivances of the God of Nature. They leave it to the genius of infidel philosophers to trace the articulations of the bones, the branchings of the veins and arteries, the properties of light, and the composition of the atmosphere, while they profess to feast their minds on more sublime and spiritual entertainments. But, surely, such astonishing displays of the wisdom and benignity of the Most High, as creation exhibits, were never intended to be treated by his intelligent offspring with apathy or indifference; and to do so, must indicate a certain degree of ingratitude towards Him whose incessant energy sustains the whole assemblage of sentient and intelligent beings, and who displays himself, in their construction and preservation, to be "wonderful in counsel, and excellent in working." Shall we imagine, that, because God stands in the gracious relation of our Redeemer, he has ceased to stand in the relation of our Creator and Preserver? Or shall we consider those subjects as unworthy of our attention, which are the theme of the praises of the heavenly host? Rev. iv. 11. Can we suppose that the Almighty displayed his infinite wisdom in the curious organization of the human eye, that man—the only being in this world who is endowed with faculties capable of appreciating its structure, and for whose use and entertainment it was intended—should overlook such a wonderful piece of Divine workmanship, and feel not gratitude for the bestowment of so admirable a gift? Shall we extol the ingenuity displayed in a clock or a watch, in a chess-player, or a steam engine, and shall we feel no sentiment of admiration at the view of millions of instances of Divine mechanism which infinitely transcend the powers of the human understanding? To act in this manner, as too many are disposed to do, is unworthy of man, both as a Christian and as an intelligent agent. Such was not the conduct of the inspired writers; their spirituality of views did not lead them to neglect the contemplation of *any* of the works of God. "I will meditate on *all* thy works," says the Psalmist, "and talk of all thy doings; I will utter abundantly the memory of thy great goodness, and speak of thy wondrous works." Accordingly we find, that the wonders of the human frame, the economy of the animal and the vegetable tribes, the scenery of the "dry land," and of the "mighty deep," and the glories of the heavens, were the frequent subjects of their devout contemplation. They consider them in relation to the unceasing agency of God, by whom they were formed and arranged, and as declaring his Wisdom, Goodness, and Omnipotence: and, with this view, ought all the scenes of the visible creation to be investigated by his intelligent creatures.

We have reason to believe, that it is owing, in part, to want of attention to the Divine wisdom and beneficence, as exhibited in the construction of the visible world, that many professed Christians entertain so vague and confused ideas respecting the wisdom and goodness of Deity, as displayed in the economy of Redemption. The terms, Wisdom, Goodness, and Beneficence, in their mouths, become words almost without meaning, to which no precise or definite ideas are attached; because they have never considered the instances and the evidence of these attributes, displayed in the material creation. And, if our minds have not been impressed with a sense of the wisdom and beneficence of God, in those objects which are presented to the external sense, we cannot be supposed to have luminous and distinct ideas of those spiritual objects and arrangements which are removed beyond the sphere of our corporeal organs. For all our ideas, in relation to Religion and its objects, are primarily derived from the intimations we receive of external objects, through the medium of our senses; and, consequently, the more clearly we perceive the agency of God, in his visible operations, the more shall we be qualified to perceive the wisdom and harmony of his dispensations, as recorded in the volume of inspiration.

We live in a world, all the arrangements of which are the effects of infinite Wisdom. [illegible]

* Those who wish to prosecute this subject, particularly that part of it which relates to the contrivances of Divine Wisdom, which appear in the animal system, will find ample gratification in Nieuwentyt's "Religious Philosopher," Vol. 1, and Dr. Paley's "Natural Theology." A variety of useful remarks on this subject will also be found in Ray's "Wisdom of God in the Creation," Derham's "Physico-Theology," and Bonnet's "Contemplation of Nature."

are surrounded with wonders on every hand; and therefore we cease to admire, or to fix our attention on any one of the wonders daily performed by God. We have never been accustomed to contemplate or to inhabit a world where benevolence and wisdom are not displayed; and, therefore, we are apt to imagine, that the circumstances of our terrestrial existence could not have been much otherwise than they actually are. We behold the sun in the morning, ascending from the east —a thousand shining globes are seen in the canopy of the sky, when he has disappeared in the west. We open our eyelids, and the myriad of objects which compose an extensive landscape are, in a moment, painted on our retina,—we wish to move our bodies, and, in an instant, the joints and muscles of our hands and feet perform their several functions. We spread out our wet clothes to dry, and in a few hours the moisture is evaporated. We behold the fields drenched with rain, and in a few days it disappears, and is dispersed through the surrounding atmosphere, to be again imbodied into clouds. These are all *common* operations, and, therefore, thoughtless and ungrateful man seldom considers the obligations he is under to the Author of his existence, for the numerous enjoyments which flow from these wise arrangements. But were the globe we inhabit, and all its appendages, to remain in their present state—and were only the principle of *evaporation* and the *refractive and reflective properties of the air* to be destroyed—we should soon feel, by the universal gloom which would ensue, and by a thousand other inconveniences we should suffer, what a miserable world was allotted for our abode. We should most sensibly perceive the wisdom and goodness we had formerly overlooked, and would most ardently implore the restoration of those arrangements for which we were never sufficiently grateful. And why should we not *now*—while we enjoy so many comforts flowing from the plans of infinite Wisdom—have our attention directed to the benevolent contrivances within us, and around us, in order that grateful emotions may be hourly arising in our hearts, to the Father of our spirits? For the essence of true religion consists chiefly in *gratitude* to the God of our life, and the Author of salvation; and every pleasing sensation we feel from the harmonies and the beauties of nature, ought to inspire us with this sacred emotion. "Hearken unto this, O man! stand still, and consider the wonderful works of God. Contemplate the balancings of the clouds, the wondrous works of Him who is perfect in knowledge."—"He hath made the earth by his power, he hath established the world by his wisdom. When he uttereth his voice, there is a noise of waters in the heavens; he causeth the vapours to ascend from the ends of the earth, and bringeth the winds out of his treasures." While it is shameful for man to be inattentive to the wonders which surround him, what can be more pleasing and congenial to a rational and devout mind, than contemplations on the works of the Most High? "What can be more gratifying," says Sturm "than to contemplate, in the heavens, in the earth, in the water, in the night and day, and indeed, throughout all nature, the proofs which they afford of the wisdom, the purity, and the goodness of our great Creator and Preserver! What can be more delightful than to recognize, in the whole creation, in all the natural world, in every thing we see, traces of the ever-working providence and tender mercy of the great Father of all!"

---

## SECTION IV.

### *On the Goodness or Benevolence of the* DEITY.

THE Benevolence of God is that perfection of his nature, by which he communicates happiness to the various ranks of sensitive and intelligent existence.

The system of Nature, in all its parts, exhibits an unbounded display of this attribute of the Divine Mind, both in relation to man, and in relation to the subordinate tribes of animated existence. In relation to *Man*—the magnificence and glory of the heavens—the variegated colouring which is spread over the scene of nature—the beautiful flowers, shrubs, and trees, with which the earth is adorned, which not only delight the eye, but perfume the air with their delicious odours—the various kinds of agreeable sounds that charm the ear—the music of the feathered songsters, which fill the groves with their melody—the thousands of pleasant images which delight the eye, in the natural embellishments of creation—the agreeable feelings produced by the contact of almost every thing we have occasion to touch—the pleasure attached to eating, drinking, muscular motion, and activity—the luxuriant profusion, and rich variety of aliments which the earth affords—and the interchanges of thought and affection—all proclaim the Benevolence of our Almighty Maker, and show that the communication of happiness is one grand object of all his arrangements. For these circumstances are not *essentially* requisite to our existence We might have lived, and breathed, and walked though every thing we touched had produced pain; though every thing we ate and drank had been bitter; though every movement of our hands and feet had been accompanied with uneasiness and fatigue; though every sound had been as harsh as the saw of the carpenter; though no birds had warbled in the groves; though no flowers had decked the fields, or filled the air with their perfumes; though one unvaried scene of dull uniformity had prevailed, and beauty and sublimity had been swept from the face of nature; though the earth had been covered with a mantle of black, and no radiant orbs had appeared in our nocturnal sky. But what a miserable world should we then have inhabited, compared with that which we now possess! Life would have passed away without enjoyment; and pain would have overbalanced the pleasure of existence. Whereas, in the existing constitution of things, all the objects around us, and every sense of which we are possessed, when preserved in its natural vigour, have a direct tendency to produce pleasing sensations, and to contribute to our enjoyment: and it is chiefly when we indulge in foolish and depraved passions, and commit immoral actions, that the benevolent intentions of the Deity are frustrated, and pain and misery produced.

If we consider, further, that the inexhaustible bounty of the Creator, and the numerous pleasures we enjoy, are bestowed upon a guilty race of men, the benevolence of the Deity will appear in a still more striking point of view. Man has dared to rebel against his Maker; he is a depraved and ungrateful creature. The great majority of our race have banished God from their thoughts, trampled upon his laws, neglected to contemplate his works, refused to pay him that tribute of reverence and adoration which his perfections demand, have been ungrateful for his favours, have blasphemed his name, and have transferred to "four-footed beasts, and creeping things," that homage which is due to him alone. It has been the chief part of their employment, in all ages, to counteract the effects of his Beneficence, by inflicting injustice, oppression, and torture, upon each other; by maiming the human frame, burning cities and villages, turning fruitful fields into a wilderness, and by every other act of violence, carrying death and destruction through the world. And if *water, air*, and the *light of heaven*, had been placed within the limits of their control, it is more than probable, that whole nations would have been occasionally deprived of these elements, so essential to human existence. Yet, notwithstanding the prevalence of such depraved dispositions, the streams of Divine benevolence towards our apostate race have never yet been interrupted. The earth has never stopped in its career, and thrown nature into a scene of confusion; the light of heaven has never ceased to illume the world; the springs of water have never been dried up, nor has the fertile soil ceased to enrich the plains with golden harvests. God "hath not left himself without a witness," to his beneficence, in any age, in that he hath unceasingly bestowed on the inhabitants of the world "rain from heaven, and fruitful seasons, filling their hearts with food and gladness." This is one of the characters of Deity which forms the most perfect contrast to the selfish and revengeful dispositions of man, which as far transcends human benevolence, as the heavens in extent surpass the earth—a character calculated to excite our highest love and admiration, and which we are called upon, in the Sacred Oracles, to imitate and revere. "Be ye merciful, as your Father who is in heaven is merciful: for he maketh his sun to rise on the evil and on the good, and sendeth rain on the just and on the unjust."— "O that men would praise the Lord for his goodness, and for his wonderful works to the children of men."

From such considerations, we learn, even from the system of nature, that *mercy* is an attribute of the Deity; for, if mercy consists in bestowing favours on those who are unworthy, or who merit punishment, the greatest sinners in all ages have shared in it, and every individual of the human race now existing enjoys a certain portion of those comforts which flow from the benevolent arrangements which the Creator has established. "He maketh the sun to rise *on the evil* and on the good." Though the nations in ancient times, as well as at present, "walked in their own way," indulging in impiety, falsehood, lewdness, war, devastations, revenge, abominable idolatries, and every other violation of his law, he still supported the functions of their animal frames, and caused the influence of the sun, the rains, and the dews, to descend upon their fields, that they might be refreshed with his bounty, and filled "with food and gladness." If mercy were not an essential attribute of the Deity, he would have cut them down in the midst of their first transgressions, shattered to pieces the globe on which they dwelt, and buried them in eternal oblivion. But whether Divine mercy will extend to the final forgiveness of sin, and the communication of eternal happiness to such beings, can be learned only from the discoveries of revelation.

In relation to the *inferior animals*—the immense multitude of living creatures with which the earth is replenished, is a striking evidence of the vast profusion of Divine Beneficence. More than a hundred thousand species of animated beings are dispersed through the different regions of the air, the water, and the earth, besides myriads which are invisible to the unassisted eye. To estimate the number of individuals belonging to any one species is beyond the power of man. What countless myriads of herrings, for example, are contained in a single shoal, which is frequently more than six miles long and three miles broad. To estimate the number of individuals in all the different species would, therefore, be as impossible as to count the grains of sand in the Arabian deserts. There is not a single spot, in any region of the globe, but what teems with animated beings. Yet, all this vast assemblage of sensitive existence is amply provided for by the bountiful Creator. "These all wait upon him, and he giveth them their meat in due season." They enjoy not only life, but also a *happy* existence. The sportive motions and gesticulations of all the animal tribes—the birds skimming through the air, warbling in the groves, and perching on the trees—the beasts of the field, bounding in the forests, and through the lawns—the fishes sporting in the waters—the reptiles wriggling in the dust, and the winged insects, by a thousand wanton mazes—all declare that they are rejoicing in their existence, and in the exercise of those powers with which the Creator has furnished them. So that, wherever we turn our eyes, we evidently perceive, that "the earth is full of the goodness of the Lord;" and that "his tender mercies are over all his works." This subject is boundless—but it would be inconsistent with the limited plan of this work, to enter into any particular details. And it is the less necessary, when we consider, that every instance of Divine Wisdom is, at the same time, an instance of *benevolence;* for it is the ultimate object of all the wise contrivances in the system of Nature, that happiness may be communicated to the various ranks of sensitive and intelligent existence. *Goodness* chooses the *end*, and *wisdom* selects the most proper *means*, for its accomplishment; so that these two attributes must always be considered in simultaneous operation. And, therefore, the instances I have already specified, of the Wisdom and Intelligence of the Creator, may also be considered, as exemplifications of Divine Benevolence. I shall, therefore, conclude this topic with the following extract from Dr. Paley.

"Contrivance proves design; and the prominent tendency of the contrivance, indicates the disposition of the designer. The world abounds with contrivances; and all the contrivances we are acquainted with, are directed to beneficial purposes. Evil, no doubt, exists; but it is never that we can perceive, the object of contrivance. Teeth are contrived to eat, not to ache; their aching now and then, is incidental to the contrivance, perhaps inseparable from it; or even, if you will, let it be called a defect in the contrivance, but it is not the *object* of it. This is a distinction which well deserves to be attended to. In describing implements of husbandry, you will hardly say of a sickle, that it is made to cut the reaper's fingers, though from the construction of the instrument, and the manner of using it, this mischief often happens. But if you had occasion to describe instruments of torture or execution, This, you would say, is to extend the sinews; this to dislocate the joints; this to break the bones; this to scorch the soles of the feet. Here pain and misery are the very *objects* of the contrivance. Now nothing of this sort is to be found in the works of nature. We never discover a train of contrivance to bring about an evil purpose. No anatomist ever discovered a system of organization calculated to produce pain and disease; or in explaining the parts of the human body, ever said, This is to irritate; this to inflame; this duct is to convey the gravel to the kidneys; this gland to secrete the humour which forms the gout. If, by chance, he come at a part of which he knows not the use, the most he can say is, that it is uselses; no one ever suspects that it is put there to incommode, to annoy, or torment. Since, then, God hath called forth his consummate wisdom to contrive and provide for our happiness, and the world appears to have been constituted with this design at first, so long as this constitution is upheld by him, we must, in reason, suppose the same design to continue."—*Paley's Moral Philosophy*, *Book* II. *Chap.* 5.

Thus, I have endeavoured, in this and the preceding section, to exhibit a few specimens of the Wisdom and Goodness of God, in the system of nature. These might have been multiplied to an indefinite extent, but the instances adduced, I presume, are sufficient to show, that the economy of the material world is not altogether a barren subject, to a pious and contemplative mind. Every intelligent believer in Revelation will readily admit, that it would be a highly desirable object, to induce upon the mass of Christians such a habit of devout attention to the visible works of creation, as would lead them, in their social and solitary walks, to recognize the agency of God, in every object they behold; to raise their thoughts to Him as the Great First Cause, and to expand their hearts with emotions of gratitude. How very different must be the sentiments and the piety of the man who looks on the scene of wisdom and magnificence around him, with a "brute unconscious gaze," as thousands of professed Christians do—and the grateful and pious emotions of him who recognizes the benevolent agency of God, in the motions of his fingers, and his eyeballs; in the pulsation of his heart; in the picture of external objects every moment formed on his retina; in the reflection of the rays of light, and the diversified colours they produce; in the drying of his clothes; in the constitution of the atmosphere; in the beauty and magnificence of the earth and the heavens; and in every other object that meets his eye, in the expanse of nature! The numberless astonishing instances of Divine agency, which every where present themselves to our view in the scene around us, seem evidently intended to arrest the mind to a consideration of an "ever-present Deity;" and I envy not the sentiments or the feelings of that man who imagines, that he stands in no need of such sensible mediums, to impress his mind with a sense of the benevolent care and *omnipresence* of God.

# CHAPTER II.

## CONTAINING A CURSORY VIEW OF SOME OF THE SCIENCES WHICH ARE RELATED TO RELIGION AND CHRISTIAN THEOLOGY.

THEOLOGY has generally been viewed as a study of a very limited range: and, hence, when it has been admitted into the circle of the sciences, a much smaller space has been allotted for its discussion, than has been devoted to almost any other department of human knowledge. When considered, however, in its most extensive sense,—in its relations to the Divine Being—to his past and present dispensations towards the human race—to the present circumstances and the future destiny of man—and to the physical and moral condition of all the sentient and intelligent beings of which we have any intimation—it ought to be viewed as the most varied and comprehensive of all the sciences; as embracing, within its extensive grasp, all the other departments of useful knowledge, both human and divine. As it has God for its object, it must include a knowledge of the universe he has formed—of the movements which are continually going on throughout the wide extent of his empire, in so far as they lie open to our inspection—of the attributes which appear to be displayed in all his operations—of the moral laws he has framed for the regulation of holy intelligences—of the merciful arrangements he has made for the restoration of fallen man—of the plans by which the knowledge of his will is to be circulated and extended in the world in which we live—of the means by which truth, and moral purity, and order, are to be promoted among our apostate race, in order to their restoration to the happiness they have lost—together with all those diversified ramifications of knowledge, which have either a more remote or a more immediate bearing on the grand object now specified. Like the lines which proceed from the circumference to the centre of an immense circle—all the *moral** arts and sciences which have been invented by men—every department of human knowledge, however far it may, at first sight, appear to be removed from religion—may be considered as having a direct bearing on Theology, as the grand central point, and as having a certain tendency to promote its important objects.

It is much to be regretted, that Theology has so seldom been contemplated in this point of view—and that the sciences have been considered rather as so many independent branches of secular knowledge, than as subservient to the elucidation of the facts and doctrines of religion and to the accomplishment of its benevolent designs. Hence, it has happened that Philosophy and Religion, instead of marching hand in hand to the portals of immortality, have frequently set themselves in hostile array; and combats have ensued equally injurious to the interests of both parties. The Philosopher has occasionally been disposed to investigate the economy of nature, without a reference to the attributes of that Almighty Being who presides over its movements, as if the universe were a self-moving and independent machine; and has not unfrequently taken occasion, from certain obscure and insulated facts, to throw out insinuations hostile to the truth and the character of the Christian Revelation. The Theologian, on the other hand, in the heat of his intemperate zeal against the infidel philosopher, has unguardedly been led to declaim against the study of science, as if it were unfriendly to religion—has, in effect, set the works of God in opposition to his word—has confounded the foolish theories of speculative minds with the rational study of the works of Deity—and has thus prevented the mass of mankind from expanding their minds, by the contemplation of the beauties and sublimities of nature.

It is now high time that a complete reconciliation were effected between these contending parties. Religion ought never to disdain to derive her supports and illustrations from the researches of science; for the investigations of philosophy into the economy of Nature, from whatever motives they may be undertaken, are nothing else than an inquiry into the plans and operations of the Eternal Mind. And Philosophy ought always to consider it as her highest honour, to walk as an handmaid in the train of that religion which points out the path to the regions of eternal bliss. By their mutual aid, and the subserviency of the one to the other, the moral and intellectual improvement of man will be promoted, and the benevolent purposes of God, in the kingdom of providence, gradually accomplished. But when set in opposition to each other, the human mind is bewildered and retarded in its progress, and the Deity is apt to be considered as set in opposition to himself—as proclaiming one system of doctrines from the economy of revelation, and another, and an opposite system, from the economy of nature. But if the Chris-

* The epithet moral is here used in its application to arts, because there are certain arts which must be considered as having an immoral tendency, such as the art of war, the art of boxing, of gambling, &c. and which, therefore, cannot have a direct tendency to promote the objects of religion.

tian Revelation and the system of the material world derived their origin from the same Almighty Being, the most complete harmony must subsist between the revelations they respectively unfold; and the apparent inconsistencies which occur must be owing chiefly to the circumstances of our present station in the universe, and to the obscure and limited views we are obliged to take of some of the grand and diversified objects they embrace. And, therefore, we have reason to believe that, when the system of nature shall be more extensively explored, and the leading objects of revelation contemplated in a clearer light, without being tinged with the false colouring of party opinions and contracted views, and when rational inquirers shall conduct their researches with a greater degree of reverence, humility and Christian temper, the beauty and harmony of all the plans and revelations of the Deity, in reference both to the physical and the moral world, will be more distinctly perceived and appreciated.

In the following cursory sketches, it forms no part of my plan to trace even an *outline* of the different sciences which are connected with religion, much less to enter into any particular details, in relation to their facts and principles. It would be comparatively easy to fill up the remaining sheets of this volume with skeletons of the different sciences; but such meager details as behooved to be brought forward, could not be interesting to the general reader, and would fail in accomplishing the object proposed. My design simply is, to select some leading facts, or general truths, in relation to some of the physical sciences, for the purpose of showing their connection with the objects of religion and the interests of rational piety. At the same time, such definite descriptions will be given as will enable common readers to appreciate the objects and bearings of the different branches of knowledge which may be presented to their view.

The first science* I shall notice is that of

### NATURAL HISTORY.

This science, taken in its most comprehensive sense, includes a knowledge and description of all the known facts in the material universe.

It is to be regretted, that most books published under the title of *Natural History*, to which common readers have access, contain nothing more than a general description of animals, as if this science were confined merely to one class of beings; whereas there is an infinite variety of other objects seldom noticed, which would appear no less interesting, and, in some instances, much more novel and gratifying to the general reader, and to the youthful mind. All the diversified forms of matter, whether existing on the surface or in the bowels of the earth, in the ocean, the atmosphere, or in the heavens, form the legitimate objects of this department of the science of nature.

Were we, therefore, to sketch a comprehensive outline of the subjects of Natural History, we might, in the first place, take a cursory survey of the globe we inhabit, in reference to its magnitude, figure, motions, and general arrangements—the form, relations, and extent of its continents—the numerous islands which diversify the surface of the ocean—the magnitude, the direction, and the extent of its rivers, and the quantity of water they pour into the ocean—the direction, elevation, and extent of the different ranges of mountains which rise from its surface—the plains, morasses, lakes, forests, dells, and sandy deserts, which diversify its aspect—the extent, the motions, the colour, and the different aspects of the ocean, and the facts which have been ascertained respecting its saltness, its depth, its bottom, and its different currents. We might next take a more particular view of some of the most remarkable objects on its surface, and give a detail of the facts which are known respecting the history of *volcanoes*—their number—the countries in which they are situated—the awful phenomena they exhibit—and the devastations they have produced; the history of *earthquakes*, their phenomena and effects, and the countries most subject to their ravages—basaltic and rocky wonders, natural bridges, precipices, cataracts, ice islands, icebergs, glaciers, whirlpools, mineral wells, reciprocating fountains, boiling springs, sulphuric mountains, bituminous lakes, volcanic islands—the various aspects of nature in the different zones, and the contrasts presented between the verdant scenes of tropical climes, and the icy cliffs of the polar regions. We would next take a survey of the subterraneous wonders which lie beneath the surface of the earth—the immense chasms and caverns which wind in various directions among the interior strata of our globe—such as the great Kentucky cavern, and the grotto of Antiparos—the mines of salt, coal, copper, lead, diamond, iron, quicksilver, tin, gold, and silver—the substances which compose the various strata, the fossil bones, shells, and petrifactions, which are imbedded in the different layers, and the bendings and disruptions which appear to have taken place in the substances which compose the exterior crust of the earth. We might next survey the *atmosphere* with which the earth is environed, and give a detail of the facts which have been ascertained respecting its specific gravity and pressure, the elementary principles of which it is compounded, its refractive

* The term *science*, in its most general and extensive sense, signifies *knowledge*, particularly that species of knowledge which is acquired by the exertion of the human faculties. In a more restricted sense, it denotes a *systematic* species of knowledge, which consists of rule and order, such as Mathematics, Astronomy, Natural Philosophy, &c.—In the discussions contained in this work, it is used in its most general sense, as denoting the various departments of human knowledge, in which sense history, both natural, civil, and sacred, may be termed *science*

and reflective powers, and the phenomena which result from its various properties and modifications—the *meteors* which appear in its different regions—thunder and lightning, winds, hail, rain, clouds, rainbows, parhelias or mock-suns, meteoric stones, the aurora borealis, luminous arches, ignes fatui, the mirage, the fata morgana, hurricanes, monsoons, whirlwinds and waterspouts, sounds and echoes.

In prosecuting our survey of sublunary nature, we would next advert to the various orders of the *vegetable tribes*—their anatomical structure—the circulation of their juices—the food by which they are nourished—the influence of light and air on their growth and motions—their male and female organs—their periods of longevity—their modes of propagation—their diseases and dissolution—their orders, genera, and species—their immense variety—their influence on the salubrity of the atmosphere—the relation which their roots, leaves, and fruits bear to the wants of man and other animals, in supplying food, clothing, and materials for constructing habitations—the gums and resinous substances they exude—the odours they exhale—the variety of colours they exhibit—the vast diversity of forms in which they appear—and the beauty and variety which they spread over the whole face of nature.

The *mineral kingdom* would next require to be surveyed. We would inquire into the facts which have been ascertained respecting the *earthy*, *saline*, *inflammable*, and *metallic* substances which are found on the surface and in the bowels of the earth—their specific and distinguishing characters—the elementary principles, or simple substances, of which they are composed—the regions of the earth where the respective minerals most frequently abound—and the ends which they are designed to accomplish in the constitution of the globe. We would consider, more particularly, the various metals, such as iron, copper, lead, tin, gold, silver, bismuth, zinc, &c. in reference to the substances with which they are united in their native ores—the changes produced upon them by the action of oxygen and the different acids—their combustibility—their combination with phosphorus, sulphur, and carbon; and the various compounds into which they may be formed—their important uses in the arts which minister to the comfort and embellishment of human life—their relation to the multifarious necessities of man—and the wisdom and goodness of the Creator, as displayed in their arrangement in the bowels of the earth, and in the admirable properties of which they are possessed. In these details, the natural history of *Iron* would hold a prominent place. In point of *utility*, it claims the highest rank in the class of metals, and is intrinsically more valuable than gold and silver, and all the diamonds of the East.—There is scarcely a mineral substance in the whole compass of nature, which affords a more striking instance of the beneficial and harmonious adaptation of things in the universal system. We would, therefore, consider it in reference to its vast abundance in all parts of the world—the numerous substances into which it enters into combination—its magnetical property—its capability of being fused and welded—the numerous useful utensils it has been the means of producing—its agency in carrying forward improvements in art and science, in the civilization of barbarous tribes, and in promoting the progress of the human mind; and the aids which it affords to the Christian missionary in heathen lands.

Having surveyed the inanimate parts of the terraqueous globe, and its appendages, we might next direct our attention to the animated tribes with which it is peopled. Beginning at *Man*, the head of the animal creation, we would detail the principal facts which have been ascertained respecting his structure and organical functions—the muscular movements of the human body, the system of bones, nerves, veins, and arteries; the process of respiration; and the organs of vision, hearing, smelling, tasting, and feeling, by which he holds a correspondence with the material world—the modifications which appear in his corporeal frame and in his mental faculties, during the periods of infancy, puberty, manhood, and old age—the causes and phenomena of sleep and dreaming—the varieties of the human race, in respect of colour, stature, and features—the deviations from the ordinary course of nature, which occasionally occur, in the case of monsters, dwarfs, and giants—the moral and intellectual faculties—and those distinguishing characteristics which prove the superiority of man over the other tribes of animated nature.

The inferior ranks of the animal creation would next demand our attention. We would take a survey of the numerous tribes of *Quadrupeds, Birds, Fishes, Serpents, Lizards, and Insects*, in reference to the characteristic marks by which the different species are distinguished,—their food and habitations—the different modes in which they display their architective faculty, in constructing places of abode for shelter and protection—the clothing with which they are furnished—their sagacity in finding out the proper means for subsistence and self-preservation—their hostilities—their artifices in catching their prey, and escaping their enemies—their modes of propagation—their transformations from one state and form to another—their migrations to different countries and climates—their various instincts—their care in rearing and protecting their young—their passions, mental characters, and social dispositions—their language, or modes of communication with each other—their capacities for instruction and improvement—their different powers of locomotion—the adaptation of all their organs to the purposes for which they seem intended—the indications they give of being possessed of moral dispositions and rational powers—their different periods of longevity, and the ends which they are intended to subserve in the system of nature. Along with these details, certain views might be exhibited of the various forms of sensitive life, and modes of existence, which obtain in those numerous species of animals which are invisible to the naked eye, and which the microscope discovers in almost every department of nature.

Having surveyed the objects which compose our sublunary system, we would next direct our view to the regions of the sky, and contemplate the facts which have been discovered in relation to the celestial orbs. We would first attend to the *apparent* motion of the sun, the different points of the horizon at which he seems to rise and set, and the different degrees of elevation to which he arrives, at different seasons of the year,—the different aspects he presents as viewed from different parts of the earth's surface, and the different lengths of days and nights in different parts of the world. We would next attend to the varied phases of the moon—the direct and retrograde motions of the planets — the apparent diurnal motion of the whole celestial sphere, from east to west—and the different clusters of stars which are seen in our nocturnal sky, at different seasons of the year. We would next consider the deductions which science has made, respecting the order and arrangement of the planets which compose the solar system—their distances from the sun, and from the earth—their magnitudes —the periods of their diurnal and annual revolutions — the secondary planets, or moons, which accompany them — their eclipses — the various phenomena which their surfaces present when viewed through telescopes—the physical influence which some of them produce on the surface of our globe—and the singular appearance of those bodies called *Comets*, which occasionally visit this part of our system. We would, in the next place, extend our views to the starry regions, and consider the number of stars which present themselves to the naked eye — the immensely greater numbers which are discovered by telescopes—the systems into which they appear to be arranged — the facts which have been ascertained respecting *new* stars—double and triple stars—stars once visible, which have now disappeared from the heavens—variable stars, whose lustre is increased and diminished at different periods of time—and the structure and position of the many hundreds of *Nebulæ*, or starry systems, which appear to be dispersed throughout the immensity of creation.

All the particulars now stated, and many others which might have been specified—*considered simply as facts* which exist in the system of Nature—form the appropriate and legitimate objects of Natural History, and demand the serious attention of every rational intelligence that wishes to trace the perfections and agency of the Almighty Creator. To investigate the *causes* of the diversified phenomena which the material world exhibits, and the principles and modes by which many of the facts now alluded to are ascertained, is the peculiar province of Natural Philosophy, Chymistry, and the Mathematical Sciences.

Amid so vast a variety of objects as Natural History presents, it is difficult to fix on any particular facts, as specimens of the interesting nature of this department of knowledge, without going beyond the limits to which I am necessarily confined in this volume. I shall content myself with a description of two objects, which have a reference chiefly to the vegetable kingdom.—The first of these is

The Banian Tree.—"This tree, which is also called the *Burr Tree*, or the *Indian Fig*, is one of the most curious and beautiful of Nature's productions, in the genial climate of India, where she sports with the greatest variety and profusion. Each tree is in itself a grove; and some of them are of an amazing size and extent, and, contrary to most other animal and vegetable productions, seem to be exempted from decay. Every branch from the main body throws out its own roots; at first, in small tender fibres, several yards from the ground; these continually grow thicker, until, by a gradual descent, they reach the surface, and there, striking in, they increase to large trunks, and become parent trees, shooting out new branches from the tops. These, in time, suspend their roots, and receiving nourishment from the earth, swell into trunks, and shoot forth other branches; thus continuing in a state of progression, so long as the earth, the first parent of them all, contributes her sustenance. A banian tree, with many trunks, forms the most beautiful walks, vistas, and cool recesses, that can be imagined. The leaves are large, soft, and of a lively green; the fruit is a small fig, when ripe of a bright scarlet, affording sustenance to monkeys, squirrels, peacocks, and birds of various kinds, which dwell among the branches.

"The Hindoos are peculiarly fond of the banian tree; they consider its long duration, its outstretching arms, and its overshadowing beneficence, as emblems of the Deity, and almost pay it divine honours. The brahmins, who thus 'find a fane in every sacred grove,' spend much of their time in religious solitude, under the shade of the banian tree; they plant it near their temples or pagodas; and in those villages where there is no structure erected for public worship, they place an image under one of these trees, and there perform a morning and evening sacrifice. The natives of all castes and tribes are fond of recreating in the cool recesses, beautiful walks, and lovely vistas of this umbrageous canopy, impervious to the hottest beams of a tropical sun. These are the trees under which a sect of naked philosophers, called Gymnosophists, assembled in Arrian's days, and this historian of Ancient Greece presents a true picture of the modern Hindoos.—'In winter,' he says, 'the Gymnosophists enjoy the benefit of the sun's rays in the open air; and in summer, when the heat becomes excessive, they pass their time in cool and moist places, under large trees, which according to the accounts of Nearchus, cover a circumference of *five acres*, and extend their branches so far, that *ten thousand men* may easily find shelter under them.

"On the banks of the river Narbuddy, in the province of Guzzerat, is a banian tree, supposed, by some persons, to be the one described by Nearchus, and certainly not inferior to it. It is distinguished by the name of Cubbeer Burr, which was given it in honour of a famous saint. High floods have, at various times, swept away a considerable part of this extraordinary tree; but what still remains, is nearly *two thousand feet* in circumference, measured round the principal stems; the overhanging branches, not yet struck down, cover a much larger space; and under it grow a number of custard-apple and other fruit trees. The large trunks of this single tree amount to *three hundred and fifty*; and the smaller ones exceed *three thousand*; every one of these is constantly sending forth branches and hanging roots, to form other trunks and become the parents of a future progeny. The Cubbeer Burr is famed throughout Hindostan, not only on account of its great extent, but also of its surpassing beauty. The Indian armies generally encamp around it; and at stated seasons, solemn Jatarras, or Hindoo festivals, to which thousands of votaries repair, from every part of the Mogul empire, are there celebrated. It is said that seven thousand persons find ample room to repose under its shade. It has long been the custom of the British residents in India, on their hunting and shooting parties, to form extensive encampments, and spend weeks together, under this delightful and magnificent pavilion, which affords a shelter to all travellers, particularly to the religious tribes of the Hindoos. It is generally filled with greenwood pigeons, doves, peacocks, and a variety of feathered songsters—with monkeys, which both divert the spectator, by their antic tricks, and interest him by the paternal affection they display to their young offspring, in teaching them to select their food, and to exert themselves in jumping from bough to bough,—and is shaded by bats of a large size, many of them measuring upwards of six feet from the extremity of one wing to the other. This tree affords not only shelter, but sustenance, to all its inhabitants, being covered, amid its bright foliage, with small figs, of a rich scarlet, on which they all regale with as much delight as the lords of creation on their more costly fare, in their parties of pleasure."

• See *Encyclopedia Britannica*, Art. *Ficus*.

This tree, which is doubtless one of the most singular and magnificent objects in the vegetable kingdom, appears to be a world in miniature, in which thousands, both of human beings and of the inferior tribes that traverse the earth and the air, may find ample accommodation and subsistence. What a striking contrast does it present to the forests of trees, or mushrooms, which are perceived by the help of the microscope, in a piece of *mouldiness*—every plant of which is several hundreds of times smaller than the point of a fine needle! Yet both are the effects of the agency of the same All-wise and Omnipotent Being. And what an immense variety of gradations is to be found in the vegetable world, between these two extremes—every part of the vast interval being filled up with flowers, herbs, shrubs, and trees of every colour, form, and size, and in such vast multitudes and profusion that no man can number them!

An object, which approximates in a certain degree to the one now described, is mentioned in "Staunton's Account of Macartney's Embassy to China," p. 70. It is called by botanists *Adansonia*, and is also known by the name of the *Monkey Bread Tree*, and was discovered in the island of St. Jago. "The circumference or girth of the base was 56 feet, which soon divided into two vast branches, the one in a perpendicular direction, whose periphery, or girth, was 42 feet, the other 26. Another, of the same species, stood near it, whose single trunk, girthing only 38 feet, was scarcely noticed."

The only other specimen I shall exhibit to the reader has a relation both to the animal and to the vegetable kingdom. It is well known that the examination of flowers, and vegetables of every description, by the microscope, opens a new and interesting field of wonders to the inquiring naturalist. Sir John Hill has given the following curious account of what appeared on his examining a carnation.

"The principal flower in an elegant bouquet was a carnation: the fragrance of this led me to enjoy it frequently and near. The sense of smelling was not the only one affected on these occasions: while that was satiated with the powerful sweet, the ear was constantly attacked by an extremely soft, but agreeable murmuring sound. It was easy to know that some animal within the covert must be the musician, and that the little noise must come from some little creature, suited to produce it. I instantly distended the lower part of the flower, and placing it in a full light, could discover troops of little insects frisking, with wild jollity, among the narrow pedestals that supported its leaves, and the little threads that occupied its centre. What a fragrant world for their habitation! What a perfect security from all annoyance, in the dusky husk that surrounded the scene of action! Adapting a microscope to take in, at one view, the whole base of the flower, I gave myself an opportunity of contemplating what they were about, and this for many days together, without giving them the least disturbance. Thus, I could discover their economy, their passions, and their enjoyments. The microscope, on this occasion, had given what nature seemed to have denied to the objects of contemplation. The base of the flower extended itself under its influence to a vast plain; the slender stems of the leaves became trunks of so many stately cedars; the threads in the middle seemed columns of massy structure, supporting at the top several ornaments; and the narrow spaces between were enlarged into walks, parterres, and terraces. On the polished bottoms of these, brighter than Parian marble, walked in pairs, alone, or in larger companies, the winged inhabitants; these from little dusky flies, for such only the naked eye would have shown them, were raised to glorious glittering animals, stained with living purple, and with a glossy gold, that would have made all the labours of the loom contemptible in the comparison. I could, at leisure, as they walked together, admire their elegant limbs, their velvet shoulders, and their silken wings; their backs vying with the empyrean in its blue; and their eyes, each formed of a thousand others, outglittering the little planes on a brilliant; above description, and too great almost for admiration. I could observe them here singling out their favourite females; courting them with the music of their buzzing wings with little songs, formed for their little organs; leading them from walk to walk, among the perfumed shades, and pointing out to their taste the drop of liquid nectar, just bursting from some vein within the living trunk—here were the perfumed groves, the more than mystic shades of the poet's fancy realized. Here the happy lovers spent their days in joyful dalliance, or, in the triumph of their little hearts, skipped after one another from stem to stem, among the painted trees, or winged their short flight to the close shadow of some broader leaf, to revel undisturbed in the heights of all felicity."

This picture of the splendour and felicity of insect life, may, to certain readers, appear somewhat overcharged. But those who have been much in the habit of contemplating the beauties of the animal and vegetable world, through microscopes, can easily enter into all the views which are here described. I have selected this example, for the purpose of illustrating the unbounded goodness of the Creator, in the vast profusion of enjoyment he has communicated, even to the lowest tribes of animal existence, and as a specimen of those invisible worlds which exist beyond the range of our natural vision. For it appears that there is a gradation of worlds downward as well as upward. However small our globe may appear when compared with the sun and with the immensity of starry systems which lie dispersed through the infinity of space, there are worlds filled with myriads of living beings, which, in point of size and extent, bear as small a proportion to the earth, as the earth bears to the vast assemblage of the celestial worlds. A single flower, a leaf, or a drop of water, may appear as large and as diversified in its structure, to some of the beings which inhabit it, as the whole earth appears to the view of man; and a thousand scenes of magnificence and beauty may be presented to their sight, of which no distinct conception can be formed by the human mind. The many thousands of transparent globes, of which their eyes are composed, may magnify and multiply the objects around them without end, so that an object scarcely visible to the eye of man may appear to them as a vast extended universe.

"Having examined," says St. Pierre, "one day, by a microscope, the flowers of thyme, I distinguished in them, with equal surprise and delight, superb flagons with a long neck, of a substance resembling the amethyst, from the gullets of which seemed to flow ingots of liquid gold. I have never made observations of the *corolla*, simply of the smallest flower, without finding it composed of an admirable substance, half transparent, studded with brilliants, and shining in the most lively colours. The beings which live under a reflex thus enriched, must have ideas very different from ours, of light, and of the other phenomena of nature. A drop of dew, filtering in the capillary and transparent tubes of a plant, presents to them thousands of cascades; the same drop fixed as a wave on the extremity of one of its prickles, an ocean without a shore; evaporated into air, a vast aerial sea. It is credible, then, from analogy, that there are animals feeding on the leaves of plants like the cattle in our meadows and on our mountains, which repose under the shades of a down imperceptible to the naked eye, and which, from goblets formed like so many suns, quaff nectar of the colour of gold and silver."

Thus it appears, that the universe extends to infinity on either hand; and that whenever matter exists, from the ponderous globes of heaven down to the invisible atom, there the Almighty Creator has prepared habitations for countless orders of existence, from the seraph to the animalcula, in order to demonstrate his boundless beneficence, and the infinite variety of modes by which he can diffuse happiness through the universal system.

"How sweet to muse upon His skill display'd
Infinite skill! in all that he has made;
To trace in nature's most minute design
The signature and stamp of power divine;
Contrivance exquisite, expressed with ease,
Where unassisted sight no beauty sees;
The shapely limb and lubricated joint,
Within the small dimensions of a point:
Muscle and nerve miraculously spun,
His mighty work who speaks and it is done;
Th' invisible in things scarce seen reveal'd;
To whom an atom is an ample field!"

*Cowper's Retirement.*

With regard to the *religious* tendency of the study of Natural History, it may be remarked—that, as all the objects which it embraces are the *workmanship of God*—the delineations and descriptions of the Natural Historian must be considered as "The history of the operations of the Creator;" or, in other words, so far as the science extends, "The history of the Creator himself:" for the marks of his incessant agency, his power, wisdom, and beneficence, are impressed on every object, however minute, throughout the three kingdoms of nature, and throughout every region of earth, air, and sky. As the Deity is invisible to mortal eyes, and cannot be directly contemplated by finite minds, without some material medium of communication—there are but two mediums with which we are acquainted, by which we can attain a knowledge of his nature and perfections. These are, either the *facts* which have occurred in the course of his providential dispensations towards our race, since the commencement of time, and the moral truths connected with them—or, the facts which are displayed in the economy of nature. The first class of facts is recorded in the Sacred Hisory, and in the Annals of Nations; the second class is exhibited in the diversified objects and motions which appear throughout the system of the visible universe. The one may be termed the *Moral History*, and the other, the *Natural History*, of the operations of the Creator. It is obviously incumbent on every rational being, to contemplate the Creator through both these mediums; for each of them conveys its distinct and peculiar revelations; and consequently our perception of Deity through the one medium does not supersede the necessity of our contemplating him through the other. While, therefore, it is our duty to contemplate the perfections, the providence, and the agency of God, as displayed in the Scripture Revelation, it is also incumbent upon us, to trace his attributes in the System of Nature, in order that we may be enable to contemplate the eternal Jehovah, *in every variety of aspect*, in which he has been pleased to exhibit himself, in the universe he has formed.

The visible creation may be considered as a permanent and sensible manifestation of Deity, intended every moment to present to our view the unceasing energies of Him "in whom we live and move." And if the train of our thoughts were directed in its proper channel, we would perceive God in every object, and in every movement: we would behold him operating in the whirlwind, and in the storm; in the subterraneous cavern, and in the depths of the ocean; in the gentle rain, and the refreshing breeze; in the rainbow, the fiery meteor, and the lightning's flash; in the splendours of the sun, and the majestic movements of the heavens; in the frisking of the lambs, the songs of birds, and the buzz of insects, in the circulation of our blood, the movements of our joints, the motion of our eyeballs, and in the rays of light which are continually darting from surrounding objects, for the purposes of vision. For these, and ten thousand other agencies in the system of nature, are nothing else but the voice of Deity, proclaiming to the sons of men, in silent but emphatic language, "Stand still, and consider the wonderful works of God."

If, then, it be admitted, that the study of Nature is the study of the Creator—to overlook the grand and beautiful scenery with which we are surrounded, or to undervalue any thing which Infinite Wisdom has formed, is to overlook and contemn the Creator himself. Whatever God has thought proper to create, and to present to our view in the visible world, it becomes man to study and contemplate, that, from thence, he may derive motives to excite him to the exercise of reverence and adoration, of gratitude and praise. In so far as any individual is unacquainted with the various facts of the history of nature, in so far does he remain ignorant of the manifestations of Deity; for every object, on the theatre of the universe, exhibits his character and designs in a different point of view. He who sees God only as he displays himself in his operations on the earth, but has never contemplated the firmament with the eye of reason, must be unacquainted with those amazing energies of eternal Power, which are displayed in the stupendous fabric and movements of the orbs of heaven. He who sees God only in the general appearances of nature, but neglects to penetrate into his minute operations, must remain ignorant of those astonishing manifestations of divine wisdom and skill which appear in the contrivances, adaptations, and functions of the animal and the vegetable kingdoms. For, the more we know of the work, the more accurate and comprehensive will be our views of the Intelligence by whom it was designed; and the farther we carry our investigations of the works of God, the more admirable and astonishing will his plans and perfections appear.

In short, a devout contemplation of the works of nature tends to ennoble the human soul, and to dignify and exalt the affections. It inspires the mind with a relish of the beauty, the harmony, and order which subsist in the universe around us—it elevates the soul to the love and admiration of that Being who is the author of our comforts, and of all that is sublime and beneficent in creation, and excites us to join with all holy beings in the chorus of praise to the God and Father of all. For they

"Whom Nature's works can charm, with God himself
Hold converse, grow familiar day by day
With his conceptions, act upon his plan,
And form to his the relish of their souls."

The man who surveys the vast field of nature with the eye of reason and devotion, will not only gain a more comprehensive view of that illimitable power which organized the universe, but will find his sources of enjoyment continually increased, and will feel an ardent desire after that glorious world, where the veil which now hides from our sight some of the grandest manifestations of Deity will be withdrawn, and the wonders of Omnipotence be displayed in all their splendour and perfection.

In conformity with these sentiments, we find the inspired writers, in numerous instances, calling our attention to the wonders of creating power and wisdom. In one of the first speeches in which the Almighty is introduced as addressing the sons of men, and the longest one in the Bible,* our attention is exclusively directed to the subjects of Natural History; — the whole address having a reference to the economy of Divine Wisdom in the arrangement of the world at its first creation—the wonders of the ocean, and of light and darkness—the phenomena of thunder and lightning, rain, hail, snow, frost, and other meteors in the atmosphere—the intellectual faculties of man, and the economy and instincts of quadrupeds, birds, fishes, and other tribes of animated existence. Indeed, the greater part of the sublime descriptions contained in the book of Job has a direct reference to the agency of God in the material creation, and to the course of his providence in relation to the different characters of men; and the reasonings of the different speakers in that sacred drama proceed on the supposition that their auditors were intimately acquainted with the varied appearances of nature, and their tendency to exhibit the character and perfections of the Omnipotent Creator. We find the Psalmist, in the 104th Psalm, employed in a devout description of similar objects, from the contemplation of which his mind is raised to adoring views of their Almighty Author—and, from the whole of his survey, he deduces the following conclusions:—"How manifold are thy works, O Lord! *In wisdom* thou hast made them all! The earth is full of thy riches; so is this great and wide sea, wherein are things creeping innumerable, both small and great beasts. The glory of the Lord shall endure for ever; the Lord shall rejoice in all his works.† I will sing unto the Lord as long as I live; I will sing praises to my God, while I have my being."

But in order to enter into the spirit of such sublime reflections, we must not content ourselves with a superficial and cursory view of the objects and operations of nature,—we must not think it sufficient to acquiesce in such vague propositions as these—"The glory of God is seen in every blade of grass, and every drop of water; all nature is full of wonders, from the dust of the earth to the stars of the firmament." We must study the works of creation with ardour, survey them with minute attention, and endeavour to acquire a *specific* and *comprehensive* knowledge of the Creator's designs. We must endeavour to acquire a knowledge of the particular modes, circumstances, contexture, configurations, adaptations, structure, functions, and relations of those objects in which benevolence and design conspicuously appear—in the animal and the vegetable world, in the ocean, the atmosphere, and the heavens; that the mind may be enabled to draw the conclusion with full conviction and intelligence—"*In wisdom thou hast made them all.*" The pointed interrogatories which Jehovah addressed to Job, evidently imply, that Job had previously acquired an intimate acquaintance with the works of nature. It seems to be taken for granted, as a matter of course, that he made himself acquainted with the general range of facts in the visible creation; and the intention of the several questions presented to his consideration evidently was to impress him with a sense of his own impotency, and to lead him to the investigation of the wonders of Creating Power which he had formerly overlooked. The conclusion which the Psalmist draws respecting the *Wisdom* displayed throughout all the works of God, plainly intimates, that he had made the different parts of nature the subject of minute examination, and of deep reflection; otherwise he could not have rationally deduced his conclusion, or felt those emotions which filled his mind with the pious rapture so beautifully expressed in that hymn of praise to the Creator of the world.

We have, therefore, reason to believe, from these and other instances, that pious men, "in the days of old," were much more accustomed than modern Christians to contemplate and admire the visible works of the Lord—and it is surely much to be regretted, that we who enjoy so many superior means of information, and who have access to the brilliant discoveries of later and more enlightened times, should manifest so much disregard to "the works of Jehovah and the operations of his hands." To enable the common mass of Christians to enter into the spirit of this delightful study and *Christian duty*, should, therefore, be one object of those periodical and other religious works which are put into their hands; so that they may be enabled, with

* Job, chap. xxxviii. xxxix. xl. xli.

† The *glory* of the Lord, in this passage, denotes the display of his perfections in the material universe: and the declaration of the inspired writer plainly intimates, that this display will continue *for ever*, and will remain as an object of unceasing contemplation to all intelligences, and as an eternal monument of his power and wisdom. For, although the earth and the aerial heavens will be changed at the close of that dispensation of Providence which respects our word, yet the general frame of the universe, in its other parts, will remain substantially the same; and not only so, but will in all probability be perpetually increasing in magnitude and grandeur. And the change which will be effected in respect to the terraqueous globe and its appendages will be such that Jehovah will have reason to "rejoice" in this as well as in all his other works.

vigour and intelligence, to form the pious resolution of Asaph, "I will meditate on all thy works, O Lord! and talk of thy doings."—"I will utter abundantly tne memory of thy great goodness, and tell of thy wondrous works."*

### GEOGRAPHY.

The next department of knowledge I shall notice is the science of Geography.

The object of this science is, to describe the world we inhabit, in reference to the continents, islands, mountains, oceans, seas, rivers, empires, and kingdoms with which it is diversified, together with the manners, customs, and religion of the different tribes which people its surface.

In order to form an accurate conception of the relative positions of objects on the surface of the earth, and to enter with intelligence on the study of this subject, it is requisite, first of all, to have an accurate idea of its figure and *magnitude*. For a long series of ages it was supposed, by the bulk of mankind, that the surface of the earth was nearly a plane, indefinitely extended, and bounded on all sides by the sky. Lactantius, and several of the fathers of the Christian church, strenuously argued that the earth was extended infinitely downwards, and established upon several foundations. The ancient philosopher Heraclitus is said to have believed that the earth was of the shape of a skiff or canoe, very much hollowed; and the philosopher Leucippus supposed it to be of the form of a cylinder or a drum. It is only within the period of the last three hundred years that the true figure of the earth has been accurately ascertained. This figure is now found to be that of an oblate spheroid, nearly approaching to the shape of a globe or sphere. To have asserted this opinion several ages ago would have been considered as a heresy in religion, and would have subjected its abettors to the anathemas of the church, and even to the peril of their lives. Historians inform us that the learned Spigelius, Bishop of Upsal, in Sweden, suffered martyrdom at the stake, in defence of the doctrine of the *Antipodes*; and we know that, for asserting the motion of the earth, the celebrated philosopher Galileo was immured in a dungeon, and condemned by an assembly of cardinals to all the horrors of perpetual imprisonment. The doctrine ne maintained, and which is now universally received by every one acquainted with the subject, was declared by those arrogant ecclesiastics to be "a proposition absurd in its very nature, false in philosophy, heretical in religion, and contrary to the Holy Scriptures." Such are some of the horrible and pernicious consequences which flow from ignorance of the phenomena of nature, and of those laws by which the Almighty governs the universe he has formed; and which prove it to be a Christian duty for every rational being to study the order and economy of the visible world.

That the earth is nearly of a globular figure, is proved by the following considerations:—1. When we stand on the seashore, while the sea is perfectly calm, we perceive that the surface of the water is not quite plain, but convex or rounded; and if we are on one side of an arm of the sea, as the Frith of Forth, and, with our eyes near the water, look towards the opposite coast, we shall plainly see the water elevated between our eyes and the opposite shore, so as to prevent our seeing the land near the edge of the water. The same experiment may be made on any portion of still water, of a mile or two in extent, when its convexity will be perceived by the eye. A little boat, for instance, may be perceived by a man who is any height above the water, but if he stoops down, and lays his eye near the surface, he will find that the fluid appears to rise, and intercept the view of the boat. 2. If we take our station on the seashore, and view the ships leaving the coast, in any direction—as they retire from our view, we may perceive the masts and rigging of the vessels when the hulls are out of sight, and, as it were, sunk in the water. On the other hand, when a ship is approaching the shore, the first part of her that is seen is the topmast; as she approaches nearer, the sails become visible, and last of all, the hull comes gradually into view.† The reason of such appearances obviously is, that the round or convex surface of the water interposes between our eye and the body of the ship, when she has reached a certain distance, while, at the same time, the sails and topmast, from their greater elevation, may be still in view. To the same cause it is owing, that the higher the eye is placed, the more extensive is the prospect; and hence it is common for sailors to climb to the tops of masts, in order to discover land or ships at a distance. The contrary of all this would take place, if the earth and waters were an extended plane. When a ship came within view, the hull would first make its appearance, being the largest object, next the sails, and, last of all, the topmast. These considerations, which hold true in all parts of the world, prove to a certainty, that the mass of the ocean is of a globular form: and if the ocean be a portion of a sphere, it follows that the *land* also is of the same general figure; for no portion of the earth's surface is elevated above four or five

* A select list of popular works on Natural History, and the other sciences noticed in the following sketches, will be found in the appendix.

† In order to make such observations to advantage, the observer's eye should be as near as possible on a level with the sea, and he should use a telescope to enable him to perceive more distinctly the upper part of the vessel.

miles above the level of the ocean. 3. That the earth is round from north to south, appears from the following circumstance:—When we travel a considerable distance from north to south, or from south to north, a number of new stars successively appear in the heavens, in the quarter to which we are advancing, and many of those in the opposite quarter gradually disappear, which would not happen if the earth were a plane in that direction. 4. That the earth is round from east to west, appears from actual experiment; for many navigators, by sailing in a westerly direction, have gone quite round it, from east to west; and were it not for the frozen seas within the polar regions, which interrupt navigation in those directions, it would, long ere now, have been circumnavigated from north to south. 5. All those proofs are confirmed and illustrated by eclipses of the moon, which present an *ocular demonstration* of the earth's rotundity. An eclipse of the moon is caused by the intervention of the body of the earth between the sun and moon; in which case the shadow of the earth falls upon the moon. This shadow is found, in all cases, and in every position of the earth, to be of a *circular* figure; which incontrovertibly proves, that the whole mass of land and water, of which the earth is composed, is nearly of a globular form. The mountains and vales which diversify its surface detract little or nothing from its globular shape; for they bear no more proportion to its whole bulk than a few grains of sand to a common terrestrial globe; the highest mountains on its surface being little more than the two-thousandth part of its diameter. Some of the mountains on the surface of the moon are higher than those on the earth, and yet that body appears, both to the naked eye and through telescopes, of a spherical figure.

To some readers, the discovery of the true figure of the earth may appear as a matter of very trivial importance in religion. I hesitate not, however, to affirm that it constitutes a most important fact in the history of Divine Providence. Had not this discovery been made, it is probable that the vast continent of America might yet have remained undiscovered; for, Columbus, who first discovered that new world, had learned, contrary to the general opinion of the times, that the earth was of a spherical figure; and, from the maps then existing, he began to conjecture, that the nearest way of sailing to the East Indies would be to sail westward. And although he missed the object of his research, he was the means of laying open to view a vast and unknown region of the earth, destined, in due time, to receive from the Eastern world the blessings of knowledge, civilization, and religion. On the knowledge of the spherical figure of the earth, the art of navigation in a great measure depends; and all the voyages of discovery, which have been made in later years, were undertaken in consequence of the knowledge of this fact. Had mankind remained unacquainted with this discovery, the circumnavigation of the globe would never have been attempted—vast portions of the habituble world would have remained unknown and unexplored—no regular intercourse would have been maintained between the various tribes of the human race; and, consequently, the blessings of Divine Revelation could never have been communicated to the greater part of the Gentile world. Besides, the knowledge of the true figure and magnitude of our sublunary world forms the groundwork of all the sublime discoveries which have hitherto been made in the regions of the firmament. For its diameter forms the *base line* of those triangles by which the distances and magnitudes of the celestial globes have been determined; without a knowledge of the extent of which, the important results which have been deduced respecting the system of the universe could not have been ascertained, and, consequently, our views of the grandeur and omnipotence of the Deity, and of the magnificence and extent of his dominions, must have been much more circumscribed than they now are. Such is the intimate connexion that subsists between every part of the chain of Divine dispensations, that if any one link had been either broken or dissolved, the state of things, in the moral and intellectual world, would have been very different from what it now is; and the plans of Providence, for accomplishing the renovation and improvement of mankind, would have been either partially or totally frustrated.

With regard to the *magnitude* of the earth—I have already stated the mode by which we may acquire the most accurate and comprehensive conception of this particular, in the course of the illustrations which were given of the omnipotence of Deity, (pp. 9—11.) It is necessary here only to remark—that, according to the latest computations, the diameter of the earth is about 7,930 miles, and its circumference 24,912 miles; and consequently, the whole surface of the land and water it contains comprehends an area of 197,552,160 miles. The proportion of land and water on its surface cannot be very accurately ascertained; but it is quite evident, from an inspection of a map of the world, that the water occupies at least two-thirds of its surface, and, of course, the land cannot occupy more than one-third. Supposing it to be only one-fourth of the earth's surface, it will contain 49,387,040 square miles, which is considerably more than what is stated in most of our late systems of geography; in some of which the extent of the land is rated at 39 millions, and in others so low as 30 millions of square miles—the former of which statements being less than one-fifth, and the latter less than one-sixth of the surface of the globe. But it is quite obvious that the extent of the land cannot be less than one-fourth of the area of the globe, and must, therefore, comprehend at least 50 millions of square miles. And if a large arctic continent, eleven hundred leagues in length, exist around the North Pole, as some French philosophers infer from Captain Parry's late discoveries*—the quantity of land on the terraqueous globe will be much greater than what has been now stated.

General Divisions of the Earth.—The surface of the earth is divided, from north to south, by two bands of earth, and two of water. The first band of earth is the ancient or Eastern Continent, comprehending Europe, Asia, and Africa; the greatest length of which is found to be in a line beginning on the east point of the northern part of Tartary, and extending from thence to the Cape of Good Hope, which measures about 10,000 miles, in a direction nearly from north-east to south-west; but if measured according to the meridians, or from north to south, it extends only 7,500 miles, from the northernmost cape in Lapland to the Cape of Good Hope. This vast body of land contains about 36 millions of square miles, forming nearly one-fifth of the whole surface of the globe. The other band of earth is what is commonly called the New Continent, which comprehends North and South America. Its greatest length lies in a line beginning at the mouth of the river Plata, passing through the island of Jamaica, and terminating beyond Hudson's Bay; and it measures about 8,000 miles. This body of land contains about 14 millions of square miles, or somewhat more than a third of the old continent.

It may not be improper here to remark, that the two lines now mentioned, which measure the greatest lengths of the two continents, divide them into two equal parts, so that an equal portion of land lies on each side of these lines, and that each of these lines has an inclination of about 30 degrees to the equator, but in opposite directions; that of the old continent extending from the north-east to the south-west, and that of the new continent from the north-west to the south-east; and that they both terminate at the same degree of northern and southern latitude. It may also be noticed, that the old and new continents are almost opposite to each other, and that the old is more extensive to the north of the equator, and the new more extensive to the south. The centre of the old continent is in the 17th degree of north latitude, and the centre of the new in the 17th degree of south latitude; so that they seem to be made to counterbalance each other, in order to preserve the equability of the diurnal rotation of the earth. There is also a singular connexion between the two continents, namely, that if they were divided into two parts, all four would be surrounded by the sea, were it not for the two small necks of land called the isthmuses of Suez and Panama.†

Between the two continents now mentioned, lie two immense bands of water, termed the Pacific and the Atlantic oceans, whose greatest length is likewise in a direction from north to south.

Besides the two bands of earth to which I have adverted, many extensive portions of land are dispersed through the ocean, which covers the remaining part of the earth's surface; particularly the extensive regions of New Holland, which occupy a space nearly as large as the whole of Europe, and the arctic continent, which probably exists within the northern polar regions, and which some French writers propose to designate by the name of *Boreasia*, is in all probability, of equal extent. There are also the extensive islands of New Guinea, Borneo, Madagascar, Sumatra, Japan, Great Britain, New Zealand, Ceylon, Iceland, Cuba, Java, and thousands of others, of different dimensions, scattered through the Pacific, the Indian, and the Atlantic oceans, and which form a very considerable portion of the habitable regions of the globe.

General Features of the Earth's Surface.—In taking a general survey of the external features of the earth, the most prominent objects that strike the eye are those huge elevations which rise above the level of its general surface, termed Hills and Mountains. These are distributed, in various forms and sizes, through every portion of the continents and islands; and, running into immense chains, form a sort of connecting band to the other portion of the earth's surface. The largest mountains are generally formed into immense chains, which extend, in nearly the same direction, for several hundreds, and even thousands of miles. It has been observed by some philosophers, that the most lofty mountains form two immense ridges, or belts, which, with some interruptions, extend around the whole globe, in nearly the same direction. One of these ridges lies between the 45th and 55th degree of north latitude. Beginning on the western shores of France and Spain, it extends eastward, including the Alps and the Pyrenees, in Europe, the Uralian and Altaic mountains, in Asia—extending from thence to the shores of Kamschatka, and after a short interruption from the sea, they rise again on the western coast of America, and terminate at Canada, near the eastern shore. It is supposed that the chain is continued completely round the globe, through the space that is covered by the Atlantic ocean, and that the Azores, and other islands in that direction, are the only summits that are visible, till we come to the British isles, The other ridge runs along the Southern hemi-

* See Monthly Magazine, April, 1823, p. 259.

† See Buffon's Natural History, vol. I.

sphere, between the 50th and 30th degrees of south latitude, of which detached portions are found in the mountains of Tucuman, and of Paraguay, in South America,—of Monomotapa and Caffraria, in Africa; in New Holland, New Caledonia, the New Hebrides, the Friendly, the Society, and other islands in the Pacific ocean. From these ridges flows a variety of ramifications, in both hemispheres, towards the Equator, and the Poles, which altogether present a magnificent scenery, which diversifies and enlivens the surface of our globe.

The highest mountains in the world, according to some late accounts published in the "Transactions of the Asiatic Society," are the *Himalaya* chain, north of Bengal, on the borders of Thibet. The highest mountain in this range is stated to be about 27,000 feet, or a little more than five miles, in perpendicular height, and is visible at the distance of 230 miles. Nineteen different mountains in this chain are stated to be above four miles in perpendicular elevation. Next to the Himalayas, are the Andes, in South America, which extend more than 4000 miles in length, from the province of Quito to the straits of Magellan. The highest summit of the Andes is Chimborazo, which is said to be 20,600 feet, or nearly four miles, above the level of the sea. The highest mountains in Europe, are the Alps, which run through Switzerland and the north of Italy,—the Pyrenees, which separate France from Spain, and the Dofrafeld, which divide Norway from Sweden. The most elevated ridges in Asia, are Mount Taurus, Imaus, Caucasus, Ararat, the Uralian, Altaian, and the mountains of Japan—in Africa, Mount Atlas, and the mountains of the Moon. Some of the mountains in these ranges are found to contain immense caverns or perforations, of more than two miles in circumference, reaching from their summits to an immeasurable depth into the bowels of the earth. From these dreadful openings are frequently thrown up, to an immense height, torrents of fire and smoke, rivers of melted metals, clouds of ashes and cinders, and sometimes red-hot stones and enormous rocks, to the distance of several miles, accompanied with thunders, lightnings, darkness, and horrid subterraneous sounds—producing the most terrible devastations through all the surrounding districts. The most noted mountains of this kind in Europe, are mount Hecla, in Iceland; Etna, in Sicily; and Vesuvius, near the city of Naples, in Italy. Numbers of volcanoes are also to be found in South America, in Africa, in the islands of the Indian ocean, and in the Empire of Japan.*

We who live in Great Britain, where the highest mountain is little more than three-quarters of a mile in perpendicular elevation, can form no adequate idea of the magnificence and awful sublimity of the mountain scenery in some of the countries now mentioned; especially when the volcano is belching forth its flames with a raging noise, and spreading terror and desolation around its base. From the tops of the lofty ridges of the Andes, the most grand and novel scenes sometimes burst upon the eye of the astonished traveller. He beholds the upper surface of the clouds far below him, covering the subjacent plain, and surrounding, like a vast sea, the foot of the mountain; while the place on which he stands appears like an island in the midst of the ocean. He sees the lightnings issuing from the clouds, and hears the noise of the tempest, and the thunders rolling far beneath his feet, while all is serene around him, and the blue vault of heaven appears without a cloud. At other times, he contemplates the most sublime and extensive prospects—mountains ranged around him, covered with eternal snows, and surrounding, like a vast amphitheatre, the plains below—rivers winding from their sources towards the ocean—cataracts dashing headlong over tremendous cliffs—enormous rocks detached from their bases, and rolling down the declivity of the mountains with a noise louder than thunder—frightful precipices impending over his head—unfathomable caverns yawning from below—and the distant volcano sending forth its bellowings, with its top enveloped in the fire and smoke.—Those who have studied nature on a grand scale, have always been struck with admiration and astonishment at the sublime and awful exhibition of wonders which mountainous regions exhibit and, perhaps, there is no *terrestrial* scene which presents, at one view, so many objects of overpowering magnitude and grandeur, and which inspires the mind with so impressive an idea of the power of that Almighty Being, who "weigheth the mountains in scales, and taketh up the isles as a very little thing."

THE OCEAN.—The ocean surrounds the earth on all sides, and penetrates into the interior parts of different countries; sometimes by large openings, and frequently by small straits. Could the eye take in this immense sheet of waters at one view, it would appear the most august object under the whole heavens. It occupies a space on the surface of the globe at least three times greater than that which is occupied by the land; comprehending an extent of 148 millions of square miles. Though the ocean, strictly speaking, is but *one* immense body of waters extending in different directions, yet different names have been appropriated to different portions of its surface. That portion of its waters which rolls between the western coast of America and the eastern of Asia, is called the *Pacific* ocean; and that portion which separates Europe and Africa from America, the *Atlantic* ocean. Other portions are

* A more particular description of the phenomena of these terrific objects will be found in Chap. iv. Sect. 2.

termed the *Northern*, *Southern*, and *Indian* oceans. When its waters penetrate into the land, they form what are called gulfs, and mediterranean seas. But without following it through all its windings and divisions, I shall state a few general facts.

With regard to the *depth* of this body of water, no certain conclusions have yet been formed. Beyond a certain depth, it has hitherto been found unfathomable. We know, in general, that the depth of the sea increases gradually as we leave the shore; but we have reason to believe that this increase of depth continues only to a certain distance. The numerous islands scattered every where through the ocean, demonstrate, that the bottom of the waters, so far from uniformly sinking, sometimes rises into lofty mountains. It is highly probable, that the depth of the sea is somewhat in proportion to the elevation of the land; for there is some reason to conclude, that the present bed of the ocean formed the inhabited part of the ancient world, previous to the general deluge, and that we are now occupying the bed of the former ocean; and, if so, its greatest depth will not exceed four or five miles; for there is no mountain that rises higher above the level of the sea. But the sea has never been actually sounded to a greater depth than a mile and sixty-six feet. Along the coast its depth has always been found proportioned to the height of the shore; where the coast is high and mountainous, the sea that washes it is deep; but where the coast is low, the water is shallow. To calculate the *quantity of water* it contains, we must therefore suppose a medium depth. If we reckon its average depth at two miles, it will contain 296 millions of cubical miles of water. We shall have a more specific idea of this enormous mass of water, if we consider, that it is sufficient to cover the whole globe, to the height of more than eight thousand feet; and if this water were reduced to one spherical mass, it would form a globe of more than 800 miles in diameter.

With regard to its *bottom*—As the sea covers so great a part of the globe, we should, no doubt, by exploring its interior recesses, discover a vast number of interesting objects. So far as the bed of the ocean has been explored, it is found to bear a great resemblance to the surface of the dry land; being, like it, full of plains, caverns, rocks, and mountains, some of which are abrupt and almost perpendicular, while others rise with a gentle acclivity, and sometimes tower above the water, and form islands. The materials, too, which compose the bottom of the sea, are the same which form the basis of the dry land. It also resembles the land in another remarkable particular;—many fresh springs, and even rivers, rise out of it; an instance of which appears near Goa, on the western coast of Hindostan, and in the Mediterranean sea, not far from Marseilles. The sea sometimes assumes *different colours*. The materials which compose its bottom cause it to reflect different hues in different places; and its appearance is also affected by the winds and by the sun, while the clouds that pass over it communicate all their varied and fleeting colours. When the sun shines, it is green; when he gleams through a fog, it is yellow; near the poles, it is black, while, in the torrid zone, its colour is often brown; and, on certain occasions, it assumes a luminous appearance, as if sparkling with fire.

The ocean has *three kinds of motion*. The first is that undulation which is produced by the wind, and which is entirely confined to its surface. It is now ascertained that this motion can be destroyed, and its surface rendered smooth, by throwing oil upon its waves. The second motion is, that continual tendency which the whole water in the sea has towards the west, which is greater near the equator than towards the poles. It begins on the west side of America, where it is moderate; but as the waters advance westward, their motion is accelerated; and, after having traversed the globe, they return, and strike with great violence on the *eastern* shore of America. Being stopped by that continent, they rush, with impetuosity, into the Gulf of Mexico, thence they proceed along the coast of North America, till they come to the south side of the great bank of Newfoundland, when they turn off and run down through the Western Isles. This motion is most probably owing to the diurnal revolution of the earth on its axis, which is in a direction contrary to the motion of the sea. The third motion of the sea is the *tide*, which is a regular swell of the ocean every 12½ hours. The motion is now ascertained to be owing to the attractive influence of the moon, and also partly to that of the sun. There is always a flux and reflux at the same time, in two parts of the globe, and these are opposite to each other; so that when our antipodes have high water we have the same. When the attractive powers of the sun and moon act in the same direction, which happens at the time of new and full moon, we have the highest, or *spring tides*; but when their attraction is opposed to each other, which happens at the quarters, we have the lowest, or *neap tides*.

Such is the ocean,—a most stupendous scene of Omnipotence, which forms the most magnificent feature of the globe we inhabit. When we stand on the seashore, and cast our eyes over the expanse of waters, till the sky and the waves seem to mingle, all that the eye can take in at *one* survey, is but an inconsiderable *speck*, less than the hundred-thousandth part of the whole of this vast abyss. If every drop of water can be divided into 26 millions of distinct parts, as some philosophers have demonstrated,* what an immense assemblage of watery particles must be contained in the unfathomable caverns of the ocean! Here the powers of calculation are completely set at defiance; and an image of infinity, immensity, and endless duration is presented to the mind. This mighty expanse of waters is the grand reservoir of nature, and the source of evaporation, which enriches the earth with fertility and verdure. Every cloud which floats in the atmosphere, and every fountain, and rivulet, and flowing stream, are indebted to this inexhaustible source for those watery treasures which they distribute through every region of the land. In fine, whether we consider the ocean as rearing its tremendous billows in the midst of the tempest, or as stretched out into a smooth expanse—whether we consider its immeasurable extent, its mighty movements, or the innumerable beings which glide through its rolling waves—we cannot but be struck with astonishment at the grandeur of that Omnipotent Being who holds its waters "in the hollow of his hand," and who has said to its foaming surges, "Hitherto shalt thou come, and no farther, and here shall thy proud waves be stayed."

Rivers.—The next feature of the earth's surface which may be noticed, is, the rivers with which it is indented in every direction. These are exceedingly numerous, and seem to form as essential a part in the constitution of our globe, as the mountains from which they flow, and as the ocean to which they direct their course. It is reckoned, that in the old continent there are about 430 rivers which fall directly into the ocean, or into the Mediterranean and the Black seas; but in the new continent, there are only about 145 rivers known, which fall directly into the sea. In this enumeration, however, only the great rivers are included, such as the Thames, the Danube, the Wolga, and the Rhone. Besides these, there are many thousands of streams of smaller dimensions, which, rising from the mountains, wind in every direction, till they fall into the large rivers, or are carried into the ocean. The largest rivers in Europe are—the Wolga, which, rising in the northern parts of Russia, runs a course of 1700 miles, till it falls into the Caspian Sea—the Danube, whose course is 1300 miles, from the mountains of Switzerland to the Black Sea—and the Don, which runs a course of 1200 miles. The greatest rivers in Asia are—the Hoanho, in China, whose course is 2400 miles—the Boorhampooter, the Euphrates, and the Ganges. The longest river in Africa is the Nile, the course of which is estimated at 2000 miles. In the continent of America, the rivers appear to be formed on the grandest scale, both as to the length of their course, and the vast body of waters which they pour into the ocean. The Amazon, the largest river in the world, runs a course of above 3000 miles across the continent of South America, till it falls into the Atlantic ocean, where it discharges a body of waters 150 miles in breadth. Next to this is the river St. Lawrence, which is more than 2400 miles from its mouth through the lake Ontario to the Lake Alempigo and the Assiniboils; and the rivers La Plata and Mississippi, each of whose courses is not less than 2000 miles.

When we consider the number and the magnitude of these majestic streams, it is evident that an enormous mass of water is continually pouring into the ocean, from every direction. From observations which have been made on the river Po, which runs through Lombardy, and waters a tract of land 380 miles long and 120 broad, it is found, that it moves at the rate of four miles an hour, is 1000 feet broad, and 10 feet in depth, and, consequently, supplies the sea with 5068 millions of cubical feet of water in a day, or a cubical mile in 29 days. On the supposition that the quantity of water which the sea receives from the great rivers in all countries is proportional to the extent and surface of those countries, it will follow, that the quantity of waters carried to the sea by all the other rivers on the globe is 1083 times greater than that furnished by the Po, (supposing the land, as formerly stated, to contain about 49 millions of square miles,) and will supply the ocean with 13,630 cubical miles of water in a year. Now reckoning the ocean, as formerly, to contain 296 millions of cubical miles of water, this last number, divided by the former, will give a quotient of 21,716. Hence it appears, that, were the ocean completely drained of its waters, it would require more than *twenty thousand years*† before its caverns could be again completely filled by all the rivers in the world running into it at their present rate.

Here, two questions will naturally occur—Whence do the rivers receive so constant a supply of waters? and why has not the ocean long ago overflowed the world? since so prodigious a mass of water is continually flowing into its abyss. This was a difficulty which long puzzled philosophers; but it is now satisfactorily solved from a consideration of the effects of evaporation. By the heat of the sun the particles of water are drawn up into the atmosphere

* The demonstration of this proposition may be seen in Nieuwentyt's Religious Philosopher, vol. iii. p. 852.

† Buffon makes this result to be 812 years, in which he is followed by Goldsmith, and most subsequent writers; but he proceeds on the false assumption, that the ocean covers only half the surface of the globe, and that it contains only 85 millions of square miles, and he estimates the average depth of the ocean to be only 440 yards, or one-fourth of a mile.

from the surface of the ocean, and float in the air in the form of clouds or vapour. These vapours are carried, by the winds, over the surface of the land, and are again condensed into water on the tops and the sides of mountains, which, gliding down into their crevices and caverns, at length break out into springs, a number of which meeting in one common valley becomes a river; and many of these united together at length form such streams as the Tay, the Thames, the Danube, and the Rhine. That evaporation is sufficient to account for this effect, has been demonstrated by many experiments and calculations. It is found that, from the surface of the Mediterranean sea, which contains 762,000 square miles, there are drawn up into the air, every day, by evaporation, 5280 millions of tons of water, while the rivers which flow into it yield only 1827 millions of tons in the same time; so that there is raised in vapour from the Mediterranean nearly *three times* the quantity of water which is poured into it by all its rivers. One third of this falls into the sea before it reaches the land; another part falls on the low lands, for the nourishment of plants; and the other third part is quite sufficient to supply the sources of all the rivers which run into the sea. This is in full conformity to what was long ago stated by an inspired naturalist: "All the rivers run into the sea, and yet the sea is not full; unto the place from whence the rivers came, thither do they return again;" but, before they regain their former place, they make a circuit over our heads through the regions of the atmosphere.

Such are the varied movements and transformations which are incessantly going on in the rivers, the ocean and the atmosphere, in order to preserve the balance of nature, and to supply the necessities of the animal and the vegetable tribes; all under the agency and direction of Him who "formed the sea and the dry land," and who has arranged all things in number, weight, and measure, to subserve the purposes of his will.

Rivers serve many important purposes in the economy of our globe. They carry off the redundant waters which fall in rains, or which ooze from the springs, which might otherwise settle into stagnant pools; they supply to the seas the loss of waters occasioned by their daily evaporation; they cool the air and give it a gentle circulation; they fertilize the countries through which they flow; their waters afford a wholesome drink, and the fishes they contain a delicious food, for the nourishment of man; they facilitate commerce, by conveying the productions of nature and art from the inland countries to the sea; they form mechanical powers for driving machinery of different kinds; they enliven and diversify the scenery of the countries through which they pass; and the cataracts which they frequently form among the mountains present us with scenes the most picturesque and sublime; so that every part of the constitution of nature is rendered subservient both to utility and to pleasure.

Waiving the consideration of other particulars, I shall simply state some of the artificial divisions of the earth, and two or three facts respecting its inhabitants.

The land has generally been divided into four parts, Europe, Asia, Africa, and America, to which has been lately added the division called Australasia, which comprehends New Holland, New Guinea, New Zealand, Van Dieman's land, and several other islands in the Pacific ocean. *Europe* comprehends the following countries, Norway, Sweden, Denmark, Russia, Prussia, Germany, Austria, Turkey, Italy, Switzerland, France, Holland, or the Netherlands, Spain, Portugal, and Great Britain and Ireland, together with the islands of Sicily, Malta, Candia, Corsica, Sardinia, Majorca, Minorca, Ivica, Zealand, Funen, Gothland, Iceland, and several others of smaller note.—*Asia*, the largest and most populous division of the ancient continent, contains the Empires of China and Japan, Chinese Tartary, Thibet, Hindostan, or British India, the Burman Empire, Persia, Arabia, Turkey in Asia, Siberia, Independent Tartary, and a variety of territories inhabited by tribes with which we are very imperfectly acquainted; together with the immense islands of Borneo, Sumatra, Java, Ceylon, Segalien, the Philippines, and thousands of others of smaller dimensions. It was in Asia where the human race was first planted; it became the nursery of the world after the universal deluge, and it was the scene in which the most memorable transactions recorded in the sacred history took place. But its inhabitants are now immersed in Mahometan and Pagan darkness; and the Christian religion, except in a few insulated spots, is almost unknown among its vast population. It is the richest and most fruitful part of the world, and produces cotton, silks, spices, tea, coffee, gold, silver, pearls, diamonds, and precious stones: but despotism, in its worst forms, reigns uncontrolled over every part of this immense region.

*Africa* comprehends the following kingdoms,—Morocco, Algiers, Tunis, Tripoli, Egypt, Zaara, Negroland, Guinea, Nubia, Abyssinia, Caffraria, Dahomey, Benin, Congo, Angola, and various other territories. By far the greater part of Africa remains hitherto unexplored, and, consequently, we are possessed of a very slender portion of information respecting the numerous tribes that may inhabit it. This quarter of the world, which once contained several flourishing kingdoms and states, is now reduced to a general state of barbarism. That most abominable traffic, the slave trade, is carried on to an unlimited extent on its eastern coasts, by a set of European ruffians, whose villanies are a disgrace to human nature. Its most striking features are those immense deserts, near its northern parts, which comprise nearly one-third of its surface. The deserts of Zaara are 1500 miles long, and 800 broad.

*America* is divided into North and South. It remained unknown to the inhabitants of the eastern hemisphere till the year 1492, when it was discovered by Columbus, who first landed on Guanahani, or *Cat island*, one of the Bahama isles. North America comprehends the following countries: The United States, New and Old Mexico, Upper and Lower Canada, Nova Scotia, New Brunswick, and Labrador. South America comprehends the immense districts called Terra Firma, Peru, Guiana, Amazonia, Paraguay, Brazil, Chili, and Patagonia.—Between N. and S. America lie the islands of Cuba, St. Domingo, Jamaica, and Porto Rico, known by the name of the *West Indies*. Besides these, there are connected with America, the Bahama and Carribbee islands, Newfoundland, Cape Breton, Tobago, Trinidad, Terra del Fuego, &c. America is distinguished by its numerous and extensive lakes, which resemble large inland seas. Its rivers, also, form one of its grand and distinguishing features, being the largest on the globe. It is likewise diversified with lofty and extensive ranges of mountains. When first discovered it was almost wholly covered with immense forests, and thinly peopled with a number of savage tribes. Its mingled population of Aborigines and Europeans is now making rapid advances in knowledge, civilization, and commerce.

In regard to the *human inhabitants* that occupy the different regions now specified—they have been divided by some geographers into the six following classes—1. The dwarfish inhabitants of the polar regions; as the Laplanders, the Greenlanders, and the Esquimaux.—2. The flat-nosed olive-coloured tawny race; as the Tartars, the Chinese, and the Japanese.—3. The blacks of Asia with European features. Of this description are the Hindoos, the Burmans, and the inhabitants of the islands in the Indian ocean.—4. The woolly-haired negroes of Africa, distinguished by their *black* colour, their flat noses, and their thick lips.—5. The copper-coloured native Americans, distinguished likewise by their black hair, small black eyes, high cheek-bones, and flat noses.—6. The sixth variety is the white European nations, as the British, the French, the Italians, and the Germans.

The *number of inhabitants* which people the earth at one time may be estimated to amount to at least *eight hundred millions;* of which 500 millions may be assigned to Asia; 80 millions to Africa; 70 millions to America; and 150 millions to Europe.—With regard to their religion, they may be estimated as follows:

| | |
|---|---|
| Pagans, . . . . | 490,000,000 |
| Mahometans, . . . | 130,000,000 |
| Roman Catholics, . . | 100,000,000 |
| Protestants, . . . | 43,000,000 |
| Greeks and Arminians, . | 30,000,000 |
| Jews, . . . . . | 7,000,000 |
| | 800,000,000 |

From this estimate it appears, that there are more than four Pagans and Mahometans to one Christian, and only one Protestant to 17 of all the other denominations. Although all the Roman Catholics, Greeks, and Protestants were reckoned true Christians, there still remain more than 620 millions of our fellow men ignorant of the true God, and of his will as revealed in the Sacred Scriptures; which shows what a vast field of exertion still lies open to Christian benevolence, before the blessings of civilization, mental improvement, rational liberty, and Christianity be fully communicated to the Pagan and Mahometan world.

If we suppose that the earth, at an average, has always been as populous as it is now, and that it contains 800 millions of inhabitants, as above stated, and if we reckon 32 years for a generation, at the end of which period the whole human race is renewed; it will follow, that 145 thousand millions of human beings have existed on the earth since the present system of our globe commenced, reckoning 5829 years from Adam to the present time.* And, consequently, if mankind had never died, there would have been 182 times the present number of the earth's inhabitants now in existence. It follows from this statement, that 25 millions of mankind die every year, 2853 every hour, and 47 every minute, and that at least an equal number, during these periods, are emerging from non-existence to the stage of life; so that almost every moment, a rational and immortal being is ushered into the world, and another is transported to the invisible state. Whether, therefore, we contemplate the world of matter, or the world of mind, we perceive incessant changes and revolutions going on, which are gradually carrying forward the earth and its inhabitants to some important consummation.—If we suppose that, before the close of time,

* This calculation proceeds on the supposition, that only 4004 years elapsed between the Mosaic creation and the birth of Christ, according to the Hebrew chronology. But Dr. Hales, in his late work on Scripture chronology, has proved, almost to a demonstration, that, from the creation to the birth of Christ are to be reckoned 5411 years; and this computation nearly agrees with the Samaritan and Septuagint chronology, and with that of Josephus. According to this computation, 7235 years are to be reckoned from the creation to the present time; and, consequently, 220 thousand millions of human beings will have existed since the creation which is more than 22 times the number of inhabitants presently existing.

as many human beings will be brought into existence, as have already existed, during the bypast ages of the world, there will, of course, be found, at the general resurrection, 290,000,000,000 of mankind. Vast as such an assemblage would be, the whole of the human beings here supposed, allowing six square feet for every individual, could be assembled within the space of 62,400 square miles, or on a tract of land not much larger than that of England, which contains, according to the most accurate calculations, above 50,000 square miles.

Our world is capable of sustaining a much greater number of inhabitants than has ever yet existed upon it at any one time. And since we are informed in the Sacred Oracles, that God "created it not in vain, but *formed it to be* inhabited," we have reason to believe, that, in future ages, when the physical and moral energies of mankind shall be fully exerted, and when Peace shall wave her olive branch over the nations, the earth will be much more populous than it has ever been, and those immense deserts, where ravenous animals now roam undisturbed, will be transformed into scenes of fertility and beauty. If it be admitted, that the produce of twelve acres of land is sufficient to maintain a family consisting of six persons, and if we reckon only one-fourth of the surface of the globe capable of cultivation, it can be proved, that the earth could afford sustenance for 16,000 millions of inhabitants, or *twenty times the number* that is presently supposed to exist. So that we have no reason to fear that the world will be overstocked with inhabitants for many ages to come; or that a period may soon arrive when the increase of population will surpass the means of subsistence, as some of the disciples of Malthus have lately insinuated. To suppose, as some of these gentlemen seem to do, that wars and diseases, poverty and pestilence, are necessary evils, in order to prevent the increase of the human race beyond the means of subsistence which nature can afford—while the immense regions of New Holland, New Guinea, Borneo, and the greater part of Africa and America are almost destitute of inhabitants—is both an insult on the dignity of human nature, and a reflection on the wisdom and beneficence of Divine Providence. The Creator is benevolent and bountiful, and "his tender mercies are over all his works;" but man, by his tyranny, ambition, and selfishness, has counteracted the streams of Divine beneficence, and introduced into the social state poverty, disorder, and misery, with all their attendant train of evils; and it is not before such demoralizing principles be in some measure eradicated, and the principles of Christian benevolence brought into active operation, that the social state of man will be greatly meliorated, and the bounties of heaven fully enjoyed by the human race. If, in the present deranged state of the social and politica world, it be found difficult, in any particular country, to find sustenance for its inhabitants, emigration is the obvious and natural remedy and the rapid emigrations which are now taking place to the Cape of Good Hope, New Holland Van Dieman's Land, and America, are, doubtless, a part of those arrangements of Providence, by which the Creator will accomplish his designs, in peopling the desolate wastes of our globe, and promoting the progress of knowledge and of the true religion among the scattered tribes of mankind.

---

With that branch of knowledge to which I have now adverted, every individual of the human race ought to be, in some measure, acquainted. For it is unworthy of the dignity of a rational being, to stalk abroad on the surface of the earth, and enjoy the bounty of his Creator, without considering the nature and extent of his sublunary habitation, the variety of august objects it contains, the relation in which he stands to other tribes of intelligent agents, and the wonderful machinery which is in constant operation for supplying his wants, and for producing the revolutions of day and night, spring and autumn, summer and winter. In a religious point of view, geography is a science of peculiar interest. For "the salvation of God," which Christianity unfolds, is destined to be proclaimed in every land, in order that men of all nations and kindreds and tongues may participate in its blessings. But, without exploring every region of the earth, and the numerous islands which are scattered over the surface of the ocean, and opening up a regular intercourse with the different tribes of human beings which dwell upon its surface, we can never carry into effect the purpose of God, by "making known his salvation to the ends of the earth." As God has ordained, that "all flesh shall see the salvation" he has accomplished, and that human beings shall be the agents for carrying his designs into effect—so we may rest assured that he has ordained every mean requisite for accomplishing this end; and, consequently, that it is his will that men should study the figure and magnitude of the earth, and all those arts by which they may be enabled to traverse and explore the different regions of land and water, which compose the terraqueous globe—and that it is also his will, that every one who feels an interest in the present and eternal happiness of his fellow men, should make himself acquainted with the result of all the discoveries in this science that have been, or may yet be made, in order to stimulate his activity, in conveying to the wretched sons of Adam, wherever they may be found, "the unsearchable riches of Christ."

To the missionary, and the directors of Bible and Missionary Societies, a minute and comprehensive knowledge of the science, and of all the facts connected with it, is essentially requisite; without which they would often grope in the dark, and spend their money in vain, and "their labour for that which doth not profit." They must be intimately acquainted with the extensive field of operation which lies before them, and with the physical, the moral, and the political state of the different tribes to which they intend to send the message of salvation; otherwise their exertions will be made at random, and their schemes be conducted without judgment or discrimination. To attempt to direct the movements of Missionary Societies, without an intimate knowledge of this subject, is as foolish and absurd as it would be for a land surveyor to lay down plans for the improvement of a gentleman's estate, before he had surveyed the premises, and made himself acquainted with the objects upon them, in their various aspects, positions, and bearings. If all those who direct and support the operations of such societies, were familiarly acquainted with the different fields for missionary exertions, and with the peculiar state and character of the diversified tribes of the heathen world, so far as they are known, injudicious schemes might be frustrated before they are carried into effect, and the funds of such institutions preserved from being wasted to no purpose. In this view, it is the duty of every Christian, to mark the progress and results of the various geographical expeditions which are now going forward in quest of discoveries, in connexion with the moral and political movements which are presently agitating the nations: for every navigator who ploughs the ocean in search of new islands and continents, and every traveller who explores the interior of unknown countries, should be considered as so many pioneers, sent beforehand, by Divine Providence, to prepare the way for the labours of the missionary, and for the combined exertions of Christian benevolence.*

But even to every private Christian, geography is an interesting branch of study, without some knowledge of which his prayers and his Christian sympathies cannot be judiciously and extensively directed. We occasionally hear the ministers of religion, at the commencement of public worship, on the first day of the week, imploring the Divine blessing on their brethren throughout the Christian church, who are commencing the same exercises; and at the close of worship in the afternoon, that the same blessing may seal the instructions which have been delivered in all the churches of the saints; as if all the public religious services of the universal church were, at that moment, drawing to a close. This is all very well, so far as it goes: the expression of such benevolent wishes is highly becoming, and congenial to the spirit of Christianity. But a very slight acquaintance with geographical science will teach us, that, when we in this country are commencing the religious services of the first day of the week, our Christian brethren in the East Indies, who live under a very different meridian, have finished theirs; those in Russia, Poland, Greece, Palestine, and on the banks of the Caspian sea, have performed one-half of their public religious worship and instructions; and those in New Holland and Van Dieman's Land have retired to rest, at the close of their Sabbath. On the other hand, our friends in the West India islands and in America, at the close of our worship, are only about to commence the public instructions of the Christian Sabbath. If, then, it be submitted, that our prayers, in certain cases, ought to be *specific*, to have a reference to the particular cases and relations of certain classes of individuals, there can be no valid reason assigned, why they should not have a reference to the geographical positions of the different portions of the Christian church, as well as to those who live on or near our own meridian: that, for example, in the beginning of our public devotions, we might implore that the blessing of God may accompany the instructions which have been delivered in the eastern parts of the world; and at the close of worship, that the same agency may direct in the exercises of those in the western hemisphere, who are about to enter on the sacred services of that day. On the same principle, we may perceive the absurdity of those "*concerts*"† for prayer in different places *at the*

* On this subject the author feels great pleasure in referring his readers to a small volume, lately published, by James Douglas, Esq. of Cavers, entitled, "Hints on Missions,"—a work which deserves the attentive perusal, both of the philosopher, the politician, and the Christian, and particularly of the directors of Missionary Societies; and which is characterized by a spirit of enlightened philanthropy, and *a condensation of thought*, which has seldom been equalled in the discussion of such topics. It concentrates, as it were, into a focus, the light which has been reflected from hundreds of volumes; and the original hints it suggests claim the serious consideration of the superintendents of missionary schemes; without an attention to some of which, the beneficial effects resulting from such undertakings will be few and unimportant. Should this note happen to strike the eye of the worthy author, it is submitted, with all due deference, whether a more extensive circulation of the substance of this volume, in a less expensive form, and with a few modifications, to bring it within the range of thought possessed by general readers, would not have a tendency to promote its benevolent objects.

† The author does not seem to mean, that it is *absurd* for Christians in every part of the earth to assemble on the same day in their respective places of devotion, to pray for a universal extension of Christianity. This objection would lie with equal weight against the Sabbath. His only objection appears to be against the *supposition*, that Christians, meeting in different parts of the earth at the same hour of the day, are praying in all places *at the same moment.—American Editor.*

same hour, which were lately proposed, and attempted by a certain portion of the religious world. Even within the limits of Europe, this could not be attempted, with the prospect of Christians joining in devotion at one and the same time; for, when it is six o'clock in one part of Europe, it is eight at another, and five o'clock at a third place; much less could such a concert take place throughout Europe, Asia, and America. So that science, and a calm consideration of the nature and relations of things, may teach us to preserve our devotional fervour and zeal within the bounds of reason and propriety; and, at the same time, to direct our reflections, and our Christian sympathies, to take a wider range than that to which they are usually confined.

Besides the considerations now suggested, a serious contemplation of the physical objects and movements which this science exhibits, has a tendency to excite pious and reverential emotions. To contemplate this huge globe of land and water, flying with rapidity through the voids of space, conveying its vast population from one region to another at the rate of fifteen hundred thousand miles in a day, and whirling round its axis at the same time, to produce the constant succession of day and night,—to contemplate the lofty ridges of mountains that stretch around it in every direction; the flaming volcanoes; the roaring cataracts; the numerous rivers, incessantly rolling their watery treasures into the seas; the majestic ocean, and its unfathomable caverns; the vapours rising from its surface, and replenishing the springs and rivers; the avalanche hurling down the mountain's side with a noise like thunder; the luxuriant plains of the torrid zone; the rugged cliffs and icebergs of the polar regions; and thousands of other objects of diversified beauty and sublimity,—has an evident tendency to expand the conceptions of the human mind, to increase its sources of animal enjoyment, and to elevate the affections to that all-powerful Being who gave birth to all the sublimities of Nature, and who incessantly superintends all its movements.

In fine, from the numerous *moral* facts, which geography unfolds, we learn the vast depth and extent of that moral degradation into which the human race has fallen—the ferocious tempers, and immoral practices, which are displayed in the regions of pagan idolatry—the horrid cruelties, the vile abominations, that are daily perpetrated under the sanction of what is termed religion—the wide extent of population, over which the prince of darkness sways his sceptre—the difficulties which require to be surmounted before the "gospel of salvation" can extend its full influence throughout the pagan world—and the vast energies which are requisite to accomplish this glorious event. All these portions of information are calculated to confirm and illustrate the scriptural doctrine of the universal depravity of man—to exercise the faith of the Christian, on the promises of Jehovah, in reference to the conversion of the benighted nations—to rouse his sympathies towards his degraded brethren of mankind, to excite his intercession in their behalf, and to direct his benevolence and activity in devising and executing schemes for enlightening the people who are sitting "in darkness, and in the shadow of death."

## GEOLOGY.

Another subject intimately related to the former, is the science of Geology.

This science has for its object, to investigate and describe the *internal structure* of the earth, the arrangement of the materials of which it is composed, the circumstances peculiar to its original formation, the different states under which it has existed, and the various changes which it appears to have undergone, since the Almighty created the substance of which it is composed. From a consideration of the vast quantity of materials contained in the internal structure of our globe, and of the limited extent to which men can carry their operations, when they attempt to penetrate into its bowels, it is obvious, that our knowledge of this subject must be very shallow and imperfect. The observations, however, which have been made on the structure of our globe during the last half century, and the conclusions deduced from them, are highly interesting, both to the philosopher and to the Christian. Before the facts, on which this branch of natural history is founded, were accurately ascertained, a variety of objections to the Mosaic history of the creation were started by certain skeptical philosophers, founded on partial and erroneous views of the real structure and economy of the earth. But it is now found, that the more accurately and minutely the system of nature is explored, the more distinctly do we perceive the harmony that subsists between the records of Revelation, and the operations of the Creator in the material world. If both be admitted as the effects of the agency of the same Almighty and Eternal Being, they must, in the nature of things, completely harmonize, and can never be repugnant to each other—whether we be capable, in every instance, of perceiving their complete coincidence, or not. If any facts could be produced in the visible creation which directly contradict the records of the Bible, it would form a proof, that the oracles which we hold as divine were not dictated by the Creator and Governor of the universe. But, although some garbled facts have been triumphantly exhibited in this view, it is now ascertained, from the discoveries which have been lately made in relation to the structure and formation of the earth, that the truth of the facts detailed in sacred history rests on a solid and immutable basis; and that the Supreme Intelligence who arranged the fabric of heaven and earth, and he alone, communicated to the inspired writers the doctrines and the facts they have recorded; and we have reason to believe, that, as geologists proceed in their researches and investigations, still more sensible proofs of the authenticity of Revelation will be brought to light.

Geology has, of late, become an interesting object of inquiry to the student of general science, and is now prosecuted with ardour by many distinguished philosophers. The observations which have been made in various parts of the world, by late navigators; the facts which have been ascertained by Pallas, Saussure, De Luc, Humboldt, and other intelligent travellers; and the discoveries which have been brought to light by modern chymists and mineralogists, have all conspired to facilitate geological inquiries, to render them more enlightened and satisfactory, and to prepare the way for future ages establishing a rational, scriptural, and substantial theory of the earth. The man who engages in such inquiries has always at hand a source of rational investigation and enjoyment. The ground on which he treads—the aspect of the surrounding country—the mines, the caves, and the quarries which he explores—every new country in which he travels, every mountain he climbs, and every new surface of the earth that is laid open to his inspection, offer to him novel and interesting stores of information. On descending into mines, we are not only gratified by displays of human ingenuity, but we also acquire views of the strata of the earth, and of the revolutions it has undergone since the period of its formation. Our researches on the surface of the earth, amidst abrupt precipices and lofty mountains, introduce us to the grandest and most sublime works of the Creator, and present to our view the effects of stupendous forces, which have overturned mountains, and rent the foundations of nature. "In the midst of such scenes, the geologist feels his mind invigorated; the magnitude of the appearances before him extinguishes all the little and contracted notions he may have formed in the closet; and he learns, that it is only by visiting and studying those stupendous works, that he can form an adequate conception of the great relations of the crust of the globe, and of its mode of formation."*

The upper crust, or surface of the earth, is found to be composed of different *strata*, or beds placed one above another. These strata, or layers, are very much mixed, and their direction, matter, thickness, and relative position, vary considerably in different places. These strata are divided into seven classes, as follows:—black earth, clay, sandy earth, marl, bog, chalk, and scabeous or stony earth. The surface of the globe, considered in relation to its inequalities, is divided into highland, lowland, and the bottom of the sea. Highland comprises Alpine land, composed of mountain groups, or series of mountain chains: lowland comprises those extensive flat tracts which are almost entirely destitute of small mountain groups. To the bottom of the sea belong the flat, rocky bottom, shoals, reefs, and islands.

At first sight, the solid mass of the earth appears to be a confused assemblage of rocky masses, piled on each other without regularity or order, where none of those admirable displays of skill and contrivance are to be observed, which so powerfully excite attention in the structure of animals and vegetables. But, on a nearer and more intimate view, a variety of beautiful arrangements has been traced by the industry of geologists, and the light of modern discoveries; by which they have been enabled to classify these apparent irregularities of nature. The materials of which the solid crust of the earth is composed, have been arranged into the four following classes:—1. Those rocks which contain neither any animal nor vegetable remains themselves, nor are intermixed with rocks which do contain them, and are therefore termed *primitive*, or *primary* rocks; the period of whose formation is considered as antecedent to that of the creation of organic beings. These are granite, gneiss, mica slate, and clay slate, which occur abundantly in all regions of the globe, with quartz rock, serpentine, granular limestone, &c. which occur more sparingly. 2. Rocks containing organic remains, or generally associated with other rocks in which such substances are found, and which, as having been formed posterior to the existence of organized beings, are termed *secondary*. These are greywacke, sandstone, limestone, and gypsum of various kinds, slate clay, with certain species of trap, and they are found lying above the primary or older rocks. 3. Above these secondary rocks, beds of gravel, sand, earth, and moss are found, which have been termed *alluvial rocks* or *formations*. This class comprehends those rocky substances formed from previously existing rocks, of which the materials have been broken down by the agency of water and air; they are therefore generally loose in their texture, and are never covered with any real solid and rocky secondary strata. 4. *Volcanic rocks;* under which class are comprehended all those rocks, beds of lava, scoriæ, and other matter, thrown out at certain points of the earth's surface by the action of subterraneous fire.

"The phenomena of geology show, that the original formation of the rocks has been accompanied, in nearly all its stages, by a process of waste, decay, and recomposition. The rocks as they were successively deposited, were acted

* Edinburgh Encyclop. Art. *Mineralogy*.

upon by air and water, heat, &c. broken into fragments, or worn down into grains, out of which new strata were formed. Even the newer secondary rocks, since their consolidation, have been subject to great changes, of which very distinct monuments remain. Thus, we have single mountains which, from their structure, can be considered only as remnants of great formations, or of great continents no longer in existence. Mount Meisner, in Hesse, six miles long and three broad, rises about 1800 feet above its base, and 2100 above the sea, overtopping all the neighbouring hills from 40 to 50 miles round. The lowest part of the mountain consists of the same shell, limestone, and sandstone, which exist in the adjacent country. Above these are, first, a bed of sand, then a bed of fossil wood, 100 feet thick at some points, and the whole is covered by a mass of basalt, 500 feet in height. On considering these facts, it is impossible to avoid concluding, that this mountain which now overtops the neighbouring country, occupied at one time, the bottom of a cavity in the midst of higher lands. The vast mass of fossil wood could not all have grown there, but must have been transported by water from a more elevated surface, and lodged in what was then a hollow. The basalt which covers the wood must also have flowed in a current from a higher site; but the soil over which both the wood and the basalt passed, has been swept away leaving this mountain as a solitary memorial to attest its existence. Thus, also, on the side of Mount Jura next the Alps, where no other mountain interposes, there are found vast blocks of granite (some of 1000 cubic yards) at the height of more than 2000 feet above the lake of Geneva. These blocks are foreign to the rocks among which they lie, and have evidently come from the opposite chain of the Alps; but the land which constituted the inclined plane over which they were rolled or transported, has been worn away, and the valley of lower Switzerland, with its lakes, now occupies its place. Transported masses of primitive rocks, of the same description, are found scattered over the north of Germany, which Van Buch ascertained by their characters to belong to the mountains of Scandinavia; and which, therefore, carry us back to a period when an elevated continent, occupying the basin of the Baltic, connected Saxony with Norway.—*Supp. to Ency. Brit.* vol. 6.

The production of a bed for *vegetation* is effected by the decomposition of rocks. This decomposition is effected by the expansion of water in the pores or fissures of rocks, by heat or congelation—by the solvent power of moisture—and by electricity, which is known to be a powerful agent of decomposition. As soon as the rock begins to be softened, the seeds of *lichens*, which are constantly floating in the air, make it their resting place. Their generations occupy it till a finely divided earth is formed, which becomes capable of supporting mosses and heath; acted upon by light and heat, these plants imbibe the dew, and convert constituent parts of the air into nourishment. Their death and decay afford food for a more perfect species of vegetable; and, at length, a mould is formed, in which even the trees of the forest can fix their roots, and which is capable of rewarding the labours of the cultivator. The decomposition of rocks tends to the *renovation* of soils, as well as their cultivation. Finely divided matter is carried by rivers from the higher districts to the low countries, and alluvial lands are usually extremely fertile. By these operations, the quantity of habitable surface is constantly increased; precipitous cliffs are generally made gentle slopes, lakes are filled up, and islands are formed at the mouths of great rivers; so that as the world grows older, its capacity for containing an increased number of inhabitants is gradually enlarging.

Of all the memorials of the past history of our globe, the most interesting are those myriads of remains of organized bodies which exist in the interior of its outer crusts. In these, we find traces of innumerable orders of beings existing under different circumstances, succeeding one another at distant epochs, and varying through multiplied changes of form. "If we examine the secondary rocks, beginning with the most ancient, the first organic remains which present themselves, are those of aquatic plants and large reeds, but of species different from ours. To these succeed madrepores, encrenities, and other aquatic zoophites, living beings of the simplest forms, which remain attached to one spot, and partake, in some degree, of the nature of vegetables. Posterior to these, are ammonites, and other mollusci, still very simple in their forms, and entirely different from any animals now known. After these, some fishes appear; and plants, consisting of bamboos and ferns, increase, but still different from those which exist. In the next period, along with an increasing number of extinct species of shells and fishes, we meet with amphibious and viviparous quadrupeds, such as crocodiles and tortoises, and some reptiles, as serpents, which show that dry land now existed. As we approach the newest of the solid rock formations, we find lamantins, phocæ, and other cetaceous and mammiferous sea animals, with some birds. And in the newest of these formations, we find the remains of herbiferous land animals of extinct species, the paleotherium, anaplotherium, &c. and of birds, with some fresh water shells. In the lowest beds of loose soil, and in peat bogs, are found the remains of the elephant, rhinoceros, hippopotamus, elk, &c. of different species from those which now exist, but belonging to the same genera. Lastly, the bones of the species which are apparently the same with those now existing alive, are never found except in the very latest alluvial depositions, or those which are either formed in the sides of rivers, the bottoms of ancient lakes and marshes now dried up, in peat beds, in the fissures and caverns of certain rocks, or at small depths below the present surface, in places where they may have been overwhelmed by debris, or even buried by man. Human bones are never found except among those of animal species now living, and in situations which show, that they have been, comparatively speaking, recently deposited."—*Supp. to Ency. Brit.* vol. 6.

More than thirty different species of animals have been found imbedded in the secondary strata—no living examples of which are now to be found in any quarter of the globe. Among the most remarkable of these are the following.—

1. The *Mammoth*, which bears a certain resemblance to the Elephant, but is much larger, and differs considerably in the size and form of the tusks, jaws, and grinders. The fossil remains of this animal are more abundant in Siberia than in other countries; there being scarcely a spot, from the river Don to Kamtschatka, in which they have not been found. Not only single bones and perfect skeletons of this animal are frequently to be met with; but, in a late instance, the whole animal was found preserved in ice. This animal was discovered on the banks of the frozen ocean, near the mouth of the river Jena, in 1799; and in 1805, Mr. Adams got it conveyed over a space of 7000 miles to Petersburgh, where it is deposited in the Museum. The flesh, skin, and hair were completely preserved, and even the eyes were entire. It was provided with a long mane, and the body was covered with hair. This hair was of different qualities. There were stiff black bristles from 12 to 15 inches long, and these belonged to the tail, mane, and ears. Other bristles were from 9 to 10 inches long, and of a brown colour; and besides these, there was a coarse wool, from 3 to 5 inches long, of a pale yellow colour. This mammoth was a male: it measured 9 feet 4 inches in height, and was 16 feet 4 inches long without including the tusks. The tusks, measuring along the curve, are 9 feet 6 inches; and the two together weigh 360 lbs. avoirdupois. The head alone without the tusks, weighs 414 lbs. avoirdupois. The remains of this animal have been found likewise in Iceland, Norway, Scotland, England, and in many places through the continent onwards to the Arctic ocean.

2. The *Megatherium.* A complete skeleton of this colossal species was found in diluvial soil, near Buenos Ayres, and sent to Madrid. The specimen is 14 feet long, and 7 Spanish feet in height.

3. The great *Mastodon* of the Ohio. This species appears to have been as tall as the elephant, but with longer and thicker limbs. It had tusks like the elephant, and appears to have lived on roots. Its remains abound in America, particularly on the banks of the Ohio.

4. The *Tapir*, which also abounds in America. The one named *Gigantic Tapir*, is about 18 feet long, and 12 feet high.

5. The *Irish Elk*, or Elk of the Isle of Man. This gigantic species, now apparently extinct, occurs in a fossil state, in Ireland, Isle of Man, England, Germany, and France. The most perfect specimen of this species, which was found in the Isle of Man, may be seen in the Museum of the University of Edinburgh. It is 6 feet high, 9 feet long, and in height to the tip of the right horn, 9 feet 7½ inches. An engraving of this skeleton may be seen in vol. 6 of *Supp. to Ency. Brit.*

From a consideration of the phenomena above described, geologists have been led to conclude, "that rocks now buried at a great depth, constituted, at one time, the surface of continents, and the seat of organic life; and that many orders of beings have been called into existence, and afterwards destroyed by great revolutions, which introduced new classes of mineral deposits, accompanied with new tribes of organic beings." It has also been concluded by some, that the appearance of man upon the face of the globe, is, geologically speaking, a very recent event; before which the earth had been inhabited thousands of years by various families of plants and tribes of animals, which had been destroyed and renewed in a long series of successions. Whether these conclusions be *necessary inferences* from the phenomena of organic remains and other geological facts, I shall not, at present, stop to inquire. It is sufficient for the Christian philosopher to show, that though they should be admitted in their full extent, they are not inconsistent with the records of sacred history, as some divines have been disposed to maintain. Though it could be proved to a demonstration, that the *materials* of which the present system of our globe is composed, have existed for millions of years, it would not, in the least, invalidate the Mosaic account of the arrangement of our world. For Moses no where affirms, that the *materials* or *substance* of the earth were created, or brought from nothing into existence, *at the period* when his history commences. His language, on the contrary, evidently implies, that the materials which enter into the constitution of our globe *did exist*, at the epoch at which he commences his narration. "The earth *was* without form, and void; and darkness *was* upon the face of the deep." This passage plainly implies the following things—1. That the original atoms, or materials, out of which the terraqueous globe in its present state, was formed, were then *in existence*, or had been previously created. *How long* they had been in existence is not stated. We may suppose them to have existed for a year, a thousand years, or a million of years, just as geological phenomena seem to warrant, without in the least invalidating the authority of the sacred historian, who states nothing contrary to the truth of either supposition. 2. That the materials of our globe, as then existing, were in a *chaotic* state. Instead of that order and beauty which we perceive on the face of nature, the whole mass presented a scene of confusion and disorder—such a scene, perhaps, as would be presented, were the earth stripped of its verdure, were its strata universally disrupted, its mountains hurled into the plains, and its rivers and seas, by some terrible convulsion, to forsake their ancient channels. 3. The passage seems to imply, that the whole, or the greater portion of the earth, as it then existed, was covered with a deluge of water: "Darkness covered the face of the *deep*," or the *abyss*.

Such was the state of the terrestrial system at the period when Moses commences his narration; no intimation being given of the period of its duration in this condition; and, consequently, nothing asserted to militate against any geological system which is founded on the facts which have been discovered respecting the organic remains which are found in the strata of our globe. It is a mistake into which too many have been apt to fall, to suppose, that Moses begins his history *at the period* when the first portions of material existence were created out of nothing; and that it was his design to mark the *precise epoch* when the whole assemblage of created beings throughout the universe was brought into existence. His primary, if not his sole intention evidently was, to detail the progress of those arrangements by which the earth was gradually reduced to that form and order in which we now behold it, from the chaotic materials which previously existed. And, as an emphatic and appropriate introduction to his narration, he states this important truth: "In the beginning God created the heaven and the earth." This passage, being of a general and comprehensive nature, decides nothing with regard to the *period*, or precise epoch, at which the different bodies in the universe were called into being; but is evidently intended to convey the following important truth, in opposition to all fanciful, chimerical, and atheistical notions respecting the origin of the world; namely, "That, at what period soever, in the lapse of duration, any object was brought into existence, it derived that existence from the God of Israel, the self-existent and eternal Jehovah."—"In the beginning *God* created the heaven and the earth." As the language of the sacred historian, therefore, decides nothing with regard to *time*—to limit the creation of every portion of the material system within the period of six thousand years, is to make an unnecessary concession to the infidel philosopher, which may afterwards be found inconsistent with certain facts which exist in the material world.

But, whatever may be said with respect to the state and duration of the earth prior to the period at which Moses commences his narration, it is admitted by every geologist, that our globe, *as to its present form and arrangement*, has been, comparatively, of but short duration. Cuvier, one of the most enlightened geologists of the age, deduces, from certain progressive changes on the earth's surface, as well as from the concurrent traditions of many nations, that the first appearance of man upon the face of the globe, or, at least, the renewal of the human race after some great catastrophe, cannot be referred to a period farther back than 5000 or 6000 years from the present time. Geologists, too, of every description, however different the systems or theories they have adopted, have all been constrained, from the evidence of fact, to admit this conclusion, "*That every part of the dry land was once covered by the ocean*;" thus confirming the scriptural account of that stupendous event, *the universal deluge*. This event, from its very nature, must have been accompanied with the most terrible convulsions, both on the exterior surface, and in the interior strata of the globe. Accordingly we find, that traces of this awful catastrophe exist in every region of the earth. Mr. Parkinson describes the whole island of Great Britain, as having, since its completion, "suffered considerable disturbance from some prodigious and mysterious power. By this power all the known strata, to the greatest depths that have been explored, have been more or less broken and displaced, and, in some places, have been so lifted, that some of the lowest of them have been raised to the surface; while portions of others, to a very considerable depth and extent, have been entirely carried away." The whole of the Alpine region in Switzerland, and the north of Italy, considered as one mass, shows the most evident marks of dislocation. At the height of 3500 feet above the level of the sea, M. Saussure met with a chasm a hundred feet wide, and so deep that he saw no bottom. All travellers on the Alps have regarded them with horror. They mark the most evident convulsions, but show no signs of having been occasioned by attrition. Mr. Townsend, speaking of the Pyrenees, which he personally inspected, says, "What is most remarkable is, to see four enormous chasms, almost perpendicular, which divided both mountains and their valleys, and which appear as if they had just been rent asunder." Throughout the ranges of the Andes, and in every other mountainous region, similar chasms and disruptions, indicating the former operation of some tremendous power, are frequently observed by those who visit such scenes of grandeur.—In some of the coal mines in our country, the coal is in some places lifted up or thrown down several hundreds of feet from the places it appears originally to have occupied. "Two miles north of Newcastle," says Mr. Townsend, "one great *dyke* or *fault* throws down the coal 540 feet—at the distance of 3 miles it is cut off, and thrown down again 240 feet."

An evidence of the effects which could be produced only by a general deluge, is also afforded by those organic remains to which I have already adverted, and particularly by those immense quantities of *marine shells*, which have been discovered in situations so elevated, and in places so far removed from the sea, as to prove that they were left there by a flood extending over the whole globe. At Touraine, in France, a hundred miles from the sea, is a bed of shells stretching 9 leagues in extent, and 20 feet in depth, and including shells not known to belong to the neighbouring sea. Humboldt found sea shells on the Andes at an elevation of 14,120 feet above the level of the sea. The slaty mountain of La Bolca, near Verona, is famous for petrifactions, among which are enumerated more than one hundred species of fish, natives of Europe, Asia, Africa, and America, *here assembled in one place.*

It appears, therefore, that the researches of geology confirm the fact of a universal deluge, and thus afford a *sensible* proof of the credibility of the sacred historian, and, consequently, of the truth of the doctrines of Divine Revelation. But, besides the testimony which this science bears to the authenticity of Scripture History, it exhibits some of the grandest objects in the history of the physical operations of Divine Providence. It presents to our view, in a most impressive form, the majestic agency of God, in convulsing and disarranging the structure of our globe, which at first sprung from his hand in perfect order and beauty. When we contemplate the objects which this science embraces, we seem to be standing on the ruins of a former world. We behold "hills" which "have melted like wax at the presence of the Lord," and "mountains" which "have been carried into the midst of the sea." We behold rocks of enormous size, which have been rent from their foundations, and rolled from one continent to another—the most solid strata of the earth bent under the action of some tremendous power, and dispersed in fragments through the surrounding regions. We behold the summits of lofty mountains, over which the ocean had rolled its mighty billows—confounding lands and seas in one universal devastation—transporting plants and forests from one quarter of the world to another, and spreading universal destruction among the animated inhabitants of the water and the earth. When we enter the wild and romantic scene of a mountainous country, or descend into the subterraneous regions of the globe, we are every where struck with the vestiges of operations carried on by the powers of nature, upon a scale of prodigious magnitude, and with the exertion of forces, the stupendous nature of which astonishes and overpowers the mind. Contemplating such scenes of grandeur, we perceive the force and sublimity of those descriptions of Deity contained in the volume of inspiration: "The Lord reigneth, he is clothed with majesty; in his hand are the deep places of the earth, the strength of the hills is his also. He removeth the mountains, and they know not: he overturneth them in his anger; he shaketh the earth out of her place, and the pillars thereof tremble. At his presence the earth shook and trembled: the foundations also of the hills moved, and were shaken, because he was wrath."—"Thou coveredst the earth with the deep, as with a garment; the waters stood above the mountains At thy rebuke they fled; at the voice of thy thunder they hastened away." While retracing such terrific displays of omnipotence, we are naturally led to inquire into the *moral* cause which induced the benevolent Creator to inflict upon the world such overwhelming desolations. For reason, as well as revelation, declares that a *moral* cause must have existed. Man must have violated the commands of his Maker, and frustrated the end of his creation; and to this conclusion the sacred historian bears ample testimony.—"God saw that the wickedness of man was great in the earth, and that every imagination of the thoughts of his heart was only evil continually: and Jehovah said, I will destroy man whom I have created, from the face of the earth, both man and beast, and the creeping thing, and the fowls of the air."

### ASTRONOMY.

Another science which stands in an intimate relation to religion, is Astronomy.

This sublime science teaches us the magnitudes and distances of the heavenly bodies, their arrangement, their various motions and phenomena, and the laws by which their movements are regulated. It presents to our view objects the most wonderful and sublime; whether we consider the *vast magnitude* of the bodies about which it is conversant—their immense *number*—the *velocity* of their motions—the *astonishing forces* requisite to impel them in their rapid career through the regions of the sky—the *vast spaces* which surround them, and in which they perform their revolutions—the *magnificent circles* they describe—the *splendour* of their appearance—or the *important ends* they are destined to serve in the grand system of the universe. Having adverted to this subject, when illustrating the omnipotence of the Deity, I shall here simply state a few additional facts with respect to the general appearance of the heavens, the bodies which compose the planetary system, and the discoveries which have been made in the region of the stars.

When we lift our eyes towards the sky, we perceive an apparent hollow hemisphere, placed at an indefinite distance, and surrounding the earth on every hand. In the day time, the principal object which appears in the hemisphere, is the sun. In the morning, we see him rise above the distant mountains, or from the extremity of the ocean; he gradually ascends the vault of heaven, and then declines, and disappears in the opposite quarter of the sky. In the northern parts of the globe, where we reside, if about the 21st of March, we place ourselves on an open plain, with our face towards the south, the sun will appear to rise on our left, or due east, about six in the morning, and about the same hour in the evening, he will set due west. In the month of June he rises to our left, but somewhat behind us, in a direction towards the north-east, ascends to a greater height at noon than in the month of March, and, after describing a large arc of the heavens, sets on our right, and still behind us, in the north-western quarter of the sky. In the month of December, if we stand in the same position, we may observe, without turning ourselves, both his rising and setting. He rises in the south-east, ascends to a small elevation at noon, and sets in the south-west, after having described a very small arc of the heavens. Every day he appears to move a little towards the *east*, or contrary to his apparent diurnal motion; for the stars which are seen to the eastward of him, appear every succeeding day to make a nearer approach to the place in which he is seen. All the variety of these successive changes is accomplished within the period of 365 days 6 hours, in which time he appears to have made a complete revolution round the heavens from *west* to *east*.

The moon is the next object in the heavens which naturally attracts our attention; and she is found to go through similar variations in the course of a month. When she first becomes visible at new moon, she appears in the western part of the heavens, in the form of a crescent, not far from the setting sun. Every night she increases in size, and removes to a greater distance from the sun, till at last, she appears in the eastern part of the horizon, just as the sun disappears in the western; at which time she presents a round full-enlightened face. After this, she gradually moves farther and farther eastward, and her enlightened part gradually decreases, till at last she seems to approach the sun as nearly in the east as she did in the west, and rises only a little before him in the morning, in the form of a crescent. All these different changes may be traced by attending to her apparent positions, from time to time, with respect to the fixed stars.

A dark shadow is occasionally seen to move across the face of the moon, which obscures her light, and gives her the appearance of tarnished copper. Sometimes this shadow covers only a small portion of her surface; at other times it covers the whole of her disk for an hour or two, and its margin always appears of the figure of a segment of a circle. This phenomenon, which happens, at an average, about twice every year, is termed an *eclipse* of the moon. It is produced by the shadow of the earth falling upon the moon, when the sun, the earth, and the moon, are nearly in a straight line; and can happen only at the time of *full moon*. Sometimes the moon appears to pass across the body of the sun, when her dark side is turned towards the earth, covering his disk either in whole or in part, and intercepting his rays from a certain portion of the earth. This is called an *eclipse of the sun*, and can happen only at the time of *new moon*. In a total eclipse of the sun, which seldom happens, the darkness is so striking, that the planets, and some of the larger stars, are distinctly seen, and the inferior animals appear struck with terror.

Again, if, on a winter's evening, about six o'clock, we direct our view to the eastern quarter of the sky, we shall perceive certain stars just risen above the horizon; if we view the same stars about midnight, we shall find them at a considerable elevation in the south, having apparently moved over a space equal to one half of the whole hemisphere. On the next morning, about six o'clock, the same stars will be seen setting in the western part of the sky. If we turn our eyes towards the north, we shall perceive a similar motion in these twinkling orbs, but with this difference, that a very considerable number of them neither rise nor set, but seem to move round an immoveable point, called the north pole. Near this point is placed the polar star, which seems to have little or no apparent motion, and which, in our latitude, appears elevated a little more than half way between the northern part of our horizon and the *zenith* or point above our heads. A person who has directed his attention to the heavens for the first time, after having made such observations, will naturally inquire—Whence come those stars which begin to appear in the east? Whither have those gone, which have disappeared in the west? and, what becomes, during the day, of the stars which are seen in the night?—It will soon occur to a rational observer, who is convinced of the roundness of the earth, that the stars which rise above the eastern horizon come from another hemisphere, which we are apt to imagine below us, and when they set, return to that hemisphere again; and, that the reason why the stars are not seen in the day-time, is, not because they are absent from our hemisphere, or have ceased to shine, but because their light is obscured by the more vivid splendour of the sun.* From such

* This is put beyond all doubt, by the invention of the telescope; by which instrument, adapted to an equatorial motion, we are enabled to see many of the stars even at noon-day. The Author of this

observations we are led to conclude, that the globe on which we tread is suspended in empty space—is surrounded on all sides by the celestial vault—and that the whole sphere of the heavens has an *apparent* motion round the earth every twenty-four hours. Whether this motion be real, or only apparent, must be determined by other considerations.

Such general views of the nocturnal heavens, which every common observer may take, have a tendency to expand the mind, and to elevate it to the contemplation of an invisible power, by which such mighty movements are conducted. Whether we consider the vast concave, with all its radiant orbs, moving in majestic grandeur around our globe, or the earth itself whirling round its inhabitants in an opposite direction—an idea of sublimity, and of Almighty energy, irresistibly forces itself upon the mind, which throws completely into the shade the mightiest efforts of human power. The most powerful mechanical engines that were ever constructed by the agency of man, can scarcely afford us the least assistance in forming a conception of that incomprehensible power, which, with unceasing energy, communicates motion to revolving worlds. And yet such is the apathy with which the heavens are viewed by the greater part of mankind, that there are thousands who have occasionally gazed at the stars, for the space of fifty years, who are still ignorant of the fact, that they perform an *apparent* diurnal revolution round our globe.

Again, if we contemplate the heavens with some attention, for a number of successive nights, we shall find, that by far the greater part of the stars never vary their positions with respect to each other. If we observe two stars at a certain apparent distance from each other, either north or south, or in any other direction, they will appear at the same distance, and in the same relative position to each other, the next evening, the next month, and the next year. The stars, for instance, which form the *sword* and *belt* of *Orion*, present to our eye the same figure and relative aspect, during the whole period they are visible in winter, and from one year to another: and the same is the case with all the fixed stars in the firmament. On examining the sky a little more minutely however, we perceive certain bodies which regularly shift their positions. Sometimes they appear to move towards the east, sometimes towards the west, and at other times seem to remain in a stationary position. These bodies have obtained the name of *planets*, or wandering stars; and, in our latitude, are most frequently seen, either in the eastern and western, or in the southern parts of the heavens. Ten of these planetary orbs have been discovered; six of which are, for the most part, invisible to the naked eye. By a careful examination of the motions of these bodies, and their different aspects, astronomers have determined, that they all move round the sun as the centre of their motions, and form, along with the earth and several smaller globes, one grand and harmonious system. This assemblage of planetary bodies is generally termed the solar system, of which I shall now endeavour to exhibit a brief outline.

### THE SOLAR SYSTEM.

Of this system, the sun is the centre and the animating principle, and by far the largest body that exists within its limits. The first thing that strikes the mind when contemplating this glorious orb, is its astonishing magnitude. This vast globe is found to be about 880,000 miles in diameter, and, consequently, contains a mass of matter equal to *thirteen hundred thousand globes* of the size of the earth. Were its central parts placed adjacent to the surface of the earth, its circumference would reach two hundred thousand miles beyond the moon's orbit on every

work, about eleven years ago, made a number of observations, by means of an *equatorial telescope*, to determine the following particulars:—What stars and planets may be conveniently seen in the day-time, when the sun is above the horizon? What degrees of magnifying power are requisite for distinguishing them? How near their conjunction with the sun they may be seen;—and, whether the diminution of the aperture of the telescope, or the increase of magnifying power, conduces most to render a star or planet visible in day-light. The results of several hundreds of observations on these points, accompanied with some original deductions and remarks, are inserted in "Nicholson's Philosophical Journal," for October, 1813, vol. 36, p. 109—128. The following are some of the results which were deduced from the observations:—That a star of the *first* magnitude may be distinguished at any time of the day, with a magnifying power of 30 times, but that a higher magnifying power is preferable—That most of the stars of the second magnitude may be seen with a power of 100; and with a power of 60 times, when the sun is not much more than two hours above the horizon—That the planet Jupiter, when not within 30 or 40 degrees of the sun, may be seen with a power of 15 times;—and that Venus may, in most instances, be seen with a power of from 7 to 100 times, and upwards—That Jupiter can scarcely be distinguished in the day-time, when within 26 degrees of the sun; but that Venus may be distinctly perceived near her superior conjunction, when only one degree and 27 minutes from the sun's margin; and, consequently, may be visible at the time of that conjunction, when her geocentric latitude equals or exceeds 1 degree 43 minutes—That she may be perceived, like a fine, slender crescent, within 35 hours after passing her *inferior* conjunction, &c. &c. One practical purpose to which such observations on Venus, at the time of her *superior* conjunction, may be applied, is, to determine the difference (if any) between her polar and equatorial diameters. For, it is only at that conjunction that she presents to the earth a full enlightened hemisphere; and in no other position can the measure of both diameters be taken, except when she makes a *transit* across the sun's disk. As the Earth, Mars, Jupiter, and Saturn, are found to be spheroids, it is highly probable that Venus is of a similar figure; but this point has never yet been ascertained by actual observation. See also "The Edinburgh Philos. Journal," No. 5, for July 1820, p. 191; and No. 13, for July, 1822—"The Scots Mag." for Feb. 1814, p. 84.—"Monthly Mag." Feb. 1814, and August 1820, p. 62.

side, filling a cubical space of 681,472,000,000,-000,000 miles. If it would require 18,000 years to traverse every square mile on the earth's surface, at the rate of thirty miles a day, (see p. 9,) it would require more than *two thousand millions of years* to pass over every part of the sun's surface, at the same rate. Even at the rate of 90 miles a day it would require more than 80 years to go round its circumference. Of a body so vast in its dimensions, the human mind, with all its efforts, can form no adequate conception. It appears an extensive universe in itself; and, although no other body existed within the range of infinite space, this globe alone would afford a powerful demonstration of the omnipotence of the Creator. Were the sun a hollow sphere, surrounded by an external shell, and a luminous atmosphere; were this shell perforated with several hundreds of openings into the internal part; were a globe as large as the earth placed at its centre, and another globe as large as the moon, and at the same distance from the centre as the moon is from us, to revolve round the central globe,—it would present to the view a universe as splendid and glorious as that which now appears to the vulgar eye,—a universe as large and extensive as the whole creation was conceived to be, by our ancestors, in the infancy of astronomy. And who can tell, but that Almighty Being, who has not left a drop of water in a stagnant pool without its inhabitants, has arranged a number of worlds within the capacious circuit of the sun, and peopled them with intelligent beings in the first stages of their existence, to remain there for a certain period, till they be prepared for being transported to a more expansive sphere of existence? It is easy to conceive, that enjoyments as exquisite, and a range of thoughts as ample as have ever yet been experienced by the majority of the inhabitants of our world, might be afforded to myriads of beings thus placed at the centre of this magnificent luminary. This supposition is, at least, as probable as that of the celebrated Dr. Herschel, who supposed that the *exterior* surface of the sun was peopled with inhabitants. For, if this were the case, the range of view of these inhabitants would be confined within the limits of two or three hundred miles, and no celestial body, but an immense blaze of light, would be visible in their hemisphere. Such is the variety which appears among the works of God, and such is the diversity of situations in which sensitive beings are placed, that we dare not pronounce it impossible that both these suppositions may be realized.

Though the sun seems to perform a daily circuit around our globe, he may be said, in this respect, to be fixed and immoveable. This motion is not *real*, but only *apparent*, and is owing to the globe on which we are placed moving round its axis from west to east; just as the objects on the bank of the river seem to move in a contrary direction, when we are sailing along its stream in a steamboat. The only motion which is found to exist in the sun is, a motion of *rotation*, like that of a globe or ball twirled round a pivot or axis, which is performed in the space of 25 days and 10 hours. This motion has been ascertained by means of a variety of dark spots which are discovered by the telescope on the sun's disk; which first appear on his eastern limb, and, after a period of about thirteen days, disappear on his western, and, after a similar period, reappear on his eastern edge. These spots are various, both in number, in magnitude, and in shape: sometimes 40 or 50, and sometimes only one or two are visible, and at other times the sun appears entirely without spots.—Most of them have a very dark nucleus, or central part, surrounded by an umbra, or fainter shade. Some of the spots are as large as would cover the whole continent of Europe, Asia, and Africa, others have been observed of the size of the whole surface of the earth; and one was seen, in the year 1779, which was computed to be more than *fifty thousand miles* in diameter.

With regard to the nature of this globe—it appears highly probable, from the observations of Dr. Herschel, that the sun is a solid and opaque body, surrounded with luminous clouds which float in the solar atmosphere, and that the dark nucleus of the spots is the opaque body of the sun appearing through occasional openings in this atmosphere. The height of the atmosphere, he computes to be not less than 1843, nor more than 2765 miles, consisting of two regions; that nearest the sun being opaque, and probably resembling the clouds of our earth; the outermost emitting vast quantities of light, and forming the apparent luminous globe we behold.

The sun is the grand source of light and heat, both to the earth and to all the other planetary bodies. The heat he diffuses animates every part of our sublunary system, and all that variety of colouring which adorns the terrestrial landscape is produced by his rays. It has been lately discovered, that the rays of light, and the rays of heat, or *caloric*, are distinct from each other; for, it can be demonstrated, that some rays from the sun produce heat, which have no power of communicating light or colour. The greatest heat is found in the *red* rays, the least in the *violet* rays; and in a space beyond the red rays, where there is no light, the temperature is greatest. The rays of the sun have also been found to produce different chymical effects. The white muriate of silver is blackened in the violet ray, in the space of 15 seconds, though the red will not produce the same effect in less than 20 minutes. Phosphorus is kindled in the vicinity of the red ray, and extinguished in the vicinity of the violet. The solar light, therefore, consists of *three* different orders of rays, one producing *colour*, a second producing *heat*, and a third *chymical* effects. Euler has computed that the light of the sun is equal to 6500 candles at a foot distance, while the moon would be as one candle at 7½ feet; Venus at 421 feet; and Jupiter at 1320 feet.—That this immense luminary appears so small to our eyes, is owing to its vast distance, which is no less than ninety-five millions of miles. Some faint idea of this distance may be obtained, by considering, that a steam-boat, moving at the rate of 200 miles a day, would require *thirteen hundred years* before it could traverse the space which intervenes between us and the sun.

"Hail sacred source of inexhausted light!
Prodigious instance of creating might!
His distance man's imagination foils;
Numbers will scarce avail to count the miles.
As swift as thought he darts his radiance round
To distant worlds, his system's utmost bound."
*Brown.*

*The Planet Mercury.*—Mercury is the nearest planet to the sun that has yet been discovered. He is about 37 millions of miles distant from the sun, and revolves around him in 88 days. His diameter is about 3200 miles. Before the discovery of the four new planets, Ceres, Pallas, Juno, and Vesta, in the beginning of the present century, this globe was considered as the smallest primary planet in the system. His surface, however, contains above 32 millions of square miles, which is not much less than all the habitable parts of our globe. On account of his nearness to the sun, he is seldom seen by the naked eye; being always near that quarter of the heavens where the sun appears; and therefore, few discoveries have been made on his surface, by the telescope. M. Schroeter concludes, from certain observations, that this planet revolves round its axis in 24 hours and five minutes. The sun will appear to an inhabitant of Mercury seven times larger than to an inhabitant of the earth; and, if the degree of heat be in proportion to a planet's nearness to the sun, the heat in this planet will be seven times greater than on the surface of our globe; and, consequently, were the earth placed in the same position, all the water on its surface would boil, and soon be turned into vapour. But the All-wise Creator has, doubtless, attempered the surface of this globe, and the constitution of the beings that may occupy it, to the situation in which they are placed.*

*Venus,* the next planet in order from the sun, revolves around him in 224 days, at the distance of 68 millions of miles, and its diameter is about seven thousand seven hundred miles, or nearly the size of the earth; and it turns round its axis in the space of 23 hours and 20 minutes. This planet is the most brilliant orb which appears in our nocturnal heavens, and is usually distinguished by the name of the morning and evening star. When it approaches nearest to the earth, it is about 27 millions of miles distant; and at its greatest distance, it is no less than 163 millions of miles from the earth. Were the whole of its enlightened surface turned towards the earth, when it is nearest, it would exhibit a light and brilliancy twenty-five times greater than it generally does, and appear like a small brilliant moon; but at that time, its dark hemisphere is turned towards our globe. Both Venus and Mercury, when viewed by a telescope, appear to pass successively through all the shapes and appearances of the moon; sometimes assuming a gibbous phase, and at other times the form of a half moon, or that of a crescent; which proves that they are dark bodies in themselves, and derive their light from the sun. The most distinct and beautiful views of Venus, especially when she appears as a crescent, are to be obtained *in the day time*, by means of an equatorial telescope.—From a variety of observations which the author has made with this instrument, it has been found that Venus may be seen every clear day without interruption, during a period of 583 days, with the occasional exception of 13 days in one case, and only 3 days in another—a circumstance which cannot be affirmed of any other celestial body, the sun only excepted.† M. Schroeter

* From a variety of facts which have been observed in relation to the production of *caloric*, it does not appear probable, that the degree of heat on the surfaces of the different planets is inversely proportional to the squares of their respective distances from the sun. It is more probable, that it depends chiefly on the distribution of the *substance of caloric* on the surfaces and throughout the atmospheres of these bodies—in different quantities, according to the different situations they occupy in the solar system; and that these different quantities of caloric are put into action by the influence of the solar rays, so as to produce that degree of *sensible* heat requisite for each respective planetary globe. On this hypothesis—which is corroborated by a very great variety of facts and experiments—there may be no more sensible heat felt on the surface of the planet Mercury, than on the surface of Herschel, although one of these bodies is nearly 50 times nearer the sun than the other. We have only to suppose that a small quantity of caloric exists in Mercury, and a larger quantity in Herschel, proportionate to his distance from the centre of the system. On this ground, we have no reason to believe, either that the planets nearest the sun are parched with excessive heat, or that those that are most distant are exposed to all the rigours of insufferable cold, or that the different degrees of temperature which may be found in these bodies render them unfit for being the abodes of sensitive and intellectual beings.

† See Edin. Phil. Journ. No. V. July, 1820, and No. XIII. July 1822.—I have found from observation, that this planet may be seen in the day-time, when only 1° 43′ from the sun's centre; and consequently when its geocentric latitude at the time of the superior conjunction exceeds that quantity, it may be distinctly seen during the whole period of 583 days, excepting about 35 hours before and after its *inferior* conjunction. It is well known to astronomers, that there has been a difference of opinion with respect to the *period* of the rotation of this planet. Cassini, from observations on a bright spot which advanced

affirms, that he has discovered mountains on the surface of this globe, one of which is 10, another 11, and a third 22 miles high. It appears also to be encompassed with an atmosphere, the densest part of which is about 16,000 feet high. About twice in the course of a century, this planet appears to pass, like a dark spot, across the sun's disk. This is termed the *transit* of Venus. The last transit happened June 3, 1769; the next will happen on December 8, 1874, which will be invisible in Europe. Another will happen on the 6th of December, 1882, which will be partly visible in Great Britain.

*The Earth* is the next planet in the system. It moves round the sun in 365 days, 5 hours, and 49 minutes, at the distance of 95 millions of miles, and round its axis in 23 hours, 56 minutes, 4 seconds. The former is called its *annual*, and the latter, its *diurnal* motion. That the earth is, in reality, a moving body, is a fact which can no longer be called in question; it is indeed susceptible of the clearest demonstration. But my limits will not permit to enter into a detail of the arguments by which it is suppprted. I have already adverted to one consideration, from which its diurnal rotation may be inferred. (See p. 23.) Either the earth moves round its axis every day, or *the whole universe* moves round it in the same time. To suppose the latter case to be the fact, would involve a reflection on the wisdom of its almighty Author, and would form the only exception that we know to that beautiful proportion, harmony, and simplicity, which appear in all the works of nature. Were it possible to construct a machine as large as the city of London, and to apply to it mechanical powers sufficient to make it revolve on an axis, so as to carry round a furnace for the purpose of roasting a joint of mutton, suspended in the centre of its motion—while we might admire the ingenuity and the energies displayed in its construction—all mankind would unite in condemning it as a display of consummate folly. But such an extravagant piece of machinery would not be half so preposterous as to suppose, that the vast universe is daily revolving around our little globe, and that all the planetary motions have an immediate respect to it. And shall we dare to ascribe to him who is "the only wise God," contrivances which we would pronounce to be the perfection of folly in mankind? It is recorded of the astronomer Alphonsus, king of Castile, who lived in the 13th century, that, after having studied the Ptolemaic system, which supposes the earth at rest in the centre of the universe, he uttered the following *impious* sentence: "If I had been of God's privy council, when he made the world, I would have advised him better." So that false conceptions of the system of nature, lead to erroneous notions of that adorable Being who is possessed of infinite perfection. We find that bodies much larger than the earth have a similar rotation. The planet Jupiter, a globe 295,000 miles in circumference, moves round his axis in less than ten hours; and all the other planetary bodies, on which spots have been discovered, are found to have a diurnal motion. Besides, it is found to be a universal law of nature that smaller globes revolve round larger; but there is no example in the universe, of a larger body revolving around a smaller. The moon revolves around the earth, but she is much smaller than the earth; the moons which move around Jupiter, Saturn, and Herschel, are all less than their primaries, and the planets which perform their revolutions around the sun are much less than that central luminary.

With regard to the *annual* revolution of the earth, if such a motion did exist, the planetary system would present a scene of inextricable confusion. The planets would sometimes move backwards, sometimes forwards, and at other times remain stationary; and would describe looped curves, so anomalous and confused, that no man in his senses could view the all-wise Creator as the author of so much confusion. But, by considering the earth as revolving in an orbit between Venus and Mars, (which all celestial observations completely demonstrate,) all the apparent irregularities of the planetary motions are completely solved and accounted for; and the solar system presents a scene of beauty, harmony and grandeur, combined with a simplicity of design which characterizes all the works of Omnipotence.

*The Moon.*—Next to the sun, the moon is to us the most interesting of all the celestial orbs. She is the constant attendant of the earth, and revolves around it in 27 days, 8 hours; but the period from one new or full moon to another is about 29 days, 12 hours. She is the nearest of all the heavenly bodies; being only about two hundred and forty thousand miles distant from the earth. She is much smaller than the earth; being only 2,180 miles in diameter. Her surface, when viewed with a telescope, presents an inte

20 degrees, in 24 hours, 34 minutes, determined the time of its rotation to be 23 hours and 20 minutes. On the other hand, Bianchini, from similar observations, concluded, that its diurnal period was 24 days and 8 hours. The difficulty of deciding between these two opinions, arises from the short time in which observations can be made on this planet, either before sun-rise or after sun-set, which prevents us from tracing, with accuracy, the progressive motion of its spots for a sufficient length of time. And although an observer should mark the position of the spots, at the same hour, on two succeeding evenings, and find they had moved forward about 20 degrees in 24 hours, he would still be at a loss to determine, whether they had moved 20 degrees *in all*, since the preceding observation, or had finished a revolution, and 20 degrees more.—In "Nicholson's Philosophical Journal," vol 36. I endeavoured to show how this point may be determined by observations on Venus in the day-time, by which, in certain cases, the progressive motion of her spots might be traced, without interruption, for 12 hours or more, which would completely settle the period of rotation.

resting and a variegated aspect; being diversified with mountains, valleys, rocks, and plains, in every variety of form and position. Some of these mountains form long and elevated ridges, resembling the chains of the Alps and the Andes; while others, of a conical form, rise to a great height, from the middle of level plains, somewhat resembling the Peak of Teneriffe. But the most singular feature of the moon, is, those circular ridges and cavities which diversify every portion of her surface. A range of mountains of a circular form, rising three or four miles above the level of the adjacent districts, surrounds, like a mighty rampart, an extensive plain; and, in the middle of this plain or cavity, an insulated conical hill rises to a considerable elevation. Several hundreds of these circular plains, most of which are considerably below the level of the surrounding country, may be perceived, with a good telescope, on every region of the lunar surface. They are of all dimensions, from two or three miles to forty miles in diameter; and, if they be adorned with verdure, they must present to the view of a spectator, placed among them, a more variegated, romantic, and sublime scenery than is to be found on the surface of our globe. An idea of some of these scenes may be acquired by conceiving a plain of about a hundred miles in circumference, encircled with a range of mountains, of various forms, three miles in perpendicular height, and having a mountain near the centre, whose top reaches a mile and a half above the level of the plain. From the top of this central mountain, the whole plain, with all its variety of objects, would be distinctly visible; and the view would appear to be bounded on all sides by a lofty amphitheatre of mountains, in every diversity of shape, rearing their summits to the sky. From the summit of the circular ridge, the conical hill in the centre, the opposite circular range, the plain below, and some of the adjacent plains, which encompass the *exterior* ridge of the mountains, would form another variety of view; and a third variety would be obtained from the various aspects of the central mountain, and the surrounding scenery, as viewed from the plains below.

The lunar mountains are of all sizes, from a furlong to five miles in perpendicular elevation. Certain luminous spots, which have been occasionally seen on the dark side of the moon, seem to demonstrate that fire exists in this planet. Dr. Herschel and several other astronomers suppose, that they are volcanoes in a state of eruption. It would be a more pleasing idea, and perhaps as nearly corresponding to fact, to suppose, that these phenomena are owing to some occasional splendid illuminations, produced by the lunar inhabitants, during their long nights. Such a scene as the burning of Moscow, the conflagration of an extensive forest, or the splendid illumination of a large city with gas-lights, might present similar appearances to a spectator in the moon. The bright spots of the moon are the mountainous regions; the dark spots are the plains, or more level parts of her surface. There may probably be rivers or small lakes on this planet; but there are no seas or large collection of water. It appears highly probable, from the observations of Schroeter, that the moon is encompassed with an atmosphere; but no clouds, rain, nor snow seem to exist in it. The illuminating power o the light derived from the moon, according to the experiments made by Professor Leslie, is about the *one hundred and fifty thousandth part* of the illuminating power of the sun. According to the experiments of M. Boguer, it is only as 1 to 300,000.

The Moon always presents the same face to us; which proves, that she revolves round her axis in the same time that she revolves round the earth. As this orb derives its light from the sun, and reflects a portion of it upon the earth, so the earth performs the same office to the moon. A spectator on the lunar surface would behold the earth, like a luminous orb, suspended in the vault of heaven, presenting a surface about 13 times larger than the moon does to us, and appearing sometimes gibbous, sometimes horned, and at other times with a round full face. The light which the earth reflects upon the dark side of the moon may be distinctly perceived by a common telescope, from three to six or eight days after the change. The lunar surface contains about 15 millions of square miles, and is, therefore, capable of containing a population equal to that of our globe, allowing only about 53 inhabitants to every square mile. That this planet is inhabited by sensitive and intelligent beings, there is every reason to conclude, from a consideration of the sublime scenery with which its surface is adorned, and of the general beneficence of the Creator, who appears to have left no large portion of his material creation without animated existences; and it is highly probable, that *direct proofs* of the moon's being inhabited may hereafter be obtained, when all the varieties on her surface shall have been more minutely explored.*

*The planet Mars.*—Next to the earth and moon, the planet Mars performs his revolution round the sun, in one year and ten months, to the distance of 145 millions of miles. His diameter is about 4,200 miles, and he is distinguished from all the other planets, by his *ruddy* appearance, which is owing to a *dense atmosphere* with which he is environed. With a good telescope, his surface appears diversified by a variety of spots; by the motion of which it is found, that he turns round his axis in 24 hours and 40 minutes. The inclination of his axis to the plane of his orbit being about 28° 42′, the

* See Appendix, No. III.

days and nights, and the different seasons in this planet, will bear a considerable resemblance to those we experience in our terrestrial sphere.*

At his nearest approach to the earth, his distance from us is about 50 millions of miles; and, at his greatest distance, he is about 240 millions of miles; so that in the former case he appears nearly 25 times larger than in the latter. To a spectator in this planet, our earth will appear, alternately, as a morning and evening star, and will exhibit all the phases of the moon, just as Venus does to us, but with a less degree of apparent magnitude and splendour. A luminous zone has been observed about the poles of Mars, which is subject to successive changes. Dr. Herschel supposes that it is produced by the reflection of the sun's light from his frozen regions, and that the melting of these masses of polar ice is the cause of the variation in its magnitude and appearance. This planet moves, in its orbit, at the rate of fifty-five thousand miles an hour.

*The new planets.*—Between the orbits of Mars and Jupiter, four planetary bodies have been lately discovered, accompanied with circumstances somewhat different from those of the other bodies which compose our system. They are named *Ceres*, *Pallas*, *Juno*, and *Vesta*. The planet *Ceres* was discovered at Palermo, in Sicily, by M. Piazzi, on the first day of the present century. It is of a ruddy colour, and appears abour the size of a star of the 8th magnitude, and is consequently invisible to the naked eye. It performs its revolution in 4 years and 7 months, at the distance of 260 millions of miles from the sun, and is reckoned, by some astronomers, to be about 1624 miles in diameter, or about half the diameter of Mercury. It appears to be surrounded with a large dense atmosphere. —*Pallas* was discovered the following year, namely, on the 28th of March, 1802, by Dr. Olbers of Bremen. It is supposed to be about 2000 miles in diameter, or nearly the size of the moon. It revolves about the sun in 4 years and 7 months, or nearly in the same time as Ceres, at the distance of 266 millions of miles; and is surrounded with a nebulosity or atmosphere, above 400 miles in height, similar to that of Ceres.—The planet *Juno* was discovered on the 1st September, 1804, by Mr. Harding of Bremen. Its mean distance from the sun is about 253 millions of miles; its revolution is completed in 4 years and 130 days, and its diameter is computed to be about 1425 miles. It is free from the nebulosity which surrounds Pallas, and is distinguished from all the other planets by the great eccentricity of its orbit; being, at its least distance from the sun, only 189 millions of miles, and at its greatest distance 316 millions.—*Vesta* was discovered by Dr. Olbers on the 29th March, 1807. It appears like a star of the 5th or 6th magnitude, and may sometimes be distinguished by the naked eye. Its light is more intense and white than any of the other three, and it is not surrounded with any nebulosity. It is distant from the sun about 225 millions of miles, and completes its revolution in 3 years and 240 days. Its diameter has not yet been accurately ascertained; but from the intensity of its light, and other circumstances, it is concluded, that it exceeds in magnitude both Pallas and Juno.

These planetary globes present to our view a variety of anomalies and singularities, which appear incompatible with the regularity, proportion, and harmony which were formerly supposed to characterize the arrangements of the solar system.—They are bodies *much smaller* in size than the other planets—they revolve *nearly at the same distances* from the sun, and perform their revolutions in *nearly the same periods*—their orbits are *much more eccentric*, and have a *much greater degree of inclination* to the ecliptic, than those of the old planets—and, what is altogether singular, (except in case of comets,) *their orbits cross each other*; so that there is a *possibility* that two of these bodies might happen to interfere, and to strike each other, in the course of their revolutions. The orbit of Ceres crosses the orbit of Pallas. Vesta may sometimes be at a greater distance from the sun than either Ceres, Pallas or Juno, although its mean distance is less than that of either of them, by several millions of miles; so that the orbit of Vesta crosses the orbits of all the other three. From these and other circumstances, it has, with a high degree of probability, been concluded—that these four planets are the fragments of a large celestial body which once revolved between Mars and Jupiter, and which had been burst asunder by some immense irruptive force. This idea seems to have occurred to Dr. Olbers after he had discovered the planet Pallas, and he imagined that other fragments might possibly exist. He concluded, that, if they all diverged from the same point, "they ought to have two common points of reunion, or two nodes in opposite regions of the heavens, through which all the planetary fragments must sooner or later pass." One of these nodes he found to be in the constellation Virgo, and the other in the Whale; and it is a remarkable coincidence, that it was in the latter of these regions that the planet Juno was discovered by Mr. Harding. In order to detect the remaining fragments (if any existed) Dr. Olbers examined, three times every year, all the small stars in Virgo and the Whale; and it was actually in the consellation Virgo, that he discovered the planet Vesta. It is not unlikely

* The inclination of the earth's axis to the ecliptic, or, in other words, to the plane of its annual orbit, is 23 degrees and 28 minutes, which is the cause of the diversity of seasons, and of the different length of days and nights. Were the axis of the earth perpendicular to its orbit, as is the case with the planet Jupiter, there would be no diversity of seasons.

that other fragments of a similar description may be discovered. Dr. Brewster attributes the fall of meteoric stones* to the smaller fragments of these bodies happening to come within the sphere of the earth's attraction. His ingenious reasonings on this subject, and in support of Dr. Olbers' hypothesis above stated, may be seen in *Edin. Ency.* vol. ii. p. 641, and in his "Supplementary chapters to Ferguson's Astronomy."

The facts to which I have now adverted seem to unfold a new scene in the history of the dispensations of the Almighty, and to warrant the conclusion, that the earth is not the only globe in the universe which is subject to physical changes and moral revolutions.

*The Planet Jupiter.*—This planet is 490 millions of miles distant from the sun, and performs its annual revolution in nearly twelve of our years, moving at the rate of twenty-nine thousand miles an hour. It is the largest planet in the solar system; being 89,000 miles in diameter, or about *fourteen hundred times* larger than the earth. Its motion round its axis is performed in nine hours and fifty-six minutes; and, therefore, the portions of its surface about the equator move at the rate of 28,000 miles an hour, which is nearly twenty-seven times swifter than the earth's diurnal rotation. The figure of Jupiter is that of an oblate spheroid, the axis, or diameter passing through the poles, being about 6000 miles shorter than that passing through the equator. The Earth, Saturn, and Mars are also spheroids; and it is highly probable that Mercury, Venus, and Herschel are of a similar figure, though the fact has not yet been ascertained by actual observation. When viewed with a telescope, several spots have been occasionally discovered on the surface of this planet, by the motion of which, its rotation was determined.

But what chiefly distinguishes the surface of Jupiter is several streaky appearances, or dusky strips, which extend across his disk, in lines parallel to his equator. These are generally termed his *belts*. Three of these belts, or zones nearly equi-distant from each other, are most frequently observed; but they are not regular or constant in their appearance.† Sometimes only one is to be seen, sometimes five, and sometimes seven or eight have been distinctly visible; and, in the latter case, two of them have been known to disappear during the time of observation. On the 28th May, 1780, Dr. Herschel perceived "the *whole surface of Jupiter* covered with small curved belts, or rather lines, that were not continuous across his disk." Though these belts are generally parallel to each other, yet they are not always so. Their breadth is likewise variable; one belt having been observed to grow narrow, while another in its neighbourhood has increased in breadth, as if the one had flowed into the other. The time of their continuance is also uncertain; sometimes they remain unchanged for several months, at other times, new belts have been formed in an hour or two. What these belts or variable appearances are it is difficult to determine. Some have regarded them as strata of clouds floating in the atmosphere of Jupiter; while others imagine, that they are the marks of great physical revolutions which are perpetually changing the surface of that planet. The former opinion appears the most probable. But, whatever be the nature of these belts, the sudden changes to which they are occasionally subject, seem to indicate the rapid operation of some powerful physical agency; for some of them are more than five thousand miles in breadth; and since they have been known to disappear in the space of an hour or two, and even during the time of a casual observation—agents more powerful than any with which we are acquainted must have produced so extensive an effect.

Jupiter is attended by four satellites or moons, which present a very beautiful appearance when viewed through a telescope. The first moon, or that nearest the planet, is 230,000 miles distant from its centre, and goes round it in 42½ hours; and will appear from its surface four times larger than our moon does to us. The second moon, being farther distant, will appear about the size of ours; the third, somewhat less; and the fourth, which is a million of miles distant from Jupiter, and takes sixteen days to go round him, will appear only about one-third the diameter of our moon. These moons suffer frequent eclipses from passing through Jupiter's shadow, in the same way as our moon is eclipsed by passing through the shadow of the earth. By

* Meteoric stones, or, what are generally termed *aerolites*, are stones which sometimes fall from the upper regions of the atmosphere, upon the earth.—The substance of which they are composed is, for the most part, *metallic;* but the ore of which they consist is not to be found *in the same constituent proportions* in any terrestrial substances. Their fall is generally preceded by a luminous appearance, a hissing noise, and a loud explosion; and, when found immediately after their descent, are always hot.—Their size differs, from small fragments, of inconsiderable weight, to the most ponderous masses. Some of the largest portions of these stones have been found to weigh from 300 lbs. to several tons; and they have often descended to the earth with a force sufficient to bury them many feet under the soil.—Some have supposed that these bodies are projected from volcanoes in the moon; others, that they proceed from volcanoes on the earth; while others imagine that they are generated in the regions of the atmosphere; but the true cause is, probably, not yet ascertained. In some instances, these stones have penetrated through the roofs of houses, and proved destructive to the inhabitants.

† A representation of these belts, in the positions in which they most frequently appear, is exhibited in the engraving, Fig. 2. Fig. 1. represents the double ring of Saturn, as it appears when viewed through a powerful telescope—Figures 1, 2, 3, 4, and 5, represent Saturn, Jupiter, Herschel, the Earth and Moon, *in their relative sizes and proportions.*

the eclipse of these moons, the motion of light was ascertained; and they are found to be of essential use in determining the longitude of places on the surface of our globe. This planet, if seen from its nearest moon, will present a surface a thousand times as large as our moon does to us, and will appear in the form of a crescent, a half-moon, a gibbous phase, and a full-moon, in regular succession, every 24 hours. Jupiter's axis being nearly perpendicular to his orbit, he has no sensible change of seasons, such as we experience on the earth. Were we placed on the surface of this planet, with the limited powers of vision we now possess, our earth and moon would entirely disappear, as if they were blotted out from the map of creation; and the inhabitants of these regions must have much better eyes than ours, if they know that there is such a globe as the earth in the universe.

*The planet Saturn.*—This planet is 900 millions of miles distant from the sun, being nearly double the distance of Jupiter. Its diameter is 79,000 miles, and, consequently, it is more than *nine hundred times* the bulk of the earth. It takes 29½ years to complete its revolution about the sun; but its diurnal motion is completed in ten hours and sixteen minutes; so that the year in this planet is nearly thirty times the length of ours, while the day is shorter, by more than one-half. The year, therefore, contains about twenty-five thousand one hundred and fifty *days*, or periods of its diurnal rotation, which is equal to 10,759 of our days. Saturn is of a spheroidal figure, or somewhat of the shape of an orange; his equatorial being more than six thousand miles longer than his polar diameter. His surface, like that of Jupiter, is diversified with belts and dark spots. Dr. Herschel, at certain times, perceived five belts on his surface, three of which were dark, and two bright. The dark belts had a yellowish tinge, and generally covered a larger zone of the disk of Saturn, than the belts of Jupiter occupy upon his surface. On account of the great distance of this planet from the sun, the light it receives from that luminary is only the *ninetieth part* of what we enjoy; but, by calculation, it is found, that this quantity is a thousand times greater than the light which the full moon affords to us. Besides, it is surrounded by no fewer than seven moons, which supply it with light in the absence of the sun. Five of these moons were discovered during the seventeenth century, by Huygens and Cassini; and the sixth and seventh were discovered by Dr. Herschel, in 1789, soon after his large forty feet reflecting telescope was constructed. These moons, and also those which accompany Jupiter, are estimated to be not less than the earth in magnitude, and are found, like our moon, to revolve round their axis in the same time in which they revolve about their respective primaries.

*Rings of Saturn.*—The most extraordinary circumstance connected with this planet, is, the phenomenon of a *double ring*, which surrounds its body, but no where touches it, being thirty thousand miles distant from any part of the planet, and is carried along with the planet in its circuit round the sun. This is the most singular and astonishing object in the whole range of the planetary system; no other planet being found environed with so wonderful an appendage; and the planets which may belong to other systems, being placed beyond the reach of our observations, no idea can be formed of the peculiar apparatus with which any of them may be furnished. This double ring consists of two concentric rings, detached from each other; the innermost of which is nearly three times as broad as the outermost. The outside diameter of the *exterior* ring is 204,000 miles; and, consequently, its circumference will measure *six hundred and forty thousand miles*, or eighty times the diameter of our globe. Its breadth is 7,200 miles, or nearly the diameter of the earth. Were four hundred and fifty globes, of the size of the earth, placed close to one another, on a plane, this immense ring would enclose the whole of them, together with all the interstices, or open spaces between the different globes. The outside diameter of the *innermost* ring is 184,000 miles, and its breadth twenty thousand miles, or about 2½ times broader than the diameter of the earth. The dark space, or interval, between the two rings, is 2,800 miles. The breadth of both the rings, including the dark space between them, is thirty thousand miles, which is equal to the distance of the innermost ring from the body of Saturn.

The following figure represents a view of Saturn and his rings, as they would appear, were our eye perpendicular to one of the planes of those rings; but our eye is never so much elevated above either plane, as to have the visual ray standing at right angles to it; it is never elevated more than 30 degrees above the planes of the rings. When we view Saturn through a telescope, we always see the ring at an oblique angle, so that it appears of an *oval* form, the outward circular rim being projected into an ellipsis more or less oblong, according to the different degrees of obliquity with which it is viewed, as will be seen in the figure of Saturn in the copperplate engraving.

These rings cast a deep shadow upon the planet, which proves that they are not shining *fluids*, but composed of *solid* matter. They appear to be possessed of a higher reflective power than the surface of Saturn; as the light reflected by them is more brilliant than that of the planet. One obvious use of this double ring is, to reflect light upon the planet, in the absence of the sun; what other purposes it may be intended to subserve, in the system of Saturn, is, at present, to us unknown. The sun illuminates

one side of it during fifteen years, or one-half of the period of the planet's revolution; and during the next fifteen years, the other side is enlightened in its turn. Twice in the course of thirty years, there is a short period, during which neither side is enlightened, and when, of course, it ceases to be visible;—namely, at the time when the sun ceases to shine on one side, and is about to shine on the other. It revolves round its axis, and, consequently, around Saturn, in ten hours and a half, which is at the rate of a thousand miles in a minute, or fifty-eight times swifter than the earth's equator. When viewed from the middle zone of the planet, in the absence of the sun, the rings will appear like vast luminous arches, extending along the canopy of heaven, from the eastern to the western horizon; having an apparent breadth equal to a hundred times the apparent diameter of our moon, and will be seen darkened about the middle, by the shadow of Saturn.*

There is no other planet in the solar system, whose firmament will present such a variety of splendid and magnificent objects, as that of Saturn. The various aspects of his seven moons, one rising above the horizon, while another is setting, and a third approaching to the meridian; one entering into an eclipse, and another emerging from it; one appearing as a crescent, and another with a gibbous phase; and sometimes the whole of them shining in the same hemisphere, in one bright assemblage; the majestic motions of the rings,—at one time illuminating the sky with their splendour, and eclipsing the stars; at another, casting a deep shade over certain regions of the planet, and unveiling to view the wonders of the starry firmament—are scenes worthy of the majesty of the Divine Being to unfold, and of rational creatures to contemplate. Such magnificent displays of wisdom and omnipotence lead us to conclude that the numerous splendid objects connected with this planet were not created merely to shed their lustre on naked rocks and barren sands; but that an immense population of intelligent beings is placed in those regions, to enjoy the bounty and to adore the perfections of their great Creator. The double ring of Saturn, when viewed through a good telescope, generally appears like a luminous handle on each side of the planet, with a dark interval between the interior edge of the ring and the convex body of Saturn; which is owing to its oblique position with respect to our line of vision. When its outer edge is turned directly towards the earth, it becomes invisible, or appears like a dark stripe across the disk of the planet. This phenomenon happens once every fifteen years.

*The planet Herschel.*—This planet, which is also known by the names of *the Georgium Sidus*, and *Uranus*, was discovered by Dr. Herschel on the 13th March, 1781. It is the

* See the engraving, fig. 7, which represents a view of the appearance which the rings and moons of Saturn will exhibit, in certain cases, about midnight, when beheld from a point 20 or 30 degrees north from his equator. The shade on the upper part of the rings represents the shadow of the body of Saturn. The shadow will appear to move gradually to the west as the morning approaches.

most distant planet from the sun, that has yet been discovered; being removed at no less than 1800 millions of miles from that luminary, which is nineteen times farther than the earth is from the sun—a distance so great, that a cannon ball, flying at the rate of 480 miles an hour, would not reach it in 400 years. Its diameter is about 35,000 miles; and, of course, it is about eighty times larger than the earth. It appears like a star of the sixth magnitude; but can seldom be distinguished by the naked eye. It takes about 83 years and a half to complete its revolution round the sun; and, though it is the slowest moving body in the system, it moves at the rate of 15,000 miles an hour. As the degree of sensible heat in any planet does not appear to depend altogether on its nearness to the sun, the temperature of this planet may be as mild as that which obtains in the most genial climate of our globe.* The diameter of the sun, as seen from Herschel, is little more than the apparent diameter of Venus, as seen by the naked eye; and the light which it receives from that luminary, is 360 times less than what we experience; yet this proportion is found by calculation to be equal to the effect which would be produced by 248 of our full moons; and, in the absence of the sun, there are *six moons* which reflect light upon this distant planet, all of which were discovered likewise by Dr. Herschel. Small as the proportion of light is, which this planet receives from the sun, it is easy to conceive, that beings similar to man, placed on the surface of this globe, with a slight modification of their organs of vision, might be made to perceive objects with a clearness and distinctness even superior to what we can do. We have only to suppose, that the Creator has formed their eyes with *pupils* capable of a much larger expansion than ours; and has endued their *retina* with a much greater degree of nervous sensibility. At all events, we may rest assured, that He who has placed sentient beings in any region, has, by laws with which we are partly unacquainted, adapted the constitution of the inhabitant to the nature of the habitation.

"Strange and amazing must the difference be,
'Twixt this dull planet and *bright Mercury*;
Yet reason says, nor can we doubt at all,
Millions of beings dwell on either ball,
With constitutions fitted for that spot
Where Providence, all-wise, has fixed their lot."
*Baker's Universe.*

The celestial globes which I have now described, are all the planets which are at present known to belong to the solar system. It is probable that other planetary bodies may yet be discovered between the orbits of Saturn and Herschel, and even far beyond the orbit of the latter; and it is also not improbable that planets may exist in the immense interval of 37 millions of miles between Mercury and the Sun.† These (if any exist) can be detected only by a series of *day observations*, made with equatorial telescopes; as they could not be supposed to be seen, after sunset, on account of their proximity to the sun. Five *primary*‡ planets, and eight *secondaries*, have been discovered within the last 42 years, and, therefore, we have no reason to conclude, that all the bodies belonging to our system have yet been detected, till every region of the heavens be more fully explored.

*Comets.*—Besides the planetary globes to which I have now adverted, there is a class of celestial bodies which occasionally appear in the heavens, to which the name of *comets* has been given. They are distinguished from the other celestial bodies, by their ruddy appearance, and by a long train of light, called the *tail*, which sometimes extends over a considerable portion of the heavens, and which is so transparent, that the stars may be seen through it. The tail is always directed to that part of the heavens which is opposite to the sun, and increases in size as it approaches him, and is again gradually diminished, as the comet flies off to the more distant regions of space. Their apparent magnitude is very different: sometimes they appear only of the bigness of the fixed stars; at other times they equal the diameter of Venus; and sometimes they have appeared nearly as large as the moon. They traverse the heavens in all directions, and cross the orbits of the planets. When examined through a telescope, they appear to consist of a dark central nucleus, surrounded by a dense atmosphere, or mass of vapours. They have been ascertained to move in long narrow *ellipses* or *ovals*, around the sun; some of them, on their nearest approach to him, having been within a million of miles of his centre; and then fly off to a region several thousands of millions of miles distant. When near the sun, they move with amazing velocity. The velocity of the comet which appeared in 1680, according to Sir Isaac Newton's calculation, was eight hundred and eighty thousand miles an hour. They appear to be bodies of no great density, and their

* See Note, page 82.

† The Author, some years ago, described a method by which the planets (if any) within the orbit of Mercury, may be discovered in the day-time, by means of a simple contrivance for intercepting the solar rays, and by the frequent application, by a number of observers, of powerful telescopes, to a certain portion of the sky, in the vicinity of the sun. The details of this plan have not yet been published; but the reader will see them alluded to in No. V. of the Edinburgh Philosophical Journal, for July 1820, p. 191.

‡ A primary planet is that which revolves round the sun as a centre; as Mars, Jupiter, and Saturn. A *secondary* planet is one which revolves round a primary planet as its centre; as the Moon, and the satellites of Jupiter and Saturn. The primary planets are distinguished from the fixed stars by the steadiness of their light; not having a *twinkling* appearance, as the stars exhibit.

size seldom exceeds that of the moon. The length of the tails of some comets has been estimated at fifty millions of miles. According to Dr. Herschel's computations, the solid nucleus or central part of the comet which appeared in 1811, was only 428 miles in diameter; but the real diameter of the head, or nebulous portion of the comet, he computed to be about 127 thousand miles. The length of its tail he computed to be above one hundred millions of miles, and its breadth nearly fifteen millions. It was nearest to the earth on the 11th of October, when its distance was 113 millions of miles. The number of comets which have occasionally been seen within the limits of our system, since the commencement of the Christian era, is about 500, of which the paths or orbits of 98 have been calculated.

As these bodies cross the paths of the planets in every direction, there is a possibility, that some of them might strike against the earth in their approach to the sun; and, were this to happen, the consequences would be awful beyond description. But we may rest assured that that Almighty Being who at first launched them into existence, directs all their motions, however complicated; and that the earth shall remain secure against all such concussions from celestial agents, till the purposes of his moral government in this world shall be fully accomplished. What regions these bodies visit, when they pass beyond the limits of our view; upon what errands they are sent, when they again revisit the central parts of our system; what is the difference in their physical constitution, from that of the sun and planets; and what important ends they are destined to accomplish, in the economy of the universe, are inquiries which naturally arise in the mind, but which surpass the limited powers of the human understanding at present to determine. Of this, however, we may rest assured, that they were not created in vain; that they subserve purposes worthy of the infinite Creator; and that wherever he has exerted his power, there also he manifests his wisdom and beneficence.*

Such is a general outline of the leading facts connected with that system of which we form a part. Though the energies of divine power had never been exerted beyond the limits of this system, it would remain an eternal monument of the wisdom and omnipotence of its Author. Independent of the sun, which is like a vast universe in itself, and of the numerous comets which are continually traversing its distant regions, it contains a mass of material existence, arranged in the most beautiful order, two thousand five hundred times larger than our globe. From late observations, there is the strongest reason to conclude, that the sun, along with all this vast assemblage of bodies, is carried through the regions of the universe, towards some distant point of space, or around some wide circumference, at the rate of more than sixty thousand miles an hour; and if so, it is highly probable, if not absolutely certain, that we shall never again occupy that portion of *absolute space*, through which we are this moment passing, during all the succeeding ages of eternity.

Such a glorious system must have been brought into existence, to subserve purposes worthy of the infinite wisdom and benevolence of the Creator. To suppose that the distant globes, of which it is composed, with their magnificent apparatus of rings and moons, were created merely for the purpose of affording a few astronomers, in these latter times, a peep at them through their glasses, would be inconsistent with every principle of reason; and would be charging Him, who is the source of wisdom, with conduct which we would pronounce to be folly in the sons of men. Since it appears, so far as our observation extends, that matter exists solely for the sake of sensitive and intelligent beings, and that the Creator made nothing in vain; it is a conclusion to which we are necessarily led, that the planetary globes are inhabited by various orders of intellectual beings, who participate in the bounty, and celebrate the glory o. their Creator.

When this idea is taken into consideration, it gives a striking emphasis to such sublime declarations of the sacred volume as these:—"All nations before him are as nothing—He sitteth upon the circle of the earth, and the inhabitants thereof are as grasshoppers—The nations are *as the drop of a bucket*—All the inhabitants of the world *are reputed as nothing* in his sight; and he doth according to his will in the army of heaven, and among the inhabitants of the earth—Thou hast made heaven, and the heaven of heavens, with all their host; and thou preservest them all, and *the host of heaven worshippeth thee*—When I consider thy heavens, *what is man*, that thou art mindful of him!" If the race of Adam were the principal intelligences in the universe of God, such passages would be stripped of all their sublimity, would degenerate into mere hyperboles, and be almost without meaning. If man were the only rational being who inhabited the *material world*, as some arrogantly imagine, it would be no wonder at all, that God should be "mindful of him;" nor could "all the inhabitants of this world," with any propriety, be compared to

* A comet has lately been discovered, whose periodical revolution is found to be only 3 years and 107 days. At its greatest distance from the sun, it is within the orbit of Jupiter, and it possesses this peculiar advantage for observation, that it will become visible ten times in thirty-three years. It was last seen in June, 1822, by the astronomers in the observatory of Paramatta, New Holland, in positions very near to those which had been previously calculated by Mr Enke. It is probable, that the observations which may hereafter be made on this comet, will lead to more definite and accurate views of the nature and destination of these singular bodies.

"a drop of a bucket," and be "reputed as nothing in his sight." Such declarations would be contrary to fact, if this supposition were admitted; for it assumes that man holds the *principal station* in the visible universe. The expressions—"The heavens, the heaven of heavens," and "the host of heaven worshipping God," would also, on this supposition, degenerate into something approaching to mere inanity. These expressions, if they signify any thing that is worthy of an inspired teacher to communicate, evidently imply, that the universe is vast and extensive, beyond the range of human comprehension—that it is peopled with myriads of inhabitants—that these inhabitants are possessed of intellectual natures, capable of appreciating the perfections of their Creator—and that they pay him a tribute of rational adoration. "The host of heaven worshippeth thee." So that the language of scripture is not only consistent with the doctrine of a plurality of worlds, but evidently supposes their existence to all the extent to which modern science can carry us. However vast the universe now appears—however numerous the worlds and systems of worlds, which may exist within its boundless range—the language of scripture is sufficiently comprehensive and sublime, to express all the emotions which naturally arise in the mind, when contemplating its structure—a characteristic which will apply to no other book, or pretended revelation. And this consideration shows not only the harmony which subsists between the discoveries of revelation and the discoveries of science, but also forms by itself a strong presumptive evidence, that the records of the Bible are authentic and divine.* Vast as the solar system, we have now been contemplating, may appear, it is but a mere point in the map of creation. To a spectator placed in one of the stars of the seventh magnitude, not only the glories of this world, and the more resplendent scenes of the planet Saturn, but even the sun himself would entirely disappear, as if he were blotted out of existence. "Were the sun," says Mr. Addison, "which enlightens this part of the creation, with all the host of the planetary worlds that move about him, utterly extinguished and annihilated, they would not be missed by an eye that could take in the whole compass of nature, more than a grain of sand upon the seashore. The space they possess is so exceedingly little, in comparison of the whole, that it would scarce make a blank in creation."

*The Fixed Stars.*—When we pass from the planetary system to other regions of creation, we have to traverse, in imagination, a space so immense, that it has hitherto baffled all the efforts of science to determine its extent. In these remote and immeasurable spaces, are placed those immense luminous bodies usually denominated the *fixed stars*. The nearest stars are, on good grounds, concluded to be at least *twenty billions* of miles distant from our globe—a distance through which *light* (the swiftest body in nature) could not travel in the space of three years; and which a ball, moving at the rate of 500 miles an hour, would not traverse in four millions five hundred thousand years, or 750 times the period which has elapsed since the Mosaic creation.—But how far they may be placed beyond this distance, no astronomer will pretend to determine. The following consideration will prove, to those unacquainted with the mathematical principles of astronomy, that the stars are placed at an immeasurable distance. When they are viewed through a telescope which magnifies objects a thousand times, they appear no larger than to the naked eye; which circumstance shows, that though we were placed at the thousandth part of the distance from them at which we now are, they would still appear only as so many shining *points;* for we should still be distant from the nearest of them, twenty thousand millions of miles: or, in other words, were we transported several thousands of millions of miles from the spot we now occupy, though their numbers would appear exceedingly increased, they would appear nc 'aiger than they do from our present station; anu ve behooved to be carried forward thousands of millions of miles further in a long succession, before their disks appeared to expand into large circles, like the moon. Dr. Herschel viewed the stars with telescopes, magnifying *six thousand times*, yet they still appeared only as brilliant points, without any sensible disks, or increase of diameter. This circumstance incontestably proves the two following things:—1. That the stars are *luminous bodies*, which shine by their own native light; otherwise they could not be perceived at such vast distances. 2. That they are bodies of an immense size, not inferior to the sun; and many of them, it is probable, far exceed that luminary in bulk and splendour.

The stars, on account of the difference in their apparent magnitudes, have been distributed into several classes or orders. Those which appear largest are called stars of the *first* magnitude; next to those in lustre, stars of the *second* magnitude, and so on to stars of the *sixth* magnitude, which are the smallest that can be distinguished by the naked eye. Stars of the 7th, 8th, 9th, 10th, &c. magnitudes, which cannot be seen by the naked eye, are distinguished by the name of *telescopic* stars. Not more than a thousand stars can be distinguished by the naked eye, in the clearest winter's night; but, by means of the telescope, millions have been discovered. (See p. 11.) And, as it is probable that by far the greater part lie beyond the reach of the best glasses which have been or ever will be constructed by man—

* See Appendix, No VI.

the real number of the stars may be presumed to be beyond all human calculation or conception, and perhaps beyond the grasp of an angelic comprehension.

In consequence of recent discoveries, we have now the strongest reason to believe, that all the stars in the universe are arranged into clusters, or groups, which astronomers distinguish by the name of *Nebulæ* or *Starry Systems*, each nebula consisting of many thousands of stars. The nearest nebula is that whitish space or zone, which is known by the name of the *Milky Way*, to which our sun is supposed to belong. It consists of many hundreds of thousands of stars.—When Dr. Herschel examined this region, with his powerful telescopes, he found a portion of it only 15 degrees long and 2 broad, which contained *fifty thousand* stars large enough to be distinctly counted; and he suspected twice as many more, which, for want of sufficient light in his telescope, he saw only now and then. More than two thousand five hundred nebulæ have already been observed; and, if each of them contain as many stars as the Milky Way, several hundreds of millions of stars must exist, even within that portion of the heavens which lies open to our observation.

It appears, from numerous observations, that *various changes* are occasionally taking place in the regions of the stars. Several stars have appeared for a while in the heavens, and then vanished from the sight. Some stars which were known to the ancients, cannot now be discovered; and stars are now distinctly visible, which were to them unknown. A few stars have gradually increased in brilliancy, while others have been constantly diminishing in lustre. Certain stars, to the number of 15, or upwards, are ascertained to have a periodical increase and decrease of their lustre, sometimes appearing like stars of the 1st or 2d magnitude, sometimes diminishing to the size of the 4th or 5th magnitude, and sometimes altogether disappearing to the naked eye. It also appears, that changes are taking place among the nebulæ—that several nebulæ are formed by the decomposition of larger nebulæ, and that many nebulæ of this kind are at present detaching themselves from the nebula of the milky way. These changes seem to indicate, that mighty movements and vast operations are continually going on in the distant regions of creation, under the superintendence of the Sovereign of the Universe, upon a scale of magnitude and grandeur which overwhelms the human understanding.

To explore, more extensively, the region of the starry firmament; to mark the changes that are taking place; to ascertain all the changeable stars; to determine the periodical variations of their light; the revolutions of double and triple stars; and the motions, and other phenomena peculiar to these great bodies, will furnish employment for future enlightened generations and will, perhaps, form a part of the studies and investigations of superior intelligences, in a higher sphere of existence, during an indefinite lapse of ages.

If every one of these immense bodies be a *Sun*, equal or superior to ours, and encircled with a host of planetary worlds, as we have every reason to conclude, (see pp. 11, 31,) how vast must be the extent of creation! how numerous the worlds and beings which exist within its boundless range! and, how great, beyond all human or angelic conception, must be the power and intelligence of that glorious Being, who called this system from nothing into existence, and continually superintends all its movements! The mind is bewildered and confounded when it attempts to dwell on this subject; it feels the narrow limits of its present faculties; it longs for the powers of a seraph, to enable it to take a more expansive flight, into those regions which "eye hath not seen;" and, while destitute of these, and chained down to this obscure corner of creation, it can only exclaim, in the language of inspiration, "Who can by searching find out God?—Great is our Lord, and of great power; his understanding is infinite!—Great and marvellous are thy works, Lord God Almighty!—Who can utter the mighty acts of Jehovah—who can show forth all his praise!"

After what has been now stated in relation to the leading facts of astronomy, it would be needless to spend time in endeavouring to show its connexion with religion. It will be at once admitted, that all the huge globes of luminous and oqaque matter, to which we have adverted, are the workmanship of Him "who is wonderful in counsel and excellent in working;" and form a part of the dominions of that august Sovereign, "whose kingdom ruleth over all." And shall it ever be insinuated, that this subject has no relation to the great object of our adoration? and that it is of no importance in our views of the Divinity, whether we conceive his dominions as circumscribed within the limits of little more than 25,000 miles, or as embracing an extent which comprehends innumerable worlds? The objects around us in this sublunary sphere strikingly evince the superintendency, the wisdom, and benevolence of the Creator; but this science demonstrates, beyond all other departments of human knowledge, the *grandeur and magnificence* of his operations: and raises the mind to sublimer views of his attributes than can be acquired by the contemplation of any other objects. A serious contemplation of the sublime objects which astronomy has explored, must, therefore, have a tendency to inspire us with profound veneration of the eternal Jehovah—to humble us in the dust before his august presence—to excite admiration of his condescension and grace in the work of redemption—to show us the littleness of this world, and the insignificancy of those riches and honours to which ambitious men aspire with so much labour and anxiety of mind—to demonstrate the glory and magnificence of God's universal kingdom—to convince us of the infinite sources of varied felicity which he has in his power to communicate to holy intelligences—to enliven our hopes of the splendours of that "exceeding great and eternal weight of glory" which will burst upon the spirits of good men, when they pass from this region of mortality—and to induce us to aspire with more lively ardour after that heavenly world, where the glories of the Deity and the magnificence of his works will be more clearly unfolded.

If, then, such be the effects which the objects of astronomy have a tendency to produce on a devout and enlightened mind—to call in question the propriety of exhibiting such views in religious publications, or in the course of religious instruction, would be an approach to impiety, and an attempt to cover with a veil the most illustrious visible displays of divine glory. It forms a striking evidence of the depravity of man, as well as of his want of true taste, and of a discernment of what is excellent, that the grandeur of the nocturnal heavens, and the perfections of Deity they proclaim, are beheld with so much apathy and indifference by the bulk of mankind. Though "the heavens declare the glory of God," in the most solemn and impressive language, adapted to the comprehension of every kindred and every tribe, yet "a brutish man knoweth not, neither doth a fool understand this." They can gaze upon these resplendent orbs with as little emotion as the ox that feeds on the grass, or as the horse that drags their carcasses along in their chariots. They have even attempted to ridicule the science of the heavens, to caricature those who have devoted themselves to such studies, and to treat with an indifference, mingled with contempt, the most august productions of Omnipotence. Such persons must be considered as exposing themselves to that divine denunciation—"Because they regard not the works of Jehovah, neither consider the operations of his hands, he will destroy them and not build them up." If the structure of the heavens, and the immensity of worlds and beings they contain, were intended by the Creator to *adumbrate*, in some measure, his invisible perfections, and to produce a sublime and awful impression on all created intelligences, (see pp. 22, 26, 28,) it must imply a high degree of disrespect to the Divinity wilfully to overlook these astonishing scenes of Power and Intelligence. It is not a matter of mere taste or caprice, whether or not we direct our thoughts to such subjects, but an imperative duty to which we are frequently directed in the word of God; the *wilful neglect* of which, where there is an opportunity of attending to it, must subject us to all that is included in the threatening now specified, if there be any meaning in language.

That the great body of professed Christians are absolute strangers to the sublime sentiments which a serious contemplation of the heavens inspires, must be owing, in part, to the minds of Christian parents and teachers not having been directed to such subject, or to the views they entertain respecting the relation of such contemplations to the objects of religion. In communicating religious instructions in reference to the attributes of God, the heavens are seldom referred to, except in such a vague and indefinite manner as can produce no deep nor vivid impression on the mind; and many pious persons, whose views have been confined to a narrow range of objects, have been disposed to declaim against such studies, as if they had a tendency to engender pride and self-conceit, and as if they were even dangerous to the interests of religion and piety. How very different were the feelings and the conduct of the sacred writers! They call upon every one of God's intelligent offspring to "stand still, and consider the wondrous works of the Most High;" and describe the profound emotions of piety which the contemplation of them produced on their own minds; "Lift up your eyes on high and behold! Who hath created these things! The heavens declare the glory of God, and the firmament showeth his handy-work. —When I *consider* thy heavens, the work of thy fingers, the moon and the stars which thou hast ordained—what is man that thou art mindful of him, and the son of man that thou visitest him! Thou, even thou, art Lord alone; thou hast made heaven, and the heaven of heavens, with all their host; and thou preservest them all; and the hosts of heaven worship thee. All the gods of the nations are idols; but the Lord *made the heavens:* Honour and Majesty are before him. Jehovah hath prepared his *throne* in the heavens: and his kingdom ruleth over all. Sing praises unto God, ye kingdoms of the earth, to him that rideth on the heaven of heavens. Ascribe ye *power* to our God; for his strength is in the heavens. Praise him for his mighty acts, praise him *according to his excellent greatness.*" If we would enter, with spirit, into such elevated strains of piety, we must not content ourselves with a passing and vacant stare at the orbs of heaven, as if they were only so many brilliant *studs* fixed in the canopy of the sky; but must "*consider*" them, with fixed attention, in all the lights in which revelation and science have exhibited them to our view, if we wish to praise God for his mighty works, and "*according to his excellent greatness.*" And, for this purpose, the conclusions deduced by those who have devoted themselves to celestial investigations, ought to be presented to the view of the intelligent Christian, that he may be enabled to "speak of the glory of Jehovah's kingdom, and to talk of his power."

Having, in the preceding sketches, considerably exceeded the limits originally prescribed for this department of my subject, I am reluctantly compelled to despatch the remaining sciences with a few brief notices.

### NATURAL PHILOSOPHY.

The object of *Natural Philosophy* is, to observe and describe the phenomena of the material universe, with a view to discover their causes, and the laws by which the Almighty directs the movements of all bodies in heaven and on earth. It embraces an investigation of the laws of gravitation, by which the planets are directed in their motions—the laws by which water, air, light, and heat are regulated, and the effects they produce in the various states in which they operate—the nature of colours, sounds, electricity, galvanism, and magnetism, and the laws of their operation—the causes which operate in the production of thunder, lightning, luminous and fiery meteors, hail, rain, snow, dew, and other atmospherical phenomena. In short, it embraces all the objects of Natural History formerly alluded to, with a view to ascertain the causes of their varied appearances, and the principles that operate in the changes to which they are subject; or, in other words, the laws by which the diversified phenomena of universal nature are produced and regulated. One subordinate use of the knowledge derived from this science, is, to enable us to construct all those mechanical engines which facilitate human labour, and increase the comforts of mankind, and all those instruments which tend to enlarge our views of the operations of nature. A still higher and nobler use to which philosophy is subservient, is, to demonstrate the wisdom and intelligence of the Great First Cause of all things, and to enlarge our conceptions of the admirable contrivance and design which appear in the different departments of universal nature. In this view, it may be considered as forming a branch of *Natural Theology*, or, in other words, a branch of the religion of angels, and of all other holy intelligences.

This department of Natural Science has generally been divided into the following branches:

I. *Mechanics.*—This branch, considered in its most extensive range, includes an investigation of the general properties of matter; such as solidity, extension, divisibility, motion, attraction, and repulsion—the laws of gravitation, and of central forces, as they appear to operate in the motions of the celestial bodies, and on the surface of our globe, in the phenomena of falling bodies, the motions of projectiles, the vibration of pendulums, &c.—the theory of machines, the principles on which their energy depends; the properties of the mechanical powers—the *lever*, the *wheel and axle*, the *pulley*, the *inclined plane*, the *wedge*, and the *screw*—and the effects resulting from their various combinations. From the investigations of philosophers on these subjects, we learn the laws by which the great bodies of the universe are directed in their motions; the laws which bind together the different portions of matter on the surface of the earth, and which regulate the motions of animal, vegetable, and inanimate nature; and the principles on which cranes, mills, wheel-carriages, pile-engines, threshing-machines, and other engines, are constructed; by means of which, man has been enabled to accomplish operations far beyond the limits of his own physical powers.

Without a knowledge of the laws of motion, and assistance from the combined effects of the mechanical powers, man would be a very limited being, his enjoyments would be few, and his active energies confined within a very narrow range. In a savage state, ignorant of manufactures, agriculture, architecture, navigation, and the other arts which depend upon mechanical combinations, he is exposed, without shelter, to the inclemencies of the season; he is unable to transport himself beyond seas and oceans, to visit other climes and other tribes of his fellow men; he exists in the desert, comfortless and unimproved; the fertile soil, over which he roams, is covered with thorns, and briers, and thickets, for the haunt of beasts of prey; his enjoyments are little superior to those of the lion, the hyæna, and the elephant, while he is much their inferior in point of agility and physical strength. But when philosophy has once demonstrated the principles of mechanics, and introduced the practice of the useful arts, "the wilderness and the solitary place are made glad, and the desert rejoices and blossoms as the rose." Cities are founded, and gradually rise to opulence and splendour; palaces and temples are erected; the damp cavern and the rush-built hut are exchanged for the warm and comfortable apartments of a substantial mansion; ships are built, and navigated across the ocean; the treasures of one country are conveyed to another, an intercourse is carried on between the most distant tribes of mankind; commerce flourishes, and machinery of all kinds is erected, for facilitating human labour, and promoting the enjoyments of man. And when the principles and the practice of "pure and undefiled religion" accompany these physical and mechanical operations, love and affection diffuse their benign influence; the prospect brightens as years roll on, and man advances with pleasure and improvement to the scene of his high destination.

II. *Hydrostatics* treats of *the pressure and equilibrium of fluids.* From the experiments which have been made in this branch of philosophy, the following important principles, among many others have been deduced:—

(1.) *That the surface of all waters which have a communication, whilst they are at rest, will be perfectly level.* This principle will be more clearly understood by an inspection of the following figures. If water be poured into the tube A, (Fig. 1.) it will run through the horizontal tube E, and rise in the opposite tube B, to the same

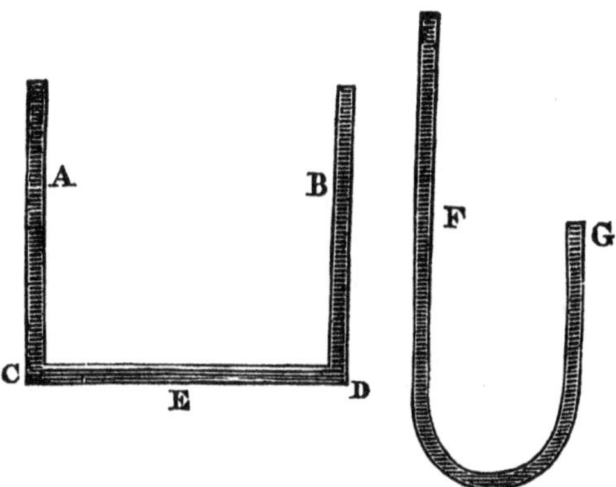


height at which it stands at A. It is on this principle that water is now conveyed under ground, through conduit pipes, and made to rise to the level of the fountain whence it is drawn. The city of Edinburgh, a considerable part of which is elevated above the level of the surrounding country, is supplied with water from a reservoir on the Pentland hills, several miles distant. The water is conveyed in leaden pipes down the declivity of the hill, along the interjacent plain, and up to the entrance of the castle, whence it is distributed to all parts of the city. If the point A represent the level of the reservoir, C D will represent the plain along which the water is conveyed, and B the elevation to which it rises on the castle hill. On the same principle, and in a similar manner, the city of London is supplied with water from the water-works at London bridge. Had the ancients been acquainted with this simple but important principle, it would have saved them the labour and expense of rearing those stupendous works of art, the *aqueducts*, which consisted of numerous arches of a vast size, and sometimes piled one above another.

Fig. 2. represents the *syphon*, the action of which depends upon the pressure of the atmosphere. If this instrument be filled with water, or any other liquid, and the shorter leg, G, plunged to the bottom of a cask, or other vessel, containing the same liquid, the water will run out at the longer leg, F, till the vessel be emptied, in consequence of the atmospheric pressure upon the surface of the liquid. On this principle, water may be conveyed over a rising ground to any distance, provided the perpendicular height of the syphon above the surface of the water in the fountain does not exceed 32 or 33 feet. On the same principle are constructed the *fountain at command*, the *cup of Tantalus*, and other entertaining devices. The same principle, too, enables us to account for springs which are sometimes found on the tops of mountains, and for the phenomena of *intermitting* springs, or those which flow and stop by regular alternations.

(2.) *Any quantity of fluid, however small, may be made to counterpoise any quantity, however large.* This is what has generally been termed the Hydrostatical Paradox; and from this principle it follows, that a given quantity of water may exert a force several hundred times greater or less, according to the manner in which it is employed. This force depends on the *height* of the column of water, independent of its quantity; for its *pressure* depends on its perpendicular height. By means of water conveyed through a very small perpendicular tube, of great length, a very strong hogshead has been burst to pieces, and the water scattered about with incredible force. On this principle, the *hydrostatic press*, and other engines of immense power, have been constructed.

(3.) *Every body which is heavier than water, or which sinks in it, displaces so much of the water as is equal to the bulk of the body immersed in the water.* On this principle, the specific gravities, or comparative weight, of all bodies are determined. It appears to have been first ascertained by Archimedes, and, by means of it, he determined that the golden crown of the king of Syracuse had been adulterated by the workmen. From this principle we learn, among many other things, the specific gravity of the human body; and that four pounds of cork will preserve a person weighing 135 pounds from sinking, so that he may remain with his head completely above water.

*Hydraulics*, which has sometimes been treated as a distinct department of mechanical philosophy, may be considered as a branch of hydrostatics. It teaches us what relates to the *motion of fluids*, and how to estimate their velocity and force. On the principles of this science, all machines worked by water are constructed—as steam-engines, water-mills, common and forcing pumps, syphons, fountains, and fire-engines.

III. *Pneumatics.*—This branch of philosophy treats of the nature and properties of the atmosphere, and of their effects on solid and fluid bodies. From this science we learn, that air has *weight*, and presses on all sides, like other fluids; that the pressure of the atmosphere upon the top of a mountain is less than on a plain beneath; that it presses upon our bodies with a weight of several thousand pounds more at one time than at another; that air can be compressed into forty thousand times less space than it naturally occupies; that it is of an elastic or expansive nature, and that the force of its spring is equal to its weight; that its elasticity is increased by heat; that it is necessary to the production of sound, the support of flame and animal life, and the germination and growth of all kinds of vegetables.

These positions are proved and illustrated by such experiments as the following:—The general *pressure* of the atmosphere is proved by such experiments as those detailed in No. II. of the *Appendix*. The following experiment proves that air is *compressible*. If a glass tube, open at one end, and closed at the other, be plunged, with the open end downwards, into a tumbler of water, the water will rise a little way in the tube; which shows, that the air which filled the tube is compressed by the water into a smaller space. The *elasticity* of air is proved by tying up a bladder, with a very small quantity of air within it, and putting it under the receiver of an air-pump, when it will be seen gradually to inflate, till it becomes of its full size. A similar effect would take place, by carrying the bladder to the higher regions of the atmosphere. On the compression and elasticity of the air, depends the construction of that dangerous and destructive instrument, the air-gun.

That it is capable of being rarified by heat, is proved by holding to the fire a half-blown bladder, tightly tied at the neck, when it will dilate to nearly its full size; and if either a *full-blown* bladder, or a thin glass bubble filled with air is held to a strong fire, it will burst. The elasticity of the air is such, that Mr. Boyle, by means of an air-pump, caused it to dilate till it occupied fourteen thousand times the space that it usually does. That air is necessary to sound, flame, animal and vegetable life, is proved by the following experiments: When the receiver of an air-pump is exhausted of its air, a cat, a mouse, or a bird, placed in it, expires in a few moments, in the greatest agonies. A bell rung in the same situation produces no sound; and a lighted candle is instantly extinguished. Similar experiments prove that air is necessary for the flight of birds the ascent of smoke and vapours, the explosion of gunpowder, and the growth of plants; and that all bodies descend equally swift in a place void of air; a guinea and a feather being found to fall to the bottom of an exhausted receiver at the same instant.

On the principles which this science has established, have been constructed the air-pump, the barometer, the thermometer, the diving-bell, the hygrometer, the condenser, and various other instruments, which have contributed to the comfort of human life, and to the enlargement of our knowledge of the constitution of nature.

IV. *Acoustics.*—This science treats of the nature, the phenomena, and the laws of *sound*, and the theory of musical concord and harmony. From the experiments which have been made on this subject, we learn, that air is essential to the production of sound; that it arises from *vibrations* in the air, communicated to it by vibrations of the sounding body; that these vibrations, or aerial pulses, are propagated all around in a spherical undulatory manner; that their density decreases, as the squares of the distances from the sounding body increase; that they are propagated together in great numbers from different bodies, without disturbance or confusion, as is evident from concerts of musical instruments; that water, timber, and flannel, are also good conductors of sound; that sound travels at the rate of 1142 feet in a second, or about thirteen miles in a minute; that the softest whisper flies as fast as the loudest thunder; and that the utmost limits, within which the loudest sounds produced by artificial means can be heard, is 180 or 200 miles;* that sound striking against an obstacle, as the wall of a house, may, like light, be reflected, and produce another sound, which is called an *echo;* and that, after it has been reflected from several places, it may be collected into one point or focus, where it will be more audible than in any other place. On these principles, whispering galleries, speaking trumpets, and other acoustic instruments, are constructed.

V. *Optics.*—This branch of philosophy treats of vision, light, and colours, and of the various phenomena of visible objects produced by the rays of light, reflected from mirrors, or transmitted through lenses. From this science we

* In the war between England and Holland, in 1672, the noise of the guns was heard in those parts of Wales which were estimated to be two hundred miles distant from the scene of action. But the sounds produced by volcanoes have been heard at a much greater distance; some instances of which are stated in Chap. IV. Sect. 2. Several other facts in relation to sound are detailed in Chap. III. Art *Acoustic Tunnels*.

learn, that light flies at the rate of nearly twelve millions of miles every minute—that it moves in straight lines—that its particles may be several thousands of miles distant from each other—that every visible body emits particles of light from its surface, in all directions—that the particles of light are *exceedingly small*; for a lighted candle will fill a cubical space of two miles every way with its rays, before it has lost the least sensible part of its substance; and millions of rays, from a thousand objects, will pass through a hole not larger than the point of a needle, and convey to the mind an idea of the form, position, and colour of every individual object—that the intensity or degree of light decreases, as the square of the distance from the luminous body increases; that is, at two yards' distance from a candle, we shall have only the fourth part of the light we should have at the distance of one yard; at three yards' distance, the ninth part; at four yards, the sixteenth part, and so on—that glass *lenses* may be ground into the following forms, *plano-convex*, *plano-concave*, *double convex*, *double concave*, and *meniscus*, that is, convex on one side, and concave on the other—that specula, or mirrors, may be ground into either a spherical, parabolical, or cylindrical form—that, by means of such mirrors and lenses, the rays of light may be so modified as to proceed either in a *diverging*, *converging*, or *parallel* direction, and the images of visible objects represented in a variety of new *forms*, *positions*, and *magnitudes*—that every ray of white light may be separated into seven primary colours: *red*, *orange*, *yellow*, *green*, *blue*, *indigo*, and *violet*—that the variegated colouring which appears on the face of nature is not in the objects themselves, but in the light which falls upon them—that the *rainbow* is produced by the refraction and reflection of the solar rays in the drops of falling rain—that the rays of light are refracted, or bent out of their course, when they fall upon glass, water, and other mediums—that the light of the sun may be collected into a point or focus, and made to produce a heat more intense than that of a furnace*—that the rays from visible objects, when reflected from a concave mirror, converge to a focus, and paint an image of the objects before it, and that when they pass through a convex glass, they depict an image behind it.

On these and other principles demonstrated by this science, the Camera Obscura, the Magic Lantern, the Phantasmagoria, the Kaleidoscope, the Heliostata, the Micrometer—Spectacles, Opera-Glasses, Prisms, single, compound, lucernal, and solar Microscopes, reflecting and refracting Telescopes, and other optical instruments, have been constructed by means of which the natural powers of human vision have been wonderfully increased, and our prospects into the works of God extended far beyond what former ages could have conceived.

VI. *Electricity*.—This name has been given to a science which explains and illustrates the operations of a very subtile fluid called *the electric fluid*, which appears to pervade every part of nature, and to be one of the chief agents employed in producing many of the phenomena of the material world. If a piece of amber, sealing wax, or sulphur, be rubbed with a piece of flannel, it will acquire the power of attracting small bits of paper, feathers, or other light substances. If a tube of glass, two or three feet in length, and an inch or two in diameter, be rubbed pretty hard, in a dark room, with a piece of dry woollen cloth, besides attracting light substances, it will emit flashes of fire, attended with a crackling noise. This luminous matter is called electricity, or the *electric fluid*. If a large globe or cylinder of glass be turned rapidly round, and made to rub against a cushion, streams and large sparks of bluish flame will be elicited, which will fly round the glass, attract light bodies, and produce a pungent sensation if the hand be held to it. This glass, with all its requisite apparatus, is called an *electrical machine*. It is found, that this fluid will pass along some bodies, and not along others. The bodies over which it passes freely are, water, and most other fluids, except oil and the aerial fluids; iron, copper, lead, and in general all the metals, semimetals, and metallic ores; which are, therefore, called *conductors* of electricity. But it will not pass over glass, resin, wax, sulphur, silk, baked woods, or dry woollen substances; nor through air, except by force, *in sparks*, to short distances. These bodies are, therefore, called *non-conductors*.

The following facts among others, have been ascertained respecting this wonderful agent:—That all bodies with which we are acquainted possess a greater or less share of this fluid—that the quantity usually belonging to any body produces no sensible effects; but when any surface

* This is produced by means of lenses, or mirrors of a large diameter, called burning-glasses. By these instruments the hardest metals, on which common fires, and even glass-house furnaces, could produce no effect, have been melted in a few seconds. M. Villette, a Frenchman, nearly a century ago, constructed a mirror, three feet eleven inches in diameter, and three feet two inches in focal distance, which melted *copper ore* in eight seconds, *iron ore* in twenty-four seconds, a fish's tooth in thirty-two seconds, *cast iron* in sixteen seconds, a silver sixpence in seven seconds, and *tin* in three seconds. This mirror condensed the solar rays 17,257 times, a degree of heat which is about *four hundred and ninety times* greater than common fire. Mr. Parker, of London, constructed a lens three feet in diameter, and six feet eight inches focus, which weighed 212 pounds. It melted twenty grains of gold in four seconds, and ten grains of platina in three seconds. The power of burning glasses is *as the area of the lens directly, and the square of the focal distance inversely*—or, in other words, the broader the mirror or lens, and the shorter the focal distance, the more intense is the heat produced by such instruments. A globular decanter of water makes a powerful burning-glass; and house furniture has been set on fire by incautiously exposing it to the rays of the sun.

becomes possessed of *more* or *less* than its natural share, it exhibits certain appearances, in the form of light, sound, attraction, or repulsion, which are ascribed to the power called *electric*—that there are two different species of the electrical fluid, or, at least two different modifications of the same general principle, termed *positive* and *negative* electricity—that positive and negative electricity always accompany each other; for if a substance acquire the one, the body with which it is rubbed acquires the other—that it moves with amazing rapidity; having been transmitted through wires of several miles in length, without taking up any sensible space of time; and, therefore, it is not improbable, that were an insulated conducting substance extended from one continent to another, it might be made to fly to the remotest regions of the earth in a few seconds of time—that it has a power of suddenly contracting the muscles of animals, or of giving a *shock* to the animal frame—that this shock may be communicated, at the same instant, to a hundred persons, or to an indefinite number who form a circle, by joining their hands together—that it may be accumulated to such a degree as to kill the largest animals—that vivid sparks of this fluid, attended with a crackling noise, may be drawn from different parts of the human body, when the person is *insulated*, or stands upon a stool, supported by glass feet—that electricity sets fire to gunpowder, spirits of wine, and other inflammable substances—that it melts iron wire, and destroys the polarity of the magnetic needle—that it augments the natural evaporation of fluids, promotes the vegetation of plants, and increases the insensible perspiration of animals, and can be drawn from the clouds by means of electrical kites, and other elevated conductors. By means of the electrical power, small models of machinery have been set in action: orreries to represent the movements of the planets, have been put in motion; and small bells have been set a ringing for a length of time; and, in consequence of the knowledge we have acquired of the mode of its operation in the system of nature, the lightnings of heaven have been arrested in their course, and constrained to descend to the earth, without producing any injurious effects.

From these, and a variety of other facts and experiments, it is now fully ascertained, that *lightning* and electricity are identical; and that it is the prime agent in producing the awful phenomena of a thunder-storm; the lightning being the rapid motion of vast masses of electric matter, and *thunder* the *noise*, with its echoes, produced by the rapid motion of the lightning through the atmosphere. There can be little doubt that, in combination with steam, the gases, and other agents, it also produces many of the terrific phenomena of earthquakes, volcanoes, whirlwinds, water-spouts, and hurricanes, and the sublime coruscations of the *aurora borealis*. In the operations of this powerful fluid we behold a striking display of the sovereignty and majestic agency of God. In directing its energies, "his way is in the whirlwind and the storm, and the clouds are the dust of his feet; the heavens are covered with sackcloth, the mountains quake before him, the hills melt, the earth is burned at his presence, and the rocks are thrown down by him:" Nah. i. 3—6. It is easy to conceive, that, by a few slight modifications produced by the hand of Omnipotence, this powerful fluid might become the agent of producing either the most awful and tremendous, or the most glorious and transporting scenes, over every region of our globe. As it now operates, it is calculated to inspire us rather with awe and terror than with admiration and joy; and to lead our thoughts to a consideration of the state of man as a depraved intelligence, and a rebel against his Maker.

VII. *Galvanism* is intimately connected with electricity, though it is generally considered as a branch of chymistry. It is only another mode of exciting electrical action. In electricity the effects are produced chiefly by *mechanical* action; but the effects of galvanism are produced by the *chymical* action of bodies upon each other. If we take a piece of zinc, and place it under the tongue, and lay a piece of silver, as big as a half-crown, above it; by bringing the outer edges of these pieces in contact, we shall immediately experience a peculiar and disagreeable tase, like that of copper. The same thing may be noticed with a guinea and a piece of charcoal. If a person, in the dark, put a slip of tinfoil upon one of his eyes, and a piece of silver in his mouth, by causing these pieces to communicate, a faint flash will appear before his eyes. If a living frog or fish, having a slip of tinfoil pasted upon its back, be placed upon a piece of zinc, by forming a communication between the zinc and tinfoil, the spasms of the muscles are excited. These and similar effects are produced by that modification of electricity which has been termed *galvanism*. Three different conductors, or what is called *a galvanic circle*, are requisite to produce such effects. A piece of copper, a piece of flannel, moistened with water or acid, and a piece of zinc, laid upon one another, form a circle; and if this circle be repeated a number of times, a galvanic pile or battery may be formed capable of giving a powerful shock. The most common and convenient form, however, of a battery, is found to be a trough of baked wood, three or four inches deep and as many wide. In the sides are grooves, opposite to each other, into each of which is placed a double metallic plate, of zinc and copper soldered together, and the cells are then filled either with salt and water, or with a solution of nitrous acid and water.

By means of the galvanic agency, a variety of surprising effects have been produced. Gunpowder, cotton, and other inflammable sub stances, have been inflamed—charcoal has been made to burn with a most brilliant and beautiful white flame—water has been decomposed into its elementary parts—metals have been melted and set on fire—fragments of diamond, charcoal, and plumbago, have been dispersed, as if they had been evaporated—platina, the hardest and heaviest of the metals, has been melted as readily as wax in the flame of a candle—the sapphire, quartz, magnesia, lime, and the firmest compounds in nature, have been made to enter into fusion. Its effects on the animal system are no less surprising. When applied to a fowl or a rabbit, immediately after life is extinct, it produces the most strange and violent convulsions on the nervous and muscular system, as if the vital functions were again revived, and when applied to the human body after death, the stimulus has produced the most horrible contortions and grimaces in the muscles of the head and face, and the most rapid movements in the hands and feet.

The galvanic agency enables us to account for the following among other facts:—Why porter has a different and more pleasant taste, when drunk out of a pewter vessel, than out of glass or earthenware,—why a silver spoon is discoloured when used in eating eggs,—why the limbs of people, under amputation, are sometimes convulsed by the application of the instruments,—why pure mercury is oxydized when amalgamated with tin,—why works of metal, which are soldered together, soon tarnish in the places where the metals are joined,—and why the copper sheathing of ships, when fastened with iron nails, is soon corroded about the place of contact. In all these cases a galvanic circle is formed, which produces the effects. We have reason to believe, that, in combination with the discoveries which modern chymistry is daily unfolding, the agencies of this fluid will enable us to carry the arts forward towards perfection, and to trace the secret causes of some of the sublimest phenomena of nature.

VIII. *Magnetism.*—This department of philosophy describes the phenomena and the properties of the *loadstone*, or natural magnet. The natural magnet is a hard dark-coloured mineral body, and is usually found in iron mines. The following are some of its characteristic properties:—1. It attracts iron and steel, and all substances which contain iron in its metallic state. 2. If a magnet be suspended by a thread, or nicely poised on a pivot, or placed on a piece of wood, and set to float in a basin of water, one end will constantly point nearly towards the north pole of the earth, and the other towards the south; and hence those parts of the magnet have been called the *north* and *south poles*. 3. When the north pole of one magnet is presented near to the south pole of another, they will *attract* each other; but if the north pole of one be presented to the north pole of another, or a south pole to a south, they will *repel* each other. 4. A magnet placed in such a manner as to be entirely at liberty, inclines one of its poles to the horizon, and of course elevates the other above it. This property is called the *dipping* of the magnet. 5. Magnets do not point directly north and south; but in different parts of the world with a different *declination* eastward or westward of the north; it is also different at the same place at different times. In London, and in most places of Great Britain, the magnetic needle, at present, points about 24 degrees to the west of north. For more than 160 years it has been gradually declining from the north to the west: but seems of late to have begun its declination to the eastward. 6. Any magnet may be made to communicate the properties now mentioned to any piece of iron or steel. For example, by gently rubbing a penknife with a magnet, it will be immediately invested with the property of attracting needles, or small pieces of iron or steel. 7. Heat weakens the power of a magnet, and the gradual addition of weight increases the magnetic power. 8. The properties of the magnet are not affected either by the presence or the absence of air; and the magnetic attraction is not in the least diminished by the interposition of any bodies except iron. A magnet will equally affect the needle of a pocket compass when a thick board is placed between them as when it is removed. It has been lately discovered, that the *violet rays of the solar spectrum*, when condensed with a convex glass, and made to pass along a piece of steel, have the power of communicating to it the magnetic virtue.

The cause which produces these singular properties of the magnet has hitherto remained a mystery; but the knowledge of the *polarity* of the magnet has been applied to a most important practical purpose. By means of it, man has now acquired the dominion of the ocean, and has learned to trace his course through the pathless deep to every region of the globe. There can be little doubt that magnetism has an intimate connexion with electricity, galvanism, light, heat, and chymical action; and the discoveries which have been lately made, and the experiments which are now making by Morichini, Oersted, Abraham, Hansteen, Barlow, Beaufoy, and Scoresby, promise to throw some light on this mysterious agent, and on the phenomena of nature with which it is connected.

Such is a faint outline of some of the interesting subjects which natural philosophy embraces. Its relation to religion will appear from the following considerations:

1. Its researches have led to the invention of machines, engines, and instruments of various kinds, which augment the energies, increase the comforts, and promote the general improvement of mankind; and these objects are inseparably connected with the propagation of Christianity

through the world. If we admit, that, in future ages, the religion of the Bible will shed its benign influence over all nations—that the external condition of the human race will then be prosperous and greatly meliorated beyond what it has ever been—and, that no *miraculous interposition* of Deity is to be expected to bring about such desirable events—it will follow, that such objects can be accomplished only in the ordinary course of Providence, by rational investigations into the principles and powers of nature, and the application of the inventions of science to the great objects of religion and of human improvement, as I shall endeavour briefly to illustrate in the following chapter. As the destructive effects of many physical agents, in the present condition of our globe, are, doubtless, a consequence of the sin and depravity of man; we have reason to believe that, when the economy of nature shall be more extensively and minutely investigated, and the minds of men directed to apply their discoveries to philanthropic and religious objects, they will be enabled to counteract, in a great measure, those devastations and fatal effects which are now produced by several of the powers of nature. The general happiness of all ranks, which will be connected with the universal extension of Christianity, necessarily supposes that this object will be accomplished; for, were a dread of destruction from the elements of nature frequently to agitate the mind, as at present, no permanent tranquillity would be enjoyed; nor would that ancient prediction, in reference to this era, receive its full accomplishment, that "there shall be *nothing to hurt or destroy* in all God's holy mountain, when the earth shall be full of the knowledge of the Lord." And since miraculous interpositions are not to be expected, to what quarter can we look for those subordinate agencies by which this object is to be effected, but to the discoveries and inventions of philosophical science?

Science has already enabled us to remedy many of those evils which are the accidental effects of the operation of physical agents. For example—the discoveries of the philosopher, with respect to the nature of the electric fluid, have enabled us to construct conductors for preserving buildings from the stroke of *lightning:* and we have every reason to hope, that in the progress of electric, galvanic, and chymical science, more complete thunder-guards, applicable to all the situations in which a person may be exposed, will be invented. Nay, our increasing knowledge of the electric fluid, and of the chymical agents which concur in its operation, may enable us to dissipate thunder-storms altogether, by disturbing the electricity of the clouds by means of a series of elevated artificial conductors. This is not only possible, but has already been in some degree effected. The celebrated Euler informs us, in his "Letters to a German Princess," that he corresponded with a Moravian priest named *Divisch*, who assured him "that he had averted, during a whole summer, every thunder storm which threatened his own habitation and the neighbourhood, by means of a machine constructed on the principles of electricity—that the machinery sensibly attracted the clouds, and constrained them to descend quietly in a distillation, without any but a very distant thunder-clap." Euler assures us that "the fact is undoubted, and confirmed by irresistible proof." Yea, not only may the destructive effects of lightning be averted by the inventions of philosophy, but its agency may be rendered subservient to human industry, and made to act as a mechanical power. This effect, too, has been partially accomplished. About the year 1811, in the village of Philipsthal, in Eastern Prussia, an attempt was made to split an immense stone into a multitude of pieces, by means of lightning. A bar of iron, in the form of a conductor, was previously fixed to the stone, and the experiment was attended with the most complete success; for, during the very first thunder-storm, the lightning burst the stone without displacing it.*

It is, therefore, probable, that in the future ages of the world, this terrific meteor, and other destructive agents, which now produce so much alarm, and so many disastrous effects, may, by the aid of philosophy, be brought under the control of man, and be made to minister to his enjoyment.

The electric fluid has also been, in many instances, successfully applied in curing palsies, rheumatisms, spasms, obstructions, and inflammation; and it is known to have a peculiar effect on the nervous system. Lightning has been known to restore the blind to a temporary enjoyment of sight. Mr. Campbell, of Succoth, in Dumbartonshire, who had been blind for several years, was led by his servant one evening through the streets of Glasgow, during a terrible thunder-storm. The lightning sometimes fluttered along the streets for a quarter of a minute without ceasing. While this fluttering lasted, Mr. C. saw the street distinctly, and the changes which had been made in that part by taking down one of the city gates. When the storm was over, his entire blindness returned. A still more remarkable instance is stated, along with this, under the article *Thunder*, in Dr. Gleig's *Supp. to Ency. Brit.* which was written by the late Professor Robison. It is also possible that barren deserts might be enriched with fertility, and immense portions of the desolate wastes of our globe prepared for the support and accommodation of human beings, by arresting the clouds, and drawing down their electrical virtue and their watery treasures by means of an extended series of elevated metallic conductors. What has been now

* See Monthly Magazine, vol. 32, p. 162

stated is only one instance, out of many, which might be adduced, of the extensive and beneficial effects which may be produced, in future ages, by the application of the discoveries of natural science.

2. A knowledge of natural philosophy enables us to detect *pretended* miracles, and to discriminate between those phenomena which are produced by the powers of nature, and the supposed effects of diabolical influence. It has been chiefly owing to ignorance of the principles of natural science, that mankind, in all ages, have been so easily imposed upon by pretenders to supernatural powers. It is owing to the same cause, that superstitious notions and vain alarms have spread their influence so extensively among the lower ranks of the population of every country. The pretended miracles by which Pagan and Popish priests endeavour to support the authority of their respective religious systems, and every species of degrading superstition, vanish into smoke, when examined by the light of modern science; and there can be no question that an enlightened missionary would, in many instances, find the principles and the instruments of natural philosophy important auxiliaries in undermining the fabric of heathen idolatry and priestcraft. They tend to dissipate a thousand idle terrors which haunt and agitate the human mind; to detect a thousand kinds of imposture by which it has been held in cruel bondage, and to prevent the perpetration of those deeds of cruelty which have uniformly marked the reign of superstition.* Had our forefathers connected a knowledge of this subject with their study of the Scriptures, they would not have brought upon themselves that indelible disgrace which now attaches to their memories, on account of their having condemned and burned at the stake hundreds of unhappy women, accused of crimes of which they could not possibly have been guilty. In New-England, towards the close of the 17th century, the witchcraft phrensy rose so high, that the execution of witches became a calamity more dreadful than the sword or the pestilence. Not only old women, but children of ten years, were put to death; young girls were stripped naked, and the marks of witchcraft searched for upon their bodies with the most indecent curiosity; and those spots of the scurvy which age impresses upon the bodies of old men, were taken for evident signs of infernal power. So that ignorance of the laws and phenomena of nature has led even Christians to commit acts of injustice and horrid cruelty. For, let it be remembered, that it was ***Christian*** magistrates and ministers, under a pretended zeal for the honour of God, who sanctioned such cruel and unrighteous decrees. This consideration, viewed in connexion with many others, tends to show, that the Christian revelation, considered abstractly by itself, without a reference to the visible system of the universe, is not sufficient for all the purposes for which it was intended; as, on the other hand, the study of the works of nature is not sufficient of itself to lead the mind to the true knowledge of God, without the aid of the discoveries derived from the sacred oracles. For, although the Bible has been in the hands of Protestant Christians ever since the reformation, yet it is only since the light of modern science began to diffuse its influence, that the superstitions of the dark ages, and the vulgar notions respecting witchcraft, necromancy, and other species of infernal agency, began to vanish, even from the minds of Christian teachers; as is evident from the writings of many eminent divines who flourished during the 16th and 17th centuries. As the two revelations which God has given us throw a mutual lustre on each other; the one must always be considered as incomplete without the other. Both are necessary in order "to make the man of God perfect," and to enable him to prosecute, with intelligence and success, the great objects of religion; and the Christian minister who affects to despise the aids of science in the cause of religion, has yet much to learn with respect to some of the grand bearings of the Christian system.

3. The investigations of natural philosophy *unfold to us the incessant agency of God*, and the plans by which his wise and benevolent designs in the system of nature are accomplished. From the immeasurable globes of heaven, down to the minutest atoms, we perceive a regular chain of causes and effects, conspiring, in a thousand different modes, to accomplish the purposes of infinite wisdom and goodness. The operation of central forces and of the law of gravitation on the earth and in the heavens—the hydrostatical laws which regulate the pressure and the motion of fluids—the chymical properties of the atmosphere, its undulatory, refractive, and reflective powers—the motion of the rays of light, and the infinite variety of effects they produce—the process of evaporation—the agencies of electricity and galvanism—the proportion of the magnet,

* Mr. Douglas, in his "Hints on Missions," formerly referred to, when speaking of the facilities which Christians now possess for extensive missionary exertions, suggests, that natural philosophy might be an important auxiliary to Christian missionaries. "All the ancient 'war weapons of victory,' excepting miracles, are at their disposal; and new instruments of still greater potency, which the science of the latter days has been accumulating for a universal revolution of the mind, are ready to be brought into action, upon a scale of overpowering magnitude. Even the single resource which is lost may yet be recompensed by equivalents, and a substitute, in many respects, may be found for miracles. The first effect of a miracle is, to rouse the attention, and to overawe opposing prejudices: the second to afford a proof of the religion of which it is a sealing accompaniment. *The first object might be gained by the natural magic of experimental philosophy:* and as to the second, the difference in the proof from miracles lies rather in its being more circuitous, than in its being less conclusive at the present day than in the times of the apostles."

and the chymical action of acids and alkalies, and of the minutest particles of matter upon each other—ought to be viewed as so many modifications of the agency of Deity, and as manifestations of his wisdom, in carrying forward those plans which regard the interests of his universal kingdom; just as we consider the rise and fall of empires, the revolutions of nations, and the circulation of the Scriptures in heathen lands, as so many acts of his moral administration as the Governor of mankind. For let it be carefully remembered, that all these physical agencies have ultimately a moral and intellectual bearing; and are essentially connected with every other part of God's providential procedure. Though we may be apt to consider them as so many detached and insulated pieces of machinery, with which we have little concern, or may even disdain to notice their mode of operation; yet, in the all-comprehensive mind of Him who takes in, at one glance, the whole chain of causes and effects, they are as essentially connected with his ultimate purposes, and the eternal destiny of man, as are the revelations of his word. Were a single principle or motion which now animates the system of nature to cease—were the agencies of electricity, for example, or the principle of evaporation, to be destroyed—the physical constitution of our globe would instantly be deranged; nature would be thrown into confusion; and the sentient and intellectual beings that now inhabit the earth would either be destroyed, or plunged into an abyss of misery. If, therefore, we admit that the *moral* agency of God is worthy of our contemplation, we ought to consider his physical operations also as no less worthy of our study and investigation; since they form the groundwork of all his other manifestations.

There is nothing, however, which so strikingly characterizes the bulk of mankind, and even the great mass of the Christian world, as that apathy and indifference with which they view the wonders of creation which surround them. They can look on all that is grand, and beautiful, and beneficent in nature, without feeling the least sentiment of admiration, or of gratitude to that Being who is incessantly operating within them and around them; and they are disposed to consider the experiments of philosophers, by which the wonderful agency of God is unveiled, as only so many toys and amusements for the entertainment of children. They would prefer the paltry entertainments of a card-table, of a ball-room, or of a gossipping party, to the inspection of the nicest pieces of divine mechanism, and to the contemplation of the most august scene in nature. However lightly some religionists may be disposed to treat this subject, that spirit of indifference with which the visible works of God are treated must be considered as flowing from the same *depraved principle* which leads multitudes to reject the revelations of the Bible, and to trifle with their everlasting interests. "Man," say Rollin, "lives in the midst of a world of which he is the sovereign, as a stranger, who looks with indifference upon all that passes in it, and as if it was not his concern. The universe, in all its parts, declares and points out its Author; but, for the most part, to the deaf and blind, who have neither ears to hear, nor eyes to see. One of the greatest services that philosophy can do us, is to awaken us from this drowsiness, and rouse us from this lethargy, which is a dishonour to humanity, and in a manner reduces us below the beasts, whose stupidity is the consequence of their nature, and not the effect of neglect or indifference. It awakens our curiosity, it excites our attention, and leads us as it were by the hand, through all the parts of nature, to induce us to study and search out the wonderful works of it." —*Belles Lettres*, vol. 4.

Since, therefore, the science of natural philosophy is conversant about the works of the Almighty, and its investigations have a direct tendency to illustrate the perfections of his nature, to unveil the plan of his operations, to unfold the laws by which he governs the kingdom of universal nature, and to display the order, symmetry, and proportion, which reign throughout the whole—it would be needless to enter into any further process of reasoning, to show that the study of it is connected with the great objects of religion. Whatever studies tend to raise our minds to the Supreme Ruler of all worlds—to expand our views of his infinite knowledge and wisdom—to excite our gratitude and our admiration of the beneficent designs which appear in all his arrangements—to guard us against erroneous conceptions of his providential procedure—and to furnish us with important auxiliaries for extending the influence of his religion through the world; must always be interesting to every Christian who wishes to enlarge his intellectual views, and to make progress in the knowledge of God.

### CHYMISTRY.

This science, which is intimately related to the preceding, has for its object to ascertain the ingredients, or first principles, of which all matter is composed—to examine the compounds formed by the combination of these ingredients—to investigate those changes in natural bodies, which are not accompanied with *sensible* motion, and the nature of the power which produces these combinations and changes.

Within the limits of the last half century, the empire of chymistry has been wonderfully extended. From an obscure and humble place among the objects of study, it has risen to a high and dignified station among those sciences which improve and adorn the human mind. No longer confined to the paltry and mercenary object of searching for the philosopher's stone, or of furnishing a little amusement, it now extends its sway over all the arts which minister to the comfort and improvement of social life, and over every species of animate and inanimate matter, within the range of human investigation. "The forms and appearances," (says Sir Humphrey Davy,) "of the beings aud substances of the external world, are almost infinitely various, and they are in a state of continued alteration. Even the earth itself, throughout its whole surface, undergoes modifications. Acted on by moisture and air, it affords the food of plants; an immense number of vegetable productions arise from apparently the same materials; these become the substance of animals; one species of animal matter is converted into another; the most perfect and beautiful of the forms of organized life ultimately decay, and are resolved into inorganic aggregrates; and the same elementary substances, differently arranged, are contained in the inert soil, or bloom and emit fragrance in the flower, or become in animals the active organs of mind and intelligence. In artificial operations, changes of the same order occur; substances having the characters of earth, are converted into metals; clays and sands are united, so as to become porcelain; earths and alkalies are combined into glass; acrid and corrosive matters are formed from tasteless substances; colours are fixed upon stuffs, or changed, or made to disappear; and the productions of the vegetable, mineral, and animal kingdoms are converted into new forms, and made subservient to the purposes of civilized life. To trace, in detail, these diversified and complicated phenomena; to arrange them, and deduce general laws from their analogies, is the business of chymistry."—*Elements of Chymical Philosophy.*

Chymists have arranged the *general forms of matter* into the four following classes. The *first* class consists of *Solids*, which form the principal parts of the globe, and which differ from each other in hardness, colour, opacity, transparency, density, and other properties. The *second* class consists of *Fluids*, such as water, oils, spirits, &c., whose parts possess freedom of motion, and require great mechanical force to make them occupy a smaller space. The *third* class comprehends *Elastic Fluids*, or *Gases*, which exist freely in the atmosphere; but may be confined by solids and fluids, and their properties examined. Their parts are highly moveable, compressible, and expansive; they are all transparent; they present two or three varieties of colour; and they differ greatly in density. The *fourth* class comprehends *Ethereal Substances*, which are known to us only in their states of motion, when acting upon our organs of sense, and which are not susceptible of being confined. Such are the *rays of light*, and *radiant heat*, which are incessantly in motion, throughout the spaces that intervene between our globe and the sun and the stars. Chymists divide the substances in nature also into *simple* and *compound*. *Simple Substances* are those which have never yet been decomposed, nor formed by art. *Compound Substances* are those which are formed by the union of two or more simple substances. The following are all the *simple* substances, with which we are at present acquainted: *Caloric, Light, Oxygen, Nitrogen, Carbon, Hydrogen, Sulphur, Phosphorus,* the *Metals,* and some of the *Earths.* All that I propose, under this article, is, simply to state some of the properties of two or three of these simple substances.

*Caloric*, or elementary fire, is the name now given by chymists to that element or property which, combined with various bodies, produces the sensation of *heat*, while it is passing from one body to another. This substance appears to pervade the whole system of nature. There are six different sources, from whence caloric may be procured. It may be produced by *combustion*, in which process the oxygen gas of the atmosphere is decomposed, and caloric, one of its component parts, set at liberty—by *friction*, or the rubbing of two substances against each other—by *percussion*, as the striking of steel against a piece of flint—by *the mixture of two or more substances*; as when sulphuric acid is poured upon water or magnesia—by *electricity* and *galvanism*. The discharge of an electric or galvanic battery will produce a more intense degree of heat than any other means whatever. But the principal, and probably the original source of caloric, is the *Sun*, which furnishes the earth with a regular supply for the support and nourishment of the animal and vegetable tribes. From this source it moves at the rate of 195,000 miles in a second of time; for it has been already stated, that the sun sends forth rays of heat, which are distinct from those which produce illumination, and which accompany them in their course through the ethereal regions.

Caloric is the cause of *fluidity*, in all substances which are capable of becoming fluid. A certain portion, or *dose* of it, reduces a solid body to the state of an incompressible fluid; a larger portion brings it to the state of an aeriform or gaseous fluid. Thus, a certain portion of caloric reduces ice to a state of water; a larger portion converts it into steam or vapour. There is reason to believe that the hardest rocks, the densest metals, and every solid substance on the face of the earth, might be converted into a fluid, and even into a gas, were they submitted to the action of a very high temperature. This substance is called *sensible* caloric, when it produces the sensation of *heat*; and *latent* caloric, when it forms an insensible part of the substance of bodies. All bodies are, in a greater or less degree, *conductors* of caloric. Metals and liquids are good conductors of heat, but silk, cotton, wool, wood, &c. are bad conductors of it. For example, if we put a short poker into the fire at one end, it will soon become hot at the other; but this will not happen with a piece of wood of the same length, and under the same circumstances. A person with a silken purse, containing metal coin, may stand so near the fire, as to make the metal almost too hot to touch, though the temperature of the purse will apparently be scarcely altered. If a hand be put upon a hot body, part of the caloric leaves the hot body and enters the hand, producing the sensation of heat. On the contrary, if a hand be put on a cold body, as a piece of iron, or another cold hand, part of the caloric contained in the hand leaves it to unite with the colder body, producing the sensation of cold. In short, caloric is diffused throughout all bodies, and enters into every operation in nature; and were it not for the influence of this subtile fluid, there is reason to believe, that the whole matter of the universe would be condensed into a solid mass.

*Oxygen* is a very pure, subtile, and elastic substance, generally diffused throughout nature; but is never found unless in combination with other substances. It is one of the most important agents in nature; there being scarcely a single process, whether natural or artificial, in which oxygen has not some important share. When combined with caloric, it is called *oxygen gas*, which forms one of the constituent parts of the atmosphere. In this state, it forms the principle of *combustion;* producing the most rapid deflagration of all combustible substances. If a lighted taper be let down into a jar of oxygen gas, it burns with such splendour, that the eye can scarcely bear the glare of light; and at the same time produces a much greater heat than when burning in common air. If a steel wire, or a thin file, having a sharp point, armed with a bit of wood in inflammation, be introduced into a jar filled with this gas, the steel will take fire, and its combustion will continue, producing a most brilliant phenomenon. It has been proved, by numerous experiments, that this gas is so *essential* to combustion, that no substance will burn in common air, which has been previously deprived of its oxygen. It is also essential to animal life; so that man, and all the inferior ranks of animated nature, may be said to depend upon this fluid for their existence. Its basis gives the *acid* character to all mineral and vegetable salts: and the *calcination* of metals is altogether effected by their union with oxygen. It constitutes the basis both of the atmosphere which surrounds the earth, and of the water which forms its rivers, seas, and oceans. It pervades the substance of all the vegetable tribes, and enables them to perform their functions; and, in combination with the different metals, serves the most important purposes in the useful arts. In the operation of this elementary principle, we perceive a striking display of the agency of the Creator, and of the admirable means which his wisdom has contrived for preserving, in due order, the system of nature. And, as this wonderful substance is so essentially necessary to animal and vegetable existence, every thing is so arranged as to produce a regular supply of it, notwithstanding its incessant changes, and the multifarious combinations into which it is continually entering.

One of the most extraordinary effects of oxygen appears, when it is combined in a certain proportion with nitrogen, so as to form the gaseous oxide of nitrogen, or what is commonly called *nitrous oxide.* This gas consists of 63 parts nitrogen, and 37 oxygen, by weight. When inhaled into the lungs, it produces an extraordinary elevation of the animal spirits, a propensity to leaping and running, involuntary fits of laughter, a rapid flow of vivid ideas, and a thousand delightful emotions; without being accompanied with any subsequent feelings of debility. This circumstance shows what a variety of delightful or pernicious effects might flow from the slightest change in the constitution of the atmosphere, were the hand of the Almighty to interpose in altering the proportion of its constituent parts: for atmospheric air is composed of 79 parts of nitrogen, and 21 of oxygen, which is not a very different proportion from the above. Another gas called *nitric* oxide, composed of 56 parts oxygen, and 44 nitrogen, produces instant suffocation in all animals that attempt to breathe it. One of the most corrosive acids, the *nitrous* acid, or aquafortis, is composed of 75 parts oxygen and 25 parts nitrogen; so that we are every moment breathing a certain substance, which, in another combination, would produce the most dreadful pain, and cause our immediate destruction. What a striking proof does this afford of the infinite comprehension of the divine mind, in foreseeing all the consequences of the elements of nature, and in directing their numerous combinations in such a manner as to promote the happiness of animated beings!

*Nitrogen,* or *azote,* is a substance generally diffused throughout nature, and particularly in animated bodies. It is not to be found in a solid or liquid state, but, combined with caloric, it forms *nitrogen gas,* which is one of the ingredients of the atmosphere. It is capable of supporting either flame or animal life. This is proved by introducing an animal, or a burning candle, into a vessel full of this gas: in which case, the animal is suddenly suffocated, and the candle instantly extinguished. It is this gas which is expelled from the lungs at every respiration, and, rising over our heads, soon enters into new combinations. Though it is destructive to animal life, it appears to be favourable to plants, which vegetate freely when surrounded with nitrogen.

*Hydrogen* is another elementary substance, abundant in nature, and, when united to caloric forms hydrogen gas. It is one of the constituent parts of *water*; for it has been completely demonstrated by experiment, that water is composed of 85 parts by weight of oxygen, and 15 of hydrogen, in every hundred parts of the fluid. This gas was formerly known by the name of *inflammable air*. It is distinguished among miners by the name of *fire-damp*; it abounds in coal-mines, and sometimes produces the most tremendous explosions. It is incapable, by itself, of supporting combustion, and cannot be breathed without the most imminent danger. It is the chief constituent of oils, fats, spirits, ether, coals, and bitumen; and is supposed to be one of the agents which produce the *ignes fatui* and the *northern lights*. It is the *lightest* of all ponderable bodies; being from twelve to fifteen times lighter than common air. A hundred cubic inches of it weigh about 2¼ grains. On account of its great levity it is used for filling *air-balloons*. In contact with atmospheric air, it burns with a pale blue colour. When mixed with oxygen gas, it may be exploded like gunpowder, with a violent report. *Carburetted hydrogen gas*, which is *carbon* dissolved in hydrogen, is that beautiful gas, which is now employed in lighting our streets, shops, and manufactories.

*Carbon* is another simple substance extensively diffused throughout nature. It is found pure and solid only in the *diamond*; but it may be procured in the state of *charcoal*, by burning a piece of wood closely covered with sand, in a crucible. Carbon enters into the composition of bitumen and pit coal, and of most animal and some mineral substances; and it forms nearly the whole of the solid basis of all vegetables, from the most delicate flower to the stately oak. It is also a component part of sugar, and of all kinds of wax, oils, gums, and resins. It combines with iron in various proportions, and the results are cast iron and steel. Black lead is a composition of nine parts of carbon to one of iron; and is, therefore, called a *carburet* of iron. Carbon is *indestructible* by age, and preserves its identity in all the combinations into which it enters. *Carbonic acid gas* is a combination of carbon and oxygen. It is found in a state of combination with lime, forming limestone, marble, and chalk; and may be separated from them by heat, or by means of the mineral acids. This gas, which was formerly called *fixed air*, is found in mines, caves, the bottoms of wells, wine cellars, brewers' vats, and in the neighbourhood of lime-kilns. It is known to miners by the name of the *choke-damp*, and too frequently runs on deadly errands. It extinguishes flame and animal life. It is the heaviest of all the gases; being nearly twice the weight of common air, and twenty times the weight of hydrogen. It may, therefore, be poured from one vessel to another; and if a small quantity of it be poured upon a lighted taper, it will be instantly extinguished. It is a powerful *antiseptic*, or preserver from putrefaction. Meat which has been sealed up in it (says Mr. Parkes) has been known to have preserved its texture and appearance for more than twenty years. There is no substance of more importance in civilized life than the different forms of *Carbon*. "In nature," says Sir. H. Davy, "this element is constantly active in an important series of operations. It is evolved in fermentation and combustion, in carbonic acid; it is separated from oxygen in the organs of plants; it is a principal element in animal structures; and is found in different forms in almost all the products of organized beings."

*Sulphur* is a substance which has been known from the earliest ages. It was used by the ancients in medicine, and its fumes have, for more than 2000 years, been employed in bleaching wool. It is found combined with many mineral substances, as arsenic, antimony, copper, and most of the metallic ores. It exists in many mineral waters, and in combination with vegetable and animal matters, but is most abundant in volcanic countries, particularly in the neighbourhood of Vesuvius, Etna, and Hecla in Iceland. It is a solid, opaque, combustible substance, of a pale yellow colour, very brittle, and almost without taste or smell. Its specific gravity is nearly twice that of water; it is a con-conductor of electricity, and, of course, becomes electric by friction. When heated to the temperature of 170° of Fahrenheit's thermometer, it rises up in the form of a fine powder, which is easily collected in a proper vessel, and is named the *flowers of sulphur*. It is insoluble in water, but may be dissolved in oils, in spirit of wine, and in hydrogen gas. When sulphur is heated to the temperature of 302° in the open air, it takes fire spontaneously, and burns with a pale blue flame, and emits a great quantity of fumes of a strong suffocating odour. When heated to the temperature of 570°, it burns with a bright white flame, and emits a vast quantity of fumes. When these fumes are collected, they are found to consist entirely of *sulphuric acid*; so that sulphur, by combustion, is converted into an *acid*. It is the base of several compound substances. It unites with oxygen, hydrogen, nitrogen, phosphorus, the alkalies, the metals, and some of the earths. This substance is of great importance in medicine, as it is found to penetrate to the extremities of the most minute vessels, and to impregnate all the secretions. It is also used in the arts, particularly in bleaching and dying; it forms a very large proportion of gunpowder; and one of its most common, but not least useful properties, is that of its *combustibility*, by which, with the help of a tinder-box, light is almost instantaneously produced. As this substance has not yet been decomposed, it is considered by chymists, in the mean time, as one of the simple substances.

*Phosphorus* is another simple combustible substance, but is never found in a pure state in nature. It is commonly united to oxygen in a state of phosphoric acid, which is found in different animal, vegetable, and mineral substances. It was first discovered by Brandt, a chymist of Hamburgh, in the year 1667, and afterwards by the Honourable Mr. Boyle, in 1679. It was formerly obtained by a disgusting process; but it is now extracted from the *bones* of animals, by burning them, and then reducing them to a fine powder, and afterwards pouring sulphuric acid upon them. This substance, when pure, resembles bees' wax, being of a clear, transparent, yellowish colour; it is insoluble in water; it may be cut with a knife, or twisted to pieces with the fingers; and it is about double the specific gravity of water. Its most remarkable property is its very strong attraction for oxygen, from which circumstance, it burns spontaneously in the open air at the temperature of 43°; that is, it attracts the oxygen gas from the atmosphere, and heat and flame are produced. It gradually consumes when exposed to the common temperature of air, emits a whitish smoke, and is luminous in the dark; for this reason it is kept in phials of water; and as the heat of the hand is sufficient to inflame it, it should seldom be handled except under water. At the temperature of 99° it melts; it evaporates at 219°, and boils at 554°. When heated to 148° it takes fire, and burns with a very bright flame, and gives out a very large quantity of white smoke, which is luminous in the dark; at the same time it emits an odour, which has some resemblance to that of garlic; and this smoke, when collected, is proved to be an *acid*. It burns with the greatest splendour in oxygen gas, and when taken internally, it is found to be poisonous. If any light substance, capable of conducting heat, be placed upon the surface of boiling water, and a bit of phosphorus be laid upon it, the heat of the water will be sufficient to set the phosphorus on fire. If we write a few words on paper with a bit of phosphorus fixed in a quill, when the writing is carried into a dark room it will appear beautifully luminous. If a piece of phosphorus, about the size of a pea, be dropped into a tumbler of hot water, and a stream of oxygen gas forced directly upon it, it will display the most brilliant combustion under water that can be imagined. All experiments with phosphorus, however, require to be performed with *great caution*. This substance is used in making phosphorus match-bottles, phosphoric oil, phosphoric tapers, and various phosphoric fireworks. *Phosphorized hydrogen* gas is produced by bits of phosphorus remaining some hours in hydrogen gas. It is supposed to be this gas which is often seen hovering on the surface of burial grounds and marshes, known in Scotland by the name of *spunkie*, and in England by that of *will-o-the-wisp*.

Some animals, as the *glow-worm* and the *fire-fly*, and fish in a putrescent state, exhibit phosphorescent qualities. M. Peron describes a singular instance of this kind in an animal which he calls the *pyrosoma atlanticum*, which he observed in his voyage from Europe to the Isle of France. The darkness was intense when it was first discovered; and all at once there appeared at some distance, as it were, a vast sheet of phosphorus floating on the waves, which occupied a great space before the vessel. When the vessel had passed through this inflamed part of the sea, it was found that this prodigious light was occasioned by an immense number of small animals, which swam at different depths, and appeared to assume various forms. Those which were deepest looked like great red-hot cannon balls, while those on the surface resembled cylinders of red-hot iron. Some of them were caught, and were found to vary in size from three to seven inches. All the exterior surface of the animal was bristled with thick long tubercles, shining like so many diamonds; and these seemed to be the principal seat of its wonderful phosphorescence.

Such is a brief description of the principal elementary substances, which, in a thousand diversified forms, pervade the system of nature, and produce all that variety which we behold in the atmosphere, the waters, the earth, and the various processes of the arts. It is probable that some of these substances are compounds, though they have not yet been decomposed. Yea, it is possible, and not at all improbable, that there are but two, or at most three, elementary substances in nature, the various modifications of which produce all the beauties and sublimities in the universe. Perhaps caloric, oxygen, and hydrogen, may ultimately be found to constitute all the elementary principles of nature. Without prosecuting this subject farther, I shall conclude this article with a few cursory reflections, tending to illustrate its connexion with religion.

The remarks which I have already thrown out in reference to natural philosophy will equally apply to the science of chymistry; and, therefore, do not require to be repeated. In addition to these, the following observations may be stated:—

1. This science displays, in a striking point of view, the wisdom and goodness of God, *in producing, by the most simple means, the most astonishing and benevolent effects.* All the varied phenomena we perceive, throughout the whole system of sublunary nature, are produced by a combination of six or seven simple substances. I formerly adverted to the infinite variety which exists in the vegetable kingdom. (see pp. 37, 38.) About fifty-six thousand different species of plants have already been discovered by botanists. All these, from the humble shrub to the cedar of Lebanon, which adorn the surface of the globe, in every clime, with

such a diversity of forms, shades, and colours, are the result of the combinations of "four or five natural substances—caloric, light, water, air, and carbon." "When we consider," says Mr. Parkes, "that the many thousand tribes of vegetables are not only all formed from a few simple substances, but that they all enjoy the same sun, vegetate in the same medium, and are supplied with the same nutriment, we cannot but be struck with the rich economy of Nature, and are almost induced to doubt the evidence of those senses with which the God of nature has furnished us. That it should be possible so to modify and intermingle a few simple substances, and thence produce all the variety of form, colour, odour, &c. which are observable in the different families of vegetables, is a phenomenon too astonishing for our comprehension. Nothing short of Omnipotence could have provided such a paradise for man."—*Chymical Catechism*, chap. 9.

> Soft roll your incense, herbs, and fruits, and flowers,
> In mingled clouds to Him, whose sun exalts,
> Whose breath perfumes you, and whose pencil paints."
> *Thomson.*

What an admirable view is here opened up of the economy of divine wisdom, and of the beneficent care which has been taken to secure the comfort and happiness of every living creature: and how ungrateful a disposition must it indicate in rational beings to overlook such benevolent arrangements! It is highly probable, that in all other worlds disposed throughout the universe an infinite diversity of scenery exists, and that no one globe or system exactly resembles another; and yet, it is probable, that the primary elements of matter, or the few *simple substances* of which our world is composed, may be of the same nature as those which form the constituent parts of every other system; and may give birth to all the variety which exists throughout the wide extent of creation, and to all the changes and revolutions through which the different systems may pass, during every period of infinite duration.

2. From this science we have every reason to conclude, that matter is indestructible. In the various changes that take place in material substances, the particles of matter are not destroyed, but only assume new forms, and enter into new combinations. When a piece of wood, for example, is burned to ashes, none of its principles are destroyed; the elementary substances of which it was composed are only separated from one another, and formed into new compounds. Carbon, as already stated, appears to be indestructible by age, and to preserve its essential properties in every mode of its existence. That Being, indeed, who created matter at first, may reduce it to nothing when he pleases; but it is highly improbable that his power will ever be interposed to produce this effect; or that any particle of matter which now exists will ever be annihilated, into whatever new or varied combinations it may enter. When any particular world, or assemblage of material existence, has remained in its original state for a certain period of duration, and accomplished all the ends it was intended to subserve in that state, the materials of which it is composed will, in all probability, be employed for erecting a new system, and establishing a new series of events, in which new scenes, and new beauties and sublimities, will arise from new and varied combinations. For the Creator does nothing in vain. But to annihilate, and again to create, would be operating in vain; and we uniformly find, that in all the arrangements of Deity in the present state of things, Nature is frugal and economical in all her proceedings; so that there is no process, when thoroughly investigated, that appears unnecessary or superfluous.

From the fact, that matter appears to be indestructible, we may learn, that the Creator may, with the self-same materials which now exist around us, new-model and arrange the globe we inhabit, after the general conflagration, so as to make a more glorious world to arise out of its ashes; purified from those physical evils which now exist; and fitted for the accommodation either of renovated men, or of other pure intelligences. From the same fact, combined with the consideration of the infinite diversity of effects which the simple substances of nature are capable of producing, we may be enabled to form a conception of the ease with which the Creator may new-model our bodies, after they have been dissolved in the dust; and how, from the same original atoms, he may construct and adorn them with more glorious forms and more delightful and exquisite senses than they now possess.

In short, the rapid progress which chymical science is now making, promises, ere long, to introduce improvements among the human race, which will expand their views of the agency of God, counteract many physical evils, and promote, to an extent which has never yet been experienced, their social and domestic enjoyment. The late discoveries of chymistry tend to convince us, that the properties and powers of natural subjects are only beginning to be discovered. Who could have imagined, a century ago, that an invisible substance is contained in a piece of coal, capable of producing the most beautiful and splendid illumination—that this substance may be conveyed, in a few moments, through pipes of several miles in length—and that a city, containing several hundred thousands of inhabitants, may be instantly lighted up by it, without the aid of either wax, oil, or tallow? Who could have imagined, that one of the ingredients of the air we breathe is the principle of combustion—that a rod of iron may be made to burn with a brilliancy that dazzles the eyes—that a piece of charcoal may be made to burn with a white and splendid light, which is inferior only to the solar rays—and that the *diamond* is nothing more than *carbon* in a crystallized state, and differs only in a slight degree from a bit of common charcoal? Who could have surmised, that a substance would be discovered, of such a degree of levity, as would have power sufficient to buoy up a number of men to the upper parts of the atmosphere, and enable them to swim, in safety, above the regions of the clouds? These are only specimens of still more brilliant discoveries which will, doubtless, be brought to light by the researches of future generations. We have reason to believe, that the investigations of this science will, in due time, enable us to counteract most of the diseases incident to the human frame; and to prevent many of those fatal accidents to which mankind are now exposed. Davy's *safety lamp* has already preserved many individuals from destruction, when working in coal mines; and thousands, in after ages, will be indebted to this discovery, for security from the dreadful explosions of hydrogen gas. And, we trust, that the period is not far distant, when specific antidotes to the diseases peculiar to the different trades and occupations in which mankind are employed will be discovered; and the health and vigour of the mass of society be preserved unimpaired, amidst all the processes in which they may be engaged. In fine, the rapid progress of chymical discovery carries forward our views to a period, when man, having thoroughly explored the powers of nature, and subjected them, in some measure, to his control, will be enabled to ward off most of those physical evils with which he is now annoyed, and to raise himself, in some degree, to the dignity and happiness he enjoyed before moral evil had shed its baleful influence on our terrestrial system. Such a period corresponds to many of the descriptions contained in the Sacred Oracles of the millenial state of the church; when social, domestic, moral, and intellectual improvement shall be carried to the utmost perfection which our sublunary station will permit; when wars shall cease; when the knowledge of Jehovah shall cover the earth; when every man shall sit under his vine and fig-tree, without being exposed to the least alarm; and when there shall be nothing to hurt nor destroy throughout the church of the living God. And, therefore, we ought to consider the various discoveries and improvements now going forward in this and other departments of science, as preparing the way for the introduction of this long-expected and auspicious era.

### ANATOMY AND PHYSIOLOGY.

The general object of both these sciences is to investigate and describe the structure and economy of the animal frame. *Anatomy* dissects *dead* bodies, *physiology* investigates the functions of those that are *living*. The former examines the fluids, muscles, viscera, and all the other parts of the human body, in a state of *rest*, the latter considers them in a state of *action*.

The parts of the human body have been distinguished into two different kinds—solids and fluids. The solid parts are *bones*, *cartilages*, *ligaments*, *muscles*, *tendons*, *membranes*, *nerves*, *arteries*, *veins*, *hair*, *nails*, and *ducts*, or fine tubular vessels of various kinds. Of these solid parts, the following compound organs consist; the *brain* and *cerebellum*; the *lungs*; the *heart*, the *stomach*; the *liver*; the *spleen*; the *pancreas*; the *glands*; the *kidneys*; the *intestines*; the *mesentery*; the *larynx*; and the organs of sense—the *eyes*, *ears*, *nose*, and *tongue*. The fluid parts are, the *saliva*, or spittle, *phlegm*, *serum*, the *chyle*, *blood*, *bile*, *milk*, *lympha*, *urine*, the *pancreatic juice*, and the *aqueous humour* of the eyes. The human body is divided into three great cavities—the *head*; the *thorax*, or breast; and the *abdomen*, or belly. The *head* is formed of the bones of the cranium, and encloses the brain and cerebellum. The *thorax* is composed of the vertebræ of the back, the sternum, and true ribs; and contains the *heart*, the *pericardium*, the *breast*, and the *lungs*. The *abdomen* is separated from the thorax by means of the *diaphragm*, which is a fleshy and membranous substance, composed, for the most part, of muscular fibres. This cavity is formed by the lumbar vertebræ, the os sacrum, the ossa innominata, the false ribs, the peritonæum, and a variety of muscles. It encloses the stomach, intestines, omentum, or caul, the liver, pancreas, spleen, kidneys, and urinary bladder. Without attempting any technical description of these different pars, which could convey no accurate ideas to a general reader, I shall merely state two or three facts in relation to the system of bones, muscles, and blood-vessels, as *specimens* of the wonderful structure of our bodily frame.

The *Bones* may be regarded as the prop-work or basis on which the human body is constructed. They bear the same relation to the animal system, as the wood-work to a building. They give shape and firmness to the body; they support its various parts, and prevent it from sinking by its own weight; they serve as levers for the muscles to act upon, and to defend the brain, the heart, the lungs, and other vital parts, from external injury. Of the bones, some are *hollow*, and filled with marrow; others are *solid* throughout; some are very *small* — others very *large*; some are round, and others *flat*; some are *plane*, and others *convex* or *concave*;—and all these several forms are requisite for the situations they occupy, and the respective functions they have to perform. The *spine*, or back-bone, consists of 24 vertebræ, or small bones connected together by cartilages, articulations, and ligaments; of which seven belong to the neck, twelve to the back, and five to the loins. In the centre of each vertebra there is a hole for the lodgment and continuation of the spinal marrow, which extends from the brain to the rump. From these vertebræ the arched bones called *ribs* proceed; and seven of them join the breast-bone on each side, where they terminate in cartilages, and form the cavity of the thorax or chest. The five lower ribs, with a number of muscles, form the cavity of the abdomen, as above stated. The spine is one of the most admirable mechanical contrivances in the human frame. Had it consisted of only three or four bones, or had the holes in each bone not exactly corresponded and fitted into each other, the spinal marrow would have been bruised, and life endangered at every bending of the body. The skull is composed of ten bones, and about 51 are reckoned to belong to the face, the orbits of the eyes, and the jaws in which the teeth are fixed. There are seldom more than 16 teeth in each jaw, or 32 in all. The number of bones in a human body is generally estimated at about 245; of which there are reckoned, in the skull, head, and face, 61; in the trunk, 64; in the arms, and hands, 60, in the legs, and feet, 60. The bones are provided with *ligaments* or hinges, which bind and fasten them together, and prevent them from being displaced by any violent motion; and, that the ligaments may work smoothly into one another, the joints are separated by *cartilages* or gristles, and provided with a gland for the secretion of oil or *mucus*, which is constantly exuding into the joints; so that every requisite is provided by our benevolent Creator, to prevent pain, and to promote facility of motion. "In considering the joints," says Dr. Paley, "there is nothing, perhaps, which ought to move our gratitude more than the reflection, *how well they wear*. A limb shall swing upon its hinge or play in its socket many hundred times in an hour, for 60 years together, without diminution of agility; which is a long time for any thing to last—for any thing so much worked as the joints are."

*The Muscular System.*—A *muscle* is a bundle of fleshy, and sometimes of tendinous fibres. The fleshy fibres compose the body of the muscle; and the tendinous fibres the extremities. Some muscles are long and round; some plain and circular; some are *spiral*, and some have *straight* fibres. Some are double, having a tendon running through the body from head to tail; some have two or more tendinous branches running through, with various rows and orders of fibres. All these, and several other varieties, are essentially requisite for the respective offices they have to perform in the animal system. The muscles constitute the fleshy part of the human body, and give it that varied and beautiful form we observe over all its surface. But their principal design is to serve as *the organs of motion*. They are inserted, by strong tendinous extremities, into the different bones of which the skeleton is composed; and, by their contraction and distention, give rise to all the movements of the body. The muscles, therefore, may be considered as so many cords attached to the bones, and the Author of nature has fixed them according to the most perfect principles of mechanism, so as to produce the fittest motions in the parts for the movement of which they are intended.

One of the most wonderful properties of the muscles is, the *extraordinary force they exert*, although they are composed of such slender threads or fibres. The following facts, in relation to this point, are demonstrated by the celebrated *Borelli*, in his work, "*De Motu Animalium.*" When a man lifts up with his teeth a weight of 200 pounds, with a rope fastened to the jaw-teeth, the muscles named *temporalis* and *masseter*, with which people chew, and which perform this work, exert a force of above 15,000lbs. weight. If any one hanging his arm directly downwards lifts a weight of 20 pounds, with the third or last joint of his thumb, the muscle which bends the thumb and bears that weight exerts a force of about *three thousand pounds*. When a man, standing upon his feet, leaps or springs upwards to the height of two feet, if the weight of such a man be 150 pounds, the muscles employed in that action will exert a force 2000 times greater; that is to say, a force of about *three hundred thousand pounds*. The *heart*, at each pulse or contraction, by which it protrudes the blood out of the arteries into the veins, exerts a force of above *a hundred thousand pounds*. Who can contemplate this amazing strength of the muscular system, without admiration of the power and wisdom of the Creator, who has thus endued a bundle of threads, each of them smaller than a hair, with such an astonishing degree of mechanical force! There have been reckoned about 446 muscles in the human body, which have been dissected and distinctly described; every one of which is essential to the performance of some one motion or other, which contributes to our ease and enjoyment; and, in most instances, a great number of them is required to perform their different functions at the same time. It has been calculated, that about *a hundred muscles* are employed every time we breathe. "Breathing with ease," says Dr. Paley, "is a blessing of every moment; yet, of all others, it is that which we possess with the least consciousness. A man in an asthma is the only man who knows how to estimate it."

*The Heart and Blood-vessels.*—The heart is a hollow muscular organ, of a conical shape, and consists of four distinct cavities. The two largest are called *ventricles*, and the two smallest *auricles*. The ventricles *send out* the blood to the arteries; the auricles *receive* it from the veins. The heart is enclosed in the *pericardium*, a membranous bag, which contains a quantity of water, or lymph. This water lubricates the heart, and facilitates all its motions. The heart is the general reservoir of the blood. When the heart contracts, the blood is propelled from the *right ventricle* into the lungs, through the pulmonary arteries, which, like all the other arteries, are furnished with *valves* that play easily forward, but admit not the blood to return toward the heart. The blood, after circulating through the lungs, and having there been revivified by coming in contact with the air, and imbibing a portion of its oxygen, returns into the *left auricle* of the heart, by the pulmonary vein. At the same instant, the *left ventricle* drives the blood into the *aorta*, a large artery which sends off branches to supply the head and arms. Another large branch of the aorta descends along the inside of the back-bone, and detaches numerous ramifications to nourish the bowels and inferior extremities. After serving the most remote extremities of the body, the arteries are converted into *veins*, which, in their return to the heart, gradually unite into larger branches, till the whole terminate in one great trunk, called the *vena cava*, which discharges itself into the *right auricle* of the heart, and completes the circulation. Each ventricle of the heart is reckoned to contain about one ounce, or two tablespoonsfull of blood. The heart contracts 4000 times every hour; and, consequently, there passes through it 250 pounds of blood in one hour. And if the mass of blood in a human body be reckoned at an average of twenty-five pounds, it will follow that *the whole mass of blood passes through the heart*, and consequently through the thousands of ramifications of the veins and arteries, *fourteen times every hour*, or about once every four minutes. We may acquire a rude idea of the force with which the blood is impelled from the heart, by considering the velocity with which water issues from a syringe, or from the pipe of a fire-engine. Could we behold these rapid motions incessantly going on within us, it would overpower our minds with astonishment, and even with terror. We should be apt to feel alarmed on making the smallest exertion, lest the parts of this delicate machine should be broken or deranged, and its functions interrupted. The arteries, into which the blood is forced, branch in every direction through the body, like the roots and branches of a tree; running through the substance of the bones, and every part of the animal frame, till they are lost in such fine tubes as to be wholly invisible. In the parts where the arteries are lost to the sight, the veins take their rise, and in their commencement are also imperceptible.

*Respiration.*—The organs of respiration are the *lungs*. They are divided into five lobes; three of which lie on the right, and two on the left side of the thorax. The substance of the lungs is chiefly composed of infinite ramifications of the trachea, or windpipe, which, after gradually becoming more and more minute, terminate in little cells, or vesicles, which have a free communication with one another. At each inspiration, these pipes and cells are filled with air, which is again discharged by expiration. In this manner, a circulation of air, which is necessary to the existence of men and other animals, is constantly kept up as long as life remains. The air-cells of the lungs open into the windpipe, by which they communicate with the external atmosphere. The whole internal structure of the lungs is lined by a transparent membrane, estimated at only the thousandth part of an inch in thickness; but whose surface, from its various convolutions, measures fifteen square feet, which is equal to the external surface of the body. On this thin and extensive membrane innumerable veins and arteries are distributed, some of them finer than hairs; and through these vessels all the blood of the system is successively propelled, by a most curious and admirable mechanism. It has been computed, that the lungs, on an average, contain about 280 cubic inches, or about five English quarts of air. At each inspiration, about forty cubic inches of air are received into the lungs, and the same quantity discharged at each expiration. On the supposition that 20 respirations take place in a minute, it will follow, that, in one minute we inhale 800 cubic inches; in an hour, 48,000; and in a day, one million, one hundred and fifty-two thousand cubic inches—a quantity which would fill seventy-seven wine hogsheads, and would weigh fifty-three pounds troy. By means of this function, a vast body of air is daily brought into contact with the mass of blood, and communicates to it its vivifying influence; and, therefore, it is of the utmost importance to health, that the air, of which we breathe so considerable a quantity, should be pure, and uncontaminated with noxious effluvia.

*Digestion.*—This process is performed by the *stomach*, which is a membranous and muscular bag, furnished with two orifices. By the one, it has a communication with the gullet, and by the other, with the bowels. The food, after being moistened by the saliva, is received into the stomach, where it is still farther diluted by the *gastric juice*, which has the power of dissolving every kind of animal and vegetable substance. Part of it is afterwards absorbed by the *lymphatic* and *lacteal* vessels, and carried into the circulating system, and converted into blood for supplying that nourishment which the perpetual waste of our bodies demands.

*Perspiration* is the evacuation of the juices of the body through the pores of the skin. It has been calculated that there are above *three hundred thousand millions of pores* in the glands of the skin which covers the body of a middle-sized man. Through these pores, more than one-half of what we eat and drink passes off by *insensible* perspiration. During a night of seven hours' sleep, we perspire about forty ounces, or two pounds and a half. At an average, we may estimate the discharge from the surface of the body, by sensible and insensible perspiration, at from half an ounce to four ounces an hour. This is a most wonderful part of the animal economy, and is absolutely necessary to our health, and even to our very existence. When *partially* obstructed, colds, rheumatisms, fevers, and other inflammatory disorders, are produced; and were it completely obstructed, the vital functions would be clogged and impeded in their movements, and death would inevitably ensue.

*Sensation.*—The *nerves* are generally considered as the instruments of sensation. They are soft white cords which proceed from the brain and spinal marrow. They come forth originally by pairs. Ten pair proceed from the medullary substance of the brain, which are distributed to all parts of the head and neck. Thirty pair proceed from the spinal marrow, through the vertebræ, to all the other parts of the body; being forty in all. These nerves, the ramifications of which are infinitely various and minute, are distributed upon the heart, lungs, blood-vessels, bowels, and muscles, till they terminate on the skin or external covering of the body. Impressions of external objects are received by the brain from the adjacent organs of sense, and the brain exercises its commands over the muscles and limbs by means of the nerves.

Without prosecuting these imperfect descriptions farther, I shall conclude this very hasty sketch with the following summary of the parts of the body, in the words of Bonnet. "The *bones*, by their joints and solidity, form the foundation of this fine machine: the *ligaments* are strings which unite the parts together: the *muscles* are fleshy substances, which act as elastic springs to put them in motion: the *nerves*, which are dispersed over the whole body, connect all the parts together: the *arteries* and *veins*, like rivulets, convey life and health throughout: the *heart*, placed in the centre, is the focus where the blood collects, or the acting power by means of which it circulates and is preserved: the *lungs*, by means of another power, draw in the external air, and expel hurtful vapours: the *stomach* and *intestines* are the magazines where every thing that is required for the daily supply is prepared: the *brain*, that seat of the soul, is formed in a manner suitable to the dignity of its inhabitant: the *senses*, which are the soul's ministers, warn it of all that is necessary either for its pleasure or use.* Adorable Creator! with what wonderful art hast thou formed us! Though the heavens did not exist to proclaim thy glory; though there were no created being on earth but myself, my own body might suffice to convince me that thou art a God of unlimited power and infinite goodness."

This subject suggests a variety of moral and religious reflections, but the limits to which I am confined will permit me to state only the following:—

1. The economy of the human frame, when seriously contemplated, has a tendency to excite admiration and astonishment, and to *impress us with a sense of our continual dependence on a superior power.* What an immense multiplicity of machinery must be in action to enable us to breathe, to feel, and to walk! Hundreds of bones, of diversified forms, connected together by various modes of articulation: hundreds of muscles to produce motion, each of them acting in at least ten different capacities, (see p. 40;) hundreds of tendons and ligaments to connect the bones and muscles; hundreds of arteries to convey the blood to the remotest part of the system; hundreds of veins to bring it back to its reservoir the heart; thousands of glands secreting humours of various kinds from the blood; thousands of lacteal and lymphatic tubes, absorbing and conveying nutriment to the circulating fluid; millions of pores, through which the perspiration is continually issuing; an infinity of ramifications of nerves, diffusing sensation throughout all the parts of this exquisite machine; and the heart at every pulsation exerting a force of a hundred thousand pounds, in order to preserve all this complicated machinery in constant operation! The whole of this vast system of mechanism must be in action before we can walk across our apartments! We admire the operation of a steam-engine, and the force it exerts. But, though it is constructed of the hardest materials which the mines can supply, in a few months some of its essential parts are worn and deranged, even though its action should be frequently discontinued. But the animal machine, though constructed, for the most part, of the softest and most flabby substances, can go on without intermission in all its diversified movements, by night and by day, for the space of eighty or a hundred years; the heart giving ninety-six thousand strokes every twenty-four hours, and the whole mass of blood rushing through a thousand pipes of all sizes every four minutes! And is it *man* that governs these nice and complicated movements? Did *he* set the heart in motion, or endue it with the muscular force it exerts? And when it has ceased to beat, can *he* command it again to resume its functions? Man knows neither the secret springs of the machinery within him, nor the half of the purposes for which they serve, or of the movements they perform. Can any thing more strikingly demonstrate our dependence

* Contemplation of Nature, vol. I. p. 64.

every moment on a superior Agent, and that it is "*in God* we live, and move, and have our being? Were a single pin of the machinery within us, and over which we have no control, either broken or deranged, a thousand movements might instantly be interrupted, and our bodies left to crumble into the dust.

It was considerations of this kind that led the celebrated physician Galen, who was a skeptic in his youth, publicly to acknowledge that a Supreme Intelligence must have operated in ordaining the laws by which living beings are constructed. And he wrote his excellent treatise "On the uses of the parts of the human frame," as a solemn hymn to the Creator of the world. "I first endeavour from His works," he says, "to know him myself, and afterwards, by the same means, to show him to others; to inform them, how great is his wisdom, his goodness, his power." The late Dr. Hunter has observed, that astronomy and anatomy are the studies which present us with the most striking view of the two most wonderful attributes of the Supreme Being. The first of these fills the mind with the idea of his immensity, in the largeness, distances, and number of the heavenly bodies; the last astonishes us with his intelligence and art, in the variety and delicacy of animal mechanism.

2. The study of the animal economy has a powerful tendency *to excite emotions of gratitude.* Man is naturally a thoughtless and *ungrateful* creature. These dispositions are partly owing to *ignorance* of the wonders of the human frame, and of the admirable economy of the visible world; and this ignorance is owing to the want of those specific instructions which ought to be communicated by parents and teachers, in connexion with religion. For, there is no rational being who is acquainted with the structure of his animal system, and reflects upon it with the least degree of attention, but must feel a sentiment of admiration and gratitude. The science which unfolds to us the economy of our bodies, shows us on what an infinity of springs and motions, and adaptations, our life and comfort depend. And when we consider, that all these movements are performed without the least care or laborious effort on our part, if we be not altogether brutish, and insensible of our dependence on a superior Power, we must be filled with emotions of gratitude towards Him "whose hands have made and fashioned us, and who giveth us life, and breath, and all things." Some of the motions to which I have adverted depend upon our will; and with what celerity do they obey its commands? Before we can rise from our chair, and walk across our apartment, a hundred muscles must be set in motion; every one of these must be relaxed or constricted, just to a certain degree, and no more; and all must act harmoniously at the same instant of time; and, at the command of the soul, all these movements are instantaneously performed. When I wish to lift my hand to my head, every part of the body requisite to produce the effect is put in motion: the nerves are braced, the muscles are stretched or relaxed, the bones play in their sockets, and the whole animal machine concurs in the action, as if every nerve and muscle had heard a sovereign and resistless call. When I wish the next moment to extend my hand to my foot, all these muscles are thrown into a different state, and a new set are brought along with them into action: and thus we may vary, every moment, the movements of the muscular system, and the mechanical actions it produces, by a simple change in our volition. Were we not daily accustomed to such varied and voluntary movements, or could we contemplate them in any other machine, we should be lost in wonder and astonishment.

Besides these voluntary motions, there are a thousand important functions which have no dependance upon our will. Whether we think of it or not, whether we are sleeping or waking, sitting or walking—the heart is incessantly exerting its muscular power at the centre of the system, and sending off streams of blood through hundreds of pipes; the lungs are continually expanding and contracting their thousand vesicles, and imbibing the vital principle of the air; the stomach is grinding the food; the lacteals and lymphatics are extracting nourishment for the blood; the liver and kidneys drawing off their secretions; and the perspiration issuing from millions of pores. These, and many other important functions with which we are unacquainted, and over which we have no control, ought to be regarded as the immediate agency of the Deity within us, and should excite our incessant admiration and praise.

There is one peculiarity in the constitution of our animal system, which we are apt to overlook, and for which we are never sufficiently grateful, and that is, *the power it possesses of self-restoration.* A wound heals up of itself; a broken bone is made firm again by a callus; and a dead part is separated and thrown off. If all the wounds we have ever received were still open and bleeding afresh, to what a miserable condition should we be reduced? But by a system of internal powers, beyond all human comprehension as to the mode of their operation, such dismal effects are effectually prevented. In short, when we consider that health depends upon such a numerous assemblage of moving organs, and that a single spring out of action might derange the whole machine, and put a stop to all its complicated movements, can we refrain from joining with the psalmist, in his pious exclamation, and grateful resolution, "How precious are thy wonderful contrivances concerning me, O God! how great is the sum of them! I will praise thee, for I am fearfully and wonderfully made. Marvellous are thy works, and that my soul knoweth right well."

Omitting the consideration of several other departments of science, I shall in the mean time notice only another subject connected with religion, and that is History.

### HISTORY.

History embraces a record and description of past facts and events, in reference to all the nations and ages of the world, in so far as they are known, and have been transmitted to our times. As natural history contains a record of the operations of the Creator in the material world, so sacred and civil history embraces a record of his transactions in the moral and intellectual world, or, in other words, a detail of the plans and operations of his providence, in relation to the inhabitants of our globe. Through the medium of Sacred History, we learn the period and the manner of man's creation—the reason of his fall from the primitive state of integrity in which he was created, and the dismal consequences which ensued; the various movements of Providence in order to his recovery, and the means by which human redemption was achieved; the manner in which the gospel was at first promulgated, the countries into which it was carried, and the important effects it produced. Through the medium of Civil History we learn the deep and universal depravity of mankind, as exhibited in the wars, dissensions, and ravages, which have desolated our fallen race, in every period, and in every land; we learn the desperate wickedness of the human heart, in the more private acts of ferocity, cruelty, and injustice, which, in all ages, men have perpetrated upon each other; we behold the righteousness of the Supreme Ruler of the world, and the equity of his administration, in the judgments which have been inflicted on wicked nations—and the improbability, nay, the *impossibility*, of men being ever restored to moral order and happiness, without a more extensive diffusion of the blessings of the gospel of peace, and a more cordial acquiescence in the requirements of the divine laws.

Such being some of the benefits to be derived from history, it requires no additional arguments to show, that this branch of knowledge should occasionally form a subject of study to every intelligent Christian. But in order to render the study of history subservient to the interests of religion, it is not enough merely to gratify our curiosity and imagination, by following out a succession of memorable events, by tracing the progress of armies and of battles, and listening to the groans of the vanquished, and the shouts of conquerors. This would be to study history merely as skeptics, as atheists, or as writers of novels. When we contemplate the facts which the historian presents to our view, we ought to raise our eyes to Him who is the Governor among the nations, "who doth according to his will in the armies of heaven, and among the inhabitants of the earth," and who overrules the jarring interests of mortals, for promoting the prosperity of that kingdom which shall never be moved. We should view the immoral propensities and dispositions of mankind as portrayed in the page of history, as evidences of the depravity of our species, and as excitements to propagate, with unremitting energy, the knowledge of that religion, whose sublime doctrines and pure precepts alone can counteract the stream of human corruption, and unite all nations in one harmonious society. We should view the contests of nations, and the results with which they are accompanied, as guided by that invisible Hand, which "mustereth the armies to the battle;" and should contemplate them either as the accomplishment of divine predictions, as the inflictions of retributive justice, as paving the way for the introduction of rational liberty and social happiness among men, or as ushering in that glorious period, when "the knowledge of the Lord shall cover the earth," and the nations shall learn war no more.

Thus I have taken a very cursory survey of some of those sciences which stand in a near relation to the objects of religion; and which may, indeed, be considered as forming so many of its subordinate branches. There are many other departments of knowledge, which, at first view, do not seem to have any relation to theological science; and yet, on a closer inspection, will be found to be essentially connected with the several subjects of which I have been treating For example—some may be apt to imagine that arithmetic, geometry, trigonometry, and other branches of mathematics, can have no relation to the leading objects of religion. But if these sciences had never been cultivated, the most important discoveries of astronomy, geography, natural philosophy, and chymistry, would never have been made; ships could not have been navigated across the ocean; distant continents, and the numerous "isles of the sea," would have remained unexplored, and their inhabitants left to grope in the darkness of heathenism; and most of those instruments and engines by which the condition of the human race will be gradually meliorated, and the influence of Christianity extended, would never have been invented. Such is the dependence of every branch of useful knowledge upon another, that were any one portion of science, which has a practical tendency, to be discarded, it would prevent, to a certain degree, the improvement of every other. And, consequently, if any one science can be shown to have a connexion with religion, all the rest must likewise stand in a certain relation to it. It must, therefore, have a pernicious effect on the minds of the mass of the Christian world, when preachers, in their sermons, endeavour to undervalue scientific knowledge, by attempting to contrast it with the doctrines of revelation. It would be just as reasonable to attempt to contrast the several doctrines, duties, and facts recorded in the New Testament with each other, in order to determine their relative importance, and to show which of them might be altogether overlooked and discarded. The series of facts and of divine revelations comprised in the bible; the moral and political events which diversify the history of nations; and the physical operations that are going on among the rolling worlds on high, and in the chymical changes of the invisible atoms of matter, are all parts of *one* comprehensive system, under the direction of the Eternal Mind; every portion of which must have a certain relation to the whole.

And, therefore, instead of attempting to degrade one part of the divine fabric in order to enhance another, our duty is to take an expansive view of the whole, and to consider the symmetry and proportion of its parts, and their mutual bearings and relations—in so far as our opportunities, and the limited faculties of our minds, will permit.

If the remarks which have been thrown out in this chapter, respecting the connexion of the sciences with religion, have any foundation, it will follow—that sermons, lectures, systems of divinity, and religious periodical works, should embrace occasional illustrations of such subjects, for the purpose of expanding the conceptions of professed Christians, and of enabling them to take large and comprehensive views of the perfections of the providence of the Almighty. It is much to be regretted, that so many members of the Christian church are absolute strangers to such studies and contemplations; while the time and attention that might have been devoted to such exercises, have, in many cases, been usurped by the most grovelling affections, by foolish pursuits, by gossiping chit-chat, and slanderous conversation. Shall the most trifling and absurd opinions of ancient and modern heretics be judged worthy of attention, and occupy a place in religious journals, and even in discussions from the pulpit, and shall "the mighty acts of the Lord," and the visible wonders of his power and wisdom, be thrown completely into the shade? To survey, with an eye of intelligence, the wide-extended theatre of the divine operations—to mark the agency of the Eternal Mind in every object we behold, and in every movement within us and around us, are some of the noblest attainments of the rational soul; and, in conjunction with every other Christian study and acquirement, are calculated to make "the man of God perfect, and thoroughly furnished unto every good work." By such studies, we are, in some measure, assimilated to the angelic tribes, whose powers of intellect are for ever employed in such investigations—and are gradually prepared for bearing a part in their immortal hymn—"Great and marvellous are thy works, Lord God Almighty; just and true are thy ways, thou King of saints. Thou art worthy to receive glory, and honour, and power; for thou hast created all things, and for thy pleasure they are and were created."

---

# CHAPTER III.

## THE RELATION WHICH THE INVENTIONS OF HUMAN ART BEAR TO THE OBJECTS OF RELIGION.

In this chapter, I shall briefly notice a few philosophical and mechanical inventions which have an obvious bearing on religion, and on the general propagation of Christianity among the nations.

The first, and perhaps the most important, of the inventions to which I allude, is the *Art of Printing*. This art appears to have been invented (at least in Europe) about the year 1430, by one Laurentius, or Lawrence Koster, a native of Haerlem, a town in Holland. As he was walking in a wood near the city, he began to cut some letters upon the rind of a beach tree, which, for the sake of gratifying his fancy, being impressed on paper, he printed one or two lines as a specimen for his grandchildren to follow. This having succeeded, he meditated greater things; and, first of all, invented a more glutinous writing ink; because he found the common ink sunk and spread; and thus formed whole pages of wood, with letters cut upon them.* By the gradual

*I am aware, that the honour of this invention has been claimed by other cities besides Haerlem, particularly by Strasburg, and Mentz, a city of Germany; and by other individuals besides Laurentius, chiefly by one *Fust*, commonly called Dr. Faustus; by Schoeffer, and by Gutenberg. It appears that the art, with many of its implements, was stolen from Laurentius by one of his servants, whom he had bound, by an oath, to secrecy, who fled to Mentz, and first commenced the process of printing in that city. Here the art was improved by Fust and Schoeffer, by their invention of *metallic*, instead of *wooden* types, which were first used. When Fust was in Paris, disposing of some bibles he had printed, at

improvement of this art, and its application to the diffusion of knowledge, a new era was formed in the annals of the human race, and in the progress of science, religion, and morals. To it we are chiefly indebted for our deliverance from ignorance and error, and for most of those scientific discoveries and improvements in the arts which distinguish the period in which we live. Without its aid, the Reformation from Popery could scarcely have been achieved; for, had the books of Luther, one of the first reformers, been multiplied by the slow process of handwriting and copying, they could never have been diffused to any extent; and the influence of bribery and of power might have been sufficient to have arrested their progress, or even to have erased their existence. But, being poured forth from the press in thousands at a time, they spread over the nations of Europe like an inundation, and with a rapidity which neither the authority of princes, nor the schemes of priests and cardinals, nor the bulls of popes, could counteract or suspend. To this noble invention it is owing that copies of the bible have been multiplied to the extent of many millions—that ten thousands of them are to be found in every Protestant country—and that the poorest individual who expresses a desire for it, may be furnished with the "word of life" which will guide him to a blessed immortality. That divine light which is destined to illuminate every region of the globe, and to sanctify and reform men of all nations, and kindreds, and tongues, is accelerated in its movements, and directed in its course through the nations, by the invention of the art of printing; and ere long it will distribute among the inhabitants of every land, the "law and the testimony of the Most High," to guide their steps to the regions of eternal bliss. In short, there is not a more powerful engine in the hands of Providence, for diffusing the knowledge of the nature and the will of the Deity, and for accomplishing the grand objects of revelation, than the art of multiplying books, and of conveying intelligence through the medium of the press. Were no such art in existence, we cannot conceive how an extensive and universal propagation of the doctrines of revelation could be effected, unless after the lapse of an indefinite number of ages. But, with the assistance of this invention, in its present improved state, the island of Great Britain alone, within less than a hundred years, could furnish a copy of the Scriptures to every inhabitant of the world, and would defray the expense of such an undertaking, with much more ease, and with a smaller sum, than were necessary to furnish the political warfare in which we were lately engaged.

These considerations teach us, that the ingenious inventions of the human mind are under the direction and control of the Governor of the world—are intimately connected with the accomplishment of the plan of his providence, and have a tendency, either directly or indirectly, to promote, over every region of the earth, the progress and extension of the kingdom of the Redeemer. They also show us, from what small beginnings the most magnificent operations of the divine economy may derive their origin. Who could have imagined that the simple circumstance of a person amusing himself by cutting a few letters on the bark of a tree, and impressing them on paper, was intimately connected with the mental illumination of mankind; and that the art which sprung from this casual process was destined to be the principal means of illuminating the nations, and of conveying to the ends of the earth, "the salvation of our God?" But, "He who rules in the armies of heaven, and among the inhabitants of the earth," and who sees "the end from the beginning," overrules the most minute movement of all his creatures, in subserviency to his ultimate designs, and shows himself, in this respect, to be "wonderful in counsel, and excellent in working."

*The Mariner's Compass.*—Another invention which has an intimate relation to religion, is, *the art of Navigation, and the invention of the Mariner's Compass.* Navigation is the art of

the low price (as was then thought) of sixty crowns, the number and the uniformity of the copies he possessed created universal agitation and astonishment. Informations were given to the police against him as a magician, his lodgings were searched, and a great number of copies being found, they were seized; the red ink with which they were embellished was said to be his blood; it was seriously adjudged, that he was in league with the devil; and if he had not fled from the city, most probably he would have shared the fate of those whom ignorant and superstitious judges, at that time, condemned for witchcraft. From this circumstance, let us learn to beware how we view the inventions of genius, and how we treat those whose ingenious contrivances may afterwards be the means of enlightening and meliorating mankind. See *Appendix*, No. VII.

Various improvements have been made, of late years, in the art of printing. That which has lately been announced by Dr. Church of Boston, is the most remarkable; and, if found successful, will carry this art to a high degree of perfection. A principal object of this improvement is, to print constantly from new types, which is effected by simplifying the process for casting and composing. The type is delivered perfect by machinery, and laid as it is cast, in separate compartments, with unerring order and exactness. The composition is then effected by other apparatus, directed by keys like those of a piano-forte, and the type may then be arranged in words and lines, as quickly as in the performance of notes in music. No error can arise except from touching the wrong key: and hence an expert hand will leave little labour for the reader. It is then found less expensive under Dr. Church's economical system of re-casting, to re-melt the types, and re-cast them, than to perform the tedious operation of distribution. The melting takes place without atmospheric exposure, by which oxydation and waste of metal are avoided. It is calculated that two men can produce 75,000 new types per hour, and in re-composing, one man will perform as much as three or four compositors. In the production of types, the saving is ninety-nine parts in a hundred; and in the composition, distribution, and reading, is three parts in four. In regard to press-work, Dr. C. has invented a machine to work with plattens, instead of cylinders, from which he will be enabled to take 80 fine impressions per minute.

conducting a ship through the sea, from one port to another. This art was partly known and practised in the early ages of antiquity, by the Phenicians, the Carthaginians, the Egyptians, the Romans, and other nations of Europe and Asia. But they had no guide to direct them in their voyages, except the sun in the day-time, and the stars by night. When the sky was overcast with clouds, they were thrown into alarms, and durst not venture to any great distance from the coast, lest they should be carried forward in a course opposite to that which they intended, or be driven against hidden rocks, or unknown shores. The danger and difficulty of the navigation of the ancients, on this account, may be learned from the deliberations, the great preparations, and the alarms of Homer's heroes, when they were about to cross the Egean sea, an extent of not more than 150 miles; and the expedition of the Argonauts under Jason, across the sea of Marmora and the Euxine, to the island of Colchis, a distance of only four or five hundred miles, was viewed as a most wonderful exploit, at which even the gods themselves were said to be amazed. The same thing appears from the narration we have in the Acts of the Apostles, of Paul's voyage from Cesarea to Rome.—"When," says Luke, "neither sun nor stars in many days appeared, and no small tempests lay on us, all hope that we should be saved was then taken away." Being deprived of these guides, they were tossed about in the Mediterranean, not knowing whether they were carried to the north, south, east, or west. So that the voyages of antiquity consisted chiefly in creeping along the coast, and seldom venturing beyond sight of land: they could not, therefore, extend their excursions by sea to distant continents and nations; and hence, the greater portion of the terraqueous globe and its inhabitants were to them altogether unknown. It was not before the invention of the *mariner's compass*, that distant voyages could be undertaken, that extensive oceans could be traversed, and an intercourse carried on between remote continents and the islands of the ocean.

It is somewhat uncertain at what precise period this noble discovery was made; but it appears pretty evident, that the mariner's compass was not commonly used in navigation before the year 1420, or only a few years before the invention of printing.* The loadstone, in all ages, was known to have the property of attracting iron; but its tendency to point towards the north and south seems to have been unnoticed till the beginning of the twelfth century. About that time some curious persons seem to have amused themselves by making to swim, in a basin of water, a loadstone suspended on a piece of cork; and to have remarked, that, when left at liberty, one of its extremities pointed to the north. They had also remarked, that, when a piece of iron is rubbed against the loadstone, it acquires also the property of turning towards the north, and of attracting needles and filings of iron. From one experiment to another, they proceeded to lay a needle, touched with the magnet, on two small bits of straw floating on the water and to observe that the needle invariably turned its point towards the north. The first use they seem to have made of these experiments, was, to impose upon simple people by the appearance of *magic*. For example, a hollow swan, or the figure of a mermaid, was made to swim in a basin of water, and to follow a knife with a bit of bread upon its point, which had been previously rubbed on the loadstone. The experimenter convinced them of his power, by commanding, in this way, a needle laid on the surface of the water to turn its point from the north to the east, or in any other direction. But some geniuses, of more sublime and reflective powers of mind, seizing upon these hints, at last applied these experiments to the wants of navigation, and constructed an instrument, by the help of which the mariner can now direct his course to distant lands, through the vast and pathless ocean.

In consequence of the discovery of this instrument, the coasts of almost every land on the surface of the globe have been explored, and a regular intercourse opened up between the remotest regions of the earth. Without the help of this noble invention, America, in all probability, would never have been discovered by the eastern nations—the vast continent of New-Holland—the numerous and interesting islands in the Indian and Pacific oceans—the isles of Japan, and other immense territories inhabited by human beings, would have remained as much unknown and unexplored as if they had never existed And as the nations of Europe and the western parts of Asia were the sole depositories of the records of revelation, they could never have conveyed the blessings of salvation to remote countries and to unknown tribes of mankind, of whose existence they were entirely ignorant. Even although the whole terraqueous globe had been sketched out before them, in all its aspects and bearings, and ramifications of islands, continents, seas, and oceans, and the moral and political state of every tribe of its inhabitants

* The invention of the compass is usually ascribed to Falvio Gioia, of Amalfi, in Campania, about the year 1302; and the Italians are strenuous in supporting this claim. Others affirm, that Marcus Paulus, a Venetian, having made a journey to China, brought back the invention with him in 1260. The French also lay claim to the honour of this invention, from the circumstance, that all nations distinguish the *north* point of the card by a *fleur-de-lis*, and, with equal reason, the English have laid claim to the same honour, from the name *compass*, by which most nations have agreed to distinguish it. But whoever were the inventors, or at whatever period this instrument was first constructed, it does not appear that it was brought into general use before the period mentioned in the text.

displayed to view · without a guide to direct their course through the billows of the ocean, they could have afforded no light and no relief to cheer the distant nations "who sit in darkness, and in the shadow of death." Though the art of printing had been invented; though millions of bibles were now prepared, adequate to the supply of all the "kindreds of the heathen;" though ships in abundance were equipped for the enterprise, and thousands of missionaries ready to embark, and to devote their lives to the instruction of the pagan world—all would be of no avail, and the "salvation of God" could never be proclaimed to the ends of the world, unless they had a mariner's compass to guide their course through the trackless ocean.

In this invention, then, we behold a proof of the agency of Divine Providence, in directing the efforts of human genius to subserve the most important designs, and contemplate a striking specimen of the "manifold wisdom of God." When the pious and contemplative Israelite reflected on the declaration of the prophets, that "the glory of Jehovah would be revealed, and that all flesh would see it together;"—from the state of the arts which then existed, he must have felt many difficulties in forming a conception of the *manner* in which such predictions could be realized. "The great and wide sea," now termed the Mediterranean, formed the boundary of his view, beyond which he was unable to penetrate. Of the continents, and "the isles afar off," and of the far more spacious oceans that lay between, he had no knowledge; and how "the ends of the earth" were to be reached, he could form no conception; and, in the midst of his perplexing thoughts, he could find no satisfaction but in the firm belief, that "with God all things are possible." But now we are enabled not only to contemplate the grand designs of the divine economy, but the principal means by which they shall all, in due time, be accomplished, in consequence of the progress of science and art, and of their consecration to the rearing and extension of the Christian church.

The two inventions to which I have now adverted, may perhaps be considered as among the most striking instances of the connexion of human art with the objects of religion. But there are many other inventions, which, at first view, do not appear to bear so near a relation to the progress of Christianity, and yet have an ultimate reference to some of its grand and interesting objects.

*The Telescope.*—We might be apt to think, on a slight view of the matter, that there can be no immediate relation between the grinding and polishing of an optic glass, and fitting two or more of them in a tube, and the enlargement of our views of the operation of the Eternal Mind. Yet the connexion between these two objects, and the dependence of the latter upon the former, can be fairly demonstrated. The son of a spectacle-maker of Middleburg in Holland, happening to amuse himself in his father's shop, by holding two glasses between his finger and his thumb, and varying their distance, perceived the weathercock of the church spire opposite to him much larger than ordinary, and apparently much nearer, and turned upside down. This new wonder excited the amazement of the father; he adjusted two glasses on a board, rendering them moveable at pleasure; and thus formed the first rude imitation of a perspective glass, by which distant objects are brought near to view. Galileo, a philosopher of Tuscany, hearing of the invention, set his mind to work, in order to bring it to perfection. He fixed his glasses at the end of long organ-pipes, and constructed a telescope, which he soon directed to different parts of the surrounding heavens. He discovered four moons revolving around the planet Jupiter—spots on the surface of the sun, and the rotation of that globe around its axis—mountains and valleys in the moon—and numbers of fixed stars where scarcely one was visible to the naked eye. These discoveries were made about the year **1610**, a short time after the first invention of the telescope. Since that period this instrument has passed through various degrees of improvement, and, by means of it, celestial wonders have been explored in the distant spaces of the universe, which, in former times, were altogether concealed from mortal view. By the help of telescopes, combined with the art of measuring the distances and magnitudes of the heavenly bodies, our views of the grandeur of the Almighty, of the plenitude of his power, and of the *extent* of his universal empire, are extended far beyond what could have been conceived in former ages. Our prospects of the range of the divine operaions are no longer confined within the limits of the world we inhabit; we can now plainly perceive, that the kingdom of God is not only "an everlasting dominion," but that it extends through the unlimited regions of space, comprehending within its vast circumference thousands of suns, and tens of thousands of worlds, all ranged in majestic order, at immense distances from one another, and all supported and governed "by Him who rides on the Heaven of heavens," whose greatness is unsearchable, and whose understanding is infinite.

The telescope has also demonstrated to us the *literal truth* of those scriptural declarations which assert that the stars are "innumerable." Before the invention of this instrument, not more than about two thousand stars could be perceived by the unassisted eye in the clearest night. But this invention has unfolded to view not only thousands, but hundreds of thousands, and millions, of those bright luminaries, which lie dispersed in every direction throughout the boundless dimensions of space. And the higher the magnifying powers of the telescope are, the more numerous those celestial orbs appear; leaving us no room to doubt, that countless myriads more lie hid in the distant regions of creation, far beyond the reach of the finest glasses that can be constructed by human skill, and which are known only to Him "who counts the number of the stars, and calls them by their names."

In short, the telescope may be considered as serving the purpose of a vehicle for conveying us to the distant regions of space. We would consider it as a wonderful achievement, could we transport ourselves two hundred thousand miles from the earth, in the direction of the moon, in order to take a nearer view of that celestial orb. But this instrument enables us to take a much nearer inspection of that planet, than if we had actually surmounted the force of gravitation, traversed the voids of space, and left the earth 230,000 miles behind us. For, supposing such a journey to be accomplished, we should still be ten thousand miles distant from that orb. But a telescope which magnifies objects 240 times, can carry our views within *one* thousand miles of the moon; and a telescope, such as Dr. Herschel's 40 feet reflector, which magnifies 6000 times, would enable us to view the mountains and vales of the moon, as if we were transported to a point about 40 miles from her surface.* We can view the magnificent system of the planet Saturn, by means of this instrument, as distinctly, as if we had performed a journey eight hundred millions of miles in the direction of that globe, which at the rate of 50 miles an hour, would require a period of more than eighteen hundred years to accomplish. By the telescope, we can contemplate the region of the fixed stars, their arrangement into systems, and their immense numbers, with the same distinctness and amplitude of view, as if we had actually taken a flight of ten hundred thousand millions of miles into those unexplored and unexplorable regions, which could not be accomplished in several millions of years, though our motion were as rapid as a ball projected from a loaded cannon. We would justly consider it as a noble endowment for enabling us to take an extensive survey of the works of God, if we had the faculty of transporting ourselves to such immense distances from the sphere we now occupy but, by means of the telescopic tube, we may take nearly the same ample views of the dominions of the Creator, without stirring a foot from the limits of our terrestrial abode. This instrument may, therefore, be considered as a providential gift, bestowed upon mankind, to serve, in the mean time, as a *temporary substitute* for those powers of rapid flight with which the seraphim are endowed, and for those superior faculties of motion with which man himself may be invested, when he arrives at the summit of moral perfection.*

*The Microscope.*—The *microscope* is another instrument constructed on similar principles, which has greatly expanded our views of the "manifold wisdom of God." This instrument, which discovers to us small objects, invisible to the naked eye, was invented soon after the invention and improvement of the telescope. By means of this optical contrivance, we peceive a variety of wonders in almost every object in the animal, the vegetable, and the mineral kingdoms. We perceive that every particle of matter, however minute, has a determinate form—that the very scales of the skin of a haddock are all beautifully interwoven and variegated, like pieces of net-work, which no art can imitate—that the points of the prickles of vegetables, though magnified a thousand times, appear as sharp and well polished as to the naked eye—that every particle of the dust on the butterfly's wing is a beautiful and regularly organized feather—that every hair of our head is a hollow tube, with bulbs and roots, furnished with a variety of threads or filaments—and that the pores in our skin, through which the sweat and perspiration flow, are so numerous and minute, that a grain of sand would cover a hundred and twenty-five thousand of them. We perceive animated beings in certain liquids, so small, that fifty thousand of them would not equal the size of a mite; and yet each of these creatures is furnished with a mouth, eyes, stomach, blood-vessels, and other organs for the performance of animal functions. In a stagnant pool which is covered with a greenish scum during the summer months, every drop of the water is found to be a world teeming with thousands of inhabitants. The mouldy substance which usually adheres to damp bodies exhibits a forest of trees and plants, where the branches, leaves, and fruit, can be plainly dis-

* Though the highest magnifying power of Dr. Herschel's large telescope was estimated at six thousand times, yet it does not appear that the doctor ever applied this power with success, when viewing the moon and the planets. The deficiency of light, when using so high a power, would render the view of these objects less satisfactory than when viewed with a power of one or two thousand times. Still, it is quite certain, that if any portions of the moon's surface were viewed through an instrument of such a power, they would appear as *large* (but *not nearly so bright and distinct*) as if we were placed about 40 miles distant from that body. The enlargement of the angle of vision, in this case, or, the apparent distance at which the moon would be contemplated, is found by dividing the moon's distance—240,000 miles by 6000, the magnifying power of the telescope, which produces a quotient of 40—the number of miles at which the moon would appear to be placed from the eye of the observer. Dr. Herschel appears to have used the highest power of his telescopes, only, or chiefly, when viewing some very minute objects in the region of the stars. The powers he generally used, and with which he made most of his discoveries were, 227, 460, 754, 932, and occasionally 2010, 3168, and 6450, when inspecting double and triple stars, and the more distant nebulæ.

* See Appendix, No VIII.

tinguished. In a word, by this admirable instrument we behold the same Almighty Hand which rounded the spacious globe on which we live, and the huge masses of the planetary orbs, and directs them in their rapid motions through the sky,—employed, at the same moment, in rounding and polishing ten thousand minute transparent globes in the eye of a fly; and boring and arranging veins and arteries, and forming and clasping joints and claws, for the movements of a mite! We thus learn the admirable and astonishing effects of the wisdom of God, and that the divine care and benevolence are as much displayed in the construction of the smallest insect, as in the elephant or the whale, or in those ponderous globes which roll around us in the sky. These, and thousands of other views which the microscope exhibits, would never have been displayed to the human mind, had they not been opened up by this admirable invention.

In fine, by means of the two instruments to which I have now adverted, we behold Jehovah's empire extending to infinity on either hand. By the telescope we are presented with the most astonishing displays of his *omnipotence*, in the immense number, the rapid motions, and the inconceivable magnitudes of the celestial globes; and, by the microscope, we behold, what is still more inconceivable, a display of his unsearchable wisdom in the divine mechanism by which a drop of water is peopled with myriads of inhabitants—a fact which, were it not subject to ocular demonstration, would far exceed the limits of human conception or belief. We have thus the most striking and sensible evidence, that, from the immeasurable luminaries of heaven, and from the loftiest seraph that stands before the throne of God, down to this lower world, and to the smallest microscopic animalcula that eludes the finest glass, *He* is every where present, and, by his power, intelligence, and agency, animates, supports, and directs the whole. Such views and contemplations naturally lead us to advert to the character of God as delineated by the sacred writers, that "He is of great power, and mighty in strength;" that "His understanding is infinite;' that "His works are wonderful;" that "His operations are unsearchable and past finding out;" and they must excite the devout mind to join with fervour in the language of adoration and praise.

When thy amazing works, O God!
My mental eye surveys,
"Transported with the view, I'm lost
In wonder, love, and praise."

*Steam Navigation.*—We might have been apt to suppose that the chymical experiments that were first made to demonstrate the force of *steam* as a mechanical agent, could have little relation to the objects of religion, or even to the comfort of human life and society. Yet it has now been applied to the impelling of ships and large boats along rivers and seas, in opposition to both wind and tide, and with a velocity which, at an average, exceeds that of any other conveyance. We have no reason to believe that this invention has hitherto approximated to a state of perfection; it is yet in its infancy, and may be susceptible of such improvements, both in point of expedition and of safety, as may render it the most comfortable and speedy conveyance between distant lands, for transporting the volume of inspiration and the heralds of the gospel of peace to "the ends of the earth." By the help of his compass the mariner is enabled to steer his course in the midst of the ocean, in the most cloudy days, and in the darkest nights, and to transport his vessel from one end of the world to another. It now only remains, that navigation be rendered safe, uniform, and expeditious, and not dependent on adverse winds, or the currents of the ocean; and, perhaps the art of propelling vessels by the force of steam, when arrived at perfection, may effectuate those desirable purposes. Even at present, as the invention now stands, were a vessel to be fitted to encounter the waves of the Atlantic, constructed of a proper figure and curvature, having a proper disposition of her wheels, and having such a description of fuel, as could be easily stowed, and in sufficient quantity for the voyage—at the rate of ten miles an hour, she could pass from the shores of Britain to the coast of America, in less than thirteen days;—and, even at eight miles an hour, the voyage could be completed in little more than fifteen days; so that intelligence might pass and repass between the eastern and western continents within the space of a single month—a space of time very little more than was requisite, sixty years ago, for conveying intelligence between Glasgow and London. The greatest distance at which any two places on the globe lie from each other, is about 12,500 miles; and, therefore, if a direct portion of water intervene between them, this space could be traversed in fifty-four or sixty days. And, if the isthmus of Panama, which connects North and South America, and the isthmus of Suez, which separates the Mediterranean from the Red sea, were cut into wide and deep canals, (which we have no doubt will be accomplished as soon as civilized nations have access to perform operations in those territories,) every country in the world could then be reached from Europe, in nearly a direct line, or at most by a gentle curve, instead of the long, and dangerous, and circuitous route which must now be taken, in sailing for the eastern parts of Asia, and the north-western shores of America. By this means, eight or nine thousand miles of sailing would be saved in a voyage from England to Nootka sound, or the peninsula of California; and more than six thousand miles, in passing from London to Bombay in the East Indies; and few places on the earth would be farther distant from each other by water than 15,000 miles; which space might be traversed, at the rate mentioned above, in a period of from sixty-two to seventy-seven days.*

But we have reason to believe, that when this invention, combined with other mechanical assistances, shall approximate nearer to perfection, a much more rapid rate of motion will be effected; and the advantages of this, in a religious as well as in a commercial point of view, may be easily appreciated, especially at the present period, when the Christian world, now aroused from their slumbers, have formed the grand design of sending a bible to every inhabitant of the globe. When the empire of the prince of darkness shall be shaken throughout all its dependencies, and the nations aroused to inquire after light, and liberty, and divine knowledge—intelligence would thus be rapidly communicated over every region, and between the most distant tribes. "Many would run to and fro, and knowledge would be increased." The ambassadors of the Redeemer, with the oracles of heaven in their hands, and the words of salvation in their mouths, would quickly be transported to every clime, "having the everlasting gospel to preach to every nation, and kindred, and tongue, and people."

*Air Balloons.*—Similar remarks may be applied to the *invention of Air Balloons.* We have heard of some pious people who have mourned over such inventions, and lamented the folly of mankind in studying their construction, and witnessing their exhibition. Such dispositions generally proceed from a narrow range of thought, and a contracted view of the divine economy and arrangements in the work of redemption. Though the perversity of mankind has often applied useful inventions to foolish, and even to vicious purposes, yet this forms no reason why such inventions should be decried; otherwise the art of printing, and many other useful arts, might be regarded as inimical to the human race. We have reason to believe that air balloons may yet be brought to such perfection, as to be applied to purposes highly beneficial to the progress of the human mind, and subservient, in some degree, for effecting the purposes of providence in the enlightening and renovation of mankind. For this purpose, it is only requisite that some contrivance, on chymical or mechanical principles, be suggested, analogous to the sails or rudder of a ship, by which they may be moved in any direction, without being directed solely by the course of the wind; and, there can be little doubt that such a contrivance is *possible* to be effected. It requires only suitable encouragement to be given to ingenious experimental philosophers, and a sufficient sum of money to enable them to prosecute their experiments on an extensive scale. To the want of such prerequisites, it is chiefly owing, that the hints on this subject, hitherto suggested, have either failed of success or have never been carried into execution. A more simple and expeditious process for filling balloons has lately been effected—the use of the *parachute*, by which a person may detach himself from the balloon, and descend to the earth, has been successfully tried,—the lightning of heaven has been drawn from the clouds, and forced to act as a mechanical power in splitting immense stones to pieces,—the atmosphere has been analyzed into its component parts, and the wonderful properties of the ingredients of which it is composed exhibited in their separate state: and why, then, should we consider it as at all improbable that the means of producing a horizontal direction in aerial navigation may soon be discovered? Were this object once effected, balloons might be applied to the purpose of surveying and exploring countries hitherto inaccessible, and of conveying the messengers of divine mercy to tribes of our fellow men, whose existence is as yet unknown.

We are certain that every portion of the inhabited world must be thoroughly explored, and its inhabitants visited, before the salvation of God can be carried fully into effect; and, for the purpose of such explorations, we must, of course, resort to the inventions of human genius in art and science. Numerous tribes of the sons of Adam are, doubtless, residing in regions of the earth with which we have no acquaintance, and to which we have no access by any of the modes of conveyance presently in use. More than one-half of the interior parts of Africa and Asia, and even of America, are wholly unknown to the inhabitants of the civilized world. The vast regions of Chinese Tartary, Thibet, Siberia, and the adjacent districts; almost the whole interior of Africa, and the continent of New Holland—the extensive isles of Borneo, Sumatra, New Guinea, and Japan, the territory of the Amazons, and the internal parts of North America, remain, for the most part, unknown and unexplored. The lofty and impassable ranges of mountains, and the deep and rapid rivers, which intervene between us and many of those regions, together with the savage and plundering hordes of men, and the tribes of ravenous beasts, through which the traveller must push his way, present to European adventurers barriers which they cannot expect to surmount by the ordinary modes of conveyance, for a lapse of ages. But by balloons constructed with an apparatus for directing their motions, all such obstructions would at once be surmounted. The most impenetrable regions, now hemmed in by streams and marshes, and lofty mountains, and a barbarous population, would be quickly laid open

* See Appendix, No. IX.

and cities and nations, lakes and rivers, and fertile plains, to which we are now entire strangers, would soon burst upon the view. And the very circumstance, that the messengers of peace and salvation *descended upon such unknown tribes from the regions of the clouds*, might arouse their minds, and excite their attention and regard to the message of divine mercy which they came thither to proclaim.* Such a scene (and it may probably be realized) would present a literal fulfilment of the prediction of "*angels flying through the midst of*" the aerial "*heaven*, having the everlasting gospel to preach to them that dwell upon the earth, and to every kindred and nation."

That the attention of the philosophical world is presently directed to this subject, and that we have some prospect of the views above suggested being soon realized, will appear from the following notice, which lately made its appearance in the London scientific journals:—"A prize being offered for the discovery of a horizontal direction in aerostation, M. Mingreli of Bologna, M. Pietripoli of Venice, and M. Lember of Nuremberg, have each assumed the merit of resolving this problem. It does not appear that any one of these has come forward to establish, by practical experiment, the validity of his claim; but a pamphlet has lately been reprinted at Paris (first printed at Vienna) on this subject, addressed to all the learned societies in Europe. The following passage appears in the work:—"Professor Robertson proposes to construct an aerostatic machine, 150 feet in diameter, to be capable of raising 72,954 kilograms, equivalent to 149,037 lbs. weight, (French,) to be capable of conveying all the necessaries for the support of sixty individuals, scientific characters, to be selected by the academicians, and the aerial navigations to last for some months, exploring different heights and climates, &c. in all seasons. If, from accident, or wear, the machine, elevated above the ocean, should fail in its functions, to be furnished with a ship that will ensure the return of the aeronauts."

Should any one be disposed to insinuate, that the views now stated on this subject are chimerical and fallacious, I beg leave to remind them, that, not more than twenty years ago, the idea of a large vessel, without oars and sails, to be navigated against the wind, with the rapidity of ten miles an hour, would have been considered as next to an impossibility, and a mere fanciful scheme, which could never be realized. Yet we now behold such vehicles transporting whole villages to the places of their destination, with a degree of ease, comfort, and expedition, formerly unknown. And little more than forty years have elapsed, since it would have been viewed as still more chimerical to have broached the idea, that a machine might be constructed, by which human beings might ascend more than two miles above the surface of the earth, and fly through the region of the clouds at the rate of seventy miles an hour, carrying along with them books, instruments, and provisions. Yet both these schemes have been fully realized, and, like many other inventions of the human intellect, are doubtless intended to subserve some important ends in the economy of divine providence.†

* In this point of view, we cannot but feel the most poignant regret at the conduct of the Spaniards, after the discovery of America, towards the natives of that country. When those untutored people beheld the ships which had conveyed Columbus and his associates from the eastern world, the dresses and martial order of his troops, and heard their music, and the thunder of their cannon, they were filled with astonishment and wonder at the strange objects presented to their view; they fell prostrate at their feet, and viewed them as a superior race of men. When *Cortes* afterwards entered the territories of Mexico, the same sentiments of reverence and admiration seemed to pervade its inhabitants. Had pure Christian motives actuated the minds of these adventurers, and had it been their ruling desire to communicate to those ignorant tribes the blessings of the gospel of peace, and to administer to their external comfort, the circumstances now stated would have been highly favourable to the success of missionary exertion, and would have led them to listen with attention to the message from heaven. But, unfortunately for the cause of religion, treachery, lust, cruelty, selfishness, and the cursed love of gold, predominated over every other feeling, affixed a stigma to the Christian name, and rendered them curses instead of blessings, to that newly-discovered race of men. It is most earnestly to be wished, that, in future expeditions in quest of unknown tribes, a few intelligent and philanthropic missionaries may be appointed to direct the adventurers in their moral conduct and intercourse with the people they visit, in order that nothing inconsistent with Christian principle make its appearance. The uniform manifestation of Christian benevolence, purity, and rectitude, by a superior race of men, would win the affections of a rude people far more effectually than all the pomp and ensigns of military parade.

† Balloons were first constructed in the year 1783, by Messrs. S. and J. Mongolfier, paper manufacturers at Annonay, in France. A sheep, a cock, and a duck, were the first animals ever carried up into the air by these vehicles. At the end of their journey, they were found perfectly safe and unhurt, and the sheep was even feeding at perfect ease. The first *human* being who ascended into the atmosphere in one of these machines, was M. Pilatre de Rozier. This adventurer ascended from amidst an astonished multitude assembled in a garden in Paris, on the 15th October, 1783, in a balloon, whose diameter was 48 feet, and its height about 74; and remained suspended above the city about four hours. Mr. Lunardi, an Italian, soon after, astonished the people of England and Scotland, by his aerial excursions. Dr. G. Gregory gives the following account of his ascent:—"I was myself a spectator of the flight of Lunardi, and I never was present at a sight so interesting and sublime. The beauty of the gradual ascent, united with a sentiment of terror, on account of the danger of the man, and the novelty and grandeur of the whole appearance, are more than words can express. A delicate woman was so overcome with the spectacle, that she died upon the spot, as the balloon ascended; several fainted; and the silent admiration of the anxious multitude was beyond any thing I had ever beheld."

Balloons have been generally made of varnished silk, and of the shape of a globe or a spheroid, from thirty to fifty feet in diameter. They are filled with hydrogen gas, which, as formerly stated, is from twelve to fifteen times lighter than common air

*Acoustic Tunnels.*—By means of the inventions just now adverted to, when brought to perfection, mankind may be enabled to transport themselves to every region of the globe, with a much greater degree of rapidity that has hitherto been attained. By the help of the microscope, we are enabled to contemplate the invisible worlds of life, and by the telescope we can penetrate into regions far beyond the range of the unassisted eye. By the arts of writing and printing, we can communicate our sentiments, after a certain lapse of time, to every quarter of the world. In the progress of human knowledge and improvement, it would obviously be of considerable importance, *could we extend the range of the human voice*, and communicate intelligence to the distance of a thousand miles, in the course of two or three hours; or could we hold an occasional conversation with a friend at the distance of 20 or 30 miles. From the experiments which have been lately made, in reference to the conveyance of sound, we have some reason to believe, that such objects may not be altogether unattainable. It has been long known, that wood is a good conductor of sound. If a watch be laid on the end of a long beam of timber, its beating will be distinctly heard, on applying the ear to the other end, though it could not be heard at the same distance through the air. In "Nicholson's Philosophical Journal" for February, 1803, Mr. E. Walker describes a simple apparatus, connected with a speaking trumpet, by means of which, at the distance of 17½ feet, he held a conversation with another in whispers, too low to be heard through the air at that distance. When the ear was placed in a certain position, the words were heard as if they had been spoken by an invisible being within the trumpet. And what rendered the deception still more pleasing, the words were more distinct, softer, and more musical, than if they had been spoken through the air.

About the year 1750, a merchant of Cleves, named Jorisen, who had become almost totally deaf, sitting one day near a harpsichord, while some one was playing, and having a tobacco-pipe in his mouth, the bowl of which rested accidentally against the body of the instrument, he was agreeably and unexpectedly surprised to hear all the notes in the most distinct manner. By a little reflection and practice, he again obtained the use of this valuable sense; for he soon learned, by means of a piece of hard wood, one end of which he placed against his teeth, while another person placed the other end on his teeth, to keep up a conversation, and to be able to understand the least whisper. In this way, two persons who have stopped their ears may converse with each other, when they hold a long stick or a series of sticks between their teeth, or rest their teeth against them. The effect is the same, if the person who speaks rests the stick against his throat, or his breast, or when one rests the stick which he holds in his teeth against some vessel into which the other speaks; and the effect will be greater, the more the vessel is capable of tremulous motion. These experiments demonstrate the facility with which the softest whispers may be transmitted. Water also is found to be a good conductor of sound. Dr. Franklin assures us, that he has heard under water, at the distance of half a mile, the sound of two stones struck against each other. It has been also observed, that the *velocity* of sound is much greater in solid bodies, than in the air. By a series of experiments, instituted for the purpose of determining this point, Mr. Chladni found that the velocity of sound, in certain solid bodies, is 16 or 17 times as great as in air.

But what has a more particular bearing on the object hinted at above, is, the experiments lately made by M. Biot, "on the transmission of sound through solid bodies, and through air, in very long tubes." These experiments were made by means of long cylindrical pipes, which were constructing for conduits and aqueducts, to embellish the city of Paris. With regard to the *velocity* of sound, it was ascertained that "its transmission through cast iron is 10½ times as quick as through air." The pipes by which he wished to ascertain at what distance sounds are audible, were 1,039 yards, or nearly five furlongs, in length. M. Biot was stationed at the one end of this series of pipes, and Mr. Martin, a gentleman who assisted in the experiments, at the other. They heard the lowest voice, so as perfectly to distinguish the words, and to keep up a conversation on all the subjects of the experiments. "I wished," says M. Biot, "to determine the point at which the human voice ceases to be audible, but could not accomplish it: words spoken as low as when we whisper a secret in another's ear, were heard and understood; so that not to be heard, there was but one resource, that of not speaking at all. This mode of conversing with an invisible neighbour is so singular, that we cannot help being surprised, even though acquainted with the cause. Between a question and answer, the interval was not greater than was necessary for the transmission of sound. For Mr. Martin and me, at the distance of 1,039 yards, the time was about 5½ seconds." Reports of a pistol fired at one end, occasioned

and they rise into the atmosphere, on the same principle as a piece of cork ascends from the bottom of a pail of water. The aerial travellers are seated in a basket below the balloon, which is attached to it by means of cords. The *parachute* is an invention, by which the voyager, in cases of alarm, may be enabled to desert his balloon in mid-air, and descend, without injury, to the ground. They resemble an umbrella, but are of far greater extent. With one of these contrivances, twenty-three feet in diameter, M. Garnerin, having detached himself from his balloon, descended from a height of more than 4000 feet, and landed without shock or accident.

considerable explosion at the other. The air was driven out of the pipe with sufficient force to give the hand a smart blow, to drive light substances out of it to the distance of half a yard, and to extinguish a candle, though it was 1,039 yards distant from the place where the pistol was fired. A detailed account of these experiments may be seen in *Nicholson's Phil. Jour. for October*, 1811. Don Gautier, the inventor of the telegraph, suggested also the method of conveying articulate sounds to a great distance. He proposed to build horizontal tunnels, widening at the remoter extremity, and found that at the distance of 400 fathoms, or nearly half a mile, the ticking of a watch could be heard far better than close to the ear. He calculated that a series of such tunnels would convey a message 900 miles in an hour,

From the experiments now stated, it appears highly probable, that sounds may be conveyed to an indefinite distance. If one man can converse with another at the distance of nearly three quarters of a mile, *by means of the softest whisper*, there is every reason to believe, that they could hold a conversation at the distance of 30 or 40 miles, provided the requisite tunnels were constructed for this purpose. The latter case does not appear more wonderful than the former. Were this point fully determined, by experiments conducted on a more extensive scale, a variety of interesting effects would follow, from a practical application of the results. A person at one end of a large city, at an appointed hour, might communicate a message, or hold a conversation with his friend, at another; friends in neighbouring, or even in distant towns, might hold an occasional correspondence by articulate sounds, and recognize each other's identity by their tones of voice. In the case of sickness, accident, or death, intelligence could thus be communicated, and the tender sympathy of friends instantly exchanged. A clergyman sitting in his own room in Edinburgh, were it at any time expedient, might address a congregation in Musselburgh or Dalkeith, or even in Glasgow. He might preach the same sermon to his own church, and the next hour to an assembly at forty miles distant. And surely there could be no valid objection to trying the effect of an *invisible preacher* on a Christian audience. On similar principles, an apparatus might be constructed for augmenting the strength of the human voice, so as to make it extend its force to an assembled multitude, composed of fifty or a hundred thousand individuals; and the utility of such a power, when the mass of mankind are once thoroughly aroused to attend to rational and religious instruction, may be easily conceived. In short, intelligence respecting every important discovery, occurence, and event, might thus be communicated, through the extent of a whole kingdom, within the space of an hour after it had taken place.

Let none imagine that such a project is either chimerical or impossible. M. Biot's experiment is decisive, so far as it goes, that the *softest whisper*, without any diminution of its intensity, may be communicated to the distance of nearly three quarters of a mile; and there is nothing but actual experiment wanting to convince us, that the ordinary tones of the human voice may be conveyed to at least twenty times that distance. We are just now acting on a similar principle, in distributing illumination through large cities. Not thirty years ago, the idea of lighting our apartments by an invisible substance, produced at ten miles' distance, would have been considered as chimerical, and as impossible to be realized, as the idea of two persons conversing together, by articulate sounds, at such a distance. It appears no more wonderful, that we should be able to *hear* at the distance of five or six miles, than that we should be enabled to *see* objects at that distance by the telescope, as distinctly as if we were within a few yards of them. Both are the effects of those principles and laws which the Creator has interwoven with the system of the material world; and when man has discovered the mode of their operation, it remains with himself to apply them to his necessities. What the telescope is to the eye, acoustic tunnels would be to the ear; and thus, those senses on which our improvement in knowledge and enjoyment chiefly depends, would be gradually carried to the utmost perfection of which our station on earth will permit. And, as to the *expense* of constructing such communications for sound, the *tenth part* of the millions of money expended in the twenty-two years' war in which we were lately engaged, would, in all probability, be more than sufficient for distributing them, in numerous ramification, through the whole island of Great Britain. Even although such a project were partially to fail of success, it would be a far more honourable and useful national undertaking, than that which now occupies the attention of the despots on the continent of Europe, and might be accomplished with far less expenditure, either of blood or of money. Less than the fourth part of a million of pounds would be sufficient for trying an experiment of this kind, on an extensive scale; and such a sum is considered as a mere *item*, when fleets and armies are to be equipped for carrying destruction through sea and land. When will the war madness cease its rage! When will men desist from the work of destruction, and employ their energies and their treasures in the cause of human improvement! The most chimerical projects that were ever suggested by the most enthusiastic visionary, are not half so ridiculous, and *degrading* to the character of man, as those ambitious and despotic schemes, in which the powers of the earth in all ages have been chiefly engaged. But on this topic it is needless to enlarge, till more extended experiments shall have been undertaken.

In the preceding sketches I have presented a few specimens of the relation which the inventions of human ingenuity bear to religious objects I intended to have traced the same relation in several other instances; in the invention of the electrical machine, the air-pump, mills, clocks and watches, gas-lights, chymical fumigations, inventions for enabling us to walk upon the water, to prevent and alleviate the dangers of shipwreck, &c. &c. But, as my prescribed limits will not permit farther enlargement, I trust that what has been already stated will be sufficient to establish and illustrate my general position. From this subject we may learn—

1st. That the various processes of art, and the exertions of human ingenuity, are under the special direction of Him who arranges all things "according to the counsel of his will." As "the king's heart is in the hand of the Lord, and, as the rivers of waters, he turns it whithersoever he pleases," so all the varied schemes and movements of the human mind, the discoveries of science, and the diversified experiments of mechanics, chymists, and philosophers, are directed in such channels as may issue in the accomplishment of His eternal purposes, in respect to the present and future condition of the inhabitants of our world. This truth is also plainly taught us in the records of inspiration. "Doth the ploughman plough all day to sow? Doth he open and break the clods of his ground? When he hath made plain the face thereof, doth he not cast abroad the fitches, and scatter the cummin,* and cast in the wheat in the principal [place,] and the barley in the appointed place, and the rye in its proper place? *For his God doth instruct him to discretion, and doth teach him.* This also cometh forth from the Lord of hosts, who is wonderful in counsel, and excellent in working." Agriculture has, by most nations, been attributed to the suggestions of Deity; for "every good and perfect gift cometh down from the Father of lights." It is he who hath taught men to dig from the bowels of the earth iron, copper, lead, silver, and gold, and to apply them to useful purposes in social life; and who hath given them "wisdom and understanding" to apply the animal and vegetable productions of nature to the manufacture of cloths, linen, muslin, and silk, for the use and ornament of man." For "all things are of God." "Both riches and honour come from him, and he reigneth over all, and in his hand is power and might; and in his hand it is to make great, and to give strength to all." When the frame of the Mosaic tabernacle and all its curious vessels were to be constructed, the mind of Bezaleel "was filled with the spirit of God, in wisdom and understanding, and in knowledge, and in all manner of workmanship, to devise curious works in gold, and in silver, and in brass." And, when the fabric of the New Testament church is to be reared, and its boundaries extended, artificers of every description, adequate for carrying on the different parts of the work are raised up, and inspired with the spirit of their respective departments—some with the spirit of writing, printing, and publishing; some with the spirit of preaching, lecturing, and catechising; some with the spirit of fortitude, to make bold and daring adventures into distant and barbarous climes; and others with the spirit of literature, of science, and of the mechanical arts—all acting as pioneers "to prepare the way of the Lord," and as builders for carrying forward and completing the fabric of the Christian church.

2dly. All the mechanical contrivances to which I have adverted, all the discoveries of science, and all the useful inventions of genius which may hereafter be exhibited, ought to be viewed as preparing the way for the *millennial era* of the church, and as having a certain tendency to the melioration of the external condition of mankind during its continuance. We are certain, from the very nature of things, as well as from scriptural predictions, that, when this period advances towards the summit of its glory, the external circumstances of this world's population will be comfortable, prosperous, and greatly meliorated beyond what they have ever been in the ages that are past. "Then shall the earth yield her increase, and God, even our own God, shall bless us. Then shall he give the rain of thy seed, that thou shalt sow thy ground withal; and bread of the increase of the earth; and it shall be fat and plenteous. In that day shall thy cattle feed in large pastures; the oxen likewise and the young asses that ear the ground shall eat savoury provender, which hath been winnowed with the shovel and with the fan. And the inhabitants shall not say, I am sick. They shall build houses and inhabit them, and plant vineyards, and eat the fruit of them. They shall not build, and another inhabit; they shall not plant, and another eat; for *as the days of a tree are the days of my people*, and mine elect shall *long enjoy* the work of their hands. They shall not labour in vain, nor bring forth for trouble; for they are the seed of the blessed of the Lord, and their offspring with them. The seed shall be prosperous, the vine shall give her fruit, and the ground shall give her increase, and the heavens shall give their dew; the evil beasts shall cease out of the land, and they shall sit every man under his vine, and under his fig-tree, and none shall make him afraid; for wars shall cease to the ends of the world, and the knowledge of the

* *Fitches* is a kind of seed frequently sown in Judea, for the use of cattle: and *cummin* is the seed of a plant somewhat like fennel.

Lord shall cover the earth as the waters cover the sea."* Diseases will be, in a great measure, banished from the world, and the life of man extended far beyond its present duration—agriculture will be brought to perfection—commodious habitations erected for the comfortable accommodation of all ranks—cities built on elegant and spacious plans, adapted to health, ornament, and pleasure; divested of all the filth, and darkness, and gloom, and narrow lanes, which now disgrace the abodes of men—roads will be constructed on improved principles, with comfortable means of retreat for shelter and accommodation at all seasons; and conveyances invented for the ease, and safety, and rapid conveyance of persons and property from one place to another. Either the climates of the earth will be meliorated, by the universal cultivation of the soil, so that storms and tempests, thunders and lightnings, shall no longer produce their present ravages, or chymical and mechanical contrivances will be invented to ward off their destructive effects. The landscape of the earth will be adorned with vegetable and architectural beauty; and, instead of horse-racing, demoralizing plays, routs and masquerades, boxing and bull-baits—artificial displays of scenery will be exhibited, more congenial to the dignity of rational, renovated, and immortal minds. For "the knowlege of the Lord," and the "beauties of holiness," will pervade men of all ranks and ages, "from the least even to the greatest."†

Now, as we have no reason to expect any *miraculous interference*, we must regard the past and the future useful inventions of philosophy and mechanics, as having a bearing on this glorious period, and a tendency to promote the improvement and the felicity of those who shall live during this era of Messiah's reign. If diseases are to be generally abolished, it will be owing to the researches of the scientific physician in discovering certain antidotes against every disorder, and to the practice of temperance, meekness, equanimity of mind, and every other mean of preserving the vigour of the animal frame. If the earth is to produce its treasures in abundance, and with little labour, it will be owing in part to the improvement of agricultural science and of the instruments by which its operations are conducted. If the lightnings of heaven shall no longer prove destructive to man and to the labours of his hands, it will be effected either by machinery for drawing off the electricity of a stormy cloud, or by the invention of *thunder-guards*, which shall afford a complete protection from its ravages. In these, and numerous other instances, the inventions of men, under the guidance of the Spirit of wisdom, will have a tendency to remove a great part of the *curse* which has so long hung over our sinful world. And since the inventions of human skill and ingenuity for the melioration of mankind, and for the swift conveyance of intelligence, have, of late years, been rapidly increasing, *at the same time* when the Christian world is roused to increased exertions in disseminating the Scriptures throughout all lands, when general knowledge is increasingly diffused, and when the fabric of superstition and despotism is shaking to its foundations—these combined and simultaneous movements seem plainly to indicate, that that auspicious era is fast hastening on, when "the glory of Jehovah shall be revealed, and all flesh shall see it together," when "righteousness and praise shall spring forth before all nations," and when "holiness to the Lord" shall be inscribed on all the pursuits, and implements, and employments of men.

Lastly,—If the remarks suggested above be well founded, we may conclude, that the mechanical and philosophical inventions of genius are worthy of the attentive consideration of the enlightened Christian, particularly in the relation they may have to the accomplishment of religious objects. He should contemplate the experiments of scientific men, not as a waste of time, or the mere gratification of an idle curiosity, but as imbodying the germs of those improvements, by which civilization, domestic comfort, knowledge, and moral principle may be diffused among the nations. To view such objects with apathy and indifference, as beneath the regard of a religious character, argues a weak and limited understanding, and a contracted view of the grand operations of a superintending Providence.

* Psalm lxvii. Isaiah xxx. 23, 24, xxxiii. 24. lxv. 21, 23, &c.

† The various circumstances above stated may be considered as the *natural results* of a state of society on which the light of science and of revelation has diffused its full influence, and where the active powers of the human mind are invariably directed by the pure principles and precepts of Christianity. That the duration of human life, at the era referred to, will be extended beyond its present boundary, appears to be intimated in some of the passages above quoted particularly the following—"*As the days of a tree shall be the days of my people*, and mine elect shall *long* enjoy the work of their hands." And, if the life of man will be thus protracted to an indefinite period, it will follow, that those *diseases* which now prey upon the human frame, and cut short its vital action, will be in a great measure extirpated. Both these effects may be viewed (without supposing any miraculous interference) as the natural consequence of that happiness and equanimity of mind which will flow from the practice of Christian virtues, from the enlargement of our knowledge of the principles of nature, and from the physical enjoyments which such a state of society will furnish

# CHAPTER IV.

## SCRIPTURAL DOCTRINES AND FACTS ILLUSTRATED FROM THE SYSTEM OF NATURE.*

WITHOUT spending time in any introductory observations on this subject, it may be remarked in general,

I.—*That scientific knowledge, or an acquaintance with the system of nature, may frequently serve as a guide to the true interpretation of Scripture.*

It may be laid down as a universal principle, that there can be no real discrepancy between a just interpretation of Scripture and the facts of physical science; and on this principle, the following canon is founded, which may be considered as an infallible rule for Scripture interpretation, namely,—*That no interpretation of Scripture ought to be admitted which is inconsistent with any well-authenticated facts in the material world.* By *well-authenticated facts*, I do not mean the theories of philosophers, or the deductions they may have drawn from them, nor the confident assertions or plausible reasonings of scientific men in support of any prevailing system of natural science; but those facts which are universally admitted, and the reality of which every scientific inquirer has it in his power to ascertain: such as that the earth is not an extended plane, but a round or globular body, and that the rays of the sun, when converged to a focus by a large convex glass, will set fire to combustible substances. Such facts, when ascertained, ought to be considered as a revelation from God, as well as the declarations of his word. For they make known to us a portion of his character, of his plans and his operations.—This rule may be otherwise expressed as follows:—*Where a passage of Scripture is of doubtful meaning, or capable of different interpretations, that interpretation ought to be preferred which will best agree with the established discoveries of science.* For since the Author of revelation and the Author of universal nature is one and the same infinite being,—there must exist a complete harmony between the revelations of his word, and the facts or relations which are observed in the material universe. To suppose the contrary, would be to suppose the Almighty capable of inconsistency a supposition which would go far to shake our confidence in the theology of nature, as well as of revelation. If, in any one instance, a record claiming to be a revelation from heaven were found to contradict a well-known fact in the material world; if, for example, it asserted, in express terms, to be literally understood, that the earth is a *quiescent* body in the centre of the universe, or that the moon is no larger than a mountain; it would be a fair conclusion, either that the revelation was not divine, or that the passages imbodying such assertions are interpolations, or that science, in reference to these points, has not yet arrived at the truth. The example, we are aware, is inapplicable to the the Christian revelation, which rests securely on its own basis, and to which science is graduually approximating, as it advances in the amplitude of its views, and the correctness of its deductions;—but it shows us how necessary it is, in interpreting the *word* of God, to keep our eye fixed upon his *works;* for we may rest assured, that *truth* in the one will always correspond with fact in the other.

To illustrate the rule now laid down, an example or two may be stated. If it be a fact that geological research has ascertained that the materials of the strata of the earth are of a more ancient date than the Mosaic account of the commencement of the present race of men; the passages in the first chapter of Genesis, and other parts of Scripture, which refer to the origin of our world, must be explained as conveying the idea, that the earth was then merely *arranged* into its present form and order, out of the materials which *previously existed* in a confused mass, and which had been created by the Almighty at a prior period in duration. For Moses no where asserts, that the materials of our globe were created, or brought into existence out of nothing, at the time to which his history refers; but insinuates the contrary. "For the earth" says he, prior to its present constitution, "*was* without form and void," &c. Again, if it be a fact that the universe is indefinitely extended, that, of many millions of vast globes which diversify the voids of space, only two or three have any immediate connexion with the earth, then it will appear most reasonable to conclude, that those expressions in the Mosaic history of the creation, which refer to the creation of the fixed stars, are not to be understood as referring

* Under this head, it was originally intended to embrace an elucidation of a considerable variety of the facts recorded in sacred history, and of the allusions of the inspired writers to the system of nature; but as the volume has already swelled beyond the limits proposed, I am reluctantly compelled to confine myself to the illustration of only two or three topics

to the *time* when they were brought into existence, as if they had been created about the same time with our earth; but, as simply declaring the fact, that, at what period soever in duration they were created, *they derived their existence from God.* That they did not all commence their existence at that period, is demonstrable from the fact, that, within the space of 2000 years past, and even within the space of the two last centuries, new stars have appeared in the heavens which previously did not exist in the concave of the firmament; which, consequently, have been created since the Mosaic period; or, at least, have undergone a change analogous to that which took place in our globe, when it emerged from a chaotic state to the form and order in which we now behold it. Consequently, the phrase, "God rested from all his works," must be understood not absolutely, or in reference to the whole system of nature, but merely in relation to our world; and as importing, that the Creator then ceased to form any new species of beings *on the terraqueous globe.* The same canon will direct us in the interpretation of those passages which refer to the last judgment, and the destruction of the present constitution of our globe. When, in reference to these events, it is said, "that the stars shall fall from heaven," that "the powers of heaven shall be shaken," and that "the earth and the heaven shall flee away," our knowledge of the system of nature leads us to conclude, either that such expressions are merely metaphorical, or that they describe only the *appearance*, not the *reality* of things. For it is impossible that the stars can ever fall to the earth, since each of them is of a size vastly superior to our globe, and could never be attracted to its surface, without unhinging the laws and the fabric of universal nature. The *appearance,* however, of the "heaven fleeing away," would be produced, should the earth's diurnal rotation at that period be suddenly stopped, as will most probably happen; in which case, all nature, in this sublunary system, would be thrown into confusion, and the heavens, with all their host, would *appear* to flee away.

Now, the scientific student of Scripture alone can judiciously apply the canon to which I have adverted; he alone can appreciate its utility in the interpretation of the sacred oracles; for he knows the facts which the philosopher and the astronomer have ascertained to exist in the system of nature; from the want of which information, many divines, whose comments on Scripture have, in other respects, been judicious, have displayed their ignorance, and fallen into egregious blunders, when attempting to explain the first chapters of Genesis, and several parts of the book of Job, which have tended to bring discredit on the oracles of heaven.

II.—*The system of nature confirms and illustrates the scriptural doctrine of the* DEPRAVITY OF MAN.

In the preceding parts of this volume, I have stated several striking instances of divine benevolence, which appear in the construction of the organs of the animal system, in the constitution of the earth, the waters, and the atmosphere, and in the *variety* of beauties and sublimities which adorn the face of nature; all which proclaim, in language which can scarcely be mistaken, that the Creator has a special regard to the happiness of his creatures. Yet the Scriptures uniformly declare, that man has fallen from his primeval state of innocence, and has violated the laws of his Maker; that "his heart is deceitful above all things, and desperately wicked;" and that "destruction and misery are in his ways." Observation and experience also demonstrate, that a moral disease pervades the whole human family, from the most savage to the most civilized tribes of mankind; which has displayed its virulence in those wars and devastations which have, in all ages, convulsed the world; and which daily displays itself in those acts of injustice, fraud, oppression, malice, tyranny, and cruelty, which are perpetrated in every country, and among all the ranks even of civilized life. That a world inhabited by moral agents of this description would display, in its physical constitution, certain indications of its Creator's displeasure, is what we should naturally expect, from a consideration of those attributes of his nature with which we are acquainted. Accordingly, we find, that, amidst all the evidences of benevolence which our globe exhibits, there are not wanting certain displays of "the wrath of Heaven against the ungodliness and unrighteousness of men," in order to arouse them to a sense of their guilt, and to inspire them with reverence and awe of that Being whom they have offended. The following facts, among many others, may be considered as corroborating this position.

In the first place, *the present state of the interior strata of the earth* may be considered as a presumptive evidence, that a moral revolution has taken place since man was placed upon the globe. When we penetrate into the interior recesses of the earth, we find its different strata bent into the most irregular forms; sometimes lying horizontally, sometimes projecting upwards, and sometimes downwards, and thrown into confusion; as if some dreadful concussion had spread its ravages through every part of the solid crust of our globe. This is visible in every region of the earth. Wherever the miner penetrates among its subterraneous recesses, wherever the fissures and caverns of the earth are explored, and wherever the mountains lay bare their rugged cliffs, the marks of ruin, convulsion, and disorder meet the eye of the beholder. Evidences of these facts are to be found in the records of all intelligent travellers and geologists who have visited Alpine districts, or explored the subterraneous regions of the earth; of which I have already stated a few instances, in the article of *Geology*, pp. 74, 75, 77. These facts seem evidently to indicate that the earth is not now in the same state in which it originally proceeded from the hand of its Creator; for such a scene of disruption and derangement appears incompatible with that order, harmony, and beauty which are apparent in the other departments of nature. We dare not assert, that such terrible convulsions took place by chance, or independent of the will of the Creator; nor dare we insinuate, that they were the effects of a random display of Almighty Power; and therefore, we are necessarily led to infer, that a *moral* cause, connected with the conduct of the rational inhabitants of the globe, must have existed, to warrant so awful an interposition of divine power; for the fate of the animated beings which then peopled the earth was involved in the consequences which must have attended this terrible catastrophe. The volume of revelation, on this point, concurs with the deductions of reason, and assigns a cause adequate to warrant the production of such an extraordinary effect. "The wickedness of man was *great* upon the earth; the earth was *filled with violence;* every purpose and desire of man's heart was *only evil continually*. Man had frustrated the end of his existence; the earth was turned into a habitation of demons; the long period to which his life was protracted only served to harden him in his wickedness, and to enable him to carry his diabolical schemes to their utmost extent, till the social state of the human race became a scene of unmixed depravity and misery. And the physical effects of the punishment of this universal defection from God are presented to our view in every land, and will remain to all ages, as a visible memorial that man has rebelled against the authority of his Maker.

2. *The existence of Volcanoes, and the terrible ravages they produce*, bear testimony to the state of man as a depraved intelligence. A volcano is a mountain, generally of an immense size, from whose summit issue fire, smoke, sulphur, and torrents of melted lava, (see p. 66.) Previous to an eruption, the smoke, which is continually ascending from the *crater*, or opening in the top, increases and shoots up to an immense height; forked lightning issues from the ascending column; showers of ashes are thrown out to the distance of forty or fifty miles; volleys of red-hot stones are discharged to a great height in the air; the sky appears thick and dark; the luminaries of heaven disappear; and these terrible forebodings are accompanied with thunder, lightning, frequent concussions of the earth, and dreadful subterraneous bellowings. When these alarming appearances have continued sometimes four or five months, the lava begins to make its appearance, either boiling over the top, or forcing its way through the side of the mountain. This fiery deluge of melted minerals rolls down the declivity of the mountain, forming a dismal flaming stream, sometimes fourteen miles long, six miles broad, and 200 feet deep. In its course, it destroys orchards, vineyards, cornfields, and villages; and sometimes cities, containing twenty thousand inhabitants, have been swallowed up and consumed. Several other phenomena, of awful sublimity, sometimes accompany these eruptions. In the eruption of Vesuvius, in 1794, a shock of an earthquake was felt; and, at the same instant, a fountain of bright fire, attended with the blackest smoke, and a loud report, was seen to issue, and to rise to a great height from the cone of the mountain; and was soon succeeded by fifteen other fiery fountains, all in a direct line extending for a mile and a half downwards. This fiery scene was accompanied with the loudest thunder, the incessant reports of which, like those of a numerous heavy artillery, were attended by a continued hollow murmur, similar to that of the roaring of the ocean during a violent storm. The houses in Naples, at seven miles' distance, were for several hours in a constant tremor; the bells ringing, and doors and windows incessantly rattling and shaking. The murmur of the prayers and lamentations of a numerous population added to the horrors of the scene. All travellers, who have witnessed these eruptions, seem to be at a loss to find words sufficiently emphatic to express the terrors of the scene. "One cannot form a juster idea," says Bishop *Berkley*, "of the *noise* emitted by the mountain, than by imagining a mixed sound made up of the raging of a tempest, the murmur of a troubled sea, and the roaring of thunder and artillery, confused altogether. Though we heard this at the distance of twelve miles, yet it was *very terrible*." In 1744, the flames of Cotopaxi, in South America, rose 3,000 feet above the brink of the crater, and its roarings were heard at the distance of *six hundred miles*. "At the port of Guayaquil, 150 miles distant from the crater," says Humboldt, "we heard, day and night, the noise of this volcano, like continued discharges of a battery, and we distinguished these tremendous sounds even on the Pacific ocean."

The *ravages* produced by volcanoes are in proportion to the terror they inspire. In the eruption of Ætna, in 1669, the stream of lava destroyed, in 40 days, the habitations of 27,000 persons; and of 20,000 inhabitants of the city of Catania, only 3,000 escaped. In the year 79, the celebrated cities of Pompeii and Herculaneum were completely overwhelmed and buried under ground by an eruption of Vesuvius, and the spots on which they stood remained unknown for 1600 years. Since that period, about 40 eruptions have taken place, each of them producing the most dreadful ravages. But the volcanoes of Asia and America are still more terrible and destructive than those of Europe. The volcanic mountain Pichinca, near Quito, caused, on one occasion, the destruction of 35,000 inhabitants. In the year 1772, an eruption of a mountain in the island of Java destroyed 40 villages, and several thousands of the inhabitants; and in October, 1822, eighty-eight hamlets, and above 2000 persons, were destroyed in the same island, by a sudden eruption from a new volcano. The eruption of Tomboro, in the island of Sumbawa, in 1815, was so dreadful, that all the Moluccas, Java, Sumatra, and Borneo, to the distance of a thousand miles from the mountain, felt tremulous motions, and heard the report of explosions. In Java, at the distance of 340 miles, the clouds of ashes from the volcano produced utter darkness.

Volcanoes are more numerous than is generally imagined. They are to be found in every quarter of the world, from the icy shores of Kamtschatka to the mountains of Patagonia. Humboldt enumerates 40 volcanoes constantly burning, between Cotopaxi and the Pacific ocean; 20 have been observed in the chain of mountains that stretches along Kamtschatka; and many of them are to be seen in the Phillippines, the Moluccas, the Cape de Verd, the Sandwich, the Ladrone, and other islands in the Indian and Pacific oceans. It is stated in vol. 6th of *Sup. to Ency. Brit.* lately published, that about 205 volcanoes are known, including only those which have been active within a period to which history or tradition reaches. Europe contains 14; and, of the whole number, it is computed, that 107 are in islands and 98 on the great continents.

Can we then suppose, that so many engines of terror and destruction, dispersed over every quarter of the globe, are consistent with the conduct of a benevolent Creator towards an *innocent* race of men? If so, we must either admit that the Creator had it not in his power, when arranging our terrestrial system, to prevent the occasional action of these dreadful ravagers, or that he is indifferent to the happiness of his innocent offspring. The former admission is inconsistent with the idea of his omnipotence, and the latter with the idea of his universal benevolence. It is not therefore, enthusiasm, but the fairest deduction of reason to conclude, that they are indications of God's displeasure against a race of transgressors who have apostatized from his laws.

3. The same reasoning will apply to the ravages produced by *earthquakes*. Next to volcanoes, earthquakes are the most terrific phenomena of nature, and are even far more destructive to man, and to the labours of his hands. An earthquake, which consists in a sudden motion of the earth, is generally preceded by a rumbling sound, sometimes like that of a number of carriages driving furiously along the pavement of a street, sometimes like the rushing noise of a mighty wind, and sometimes like the explosions of artillery. Their effect on the surface of the earth is various. Sometimes it is instantaneously heaved up in a perpendicular direction, and sometimes it assumes a kind of rolling motion, from side to side. The ravages which earthquakes have produced, are terrible beyond description; and are accomplished almost in a moment. In 1692, the city of Port-Royal, in Jamaica, was destroyed by an earthquake, in the space of two minutes, and the houses sunk into a gulf forty fathoms deep. In 1693, an earthquake happened in Sicily, which either destroyed, or greatly damaged, fifty-four cities, and an incredible number of villages. The city of Catania was utterly overthrown: the sea all of a sudden began to roar; mount Ætna to send forth immense spires of flame; and immediately a shock ensued, as if all the artillery in the world had been discharged. The birds flew about astonished; the sun was darkened; the beasts ran howling from the hills; a dark cloud of dust covered the air; and, though the shock did not last three minutes, yet nineteen thousand of the inhabitants of the city perished in the ruins. This shock extended to a circumference of 7000 miles.

Earthquakes have been producing their ravages in various parts of the world, and in every age. Pliny informs us, that 12 cities in Asia Minor were swallowed up in one night. In the year 115, the city of Antioch, and a great part of the adjacent country, were buried by an earthquake. About 300 years after, it was again destroyed, along with 40,000 inhabitants; and, after an interval of only 60 years, it was a third time overturned, with the loss of not less than 60,000 souls. In 1755, Lisbon was destroyed by an earthquake, and it buried under its ruins above 50,000 inhabitants. The effects of this terrible earthquake were felt over the greater part of Europe and Africa, and even in the midst of the Atlantic ocean; and are calculated to have extended over a space of not less than four millions of square miles. In August, 1822, two-thirds of the city of Aleppo, which contained 40,000 houses, and 200,000 inhabitants, were destroyed by an earthquake, and nearly thirty thousand inhabitants were buried under the ruins. To suppose that the human beings who have been victims to the ravages of earthquakes and volcanoes, "were sinners above all those who dwelt around them," would be t height of impiety and presumption. But, fact that thousands of rational beings have been swept from existence, in a manner so horrible and tremendous, seems plainly to indicate, that they belonged to a race of apostate intelligences, who had violated the commands of their Creator. Such visitations are quite accordant to the idea of man being in the condition of a transgressor; but, if he were an *innocent* creature, they would be altogether unaccountable, as happening under the government of a Being of unbounded benevolence.

4. The phenomena of *thunder-storms, tempests, and hurricanes*, and the ravages they produce, are also presumptive proofs that man is a depraved intelligence. In that season of the year when Nature is arrayed in her most beautiful attire, and the whole terrestrial landscape tends to inspire the mind with cheerfulness—suddenly a sable cloud emerges from the horizon—the sky assumes a baleful aspect—a dismal gloom envelopes the face of nature—the lightnings flash from one end of the horizon to another—the thunders roll with awful majesty along the verge of heaven, till at length they burst over head in tremendous explosions. The sturdy oak is shattered and despoiled of its foliage; rocks are rent into shivers; and the grazing herds are struck into a lifeless group. Even *man* is not exempted from danger in the midst of this appalling scene. For hundreds in every age have fallen victims either to the direct stroke of the lightning, or to the concussions and conflagrations with which it has been attended. In tropical countries, the phenomena of thunderstorms are more dreadful and appalling, than in our temperate climate. The thunder frequently continues for days and weeks in almost one incessant roar; the rains are poured down in torrents; and the flashes of lightning follow each other in so rapid a succession, that the whole atmosphere and the surrounding hills seem to be in a blaze. In some instances, the most dreadful effects have been produced by the bursting of an electrical cloud. In 1772, a bright cloud was observed at midnight to cover a mountain in the island of Java; it emitted globes of fire so luminous, that the night became as clear as day. Its effects were astonishing. Every thing was destroyed for 7 leagues round; houses were demolished; plantations buried in the earth; and 2140 people lost their lives, besides 1500 head of cattle, and a vast number of horses and other animals.—*Ency. Brit.* Art. *Cloud.*

Is it not reasonable, then, to conclude, that such awful phenomena as storms, volcanoes, and earthquakes, are so many occasional indications of the frown of an offended Creator upon a race of transgressors, in order to arouse them to a sense of their apostacy from the God of heaven? We cannot conceive that such physical operations, accompanied by so many terrific and destructive effects, are at all compatible with the idea that man is at present in a *paradisaical* state, and possessed of that moral purity in which he was created. Such appalling displays of almighty power are in complete unison with the idea, that man is a transgressor, and that the present dispensations of God are a mixture of mercy and of judgment; but if he belong to an innocent race of moral intelligences, they appear quite anomalous, and are altogether inexplicable, on the supposition, that a Being of infinite benevolence and rectitude directs the operations of the physical and moral world; more especially when we consider the admirable care which is displayed in the construction of animal bodies, in order to prevent pain, and to produce pleasurable sensations. When man was first brought into existence, his thoughts and affections, we must suppose, were in unison with the will of his Creator; his mind was serene and unruffled; and, consequently, no foreboding apprehensions of danger would, in such a state, take possession of his breast. But after he had swerved from the path of primeval rectitude, and especially after the deluge had swept away the inhabitants of the antediluvian world, the constitution of the earth and the atmosphere seems to have undergone a mighty change, corresponding to the degraded state into which he had fallen; so that those very elements which may have formerly ministered to his enjoyment—by being formed into different combinations—now conspire to produce terror and destruction.

The same important conclusion might have been deduced, from a consideration of the immense deserts of marshes and barren sands which are dispersed over the globe—the vast and frightful regions of ice around the poles—the position of the mineral strata, and the vast disproportion which the extent of the dry land bears to the expanse of the ocean—all which circumstances, and many others, in conjunction with the facts above stated, conspire to show, that man no longer stands in the rank of a pure intelligence; and that his habitation corresponds, in some degree, to his state of moral degradation. By overlooking this consideration, St. Pierre and other naturalists have found themselves much at a loss, when attempting to vindicate the wisdom and equity of Providence, in the physical disorders which exist in the present constitution of our globe. The circumstance, that man is a fallen creature, appears the only clue to guide us in unravelling the mysteries of Providence, and to enable us to perceive the *harmony* and *consistency* of the divine operations in the system of nature; and no other consideration will fully account for the disorders which exist in the present economy of our world.

But it is a most consoling consideration, that, amidst all the physical evils which abound, the benevolence and mercy of God are admirably blended with the indications of his displeasure.

Thunder-storms and tempests contribute to the purification of the atmosphere; and volcanoes are converted into funnels for vomiting up those fiery materials which produce earthquakes, and which might otherwise swallow up whole provinces in one mighty gulf. In the *ordinary course* of things, such phenomena are more terrific than destructive; and are calculated rather to rouse an unthinking world to consideration, than to prove the instruments of human destruction. Compared with the miseries which men have voluntarily inflicted on one another, the destructive effects of the elements of nature dwindle into mere temporary and trifling accidents. We have reason to believe, that a much greater destruction of human beings has been produced by two or three of the late battles in modern Europe, such as those of Waterloo, Borodina, and Smolensko, than has been produced by all the electrical storms, earthquakes, and volcanic eruptions, which have raged for the space of a hundred years. It has been calculated, that during the Russian campaign of 1812, including men, women, and children, belonging to the French and Russians, there were not less than five hundred thousand human victims sacrificed to the demon of war. It is probable, that the destruction produced among the human race, by the convulsions of nature, since the commencement of time, (the deluge only excepted,) does not amount to above four or five millions of lives; but were we take into account the destruction of human life produced by ambition, tyranny, oppression, superstition, wars, devastations, murders, and horrid cruelties, in every period of the world, it would, doubtless, amount to several hundreds of millions. So that, amidst the most terrible displays of the displeasure of God against the sins of men, *mercy* is mingled with judgment; and while man is the greatest enemy and destroyer of his own species, benevolence is the *prominent* feature of all the arrangements of the Deity in the physical world. For "his tender mercies are over all his works."*

III.—*The discoveries which have been made in the system of nature, illustrate the doctrine of the* RESURRECTION OF THE DEAD.

The doctrine of a resurrection from the dead, at first view, appears to involve in it a variety of difficulties, and apparent contradictions. That a complex organical machine, as the human body is, consisting of thousands of diversified parts for the performance of its functions, after it has been reduced to atoms, and those atoms dispersed to "the four winds of heaven"—should be again reared up with the same materials, in a new and more glorious form—is an idea which seems to baffle the human comprehension; and, in all probability, would never have entered the mind of man, had it not been communicated by divine revelation. Accordingly we find, that the philosophers of antiquity, though many of them believed in the doctrine of a future state, never once dreamed, that the bodies of men, after they had been committed to the dust, would ever again be reanimated; and hence, when the apostle Paul proposed this doctrine to the Athenian philosophers, they scouted the idea, as if it had been the reverie of a madman. And, indeed, without a strong conviction, and a lively impression of the infinite power and intelligence of God, the mind cannot rely with unshaken confidence on the declaration of a future fact so widely different from all the obvious phenomena of nature, and from every thing that lies within the range of human experience. "If a man die," says Job, "shall he live again? There is hope of a tree, if it be cut down, that it will sprout again, and bring forth boughs like a plant. But man dieth and wasteth away; yea, man giveth up the ghost, and where is he?" When the mind, however, is frequently exercised in contemplations on the stupendous works of the Almighty, it must feel an impressive conviction, that "nothing can be too hard for Jehovah." When we endeavour to draw aside the veil which conceals many of the scenes of nature from the vulgar eye, we perceive a variety of operations and analogies, which tend to assist us in forming a conception, not only of the *possibility* of a resurrection, but also of the *manner* in which it may probably be effected, when the power of Omnipotence is interposed.

The transformations of insects afford us a beautiful illustration of this subject. All the butterflies which we see fluttering about in the summer months, were originally caterpillars. Before they arrive at that highest stage of their existence, they pass through four different transformations. The first state of a butterfly is that of an *egg*; it next assumes the form of a loathsome crawling *worm*; after remaining some time in this state, it throws off its caterpillar skin; languishes; refuses to eat; ceases to move, and is shut up, as it were, in a tomb. In this state, the animal is termed a *chrysalis*; it is covered with a thin crust or shell, and remains sometimes for six or eight months without motion, and apparently without life. After remaining its allotted time in this torpid condition, it begins to acquire new life and vigour; it bursts its imprisonment, and comes forth a butterfly with wings tinged with the most beautiful colours. It mounts the air; it ranges from flower to flower, and seems to rejoice in its new and splendid existence. How very different does it

*The facts stated in this section are expressed for the most part in the author's own words, for the sake of compression. His authorities are, Goldsmith's "Natural History," Humboldt's "Travels," Brydon's, "Tour," Sir W. Hamilton's "Observations," Raffles' "History of Java," *Ency. Brit.* Art. *Etna, Volcano, Earthquake, Antioch, Cloud;* The Literary and Scientific Journals for 1822, &c

appear in this state from what it did in the preceding stages of its existence! How unlikely did it seem that a rough, hairy, *crawling* worm, which lay for such a length of time in a death-like torpor, and enshrouded in a tomb, should be reanimated, as it were, and changed into so beautiful a form, and endowed with such powers of rapid motion! Perhaps the change to be effected on the bodies of men, at the general resurrection, may not be greater, nor more wonderful in its nature, than are the changes which take place from the first to the last stage of a caterpillar's existence. In such transformations, then, we behold a lively representation of the death and resurrection of a righteous man. "A little while he shall lie in the ground, as the seed lies in the bosom of the earth; but he shall be raised again, and shall never die any more."

There is another illustration, taken from a consideration of the chymical changes of matter, which has a still more direct bearing on the doctrine of a resurrection. We know, that substances which are invisibly incorporated with air, water, and other fluids, and which seem to be destroyed, may be made to reappear in their original form by the application of certain chymical agents. For example; put a small piece of solid camphor into a phial half filled with alcohol or spirits of wine; in a short time the camphor will be dissolved in the fluid, and the spirit will be as transparent as at first. If water be now added, it will unite with the ardent spirit, and the camphor will be separated and fall to the bottom of the phial. In this way the camphor may be nearly all recovered as at first; and, by distillation, the alcohol may also be separated from the water, and exhibited in a separate state. I have already noticed, that *carbon*, which forms an essential part of all animal and vegetable substances, is found to be not only indestructible by age, but in all its combinations, which are infinitely diversified, it still preserves its *identity*. In the state of carbonic acid it exists in union with earths and stones in unbounded quantities; and though buried for thousands of years beneath immense rocks, or in the centre of mountains, it is still carbonic acid; for no sooner is it disengaged from its dormitory than it rises with all the life and vigour of recent formation, not in the least impaired by its torpid inactivity during a lapse of ages. The beams of the theatre at Herculaneum were converted into *charcoal* (which is one of the compounds of carbon) by the lava which overflowed that city, during an eruption of Mount Vesuvius; and during the lapse of 1700 years, the charcoal has remained as entire as if it had been formed but yesterday, and it will probably continue so to the end of the world. In addition to these facts it may be stated, that provision has been made for the restoration of the fallen leaves of vegetables which rot upon the ground, and, to a careless observer, would appear to be lost for ever. It has been shown by experiment, that whenever the soil becomes charged with such matter, the oxygen of the atmosphere combines with it, and converts it into carbonic acid gas. The consequence of which is, that *this very same carbon* is, in process of time, absorbed by a new race of vegetables, which it clothes with a new foliage, and which is itself destined to undergo similar putrefaction and renovation to the end of time."*

These facts and others of a similar description which might have been stated, demonstrate, that one of the constituent parts of animal bodies remains unalterably the same, amidst all the revolutions of time, and all the changes and decompositions which take place in the system of nature: and, consequently, that though human bodies may remain in a state of putrefaction for ages in the earth and in the waters, yet their component parts remain unchanged, and in readiness to enter into a new and more glorious combination, at the command of that *Intelligence* to whom all the principles of nature and all their diversified changes are intimately known; and whose *Power* is able to direct their combinations to the accomplishment of his purposes.— Though such considerations as these may have no weight on certain unreflecting minds, that never meet with any difficulties in the economy either of nature or of redemption; yet, the man of deep reflection, who has frequently had his mind distracted with the apparent improbability of the accomplishment of certain divine declarations, will joyfully embrace such facts in the economy of nature, as a *sensible support* to his faith in the promises of his God; and will resign his body to dust and putrefaction, in the firm hope of emerging from the tomb to a future and more glorious transformation.

## IV. *The discoveries of science tend to illustrate the doctrine of the* GENERAL CONFLAGRATION.

We are informed, in the Sacred Oracles, that a period is approaching, when "the elements shall melt with fervent heat, and the earth, and the works that are therein, shall be burned up." Science has ascertained certain facts in the constitution of nature, which lead us to form some conception of the *manner* in which this awful catastrophe may probably be effected, and also of the ease with which it may be accomplished, when the destined period shall have arrived. It was formerly stated, (pp. 35, 104,) that the atmosphere, or the air we breathe, is a compound substance, composed of two very different and opposite principles, termed *oxygen* and *nitrogen*. The oxygen, which forms about a fifth part of the atmosphere, is now ascertained to be the principle of flame; a lighted taper immersed in this gas, burns with a brilliancy too

* Parkes's "Chym. Catechism," p. 266, and the additional notes.

great for the eye to bear; and even a rod of iron or steel is made to blaze under its energy.

The modern infidel, like the scoffers of old, scouts the idea of the dissolution of the world, and of the restitution of the universe, "because all things continue as they were from the beginning of the creation; not knowing the Scriptures, nor the power of God;" and not considering the principles and facts in the system of nature, which indicate the possibility of such an event. But, from the fact now stated, we may learn how easily this effect may be accomplished, even in conformity with those laws which now operate in the constitution of our globe. For should the Creator issue forth his almighty fiat—"Let the nitrogen of the atmosphere be completely separated from the oxygen, and let the oxygen exert its native energies without control, wherever it extends;"—from what we know of its nature, we are warranted to conclude, that instantly a universal conflagration would commence throughout all the kingdoms of nature—not only wood, coals, sulphur, bitumen, and other combustible substances, but even the hardest rocks and stones, and all the metals, fossils, and minerals, and water itself, which is a compound of two inflammable substances, would blaze with a rapidity which would carry destruction through the whole expanse of the terraqueous globe, and change its present aspect into that of a new world:—at the same time, all the other laws of nature might still operate as they have hitherto done since the creation of the world.

I do not mean positively to assert, that this is the agent which the Almighty will certainly employ for accomplishing this terrible catastrophe, (though we think it highly probable,) since Infinite Power is possessed of numerous resources for accomplishing its objects, which lie beyond the sphere of our knowledge and comprehension. But I have brought forward this fact, to show with what infinite ease this event may be accomplished, when Almighty Power is interposed. By means of the knowledge we have acquired of the constitution of the atmosphere, and by the aid of chymical apparatus, we can perform experiments on a *small scale*, similar in kind, though infinitely inferior in degree, to the awful event under consideration. And, therefore, we can easily conceive that He who formed the expansive atmosphere which surrounds us, and who knows the native energy of its constituent principles, may, by a simple volition, make that invisible fluid, in a few moments, the cause of the destruction of the present constitution of our world, and, at the same time, the means of its subsequent renovation. For, as fire does not annihilate, but only changes, the forms of matter, this globe on which we now tread, and which bears the marks of ruin and disruption in several parts of its structure, may come forth from the flames of the general conflagration, purified from all its physical evils, adorned with new beauties and sublimities, and rendered a fit habitation for pure intelligences, either of our own species or of another order. For, though the "heavens," or the atmosphere, "shall be dissolved, and the elements melt with fervent heat;" "yet," says the Apostle Peter, "we, according to his promise, look for new heavens and a new earth, wherein dwelleth righteousness." Whether, after being thus renovated it shall be allotted as the residence of the redeemed inhabitants of our world, is beyond our province at present to determine. But if not, it will, in all probability, be allotted as the abode of other rational beings, who may be transported from other regions, to contemplate a new province of the divine empire, or who may be immediately created for the purpose of taking possession of this renovated world. For we have reason to believe, that the energies of creating power will be continually exerted, in replenishing the boundless universe, throughout all the ages of infinite duration, and that no substances or worlds which God has created, will ever be suffered to fall into annihilation—at least, that the original atoms of matter will never be destroyed, whatever new forms they may assume, and however varied the combinations into which they may enter.

The above are only a few examples out of many which were intended to be specified, of the illustrations which the system of nature affords of the doctrines and facts of revelation, but the narrow limits of this volume prevent further enlargement.

It was also intended to follow up the preceding discussions with particular illustrations of the following topics:—The views which science affords of the *incessant energies of creating power*—the changes and revolutions which appear to have happened, and which are still going on in the distant regions of the universe, *as tending to amplify our views of the grand and multifarious objects over which Divine Providence presides—the connexion of science with a future state*—the aids which the discoveries of science afford, in enabling us to form a conception of the scenes of future felicity—of the employments of the heavenly inhabitants, and of their perpetual advances in knowledge and happiness, and in their views of the perfections of Deity—the *moral relations of intelligent beings* to their Creator, and to each other; and the *physical grounds* or *reason* of those moral laws which the Deity has promulgated for regulating the conduct, and for promoting the harmony and order of intelligent agents—illustrations of the allusions of the sacred writers to the system of the material world

—the *simultaneous progress of science and religion*, considered as an evidence of the connexion of the one with the other—the *moral effects* of the study of science in connexion with religon—replies to objections and insinuations which have been thrown out against the idea of combining the discoveries of science with the discoveries of revelation, &c. But, as illustrations of these, and various other topics connected with them, would occupy two or three hundred pages, they must, in the mean time, be postponed.*

* A work, embracing illustrations of some of the topics here stated, is preparing for the press, under the title of "*The Philosophy of Religion;* or, an illustration of the Moral Laws of the Universe, on the principles of Reason and Divine Revelation." In this work, an original, and, at the same time, a popular train of thought will be prosecuted, and the different topics will be enlivened with illustrative facts, borrowed from the scenery of nature and the moral history of mankind.

---

# CHAPTER V.

## BENEFICIAL EFFECTS WHICH MIGHT RESULT TO CHRISTIAN SOCIETY FROM CONNECTING THE DISCOVERIES OF SCIENCE WITH THE OBJECTS OF RELIGION.

I.—THE VARIETY OF TOPICS *which would be introduced into Christian instructions, by connecting them with the manifestations of Deity in the system of nature,* WOULD HAVE A TENDENCY TO ALLURE THE ATTENTION OF THE YOUNG TO RELIGIOUS SUBJECTS, *and to afford mental entertainment and moral instruction to intelligent minds of every description.*

NOVELTY and *variety* appear to be essentially requisite in order to rouse the attention, not only of the more ignorant, but even of the more intelligent class of mankind, and to excite them to make progress in the path of intellectual and moral improvement. The principle of *curiosity*, which appears at a very early period of life, and which variegated scenery and novel objects tend to stimulate and to gratify—so far from being checked and decried, in a religious point of view, as some have been disposed to do, ought to be encouraged and cultivated in the minds both of the old and of the young. As it is a principle which God himself has implanted in our natures, for wise and important purposes, it requires only to be chastened, and directed in a proper channel, in order to become one of the most powerful auxiliaries in the cause of religion, and of intellectual improvement. To gratify this principle, and to increase its activity, the Creator has adorned our globe with a combination of beauties and sublimities, strewed in endless variety over all its different regions. The hills and dales, the mountains and plains; the seas, the lakes, the rivers, the islands of every form and size which diversify the surface of the ocean; the bays, the gulfs, and peninsulas; the forests, the groves, the deep dells, and towering cliffs; the infinite variety of trees, plants, flowers, and vegetable productions of every hue, so profusely scattered over the face of nature; the diversified productions of the mineral kingdom; the variegated colouring spread over the face of nature; together with the many thousands of different species of animated beings which traverse the air, the waters, and the earth—afford so many stimuli to rouse this principle into exercise, and to direct the mind to the contemplation of the Creator. And as the earth displays an endless diversity of objects, so the heavens, in so far as they have been explored, exhibit a scenery both grand and variegated. There is not a planet in the solar system but differs from another, in its magnitude, in its distance from the central luminary about which it revolves, in the velocity of its motion, in the extent of the circle it describes around the sun, in the period of time in which its revolution is completed, in its rotation round its axis, in the number of moons with which it is attended, in the inclination of its axis to the plane of its orbit, and the diversity of seasons which results from this circumstance; in the density of its atmosphere, and the various appearances which diversify its surface. And if we were favoured with a nearer view of these majestic orbs, we should, doubtless, behold a similar variety in every part of their internal arrangements. The surface of the moon presents a variegated prospect of mountains and vales, but so very different in their form, position, and arrangement, from what obtains on the surface of our globe, that it would exhibit a scenery altogether new and uncommon to an inhabitant of this world, were he placed on the surface of that planet. Every comet, too, is distinguished from another, by its magnitude, the extent of its atmosphere, the length of its blazing tail, the rapidity of its motion, and the figure of the curve it describes around the sun. With regard to the fixed stars, which are distributed, of every size, and in every direction, through the immensity of space, our senses, as well as the declaration of an inspired writer, convince us, that, in point of brilliancy, colour, and magnitude, "one star differeth from another star in glory."

And as the system of nature in all its parts presents a boundless variety of scenery, to arouse the attention, and to gratify the desire for novelty, so the revelation of God contained in the Sacred Records displays a diversified combination of the most sublime and interesting subjects and events. Were we to form an opinion of the compass of divine revelation, from the range of subjects to which the minds of some professing Christians are confined, it might all be comprehended within the limits of five or six chapters of the New Testament; and all the rest might be thrown aside, as a dead-weight upon the Christian system. But here, as in all the other displays of the Almighty, divine perfection and providence are exhibited in the most diversified aspects. Here we have recorded a history of the creation and arrangement of our globe,—of the formation of the first human pair,—of their primeval innocence, temptation, and fall,—of the arts which were cultivated in the first ages of the world,—of the increase of human wickedness,—of the building of the ark,—of the drowning of the world by a universal deluge,—of the burning of Sodom by fire from the clouds,—of the origin of languages,—of the dividing of the Red sea,—of the journeying of the tribes of Israel through the deserts of Arabia,—of their conquest of the promised land, and their wars with the nations of Canaan,—of the corporeal translation of Elijah from earth to heaven,—of the manifestation of the son of God in human flesh, the benevolent miracles he performed, and the triumphs he obtained over all the powers of hell and earth. We are here presented with the most interesting and affecting narratives, elegies, dramatic poems, and triumphal songs,—with views of society in the earliest ages of the world, when the lives of men were prolonged to nearly a thousand years,—with splendid miracles performed in the land of Egypt, in the wilderness of Horeb, and in the "field of Zoan," when "the sun and moon stood still in their habitation;" when the waters of the great deep were divided, and mountains shook and trembled "at the presence of Jehovah,"—with the glorious marching of a whole nation through the Arabian deserts, under the guidance of a miraculous pillar of cloud and fire,—with the visits of celestial messengers, and the visible symbols of "a present Deity,"—with prophetical delineations of the present and future condition of the race of Adam,—with descriptions of the power, wisdom, love, and majesty of the Almighty, and of his operations in heaven and earth,—with the results and bearing of the economy of redemption,—with divine songs, odes, and hymns, composed by angels and inspired men,—with maxims of moral wisdom, examples of sublime eloquence, of strength of reasoning, and of manly boldness of reproof,—with proverbs, parables, allegories, exhortations, promises, threatenings, and consolatory addresses. In short, we have here detailed, in the greatest variety, history, antiquities, voyages, travels, philosophy, geography, natural and moral science, biography, arts, epic poetry, epistles, memoirs, delineations of nature, sketches of human character, moral precepts, prophecies, miracles, narrations, wonderful providences, marvellous deliverances, the phenomena of the air, the waters, and the earth; the past, the present, and the future scenes of the world—all blended together in one harmonious system, without artificial order, but with a majesty and grandeur corresponding to the style of the other works of God,—and all calculated to gratify the principle of curiosity—to convey "reproof, correction, and instruction in righteousness," and "to make the man of God perfect, and thoroughly furnished to every good work."

And, as the scenes of nature, and the scenes of revelation, are thus wonderfully diversified, in order to excite the attention of intelligent beings, and to gratify the desire for variety, so we have every reason to believe, that the scenes, objects, and dispensations, which will be displayed in the heavenly world, will be incomparably more grand and diversified. When we consider the immensity of God's universal kingdom, and the numerous systems, and worlds, and beings comprehended within its vast circumference, and that the energies of creating power may be for ever exerted in raising new worlds into existence—we may rest assured, that the desire of variety and of novelty, in holy intelligences, will be completely gratified throughout an endless succession of existence; and that the most luxuriant imagination, in its boldest excursions, can never go beyond the reality of those scenes of diversified grandeur which the heaven of heavens will display.

Now, since the book of nature, and the book of revelation, since all the manifestations of the Creator in heaven and earth, are characterized by their sublime and diversified aspect; we would ask, why should we not be imitators of God, in displaying the diversified grandeur of his kingdom of providence and of grace, before the minds of those whom we profess to instruct? Why should we confine our views to a few points in the Christian system, to a few stones in the fabric of the divine operations, when "a wide and unbounded prospect lies before us?" Why should we not rather attempt to rouse the moral and intellectual energies of mankind, from the press, in the school-room, and in the family circle, by exhibiting the boundless variety of aspect which the revelations of heaven present, and the holy tendencies of devout contemplation on the works and the ways of God? that they may learn, with intelligence, to "meditate on *all* the works of the Lord, and to talk of *all* his doings." By enlarging and diversifying the topics of religious discussion, according to the views now stated, we have it in our power to spread out an intellectual feast to allure and to gratify every variety of taste,—the young and the old, the learned and the unlearned; yea, even the careless and the ignorant, the skeptical and the dissipated, might frequently be allured by the selection of a judicious variety of striking and impressive objects and descriptions, to partake of those mental enjoyments which might ultimately issue in the happiest results. The man of an inquisitive turn of mind, who now throws aside every thing that has the appearance of religion, on account of its dulness, might have his curiosity gratified amidst such a variety as that to which I allude; and, from perceiving the bearing of every discussion on the great realities of religion and a future state, might be led to more serious inquiries after the path that leads to immortality. In a word, to associate and to amalgamate, as it were, the arts and sciences, and every department of useful knowledge, with divine subjects, is to consecrate them to their original and legitimate ends, and to present religion to the eyes of men, in its most sublime, and comprehensive, and attractive form, corresponding to what appears to be the design of the Creator, in all the manifestations he has given of himself, in the system of nature, in the operations of Providence, and in the economy of redemption.

II.—*By connecting science with religion, Christians would be enabled to take* AN EXTENSIVE SURVEY OF THE KINGDOM OF GOD.

How very narrow and limited are the views of most professors of religion respecting the universal kingdom of Jehovah, and the range of his operations! The views of some individuals are confined chiefly within the limits of their own parish, or at farthest, extend only to the blue mountains that skirt their horizon, and form the boundary of their sight. Within this narrow circle, all their ideas of God, of religion, and of the relations of intelligent beings to each other, are chiefly confined. There are others, who form an extensive class of our population, whose ideas are confined nearly to the county in which they reside, and to the adjacent districts; and there are few, comparatively, whose views extend beyond the confines of the kingdom to which they belong—though the whole island in which we reside is less than the two-thousandth part of the globe we inhabit. Of the vast extent of this earthly ball, of its figure and motions of its continents, seas, islands, and oceans, of its volcanoes and ranges of mountains, of its numerous and diversified climates and landscapes; of the various nations and tribes of mankind that people its surface, and of the moral government of God respecting them,—they are almost as completely ignorant as the untutored Greenlander, or the roving savage. With regard to the objects which lie beyond the boundary of our world, they have no precise and definite conceptions. When the moon is "walking in brightness" through the heavens, they take the advantage of her light to prosecute their journeys; and, when the sky is overcast with clouds, and they are anxious to travel a few miles to their destined homes, they will lift up their eyes to the heavens to see if any of the stars are twinkling through the gloom, that their footsteps may be directed by their glimmering rays. Beyond this they seldom soar. What may be the nature of the vast assemblage of shining points which adorn the canopy of their habitation, and the ends they are destined to accomplish in the plan of the Creator's operations, they consider as no part of their province to inquire.

"Their minds, fair science never taught to stray
Far as the solar worlds, or milky way."

How very different, in point of variety, of grandeur, and of extent, are the views of the man who connects all the different departments of knowledge, and the discoveries of science, with his prospects of God's universal dominion and government? With his mental eye he can traverse the different regions of the earth, and penetrate into the most distant and retired recesses where human beings have their residence. —He can contemplate and adore the conduct of divine sovereignty, in leaving so many nations to grope amidst the darkness of heathen idolatry,—he can trace the beams of the Sun of righteousness, as they gradually rise to illumine the benighted tribes of men,—he can direct his prayers, with intelligence and fervour, in behalf of particular kindreds and people,—he can devise, with judgment and discrimination, schemes for carrying the "Salvation of God" into effect, —he can realize, in some measure, to his mental sight, the glorious and happy scenes which will be displayed in the future ages of time, when "the kingdoms of this world shall become the kingdom of our Lord, and of his Christ," and when the "everlasting gospel" shall be published, and its blessings distributed among all who dwell upon the face of the earth. He can bound from this earth to the planetary worlds and survey far more spacious globes, peopled with a higher order of intelligences, arranged and superintended by the same Almighty Sovereign, who "doth according to his will among the inhabitants of the earth." He can wing his way beyond the visible region of the sky, till he find himself surrounded on every hand with suns and systems of worlds, rising to view in boundless perspective, throughout the tracts of immensity—diversified with scenes of magnificence, and with beings of every order—all under the government and the wise direction of Him who "rules among the armies of heaven," and who "preserveth them all," and whom the "host of heaven worship" and adore. He can soar beyond them all to the throne of God, where angels and archangels, cherubim and seraphim, celebrate the praises of their Sovereign Lord, and stand ready to announce his will, by their rapid flight to the most distant provinces of his empire. He can descend from that lofty eminence to this terrestrial world, allotted for his temporary abode, and survey another unbounded province of the empire of God, in those living worlds which lie hid from the unassisted sight, and which the microscope alone can descry. He can here perceive the same Hand and Intelligence which direct the rolling worlds above, and marshal all the angelic tribes—organizing, arranging, and governing the countless myriads of animated existence which people the surface of a muddy pool. He can speed his course from one of these departments of Jehovah's kingdom to another, till, astonished and overwhelmed with the order, the grandeur, and extent of the wondrous scene, he is constrained to exclaim, "Great and marvellous are thy works, Lord God Almighty!" "Thine understanding is infinite!" The limits of thy dominions are "past finding out!"

By taking such extensive surveys of the empire of Jehovah, we are enabled to perceive the spirit and references of those sublime passages in the sacred writings which proclaim the majesty of God, and the glory of his kingdom. Such passages are diffusely scattered through the inspired volume, and have evidently an extent of reference far beyond what is generally conceived by the great mass of the Christian world. The following may suffice as a specimen:—

"Thine, O Lord! is the greatness, and the glory, and the majesty; for all in heaven and earth is thine! Thine is the kingdom, O Lord! Thou art exalted above all, thou reignest over all, and in thine hand is power and might.—Behold, the heaven, and the heaven of heavens, is the Lord's; the earth also, with all that therein is. —Ascribe ye greatness to our God; for there is none like unto the God of Israel, who rideth upon the heavens in his strength, and in his excellency on the sky. Thou, even thou, art Lord alone; thou hast made heaven, the heaven of heavens, with all their host; the earth, and all things that are therein; the sea, and all that is therein; and thou preservest them all, and the host of heaven worshippeth thee.—He divideth the sea by his power; by his Spirit he hath garnished the heavens: Lo! these are only parts of his ways; but how little a portion is heard of him, and the thunder of his power who can understand?—The Lord hath prepared his throne in the heavens, and his kingdom ruleth over all.—O Lord our God! how excellent is thy name in all the earth! who hast set thy glory above the heavens. When I consider thy heavens, the work of thy fingers, the moon and the stars, which thou hast ordained; what is *man*, that thou art mindful of him!—His kingdom is an everlasting kingdom honour and majesty are before him; *all the inhabitants of the earth are reputed as nothing in his sight*, and he doth according to his will in the army of heaven, and among the inhabitants of the earth.—He measures the waters in the hollow of his hand; he meteth out heaven with a span, and comprehendeth the dust of the earth in a measure.—He sitteth upon the circle of the earth, and the inhabitants thereof are as grasshoppers.—I have made the earth, and created man upon it; I, even my hands, have stretched out the heavens, and all their host have I commanded.—The Most High dwelleth not in temples made with hands; for the heaven is his throne, and the earth is his footstool.—With God is awful majesty.—Great things doth He, which we cannot comprehend; yea, the Lord sitteth King for ever.—Praise ye the Lord in the heavens; praise him in the heights; praise him, all his angels; praise ye him, all his hosts. Praise him, sun and moon; praise him, all ye stars of light; praise him, ye heaven of heavens. Praise him, ye kings of the earth, and all people, princes and judges of the earth; both young men and maidens; old men and children—let them praise the name of the Lord; for his name alone is excellent, his glory is above the earth and heaven."

These sublime descriptions of the supremacy of God, and of the grandeur of his kingdom, must convince every reflecting mind, of the inconceivable magnificence and extent of that dominion "which ruleth over all." It is quite evident, that we can never enter, with intelligence, into the full import and the grand references of such exalted language employed by inspired writers, unless we take into view all the discoveries which science has made, both in the earth and in the heavens, respecting the variety and extent of the dominions of the Creator. If the "kingdom of the most High" were as limited in its range as most Christians seem to conceive, such descriptions might be considered as mere hyperboles, or bombast, or extravagant declamation, which far exceeds the bounds of "truth and soberness." But we are certain, that the conceptions and the language of mortals can never go beyond the reality of what actually exists within the boundless precincts of Jehovah's empire. For "who can utter the mighty acts of the Lord?" or "who can show forth *all* his praise?" The language and descriptions to which we have now adverted, seem to have had a prospective reference to later and more enlightened times, when more extensive prospects of God's dominions would be opened up by the exertions of human intellect. And were we to search the records of literature, in ancient or modern times, we should find no descriptions nor language of such dignified nature as to express the views and feelings of an enlightened Christian philosopher, when he contemplates the sublimity and extent of divine operations—except those which are to be found in the inspired volume—the strength, and majesty, and comprehension of which no human language can ever exceed.

Again, by familiarizing our minds to such extended prospects of God's universal kingdom, we shall be qualified and disposed to comply with the injunctions of Scripture, which represent it as an imperious duty, *to communicate to the minds of others such elevated conceptions.* This duty is enjoined in numerous passages of Sacred Scripture, particularly in the book of Psalms: "Declare his glory among the heathen, and his wonders among all people.—I will extol thee, my God, O King.—One generation shall praise thy works to another, and shall declare thy mighty acts.—I will speak of the glorious honour of thy majesty, and of thy wondrous works. And men shall speak of the might of thy terrible acts; and shall declare thy greatness. All thy works shall praise thee, O Lord; and thy saints shall bless thee. *They shall speak of the glory of thy kingdom, and talk of thy power; to make known to the sons of men thy mighty acts, and the glorious majesty of thy kingdom.*"* When we look around us in the world, and in the visible church, and mark the conceptions and the conversation of the members of religious societies, we need scarcely say how little this ennobling duty is attended to by by the mass of those who bear the Christian name. We hear abundance of idle chat about the fashions and the politics of the day—how Miss A. danced so gracefully at the ball, and how Miss B. sung so sweetly at the concert; how Mr. C. acted his part so well in the character of Rob Roy, and how Mr. D. made such a flaming speech at the corporation dinner. We listen to slanderous conversation, and hear abundance of mean, and base, and uncharitable insinuations against our neighbours; which indicate the operation of malice, hatred, envy, and other malevolent tempers. We spend whole hours in boisterous disputations about metaphysical subtleties in religion, and questions "which gender strife rather than godly edifying;" but "to speak of the glory of God's kingdom, and to talk of his *power*," with the view of "making known to the sons of men his mighty works," is a duty which remains yet to be learned by a majority of those who profess the religion of Jesus. And how can they be supposed to be qualified to enter into the spirit of this duty, and to proclaim to others "the glorious majesty of God's kingdom," unless such subjects be illustrated in *minute detail*, and proclaimed with becoming energy, both from the pulpit and from the press? These powerful engines, when conducted with judgment and discrimination, are capable of producing on the mass of mankind a tone of thinking, and an enlargement of conception, on such subjects, which no other means can easily effect; and it is to be hoped, that more precise and luminous details, and more vigour and animation, will soon be displayed, in this respect, than in the ages that are past.

There is a certain principle of *selfishness* which pervades the minds of many professed religionists, which leads them to conclude, that, if they can but secure their own *personal salvation*, they need give themselves no trouble about the glory and extent of the kingdom of the Most High. "What need we care," say they, "about nations in the far-distant parts of the world, and about the planets and the stars; our business is to attend to the spiritual interests of our souls." Such persons seem neither to understand in what salvation really consists, and what is conducive to their spiritual interests, nor to appreciate those tempers and habits which will qualify them for the enjoyment of eternal life. It forms but a very slender evidence of their possessing any spark of Christianity at all, if they wish to rest satisfied with the most vague and grovelling conceptions, and if they do not ardently aspire after a more enlarged view of the attributes of God, of the glory of his empire, and of whatever may tend to expand their conceptions of "the inheritance of the saints in light." We have often been astonished at the opinions of some of those who move in a higher sphere of intelligence, who seem to consider it as a matter of *pure indifference*, whether or not Christians should attain to the highest conception in their power of the God whom they worship, and of his boundless dominions; because they conceive that such views are not essentially connected with salvation? Though they may not have been essential to the salvation of men in the dark ages that are past, or to obscure tribes of people at present, who have no access to the proper sources of information, yet, since God, in the course of his providence, which guides all human inventions and discoveries, has disclosed to us a far more expansive view of the "glory of his kingdom," than former ages could obtain, for the purpose of illustrating the revelations of his word—who will dare to assert, that the man who has access, by his studious efforts, to contemplate this wondrous scene, and to display its grandeur to others, and yet wilfully shuts his eyes on the divine glory therein displayed, does not thereby hazard the

* Psalm cxlv. and xcvi. 3, 4

divine displeasure? In this point of view, the following passage deserves a serious consideration: "Because they regard not the works of the Lord, nor the operations of his hands, he shall destroy them, and not build them up." We have no hesitation in admitting, that persons may have obtained salvation who never saw more of the sacred writings than what is contained in the gospel of Mark, or in one of Paul's epistles; but what would we say of the man who had access to all the revelations of heaven we now possess, and yet confined his attention solely to a chapter or two in the New Testament, and would not deign to look into any other part of the inspired volume? We should not hesitate at once to pronounce that such a person was grossly deficient in his duty, and devoid of that reverence and submission which are due to the oracles of God. And, if it be admitted, that the person who has access to the bible, and who refuses to peruse its important contents, is guilty of a criminal neglect, we do not see how the man, who has free access to the other volume of God's revelation, and views it as a matter of mere indifference whether he looks into into it or not, can be deemed, in this respect, entirely innocent. If it be understood, that we shall be judged according to the light and privileges we enjoy, and the use we make of them, in our improvement in the knowledge of God—we would deem it a hazardous position for any one to support, that "inattention to the visible glories of the kingdom of God, and to the 'declaration of his wonders among the people,' is a matter either of indifference or of trivial importance."

For, let it be considered, further—*that on the extent of our views respecting the universal kingdom of God depends our conceptions of the majesty and glory of the Creator himself.* We become acquainted with the nature of God, only in so far as he has manifested himself to us by external operations,* and in so far as we form just conceptions of these operations. If we conceive his empire as included within the bounds of eighty or ninety thousand miles, our conceptions of the Sovereign of that empire will be circumscribed within nearly the same limits. The mind of every reasonable man must, indeed, admit the abstract proposition, "That the Divine Being is infinite, and, consequently, fills all space with his presence." But this infinity, in our view, is nothing more than *a vague conception of empty space, extending a little way beyond the sphere of his visible operations.* The mind must have some material, visible, or tangible objects to rest upon, and to guide it in its excursions, when it would attempt to form the most definite and comprehensive conceptions of an infinite, eternal, and invisible existence. For however much we may talk about purely *spiritual ideas*, it is quite evident, from the nature of things, and from the very constitution of man, that we can have no ideas at all without the intervention of *sensible objects.* And, therefore, if we would wish to form the most sublime conceptions of God himself, we must endeavour, in the first place, to take the most extensive views which science and revelation exhibit, of his vast dominions. We must endeavour to form some adequate idea of the wide extent of the globe on which we dwell, its diversified scenery, and the numerous tribes of human beings, and other animated existences, visible and invisible, which people its different provinces. We must explore the vast regions of the planetary system, and compare the bulk of the earth, large as it is, with some of those more magnificent globes, which would contain a thousand worlds as large as ours. We must next wing our way, in imagination, over a space which a cannon-ball, flying five hundred miles every hour, would not traverse in ten hundred thousand years, till we arrive at the nearest fixed stars, and find ourselves in the centre of thousands of systems and worlds, arranged at immeasurable distances from one another. We must pass from one nebula, or cluster of systems, to another; continuing our excursions as far as the eye or the telescope can direct our view; and, when the aid of artificial instruments begins to fail, our imagination must still take its flight far beyond the boundaries of mortal vision, and add system to system, and nebula to nebula, through the boundless regions of space, till we arrive at the grand centre of the universe, the throne of God, around which all worlds and beings revolve, where "thousands thousands" of bright intelligences "minister to Him, and ten thousand times ten thousand stand before him." We must consider all this magnificent assemblage of objects, not merely as so many masses of inert matter, or as a grand raree-show, to dazzle the eyes of a few hundreds of human spectators,—but as destined for purposes worthy of the plans and the intelligence of Him who is "the only wise God,"—as peopled with numerous orders of intelligent beings, whose physical and moral economy is superintended and directed by Him, who, at the same time, rules amidst the tumults of human revolutions, and governs the living myriads which people a drop of water.

In this way, then, do we come to acquire the most extensive views of the amplitude and glory of the kingdom of the Most High; and it is only by the same process of thought that we can ever attain the most exalted conceptions of the attributes of its almighty Sovereign. For our views of the Sovereign of the universe must always correspond with our views of the extent and magnificence of those dominions which sprung from his creating hand, and over which he every moment presides. His essence must for ever remain im-

* Here I include the manifestations of Deity, as exhibited both in divine revelation, and in the system of nature.

perceptible to finite minds; for he is "the King eternal, immortal, and *invisible*, dwelling in that light which no man can approach unto, whom no man hath seen, or *can see*." From his nature, as a spiritual uncompounded substance, and from his immensity, as filling infinite space with his presence, it appears impossible, in the very nature of things, that the glory of his perfections can be displayed in any other way than through the medium of the visible operations of his hands, or in the dispensations of his providence towards particular worlds or classes of intelligences. And if, in the future world, the souls of good men will enjoy a more glorious display than at present, of the attributes of Deity, it will be owing chiefly to their being placed in more favourable circumstances than they now are, for contemplating this display; to their faculties being more invigorated; and every physical and moral impediment to their exercise being completely removed; so as to enable them to perceive more clearly than they now do, the unbounded displays he has given of his power, wisdom, and benevolence. And, if we expect to be introduced to this state of enlarged vision, when we pass from the scenes of mortality, it cannot be a matter of *mere indifference*, even now, whether or not our minds are prepared for such exalted employments, by endeavouring to form the most ample conceptions of the attributes of God which can be obtained through the medium of his word, and by a contemplation of the variety and magnificence of his works. In the prospect of that world where we hope to spend an interminable existence, it must also be interesting to ascertain, whether or not the dominions of the universal Sovereign present such an extent of empire, and such a variety of objects, that new scenes of wonder and glory may be expected to be displayed in continual succession, for the contemplation and entertainment of holy beings, while eternal ages are rolling on. And, on this point, the discoveries of science confirm and illustrate the notices of heavenly glory and felicity recorded in the inspired volume, and lead us to rest with full assurance on the prophetic declaration, that "eye hath not seen, nor ear heard, nor hath it entered into the heart of man to conceive, the things which God hath prepared for them that love him."

III.—*By connecting the discoveries of science with religion, the minds of Christians would be enabled to take a more minute and comprehensive survey of the* OPERATIONS OF PROVIDENCE.

Providence is that superintendence and care which God exercises over all creatures and events, in order to accomplish the eternal purposes of his will. In *creation*, God brought the universe out of nothing, and arranged all its provinces and inhabitants in due order. By his *providence* he supports and governs all the movements of the mat rial system, and the sensitive and rational beings with which it is peopled. It is evident, that, in proportion as our views of the Creator's dominions are extended, our views of his providence will, to a certain extent, be proportionably enlarged. For wherever worlds and beings exist, there will God be found, preserving, superintending, and governing the movements of all creatures and events. It is chiefly, however, in the world in which we reside, that the diversified dispensations of Providence can be distinctly traced. Now an acquaintance with the prominent parts of the different branches of knowledge to which I have already adverted, would enable us to take a particular and comprehensive view, not only of the ways of God to man, but also of his arrangements in reference to all subordinate creatures and events.

From the inspired history of the Old Testament, we can trace the prominent lines of the dispensations of God towards man, particularly in regard to the Israelites and the surrounding nations—from the creation to a period about 400 years before the coming of Christ. But in order to perceive the farther progress and bearings of these lines till the commencement of the New Testament economy, we must have recourse to the most authentic records of profane history. From the era of the birth of Christ to near the close of the first century, we can acquire, from the evangelists and the history of the apostles, a particular account of the life of Christ, of the events which preceded and accompanied the finishing of the work of redemption, and of the progress of the gospel through Judea and the adjacent countries. But after this period we have no *inspired* guide to direct us in tracing the divine dispensations towards the various nations of the earth; and, therefore, we must have recourse to the annals, memoirs, chronicles, and other records of the history of nations, down to the period in which we live; otherwise we could never contemplate the continued series of events in the divine economy towards the inhabitants of our world. Unless men of learning and of observation had recorded the prominent facts which have occurred in the history of nations, for 1700 years past, we must have remained almost as ignorant of the dispensations of God towards our race, during that period, as the inhabitants of the planet Saturn: and unless we study the events thus recorded in the writings of the historian, and contemplate their varied aspects and bearings in the light of divine revelation, we must still remain ignorant of the grand movements and tendencies of divine providence. This single circumstance shows, in the clearest light, that it is the intention of God, that we should learn the operations of his providence from the researches of science and history, as well as from the records of revelation; and that the scriptures, though they contain every *supernatural* discovery requisite to our happiness, are not of themselves sufficient to present us with a connected view of the prominent dispensations of heaven, from the creation to the period in which we live.

From the science of *geography* we acquire a knowledge of the extent of the surface of the earth—of the various tribes of human inhabitants with which it is peopled—of the physical aspect of the different climates they inhabit—of their arts, manners, customs, laws, religion, vices, wars, and political economy: and, consequently, we can, in these and similar respects, trace some of the aspects of Divine Providence towards them in relation to their present and future condition. From the same source, we learn the number of human beings which the Governor of the world has under his direction at one time, which is nearly a thousand millions, or five hundred times the number of the inhabitants of Scotland. From the data afforded by this science, we may also form an estimate of the number of disembodied spirits that have passed from this world since the creation, and are now under the superintendence of the Almighty in the invisible state, which cannot be much less than 145,000 millions; and on similar grounds we may also learn the number of rational beings that are coming forward into existence, and passing into the eternal world every day, which is at least 68,000, and, consequently, nearly 50 during each passing minute,—every individual of which, the Supreme Disposer of events superintends at his entrance into life; and, at his departure from it, directs to his respective and eternal state of destination. All which circumstances, and many others of a similar kind, must be taken into account, in order to our forming a comprehensive conception of the numerous bearings and the incessant agency of a Superintending Providence.

From *natural history* we learn the immense number and variety of the subordinate tribes of animated beings which inhabit the different regions of earth, air, and sea—their economy and instincts—their modes of existence, and the manner in which the Creator provides for their various necessities. From an acquaintance with the *history of the arts and mechanical inventions*, we learn the gradual manner in which God directs the movements of the human mind, in making those improvements and discoveries which have a bearing upon the accomplishment of his eternal plans of mercy, and which tend to enlarge our views of the amplitude and the glories of his kingdom. From *natural philosophy* and *chymistry*, we learn the secondary causes or subordinate laws by which the Almighty supports and directs the natural constitution of the world —the wonderful manner in which our lives are every moment supported—and the agencies by which fire, air, light, heat, and fertility are distributed through the globe, for promoting the comfort and happiness "of every thing that lives." From *anatomy* and *physiology*, we learn, how "fearfully and wonderfully we are made and preserved"—that our health and comfort depend upon the regular action of a thousand organical parts and functions, over which we have no control—and that our very existence every moment is dependent on the superintendence of a Superior Power, "in whose hand our breath is, and whose are all our ways."

By an occasional study, then, of the subjects to which we have now alluded, we would gradually expand our conceptions of the range and operations of Divine Providence. Every geographical exploration of a new region of the globe—every scientific improvement and discovery—every useful invention—every eruption of a volcano—every shock of an earthquake—every hurricane, and storm, and tempest—every battle of the warrior—every revolution among the nations—and every detail in the newspapers we daily read, would lead us to form some conceptions of the providential purposes of Him who is the Supreme Disposer of all events.—Even the arrangements of Divine Wisdom, with regard to the economy of the lower animals, ought not to be overlooked in such a survey. When we consider the immense number and variety of animated beings—that there are 500 species of quadrupeds, every species containing, perhaps, many millions of individuals; 4000 species of birds; 2500 species of fishes; 700 species of reptiles; and 44,000 different kinds of insects, besides many thousands of species altogether invisible to the unassisted sight—when we consider that the structure and organization of all these different species are different from each other, and exactly adapted to their various situations and modes of existence, and that their multifarious wants, in regard to food and habitation, are all provided for, and amply supplied by Him, who, at the same time, arranges and governs the affairs of ten thousand worlds—we must be lost in astonishment at the greatness of that Intelligence which formed them, and at the exuberance of that Bounty which spreads so full a table for so immense an assemblage of living beings! And were we transported to other worlds, we should, doubtless, behold still more ample displays of Divine Beneficence.

We are here presented with a striking commentary on such passages of the sacred volume as these: "The eyes of all look unto Thee, O Lord! and thou givest them their meat in due season. Thou openest thy hand liberally, and satisfiest the desire of every living thing. The earth is full of thy riches, O Lord! so is the great and wide sea, wherein are things creeping innumerable, both great and small beasts. These all wait upon thee, and thou givest them their meat in due season. That which thou givest them they gather: Thou openest thy hand, they are filled with good."—"O Lord, thou preservest man and beast! How excellent is thy loving-kindness! Therefore the children of men shall put their trust under the shadow of thy wings: They shall be abundantly satisfied with the fatness of thy house,"* (of the table thou hast spread in thy world for all thine offspring,) "and thou shall make them drink of the river of thy pleasures." One excellent practical effect which might flow from such contemplations would be, to inspire us with feelings of humanity towards the inferior order of animals, and to prevent us from wantonly and unnecessarily torturing, or depriving them of existence. For since the Creator and Preserver of all has so curiously organized their bodies, and fitted them for the different regions in which they reside, and so carefully provided for all their wants, it must be His will that they should enjoy happiness according to the extent of their capacities; and, therefore, they ought to be considered as necessary parts of our sublunary system. Another practical lesson we may derive from such surveys, is, to place an unshaken dependence upon God for our temporal subsistence, while we, at the same time, exert all our faculties in the line of active duty. "Blessed is the man who trusteth in him; for there is no want to them that fear him. The young lions may suffer hunger, but they that fear the Lord shall not want any good thing." He who decks the lily of the vale, and spreads out a plentiful table to the fowls of heaven, to the beasts of the forests, to the creeping insects, and even to the microscopic animalculæ, will never fail to supply the necessary wants of those who "do His will, and hearken to the voice of his commandments." And if, at any time, we be found destitute of daily food, and pining away in penury and squalid disease, we have too much reason to conclude, that in one way or another, either our deviation from the path of rectitude, or our distrust of divine providence, or our want of prudence and economy, has procured for us these things.

I have said, that it is chiefly in the world in which we dwell, that the dispensations of Providence can be distinctly traced. But we must nevertheless admit that the care and superintendence of God are as minutely exercised in the distant regions of the universe as in our terrestrial sphere; though we are not permitted, at present, to inspect the particular details of His procedure in reference to other orders of intelligences. We are not, however, altogether ignorant of some prominent features of the physical and moral economy of other worlds, in consequence of the discoveries of modern astronomical science.

With respect to their *physical* economy, we behold a striking variety in the divine arrangements. We perceive one planetary world surrounded by two splendid and magnificent rings, one of them 204,000, and the other 184,000 miles in diameter, stretching across its celestial canopy from one end of the heavens to another—moving with majestic grandeur around its inhabitants every ten hours, and diffusing a light equal to several thousands of moons like ours—which may be considered as a visible and permanent emblem of the majesty and glory of their Creator. We perceive connected with the same globe, seven moons, all larger than ours, of different magnitudes, and placed at different distances, and revolving in different periods of time around that spacious world. The diversified aspects of these rings, as viewed from the different regions of the planet at different times, and the variety of appearances produced by the alternate rising and setting, culmination, and frequent eclipses, and other aspects of the moons, must present to the inhabitants a very grand and varied and magnificent scene of divine operation.* On the other hand, we behold another planetary globe, destitute both of rings and moons, but which has the starry heavens presented to view nearly in the same aspect in which we behold them. We perceive a third globe much larger than them both, capable of containing 200 times the number of the inhabitants of our world—accompanied in its course with four moons to diffuse light in the absence of the sun, and to diversify the aspect of its sky. In some of these worlds, the succession of day and night is accomplished within the space of ten hours; in others, this revolution is not completed till after the lapse of twenty-four hours, or of as many days. In some, the days and nights are nearly equal on every part of their surface, and they have little variety of seasons; in others, the variety in the length of the days, and the vicissitudes of the seasons, are nearly the same as those we experience in our terrestrial world. Around some there appears a dense atmosphere, while others are environed with atmospheres more rare and transparent. Some move in the vicinity of the sun, and enjoy an abundant efflux of light and heat, while others are removed to the distance of eighteen hundred millions of miles from that central luminary. Some finish the revolution of their year in a few months; while others require twelve, thirty, or even eighty of our years to complete their annual round. Some appear

* This, and several other similar passages, may be considered as more especially applicable to the bounty of providence which God has provided for all his creatures. The practice of *spiritualizing* such passages, as it is termed, has a tendency to caricature Scripture, and to twist it from its precise and sublime references, to accord with the vague fancies of injudicious minds. The literal meaning of Scripture is always the most appropriate, emphatic, and sublime; but it may, in some cases, be used by way of accommodation, in illustrating divine subjects, when it is applied with judgment and discrimination.

* See the plate, Fig. 7

adorned with majestic mountain scenery, and others seem to have great changes occasionally taking place in their atmosphere, or on their surfaces. There are four planetary bodies lately discovered, which, there is every reason to believe, once formed the component parts of a large globe; but by some mighty catastrophe in the dispensations of heaven, it appears to have been burst asunder into the fragments we now behold. If the general proposition illustrated in section 2. of the preceding chapter be admitted, such a fact would seem to indicate that a moral revolution has taken place among the intelligent beings who had originally been placed in those regions; and that their fate was involved in the dreadful shock which burst asunder the globe they inhabited; just as the fate of the antediluvians was involved in the shock by which the solid crust of our globe was disrupted, at the period of the universal deluge.

These are some outlines in the economy of Providence which we can trace with regard to the arrangements of other worlds; but beyond such general aspects we are not permitted to penetrate, so long as we sojourn in tabernacles of clay. But even such general views afford some scope to the contemplative mind, for forming enlarged conceptions of the grandeur and diversity of the dispensations of God, in the worlds which roll in the distant regions of space.

With regard to their *moral economy*—we may rest assured that the prominent outlines of it are materially the same as of that economy which relates to the inhabitants of our world. The fundamental principles of the moral laws given to men, and which it is the great object of revelation to support and illustrate, are, "Thou shalt love the Lord thy God with all thy heart and understanding," and, "Thou shalt love thy neighbour as thyself." On these two commandments hang all the law and the prophets. Now, we must admit, from the nature of the Divine Being, and from the relations in which rational beings stand to Him and to one another, that the Creator has enacted these laws, as the great governing principles by which the actions of all intelligences in heaven, as well as upon earth, are to be directed. For the Governor of the world can never be supposed to issue a law to any order of rational creatures, which would permit them to *hate* their Creator, or to hate those whom he has formed after his own image. Such a supposition would be inconsistent with the eternal rules of rectitude, and with the perfections of Deity—and the fact supposed, (if it could exist,) would introduce confusion and misery throughout the whole intelligent universe. And, therefore, we must necessarily admit, that the laws to which I now advert, are binding upon all the rational inhabitants which exist throughout Jehovah's dominions; and that it is by these that the moral order of all the principalities and powers of heaven is preserved and directed. In those worlds where there is no change in the succession of their inhabitants—or, in other words, where there is no death, or where they are not produced by any process analogous to generation, but have a fixed and permanent residence, there will be no need for moral precepts corresponding to the fifth and the seventh commandments of our moral law; and in those worlds where property is common, and the bounties of the Creator are equally enjoyed by all, there will be no necessity for a law corresponding to the eighth commandment; but the general principles on which these laws are founded, will be applicable to all the other circumstances and relations which actually exist; so that the *principle*, and *spirit*, and *essence* of our religion must be common to all the holy inhabitants of the universe. And, therefore, it will follow, that every intelligent being that is animated and directed by such principles and affections, will be qualified for holding delightful intercourse with all holy beings throughout the universe of God, in whatever province of the Creator's empire he may hereafter be placed; and, to qualify us for such harmonious and affectionate intercourse, is one great end of the salvation exhibited in the gospel. So that, although we cannot, in our present state, acquire a minute and comprehensive knowledge of the moral history of other worlds, of the special interpositions or manifestations of Deity in relation to them, or of the means by which they are carried forward in moral and intellectual improvement—yet we can trace the *general* principles or laws which form the basis of their moral and religious economy. For as the laws of optics, and the principle of gravitation, pervade the whole material system, as far as the universe is visible to our assisted vision, so the principle of supreme love to God, and sincere affection to fellow-intelligences, must pervade the *intellectual* universe, wherever it extends; and, if any intelligent agents besides men, have violated these laws, they must experience pain, and misery, and disorder, analogous to those which are felt by the inhabitants of our apostate world.

Thus I have endeavoured to show, that the combination of science with religion would tend to expand our views of divine providence—in the various arrangements of God, in relation to the human race, and to the subordinate tribes of sensitive beings—and in reference to some of the prominent features of his administration in distant worlds. And, therefore, though the Christian ought never to overlook the ways of Providence in relation to himself, and to his spiritual and domestic concerns, yet it would argue a selfishness and a sottishness altogether inconsistent with the noble and expansive spirit of Christianity, to overlook all the other parts of the theatre of divine dispensations, when a very slight degree of labour and research might be instrumental in unfolding them to his view.

IV.—*The connexion of science with religion would have a tendency to induce upon Christians* A SPIRIT OF LIBERALITY, OF CANDOUR, *and of* ACCURACY IN JUDGING OF THE OPINIONS AND ACTIONS OF MEN, *and of* THE DIVINE PROCEDURE AND OPERATIONS.

Who is the most candid and liberal Being in the Universe? *God.*—And why is God to be considered as the most liberal intelligence that exists? Because he embraces a minute, a full, and comprehensive view of all the circumstances, connexions, relations, habits, motives, temptations, modes of thinking, educational biases, physical affections, and other causes, that may influence the sentiments or the conduct of any of his creatures.—Who among created intelligences may be viewed as endowed with these qualities in the next degree? The loftiest seraph that God has created, who has winged his way to numerous worlds, and taken the most extensive survey of the dispensations of the Almighty, and of all creatures and events.—Who, among the sons of men, is the most illiberal and inaccurate in judging of opinions, of persons, and of things? The man who has lived all his days within the smoke of his father's chimney, or within the confines of his native village—who has never looked beyond the range of his own religious party—whose thoughts have always run in one narrow track—whose reading has been confined to two or three musty volumes, which have lain for ages on the same smoky shelf—who cares for nothing either in the heavens or the earth, but in so far as it ministers to his convenience, his avarice, or his sensual enjoyment—who will admit no sentiment to be true, but what he may have heard broached by his parson—and whose conversation seldom rises beyond mere gossipping chit-chat, and the slanderous remarks which are circulated among his neighbours.—Such characters are entirely unqualified for forming a correct judgment, either of the sentiments and the actions of men, or of the works and the ways of God; for they are completely destitute of the requisite *data* whereon to form a rational decision in relation to either of these subjects.

It may be admitted as a kind of axiom, in our estimate of human character, that in proportion to the ignorance and the narrow range of view which characterize any individual, in a similar proportion will be his want of candour and his unfitness for passing a sound judgment on any subject that is laid before him,—and that the man who has taken excursions through the widest range of thought, accompanied with a corresponding improvement of his moral powers, will always be the most liberal and candid in his decisions on the moral and intellectual qualities of others. To these maxims few exceptions will generally be found.—In forming an enlightened judgment in regard to any action or object, it is essentially requisite, that we contemplate it in all its different features and aspects, and in all its minute circumstances, bearings, and relations. We would not hesitate for a moment to determine who is best qualified to give an accurate description of a city,—he who has only viewed its spires from a distance, while in rapid motion in his chariot—or he who has minutely surveyed all its streets, lanes, squares, public edifices, and surrounding scenery, in every variety of aspect; or, who appears most likely to form the most accurate and enlightened judgment in relation to any particular kingdom—he who has just skirted along a few miles on one of its coasts, or he who has traversed its length and breadth in all directions, and mingled with every class of its inhabitants. On the same principle, it must be admitted, that he who has viewed religion in all its aspects and bearings, who has taken the most extensive survey of the manifestations of God, and of the habits and relations of men, is the best qualified to pronounce a candid and accurate decision on all the intellectual and moral cases that may come before him.

If the spirit of the above stated sentiments be founded on reason and on fact, it will follow, that the more we resemble God in the amplitude of our intellectual views and benevolent affections, the more candid, and liberal, and accurate will our judgments be in reference to all the actions, objects, and relations we contemplate.—On the other hand, the man who is confined to a narrow range of thought and prospect is continually blundering in the estimates he forms, both in respect to physical facts, to general principles, and to moral actions. He forms a premature and uncharitable opinion on every slander and report against his neighbour. He condemns, without hesitation, and throws an unmerited odium on whole bodies of men, because one or two of their number may have displayed weakness or folly. He hates and despises men and their opinions, because they belong not to his political or religious party. He pronounces his decisions on the motives of men, with as much confidence as if he had surveyed their hearts with the eye of omniscience. He cannot hear an objection against his favourite opinions with patience, nor an apology for any set of opinions but his own. He is arrogant and dogmatical in his assertions, and will make no concessions to the superior wisdom of others. He sets himself, with violence, against every proposal for reformation in the church, because his forefathers never thought of it, and because such "innovations" do not suit his humour and preconceived opinions. He decides, in the most confident tone, on what God *can* and *cannot* do, as if he had taken the gauge of infinite perfection; and he frets at the divine dispensations when they do not exactly quadrate with his own humours and selfish views.

With regard to the operations of the Most High, he also forms the most foolish, and vague, and contradictory conceptions. Tell him of the vast dimensions of the planetary system, of the men and animals that live on the opposite side of the globe, of the annual and diurnal motion of the earth—that this world and its inhabitants are moving through the regions of space many thousands of miles every hour—that one of the planets is so large that it would contain 1400 worlds as spacious as ours—that another is flying through the tracts of immensity, at the rate of a hundred thousand miles in an hour—and that light is darted from the sun with a velocity of 195,000 miles in a moment of time—he will stare at you with astonishment at such extravagant assertions, and will sooner believe the stories of giants 100 feet high, and of fairies that can enter in crowds through the key-hole of his door. Instead of frankly acknowledging that "He is ignorant of such subjects, and of the grounds of such conclusions,—that those who have studied them with intelligence are best capable of judging,—that, if true, they must fill us with admiration of the glory of God,—but that, as he has hitherto had no opportunity of examining such matters, he must suspend his assent till he inquire into the reasons which can be given for such amazing deductions;"—instead of such concessions, which are the dictates of modesty and of common sense—he will tell you at once, without hesitation, and without a blush at his presumptuous decisions, that "it is all extravagance, and folly, and idle romance, contrary to Scripture, and reason, and common sense;" and will not hesitate to brand you as a heretic, for endeavouring to break loose his intellectual trammels!—thus tacitly declaring, that he is far better qualified to pronounce a decision on such topics, than all the philosophers and divines, and all the brightest geniuses who have appeared in the world for ages past; though he will at the same time admit, that he never gave himself the trouble to examine into such matters.

His views of the providential dispensations of God are equally partial and distorted. If disease, or poverty, or misfortune, happen to his neighbour, especially if he had withdrawn from the religious party to which he belongs, it is considered as a penal judgment for his error and apostacy. If prosperous circumstances attend his family or his religious party, it is viewed as a sign of divine approbation. He seldom views the hand of God, except in uncommon occurrences; and then, he imagines that a miracle is performed, and that the wheels of nature are stopped in order to accomplish the event. He seldom looks beyond the precincts of his own church or nation, to observe the movements of the divine footsteps towards other tribes of his fallen race. He overlooks the traces of divine operation which are every moment to be seen above and around him—and yet, in the midst of all such partial and contracted views, he will sometimes decide on the wisdom and rectitude of the ways of God, with as much confidence, as if he had entered into the secret counsels of the Eternal, and surveyed the whole plan of his procedure.

Such are a few prominent outlines of the character of thousands whose names are enrolled as members of the visible church—whose illiberality and self-conceit are owing to the contracted notions they have formed of God and of religion. And, surely, it must appear desirable to every enlightened Christian, that all proper means should be used to prevent rational immortal beings from remaining enchained in such mental thraldom.

On the other hand, the man who takes an enlightened view of all the works and dispensations of God, and of all the circumstances and relations of subordinate beings, necessarily acquires a nobleness and liberality of mind, and an accuracy in judging of things human and divine, which no other person can possess. He does not hastily take up an evil report against his neighbour; for he considers how unfounded such reports often are, and how much they are owing to the insinuations of envy or of malice. And when he can no longer doubt of an evil action being substantiated against any one, he does not triumph over him in the language of execration; for he considers all the circumstances, relations, feelings, and temptations with which he may have been surrounded; he considers, that he himself is a frail sinful creature, and might possibly have fallen in a similar way, had he been placed in the same situation. He does not trumpet forth the praises of a man who has performed *one* brilliant benevolent deed, as if he were a character to be admired and eulogized—while the general course of his life is marked with vice, and an utter forgetfulness of God and religion; nor does he fix a stigma of immorality upon the person who may have acted foolishly or sinfully, in one or two instances, while the general tenor of his conduct has been marked by purity and rectitude: for, in both cases, he considers, that it is not an *insulated action*, but *general habits*, which determine the character of any individual. He esteems the wise and the good, and holds friendly intercourse with them, to whatever political or religious party they belong. He can bear, with affability and candour, to have his opinions contradicted, and can differ from his neighbour in many disputed points, while, at the same time, he values and esteems him. He will not brand a man as a heretic or a Deist, because he takes a view of some dogmas in theology, in a different light from what he himself does; for he considers the difference of habits, studies, pursuits, and educational prejudices which must have influenced his opinions; and makes due allowance for the range of thought to which he may have been accustomed. He is always disposed to attribute the actions of others to good motives, when he has no proof of the contrary. He uses no threats nor physical force to support his opinions, or to convince gainsayers; for he knows that no external coercion can illuminate the mind, and that the strength of arguments, and the force of truth, can alone produce conviction. He is convinced how ignorant he is, notwithstanding all his study, observations, and researches; and presses forward, as long as he lives, to higher degrees of knowledge and of moral improvement.

He is an active promoter of every scheme that tends to enlighten and meliorate mankind, and to extend the knowledge of salvation to the ends of the earth; for he considers that it is not by *miracles*, but by the subordinate agency of intelligent beings, that God will effectuate the illumination and the moral renovation of our apostate race. He views the special agency of God in all the movements of the scientific, the religious, and the political world, and perceives Him accomplishing his purpose in the inventions of human genius, and in the economy of the minutest insect, as well as in the earthquake, the storm, and the convulsions of nations; for he considers the smallest atom, and the hosts of heaven, as equally directed by eternal wisdom, and equally necessary in the universal chain of creatures and events. He displays a becoming *modesty* in speaking of the ways and the works of God. When he meets with any dark and afflictive dispensation in the course of Providence, he does not fret and repine, but is calm and resigned, conscious that he perceives only a small portion of the chain of God's dispensations, and is, therefore, unable to form a just comparison of the connexion of any one part with the whole. When he contemplates the depraved and wretched condition of the greater part of the world, at present, and for thousands of years past, notwithstanding the salvation which has been achieved for sinners of mankind, he is far from arraigning the divine goodness and rectitude, in leaving so many nations "to walk in their own ways;" for he knows not what relation this dismal scene may bear, what influence it may have, or what important impressions it may produce, on worlds and beings with which we are at present unacquainted.

He is cautious in pronouncing decisively respecting the dispensations of God, *in regard to the universe at large*. He does not, for example, assert, with the utmost confidence, as some have done, "that there never was, and never will be, to all the ages of eternity, such a bright display of the divine glory as in the cross of Christ." He admires and adores the condescension and the love of God, in the plan of salvation, which the gospel exhibits, and feels an interest in it far beyond that of any other special manifestation of Deity; but he dares not set limits to the divine attributes and operations. He considers himself at present, with regard to the grand system of the universe, in a situation similar to that of a small insect on one of the stones of a magnificent edifice, which sees only a few hair-breadths around it, and is altogether incapable of surveying the symmetry, the order, and beauty of the structure, and of forming an adequate conception of the whole. He considers that he has never yet surveyed the millionth part of Jehovah's empire, and therefore, cannot tell what the eternal Sovereign has been pleased to exhibit in its numerous provinces; and, least of all, can he ever presume to dive into the depths of interminable ages, and boldly declare what the Almighty will, or will not do, through eternity to come. He, therefore views it as presumption, while he has no dictate of revelation for his warrant, to pronounce decisively, either on the one side or the other, of such a deep and important question, which seems above the reach of the loftiest seraph to determine.* In short, he endeavours to take a view of all the manifestations of Deity within his reach, from every source of information which lies before him, and as far as his limited faculties will permit. He does not call in question the discoveries of science, because they bring to his ears most astonishing reports of the wisdom and omnipotence of Jehovah, and of the boundless extent of his kingdom; but rejoices to learn, that the grandeur of his dominions is actually found to correspond with the lofty descriptions of divine majesty and glory recorded in the volume of inspiration, and is thereby inspired with nobler hopes of the glory and felicity of that heavenly world where he expects to spend an endless existence.

If, then, such be some of the features in the character of the enlightened Christian; if liberality and candour, and accurate investigation, mark the judgments he pronounces on the sentiments and the actions of men, and on the works and the ways of God; and if such views and feelings ought to be considered as more congenial to the noble and benevolent spirit of our religion, than the narrow and distorted notions of a contracted mind, it must be an object much to be desired, that the mass of the Christian world be led into such strains of thought, as might imbue their minds with a larger proportion of this spirit. And, if diversified and occasional discussions on the topics to which we have adverted would have a tendency to produce this desirable

* See Appendix, No. X.

effect, it is obvious, that such branches of knowledge as are calculated to enlarge the capacity of the mind, and to throw a light over the revelations and the works of God, should no longer be overlooked in the range of our religious contemplations.

V.—*The extensive range of thought which the diversified objects in nature present,* WOULD HAVE A TENDENCY TO INSPIRE US WITH A SPIRIT OF PIETY, AND OF PROFOUND HUMILITY.

It is owing, in many instances, to want of attention to the impressive displays of wisdom and omnipotence in the material world, that our pious feelings and devotional exercises are so cold and languid. We stalk about on the surface of the earth, and pass from one day to another, without reflecting on the grand and complicated machinery around us, which is carrying us along through the regions of space, and from one portion of duration to another, as if the mighty energies of the Eternal Mind, exerted in our behalf, were unworthy of our acknowledgement or regard. How few, for example, reflect, when they open their eyes in the morning, and perceive the first beams of the rising sun, that since they lay down to sleep, the divine power has been exerted in carrying them more than four thousand miles round to the eastward, in order that they might again be cheered with the morning light; and that, during the same period, they, along with the earth and its vast population, have been carried forward 476,000 miles from that portion of space which they occupied seven hours before! Or, if they have no idea of the motion of the earth, and attach no belief to such an opinion, how is it they do not reflect, that after night has thrown its shades around them, the sun, and ten thousand other vast globes, must move several hundreds of millions of miles before their eyes can again behold the light of day? Either the one or the other of these cases *must be the fact;* and, in either case, there is presented to our view a display of the omnipotence and the superintendence of Him in whom we live and move, which demands our gratitude, our admiration, and praise. And can it ever be supposed, that such reflections, combined with all the other excitements to reverence and gratitude, will not tend to elevate our contemplations, and to raise our pious feelings to a higher pitch of devotion? Whether the psalmist entertained any views of this kind when he composed the ninety-second Psalm, we cannot certainly determine; but I presume, the pious and contemplative mind, when awaking from the slumbers of the night, under such impressions, might sing the first part of that song of praise with peculiar emphasis and delight—"It is a good thing to give thanks to Jehovah, and to sing praise to thy name, O thou Most High! to show forth thy loving kindness in the morning. For thou, Lord, hast made me glad through thy work," (or thy powerful energy:) "I will triumph in the works of thy hands. O Lord! *how great are thy works!* and thy thoughts" (or contrivances) "are very deep! A brutish man knoweth not, neither doth a fool understand this."



An extensive acquaintance with nature and science, combined with Christian principle, would also induce *profound humility.* The man who has made excursions through the most diversified regions of thought, is deeply sensible of the little progress he has attained, and of the vast and unbounded field of divine science which still remains to be explored. When he considers the immense variety of sublime subjects which the volume of inspiration exhibits, and of which he has obtained but a very faint and imperfect glimpse—the comprehensive extent, and the intricate windings of the operations of Providence, and the infinite number of beings over which it extends—the amplitude and magnificence of that glorious universe over which Jehovah presides, and how small a portion of it lies open to his minute inspection—he is humbled in the dust at the view of his own insignificance; he sees himself to be a very babe in knowledge; and, as it were, just emerging from the gloom of ignorance into the first dawnings of light and intelligence. He feels the full force and spirit of the poet's sentiments—

"Much learning shows *how little* mortals know."

When he considers the comprehensive extent of the divine law, and its numerous bearings on every part of his conduct, and on all the diversified relations in which he stands to his God, and to his fellow men; and when he reflects on his multiplied deviations from that eternal rule of rectitude, he is ashamed and confounded in the presence of the Holy One of Israel; and, on a review of his former pride and self-conceit, is constrained to adopt the language of Agur and of Asaph—"Surely I am more brutish than any man, and have not the understanding of a man." "So foolish was I, and *ignorant,* I was as a beast before thee." He views the meanest and the most ignorant of his species, as but a very few degrees below him in the scale of intelligence, and sees no reason why he should glory over his fellows.

This sentiment might be illustrated from the example of some of the most eminent men, in whose minds science and religion were combined. The Honourable Mr. *Boyle* was the most unwearied and successful explorer of the works of God, in the age in which he lived, and all his philosophical pursuits were consecrated to the service of religion. Among other excellent traits in his character, *humility* was the most conspicuous. "He had about him," says Bishop

Burnet, "all that unaffected neglect of pomp in clothes, lodging, furniture, and equipage, which agreed with his grave and serious course of life," and was courteous and condescending to the meanest of his fellow men. "He had," says the same author, "the profoundest veneration for the great God of heaven and earth, that I ever observed in any person. The very *name* of God was never mentioned by him without a pause, and a visible stop in his discourse;" and the tenor of his philosophical and theological writings is in complete unison with these traits of character. Sir *Isaac Newton*, too, whose genius seemed to know no limits but those of the visible universe, was distinguished by his *modesty*, *humility*, and *meekness* of temper. He had such an *humble* opinion of himself, that he had no relish of the applause which was so deservedly paid him. He would have let others run away with the glory of his inventions, if his friends and countrymen had not been more jealous of his honour than he was himself. He said, a little before his death, "I do not know what I may appear to the world, but to myself I seem to have been only like a boy playing on the sea-shore, and diverting myself in now and then finding a pebble or a prettier shell than ordinary, whilst the great ocean of truth lay all undiscovered before me."

The same sentiment might have been illustrated from the lives of Bacon, Locke, Dr. Boerhaave, Hervey, Nieuwentyt, Ray, Derham, the Abbe Pluche, Bonnet, and other eminent characters, who devoted their stores of knowledge to the illustration of the Christian system. For an *extensive* knowledge of the operations of God has a *natural tendency* to produce humility and veneration; and wherever it is combined with pride and arrogance, either among philosophers or divines, it indicates a lamentable deficiency, if not a complete destitution of Christian principle, and of all those tempers which form the bond of union among holy intelligences. After the attention of Job had been directed to the works of God, and when he had contemplated the inexplicable phenomena of the divine agency in the material world, he was ashamed and confounded at his former presumption; and, in deep humility, exclaimed, "I have heard of thee by the hearing of the ear; but now mine eye seeth thee; wherefore I abhor myself, and repent in dust and ashes." In accordance with what has been now stated, we find that the most exalted intelligences, who, of course, possess the most extensive views of the works and providential arrangements of God, are represented as also the most humble in their deportment and as displaying the most profound reverence in their incessant adorations. They "*fall down* before Him who sits upon the throne: and *cast their crowns before the throne*, saying, Thou art worthy, O Lord, to receive glory, and honour, and power; for thou hast created all things, and for thy pleasure they are and were created." Their moral conduct evinces the same lowly temper of mind. They wait around the throne, in the attitude of motion, with wings outspread ready to fly, on the first signal of their Sovereign's will; they "do his commandments, hearkening to the voice of his word," and do not disdain to perform important services, in our wretched world, to the meanest human being who is numbered among "the heirs of salvation." In like manner, were *we* endued with the grasp of intellect, the capacious minds, the extensive knowledge, and the moral powers which they possess, we would also display the same humble and reverential spirit, and feel ashamed of those emotions of vanity and pride, which dispose so many of the human family to look down with contempt on their fellow mortals.

---

If the leading train of sentiment which pervades this volume be admitted, the following *general conclusions* may be adduced:—That, in conducting the religious instruction of the young, the works of God in the material world, and the most striking discoveries which have been made as to their magnitude, variety, and mechanism, should be frequently exhibited to their view *in minute detail;* as illustrations of the attributes of the Deity, and of those descriptions of his nature and operations contained in the volume of inspiration;—that the books put into their hands should contain, among other subjects, popular and striking descriptions of the facts and appearances of nature;—that seminaries should be established for the occasional instruction of young persons, from the age of 15 to the age of 20 or 30, or upwards, in all those popular branches of natural and moral science which have a tendency to enlarge the capacity of their minds, and to expand their conceptions of the incessant agency of God;—and that the ministers of religion, in their public instructions, should frequently blend their discussions of divine topics with illustrations derived from the scenes of creation and providence.

# APPENDIX,

CONTAINING

# NOTES AND ILLUSTRATIONS.

No. I. p. 23 —*Illustration of the Rate of Motion in the Heavenly Bodies, on the supposition that the earth is at rest.*

THE distance of the sun is about 95 millions of miles; consequently, the diameter of the circle he would describe around the earth would be 190 millions, and its circumference 597,142,857, which forms the extent of the circuit through which he would move in 24 hours, if the earth were at rest. This number divided by 24, gives 25,880,952, the number of miles he would move in an hour; and this last number, divided by 60, gives 414,682, the number of miles he would move in a minute. The nearest star is reckoned to be at least 20,000,000,000,000, or twenty billions of miles distant from the earth; consequently, its daily circuit round our globe would measure more than 125,000,000,000,000 miles. This sum divided by 86,400, the number of seconds in a day, would give 1,454,861,111, or somewhat more than one thousand four hundred millions of miles, for its rate of motion in a second of time—a motion which, were it actually existing, would, in all probability, shatter the universe to atoms.

The unlearned reader may, perhaps, acquire a more distinct idea of this explanation from the following figure:

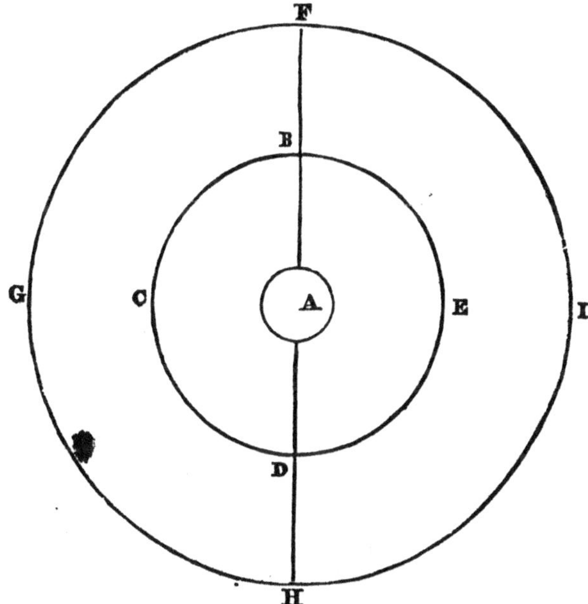


Let the small circle A, in the centre, represent the earth, and the circle B C D E the orbit of the sun, on the supposition that he moves round the earth every 24 hours. The line A B will represent the distance of the sun from the earth, or 95 millions of miles; the line B D the *diameter* of the orbit he would describe; and the circle B C D E the circumference along which he would move every day, or 597 millions of miles, which is somewhat more than three times the diameter. If the line A F represent the distance of the nearest star, the circle F G H I will represent the circuit through which it would move every 24 hours, if the earth were at rest. It is obvious, from the figure, that since the stars are at a greater distance from the earth than the sun, the circle they would describe around the earth would be larger in proportion, and, consequently, their velocities would be proportionably more rapid; since they would move through their larger circles in the same time in which the sun moved through his narrow sphere. But the supposition that the earth is the centre of all the celestial motions, and that the different stars are daily moving around it with different velocities, and the slowest of these motions is so inconceivably rapid—is so wild and extravagant, that it appears altogether inconsistent with the harmony of the universe, with the wisdom and intelligence of the Deity, and with all the other arrangements he has made in the system of nature.

No. II. p. 34.—*Experimental illustrations of the Pressure of the Atmosphere.*

The pressure of the atmosphere is most strikingly illustrated by means of the air-pump. But as few persons, comparatively, possess this instrument, the following experiments, which any person may perform at pleasure, are sufficiently convincing on this point. Take a common wine-glass, and fill it with water; apply a piece of paper over the mouth of the glass; press the paper to the rim of the glass with the palm of the hand; turn the glass upside down; withdraw the hand from the paper, and the water will be supported by the pressure of the atmosphere. That it is the atmospherical pressure, and not the paper, which supports the water, is evident; for the paper, instead of being pressed down by the weight of the water, is pressed upward by the pressure of the atmosphere, and appears *concave*, or hollow in the middle. If the flame of a candle be applied to the paper, it may be held, for an indefinite length of time, close to the paper, without setting fire to it. The same fact is proved by the following experiment:—Take a glass tube, of any length, and of a narrow bore; put one end of it in a basin of water; apply the mouth to the other end, and draw out the air by suction; the water will immediately rise toward the top of the tube; and if the finger or thumb be applied to the top of the tube, to prevent the admission of air, and the tube removed from the basin of water, the water in the tube will be supported by the pressure of the atmosphere on the lower end. Again:—Take a wine-glass, and burn a small bit of paper in it; and when the paper is burning press the palm of the hand upon the mouth of the glass, and it will adhere to the hand with considerable force. In this case, the pressure of the atmosphere will be *sensibly* felt: for it will sometimes require considerable force to detach the glass from the hand.

The pressure of the atmosphere explains a variety of common phenomena. When we take a draught of water out of a basin, or a running stream, we immerse our mouths in the water, and make a vacuum by drawing in the air; the pressure of the atmosphere upon the external surface of the water then forces it into the mouth. The same cause explains the process of a child sucking its mother's breasts—the action of a boy's sucker, in lifting large stones—the rise of water in pumps—the effects produced by *cements*—the firm adhesion of snails and periwinkles to rocks and stones—the scarcity of water in the time of hard frosts—and the fact that a cask will not run by the cock, unless a hole be opened in some other part of the cask.

---

No. III. p. 118.—*On the means by which it may probably be ascertained whether the Moon be a Habitable World.*

About six years ago, the author published, in the Monthly Magazine, a few observations on the surface of the moon, in which a few remarks were offered on this subject. The following is an extract from that communication:—

"If we be ever to obtain an ocular demonstration of the habitability of any of the celestial orbs, the moon is the only one, where we can expect to trace, by our telescopes, indications of the agency of sentient or intelligent beings; and I am pretty much convinced, that a long continued series of observations on this planet, by a number of individuals in different places, might completely set at rest the question, 'Whether the moon be a habitable world?' Were a vast number of persons, in different parts of the world, to devote themselves to a particular survey of the moon—were different portions of her surface allotted to different individuals, as the object of their particular research—were every mountain, hill, cavern, cliff, and plain accurately inspected—and every change and modification in the appearance of particular spots carefully marked and represented in a series of delineations, it might lead to some certain conclusions, both as to her physical constitution, and her ultimate destination. It can be demonstrated, that a telescope which magnifies 100 times, will show a spot on the moon's surface, whose diameter is 1223 yards; and one which magnifies a thousand times, will, of course, enable us to perceive a portion of her surface, whose size is only 122 yards: and, consequently, an object, whether natural or artificial, of no greater extent than one of our large edifices, (for example, St. Paul's church, London,) may, by such an instrument, be easily distinguished. Now, if every minute point on the lunar surface were accurately marked by numerous observers, it might be ascertained whether any changes are taking place, either from physical causes, or from the operations of intelligent agents. If a large forest were cutting down—if a city were building in an open plain, or extending its former boundaries—if a barren waste were changing into a scene of vegetation—or, if an immense concourse of animated beings were occasionally assembled on a particular spot, or shifting from one place to another—such changes would be indicated by certain modifications of shade, colour, or motion; and, consequently, would furnish a direct proof of the agency of intelligent beings analogous to man, and of the moon being a habitable globe. For although we may never be able to distinguish the *inhabitants* of the moon, (if any exist,) yet if we can trace those *effects* which can flow only from the operations of intelligent agents, it would form a complete demonstration of their existence, on the same ground on which a navigator concludes an unknown island to be inhabited, when he perceives human habitations, and cultivated fields.

"That changes occasionally happen on the lunar hemisphere next the earth, appears from the observations of Herschel and Schroeter, particularly from those of the latter. In the transactions of the 'Society of Natural Philosophy,' at Berlin, Schroeter relates, that on the 30th December, 1791, at five o'clock, P. M. with a seven feet reflector, magnifying 161 times, he perceived the commencement of a small crater on the south-west declivity of the volcanic mountain in the *Mare Crisium*, having a shadow of at least 2'' 5. On the 11th January, at twenty minutes past five, on looking at this place again, he could see neither the new crater nor its shadow. Again, on the 4th January, 1792, he perceived, in the eastern crater of Helicon, a central mountain, of a clear gray colour, 3'' in diameter, of which, during many years' observations, he had perceived no trace. 'This appearance,' he adds, 'is remarkable, as probably from the time of Hevelius, the western part of Helicon has been forming into its present shape, and nature seems, in that district, to be particularly active.'—In making such minute observations as those to which I allude, it would be proper, along with an inspection of the moon's luminous disk, to mark the appearances of different portions of her dark hemisphere, when it is partially enlightened by the reflected light from the earth, soon after the appearance of new moon. These researches would require a *long-continued* series of the most minute observations, by numerous observers in different regions of the globe, which could be effected only by exciting, among the bulk of mankind, a general attention to such investigations. But were this object accomplished, and were numerous observations made from the tops of mountains, and in the serene sky of southern climes, where the powers of the telescope are not counteracted by dense vapours, there can be little doubt that direct proofs would be obtained that the moon is a habitable world; or, at least, that the question in relation to this point would be completely set at rest."

### No. IV.—*Remarks on the late pretended discovery of a Lunar Fortification.*

The British public was lately amused by the announcement of a discovery said to have been made by Professor Frauenhofer, of Munich. This gentleman was said to have discovered a *fortification* in the moon, and to have distinguished several lines of road, supposed to be the work of the lunar inhabitants. It is scarcely necessary to say, that such announcements are obviously premature. To perceive distinctly the shape of an object in the moon, which resembles a fortification, it is requisite, that that object be of a much larger size than our terrestrial ramparts. Besides, although an object resembling one of our fortifications were perceived on the surface of the moon, there would be no reason to conclude, that it served the same purpose as fortifications do among us. We are so much accustomed to *war* in our terrestrial system, and reflect so little on its diabolical nature, that we are apt to imagine that it must form a necessary employment even in other worlds. To be assured that a fortification existed in the moon for the same purpose as with us, would indeed be dismal tidings from another world; for it would be a necessary conclusion, from such intelligence, that the inhabitants of that globe are actuated by the same principles of depravity, ambition, and revenge, which have infected the moral atmosphere of our sublunary world. With regard to the pretended discovery of the lunar *roads*, it may not be improper to remark, that such roads behooved to be at least 400 feet broad, or ten times the breadth of ours, in order to be perceived as faint lines through a telescope which magnifies a thousand times; which is a higher power, I presume, than Frauenhofer can apply with *distinctness* to any of his telescopes. It is not at all likely that the lunar inhabitants are of such a gigantic size, or employ carriages of such an enormous bulk, as to require roads of such dimensions, since the whole surface of the moon is only the thirteenth part of the area of our globe.

Schroeter conjectures the existence of a great city to the north of *Marius*, (a spot in the moon,) and of an extensive canal towards *Hygena*, (another spot,) and he represents part of the spot named *Mare Imbrium*, to be as fertile as the Campania. See *Edin. Phil. Jour. No.* 21, *for July*, 1824. Similar remarks to those now stated will apply to these conjectures of Schroeter. We are too apt to imagine, that the objects we perceive in the moon must bear a certain resemblance to those with which we are acquainted on the earth; whereas, there is every reason to believe, from the variety we perceive in nature, that no one world resembles another, except in some of its more prominent and *general* arrangements. The moon bears a general resemblance to the earth, in its being diversified with mountains and valleys; but the positions and arrangement of these objects in the moon, and the scenery they exhibit, are materially different from what appears on the surface of the terraqueous globe.

No. V.—*On the ideas of Magnitude, Motion, and Duration, as expressed by numbers. See pp.* 44, 46.

In the pages referred to, and other parts of this volume, some very large numbers are expressed in *figures*. Some readers have insinuated, that it would have been better to have expressed such numbers in *words*. The author, however, is of a different opinion; because to some readers, not much acquainted with *numeration*, a thousand *trillions* would convey nearly the same idea as a thousand *nonilions*, though the one number contains 58 places of figures, and the other only 22. It is chiefly the number of figures, or ciphers, in such large sums, that leads us to form a comparative estimate of their value or extent. Our ideas of magnitude and extension, conveyed by such numbers, must, of course, be very vague and undefined. If we have been accustomed to travelling, we have a tolerable clear conception of a *hundred*, and even of a *thousand* miles; but we have no clear nor *adequate* conception of a body, or a portion of space, ten hundred thousand, ten hundred millions, or ten hundred billions of miles in extent. The mind, however, may be assisted in its conceptions, and in its comparative estimate of different numbers, by fixing on some particular number as a standard. If, according to the common reckoning, we suppose, that 5828 years have elapsed since the commencement of time, the number of seconds, or moments, in this period, will amount to 183,913,782,212, or one hundred and eighty-three thousand nine hundred and thirteen millions, seven hundred and eighty-two thousand, two hundred and twelve, which is less than the fifth part of a billion. If the distance of the nearest stars from the earth be at least 20 billions of miles, then this distance may be otherwise expressed, by saying, that the number of miles which intervene between us and these bodies is more than *a hundred times greater* than the number of moments which have elapsed since the creation; and, by a similar comparison, it will be found that the number of cubical miles within the limits of the planetary system, is 130,000,000,000,000,000, or one hundred and thirty thousand billions of times greater than the number of moments in 5828 years.

It has been computed, that the earth, supposing it a solid globe, contains about 30,000,000,000,000,000,000,000,000,000,000, or thirty septillions of grains of sand, supposing a hundred grains of sand to be equal in length to an inch, and, consequently, a million of such grains for every cubical inch. If we use this number as a standard for estimating the number of *cubical* miles contained within the space which intervenes between us and the nearest stars, shall find that the number of *cubical miles* comprehended within this space, is more than ten thousand millions of times greater than the number of the grains of sand contained in the globe on which we dwell.

Though the human mind can form no definite conceptions of such numbers and magnitudes, yet it may be useful, occasionally, to ruminate on such subjects; as it is the only, or, at least, the principal mode by which limited minds like ours can approximate to an idea of the *infinity* of the Creator. And if an *image* of infinity is presented to the mind in the spaces comprehended within the limits of our system, how overpowering the conception of innumerable systems, to which ours bears no more proportion than a drop of water to the mighty ocean! How ineffably glorious must be the attributes of that incomprehensible Being who pervades every part of this vast universe, and who continually superintends all its minute and diversified movements!

No. VI. p. 91.—*On a Plurality of Worlds.*

The doctrine of a plurality of worlds is now admitted as highly probable both by philosophers and by enlightened divines. But it has been admitted by many persons on grounds that are too general and vague, and consequently, a *full conviction* of its truth is seldom produced in the mind. In different parts of the preceding volume, I have all along taken it for granted, because I consider it as susceptible of a moral *demonstration*. The following heads of argument, were they fully illustrated, would go far to carry demonstration to the mind on this subject: namely, That there are numerous bodies in the universe of a bulk sufficient to contain myriads of intelligent beings, and to afford them enjoyment—that there appears, in the constitution of many of these bodies, a variety of arrangements evidently adapted to this end—that, in relation to the planets of our system, there are many circumstances which bear a striking resemblance to the constitution of our globe and its appendages. they have annual and diurnal motions, moons, atmospheres, mountains, and vales—that light, and heat, and colour, appear to be distributed throughout the regions of immensity; and that these agents can have a relation only to the necessities and the happiness of organized intelligences—that every part of nature, so far as our observations on the surface of this globe extend, appears to exist solely for the sake of sentient beings—that this doctrine is more worthy of the Infinite Creator, and gives a more glorious and magnificent idea of his nature, than to suppose his benevolent regards confined to the globe on which we dwell. When these and a variety of other arguments are considered, in connexion with the *wisdom* and other attributes of the Deity, they amount not only to a high degree of probability, but to something approaching to a moral demonstration. But to illustrate these arguments in a minute detail, so as to make a convincing impression on the mind, would require a volume of a considerable size. The author flatters himself he has some original thoughts on this subject, which may probably see the light should the present work meet with public acceptance. There is no work in our language which takes an extensive view of this subject, in connexion with the attributes of the Deity, and the intimations contained in divine revelation. Fontenelle's "Plurality of Worlds" contains a number of ingenious reasonings; but he treats the subject in too light and flippant a manner, and without the least reference to a Supreme Intelligence. The celebrated Huygens, in his "*Cosmotheoros*," instead of attempting to prove the doctrine of a plurality of worlds, takes it for granted, and indulges chiefly in conjectures respecting the original structure and faculties of their inhabitants.

That the scriptures are silent on this head, has been assumed by some as a presumptive argument that this doctrine is without a solid foundation. I have already endeavoured to show that this assumption is unfounded; (see page 90.) A plurality of worlds is more than once asserted in scripture, and in numerous passages is evidently taken for granted. Celestial intelligences are represented as ascribing "glory, honour, wisdom, and power" to the king of heaven, "because he hath created all things," and because they perceive his works to be "great and marvellous." But if all the great globes in the firmament were only so many frightful deserts, destitute of inhabitants, such a universe could never inspire superior intelligences with admiration of the *wisdom* of the Creator. For wisdom consists in proportioning *means* to *ends*; but, in the case supposed, there would be no proportion between the means and the end. The means are indeed great and astonishing; but no end appears to justify such a display of creating energy. The psalmist, when he contemplated the heavens, was so affected with the idea of the immense population of the universe, that he seems to have been almost afraid lest he should be overlooked amidst the immensity of beings that are under the superintendence of God. "When I consider thy heavens—what is man that thou art mindful of him!" There would be no propriety nor emphasis in this exclamation, if the heavenly orbs were devoid of inhabitants; for if no intelligent beings exist beside man, and a colony of angels, it would not appear wonderful that the Creator should exercise a particular care over the one-half of his intelligent offspring. But, if we conceive the universe as composed of ten thousand times ten thousand worlds, peopled with myriads of intellectual beings of various orders, the sentiment of admiration implied in the passage is extremely natural and emphatic, and conveys to us an impressive idea of the intelligence, the beneficence, and the condescension of the Founder and Governor of all worlds.

### No. VII. pp. 114, 115.—*On the first Inventor of Printing.*

Mr. Ireland, in his "Picturesque Tour through Holland, Brabant, and part of France, in 1789," gives the following account of the inventor of printing, when describing the city of Haerlem.

"Haerlem claims the invention of the art of printing. It is attributed to Lawrence Koster, an alderman of this city, in 1440; whose house is yet standing in the market-place opposite the church. Amusing himself one day in the neighbouring wood, with cutting the bark of trees into the letters that formed the initials of his name, he is said to have laid them on paper, and falling asleep, when he awoke, observed, that from the dew, their form was impressed on the paper. This accident induced him to make further experiments: he next cut his letters in wood, and, dipping them in a glutinous liquid, impressed them on paper, which he found an improvement; and, soon after, substituting leaden and pewter letters, erected a press in his house; thus laying the foundation of this noble art, which has thence gradually risen to its present excellence. The art, it is said, was stolen from him by his servant, John Faustus, who conveyed it to Mentz, and, from the novelty of the discovery, soon acquired the title of doctor and conjuror. The original specimens are now shown at the library in the Town Hall. The first is on a leaf of parchment, and the second and third on paper, printed only on one side, and the corners left blank for capitals. At the top are wooden cuts, representing the creation, and, as it is called, Lucifer's Fall."—Pp. 109—1 '.

No. VIII. p. 118.—*On Telescopes; with a brief notice of a* NEW REFLECTING TELESCOPE, *constructed by the author.*

It is doubtful to what particular individual we owe the invention of the telescope. Some have supposed that Roger Bacon and Baptista Porta invented this instrument. Borelli ascribes the invention to Zacharias Jansen, a native of Middleburgh. Perhaps the account given in the article to which this note refers, and which is stated by a variety of authors, may be as probable as any other. It is certain that the telescope was not in general use until the beginning of the 17th century, and that no discoveries in the heavens were made with it, till the year 1609.

There are two kinds of telescopes, *refracting* and *reflecting*. In refracting telescopes, the rays of light pass through convex or concave glasses or lenses. The object-glass is always convex, and forms an image or picture of the object in an inverted position in its focus; which image is viewed by the eye-glass; and the magnifying power is in the proportion of the focal distance of the object-glass to that of the eye-glass. The focal distance of a convex glass may be ascertained by holding it in the rays of the sun, opposite to a piece of white paper, and measuring the distance between the glass and the white spot, or burning point, formed on the paper. An astronomical telescope for viewing celestial objects may be constructed with only two glasses. If an object-glass, 30 inches focal distance, be fixed in the end of a tube, and an eye-glass of one inch focus be placed at the other end, at the distance of 31 inches from the object-glass, a telescope will be formed, which will magnify in the proportion of one to thirty, or 30 times; that is, objects seen through such a telescope will appear thirty times larger in diameter, or thirty times nearer, than to the naked eye. By such an instrument, the inequalities on the moon's surface, and some of the satellites of Jupiter, may be perceived; but when directed to land objects they will appear inverted, or turned upside down. In order to reverse the appearance of the object, two other eye-glasses are required; or, if a *concave* eye-glass of a similar focus be placed at 29 inches from the object-glass, the object will appear in its natural position, and the magnifying power will be the same; but the field of view will be much smaller. Astronomical telescopes of this construction were formerly made of 120, and even of 200 feet in length, and were used without a tube; the object-glass being placed on the top of a long pole; but these are now entirely superseded by *achromatic* telescopes. In the achromatic telescope, the object-glass is compounded of two, and sometimes of three lenses, placed close to each other, one of which is a double concave of white flint glass, and the other a double convex of crown glass. By this means an image is formed without being blended with the prismatic colours; and it will, therefore, bear a much greater magnifying power than a common refractor. An achromatic telescope four feet long will magnify objects as much as a common refractor 100 feet long.

In *reflecting* telescopes the images of objects are formed by speculums or mirrors, instead of lenses. They are of two kinds, the *Gregorian* and the *Newtonian*. The Gregorian reflector consists of a tube, in which a concave mirror, having a hole in its centre, is placed. The rays of light from distant objects falling upon this mirror, form an image before it, in its centre or focus. This image is intercepted by a smaller mirror, which reflects it back through the hole in the large mirror, to an eye-glass, through which the observer views the object. In the Newtonian reflector, a plane mirror, placed at an angle of 45 degrees, is substituted in place of the small mirror in the Gregorian construction, and the observer looks down upon the object through the side of the tube. Dr. Brewster has suggested an interesting improvement in the construction of this instrument, which is described in *the Edinburgh Ency.* Art. *Optics*, p. 644.

*New Reflector.*—About three years ago, the author commenced a series of experiments on reflecting telescopes; and has lately constructed several on a new plan and principle. In this construction, there is no *small* speculum, either plane, convex, or concave; there is no tube, except a short one of two or three inches in length, for holding the speculum. The observer sits with his back to the object, and views the image formed by the speculum through an eye-piece, which requires to be nicely directed and adjusted. Three or four instruments of this construction have been fitted up, with specula of 5, 8, 16, 28, 35, and 49 inches focal distance. One of them, having a speculum of eight inches focus, and two inches diameter, with a terrestrial eye-piece, magnifying about 25 times, forms an excellent parlour telescope for viewing land objects, and exhibits them in a brilliant and novel aspect. When compared with a Gregorian of the same size and magnifying power, the quantity of light upon the object appears nearly doubled, and the image *is equally distinct*. It represents objects in their natural colours, without that dingy and yellowish tinge which appears when looking through a Gregorian. Another of these instruments, having a speculum of 28 inches focal distance, and an eye-piece producing a magnifying power of about 100 times, serves as an excellent astronomical telescope. By this instrument the belts and satellites of Jupiter, the ring of Saturn, and the mountains and cavities of the moon, may be contemplated with great ease and distinctness. By placing the pedestal on the floor of the apartment, when the object is at a high elevation, we can view celestial phenomena with the same ease as if we were sitting at a writing desk reading a book. With a magnifying power of about 40 or 50 times applied to this telescope, terrestrial objects appear extremely bright and well defined. A speculum of 49 inches focal distance, and 6½ inches diameter, has lately been fitted up on the same principle. With magnifying powers of from 100 to 160 times, it exhibits distinct and interesting views of the moon's surface, and of the ring of Saturn, and with a power of 56 times it affords a beautiful view of land objects. The specula used in these instruments are far from being good; being of a yellowish colour, and scarcely half polished, and having large holes in the centre; as they were originally intended for Gregorian reflectors; yet the brightness of vision approaches nearly to that of achromatic telescopes. The experiments which have been made on this subject demonstrate, that a *tube* is not necessary for a reflecting telescope, when viewing either celestial or terrestrial objects; and, therefore, this construction of the instrument may be denominated, *The Aerial Reflector*. The simplicity of the construction, and the excellence of the performance of these instruments, have been much admired by several scientific gentlemen to whom they have been exhibited. A *caveat* has lately been lodged at the Patent Office, in the view of taking out a patent for this construction of reflecting telescopes; and a more detailed account of it will probably soon appear in some of the scientific journals.

In the system of *Optics*, lately published in the Edinburgh Encyclopædia, (one of the most luminous and comprehensive treatises which has yet appeared on this subject,) the writer, in his introduction to the account of Dr. Brewster's improvement on the Newtonian telescope, remarks:—"If we could dispense with the use of the small specula in telescopes of moderate length, by inclining the great speculum, and using an oblique, and, consequently, a *distorted* reflection, as proposed first by La Maire, we should consider the Newtonian telescope as perfect; and on a large scale, or when the instrument exceeds 20 feet, it has undoubtedly this character, as nothing can be more simple than to magnify, by a single eyeglass, the image formed by a single speculum. —As the *front view* is quite *impracticable*, and, indeed, *has never been attempted* in instruments of a small size, it becomes of great practical consequence to remove as much as possible the evils which arise from the use of a small speculum," &c.—The instruments noticed above have effectuated the desirable object alluded to by this respectable writer; and the principle of the construction is neither that of Dr. Herschel's *front view*, nor does it coincide with that proposed by La Maire, which seems to have been a mere hint, which was never put into execution.

No. IX. p. 256.—*On Steam Navigation.*

The application of steam, as a mechanical power for impelling vessels along rivers and seas, is one of the most brilliant and useful achievements of art which distinguish the present age and seems destined to produce an important and interesting change in the general intercourse of nations. From the "Report of a Committee of Parliament," published in 1822, it appears, that the first application of steam to the impelling of vessels was made by an Englishman, of the name of Hull, who, in 1736, obtained a patent for the invention of a steam-boat, to be moved with a crank and paddles. But it was only in 1807, that the invention was fairly brought into practical use, by Mr. Fulton, an American, who had the assistance and advice of Mr. Bell, a Scots engineer. There are now, according to Mr. Perkins' statement, about 300 steam-boats on the rivers, bays, and coasts of the United States, varying in their size from 100 to 700 tons. In Britain, the first successful application of steam to vessels was made by the above-mentioned Mr. Bell,* who built the Comet of 25 tons, and four horses' power, to ply on the Clyde. There are now reckoned about 150 steam-boats, from 40 to 500 tons, plying on the rivers and coasts of the British isles. Glasgow, which had the honour of introducing steam navigation on this side of the Atlantic, is still the seat of its greatest activity. According to a statement given in the "Edinburgh Philosophical Journal," published in July, 1822, there were then no less than 36 steam-boats, of various sizes, plying on the Clyde. Some of these, besides performing regular voyages to Inverary, Campbelton, Belfast, Liverpool, and other places, are also performing tours, during the summer months, to the Giant's Causeway, Staffa, Skye, and other ports of the Western isles, and to Inverness by the Caledonian canal. Steam-boats are also plying between Aberdeen and Leith—between Newhaven and Aberdour, Bruntisland, Kinghorn, Kirkaldy, and Dysart; and to Queensferry, Alloa, Grangemouth, and Sterling—between Leith and London—Dover and Calais. One has been plying for several years on Loch-Lomond, which enables the traveller, at a small expense, to take an interesting view of the diversified scenery of that beautiful lake. Five are just now plying on the Tay; two of which, with engines of 30 and 40 horse powers, and fitted up with elegant accommodations ply daily between Perth and Dundee; each of them, during

* It is much to be regretted, and it is certainly not congenial to the liberal spirit of the age, that this gentleman, who was among the first inventors of steam navigation, and who has done so much to promote its success in the neighbourhood of Glasgow, has never received any public reward for his exertions, and has been left to sink into a state approaching to poverty.

most of the summer months, transporting nearly a hundred passengers at every trip.

Steam navigation, though less understood on the Continent than with us, is now beginning to make considerable progress. There are 8 steam-boats on the Garonne, and several on the Seine. There are two on the Lake of Geneva, and two are about to be established on the Lake Constance, and there are, besides, one or two on the Danube. It is likely, that in the course of a few years such conveyances will be established on all our friths and rivers, and the period is, no doubt, hastening on, when excursions will be taken, in such vehicles, between Europe and America. A steam-boat of 700 tons burden, and 100 horse power, has sailed regularly, summer and winter, for three or four years, between New-York and New-Orleans, a distance of 2000 miles, in an open sea, exposed to great storms; and, by many, she is preferred to the packets, not only for the certainty of making shorter voyages, but *on account of greater safety*. In America, steam vessels are fitted up with every accommodation and elegancy which art can devise; so as to produce, if possible, as great a variety of enjoyment to passengers on sea as on land. Mr. Church, the American consul in France, has invented a paddle, which revolves on the paddle wheel, by very simple mechanism, which is found to save power. In the United States, a new mode of constructing cabins has been lately introduced, so as to place them beyond the reach of injury from explosions of the boiler. A steam vessel of a large size has lately been fitted up, which is intended to sail between London and Calcutta.

"Steam vessels have been built in this country of from 10 to 500 tons, and from 3 or 4 to 110 horse power. The length of the City of Edinburgh, on the upper deck, is 143 feet; and some have lately been constructed of still larger dimensions. The American steam-boats are larger than ours, and are much more used for the conveyance of merchandise. The Frontinac, which plies on the Canadian side of Lake Ontario, is 170 feet long on deck, and 32 feet broad; and the Chancellor Livingston, which plies on the Hudson, is of the same size. The velocity aimed at is generally 8 or 9 miles an hour. The proportion is, on an average, about one horse power for every four tons of burden, computed in the usual way. The velocity is found to be nearly as the square root of the power, so that an 80 horse power engine will produce only *twice* the velocity of one of 20 horse power. Something depends also on the make and size of the vessel. The "Sovereign," of 210 tons, and 80 horse power, goes 9¾ miles an hour in still water; and the "James Watt," of 448 tons, and 100 horse power, is stated to go 10 miles. For the paddle-boards, the rule is, that 3–10ths of a square foot of surface should be immersed in the water for each horse power. The paddle wheels vary from 10 to 15 feet in diameter, dip from 12 to 20 inches in the water, and have about one foot in breadth for each 10 horse power. Mr. Gladstone affirms, that so much power is wasted in displacing the water by the stroke of the board, that the velocity of the ship is only about one-half of that of the outer surface of the paddle-wheel.

"There are two sources of apprehension in steam-boats—fire, and the bursting of the boiler. With regard to the latter, when the boiler is of low pressure, it is satisfactorily established that not the smallest danger exists. And in the best constructed vessels, the danger from fire is completely obviated, by separating the furnace from the sides of the vessels by five inches of water."

The power of steam is now rendered subservient to the breaking of stones for the construction of roads. The stones are put into a kind of hopper above, and pushed down with a rake, and the machine is worked by a rotatory motion of one horse power; and will break a ton of hard pebbles completely, in from six to eight minutes. A steam machine has also been invented for the dressing of woollen cloth, which does as much work in 50 minutes as two men could do in two days. *Mon. Mag. Aug.* 1823, p. 71.—A steam carriage, for conveying goods and passengers on land, was lately constructing by Mr. Griffiths. Its rate of motion, on common roads, is estimated at five miles an hour, at an average; about three miles when going up hill, and above seven when running down. But pecuniary embarrassments, or other impediments, have, hitherto, prevented the completion of his design.

Mr. Perkins has lately made improvements on the steam engine, which promise to carry its powers to a high degree of perfection. The engine he has lately constructed is calculated to a ten horse power, though the cylinder is no more than two inches in diameter, and 18 inches long, with a stroke of only 12 inches. Although the space occupied by the engine is not more than six feet by eight, yet Mr. P. considers the apparatus (with the exception of the working cylinder and piston) as perfectly sufficient for a thirty horse engine. When the engine performs full work, it consumes only two bushels of coal in the day. Mr. Perkins has also announced a discovery still more extraordinary, viz. that he has been able "to arrest the heat, after it has performed its mechanical functions, and actually pump it back to the generator, to unite with a fresh portion of water, and renew its useful labours." A particular account of Perkins's engine, accompanied with an engraving, is given in the Edin. Philos. Journal, No. 17, for July 1823. The pretensions of Mr. Perkins, however, have not yet been so fully substantiated by experiment as to satisfy the anxious expectation of the public.

An interesting report has lately been published of a series of experiments, made with *a new steam engine*, invented by an American machinist, called the *capillary steam engine.* Three great objects are said to be accomplished by this invention, *lightness*, *safety*, and *economy of fuel.* In an engine calculated for a four horse power, the *generator* is formed of a copper tube ¼ inch in diameter, and 100 feet long, which weighs about 16lbs. It is arranged in coils, one above another, in the form of a sugar loaf, 30 inches high; the bottom coil being 18 inches in diameter, and the top one considerably less. The wood is prepared as is usual for a stove, and put within the coils. The *steam cylinder* is formed of sheet copper, three inches in diameter, 27 inches in stroke, and, with all its appendages, weighs about 25lbs. It has been ascertained, that the generator and main cylinder, with their contents and appendages, exclusive of fuel, need not weigh more than 20lbs. to the horse power. *No harm can be done by the bursting of boilers*—even a safety-valve is considered as useless. In the course of the experiments, the experimenters several times burst the tube; but, so far from doing any injury, it could not always be perceived by the spectators. To ascertain what may be done towards *aerial navigation*, by steam, experiments were made on the power of wings in the air, and on the power necessary to work them. The result is, that it requires a horse power to carry 30lbs. in the air; so that a flying engine, to be worked by charcoal, would weigh about 30lbs. to the horse power, wings, condenser and fuel included. It was also ascertained by experiments and calculations, that a balloon could be made to carry a man with an engine, which would push it at the rate of 15 miles an hour in the air. A more particular detail of these experiments may be seen in the "London Mechanics' Magazine," No. 60, for 16th October, 1824.

No. X. p. 146.—*Strictures on a certain sentiment respecting the work of Human Redemption.*

The sentiment referred to in this paragraph, "That there never was, nor ever will be, through all the ages of eternity, so wonderful a display of the divine glory, as in the cross of Christ," has been reiterated a thousand times, in sermons and in systems of divinity, and is still repeated by certain preachers, as if it were an incontrovertible axiom, which ought never to be called in question; and is, no doubt, intended to magnify the divine attributes, and the work of redemption.* But it is nothing more than a presumptuous assumption, which has a tendency to *limit* the perfections of Deity, and to present a partial and distorted view of the economy of human redemption. For, in the first place, *it has no foundation in Scripture.* There is not a single passage from which it can be legitimately deduced. The *onus probandi*, on this point, rests with those who make the assertion. A gentleman, when lately conversing on this subject, brought forward the following interrogation, as a demonstrative argument in proof of the position in question: "Is not redemption declared in Scripture to be *the chief of all the works of God?*" but he was not a little surprised, when he was informed that the passage, which he had partly misquoted, is applied to the behemoth or the elephant, as stated in Job xl. 19.—2dly, the assertion is as presumptuous as it is unfounded. It takes for granted, that we know all the events which have already happened, and which are now taking place throughout the whole range of God's universal empire. This empire appears unbounded; and that portion of it which we can minutely explore, is but as a point in comparison

* It is not important to determine how often the sentiment here expressed has been "reiterated in sermons and systems of divinity." We cannot, however, believe that it has been repeated with the same frequency as the author's language seems to imply. That there are instances, in which it was designed to express all the meaning here attributed to it, cannot be denied. But why may it not have been sometimes used to distinguish the work of mediation from all the other favours which God has conferred on our race? In his History of Redemption, p. 342, President Edwards says, "From what has been said, one may argue, that the work of redemption is the greatest of all God's works, of which we have any notice, and it is the end of all his other works." This view of the subject accords with the scriptures. Though it cannot be asserted, that in a single instance they directly affirm the work of redemption to be the greatest of all the works of God, yet they give it such an importance and prominency, as are conceded to no other of His dispensations. In this light the apostles seem to have regarded it. Paul counted all the distinctions and honours and advantages which he had acquired among the Jews, as loss in comparison with the glory of the gospel. He went even farther. He declared that he counted *all things* but loss for the excellency of the knowledge of Christ Jesus his Lord. In this view of the subject there is no presumption and no limitation of the "divine perfections and operations." It has no tendency either to damp the hopes, or obscure the prospects of immortal beings.

On the other hand, who, that is not presumptuous beyond endurance, will suppose, that he now understands the full extent of the love of Christ, and its bearings on all the other divine operations? Who will dare to assert, that this theme will not be sufficient for ever to employ the meditations and the songs of the redeemed? Has any one ascertained, that it is so limited, as to be soon exhausted? On these topics the author is happily silent; or rather he "pronounces nothing decisively;" but affirms, that were he "to hazard a conjecture," he should say, that the converse of the proposition" under consideration "is true." But for ourselves "we feel chained down to an obscure corner of God's domains," and possess no light except that which he has given us. In our present condition *we dare* not launch with the author into the ocean of conjecture. Guided by the revelation which God has made, we are compelled to regard the work of redemption as the greatest of all the divine works of which we have any knowledge; and we are satisfied, that the development of the relations and bearings and effects of this stupendous work will be sufficient to employ all our powers of comprehension, and ever to minister to us new and constant delight.—*Am. Editor*

of the whole. But before we can, on good grounds, hazard such an assertion as that under consideration, we must have explored *all* the dispensations of God, through every portion of his vast dominions; and be able to form a comparison between the different displays of divine glory, made to all the different classes of intellectual beings, under the government of the Creator. And who, among the sons of Adam, can lay claim to such high qualifications for pronouncing so sweeping a decision on this point? 3dly, *It sets limits to the divine perfections and operations.* For although it could be proved, (which it cannot be,) that no such displays have hitherto been made to any other beings, yet who can take upon him to assert, that displays of divine perfection far more glorious and astonishing will not be exhibited during the countless ages of eternity which are yet to come? To set limits to the operations of almighty power and boundless benevolence, during the lapse of infinite duration, is not the province of any created intelligence, and far less of man, who stands so low in the scale of universal being. 4thly, *It tends to damp the hopes and prospects of immortal beings*, when looking forward to an interminable existence. For this sentiment leads them to conclude, that they are already acquainted with the greatest display of divine glory which can be made; and that whatever scenes of wonder may be exhibited in the future world, they must, of course, be all inferior to this, in point of extent and grandeur.

The redemption of the human race, as displayed in the Christian revelation, is a theme sufficiently grand, astonishing, and interesting, to command the attention of all who are convinced that they belong to an apostate race of intelligences, and to excite the admiration and gratitude of all who have experienced its benefits; and it stands in no need of such unfounded and extravagant assertions, to display its riches and glory. "Will a man speak deceitfully for God? Shall not his excellency make you afraid, and his dread fall upon you?"—We pronounce nothing decisively on this subject. We feel ourselves chained down to an obscure corner of God's dominions, to be in the very infancy of our knowledge, and withal, to be connected with a race of beings whose "understandings are darkened by reason of sin;" and are therefore unable to pronounce an infallible decision on what God will or will not do. Were we to hazard a conjecture on this subject, we would say, that the converse of the proposition under consideration is more probable than the proposition itself. We can conceive of worlds ten thousand times more populous than ours, and peopled with a higher order of intellectual beings, towards whom a similar display of benevolence and mercy, were it necessary, may be made; and, therefore, in point of *the extent* of its objects, we can conceive the love of God more illustriously manifested than even to the inhabitants of our globe. But whether such an event shall ever take place it would be presumption in us to determine. For the thoughts and the ways of God as far transcend ours, "as the heavens are high above the earth." It demands our highest tribute of grateful adoration, that the Almighty condescended to "regard us in our low estate," and to deliver us from the moral degradation into which we had fallen; but, surely, it would be unreasonable to conclude, from this consideration, that of all the rational tribes which people the universe, *man* is the only favourite of the Most High, "when thousand worlds are round." Though myriads of other intelligences were to share in similar favours, it would not lessen the happiness conferred on us, nor ought it in the least to detract from our admiration of "the love of God, which is in Christ Jesus our Lord."

There are a great many other vague and untenable notions which are entertained and reiterated by certain commentators and divines, as indisputable axioms, which it would be of importance to the cause of religion to discard such as—that angels are pure *immaterial* substances*—that they were formed on the first day of the Mosaic creation—that the *wisdom* of God is no where so illustriously displayed throughout the universe as in the scheme of redemption†—that the chief employment of the future world will be to pry into the *mysteries* of salvation‡—that sin is an *infinite* evil§—that the

* In the Scriptures angels are called *spirits.* And till some evidence is offered of their materiality, we shall see no reason to abandon the opinion, that they are *pure spirits.—Ed.*

† To show that it is important to discard this sentiment, the author ought at least to have stated some good reason for believing it to be without foundation. Until something more decisive of this point shall be made to appear, there cannot be the least occasion to abandon the sentiment in question.—*Ed.*

‡ Here substantially the same reply may be made as in the preceding instance. Prove that this will not be the chief employment of heaven—Show that any thing else will, for the most part, occupy the attention of the spirits of just men made perfect in glory, and the sentiment under consideration will be readily renounced. Till then we shall claim the right to believe, and maintain, that the employment of the redeemed in glory will consist, to a great extent, in beholding, admiring, and adoring Him, who hath loved them and died for them.—*Ed.*

§ Infinite is once used in the scriptures to qualify the term iniquity, Job xxii. 5. *Is not thy wickedness great and thine iniquities infinite?* But not to insist on perhaps a too literal interpretation of the term, it will be sufficient to show what it is ordinarily used to denote.

Some authors, regarding only the very limited faculties and powers of human beings, deem it impossible, that any of their deeds can be an *infinite evil.*

Others, considering only the infinity of the Being against whom sin is committed, find no difficulty in convincing themselves, that *it is* an *infinite evil.*

There is also a third class, who, taking the word of God for their guide, and learning that sin exposes men to *everlasting punishment*, do not hesitate to denominate that an *infinite evil*, which brings on its guilty victim sufferings infinite in duration. Understood in this last sense, we can feel no obligation to

whole material universe was brought into existence *at the same time* with our earth—that the Creator ceased to create any new order of beings in the universe, after arranging the fabric of our globe—that the whole system of material nature in heaven and earth will be destroyed at the period of the dissolution of our world—that our thoughts and affections should be completely detached from all *created* things, &c. &c.—Several vague notions of this description are founded on the false assumption, that the globe we inhabit, and the rational beings that have appeared on its surface from age to age, are the *chief objects* of God's superintendence and care—and that the Scriptures are *the only medium* through which we can view the plans and operations of the Deity—assumptions, which are contrary to reason, which are unwarranted in revelation, nay, which are directly contradicted in numerous passages of Scripture, some of which have already been referred to in the course of this volume. It would be of essential service to the cause of Christianity, that its doctrines, facts, and moral requisitions were uniformly exhibited in their native simplicity and grandeur, without being obscured and distorted by the vague and extravagant representations with which they are too frequently blended by injudicious minds.

## No. XI.

As authority has a considerable degree of weight on some minds, I shall conclude with an extract on the subject of this volume, from that respectable and enlightened divine, Dr. Dwight, late president of Yale college:—"The works of God were by him intended to be, and are, in fact, manifestations of himself; proofs of his character, presence, and agency. In this light he requires men continually to regard them: and to refuse this regard is considered by him as grossly wicked, and highly deserving of punishment, Psalm xxviii. 5. Isa. v. 12—14. I am apprehensive, that even good men are prone to pay less attention to the works of creation and providence than piety demands, and the scriptures require. We say and hear so much concerning the insufficiency of these works to unfold the character of God, and the nature of genuine religion, that we are prone to consider them as almost uninstructive in moral things, and, in a great measure, useless to the promotion of piety. This, however, is a palpable and dangerous error. The works *alone*, without the aid of the scriptures, would, I acknowledge, be far less instructive than they now are, and utterly insufficient to guide us in the way of righteousness. The scriptures were designed to be a comment on these works; to explain their nature, and to show us the agency, purposes, wisdom, and goodness of God in their formation. Thus explained, thus illuminated, they become means of knowledge, very extensive and eminently useful. He who does not find in the various, beautiful, sublime, awful, and astonishing objects presented to us in creation and providence, irresistible and glorious reasons for admiring, adoring, loving, and praising his Creator, has not a claim to evangelical piety."—*System of Theology*, vol. iii. p. 477.

reject it. It must, however, be admitted that it is not always used in this manner, and that it is sometimes an occasion of ambiguity.—*Ed.*

No. XII.—*List of Popular Works on the different Sciences treated of in this volume, with occasional remarks.*

### SELECT BOOKS ON NATURAL HISTORY.

"Goldsmith's History of the Earth, and animated nature," with notes by T. Brown, Esq. published at Manchester, 6 vols. 8vo. The copious notes appended to this edition, contain an account of the latest discoveries, and form a valuable addition to the original work—"The Gallery of Nature and Art," by Dr. Mason Good, and others, 6 vols. 8vo.—"*Spectacle de la Nature*," or Nature Displayed, 7 vols. 12mo. —"Nature Displayed," by Dr. Simeon Shaw, 3 vols. 8vo. or in 6 vols. 12mo. This work, though chiefly a compilation, imbodies a great variety of interesting and popular descriptions of the most remarkable facts in the system of nature, which are illustrated with numerous engravings, both plain and coloured.—Clarke's "Hundred Wonders of the World," one vol. 12mo. and Platt's "Book of Curiosities," contain a number of interesting selections on this subject.—Smellie's "Philosophy of Natural History," 2 vols. 4to. and his translation of "Buffon's Natural History."—Works entitled, "System" and "Elements" of "Natural History," are numerous; but the greatest part of them is confined to descriptions of the forms, habits, and instinct of animals. On this department of natural science, a work is just now in course of publication, by the celebrated Cuvier, entitled "*The Animal Kingdom*," with engravings, chiefly from the living subjects in the Museum of Natural History at Paris.—A popular and comprehensive history of the facts which have been ascertained respecting the earth, the atmosphere, the meteors, the heavens, &c. calculated for general readers, and interspersed with appropriate moral and religious reflections, is still a *desideratum*. The facts of natural history, next to the facts recorded in the sacred volume, are the first subjects to which the minds of the young should be directed in the course of a general education.

SELECT BOOKS ON GEOGRAPHY.

Pinkerton's Modern Geography, 2 vols. 4to. and the Abridgment, one vol. 8vo.—Guthrie's Geographical Grammar.—The Glasgow Geography, in 5 vols. 8vo. This work comprehends an immense mass of information, on the historical and descriptive parts of geography. It also contains comprehensive compends of astronomy, geology, meteorology, &c.—Malte Brun's "System of Geography," 8vo. The English translation of this work, when completed, will comprise the fullest and most comprehensive view of universal geography that has yet appeared in our language, including details of the most recent discoveries. Five volumes of the English translation have already appeared. The first volume contains a luminous and comprehensive outline of the science of Geology, and Physical and Mathematical Geography.—Myer's "System of Modern Geography," with maps, views, engravings representing costumes, &c. 2 large vols. 4to.—Cooke's "System of Universal Geography," in 2 very large quarto vols. closely printed, contains a great variety of interesting sketches in relation to ***Descriptive*** Geography, extracted from the writings of modern voyagers and travellers; the details of incidents, &c. being related for the most part, in the words of the respective authors from whom the information is collected.—Winterbotham's "Geographical and Historical view of the United States of America, &c." 4 vols. 8vo. —Morse's American Geography," 8vo.—Goldsmith's "Geography on a popular plan," contains an interesting account of the manners and customs of nations, for the entertainment and instruction of the young, illustrated with above 60 engravings. Of smaller systems, there is a great abundance in the English language, but most of them are extremely deficient, particulary in what relates to *General* Geography.—On *Sacred* Geography, Wells's Geography, modernized by the editor of Calmet's Dictionary, is the most complete work of its kind.—On ***Physical*** or *General* Geography—Playfair's System of Geography, vol. I. and Varenius's General Geography. A *Modern* system of Geography, in a separate form, on the plan of Varenius, is a *desideratum.* —Edin. Ency. Art. *Geography.*—Sup. to Ency. Brit. Art. *Physical Geography*, &c. &c. Books of Voyages and Travels, generally contain the most circumstantial details of the physical aspects of the different countries, and of the dispositions and customs of their inhabitants; and present to the view of the Christian philanthropist, those facts and incidents, from which the ***moral*** state and character of the various tribes of human beings may be inferred. The following works contain comprehensive abridgments of the most celebrated voyages and travels.—"Pinkerton's General Collection of Voyages and Travels in all parts of the World," 17 vols 4to —"Mavor's Voyages," &c. 28 vols. 18mo.—"The World Displayed," 18 vols. 18mo.—"Philips's Collection of Voyages and Travels," &c.

The following are among the most respectable modern publications on this subject, arranged according to the different quarters of the world. ASIA.—"Valencia's Travels in India, Arabia," &c.—"Porter's Travels in Georgia, Armenia," &c.—"Golownin's Travels in Japan."—"Staunton's Account of Macartney's Embassy to China."—"Raffle's Travels in Java."—"Clarke's Travels in Asia Minor, and the Holy Land."—"Chateaubriand's Travels in Palestine."—"Ali Bey's Travels in Arabia."—"Morier's Travels through Persia," &c. AFRICA.—"Lyon's Travels in Northern Africa."—Burckhard's Travels in Nubia.—Bruce's Travels in Abyssinia.—Salt's Travels in Abyssinia.—Bowdich, Hutton, and Dupuis's Account of *Ashantee.*—Leigh's Jour. in Egypt.—Belzoni's Travels in Egypt.—Sonini's Travels in Egypt.—Barrow's, Burchell's, and Campbell's Travels in Southern Africa, &c. &c. AMERICA.—Howison's Sketches of Upper Canada. Fearon's Sketches of the United States.—Miss Wright's Views of Society in the United States.—Humboldt's Travels in South America.—Duncan's Travels in the United States.—Luccock's, Vidal's, Kosters's, and Hall's Travels in South America, &c. EUROPE.—Henderson's and Mackenzie's Travels in Iceland.—Thompson's Travels in Sweden.—Carr's Travels in Russia, Denmark, &c —Pallas's Travels in Russia.—Wraxhall's, Neale's, Coxe's, and Lemaistre's Tours through France, Switzerland, Germany, &c.—Bourgoing's and Jacob's Travels in Spain.—Brydon's Tour in Sicily, &c.—Von Buch's Travels in Norway and Lapland.—Cochrane's Travels in Siberia, &c.—Cook's, Anson's, Byron's, Perouse's, and Bougainville's Voyages round the World, &c.—Prior's Universal Traveller, one thick vol. 12mo. closely printed, with one hundred engravings.

SELECT BOOKS ON GEOLOGY.

Kirwan's "Mineralogy," and his "Geological Essays."—De Luc's "Geology," and his "Geological Travels."—Parkinson's "Organic Remains of a former World," 3 vols. 4to.—"The Fossils of the South Downs, or Illustrations of the Geology of Sussex, by G. Mantel, F. L. S." The preliminary essay to this splendid work contains several excellent remarks respecting the connexion of geology with religion, which are calculated to advance the interests of both. —Cuvier's "Essay on the Theory of the Earth,' with illustrations by Professor Jameson; 4th edition.—Playfair's illustrations of the Huttonian Theory of the Earth.—Transactions of the

Geological and Wernerian Societies.—Jameson's Mineralogy.—Buckland's Account of the Discovery of a Den of Hyenas in a cavern in Yorkshire.—Philips's "Outlines of Mineralogy and Geology," 12mo. This last work forms a good introduction to the study of Geology, for those who are just commencing their inquiries on this subject. The object of this science, in the mean time, should be chiefly to *the collecting of facts* in reference to the structure of the earth, and the changes it has undergone. The exterior aspect of our globe, and its internal recesses, must be still more extensively explored, before any theory of the earth can be established on a broad and solid foundation. It should be left to future ages to build a system with the materials we are now preparing.

#### POPULAR WORKS ON ASTRONOMY.

Brewster's "Ferguson's Astronomy," 2 vols. 8vo. with a vol. of plates. The notes and supplementary chapters of this work, written by Dr. Brewster, contain a full and comprehensive detail of all the modern discoveries in this science.—"Bonnycastle's Introduction to Astronomy," 1 vol. 8vo.—La Place's "System of the World," 2 vols. 8vo. Dr. Olinthus Gregory's Astronomy, 1 vol. 8vo.—Mrs. Bryan's "System of Astronomy," 8vo.—Dr. Mylne's "Elementary Treatise on Astronomy," 8vo.—Adam's "Astronomical and Geographical Essays," 8vo. —Philips's "Eight Familiar Lectures on Astronomy," 12mo.—Squire's "Grammar of Astronomy," 1 thick vol. 18mo. closely printed and illustrated with 35 plates.—The "Wonders of the Heavens," 12mo. This work contains a popular view of the principal facts of Astronomy, and is illustrated with 50 elegant engravings, of a variety of interesting objects connected with the scenery of the heavens; but its discussions are too frequently blended with the peculiarities of a modern physical theory.—Martin's "Gentleman and Lady's Philosophy," vol. 1.—Derham's "Astro-Theology," and Whiston's "Astronomical principles of Religion," 8vo.—Baxter's "Matho," 2 vols. &c.—An elegant and comprehensive outline of the leading facts of Astronomy, in their relation to revealed Religion, will be found in Dr. Chalmers's "Discourses on the Christian Revelation, viewed in connection with the Modern Astronomy," 8vo.—The general reader in commencing his study of this science, will find Bonnycastle's "Introduction" a very interesting work. It is written in an elegant and animated style, and is agreeably interspersed with a number of appropriate reflections; but it is deficient in the detail of modern discoveries. He might next proceed to the perusal of Ferguson, Gregory, Squire, &c. La Place's work contains a beautiful exposition of the Newtonian system, but it is glaringly deficient in a reference to the wisdom and agency of a Supreme Intelligence. "An undevout astronomer is mad." Baxter's "Matho," contains a popular and interesting view of this subject, and forms a striking contrast to the apathy of La Place, who carefully keeps out of view the agency of the Creator—the main design of this author being to connect the phenomena of the heavens and the earth with the attributes of Deity, and the high destination of immortal minds. Though this work passed through three editions, it does not seem to have been appreciated according to its merits. As it has now become scarce, a new edition, with *notes*, containing a detail of modern discoveries, might be an acceptable present to the public. Those who wish to prosecute this subject to a greater extent, may be referred to "Long's Astronomy," 2 vols. 4to.—Robinson's "Mechanical Philosophy," vol. 1.—Vince's "Complete System of Astronomy," 3 vols. 4to.—"La Lande *Astronomie*," 3 vols. 4to.—and Biot's "Traite Elémentaire d'Astronomie Physique." A comprehensive work on *Descriptive Astronomy*, detailing, in a popular manner, all the facts which have been ascertained respecting the scenery of the heavens, accompanied with a variety of striking delineations, and interspersed with appropriate reflections, accommodated to the general reader, is a *desideratum*.

#### SELECT BOOKS ON NATURAL PHILOSOPHY.

Hauy's "Elementary treatise on Natural Philosophy," translated by Dr. O. Gregory, 2 vols. 8vo. This translation contains a number of valuable notes by the translator.—Ferguson's "Lectures on Select Subjects in Mechanics," &c. by Dr. Brewster, 2 vols. 8vo with a volume of plates. The *Appendix* to this work, by Dr. Brewster, contains a mass of valuable information on Mechanics, Hydraulics, Dialling, and the construction of *Optical Instruments;* besides a variety of illustrative notes interspersed through the body of the work. A new edition of this work, comprising a detailed account of the recent discoveries in Experimental Philosophy, has been lately published.—Nicholson's "Introduction to Natural Philosophy," 2 vols. 8vo.—Cavallo's "Complete Treatise on Natural and Experimental Philosophy," 4 vols. 8vo.—Martin's "Philosophia Britannica," 3 vols. 8vo. His "Gentleman and Lady's Philosophy," 3 vols. 8vo. and his "Philosophical Grammar," 1 vol. 8vo.—Gregory's "Economy of Nature," 3 vols. 8vo. and his "Lectures on Experimental Philosophy, Astronomy, and Chymistry," 2 vols. 12mo.—Joyce's "Letters on Experimental Philosophy," 2 vols. 12mo. and his "Scientific Dialogues," 6 vols. 18mo.—Adam's "Lectures on Natural and Experimental Philosophy," 4 vols. 8vo. with a volume of plates.—Young's

' Lectures on Natural Philosophy;" 2 vols. 8vo. —Walker's system of "Familiar Philosophy," 4to. in 12 lectures, with 47 quarto engravings. —Conversations on Natural Philosophy, by the author of Conversations on Chymistry, 1 thick vol. 12mo. with 23 engravings.—Blair's "Grammar of Natural and Experimental Philosophy," especially the late editions, contains (at a small price) a comprehensive view of the principal departments of Philosophy, including Astronomy, Geology, Chymistry, Meteorology, &c.—Euler's "Letters to a German Princess," 2 vols. 8vo. contains a popular view of the most interesting subjects connected with Natural and Experimental Philosophy, Logic, and Ethics. This work is distinguished by a vein of dignified and scriptural piety, which runs through every part of it. Euler was one of the most distinguished philosophers and mathematicians of his day. He died in 1783, at the age of 77. A new edition of this work, *with notes by Dr. Brewster*, has been lately published. These notes are excellent, so far as they extend; but it is to be regretted that they are so sparingly distributed, and that the passages suppressed by M. Condorcet, and De la Croix, which were restored by Dr. Hunter, who translated the work, and the notes of the French and English editors, are, for the most part, discarded. Notwithstanding the numerous excellent treatises which are to be found on this subject, a comprehensive work on experimental philosophy, blended with sketches of those parts of natural history, which are connected with it, and enlivened with appropriate reflections on the peculiar agencies of the Deity, which appear in the various processes of nature—is still wanting to interest the general reader, and to attract his attention to this department of knowledge. Were philosophers, in their discussions of natural science, more frequently to advert to the agency of the Deity, and to point out the religious and philanthropic purposes to which modern discoveries might be applied, they might be the means of promoting, at the same time, the interests both of science and of religion; by alluring general readers to direct their attention to such subjects; and by removing those groundless prejudices which a great proportion of the Christian world still entertain against philosophical studies. About the period when Boyle, Ray, Derham, Nieuwentyt, Whiston, Addison, the Abbe Pluche, and other Christian philosophers flourished, more attention seems to have been paid to this object than at present. Since the middle of the last century, the piety of philosophers appears to have been greatly on the decline. It is to be hoped that it is now beginning to experience a revival. But, whatever may be the varying sentiments and feelings of mere philosophers, in reference to the agencies of the material system—"all the works of God *invariably* speak of their Author," to the humble and enlightened Christian; and if he be directed to contemplate the order of nature, with an eye of intelligence, he will never be at a loss to trace the footsteps and the attributes of his Father and his God.

### SELECT BOOKS ON CHYMISTRY

Davy's Elements of Chymical Philosophy, 8vo.—Ure's Dictionary of Chymistry, on the basis of Mr. Nicholson's, 1 large vol. 8vo. Henry's Epitome of Chymistry, 2 vols. 8vo.—Accum's Chymistry, 2 vols. 8vo.—Thomson's System of Chymistry, 4 vols. 8vo.—Murray's System of Chymistry, 4 vols. 8vo. and Appendix.—Kerr's translation of Lavoisier's Elements of Chymistry, 8vo.—Chaptal's Chymistry, applied to the Arts, 4 vols. 8vo.—Fourcroy's Chymistry, 4 vols.—Accum's "Chymical Amusements," and Griffin's "Chymical Recreations," contain a description of a variety of interesting chymical facts and amusing experiments.—Gurney's Lectures on the Elements of Chymical Science, 8vo.—Mackenzie's One Thousand Experiments in Chymistry, &c.—Mitchell's Dictionary of Chymistry.—Conversations on Chymistry, by a Lady, 2 vols. 12mo.—Joyce's Dialogues on Chymistry, 2 vols. 18mo.—Parker's Rudiments of Chymistry, 18mo. and his Chymical Catechism, 8vo. The four works last mentioned may be recommended as popular introductions to the study of this science. Parker's Rudiments and Catechism are distinguished by their constant reference to the agency of the Deity, and by the anxiety which the author displays to fix the attention of his readers on the evidences of benevolent design which appear in the constitution of nature. The numerous notes appended to the Chymical Catechism, imbody a great variety of interesting facts in reference to the economy of nature, and the processes of the arts. To this amiable and intelligent writer I feel indebted for several of the chymical facts stated in this volume.

www.ingramcontent.com/pod-product-compliance
Lightning Source LLC
LaVergne TN
LVHW010513100826
845148LV00001B/6

* 9 7 8 1 4 2 5 5 7 4 0 2 4 *